WISCONSIN
· BLUE BOOK ·

2023 · 2024

Published biennially by
the Wisconsin Legislative Reference Bureau

To view a pdf of the 2023–2024 *Wisconsin Blue Book*, go to
http://legis.wisconsin.gov/lrb/blue-book

Wisconsin Legislative Reference Bureau
One East Main Street, Suite 200, Madison, WI 53703
http://legis.wisconsin.gov/lrb
©2023 Joint Committee on Legislative Organization, Wisconsin Legislature
All rights reserved. Published 2023.
Printed in the United States of America.

ISBN: 978-1-7333817-2-7

Sold and distributed by:
Document Sales Unit
Department of Administration
2310 Darwin Road
Madison, WI 53704
608-243-2441, 800-362-7253
DOADocumentSalesInformation@wisconsin.gov

Front cover: Sunlight illuminates "Wisconsin" on an otherwise cloudy summer day. For over a century, this statue, sculpted by Daniel Chester French, has graced the capitol dome. Standing over 15 feet tall and weighing over three tons, she holds an outstretched arm towards Lake Monona. Her massive size prompted both excitement and anxiety among those who assembled at the capitol square to watch her ascension atop the dome on July 20, 1914. The Wisconsin State Journal reported that thousands of spectators emitted "an audible sigh of relief" when the operation was carried out successfully.
JAY SALVO, LEGISLATIVE PHOTOGRAPHER

Back cover: During the 1899 legislative session, reporters covering the Wisconsin State Assembly sit at two semicircular desks situated between the assembly chief clerk and a row of freshman representatives. They shared this tight space with a handful of boys who served as assembly pages. Apart from these desks, reporters had no home base in the capitol building until 1947 Senate Joint Resolution 20 dedicated a small room in the south wing for use as a pressroom. Since then, the pressroom has become essential to the work of the capitol press corps, and 1997 Wisconsin Act 237 guaranteed reporters' use of the pressroom under statute. See the feature article beginning on p. 278 for a profile of the people and stories that have animated the pressroom over the past 50 years. WHS IMAGE ID 23448

Tony Evers
Office of the Governor

July 2023

Dear Readers:

In 2023, we will celebrate Wisconsin's 175th birthday, and never in 175 years of statehood has our state been in a better fiscal position than it is today. We've made critical, strategic investments to recover from the worst pandemic in a century and the worst economic crisis in a decade, and our state's economy shows it.

Our unemployment recently hit record lows; we have had the highest number of people employed ever; and our general and "rainy day" funds ended the last fiscal year at the highest levels ever. Today, Wisconsin has a historic surplus, and with it, historic opportunity and historic responsibility: we have roads and bridges to fix; schools to fund; kids to support; communities to keep safe; water to keep clean; and a future we've built together after years of neglect that, today, we must work to protect. Preparing our state for the twenty-first century and building the future we want for our kids is only possible if we're willing to do the work together.

The Wisconsin Blue Book always reflects upon a moment of our state's history, and the 2023–24 *Wisconsin Blue Book* is no exception. This is a breakthrough biennium that will determine the trajectory of our state for generations. We face much work ahead of us, but there is also much opportunity. We can achieve big things in our next four years together. And if we are inspired, not by power, but by partnership; if we are dedicated, not to selfish interests, but to self-sacrifice; if we can forge new paths, not through conflict, but through collaboration, then together we will.

Happy reading, and On, Wisconsin!

Sincerely,

Tony Evers
Governor

INTRODUCTION

In an oft-quoted letter to the Marquis de Lafayette in 1823, Thomas Jefferson wrote that "the only security of all is in a free press." Since early statehood, Wisconsin has been fortunate in having a capitol press corps committed to this principle. Those who have served in the capitol press corps in the last 175 years have provided thorough, timely, and objective reporting on the state legislature and all of state government. Wisconsinites know of the actions of their state elected officials through capitol reporters and, with that knowledge, may become more informed citizens.

The 2023–24 *Wisconsin Blue Book* feature article, "On the Capitol Beat," focuses on the men and women who report the news, illuminating the unique challenges and rewards that their work entails. The article draws from interviews with current and past members of the capitol press corps that the Legislative Reference Bureau began conducting in January 2022. This undertaking is part of a larger LRB oral history project to preserve the recollections of legislators and other key actors in state government. Members of the capitol press corps are among these key actors. From these interviews, Managing Legislative Analyst Jillian Slaight has compiled a narrative account of the people, stories, and outlets that keep Wisconsinites informed.

The 2023–24 *Blue Book* also contains the biographies of statewide elected officials, descriptions of legislative, executive, and judicial branch agencies and responsibilities, and vital statistics on Wisconsin. The *Blue Book* is an introduction to Wisconsin state and local government and the most comprehensive source for information about the State of Wisconsin. Composing the Blue Book requires agency-wide collaboration, involving all LRB staff, to write essays, update tables, and assemble and organize material about the legislature and state and local government. The LRB's legal and research expertise is unmatched, and two people deserve special recognition: Nancy Warnecke and Kira Langoussis Mochal. Their leadership has been invaluable. In addition, I am especially grateful for the contributions of Stefanie Rose, Jessie Gibbons, Jillian Slaight, and Madeline Kasper.

Richard A. Champagne

Richard A. Champagne, Director and General Counsel
Wisconsin Legislative Reference Bureau

TABLE OF CONTENTS

Governor's letter iii
Introduction iv

1 ELECTED OFFICIALS

Index of biographies 2
State executive officers 4
State supreme court justices 8
U.S. congressional delegation 12
State legislature 20

2 UNITS OF STATE GOVERNMENT

The Legislature 124
Overview 125
Apparatus for conducting business ... 126
How a bill becomes a law 131
Senate standing committees 137
Assembly standing committees 139
Joint legislative committees and commissions 142
Legislative service agencies 160

The Executive 166
Office of the Governor 166
Office of the Lieutenant Governor ... 176
Department of Administration 177
Department of Agriculture, Trade and Consumer Protection 185
Department of Children and Families 187
Department of Corrections 189
Educational Communications Board 192
Elections Commission 192
Department of Employee Trust Funds 193

Ethics Commission 195
Department of Financial Institutions 196
Department of Health Services 198
Higher Educational Aids Board 201
State Historical Society of Wisconsin 202
Office of the Commissioner of Insurance 205
State of Wisconsin Investment Board 206
Department of Justice 207
Department of Military Affairs 209
Department of Natural Resources 211
Office of the State Public Defender ... 217
Department of Public Instruction 217
Board of Commissioners of Public Lands 220
Public Service Commission 220
Department of Revenue 223
Department of Safety and Professional Services 224
Office of the Secretary of State 229
Office of the State Treasurer 229
Technical College System 229
Department of Tourism 230
Department of Transportation 233
University of Wisconsin System 234
Department of Veterans Affairs 240
Department of Workforce Development 241
Authorities 244
Nonprofit corporations 246
Regional planning commissions 247

Other regional entities	250
Interstate compacts	252

The Judiciary **261**

Wisconsin Supreme Court	261
Wisconsin Court of Appeals	263
Circuit court	265
Municipal court	269
Auxiliary entities	270

3 ABOUT WISCONSIN

Feature article: On the Capitol Beat	278
Elections in Wisconsin	318
Local government in Wisconsin	340
Public education in Wisconsin	348
The legislature and the state budget	357
Significant enactments of the 2021 Legislature	364
Survey of significant Wisconsin court decisions	385
Special sessions of the Wisconsin Legislature	422
Extraordinary sessions of the Wisconsin Legislature	435

4 STATISTICS AND REFERENCE

Wisconsin state symbols	454
Significant events in Wisconsin history	460
Historical lists	480
Population and political subdivisions	526
Elections	570
Officials and employees	634
Public finance	659
Commerce and industry	675
Employment and income	681
Social services	686
Correctional and treatment facilities	691
Military and veterans affairs	693
Education	697
Agriculture	706
Conservation	712
Transportation	717
News media	726
The Wisconsin Constitution	727
Index	763

1
ELECTED OFFICIALS

INDEX OF BIOGRAPHIES

Agard, Melissa 67
Allen, Scott 118
Anderson, Clinton 66
Anderson, Jimmy 68
Andraca, Deb 44
Armstrong, David 95
August, Tyler 53

Baldeh, Samba 69
Baldwin, Tammy 12
Ballweg, Joan 61
Bare, Mike 101
Behnke, Elijah 110
Billings, Jill 116
Binsfeld, Amy 48
Blazel, Edward (Ted) A. 122
Bodden, Ty 80
Born, Mark 60
Bradley, Ann Walsh 8
Bradley, Marc Julian 103
Bradley, Rebecca Grassl 9
Brandtjen, Janel 44
Brooks, Robert 81
Byers, Anne Tonnon 122

Cabral-Guevara, Rachael 76
Cabrera, Marisabel 30
Callahan, Calvin 56
Carpenter, Tim 28
Clancy, Ryan 41
Conley, Sue 65
Considine, Dave 102
Cowles, Robert L. 25

Dallet, Rebecca Frank 9
Dallman, Alex 62
Dittrich, Barbara 59
Donovan, Bob 105
Doyle, Steve 116
Drake, Dora 32
Duchow, Cindi S. 120

Edming, James W. 108
Emerson, Jodi 113
Engels, Tom 121
Evers, Tony 4

Felzkowski, Mary J. 55
Feyen, Dan 73
Fitzgerald, Scott 16

Gallagher, Mike 17
Godlewski, Sarah 7
Goeben, Joy 26
Goyke, Evan 39
Green, Chanz 95
Grothman, Glenn 16
Gundrum, Rick 80
Gustafson, Nathaniel Lee 77

Hagedorn, Brian 10
Haywood, Kalan 38
Hesselbein, Dianne 100
Hong, Francesca 98
Hurd, Karen 89
Hutton, Rob 34

Jacobson, Jenna 65
Jacque, André 22
Jagler, John 58
James, Jesse 88
Joers, Alex 101
Johnson, LaTonya 37
Johnson, Ron 12
Johnson, Scott 54

Kapenga, Chris 118
Karofsky, Jill J. 10
Katsma, Terry 47
Kaul, Joshua L. 5
Kitchens, Joel C. 23
Knodl, Dan 43
Krug, Scott S. 93
Kurtz, Tony 71

Larson, Chris 40
Leiber, John 6
LeMahieu, Devin 46

Macco, John J. 110
Madison Jr., Darrin B. 32
Magnafici, Gae 50
Marklein, Howard 70
Maxey, Dave 36

Index of Biographies

McGuire, Tip 86
Michalski, Tom 35
Moore, Gwendolynne S. 15
Moore Omokunde, Supreme 38
Moses, Clint 50
Murphy, Dave 77
Mursau, Jeffrey L. 57
Myers, LaKeshia N. 33

Nass, Stephen L. 52
Nedweski, Amanda 83
Neubauer, Greta 87
Neylon, Adam 119
Novak, Todd 72

O'Connor, Jerry 74
Ohnstad, Tod 86
Oldenburg, Loren 117
Ortiz-Velez, Sylvia 29

Palmeri, Lori 75
Penterman, William 59
Petersen, Kevin 62
Petryk, Warren 114
Pfaff, Brad 115
Plumer, Jon 63
Pocan, Mark 14
Pronschinske, Treig E. 113
Protasiewicz, Janet Claire 11

Queensland, Michael J. 121
Quinn, Romaine 94

Ratcliff, Melissa 68
Rettinger, Nik 104
Riemer, Daniel G. 29
Rodriguez, Jessie 42
Rodriguez, Sara 5
Roys, Kelda Helen 97
Rozar, Donna 90

Sapik, Angie 95
Schmidt, Peter 27
Schraa, Michael 74
Schutt, Ellen 53
Shankland, Katrina 92
Shelton, Kristina 111

Sinicki, Christine 41
Smith, Jeff 112
Snodgrass, Lee 78
Snyder, Patrick 107
Sortwell, Shae 23
Spiros, John 107
Spreitzer, Mark 64
Stafsholt, Rob 49
Steffen, David 26
Steil, Bryan 14
Stroebel, Duey 79
Stubbs, Shelia 98
Subeck, Lisa 99
Summerfield, Rob 89
Swearingen, Rob 56

Taylor, Lena C. 31
Testin, Patrick 91
Tiffany, Tom 17
Tittl, Paul 47
Tomczyk, Cory 106
Tranel, Travis 71
Tusler, Ron 24

Underly, Jill 6

VanderMeer, Nancy Lynn 92
Van Orden, Derrick 15
Vining, Robyn Dorianne Beckley 35
Vos, Robin J. 84

Wanggaard, Van H. 82
Wichgers, Chuck 104
Wimberger, Eric 109
Wirch, Robert W. 85
Wittke Jr., Robert O. 83

Ziegler, Annette Kingsland 8
Zimmerman, Shannon 51

STATE EXECUTIVE OFFICERS

Tony Evers, Governor
Democrat

Personal: Born Plymouth, Wisconsin, November 5, 1951; married; 3 children, 9 grandchildren.

Education: Plymouth High School 1969; BS University of Wisconsin–Madison 1973; MS University of Wisconsin–Madison 1976; PhD University of Wisconsin–Madison 1986.

Occupation: Former educator; technology coordinator; principal, Tomah; superintendent of schools, Oakfield, Verona; CESA 6 administrator, Oshkosh; deputy state superintendent of public instruction.

Former member: Wisconsin Association of CESA Administrators; Wisconsin Association of School District Administrators; University of Wisconsin Board of Regents; Wisconsin Technical College System Board; Council of Chief State School Officers.

Previous office: Elected state superintendent of public instruction 2009–17.

Current office: Elected governor 2018. Reelected 2022.

Contact: eversinfo@wisconsin.gov; 608-266-1212; PO Box 7863, Madison, WI 53707-7863.

Sara Rodriguez, Lieutenant Governor
Democrat

Personal: Born Milwaukee, Wisconsin, July 25, 1975; married; 2 children.

Education: Brookfield East High School 1993; BA in Neuroscience, Illinois Wesleyan University 1997; BS in Nursing, Johns Hopkins University 2002; MPH and MS in Nursing, Johns Hopkins University 2003.

Occupation: Owner, health care consulting company. Former health care executive for health care systems, health technology firms, and public health departments; epidemic intelligence service officer for the Centers for Disease Control and Prevention; registered nurse; Peace Corps volunteer.

Previous office: Elected to Assembly, 13th District 2020.

Current office: Elected lieutenant governor 2022.

Contact: ltgov@wisconsin.gov; 608-266-3516; PO Box 2043, Madison, WI 53701.

Joshua L. Kaul, Attorney General
Democrat

Personal: Born Mount Lebanon, Pennsylvania, February 2, 1981; married; 2 children.

Education: Goodrich High School (Fond du Lac) 1999; BA in Economics and History, Yale University 2003; JD Stanford Law School 2006.

Occupation: Former attorney; Assistant United States Attorney; president of Stanford Law Review.

Current office: Elected attorney general 2018. Reelected 2022. Member ex officio: Board of Commissioners of Public Lands.

Contact: 608-266-1221; PO Box 7857, Madison, WI 53707-7857.

Jill Underly, State Superintendent of Public Instruction
nonpartisan office

Personal: Born Hammond, Indiana, August 2, 1977; married; 2 children.

Education: Munster High School (Munster, Indiana) 1995; BA in History and Sociology, Indiana University 1999; MA in Secondary Education Curriculum and Instruction, Indiana University–Purdue University, (Indianapolis); PhD in Educational Leadership and Policy Analysis, University of Wisconsin–Madison 2012.

Occupation: Former school superintendent, middle school principal, high school principal, elementary principal, and director of instruction at Pecatonica Area School District (Blanchardville); assistant director and education consultant, Wisconsin Department of Public Instruction; senior student services coordinator, College of Letters & Science, University of Wisconsin–Madison; high school social studies teacher, Munster High School (Munster, Indiana) and Community Schools of Frankfort (Frankfort, Indiana).

Member: Iowa County Humane Society; Trinity Episcopal Church (Mineral Point); American Association of School Administrators; Council of Chief School State Officials.

Former member: Wisconsin Association of School District Administrators (executive board); Wisconsin Association of Business Officials; Vestry, Trinity Episcopal Church (Mineral Point); Fitchburg Optimists Club.

Current office: Elected state superintendent 2021. Member ex officio: University of Wisconsin Board of Regents; Wisconsin Technical College System Board; Education Commission of the States.

Contact: dpistatesuperintendent@dpi.wi.gov; 608-266-3390; 125 South Webster Street, Madison, WI 53703.

John S. Leiber, State Treasurer
Republican

Personal: Born San Jose, California, October 17, 1977; married; 3 children.

Voting address: Cottage Grove, Wisconsin.

Education: The Prairie School (Wind Point, Wisconsin) 1996; BA in History, University of Wisconsin–Parkside 2000; JD University of Wisconsin Law School 2021.

Occupation: Attorney. Former legislative staff in Wisconsin State Senate and Assembly; substitute teacher.

Elected officials: Executive | 7

Member: National Association of State Treasurers; State Financial Officers Foundation.

Former member: Caledonia Parks and Recreation Commission (president); Housing Authority of Racine County (commissioner).

Current office: Elected State Treasurer 2022. Member ex officio: Board of Commissioners of Public Lands.

Contact: treasurer@wisconsin.gov; 608-266-1714; Room B38 West, State Capitol, PO Box 7871, Madison, WI 53707-7871.

Sarah Godlewski, Secretary of State
Democrat

Personal: Born Eau Claire, Wisconsin, November 9, 1981; married; 1 child.

Education: Eau Claire Memorial High School 2000; BA in Peace and Conflict Resolution, George Mason University 2004; Master of Public Administration candidate, University of Pennsylvania; National Security Fellow, Air War College 2013; Certificates in Public Treasury Management and Finance, Pepperdine Graziadio Business School and National Institute of Public Finance 2017.

Occupation: Former national security project manager; director of strategy and performance; investor; entrepreneur.

Former member: UNICEF Advocacy Leadership Committee (chair); Congressional Bipartisan Post Traumatic Stress Disorder Task Force; U.S. Fund for UNICEF (board member); Arlington Academy of Hope (board secretary); George Mason University College of Visual and Performance Arts (board member).

Previous office: Elected state treasurer 2018.

Current office: Appointed secretary of state March 2023 following resignation of Douglas La Follette. Member ex officio: Board of Commissioners of Public Lands (chair 2023, 2021, 2019).

Contact: statesec@wisconsin.gov; 608-266-8888; Room B41 West, State Capitol, PO Box 7848, Madison, WI 53707-7848.

■ ■ ■

STATE SUPREME COURT JUSTICES

Ann Walsh Bradley

Personal: Born Richland Center, Wisconsin, July 5, 1950; married; 4 children.

Education: Richland Center High School; BA Webster College (St. Louis, Missouri); JD University of Wisconsin Law School (Knapp Scholar) 1976.

Occupation: Former high school teacher; practicing attorney.

Member: International Association of Women Judges (chair of the Board of Managerial Trustees); Global Network on Electoral Justice (founding member); American Law Institute (elected member); state coordinator for iCivics; Wisconsin Bench Bar Committee; University of Wisconsin Law School Board of Visitors; American Bar Association; State Bar of Wisconsin; lecturer for the American Bar Association's Asian Law Initiative, International Judicial Academy, U.S. Department of State, and Institute of International Education.

Former member: International Judicial Academy (board of directors and vice chair); National Association of Women Judges (board of directors); American Judicature Society; National Conference on Uniform State Laws; Wisconsin Judicial College (associate dean and faculty); Wisconsin Rhodes Scholarship Committee (chair); Judicial Council; Wisconsin Equal Justice Task Force; Judicial Conference (executive committee, legislative committee, judicial education committee); Civil Law Committee (executive committee); Task Force on Children and Families; Wisconsin State Public Defender (board of directors); Committee on the Administration of Courts; Federal-State Judicial Council.

Previous office: Elected Marathon County Circuit Court judge.

Current office: Elected to Supreme Court 1995. Reelected 2005 and 2015.

Annette Kingsland Ziegler, Chief Justice

Personal: Born Grand Rapids, Michigan, March 6, 1964; married with children.

Education: Forest Hills Central High School; BA in Business Administration and Psychology, Hope College (Holland, Michigan) 1986; JD Marquette University Law School 1989.

Occupation: Former practicing attorney (civil litigation) 1989–95; pro bono special assistant district attorney, Milwaukee County 1992, 1996; assistant U.S. attorney, Eastern District of Wisconsin 1995–97; judicial faculty at various seminars.

Member: State Bar of Wisconsin; American Bar Association; American Law Institute (elected member); American Bar Foundation (fellow); International Women's Forum; Washington County Bar Association; Milwaukee County Bar Association; Eastern District of Wisconsin Bar Association; Boys & Girls Club of Washington County (trustee board president); Marquette University Law School Advisory Board; Rotary Club West Bend.

Former member: Uniform State Laws Commission; Judicial Council; State Bar of Wisconsin Bench & Bar Committee; Governor's Juvenile Justice Commission; Criminal Benchbook Committee; Criminal Jury Instruction Committee; Legal Association for Women; James E. Doyle American Inn of Court.

Previous office: Washington County Circuit Court judge (appointed 1997, elected 1998–2004); Court of Appeals judge, District II (Judicial Exchange Program 1999); deputy chief judge, Third Judicial District.

Current office: Elected to Supreme Court 2007. Reelected 2017. Elected chief justice 2023, 2021.

Rebecca Grassl Bradley

Personal: Born Milwaukee, Wisconsin.

Education: Divine Savior Holy Angels High School; Honors BS in Business Administration and Business Economics, Marquette University 1993; JD University of Wisconsin Law School 1996.

Occupation: Former practicing attorney 1996–2012.

Member: Supreme Court Judicial Education Committee; Supreme Court Finance Committee; Supreme Court Legislative Committee; Board of Advisors, Federalist Society, Milwaukee Lawyers Chapter.

Former member: Wisconsin State Advisory Committee, U.S. Commission on Civil Rights; Board of Governors, St. Thomas More Lawyers Society; Wisconsin Juvenile Jury Instructions Committee; Wisconsin Juvenile Benchbook Committee; Milwaukee Trial Judges Association; Wisconsin Trial Judges Association; State Bar of Wisconsin (chair, Business Law section); American Arbitration Association arbitrator.

Previous office: Milwaukee County Circuit Court judge (appointed 2012, elected 2013); Court of Appeals judge, District I (appointed 2015).

Current office: Appointed to Supreme Court October 2015 to fill vacancy created by death of Justice N. Patrick Crooks. Elected to full term 2016.

Rebecca Frank Dallet

Personal: Born Cleveland, Ohio, July 15, 1969; married; 3 children.

Education: BA in Economics, summa cum laude with honors, The Ohio State University 1991; JD, summa cum laude, Case Western Reserve University School of Law 1994; LLM Duke Law School anticipated 2025.

Occupation: Former law clerk for U.S. Magistrate Judge Aaron Goodstein; assistant district attorney, Milwaukee County; special assistant U.S. attorney, Eastern District of Wisconsin; adjunct law professor, Marquette University Law School; presiding court commissioner, Milwaukee County.

Member: Race Equity, Inclusion, and Access Subcommittee of the Wisconsin Criminal Justice Coordinating Council (cochair); Access to Justice Commission (court liaison); American Law Institute; National Board of Trial Advocacy.

Former member: Wisconsin Criminal Jury Instruction Committee; Wisconsin Judicial College (associate dean); Association of Women Lawyers (secretary); Milwaukee Trial Judges' Association (president); Eastern District of Wisconsin Bar Association (ex officio director); Milwaukee Jewish Federation (board member); Congregation Shalom (board member, youth leader, and educator).

Previous office: Elected Milwaukee County Circuit Court judge.

Current office: Elected to Supreme Court 2018.

Brian Hagedorn

Personal: Born Brookfield, Wisconsin, January 21, 1978.

Education: Wauwatosa West High School 1996; BA in Philosophy, Trinity International University 2000; JD Northwestern University School of Law 2006.

Occupation: Former attorney in private practice 2006–9; Wisconsin Supreme Court law clerk 2009–10; Assistant Attorney General at Wisconsin Department of Justice 2010–11; Chief Legal Counsel for the Office of Governor Scott Walker 2011–15.

Member: Wisconsin Judicial Council; State Bar of Wisconsin Bench Bar Committee; Claims Board; Judicial Commission; Federalist Society.

Previous office: Court of Appeals judge, District II (appointed 2015, elected 2017).

Current office: Elected to Supreme Court 2019.

Jill J. Karofsky

Personal: Born Madison, Wisconsin, July 15, 1966; 2 children.

Education: Middleton High School 1984; BA in Political Science and Spanish, Duke University 1988; MA University of Wisconsin Robert M. La Follette School of Public Affairs 1992; JD University of Wisconsin Law School 1992.

Occupation: Former assistant district attorney and deputy district attorney for Dane County 1992–2001; general counsel and director of education and human resources for the National Conference of Bar Examiners 2001–10; adjunct law professor at University

Elected officials: Supreme Court | 11

of Wisconsin 2005–14; assistant state attorney general and Wisconsin's first Violence Against Women Prosecutor 2010–11; executive director of Office of Crime Victim Services at Wisconsin Department of Justice 2011–17.

Member: Violence Against Women STOP (Services, Training, Officers, and Prosecutors) Grant committee; Wisconsin State Bar; Dane County Bar Association.

Former member: Governor's Council on Domestic Abuse; Wisconsin Child Abuse and Neglect Prevention Board; Wisconsin Crime Victims Council; Dane County Big Brothers/Big Sisters Board of Directors; Wisconsin Attorney General's Sexual Assault Response Team (cochair); James E. Doyle Inn of Court; Wisconsin Attorney General's Child Maltreatment Task Force; Madison Metropolitan School District Guiding Coalition Committee; Wisconsin Celebrate Children's Foundation; Wisconsin Legislative Committee on Criminal Penalties; Wisconsin Child Abuse Network Leadership Committee; Wisconsin Child Death Review Council; Wisconsin Task Force on Children in Need; Safe Harbor of Dane County; Judicial Education Committee.

Previous office: Elected Dane County Circuit Court judge 2017–20.

Current office: Elected to Supreme Court 2020.

Janet Claire Protasiewicz

Personal: Born Milwaukee, Wisconsin, December 3, 1962; married.

Education: Pius XI High School 1981; BA in History, University of Wisconsin–Milwaukee 1985; JD Marquette University Law School 1988.

Occupation: Former assistant district attorney for Milwaukee County 1988–2014; adjunct professor of law, Marquette University Law School; instructor, U.S. Department of Justice National Advocacy Center.

Member: Wisconsin State Bar; Milwaukee Bar Association; Rotary Club of Milwaukee; Fairchild Inns of Court; Serjeants' Inns of Court; Woman's Club of Wisconsin; Professional Dimensions; TEMPO; Association of Women Lawyers; Polish Heritage Alliance Board of Directors; Wisconsin Law Fellow; Milwaukee Women Inc.; Tuckaway Country Club; Association of Marquette University Women (board member).

Former member: American Red Cross of Southeastern Wisconsin (board member); Marquette University Law School Alumni Board (president).

Previous office: Elected Milwaukee County Circuit Court judge 2014–23.

Current office: Elected to Supreme Court 2023.

■ ■ ■

U.S. CONGRESSIONAL DELEGATION

Tammy Baldwin, U.S. Senator
Democrat

Personal: Born Madison, Wisconsin, February 11, 1962.

Voting address: Madison, Wisconsin.

Education: Madison West High School; AB in Mathematics and Government, Smith College (Massachusetts) 1984; JD University of Wisconsin Law School 1989.

Occupation: Former practicing attorney 1989–92.

Previous office: Elected to City of Madison Common Council 1986; Dane County Board of Supervisors 1986–94; 78th State Assembly District 1992–96 (served until January 4, 1999); U.S. House of Representatives 1998–2010.

Current office: Elected to U.S. Senate 2012. Reelected 2018. Committee assignments 118th Congress: Appropriations; Commerce, Science, and Transportation; Health, Education, Labor and Pensions.

Contact: Washington—202-224-5653; 141 Hart Senate Office Building, Washington, D.C. 20510. Eau Claire—715-832-8424; 500 South Barstow Street, Suite LL2, Eau Claire, WI 54701. Green Bay—920-498-2668; 1039 West Mason Street, Suite 119, Green Bay, WI 54303. La Crosse—608-796-0045; 210 7th Street South, Suite 203, La Crosse, WI 54601. Madison—608-264-5338; 30 West Mifflin Street, Suite 700, Madison, WI 53703. Milwaukee—414-297-4451; 633 West Wisconsin Avenue, Suite 1300, Milwaukee, WI 53203. Ladysmith—715-832-8424; PO Box 401, Ladysmith, WI 54848.

Website: www.baldwin.senate.gov

Ron Johnson, U.S. Senator
Republican

Personal: Born Mankato, Minnesota, April 8, 1955; 3 children.

Voting address: Oshkosh, Wisconsin.

Education: Edina High School 1973; BSB University of Minnesota 1977.

Occupation: Former CEO, plastics manufacturing company.

Former member: Partners in Education Council; Oshkosh Chamber of Commerce (business cochair);

Oshkosh Opera House Foundation (treasurer); Lourdes Foundation (board president); Diocese of Green Bay Finance Council; Oshkosh Chamber of Commerce Board of Directors; Oshkosh Area Community Foundation Investment Council.

Current office: Elected to U.S. Senate 2010. Reelected since 2016. Committee assignments 118th Congress: Budget; Finance; Homeland Security and Governmental Affairs.

Contact: Washington—202-224-5653; 328 Hart Senate Office Building, Washington, D.C. 20510. Milwaukee—414-276-7282; 517 East Wisconsin Avenue, Suite 408, Milwaukee, WI 53202. Oshkosh—920-230-7250; 219 Washington Avenue, Suite 100, Oshkosh, WI 54901. Madison—608-240-9629; 5315 Wall Street, Suite 110, Madison, WI 53718.

Website: www.ronjohnson.senate.gov

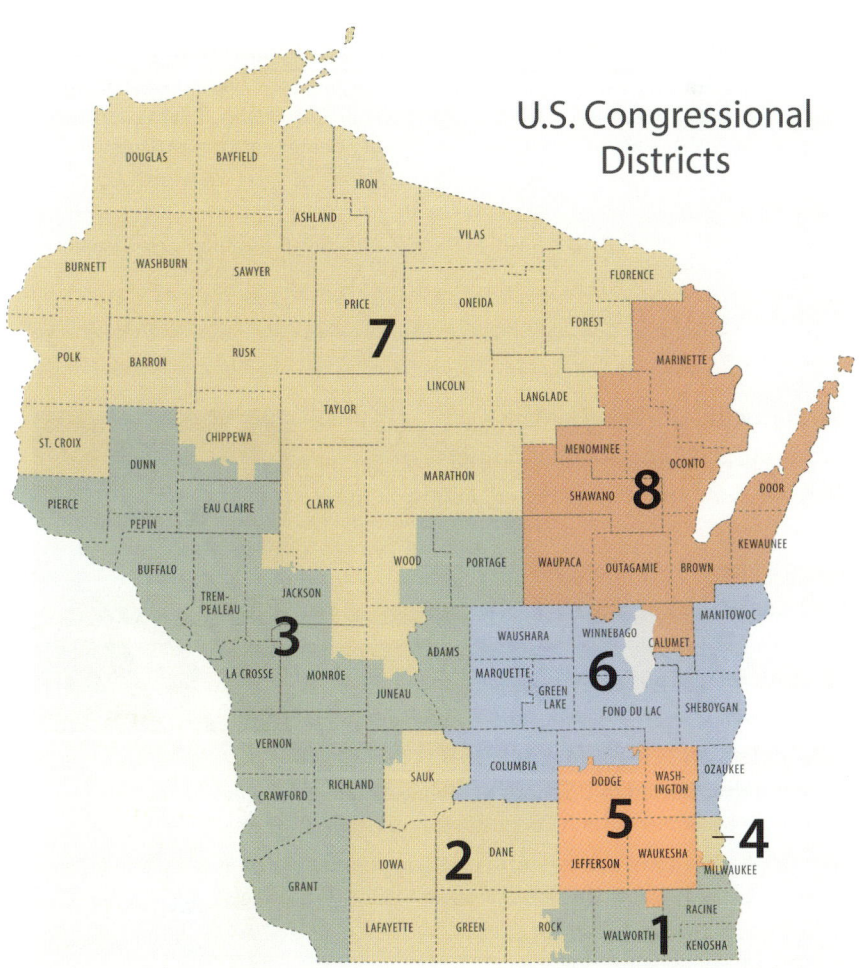

Bryan Steil, U.S. Representative
Republican, 1st Congressional District

Personal: Born Janesville, Wisconsin, March 3, 1981.

Voting address: Janesville, Wisconsin.

Education: Janesville Craig High School; BS in Business Administration, Georgetown University 2003; JD University of Wisconsin Law School 2007.

Occupation: Former attorney; businessman.

Member: St. John Vianney Parish.

Former member: University of Wisconsin Board of Regents.

Current office: Elected to U.S. House of Representatives 2018. Reelected since 2020. Committee assignments 118th Congress: Financial Services; House Administration (chair).

Contact: Washington—202-225-3031; 1526 Longworth House Office Building, Washington, D.C. 20515. Janesville—608-752-4050; 20 South Main Street, Suite 10, Janesville, WI 53545. Kenosha—262-654-1901; Kenosha County Center, 19600 75th Street, Room 177, Bristol, WI 53104. Beloit—100 State Street, Beloit, WI 53511. Walworth County—Matheson Memorial Library, Mary Bray Room, 101 North Wisconsin Street, Elkhorn, WI 53121. Racine—262-637-0510; Racine County Courthouse, Room 101, 730 Wisconsin Avenue, Racine, WI 53403.

Website: https://steil.house.gov

Mark Pocan, U.S. Representative
Democrat, 2nd Congressional District

Personal: Born Kenosha, Wisconsin, August 14, 1964; married.

Voting address: Town of Vermont, Wisconsin.

Education: Mary D. Bradford High School (Kenosha); BA University of Wisconsin–Madison 1986.

Occupation: Small business owner.

Previous office: Elected to 78th State Assembly District 1998–2010.

Current office: Elected to U.S. House of Representatives 2012. Reelected since 2014. Committee assignments 118th Congress: Appropriations.

Contact: Washington—202-225-1026; 1026 Longworth House Office Building, Washington, D.C. 20515. Madison—608-258-9800; 10 East Doty Street, Suite 405, Madison, WI 53703.

Website: http://pocan.house.gov

Elected officials: Congress | 15

Derrick Van Orden, U.S. Representative
Republican, 3rd Congressional District

Personal: Born September 15, 1969; married; 4 children, 8 grandchildren.

Voting address: Prairie du Chien, Wisconsin.

Education: Excelsior University.

Occupation: Navy SEAL (26 years).

Current office: Elected to U.S. House of Representatives 2022. Committee assignments 118th Congress: Agriculture; Transportation and Infrastructure; Veterans' Affairs.

Contact: Washington—202-225-5506; 1513 Longworth House Office Building, Washington, D.C. 20515. La Crosse—608-782-2558; 210 7th Street South, Suite 204, La Crosse, WI 54601. Eau Claire—715-831-9214; Eau Claire Federal Building and U.S. Courthouse, 500 South Barstow Street, Suite B7, Eau Claire, WI 54701.

Website: https://vanorden.house.gov

Gwendolynne S. Moore, U.S. Representative
Democrat, 4th Congressional District

Personal: Born Racine, Wisconsin, April 18, 1951; 3 children.

Voting address: Milwaukee, Wisconsin.

Education: North Division High School (Milwaukee); BA in Political Science, Marquette University 1978; certification in Credit Union Management, Milwaukee Area Technical College 1983.

Occupation: Former housing officer with Wisconsin Housing and Economic Development Authority; development specialist with Milwaukee City Development; program and planning analyst with Wisconsin Departments of Employment Relations and Health and Social Services.

Member: National Black Caucus of State Legislators; National Conference of State Legislatures—Host Committee, Milwaukee 1995; National Black Caucus of State Legislators—Host Committee (chair) 1997; Wisconsin Legislative Black and Hispanic Caucus (chair since 1997).

Previous office: Elected to 7th State Assembly District 1988–90; 4th State Senate District 1992–2000. Senate President Pro Tempore 1997, 1995 (effective 7/15/96).

Current office: Elected to U.S. House of Representatives 2004. Reelected since 2006. Committee assignments 118th Congress: Ways and Means; Joint Economic Committee.

Contact: Washington—202-225-4572; 2252 Rayburn House Office Building, Washington,

D.C. 20515. Milwaukee—414-297-1140; 250 East Wisconsin Avenue, Suite 950, Milwaukee, WI 53202.

Website: https://gwenmoore.house.gov

Scott Fitzgerald, U.S. Representative
Republican, 5th Congressional District

Personal: Born Chicago, Illinois; married; 3 children.

Voting address: Juneau, Wisconsin.

Education: Hustisford High School 1981; BS in Journalism, University of Wisconsin Oshkosh 1985; U.S. Army Armor Officer Basic Course 1985; U.S. Army Command and General Staff College.

Occupation: Former associate newspaper publisher; U.S. Army Reserve Lieutenant Colonel (retired).

Member: Dodge County Republican Party (chair 1992–94); Juneau Lions Club; Reserve Officers Association; Knights of Columbus.

Previous office: Elected to 13th State Senate District 1994–2018. Majority Leader 2019, 2017, 2015, 2013, 2011 (through 7/24/12); Minority Leader 2011 (effective 7/24/12), 2009, 2007; Majority Leader 9/17/04 to 11/10/04.

Current office: Elected to U.S. House of Representatives 2020. Reelected 2022. Committee assignments 118th Congress: Financial Services; Judiciary.

Contact: Washington—202-225-5101; 1507 Longworth House Office Building, Washington, D.C. 20515. Oconomowoc—262-784-1111; 175 East Wisconsin Avenue, Suite H (2nd Floor), Oconomowoc, WI 53066.

Website: https://fitzgerald.house.gov

Glenn Grothman, U.S. Representative
Republican, 6th Congressional District

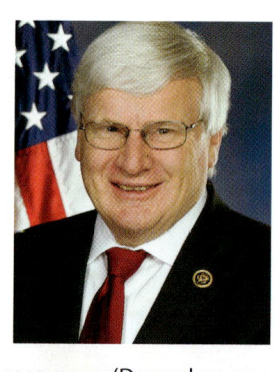

Personal: Born Milwaukee, Wisconsin, July 3, 1955.

Voting address: Glenbeulah, Wisconsin.

Education: Homestead High School (Mequon); BBA University of Wisconsin–Madison; JD University of Wisconsin Law School.

Occupation: Former practicing attorney.

Member: ABATE of Wisconsin; Rotary Club of Fond du Lac.

Previous office: Elected to 59th State Assembly District 1993–2000 (December 1993 special election), 58th district 2002; 20th State Senate District 2004–12. Assistant Majority

Elected officials: Congress | 17

Leader 2013, 2011; Assistant Minority Leader 2009; Minority Caucus Chair 2007; Majority Caucus Vice Chair 2003, 2001, 1999.

Current office: Elected to U.S. House of Representatives 2014. Reelected since 2016. Committee assignments 118th Congress: Budget; Education and the Workforce; Oversight and Accountability.

Contact: Washington—202-225-2476; 1511 Longworth House Office Building, Washington, D.C. 20515. Fond du Lac—920-907-0624; 525 North Peters Avenue, Suite 700, Fond du Lac, WI 54937.

Website: https://grothman.house.gov

Tom Tiffany, U.S. Representative
Republican, 7th Congressional District

Personal: Born Wabasha, Minnesota, December 30, 1957; married; 3 children.

Voting address: Town of Minocqua, Wisconsin.

Education: Elmwood High School 1976; BS in Agricultural Economics, University of Wisconsin–River Falls 1980.

Occupation: Dam tender, Wisconsin Valley Improvement Company.

Member: NRA; Ruffed Grouse Society.

Previous office: Elected to Town of Little Rice Board (supervisor) 2009–13; 35th State Assembly District 2010; 12th State Senate District 2012–16.

Current office: Elected to U.S. House of Representatives in May 2020 special election. Reelected since November 2020. Committee assignments 118th Congress: Judiciary; Natural Resources.

Contact: Washington—202-225-3365; 451 Cannon House Office Building, Washington, D.C. 20515. Wausau—715-298-9344; 2620 Stewart Avenue, Suite 312, Wausau, WI 54401.

Website: https://tiffany.house.gov

Mike Gallagher, U.S. Representative
Republican, 8th Congressional District

Personal: Born Green Bay, Wisconsin, March 3, 1984.

Voting address: Green Bay, Wisconsin.

Education: AB Princeton University; master's degree in Security Studies, Georgetown University; PhD in International Relations, Georgetown University.

Occupation: Iraq War Veteran, intelligence officer, served in U.S. Marine Corps 2006–13. Former staffer, U.S. Senate

Foreign Relations Committee; senior global market strategist at a fuel management services company.

Current office: Elected to U.S. House of Representatives 2016. Reelected since 2018. Committee assignments 118th Congress: Armed Services.

Contact: Washington—202-225-5665; 1211 Longworth House Office Building, Washington, D.C. 20515. De Pere—920-301-4500; 1702 Scheuring Road, Suite B, De Pere, WI 54115.

Website: https://gallagher.house.gov

■ ■ ■

STATE LEGISLATURE

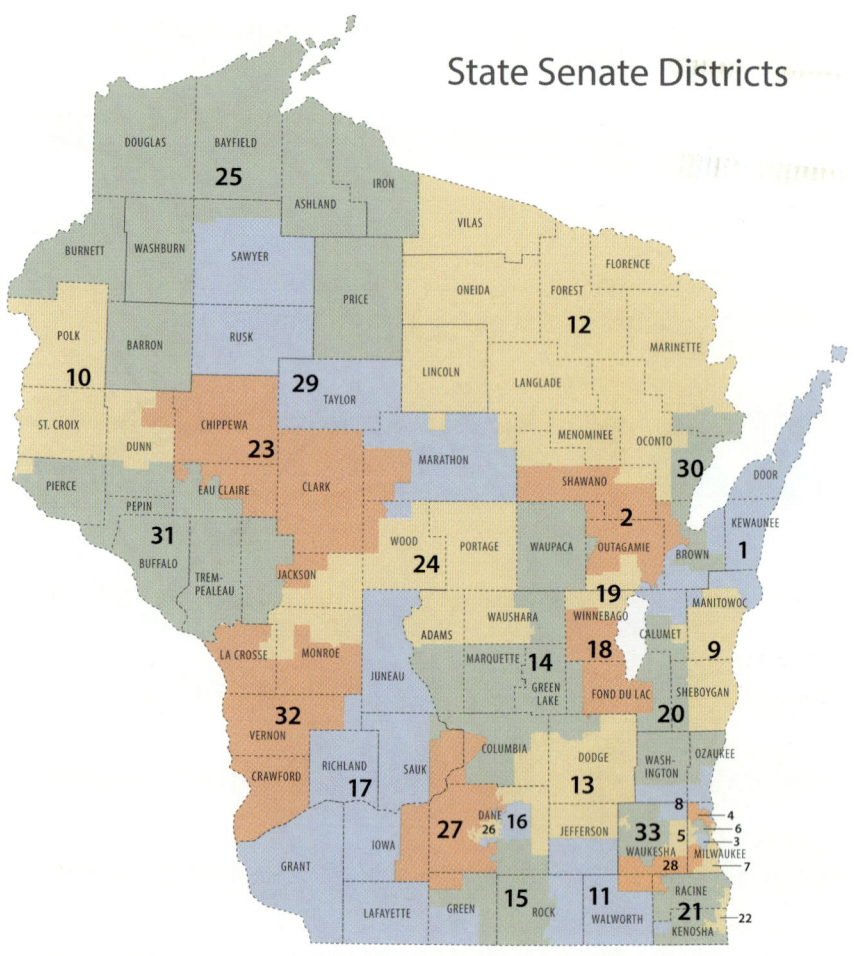

The Wisconsin Constitution requires the state assembly and senate districts be redrawn, based on population, following each U.S. Census. The Constitution additionally requires that senate districts be "convenient contiguous territory" and that "no assembly district [be] divided in the formation of a senate district." In 2022, the Wisconsin Supreme Court established the current districts in *Johnson v. Wisconsin Elections Commission*, using maps based on data from the 2020 U.S. Census. Under that ruling, each senate district comprises three whole and contiguous assembly districts, numbered in consecutive order: for example, Senate District 1 comprises Assembly Districts 1, 2, and 3.

Elected officials: Legislature | 21

2023 State Senate Officers

President Kapenga

President Pro Tempore Testin

Majority Leader LeMahieu

Assistant Majority Leader Feyen

Minority Leader Agard

Assistant Minority Leader Smith

Chief Clerk Queensland

Sergeant at Arms Engels

2023 State Assembly Officers

Speaker Vos

Speaker Pro Tempore Petersen

Majority Leader August

Assistant Majority Leader Plumer

Minority Leader Neubauer

Assistant Minority Leader Haywood

Chief Clerk Blazel

Sergeant at Arms Tonnon Byers

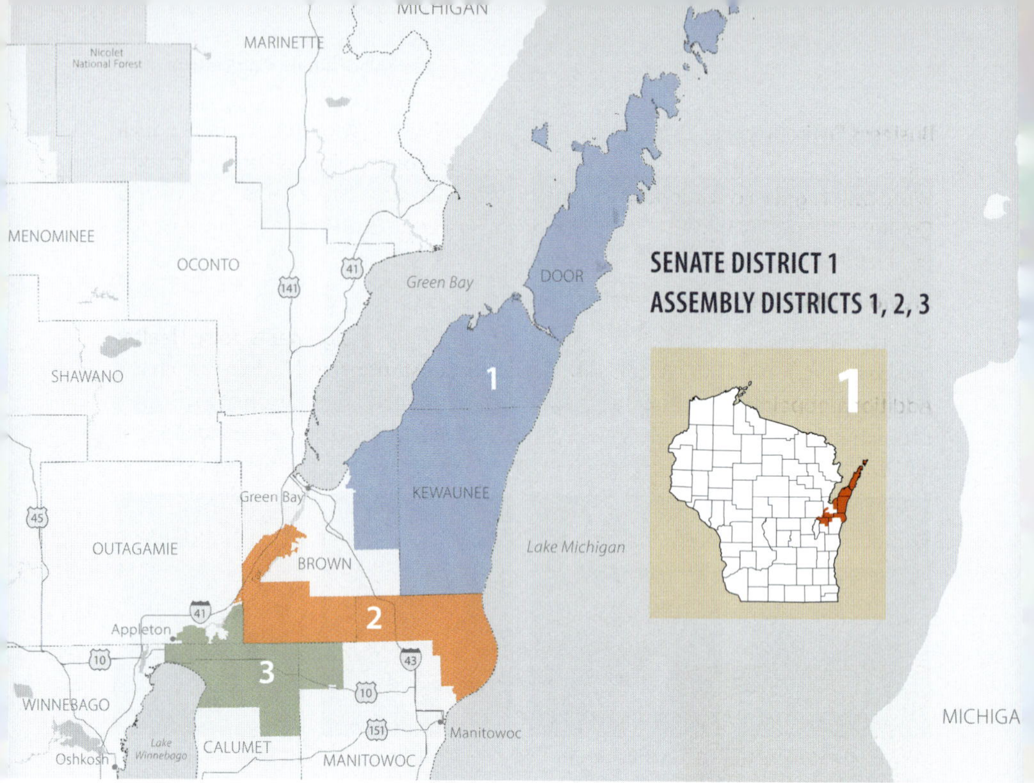

SENATE DISTRICT 1
ASSEMBLY DISTRICTS 1, 2, 3

André Jacque, Senate District 1
Republican

Personal: Born Beaver Dam, Wisconsin, October 13, 1980; married; 6 children.

Voting address: De Pere, Wisconsin.

Education: Green Bay Southwest High School; BS University of Wisconsin–Madison; graduate certificate UW–Madison La Follette School of Public Affairs.

Occupation: Environmental consultant. Former communications and planning director; municipal and county grant writer.

Member: Wisconsin Council on Domestic Abuse; Education Commission of the States; Council on Workforce Investment; Legislative State Supported Programs Study and Advisory Committee; Wisconsin Artistic Endowment Foundation; Great Lakes/St. Lawrence River Legislative Caucus (chair); National Caucus of Environmental Legislators (state lead); Family & Childcare Resources of Northeast Wisconsin (vice president); Green Bay Area Crime Stoppers (board member); Van Handel Foundation for Families of Children with Special Needs (board member); VFW Auxiliary; Knights of Columbus.

Former member: Wisconsin Housing and Economic Development Authority (board member); Small Business Regulatory Review Board (former chair); Wisconsin Small

Business Environmental Council; Child Abuse and Neglect Prevention Board; Council on Tourism; Golden House Domestic Abuse Shelter Community Leadership Council; Wisconsin Higher Educational Aids Board; Wisconsin Association of Municipal and County Assistant Managers; National Association of Local Government Environmental Professionals Grants Management Taskforce.

Previous office: Elected to Assembly 2010–16.

Current office: Elected to Senate since 2018. Committee assignments 2023: Health; Judiciary and Public Safety (vice chair); Licensing, Constitution and Federalism (chair). Additional appointments: Building Commission; Education Commission of the States; Legislative State Supported Programs Study and Advisory Committee; State Capitol and Executive Residence Board; Transportation Projects Commission; Wisconsin Artistic Endowment Foundation.

Contact: sen.jacque@legis.wisconsin.gov; 608-266-3512; Room 7 South, State Capitol, PO Box 7882, Madison, WI 53707-7882.

Joel C. Kitchens, Assembly District 1
Republican

Personal: Born Washington, D.C., September 20, 1957; married; 3 children, 2 grandchildren.

Voting address: Sturgeon Bay, Wisconsin.

Education: Ballard High School (Louisville, Kentucky) 1975; BS Ohio State University 1979; DVM Ohio State University 1983.

Occupation: Large animal veterinarian.

Member: Sturgeon Bay Moravian Church; Door County Medical Center (board member); Wisconsin Veterinary Medical Association; American Veterinary Medical Association; Sturgeon Bay Rotary Club; Wisconsin Coastal Management Council.

Previous office: Elected to Sturgeon Bay Board of Education 2000–14.

Current office: Elected to Assembly since 2014. Committee assignments 2023: Agriculture; Education (chair); Environment (vice chair); Tourism.

Contact: rep.kitchens@legis.wisconsin.gov; 608-237-9101; 888-482-0001 (toll free); 920-743-7990 (district); Room 314 North, State Capitol, PO Box 8952, Madison, WI 53708-8952.

Shae Sortwell, Assembly District 2
Republican

Personal: Born Saratoga Springs, New York, 1985; married; 6 children.

Voting address: Gibson, Wisconsin.

Education: BA in Public Administration, University of Wisconsin–Green Bay 2006; Hazmat Tech certified, U.S. Army Chemical School 2012.

Occupation: Truck driver. Former U.S. Army Sergeant, U.S. Army Reserve Chemical Corps 2009–18; Hazmat Technician and Emergency Response Team Member.

Member: Disabled American Veterans; American Legion.

Previous office: Elected to Gibson Town Board (supervisor); Green Bay City Council.

Current office: Elected to Assembly since 2018. Committee assignments 2023: Criminal Justice and Public Safety; Energy and Utilities; Judiciary; Regulatory Licensing Reform (chair); Sporting Heritage; Veterans and Military Affairs.

Contact: rep.sortwell@legis.wisconsin.gov; 608-237-9102; 888-534-0002 (toll free); Room 214 North, State Capitol, PO Box 8953, Madison, WI 53708-8953.

Ron Tusler, Assembly District 3
Republican

Personal: Born Appleton, Wisconsin, March 21, 1984; married; 2 children.

Voting address: Harrison, Wisconsin.

Education: Neenah High School 2002; degree in Urban Education and History with honors from University of Wisconsin–Milwaukee 2007; JD Marquette University Law School 2010.

Occupation: Small business owner, law practice; attorney, private practice clients and Outagamie County Public Defender's Office. Former attorney for Winnebago County District Attorney's Office and Outagamie County District Attorney's Office; student teacher, Milwaukee Public Schools.

Member: Appleton Area Jaycees (chair, president, treasurer); Heart of the Valley Chamber of Commerce; Republican Party of Outagamie County (former chair, vice chair, communications director).

Former Member: St. Thomas More Society (vice president); Native American Law Society (treasurer); Boy Scouts of America–Gathering Waters District (membership chair, executive officer).

Current office: Elected to Assembly since 2016. Committee assignments 2023: Campaigns and Elections; Forestry, Parks and Outdoor Recreation; Insurance; Judiciary (chair). Additional appointment: Commission on Uniform State Laws (chair).

Contact: rep.tusler@legis.wisconsin.gov; 608-237-9103; 888-534-0003 (toll free); 920-749-0400 (district); Room 22 West, State Capitol, PO Box 8953, Madison, WI 53708-8953.

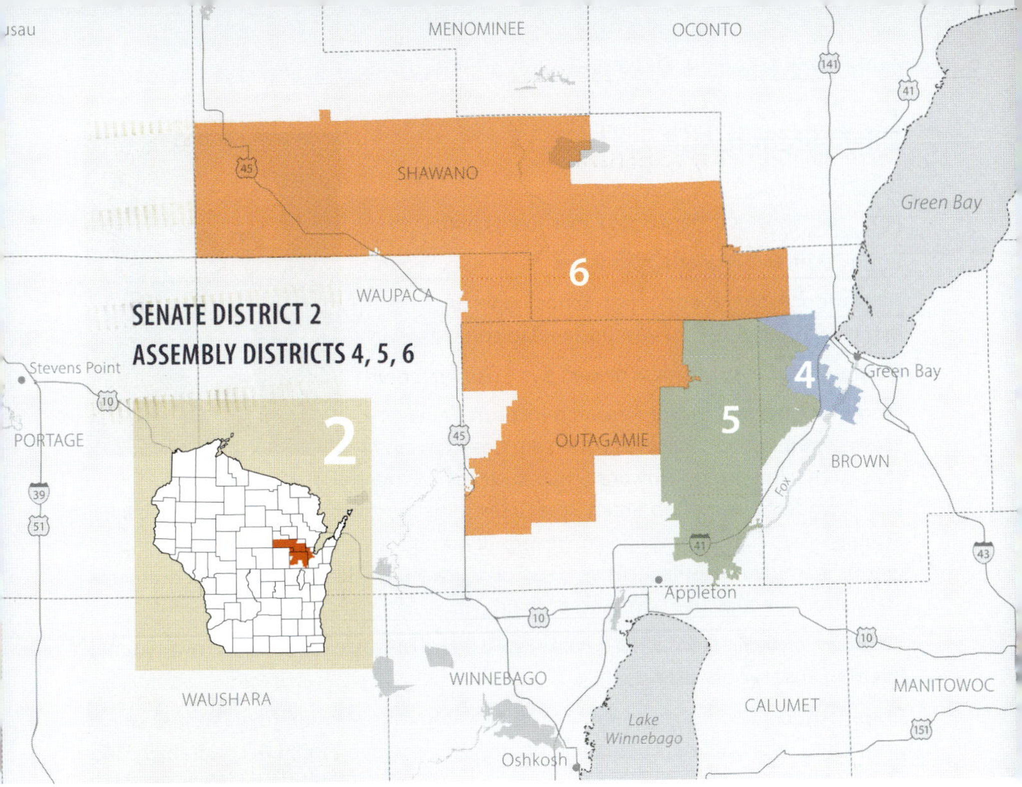

Robert L. Cowles, Senate District 2
Republican

Personal: Born Green Bay, Wisconsin, July 31, 1950.

Voting address: Green Bay, Wisconsin.

Education: BS University of Wisconsin–Green Bay 1975; graduate work University of Wisconsin–Green Bay.

Occupation: Small business owner and legislator. Former director of an alternative energy division for a communications construction company.

Member: Kiwanis Club of Greater Green Bay; Friends of Whitefish Dunes State Park; Green Bay/Brown County Professional Football Stadium District Board; National Caucus of Environmental Legislators; Salvation Army Volunteer; Trout Unlimited.

Previous office: Elected to Assembly 1982–86 (resigned 4/21/87).

Current office: Elected to Senate in April 1987 special election. Reelected since 1988. Committee assignments 2023: Economic Development and Technical Colleges; Natural Resources and Energy (chair); Transportation and Local Government (vice chair); Joint Survey Committee on Retirement Systems. Additional appointment: Transportation Projects Commission.

Contact: sen.cowles@legis.wisconsin.gov; 608-266-0484; 800-334-1465 (toll free); 920-448-5092 (district); Room 118 South, State Capitol, PO Box 7882, Madison, WI 53707-7882.

David Steffen, Assembly District 4
Republican

Personal: Born October 12, 1971; married; 1 child.

Voting address: Howard, Wisconsin.

Education: Ashwaubenon High School 1990; BA in Political Science, University of Wisconsin–Madison 1995.

Occupation: Small business owner.

Member: McPherson Eye Research Institute (advisory council member); U.S. Global Leadership Coalition (advisory council member); Howard Small Business Partnership (founder); Howard Go Green Save Green Initiative (founder, chair); Ashwaubenon Business Association (president); Prevent Blindness—Northeastern Wisconsin (president); Team Lambeau (executive director); Green Bay Area Chamber of Commerce State and Federal Issues Committee (chair).

Previous office: Elected to Village of Howard Board of Trustees 2007–15; Brown County Board of Supervisors 2012–15.

Current office: Elected to Assembly since 2014. Committee assignments 2023: Criminal Justice and Public Safety; Energy and Utilities (chair); Government Accountability and Oversight (vice chair).

Contact: rep.steffen@legis.wisconsin.gov; 608-237-9104; 888-534-0004 (toll free); Room 323 North, State Capitol, PO Box 8953, Madison, WI 53708-8953.

Joy Goeben, Assembly District 5
Republican

Personal: Born Green Bay, Wisconsin, October 16, 1972; married; 4 children.

Voting address: Hobart, Wisconsin.

Education: Green Bay East High School 1990; BS in Elementary Education, University of Wisconsin–Green Bay 1997; MS in Education, Walden University 2009.

Occupation: Elementary school teacher, Ashwaubenon School District. Former owner of a child care center.

Member: Green Bay Area Christian Homeschoolers (former board member); Christ Alone Church (former deacon and church elder); Kaukauna Sportsman Club; NRA.

Current office: Elected to Assembly 2022. Committee assignments 2023: Children and Families (vice chair); Colleges and Universities; Housing and Real Estate; Regulatory Licensing Reform.

Contact: rep.goeben@legis.wisconsin.gov; 608-237-9105; 888-534-0005 (toll free); Room 209 North, State Capitol, PO Box 8952, Madison, WI 53708-8952.

Peter Schmidt, Assembly District 6
Republican

Personal: Born Shawano, Wisconsin, July 3, 1992; single.

Voting address: Bonduel, Wisconsin.

Education: Bonduel High School 2010; BA in Political Science and Spanish, University of Wisconsin–Stevens Point 2013.

Occupation: Dairy farmer.

Member: Shawano County Farm Bureau (former board member); NRA; United States Concealed Carry Association; Brown, Outagamie, Shawano, Waupaca County Republican Party.

Former member: Wisconsin Counties Association 2018–20; National Association of Counties 2018–20.

Previous office: Elected to Shawano County Board of Supervisors 2018–20.

Current office: Elected to Assembly 2022. Committee assignments 2023: Agriculture; Consumer Protection; Environment; Rural Development (vice chair); Transportation.

Contact: rep.schmidt@legis.wisconsin.gov; 608-237-9106; 888-529-0006 (toll free); Room 409 North, State Capitol, PO Box 8953, Madison, WI 53708-8953.

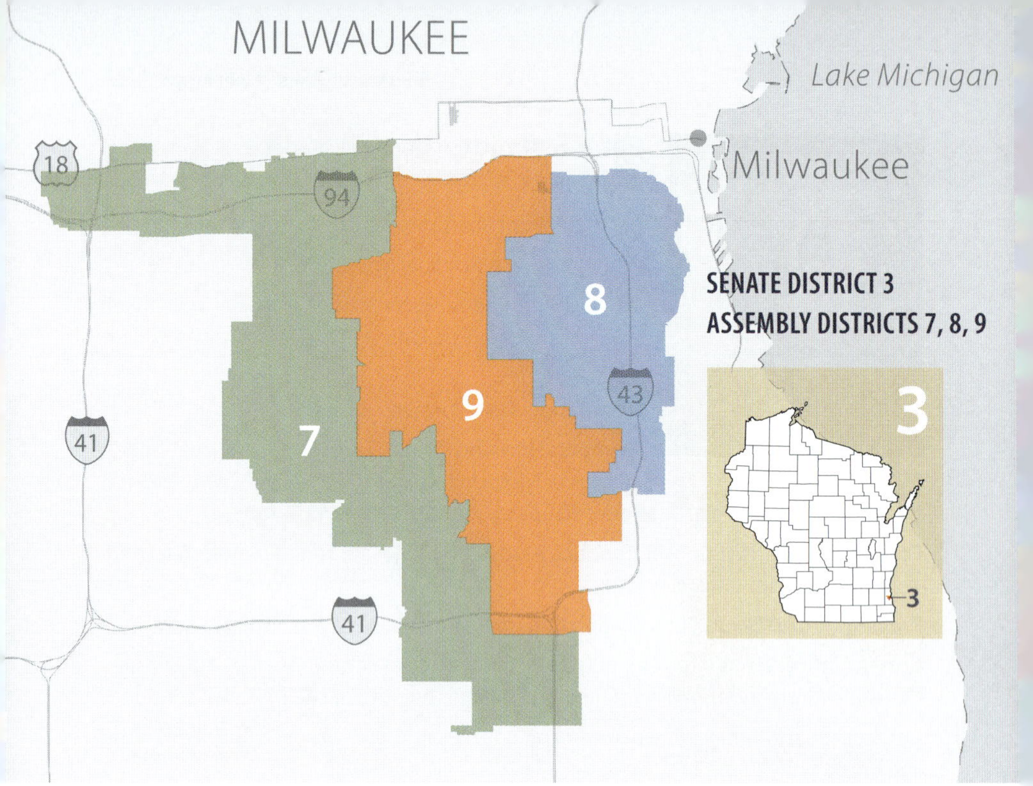

MILWAUKEE

SENATE DISTRICT 3
ASSEMBLY DISTRICTS 7, 8, 9

Tim Carpenter, Senate District 3
Democrat

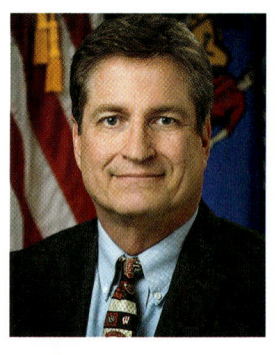

Personal: Born St. Francis Hospital, Milwaukee, Wisconsin; lifelong South Side resident.

Voting address: Milwaukee, Wisconsin.

Education: Pulaski High School; BA in Political Science and History, University of Wisconsin–Milwaukee; MA in Public Policy and Public Administration, La Follette School of Public Affairs, University of Wisconsin–Madison; Milwaukee Police Department Citizen Academy 2018.

Member: Menominee Valley Partners; Friends of Hank Aaron State Trail; Sierra Club; Jackson Park Neighborhood Association; Milwaukee VA Soldiers Home Advisory Council; Wisconsin Humane Society; Friends of the Mitchell Park Domes; Human Rights Campaign; Democratic Party of Wisconsin.

Previous office: Elected to Assembly 1984–2000.

Current office: Elected to Senate since 2002. Leadership positions: Senate President Pro Tempore 2013, 2011; Assembly Speaker Pro Tempore 1993–94. Committee assignments 2023: Health; Labor, Regulatory Reform, Veterans and Military Affairs; Licensing,

Constitution and Federalism; Transportation and Local Government; Joint Legislative Audit Committee. Additional appointments: State Fair Park Board; Transportation Projects Commission.

Contact: sen.carpenter@legis.wisconsin.gov; 608-266-8535; Room 109 South, State Capitol, PO Box 7882, Madison, WI 53707-7882.

Daniel G. Riemer, Assembly District 7
Democrat

Personal: Born Milwaukee, Wisconsin, December 10, 1986; married; 2 children.

Voting address: Milwaukee, Wisconsin.

Education: Rufus King High School (Milwaukee) 2005; BA University of Chicago 2009; JD University of Wisconsin Law School 2013.

Occupation: Attorney. Captain, United States Army Reserve; Judge Advocate General's Corp.

Member: Wisconsin State Bar Association; World Economic Forum: Global Shapers Alumni, Milwaukee Hub; Eisenhower Fellows; Milwaukee Jewish Federation—Weinstein Fellowship.

Current office: Elected to Assembly since 2012. Committee assignments 2023: Health, Aging and Long-Term Care; Insurance; Veterans and Military Affairs; Ways and Means.

Contact: rep.riemer@legis.wisconsin.gov; 608-237-9107; 888-529-0007 (toll free); Room 104 North, State Capitol, PO Box 8953, Madison, WI 53708-8953.

Sylvia Ortiz-Velez, Assembly District 8
Democrat

Personal: Born Milwaukee, Wisconsin; widowed.

Voting address: Milwaukee, Wisconsin.

Education: BA in Political Science, University of Wisconsin–Milwaukee.

Occupation: Real estate broker.

Current office: Elected to Assembly since 2020. Committee assignments 2023: Consumer Protection; Housing and Real Estate; Judiciary; Transportation; Veterans and Military Affairs.

Contact: rep.ortiz-velez@legis.wisconsin.gov; 608-237-9108; 888-534-0008 (toll free); Room 307 West, State Capitol, PO Box 8953, Madison, WI 53708-8953.

Marisabel Cabrera, Assembly District 9
Democrat

Personal: Born Milwaukee, Wisconsin, December 12, 1975; single.

Voting address: Milwaukee, Wisconsin.

Education: Nathan Hale High School 1993; BA in Spanish and BA in Latin American Iberian Studies, University of Wisconsin–Madison 1998; JD Michigan State University College of Law 2002.

Occupation: Small business owner; immigration attorney.

Member: National Hispanic Caucus of State Legislators (vice chair, Immigration Task Force); National Association of Elected and Appointed Officials; Milwaukee Delegation of Democratic State Legislators; Wisconsin Legislative Latino Caucus; Wisconsin Legislative LGBT Caucus; Wisconsin Democratic Labor Workgroup; Voces de la Frontera; Democratic Party of Wisconsin (vice chair, Latino Caucus); Democratic Party of Milwaukee County; State Bar of Wisconsin; State Bar of Florida.

Former member: City of Milwaukee Fire and Police Commission (chair); Centro Hispano of Milwaukee Board of Directors.

Current office: Elected to Assembly since 2018. Committee assignments 2023: Consumer Protection; Corrections; Family Law; State Affairs.

Contact: rep.cabrera@legis.wisconsin.gov; 608-237-9109; 888-534-0009 (toll free); Room 18 North, State Capitol, PO Box 8952, Madison, WI 53708-8952.

SENATE DISTRICT 4
ASSEMBLY DISTRICTS 10, 11, 12

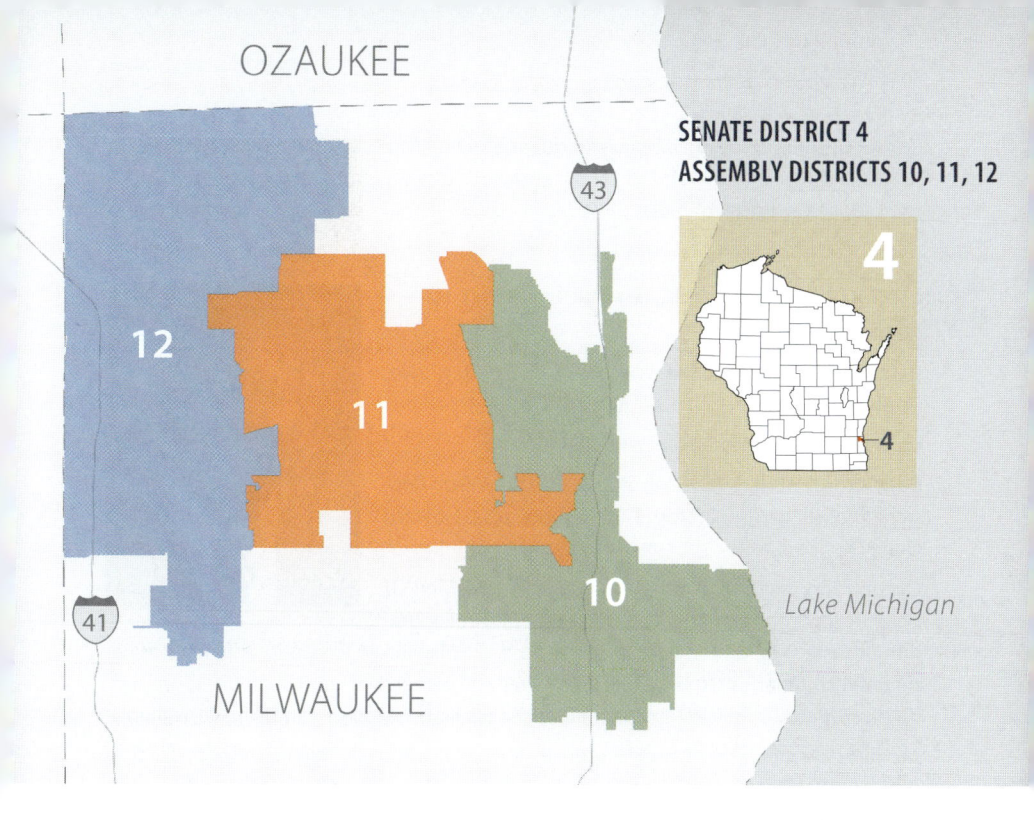

Lena C. Taylor, Senate District 4
Democrat

Personal: Born Milwaukee, Wisconsin, July 25, 1966; 1 child.

Voting address: Milwaukee, Wisconsin.

Education: Rufus King High School (Milwaukee) 1984; BA in English, University of Wisconsin–Milwaukee 1990; JD Southern Illinois University–Carbondale 1993.

Occupation: Practicing Wisconsin attorney 1993–present; founding partner, Taylor & Associates Law Office, 1996–present.

Member: Alpha Kappa Alpha Sorority Incorporated (former Wisconsin state connection coordinator); National Organization of Black Elected Legislative Women; National Black Caucus of State Legislators; NAACP.

Previous office: Elected to Assembly in April 2003 special election.

Current office: Elected to Senate since 2004. Committee assignments 2023: Economic Development and Technical Colleges; Insurance and Small Business; Judiciary and Public Safety; Joint Review Committee on Criminal Penalties; Joint Survey Committee on Tax Exemptions. Additional appointments: Historical Society of Wisconsin Board of Curators; Commission on Uniform State Laws.

Contact: sen.taylor@legis.wisconsin.gov; 608-266-5810; 414-342-7176 (district); Facebook: Senator Lena Taylor; Twitter: @sentaylor; Room 5 South, State Capitol, PO Box 7882, Madison, WI 53707-7882.

Darrin B. Madison Jr., Assembly District 10
Democrat

Personal: Born Milwaukee, Wisconsin, February 1, 1997; single.

Voting address: Milwaukee, Wisconsin.

Education: Pulaski High School 2012; Ronald Wilson Reagan (IB) College Preparatory High School 2015; Howard University 2016.

Occupation: National Youth Alliance For Boys & Men Of Color (fellow); City of Milwaukee Environmental Collaboration Office (eco-neighborhoods specialist 2017–18); Milwaukee Turners (program coordinator); African American Roundtable (democracy organizer 2021–22); Urban Underground/Youth Justice Milwaukee (program manager 2018–21); freelance campaign consultant.

Member: Democratic Party of Wisconsin; Milwaukee Turners; Democratic Socialists of America; National Youth Alliance For Boys & Men Of Color (fellow); African American Roundtable; Urban Ecology Center.

Former member: Democratic Party of Milwaukee County (4CD vice chair); Americorps Public Allies (alumnus); ACLU Milwaukee (board member); Grow2Learn (lead organizer); Opportunity Youth United (Community Action Team coordinator).

Current office: Elected to Assembly 2022. Committee assignments 2023: Children and Families; Corrections; Criminal Justice and Public Safety; Workforce Development and Economic Opportunities. Additional appointment: Milwaukee Child Welfare Partnership Council.

Contact: rep.madison@legis.wisconsin.gov; 608-237-9110; 888-534-0010 (toll free); Room 21 North, State Capitol, PO Box 8953, Madison, WI 53708-8953.

Dora Drake, Assembly District 11
Democrat

Personal: Born Milwaukee, Wisconsin.

Education: Eastbrook Academy (Milwaukee) 2011; BA Marquette University 2015.

Occupation: Social worker; trauma-informed response facilitator; sales representative.

Member: Young Democrats of Wisconsin; Emerge Wisconsin, Class of 2020; Wisconsin Legislative Black Caucus (2023 chair).

Former member: Wisconsin Delegate for Young Democrats of America; Milwaukee Area Professionals Chapter of National Society of Black Engineers.

Current office: Elected to Assembly since 2020. Committee assignments 2023: Criminal Justice and Public Safety; Energy and Utilities; Health, Aging and Long-Term Care; Transportation.

Contact: rep.drake@legis.wisconsin.gov; 608-237-9111; 888-534-0011 (toll free); Room 19 North, State Capitol, PO Box 8952, Madison, WI 53708-8952.

LaKeshia N. Myers, Assembly District 12
Democrat

Personal: Born Milwaukee, Wisconsin, May 21, 1984; single.

Voting address: Milwaukee, Wisconsin.

Education: Rufus King High School 2002; BA in Political Science, Alcorn State University 2006; MEd Strayer University 2009; EdD Argosy University 2016.

Occupation: Educator; small business owner. Former subcommittee clerk, U.S. House of Representatives; legislative aide, Wisconsin State Senate.

Member: Alcorn State University National Alumni Association (Milwaukee Chapter vice president); Alpha Kappa Alpha Sorority, Inc.; Democratic Party of Wisconsin; Historically Black College/University Alumni United (president); Milwaukee Metropolitan Alliance of Black School Educators; American Federation of Teachers; NAACP; African American Chamber of Commerce of Wisconsin; The Links, Incorporated; The Junior League of Milwaukee.

Former member: College Democrats of America (national membership director, 2005–6); Phi Delta Kappa International; National Education Association; National Council of Negro Women; Girl Scouts of the USA.

Current office: Elected to Assembly since 2018. Committee assignments 2023: Agriculture; Education; Tourism.

Contact: rep.myers@legis.wisconsin.gov; 608-237-9112; 888-534-0012 (toll free); 262-297-3291 (district); Room 6 North, State Capitol, PO Box 8953, Madison, WI 53708-8953.

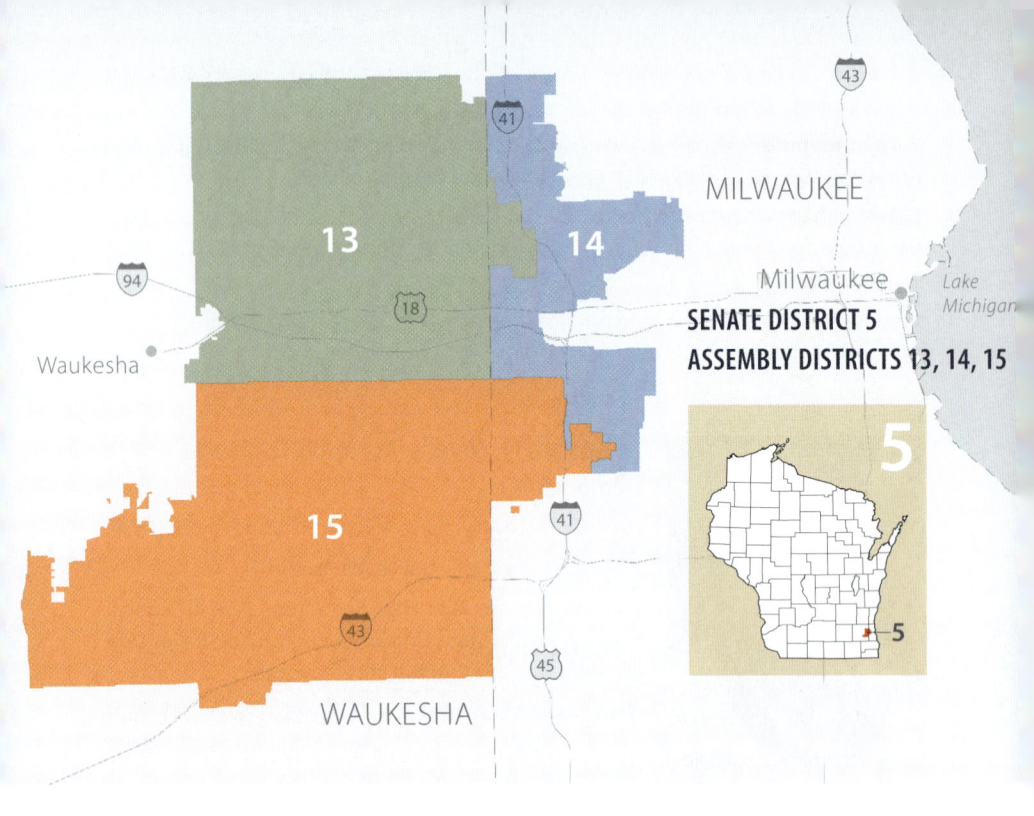

Rob Hutton, Senate District 5
Republican

Personal: Born Milwaukee, Wisconsin, April 7, 1967; married; 4 children.

Voting address: Brookfield, Wisconsin.

Education: Brookfield East High School 1985; BA in History, University of Wisconsin–Whitewater 1990.

Occupation: 25 years executive and business owner experience.

Previous office: Elected to Waukesha County Board of Supervisors 2005–12; Assembly 2012–18.

Current office: Elected to Senate 2022. Committee assignments 2023: Insurance and Small Business (vice chair); Judiciary and Public Safety; Transportation and Local Government; Universities and Revenue (chair); Joint Review Committee on Criminal Penalties (cochair). Additional appointment: Council on Highway Safety.

Contact: sen.hutton@legis.wisconsin.gov; 608-266-2512; Room 313 South, State Capitol, PO Box 7882, Madison, WI 53707-7882.

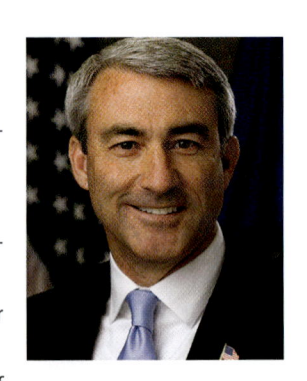

Tom Michalski, Assembly District 13
Republican

Personal: Born Milwaukee, Wisconsin, June 27, 1951; married; 1 child, 2 grandchildren.

Voting address: Elm Grove, Wisconsin.

Education: Greenfield High School 1969; bachelor's degree in Business Administration, University of Wisconsin–Milwaukee 1976.

Occupation: Elm Grove Fire Department since 2006. Former I.T. professional, Marquette University 1976–2006. Served in the U.S. Air Force 1970–1976.

Member: Elmbrook Rotary; Waukesha County Technical College Board of Trustees.

Previous office: Elected to Village of Elm Grove Board of Trustees 2009–present; Waukesha County Board of Supervisors (executive committee member) 2012–present.

Current office: Elected to Assembly 2022. Committee assignments 2023: Colleges and Universities; Government Accountability and Oversight; Local Government; Veterans and Military Affairs; Workforce Development and Economic Opportunities (vice chair).

Contact: rep.michalski@legis.wisconsin.gov; 608-237-9113; 888-534-0013 (toll free); Room 9 West, State Capitol, PO Box 8953, Madison, WI 53708-8953.

Robyn Dorianne Beckley Vining
Assembly District 14
Democrat

Personal: Born Wright Patterson Air Force Base, Ohio, November 11, 1976; married; 2 children.

Voting address: Wauwatosa, Wisconsin.

Education: Attended Westlake High School (Austin, Texas); graduated James Madison High School (Vienna, Virginia) 1995; BA in Psychology and BA in Studio Art, James Madison University 1999; MA in Religion, Trinity Evangelical Divinity School 2002.

Occupation: Small business owner; photographer. Former pastor; church planter; youth minister.

Member: Milwaukee Delegation (chair); Wisconsin Legislative Children's Caucus; Trails Caucus; Reproductive Rights Work Group; Labor Work Group; Climate Work Group; Wisconsin Coalition for Gun Safety; Healthy School Meals for All Coalition; cofounder of organization that combats child sex trafficking.

Current office: Elected to Assembly since 2018. Committee assignments 2023: Children and Families; Family Law; Health, Aging and Long-Term Care; Jobs, Economy and Small Business Development; Mental Health and Substance Abuse Prevention.

Contact: rep.vining@legis.wisconsin.gov; 608-237-9114; 888-534-0014 (toll free); Room 107 North, State Capitol, PO Box 8953, Madison, WI 53708-8953.

Dave Maxey, Assembly District 15
Republican

Personal: Born Oconomowoc, Wisconsin, January 15, 1973; married; 3 children.

Voting address: New Berlin, Wisconsin.

Education: Brookfield East High School 1991; associate degree in Marketing, Waukesha County Technical College 2002; Certificate in Social Media Marketing, Waukesha County Technical College 2017.

Occupation: Served in U.S. Navy 1991–94.

Member: Poplar Creek Church; New Berlin City Council.

Previous office: Elected to New Berlin City Council (president) 2019–present; New Berlin School Board 2008–17 (president 2011–17).

Current office: Elected to Assembly 2022. Committee assignments 2023: Campaigns and Elections (vice chair); Corrections; Local Government; Transportation.

Contact: rep.maxey@legis.wisconsin.gov; 608-237-9115; 888-534-0015 (toll free); Room 412 North, State Capitol, PO Box 8953, Madison, WI 53708-8953.

SENATE DISTRICT 6
ASSEMBLY DISTRICTS 16, 17, 18

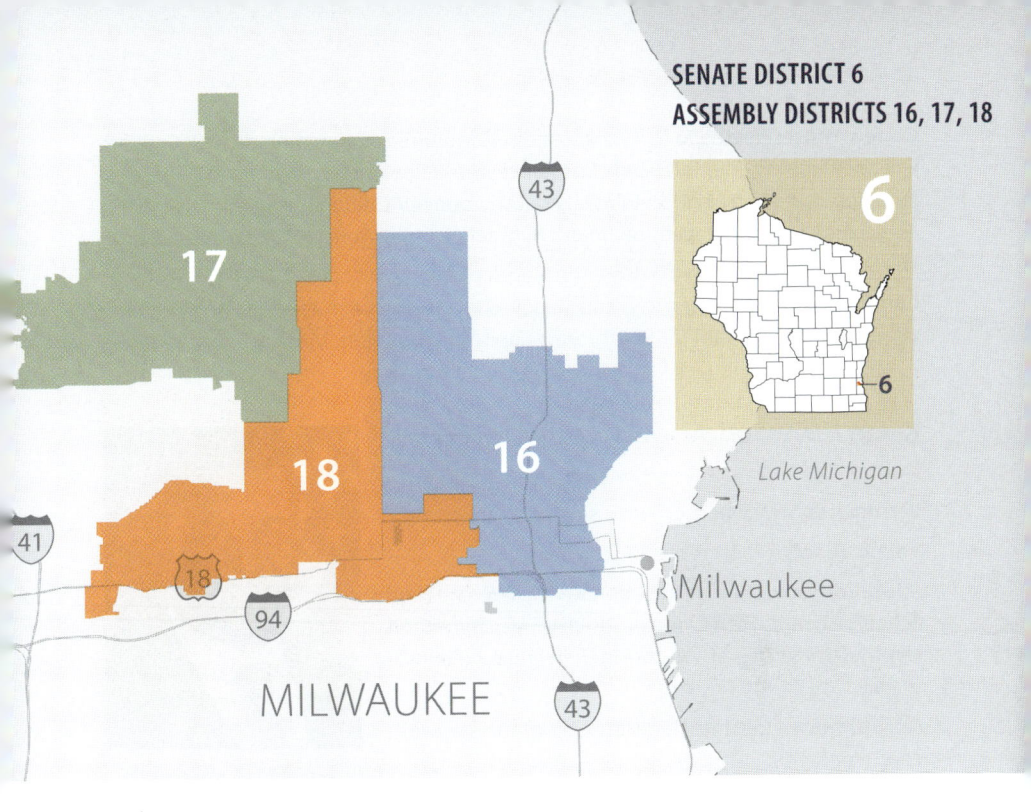

LaTonya Johnson, Senate District 6
Democrat

Personal: Born Somerville, Tennessee, June 22; 1 child.

Voting address: Milwaukee, Wisconsin.

Education: Bay View High School 1990; BS in Criminal Justice, Tennessee State University 1997; attended University of Wisconsin–Milwaukee 1990–92.

Occupation: Full-time legislator. Former family child care provider and owner 2002–12; insurance agent 2000–2; financial employment planner 1997–2000.

Member: American Federation of State, County and Municipal Employees (AFSCME) Wisconsin Child Care Providers Together Local 502 (former president); AFSCME District Council 32 (former vice president); AFSCME People; Emerge Wisconsin, Class of 2012; Milwaukee Democratic Legislative Caucus (former chair); Wisconsin Legislative Black Caucus; University of Wisconsin Population Health Institute (advisory board member); Wisconsin Legislative Children's Caucus (cochair); BLOC (Black Leaders Organizing for Communities) cofounder; College Savings Program Board; NAACP.

Former Member: African American Chamber of Commerce; Wisconsin Women in Government (board member); Coalition of Black Trade Unionists (CBTU); Midwestern Legislative Conference (executive committee member).

Previous office: Elected to Assembly 2012–14.

Current office: Elected to Senate since 2016. Committee assignments 2023: Education; Finance; Housing, Mental Health, Substance Abuse Prevention, Children and Families; Joint Committee on Finance; Joint Legislative Council. Additional appointments: Child Abuse and Neglect Prevention Board; Milwaukee Child Welfare Partnership Council; Wisconsin Center District Board.

Contact: sen.johnson@legis.wisconsin.gov; 608-266-2500; 877-474-2000 (toll free); 414-313-1241 (district); Room 106 South, State Capitol, PO Box 7882, Madison, WI 53707-7882.

Kalan Haywood, Assembly District 16
Democrat

Personal: Born Milwaukee, Wisconsin, June 5, 1999; single.

Voting address: Milwaukee, Wisconsin.

Education: Rufus King International Baccalaureate High School 2017; attended Cardinal Stritch University; attending the University of Wisconsin–Milwaukee (Finance major).

Occupation: Full-time legislator. Former nonprofit consultant.

Member: Milwaukee Metropolitan Sewerage District Board of Directors; Young Elected Officials Network; National Black Caucus of State Legislators; National Caucus of State Legislators (NCSL); City of Milwaukee Black Male Achievement Advisory Council.

Former member: City of Milwaukee Youth Council (president); City of Milwaukee Restorative Justice Advisory Committee (chair); BlackCEO Milwaukee Chapter (vice president); Determined Young Investors (president).

Current office: Elected to Assembly since 2018. Leadership positions: Assistant Minority Leader 2023, 2022; Minority Caucus Sergeant at Arms 2021. Committee assignments 2023: Assembly Organization; Energy and Utilities; Housing and Real Estate; Rules; Transportation; Joint Committee on Legislative Organization; Joint Legislative Council. Additional appointments: Wisconsin Center District Board; Wisconsin Housing and Economic Development Authority.

Contact: rep.haywood@legis.wisconsin.gov; 608-237-9116; 888-534-0016 (toll free); 608-266-3487 (district); Room 119 North, State Capitol, PO Box 8952, Madison, WI 53708-8952.

Supreme Moore Omokunde, Assembly District 17
Democrat

Personal: Born Milwaukee, Wisconsin, August 22, 1979; single.

Voting address: Milwaukee, Wisconsin.

Education: Riverside University High School (Milwaukee) 1997; attended Marquette University 1997–2000 and University of Wisconsin–Milwaukee.

Occupation: Full-time legislator. Former youth worker, Boys and Girls Club and YMCA; community organizer, Sherman Park Community Association; health care organizer, Citizen Action of Wisconsin.

Member: Milwaukee Area Technical College Board of Directors; Milwaukee City County Task Force on Climate and Economic Equity (cocreator); Democratic Party of Wisconsin; Citizen Action Wisconsin (board member).

Former member: Milwaukee Public Museum Board of Directors; Milwaukee County Human Rights Commission (workgroup member); Public Allies Milwaukee; TRUE Skool Board; 2016 Democratic National Convention (delegate for Bernie Sanders).

Previous office: Elected to Milwaukee County Board of Supervisors 2015–20.

Current office: Elected to Assembly since 2020. Committee assignments 2023: Energy and Utilities; Mental Health and Substance Abuse Prevention; Regulatory Licensing Reform; Transportation.

Contact: rep.mooreomokunde@legis.wisconsin.gov; 608-237-9117; 888-534-0017 (toll free); Room 8 North, State Capitol, PO Box 8953, Madison, WI 53708.

Evan Goyke, Assembly District 18
Democrat

Personal: Born Neenah, Wisconsin, November 24, 1982; married; 1 child.

Voting address: Milwaukee, Wisconsin.

Education: Edgewood High School (Madison) 2001; BA in Political Science, St. John's University (Minnesota) 2005; JD Marquette University Law School 2009.

Occupation: Attorney. Former state public defender.

Member: Historic Concordia Neighborhood Association (former board member); Progressive Community Health Center (former board member); State Bar of Wisconsin; Eagle Scout, Boy Scouts of America; Milwaukee Democratic Delegation (former chair); Milwaukee Young Lawyers Association (former board member).

Former member: American Federation of Teachers Local 4822.

Current office: Elected to Assembly since 2012. Committee assignments 2023: Corrections; Finance; Joint Committee on Finance; Joint Legislative Council; Joint Review Committee on Criminal Penalties; Joint Survey Committee on Tax Exemptions.

Contact: rep.goyke@legis.wisconsin.gov; 608-237-9118; 888-534-0018 (toll free); Room 112 North, State Capitol, PO Box 8952, Madison, WI 53708-8952.

SENATE DISTRICT 7
ASSEMBLY DISTRICTS 19, 20, 21

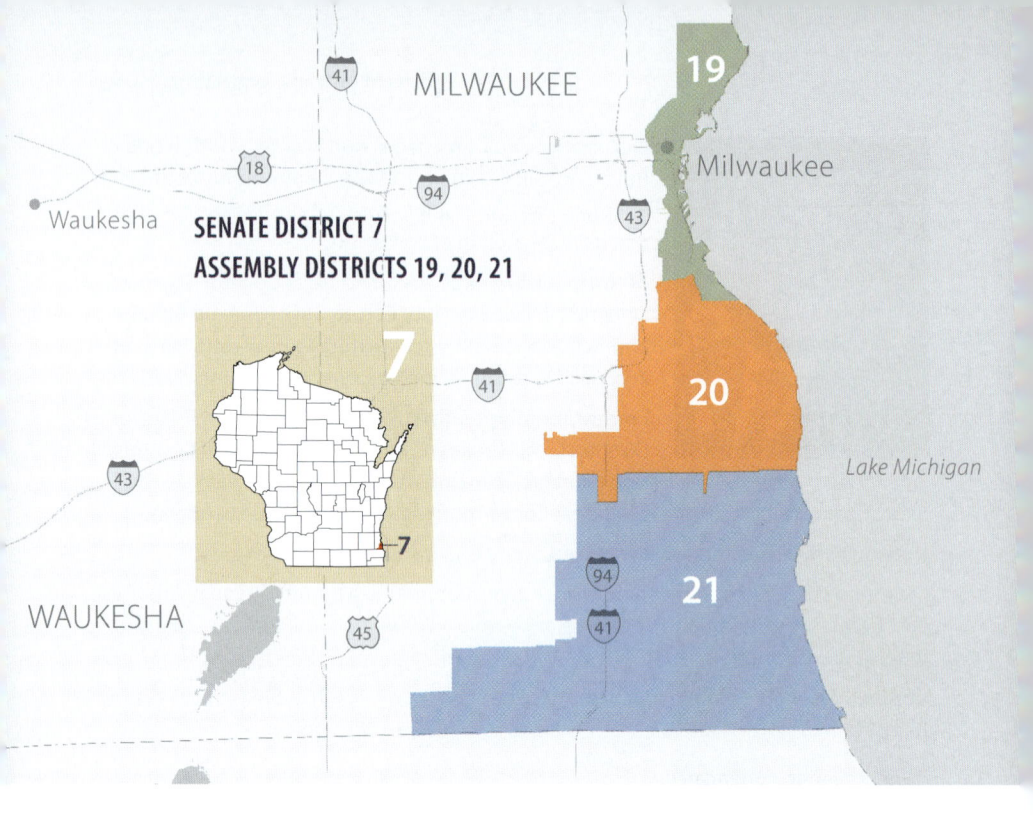

Chris Larson, Senate District 7
Democrat

Personal: Born Milwaukee County, Wisconsin, November 12, 1980; married; 2 children.

Voting address: Milwaukee, Wisconsin.

Education: Thomas More High School 1999; degree in Finance, University of Wisconsin–Milwaukee 2007.

Occupation: Full-time legislator. Former business manager.

Member: ACLU; University of Wisconsin–Milwaukee Alumni Association (former board member); League of Conservation Voters; Bay View Neighborhood Association; Planned Parenthood Advocates of Wisconsin; Sierra Club; South Side Business Club of Milwaukee; Bay View Historical Society; Arbor Day Foundation; TriWisconsin; Badgerland Striders; Bay View Lions Club; Lake Park Friends; MPTV Friends; Voces de la Frontera; Citizen Actions of Wisconsin (board of directors); Milwaukee Turners; Citizen Action of Wisconsin (board member); Climate Power (national board member); Mothers Against Drunk Driving (MADD) (Illinois/Iowa/Wisconsin advisory board); Governor's Bicycle Coordinating Council.

Former member: Airport Area Economic Development Group; Young Elected Officials; Coalition to Save the Hoan Bridge (cofounder); Wisconsin Public Interest Research Group (WISPIRG) campus intern.

Previous office: Elected to Milwaukee County Board of Supervisors 2008–10.

Current office: Elected to Senate since 2010. Leadership positions: Minority Caucus Chair 2023; Minority Leader 2013. Committee assignments 2023: Administrative Rules; Education; Universities and Revenue; Joint Committee for Review of Administrative Rules; Joint Committee on Information Policy and Technology. Additional appointment: Educational Communications Board.

Contact: sen.larson@legis.wisconsin.gov; 608-266-7505; 800-361-5487 (toll free); Room 20 South, State Capitol, PO Box 7882, Madison, WI 53707-7882.

Ryan Clancy, Assembly District 19
Democrat

Personal: Born January 9, 1977; married; 5 children.

Voting address: Milwaukee, Wisconsin.

Education: Nicolet High School 1995; BA in English, Certification in Secondary Education, Beloit College 2000; MA in Negotiation, Conflict Resolution, and Peacebuilding, California State University–Dominguez Hills 2012.

Occupation: Co-owner, Bounce Milwaukee; volunteer legal observer and team leader, ACLU; volunteer, Mass Care/Sheltering, American Red Cross. Former teacher, Milwaukee Public Schools; counselor and counselor trainer, Legacy International; owner, Trounce Records; volunteer, United States Peace Corps.

Member: Bay View Neighborhood Association; Democratic Socialists of America; Milwaukee DSA; Citizen Action; Working Families Party; Leaders Igniting Transformation (board member); ACLU of Wisconsin; Voces de la Frontera; Main Street Alliance; Progressive Restaurants and Activists of Wisconsin Network (PRAWN); Restaurants Advancing Industry Standards in Employment (RAISE); Democratic Party of Wisconsin (delegate).

Former member: Peace Action of Wisconsin (board member).

Previous office: Elected to Milwaukee County Board of Supervisors, District 4, 2020–present.

Current office: Elected to Assembly 2022. Committee assignments 2023: Audit; Corrections; Government Accountability and Oversight; Housing and Real Estate; Joint Legislative Audit Committee.

Contact: rep.clancy@legis.wisconsin.gov; 608-237-9119; 888-534-0019 (toll free); Room 21 North, State Capitol, PO Box 8952, Madison, WI 53708-8952.

Christine Sinicki, Assembly District 20
Democrat

Personal: Born Milwaukee, Wisconsin, March 28, 1960; married; 2 children.

Voting address: Milwaukee, Wisconsin.

Education: Bay View High School; Bowhay Institute Fellow, La Follette School, University of Wisconsin–Madison 2001; Flemming Fellow, Center for Policy Alternatives 2003.

Occupation: Former small business manager.

Member: Legislative Democrats Labor Workgroup (founder, cochair 2021–22); Respite Care Association of Wisconsin (board member); Bay View Historical Society; Bay View Neighborhood Association; American Council of Young Political Leaders (delegate to Israel and Palestine, 2001); Major, Wisconsin Wing, Civil Air Patrol Legislative Squadron (official Auxiliary of the U.S. Air Force).

Former member: Heroes for Healthcare 2021–23; State Committee to Celebrate the Centennial Anniversary of Wisconsin's Ratification 2019; delegate to U.S. President Electoral College 2000; State Minimum Wage Council (governor's appointee) 2005; Assembly Democratic Task Force on Working Families (chair) 2003; State Assembly Milwaukee Caucus (chair 2005, 2003); Milwaukee Committee on Domestic Violence and Sexual Assault; Milwaukee City Council Parents and Teachers Association.

Previous office: Elected to Milwaukee School Board 1991–98.

Current office: Elected to Assembly since 1998. Leadership positions: Minority Caucus Sergeant at Arms 2019, 2017; Minority Caucus Secretary 2001. Committee assignments 2023: Labor and Integrated Employment; Regulatory Licensing Reform; State Affairs; Veterans and Military Affairs; Workforce Development and Economic Opportunities. Additional appointment: State Fair Park Board.

Contact: rep.sinicki@legis.wisconsin.gov; 608-237-9120; 888-534-0020 (toll free); Room 114 North, State Capitol, PO Box 8953, Madison, WI 53708-8953.

Jessie Rodriguez, Assembly District 21
Republican

Personal: Born Puerto el Triunfo, El Salvador, July 5, 1977; married.

Voting address: Oak Creek, Wisconsin.

Education: Alexander Hamilton High School (Milwaukee) 1996; BA Marquette University 2002.

Occupation: Full-time legislator. Former analyst for a supermarket company; outreach coordinator for a nonprofit.

Member: Wisconsin Center District Board.

Current office: Elected to Assembly in November 2013 special election. Reelected since 2014. Leadership positions: Majority Caucus Secretary 2019, 2017, 2015. Committee assignments 2023: Finance; Joint Committee on Finance. Additional appointments: State Fair Park Board; Wisconsin Center District Board.

Contact: rep.rodriguez@legis.wisconsin.gov; 608-237-9121; 888-534-0021 (toll free); Room 306 East, State Capitol, PO Box 8953, Madison, WI 53708-8953.

SENATE DISTRICT 8
ASSEMBLY DISTRICTS 22, 23, 24

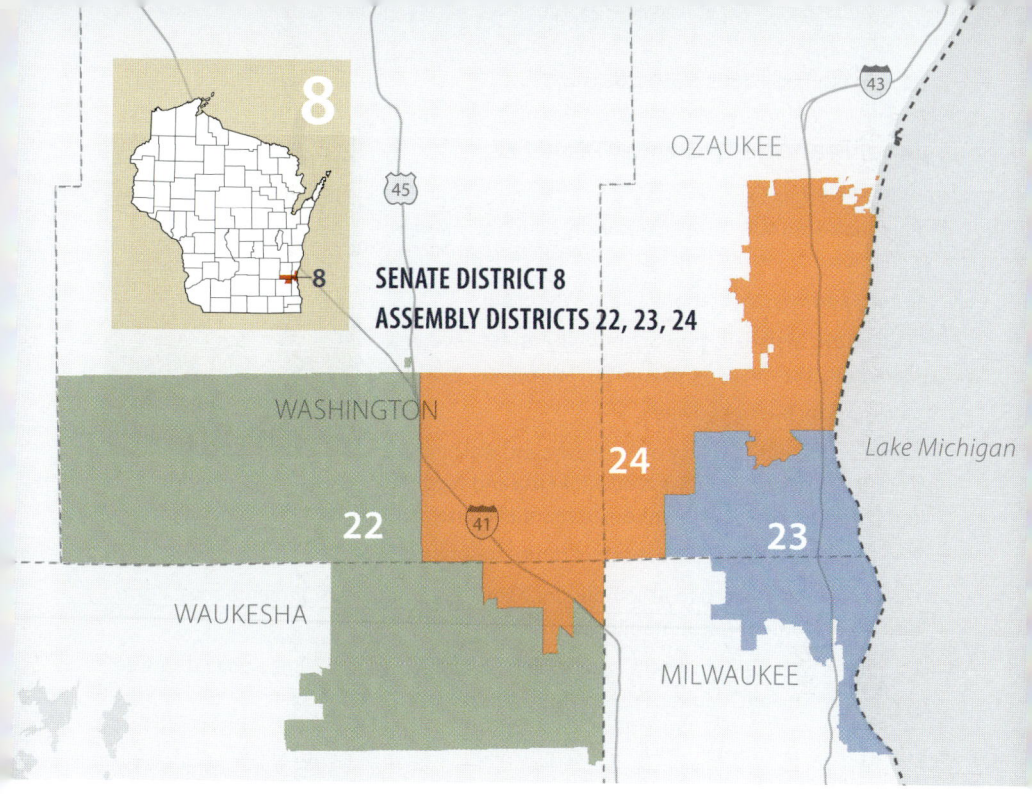

Dan Knodl, Senate District 8
Republican

Personal: Born Milwaukee, Wisconsin, December 14, 1958; 4 children, 6 grandchildren.

Voting address: Germantown, Wisconsin.

Education: Menomonee Falls East High School 1977; attended University of Wisconsin–Madison.

Occupation: Land developer.

Member: Ozaukee Washington Land Trust; Pike Lake Sportsmen's Club; Pike Lake Protection District (member 2000–present, secretary 2010–17, chair, 2017–19); Menomonee Falls Optimist Club; Knights of Columbus; St. Boniface Parish.

Previous office: Elected to Washington County Board 2006–08; Assembly 2008–22 (resigned 5/3/23).

Current office: Elected to Senate in April 2023 special election. Committee assignments 2023: Economic Development and Technical Colleges; Judiciary and Public Safety; Licensing, Constitution and Federalism; Shared Revenue, Elections and Consumer Protection (chair). Additional appointment: State Fair Park Board.

Contact: sen.knodl@legis.wisconsin.gov; 608-266-5830; Room 108 South, State Capitol, PO Box 7882, Madison, WI 53707-7882.

Janel Brandtjen, Assembly District 22
Republican

Personal: Born Milwaukee, Wisconsin, March 27; married; 2 children.

Voting address: Menomonee Falls, Wisconsin.

Education: Marshall High School; BBA in Finance and Marketing, University of Wisconsin–Milwaukee 1988.

Occupation: Business owner.

Member: Republican Party of Waukesha and Washington Counties; Republican Women of Waukesha and Washington Counties; NRA (life member); Immanuel Lutheran Church.

Previous office: Elected Waukesha County supervisor 2008–16.

Current office: Elected to Assembly since 2014. Committee assignments 2023: Corrections; Government Accountability and Oversight.

Contact: rep.brandtjen@legis.wisconsin.gov; 608-237-9122; 888-534-0022 (toll free); Room 4 West, State Capitol, PO Box 8952, Madison, WI 53708-8952.

Deb Andraca, Assembly District 23
Democrat

Personal: Born Springfield, Massachusetts, April 10, 1970; married; 2 children.

Voting address: Whitefish Bay, Wisconsin.

Education: BA in Political Science and Public Relations, Syracuse University 1992; MA in Political Management, George Washington University 1996; completed teacher licensure program, Alverno College 2018.

Occupation: Substitute teacher. Former summer school math teacher, Bruce Guadalupe Community School; substitute teacher, Whitefish Bay School District; communications director and lobbyist, Environmental Law and Policy Center of the Midwest; vice president, FleishmanHillard International Communications; executive assistant, Solar Energy Industries Association.

Member: National Caucus of Environmental Legislators; Great Lakes-St. Lawrence Legislative Caucus.

Former member: Cumberland Elementary School PTO (president); Advocates for Education of Whitefish Bay (board member); Girl Scout Leader troops 1586 and 1305; Urban Ecology Center (fundraiser chair).

Current office: Elected to Assembly since 2020. Committee assignments 2023: Education; Energy and Utilities; Forestry, Parks and Outdoor Recreation; Veterans and Military Affairs.

Contact: rep.andraca@legis.wisconsin.gov; 608-237-9123; 888-534-0023 (toll free); Room 109 North, State Capitol, PO Box 8952, Madison, WI 53708-8952.

Assembly District 24

This office was vacant at the time of publication. For complete information on the representative for this district, visit: https://docs.legis.wisconsin.gov/2023/legislators/assembly

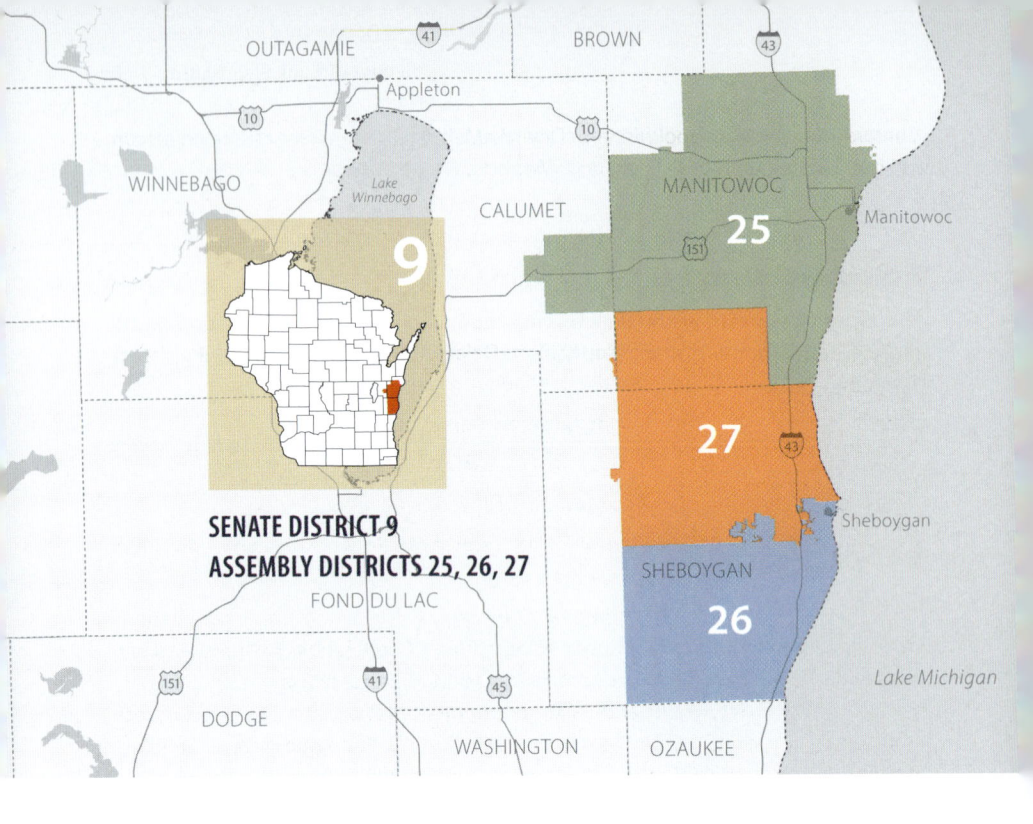

Devin LeMahieu, Senate District 9
Republican

Personal: Born Sheboygan, Wisconsin, August 8, 1972; single.

Voting address: Oostburg, Wisconsin.

Education: Sheboygan County Christian High School 1991; BA in Business Administration and Political Science, Dordt College (Sioux Center, Iowa) 1995.

Occupation: Publisher/owner, Lakeshore Weekly.

Member: Oostburg Chamber of Commerce; Sheboygan County Chamber of Commerce; Manitowoc County Chamber of Commerce; Bethel Orthodox Presbyterian Church (deacon); NRA (life member).

Previous office: Elected Sheboygan County Board supervisor 2006–15.

Current office: Elected to Senate since 2014. Leadership positions: Majority Leader 2023, 2021. Committee assignments 2023: Senate Organization (chair); Joint Committee on Employment Relations; Joint Committee on Legislative Organization; Joint Legislative Council. Additional appointments: Wisconsin Aerospace Authority Board; Wisconsin Center District Board.

Contact: sen.lemahieu@legis.wisconsin.gov; 608-266-2056, 888-295-8750 (toll free);

senatordevin.com; Facebook: Senator Devin LeMahieu; Twitter: @senatordevin; Room 211 South, State Capitol, PO Box 7882, Madison, WI 53707-7882.

Paul Tittl, Assembly District 25
Republican

Personal: Born Delavan, Wisconsin, November 23, 1961; married; 2 children, 3 grandchildren.

Voting address: Manitowoc, Wisconsin.

Education: Lincoln High (Manitowoc) 1980.

Occupation: Business owner.

Member: Faith Church Manitowoc (deacon); Lions Club of Manitowoc; NRA.

Former member: Eagles Manitowoc; Manitowoc County Home Builders Association; Economic Development Corporation; Wastewater Treatment Facility Board; Manitowoc Crime Prevention Committee; Community Development Authority; Safety Traffic and Parking Commission; Wisconsin Utility Tax Association 2009–13; Wisconsin Counties Association (WCA) Taxation and Finance Steering Committee 2010–13; WCA Judicial and Public Safety Steering Committee 2010–13.

Previous office: Elected to Manitowoc City Council 2004–8 (president 2006–7); Manitowoc County Board of Supervisors 2006–13 (chair 2010–12).

Current office: Elected to Assembly since 2012. Committee assignments 2023: Campaigns and Elections; Corrections; Energy and Utilities; Forestry, Parks and Outdoor Recreation; Mental Health and Substance Abuse Prevention (chair); Sporting Heritage (vice chair); Veterans and Military Affairs.

Contact: rep.tittl@legis.wisconsin.gov; 608-237-9125; 888-529-0025 (toll free); Room 218 North, State Capitol, PO Box 8953, Madison, WI 53708-8953.

Terry Katsma, Assembly District 26
Republican

Personal: Born Sheboygan, Wisconsin, April 23, 1958; married; 3 children, 6 grandchildren.

Voting address: Oostburg, Wisconsin.

Education: Sheboygan County Christian High School 1976; BA in Business Administration, Dordt College (Sioux Center, Iowa) 1980; MBA Marquette University 1985.

Occupation: Full-time legislator. Former community bank president and CEO.

Member: Oostburg State Bank Board of Directors (former president and CEO); Oostburg

Chamber of Commerce (former president-elect); Oostburg Christian Reformed Church; Random Lake Area Chamber of Commerce; Republican Party of Sheboygan County; NRA; Sheboygan County Chamber of Commerce; YMCA of Sheboygan County Board of Managers.

Former member: Trinity Christian College Board of Trustees (Palos Heights, Illinois—treasurer); Dordt College Board of Trustees (vice chair); Sheboygan County Christian High School (board president); Oostburg Christian School Board (secretary); Oostburg Community Education Foundation; Oostburg Kiwanis Club (president); Workbound, Inc. (president).

Current office: Elected to Assembly since 2014. Committee assignments 2023: Finance (vice chair); Financial Institutions; Joint Committee on Finance (vice chair).

Contact: rep.katsma@legis.wisconsin.gov; 608-237-9126; 888-529-0026 (toll free); Room 304 East, State Capitol, PO Box 8952, Madison, WI 53708-8952.

Amy Binsfeld, Assembly District 27
Republican

Personal: Born Sheboygan, Wisconsin, October 5, 1976; married; 2 children.

Voting address: Sheboygan, Wisconsin.

Education: Manitowoc Lutheran High School 1995; associate degree in Paralegal Studies, Lakeshore Technical College 2013.

Occupation: Full-time legislator. Formerly at Bitter Neumann 1996–2011, 2014–22; Olsen Kloet Gunderson & Conway 2012–14.

Member: St. Paul's Evangelical Lutheran Church of Howards Grove (audiovisual committee member); Westwood Condo Association (vice chair).

Current office: Elected to Assembly 2022. Committee assignments 2023: Education; Family Law (vice chair); Jobs, Economy and Small Business Development; Ways and Means. Additional appointment: State Capitol and Executive Residence Board.

Contact: rep.binsfeld@legis.wisconsin.gov; 608-237-9127; 888-529-0027 (toll free); Room 418 North, State Capitol, PO Box 8952, Madison, WI 53708-8952.

SENATE DISTRICT 10
ASSEMBLY DISTRICTS 28, 29, 30

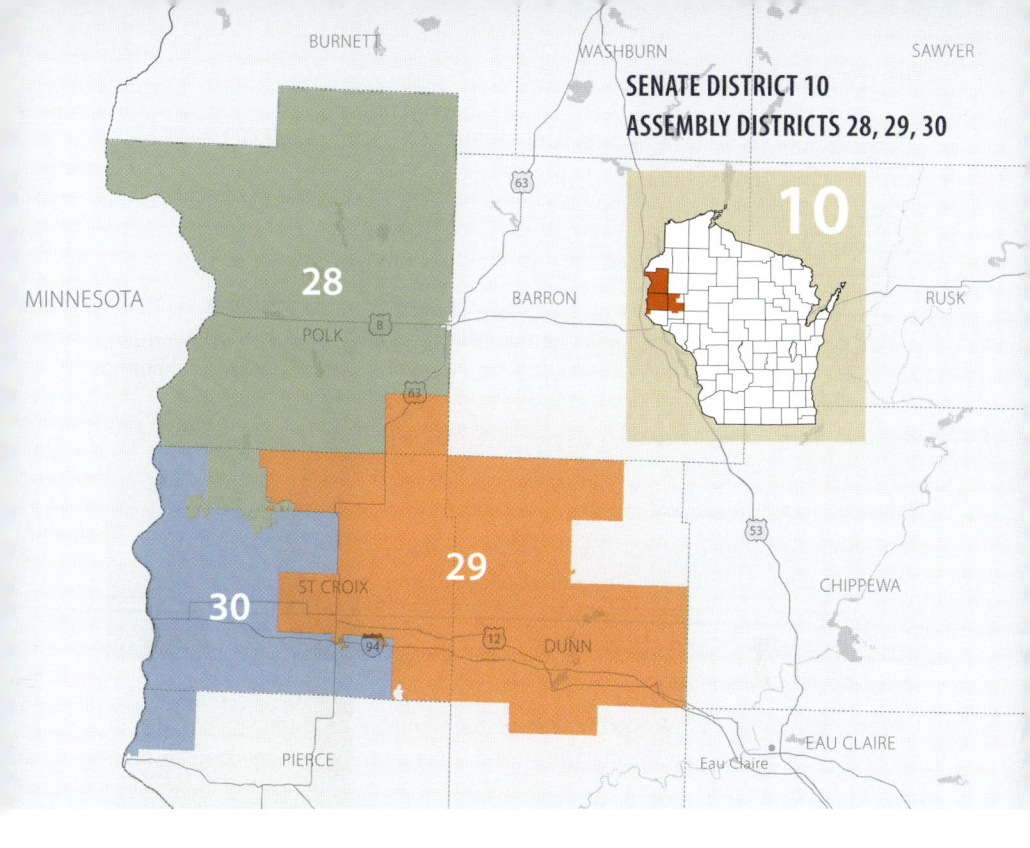

Rob Stafsholt, Senate District 10
Republican

Personal: Lifelong resident of St. Croix County, Wisconsin; 1 child.

Voting address: New Richmond, Wisconsin.

Education: New Richmond Public Schools; attended University of Wisconsin–Eau Claire and University of Wisconsin–River Falls.

Occupation: Farmer; owner of waste disposal company; owner of residential rental and real estate investment company; volunteer coach for the New Richmond-Somerset High School trap team. Former co-owner of a salad and food dressings manufacturing and sales company; mortgage loan originator.

Member: Farm Bureau; NRA (life member); New Richmond Chamber of Commerce.

Former member: Erin Prairie Township Planning Commission; Wisconsin Bear Hunters' Association (board of directors); Wisconsin Association of Mortgage Brokers.

Previous office: Elected to Assembly 2016–18.

Current office: Elected to Senate 2020. Committee assignments 2023: Economic Development and Technical Colleges (vice chair); Financial Institutions and Sporting Heritage (chair); Housing, Rural Issues and Forestry; Additional appointments: Small Business Environmental Council; Sporting Heritage Council.

Contact: sen.stafsholt@legis.wisconsin.gov; 608-266-7745; Room 15 South, State Capitol, PO Box 7882, Madison, WI 53707-7882.

Gae Magnafici, Assembly District 28
Republican

Personal: Born Amery, Wisconsin, July 14, 1952; married; 2 children, 3 grandchildren.

Voting address: Dresser, Wisconsin.

Education: Amery High School 1970; associate degree in Applied Science, Sauk Valley Community College (Dixon, Illinois) 1982.

Occupation: Small business owner. Former mental health technician; registered nurse.

Current office: Elected to Assembly since 2018. Committee assignments 2023: Health, Aging and Long-Term Care; Mental Health and Substance Abuse Prevention; Tourism (chair).

Contact: rep.magnafici@legis.wisconsin.gov; 608-237-9128; 888-529-0028 (toll free); Room 221 North, State Capitol, PO Box 8953, Madison, WI 53708-8953.

Clint Moses, Assembly District 29
Republican

Personal: Born Menomonie, Wisconsin, April 10, 1976; married; 4 children.

Voting address: Menomonie, Wisconsin.

Education: Menomonie High School 1995; BA in Psychology, University of Wisconsin–Stout 1999; BS in Human Biology, Northwestern College of Chiropractic 2001; Doctor of Chiropractic, Northwestern College of Chiropractic 2003.

Occupation: Chiropractor; small business owner; farmer.

Member: Menomonie Rotary Club (former president); Menomonie Chamber of Commerce; Wisconsin Farm Bureau.

Former member: Community Foundation of Dunn County (board president); Colfax Health & Rehabilitation Board; NRA; Boy Scouts of America (Eagle Scout and board member for the Tall Oaks District); School District of the Menomonie Area (board clerk).

Current office: Elected to the Assembly since 2020. Committee assignments 2023:

Agriculture; Colleges and Universities; Forestry, Parks and Outdoor Recreation; Health, Aging and Long-Term Care (chair); Rural Development; State Affairs.

Contact: rep.moses@legis.wisconsin.gov; 608-237-9129; 888-529-0029 (toll free); Room 12 West, State Capitol, PO Box 8953, Madison, WI 53708-8953.

Shannon Zimmerman, Assembly District 30
Republican

Personal: Born Madison, Wisconsin, March 15, 1972; married; 2 children.

Voting address: Town of Clifton, Wisconsin.

Education: Attended Augusta High School; Chippewa Valley Technical College; University of Wisconsin–Milwaukee.

Occupation: Founder and CEO, language translation company; entrepreneur, started numerous Wisconsin businesses.

Former member: University of Wisconsin–River Falls Foundation Board; University of Wisconsin–River Falls Chancellor's Advisory Committee; Rotary; Department of Workforce Development Board.

Current office: Elected to Assembly since 2016. Committee assignments 2023: Finance; Joint Committee on Finance; Joint Committee on Information Policy and Technology (cochair).

Contact: rep.zimmerman@legis.wisconsin.gov; 608-237-9130; 888-529-0030 (toll free); Room 324 East, State Capitol, PO Box 8953, Madison, WI 53708-8953.

SENATE DISTRICT 11
ASSEMBLY DISTRICTS 31, 32, 33

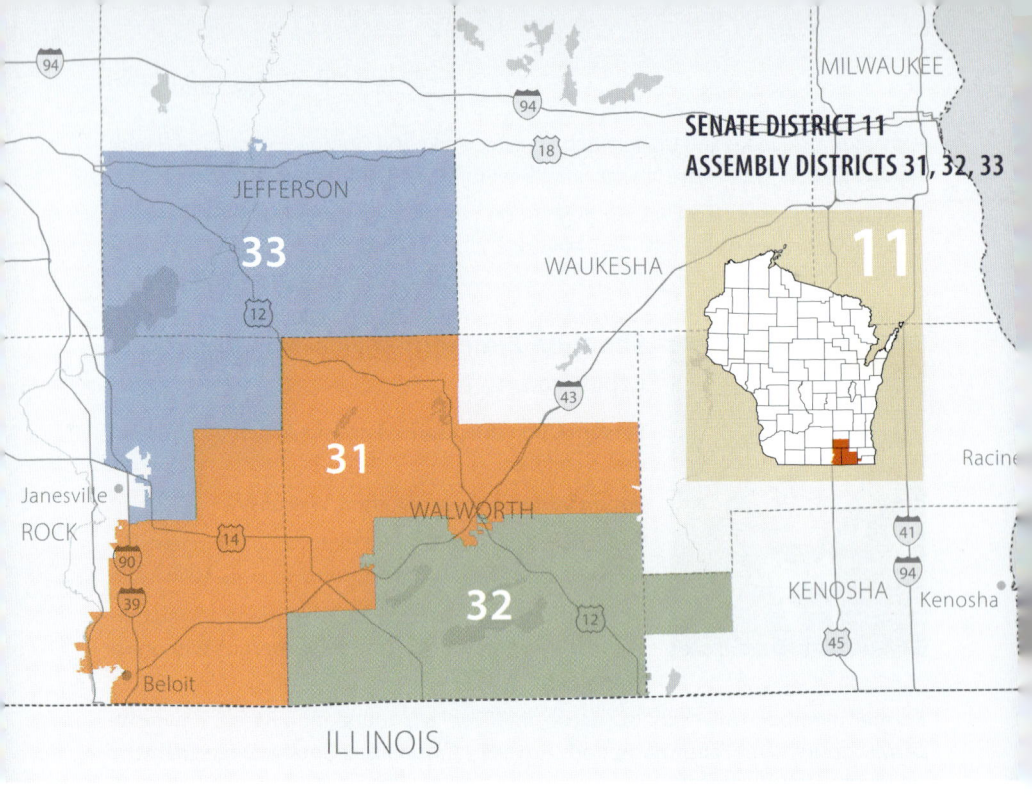

Stephen L. Nass, Senate District 11
Republican

Personal: Born Whitewater, Wisconsin, October 7, 1952.

Voting address: Whitewater, Wisconsin.

Education: Whitewater High School; BS University of Wisconsin–Whitewater 1978; MSEd in School Business Management, University of Wisconsin–Whitewater 1990.

Occupation: Owner, rental property business. Former payroll benefits analyst and information analyst/negotiator. Member of Wisconsin Air National Guard (retired, CMSgt, 33 years of service), served in Middle East in Operations Desert Shield and Desert Storm.

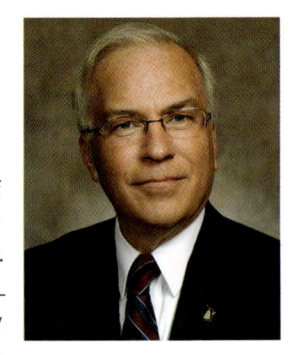

Member: American Legion; VFW.

Previous office: Elected to Whitewater City Council 1977–81; University of Wisconsin–Whitewater Board of Visitors 1979–89; Assembly 1990–2012.

Current office: Elected to Senate since 2014. Committee assignments 2023: Administrative Rules (chair); Education; Labor, Regulatory Reform, Veterans and Military Affairs (vice chair); Universities and Revenue; Joint Committee for Review of Administrative Rules (cochair). Additional appointment: Midwestern Higher Education Commission.

Contact: sen.nass@legis.wisconsin.gov; 608-266-2635; Room 10 South, State Capitol, PO Box 7882, Madison, WI 53707-7882.

Ellen Schutt, Assembly District 31
Republican

Personal: Born Janesville, Wisconsin, October 16, 1995; married.

Education: Delavan-Darien High School 2014; BA in Political Science, University of Wisconsin–Madison 2017.

Occupation: Former legislative staff member.

Member: Wisconsin Farm Bureau; Clinton Community Historical Society; Republican Party of Rock County; Walworth County Fair (lifetime member).

Current office: Elected to Assembly 2022. Committee assignments 2023: Agriculture; Colleges and Universities; Criminal Justice and Public Safety (vice chair); Health, Aging and Long-Term Care; Transportation; Joint Committee on Information Policy and Technology.

Contact: rep.schutt@legis.wisconsin.gov; 608-237-9131; 888-529-0031 (toll free); Room 316 North, State Capitol, PO Box 8953, Madison, WI 53708-8953.

Tyler August, Assembly District 32
Republican

Personal: Born Wisconsin, January 26, 1983; single.

Voting address: Lake Geneva, Wisconsin.

Education: Big Foot High School 2001; attended University of Wisconsin–Eau Claire and University of Wisconsin–Madison; completed 2012 Emerging Leader Program at University of Virginia Darden School of Business.

Occupation: Full-time legislator.

Member: Republican Party of Wisconsin (former board member); First Congressional District Republican Party (former chair); Republican Party of Walworth County (former chair, vice chair); NRA (life member).

Current office: Elected to Assembly since 2010. Leadership positions: Majority Leader 2023; Speaker Pro Tempore 2021, 2019, 2017, 2015, 2013. Committee assignments 2023: Assembly Organization (vice chair); Employment Relations; Rules (chair); Joint Committee on Employment Relations; Joint Legislative Organization; Joint Legislative Council; Joint Survey Committee on Retirement Systems (cochair); Joint Survey Committee on Tax Exemptions (cochair).

Contact: rep.august@legis.wisconsin.gov; 608-237-9132; 888-529-0032 (toll free); Room 115 West, State Capitol, PO Box 8952, Madison, WI 53708-8952.

Scott Johnson, Assembly District 33
Republican

Personal: Born Elgin, Illinois, February 12, 1954; married; 2 children, 1 grandchild.

Voting address: Jefferson, Wisconsin.

Education: Milton High School 1972; BS in Agricultural Economics, University of Wisconsin–Madison 1977; attended master's program University of Wisconsin–Whitewater School of Business Finance 1998; graduate of University of Wisconsin Extension Leadership Wisconsin.

Occupation: Farmer; farm consultant; school bus driver. Former sales and marketing for Monsanto and Ralston Purina (agricultural).

Member: Delta Theta Sigma Educational Foundation (cofounder and former president); Jefferson County Soil Builders; St. Luke's Church.

Previous office: Elected to Fort Atkinson School Board (president, vice president, treasurer, clerk) 1998–2014.

Current office: Elected to Assembly 2022. Committee assignments 2023: Colleges and Universities; Consumer Protection (vice chair); Local Government; Transportation.

Contact: rep.johnson@legis.wisconsin.gov; 608-237-9133; 888-529-0033 (toll free); Room 109 West, State Capitol, PO Box 8952, Madison, WI 53708-8952.

SENATE DISTRICT 12
ASSEMBLY DISTRICTS 34, 35, 36

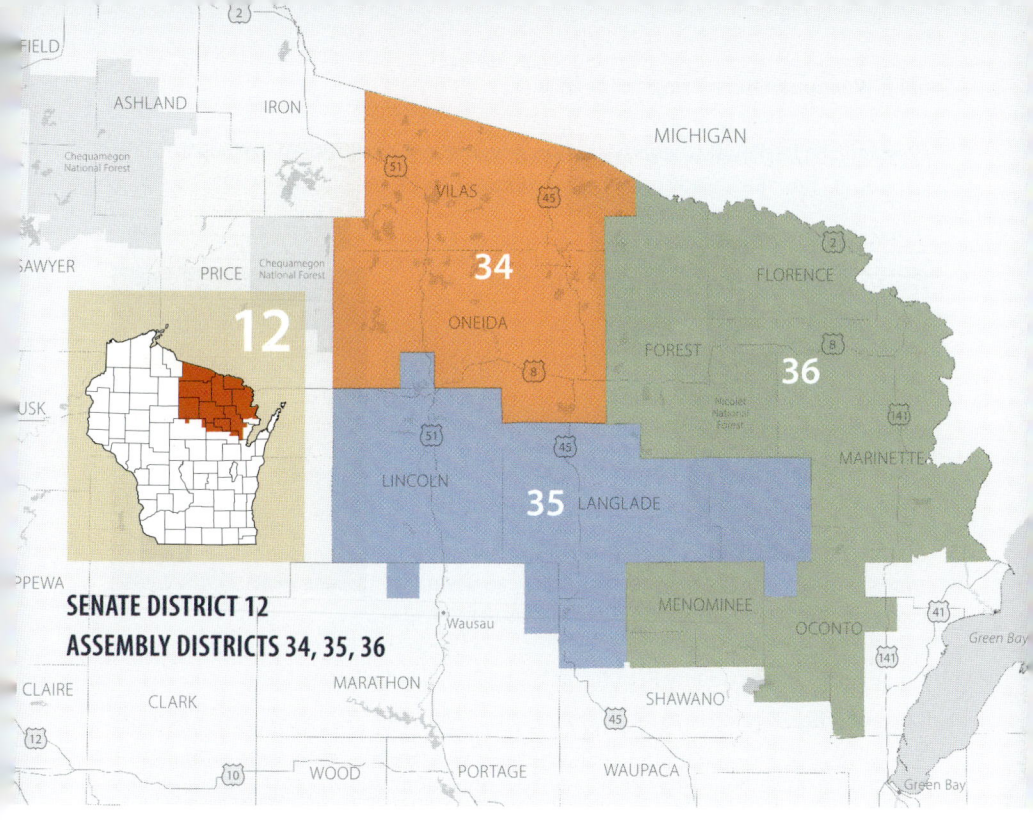

Mary J. Felzkowski, Senate District 12
Republican

Personal: Born Tomahawk, Wisconsin, September 25, 1963; married; 5 children, 4 grandchildren.

Voting address: Tomahawk, Wisconsin.

Education: Tomahawk High School 1981; BS in Finance and Economics, University of Wisconsin–River Falls 1986.

Occupation: Insurance agency owner.

Member: Tomahawk Main Street, Inc. (former president); Tomahawk Regional Chamber of Commerce; Tomahawk Child Care (former president); NRA (life member); Professional Insurance Agents of Wisconsin (former board member, secretary, treasurer, vice president, president, national director).

Former member: National Alliance for Insurance Education and Research (board member).

Previous office: Elected to Assembly 2012–18.

Current office: Elected to Senate 2020. Leadership positions: Assistant Majority Leader 2019. Committee assignments 2023: Finance; Financial Institutions and Sporting Heritage (vice chair); Health; Insurance and Small Business (chair); Joint Committee on Finance; Joint Legislative Council. Additional appintment: Small Business Regulatory Review Board.

Contact: sen.felzkowski@legis.wisconsin.gov; 608-266-2509; Room 415 South, State Capitol, PO Box 7882, Madison, WI 53707-7882.

Rob Swearingen, Assembly District 34
Republican

Personal: Born Oneida County, Wisconsin, July 23, 1963; married; 2 children.

Voting address: Rhinelander, Wisconsin.

Education: Rhinelander High School 1981.

Occupation: Restaurant owner and operator.

Member: Tavern League of Wisconsin (former president, zone vice president, district director); American Beverage Licensees (former member, board of directors); Oneida County Tavern League (former president, vice president); Rhinelander Chamber of Commerce; Oneida County Republican Party; Rhinelander Rotary Club.

Current office: Elected to Assembly since 2012. Committee assignments 2023: Forestry, Parks and Outdoor Recreation; State Affairs (chair); Tourism (vice chair); Joint Survey Committee on Retirement Systems; Joint Survey Committee on Tax Exemptions. Additional appointment: Building Commission.

Contact: rep.swearingen@legis.wisconsin.gov; 608-237-9134; 888-534-0034 (toll free); Room 123 West, State Capitol, PO Box 8953, Madison, WI 53708-8953.

Calvin Callahan, Assembly District 35
Republican

Personal: Born Wausau, Wisconsin, March 2, 1999; single.

Voting address: Tomahawk, Wisconsin.

Occupation: Full-time legislator.

Member: Lincoln County Republican Party (chairman 2018–20); Langlade County Republican Party; Marathon County Republican Party; NRA; Somo ATV Club; Somo Fish and Game Club; Wisconsin ATV/UTV Association; Wisconsin Bear Hunters Association; Wisconsin Trappers Association.

Previous office: Elected to Lincoln County Board (supervisor) 2018–present; Town of Wilson Board (supervisor) 2019–21.

Current office: Elected to Assembly since 2020. Committee assignments 2023: Consumer Protection (chair); Corrections; Forestry, Parks and Outdoor Recreation (vice chair); Insurance (vice chair); Labor and Integrated Employment; Sporting Heritage; State Affairs; Ways and Means.

Contact: rep.callahan@legis.wisconsin.gov; 608-237-9135; 888-534-0035 (toll free); Room 15 West, State Capitol, PO Box 8952, Madison, WI 53708-8952.

Jeffrey L. Mursau, Assembly District 36
Republican

Personal: Born Oconto Falls, Wisconsin, June 12, 1954; married; 4 children, 11 grandchildren.

Voting address: Crivitz, Wisconsin.

Education: Coleman High School 1972; attended University of Wisconsin Oshkosh.

Occupation: Small business owner; Cellcom agent.

Member: Crivitz Ski Cats waterski team (advisor, former president); Crivitz Lions Club; Crivitz, Wisconsin–Crivitz, Germany Sister City Organization (former director); Wings Over Wisconsin; St. Mary's Catholic Church; Fourth Degree Knights of Columbus; Friends of Governor Thompson State Park; Master Loggers Certifying Board; Governor's Task Force on Broadband Access; State Superintendent's Advisory Council on Rural Schools, Libraries, and Communities; Missing and Murdered Indigenous Women Task Force.

Previous office: Elected Crivitz Village president 1991–2004.

Current office: Elected to Assembly since 2004. Committee assignments 2023: Agriculture; Education; Forestry, Parks and Outdoor Recreation (chair); Sporting Heritage; Tourism. Additional appointments: Council on Forestry; Special Committee on State-Tribal Relations (chair).

Contact: rep.mursau@legis.wisconsin.gov; 608-237-9136; 888-534-0036 (toll free); Room 113 West, State Capitol, PO Box 8953, Madison, WI 53708-8953.

SENATE DISTRICT 13
ASSEMBLY DISTRICTS 37, 38, 39

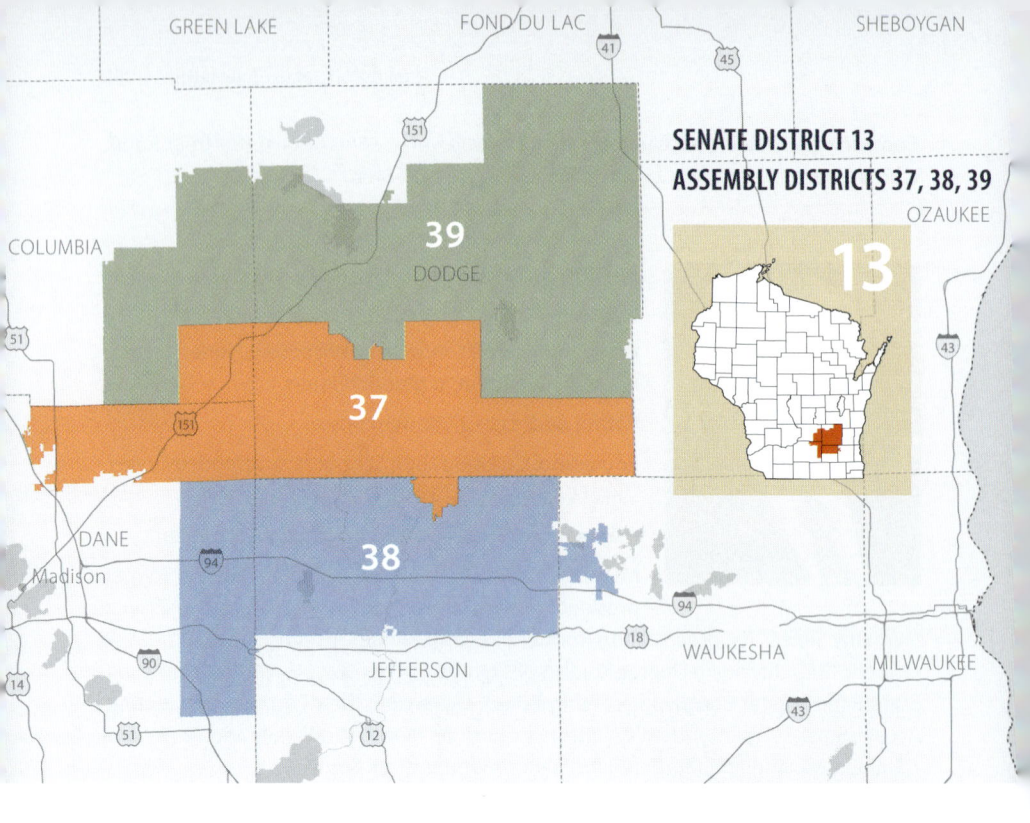

John Jagler, Senate District 13
Republican

Personal: Born Louisville, Kentucky, November 4, 1969; married; 3 children.

Voting address: Watertown, Wisconsin.

Education: Oak Creek High School 1987; Trans-American School of Broadcasting (Madison) 1989; attended University of Wisconsin–Parkside 1987–88.

Occupation: Realtor; owner, family-run natural dog treat company; owner, communications consulting company. Former radio morning show host, news anchor; communications director for Assembly Speaker Jeff Fitzgerald.

Member: Honorable Order of Kentucky Colonels; Watertown Elks Lodge #666; Watertown Moose Lodge #830.

Former member: Radio TV News Directors Association; Milwaukee Press Club.

Previous office: Elected to Assembly 2012–20 (resigned 4/23/21).

Current office: Elected to Senate in April 2021 special election. Committee assignments 2023: Education (chair); Housing, Rural Issues and Forestry (vice chair); Insurance and Small Business; Joint Legislative Council. Additional appointments: Agricultural

Education and Workforce Development Council; Committee on School District and School Financial Information Transparency.

Contact: sen.jagler@legis.wisconsin.gov; 608-266-5660; Room 131 South, State Capitol, PO Box 7882, Madison, WI 53708-7882.

William Penterman, Assembly District 37
Republican

Personal: Born Kaukauna, Wisconsin, May 18, 1996; married.

Voting address: Columbus, Wisconsin.

Education: Fox Valley Lutheran High School 2014; BA in Politics and Government, Ripon College 2018.

Occupation: Sergeant in the United States Army Reserve; substitute teacher.

Member: Dodge County Farm Bureau; Columbia County GOP Membership Chair; Columbus Kiwanis Club; Zion Lutheran Church (treasurer); Phi Beta Kappa; NRA; Adopt-A-Highway.

Current office: Elected to Assembly in July 2021 special election. Reelected 2022. Committee assignments 2023: Children and Families; Education; Housing and Real Estate (vice chair); Labor and Integrated Employment (chair); Veterans and Military Affairs. Additional appointment: Historical Society of Wisconsin Board of Curators.

Contact: rep.penterman@legis.wisconsin.gov; 608-237-9137; 888-534-0037 (toll free); Room 207 North, State Capitol, PO Box 8953, Madison, WI 53708-8953.

Barbara Dittrich, Assembly District 38
Republican

Personal: Born Milwaukee, Wisconsin, May 21, 1964; married; 3 children.

Voting address: Oconomowoc, Wisconsin.

Education: Hamilton High School (Sussex) 1982; attended Waukesha County Technical College 1983; attended University of Wisconsin–Milwaukee 1986.

Occupation: Former nonprofit leader (16 years); financial advisor (13 years); small business owner.

Member: Crosspoint Community Church; Wisconsin Legislature Trails Caucus; American Irish State Legislators Caucus; Respite Care Association of Wisconsin (board); Key Ministry (board); Independent Women's Network (chapter co-leader).

Former member: Great Lakes Hemophilia Foundation (board of directors); Christian

Council on Persons with Disabilities (board of directors); Lutheran Homes of Oconomowoc (personnel committee member); St. Catherine of Alexandria (parish council treasurer); Oconomowoc Area Chamber of Commerce (ambassador); National Organization for Rare Disorders (Rare Disease Day ambassador).

Current office: Elected to Assembly since 2018. Committee assignments 2023: Children and Families; Education (vice chair); Health, Aging and Long-Term Care; Insurance (chair); Mental Health and Substance Abuse Prevention (vice chair); Rules; Ways and Means.

Contact: rep.dittrich@legis.wisconsin.gov; 608-237-9138; 888-534-0038 (toll free); Room 317 North, State Capitol, PO Box 8952, Madison, WI 53708-8952.

Mark L. Born, Assembly District 39
Republican

Personal: Born Beaver Dam, Wisconsin, April 14, 1976; married; 1 child.

Voting address: Beaver Dam, Wisconsin.

Education: Beaver Dam High School 1994; BA in Political Science and History, Gustavus Adolphus College (St. Peter, Minnesota) 1998.

Occupation: Full-time legislator. Former corrections supervisor, Dodge County Sheriff's Department.

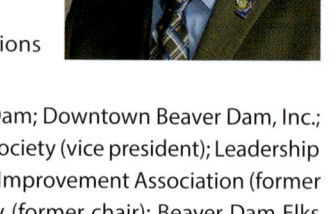

Member: Trinity Church United Methodist Beaver Dam; Downtown Beaver Dam, Inc.; Friends of Horicon Marsh; Dodge County Historical Society (vice president); Leadership Beaver Dam Steering Committee; Beaver Dam Lake Improvement Association (former vice president); Republican Party of Dodge County (former chair); Beaver Dam Elks Lodge 1540.

Previous office: Elected to Beaver Dam Fire and Police Commission 2003–05; Beaver Dam City Council 2005–09.

Current office: Elected to Assembly since 2012. Committee assignments 2023: Audit; Employment Relations; Finance (cochair); Rules; Joint Committee on Employment Relations; Joint Committee on Finance (cochair); Joint Legislative Audit Committee; Joint Legislative Council. Additional appointment: Wisconsin Hospitals and Clinics Authority Board.

Contact: rep.born@legis.wisconsin.gov; 608-237-9139; 888-534-0039 (toll free); Room 308 East, State Capitol, PO Box 8952, Madison, WI 53708-8952.

SENATE DISTRICT 14
ASSEMBLY DISTRICTS 40, 41, 42

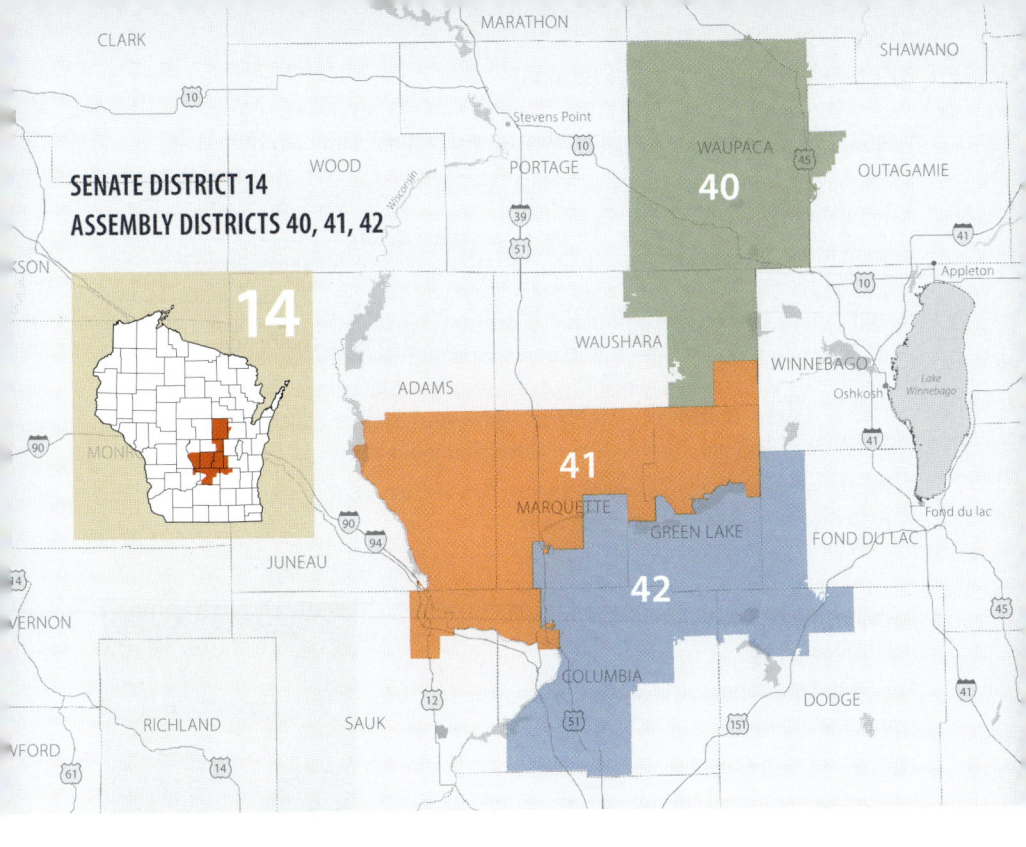

Joan Ballweg, Senate District 14
Republican

Personal: Born Milwaukee, Wisconsin, March 16, 1952; married; 3 children, 3 grandchildren.

Voting address: Markesan, Wisconsin.

Education: Nathan Hale High School (West Allis) 1970; attended University of Wisconsin–Waukesha; BA in Elementary Education, University of Wisconsin–Stevens Point 1974.

Occupation: Co-owner of farm equipment business. Former first grade teacher.

Member: Council of State Governments (chair 2021, 2020); Midwest Legislative Conference (chair 2016); Markesan Chamber of Commerce (former treasurer); Waupun Chamber of Commerce; Green Lake County Farm Bureau; Waupun Memorial Hospital (board of directors, former chair); Agnesian HealthCare Enterprises LLC management committee (former secretary); volunteer, Markesan District Schools; Markesan PTA (former president); Markesan American Field Service Chapter (hosting coordinator, president, former host family, liaison); Wisconsin Legislative Children's Caucus; Agricultural Export Advisory Council.

Former member: FEMA V Regional Advisory Council.

Previous office: Elected to Markesan City Council 1987–91; mayor of Markesan 1991–97; Assembly 2004–18.

Current office: Elected to Senate 2020. Leadership positions: Majority Caucus Vice Chair 2023. Committee assignments 2023: Agriculture and Tourism (chair); Finance; Mental Health, Substance Abuse Prevention, Children and Families; Universities and Revenue; Joint Committee on Finance. Additional appointments: Agricultural Education and Workforce Development Council; Child Abuse and Neglect Prevention Board; Council on Tourism; State Building Commission; Midwestern Higher Education Commission; Wisconsin Commission for the United States Semiquincentennial Commission.

Contact: sen.ballweg@legis.wisconsin.gov; 608-266-0751; Room 409 South, State Capitol, PO Box 7882, Madison, WI 53707-7882.

Kevin David Petersen, Assembly District 40
Republican

Personal: Born Waupaca, Wisconsin, December 14, 1964; married; 2 children.

Voting address: Waupaca, Wisconsin.

Education: Waupaca High School 1983; BSME University of New Mexico 1989.

Occupation: Co-owner of family-run electronics corporation. Served in U.S. Navy submarine service 1983–94; Persian Gulf War veteran; U.S. Naval Reserve member 1994–2008.

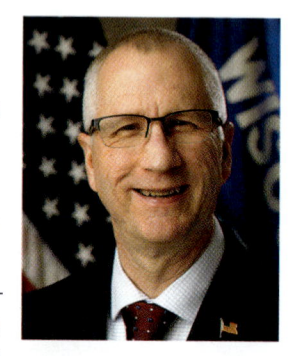

Member: Waupaca County Republican Party; Waushara County Republican Party; VFW Post 1037 (life member); AMVETS Post 1887 (life member); American Legion Post 161; Waupaca Area Chamber of Commerce; New London Area Chamber of Commerce; NRA.

Previous office: Elected to Town of Dayton Board (supervisor) 2001–07.

Current office: Elected to Assembly since 2006. Leadership positions: Speaker Pro Tempore 2023; Assistant Majority Leader 2021. Committee assignments 2023: Review of Administrative Rules (vice chair); Assembly Organization; Energy and Utilities; Rules; Joint Committee for Review of Administrative Rules; Joint Legislative Council.

Contact: rep.petersen@legis.wisconsin.gov; 608-237-9140; 888-947-0040 (toll free); Room 309 North, State Capitol, PO Box 8953, Madison, WI 53708-8953.

Alex Dallman, Assembly District 41
Republican

Personal: Born Fond du Lac, Wisconsin, May 22, 1992; single.

Voting address: Green Lake, Wisconsin.

Education: Markesan High School 2011; BS Edgewood College 2015.

Occupation: Wisconsin Interscholastic Athletic Association (WIAA) licensed basketball official. Former outreach representative for U.S. Congressman Glenn Grothman.

Member: Green Lake County Republican Party (former chair); Green Lake County Farm Bureau; Manchester Rod & Gun Club; NRA; St. John's Lutheran Church (Markesan).

Current office: Elected to Assembly since 2020. Committee assignments 2023: Finance; Joint Committee on Finance. Additional appointment: Claims Board.

Contact: rep.dallman@legis.wisconsin.gov; 608-237-9141; 888-534-0041 (toll free); Room 321 East, State Capitol, PO Box 8952, Madison, WI 53708-8952.

Jon Plumer, Assembly District 42
Republican

Personal: Born Sterling, Illinois, March 1, 1955; married; 4 children, 9 grandchildren.

Voting address: Lodi, Wisconsin.

Education: West High School 1973.

Occupation: Small business owner, Plumer Karate America. Former route salesman for Kraft Foods for 30 years.

Member: Lake Wisconsin Alliance Board Member; Lodi Knights of Columbus.

Former member: Lodi Area EMS Commission; Lodi & Lake Wisconsin Chamber of Commerce (three-term president); Lodi Optimist Club; Lodi Rotary Club.

Previous office: Elected to Columbia County Board (supervisor); Town of Lodi Board (supervisor).

Current office: Elected to Assembly in June 2018 special election. Reelected since November 2018. Leadership positions: Assistant Majority Leader 2023. Committee assignments 2023: Assembly Organization; Mental Health and Substance Abuse Prevention; Rules; Tourism; Transportation; Joint Committee on Legislative Organization; Joint Legislative Council.

Contact: rep.plumer@legis.wisconsin.gov; 608-237-9142; 888-534-0042 (toll free); Room 315 North, State Capitol, PO Box 8953, Madison, WI 53708-8953.

SENATE DISTRICT 15
ASSEMBLY DISTRICTS 43, 44, 4

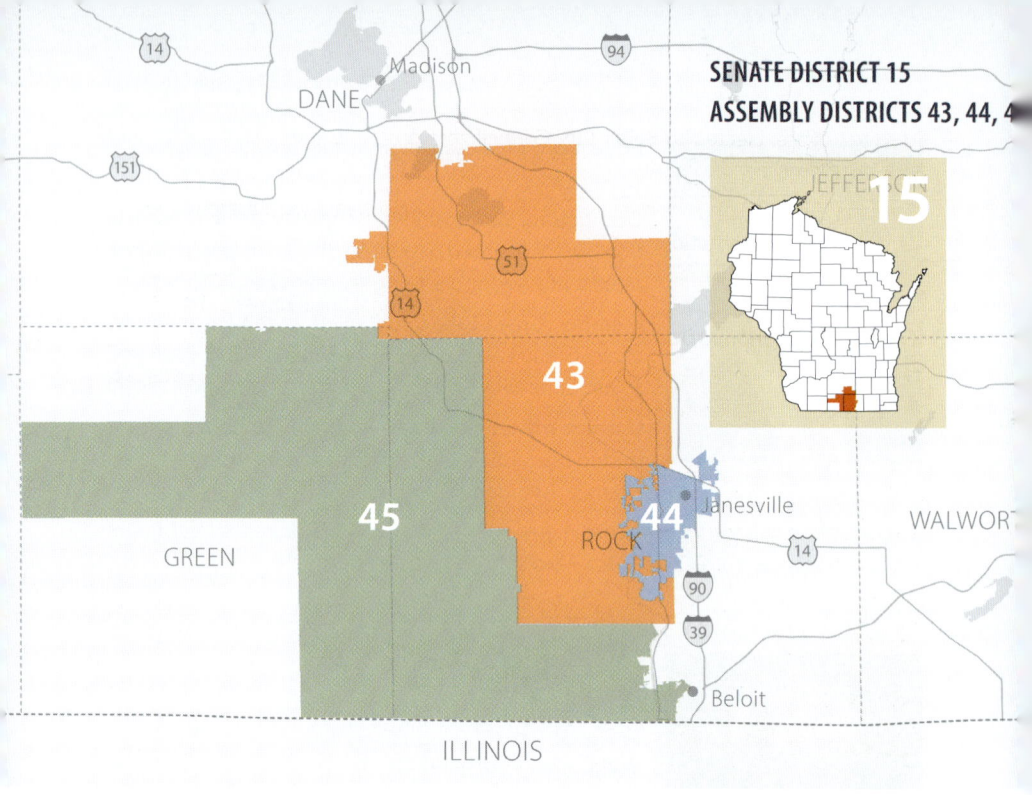

Mark Spreitzer, Senate District 15
Democrat

Personal: Born Chicago, Illinois, December 16, 1986; married.

Voting address: Beloit, Wisconsin.

Education: Northside College Preparatory High School (Chicago, Illinois) 2005; BA in Political Science, Beloit College 2009; Bowhay Institute for Legislative Leadership Development (BILLD) 2017; State Legislative Leaders Foundation Emerging Leaders Program 2017.

Occupation: Full-time legislator. Former assistant director of alumni and parent relations and annual support, Beloit College.

Member: United Church of Beloit (finance and facilities board); Welty Environmental Center (board member); National Caucus of Environmental Legislators; Great Lakes Legislative Caucus; Wisconsin Legislative LGBTQ+ Caucus; Wisconsin Legislative Sportsmen's Caucus; Major, Wisconsin Wing, Civil Air Patrol Legislative Squadron (official Auxiliary of the U.S. Air Force); Wisconsin Legislative Trails Caucus; Council of State Governments (Midwestern Legislative Conference Agriculture and Rural Affairs Committee and Midwest-Canada Relations Committee).

Former member: Community Action, Inc. of Rock and Walworth Counties (board member); City of Beloit Appointment Review Committee (chair).

Previous office: Elected to Beloit City Council 2011, 2013 (president 2014); Assembly 2014, 2016, 2018, 2020. Minority Caucus Chair 2021, 2019, 2017.

Current office: Elected to Senate 2022. Committee assignments 2023: Agriculture and Tourism; Financial Institutions and Sporting Heritage; Housing, Rural Issues and Forestry; Shared Revenue, Elections and Consumer Protection; Joint Committee on Information Policy and Technology; Joint Legislative Council. Additional appointment: Wisconsin Housing and Economic Development Authority.

Contact: sen.spreitzer@legis.wisconsin.gov; 608-266-2253; Room 126 South, State Capitol, PO Box 7882, Madison, WI 53707-7882.

Jenna Jacobson, Assembly District 43
Democrat

Personal: Born Brenham, Texas, February 4, 1982; married; 3 children.

Voting address: Oregon, Wisconsin.

Education: Frederic High School 2000; University of Wisconsin–River Falls 2003; Purdue University 2008.

Occupation: Former housing program specialist; financial analyst.

Previous office: Elected to Village of Oregon Board of Trustees 2017–22.

Current office: Elected to Assembly 2022. Committee assignments 2023: Agriculture; Consumer Protection; Financial Institutions; Workforce Development and Economic Opportunities.

Contact: rep.jacobson@legis.wisconsin.gov; 608-237-9143; 888-534-0043 (toll free); Room 11 North, State Capitol, PO Box 8952, Madison, WI 53708-8952.

Sue Conley, Assembly District 44
Democrat

Personal: Born Galesburg, Illinois, February 19, 1960; married; 3 children.

Voting address: Janesville, Wisconsin.

Education: Joseph A. Craig High School (Janesville); attended University of Wisconsin–Whitewater, University of Wisconsin–Rock County, and Blackhawk Technical College.

Occupation: Full-time legislator. Former banker; YWCA Executive Director; Community Foundation of Southern Wisconsin Executive Director; University of Wisconsin–Whitewater Rock County Foundation Executive Director.

Previous office: Elected to Janesville City Council 2017–21 (president 2020–21).

Current office: Elected to Assembly since 2020. Committee assignments 2023: Review of Administrative Rules; Family Law; Local Government; Sporting Heritage; Ways and Means; Joint Committee for Review of Administrative Rules. Additional appointment: Council on Domestic Abuse.

Contact: rep.conley@legis.wisconsin.gov; 608-237-9144; 888-947-0044 (toll free); Room 320 West, State Capitol, PO Box 8952, Madison, WI 53708-8952.

Clinton Anderson, Assembly District 45
Democrat

Personal: Born Beloit, Wisconsin, 1993; single.

Voting address: Beloit, Wisconsin.

Education: Beloit Memorial High School 2011; associate degree, University of Wisconsin–Rock County 2014; BS in Psychology, University of Wisconsin–Whitewater 2018.

Occupation: Former youth support specialist, Professional Services Group; volunteer coordinator and shelter advocate, YWCA Rock County.

Member: Beloit Meals on Wheels (board member); Young Elected Officials Network.

Previous office: Elected to Beloit City Council 2017–23 (vice president 2019–21, president 2021–22).

Current office: Elected to Assembly 2022. Committee assignments 2023: Agriculture; Campaigns and Elections; Local Government; Rural Development.

Contact: rep.canderson@legis.wisconsin.gov; 608-237-9145; 888-534-0045 (toll free); Room 17 North, State Capitol, PO Box 8952, Madison, WI 53708-8952.

SENATE DISTRICT 16
ASSEMBLY DISTRICTS 46, 47, 48

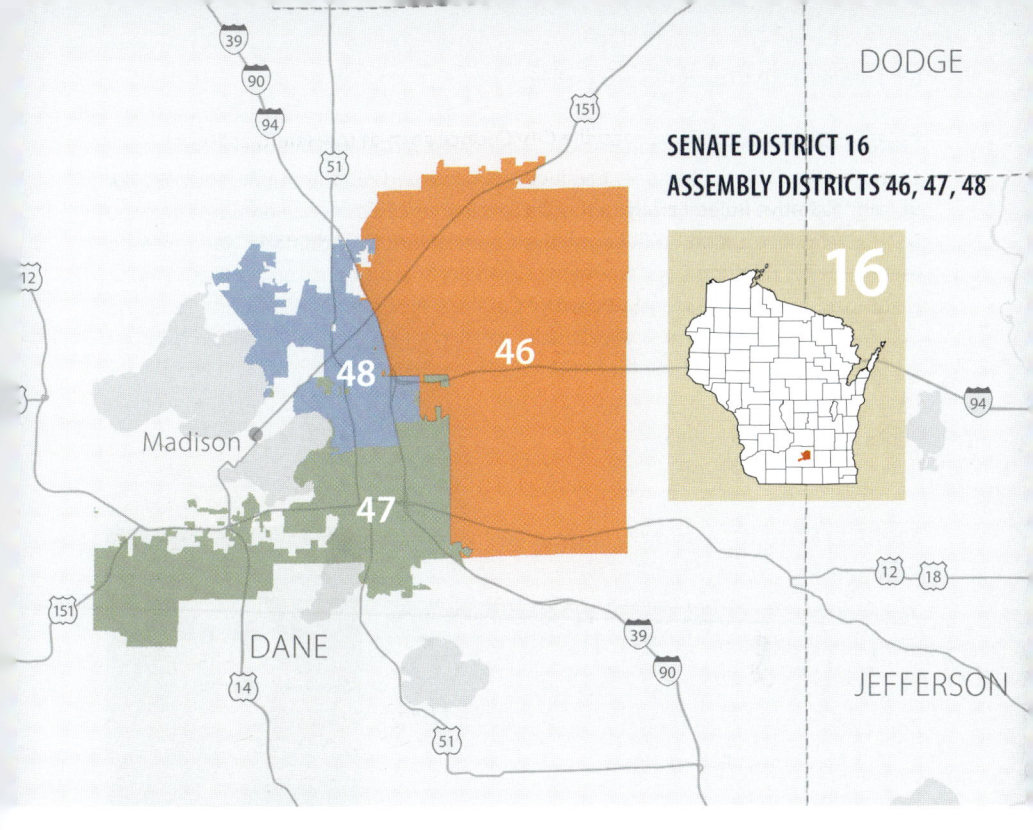

Melissa Agard, Senate District 16
Democrat

Personal: Born Madison, Wisconsin, March 28, 1969; 4 children.

Voting address: Madison, Wisconsin.

Education: Madison East High School 1987; BA University of Wisconsin–Madison 1991; Bowhay Institute for Legislative Leadership Development (BILLD) 2014; Emerging Leaders Program, University of Virginia 2014; Toll Fellowship 2015.

Occupation: Full-time legislator. Former small business owner.

Member: Women in Government; Dane County Democratic Party; Democratic Party; National Caucus of Environmental Legislators; Great Lakes-St. Lawrence Legislative Caucus.

Former member: Emerge Wisconsin (board of directors); Make Room for Youth; Boy Scouts of America Glacier's Edge Council (board of directors); Midwest Shiba Inu Dog Rescue (president); Gompers PTO (president).

Previous office: Elected to Dane County Board of Supervisors 2010–14; Assembly 2012–18.

Current office: Elected to Senate 2020. Leadership positions: Minority Leader 2023, 2021 (effective 11/16/22); Minority Caucus Vice Chair 2021. Committee assignments 2023: Senate Organization, Joint Committee on Employment Relations, Joint Committee on Legislative Organization, Joint Legislative Council, Joint Survey Committee on Retirement Systems. Additional appointments: Disability Board; Council on Domestic Abuse; Historical Society of Wisconsin Board of Curators; Presidential Preference Selection Committee; Committee on School District and School Financial Information Transparency; Wisconsin Commission for the United States Semiquincentennial Commission.

Contact: sen.agard@legis.wisconsin.gov; 608-266-9170; Room 206 South, State Capitol, PO Box 7882, Madison, WI 53707-7882.

Melissa Ratcliff, Assembly District 46
Democrat

Personal: Born Green Bay, Wisconsin, November 19, 1976; married; 2 children.

Voting address: Cottage Grove, Wisconsin.

Education: Wausau East High School 1995; Paralegal Certificate, Madison College 2000.

Occupation: Paralegal.

Member: Friends of the Cottage Grove Library; Sun Prairie Rotary Club; Madison Area Paralegal Association; Sun Prairie Area Historical Society; Cottage Grove Area Historical Society; Cottage Grove Chamber of Commerce; Sun Prairie Chamber of Commerce; Friends of Lake Kegonsa Society; Monona Grove Education Foundation Snack Pack Program; Governor's Task Force on Broadband Access; Miracle League of Dane County (founding member).

Former member: Cottage Grove Optimist Club (secretary).

Previous office: Appointed to Dane County Board of Supervisors District 36 2018; elected 2019, 2020, 2022. Elected Cottage Grove Village Board trustee 2018–22.

Current office: Elected to Assembly 2022. Committee assignments 2023: Local Government; Rural Development; Veterans and Military Affairs; Joint Committee on Information Policy and Technology.

Contact: rep.ratcliff@legis.wisconsin.gov; 608-237-9146; 888-534-0046 (toll free); Room 11 North, State Capitol, PO Box 8953, Madison, WI 53708-8953.

Jimmy Anderson, Assembly District 47
Democrat

Personal: Born El Paso, Texas, August 26, 1986; raised in Patterson, California.

Voting address: Fitchburg, Wisconsin.

Education: Patterson High School 2004; BA, summa cum laude, California State

University Monterey Bay 2008; JD University of Wisconsin Law School 2012.

Occupation: Nonprofit director; attorney.

Member: Wisconsin State Bar Association.

Current office: Elected to Assembly since 2016. Committee assignments 2023: Colleges and Universities; Environment; Financial Institutions; Health, Aging and Long-Term Care; Judiciary.

Contact: rep.anderson@legis.wisconsin.gov; 608-237-9147; 888-302-0047 (toll free); Room 9 North, State Capitol, PO Box 8952, Madison, WI 53708-8952.

Samba Baldeh, Assembly District 48
Democrat

Personal: Born Choya Village, The Gambia, September 10, 1971; married.

Voting address: Madison, Wisconsin.

Education: Armitage High School; associate degree, Madison Area Technical College 2006; attended University of The Gambia for BA in Education; masters certificate in Project Management, Information Technology, University of Wisconsin–Madison 2017; Bowhay Institute for Legislative Leadership Development (BILLD) 2021.

Occupation: Full-time legislator. Former software engineer, information technology project manager, and small business owner.

Member: 100 Black Men of Madison; Dane County Democratic Party; YALI–UW Madison (Mandela Washington fellowship program for Young African Leaders Initiative) (board member); NAACP, Dane County; University of Wisconsin–Madison Community Advisory Council; New American Leaders, Elected Advisory Council (NAL–EAC); Center for Community Stewardship (C4CS); African Association of Madison (AAM).

Previous office: Elected City of Madison alder, District 17 (Common Council president).

Current office: Elected to Assembly since 2020. Committee assignments 2023: Review of Administrative Rules; Local Government; State Affairs; Ways and Means; Joint Committee for Review of Administrative Rules; Joint Committee on Information Policy and Technology.

Contact: rep.baldeh@legis.wisconsin.gov; 608-237-9148; 888-534-0048 (toll free); Room 111 North, State Capitol, PO Box 8952, Madison, WI 53708-8952.

SENATE DISTRICT 17
ASSEMBLY DISTRICTS 49, 50, 51

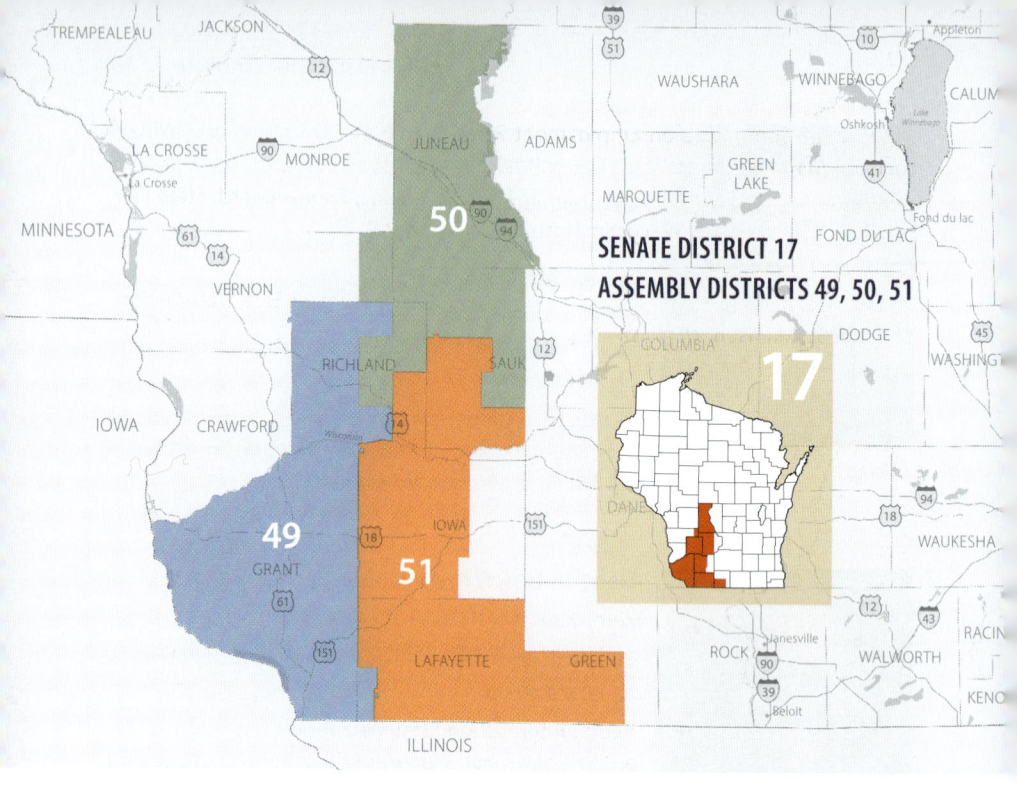

Howard Marklein, Senate District 17
Republican

Personal: Born October 3, 1954; married; 2 children, 3 stepchildren, 7 grandchildren.

Voting address: Spring Green, Wisconsin.

Education: River Valley High School (Spring Green) 1972; BBA University of Wisconsin–Whitewater 1976.

Occupation: Retired certified public accountant (CPA); retired certified fraud examiner (CFE).

Member: St. John's Catholic Church Spring Green (finance committee member); NRA; Knights of Columbus.

Former member: Taliesin Preservation Inc. Board of Trustees (treasurer); University of Wisconsin–Whitewater National Alumni Association (president); University of Wisconsin–Whitewater Foundation (board of directors president); Fort HealthCare Board of Directors (chair, treasurer); Fort Atkinson Rotary Club (president); Fort Atkinson Chamber of Commerce (president); Whitewater Chamber of Commerce (president); Dodgeville Chamber of Commerce (vice president).

Previous office: Elected to Assembly 2010–12.

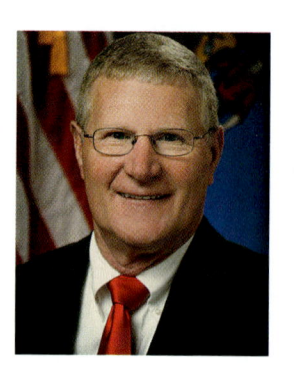

Current office: Elected to Senate since 2014. Leadership positions: Senate President Pro Tempore 2019, 2017. Committee assignments 2023: Agriculture and Tourism; Finance (chair); Joint Committee on Employment Relations; Joint Committee on Finance (cochair); Joint Legislative Audit Committee; Joint Legislative Council; Joint Survey Committee on Tax Exemptions. Additional appointments: Claims Board; State Fair Park Board; University of Wisconsin Hospitals and Clinics Authority Board; Wisconsin Mississippi River Parkway Commission.

Contact: sen.marklein@legis.wisconsin.gov; 608-266-0703; Room 316 East, State Capitol, PO Box 7882, Madison, WI 53707-7882.

Travis Tranel, Assembly District 49

Republican

Personal: Born Dubuque, Iowa, September 12, 1985; married; 5 children.

Voting address: Cuba City, Wisconsin.

Education: Wahlert Catholic High School (Dubuque, Iowa) 2004; BA Loras College (Dubuque, Iowa) 2007.

Occupation: Dairy farmer; small business owner.

Member: St. Joseph Sinsinawa Parish Council 2010–12 (president 2011–12); Wisconsin Farm Bureau; Knights of Columbus; NRA; Platteville Regional Chamber of Commerce; Grant County Republican Party.

Current office: Elected to Assembly since 2010. Committee assignments 2023: Agriculture (chair); Energy and Utilities; Insurance. Additional appointment: Council on Tourism.

Contact: rep.tranel@legis.wisconsin.gov; 608-237-9149; 888-872-0049 (toll free); Room 302 North, State Capitol, PO Box 8953, Madison, WI 53708-8953.

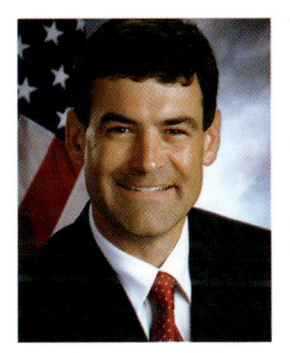

Tony Kurtz, Assembly District 50

Republican

Personal: Born Columbus, Ohio, December 23, 1966.

Voting address: Wonewoc, Wisconsin.

Education: BS in Professional Aeronautics, Embry-Riddle Aeronautical University 1989; MS in International Relations, Troy State University (Troy, Alabama) 1997.

Occupation: Organic grain farmer. Former U.S. Army attack helicopter pilot 1985–2005, retired from active duty as a Chief Warrant Officer Four (CW4); Persian Gulf War veteran; Iraq War veteran.

Member: VFW (life member); Military Officers Association of America (life member); American Legion; Wisconsin Farm Bureau; Organic Farmers Association; Juneau County Republican Party.

Current office: Elected to Assembly since 2018. Committee assignments 2023: Finance; Joint Committee on Finance.

Contact: rep.kurtz@legis.wisconsin.gov; 608-237-9150; 888-534-0050; Room 320 East, State Capitol, PO Box 8952, Madison, WI 53708-8952.

Todd Novak, Assembly District 51
Republican

Personal: Born Cobb, Wisconsin, April 23, 1965; 2 children.

Voting address: Dodgeville, Wisconsin.

Education: Iowa-Grant High School 1983; attended Southwest Technical College 1983–85.

Occupation: Former government/associate newspaper editor 1990–2014.

Member: Wisconsin League of Municipalities; NRA; Wisconsin Farm Bureau.

Former member: Iowa County Humane Society (founding member, treasurer); Wisconsin Newspaper Association; National Newspaper Association.

Previous office: Elected mayor of Dodgeville 2012–present; Southwestern Wisconsin Regional Planning Commission 2012–present.

Current office: Elected to Assembly since 2014. Committee assignments 2023: Agriculture; Criminal Justice and Public Safety; Environment; Local Government (chair); Rural Development. Additional appointment: Wisconsin Housing and Economic Development Authority.

Contact: rep.novak@legis.wisconsin.gov; 608-237-9151; 888-534-0051 (toll free); Room 310 North, State Capitol, PO Box 8953, Madison, WI 53708-8953.

SENATE DISTRICT 18
ASSEMBLY DISTRICTS 52, 53, 54

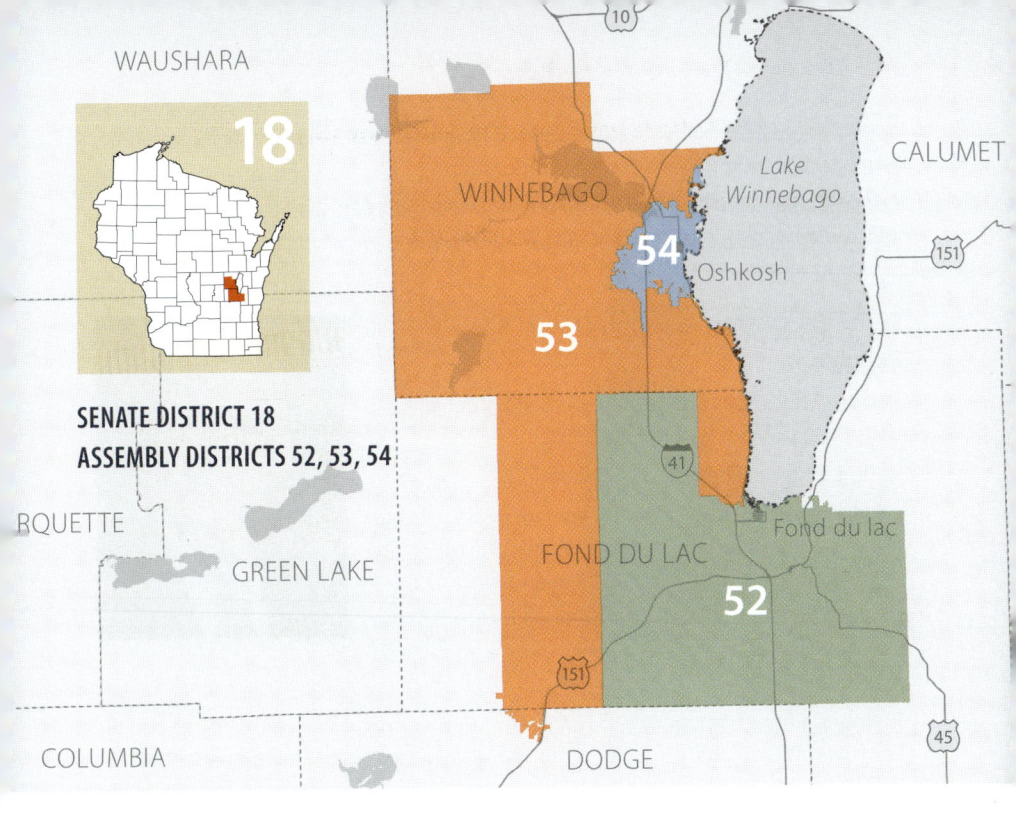

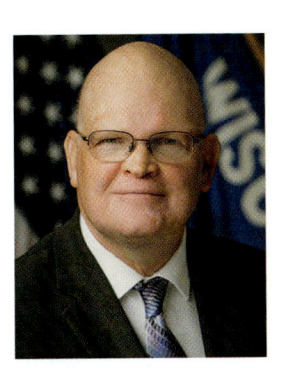

Dan Feyen, Senate District 18
Republican

Personal: Born New Holstein, Wisconsin; married; 2 children.

Voting address: Fond du Lac, Wisconsin.

Education: New Holstein High School 1986; diploma in Printing, Fox Valley Technical College 1988.

Occupation: Print and bindery coordinator.

Member: Knights of Columbus; Elks Club; Major, Wisconsin Wing, Civil Air Patrol Legislative Squadron (official Auxiliary of the U.S. Air Force); Fond du Lac County Republican Party (former chair); Fond du Lac Noon Rotary Club; Sixth District Republican Party (former chair).

Former member: Jaycees Fond du Lac County (president); Fond du Lac Advisory Parks Board.

Current office: Elected to Senate since 2016. Leadership positions: Assistant Majority Leader 2023, 2021, 2019. Committee assignments 2023: Economic Development and Technical Colleges (chair); Government Operations; Senate Organization; Shared Revenue, Elections and Consumer Protection (vice chair); Joint Committee on Legislative Organization; Joint Survey Committee on Retirement Systems (cochair). Additional appointments: Legislative State Supported Programs Study and Advisory Committee; Wisconsin Economic Development Corporation.

Contact: sen.feyen@legis.wisconsin.gov; 608-266-5300; 888-529-0052 (toll free); Room 306 South, State Capitol, PO Box 7882, Madison, WI 53707-7882.

Jerry O'Connor, Assembly District 52
Republican

Personal: Born Lone Rock, Wisconsin, September 14, 1953; married; 5 children, 4 grandchildren.

Voting address: Fond du Lac, Wisconsin.

Education: Madison West High School 1971; Pastoral Studies, Minnesota Bible College 1973; diploma from University of Wisconsin–Madison School of Banking 2001.

Occupation: Retired bank CEO and board chair. Former licensed real estate broker and insurance agent; real estate developer.

Member: Charis Pregnancy and Family Help Center Executive Board (chair); Fond du Lac Noon Rotary Club; e-Center for Hope and Vision Executive Board (treasurer).

Former member: Wisconsin Bankers Association Board (cochair); Community Bankers of Wisconsin Board (chair); Fond du Lac County Capital Markets Board; Fond du Lac County Economic Development Corporation Board; Waupun Economic Development Board (treasurer); Waupun Christmas Club (chair); Waupun Rotary Club (chair); 4-H Horse Project Advisor; church deacon.

Current office: Elected to Assembly 2022. Committee assignments 2023: Colleges and Universities; Corrections; Family Law; Financial Institutions (vice chair); Jobs, Economy and Small Business Development; Workforce Development and Economic Opportunities.

Contact: rep.o'connor@legis.wisconsin.gov; 608-237-9152; Room 17 West, State Capitol, PO Box 8953, Madison, WI 53708-8953.

Michael Schraa, Assembly District 53
Republican

Personal: Born Fort Carson, Colorado, April 17, 1961; married; 3 children.

Voting address: Oshkosh, Wisconsin.

Education: Oshkosh North High School 1979; attended University of Wisconsin Oshkosh 1980–82.

Occupation: Restaurant owner. Former stock broker/investment advisor.

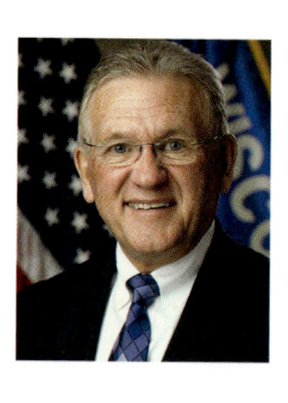

Member: Winnebago County Republican Party; Fond du Lac County Republican Party; Calvary SonRise Church (Oshkosh); Wisconsin Independent Businesses; NRA; Winnebago County Farm Bureau; Fond du Lac County Farm Bureau.

Former member: Southwest Rotary; National Federation of Independent Businesses (NFIB); Oshkosh Jaycees; Big Brothers Big Sisters; Exchange Club.

Current office: Elected to Assembly since 2012. Committee assignments 2023: Corrections (chair); Criminal Justice and Public Safety; Housing and Real Estate; Insurance; Rules; State Affairs.

Contact: rep.schraa@legis.wisconsin.gov; 608-237-9153; 888-534-0053 (toll free); Room 107 West, State Capitol, PO Box 8953, Madison, WI 53708-8953.

Lori Palmeri, Assembly District 54
Democrat

Personal: Born Takoma Park, Maryland, May 25, 1967; married; 2 children, 2 grandchildren.

Voting address: Oshkosh, Wisconsin.

Education: received GED 1985; University of Wisconsin–Fox Cities 2008; BA in Urban and Regional Studies, University of Wisconsin Oshkosh 2010; master's degree in Urban Planning, University of Wisconsin–Milwaukee 2013.

Occupation: Full-time legislator. Former mayor, City of Oshkosh 2019–23; Oshkosh Common Council 2016–23; substitute teacher, Oshkosh School District; medical courier, CS Logistics 2020–23; planning intern, City of Oshkosh 2011–12; intern, East Central Wisconsin Regional Planning Commission 2009–10; finance recruiting administrator, Kimberly Clark 2002–5.

Member: East Central Wisconsin Regional Planning Commission (commissioner); Oshkosh Redevelopment Authority (chair); Council Liaison for Parks Advisory and Bike and Pedestrian Boards; Middle Village Neighborhood Association (cofounder).

Former member: Day by Day Warming Shelter Board; Sustainability Advisory Board; Oshkosh Planning Commission; Transit Advisory Board; Diversity and Inclusion Committee; Greater Oshkosh Healthy Neighborhoods Committee.

Previous office: Elected mayor of Oshkosh 2019–23; deputy mayor of Oshkosh, 2018; Oshkosh Common Council member 2016–23.

Current office: Elected to Assembly 2022. Committee assignments 2023: Environment; Forestry, Parks and Outdoor Recreation; Mental Health and Substance Abuse Prevention; Regulatory Licensing Reform.

Contact: rep.palmeri@legis.wisconsin.gov; 608-237-9154; 888-534-0054 (toll free); Room 5 North, State Capitol, PO Box 8953, Madison, WI 53708-8953.

SENATE DISTRICT 19
ASSEMBLY DISTRICTS 55, 56, 57

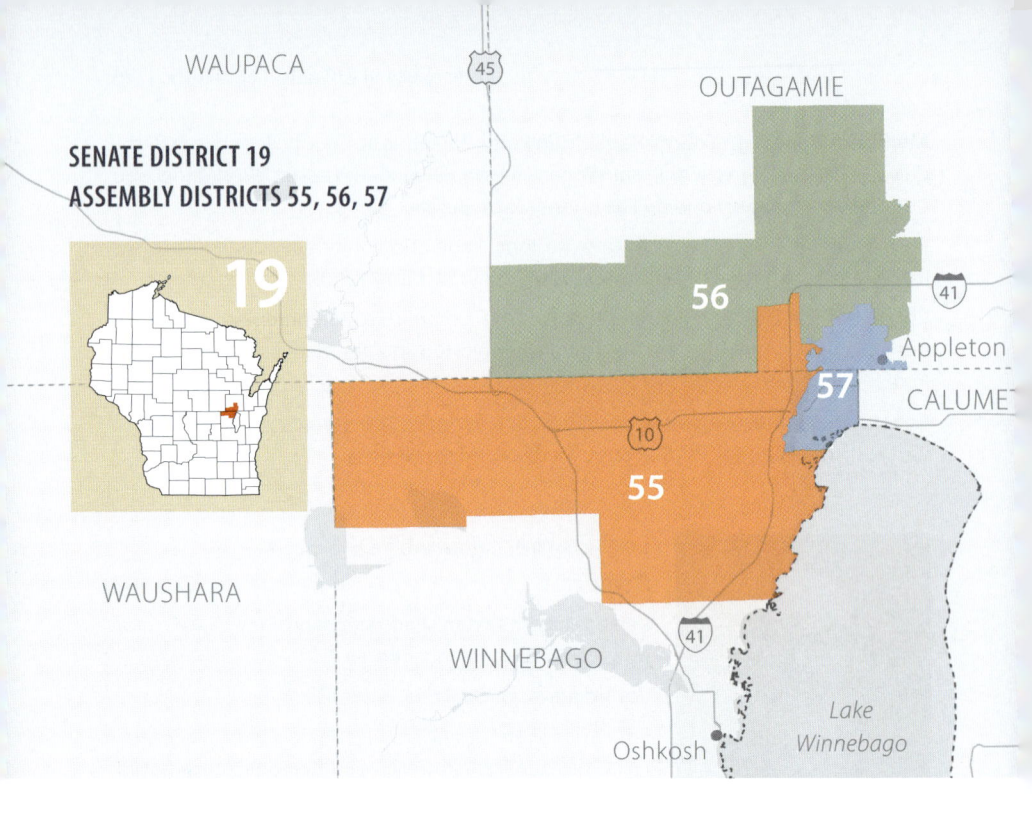

Rachel Cabral-Guevara, Senate District 19
Republican

Personal: Born Appleton, Wisconsin, August 10, 1976; divorced; 4 children.

Voting address: Appleton, Wisconsin.

Education: Machebeuf Catholic High School (Denver, Colorado); BS in Biology and Chemistry, Mount Mary University 2000; BS in Nursing, University of Wisconsin–Oshkosh 2004; MS in Nursing, University of Wisconsin–Milwaukee 2008.

Occupation: Nurse practitioner and owner of Nurse Practitioner Health Services LLC. Former senior lecturer in the College of Nursing, University of Wisconsin Oshkosh.

Member: Winnebago County Republican Party; Outagamie County Republican Party; ACES Xavier School System (parent volunteer); American Nurses Credentialing Center; Boy Scouts of America (parent volunteer); Fox Valley Health Professionals; Wisconsin Nurses Association (APRN Coalition); AANP (American Association of Nurse Practitioners); Boy Scouts of America Bay-Lakes Council (executive board); American Legion Auxiliary.

Former member: Sigma Theta Tau, Neenah Alliance School (parent volunteer), Wisconsin Express—Wisconsin AHEC (Area Health Education Centers) program; Fox Cities Morning Rotary Club.

Previous office: Elected to Assembly 2020.

Current office: Elected to Senate 2022. Committee assignments 2023: Education; Health (chair); Mental Health, Substance Abuse Prevention, Children and Families (vice chair); Universities and Revenue. Additional appointments: State Council on Interstate Compact on Educational Opportunity for Military Children; Women's Council.

Contact: sen.cabral-guevara@legis.wisconsin.gov; 608-266-0718; Room 323 South, State Capitol, PO Box 7882, Madison, WI 53707-7882.

Nathaniel Lee Gustafson,
Assembly District 55
Republican

Personal: Born Appleton, Wisconsin, February 28, 1995; single.

Voting address: Fox Crossing, Wisconsin.

Education: Neenah High School 2013; associate degree, Fox Valley Technical College 2018; attended University of Wisconsin–Fox Valley.

Occupation: Systems analyst, Outagamie County Health and Human Services.

Member: Fox River Hurling Club (general manager); Winnebago County for Freedom (cofounder and vice president); Winnebago County Republican Party (executive board); Shepherd of the Hills Lutheran Church.

Previous office: Elected Winnebago County Board supervisor 2022.

Current office: Elected to Assembly 2022. Committee assignments 2023: Judiciary; Labor and Integrated Employment; Regulatory Licensing Reform (vice chair); State Affairs; Ways and Means.

Contact: rep.gustafson@legis.wisconsin.gov; 608-237-9155; 888-534-0055 (toll free); Room 420 North, State Capitol, PO Box 8952, Madison, WI 53708-8952.

Dave Murphy, Assembly District 56
Republican

Personal: Born Appleton, Wisconsin, November 26, 1954; married; 2 children.

Voting address: Greenville, Wisconsin.

Education: Hortonville High School 1972; University of Wisconsin–Fox Valley 1972–74; Wisconsin School of Real Estate 1975.

Occupation: Full-time legislator and farmer. Former owner, fitness center and agribusiness; real estate broker.

Member: Irish Fest of the Fox Cities (board of directors); Wisconsin Family Impact Seminars (advisory board); Free Speech for Campus (board of directors); Greenville Lions Club; Immanuel Lutheran Church.

Current office: Elected to Assembly since 2012. Committee assignments 2023: Campaigns and Elections; Colleges and Universities (chair); Financial Institutions; Health, Aging and Long-Term Care; Housing and Real Estate. Additional appointment: Midwestern Higher Education Commission.

Contact: rep.murphy@legis.wisconsin.gov; 608-237-9156; 888-534-0056 (toll free); Room 318 North, State Capitol, PO Box 8953, Madison, WI 53708-8953.

Lee Snodgrass, Assembly District 57
Democrat

Personal: Born Philadelphia, Pennsylvania, February 9, 1969; single; 2 children.

Voting address: Appleton, Wisconsin.

Education: Preble High School (Green Bay) 1987; BA in English Literature, University of Wisconsin–Madison 1991.

Occupation: Full-time legislator; Livestrong Instructor, YMCA Fox Cities. Former communications director for Girl Scouts of the Northwestern Great Lakes; senior design project manager; sales manager for a paper corporation.

Member: Children's Caucus: Fox Cities Greenways; LGBTQ+ Caucus; Trails Caucus (cochair); Democratic Party of Wisconsin (second vice chair); Leaders for Climate Accountability; Outagamie County Aging Advisory Committee; Wisconsin Bike Fed; Wisconsin Women's Business Initiative Corporation Ambassador.

Current office: Elected to Assembly since 2020. Leadership positions: Minority Caucus Sergeant at Arms 2023. Committee assignments 2023: Campaigns and Elections; Children and Families; Forestry, Parks and Outdoor Recreation; Jobs, Economy and Small Business Development.

Contact: rep.snodgrass@legis.wisconsin.gov; 608-237-9157; 888-534-0057 (toll free); Room 120 North, State Capitol, PO Box 8953, Madison, WI 53708-8953.

SENATE DISTRICT 20
ASSEMBLY DISTRICTS 58, 59, 60

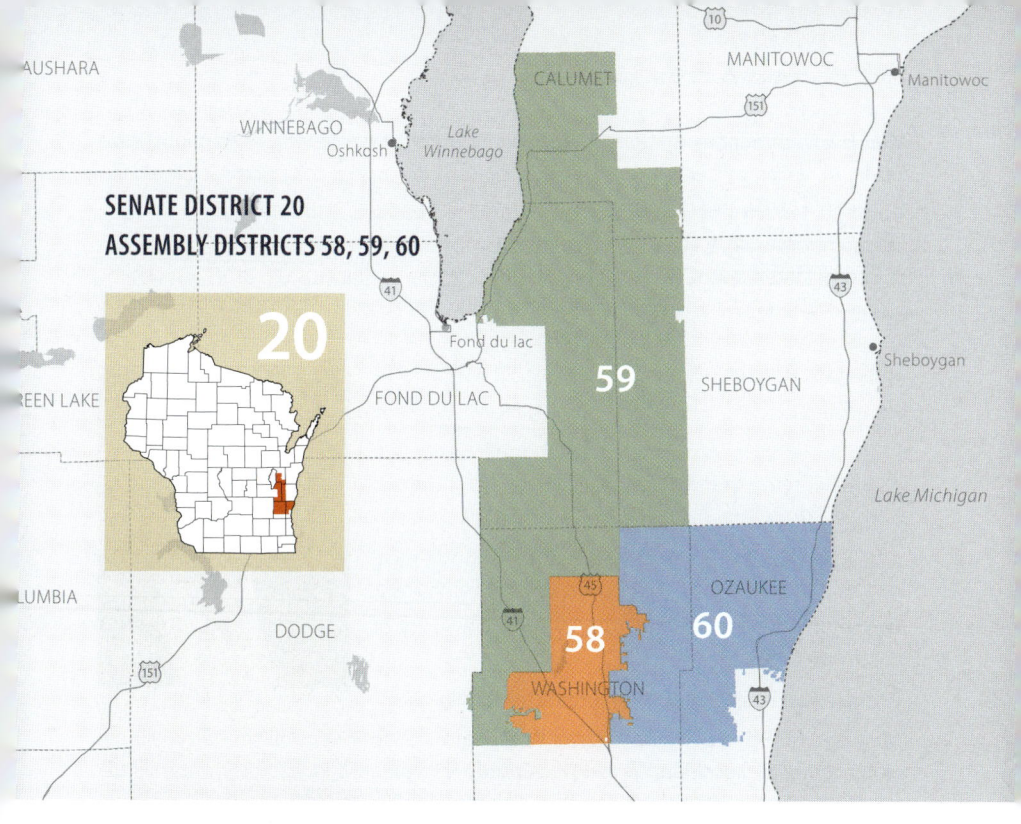

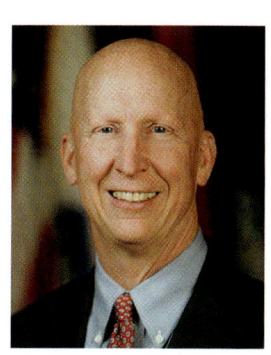

Duey Stroebel, Senate District 20
Republican

Personal: Born Cedarburg, Wisconsin, September 1, 1959; married; 8 children.

Voting address: Town of Cedarburg, Wisconsin.

Education: Cedarburg High School 1978; BBA University of Wisconsin–Madison 1984; MS University of Wisconsin–Madison 1987.

Occupation: Real estate.

Member: Lakeshore Realtors Association; Cedarburg Chamber of Commerce; Greater Cedarburg Foundation (former president); Concordia University President's Council; Farm Bureau; ABATE of Wisconsin; West Bend Chamber of Commerce; Saukville Chamber of Commerce.

Former member: City of Cedarburg Downtown Ad Hoc Committee; Ozaukee Bank and Cornerstone Bank (board of directors).

Previous office: Elected to Town of Cedarburg Parks Commission 2001–4; Town of Cedarburg Planning Commission 2003–5; Cedarburg School Board 2007–12; Assembly in May 2011 special election, reelected 2012.

Current office: Elected to Senate in April 2015 special election. Reelected since 2016. Committee assignments 2023: Administrative Rules (vice chair); Education; Finance (vice chair); Government Operations (chair); Joint Committee for Review of Administrative Rules; Joint Committee on Finance (vice chair).

Contact: sen.stroebel@legis.wisconsin.gov; 608-266-7513; 800-662-1227 (toll free); senatorstroebel.com; Facebook: Senator Duey Stroebel; Twitter: @SenStroebel; Room 18 South, State Capitol, PO Box 7882, Madison, WI 53707-7882.

Rick Gundrum, Assembly District 58
Republican

Personal: Born Nenno, Wisconsin, September 4; married; 2 stepchildren, 4 grandchildren.

Voting address: Slinger, Wisconsin.

Education: St. Kilian Catholic Grade School; Hartford Union High School; AD University of Wisconsin–Washington County; BS in Radio-TV-Film, University of Wisconsin Oshkosh.

Occupation: Business owner in broadcast media.

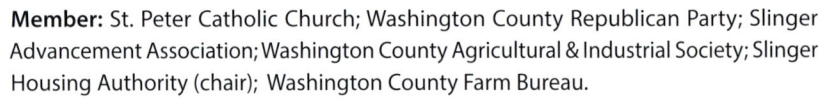

Member: St. Peter Catholic Church; Washington County Republican Party; Slinger Advancement Association; Washington County Agricultural & Industrial Society; Slinger Housing Authority (chair); Washington County Farm Bureau.

Former member: East Wisconsin Counties Railroad Consortium (chair); Washington County Aging & Disability Resource Board; Washington County Board of Health; Washington-Ozaukee County Joint Board of Health; Waukesha-Ozaukee-Washington Workforce Development Board of Directors; Wisconsin Counties Association Board of Directors; Wisconsin Counties Utility Tax Association Board of Directors.

Previous office: Elected to Village of Slinger Board of Trustees 2009–2023; Washington County Board of Supervisors 2006–18 (chair 2016–18).

Current office: Elected to Assembly in January 2018 special election. Reelected since November 2018. Committee assignments 2023: Children and Families; Health, Aging and Long-Term Care; Jobs, Economy and Small Business Development (chair); Local Government; Mental Health and Substance Abuse Prevention; Workforce Development and Economic Opportunities.

Contact: rep.gundrum@legis.wisconsin.gov; 608-237-9158; 888-534-0058 (toll free); Room 312 North, State Capitol, PO Box 8952, Madison, WI 53708.

Ty Bodden, Assembly District 59
Republican

Personal: Born Madison, Wisconsin, December 15, 1993; married; 3 children, 2 living.

Voting address: Hilbert, Wisconsin.

Education: Stockbridge High School (Stockbridge, Wisconsin) 2012; bachelor's degree in

Public Administration and Political Science, University of Wisconsin–Green Bay 2016; MPA in Public Administration, Arkansas State University 2018.

Occupation: Legislative researcher, John Birch Society; corrections sentencing associate, Taycheedah Correctional Institution; offender records associate, Kettle Moraine Correctional Institution; nonprofit manager, Cristo Rey Ranch.

Member: Stockbridge Sewer & Water Utility Commissions; Republican Party of Calumet County 2021–23.

Previous office: Elected to Stockbridge Village Board 2017–22.

Current office: Elected to Assembly 2022. Committee assignments 2023: Children and Families; Corrections (vice chair); Environment; Forestry, Parks and Outdoor Recreation; Judiciary; Sporting Heritage.

Contact: rep.bodden@legis.wisconsin.gov; 608-237-9159; 888-534-0059 (toll free); Room 304 North, State Capitol, PO Box 8952, Madison, WI 53708-8952.

Robert Brooks, Assembly District 60
Republican

Personal: Born Rockford, Illinois, July 13, 1965; married; 2 children, 2 grandchildren.

Voting address: Saukville, Wisconsin.

Education: Orfordville Parkview High School 1983; attended University of Wisconsin–La Crosse 1983–86.

Occupation: Real estate broker since 1990; restaurant/tavern owner.

Former member: Stars and Stripes Honor Flight (board of directors); Wisconsin County Mutual (board of directors); Wisconsin Board of Realtors; Ozaukee County Tavern League (board of directors).

Previous office: Elected to Ozaukee County Board 2000–14; Southeastern Wisconsin Regional Planning Commission.

Current office: Elected to Assembly since 2014. Leadership positions: Assistant Majority Leader 2017. Committee assignments 2023: Corrections; Health, Aging and Long-Term Care; Housing and Real Estate (chair); Sporting Heritage; State Affairs; Ways and Means (vice chair).

Contact: rep.rob.brooks@legis.wisconsin.gov; 608-237-9160; 888-534-0060 (toll free); Room 216 North, State Capitol, PO Box 8952, Madison, WI 53708-8952.

SENATE DISTRICT 21
ASSEMBLY DISTRICTS 62, 63, 6

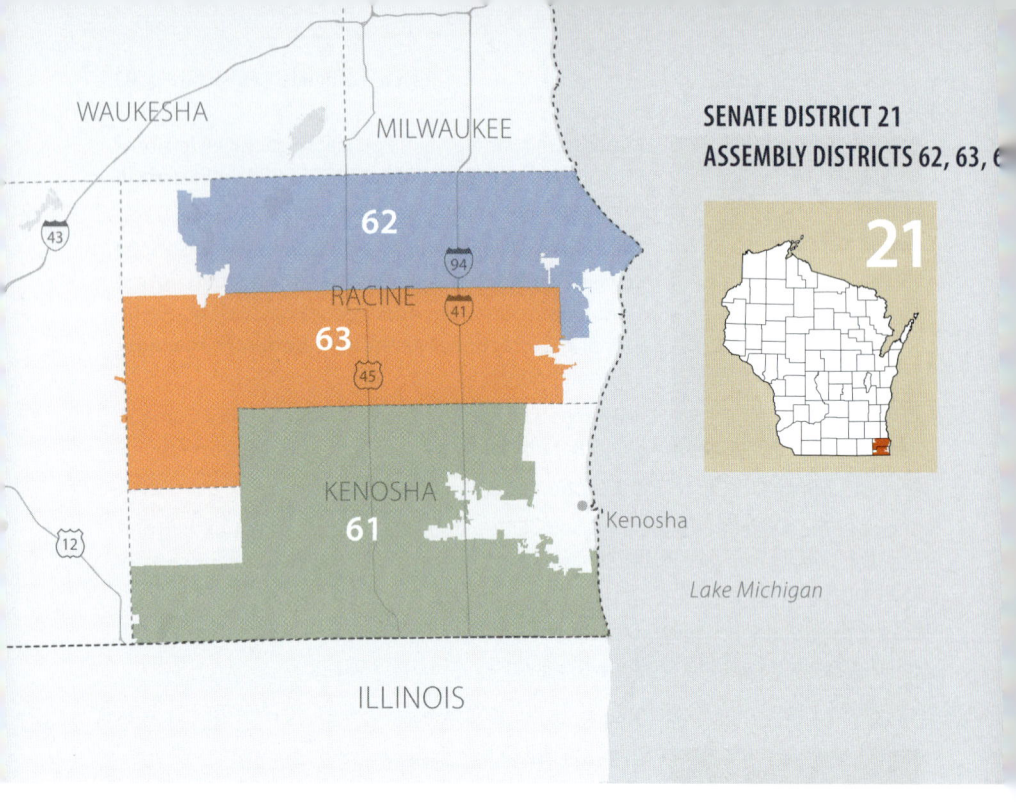

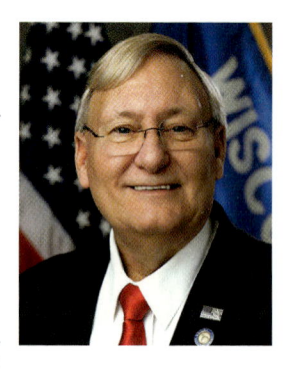

Van H. Wanggaard, Senate District 21
Republican

Personal: Born Ft. Leavenworth, Kansas, April 1952; married; 2 children, 3 grandchildren.

Voting address: Racine, Wisconsin.

Education: Racine Lutheran High School 1970; Racine Police Academy; Wisconsin State Patrol Academy Accident Investigation; Northwestern University Traffic Institute —Reconstruction; U.S. Coast Guard National Search and Rescue School; attended John F. Kennedy University (California); University of Wisconsin–Extension; University of Wisconsin–Parkside; Green Bay Technical College; Milwaukee Area Technical College; Fox Valley Technical College.

Occupation: Retired traffic investigator, Racine Police Department; adjunct instructor, Gateway Technical College and Northwestern Traffic Institute; police liaison and security, Racine Unified School District.

Member: NRA (endowment/life member); Racine County Line Rifle Club (board of directors); Racine Police Credit Union (former president, vice president); Major, Wisconsin Wing, Civil Air Patrol Legislative Squadron (official Auxiliary of the U.S. Air Force).

Former member: Racine Zoological Society (board of directors); Racine Jaycees; Racine Police Explorers (advisor); Traffic Accident Consultants, Inc. (board of directors);

Association of SWAT Personnel; Racine Innovative Youth Service (board); Hostage Negotiation Team, RAPD; Racine Junior Deputy Sheriffs Association; Racine Alateen (advisor); National Association for Search and Rescue (PSAR chair).

Previous office: Elected to Racine County Board 2002–11; Racine Police and Fire Commission 2003–13.

Current office: Elected to Senate 2010. Reelected since 2014. Leadership positions: Majority Caucus Chair 2023, 2021, 2019, 2017; Majority Caucus Vice Chair 2017, 2015. Committee assignments 2023: Judiciary and Public Safety (chair); Labor and Regulatory Reform, Veterans and Military Affairs; Utilities and Technology (vice chair). Additional appointments: Historical Society of Wisconsin Board of Curators; Judicial Council; Midwest Interstate Passenger Rail Commission; State Capitol and Executive Residence Board.

Contact: sen.wanggaard@legis.wisconsin.gov; 608-266-1832; 866-615-7510 (toll free); Room 122 South, State Capitol, PO Box 7882, Madison, WI 53707-7882.

Amanda Nedweski, Assembly District 61
Republican

Personal: Born Kenosha, Wisconsin, December 22, 1975; single; 2 children.

Voting address: Pleasant Prairie, Wisconsin.

Education: Mary D. Bradford High School (Kenosha) 1994; attended Carthage College 1994; BA in Communications, University of Wisconsin–Parkside 1998; ongoing studies, University of Wisconsin–Parkside 1998–2016.

Occupation: Senior technology consultant, Braun Consulting; senior Financial Analyst, CNH Global; self-employed business intelligence systems consultant.

Member: Moms for Liberty of Kenosha County (vice chair).

Former member: Kenosha Unified School District Audit/Budget/Finance Standing Committee.

Previous office: Elected to Kenosha County Board of Supervisors, District 16, 2022–present.

Current office: Elected to Assembly 2022. Committee assignments 2023: Colleges and Universities (vice chair); Education; Family Law; Workforce Development and Economic Opportunities.

Contact: rep.nedweski@legis.wisconsin.gov; 608-237-9161; 888-529-0061 (toll free); Room 7 West, State Capitol, PO Box 8953, Madison, WI 53708-8953.

Robert O. Wittke Jr., Assembly District 62
Republican

Personal: Born Racine, Wisconsin, September 23, 1957; married; 4 children.

Voting address: Racine, Wisconsin.

Education: William Horlick High School (Racine, Wisconsin) 1975; BA University of Wisconsin–Eau Claire 1980; Bowhay Institute for Legislative Leadership Development (BILLD) 2019.

Occupation: Tax professional for 35 years, specializing in corporate taxation.

Previous office: Elected to Racine Unified School District Board 2016–19 (former president).

Current office: Elected to the Assembly since 2018. Committee assignments 2023: Audit (chair); Colleges and Universities; Education; Joint Legislative Audit Committee (cochair). Additional appointment: Building Commission.

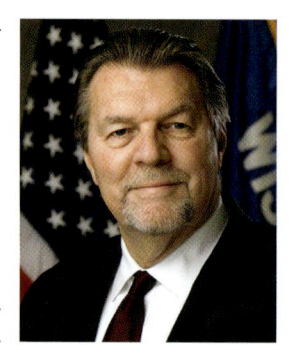

Contact: rep.wittke@legis.wisconsin.gov; 608-237-9162; 888-534-0062 (toll free); 262-417-0045 (district); Room 18 West, State Capitol, PO Box 8953, Madison, WI 53708-8953.

Robin J. Vos, Assembly District 63
Republican

Personal: Born Burlington, Wisconsin, July 5, 1968.

Voting address: Burlington, Wisconsin.

Education: Burlington High School 1986; University of Wisconsin–Whitewater 1991.

Occupation: Owner of several small businesses. Former congressional district director; legislative assistant.

Member: President of the National Conference of State Legislatures (NCSL); Vice Chair of the State Legislative Leaders Foundation; Tommy G. Thompson Center on Public Leadership; Center Rotary Club (former president); Racine/Kenosha Farm Bureau; Knights of Columbus; Racine County Republican Party; Union Grove Chamber of Commerce; Burlington Chamber of Commerce.

Previous office: Appointed to University of Wisconsin Board of Regents 1989–91. Elected to Racine County Board 1994–2004.

Current office: Elected to Assembly since 2004. Leadership positions: Speaker of the Assembly 2023, 2021, 2019, 2017, 2015, 2013; cochair of the Joint Committee on Finance 2011. Committee assignments 2023: Assembly Organization (chair); Employment Relations (cochair); Rules; Joint Committee on Employment Relations (cochair); Joint Committee on Legislative Organization (cochair); Joint Legislative Council.

Contact: rep.vos@legis.wisconsin.gov; 608-237-9163; 888-534-0063 (toll free); repvos.com; 608-282-3663 (fax); Room 217 West, State Capitol, PO Box 8953, Madison, WI 53708-8953.

SENATE DISTRICT 22
ASSEMBLY DISTRICTS 64, 65, 66

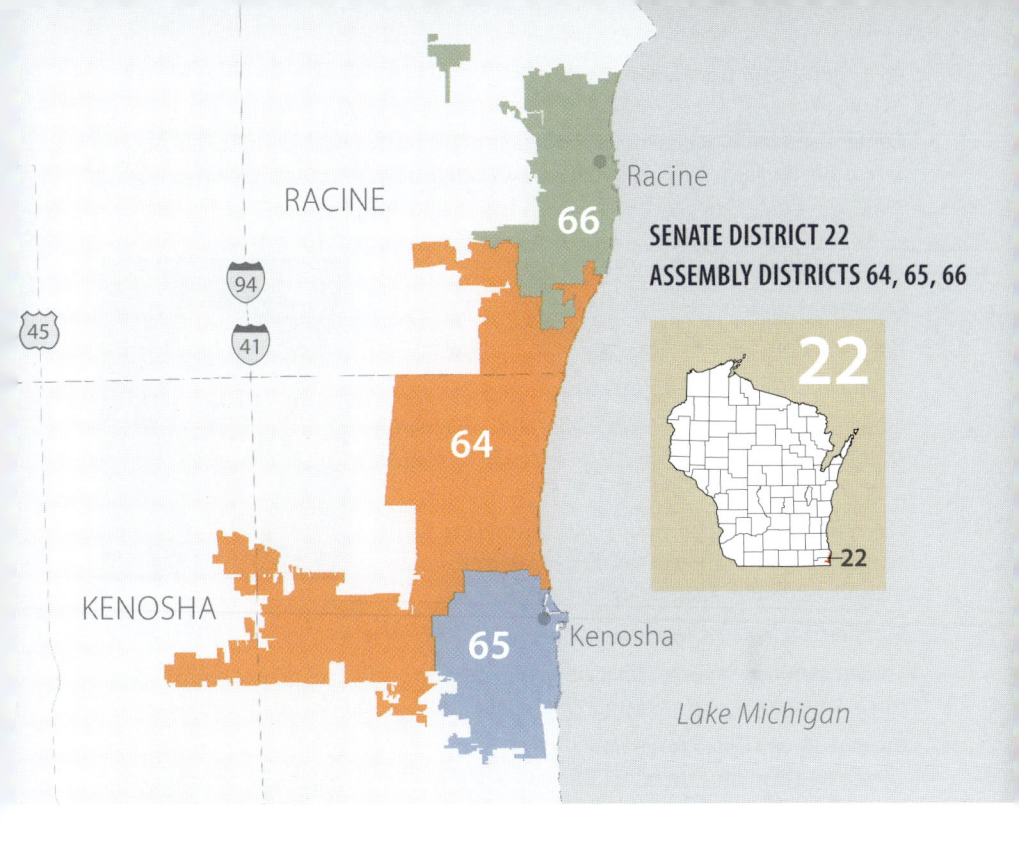

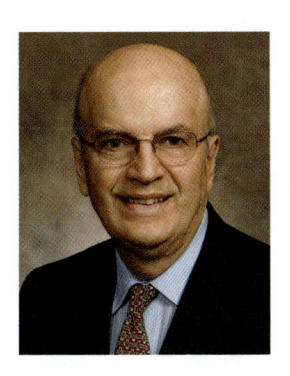

Robert W. Wirch, Senate District 22
Democrat

Personal: Born Kenosha, Wisconsin, November 16, 1943; 2 children.

Voting address: Somers, Wisconsin.

Education: Mary D. Bradford High School; BA University of Wisconsin–Parkside 1970.

Occupation: Full-time legislator. Former factory worker and liaison to Job Training Partnership Act (JPTA) programs. Served in Army Reserve 1965–71.

Member: Danish Brotherhood; Kenosha Sport Fishing and Conservation Association; Democratic Party of Wisconsin.

Former member: Kenosha Boys and Girls Club (board of directors).

Previous office: Elected Kenosha County supervisor 1986–94; Assembly 1992–94.

Current office: Elected to Senate since 1996. Leadership positions: Minority Caucus Chair 2003. Committee assignments 2023: Housing, Rural Issues and Forestry; Labor, Regulatory Reform, Veterans and Military Affairs; Licensing, Constitution and Federalism; Natural Resources and Energy. Additional appointments: Building Commission; Council on Military and State Relations; Migrant Labor Council; Sporting Heritage Council.

Contact: sen.wirch@legis.wisconsin.gov; 608-267-8979; 262-694-7379 (district); 888-769-4724 (office hotline); Room 127 South, State Capitol, PO Box 7882, Madison, WI 53707-7882.

Tip McGuire, Assembly District 64
Democrat

Personal: Born Somers, Wisconsin.

Voting address: Kenosha, Wisconsin.

Education: St. Catherine's High School (Racine) 2005; BA Marquette University 2009; JD University of Wisconsin Law School 2017.

Occupation: Attorney. Former legislative aide to Representative Peter Barca; Kenosha County special prosecutor; Milwaukee County assistant district attorney.

Member: State Bar of Wisconsin.

Former member: Kenosha Public Library Foundation Board (president of board of directors); National Alliance on Mental Illness (NAMI) of Kenosha County (board member).

Current office: Elected to Assembly in April 2019 special election. Reelected since 2020. Committee assignments 2023: Criminal Justice and Public Safety; Finance; Sporting Heritage; Joint Committee on Finance. Additional appointment: Commission on Uniform State Laws.

Contact: rep.mcguire@legis.wisconsin.gov; 608-237-9164; 888-534-0064 (toll free); Room 321 West, State Capitol, PO Box 8953, Madison, WI 53708-8953.

Tod Ohnstad, Assembly District 65
Democrat

Personal: Born Eau Claire, Wisconsin, May 21, 1952; married.

Voting address: Kenosha, Wisconsin.

Education: Altoona Public High School 1970; attended University of Wisconsin–Parkside.

Former member: UAW Local 72, 1974–2004 (Assembler, Steward, Chief Steward, Executive Board, and Bargaining Committee member).

Previous office: Elected City of Kenosha alder 2008–14.

Current office: Elected to Assembly since 2012. Committee assignments 2023: Jobs, Economy, and Small Business Development; Labor and Integrated Employment; State Affairs; Ways and Means.

Contact: rep.ohnstad@legis.wisconsin.gov; 608-237-9165; 888-534-0065 (toll free); Room 128 North, State Capitol, PO Box 8953, Madison, WI 53708-8953.

Greta Neubauer, Assembly District 66
Democrat

Personal: Born Racine, Wisconsin, September 13, 1991.

Voting Address: Racine, Wisconsin.

Education: The Prairie School 2010; BA in History, Middlebury College 2015.

Occupation: Former legislative aide to State Representative Cory Mason; Fossil Fuel Divestment Student Network (director and cofounder); 350.org (fellow).

Member: Racine Hospitality Center Board; Racine Interfaith Coalition; NAACP—Racine Branch; National Caucus of Environmental Legislators; Climate Power Advisory Board; Victory Institute; Democratic Party of Racine County.

Former Member: Joint Committee on Finance; Governor's Task Force on Climate Change; Mayor's Task Force on Police Reform.

Current office: Elected to Assembly in January 2018 special election. Reelected since November 2018. Leadership positions: Minority Leader 2023, 2021 (effective 12/20/21). Committee assignments 2023: Assembly Organization; Employment Relations; Rules; Joint Committee on Employment Relations; Joint Committee on Legislative Organization; Joint Legislative Council; Joint Survey Committee on Retirement Systems.

Contact: rep.neubauer@legis.wisconsin.gov; 608-237-9166; 888-534-0066 (toll free); Room 201 West, State Capitol, PO Box 8953, Madison, WI 53708-8953.

SENATE DISTRICT 23
ASSEMBLY DISTRICTS 67, 68, 69

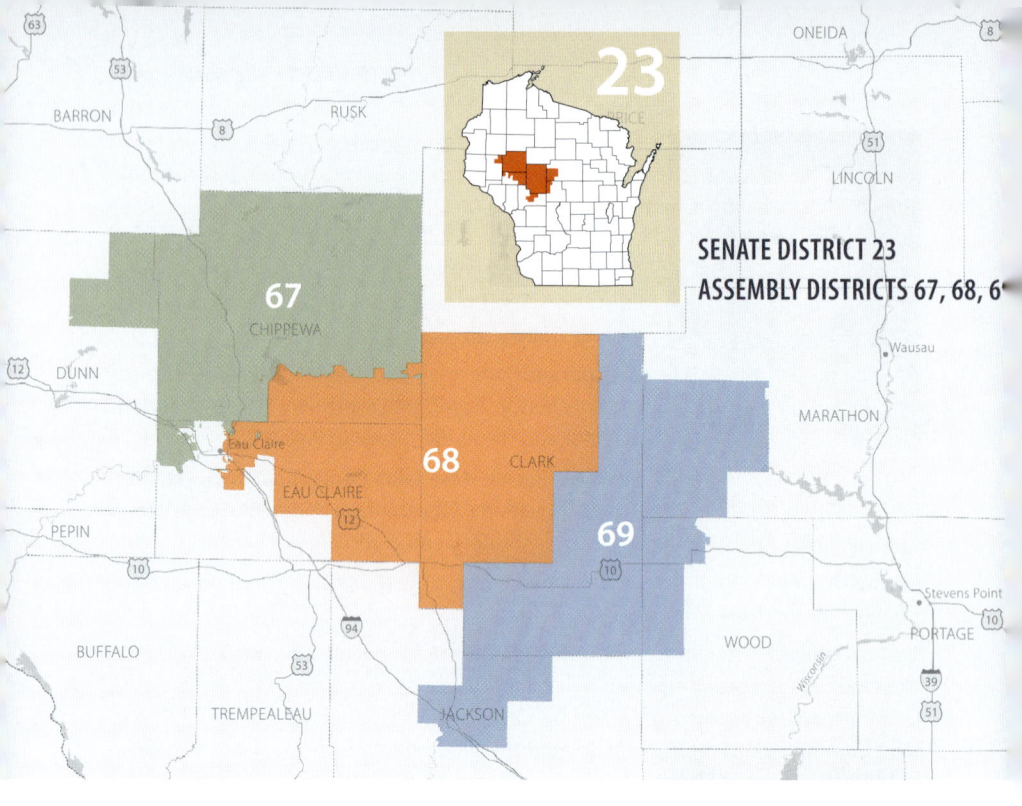

Jesse James, Senate District 23
Republican

Personal: Born Eau Claire, Wisconsin, April 16, 1972; married; 4 children, 2 grandchildren.

Voting address: Altoona, Wisconsin.

Education: Eau Claire North High School 1990; associate degree in Police Science, Chippewa Valley Technical College (Eau Claire) 2001; Emergency Medical Responder 2015; Entry level, Fire I, Fire II Firefighter 2016; University of Wisconsin–Madison Command College (Certified Public Manager) 2017; University of Virginia Darden School of Business Emerging Legislative Leaders Program Attendee 2020; Bowhay Institute for Legislative Leadership Development (BILLD) 2021.

Occupation: Small business owner; part-time police officer, Cadott Police Department; State of Wisconsin Firearms Instructor. Former warehouse specialist; SWAT team member; firefighter. Served in the U.S. Army Air Defense 1990–93; U.S. Army Reserves (Medic) 1993–96; Persian Gulf War veteran.

Member: Solis Circle Housing Project—Altoona (community representative); American Veterans Association Post 0654; American Legion Post 291 (Augusta, Wisconsin); American Legion Post 73 (Neillsville, Wisconsin); National Conference of State Legislatures Opioid Fellow, 2022.

Previous office: Elected to Assembly 2018–2020.

Current office: Elected to Senate 2022. Committee assignments 2023: Judiciary and Public Safety; Mental Health, Substance Abuse Prevention, Children and Families (chair); Universities and Revenue (vice chair); Joint Legislative Audit Committee. Additional appointments: Council on Alcohol and Other Drug Abuse; Council on Military and State Relations.

Contact: sen.james@legis.wisconsin.gov; 608-266-7511; Room 319 South, State Capitol, PO Box 7882, Madison, WI 53707-7882.

Robert Summerfield, Assembly District 67
Republican

Personal: Born Eau Claire, Wisconsin, February 24, 1980; raised in Bloomer, Wisconsin; married; 3 children.

Voting address: Bloomer, Wisconsin.

Education: Bloomer High School 1998; BS in Business Administration, University of Wisconsin–Stout 2002.

Occupation: Small business owner.

Member: Bloomer Chamber of Commerce; Bloomer Community Lake Association; Bloomer Rod & Gun; Chippewa County Tavern League; NRA; Good Shepherd Lutheran Church (Bloomer, Wisconsin).

Former member: Tavern League of Wisconsin.

Current office: Elected to Assembly since 2016. Leadership positions: Majority Caucus Chair 2023. Committee assignments 2023: Assembly Organization; Energy and Utilities (vice chair); Health, Aging and Long-Term Care; Housing and Real Estate; Rules; State Affairs; Tourism; Veterans and Military Affairs.

Contact: rep.summerfield@legis.wisconsin.gov; 608-237-9167; 888-534-0067 (toll free); Room 119 West, State Capitol, PO Box 8953, Madison, WI 53708-8953.

Karen Hurd, Assembly District 68
Republican

Personal: Born Houston, Texas, October 20, 1957; married; 5 children, 6 grandchildren.

Voting address: Fall Creek, Wisconsin.

Education: Kirkwood High School (Kirkwood, Missouri) 1976; BA in Spanish, Truman State University 1980; Diploma in Comprehensive Nutrition, Huntington College of Health Sciences 1994; MS in Biochemistry, University of Saint Joseph 2017.

Occupation: Nutritionist; owner of Karen R. Hurd Nutritional Practice 1994–present; K–12 substitute teacher, Fall Creek School System 2021–present. Served as U.S. Army Captain, Military Intelligence 1980–84.

Member: Fall Creek Valley Housing/Fall Creek Retirement Housing (board member, former president); American Legion Post 376 (color guard commander, chaplain); Fall Creek Public Library Trustee; Fall Creek Lions Club; Fall Creek Historical Society.

Former member: Faith Evangelical Free Church (director of music, worship leader, Sunday school teacher, women's bible study leader).

Previous office: Elected Fall Creek Village trustee 2021–present.

Current office: Elected to Assembly 2022. Committee assignments 2023: Agriculture; Corrections; Energy and Utilities; Family Law; Rural Development; Transportation (vice chair).

Contact: rep.hurd@legis.wisconsin.gov; 608-237-9168; 888-534-0068 (toll free); Room 15 North, State Capitol, PO Box 8952, Madison, WI 53708-8952.

Donna Rozar, Assembly District 69
Republican

Personal: Born Lancaster, Pennsylvania, February 9; single; 5 children, 6 grandchildren.

Voting address: Marshfield, Wisconsin.

Education: Virginia Baptist Hospital School of Nursing 1971; BS in Nursing, University of Tennessee 1981; MS in Nursing, Viterbo University 2008.

Occupation: Registered nurse; small business owner, residential and commercial rental property. Former nurse educator.

Member: Special Committee on State Tribal Relations.

Current office: Elected to Assembly since 2020. Committee assignments 2023: Campaigns and Elections; Education; Family Law (chair); Health, Aging and Long-Term Care (vice chair); Jobs, Economy and Small Business Development; Workforce Development and Economic Opportunities.

Contact: rep.rozar@legis.wisconsin.gov; 608-237-9169; 888-534-0069 (toll free); Room 13 West, State Capitol, PO Box 8953, Madison, WI 53708-8953.

SENATE DISTRICT 24
ASSEMBLY DISTRICTS 70, 71, 72

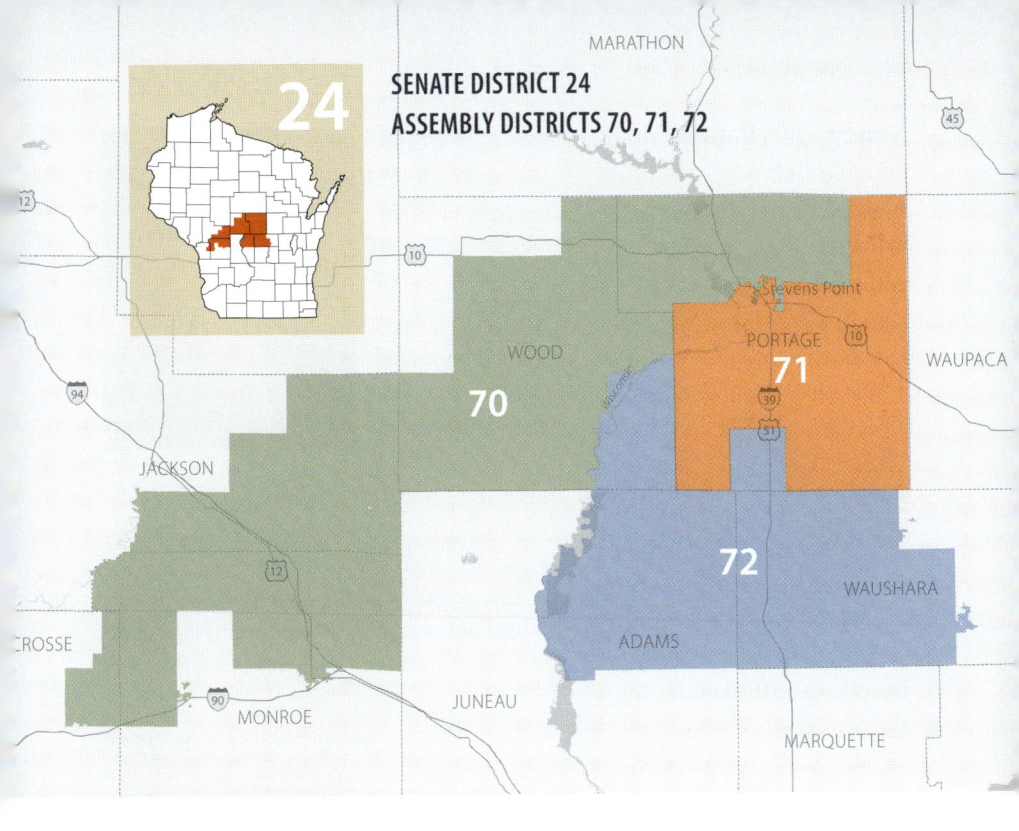

Patrick Testin, Senate District 24
Republican

Personal: Born Madison, Wisconsin, June 9, 1988; married.

Voting address: Stevens Point, Wisconsin.

Education: Marinette High School 2006; BS in Political Science, University of Wisconsin–Stevens Point 2011; Bowhay Institute for Legislative Leadership Development (BILLD) Fellow 2018.

Occupation: Sales professional for a Wisconsin-based wine distributor.

Member: Stevens Point Elk Lodge 641; Ignite Leadership Network of Portage County; Wisconsin Wing, Civil Air Patrol Legislative Squadron.

Current office: Elected to Senate since 2016. Leadership positions: President Pro Tempore 2023, 2021; Majority Caucus Vice Chair 2019, 2017. Committee assignments 2023: Agriculture and Tourism; Finance; Health (vice chair); Labor, Regulatory Reform, Veterans and Military Affairs (chair); Joint Committee on Finance; Joint Committee on Information Policy and Technology; Joint Legislative Council; Joint Survey Committee on Tax Exemptions (cochair).

Contact: sen.testin@legis.wisconsin.gov; 608-266-3123; Room 8 South, State Capitol, PO Box 7882, Madison, WI 53707-7882.

Nancy Lynn VanderMeer, Assembly District 70
Republican

Personal: Born Evergreen Park, Illinois, December 15, 1958; married.

Voting address: Tomah, Wisconsin.

Education: Evergreen Park Community High School 1976; BS in Psychology, University of Wisconsin–La Crosse 1988; Bowhay Institute for Legislative Leadership Development (BILLD) 2017; National Conference of State Legislatures Early Learning Fellow 2018.

Occupation: Small business owner; family dairy farmer. Former automobile dealer.

Member: Vietnam Veterans of America (honorary life member); Jackson County Local Emergency Planning Commission; Farm Bureau; Gloria Dei Lutheran Church (former council president); Tomah Chamber of Commerce (former member of board of directors); NRA; American Legion Auxiliary; board of directors of the nonprofit Handishop Industries; Monroe County Mental Health Coalition; American Association of University Women—Tomah Chapter.

Former member: Tomah Memorial Hospital board of directors (officer); American Business Women's Association (president).

Current office: Elected to Assembly since 2014. Committee assignments 2023: Agriculture; Health, Aging and Long-Term Care; Mental Health and Substance Abuse Prevention; Rural Development; Tourism; Transportation (chair); Veterans and Military Affairs (vice chair); Joint Legislative Council (cochair). Additional appointment: Small Business Regulatory Review Board.

Contact: rep.vandermeer@legis.wisconsin.gov; 608-237-9170; 888-534-0070 (toll free); Room 11 West, State Capitol, PO Box 8953, Madison, WI 53708-8953.

Katrina Shankland, Assembly District 71
Democrat

Personal: Born Wausau, Wisconsin, August 4, 1987; married.

Voting address: Stevens Point, Wisconsin.

Education: Wittenberg-Birnamwood High School 2005; attended University of Wisconsin–Marathon County 2004–5 and Marquette University 2005–6; BA in Political Science, University of Wisconsin–Madison 2009; MS in Community and Organizational Leadership, University of Wisconsin–Stevens Point 2019.

Occupation: Full-time legislator. Former nonprofit professional.

Member: Governor's Council on Workforce Investment; Wisconsin Legislative

Sportsmen's Caucus (cochair); Wisconsin Legislative Children's Caucus; Wisconsin Legislative Paper Caucus; National Caucus of Environmental Legislators (Wisconsin state lead); Elected Officials Protecting America National Leadership Council; Council of State Governments Henry Toll Fellow 2013; Major, Wisconsin Wing, Civil Air Patrol Legislative Squadron (official Auxiliary of the U.S. Air Force); Born Learning Advocacy and Awareness Steering Committee.

Current office: Elected to Assembly since 2012. Leadership positions: Assistant Minority Leader 2015. Committee assignments 2023: Agriculture; Colleges and Universities; Environment; Sporting Heritage; Workforce Development and Economic Opportunities. Additional appointments: Council on Forestry; Sporting Heritage Council.

Contact: rep.shankland@legis.wisconsin.gov; 608-237-9171; 888-534-0071 (toll free); Room 304 West, State Capitol, PO Box 8953, Madison, WI 53708-8953.

Scott S. Krug, Assembly District 72
Republican

Personal: Born Wisconsin Rapids, Wisconsin, September 16, 1975; married; 6 children.

Voting address: Rome, Wisconsin (Adams County).

Education: Lincoln High School 1993; attended University of Wisconsin–Stevens Point; associate degree, Mid-State Technical College 1999; BAS in Psychology, University of Wisconsin–Green Bay 2008.

Occupation: Realtor; Adams County Board of Supervisors District 18. Former Wood County Drug Court Coordinator, jail discharge planner; Juneau County Sheriff's deputy.

Member: Wisconsin Rapids Elks Lodge #693 (exalted ruler); Heart of Wisconsin Chamber of Commerce; Wisconsin Rapids Rotary.

Current office: Elected to Assembly since 2010. Committee assignments 2023: Campaigns and Elections (chair); Colleges and Universities; Housing and Real Estate; Local Government; Tourism. Additional appointment: Transportation Projects Commission.

Contact: rep.krug@legis.wisconsin.gov; 608-237-9172; 888-529-0072 (toll free); Room 223 North, State Capitol, PO Box 8952, Madison, WI 53708-8952.

SENATE DISTRICT 25
ASSEMBLY DISTRICTS 73, 74, 75

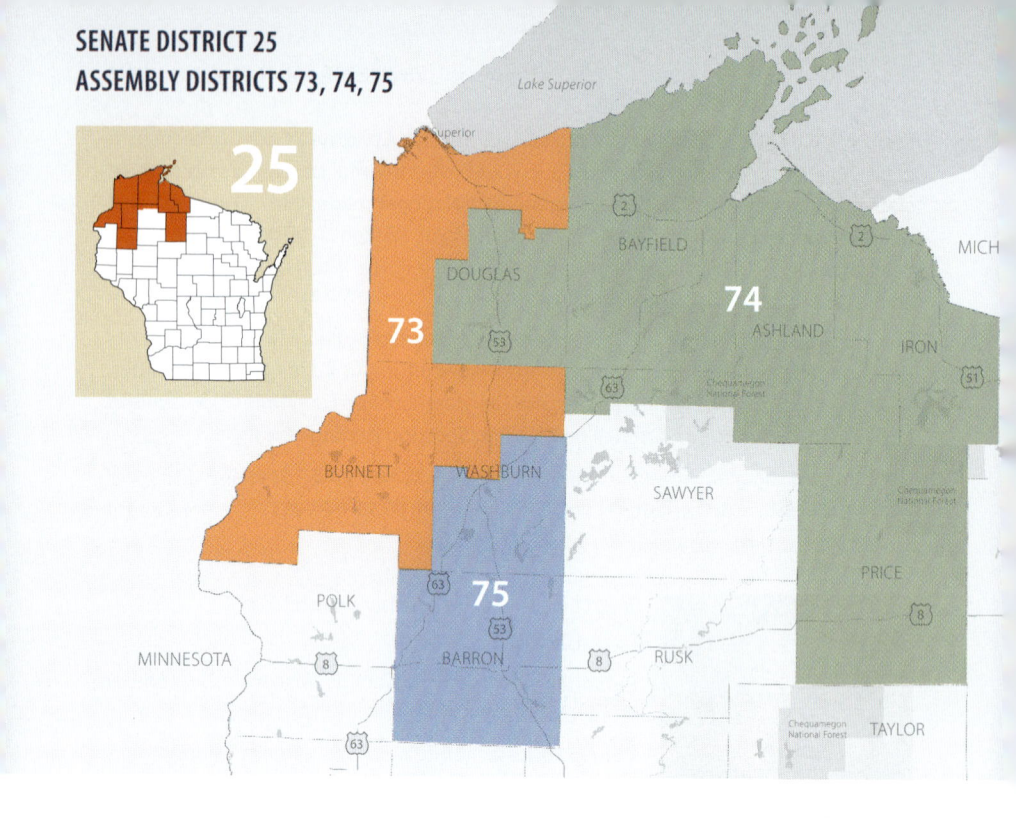

Romaine Quinn, Senate District 25
Republican

Personal: Born Rice Lake, Wisconsin, July 30, 1990.

Voting address: Cameron, Wisconsin.

Education: Rice Lake High School 2009; interdisciplinary BA in Political Science with emphasis on Public Leadership, University of Wisconsin–Green Bay 2014; attended University of Wisconsin–Barron County and University of Wisconsin–Eau Claire.

Occupation: Legislator; realtor. Former beverage salesman.

Previous office: Elected to Rice Lake City Council 2009–10; mayor of Rice Lake 2010–12; Assembly 2014–2020.

Current office: Elected to Senate 2022. Committee assignments 2023: Agriculture and Tourism; Education (vice chair); Housing, Rural Issues and Forestry (chair); Shared Revenue, Elections and Consumer Protection; Utilities and Technology; Joint Committee on Information Policy and Technology; Joint Legislative Council. Additional appointments: Council on Forestry; Educational Communications Board; Legislative State Supported Programs Study and Advisory Committee; Wisconsin Housing and Economic Development Authority.

Contact: sen.quinn@legis.wisconsin.gov; 608-266-3510; 800-469-6562 (toll free); Room 123 South, State Capitol, PO Box 7882, Madison, WI 53707-7882.

Angie Sapik, Assembly District 73
Republican

Personal: Born Grand Rapids, Minnesota, August 4, 1984; married; 2 children.

Voting address: Lake Nebagamon, Wisconsin.

Education: Northwestern High School; degree in Human Services, Duluth Business University.

Occupation: Onion broker.

Current office: Elected to Assembly 2022. Committee assignments 2023: Corrections; Health, Aging and Long-Term Care; Labor and Integrated Employment (vice chair); Workforce Development and Economic Opportunities.

Contact: rep.sapik@legis.wisconsin.gov; 608-237-9173; 888-534-0073 (toll free); Room 16 West, State Capitol, PO Box 8953, Madison, WI 53708-8953.

Chanz Green, Assembly District 74
Republican

Personal: Born Amery, Wisconsin, January 29, 1991; single.

Voting address: Mason, Wisconsin.

Education: Amery High School 2009.

Occupation: Tavern owner. Former assistant director of public works (Amery, Wisconsin); utilities manager (Ashland, Wisconsin).

Member: Wisconsin Bear Hunters Association; NRA; Hunter Nation; Wisconsin Tavern League.

Current office: Elected to Assembly 2022. Committee assignments 2023: Criminal Justice and Public Safety; Forestry, Parks and Outdoor Recreation; Rural Development; Sporting Heritage; State Affairs (vice chair).

Contact: rep.green@legis.wisconsin.gov; 608-237-9174; 888-534-0074 (toll free); Room 125 West, State Capitol, PO Box 8952, Madison, WI 53708-8952.

David Armstrong, Assembly District 75
Republican

Personal: Born St. Paul, Minnesota, October 3, 1961; married; 4 children, 3 grandchildren.

Voting address: Rice Lake, Wisconsin.

Education: St. Bernard's High School (St. Paul, Minnesota) 1979; attended Metropolitan State University (St. Paul, Minnesota).

Occupation: Executive director, Barron County Economic Development Corporation. Former owner of multiple businesses.

Member: Rice Lake Tourism Commission (board member).

Former member: Community Connections to Prosperity (vice president); Heart of the North Legislative Day (chairperson); Law Enforcement Foundation of Barron County (president); Rice Lake Cable Commission (president); Law Enforcement Foundation of Barron County (board member and president); Pioneer Village-Barron County Historical Society (board member); Rice Lake Chamber of Commerce (board member); Wisconsin Rural Partners.

Current office: Elected to Assembly since 2020. Committee assignments 2023: Housing and Real Estate; Jobs, Economy and Small Business Development (vice chair); Rural Development (chair); Ways and Means; Workforce Development and Economic Opportunities. Additional appointment: Wisconsin Economic Development Corporation.

Contact: rep.armstrong@legis.wisconsin.gov; 608-237-9175; 888-534-0075 (toll free); Room 220 North, State Capitol, PO Box 8952, Madison, WI 53708-8952.

SENATE DISTRICT 26
ASSEMBLY DISTRICTS 76, 77, 78

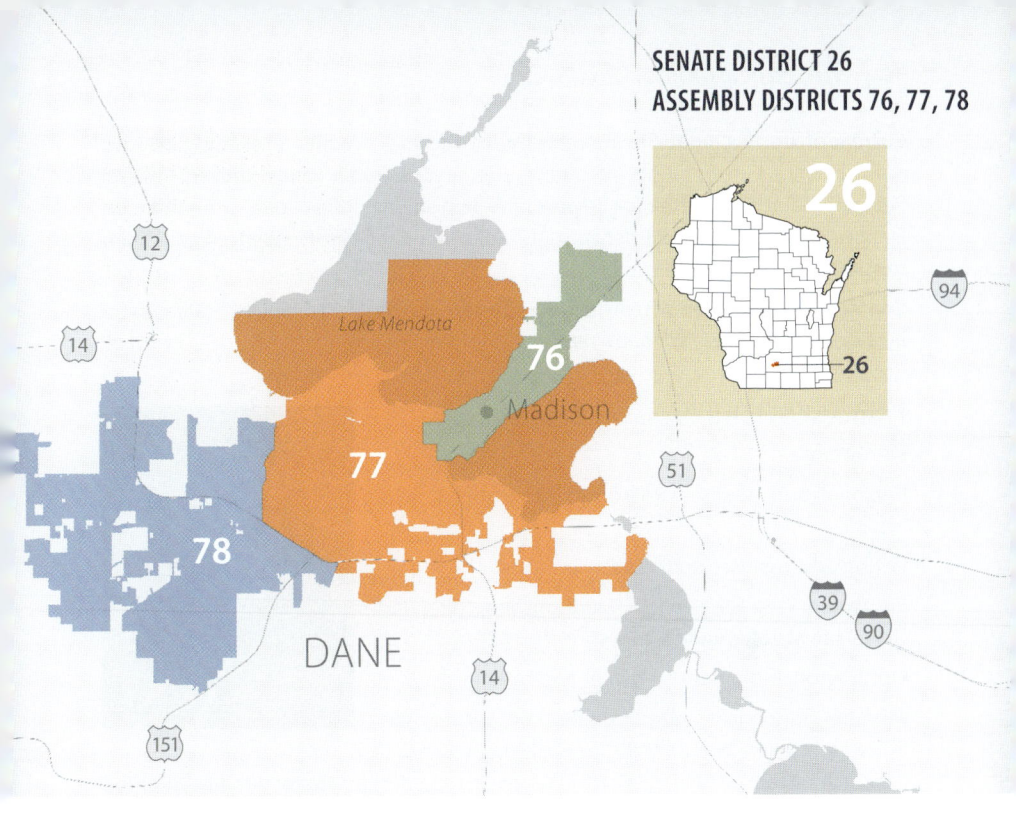

Kelda Helen Roys, Senate District 26
Democrat

Personal: Born Marshfield, Wisconsin, June 24, 1979; married; 3 children, 2 stepchildren.

Voting address: Madison, Wisconsin.

Education: BA in Drama, Politics, and Cultural Studies, magna cum laude, New York University 2000; JD, magna cum laude, University of Wisconsin Law School 2004.

Occupation: Attorney; small business owner. Former nonprofit executive.

Member: Clean Lakes Alliance (board); Legal Association for Women; State Bar of Wisconsin; TEMPO Madison (former board member, membership chair).

Former member: ACLU of Wisconsin (board); Coalition of Wisconsin Aging Groups (legislative advisory board); Citizen Action of Wisconsin (board); Common Cause of Wisconsin (board); Dane County Democratic Party (executive committee); Democratic Leadership Institute (board); Emerge Wisconsin (advisory board); Madison Repertory Theatre (board); Public Interest Law Foundation (board); Wisconsin Bar Association (legal assistance committee); Sherman Neighborhood Association (board); Women's Council (board); Public Interest Law Foundation (board).

Previous office: Elected to Assembly 2008–10. Minority Caucus Chair 2011.

Current office: Elected to Senate 2020. Committee assignments 2023: Administrative Rules; Finance; Government Operations; Judiciary and Public Safety; Universities and Revenue; Joint Committee for Review of Administrative Rules; Joint Committee on Finance. Additional appointments: State Capitol and Executive Residence Board; Commission on Uniform State Laws.

Contact: sen.roys@legis.wisconsin.gov; 608-266-1627; Room 130 South, State Capitol, PO Box 7882, Madison, WI 53707-7882.

Francesca Hong, Assembly District 76
Democrat

Personal: Born Madison, Wisconsin, November 4, 1988; 1 child.

Voting address: Madison, Wisconsin.

Education: West High School (Madison) 2007; attended University of Wisconsin–Madison.

Occupation: Restaurant co-owner and co-chef.

Member: Wisconsin United Coalition of Mutual Assistance Association (board); Main Street Alliance Wisconsin (leadership team); AAPI Coalition of Wisconsin (board, executive committee); Rooted Wisconsin (board); Dane County Food Collective (cofounder); Culinary Ladies Collective (cofounder, board president); Kennedy Heights Community Center (board).

Current office: Elected to Assembly since 2020. Committee assignments 2023: Audit; Education; Labor and Integrated Employment; State Affairs; Joint Legislative Audit Committee. Additional appointment: Wisconsin Economic Development Corporation.

Contact: rep.hong@legis.wisconsin.gov; 608-237-9176; 888-534-0076 (toll free); Room 122 North, State Capitol, PO Box 8952, Madison, WI 53708-8952.

Shelia Stubbs, Assembly District 77
Democrat

Personal: Born Camden, Arkansas, February 22, 1971; married; 6 children.

Voting address: Madison, Wisconsin.

Education: Beloit Memorial High School; BA in Political Science, Tougaloo College; BS in Criminal Justice Administration, magna cum laude, Mount Senario College; Masters of Science & Management, Cardinal Stritch University; Bowhay Institute for Legislative Leadership Development (BILLD) Fellow 2021.

Occupation: Full-time legislator. Former special education teacher; adjunct professor; probation and parole agent; match support specialist.

Member: Democratic Party of Wis.; Democratic Party of Wis. Black Caucus (former chair);

Greater Madison Convention & Visitors Bureau (board of directors); Tamara D. Grigsby Office of Equity and Inclusion (advisory board); Alliant Energy Center Redevelopment Committee; Dane Co. Youth in Government (mentor); Wis. Legislative Black Caucus (former chair); Vel Phillips Statue Advisory Taskforce; National Association of Counties (NACo); Women of NACo (secretary); Community Justice Action Fund Policy Makers for Peace (regional lead); Women's Legislative Network Governance; National Conference of State Legislatures (NCSL) Law, Criminal Justice, and Public Safety Committee and Women's Legislative Network (regional board); Bridge-Lake Point Neighborhood Association (president); Delta Sigma Theta Sorority, Madison Alumnae Chapter; NAACP Dane Co. Branch; End Time Ministries International (cofounder, ordained pastor); Wis. Women in Government (legislative board); Madison Complete Count Committee (chair); Wis. Complete Count Committee; 2022 NCSL Pretrial Policy Fellow; 2022 Fair Fight Fellow.

Previous office: Elected to Dane County Board of Supervisors.

Current office: Elected to Assembly since 2018. Committee assignments 2023: Colleges and Universities; Corrections; Criminal Justice and Public Safety; Tourism. Additional appointments: Council on Domestic Abuse; Council on Tourism.

Contact: rep.stubbs@legis.wisconsin.gov; 608-237-9177; 888-534-0077 (toll free); Room 7 North, State Capitol, PO Box 8953, Madison, WI 53708-8953.

Lisa Subeck, Assembly District 78
Democrat

Personal: Born Chicago, Illinois, June 17, 1971; single.

Voting address: Madison, Wisconsin.

Education: Rich Central High School 1989; BA University of Wisconsin–Madison 1993.

Occupation: Full-time legislator. Former early childhood education/Head Start program manager; technical college instructor; nonprofit executive director.

Member: National Foundation of Women Legislators (board); National Association of Jewish Legislators (board); National Caucus of Environmental Legislators; Great Lakes Legislative Council; Women in Government (state director).

Former member: American Federation of Teachers.

Previous office: Elected to City of Madison Common Council 2011–15.

Current office: Elected to Assembly since 2014. Leadership positions: Minority Caucus Chair 2023. Committee assignments 2023: Assembly Organization; Campaigns and Elections; Energy and Utilities; Health, Aging and Long-Term Care; Insurance; Rules. Additional appointment: State Capitol and Executive Residence Board (chair).

Contact: rep.subeck@legis.wisconsin.gov; 608-237-9178; 888-534-0078 (toll free); Room 113 North, State Capitol, PO Box 8953, Madison, WI 53708-8953.

SENATE DISTRICT 27
ASSEMBLY DISTRICTS 79, 80, 81

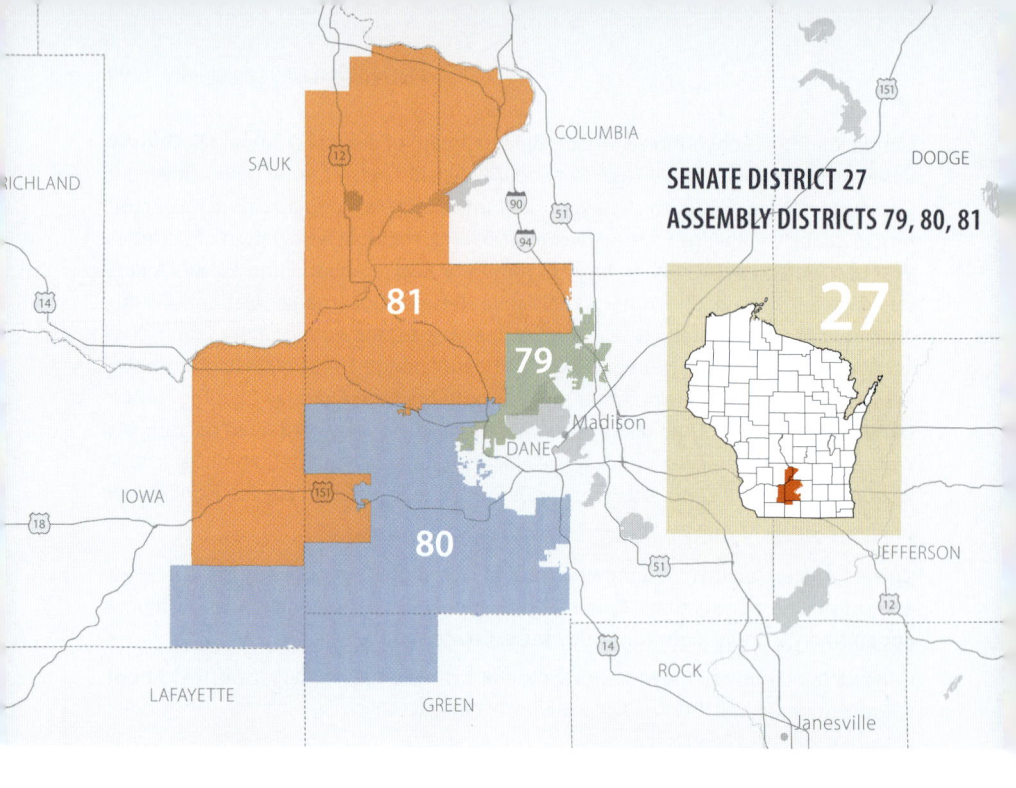

Dianne Hesselbein, Senate District 27
Democrat

Personal: Born Madison, Wisconsin, March 10, 1971; married; 3 children.

Voting address: Middleton, Wisconsin.

Education: La Follette High School (Madison) 1989; BS University of Wisconsin Oshkosh 1993; MA Edgewood College 1996.

Occupation: Full-time legislator.

Member: Dane County Democratic Party; Friends of Pheasant Branch; Middleton Action Team; VFW Auxiliary Council.

Former member: Parent Teacher Organization (president); Boy Scouts of America (cubmaster); Girl Scouts (troop leader); Monona Terrace Convention and Community Center Board.

Previous office: Elected to Middleton-Cross Plains Area Board of Education 2005–8; Dane County Board of Supervisors 2008–14; Assembly 2012–20.

Current office: Elected to Senate 2022. Leadership positions: Minority Caucus Vice Chair 2023. Committee assignments 2023: Financial Institutions and Sporting Heritage; Government Operations; Health; Mental Health, Substance Abuse Prevention, Children and Families; Natural Resources and Energy; Joint Legislative Audit Committee. Additional appointment: Women's Council.

Contact: sen.hesselbein@legis.wisconsin.gov; 608-266-6670; Room 3 South, State Capitol, PO Box 7882, Madison, WI 53707-7882.

Alex Joers, Assembly District 79
Democrat

Personal: Born Madison, Wisconsin, August 27, 1992; married; 1 child.

Voting address: Madison, Wisconsin.

Education: Middleton High School 2011; BA in Public Administration and Political Science, University of Wisconsin–La Crosse 2015.

Occupation: Small Business Manager. Former legislative aide and association executive.

Member: Dane County Democratic Party; Friends of Pheasant Branch Conservancy; New Leaders Council–Wisconsin (former fellow and board member); University of Wisconsin–La Crosse Alumni Association; Young Elected Officials Network; MCPSAD Education Foundation Board of Directors; Monona Terrace Community and Convention Center Board of Directors.

Former member: Dane County Youth Commission.

Previous office: Elected to Dane County Board of Supervisors 2020–23.

Current office: Elected to Assembly 2022. Committee assignments 2023: Colleges and Universities; Forestry, Parks and Outdoor Recreation; Rules; Tourism.

Contact: rep.joers@legis.wisconsin.gov; 608-237-9179; 888-534-0079 (toll free); Room 20 North, State Capitol, PO Box 8952, Madison, WI 53708-8952.

Mike Bare, Assembly District 80
Democrat

Personal: Born March 8, 1983, Manitowoc, Wisconsin.

Voting address: Verona, Wisconsin.

Education: Manitowoc Lincoln High School 2001; BA in Political Science, American University 2005; MA in Political Science, American University 2010.

Occupation: Co-owner, Biergarten at Olbrich Park. Former researcher and advocate, Community Advocates Public Policy Institute.

Former member: New Leaders Council–Wisconsin (chapter director); Down Syndrome Association of Wisconsin; Special Olympics of Wisconsin; Verona City Council; Verona Parks Commission; Verona Plan Commission.

Previous office: Elected to Verona City Council 2013–14; Dane County Board 2020–23.

Current office: Elected to Assembly 2022. Committee assignments 2023: Forestry, Parks and Outdoor Recreation; Housing and Real Estate; Insurance; Rules.

Contact: rep.bare@legis.wisconsin.gov; 608-237-9180; 888-534-0080 (toll free); Room 306 West, State Capitol, PO Box 8952, Madison, WI 53708-8952.

Dave Considine, Assembly District 81
Democrat

Personal: Born Janesville, Wisconsin, March 29, 1952; married; 5 children, 13 grandchildren.

Voting address: Town of Caledonia, Wisconsin.

Education: Mukwonago Union High School 1970; BS in Education, University of Wisconsin–Whitewater 1974; certificate in Emotional/Behavorial Disabilities, University of Wisconsin–Madison 1990; MA in Education, Viterbo University 2005; instructor certificate in autism spectrum and enhanced verbal skills, Crisis Prevention Institute (Milwaukee) 2008, 2010, 2013.

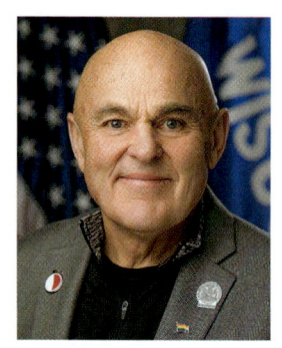

Occupation: Full-time legislator. Former dairy goat farmer; special education teacher.

Member: Columbia County Democratic Party; Sauk County Democratic Party; Pheasants Forever; Ducks Unlimited; First United Methodist Church, Baraboo.

Former member: Baraboo Education Association (president); American Dairy Goat Association (judge); Wisconsin Dairy Goat Association (president); Crisis Prevention Institute (instructor).

Current office: Elected to Assembly since 2014. Committee assignments 2023: Agriculture; Education; Mental Health and Substance Abuse Prevention; Rural Development; Transportation.

Contact: rep.considine@legis.wisconsin.gov; 608-237-9181; 888-534-0081 (toll free); Room 303 West, State Capitol, PO Box 8952, Madison, WI 53708-8952.

SENATE DISTRICT 28
ASSEMBLY DISTRICTS 82, 83, 84

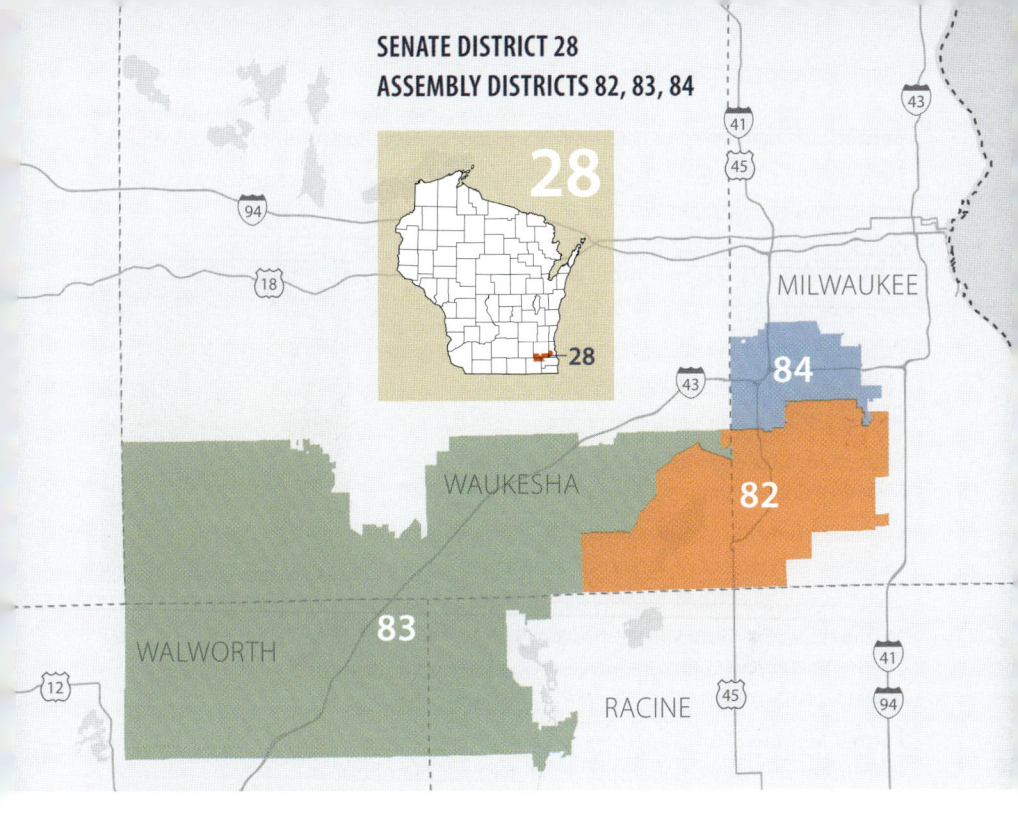

Marc Julian Bradley, Senate District 28
Republican

Personal: Born Baltimore, Maryland, February 11, 1981; moved to Wisconsin in 1992.

Voting address: Franklin, Wisconsin.

Education: Attended Temple University (Philadelphia) 2004–5; BS in Political Science, University of Wisconsin–La Crosse 2014.

Occupation: Realtor. Former operations manager for Northwestern Mutual & CenturyLink.

Member: Milwaukee County Republican Party; Waukesha County Republican Party; Walworth County Republican Party; Racine County Republican Party; NRA.

Former member: La Crosse County Republican Party (chair); 2015 Republican Party of Wisconsin Convention (chair); Third Congressional District Republican Party (vice chair); Together for Tots, Toys for Tots Drive (cofounder).

Current office: Elected to Senate 2020. Committee assignments 2023: Administrative Rules; Government Operations (vice chair); Licensing, Constitution and Federalism (vice chair); Utilities and Technology (chair); Joint Committee for Review of Administrative Rules; Joint Committee on Information Policy and Technology (cochair).

Contact: sen.bradley@legis.wisconsin.gov; 608-266-5400; Room 316 South, State Capitol, PO Box 7882, Madison, WI 53707-7882.

Chuck Wichgers, Assembly District 82
Republican

Personal: Born Milwaukee, Wisconsin, July 4, 1965; married; 8 children, grandfather.

Voting address: Muskego, Wisconsin.

Education: Muskego High School 1983; Waukesha County Technical College 1984–85.

Occupation: Works in professional sales. Former medical salesman offering conservative options for pain management. Coach for softball, basketball, football.

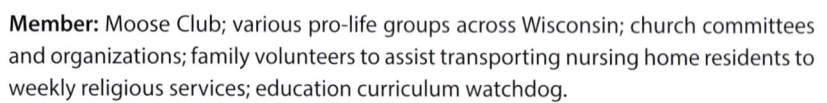

Member: Moose Club; various pro-life groups across Wisconsin; church committees and organizations; family volunteers to assist transporting nursing home residents to weekly religious services; education curriculum watchdog.

Former Member: Muskego Hoops Booster Club (cofounder); Preserve Muskego (president); Janesville Road Reconstruction Advisory Committee.

Previous office: Elected to City of Muskego Common Council 1999–2002; Waukesha County Board of Supervisors 1999–2002.

Current office: Elected to Assembly since 2016. Committee assignments 2023: Children and Families; Criminal Justice and Public Safety; Education; Mental Health and Substance Abuse Prevention.

Contact: rep.wichgers@legis.wisconsin.gov; 608-237-9182; 888-534-0082 (toll free); Room 306 North, State Capitol, PO Box 8953, Madison, WI 53708-8953.

Nik Rettinger, Assembly District 83
Republican

Personal: Born Brookfield, Wisconsin, August 6, 1990; married.

Voting address: Mukwonago, Wisconsin.

Education: Waukesha South High School 2008; AAS with Political Science Emphasis, University of Wisconsin–Waukesha 2011; BA in Political Science and History, minor in International Studies, University of Wisconsin–Milwaukee 2014.

Occupation: Former chief of staff to State Senator Andre Jacque.

Member: Mukwonago Area Chamber of Commerce; NRA; Young Republican National

Federation (board of directors); Wisconsin Young Republicans (state chairman); United States Bowling Congress.

Former member: Boy Scouts of America (Eagle Scout & Order of the Arrow Honor Society); First Congressional District Republican Party (chair); Republican Party of Waukesha County (first vice chair).

Current office: Elected to Assembly 2022. Committee assignments 2023: Consumer Protection; Financial Institutions; Insurance; Judiciary (vice chair); Workforce Development and Economic Opportunities.

Contact: rep.rettinger@legis.wisconsin.gov; 608-237-9183; 888-534-0083 (toll free); Room 8 West, State Capitol, PO Box 8953, Madison, WI 53708-8953.

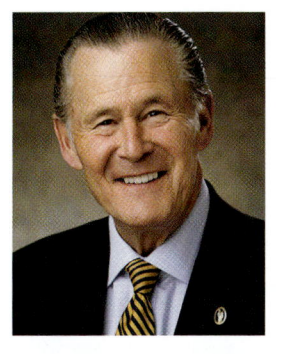

Bob Donovan, Assembly District 84
Republican

Personal: Born Milwaukee, Wisconsin, May 4, 1956; married; 5 children, 11 grandchildren.

Voting address: Greenfield, Wisconsin.

Education: Thomas More High School (Milwaukee); St. Francis De Sales Seminary; University of Wisconsin–Milwaukee.

Occupation: Former foreman, Milwaukee Solvay Coke Company; life insurance agent, Prudential Insurance.

Member: Shamrock Club of Wisconsin; Emerald Society.

Previous office: Elected to City of Milwaukee Common Council 2000–20.

Current office: Elected to Assembly 2022. Committee assignments 2023: Criminal Justice and Public Safety; Energy and Utilities; Local Government (vice chair).

Contact: rep.donovan@legis.wisconsin.gov; 608-237-9184; 888-534-0084 (toll free); Room 3 North, State Capitol, PO Box 8952, Madison, WI 53708-8952.

SENATE DISTRICT 29
ASSEMBLY DISTRICTS 85, 86, 87

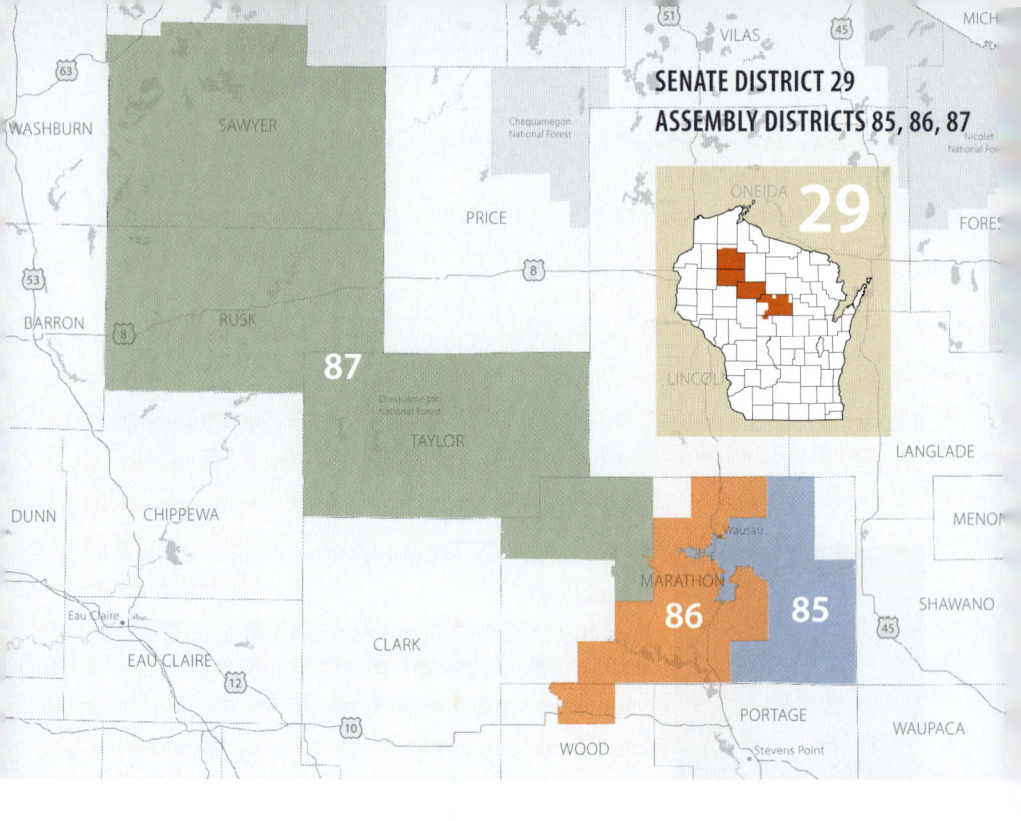

Cory Tomczyk, Senate District 29
Republican

Personal: Born Rudolph, Wisconsin, October 26, 1962; married; 2 children, 3 grandchildren.

Voting address: Town of Mosinee, Wisconsin.

Education: Lincoln High School (Wisconsin Rapids) 1980.

Occupation: Small business owner.

Member: International Secure Information Governance and Management Association (iSIGMA); Data Destruction Leadership Council; Marathon County Republican Party (former vice chair).

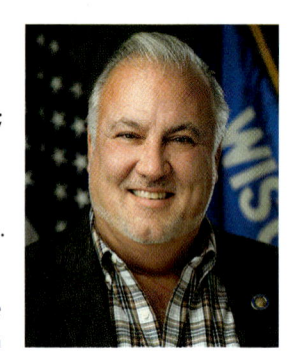

Former member: National Association for Information Destruction (NAID) Board of Directors; iSIGMA Board of Directors; NAID Complaint Resolution Committee (chair).

Previous office: Elected to Mosinee School Board 2006–19 (president 2010–15).

Current office: Elected to Senate 2022. Committee assignments 2023: Agriculture and Tourism (vice chair); Financial Institutions and Sporting Heritage; Natural Resources and Energy; Transportation and Local Government (chair). Additional appointments: Migrant Labor Council; Rustic Roads Board; Transportation Projects Commission.

Contact: sen.tomczyk@legis.wisconsin.gov; 608-266-2502; Room 310 South, State Capitol, PO Box 7882, Madison, WI 53707-7882.

Patrick Snyder, Assembly District 85
Republican

Personal: Born Boone, Iowa, October 10, 1956; married; 2 children, 5 grandchildren.

Voting address: Schofield, Wisconsin.

Education: Oelwein Community High School (Iowa) 1974; BA in Communications, University of Iowa 1978.

Occupation: Former congressional staffer for Congressman Sean Duffy; radio host for WSAU.

Member: Wausau Noon Rotary; Elks Club; United Way's Hunger Coalition and Housing and Homelessness Committee; Marathon County Health Department's Alcohol and Other Drugs (AOD) Committee.

Former member: St. Therese Parish Council; Marathon County Department of Social Services Administrative Review Panel.

Previous office: Elected City of Schofield alder.

Current office: Elected to Assembly since 2016. Committee assignments 2023: Children and Families (chair); Family Law; Government Accountability and Oversight; Veterans and Military Affairs; Ways and Means; Workforce Development and Economic Opportunities. Additional appointment: Child Abuse and Neglect Prevention Board.

Contact: rep.snyder@legis.wisconsin.gov; 608-237-9185; 888-534-0085 (toll free); Room 307 North, State Capitol, PO Box 8953, Madison, WI 53708-8953.

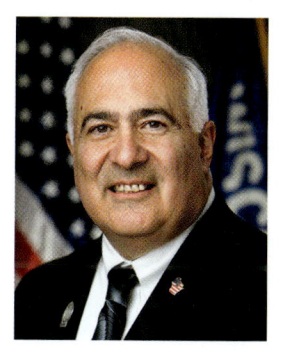

John Spiros, Assembly District 86
Republican

Personal: Born Akron, Ohio, July 28, 1961; married; 5 children, 4 grandchildren.

Voting address: Marshfield, Wisconsin.

Education: Marietta High School (Marietta, Ohio) 1979; AAS in Criminal Justice, Metropolitan Technical Community College (Omaha, Nebraska) 1985.

Occupation: Vice president, safety and claims management for a national trucking company (Marshfield, Wisconsin). Served in U.S. Air Force 1979–85, member of the Strategic Air Command "Elite" guard.

Member: Trucking Industry Defense Association (president of the board of directors

2015–17; executive committee 2013–18); Wisconsin Farm Bureau; Marshfield Elks Club; American Trucking Association.

Previous office: Elected City of Marshfield alder 2005–13.

Current office: Elected to Assembly since 2012. Committee assignments 2023: Review of Administrative Rules; Criminal Justice and Public Safety (chair); State Affairs; Transportation; Joint Committee for Review of Administrative Rules.

Contact: rep.spiros@legis.wisconsin.gov; 608-237-9186; 888-534-0086 (toll free); Room 212 North, State Capitol, PO Box 8953, Madison, WI 53708-8953.

James W. Edming, Assembly District 87
Republican

Personal: Born Ladysmith, Wisconsin, November 22, 1945; married; 3 sons, 2 granddaughters, 1 great-granddaughter.

Voting address: Glen Flora, Wisconsin.

Education: Flambeau High School (Tony, Wisconsin) 1964; Teacher's Certificate, Taylor County Teacher's College 1967; attended University of Wisconsin–Superior, University of Wisconsin–Eau Claire, University of Wisconsin–Menomonie, and University of Wisconsin–Barron County.

Occupation: Convenience store owner; metal stamping company owner; mini-storage business owner; farmer. Former frozen pizza manufacturer.

Member: 3rd degree Master Mason; 32nd degree Scottish Rite; Shriner; Sons of AMVETS Squadron 127—Ladysmith; NRA (gun instructor); Model T Ford Club; Wisconsin Self Storage Association; St. Joseph's Hospital Advisory Council (Chippewa Falls) 2018–present; Rusk County Hospital Board 1980–82, 2010–18.

Previous office: Elected to Rusk County Board of Supervisors 1976–87.

Current office: Elected to Assembly since 2014. Committee assignments 2023: Forestry, Parks and Outdoor Recreation; Labor and Integrated Employment; Rural Development; Transportation; Veterans and Military Affairs (chair).

Contact: rep.edming@legis.wisconsin.gov; 608-237-9187; 888-534-0087 (toll free); Room 129 West, State Capitol, PO Box 8952, Madison, WI 53708-8952.

SENATE DISTRICT 30
ASSEMBLY DISTRICTS 88, 89, 90

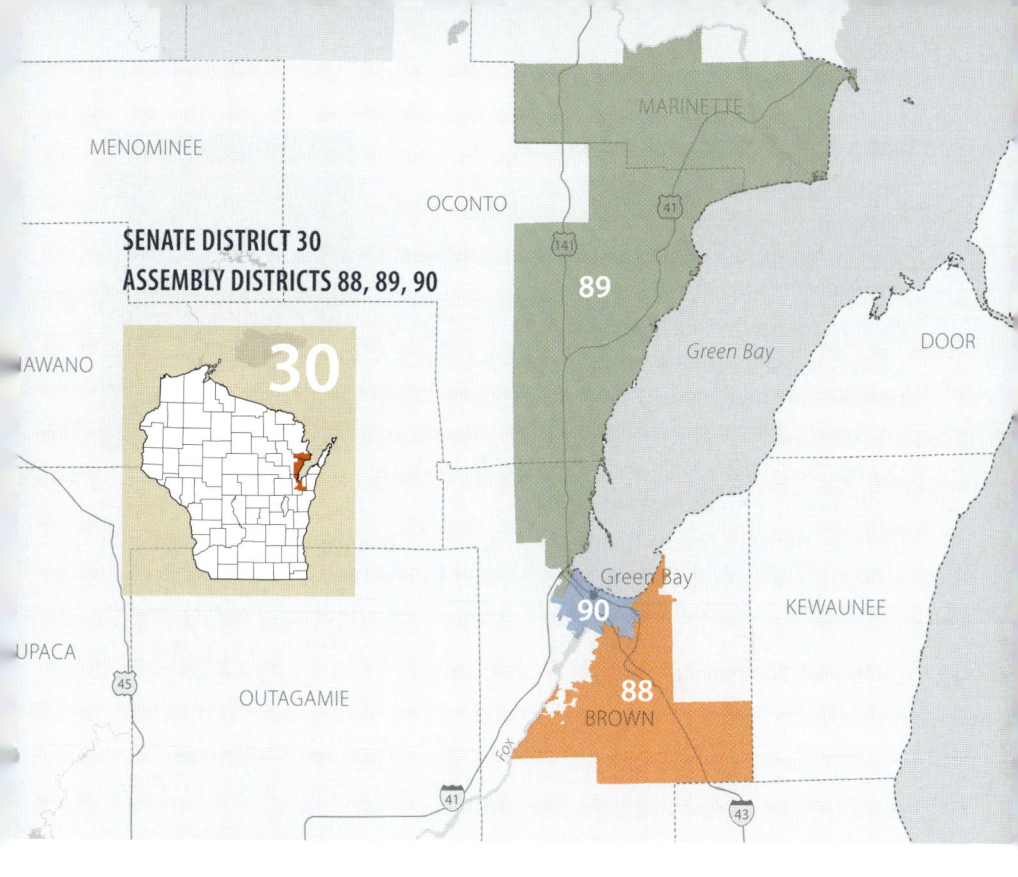

Eric Wimberger, Senate District 30
Republican

Personal: Born Green Bay, Wisconsin, April 2, 1979; single.

Voting address: Green Bay, Wisconsin.

Education: BA in Criminal Justice, St. Cloud State University 2001; JD Marquette University Law School 2005.

Occupation: Attorney and small business owner; operates family-run candy store in Lakewood and a legal practice in Green Bay. Former long-haul truck driver; bartender; factory worker. Served as Captain, U.S. Marine Corps, Judge Advocate General's Corp 2006–10.

Member: Green Bay Packers season ticket holder and shareholder; Cloud Family Foundation (board member).

Current office: Elected to Senate 2020. Committee assignments 2023: Finance; Judiciary and Public Safety; Natural Resources and Energy (vice chair); Joint Committee on Finance; Joint Legislative Audit Committee (cochair). Additional appointment: Commission on Uniform State Laws.

Contact: sen.wimberger@legis.wisconsin.gov; 608-266-5670; Room 104 South, State Capitol, PO Box 7882, Madison, WI 53707-7882.

John J. Macco, Assembly District 88
Republican

Personal: Born Green Bay, Wisconsin, September 23, 1958; widowed, remarried; 2 children, 3 stepchildren, 9 grandchildren.

Voting address: De Pere, Wisconsin.

Education: Green Bay Southwest High School 1976; attended Northeast Wisconsin Technical College and University of Wisconsin–Green Bay.

Occupation: Founder of financial planning group; founder of retail franchise; business consultant.

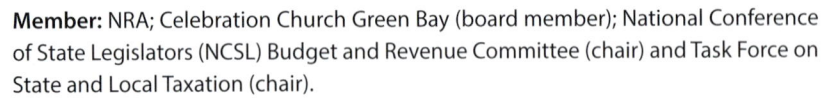

Member: NRA; Celebration Church Green Bay (board member); National Conference of State Legislators (NCSL) Budget and Revenue Committee (chair) and Task Force on State and Local Taxation (chair).

Former member: American Cancer Society of Wood County; Old Main Street Marshfield; Old Main Street De Pere; Old Main Street Green Bay; U.S. Ski Patrol; Aircraft Owners and Pilots Association.

Current office: Elected to Assembly since 2014. Committee assignments 2023: Audit (vice chair); Jobs, Economy and Small Business Development; Regulatory Licensing Reform; Ways and Means (chair); Joint Legislative Audit Committee.

Contact: rep.macco@legis.wisconsin.gov; 608-237-9188; 888-534-0088 (toll free); Room 208 North, State Capitol, PO Box 8953, Madison, WI 53708-8953.

Elijah Behnke, Assembly District 89
Republican

Personal: Born Oconto, Wisconsin, February 15, 1983; married; 2 children.

Voting address: Oconto, Wisconsin.

Education: Oconto High School 2001; associate degree in Biblical Studies, Toccoa Falls College 2005 (class chaplain).

Occupation: Entrepreneur. Former landscaper and farmer.

Member: Jacob's Well Church.

Former member: Town of Little River 4H Club (president).

Current office: Elected to Assembly in April 2021 special election. Reelected 2022. Committee assignments 2023: Consumer Protection; Environment; Mental Health and Substance Abuse Prevention.

Contact: rep.behnke@legis.wisconsin.gov; 608-237-9189; 888-534-0089 (toll free); Room 308 North, State Capitol, PO Box 8952, Madison, WI 53708-8952.

Kristina Shelton, Assembly District 90
Democrat

Personal: Born Pittsburgh, Pennsylvania, June 2, 1980; married; 2 children.

Voting address: Green Bay, Wisconsin.

Education: North Hills High School (Pittsburgh, Pennsylvania) 1998; BS in Kinesiology, Pennsylvania State University 2002; MS in Health Promotion Management, Marymount University (Arlington, Virginia) 2010.

Occupation: Former health education specialist and physical education teacher; nonprofit director; community organizer.

Member: Yoga Alliance; National Commission for Health Education Credentialing.

Former member: Wisconsin Association of School Boards; American Public Health Association; The Society of Health and Physical Educators (SHAPE America).

Previous office: Elected to Green Bay School Board (vice president).

Current office: Elected to Assembly since 2020. Leadership positions: Minority Caucus Secretary 2023. Committee assignments 2023: Education; Jobs, Economy and Small Business Development; Sporting Heritage; Workforce Development and Economic Opportunities.

Contact: rep.shelton@legis.wisconsin.gov; 608-237-9190; 888-534-0090 (toll free); Room 126 North, State Capitol, PO Box 8953, Madison, WI 53708-8953.

SENATE DISTRICT 31
ASSEMBLY DISTRICTS 91, 92, 93

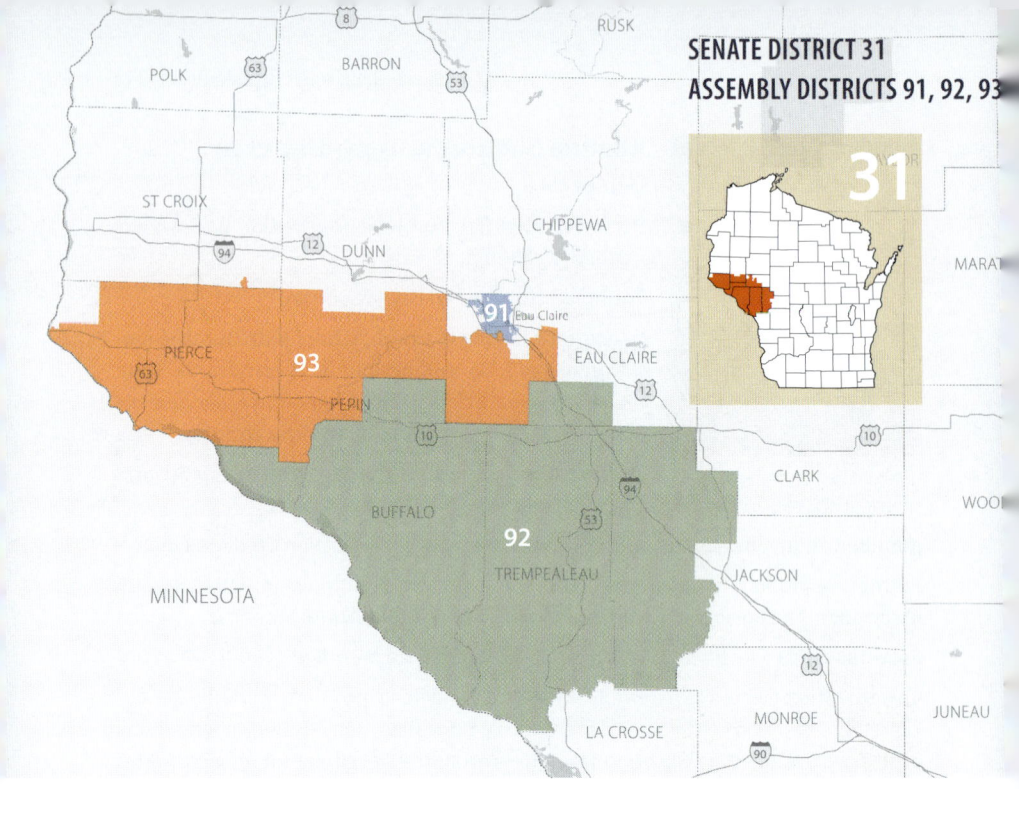

Jeff Smith, Senate District 31
Democrat

Personal: Born Eau Claire, Wisconsin, March 15, 1955; married; 2 children.

Voting address: Town of Brunswick, Wisconsin.

Education: Eau Claire North High School 1973.

Occupation: Former owner/operator of window cleaning business 1973–2011; community organizer for Western Wisconsin Organizing Cooperative of Citizen Action 2016–18.

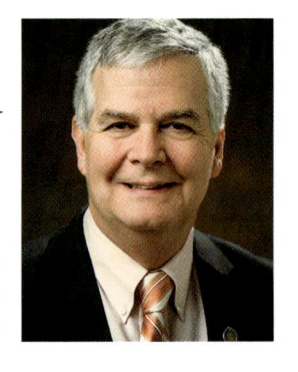

Member: Eau Claire Area Chamber of Commerce; Wisconsin Farmers Union.

Former member: Valley Gospel Choir (president); Eau Claire Male Chorus; Eau Claire Kiwanis Club; Eau Claire Area School District Parent Advisory Committee (founder and chair); Eau Claire Family Resource Center (board member); Governor's Task Force for Educational Excellence; Wisconsin PTA state board; DPI Parent Leadership Corps; Wisconsin Alliance for Excellent Schools; Township Fire Department (vice president of board of directors); Tainter-Menomin Lake Improvement Association (board member); University of Wisconsin Extension Community Partner Advisory Group.

Previous office: Elected to Town of Brunswick Board (chair) 2001–2007; Assembly 2006–10.

Current office: Elected to Senate since 2018. Leadership positions: Assistant Minority Leader 2023; Minority Caucus Chair 2021. Committee assignments 2023: Agriculture and Tourism; Senate Organization; Shared Revenue, Elections and Consumer Protection; Universities and Revenue; Utilities and Technology; Joint Committee on Legislative Organization; Joint Legislative Council. Additional appointments: Council on Alcohol and Other Drug Abuse; Council on Tourism.

Contact: sen.smith@legis.wisconsin.gov; 608-266-8546; 877-763-6636 (toll free); Room 19 South, State Capitol, PO Box 7882, Madison, WI 53707-7882.

Jodi Emerson, Assembly District 91
Democrat

Personal: Born Eau Claire, Wisconsin, August 3, 1972; married; 2 children.

Voting address: Eau Claire, Wisconsin.

Education: Eau Claire Memorial High School 1990; studied Biotechnology, University of Wisconsin–River Falls 1990–92.

Occupation: Former anti-human trafficking advocate.

Member: Wisconsin Anti-Human Trafficking Consortium; Wisconsin Women's Council; Governor's Council on Migrant Labor; Wisconsin Legislative Children's Caucus; National Foundation for Women Legislators (state director).

Former member: Wisconsin Human Trafficking Advisory Council; Wisconsin Anti-Human Trafficking Task Force; Wisconsin PTA; Girl Scouts; Eastside Hill Neighborhood Association Steering Committee.

Current office: Elected to Assembly since 2018. Committee assignments 2023: Colleges and Universities; Criminal Justice and Public Safety; Housing and Real Estate; Rural Development. Additional appointments: Migrant Labor Council; Women's Council.

Contact: rep.emerson@legis.wisconsin.gov; 608-237-9191; 888-534-0091 (toll free); 715-456-9355 (district); Room 322 West, State Capitol, PO Box 8952, Madison, WI 53708-8952.

Treig E. Pronschinske, Assembly District 92
Republican

Personal: Born Eau Claire, Wisconsin, July 7, 1978; married; 1 child.

Voting address: Mondovi, Wisconsin.

Education: Memorial High School 1996; degree in Construction Management, Chippewa Valley Technical College 1997.

Occupation: Small business owner; general construction contractor; beef herdsman.

Member: Gilmanton Community Club.

Former member: Mondovi Fire Department (volunteer firefighter); Mondovi Youth Baseball Association (president); Mondovi Ambulance Commission 2014–18; Big Brothers Big Sisters; Junior Achievement volunteer.

Previous office: Elected mayor of Mondovi 2014–18.

Current office: Elected to Assembly since 2016. Leadership positions: Majority Caucus Sergeant at Arms 2023. Committee assignments 2023: Children and Families; Consumer Protection; Forestry, Parks and Outdoor Recreation; Housing and Real Estate; Local Government; Sporting Heritage (chair).

Contact: rep.pronschinske@legis.wisconsin.gov; 608-237-9192; 888-534-0092 (toll free); Room 127 West, State Capitol, PO Box 8953, Madison, WI 53708-8953.

Warren Petryk, Assembly District 93
Republican

Personal: Born Eau Claire, Wisconsin, January 24, 1955; married with grandchildren.

Voting address: Eau Claire County, Wisconsin.

Education: Badger Boys State 1972; Boyceville High School, valedictorian, 1973; attended University of Wisconsin–Stout; BA, highest honors, University of Wisconsin–Eau Claire 1978.

Occupation: Worked 15 years in community relations for United Cerebral Palsy of West Central Wisconsin; cofounder of musical entertainment group "The Memories" (started 1972).

Member: Boy Scouts (Eagle Scout, November 1969); Eau Claire, Menomonie, Ellsworth, River Falls, and Prescott Chambers of Commerce; NRA; Eau Galle-Rush River, Ellsworth, Durand, Rock Falls, and Arkansaw Sportsmen's Clubs; Wisconsin Farm Bureau; Sons of the American Legion; Cleghorn Lions Club; Chippewa Valley Council of Boy Scouts of America (board of directors).

Current office: Elected to Assembly since 2010. Committee assignments 2023: Energy and Utilities; Financial Institutions; Insurance; Labor and Integrated Employment; Veterans and Military Affairs; Workforce Development and Economic Opportunities (chair).

Contact: rep.petryk@legis.wisconsin.gov; 608-237-9193; 888-534-0093 (toll free); Room 103 West, State Capitol, PO Box 8953, Madison, WI 53708-8953.

SENATE DISTRICT 32
ASSEMBLY DISTRICTS 94, 95, 96

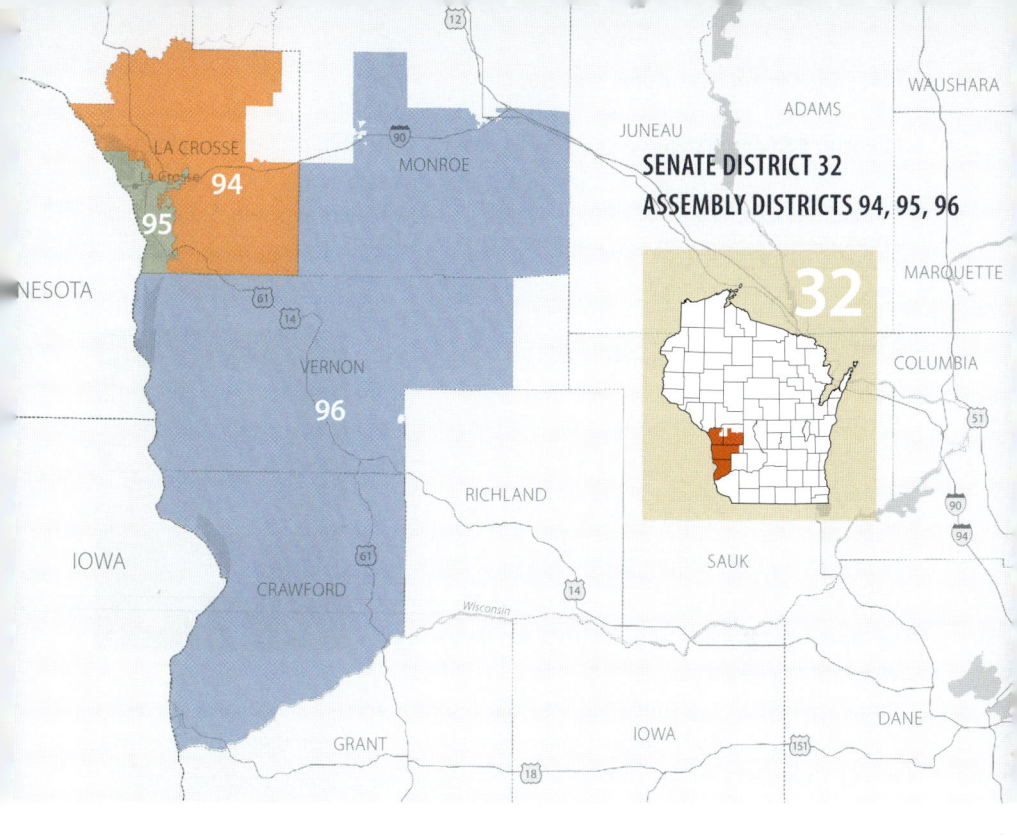

Brad Pfaff, Senate District 32
Democrat

Personal: Born La Crosse, Wisconsin, December 7, 1967; married; 2 children.

Voting address: Onalaska, Wisconsin.

Education: Melrose-Mindoro High School 1986; BS University of Wisconsin–Green Bay 1990; MPA George Mason University 2000.

Occupation: Full-time legislator. Former secretary-designee, Wisconsin Department of Agriculture, Trade and Consumer Protection; director, Business and Rural Development, Wisconsin Department of Administration; deputy administrator and state executive director, Farm Programs, U.S. Department of Agriculture, Farm Service Agency; staff of U.S. Representative Ron Kind and U.S. Senator Herb Kohl.

Member: Downtown La Crosse Rotary; Governor's Task Force on Broadband Access.

Previous office: Elected to La Crosse County Board of Supervisors 2006–9.

Current office: Elected to Senate 2020. Committee assignments 2023: Agriculture and Tourism; Economic Development and Technical Colleges; Insurance and Small Business; Transportation and Local Government; Utilities and Technology. Additional appointments: Transportation Projects Commission; Wisconsin Economic Development Corporation.

Contact: sen.pfaff@legis.wisconsin.gov; 608-266-5490; Room 22 South, State Capitol, PO Box 7882, Madison, WI 53707-7882.

Steve Doyle, Assembly District 94
Democrat

Personal: Born La Crosse, Wisconsin, May 21, 1958; married; 2 children.

Voting address: Onalaska, Wisconsin.

Education: Aquinas High School 1976; BA University of Wisconsin–La Crosse 1980; JD University of Wisconsin Law School 1986.

Occupation: Attorney. Former instructor, University of Wisconsin–La Crosse.

Former member: Family Resource Center (board member); Family and Children's Center (board member); Coulee Region Humane Society (board member, president).

Previous office: Elected to La Crosse County Board 1986–present (chair 2002–11).

Current office: Elected to Assembly in May 2011 special election. Reelected since 2012. Leadership positions: Minority Caucus Vice Chair 2019, 2017. Committee assignments 2023: Financial Institutions; Insurance.

Contact: rep.doyle@legis.wisconsin.gov; 608-237-9194; 888-534-0094 (toll free); Room 124 North, State Capitol, PO Box 8952, Madison, WI 53708-8952.

Jill Billings, Assembly District 95
Democrat

Personal: Born Rochester, Minnesota; 2 children.

Voting address: La Crosse, Wisconsin.

Education: Stewartville High School 1980; BA Augsburg College (Minneapolis, Minnesota) 1989; Bowhay Institute for Legislative Leadership Development (BILLD) Fellow 2012, Toll Fellow 2014; National Conference of State Legislatures Early Learning Fellow.

Occupation: Full-time legislator. Former teacher of English and Citizenship to Hmong adults.

Member: Council of State Governments (member of Health and Human Services Committee); National Caucus of Environmental Legislators, Mississippi River Caucus; Wisconsin Legislative Children's Caucus (cochair); Wisconsin Family Impact Seminar Advisors Committee; Viterbo University Board of Advisors; University of Wisconsin–La

Crosse Chancellor's Community Council; American Association of University Women La Crosse Branch; Preservation Alliance of La Crosse; La Crosse Alliance to HEAL (Halting the Effects of Addiction Locally); Taiwan Friendship Caucus (cochair).

Previous office: Elected to La Crosse County Board 2004–12.

Current office: Elected to Assembly in November 2011 special election. Reelected since 2012. Leadership positions: Minority Caucus Vice Chair 2023, 2021. Committee assignments 2023: Children and Families; Rules; Tourism; Joint Legislative Council. Additional appointments: Building Commission; Child Abuse and Neglect Prevention Board; Historical Society of Wisconsin Board of Curators.

Contact: rep.billings@legis.wisconsin.gov; 608-237-9195; 888-534-0095 (toll free); Room 118 North, State Capitol, PO Box 8952, Madison, WI 53708-8952.

Loren Oldenburg, Assembly District 96

Republican

Personal: Born Viroqua, Wisconsin, September 8, 1965; married.

Voting address: Viroqua, Wisconsin.

Education: Viroqua High School 1984; attended University of Wisconsin–La Crosse 1984–87.

Occupation: Small business owner; vacation rental owner; fourth-generation farmer. Former dairy farmer.

Member: Chaseburg Cenex Co-op (19 years, former president of the board); Viroqua Church of Christ (trustee).

Former member: Westby Co-op Creamery (board member and president).

Previous office: Elected to Harmony Town Board (supervisor, chair).

Current office: Elected to Assembly since 2018. Committee assignments 2023: Agriculture (vice chair); Energy and Utilities; Environment (chair).

Contact: rep.oldenburg@legis.wisconsin.gov; 608-237-9196; 888-534-0096 (toll free); Room 10 West, State Capitol, PO Box 8953, Madison, WI 53708-8953.

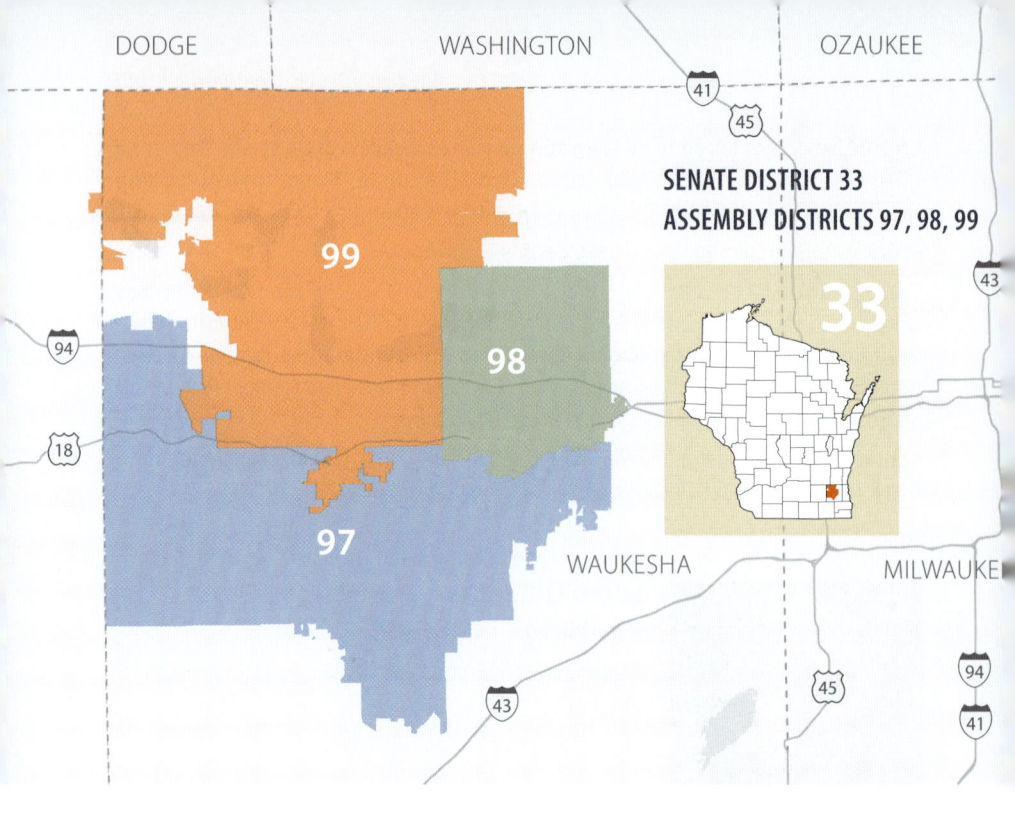

SENATE DISTRICT 33
ASSEMBLY DISTRICTS 97, 98, 99

Chris Kapenga, Senate District 33
Republican

Voting address: Delafield, Wisconsin.

Education: BS in Accountancy, Calvin University (Grand Rapids, Michigan) 1994.

Occupation: Business owner.

Previous office: Elected to Assembly 2010–14 (resigned 8/5/2015).

Current office: Elected to Senate in July 2015 special election. Reelected since 2018. Leadership positions: Senate President 2023, 2021. Committee assignments 2023: Senate Organization (vice chair); Joint Committee on Employment Relations (cochair); Joint Committee on Legislative organization (cochair); Joint Legislative Council.

Contact: sen.kapenga@legis.wisconsin.gov; 608-266-9174; 800-863-8883 (toll free); Room 220 South, State Capitol, PO Box 7882, Madison, WI 53707-7882.

Scott Allen, Assembly District 97
Republican

Personal: Born Racine, Wisconsin, December 18, 1965; married; 2 adult children.

Voting address: Waukesha, Wisconsin.

Education: Kettle Moraine High School; attended University of Wisconsin Oshkosh, University of Wisconsin–Waukesha; BA University of Wisconsin–Milwaukee; Master of Public Administration and Master of Planning, University of Southern California.

Occupation: Realtor; sales and leadership speaker, trainer, and coach; co-owner of a printing and promotional products business. Former sales director; home builder; risk management analyst. Served in U.S. Army Reserve 1984–90.

Member: Republican Party of Waukesha County; Spring Creek Church; Carroll University President's Advisory Committee; La Casa de Esperanza Advisory Board; Greater Milwaukee Association of Realtors (former board member); Wisconsin Realtors Association.

Previous office: Elected City of Waukesha alder 1998–2001; Waukesha County Community Development Block Grant Board 2010–14.

Current office: Elected to Assembly since 2014. Committee assignments 2023: Financial Institutions; Housing and Real Estate; Regulatory Licensing Reform; Veterans and Military Affairs.

Contact: rep.allen@legis.wisconsin.gov; 608-237-9197; 888-534-0097 (toll free); Room 105 West, State Capitol, PO Box 8952, Madison, WI 53708-8952.

Adam Neylon, Assembly District 98
Republican

Personal: Born Elgin, Illinois, December 30, 1984; married; 3 children.

Voting address: Pewaukee, Wisconsin.

Education: HD Jacobs High School 2003; BA Carroll University 2008.

Occupation: Full-time legislator; small business owner. Former legislative staffer for U.S. Representative Jim Sensenbrenner and Republican leadership in the Wisconsin Assembly.

Member: Republican Party of Waukesha County (former youth chair).

Former Member: President's Advisory Council at Carroll University; 100th Anniversary Capitol Commemorative Commission.

Current office: Elected to Assembly in April 2013 special election. Reelected since 2014. Committee assignments 2023: Review of Administrative Rules (chair); Energy and Utilities; Jobs, Economy and Small Business Development; Joint Committee for Review of Administrative Rules (cochair).

Contact: rep.neylon@legis.wisconsin.gov; 608-237-9198; 888-534-0098 (toll free); Room 204 North, State Capitol, PO Box 8953, Madison, WI 53708-8953.

Cindi S. Duchow, Assembly District 99
Republican

Personal: Born Waukesha, Wisconsin; married; 2 children.

Voting address: Pewaukee, Wisconsin.

Education: Catholic Memorial High School; BS University of Wisconsin–Madison.

Occupation: Former manager and fashion specialist for national retailers.

Member: St. Anthony's Church; Republican Party of Waukesha County, Leadership Circle; Volunteer Service Club of Pewaukee Lake (former president); Pewaukee Yacht Club.

Former member: Waukesha Youth Hockey Association board.

Previous office: Elected Town of Delafield supervisor 2013–16.

Current office: Elected to Assembly in September 2015 special election. Reelected since 2016. Leadership positions: Majority Caucus Vice Chair 2023, 2021. Committee assignments 2023: Criminal Justice and Public Safety; Education; Financial Institutions (chair); Insurance; Joint Legislative Council. Additional appointments: State Capitol and Executive Residence Board.

Contact: rep.duchow@legis.wisconsin.gov; 608-237-9199; 888-534-0099 (toll free); Room 210 North, State Capitol, PO Box 8952, Madison, WI 53708-8952.

■ ■ ■

CHIEF CLERKS AND SERGEANTS AT ARMS

Michael J. Queensland, Senate Chief Clerk

Personal: Born Rochester, Minnesota, July 19, 1985; married; 2 children.

Voting address: Monona, Wisconsin.

Education: Kingsland High School (Spring Valley, Minnesota) 2003; BS in Public Administration, University of Wisconsin–La Crosse 2007; JD University of Wisconsin Law School 2011.

Occupation: Former attorney, Wisconsin Legislative Council 2011–20.

Member: American Society of Legislative Clerks and Secretaries; Council of State Governments; Mason's Manual Commission; National Conference of State Legislatures, Research, Editorial, Legal and Committee Staff; State Bar of Wisconsin.

Current office: Elected Senate Chief Clerk since 2021.

Contact: 608-266-2517; Room B20 Southeast, State Capitol, PO Box 7882, Madison, WI 53707-7882.

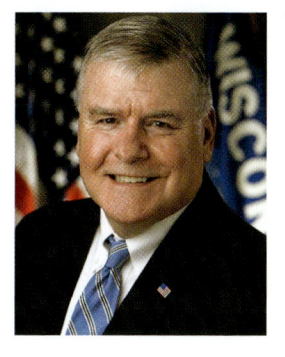

Tom Engels, Senate Sergeant at Arms

Personal: Born Shullsburg, Wisconsin, January 1964; married; 3 children.

Voting address: Cottage Grove, Wisconsin.

Education: Shullsburg High School 1982; firefighting and emergency medical service certification programs, Madison Area Technical College; BA in History, University of Wisconsin–Madison.

Occupation: Former deputy secretary, Wisconsin Department of Health Services; Health Resources and Services Administration administrator, U.S. Department of Health and Human Services; appointed member of White House Coronavirus Task Force.

Member: Experimental Aircraft Association.

Former member: Monona and Cottage Grove Volunteer Fire Departments firefighter; Monona and Deer Grove Emergency Medical Services volunteer emergency medical technician; Smithsonian Institute National Air and Space Museum volunteer.

Current office: Elected Senate Sergeant at Arms since 2021.

Contact: tom.engels@legis.wisconsin.gov; 608-266-1801; Room 315 South, State Capitol, PO Box 7882, Madison, WI 53707-7882.

Edward (Ted) A. Blazel, Assembly Chief Clerk

Personal: Born Quincy, Illinois, June 14, 1972; married; 2 children.

Voting address: Madison, Wisconsin.

Education: Quincy Senior High School 1990; BA St. Norbert College (De Pere) 1994; MA Marquette University 1998.

Member: American Society of Legislative Clerks and Secretaries.

Previous office: Elected Senate Sergeant at Arms 2003–21 (resigned 3/12/2021).

Current office: Elected Assembly Chief Clerk since 2021.

Contact: 608-266-1501; Room 401 RJC, State Capitol, PO Box 7882, Madison, WI 53707-7882.

Anne Tonnon Byers
Assembly Sergeant at Arms

Personal: Born Green Bay, Wisconsin, December 14, 1968; married; 2 children.

Voting address: McFarland, Wisconsin.

Education: Green Bay East High School 1987; attended University of Wisconsin–Green Bay; BS University of Wisconsin–Madison 1991; University of Wisconsin Certified Public Management Program 2001.

Occupation: Former Assembly Assistant Sergeant at Arms 1998–2010; office manager for Assembly Sergeant 1993–98.

Current office: Elected Assembly Sergeant at Arms since 2011.

Contact: anne.tonnonbyers@legis.wisconsin.gov; 608-266-2004; Room 411 West, State Capitol, PO Box 8952, Madison, WI 53708-8952.

■ ■ ■

2
UNITS OF STATE GOVERNMENT

THE LEGISLATURE

Officers of the Senate
President: Chris Kapenga
President pro tempore: Patrick Testin

Majority leader: Devin LeMahieu
Assistant majority leader: Dan Feyen
Majority caucus chair: Van H. Wanggaard
Majority caucus vice chair: Joan Ballweg

Minority leader: Melissa Agard
Assistant minority leader: Jeff Smith
Minority caucus chair: Chris Larson
Minority caucus vice chair: Dianne H. Hesselbein

Chief clerk: Michael Queensland
Sergeant at arms: Tom Engels

Officers of the Assembly
Speaker: Robin J. Vos
Speaker pro tempore: Kevin Petersen

Majority leader: Tyler August
Assistant majority leader: Jon Plumer
Majority caucus chair: Rob Summerfield
Majority caucus vice chair: Cindi Duchow
Majority caucus secretary: Nancy VanderMeer
Majority caucus sergeant at arms: Treig E. Pronschinske

Minority leader: Greta Neubauer
Assistant minority leader: Kalan Haywood
Minority caucus chair: Lisa Subeck
Minority caucus vice chair: Jill Billings
Minority caucus secretary: Kristina M. Shelton
Minority caucus sergeant at arms: Lee Snodgrass

Chief clerk: Edward A. Blazel
Sergeant at arms: Anne Tonnon Byers

Contact: 608-266-9960; 800-362-9472 (toll free)
Website: www.legis.wisconsin.gov
Number of employees: 200 (senate, includes the 33 senators); 315 (assembly, includes the 99 representatives)
Total budget 2021–23: $177,248,900 (includes the legislative service agencies)

Overview

Wisconsin's legislature makes the laws of the state. The legislature also controls the state's purse strings: no money can be paid out of the treasury unless the legislature enacts a law that specifically appropriates it. At the same time, the legislature is required to raise revenues sufficient to pay for the state's expenditures, and it is required to audit the state's accounts. The legislature can remove any elective office holder in state government, including the governor, from office for wrongdoing. It can also remove a judge or supreme court justice from office for any reason that, in its judgment, warrants it. The legislature can override the governor's veto of legislation. Finally, the legislature has charge of the two avenues by which the Wisconsin Constitution can be amended: the legislature can propose amendments for the people to vote on, and it can set in motion the process for calling a constitutional convention.

The legislature has two houses: the senate and the assembly. The senate is composed of 33 senators, each elected for a four-year term from a different senate district. The assembly is composed of 99 representatives, each elected for a two-year term from a different assembly district. Each senate district comprises the combined territory of three assembly districts. Elections are held in November of each

The 2023 Wisconsin Legislature convenes on January 3, 2023. Members take their oath of office on the bible used to swear in Henry Dodge as the first governor of the Wisconsin Territory in July 1836.

even-numbered year. The terms of 17 senate seats expire in alternate even-numbered years from the terms of the other 16. If a midterm vacancy occurs in the office of senator or representative, it is filled through a special election called by the governor.

A new legislature is sworn in to office in January of each odd-numbered year, and it meets in continuous session for the full biennium until its successor is convened. The 2023 legislature is the 106th Wisconsin Legislature. It convened on January 3, 2023, and will continue until January 3, 2025.

Apparatus for conducting business

Rules. The Wisconsin Constitution prescribes a number of specific procedural requirements for the legislature (for example, that each house must keep and publish a journal of its proceedings and that a roll call vote, rather than a voice vote, must be taken in certain circumstances). For the most part, however, the legislature determines for itself the manner in which it conducts its business. Each house of the legislature has adopted rules that codify its own practices, and the two houses have adopted joint rules that deal with relations between the houses and administrative proceedings common to both. Either house can change its own rules by passing a resolution, and the two houses can change the joint rules by passing a joint resolution.

Officers. Each house elects from among its members a presiding officer and an officer to stand in for the presiding officer as needed. The presiding officer or stand-in chairs the house's meetings and authenticates the house's acts, orders, and proceedings. In the senate, these officers are the president and president pro tempore; in the assembly, they are the speaker and speaker pro tempore.

Each house also elects two individuals who are not legislators to serve as the house's chief clerk and sergeant at arms. The chief clerk is the clerk for the house's meetings. The chief clerk also manages the house's paperwork, records, and general operations. The sergeant at arms maintains order in and about the house's meeting chamber and supervises the house's messengers.

Within each house, the members from each political party organize as a caucus and elect officers to coordinate their activity. The majority leader and assistant majority leader and the minority leader and the assistant minority leaders are their party's respective leaders.

The senate majority leader and the assembly speaker play major, and roughly parallel, roles in guiding the activities of their houses as a result of special responsibilities that the rules in their houses assign to their offices. These responsibilities include appointing the members of committees, determining what business will

Assembly Speaker Robin Vos (*top right*), serving as the assembly's presiding officer for his sixth session, addresses his fellow representatives during a floor session. Vos is the longest-serving assembly speaker in state history. Speaker Pro Tempore Kevin Petersen (*bottom left*) consults with Assembly Chief Clerk Ted Blazel (*bottom right*).

(*BOTH PHOTOS*) JOE KOSHOLLEK, LEGISLATIVE PHOTOGRAPHER

Senate President Chris Kapenga (*left*) confers with Senate Chief Clerk Michael Queensland (*right*). Senate President Pro Tempore Patrick Testin (*far right*) presides over floor session. Each house in the legislature elects presiding officers who ensure that business is conducted in accordance with the chamber's adopted rules.

be scheduled for the house's meetings, and making staffing and budget decisions for the house's operations.

Committees. The legislature does much of its work in committees. Legislative committees study proposed legislation to determine whether it should be given further consideration by the houses. They review the performance and expenditures of state agencies. And they conduct inquiries to inform the public and the legislature about important issues facing the state.

Each committee is assigned a general area of responsibility or a particular matter to look into and, within the scope of its assignment, can hold hearings to gather information and executive sessions (deliberative meetings) to decide what recommendations and reports it will make. Some committees can do more than make recommendations and reports. (For example, the Joint Committee on Finance can approve requests from state agencies for supplemental funding.) With rare exceptions, all committee proceedings are open to the public.

Each house has its own committees, and the two houses together have joint committees. Usually, every member of the legislature serves on at least one committee. Each house committee includes members from the two major political parties, but more of the members are from the majority party. On a joint committee, which includes members from both houses, more of the members from each house are from the majority party in that house. For some members on some committees, membership is automatic and based on another office that they hold (ex officio membership), but otherwise, committee members are appointed. The senate majority leader and the assembly speaker make the appointments in their respective houses but honor the nominations of the minority leader for the minority party appointments. They also designate the committee chairs and the joint committee cochairs, except when those positions are held ex officio.

The standing committees in each house operate through the legislature's entire biennial session. They are created under or pursuant to the rules of the house and consist exclusively of legislators from the house. Most of the standing committees have responsibility for one or more specific subject areas—for example, "transportation" or "health." However, the Committee on Senate Organization has organizational responsibilities: it schedules and determines the agendas for the senate's meetings, and it decides matters pertaining to the senate's personnel,

Senate Majority Leader Devin LeMahieu and Senate Minority Leader Melissa Agard, the Republican and Democratic Parties' respective leaders, chat while the senate stands "informal"—the official term for a temporary suspension of proceedings.

In January 2023, Representative Tyler August (*left*) stepped into a new role as assembly majority leader after serving as the assembly's speaker pro tempore for five sessions. Representative Greta Neubauer (*right*) continues to serve as assembly minority leader for a second session.

expenditures, and general operations. In the assembly, these organizational responsibilities fall, respectively, to the Assembly Committee on Rules and the Committee on Assembly Organization.

In addition to the standing committees in the houses, there are 10 joint standing committees, which likewise operate through the entire biennial session. These committees are created in the statutes rather than under the legislature's rules. Three of these committees include nonlegislators in addition to the legislators from both houses.

Special committees can also be appointed in either house or by the two houses jointly. Committees of this type are created to study a problem or conduct an investigation and report their findings to the house or the legislature. Special committees cease to exist when they have completed their assignments.

Meetings. Early in the biennial session, the legislature adopts a joint resolution to establish its session schedule. The session schedule specifies the floorperiods for the session. A floorperiod is a day or span of days that is reserved for meetings of the full houses. Committees can meet on any day, but generally do not meet on days when one or more of the full houses are meeting. When a house meets during a floorperiod, it meets in regular session.

The legislature can also call itself into extraordinary session for any day or span of days. The call requires a majority vote of the members of the committee on organization in each house, the adoption of a joint resolution in both houses, or a joint petition signed by a majority of the members of each house. In addition, the call must specify what business can be considered during the session. An extraordinary session can have the effect of extending a floorperiod so that it begins earlier or ends later than originally scheduled. An extraordinary session can also overlap a floorperiod, and a house can meet in extraordinary session and in regular session at different times during the same day.

The governor can call the legislature into special session at any time. When the legislature convenes in special session, it can act only upon the matters specified in the governor's call. Special sessions can occur during floorperiods and during extraordinary sessions, and a house can meet in special session and in regular or extraordinary session at different times during the same day.

Notices and records. Each house issues a calendar for each of its meetings. The calendar lists the business that the house will consider at the meeting.

The legislature publishes on the Internet a schedule of committee activities that indicates the time, place, and business scheduled for each committee meeting.

Each house keeps a record of its actions known as the daily journal.

The legislature issues the *Bulletin of the Proceedings of the Wisconsin Legislature* periodically during the biennial session. Each issue contains a cumulative record of actions taken on bills, resolutions, and joint resolutions; information on administrative rule changes; and a listing of statutes affected by acts.

Employees. Each house employs staff for its members and staff to take care of general administrative matters. In addition, the legislature maintains five service agencies to provide it with legal advice; bill drafting services; budgetary, economic, and fiscal analysis; public policy analysis; research and information services; committee staffing; auditing services; and information technology services.

How a bill becomes a law

A bill is a formal document that proposes to make a new law or change an existing law. For a bill to become a law, two things must happen: (1) the bill must be enacted—that is, it must be passed in identical form by both houses of the legislature and either agreed to by the governor or passed again with a two-thirds vote by both houses over the governor's veto, and (2) the enacted bill must be published.

First reading. A bill takes the first step toward becoming a law when a member or committee of the legislature introduces it in the house of the member or committee. This is done by filing the bill with the chief clerk. The chief clerk then assigns the bill its bill number (for example, Assembly Bill 15), and the presiding officer refers the bill to a standing committee or joint standing committee. Upon referral to committee, the bill is introduced.

A bill must be given three readings on three different days before the house can pass it. Each reading is followed by a different stage in the house's deliberation process. Introduction and referral to committee are considered a bill's first reading and are followed by committee review.

Committee review. When a bill is referred to a committee, it remains in the committee until the committee reports it out to the house, the bill is rereferred, or the house acts to withdraw it. The committee chair (or cochairs in a joint committee) determines whether the committee will meet to consider a bill and, if so, whether it will hold a hearing or an executive session or both. In the senate, though not in the assembly, a bill that has not received a public hearing cannot be placed on the calendar for a meeting of the full house unless the Committee on Senate Organization waives the public hearing requirement. And in both houses, a committee cannot report out a bill to the house unless it holds an executive session.

A committee holds a hearing on a bill to gather information from the public at large or from specifically invited persons. A committee holds an executive session on a bill to decide what recommendation it will make to the house. The committee can recommend passage of the bill as originally introduced, passage of the bill with amendments, passage of a substitute amendment, or rejection of the bill. Unless it recommends rejection, the committee reports out the bill, together with its recommendation, to the house. In limited circumstances (such as a tie vote), a committee can report out a bill without a recommendation.

If a bill is reported out by a committee, or if it is withdrawn from a committee by the house, it is generally sent to the house's scheduling committee—the Committee on Senate Organization or the Assembly Committee on Rules, depending on the house of origin—so that it can be scheduled for consideration at a meeting of that house. Sometimes, however, a bill is referred to another committee for that committee to review. In such cases, the bill remains in that other committee, just as it did in the previous committee, until it is reported out or withdrawn.

Scheduling. A bill that reaches a scheduling committee cannot advance further unless the scheduling committee schedules it for a meeting of the house or the house acts to withdraw it. The scheduling committee, however, is not required to schedule the bill for a meeting of the house. If the house withdraws a bill from the scheduling committee, the bill is automatically scheduled for a future meeting of the house. (In the senate, it is placed on the calendar for the senate's next succeeding meeting; in the assembly, it is placed on the calendar for the assembly's second succeeding meeting.) If a bill is scheduled for a meeting of the house, it can be given its second reading at that meeting.

Second reading. A bill's second reading is a formal announcement that the chief clerk makes just prior to the house considering the bill. Following this *(from left)* Representatives Jodi Emerson, Lee Snodgrass (minority caucus sergeant at arms), Jill Billings (minority caucus vice chair), and Kristina Shelton (minority caucus secretary) socialize before the assembly is called to order during a January floor session.

announcement, the house debates and votes on amendments and substitute amendments to the bill (any that the standing committee recommended and any that are offered by members). This stage ends if the house votes affirmatively to engross the bill. Such a vote means that the house has decided on the final form that the bill will take and is ready to consider passage of the bill in that final form. According to the house rules, the house cannot proceed to consider passage until the bill has been given its third reading—and this must be done on a different day. However, and this is often the case, the house can suspend this restriction by a unanimous voice vote or a two-thirds roll call vote. If the house suspends the restriction, the house may immediately proceed to the bill's third reading. If the house does not suspend the restriction, the bill is scheduled for a future meeting of the house. (In the senate, it is placed on the calendar for the senate's next succeeding meeting; in the assembly, it is placed on the calendar for the assembly's second succeeding meeting.)

Third reading. A bill's third reading, like its second, is a formal announcement that the chief clerk makes just prior to the house considering the bill. Following this announcement, the house debates whether the bill, in its final form previously determined by the house, should be passed. Members can speak only for or against passage; no further amendments can be offered. When debate on the bill

Senator LaTonya Johnson rises to speak as Senator Brad Pfaff listens in. Floor debate provides legislators with the opportunity to command all of their colleagues' attention.

ends, the members of the house vote. If the house passes the bill, it is ready to be messaged to the other house. Messaging occurs automatically following a reconsideration period specified in the rules of the house unless, within that period, the house chooses to reconsider its action in passing the bill. (In the senate, the reconsideration period extends through the senate's next meeting; in the assembly, it extends through the seventh order of business at the assembly's next meeting.) Generally, only a member who voted for passage can make a motion for reconsideration. Alternatively, the house can suspend its rules to message the bill immediately, by a unanimous voice vote or a two-thirds roll call vote.

Action in the second house. When the bill is received in the other house, it goes through substantially the same process as in the first house. If the second house ultimately passes the bill, which it can do with or without additional amendments, it messages the bill back to the house of origin.

Subsequent action in the houses. If the second house adopted additional amendments, the house of origin must determine whether it agrees to those amendments. If the house of origin rejects or amends the amendments, it can message the bill back to the second house. The houses can message the bill back and forth repeatedly until it has been passed in identical form by both houses. Alternatively, the houses can create a conference committee to develop a compromise version of the bill. If the conference committee proposes a compromise version, the houses can vote on it but cannot adopt additional amendments. The compromise version is considered in the second house first; if it passes in the second house, it is messaged to the house of origin.

Action by the governor. If a bill is passed in identical form by both houses, it

Senators Robert Wirch (*left*) and André Jacque (*right*) converse below two paintings by the artist Kenyon Cox (1856–1919). These and other works of art contribute to the grandeur of the senate chamber.

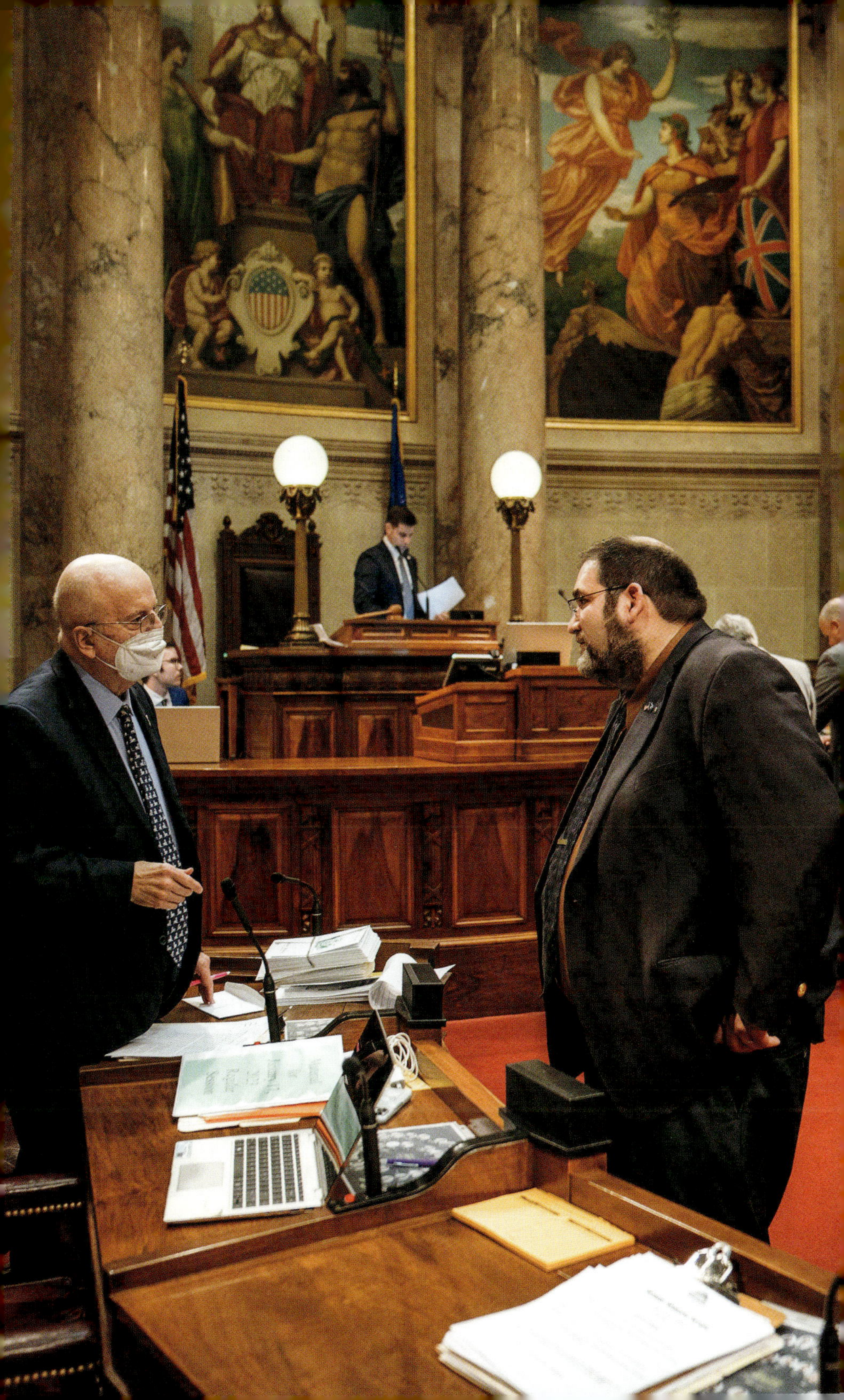

The assembly chamber welcomed 24 new members in January 2023. Representative Ellen Schutt (*top left*) and Representative Alex Joers (*top right*), both former legislative aides, sign the assembly's official register on inauguration day. Following her maiden speech, Representative Lori Palmeri (*above*) receives congratulations from fellow newcomer Representative Amanda Nedweski. For legislators in both houses, speaking on the floor for the first time is an important rite of passage.

(ALL PHOTOS THIS PAGE) JOE KOSHOLLEK, LEGISLATIVE PHOTOGRAPHER is sent to the governor. The governor has six days (excluding Sundays) in which to take action on a bill after receiving it. If the governor takes no action, the bill is enacted on the seventh day. If the governor signs the bill, the bill is enacted on the day it is signed. If the governor vetoes the bill, it goes back to the house of origin. If the governor signs the bill but vetoes part of it—which is permitted for appropriation bills—the signed part is enacted on the day it is signed, and the vetoed part goes back to the house of origin.

Publication and effective date. A bill or part of a bill that has been enacted is called an act. An act becomes a law when it is published in the manner prescribed by the legislature. The legislature has provided for the Legislative Reference Bureau to publish each act on the Internet the day after its date of enactment. An act goes into effect on the day after the Legislative Reference Bureau publishes the act, unless the act specifies that it goes into effect on a different date.

Veto override. A bill or part of a bill that the governor has vetoed can become a law if the legislature passes it again over the governor's veto. The procedure is different from when the bill was passed the first time. The only question considered is passage, and this question can be taken up immediately; the three-readings process is not repeated, and amendments cannot be offered. In addition, passage requires a two-thirds vote in each house, rather than a simple majority vote. Any action on a veto begins in the house of origin. If a vote is taken in the house of origin and two-thirds of the members present and voting agree to pass the vetoed bill or vetoed part of a bill, the bill or part is messaged to the other house. If a vote is taken in the second house and two-thirds of the members present and voting agree to pass the bill or part, the bill or part is enacted on the day the vote is taken. The enacted bill or part is then published and becomes a law in the same way as other acts. If either house fails to take a vote or to muster a two-thirds vote to override the veto, the bill or part advances no further, and the governor's veto stands.

Senate standing committees

Administrative Rules Nass, *chair;* Stroebel, *vice chair;* Bradley; Roys, *ranking minority member;* Larson

Agriculture and Tourism Ballweg, *chair;* Tomczyk, *vice chair;* Marklein; Testin; Quinn; Pfaff, *ranking minority member;* Smith; Spreitzer

Economic Development and Technical Colleges Feyen, *chair;* Stafsholt, *vice chair;* Cowles; Knodl; Pfaff, *ranking minority member;* Taylor

Education Jagler, *chair;* Quinn, *vice chair;* Nass; Stroebel; Cabral-Guevara; Larson, *ranking minority member;* L. Johnson

During a January floor session, Senator Jeff Smith (assistant minority leader) converses with his freshman colleagues, Senators Jesse James and Cory Tomczyk.

Finance Marklein, *chair*; Stroebel, *vice chair*; Felzkowski; Ballweg; Testin; Wimberger; L. Johnson, *ranking minority member*; Roys

Financial Institutions and Sporting Heritage Stafsholt, *chair*; Felzkowski, *vice chair*; Tomczyk; Spreitzer, *ranking minority member*; Hesselbein

Government Operations Stroebel, *chair*; Bradley, *vice chair*; Feyen; Roys, *ranking minority member*; Hesselbein

Health Cabral-Guevara, *chair*; Testin, *vice chair*; Felzkowski; Jacque; Hesselbein, *ranking minority member*; Carpenter

Housing, Rural Issues and Forestry Quinn, *chair*; Jagler, *vice chair*; Stafsholt; Wirch, *ranking minority member*; Spreitzer

Insurance and Small Business Felzkowski, *chair*; Hutton, *vice chair*; Jagler; Taylor, *ranking minority member*; Pfaff

Judiciary and Public Safety Wanggaard, *chair*; Jacque, *vice chair*; Wimberger; Knodl; James; Taylor, *ranking minority member*; Roys

Labor, Regulatory Reform, Veterans and Military Affairs Testin, *chair*; Nass, *vice chair*; Wanggaard; Wirch, *ranking minority member*; Carpenter

Licensing, Constitution and Federalism Jacque, *chair*; Bradley, *vice chair*; Knodl; Carpenter, *ranking minority member*; Wirch

Mental Health, Substance Abuse Prevention, Children and Families James, *chair*; Cabral-Guevara, *vice chair*; Ballweg; L. Johnson, *ranking minority member*; Hesselbein

Natural Resources and Energy Cowles, *chair;* Wimberger, *vice chair;* Tomczyk; Wirch, *ranking minority member;* Hesselbein

Senate Organization LeMahieu, *chair;* Kapenga, *vice chair;* Feyen; Agard, *ranking minority member;* Smith

Shared Revenue, Elections and Consumer Protection Knodl, *chair;* Feyen, *vice chair;* Quinn; Spreitzer, *ranking minority member;* Smith

Transportation and Local Government Tomczyk, *chair;* Cowles, *vice chair;* Hutton; Carpenter, *ranking minority member;* Pfaff

Universities and Revenue Hutton, *chair;* James, *vice chair;* Nass; Ballweg; Cabral-Guevara; Larson, *ranking minority member;* Roys; Smith

Utilities and Technology Bradley, *chair;* Wanggaard, *vice chair;* Quinn; Smith, *ranking minority member;* Pfaff

Assembly standing committees

Administrative Rules, Review of Neylon, *chair;* Petersen, *vice chair;* Spiros; Conley, *ranking minority member;* Baldeh

Agriculture Tranel, *chair;* Oldenburg, *vice chair;* Hurd; Kitchens; Moses; Mursau; Novak; Schutt; Schmidt; VanderMeer; Considine, *ranking minority member;* Shankland; Myers; Jacobson; C. Anderson

Assembly Organization Vos, *chair;* August, *vice chair;* Plumer; Petersen; Summerfield; Neubauer, *ranking minority member;* Haywood; Subeck

Audit Wittke, *chair;* Macco, *vice chair;* Born; Hong, *ranking minority member;* Clancy

Campaigns and Elections Krug, *chair;* Maxey, *vice chair;* Murphy; Rozar; Tittl; Tusler; Snodgrass, *ranking minority member;* Subeck; C. Anderson

Children and Families Snyder, *chair;* Goeben, *vice chair;* Bodden; Dittrich; Gundrum; Penterman; Pronschinske; Wichgers; Billings, *ranking minority member;* Vining; Snodgrass; Madison

Colleges and Universities Murphy, *chair;* Nedweski, *vice chair;* Moses; Wittke; Krug; Goeben; Schutt; S. Johnson; Michalski; O'Connor; Emerson, *ranking minority member;* Stubbs; Joers; Shankland; J. Anderson

Consumer Protection Callahan, *chair;* S. Johnson, *vice chair;* Behnke; Pronschinske; Rettinger; Schmidt; Ortiz-Velez, *ranking minority member;* Cabrera; Jacobson

Corrections Schraa, *chair;* Bodden, *vice chair;* Brandtjen; Brooks; Callahan; Hurd; Maxey; O'Connor; Sapik; Tittl; Stubbs, *ranking minority member;* Goyke; Cabrera; Clancy; Madison

Criminal Justice and Public Safety Spiros, *chair;* Schutt, *vice chair;* Duchow; Novak; Green; Donovan; Schraa; Steffen; Wichgers; Sortwell; Drake, *ranking minority member;* McGuire; Emerson; Stubbs; Madison

Education Kitchens, *chair;* Dittrich, *vice chair;* Binsfeld; Duchow; Mursau; Nedweski; Penterman; Rozar; Wichgers; Wittke; Shelton, *ranking minority member;* Considine; Myers; Andraca; Hong

Employment Relations Vos, *chair;* August; Born; Neubauer, *ranking minority member*

Energy and Utilities Steffen, *chair;* Summerfield, *vice chair;* Donovan; Hurd; Neylon; Oldenburg; Petersen; Petryk; Sortwell; Tittl; Tranel; Subeck, *ranking minority member;* Drake; Andraca; Moore Omokunde; Haywood

Environment Oldenburg, *chair;* Kitchens, *vice chair;* Novak; Behnke; Bodden; Schmidt; Shankland, *ranking minority member;* J. Anderson; Palmeri

Family Law Rozar, *chair;* Binsfeld, *vice chair;* Hurd; O'Connor; Nedweski; Snyder; Cabrera, *ranking minority member;* Conley; Vining

Finance Born, *chair;* Katsma, *vice chair;* Zimmerman; Rodriguez; Kurtz; Dallman; Goyke, *ranking minority member;* McGuire

Financial Institutions Duchow, *chair;* O'Connor, *vice chair;* Allen; Katsma; Murphy; Petryk; Rettinger; Doyle, *ranking minority member;* J. Anderson; Jacobson

Forestry, Parks and Outdoor Recreation Mursau, *chair;* Callahan, *vice chair;* Bodden; Edming; Green; Moses; Pronschinske; Swearingen; Tittl; Tusler; Andraca, *ranking minority member;* Bare; Joers; Palmeri; Snodgrass

Government Accountability and Oversight vacant, *chair;* Steffen, *vice chair;* Brandtjen; Michalski; Snyder; Myers, *ranking minority member;* Clancy

Health, Aging and Long-Term Care Moses, *chair;* Rozar, *vice chair;* Brooks; Dittrich; Gundrum; Magnafici; Murphy; Sapik; Schutt; Summerfield; VanderMeer; Subeck, *ranking minority member;* Riemer; J. Anderson; Vining; Drake

Housing and Real Estate Brooks, *chair;* Penterman, *vice chair;* Allen; Armstrong; Goeben; Krug; Murphy; Pronschinske; Schraa; Summerfield; Haywood, *ranking minority member;* Emerson; Ortiz-Velez; Bare; Clancy

Insurance Dittrich, *chair;* Callahan, *vice chair;* Petryk; Schraa; Tranel; Duchow; Tusler; Rettinger; Doyle, *ranking minority member;* Riemer; Subeck; Bare

Jobs, Economy and Small Business Development Gundrum, *chair;* Armstrong, *vice chair;* Binsfeld; Macco; Neylon; O'Connor; Rozar; Ohnstad, *ranking minority member;* Shelton; Snodgrass; Vining

Judiciary Tusler, *chair;* Rettinger, *vice chair;* Bodden; Gustafson; Sortwell; J. Anderson, *ranking minority member;* Ortiz-Velez

Labor and Integrated Employment Penterman, *chair;* Sapik, *vice chair;* Callahan; Edming; Gustafson; Petryk; Sinicki, *ranking minority member;* Ohnstad, Hong

Local Government Novak, *chair;* Donovan, *vice chair;* Gundrum; Maxey; Krug; Michalski; Pronschinske; S. Johnson; Baldeh, *ranking minoriy member;* Conley; C. Anderson; Ratcliff

Mental Health and Subtance Abuse Prevention Tittl, *chair;* Dittrich, *vice chair;* Behnke;

Representative David Armstrong (*left*) chairs a hearing of the Assembly Committee on Rural Development, and Representative Melissa Ratcliff (*right*) addresses her colleagues during a committee meeting. The bulk of the legislature's work occurs in committee, where legislators have an opportunity to discuss proposed bills with the public and each other.

Gundrum; Magnafici; Plumer; VanderMeer; Wichgers; Vining, *ranking minority member*; Considine; Moore Omokunde; Palmeri

Regulatory Licensing Reform Sortwell, *chair*; Gustafson, *vice chair*; Allen; Goeben; Macco; Moore Omokunde, *ranking minority member*; Sinicki; Palmeri

Rules August, *chair*; Vos, *vice chair*; Petersen; Plumer; Summerfield; Born; Tittl; Dittrich; Schraa; Neubauer, *ranking minority member*; Haywood; Subeck; Bilings; Bare; Joers

Rural Development Armstrong, *chair*; Schmidt, *vice chair*; Edming; Green; Hurd; Moses; Novak; VanderMeer; Emerson, *ranking minority member*; Considine; Ratcliff; C. Anderson

Sporting Heritage Pronschinske, *chair*; Tittl, *vice chair*; Bodden; Brooks; Callahan; Green; Mursau; Sortwell; Shelton, *ranking minority member*; Shankland; McGuire; Conley

State Affairs Swearingen, *chair*; Green, *vice chair*; Summerfield; Schraa; Brooks; Spiros; Moses; Callahan; Gustafson; Sinicki, *ranking minority member*; Ohnstad; Cabrera; Baldeh; Hong

Tourism Magnafici, *chair*; Swearingen, *vice chair*; Kitchens; Krug; Mursau; Plumer; Summerfield; VanderMeer; Billings, *ranking minority member*; Stubbs; Myers; Joers

Transportation VanderMeer, *chair*; Hurd; *vice chair*; Plumer; Spiros; Edming; S. Johnson; Schmidt; Maxey; Schutt; Considine, *ranking minority member*; Haywood; Ortiz-Velez; Moore Omokunde; Drake

Veterans and Military Affairs Edming, *chair*; VanderMeer, *vice chair*; Allen; Michalski; Penterman; Petryk; Snyder; Sortwell; Summerfield; Tittl; Riemer, *ranking minority member*; Sinicki; Andraca; Ortiz-Velez; Ratcliff

Representative Christine Sinicki—the longest serving member of the assembly, having served since 1999—engages in floor debate.

Ways and Means Macco, *chair*; Brooks, *vice chair*; Snyder; Dittrich; Armstrong; Callahan; Binsfeld; Gustafson; Conley, *ranking minority member*; Ohnstad; Riemer; Baldeh

Workforce Development and Economic Opportunities Petryk, *chair*; Michalski, *vice chair*; Gundrum; Snyder; Armstrong; Rozar; Nedweski; O'Connor; Rettinger; Sapik; Shankland, *ranking minority member*; Sinicki; Shelton; Jacobson; Madison

Joint legislative committees and commissions

Joint committees and commissions are created by statute and include members from both houses. Three joint committees include members who are not legislators. Commissions include gubernatorial appointees and, in two cases, the governor.

Commission on Uniform State Laws

Members: Representative Tusler, *chair*; Aaron Gary (designated by Legislative Reference Bureau director), *secretary*; Senators Wimberger, Roys; Representative McGuire;

Margit Kelley (designated by Legislative Council Staff director); former state senator Fred Risser, David Zvenvach (public members appointed by governor); former state representative David Cullen, former state senator Joanne B. Huelsman, Justice David T. Prosser Jr. (ULC life members appointed by commission)

Contact: lrb.legal@legis.wisconsin.gov; 608-504-5801; 1 East Main Street, Suite 200, Madison, WI 53701-2037

The Commission on Uniform State Laws examines subjects on which interstate uniformity is desirable, cooperates with the national Uniform Law Commission, and advises the legislature on uniform laws and model laws. The commission consists of four current or former legislators, two public members, and two members representing legislative service agencies. The commission may also appoint as members individuals who have attained the status of Life Members of the national Uniform Law Commission.

Joint Committee for Review of Administrative Rules

Senators: Nass, *cochair*; Stroebel, Bradley; Roys, *ranking minority member*; Larson
Representatives: Neylon, *cochair*; Petersen; Spiros; Conley, *ranking minority member*; Baldeh

The Joint Committee for Review of Administrative Rules must review proposed rules and may object to the promulgation of rules as part of the legislative oversight of the rule-making process. It also may suspend rules that have been promulgated; suspend or extend the effective period of emergency rules; and order an agency to put policies in rule form. Following standing committee review, a proposed rule must be referred to the joint committee. The joint committee must meet to review proposed rules that receive standing committee objections, and may meet to review any rule received without objection. The joint committee generally has 30 days to review the rule, but that period may be extended in certain cases. The joint committee may concur or nonconcur in the standing committee's action or may on its own accord object to a proposed rule or portion of a rule. If it objects

Senator Julian Bradley shares a laugh with colleagues during a break on the senate floor. Bradley, first elected in 2020, is the first Black Republican to serve in the Wisconsin State Senate.

or concurs in a standing committee's objection, it must introduce bills concurrently in both houses to prevent promulgation of the rule. If either bill is enacted, the agency may not adopt the rule unless specifically authorized to do so by a subsequent legislative enactment. The joint committee may also request that an agency modify a proposed rule. The joint committee may suspend a rule that was previously promulgated after holding a public hearing. Within 30 days following the suspension, the joint committee must introduce bills concurrently in both houses to repeal the suspended rule. If either bill is enacted, the rule is repealed and the agency may not promulgate it again unless authorized by a subsequent legislative action. If both bills fail to pass, the rule remains in effect. The joint committee receives notice of any action in a circuit court for declaratory judgments about the validity of a rule and may intervene in the action with the consent of the Joint Committee on Legislative Organization. The joint committee is composed of five senators and five representatives, and the membership from each house must include representatives of both the majority and minority parties.

Joint Committee on Employment Relations

Senators: Kapenga, *cochair*; LeMahieu, Marklein; Agard, *ranking minority member*
Representatives: Vos, *cochair*; August, Born; Neubauer, *ranking minority member*

The Joint Committee on Employment Relations approves all changes to the collective bargaining agreements that cover state employees represented by unions and the compensation plans for nonrepresented state employees. These plans and agreements include pay adjustments; fringe benefits; performance awards; pay equity adjustments; and other items related to wages, hours, and conditions of employment. The committee also approves the assignment of certain unclassified positions to the executive salary group ranges. The Division of Personnel Management in the Department of Administration submits the compensation plans for nonrepresented employees to the committee. One plan covers all nonrep-

Representative Rob Summerfield (majority caucus chair) listens as colleagues debate an amendment to the Wisconsin Constitution during a January floor session.

JOE KOSHOLLEK, LEGISLATIVE PHOTOGRAPHER

resented classified employees and certain officials outside the classified service, including legislators, supreme court justices, court of appeals judges, circuit court judges, constitutional officers, district attorneys, heads of executive agencies, division administrators, and others designated by law. The faculty and academic staff of the University of Wisconsin System are covered by a separate compensation plan, which is based on recommendations made by the University of Wisconsin Board of Regents. After public hearings on the nonrepresented employee plans, the committee may modify the plans, but the committee's modifications may be disapproved by the governor. The committee may set aside the governor's disapproval by a vote of six members. In the case of unionized employees, the Division of Personnel Management or, for University of Wisconsin bargaining units, the Board of Regents of the University of Wisconsin–Madison submits to the committee tentative agreements negotiated between it and certified labor organizations. If the committee disapproves an agreement, it is returned to the bargaining parties for renegotiation. When the committee approves an agreement for unionized employees it introduces those portions requiring legislative approval in bill form and recommends passage without change. If the legislature fails to pass the bill, the agreement is returned to the bargaining parties for renegotiation. The committee is composed of eight members: the presiding officers of each house; the majority and minority leaders of each house; and the cochairs of the Joint Committee on Finance. It is assisted in its work by the Legislative Council Staff and the Legislative Fiscal Bureau.

Senator Mary Felzkowski, seen here addressing colleagues on the senate floor, is a member of the powerful Joint Committee on Finance, which reviews bills related to state spending.

Joint Committee on Finance

Senators: Marklein, *cochair*; Stroebel, *vice chair*; Felzkowski, Ballweg, Testin, Wimberger; L. Johnson, *ranking minority member*; Roys

Representatives: Born, *cochair*; Katsma, *vice chair*; Zimmerman, Rodriguez, Kurtz, Dallman; Goyke, *ranking minority member*; McGuire

Assistant Senate Majority Leader Dan Feyen (*left*) and Senate Majority Leader Devin LeMahieu (*right*) determine the direction of their caucus, including assigning committee seats and making staffing decisions.

The Joint Committee on Finance examines legislation that deals with state income and spending. The committee also gives final approval to a wide variety of state payments and assessments. Any bill introduced in the legislature that appropriates money, provides for revenue, or relates to taxation must be referred to the committee. The committee introduces the biennial budget as recommended by the governor. After holding a series of public hearings and executive sessions, it submits its own version of the budget as a substitute amendment to the governor's budget bill for consideration by the legislature. At regularly scheduled quarterly meetings, the committee considers agency requests to adjust their budgets. It may approve a request for emergency funds if it finds that the legislature has authorized the activities for which the appropriation is sought. It may also transfer funds between existing appropriations and change the number of positions authorized to an agency in the budget process. When required, the committee introduces legislation to pay claims against the state, resolve shortages in funds, and restore capital reserve funds of the Wisconsin Housing and Economic Development Authority to the required level. As an emergency measure, it may reduce certain state agency appropriations when there is a decrease in state revenues. The committee is composed of the eight senators on the Senate Finance Committee and the eight representatives on the Assembly

Finance Committee. It includes members of the majority and minority parties in each house. The cochairs are appointed in the same manner as are the chairs of standing committees in their respective houses.

Joint Committee on Information Policy and Technology

Senators: Bradley, *cochair*; Testin, Quinn; Larson, *ranking minority member*; Spreitzer
Representatives: Zimmerman, *cochair*; Schutt; Baldeh, *ranking minority member*; Ratcliff: 1 vacancy

The Joint Committee on Information Policy and Technology reviews information management practices and technology systems of state and local units of government to ensure economic and efficient service, maintain data security and integrity, and protect the privacy of individuals who are subjects of the databases. It studies the effects of proposals by the state to expand existing information technology or implement new technologies. With the concurrence of the Joint Committee on Finance, it may direct the Department of Administration to report on any information technology system project that could cost $1 million or more in the current or succeeding biennium. The committee may direct the Department of Administration to prepare reports or conduct studies and may make recommendations to the governor, the legislature, state agencies, or local governments on the basis of this information. The University of Wisconsin Board of Regents is required to submit a report to the committee semiannually, detailing each information technology project in the University of Wisconsin System costing more than $1 million or deemed "high-risk" by the board. The committee may make recommendations on the identified projects to the governor and the legislature. The committee is composed of three majority and two minority party members from each house of the legislature.

Representative Cindi Duchow (majority caucus vice chair), now in her fifth term in the assembly, speaks during a floor session in January 2023. Assembly rules permit the soda that appears on Duchow's desk; the senate only recently revised its rules to permit the consumption of beverages in the chamber.

Senator Robert Cowles—the most senior Wisconsin legislator, having served since 1987—talks shop with Senator Joan Ballweg (majority caucus vice chair) while the senate stands informal.

Joint Committee on Legislative Organization

Senators: Kapenga (senate president), *cochair*; LeMahieu (majority leader), Feyen (assistant majority leader); Agard (minority leader), Smith (assistant minority leader)

Representatives: Vos (assembly speaker), *cochair*; August (majority leader), Plumer (assistant majority leader); Neubauer (minority leader), Haywood (assistant minority leader)

The Joint Committee on Legislative Organization is the policy-making body for the Legislative Audit Bureau, the Legislative Fiscal Bureau, the Legislative Reference Bureau, and the Legislative Technology Services Bureau. In this capacity, it assigns tasks to each bureau, approves bureau budgets, and sets the salary of bureau heads. The committee selects the four bureau heads, but it acts on the recommendation of the Joint Legislative Audit Committee when appointing the state auditor. The committee also selects the director of the Legislative Council Staff. The committee may inquire into misconduct by members and employees of the legislature. It oversees a variety of operations, including the work schedule for the legislative session, computer use, space allocation for legislative offices and legislative service agencies, parking on the State Capitol Park grounds, and sale and distribution of legislative documents. The committee recommends which newspaper should serve as the official state newspaper for publication of state legal notices. It advises the Elections Commission and the Ethics Commission on their operations and, upon recommendation of the Joint Legislative Audit Committee, may investigate any problems the Legislative Audit Bureau finds during its audits. The committee may employ outside consultants to study ways to improve legislative staff services and organization. The 10-member committee consists of the presiding officers and party leadership of both houses. The committee has established the Subcommittee on Legislative Services to advise it on matters pertaining to the legislative institution, including the review of computer technology purchases. The Legislative Council Staff provides staff assistance to the committee.

Joint Legislative Audit Committee

Senators: Wimberger, *cochair*; Marklein (cochair, Joint Committee on Finance), James; Hesselbein, *ranking minority member*; Carpenter

Representatives: Wittke, *cochair*; Macco, Born (cochair, Joint Committee on Finance); Hong, *ranking minority member*; Clancy

The Joint Legislative Audit Committee advises the Legislative Audit Bureau, subject to general supervision of the Joint Committee on Legislative Organization. The committee is composed of the cochairs of the Joint Committee on Finance, plus two majority and two minority party members from each house of the legislature. The committee evaluates candidates for the office of state auditor and makes recommendations to the Joint Committee on Legislative Organization, which selects

Senator Dianne Hesselbein (minority caucus vice chair), pictured addressing her colleagues in January 2023, is serving her first term in the senate. Like many of her colleagues, Hesselbein served in the assembly for several sessions before seeking election to the upper house.

GREG ANDERSON, LEGISLATIVE PHOTOGRAPHER

the auditor. The committee may direct the state auditor to undertake specific audits and review requests for special audits from individual legislators or standing committees, but no legislator or standing committee may interfere with the auditor in the conduct of an audit. The committee reviews each report of the Legislative Audit Bureau and then confers with the state auditor, other legislative committees, and the audited agencies on the report's findings. It may propose corrective action and direct that follow-up reports be submitted to it. The committee may hold hearings on audit reports, request the Joint Committee on Legislative Organization to investigate any matter within the scope of the audit, and request investigation of any matter relative to the fiscal and performance responsibilities of a state agency. If an audit report cites financial deficiencies, the head of the agency must report to the Joint Legislative Audit Committee on remedial actions taken. Should the agency head fail to report, the committee may refer the matter to the Joint Committee on Legislative Organization and the appropriate standing committees. When the committee determines that legislative action is needed, it may refer the necessary information to the legislature or a standing committee. It can also request information from a committee on action taken or seek advice of a standing committee on program portions of an audit. The committee may introduce legislation to address issues covered in audit reports.

Senator Mark Spreitzer presents an argument on the senate floor. In addition to the party caucuses, legislators are members of other caucuses; Spreitzer is a member of both the Sportsmen's Caucus and the LGBTQ+ Caucus.

Joint Legislative Council

Senators: Kapenga (senate president) *cochair*; LeMahieu (majority leader), Marklein (cochair, Joint Committee on Finance), Testin (president pro tempore), Felzkowski, Jagler, Quinn; Agard (minority leader), *ranking minority member*; Smith; L. Johnson (ranking minority member, Joint Committee on Finance); Spreitzer

Representatives: VanderMeer, *cochair*; Vos (assembly speaker), Petersen, August (majority leader), Born (cochair, Joint Committee on Finance), Duchow, Plumer (assistant majority leader); Neubauer (minority leader), *ranking minority member*;

Senator Howard Marklein and Representative Evan Goyke confer during a meeting of the Joint Legislative Council, which hears reports from the legislature's various study committees.

Haywood (assistant minority leader), Goyke (ranking minority member, Joint Committee on Finance), Billings
Legislative Council Staff: Anne Sappenfield, Rachel Letzing, Kelly Mautz
Contact: leg.council@legis.wisconsin.gov; 608-266-1304; 1 East Main Street, Suite 401, Madison, WI 53703-3382
Website: https://legis.wisconsin.gov/lc
Publications: *General Report of the Joint Legislative Council to the Legislature; State Agency Staff with Responsibilities to the Legislature; Directory of Joint Legislative Council Committees; Comparative Retirement Study; A Citizen's Guide to Participation in the Wisconsin State Legislature*; rules clearinghouse reports; staff briefs; memoranda on substantive issues considered by council committees; information memoranda and issue briefs; amendment and act memoranda.
Number of employees: 34.17
Total budget 2021–23: $8,455,200

The Joint Legislative Council creates special committees made up of legislators and members of the public to study various state and local government problems. Study topics are selected from requests presented to the council by law, joint resolution, and individual legislators. After research, expert testimony, and public hearings, the study committees draft proposals and submit them to the council, which must approve those drafts it wants introduced in the legislature as council bills. The council is assisted in its work by the Legislative Council Staff. The staff provides legal and research assistance to all of the legislature's substantive standing committees and joint statutory committees (except the Joint Committee on Finance) and assists individual legislators on request. The staff operates the rules clearinghouse to review proposed administrative rules and assists standing committees in their oversight of rulemaking. The staff also assists the legislature in identifying and responding to issues relating to the Wisconsin Retirement System. By law, the Legislative Council Staff must be strictly nonpartisan and must observe the confidential nature of the research and drafting requests it receives. The law requires that state agencies and local governments cooperate fully with the council staff to fulfill its statutory duties. The Joint Committee on Legislative Organization appoints the director of the Legislative Council Staff from outside the classified service, and the director appoints the other staff members from outside the classified service. The council consists of 22 legislators. The majority of them serve ex officio, and the remainder are appointed in the same manner as are members of standing committees. The president of the senate and the speaker of the assembly serve as cochairs, but each may designate another member to serve as cochair and each may decline to serve on the council. The council operates two permanent statutory committees and various special committees appointed to study selected subjects.

PERMANENT COMMITTEES OF THE COUNCIL REPORTING IN 2022

Special Committee on State-Tribal Relations Representative Mursau, *chair*; Senator Bewley, *vice chair*; Senator Jacque; Representatives Bowen, Edming, Rozar, Tittl, Vining; Dee Ann Allen (Lac du Flambeau Band of Lake Superior Chippewa Indians), Joey Awonohopay (Menominee Indian Tribe of Wisconsin), Ned Daniels Jr. (Forest County Potawatomi Community), Michael J. Decorah (St. Croix Chippewa Indians of Wisconsin), Lorraine Gouge (Lac Courte Oreilles Tribal Governing Board), Conroy Greendeer Jr. (Ho-Chunk Nation), Shannon Holsey (Stockbridge-Munsee Community), Lisa Liggins (Oneida Nation), Carmen McGeshick (Sokaogon Chippewa Community), Christopher D. Boyd (Red Cliff Band of Lake Superior Chippewa Indians)

State-Tribal Relations Technical Advisory Committee Tom Bellavia (Department of Justice), Cyless Peterson (Department of Transportation), David O'Connor (Department of Public Instruction), Kris M. Goodwill (Department of Natural Resources), Danielle Williams (Department of Workforce Development), Holly Wilmer (Department of Revenue), Gail Nahwahquaw (Department of Health Services), Stephanie Lozano (Department of Children and Families)

The Special Committee on State-Tribal Relations is appointed by the Joint Legislative Council each biennium to study issues related to American Indians and the Indian tribes and bands in this state and develop specific recommendations and legislative proposals relating to such issues. Legislative membership includes not fewer than six nor more than 12 members, with at least one member of the majority and the minority party from each house. The council appoints no fewer than six and no more than 11 members from names submitted by federally recog-

Units of State Government: Legislature | 153

Representative Jeffrey Mursau (*middle*), who chairs the Special Committee on State-Tribal Relations, meets with Shannon Holsey (*left*), President of the Stockbridge-Munsee Band of Mohican Indians, and Robert VanZile, Jr. (*right*), Chairman of the Sokaogan Chippewa Community, who delivered the 2023 State of the Tribes address.

nized Wisconsin Indian tribes or bands or the Great Lakes Inter-Tribal Council. The council may not appoint more than one member recommended by any one tribe or band or the Great Lakes Inter-Tribal Council. The Technical Advisory Committee, consisting of representatives of eight major executive agencies, assists the Special Committee on State-Tribal Relations.

Law Revision Committee Senators Wimberger, *cochair*; Wanggaard, Smith, Roys; Representatives August, *cochair*; Petersen, Hebl, Riemer

The Law Revision Committee is appointed each biennium by the Joint Legislative Council. The membership of the committee is not specified, but it must include majority and minority party representation from each house. The committee reviews minor, remedial changes to the statutes as proposed by state agencies and reviews opinions of the attorney general and court decisions declaring a Wisconsin statute unconstitutional, ambiguous, or otherwise in need of revision. It considers proposals by the Legislative Reference Bureau to correct statutory language and session laws that conflict or need revision, and it may submit recommendations for major law revision projects to the Joint Legislative Council. It also serves as the repository for interstate compacts and agreements and makes recommendations to the legislature regarding revision of such agreements.

SPECIAL COMMITTEES OF THE COUNCIL REPORTING IN 2022

Legislative Council Study Committee on Increasing Offender Employment Opportunities Senator Felzkowski, *chair*; Representative Schraa, *vice chair*; Senator Taylor; Representatives Goyke, Petryk, Stubbs; Jan Allman, Sadique Isahaku, Eli Rivera, Elizabeth Roddy, Reijo Wahlin

This study committee is directed to review existing impediments to employment and job training for individuals who are incarcerated or recently released and to recommend legislation following its review. The committee will explore ways to expand connections between private employers and potential employees who are incarcerated in state institutions or on extended supervision, explore vocational earned release programs for possible implementation, consider release location flexibility based on employment opportunities, and evaluate other methods for improving job prospects for the offender population.

Legislative Council Study Committee on Occupational Licenses Senator Stafsholt, *chair*; Representative Sortwell, *vice chair*; Senator Ringhand; Representative Moore Omokunde; Monica Johnson, Stanley Johnson, Jessica Ollenburg, Albert Walker, Ann Zenk

This study committee is directed to review the current occupational licensing system administered by the Department of Safety and Professional Services. The committee will review prior recommendations made by the department regarding any current laws requiring occupational credentials that may be eliminated without clearly harming or endangering the health, safety, or welfare of the public. The committee will also review whether it is necessary to implement systems of review both to determine the necessity of legislative proposals for new occupational credentials and to periodically review the appropriateness of maintaining current occupational credential requirements. Finally, the committee will review options to expand access to individuals from other states to receive a reciprocal credential to practice in Wisconsin. Following these reviews, the committee will recommend legislation on current credentials that may be eliminated, on systems for review of new and existing occupational credentials, and on the issuance of reciprocal credentials.

Legislative Council Study Committee on Shared School District Services Representative Brooks, *chair*; Senator Feyen, *vice chair*; Senator Bewley; Representative Considine; Lance Bagstad, Jeffrey Dellutri, Bobbie Guyette, Ted Neitzke, Ben Niehaus, Tara Villalobos

This study committee is directed to review current barriers to shared administrative or other services between school districts and to explore statutory changes or creation of incentives to encourage efficiencies. The committee will consider methods for sharing or consolidating services such as district-level administration and personnel, purchasing, technology and data processing, transportation, food service, and building maintenance and make recommendations for legislation. As part of its work, the committee will study school district structures employed in other states, particularly county-wide school district models.

Legislative Council Study Committee on the Commercial Building Permitting Process
Senator Stroebel, *chair*; Representative Summerfield, *vice chair*; Representatives Baldeh, Conley; Robert Brandherm, Melissa Destree, Frank Gorham, Doug Hoerth, Steve Klessig, Mark Piotrowicz, Robert Procter, Cory Scheidler, Peter Tomasi

Representative Nancy VanderMeer (majority caucus secretary) speaks on the assembly floor during a debate about a proposed constitutional amendment relating to pretrial release and bail.

JOE KOSHOLLEK, LEGISLATIVE PHOTOGRAPHER

This study committee is directed to review the current commercial building permitting process. The review will focus on the commercial plan review process within the Department of Safety and Professional Services and municipalities, timelines for environmental permitting, and the role of the Commercial Building Code Council. As part of its review, the study committee will also evaluate approaches in other states and identify innovative and exemplary policies that could serve as a model for Wisconsin. Following this review, the committee will recommend legislation to improve the commercial building permitting process.

Legislative Council Study Committee on Uniform Death Reporting Standards Senator Ballweg, *chair*; Representative James, *vice chair*; Senator L. Johnson; Representative Doyle; Lynda Biedrzycki, Tim Candahl, Sara Kohlbeck, Brian Michel, Teresa Paulus, Kerry Riemer, Tara Steininger

This study committee is directed to review the current protocols for investigating causes of death and reporting death and the uniformity of those protocols. The review willl focus on options to implement more comprehensive uniform death reporting standards across Wisconsin, including the advantages and barriers to implementation of such standards. Following review, the committee will develop

Representatives Dave Considine (*left*) and Clinton Anderson (*right*) stretch their legs during a break in assembly floor action. They serve together on the Assembly Committees on Agriculture and Rural Development.

legislation to provide minimum requirements for death investigations and reporting, particularly deaths involving homicide, suicide, child or infant death, domestic violence, maternal mortality, and substance use.

Legislative Council Study Committee on Wisconsin National Guard Sexual Misconduct Procedures Representative Kurtz, *chair*; Senator Wimberger, *vice chair*; Senator Agard; Representative Riemer; Amy Arenz, Autumn Carroll, Jacob Curtis, Adam Gerol, Gabriela Guzman, Melissa Inlow, Jade La Sage

This study committee is directed to study the Wisconsin National Guard's procedures for investigating and addressing sexual misconduct. The committee will review the findings and recommendations contained in previously completed investigations into the Wisconsin National Guard's procedures, with a particular focus on the National Guard Bureau Office of Complex Investigation's assessment of the Wisconsin National Guard's sexual assault and harassment reporting procedures, investigation protocols, and accountability measures. The committee is directed to recommend legislation that enhances oversight of the Wisconsin National Guard as it relates to sexual misconduct, ensures state law complies with relevant federal requirements, and amends the Wisconsin Code of Military Justice where necessary.

Joint Review Committee on Criminal Penalties

Senators: Hutton, *cochair;* Taylor, *ranking minority member*
Representatives: Goyke, *ranking minority member;* 1 vacancy
Other members: Josh Kaul (attorney general); Kevin A. Carr (secretary of corrections); Kelli S. Thompson (state public defender); 2 vacancies (members appointed by the supreme court); Bradley Gehring, Maury Straub (public members appointed by the governor)

The Joint Review Committee on Criminal Penalties reviews any bill that creates a new crime or revises a penalty for an existing crime when requested to do so by the chair of a standing committee in the house of origin to which the bill was referred. The presiding officer in the house of origin may also request a report from the joint committee if the bill is not referred to a standing committee. Reports of the joint committee on bills submitted for its review concern the costs or savings to public agencies; the consistency of proposed penalties with existing penalties; whether alternative language is needed to conform the proposed penalties to existing penalties; and whether any acts prohibited by the bill are already prohibited under existing law. Once a report is requested for a bill, a standing committee may not vote on the bill and the house of origin may not pass the bill before the joint committee submits its report or before the 30th day after the request is made, whichever is earlier. The joint committee includes one majority and one minority party member from each house of the legislature; the members from the majority party serve as cochairs. The attorney general, secretary of corrections, and state public defender serve ex officio. The supreme court appoints one reserve judge residing somewhere within judicial administrative districts 1 to 5 and another residing within districts 7 to 10. The governor appoints two public members—an individual with law enforcement experience and an elected county official.

Joint Survey Committee on Retirement Systems

Senators: Feyen, *cochair;* Cowles; Agard, *ranking minority member*
Representatives: August, *cochair;* Swearingen; Neubauer
Other members: Charlotte Gibson (assistant attorney general appointed by attorney general), John Voelker (secretary of employee trust funds), Nathan Houdek (insurance commissioner), Michele Stanton (public member appointed by governor)

The Joint Survey Committee on Retirement Systems makes recommendations on legislation that affects retirement and pension plans for public officers and employees, and its recommendations must be attached as an appendix to each retirement bill. Neither house of the legislature may consider such a bill until the committee submits a written report that describes the proposal's purpose, probable costs, actuarial effect, and desirability as a matter of public policy. The 10-member committee includes two majority party members and one minority party member from each house of the legislature. An experienced actuary from the Office of the Commissioner of Insurance may be designated to serve in the commissioner's place on the committee. The public member cannot be a participant in any public retirement system in the state and is expected to "represent the interests of the taxpayers." Appointed members serve four-year terms unless they lose the status upon which the appointment was based. The committee is assisted by the Legislative Council Staff in the performance of its duties, but may contract for actuarial assistance outside the classified service.

Joint Survey Committee on Tax Exemptions

Senators: Testin, *cochair*; Marklein; Taylor
Representatives: August, *cochair*; Swearingen; Goyke
Other members: Peter Barca (secretary of revenue), Brian Keenan (Department of Justice representative appointed by attorney general), Elizabeth Kessler (public member appointed by governor)

The Joint Survey Committee on Tax Exemptions considers all legislation related to the exemption of persons or property from state or local taxes. It is assisted by the Legislative Council Staff. Any legislative proposal that provides a tax exemption must be referred to the committee immediately upon introduction. Neither house of the legislature may consider the proposal until the committee has issued its report, attached as an appendix to the bill, describing the proposal's legality, desirability as public policy, and fiscal effect. In the course of its review, the committee is authorized to conduct investigations, hold hearings, and subpoena witnesses. For an executive budget bill that provides a tax exemption, the committee must prepare its report within 60 days. The committee includes two majority party members and one minority party member from each house of the legislature. The public member must be familiar with the tax problems of local government. Members' terms expire on January 15 of odd-numbered years.

State of Wisconsin Building Commission

Governor: Tony Evers, *chair*
Senators: Wirch, Jacque, Ballweg
Representatives: Swearingen, *vice chair*; Billings, Wittke
Other members: Barb Worcester (citizen member appointed by governor)
Nonvoting advisory members from Department of Administration: Naomi De Mers (administrator, Division of Facilities Development), *commission secretary*; R. J. Binau, Aaron Heintz, Kevin Trinastic, Jillian Vessely
Contact: 608-266-1855; 101 East Wilson Street, Seventh Floor, Madison, WI 53703; PO Box 7866, Madison, WI 53707-7866

The State of Wisconsin Building Commission coordinates the state building

Representative Sylvia Ortiz-Velez listens attentively during floor debate. Although they usually no longer go late into the night, floor sessions last long enough to test legislators' stamina.

program, which includes the construction of new buildings; the remodeling, renovation, and maintenance of existing facilities; and the acquisition of lands and capital equipment. The commission determines the projects to be incorporated into the building program and biennially makes recommendations concerning the building program to the legislature, including the amount to be appropriated in the biennial budget. The commission oversees all state construction, except highway development. In addition, the commission may authorize expenditures from the State Building Trust Fund for construction, remodeling, maintenance, and planning of future development. The commission has supervision over all matters relating to the contracting of state debt. All transactions for the sale of instruments that result in a state debt liability must be approved by official resolution of the commission. The eight-member commission includes three senators and three representatives. Both the majority and minority parties in each house must be represented, and one legislator from each house must also be a member of the State Supported Programs Study and Advisory Committee. The governor serves as chair. One citizen member serves at the pleasure of the governor. The Department of Administration provides staffing for the commission, and several department employees serve as nonvoting, advisory members.

Transportation Projects Commission

Governor: Tony Evers, *chair*
Senators: Cowles, Marklein; Carpenter, Pfaff

Representatives: Krug, Spiros, Spreitzer; Riemer, Plumer
Other members: Mark Servi, Allison Bussler, Timothy Hanna (citizen members appointed by governor)
Nonvoting member: Craig Thompson (transportation secretary-designee)
Commission secretary: Craig Thompson
Contact: bshp.dtim@dot.wi.gov; 608-267-9617; Bureau of State Highway Programs, 4822 Madison Yards Way, Sixth Floor South, Madison, WI 53705

Representative Jerry O'Connor (*left*), elected in 2022, speaks with Representative David Murphy (*right*), who has been a member of the assembly since 2013. Both hail from the Fox Valley area.

GREG ANDERSON, LEGISLATIVE PHOTOGRAPHER

The Transportation Projects Commission includes three majority party and two minority party members from each house of the legislature. The commission reviews Department of Transportation recommendations for major highway projects. The department must report its recommendations to the commission by September 15 of each even-numbered year, and the commission, in turn, reports its recommendations to the governor or governor-elect, the legislature, and the Joint Committee on Finance before December 15 of each even-numbered year. The department must also provide the commission with a status report on major transportation projects every six months. The commission also approves the preparation of environmental impact or assessment statements for potential major highway projects.

Legislative service agencies

Legislative Audit Bureau
State auditor: Joe Chrisman
Deputy state auditor for financial audit: Carolyn Stittleburg
Deputy state auditor for performance evaluation: Dean Swenson
Financial audit directors: Sherry Haakenson, Erin Scharlau
Assistant financial audit directors: Brian Geib, Lisa Kasel
Contact: asklab@legis.wisconsin.gov; 608-266-2818; 877-FRAUD-17 (fraud, waste, and

mismanagement toll-free hotline); 22 East Mifflin Street, Suite 500, Madison, WI 53703-2512
Website: http://legis.wisconsin.gov/lab
Publications: Audit reports of individual state agencies and programs; biennial reports.
Number of employees: 86.80
Total budget 2021–23: $18,811,900

The Legislative Audit Bureau is responsible for conducting financial and program audits to assist the legislature in its oversight function. The bureau performs financial audits to determine whether agencies have conducted and reported their financial transactions legally and properly. It undertakes program audits to analyze whether agencies have managed their programs efficiently and effectively and have carried out the policies prescribed by law. The bureau's authority extends to executive, legislative, and judicial agencies; authorities created by the legislature; special districts; and certain service providers that receive state funds. The bureau may audit any county, city, village, town, or school district at the request of the Joint Legislative Audit Committee. The bureau provides an annual audit opinion on the state's comprehensive financial statements by the Department of Administration and prepares audits and reports on the financial transactions and records of state agencies at the state auditor's discretion or at the direction of the Joint Legislative Audit Committee. The bureau maintains a toll-free number to receive reports of fraud, waste, and mismanagement in state government. Typically, the bureau's program audits are conducted at the request of the Joint Legislative Audit Committee, initiated by the state auditor, or required by legislation. The reports are reviewed by the Joint Legislative Audit Committee, which may hold hearings on them and may introduce legislation in response to audit recommendations. The director of the bureau is the state auditor, who is appointed by the Joint Committee on Legislative Organization upon the recommendation of the Joint Legislative Audit Committee. Both the state auditor and the bureau's staff are appointed from outside the classified service and are strictly nonpartisan.

STATUTORY ADVISORY COUNCIL

Municipal Best Practices Reviews Advisory Council Steve O'Malley; vacancy (representing the Wisconsin Counties Association); Mark Rohloff (representing the League of Wisconsin Municipalities); Richard Nawrocki (representing the Wisconsin Towns Association).

The Municipal Best Practices Reviews Advisory Council advises the state auditor on the selection of county and municipal service delivery practices to be reviewed by the state auditor. The state auditor conducts periodic reviews of procedures and practices used by local governments in the delivery of governmental services; identifies variations in costs and effectiveness of such services between counties and municipalities; and recommends practices to save money or provide more effective service delivery. Council members are chosen and appointed by the state auditor from candidates submitted by the organizations represented.

Legislative Council Staff

Director: Anne Sappenfield
Deputy directors: Rachel Letzing, Dan Schmidt
Rules clearinghouse director: Scott Grosz
Rules clearinghouse assistant director: Margit Kelley
Contact: leg.council@legis.wisconsin.gov; 608-266-1304; 1 East Main Street, Suite 401, Madison, WI 53703-3382
Website: http://lc.legis.wisconsin.gov

See the entry for the Joint Legislative Council, beginning on page 150.

Legislative Fiscal Bureau

Director: Robert Wm. Lang
Assistant director: David Loppnow
Program supervisors: Jere Bauer, Paul Ferguson, Charles Morgan, Sean Moran, Christa Pugh, Al Runde
Supervising analysts: Jon Dyck, Rachel Janke
Administrative assistant: Becky Hannah
Contact: fiscal.bureau@legis.wisconsin.gov; 608-266-3847; 1 East Main Street, Suite 301, Madison, WI 53703
Website: http://legis.wisconsin.gov/lfb
Publications: Biennial budget and budget adjustment summaries; summaries of state agency budget requests; cumulative and comparative summaries of the governor's proposals, Joint Committee on Finance provisions and legislative amendments, and separate summaries of legislative amendments when necessary; summary of governor's partial vetoes. Informational reports on various state programs, budget issue papers, and revenue estimates. (Reports and papers available on the Internet and upon request.)
Number of employees: 35.00
Total budget 2021–23: $8,490,400

The Legislative Fiscal Bureau develops fiscal information for the legislature, and its services must be impartial and nonpartisan. One of the bureau's principal duties is to staff the Joint Committee on Finance and assist its members. As part of this responsibility, the bureau studies the state budget and its long-range implications, reviews state revenues and expenditures, suggests alternatives to the committee and the legislature, and prepares a report detailing earmarks in the budget bill. In addition, the bureau provides information on all other bills before the committee and analyzes agency requests for new positions and appropriation supplements outside of the budget process. The bureau provides fiscal information to any legis-

At an event celebrating the start of Black History Month, (*from left*) Representatives Darrin Madison, Dora Drake, and Kalan Haywood (assistant minority leader) are joined in the capitol rotunda by Senator Lena Taylor.

lative committee or legislator upon request. On its own initiative, or at legislative direction, the bureau may conduct studies of any financial issue affecting the state. To aid the bureau in performing its duties, the director or designated employees are granted access to all state departments and to any records maintained by the agencies relating to their expenditures, revenues, operations, and structure. The Joint Committee on Legislative Organization is the policy-making body for the Legislative Fiscal Bureau, and it selects the bureau's director. The director is assisted by program supervisors responsible for broadly defined subject areas of government budgeting and fiscal operations. The director and all bureau staff are chosen outside the classified service.

Legislative Reference Bureau

Director and general counsel: Richard A. Champagne
Deputy director: Cathlene M. Hanaman
Chief counsel: Joe Kreye
Assistant chief counsel: Michael Gallagher, Fern Knepp
Managing legislative analysts: Madeline Kasper, Jillian Slaight
Administrative services manager: Wendy L. Jackson
Contact: 608-504-5801 (legal); 608-504-5802 (research and analysis); 1 East Main Street, Suite 200, Madison; PO Box 2037, Madison, WI 53701-2037
Website: http://legis.wisconsin.gov/lrb

(from left) Bob Lang, Anne Sappenfield, and Rick Champagne respectively lead the Legislative Fiscal Bureau, Legislative Council, and Legislative Reference Bureau, three of five service agencies that provide nonpartisan information and assistance to the legislature.

Publications: Wisconsin Statutes; Laws of Wisconsin; Wisconsin Administrative Code and Register; *Wisconsin Blue Book*; informational, legal, and research reports.
Number of employees: 60.00
Total budget 2021–23: $12,701,800

The Legislative Reference Bureau provides nonpartisan, confidential bill drafting and other legal services to the Wisconsin Legislature. The bureau employs a staff of attorneys and editors who serve the legislature and its members and who draft and prepare all legislation, including the executive budget bill, for introduction in the legislature. Bureau attorneys also draft legislation at the request of state agencies. The bureau publishes all laws enacted during each biennial legislative session and incorporates the laws into the Wisconsin Statutes. The bureau prints the Wisconsin Statutes every two years and continuously updates the Wisconsin Statutes on the Wisconsin Legislature website. The bureau also publishes and updates the Wisconsin Administrative Code and the Wisconsin Administrative Register on the Wisconsin Legislature website. The Legislative Reference Bureau employs research analysts who provide research and analysis services to the legislature. Bureau analysts and librarians also provide information services to the legislature and the public. The bureau publishes the *Wisconsin Blue Book* and informational, legal, and research reports. The bureau responds to inquiries from legislators, legislative staff, and the public on current law and pending legislation and the operations of the legislature and state government. The bureau operates a legislative library that contains an extensive collection of materials pertaining to Wisconsin government and politics. The bureau compiles and publishes the Assembly Rules, Senate Rules, and Joint Rules. The bureau maintains for public inspection the drafting records of all legislation introduced in the Wisconsin Legislature, beginning with the 1927 session. The Joint Committee on Legislative Organization is the policy-making body for the Legislative Reference Bureau, and it selects the bureau director. The director employs all bureau staff. The director and the bureau staff serve outside the classified service.

Legislative Technology Services Bureau

Director: Jeff Ylvisaker
Deputy director: Nate Rohan
Administration manager: Christopher Sewell
Enterprise operations manager: Matt Harned
Geographic information systems manager: Ryan Squires
Software development manager: Doug DeMuth
Technical services manager: Cade Gentry
Contact: 608-264-8582; 17 West Main Street, Suite 200, Madison, WI 53703
Website: http://legis.wisconsin.gov/ltsb
Number of employees: 43.00
Total budget 2021–23: $9,983,600

The Legislative Technology Services Bureau provides confidential, nonpartisan information technology services and support to the Wisconsin Legislature. The bureau creates, maintains, and enhances specialized software used for bill drafting, floor session activity, and committee activity, managing constituent interactions, producing the Wisconsin Statutes and the Wisconsin Administrative Code, and publishing the *Wisconsin Blue Book*. It supports the publication of legislative documents including bills and amendments, house journals, daily calendars, and the Bulletin of the Proceedings. The bureau also maintains network infrastructure, data center operations, electronic communications, desktops, laptops, printers, and other technology devices. It keeps an inventory of computer hardware and software assets and manages technology replacement schedules. It supports the redistricting project following each decennial U.S. Census and provides mapping services throughout the decade. The bureau also supports the legislature during floor sessions, delivers audio and video services, manages the technology for the Wisconsin Legislature's websites, and offers training services for legislators and staff in the use of information technology. The bureau's director is appointed by the Joint Committee on Legislative Organization and has overall management responsibilities for the bureau. The director appoints bureau staff; both the director and the staff serve outside the classified service.

THE EXECUTIVE

Governor Tony Evers delivers his inaugural address on January 3, 2023, before he is sworn in for a second term as the 46th Governor of Wisconsin.

Office of the Governor

Governor: Tony Evers
Chief of staff: Maggie Gau
Location: 115 East, State Capitol, Madison
Contact: eversinfo@wisconsin.gov; 608-266-1212; PO Box 7863, Madison, WI 53707-7863
Website: https://evers.wi.gov
Number of employees: 37.25
Total budget 2021–23: $8,474,600

The governor is the state's chief executive. Voters elect the governor and lieutenant governor on a joint ballot to a four-year term. Most of the individuals, commissions, and boards that head the major executive branch agencies are appointed by, and serve at the pleasure of, the governor, although many of these appointments require senate confirmation. The governor reviews all bills passed by the legislature and can veto an entire bill or veto parts of a bill containing an appropriation. A two-thirds vote of the members present in each house of the legislature is required to override the governor's veto. In addition, the governor can call the legislature into special session to deal with specific legislation.

If a vacancy occurs in the state senate or assembly, state law directs the governor to call a special election. Vacancies in elective county offices and judicial positions can be filled by gubernatorial appointment for the unexpired terms or until a successor is elected. The governor may dismiss sheriffs, district attorneys, coroners, and registers of deeds for cause.

Finally, the governor serves as commander in chief of the Wisconsin National Guard when it is called into state service during emergencies, such as natural disasters and civil disturbances.

Subordinate statutory boards, councils, and committees

COUNCIL ON MILITARY AND STATE RELATIONS

The Council on Military and State Relations assists the governor by working with the state's military installations, commands and communities, state agencies, and economic development professionals to develop and implement strategies designed to enhance those installations. It advises and assists the governor on issues related to the location of military installations and assists and cooperates with state agencies to determine how those agencies can better serve military communities and families. It also assists the efforts of military families and their support groups regarding quality-of-life issues for service members and their families.

COUNCIL ON VETERANS EMPLOYMENT

The Council on Veterans Employment advises the governor and state agencies on, and assists them with, the recruitment and employment of veterans so as to increase veteran employment in state government.

STATE COUNCIL ON ALCOHOL AND OTHER DRUG ABUSE

The State Council on Alcohol and Other Drug Abuse coordinates and reviews the efforts of state agencies to control and prevent alcohol and drug abuse. It evaluates program effectiveness, recommends improved programming, educates people about the dangers of drug abuse, and allocates responsibility for various alcohol and drug abuse programs among state agencies. The council also reviews and provides an opinion to the legislature on proposed legislation that relates to alcohol and other drug abuse policies, programs, or services.

Independent entities attached for administrative purposes

DISABILITY BOARD

Members: Tony Evers (governor), Annette K. Ziegler (chief justice of the supreme court), Senator Kapenga (senate president), Senator Agard (senate minority leader), Representative Vos (assembly speaker), Representative Neubauer (assembly minority leader), Robert Golden (dean, UW Medical School)

The Disability Board is authorized to determine when a temporary vacancy exists in the office of the governor, lieutenant governor, secretary of state, treasurer, state superintendent of public instruction, or attorney general because the incumbent is incapacitated due to illness or injury.

Nongovernmental entities with gubernatorial appointments

THE MEDICAL COLLEGE OF WISCONSIN, INC.

President and CEO: John R. Raymond Sr.
Contact: 414-955-8296; 8701 Watertown Plank Road, Milwaukee, WI 53226
Website: www.mcw.edu
Total state appropriation 2021–23: $22,215,000

The Medical College of Wisconsin, Inc., is a private nonprofit institution located in Milwaukee that operates a school of medicine, school of pharmacy, and graduate school of biomedical sciences. The college receives state funds for education, training, and research; for its family medicine residency program; and for cancer research. The college is required to fulfill certain reporting requirements concerning its finances, student body, and programs. The governor appoints two members to the board of trustees with the advice and consent of the senate.

WISCONSIN HUMANITIES COUNCIL

Executive director: Dena Wortzel
Contact: contact@wisconsinhumanities.org; 608-262-0706; 3801 Regent Street, Madison, WI 53705
Website: www.wisconsinhumanities.org

The Wisconsin Humanities Council is an independent affiliate of the National Endowment for the Humanities. It is supported by state, federal, and private funding. Its mission is to create and support programs that use history, culture, and discussion to strengthen community life in Wisconsin. The governor appoints six members to the council. Other members are elected by the council.

Governor Tony Evers greets Senator Tim Carpenter (*top*) and Assembly Speaker Pro Tempore Kevin Petersen (*above*) before delivering the 2023 State of the State Address on January 24, 2023. The annual speech offers the governor an opportunity to outline his policy priorities before the public and a joint session of the legislature.

Governor's special committees

The committees listed below were created by executive order to conduct studies and provide advice. Members serve at the governor's pleasure. These committees submit final reports to the governor or governor-elect prior to the beginning of a new gubernatorial term and, unless continued by executive order, expire on the fourth Monday in the January of the year in which a new gubernatorial term begins.

BICYCLE COORDINATING COUNCIL
Aligned to: Department of Transportation

Created by Governor Tommy G. Thompson in 1991 and continued most recently by Governor Evers, the Bicycle Coordinating Council's concerns include encouraging the use of the bicycle as an alternative means of transportation, promoting bicycle safety and education, promoting bicycling as a recreational and tourist activity, and disseminating information about state and federal funding for bicycle programs.

BIRTH TO THREE EARLY INTERVENTION INTERAGENCY COORDINATING COUNCIL
Aligned to: Department of Health Services
Website: https://www.dhs.wisconsin.gov/b3icc/index.htm

First established by Governor Tommy G. Thompson in 1987, reestablished by Governor Thompson in 1998, and continued most recently by Governor Evers, the Early Intervention Interagency Coordinating Council was created pursuant to federal law. The council assists the Department of Health Services in the development and administration of early intervention services commonly referred to as the "Birth to Three Program," for infants and toddlers with developmental delays and their families. The council's members include parents of children with disabilities.

The Governor's Early Childhood Advisory Council works to ensure that all children in Wisconsin have access to early childhood programs and services. Below, Governor Tony Evers—a former educator, principal, and superintendent—visits with students in a school cafeteria.

COUNCIL ON AUTISM

Aligned to: Department of Health Services
Contact: dhsautismcouncil@dhs.wisconsin.gov
Website: https://autismcouncil.wisconsin.gov

Created by Governor Jim Doyle in 2005 and continued by Governor Evers, the Council on Autism advises the Department of Health Services on strategies for implementing statewide support and services for children with autism. A majority of its members are parents of children with autism or autism spectrum disorders.

CRIMINAL JUSTICE COORDINATING COUNCIL

Aligned to: Department of Justice
Website: https://cjcc.doj.wi.gov

Created by Governor Walker in 2012, and continued by Governor Evers, the Criminal Justice Coordinating Council is tasked with assisting the governor in directing, collaborating with, and coordinating the services of state, local, and private actors in the criminal justice system to increase public safety and the system's efficiency and effectiveness. Members of the council represent various aspects of the state's criminal justice system.

EARLY CHILDHOOD ADVISORY COUNCIL

Aligned to: Department of Children and Families
Website: https://dcf.wisconsin.gov/ecac

Governor Jim Doyle created the Early Childhood Advisory Council in 2008 in accordance with federal law, and Governor Evers has continued it. The council advises the governor on the development of a comprehensive statewide early childhood development system by, among other things, conducting needs assessments, developing recommendations for increasing participation of children in early childhood services, assessing the capacity of higher education to support the development of early childhood professionals, and making recommendations for the improvement of early learning standards.

GOVERNOR'S COMMITTEE FOR PEOPLE WITH DISABILITIES

Aligned to: Department of Health Services
Website: https://www.dhs.wisconsin.gov/gcpd/index.htm

The Governor's Committee for People with Disabilities, in its present form, was established in 1976 by Governor Patrick J. Lucey and has since been continued by each succeeding governor. The committee's functions include advising the governor on a broad range of issues affecting people with disabilities, including involvement in the workforce; reviewing legislation affecting people with disabilities; and promoting public awareness of the needs and abilities of people with disabilities.

GOVERNOR'S COUNCIL ON FINANCIAL LITERACY AND CAPABILITY

Aligned to: Department of Financial Institutions
Website: https://www.wdfi.org/ofl/govcouncilfinlit

Created by Governor Jim Doyle in 2005 as the Governor's Council on Financial Literacy, this council was continued and renamed by Governor Evers. The Governor's Council on Financial Literacy and Capability works with state agencies, private entities, and nonprofit associations to improve financial literacy among Wisconsin citizens. The council promotes the financial literacy awareness and education campaign called Money Smart Week and identifies barriers to financial inclusion, such as systemic racism, in certain sectors.

GOVERNOR'S COUNCIL ON PHYSICAL HEALTH AND WELLNESS

Aligned to: Office of the Governor

Governor Anthony Earl established the Governor's Council on Physical Fitness and Health in 1983, and Governor Walker recreated it in 2012. It was continued by Governor Evers in 2019. The council develops policy recommendations to improve the status of and educate the public concerning children's health, physical fitness, and nutrition. The council also encourages obesity prevention for all state residents.

GOVERNOR'S COUNCIL ON WORKFORCE INVESTMENT

Aligned to: Department of Workforce Development
Contact: 414-874-1680
Website: www.wi-cwi.org

Governor Tommy G. Thompson created the Governor's Council on Workforce Investment in 1999. Governor Scott Walker reconstituted the council in 2015 as a result of changes to federal law, and Governor Evers continued the council in 2019. The council is charged with carrying out certain duties and functions established under federal law governing state workforce development boards, including recommending strategies that align workforce development resources to support economic development, promoting programs to increase the number of skilled workers in the workforce and to provide resources to job seekers, and developing an online statewide workforce and labor market information system.

GOVERNOR'S GREEN RIBBON COMMISSION ON CLEAN ENERGY AND ENVIRONMENTAL INNOVATION

Aligned to: Department of Administration

Governor Evers created the Governor's Green Ribbon Commission on Clean Energy and Environmental Innovation in 2023 to advise the Department of Administration and the Wisconsin Economic Development Corporation on the establishment of an environmental and clean energy fund and to gather public input relating to such a fund.

GOVERNOR'S INFORMATION TECHNOLOGY EXECUTIVE STEERING COMMITTEE
Aligned to: Department of Administration

Created by Governor Walker in 2003 and continued by Governor Evers, the Governor's Information Technology Executive Steering Committee is responsible for the effective and efficient application of information technology assets across state agencies.

GOVERNOR'S JUDICIAL SELECTION ADVISORY COMMITTEE
Aligned to: Office of the Governor

Created by Governor Walker in 2011 and continued by Governor Evers, the Governor's Judicial Selection Advisory Committee recommends candidates to the governor to fill judicial vacancies in the state courts.

GOVERNOR'S JUVENILE JUSTICE COMMISSION
Aligned to: Department of Justice
Website: https://gjjc.widoj.gov

Governor Tommy G. Thompson created the Juvenile Justice Advisory Group in 1989. In 1991, he recreated it as the Governor's Juvenile Justice Commission, which was continued most recently by Governor Evers. The commission distributes federal grant moneys for the improvement of the juvenile justice system in the state. It also advises the governor and the legislature concerning juvenile justice issues.

GOVERNOR'S PARDON ADVISORY BOARD
Aligned to: Office of the Governor
Website: https://evers.wi.gov/pages/pardon-information.aspx

Governor Lee Sherman Dreyfus originally created the Pardon Advisory Board in 1980; Governors Thompson, McCallum, and Doyle later recreated and restructured the board. Governor Evers recreated the board again in 2019. As recreated, the board consists of nine members appointed by the governor, including the governor's chief legal counsel or a designee, who serves as chair. Using applications provided by the Office of the Governor, the board receives and considers requests for clemency, as authorized under Article V, Section 6, of the Wisconsin Constitution.

GOVERNOR'S TASK FORCE ON BROADBAND ACCESS
Aligned to: Public Service Commission

Governor Evers created this task force in 2020 to research and recommend policies to address broadband needs and facilitate broadband access across the state. The task force must report to the governor and the legislature on recommendations for facilitating broadband expansion, measures for addressing gaps and inequities in broadband access, opportunities for coordination among various public and private entities, the role of broadband in specific sectors and industries, advances in broadband technology, and the extent to which certain institutions have access to federal broadband expansion funds.

GOVERNOR'S TASK FORCE ON RETIREMENT SECURITY
Aligned to: Office of the State Treasurer
Website: https://statetreasurer.wi.gov/pages/retirement.aspx

The Governor's Task Force on Retirement Security was created by Governor Evers in 2019 and is chaired by the state treasurer. It is tasked with developing recommendations for how the state can best address the retirement crisis for Wisconsinites who do not have a way to save for retirement; reducing the regulatory and operational burden on small businesses that want to offer payroll deduction retirement savings options to employees; encouraging younger Wisconsinites to save early in life; and developing other innovative reforms to help Wisconsinites retire in a financially secure manner.

HISTORICAL RECORDS ADVISORY BOARD
Aligned to: State Historical Society of Wisconsin
Website: https://wisconsinhistory.org/records/article/CS3558

Continued most recently by Governor Evers, the Historical Records Advisory Board enables the state to participate in a grant program of the National Historical Publications and Records Commission. The board also promotes the availability and use of historic records as a key to understanding American culture.

HOMELAND SECURITY COUNCIL
Contact: 608-242-3026; PO Box 14587, Madison, WI 53708-0587
Website: https://homelandsecurity.wi.gov

Created by Governor Jim Doyle in 2003 and continued by Governor Evers, the Homeland Security Council advises the governor and coordinates the efforts of state and local officials concerning the prevention of and response to potential threats to the homeland security of Wisconsin.

INDEPENDENT LIVING COUNCIL OF WISCONSIN
Contact: ilcwinfo@gmail.com; 608-206-1581; 3810 Milwaukee Street, Madison, WI 53714
Website: https://il-wis.net/independent-living-council/about-the-council/

Governor Tommy G. Thompson created the Independent Living Council of Wisconsin in 1994; Governor Jim Doyle established the council as a nonprofit entity in 2004. Governor Evers has continued it. In coordination with the Division of Vocational Rehabilitation in the Department of Workforce Development, the council maintains the state's plan for independent living services for people with disabilities. The majority of the council's members are persons with disabilities. At least one member must be a director of a center for independent living, and at least one member must represent Native American vocational rehabilitation programs.

JOINT ENFORCEMENT TASK FORCE ON PAYROLL FRAUD AND WORKER MISCLASSIFICATION
Aligned to: Department of Workforce Development
Website: https://dwd.wisconsin.gov/misclassification

The Joint Enforcement Task Force was created by Governor Evers to work with relevant agencies to coordinate the investigation and enforcement of worker misclassification issues, which can result in underpayment of wages, payroll taxes, unemployment insurance contributions, and workers' compensation insurance.

TELECOMMUNICATIONS RELAY SERVICE COUNCIL
Aligned to: Public Service Commission

Created by Governor Tommy G. Thompson in 1990 and continued most recently by Governor Evers, the Telecommunications Relay Service Council advises the state concerning telecommunications relay service, including with respect to rates and availability. The members include one speech-impaired person, one hearing-impaired person, one speech-impaired and hearing-impaired person, and one person who does not have a speech or hearing impairment.

WISCONSIN COASTAL MANAGEMENT COUNCIL
Aligned to: Department of Administration
Contact: coastal@wisconsin.gov
Website: https://doa.wi.gov/pages/localgovtsgrants/coastaladvisorycouncil.aspx

The Wisconsin Coastal Management Council was created by acting Governor Martin J. Schreiber in 1977 to comply with provisions of the federal Coastal Zone Management Act of 1972 and to implement Wisconsin's Coastal Management Program. It was continued most recently by Governor Evers. The council advises the governor with respect to Wisconsin's coastal management efforts.

WISCONSIN PFAS ACTION COUNCIL (WISPAC)
Aligned to: Department of Natural Resources
Contact: dnrpfasinquiries@wisconsin.gov
Website: https://dnr.wisconsin.gov/topic/pfas/wispac.html

Governor Evers created the PFAS Coordinating Council in 2019 to assess the public health risks of per- and polyfluoroalkyl substances (PFAS) and develop a statewide plan to address those risks. The council is now known as the Wisconsin PFAS Action Council, or WisPAC, and its tasks include developing protocols to inform and engage the public on PFAS, best practices for identifying PFAS sources, and standard testing and treatment protocols. The council must also engage academic institutions and other experts to collaborate on joint projects and explore various avenues of public and private funding to support their efforts to address PFAS.

WISCONSIN REHABILITATION COUNCIL
Aligned to: Department of Workforce Development
Contact: dvrwirehabcouncil@dwd.wisconsin.gov
Website: https://dwd.wisconsin.gov/dvr/partners/wrc

Created by Governor Tommy G. Thompson in 1999 and continued most recently by Governor Evers, the Wisconsin Rehabilitation Council advises the Department of Workforce Development on a statewide vocational rehabilitation plan for disabled individuals that is required by federal law.

WISCONSIN SHARED SERVICES EXECUTIVE COMMITTEE
Aligned to: Department of Administration

The Wisconsin Shared Services Executive Committee was created by Governor Walker in 2018 and continued by Governor Evers in 2019. The committee is charged with establishing a shared services business model to deliver high-quality human resources and payroll and benefits services to all state agencies.

WISCONSIN TECHNOLOGY COMMITTEE
Aligned to: Wisconsin Technology Council
Contact: 608-442-7557
Website: http://wisconsintechnologycouncil.com

Created by Governor Walker in 2011 and continued by Governor Evers in 2019, the Wisconsin Technology Committee consists of the members of the Wisconsin Technology Council, a nonprofit corporation that was created by state legislation but later removed from the statutes. The committee provides a means by which the council can coordinate with state government. The council assists the state in promoting the creation, development, and retention of science-based and technology-based businesses.

Office of the Lieutenant Governor

Lieutenant governor: Sara Rodriguez
Chief of staff: Justin Koestler
Location: 19 East, State Capitol, Madison

Units of State Government: Executive | 177

Contact: ltgovernor@wisconsin.gov; 608-266-3516; PO Box 2043, Madison, WI 53702
Website: www.ltgov.wisconsin.gov
Number of employees: 5.00
Total budget 2021–23: $941,000

The lieutenant governor is the state's second-ranking executive officer, a position analogous to that of the vice president of the United States. If the incumbent governor dies, resigns, or is removed from office, the lieutenant governor becomes governor for the remainder of the unexpired term. The lieutenant governor serves as acting governor while the governor is unable to perform the duties of the office due to impeachment, incapacitation, or absence from the state. If there is a vacancy in the office of lieutenant governor, the governor must nominate a successor to serve, upon confirmation by both the senate and assembly, for the remainder of the unexpired term.

Lieutenant Governor Sara Rodriguez is sworn in for her first term as the 46th Lieutenant Governor of Wisconsin on January 3, 2023.

GREG ANDERSON, LEGISLATIVE PHOTOGRAPHER

The governor may designate the lieutenant governor to represent the governor's office on any statutory board, commission, or committee on which the governor is entitled to membership; on any nonstatutory committee established by the governor; and on any intergovernmental body created to maintain relationships with federal, state, and local governments or regional agencies. The governor may ask the lieutenant governor to coordinate certain state services and programs that the governor is directed by law to coordinate.

Voters elect the governor and lieutenant governor on a joint ballot to a four-year term. Candidates are nominated independently in the partisan August primary, but voters cast a combined ballot for the two offices in the November election.

Department of Administration

Department secretary-designee: Kathy Blumenfeld
Deputy secretary: Chris Patton
Location: 101 East Wilson Street, Madison
Contact: 608-266-1741; PO Box 7864, Madison, WI 53707-7864

Website: https://doa.wi.gov
Number of employees: 1,425.78
Total budget 2021–23: $1,817,747,400

The Department of Administration is administered by a secretary who is appointed by the governor with the advice and consent of the senate.

The department provides a wide range of services to other state agencies, including personnel management, payroll, accounting systems, and legal services. The department administers the state civil service system. The department also administers the state's procurement policies and contracts, fleet transportation, and risk management. It oversees the state's buildings and leased office space, as well as statewide facilities project planning and analysis. The department also oversees the Capitol Police. It administers a low-income household energy assistance program, funded with federal and state moneys, and offers program assistance and funds to address homelessness and support affordable housing, public infrastructure, and economic development opportunities. It provides fiscal and policy analysis to the governor for development of executive budget proposals. It regulates racing, charitable gaming, and Indian gaming. The department advises the Building Commission and the governor on the issuance of state debt. It administers finances for the clean water revolving loan fund program. Finally, the department provides a variety of services to the public and state, local, and tribal governments.

Subordinate statutory boards, councils, and committees

CERTIFICATION STANDARDS REVIEW COUNCIL
Chair: Paul Junio

The Certification Standards Review Council reviews the Department of Natural Resources laboratory certification and registration program and makes recommendations on programs for testing water, wastewater, waste material, soil, and hazardous substances.

COUNCIL ON AFFIRMATIVE ACTION
Chair: Adin Palau
Contact: 608-266-5709; PO Box 7855, Madison, WI 53707-7855
Website: https://dpm.wi.gov/pages/hr_admin/state-council-on-affirmative-action-diversity-awards.aspx

The Council on Affirmative Action advises the administrator of the Division of Personnel Management, evaluates affirmative action programs throughout the classified service, seeks compliance with state and federal regulations, and recommends improvements in state affirmative action efforts.

COUNCIL ON SMALL BUSINESS, VETERAN-OWNED BUSINESS AND MINORITY BUSINESS OPPORTUNITIES (inactive)
Contact: supplierdiversity@wi.gov; PO Box 7970, Madison, WI 53707-7970

The Council on Small Business, Veteran-Owned Business and Minority Business Opportunities advises the department on how to increase the participation of small businesses, veteran-owned businesses, and minority businesses in state purchasing.

STATE EMPLOYEES SUGGESTION BOARD (inactive)

The State Employees Suggestion Board administers an awards program to encourage unusual and meritorious suggestions and accomplishments by state employees that promote economy and efficiency in government functions.

Independent entities attached for administrative purposes

BOARD FOR PEOPLE WITH DEVELOPMENTAL DISABILITIES
Chair: Gregory Meyer
Executive Director: Beth Swedeen
Contact: 608-266-7826; 101 East Wilson Street, Room 219, Madison, WI 53703
Website: https://wi-bpdd.org
Number of employees: 7.00
Total budget 2021–23: $3,468,700

The Board for People with Developmental Disabilities advises the department, other state agencies, the legislature, and the governor on matters related to developmental disabilities. The board also administers a program to foster the employment of individuals with disabilities and provide specific, targeted supports to businesses, school districts, and vocational agencies that demonstrate how coworkers can provide internal support to coworkers with disabilities.

BOARD ON AGING AND LONG-TERM CARE
Chair: James Surprise
Executive director: Jessica Trudell
Contact: boaltc@wisconsin.gov; 608-246-7013; Ombudsman Program, 800-815-0015 (toll free); Medigap Helpline, 800-242-1060 (toll free); Medigap Part D Helpline, 855-677-2783 (toll free); 1402 Pankratz Street, Suite 111, Madison, WI 53704
Website: https://longtermcare.wi.gov
Number of employees: 44.50
Total budget 2021–23: $7,436,800

The Board on Aging and Long-Term Care reports to the governor and the legislature on matters relating to long-term care for the aged and disabled. The board monitors the development and implementation of federal, state, and local laws and regulations related to long-term care facilities and investigates complaints from people receiving long-term care. The board operates the Medigap Helpline, which provides information on insurance designed to supplement Medicare.

CLAIMS BOARD
Chair: Corey Finkelmeyer
Secretary: Anne Hanson
Contact: stateclaimsboard@wisconsin.gov; PO Box 7864, Madison, WI 53707-7864
Website: https://claimsboard.wi.gov

The Claims Board investigates and makes recommendations on all money claims against the state for $10 or more. The findings and recommendations are reported to the legislature, and no claim may be considered by the legislature until the board has made its recommendation.

DIVISION OF HEARINGS AND APPEALS
Administrator: Brian Hayes
Location: 4822 Madison Yards Way, Fifth Floor North, Madison
Contact: dhamail@wisconsin.gov; 608-266-7709; PO Box 7875, Madison, WI 53707-7875
Website: https://doa.wi.gov/divisions/hearings-and-appeals

The Division of Hearings and Appeals decides contested proceedings for the Department of Natural Resources, cases arising under the Department of Justice's Crime Victim Compensation Program, and appeals related to actions of the Departments of Health Services, Children and Families, Safety and Professional Services, and Agriculture, Trade and Consumer Protection. It hears appeals from the Department of Transportation, including those related to motor vehicle dealer licenses, highway signs, motor carrier regulation, and disputes arising between motor vehicle dealers and manufacturers. The division conducts hearings for the Department of Corrections on probation, parole, and extended supervision revocation and juvenile aftercare supervision. It handles contested cases for the Department of Public Instruction, the Department of Employee Trust Funds, and the Low-Income Home Energy Assistance Program of the Department of Administration. Other agencies may request the division to conduct hearing services.

DIVISION OF TRUST LANDS AND INVESTMENTS
Executive secretary: Tom German
Deputy secretary: vacant
Contact: 608-266-1370; PO Box 8943, Madison, WI 53708-8943
Website: https://bcpl.wisconsin.gov

The Division of Trust Lands and Investments assists the Board of Commissioners of Public Lands in its work and is under the direction and supervision of that board. The division is headed by an executive secretary who is appointed by the board. See the entry for the Board of Commissioners of Public Lands on page 220.

ELECTRONIC RECORDING COUNCIL
Chair: Sharon Martin
Contact: PO Box 7864, Madison, WI 53707-7864
Website: http://ercwis.wi.gov

The Electronic Recording Council adopts standards regarding the electronic recording of real estate documents to be promulgated by rule by the department.

INCORPORATION REVIEW BOARD
Chair: Dawn Vick
Contact: wimunicipalboundaryreview@wi.gov; 608-264-6102; PO Box 1645, Madison, WI 53701
Website: https://doa.wi.gov/pages/localgovtsgrants/incorporationreviewboard.aspx

The Incorporation Review Board reviews petitions for incorporating territory as a city or village to determine whether the petition meets certain statutory standards and is in the public interest.

INTERAGENCY COUNCIL ON HOMELESSNESS
Director: Michael Basford
Website: https://doa.wi.gov/pages/aboutdoa/ich.aspx

The Interagency Council on Homelessness is tasked with establishing and periodically reviewing a statewide policy with the purpose of preventing and ending homelessness in Wisconsin.

LABOR AND INDUSTRY REVIEW COMMISSION
Chair: Michael Gillick
Location: 3319 West Beltline Highway, Madison
Contact: lirc@wisconsin.gov; 608-266-9850; PO Box 8126, Madison, WI 53708-8126
Website: https://lirc.wisconsin.gov
Number of employees: 18.70
Total budget 2021–23: $5,593,600

The Labor and Industry Review Commission reviews the decisions of the Department of Workforce Development related to unemployment insurance, fair employment, and public accommodations and decisions of the Department of Workforce Development and the Division of Hearings and Appeals related to worker's compensation. The commission also hears appeals about discrimination in postsecondary education involving a person's physical condition or developmental disability.

NATIONAL AND COMMUNITY SERVICE BOARD

Chair: Christine Beatty
Executive director: Jeanne M. Duffy
Contact: servewisconsin@wisconsin.gov; 608-261-6716; 101 East Wilson Street, Sixth Floor, Madison, WI 53703-3405
Website: https://www.servewisconsin.wi.gov

The National and Community Service Board prepares a plan for providing national service programs (which must ensure outreach to organizations serving underrepresented populations) and provides a system to recruit and place participants in national service programs. The board receives and distributes funds from governmental and private sources and acts as an intermediary between the Corporation for National and Community Service and local agencies.

OFFICE OF BUSINESS DEVELOPMENT

Contact: doaobd@wisconsin.gov
Website: https://doa.wi.gov/obd

The Office of Business Development provides administrative support to the Small Business Regulatory Review Board.

PUBLIC RECORDS BOARD

Chair: Paul Ferguson
Contact: 101 East Wilson Street, Madison, WI 53703
Website: https://publicrecordsboard.wi.gov

The Public Records Board is responsible for the preservation of important state records, the cost-effective management of records by state agencies, and the orderly disposition of state records that have become obsolete. State agencies must have written approval from the board to dispose of records they generate or receive.

SMALL BUSINESS REGULATORY REVIEW BOARD

Contact: doaobd@wisconsin.gov
Website: https://doa.wi.gov/pages/doingbusiness/sbrrb.aspx

The Small Business Regulatory Review Board reviews state agency rules and guidelines, proposed rules, and emergency rules to determine whether they place an unnecessary burden on small businesses.

STATE CAPITOL AND EXECUTIVE RESIDENCE BOARD

Members: Senator Roys, Senator Wanggaard, Senator Jacque, Representative Duchow, Representative Binsfeld, Representative Subeck, John Fernholz, Arlan Kay, Melissa Destree, Janis Ringhand, Lesley Sager, Ron Siggelkow, Marcel Maul, Christian Overland, Rafeeq Asad, Thomas List, Megan Wolf
Website: https://doa.wi.gov/pages/capitol/state-capitol-and-executive-residence-board-(scerb).aspx

The State Capitol and Executive Residence Board is responsible for approving all renovations, repairs, furnishings, and fixtures on the grounds of the Wisconsin State Capitol and the Governor's Mansion, pictured here. The mansion sits on Lake Mendota and has been the home of the governor's family for over 50 years.

The State Capitol and Executive Residence Board (SCERB) ensures the architectural and decorative integrity of the buildings, decorative furniture, furnishings, and grounds of the capitol and executive residence and directs the continuing and consistent maintenance of the properties. No renovations, repairs (except of an emergency nature), installation of fixtures, decorative items, or furnishings for the ground and buildings of the capitol or executive residence may be performed by or become the property of the state by purchase wholly or in part from state funds, or by gift, loan, or otherwise, until approved by the board as to design, structure, composition, and appropriateness.

Increasing awareness of and concern for preserving and protecting the special nature of the people's buildings led to the creation of a mechanism for ensuring that the public interest and appropriate standards be carefully considered when altering or redecorating historic facilities. Building upon the State Capitol Restoration Guidelines prepared in 1980 by the Department of Administration's Division of State Facilities, the Legislature's Joint Committee on Legislative Organization in 1987 approved the Capitol Master Plan, which envisioned a full-scale renovation of the capitol, balancing the integrity of the building with the need to maintain it as a modern, functioning seat of government. After approval of the plan by SCERB and the State of Wisconsin Building Commission, renovation of the capitol, whose construction had been completed in 1917, commenced in 1990 and concluded in 2001. The project included extensive updating and improvements to the plumbing, electrical, and heating and cooling systems and largely restored office spaces to their original décor. The board is also responsible for overseeing the upkeep of the Classical Revival home on the shores of Lake

Mendota in the Village of Maple Bluff that has served as the official residence of the governor's family for over 50 years.

STATE USE BOARD
Chair: Tracy Nelson
Contact: 608-266-5462; PO Box 7867, Madison, WI 53707-7867
Website: http://stateuseprogram.wi.gov

The State Use Board oversees state purchases of goods and services from charitable organizations or nonprofit institutions that employ individuals with severe disabilities for at least 75 percent of the direct labor used in providing the goods or services.

TAX APPEALS COMMISSION
Commissioners: Elizabeth Kessler, *chair*
Contact: dorappeals@wisconsin.gov; 101 East Wilson Street, Fifth Floor, Madison, WI 53703
Website: https://taxappeals.wi.gov

The Tax Appeals Commission hears and decides appeals of assessments and determinations made by the Department of Revenue involving state-imposed taxes and state tax assessments of manufacturing property. The commission also adjudicates disputes between taxpayers and the Department of Transportation regarding certain motor vehicle taxes and fees. In addition, the commission has jurisdiction over cases involving the reasonableness of municipally imposed fees. The commission's decisions may be appealed to circuit court.

WASTE FACILITY SITING BOARD
Chair: Dale Shaver
Executive director: Brian Hayes
Location: 4822 Madison Yards Way, Fifth Floor North, Madison
Contact: dhamail@wisconsin.gov; 608-266-7709; PO Box 7875, Madison, WI 53707-7875
Website: https://doa.wi.gov/pages/licenseshearings/dhawastefacilitysitingboard.aspx

The Waste Facility Siting Board supervises a mandated negotiation-arbitration procedure between applicants for new or expanded solid or hazardous waste facility licenses and local committees comprising representatives from the municipalities affected by proposed facilities. It is authorized to make final awards in arbitration hearings and can enforce legal deadlines and other obligations of applicants and local committees during the process.

WOMEN'S COUNCIL
Chair: Denise Gaumer Hutchison
Contact: womenscouncil@wisconsin.gov; 608-266-2219; 101 East Wilson Street, Fifth Floor, Madison, WI 53703
Website: http://womenscouncil.wi.gov

The Women's Council identifies barriers that prevent women in Wisconsin from participating fully and equally in all aspects of life. The council advises state agencies about how current and emerging state policies, laws, and rules have an impact on women; recommends changes to the public and private sectors and initiates legislation to further women's economic and social equality and improve this state's tax base and economy; and disseminates information on the status of women.

Department of Agriculture, Trade and Consumer Protection

Board of Agriculture, Trade and Consumer Protection: Doug Rebout, *chair*
Department secretary: Randy Romanski
Deputy secretary: Aileen Switzer
Location: 2811 Agriculture Drive, Madison
Contact: 608-224-5012; PO Box 8911, Madison, WI 53708-8911
Website: https://datcp.wi.gov
Number of employees: 633.29
Total budget 2021–23: $221,844,800

The Department of Agriculture, Trade and Consumer Protection is directed and supervised by the Board of Agriculture, Trade and Consumer Protection and is administered by a secretary. The members of the board and the secretary are appointed by the governor with the advice and consent of the senate.

Among many other responsibilities, the Department of Agriculture, Trade and Consumer Protection regulates food production and promotes agricultural development in Wisconsin. Below, DATCP Secretary Randy Romanski tours a farm with Venice Williams, the interim executive director of Fondy Market, a nonprofit that aims to bring healthy food and economic opportunity to Greater Milwaukee.

The department regulates agriculture, trade, and commercial activity in Wisconsin for the protection of the state's citizens. It enforces the state's primary consumer protection laws, including those relating to deceptive advertising, unfair business practices, and consumer product safety. The department oversees the enforcement of Wisconsin's animal health and disease control laws and conducts a variety of programs to conserve and protect the state's vital land, water, and plant resources. The department licenses and inspects food-related businesses to ensure the safety of food produced or sold in Wisconsin. The department administers financial security programs to protect agricultural producers, facilitates the marketing of Wisconsin agricultural products in interstate and international markets, and promotes agricultural development.

Subordinate statutory boards, councils, and committees

AGRICULTURAL PRODUCER SECURITY COUNCIL

The Agricultural Producer Security Council advises the department on the administration and enforcement of the agricultural producer security program, which reimburses grain, milk, and vegetable producers and grain warehouse keepers if a purchaser defaults on payment.

FARM TO SCHOOL COUNCIL

Contact: wifarmtoschool@wisconsin.gov

The Farm to School Council advises the department regarding the promotion and administration of farm to school programs and reports to the legislature on the needs of those programs.

FERTILIZER RESEARCH COUNCIL

Website: https://frc.soils.wisc.edu

The Fertilizer Research Council provides funding, with the department secretary's final approval, to the University of Wisconsin System for fertilizer-related research projects. The research projects are funded from a portion of the sales of fertilizer and soil or plant additives in Wisconsin.

VETERINARY EXAMINING BOARD

Chair: Hunter Lang
Contact: datcpveb@wi.gov; 608-224-4353

The Veterinary Examining Board determines the education and experience required for obtaining veterinary licenses and veterinary technician certifications and develops and evaluates examinations for obtaining these licenses and certifications. The board also establishes and enforces standards of professional conduct for veterinarians and veterinary technicians.

Independent entities attached for administrative purposes

LAND AND WATER CONSERVATION BOARD

Chair: Mark E. Cupp

The Land and Water Conservation Board advises the secretary and department regarding soil and water conservation, farmland preservation, and pollution management and abatement. It reviews and makes recommendations to the department on county land and water resource plans and funding allocations to county land conservation committees. The board also advises the University of Wisconsin System about needed research and education programs related to soil and water conservation and assists the Department of Natural Resources with issues related to runoff from agricultural and other rural sources of pollution.

LIVESTOCK FACILITY SITING REVIEW BOARD
Contact: sitingboard@wisconsin.gov; 608-224-5006

The Livestock Facility Siting Review Board may review certain decisions made by political subdivisions relating to the siting or expansion of livestock facilities such as feedlots. An aggrieved person may challenge the decision of a city, village, town, or county government approving or disapproving the siting or expansion of a livestock facility by requesting that the board review the decision. If the board determines that a challenge is valid, it must reverse the decision of the governmental body. The decision of the board is binding on the governmental body, but either party may appeal the board's decision in circuit court.

The Department of Agriculture, Trade and Consumer Protection regulates livestock facilities in Wisconsin, promulgating rules covering odor control, runoff management, and the storage of waste, among other things. Above, Governor Tony Evers (*left*) and DATCP Secretary Randy Romanski (*third from left*) talk with farmers at Peters Farm in Vernon County.

Department of Children and Families

Department secretary: Emilie Amundson
Deputy secretary: Jeff Pertl
Assistant secretary: Nadya Perez-Reyes
Location: 201 West Washington Avenue, Madison
Contact: dcfweb@wisconsin.gov; 608-422-7000; PO Box 8916, Madison, WI 53703-8916
Website: https://dcf.wisconsin.gov
Number of employees: 798.17
Total budget 2021–23: $2,883,541,900

The Department of Children and Families is administered by a secretary who is appointed by the governor with the advice and consent of the senate.

The department provides or oversees county provision of various services to assist children and families, including services for children in need of protection or services, adoption and foster care services, the licensing of facilities that provide out-of-home care for children, background investigations of child caregivers, child abuse and neglect investigations, and community-based juvenile justice services. The department administers the Wisconsin Works (W-2) public assistance program, including the Wisconsin Shares child care subsidy program, the YoungStar child care quality improvement program, the child support enforcement and paternity establishment program, and programs related to the federal Temporary Assistance for Needy Families (TANF) income support program. The department also works to ensure that families have access to high quality and affordable early childhood care and education and administers the licensing and regulation of child care centers.

Subordinate statutory boards, councils, and committees

GOVERNOR'S COUNCIL ON DOMESTIC ABUSE
Website: https://dcf.wisconsin.gov/domesticabuse

The Council on Domestic Abuse reviews applications for domestic abuse services grants, advises the department and the legislature on matters of domestic abuse policy, and, in conjunction with the Judicial Conference, develops forms for filing petitions for domestic abuse restraining orders and injunctions.

RATE REGULATION ADVISORY COMMITTEE
Contact: dcfcwlratereg@wisconsin.gov
Website: https://dcf.wisconsin.gov/ratereg

The Rate Regulation Advisory Committee advises the department regarding rates for child welfare agencies, residential care centers, and group homes.

Independent entities attached for administrative purposes

CHILD ABUSE AND NEGLECT PREVENTION BOARD
Chair: Vicki Tylka
Executive director: Rebecca K. Murray
Contact: preventionboard@wisconsin.gov; 608-266-6871; 125 South Webster Street, Madison, WI 53703
Website: https://preventionboard.wi.gov
Number of employees: 7.00
Total budget 2021–23: $6,442,400

Emilie Amundson, secretary of children and families, plays with a child during a tour of Corinne's Little Explorers in New Glarus. The department is responsible for licensing and monitoring Wisconsin's child care centers.

The Child Abuse and Neglect Prevention Board administers the Children's Trust Fund, which was created to develop and fund strategies that prevent child maltreatment in Wisconsin. In addition, the board recommends to the governor, the legislature, and state agencies changes needed in state programs, statutes, policies, budgets, and rules to reduce child abuse and neglect and improve coordination among state agencies.

MILWAUKEE CHILD WELFARE PARTNERSHIP COUNCIL
Chair: Christine Holmes
Contact: dcfmilwaukeechildwelfare@wisconsin.gov; 414-343-5500; 635 North 26th Street, Milwaukee, WI 53233
Website: https://dcf.wisconsin.gov/mcps/partnership-council

The Milwaukee Child Welfare Partnership Council makes recommendations to the department and the legislature regarding policies and plans to improve the child welfare system in Milwaukee County.

Department of Corrections

Department secretary: Kevin A. Carr
Deputy secretary: Jared Hoy

Correctional officers share congratulations after graduating from the Department of Corrections' Officer Pre-Service Academy.

Location: 3099 East Washington Avenue, Madison
Contact: 608-240-5000; PO Box 7925, Madison, WI 53707-7925
Website: https://doc.wi.gov
Number of employees: 10,261.52
Total budget 2021–23: $2,838,410,000

The Department of Corrections is administered by a secretary appointed by the governor with the advice and consent of the senate. The department administers Wisconsin's state prisons, community corrections programs, and juvenile corrections programs. It supervises the custody and discipline of all inmates and operates programs to rehabilitate offenders and reintegrate them into society. It also supervises offenders on probation, parole, and extended supervision; monitors compliance with deferred prosecution programs; and may make recommendations for pardons or commutations of sentence when requested by the governor. The department maintains the sex offender registry and monitors sex offenders and sexually violent persons who are subject to GPS tracking.

Subordinate statutory boards, councils, and committees

CORRECTIONS SYSTEM FORMULARY BOARD

The Corrections System Formulary Board establishes written guidelines, to be applied uniformly throughout the state's correctional institutions, for making therapeutic alternate drug selections for prisoners.

Independent entities attached for administrative purposes

COUNCIL ON OFFENDER REENTRY
Chair: Silvia Jackson
Website: https://doc.wi.gov/pages/aboutdoc/reentryunit.aspx (council annual reports)

The Council on Offender Reentry coordinates reentry initiatives across the state, including by promoting collaboration in the provision of transition services and training opportunities, identifying funding sources, and developing methods of information sharing.

INTERSTATE ADULT OFFENDER SUPERVISION BOARD
Chair: Joselyn López, *commissioner/compact administrator*
Contact: docdccic@wisconsin.gov, 608-240-5388 (Interstate Compact Office); 3099 East Washington Avenue, Madison, WI 53704
Website: https://doc.wi.gov/pages/aboutdoc/communitycorrections/interstatecompact.aspx; https://www.interstatecompact.org/midwest/wisconsin

The Interstate Adult Offender Supervision Board appoints the Wisconsin representative to the Interstate Commission for Adult Offender Supervision. The board advises and exercises oversight and advocacy concerning the state's participation in the Interstate Compact for Adult Offender Supervision and on the operation of the compact within this state.

PAROLE COMMISSION
Chair: Jon Erpenbach
Contact: parolecommission@wisconsin.gov; 608-240-7280; PO Box 7960, Madison, WI 53707-7960
Website: https://doc.wi.gov/pages/aboutdoc/parolecommission.aspx

The Parole Commission conducts regularly scheduled interviews to consider the parole of eligible inmates and is responsible for notifying victims and law enforcement about parole decisions.

PRISON INDUSTRIES BOARD
Chair: David Hagemeir
Contact: P.O. Box 8990, Madison, WI 53708
Website: https://www.shopbce.com; https://doc.wi.gov/pages/aboutdoc/adultinstitutions/bureauofcorrectionalenterprises.aspx

The Prison Industries Board develops a plan for the manufacture and marketing of prison industry products and the provision of prison industry services and research and development activities.

STATE BOARD FOR INTERSTATE JUVENILE SUPERVISION
Chair: Christopher Dee

Website: https://doc.wi.gov/pages/aboutdoc/juvenilecorrections/interstatecompact.aspx; https://www.juvenilecompact.org/midwest/wisconsin

The State Board for Interstate Juvenile Supervision advises and exercises oversight and advocacy concerning the state's participation in the Interstate Compact for Juveniles and on the operation of the compact within this state.

Educational Communications Board

Chair: James Zylstra
Executive director: Marta Bechtol
Location: 3319 West Beltline Highway, Madison
Contact: 608-264-9600; 3319 West Beltline Highway, Madison, WI 53713
Website: https://www.ecb.org
Number of employees: 54.18
Total budget 2021–23: $41,873,100

The Educational Communications Board oversees the statewide public broadcasting system. It maintains and operates the infrastructure necessary for the state's public radio and television networks; maintains the infrastructure and oversees the operation of the Emergency Alert System, the Amber Alert System, and National Weather Service transmitters; and provides broadcast engineering and transmission services. The board operates the statewide Wisconsin Public Radio and Wisconsin Public Television services in partnership with the University of Wisconsin–Madison and provides additional educational resources.

The Educational Communications Board maintains the infrastructure of the state's public broadcasting system, including the candelabra tower pictured above, which hosts both public and private TV and radio broadcasters.

Elections Commission

Commissioners: Don M. Millis, *chair*; Robert F. Spindell, *vice chair*; Marge Bostelmann, Ann S. Jacobs, Mark L. Thomsen, Joseph Czarnezki
Administrator: Meagan Wolfe
Location: 201 West Washington Avenue, Second Floor, Madison
Contact: elections@wi.gov; 608-266-8005; 866-VOTE-WIS (toll free voter help line); PO Box 7984, Madison, WI 53707-7984

Units of State Government: Executive | 193

Website: https://elections.wi.gov
Number of employees: 31.75
Total budget 2021–23 $11,960,200

The Elections Commission consists of six members and can include additional members in certain circumstances. The majority leader of the senate, the speaker of the assembly, and the minority leaders of the senate and assembly each appoint one member. The governor appoints two members who were formerly county or municipal clerks, selecting one each from lists prepared by the legislative leadership of the two major political parties. If another political party qualified for a separate ballot and received at least 10 percent of the vote in the most recent gubernatorial election, the governor must appoint an additional member selected from a list prepared by that party. The governor's appointees must be confirmed by a majority of the members of the senate, but they can serve on the commission prior to confirmation. The commission appoints an administrator to direct and supervise the commission's staff. This appointment must be confirmed by the senate, but the commission can select a person to serve as interim administrator while the confirmation is pending. The administrator serves as the chief election officer of the state. The commission is responsible for ensuring compliance with state election laws and with the federal Help America Vote Act of 2002, which established certain requirements regarding the conduct of federal elections in the state. In this capacity, the commission trains and certifies all municipal clerks and chief election inspectors in the state to promote uniform election procedures. In addition, the commission is responsible for the design and maintenance of the statewide voter registration system. Every municipality in the state must use this system to administer federal, state, and local elections.

Don Millis, pictured above, has served as chair of the Wisconsin Elections Commission since June 2022.

Department of Employee Trust Funds

Employee Trust Funds Board: William Ford, *chair*
Department Secretary: John Voelker
Deputy Secretary: Shirley Eckes

Location: 4822 Madison Yards Way, Eighth Floor, Madison
Contact: 608-266-3285; 877-533-5020 (toll free); PO Box 7931, Madison, WI 53707-7931
Website: https://etf.wi.gov
Number of employees: 275.20
Total budget 2021–23: $101,922,900

The Department of Employee Trust Funds is directed and supervised by the Employee Trust Funds Board. The board consists of 13 members, one of whom is the governor (or a designee). The department is administered by a secretary who is appointed by the board.

The department administers various benefit programs available to state and local public employees, including the Wisconsin Retirement System, health and life insurance programs for active and retired employees of the state and participating local governments, a deferred compensation program, and employee-funded reimbursement account plans. The department serves all state employees and teachers and most municipal employees, with the notable exceptions of employees of the City of Milwaukee and Milwaukee County.

The Employee Trust Funds Board sets policy for the department; appoints the department secretary; approves tables used for computing benefits, contribution rates, and actuarial assumptions; authorizes all annuities except for disability; approves or rejects the department's administrative rules; and generally oversees benefit programs administered by the department, except the group insurance and deferred compensation programs.

Subordinate statutory boards, councils, and committees

DEFERRED COMPENSATION BOARD

Website: https://etf.wi.gov/boards/board_dc.htm

The Deferred Compensation Board oversees the deferred compensation plans offered to state and local employees and contracts with deferred compensation plan providers.

GROUP INSURANCE BOARD

Website: https://etf.wi.gov/boards/board_gib.htm

The Group Insurance Board oversees the group health, life, income continuation, and other insurance programs offered to state employees, covered local employees, and retirees.

TEACHERS RETIREMENT BOARD

Website: https://etf.wi.gov/boards/board_tr.htm

The Teachers Retirement Board advises the Employee Trust Funds Board about retirement matters related to teachers, approves administrative rules related to teachers, authorizes the payment of disability annuities to teachers, and hears appeals of staff determinations regarding disability annuities for teacher participants.

WISCONSIN RETIREMENT BOARD
Website: https://etf.wi.gov/boards/board_wr.htm
The Wisconsin Retirement Board advises the Employee Trust Funds Board about retirement matters related to state and local general and protective employees and performs the same functions for these employees as the Teachers Retirement Board does for teachers.

Ethics Commission

Commissioners: Pat Strachota, *chair;* Andrew Weininger, Gerald Ptacek, Maryann Sumi, Carousel Bayrd, Timothy Van Akkeren
Administrator: Daniel A. Carlton Jr.
Location: 101 East Wilson Street, Suite 127, Madison
Contact: ethics@wi.gov (general agency and code of ethics questions); campaign finance@wi.gov (campaign finance); ethlobbying@wi.gov (lobbying); 608-266-8123; PO Box 7125, Madison, WI 53707-7125
Website: https://ethics.wi.gov; https://cfis.wi.gov (Campaign Finance Information System); https://lobbying.wi.gov (Eye On Lobbying); https://sei.wi.gov (Statements of Economic Interests)
Number of employees: 8.00
Total budget 2021–23: $3,017,000

The Ethics Commission consists of six members and may include additional members in certain circumstances. The majority leader of the senate, the speaker of the assembly, and the minority leaders of the senate and assembly each appoint one member. The governor appoints two members who were formerly elected judges, selecting one each from lists prepared by the legislative leadership of the two major political parties. If another political party qualified for a separate ballot and received at least 10 percent of the vote in the most recent gubernatorial election, the governor must appoint an additional member selected from a list prepared by that party. The governor's appointees must be confirmed by a majority of the members of the senate, but they can serve on the commission prior to confirmation. The commission appoints an administrator to direct and supervise the commission's staff. The senate must confirm this appointment, but the commission may select a person to serve as interim administrator while the confirmation is pending.

The commission administers Wisconsin's campaign finance laws, lobbying laws, and ethics laws. The commission is the campaign finance filing officer for political organizations that are required to file campaign finance reports with the state, and provides forms, training materials, and assistance to local campaign filing officers (municipal, county, and school district clerks). Lobbyists must obtain a license from the commission, and organizations that employ a lobbyist must register and file reports with the commission detailing the time and money they spend on lobbying. State officials, candidates, and nominees must annually file with the commission statements detailing their economic interests.

Department of Financial Institutions

Department secretary-designee: Cheryll Olson-Collins
Deputy secretary: Patti Epstein
Location: 4822 Madison Yards Way, North Tower, Madison
Contact: 608-261-9555; PO Box 8861, Madison, WI 53708-8861
Website: www.wdfi.org
Number of employees: 141.54
Total budget 2021–23: $39,086,800

The Department of Financial Institutions is administered by a secretary who is appointed by the governor with the advice and consent of the senate. The department regulates state-chartered banks, savings banks, and savings and loan associations. The department also registers securities and securities industry members and regulates securities offerings, securities industry operations, corporate takeovers, and franchise offerings. It examines and files organizational documents and annual reports for corporations, limited liability companies, and other business entities.

The Department of Financial Institutions' Office of Financial Literacy Director David Mancl (*standing*) and Secretary-designee Cheryll Olson-Collins (*seated*) speak with high school students during the annual Finance & Investment Challenge Bowl tournament.

It also licenses and regulates the mortgage banking industry and other financial service providers, including payday lenders, high-interest consumer lenders, collection agencies, check cashing services, check sellers, credit counseling and debt settlement services, and automobile sales finance companies. The department administers the Uniform Commercial Code filing system and the Wisconsin Consumer Act. It also issues notary public commissions and registers trademarks, trade names, and brands. It registers and regulates charitable organizations, persons involved with solicitations on behalf of charitable organizations, and professional employer organizations. It also issues video service franchises to cable television operators and maintains a filing system for homeowners' association notices.

Subordinate statutory boards, councils, and committees

BANKING INSTITUTIONS REVIEW BOARD

The Banking Institutions Review Board advises the Division of Banking in the department on matters related to banks, savings banks, and savings and loan associations, and reviews the division's administrative actions.

Independent entities attached for administrative purposes

COLLEGE SAVINGS PROGRAM BOARD

Administrator: Jessica Wetzel
Contact: 608-264-7899; PO Box 8861, Madison, WI 53708-8861
Website: http://529.wi.gov

The College Savings Program Board administers the Edvest and Tomorrow's Scholar programs, which provide for tax-advantaged investment accounts used to pay higher education expenses. The board also has continuing responsibility for a legacy college Tuition Units program.

OFFICE OF CREDIT UNIONS AND CREDIT UNION REVIEW BOARD

Director: Kim Santos
Contact: 608-261-9543; PO Box 14137, Madison, WI 53708-0137
Website: www.wdfi.org/fi/cu

The Office of Credit Unions regulates state-chartered credit unions. The Credit Union Review Board advises the Office of Credit Unions on matters relating to credit unions and reviews the office's administrative actions.

REMOTE NOTARY COUNCIL

The Remote Notary Council adopts standards for notaries public to perform notarial acts for remotely located individuals, and these standards are then promulgated as rules by the department.

Department of Health Services

Secretary-designee: Kirsten Johnson
Deputy secretary: Deb Standridge
Location: 1 West Wilson Street, Madison
Contact: 608-266-1865; 800-947-3529 (toll free); 1 West Wilson Street, Madison, WI 53703
Website: www.dhs.wisconsin.gov
Number of employees: 6,341.92
Total budget 2021–23: $30,163,074,200

The Department of Health Services is administered by a secretary who is appointed by the governor with the advice and consent of the senate.

The Department of Health Services administers a wide range of services to clients in the community and at state institutions; regulates certain care providers, including emergency medical services practitioners; oversees vital records, including birth, death, marriage, and divorce certificates; and supervises and consults with local public agencies. The department promotes and protects public health in Wisconsin through various services and regulations addressing environmental and occupational health, family and community health, chronic and communicable disease prevention and control, and maternal and child health. The department provides access to health care for low-income persons, the elderly, and people with disabilities and administers the Medical Assistance (Medicaid), BadgerCare Plus, SeniorCare, chronic disease aids, general relief, and FoodShare programs. Additionally, the department administers programs that provide long-term support for the elderly and people with disabilities, including Family Care, IRIS, Aging and Disability Resource Centers, and the Employment First Initiative. The department licenses and regulates programs and facilities that provide general and mental health services, long-term care, and substance abuse services, including assisted living facilities, nursing homes, home health agencies, and facilities serving people with developmental disabilities, including three state-operated centers for persons with developmental disabilities. The department administers programs to meet mental health disorder and substance abuse prevention, diagnosis, early intervention, and treatment needs in community and institutional settings, including two state-owned, inpatient mental health institutes, Mendota Mental Health Institute and Winnebago Mental Health Institute. Mendota Mental Health Institute houses a secure treatment unit to meet the mental health needs of male adolescents from the Department of Corrections' juvenile institutions. The department also operates the Wisconsin Resource Center as a maximum security facility for prison inmates whose mental health treatment needs cannot be met by the Department of Corrections and provides treatment at the Sand Ridge Secure Treatment Center for individuals civilly committed under the sexually violent persons law.

The Department of Health Services' Maternal and Child Health Program aims to strengthen health outcomes for families across Wisconsin by combatting maternal and infant mortality. At an event pictured above, DHS Chief Medical Officer Dr. Jasmine Zapata (*far right*) joins representatives from the Medical College of Wisconsin and the UW School of Medicine and Public Health to announce the recipients of $16 million in maternal and child health grant funding.

Subordinate statutory boards, councils, and committees

COUNCIL FOR THE DEAF AND HARD OF HEARING
Website: https://dhhcouncil.wisconsin.gov

The Council for the Deaf and Hard of Hearing advises the department on the provision of effective services to persons who are deaf, hard-of-hearing, or deaf-blind.

COUNCIL ON BIRTH DEFECT PREVENTION AND SURVEILLANCE
Website: https://cbdps.wisconsin.gov

The Council on Birth Defect Prevention and Surveillance makes recommendations to the department regarding the administration of the Wisconsin Birth Defects Registry, which documents diagnoses and counts the number of birth defects for children up to age two. The council advises what birth defects are to be reported and the content, format, and procedures for reporting.

COUNCIL ON BLINDNESS
Contact: dhsobvi@dhs.wisconsin.gov
Website: https://scob.wisconsin.gov

The Council on Blindness makes recommendations to the department and other state agencies on services, activities, programs, investigations, and research that affect persons who are blind or visually impaired.

COUNCIL ON MENTAL HEALTH
Contact: wcmh@wisconsin.gov

Website: https://mhc.wisconsin.gov

The Council on Mental Health advises the department, governor, and legislature on mental health programs; provides recommendations on the expenditure of federal mental health block grants; reviews the department's plans for mental health services; and serves as an advocate for those who have mental illness.

A staff member at the Wisconsin Resource Center reviews a patient's electronic health records. The center develops innovative treatment methods for state prison residents in need of specialized mental health services.

PUBLIC HEALTH COUNCIL
Contact: dhspublichealthcouncil@wisconsin.gov
Website: https://publichealthcouncil.wisconsin.gov

The Public Health Council advises the department, the governor, the legislature, and the public on progress made in the implementation of the department's 10-year public health plan and coordination of responses to public health emergencies.

TRAUMA ADVISORY COUNCIL
Contact: dhstrauma@dhs.wisconsin.gov
Website: https://stac.wisconsin.gov

The Trauma Advisory Council advises the department on developing and implementing a statewide trauma care system.

Other statutorily required advisory entities

MEDICAID PHARMACY PRIOR AUTHORIZATION ADVISORY COMMITTEE
Website: https://www.forwardhealth.wi.gov/wiportal/content/provider/pac/index.htm.spage

The Medicaid Pharmacy Prior Authorization Advisory Committee advises the department on issues related to prior authorization decisions concerning prescription drugs on behalf of Medical Assistance recipients.

NEWBORN SCREENING ADVISORY GROUP: UMBRELLA COMMITTEE
Website: http://www.slh.wisc.edu/clinical/newborn/program-information/wisconsin-newborn-screening-advisory-group

The Newborn Screening Advisory Umbrella Committee advises the department regarding a statutorily required program that generally requires that newborn infants receive blood or other diagnostic tests for congenital and metabolic disorders.

QUALITY ASSURANCE AND IMPROVEMENT COMMITTEE
Website: https://www.dhs.wisconsin.gov/regulations/qai/members.htm

The Quality Assurance and Improvement Committee makes recommendations for the disbursement of civil money penalties funds allocated for improving the quality of care in Wisconsin nursing homes.

Independent entities attached for administrative purposes

COUNCIL ON PHYSICAL DISABILITIES
Chair: Benjamin Barrett
Contact: 608-266-5364
Website: https://cpd.wisconsin.gov

The Council on Physical Disabilities develops and modifies the state plan for services to persons with physical disabilities. The council advises the secretary of health services, recommends legislation, encourages public understanding of the needs of persons with physical disabilities, and promotes programs to prevent physical disability.

EMERGENCY MEDICAL SERVICES BOARD
Chair: Jerry Biggart
Website: https://www.dhs.wisconsin.gov/ems/boards/index.htm

The Emergency Medical Services Board appoints an advisory committee of physicians to advise the department on the selection of the state medical director for emergency medical services and to review that person's performance. The board also advises the director on medical issues; reviews emergency medical service statutes and rules concerning the transportation of patients; and recommends changes to the department and the Department of Transportation.

Higher Educational Aids Board

Members: Stephen Willett, *chair*; Jennifer Kammerud, *vice chair*; Jeff Cichon, *secretary*;
  Efremn Dana, Rosa Faustino, Jennifer Garrett, Jeff Neubauer, Timothy Opgenorth,
  Susan Teerink, Justin Wesolek, Kyle M. Weatherly
Nonvoting members: Russell Swagger (president, Lac Courte Oreilles Ojibwe University)
Executive secretary: Connie Hutchison
Location: 4822 Madison Yards Way, Seventh Floor, Madison
Contact: heabmail@wisconsin.gov; 608-267-2206; PO Box 7885, Madison, WI 53707-7885

Website: https://heab.state.wi.us
Number of employees: 10.00
Total budget 2021–23: $295,822,600

The Higher Educational Aids Board consists of the superintendent of public instruction and 10 members appointed by the governor without senate confirmation. The board has added one nonvoting member to represent tribal colleges. The governor appoints the board's executive secretary. The board is responsible for administering the state's higher education student financial aid system and also enters into certain interstate agreements relating to higher education.

Independent entities attached for administrative purposes

DISTANCE LEARNING AUTHORIZATION BOARD

Members: Anny Morrobel-Sosa, *chair*; Morna Foy, *vice chair*; Rolf Wegenke, *secretary*; Russell Swagger
Website: https://heab.state.wi.us/dlab

The Distance Learning Authorization Board administers this state's participation in the State Authorization Reciprocity Agreement (SARA), an interstate agreement related to state authorization and oversight of postsecondary institutions that offer educational programs to students located in other states. As provided in SARA, the board reviews, authorizes, and monitors eligible postsecondary institutions with respect to their distance learning programs, such as online classes offered to out-of-state students.

State Historical Society of Wisconsin

Board of Curators: Angela Bartell, *president*; Donald Schott, *president-elect*; Greg Huber, *past president*; Walter Rugland, *treasurer*; Christian Overland, *secretary*; Cindy Arbiture (president, Wisconsin Council for Local History), Patrick Fee (chair, Wisconsin Historical Foundation Board of Directors), Laura Cramer (president, Friends of the Wisconsin Historical Society), Marcia Anderson, Sherman Banker, Representative Billings, Eric Borgerding, Mary Buestrin, Jeffrey Cheney, Ramona Gonzalez, Mary Jane Herber, Joanne Huelsman, Susan McCleod, Janan Najeeb, Representative Penterman, Lowell Peterson, Julie Ragland, Thomas Shriner Jr., Robert Smith, Leonard Sobczak, Senator Taylor, John Thompson, Chia Youyee Vang, Senator Wanggaard, Keene Winters, Terri Yoho, Cate Zeuske, Aharon Zorea
Director: Christian Overland
Location: 816 State Street, Madison (archives and library); 30 North Carroll Street, Madison (museum)
Contact: 608-264-6400 (general); 608-264-6535 (library); 608-264-6460 (archives); 608-264-6555 (museum); 608-261-9582 (historic preservation); 608-264-6456 (programs and outreach); 816 State Street, Madison, WI 53706

The headquarters of the Wisconsin Historical Society anchors Library Mall on the University of Wisconsin–Madison campus. It houses extensive library and archival collections, including the Wisconsin Center for Film and Theatre Research, a noteworthy collection of materials relating to the entertainment industry.

Website: www.wisconsinhistory.org
Number of employees: 177.70
Total budget 2021–23 $59,877,300

The State Historical Society of Wisconsin, also known as the Wisconsin Historical Society, is both a state agency and a membership organization. The society's Board of Curators includes eight statutory appointments and up to 30 members who are selected according to the society's constitution and bylaws. Three board members are appointed by the governor with the advice and consent of the senate. The board selects the society's director, who serves as administrative head and as secretary to the board.

The mission of the society is to help connect people to the past. The society has a statutory duty to collect and preserve historical and cultural resources related to Wisconsin and to make them available to the public. To meet these objectives, the society maintains a major history research collection in Madison and, in partnership with the University of Wisconsin System, operates 13 other area research centers, including the Northern Great Lakes Visitor Center. The society operates the Wisconsin Historical Museum in Madison and 10 other museums and historic sites throughout the state. The society also leases Circus World Museum, which is operated by the Circus World Museum Foundation. The society provides statewide school services programs and public history programming, such as National History Day; publishes a magazine and books related to Wisconsin history; and provides travelling exhibits and speakers on historical topics. The society also provides technical services and advice to approximately 400 affiliated local historical societies throughout the state. The society serves as the state's historic preservation office, which facilitates the preservation of historic structures and archaeological sites and administers the state and national registers of historic places. The society is also responsible for administering the state's Burial Sites Preservation Law and assisting the Wisconsin semiquincentennial commission in commemorating, on July 4, 2026, the 250th anniversary of the country's founding.

Independent entities attached for administrative purposes

BURIAL SITES PRESERVATION BOARD

Members: Melinda Young, *chair;* Cynthia Stiles, *vice chair;* David J. Grignon, Jennifer Haas, Christian Overland, Katherine Stevenson, Corina Williams
Nonvoting members: James Skibo, Daina Penkiunas
Contact: 816 State Street, Madison, WI 53706
Website: https://www.wisconsinhistory.org/records/article/CS3252

The Burial Sites Preservation Board assists in the administration of the state's burial sites laws. The board's duties include reviewing decisions of the Wisconsin Historical Society director to record burial sites in the catalog or to remove land from the burial sites catalog, determining which Native American tribes in Wisconsin have an interest in cataloged burial sites, approving applicants for a registry of persons having an interest in cataloged burial sites, reviewing decisions on permit applications to disturb cataloged burial sites, reviewing decisions regarding the disposition of human remains and burial objects removed from burial sites, and approving the transfer of burial sites from the state or a political subdivision to private ownership.

HISTORIC PRESERVATION REVIEW BOARD

Members: Peter Wolter, *chair;* Amy Scanlon, *vice chair;* Sergio Gonzalez, Carlen Hatala, Carol McChesney Johnson, Dan J. Joyce, Neil Prendergast, Ray Reser, Matt Sadowski, Sissel Schroeder, Valentine Schute Jr., Daniel J. Stephans, Melinda Young, Donna Zimmerman
Contact: 816 State Street, Madison, WI 53706
Website: https://www.wisconsinhistory.org/records/article/CS3564

The Historic Preservation Review Board approves nominations to the Wisconsin State Register of Historic Places and the National Register of Historic Places upon recommendation of the state historic preservation officer. The board approves the distribution of federal grants-in-aid for preservation and approves the state preservation plan; advises the State Historical Society; and requests comments from planning departments of affected cities, villages, towns, counties, local landmark commissions, and local historical societies regarding properties being considered for nomination to the state and national registers.

Office of the Commissioner of Insurance

Commissioner: Nathan Houdek
Deputy commissioner: Rachel Cissne Carabell
Location: 125 South Webster Street, Madison
Contact: 608-266-3585; 800-236-8517 (toll free); PO Box 7873, Madison, WI 53707-7873
Website: https://oci.wi.gov
Email contacts by subject: https://oci.wi.gov/pages/aboutoci/emailadd.aspx
Number of employees: 134.83
Total budget 2021–23: $520,114,200

The Office of the Commissioner of Insurance is administered by the commissioner of insurance, who is appointed by the governor with the advice and consent of the senate. The office supervises the insurance industry in Wisconsin. The office is responsible for examining insurance industry financial practices and market conduct, licensing insurance agents, reviewing policy forms for compliance with state insurance statutes and regulations, investigating consumer complaints, and providing consumer information.

The office administers two segregated insurance funds: the State Life Insurance Fund and the Injured Patients and Families Compensation Fund. The State Life Insurance Fund offers up to $10,000 of low-cost life insurance protection to any Wisconsin resident who meets prescribed risk standards. The Injured Patients and Families Compensation Fund provides medical malpractice coverage for qualified health care providers on claims in excess of a provider's underlying coverage. The office also oversees the Health Care Liability Insurance Plan, which provides liability coverage for hospitals, physicians, and other health care providers in Wisconsin.

Subordinate statutory boards, councils, and committees

BOARD OF DIRECTORS OF THE INSURANCE SECURITY FUND

Chair: Raina Zanow
Contact: wisconsin@wisf-madison.org; 608-242-9473; 844-344-5484 (toll free); 2820 Walton Commons Lane, Suite 135, Madison, WI 53718-6797
Website: https://www.wilifega.org

The Board of Directors of the Insurance Security Fund administers a fund that protects certain insurance policyholders and claimants from excessive delay and loss in the event of insurer liquidation. The fund consists of accounts for life insurance, allocated annuities, disability insurance (includes health), HMO insurers, other insurance (includes property and casualty), and fund administration. The fund supports continuation of coverage under many life, annuity, and health policies. It is financed by assessments paid by most insurers in this state.

BOARD OF GOVERNORS OF THE INJURED PATIENTS AND FAMILIES COMPENSATION FUND/ WISCONSIN HEALTH CARE LIABILITY INSURANCE PLAN
Chair: Nathan Houdek
Contact: PO Box 7873, Madison, WI 53707-7873; Injured Patients and Families Compensation Fund: ociipfcf@wisconsin.gov; 608-707-5481; Wisconsin Health Care Liability Insurance Plan: whclip@wausaumms.com; 715-841-1690
Website: https://oci.wi.gov/pages/funds/ipfcfboardofgovernors.aspx

The Board of Governors of the Injured Patients and Families Compensation Fund/Wisconsin Health Care Liability Insurance Plan oversees the health care liability plan for licensed physicians and certified registered nurse anesthetists, medical partnerships and corporations, cooperative health care associations, ambulatory surgery centers, hospitals, some nursing homes, and certain other health care providers. The board also supervises the Injured Patients and Families Compensation Fund, which pays medical malpractice claims in excess of a provider's underlying coverage.

INJURED PATIENTS AND FAMILIES COMPENSATION FUND PEER REVIEW COUNCIL
The Injured Patients and Families Compensation Fund Peer Review Council reviews, within one year of the first payment on a claim, each claim for damages arising out of medical care provided by a health care provider or provider's employee if the claim is paid by any of the following: the Injured Patients and Families Compensation Fund, the Wisconsin Health Care Liability Insurance Plan, a private health care liability insurer, or a self-insurer. The council can recommend adjustments in fees paid to the Injured Patients and Families Compensation Fund, premiums paid to the Wisconsin Health Care Liability Insurance Plan, or premiums paid to private insurers if requested by the insurer.

State of Wisconsin Investment Board

Chair: Barbara Nick
Executive director/chief investment officer: Edwin Denson
Location: 121 East Wilson Street, Madison
Contact: info@swib.state.wi.us; 608-266-2381; PO Box 7842, Madison, WI 53707-7842
Website: www.swib.state.wi.us
Number of employees: 236.00
Total budget 2021–23: $135,329,400

The State of Wisconsin Investment Board consists of the secretary of administration or his or her designee and eight other members, six of whom are appointed by the governor with the advice and consent of the senate. The board appoints the executive director.

The board is responsible for investing the assets of the Wisconsin Retirement System and the State Investment Fund. The board's investments are managed by its own professional staff and by outside money managers. As of December 31, 2021, the board managed nearly $166 billion in assets. The largest portion of the assets managed by the board, more than $147 billion, is the trust funds of the Wisconsin Retirement System. For purposes of investment, the retirement system's assets are divided into two funds: the core fund, which is a broadly diversified portfolio that includes stocks, bonds, and other assets, and the variable fund, which is an all-stock fund. As of December 31, 2021, more than $20 billion of the assets under management by the board are in the State Investment Fund, which is the state's cash management fund, and which is also available to local units of government through the Local Government Pooled-Investment Fund, a separate fund within the State Investment Fund. The board also manages the assets of the following trust funds, which together account for less than 1 percent of the board's total assets under management: the State Life Insurance Fund, the Historical Society Trust Fund, the Injured Patients and Families Compensation Fund, and the UW System Trust Funds.

Department of Justice

Attorney general: Joshua L. Kaul
Deputy attorney general: Eric Wilson
Location: 114 East, State Capitol (attorney general's office); 17 West Main Street, Madison (Department of Justice)
Contact: 608-266-1221; PO Box 7857, Madison, WI 53707-7857
Website: https://www.doj.state.wi.us
Number of employees: 712.14
Total budget 2021–23: $314,712,100

The Department of Justice is headed by the attorney general, a constitutional officer who is elected on a partisan ballot to a four-year term. The department provides legal advice and representation, investigates criminal activity, and provides various law enforcement services for the state. The department appears for the state and prosecutes or defends civil and criminal actions and proceedings in the court of appeals or the supreme court in which the state is interested or a party. The department prosecutes or defends all civil cases sent or remanded to any circuit court in which the state is a party. The department also represents the

Attorney General Josh Kaul delivers remarks after being sworn in for a second term as Wisconsin's 45th attorney general.

state in criminal cases on appeal in federal court.

Subordinate statutory boards, councils, and committees

CRIME VICTIMS COUNCIL

Members: Lindsay Anderson, Tania M. Bonnett, Jessica Bryan, Veronica Figueroa Velez, Jane E. Graham Jennings, Heather Haeflinger, Kurt Heuer, Scott Horne, Heidi Kilbourn, Connie Klick, David Lasee, Jennifer L. Noyes, Mallory E. O'Brien, Kari Sasso, Amy Severt
Contact: ocvs@doj.state.wi.us
Website: https://www.doj.state.wi.us/ocvs/not-crime-victim/crime-victims-council

The Crime Victims Council provides advice and recommendations to the attorney general on the rights of crime victims, how to improve the criminal justice response to victims, and other issues affecting crime victims.

Independent entities attached for administrative purposes

CRIME VICTIMS RIGHTS BOARD

Operations Director: Julie Braun
Members: Jen Dunn, Adam Gerol, Christine Nolan, Nela Kalpic, Andre Sayles
Contact: cvrb@doj.state.wi.us
Website: https://www.doj.state.wi.us/ocvs/victim-rights/crime-victims-rights-board

The Crime Victims Rights Board has the authority to review complaints filed by a crime victim that allege that a public official, public employee, or public agency violated the victim's rights. The board may issue a private or public reprimand for a violation, seek appropriate equitable relief on behalf of a victim, or bring a civil action to assess a forfeiture for an intentional violation. The board may issue a report or recommendation concerning the rights of crime victims and the provision of services to crime victims.

LAW ENFORCEMENT STANDARDS BOARD

Chair: Christopher Domagalski

Members: Kalvin Barrett, Benjamin Bliven, Robert Botsch, Timothy Carnahan, Jean Galasinski, Timothy Gruenke, Casey Krueger, Jessie Metoyer, Nicole Miller, Katie Rosenberg, James Small, Charles Tubbs, Steven Wagner, 2 vacancies
Contact: wilenet@doj.state.wi.us
Website: https://wilenet.widoj.gov

The Law Enforcement Standards Board sets minimum education and training standards for law enforcement, tribal law enforcement, and jail and juvenile detention officers. The board certifies persons who meet professional standards as qualified to be law enforcement, tribal law enforcement, jail, or juvenile detention officers. The board consults with other government agencies regarding the development of training schools and courses, conducts research to improve law enforcement and performance, and evaluates governmental units for compliance with board standards.

The Curriculum Advisory Committee advises the Law Enforcement Standards Board on the establishment of curriculum requirements for training of law enforcement, tribal law enforcement, and jail and juvenile detention officers.

Department of Military Affairs

Commander in chief: Tony Evers (governor)
Adjutant general: Major General Paul E. Knapp
Deputy adjutant general for civil authority support: Brigadier General Timothy D. Covington
Deputy adjutant general for army: Brigadier General Matthew J. Strub
Deputy adjutant general for air: Brigadier General David W. May
Administrator, Division of Emergency Management: Greg Engle
Location: 2400 Wright Street, Madison
Contact: 608-242-3000 (general); 800-335-5147 (toll free public affairs); 800-943-0003 (toll free 24-hour duty officer); PO Box 7865, Madison, WI 53707-7865
Website: http://dma.wi.gov (Department of Military Affairs and Wisconsin National Guard)
Number of state employees: 556.50
Total state budget 2021–23: $283,263,900 (Additional federal funding pays for National Guard salaries, benefits, and training.)

The governor is the commander in chief of the state's military forces, which are organized as the Wisconsin National Guard within the Department of Military Affairs. The department is directed by an adjutant general who is appointed by the governor without senate advice and consent. The department also includes the Division of Emergency Management, which is headed by an administrator who is appointed by the governor with the advice and consent of the senate.

The Wisconsin National Guard is maintained by both the federal and the (*top*) The Wisconsin Air National Guard's 115th Fighter Wing pays tribute to the legacy of the F-16 Fighting Falcon aircraft during a ceremony held at Truax Field in Madison. (*bottom*) Members of the Wisconsin National Guard's 54th Civil Support Team plan their entrance into a building during a hazardous materials training exercise in Poynette.

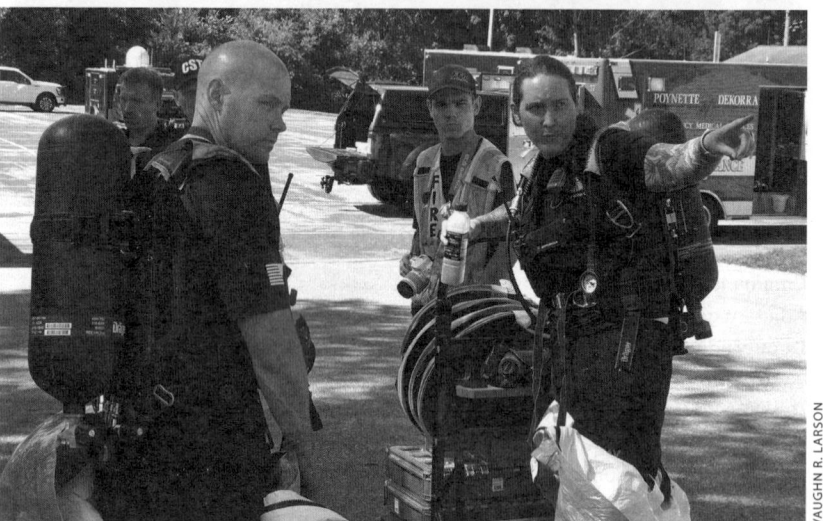

state governments. When it is called up for active federal duty, the president of the United States, rather than the governor, becomes its commander in chief. The federal mission of the National Guard is to provide trained units to the U.S. Army and U.S. Air Force in time of war or national emergency. Its state mission is to assist civil authorities; protect life and property; and preserve peace, order, and public safety in times of natural or human-caused emergencies. The federal government provides the National Guard with arms and ammunition, equipment and uniforms, and major outdoor training facilities and pays for military and support personnel, training, and supervision. The state provides personnel; conducts training as required under the National Defense Act; and shares the cost of constructing, maintaining, and operating armories and other military facilities.

The Division of Emergency Management coordinates the development and implementation of the state emergency operations plan; provides assistance to local jurisdictions in the development of their programs and plans; administers private and federal disaster and emergency relief funds; administers the Wisconsin Disaster Fund; and maintains the state's 24-hour duty officer reporting and response system. The division also conducts training programs in emergency planning for businesses and state and local officials, as well as educational programs for the general public. It also prepares for off-site radiological emergencies at nuclear power plants and provides assistance for various emergencies such as prison disturbances and natural disasters.

Independent entities attached for administrative purposes

INTEROPERABILITY COUNCIL
Chair: Matthew Joski
Website: https://oec.wi.gov/interop

The Interoperability Council develops strategies and makes recommendations on how to achieve and operate a statewide public safety interoperable communication system.

Department of Natural Resources

Natural Resources Board: Bill Smith, *chair*
Secretary-designee: Adam Payne
Deputy secretary: Sarah Barry
Location: 101 South Webster Street, Madison
Contact: 888-936-7463 (toll free); PO Box 7921, Madison, WI 53707-7921
Website: https://dnr.wi.gov
Number of employees: 2,510.93
Total budget 2021–23: $1,123,846,500

The Department of Natural Resources is directed and supervised by the Natural Resources Board and is administered by a secretary. The members of the board and the secretary are appointed by the governor with the advice and consent of the senate.

The department is responsible for implementing state and federal laws that protect and enhance Wisconsin's natural resources, including its air, land, water, forests, wildlife, fish, and plants. It coordinates the many state-administered programs that protect the environment and provides a full range of outdoor recreational opportunities for Wisconsin residents and visitors.

Subordinate statutory boards, councils, and committees

COUNCIL ON FORESTRY

The Council on Forestry advises the governor, legislature, department, and other state agencies on topics relating to forestry in Wisconsin, including protection from fire, insects, and disease; sustainable forestry; reforestation and forestry genetics; management and protection of urban forests; increasing the public's knowledge and awareness of forestry issues; forestry research; economic development and marketing of forestry products; legislation affecting forestry; and staff and funding needs for forestry programs.

DRY CLEANER ENVIRONMENTAL RESPONSE COUNCIL (inactive)

The Dry Cleaner Environmental Response Council advises the department on matters relating to the Dry Cleaner Environmental Response Program, which is administered by the department and which provides awards to dry cleaning establishments for assistance in the investigation and cleanup of environmental contamination.

METALLIC MINING COUNCIL (inactive)

The Metallic Mining Council advises the department on matters relating to the reclamation of mined land and the disposal of metallic mine-related waste.

NATURAL AREAS PRESERVATION COUNCIL

The Natural Areas Preservation Council advises the department on matters pertaining to the protection of natural areas that contain native biotic communities and habitats for rare species. It also makes recommendations about gifts or purchases for the state natural areas system.

NONMOTORIZED RECREATION AND TRANSPORTATION TRAILS COUNCIL

The Nonmotorized Recreation and Transportation Trails Council carries out studies and advises the governor, the legislature, the department, and the Department of Transportation on matters relating to nonmotorized recreation and transportation trails.

OFF-HIGHWAY MOTORCYCLE COUNCIL

The Off-Highway Motorcycle Council makes recommendations to the department on matters relating to off-highway motorcycle corridors and routes and the operation of off-highway motorcycles.

OFF-ROAD VEHICLE COUNCIL

The Off-Road Vehicle Council advises the department, the Department of Transportation, the governor, and the legislature on all matters relating to all-terrain vehicle trails and routes.

SMALL BUSINESS ENVIRONMENTAL COUNCIL

The Small Business Environmental Council advises the department on the effectiveness of assistance programs to small businesses that enable the businesses to comply with the federal Clean Air Act. It also advises on the fairness and effectiveness of air pollution rules promulgated by the department and the U.S. Environmental Protection Agency regarding their impact on small businesses.

SNOWMOBILE RECREATIONAL COUNCIL

The Snowmobile Recreational Council carries out studies and makes recommendations to the governor, the legislature, the department, and the Department of Transportation regarding all matters affecting snowmobiling.

SPORTING HERITAGE COUNCIL

The Sporting Heritage Council advises the governor, the legislature, and the Natural Resources Board about issues relating to hunting, trapping, fishing, and other types of outdoor recreation activities.

STATE TRAILS COUNCIL

The State Trails Council advises the department about the planning, acquisition, development, and management of state trails.

WETLAND STUDY COUNCIL

The Wetland Study Council conducts research and develops recommendations on a range of topics involving wetland policy, procedures, regulations, and financing, including the implementation and effectiveness of statewide wetland mitigation programs; statewide incentive programs for creating, restoring, and enhancing wetlands; providing statewide wetland trainings; and methods of financing wetland mitigation requirements for local units of government.

Other advisory entities

FIRE DEPARTMENT ADVISORY COUNCIL

The Fire Department Advisory Council was chartered in 1994 as an official advisory council to the state forester. The purpose of the council is to strengthen partnerships between the department and the rural fire service in Wisconsin. The council advises and assists the state forester on operational issues relating to the department's forest fire management program to provide for an effective

In 2022, the Department of Natural Resources issued more than 800,000 hunting licenses and over one million fishing licenses, including around 13,000 sturgeon spearing licenses. Above, two hunters hike through the woods (*left*), and a spearer poses with the fish she harvested during the 2023 sturgeon spearing season (*right*).

rural community fire protection program. In addition, the council provides fundamental guidance on the administration of the Forest Fire Protection Grant.

URBAN FORESTRY COUNCIL

The Urban Forestry Council advises the state forester and the department on the best ways to preserve, protect, expand, and improve Wisconsin's urban and community forest resources. The council gives awards to outstanding individuals, organizations, and communities that further urban forestry in Wisconsin.

Independent entities attached for administrative purposes

GROUNDWATER COORDINATING COUNCIL
Chair: James Zellmer

The Groundwater Coordinating Council advises state agencies on the coordination of nonregulatory programs relating to groundwater management. Member agencies exchange information regarding groundwater monitoring, budgets for groundwater programs, data management, public information efforts, laboratory analyses, research, and state appropriations for research.

COUNCIL ON RECYCLING
Chair: Mark Walter

The Council on Recycling promotes implementation of the state's solid waste reduction, recovery, and recycling programs; helps public agencies coordinate recycling programs and exchange information; advises state agencies about creating administrative rules and establishing priorities for market development; and advises the department and the University of Wisconsin System about education and research relating to solid waste recycling. The council also works with the packaging industry on standards for recyclable packaging and works with counties, municipalities, and the auto service industry to promote the recycling of oil filters. The council advises the department about statewide public information activities and advises the governor and the legislature.

INVASIVE SPECIES COUNCIL
Chair: Thomas Buechel
The Invasive Species Council conducts studies relating to controlling invasive species and makes recommendations to the department regarding a system for classifying invasive species under the department's statewide invasive species control program and regarding procedures for awarding grants to public and private agencies engaged in projects to control invasive species.

LAKE MICHIGAN COMMERCIAL FISHING BOARD
Members: Charles W. Henriksen, Richard R. Johnson, Michael LeClair, Mark Maricque, Dan Pawlitzke, Brett Schwarz, Todd Stuth
The Lake Michigan Commercial Fishing Board reviews applications for transfers of commercial fishing licenses between individuals, establishes criteria for allotting catch quotas to individual licensees, assigns catch quotas when the department establishes special harvest limits, and assists the department in establishing criteria for identifying inactive license holders.

LAKE SUPERIOR COMMERCIAL FISHING BOARD
Members: Bill Bodin, Maurine Halvorson, Craig Hoopman, Christopher Boyd, Bryan Bainbridge
The Lake Superior Commercial Fishing Board reviews applications for transfers of commercial fishing licenses between individuals, establishes criteria for allotting catch quotas to individual licensees, assigns catch quotas when the department establishes special harvest limits, and assists the department in establishing criteria for identifying inactive license holders.

LOWER WISCONSIN STATE RIVERWAY BOARD
Chair: Gigi La Budde
Executive Director: Mark E. Cupp
Contact: PO Box 187, Muscoda, WI 53573
Website: http://lwr.state.wi.us/index.asp
Number of employees: 2.00
Total budget 2021–23: $513,200

The Lower Wisconsin State Riverway Board is responsible for protecting and preserving the scenic beauty and natural character of the Lower Wisconsin River. The board reviews permit applications for buildings, walkways and stairways, timber harvests, nonmetallic mining, utility facilities, public access sites, bridges, and other structures in the riverway and issues permits for activities that meet established standards.

WISCONSIN WATERWAYS COMMISSION
Chair: Roger Walsh

The Wisconsin Waterways Commission conducts studies to determine the need for recreational boating facilities; approves financial aid to local governments for the development of recreational boating projects, including the acquisition of weed harvesters; and recommends administrative rules for the recreational facilities boating program.

Affiliated entity

CONSERVATION CONGRESS

The Conservation Congress is a publicly elected citizen advisory group, and its district leadership council advises the Natural Resources Board on all matters under the board's jurisdiction.

The Lower Wisconsin Riverway, pictured below, extends 92.3 miles from below the dam at Prairie du Sac to the confluence with the Mississippi River near Prairie du Chien.

Office of the State Public Defender

Public Defender Board: James M. Brennan, *chair*
State public defender: Kelli S. Thompson
Deputy state public defender: Katie York
Location: 17 South Fairchild Street, Fifth Floor, Madison
Contact: 608-266-0087; PO Box 7923, Madison, WI 53707-7923
Website: www.wispd.gov
Number of employees: 619.85
Total budget 2021–23: $227,505,200

The Office of the State Public Defender provides legal representation to indigent persons and to persons otherwise entitled to such representation. The state public defender, who must be a member of the state bar, serves at the pleasure of the Public Defender Board. Board members are appointed by the governor with the advice and consent of the senate.

The state public defender assigns attorneys to persons charged with a crime that may be sentenced with imprisonment and to other cases, such as cases involving paternity determinations, termination of parental rights, juvenile delinquency proceedings, emergency detentions, involuntary commitments, modification of bifurcated sentences, and certain appeals.

Department of Public Instruction

State superintendent of public instruction: Jill Underly
Deputy state superintendent: John Johnson
Location: 125 South Webster Street, Madison
Contact: 608-266-3390; 800-441-4563 (toll free); PO Box 7841, Madison, WI 53707-7841
Website: www.dpi.wi.gov
Number of employees: 644.00
Total budget 2021–23: $16,249,627,000

The Department of Public Instruction is headed by the state superintendent of public instruction, a constitutional officer who is elected on the nonpartisan spring ballot for a term of four years. The department provides guidance and technical assistance to support public elementary and secondary education in Wisconsin. The department also administers the Milwaukee, Racine, and Statewide Parental Choice Programs; the Special Needs Scholarship Program; the open enrollment program; and a number of educational and other services for children and their families.

The department offers a broad range of programs and professional services to local school administrators and staff. It also reviews and approves educator preparation programs and licenses teachers, pupil services personnel, administrators,

Wisconsin State Superintendent of Public Instruction Jill Underly (*far right*) poses with the 2023 Teachers of the Year. Each year, the agency selects five outstanding teachers to represent the state's elementary schools, middle schools, and high schools on the Teacher of the Year Council.

and library professionals. The department distributes state and federal aids to supplement local tax revenue, improve curriculum and school operations, ensure education for children with disabilities, offer professional guidance and counseling, and develop school and public library resources. The department also administers the Wisconsin Educational Services Program for the Deaf and Hard of Hearing and the Wisconsin Center for the Blind and Visually Impaired.

Finally, the department provides assistance for the development and improvement of public and school libraries. The department fosters interlibrary cooperation and resource sharing and promotes information and instructional technology in schools and libraries. The department also acts as a state-level clearinghouse for interlibrary loan requests and administers BadgerLink (https://badgerlink.dpi.wi.gov), the statewide full-text database project that allows access to thousands of magazines, newsletters, newspapers, pamphlets, and historical documents.

Subordinate statutory boards, councils, and committees

BLIND AND VISUAL IMPAIRMENT EDUCATION ADVISORY COUNCIL

Website: https://www.wcbvi.k12.wi.us/resources/advisory-council

The Blind and Visual Impairment Education Advisory Council provides advice on statewide activities that will benefit students who are blind or visually impaired; makes recommendations for improvements in services provided by the Wisconsin Center for the Blind and Visually Impaired; and proposes ways to improve the preparation of teachers and staff and coordination between the department and other agencies that offer services to the visually impaired.

COUNCIL ON LIBRARY AND NETWORK DEVELOPMENT
Website: https://dpi.wi.gov/coland
The Council on Library and Network Development advises the state superintendent and the Division for Libraries and Technology to ensure that all state citizens have access to library and information services.

COUNCIL ON SPECIAL EDUCATION
Website: https://dpi.wi.gov/sped/council
The Council on Special Education advises the state superintendent on matters related to meeting the needs and improving the education of children with disabilities.

DEAF AND HARD-OF-HEARING EDUCATION COUNCIL
Website: http://wesp-dhh.wi.gov/advisory-council
The Deaf and Hard-of-Hearing Education Council advises the state superintendent on issues related to pupils who are hearing impaired and informs the state superintendent about services, programs, and research that could benefit those pupils.

PROFESSIONAL STANDARDS COUNCIL
Website: https://dpi.wi.gov/licensing/programs/psc
The Professional Standards Council advises the state superintendent regarding licensing and evaluating teachers; the evaluation and approval of teacher education programs; the status of teaching in Wisconsin; school board practices to develop effective teaching; peer mentoring; evaluation systems; alternative dismissal procedures; and alternative procedures for the preparation and licensure of teachers.

SCHOOL DISTRICT BOUNDARY APPEAL BOARD
Website: https://dpi.wi.gov/sms/school-district-boundary-appeal-board
Panels consisting of three or seven members of the School District Boundary Appeal Board hear appeals related to school district creation and dissolution, annexation, and boundary disputes.

STATE SUPERINTENDENT'S ADVISORY COUNCIL ON ALCOHOL AND OTHER DRUG ABUSE PROBLEMS
Website: https://dpi.wi.gov/sspw/aoda/wi-dpis-state-superintendents-aoda
The council advises the state superintendent, the department, school districts, and other education-related agencies about programs to prevent or reduce alcohol, tobacco, and other drug abuse.

Board of Commissioners of Public Lands

Members: Sarah Godlewski (secretary of state), *chair*; Joshua L. Kaul (attorney general); John Leiber (state treasurer)
Division of Trust Lands and Investments: Tom German, *executive secretary*; Richard Sneider, *chief investment officer*
Location: 101 East Wilson Street, Second Floor, Madison
Contact: 608-266-1370 (Madison); 715-277-3366 (Lake Tomahawk); PO Box 8943, Madison, WI 53708-8943
Website: https://bcpl.wisconsin.gov
Number of employees: 9.50
Total budget 2021–23: $3,313,400

The Board of Commissioners of Public Lands is a body established in the Wisconsin Constitution. The board is composed of the secretary of state, state treasurer, and attorney general. The board manages the state's remaining trust lands, manages trust funds primarily for the benefit of public education, and maintains the state's original 19th-century land survey and land sales records. The board is assisted in its work by the Division of Trust Lands and Investments, an entity attached to the Department of Administration for administrative purposes.

The board holds title to nearly 77,000 acres of school trust lands. These lands are managed for timber production, natural area preservation, and public use. The board manages four trust funds, totaling over $1.4 billion in assets. The largest of these is the Common School Fund. The principal of this fund continues to grow through the collection of fees, fines, and forfeitures that accrue to the state. The board invests the moneys of this fund in various asset classes, including state and municipal bonds. It also loans moneys from this fund directly to Wisconsin municipalities and school districts through the State Trust Fund Loan Program. These loans are used for economic development, school repairs and improvements, local infrastructure and utilities, and capital equipment and vehicles. The net earnings of the Common School Fund are distributed annually by the Department of Public Instruction to all of Wisconsin's public school districts and provide the sole source of state aid for public school library media and resources.

Public Service Commission

Commissioners: Rebecca Cameron Valcq, *chair*; Tyler Huebner, Summer Strand
Executive assistant to the chair: Heather Young
Location: 4822 Madison Yards Way, North Tower, Sixth Floor, Madison
Contact: pscrecordsmail@wisconsin.gov (general); pscpublicrecordsrequest@wisconsin. gov (public records requests); 608-266-5481; 888-816-3831 (toll free); 608-266-2001

Wisconsin's Public Service Commission is responsible for regulating more than 1,100 public utilities, which provide electric, gas, water, sewer, and telephone services to households and businesses across the state. Above, Chairperson Rebecca Valcq (*second from left*) tours the Bay Front Generating Station, a biomass facility that produces renewable energy in Ashland County.

(consumer complaints); 800-225-7729 (consumer complaints, toll free); PO Box 7854, Madison, WI 53707-7854
Website: https://psc.wi.gov
Number of employees: 154.75
Total budget 2021–23: $64,390,800

The Public Service Commission consists of three commissioners appointed to six-year terms by the governor with the advice and consent of the senate. The governor appoints one of the commissioners as chair for a two-year term. A commissioner may not have a financial interest in a railroad, public utility, or water carrier; may not be a candidate for public office; and is subject to certain restrictions regarding political activity.

The commission is responsible for regulating Wisconsin's public utilities and ensuring that utility services are provided to customers safely, reliably, and at prices reasonable to both ratepayers and utility owners. The commission also regulates the rates and services of electric, natural gas distribution, water, and municipal combined water and sewer utilities. The commission's responsibilities include determining levels for adequate and safe service; overseeing compliance with renewable energy and energy conservation and efficiency requirements; approving public utility bond sales and stock offerings; and approving mergers, consolidations, and ownership changes regarding public utilities. The commission also considers applications for major construction projects, such as power plants, transmission lines, and wind farms. In addition to ensuring public utility compliance with statutes, administrative codes, and record-keeping requirements, commission staff investigates and mediates consumer complaints.

The commission has limited jurisdiction over landline telecommunications providers and services. The commission certifies various types of telecommunications providers; manages the Universal Service Fund; handles some wholesale disputes between telecommunications providers; and administers telephone numbering resources. In general, the commission has no jurisdiction over electric cooperatives, liquefied petroleum gas, fuel oil, wireless telephone, or cable television. Although the commission has no jurisdiction over Internet service, it does provide oversight for statewide broadband mapping and planning and makes grants for constructing broadband infrastructure in underserved areas. Also, the commission has the authority to enforce Digger's Hotline requirements involving natural gas or other hazardous materials.

Subordinate statutory boards, councils, and committees

UNIVERSAL SERVICE FUND COUNCIL

Contact: PO Box 7854, Madison, WI 53707-7854

The Universal Service Fund Council advises the commission on the administration of the Universal Service Fund. The purposes of the fund include assisting low-income customers, customers in areas where telecommunications service costs are relatively high, and customers with disabilities in obtaining affordable access to basic telecommunications services. The Universal Service Fund director acts as the liaison between the Public Service Commission and the council.

WIND SITING COUNCIL

The Wind Siting Council advises the commission on the promulgation of rules relating to restrictions that a political subdivision may impose on the installation or use of a wind energy system, including setback requirements that provide reasonable protection from any health effects. The council also surveys the peer-reviewed scientific research regarding the health impacts of wind energy systems and studies state and national regulatory developments regarding the siting of wind energy systems.

Independent entities attached for administrative purposes

OFFICE OF THE COMMISSIONER OF RAILROADS

Commissioner of railroads: Yash P. Wadhwa

Contact: 608-261-8221; ocr@wisconsin.gov; PO Box 7854, Madison, WI 53707-7854

Website: https://ocr.wi.gov

The governor appoints the commissioner of railroads with the advice and consent of the senate for a six-year term. The commissioner may not have a financial interest in railroads or water carriers and may not serve on or under any committee of a political party. The Office of the Commissioner of Railroads enforces regulations related to railway safety and determines the safety of highway crossings, including the adequacy of railroad warning devices. The office also has authority over the rates and services of intrastate water carriers.

Department of Revenue

Department secretary: Peter Barca
Deputy secretary: Maria Guerra Lapacek
Location: 2135 Rimrock Road, Madison
Contact: 608-266-2772 (office phone); 608-266-2486 (individuals); 608-266-2776 (businesses); PO Box 8949, Madison, WI 53708-8949
Website: www.revenue.wi.gov
Number of employees: 1,178.00
Total budget 2021–23: $476,631,000

The Department of Revenue is administered by a secretary who is appointed by the governor with the advice and consent of the senate. The department administers all major state tax laws except the insurance premiums tax and enforces the state's alcohol beverage and tobacco laws. It estimates state revenues, forecasts state economic activity, helps formulate tax policy, and administers the Wisconsin Lottery. The department also determines the equalized value of taxable property and assesses manufacturing and telecommunications company property for property tax purposes. It administers the tax incremental financing program, shared revenue, and other local financial assistance programs and assists local governments in their property assessments and financial management. The department also oversees Wisconsin's Unclaimed Property program, which matches taxpayers with unclaimed financial assets.

Subordinate statutory boards, councils, and committees

FARMLAND ADVISORY COUNCIL

The Farmland Advisory Council advises the department on assessing agricultural land, implementing use-value assessment of agricultural land, and reducing the expansion of urban sprawl. It reports annually to the legislature on the usefulness of use-value assessment as a way to preserve farmland and reduce the conversion of farmland to other uses. The council also recommends changes to the shared revenue formula to compensate local governments and school districts adversely affected by use-value assessment.

STATE BOARD OF ASSESSORS

The State Board of Assessors investigates objections filed by manufacturers and municipalities to the amount, valuation, or taxability of real or personal manufacturing property, as well as objections to the penalties issued for late filing or nonfiling of required manufacturing property report forms.

Independent entities attached for administrative purposes

INVESTMENT AND LOCAL IMPACT FUND BOARD (inactive)
Website: https://www.revenue.wi.gov/pages/governments/ilif-board-home.aspx

The Investment and Local Impact Fund Board administers the Investment and Local Impact Fund, created to help municipalities alleviate costs associated with social, educational, environmental, and economic impacts of metalliferous mineral mining. The board certifies to the Department of Administration the amount of the payments to be distributed to municipalities from the fund. It also provides funding to local governments throughout the development of a mining project and distributes federal mining revenue received by the state to municipalities that are affected by mining on federal land.

Department of Safety and Professional Services

Secretary-designee: Dan Hereth
Deputy secretary: Donna V. Moreland
Location: 4822 Madison Yards Way, Madison
Contact: dsps@wisconsin.gov; 608-266-2112; 4822 Madison Yards Way, Madison, WI 53705
Website: http://dsps.wi.gov
Number of employees: 244.14
Total budget 2021–23: $127,482,600

The Department of Safety and Professional Services is administered by a secretary who is appointed by the governor with the advice and consent of the senate.

The department administers and enforces laws to ensure safe and sanitary conditions in public and private buildings, including by reviewing plans and performing inspections of commercial buildings and certain components and systems therein.

The department is also responsible for ensuring the safe and competent practice of various licensed occupations and businesses in Wisconsin. The department provides direct regulation or licensing of certain occupations and businesses. In addition, numerous boards are attached to the department that are responsible for regulating other occupations and businesses. In general, these boards determine the education and experience required for credentialing, develop and evaluate examinations, and establish standards for professional conduct. The department or the relevant board may reprimand a credential holder in a field that it regulates; limit, suspend, or revoke the credential of a practitioner who violates laws or rules; and, in some cases, impose forfeitures. The department provides administrative services to the boards and policy assistance in such areas as evaluating and establishing new professional licensing programs, creating routine procedures for legal proceedings, and adjusting policies in response to public needs. The department also investigates and prosecutes complaints against credential holders and assists with drafting administrative rules.

Under its Educational Approval Program, the department is also responsible for approving and overseeing most private, for-profit postsecondary schools offering educational programs or occupational training in this state; in-state private, nonprofit colleges and universities incorporated after 1991; and out-of-state postsecondary institutions offering distance education to Wisconsin residents if the institution is not located in a state participating in the State Authorization Reciprocity Agreement (see Distance Learning Authorization Board for more information on the agreement).

Subordinate statutory boards, councils, and committees

AUTOMATIC FIRE SPRINKLER SYSTEM CONTRACTORS AND JOURNEYMEN COUNCIL

The Automatic Fire Sprinkler System Contractors and Journeymen Council advises the department on rules for credentials required for installing and maintaining automatic fire sprinkler systems.

COMMERCIAL BUILDING CODE COUNCIL

The Commercial Building Code Council advises the department on rules relating to public buildings and buildings that are places of employment. The council also reviews and makes recommendations pertaining to the department's rules for constructing, altering, adding to, repairing, and maintaining those types of buildings.

CONTROLLED SUBSTANCES BOARD

The Controlled Substances Board classifies controlled substances into schedules that regulate the prescription, use, and possession of controlled substances. The board also approves special use permits for controlled substances.

CONVEYANCE SAFETY CODE COUNCIL

The Conveyance Safety Code Council makes recommendations to the department pertaining to safety standards for elevators, escalators, and similar conveyances.

MANUFACTURED HOUSING CODE COUNCIL
The Manufactured Housing Code Council makes recommendations to the department pertaining to standards for the construction, installation, and sale of manufactured homes.

PLUMBERS COUNCIL
The Plumbers Council advises the department on rules for credentials required for plumbing.

UNIFORM DWELLING CODE COUNCIL
The Uniform Dwelling Code Council reviews and makes recommendations for department rules regarding the construction and inspection of one-family and two-family dwellings and regarding continuing education, examinations, and financial responsibility for building contractors. The council also reviews complaints about building inspectors and recommends disciplinary action to the department. In addition, the council reviews and makes recommendations for department rules regarding modular homes.

Independent entities attached for administrative purposes
These are the occupation and business regulating boards described in the write-up of the department given above. (In each case, the occupations or businesses regulated are indicated by the entity's name.)

ACCOUNTING EXAMINING BOARD
Chair: Michael E. Friedman

ATHLETIC TRAINERS AFFILIATED CREDENTIALING BOARD (affiliated to Medical Examining Board)
Chair: Kurt A. Fielding

AUCTIONEER BOARD
Chair: Jerry L. Thiel

BOARD OF NURSING
Chair: Robert W. Weinman

CEMETERY BOARD
Chair: E. Glen Porter III

CHIROPRACTIC EXAMINING BOARD
Chair: Amy L. Heffernan

COSMETOLOGY EXAMINING BOARD
Chair: Megan A. Jackson

DENTISTRY EXAMINING BOARD
Chair: Matthew R. Bistan

DIETITIANS AFFILIATED CREDENTIALING BOARD (affiliated to Medical Examining Board)
Chair: Tara L. LaRowe

EXAMINING BOARD OF ARCHITECTS, LANDSCAPE ARCHITECTS, PROFESSIONAL ENGINEERS, DESIGNERS, PROFESSIONAL LAND SURVEYORS, AND REGISTERED INTERIOR DESIGNERS
Chair: Rosheen Styczinski
Architect section chair: Steven L. Wagner
Designer section chair: Michael J. Heberling
Engineer section chair: Kristine A. Cotharn
Landscape architect section chair: Rosheen M. Styczinski
Land surveyor section chair: Daniel Fedderly
Registered interior design section chair: Robin A. Stroebel

EXAMINING BOARD OF PROFESSIONAL GEOLOGISTS, HYDROLOGISTS AND SOIL SCIENTISTS
Chair: Trevor W. Nobile
Geologist section chair: Trevor W. Nobile
Hydrologist section chair: Ann D. Hirekatur
Soil scientist section: (all seats currently vacant)

FUNERAL DIRECTORS EXAMINING BOARD
Chair: Joseph B. Schinkten

HEARING AND SPEECH EXAMINING BOARD
Chair: Kathleen A. Pazak

GENETIC COUNSELORS AFFILIATED CREDENTIALING BOARD
Chair: vacant

MARRIAGE AND FAMILY THERAPY, PROFESSIONAL COUNSELING, AND SOCIAL WORK EXAMINING BOARD
Chair: Tammy H. Scheidegger
Marriage and family therapist section chair: Patrick J. Stumbras
Professional counselor section chair: vacant
Social worker section chair: Sheng B. Lee Yang

MASSAGE THERAPY AND BODYWORK THERAPY AFFILIATED CREDENTIALING BOARD (affiliated to Medical Examining Board)
Chair: Jaime L. Ehmer

MEDICAL EXAMINING BOARD
Chair: Sheldon A. Wasserman

Advisory councils assisting the board: Council on Anesthesiologists Assistants, Michael L. Bottcher, *chair*; Perfusionists Examining Council, Shawn E. Mergen, *chair*; Respiratory Care Practitioners Examining Council, Chris R. Becker, *chair*

NATUROPATHIC MEDICINE EXAMINING BOARD
Chair: Jill Crista

NURSING HOME ADMINISTRATOR EXAMINING BOARD
Chair: David L. Larson

OCCUPATIONAL THERAPISTS AFFILIATED CREDENTIALING BOARD (affiliated to Medical Examining Board)
Chair: Laura O'Brien

OPTOMETRY EXAMINING BOARD
Chair: Robert C. Schulz

PHARMACY EXAMINING BOARD
Chair: John G. Weitekamp

PHYSICAL THERAPY EXAMINING BOARD
Chair: John F. Greany

PHYSICIAN ASSISTANT AFFILIATED CREDENTIALING BOARD (affiliated to Medical Examining Board)
Chair: Jennifer L. Jarrett

PODIATRY AFFILIATED CREDENTIALING BOARD (affiliated to Medical Examining Board)
Chair: Robert M. Sage

PSYCHOLOGY EXAMINING BOARD
Chair: Daniel A. Schroeder

RADIOGRAPHY EXAMINING BOARD
Chair: Donald A. Borst

REAL ESTATE APPRAISERS BOARD
Chair: Daniel J. Figurski

REAL ESTATE EXAMINING BOARD
Chair: Thomas J. Richie
Advisory councils assisting the board: Council on Real Estate Curriculum and Examinations, Robert Blakely, *chair*; Real Estate Contractual Forms Advisory Council, Sonya G. Mays, *chair*

Office of the Secretary of State

Secretary of state: Sarah Godlewski
Location: B41 West, State Capitol, Madison
Contact: statesec@wi.gov; 608-266-8888; PO Box 7848, Madison, WI 53707-7848
Website: https://sos.wi.gov
Number of employees: 2.00
Total budget 2021–23: $562,800

The secretary of state is a constitutional officer elected for a four-year term by partisan ballot in the November general election. The secretary of state maintains the official acts of the legislature and governor and keeps the Great Seal of the State of Wisconsin, affixing it to all official acts of the governor. Along with the attorney general and the state treasurer, the secretary of state serves on the Board of Commissioners of Public Lands. The secretary of state may also be called upon to act as governor under certain circumstances, such as if the sitting governor dies or resigns and there is a vacancy in the office of lieutenant governor.

Office of the State Treasurer

State treasurer: John S. Leiber
Location: Room B38 West, State Capitol, Madison
Contact: treasurer@wisconsin.gov; 608-266-1714; PO Box 7871, Madison, WI 53707
Website: https://statetreasurer.wi.gov
Number of employees: 1.00
Total budget 2021–23: $253,600

The state treasurer is a constitutional officer elected for a four-year term by partisan ballot in the November general election. The state treasurer signs certain checks and financial instruments and helps to promote the state's unclaimed property program. Along with the attorney general and secretary of state, the state treasurer serves on the Board of Commissioners of Public Lands.

Technical College System

Technical College System Board: Rodney Pasch, *president*
System president: Morna K. Foy
Location: 4622 University Avenue, Madison
Contact: 608-266-5311; PO Box 7874, Madison, WI 53707-7874
Website: https://wtcsystem.edu
Number of employees: 55.00
Total budget 2021–23: $1,221,629,400

The Technical College System Board is the agency that oversees the Technical

College System. The governor, with the advice and consent of the senate, appoints 10 of the board's 13 members, nine to serve six-year terms and a technical college student to serve a two-year term. Of the nine nonstudent appointees, there must be at least one employer, one nonmanagerial employee, and one farmer. The three remaining board members are the state superintendent of public instruction, the secretary of workforce development, and the president of the Board of Regents of the University of Wisconsin System (but each of these officers may designate another individual to serve in his or her place).

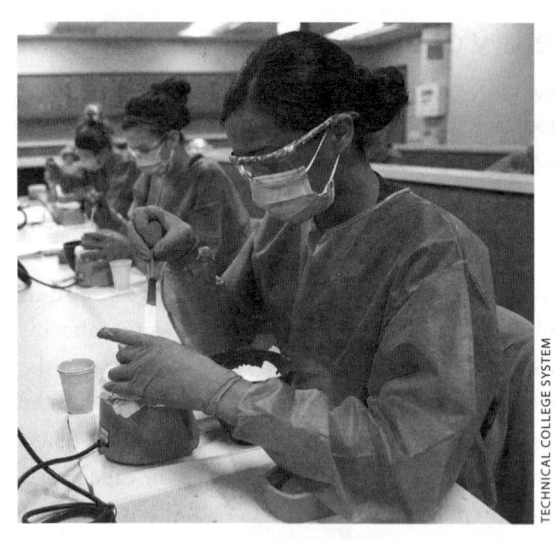

The Wisconsin Technical College System prepares students for a variety of careers. Above, students at Blackhawk Technical College who are training to become dental technicians practice mixing materials for dental molds.

The board establishes statewide policies for the educational programs and services provided by the state's 16 technical college districts. Each technical college district is governed by a district board that is responsible for the direct operation of that technical college, including setting academic and grading standards and hiring instructional staff for its programs.

The board defines, approves, evaluates, and reviews educational programs; provides guidance to the technical college districts in developing financial policies and standards; distributes state and federal aid; sets student fees; sets standards for and approves building projects; oversees district budgets and enrollments; coordinates state and federal grant programs and student financial aid; and supports services for students. The board also coordinates with the University of Wisconsin System on programming and college transfer courses and with other state agencies on vocational and technical education programs and apprentice training.

Department of Tourism

Secretary: Anne Sayers
Location: 3319 West Beltline Highway, Madison
Contact: tourinfo@travelwisconsin.com; 800-432-8747 (toll free); 608-266-2161; PO Box 8690, Madison, WI 53708-8690

Units of State Government: Executive | 231

Website: www.travelwisconsin.com (information for tourists); https://www.industry.travelwisconsin.com (information for the tourism industry)
Number of employees: 34.00
Total budget 2021–2023: $37,103,600

The Department of Tourism is administered by a secretary who is appointed by the governor with the advice and consent of the senate. The department formulates and implements a statewide marketing strategy to promote travel to Wisconsin's scenic, historic, natural, agricultural, educational, and recreational attractions. The department coordinates its efforts with public and private organizations and provides assistance to travel-related and recreational industries and their consumers. The department also does the following: (1) makes grants to local governments, American Indian organizations, and nonprofits for tourist information centers and marketing projects; (2) provides marketing services to state agencies; and (3) coordinates its economic development activities with the Wisconsin Economic Development Corporation and makes annual reports to the legislature assessing those activities.

Wisconsin's public murals, monuments, sculptures, statues, and historical markers attract visitors from across the Midwest. Below, friends pose for a photo at the Waves of Giving Mural in Janesville.

Subordinate statutory boards, councils, and committees

ARTS BOARD
Chair: Brian Kelsey
Executive director: George Tzougros
Contact: artsboard@wisconsin.gov; 608-266-0190; PO Box 8690, Madison, WI 53708-8690
Website: https://artsboard.wisconsin.gov

The Arts Board studies and assists artistic and cultural activities in the state, assists communities in developing their own arts programs, and plans and implements financial support programs for individuals and organizations engaged in the arts, including creation and presentation grants, folk arts apprenticeships, creative communities grants, and challenge grants to organizations that exceed fundraising goals. The board also provides matching grants to local arts agencies and municipalities through the Wisconsin Regranting Program.

COUNCIL ON TOURISM
Chair: Ben Popp
Website: https://www.industry.travelwisconsin.com/about-us/tourism-council-committees/wisconsin-council-on-tourism

The Council on Tourism advises the secretary on tourism, including assisting in the formulation of the statewide marketing strategy. The council also develops and adopts a plan for encouraging Wisconsin-based companies to promote the state in their advertisements.

Independent entities attached for administrative purposes

KICKAPOO RESERVE MANAGEMENT BOARD
Chair: Scott Lind
Executive director: Lynn Kronschnabel
Contact: kickapoo.reserve@krm.state.wi.us; 608-625-2960; S3661 State Road 131, La Farge, WI 54639
Website: http://kvr.state.wi.us
Number of employees: 4.00
Total budget 2021–23: $2,069,600

The Kickapoo Reserve Management Board manages the approximately 8,600-acre Kickapoo Valley Reserve through a joint management agreement with the Ho-Chunk Nation. The Kickapoo Valley Reserve exists to preserve and enhance the area's environmental, scenic, and cultural features and provides facilities for the use and enjoyment of visitors. Subject to the approval of the governor, the board may purchase land for inclusion in the reserve and may trade land in the reserve under certain conditions. The board also may lease land for purposes consistent with the management of the reserve or for agricultural purposes.

STATE FAIR PARK BOARD
Chair: John Yingling
Chief executive officer: Shari Black
Contact: wsfp@wistatefair.com; 414-266-7000; 414-266-7100 (ticket office); 640 South 84th Street, West Allis, WI 53214
Website: https://wistatefair.com/wsfp
Number of employees: 47.00
Total budget 2021–23: $45,570,100

The State Fair Park Board manages the Wisconsin State Fair Park, including the development of new facilities. The park provides a permanent location for the annual Wisconsin State Fair and for major sports events, agricultural and industrial expositions, and other programs of civic interest.

Department of Transportation

Secretary: Craig Thompson
Deputy secretary: Paul Hammer
Location: 4822 Madison Yards Way, Madison, WI 53705
Contact: opa.exec@dot.wi.gov, 608-266-3581 (Office of Public Affairs); information.dmv@dot.wi.gov, 608-264-7447 (Driver Services and Vehicle Services); PO Box 7910, Madison, WI 53707-7910
Website: https://wisconsindot.gov
Number of employees: 3,238.91
Total budget 2021–23: $6,600,533,600

The Department of Transportation is administered by a secretary who is appointed by the governor with the advice and consent of the senate. The department is responsible for the planning, promotion, and protection of all transportation systems in the state. Its major responsibilities involve highways, motor vehicles, motor carriers, traffic law enforcement, railroads, waterways, mass transit, and aeronautics. The department issues vehicle titles and registrations and individual identification cards; it also examines and licenses drivers. The department works with several federal agencies in the administration of federal transportation aids. It also cooperates with departments at the state level in travel promotion, consumer protection, environmental analysis, and transportation services for elderly and handicapped persons.

Subordinate statutory boards, councils, and committees

COUNCIL ON HIGHWAY SAFETY
Acting chair: John Mesich
The Council on Highway Safety advises the governor and the department secretary about highway safety matters.

COUNCIL ON UNIFORMITY OF TRAFFIC CITATIONS AND COMPLAINTS
Chair: Sharon Olson
The Council on Uniformity of Traffic Citations and Complaints recommends forms used for traffic violations citations.

RUSTIC ROADS BOARD
Chair: Marion Flood
Contact: wirusticroads@dot.wi.gov; 608-267-3614; PO Box 7913, Madison, WI 53705
Website: https://wisconsindot.gov/pages/travel/road/rustic-roads/create.aspx

Wisconsin's Rustic Roads program was established in 1973 to help citizens and local governments preserve the state's remaining scenic country roads. Above, cyclists enjoy a winding ride on State Highway 42 in Door County.

The Rustic Roads Board oversees the application and selection process of locally nominated county highways and local roads for inclusion in the Rustic Roads network system. The Rustic Roads program is a partnership between local officials and state government to showcase some of Wisconsin's most picturesque and lightly traveled roadways for the leisurely enjoyment of hikers, bikers, and motorists.

University of Wisconsin System

Board of Regents: Angela Adams, Robert Atwell, Amy Blumenfeld Bogost, Evan Brenkus, Héctor Colón, Mike Jones, Jim Kreuser, Edmund Manydeeds III, John W. Miller, Rodney Pasch, Cris Peterson, Joan Prince, Ashok Rai, Jennifer Staton, Jill Underly, Dana Wachs, Karen Walsh, Kyle M. Weatherly
Executive director and corporate secretary: Megan Wasley
System Administration: Jay Rothman, *president*
Contact: 608-262-2321; 1860 Van Hise Hall, 1220 Linden Drive, Madison, WI 53706
Website: www.wisconsin.edu
Number of employees: 35,672.25
Total budget 2021–23: $12,931,895,300

The University of Wisconsin System is governed by an 18-member Board of Regents, which consists of 14 citizen members, 2 student members, the president of the Technical College System Board or his or her designee, and the state superintendent of public instruction. The citizen and student members are appointed by the governor subject to senate confirmation. The Board of Regents appoints the president of the UW System, who has executive responsibility for system operation and management, and the chancellors for each four-year university.

The prime responsibilities of the UW System are teaching, public service, and research. The system provides postsecondary academic education for approximately 160,000 students, including approximately 140,000 undergraduates. The system consists of 13 four-year universities, an additional 13 branch campuses, and a statewide extension network with offices in every county. All of the four-year universities offer bachelor's degrees. Two of the four-year universities (UW–Madison and UW–Milwaukee) offer comprehensive master's and doctoral degree programs, including professional doctorate degrees. The remaining four-year universities (UW–Eau Claire, UW–Green Bay, UW–La Crosse, UW Oshkosh, UW–Parkside, UW–Platteville, UW–River Falls, UW–Stevens Point, UW–Stout, UW–Superior, and UW–Whitewater) offer more limited master's degree programs, and some also offer associate degrees and clinical or professional doctorate degrees in select areas. The 13 branch campuses, aligned with seven of the four-year universities, offer Associate of Arts and Sciences (AAS) degrees, as well as transfer programs for students wishing to satisfy general education requirements and then transfer to a four-year university. Many branch campuses also offer bachelor's degrees in certain fields of study through collaboration with a four-year university. The system provides extension services, including access to system resources and research, through UW–Madison and the UW System administration.

A new simulation center is ready to train the next generation of nurses at UW-Milwaukee. Melissa Melcher (*left*), a clinical assistant professor, and Bayan Alqam (*right*), a PhD nursing student and teaching assistant, prepare a mannequin before class.

UWM PHOTO/ELORA HENNESSEY

UW–EAU CLAIRE
Chancellor: James Schmidt
Contact: 715-836-4636; 105 Garfield Avenue, Eau Claire, WI 54701
Website: www.uwec.edu

UW–GREEN BAY
Chancellor: Michael Alexander
Contact: 920-465-2000; 2420 Nicolet Drive, Green Bay, WI 54311
Website: www.uwgb.edu

UW–LA CROSSE
Chancellor: Joe Gow
Contact: 608-785-8000; 1725 State Street, La Crosse, WI 54601
Website: www.uwlax.edu

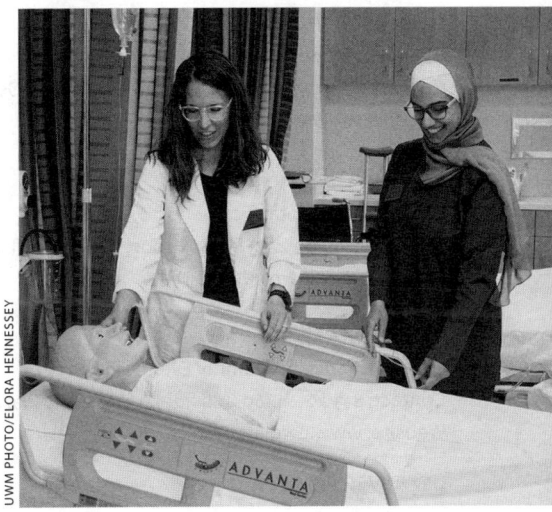

Participants in UW–Stout's Stoutward Bound program attempt the campus ropes course. The program, which received the Ann Lydecker Educational Diversity Award in 2022, supports students each year from historically underrepresented and underserved backgrounds.

UW–MADISON
Chancellor: Jennifer L. Mnookin
Contact: 608-262-9946; 500 Lincoln Drive, Madison, WI 53706
Website: www.wisc.edu

UW–MILWAUKEE
Chancellor: Mark Mone
Contact: 414-229-4331; PO Box 413, Milwaukee, WI 53201
Website: www.uwm.edu

UW OSHKOSH
Chancellor: Andrew J. Leavitt
Contact: 920-424-1234; 800 Algoma Boulevard, Oshkosh, WI 54901
Website: www.uwosh.edu

UW–PARKSIDE
Chancellor: Deborah Ford
Contact: 262-595-2211; PO Box 2000, Kenosha, WI 53141-2000
Website: www.uwp.edu

UW–PLATTEVILLE
Interim Chancellor: Tammy Evetovich
Contact: 833-200-6869 (toll free); 1 University Plaza, Platteville, WI 53818
Website: www.uwplatt.edu

UW–RIVER FALLS
Interim Chancellor: Maria Gallo

Contact: 715-425-3911; 410 South Third Street, River Falls, WI 54022
Website: www.uwrf.edu

UW–STEVENS POINT
Chancellor: Thomas Gibson
Contact: 715-346-0123; 2100 Main Street, Stevens Point, WI 54481
Website: www.uwsp.edu

UW–STOUT
Chancellor: Katherine P. Frank
Contact: 715-232-1122; 712 South Broadway, Menomonie, WI 54751
Website: www.uwstout.edu

UW–SUPERIOR
Chancellor: Renée Wachter
Contact: 715-394-8101; P. O. Box 2000, Superior, WI 54880
Website: www.uwsuper.edu

UW–WHITEWATER
Interim Chancellor: Corey A. King
Contact: 262-472-1234; 800 West Main Street, Whitewater, WI 53190
Website: www.uww.edu

Programs required by statute

AREA HEALTH EDUCATION CENTERS
Director: Elizabeth Bush
Contact: ahec@ahec.wisc.edu; 608-263-1712; 4251 Health Sciences Learning Center, 750 Highland Avenue, Madison, WI 53705
Website: www.ahec.wisc.edu

GEOLOGICAL AND NATURAL HISTORY SURVEY
Interim director and state geologist: Eric Carson
Contact: 608-262-1705; 3817 Mineral Point Road, Madison, WI 53705
Website: http://wgnhs.wisc.edu

INSTITUTE FOR URBAN EDUCATION
Chair: Denise Ross
Contact: iue-info@uwm.edu; 414-251-9490; UW–Milwaukee, 2400 East Hartford Avenue, Room 568, Milwaukee, WI 53211
Website: https://uwm.edu/education/institute-urban-edu

JAMES A. GRAASKAMP CENTER FOR REAL ESTATE
Executive director: Mark Eppli
Contact: Grainger Hall, 975 University Avenue, Madison, WI 53706
Website: https://bus.wisc.edu/centers/james-a-graaskamp-center-for-real-estate

OFFICE OF THE STATE CARTOGRAPHER
State cartographer: Howard Veregin
Contact: sco@wisc.edu; 608-262-3065; 384 Science Hall, 550 North Park Street, Madison, WI 53706
Website: www.sco.wisc.edu

PSYCHIATRIC HEALTH-EMOTIONS RESEARCH INSTITUTE
Director: Ned Kalin
Contact: 608-232-3171; 6001 Research Park Boulevard, Madison, WI 53719
Website: www.psychiatry.wisc.edu/research/heri

ROBERT M. LA FOLLETTE SCHOOL OF PUBLIC AFFAIRS
Director: Susan Yackee
Contact: info@lafollette.wisc.edu; 608-262-3581; 1225 Observatory Drive, Madison, WI 53706
Website: www.lafollette.wisc.edu

SCHOOL OF VETERINARY MEDICINE
Dean: Mark D. Markel
Contact: 608-263-6716; 2015 Linden Drive, Madison, WI 53706
Website: www.vetmed.wisc.edu

STATE SOILS AND PLANT ANALYSIS LABORATORY
Lab Manager: Andrew Stammer
Contact: soil-lab@mailplus.wisc.edu; 608-262-4364; 4702 University Avenue, Madison, WI 53703
Website: https://uwlab.soils.wisc.edu

UW CENTER FOR AGRICULTURAL SAFETY AND HEALTH
Safety Engineering and Agricultural Health Specialist: John Shutske
Contact: 608-265-0568; 460 Henry Mall, Madison, WI 53706
Website: http://fyi.extension.wisc.edu/agsafety

WISCONSIN CENTER FOR ENVIRONMENTAL EDUCATION
Contact: wcee@uwsp.edu; 715-346-4854; 110 Trainer Resources Building, 800 Reserve Street, Stevens Point, WI 54481
Website: www.uwsp.edu/cnr-ap/wcee

WISCONSIN STATE HERBARIUM
Director: Kenneth Cameron
Contact: 608-262-2792; Birge Hall, 430 Lincoln Drive, Madison, WI 53706
Website: http://herbarium.wisc.edu

Subordinate statutory boards, councils, and committees
LABORATORY OF HYGIENE BOARD
Members: Gregory Pils, *chair*; Robert Corliss, *vice chair;* Anjon Audhya, Jessica Blahnik,

Jennifer Buchholz, Gina Green-Harris, Gil Kelley, Jeff Kindrai, Jon Meiman, Christopher Strang, Mark Werner
Nonvoting member and laboratory director: James Schauer
Contact: WSLHBoard@slh.wisc.edu; 608-890-0288
Website: http://www.slh.wisc.edu/about/board

The Laboratory of Hygiene Board oversees the Laboratory of Hygiene, which provides laboratory services in the areas of water quality, air quality, public health, and contagious diseases for state agencies, local health departments, physicians, veterinarians, and others to prevent and control diseases and environmental hazards. Attached to UW–Madison, the laboratory provides facilities for teaching and research in the fields of public health and environmental protection.

RURAL HEALTH DEVELOPMENT COUNCIL
Contact: 800-385-0005 (toll free), Ext. 2; Wisconsin Office of Rural Health, 310 North Midvale Boulevard, Suite 301, Madison, WI 53705
Website: http://www.worh.org/rhdc

The Rural Health Development Council consists of 17 members appointed by the governor, with the advice and consent of the senate, for five-year terms and the secretary of health services or his or her designee. The council advises the Board of Regents on matters related to loan assistance programs for physicians, dentists, and other health care providers.

Independent entities attached for administrative purposes

PUBLIC LEADERSHIP BOARD
Members: Scott Jensen, Kimber Liedl, Gerard Randall, Dean Stensberg, Jason Thompson, Robin Vos
Thompson Center Director: Alexander Tahk
Contact: thompsoncenter@wisc.edu; 608-265-4087; 445 Henry Mall, Madison, WI 53706
Website: https://thompsoncenter.wisc.edu/people

The Public Leadership Board appoints, upon joint recommendation of UW–Madison's chancellor and its dean of the College of Letters and Science, the director of the Tommy G. Thompson Center on Public Leadership at UW–Madison. The mission of the center, to be carried out in all the universities of the UW System, is to facilitate research, teaching, outreach, and policy reform regarding effective public leadership that improves American government. The board approves the center's budget and must allocate at least $500,000 annually for speaking engagements at campuses other than UW–Madison.

VETERINARY DIAGNOSTIC LABORATORY BOARD
Members: Laurence Bauman, Kristen Bernard, Barry Kleppe, Darlene Konkle, Paul Kunde, Sandra Madland, Mark Markel, Rory Meyer, Rebecca Suchla

Nonvoting member and laboratory director: Keith Poulsen
Contact: 608-262-5432; 800-608-8387 (toll free); 445 Easterday Lane, Madison, WI 53706
Website: https://www.wvdl.wisc.edu/index.php/about-wvdl/board-of-directors

The Veterinary Diagnostic Laboratory Board oversees the Veterinary Diagnostic Laboratory, which provides animal health testing and diagnostic services on a statewide basis for all types of animals. The laboratory may also participate in research, education, and field services related to animal health.

Department of Veterans Affairs

Department secretary-designee: James Bond
Deputy secretary: Christopher J. McElgunn
Board of Veterans Affairs: William Schrum, *chair*
Location: 2135 Rimrock Road, Madison
Contact: 1-800-WIS-VETS (toll free); 608-266-0517 (media inquiries); PO Box 7843, Madison, WI 53707-7843
Website: https://dva.wi.gov
Number of employees: 1,242.43
Total budget 2021–23: $288,243,000

The Department of Veterans Affairs is administered by a secretary who must be a veteran and who is appointed by the governor with the advice and consent of the senate. The department includes the Board of Veterans Affairs, consisting of nine members who must be veterans and who are appointed by the governor with the advice and consent of the senate. The board advises the secretary on the promulgation of administrative rules necessary to carry out the powers and duties of the department.

The department administers an array of grants, benefits, programs, and services for eligible veterans, their families, and organizations that serve veterans. It operates the Wisconsin veterans homes at Chippewa Falls, King, and Union Grove, which provide short-term rehabilitation and long-term skilled nursing care to eligible veterans (and, to the extent of their resources, to the spouses and parents of veterans). The department also operates the Southern Wisconsin Veterans Memorial Cemetery at Union Grove, the Northern Wisconsin Veterans Memorial Cemetery near Spooner, and the Central Wisconsin Veterans Memorial Cemetery at King. Finally, the department operates the Wisconsin Veterans Museum in Madison.

Subordinate statutory boards, councils, and committees

COUNCIL ON VETERANS PROGRAMS
Chair: Larry Hill

Website: https://dva.wi.gov/pages/aboutwdva/councilonveteransprograms.aspx

The Council on Veterans Programs studies and presents policy alternatives and recommendations to the Board of Veterans Affairs and the Department of Veterans Affairs.

WISCONSIN COMMISSION FOR THE UNITED STATES SEMIQUINCENTENNIAL COMMISSION

Chair: Chris Kolakowski

The Wisconsin Commission for the United States Semiquincentennial Commission is responsible for planning, coordinating, and implementing a program to commemorate the 250th anniversary of the founding of the United States, specifically highlighting the role of Wisconsin in that event.

Department of Workforce Development

Department secretary-designee: Amy Pechacek
Deputy secretary: Pamela McGillivray
Location: 201 East Washington Avenue, Madison
Contact: 608-266-3131; PO Box 7946, Madison, WI 53707-7946
Website: https://dwd.wi.gov
Number of employees: 1,610.45
Total budget 2021–23: $732,400,700

The Department of Workforce Development is administered by a secretary who is appointed by the governor with the advice and consent of the senate.

The department administers the unemployment insurance program and

The Wisconsin Veterans Museum, an educational enterprise of the Department of Veterans Affairs, preserves and shares the stories of Wisconsin veterans dating back to the Civil War.

oversees the worker's compensation program. The department also operates the state's job center network (https://jobcenterofwisconsin.com); manages the Fast Forward worker training grant program (https://wisconsinfastforward.com); operates adult and youth apprenticeship programs; collects, analyzes, and distributes labor market information; monitors migrant workers services; provides vocational rehabilitation services to help people with disabilities achieve their employment goals; and offers comprehensive employment and training programs and services to youth and adults, including veterans with service-connected disabilities. Finally, the department enforces wage and hour laws; leave and benefits laws; child labor laws; civil rights laws; plant closing laws; and laws regulating migrant labor contractors and camps.

Subordinate statutory boards, councils, and committees

GOVERNOR'S COUNCIL ON MIGRANT LABOR
Contact: dwddet@dwd.wisconsin.gov; 608-266-0327; PO Box 7972, Madison WI 53707
Website: https://dwd.wisconsin.gov/jobservice/msfw/Migrant-Labor-Council-description.htm

The Governor's Council on Migrant Labor advises the department and other state officials about matters affecting migrant workers.

HEALTH CARE PROVIDER ADVISORY COMMITTEE
Chair: Steve Peters
Contact: 608-266-1340; dwddwc@dwd.wisconsin.gov; 201 East Washington Avenue, Madison, WI 53703
Website: https://dwd.wisconsin.gov/wc/councils/wcac//hcpac

The Health Care Provider Advisory Committee advises the department and the Council on Worker's Compensation on the standards that the department uses when it determines whether treatment provided to an injured employee was necessary treatment that is compensable by worker's compensation insurance.

SELF-INSURERS COUNCIL
Contact: dwddwc@dwd.wisconsin.gov; 608-266-1340; PO Box 7901, Madison, WI 53707-7901
Website: https://dwd.wisconsin.gov/wc/councils/self-insured

The Self-Insurers Council assists the department in administering the self-insurance program, under which an employer may be allowed to cover its worker's compensation costs directly rather than by purchasing insurance. The council ensures that those employers applying for self-insurance are financially viable and monitors the financial status of employers in the self-insurance pool.

UNEMPLOYMENT INSURANCE ADVISORY COUNCIL
Chair: Janell Knutson
Contact: 608-267-1405; PO Box 8942, Madison, WI 53708-8942
Website: https://dwd.wisconsin.gov/uibola/uiac

The Unemployment Insurance Advisory Council provides advice and counsel to the department and the legislature about unemployment insurance matters, including by providing advice and recommendations with respect to proposed changes to the unemployment insurance law.

WISCONSIN APPRENTICESHIP ADVISORY COUNCIL
Cochairs: Henry Hurt, Corey Gall
Website: https://dwd.wisconsin.gov/apprenticeship/advisory-council.htm

The Wisconsin Apprenticeship Advisory Council advises the department on matters pertaining to Wisconsin's apprenticeship system.

WORKER'S COMPENSATION ADVISORY COUNCIL
Chair: Steve Peters
Contact: 608-266-1340; dwddwc@dwd.wisconsin.gov; 201 East Washington Avenue, Madison, WI 53703
Website: https://dwd.wisconsin.gov/wc/councils/wcac

The Council on Worker's Compensation provides advice and counsel to the department and the legislature about worker's compensation matters, including by providing advice and recommendations with respect to proposed changes to the worker's compensation law.

Independent entities attached for administrative purposes

EMPLOYMENT RELATIONS COMMISSION
Chair: James J. Daley
Location: 2418 Crossroads Drive, Suite 1000, Madison, WI 53718-7896
Contact: werc@werc.state.wi.us; 608-243-2424
Website: http://werc.wi.gov
Number of employees: 6.00
Total budget 2021–23: $2,006,000

The Employment Relations Commission promotes collective bargaining and peaceful labor relations in the private and public sectors. The commission determines various types of labor relations cases and issues decisions arising from state employee civil service appeals. The commission also provides mediation and grievance arbitration services as well as training and assistance to parties interested in labor-management cooperation and a consensus approach to resolving labor relations issues.

Authorities

Fox River Navigational System Authority
Board of directors chair: Ron Van De Hey
Executive director: Phil Ramlet
Contact: 920-455-9174; 1008 Augustine Street, Kaukauna, WI 54130-1608
Website: www.foxlocks.org
Total state appropriation 2021–23: $250,800

The Fox River Navigational System Authority is a public corporation that is responsible for the rehabilitation, repair, and management of the navigation system on or near the Fox River, and it may enter into contracts with third parties to operate the system. The authority may charge fees for services provided to watercraft owners and users of navigational facilities, enter into contracts with nonprofit organizations to raise funds, and contract debt, but it may not issue bonds. Annually, the authority must submit an audited financial statement to the Department of Administration. The authority is governed by a nine-member board of directors. The nine members include six appointees of the governor, who appoints two each from Brown, Outagamie, and Winnebago Counties.

Lower Fox River Remediation Authority (inactive)

The Lower Fox River Remediation Authority is a public corporation that is authorized to issue assessment bonds for eligible waterway improvement costs, which generally include environmental investigation and remediation of the Fox River extending from Lake Winnebago to the mouth of the river in Lake Michigan, including any portion of Green Bay in Lake Michigan that contains sediments discharged from the river.

University of Wisconsin Hospitals and Clinics Authority
Board of directors chair: Paul W. Seidenstricker
Chief executive officer: Alan Kaplan
Contact: 608-263-6400; 800-323-8942 (toll free); corporategovernance@uwhealth.org; 600 Highland Avenue, Madison, WI 53792
Website: www.uwhealth.org

The University of Wisconsin Hospitals and Clinics Authority is a public corporation governed by a 16-member board of directors that includes the cochairs of the Joint Committee on Finance and six appointees of the governor. The authority operates the UW Hospital and Clinics, including the American Family Children's Hospital, and related clinics and health care facilities. Through the UW Hospital and Clinics and its other programs, the authority delivers health care, including care for the indigent; provides an environment for instruction of physicians, nurses, and other health-related disciplines; sponsors and supports health care research; and assists health care programs and personnel throughout the state. The authority is self-financing. It derives much of its income from charges for clinical and hospital services. The authority also may issue bonds to support its operations, which, however, do not create a debt of the state, and may seek financing from the Wisconsin Health and Educational Facilities Authority.

Wisconsin Aerospace Authority (inactive)

The Wisconsin Aerospace Authority is directed to promote and develop the state's space-related industry and coordinate these activities with governmental entities, the aerospace industry, businesses, educational organizations, and the Wisconsin Space Grant Consortium.

Wisconsin Economic Development Corporation

Board of directors chair: Henry C. Newell
Chief executive officer: Missy Hughes
Chief operating officer: Sam Rikkers
Location: 201 West Washington Avenue, Madison
Contact: 855-INWIBIZ (855-469-4249, toll free); PO Box 1687, Madison, WI 53701
Website: https://wedc.org
Total state appropriation 2021–23 $83,101,400

The Wisconsin Economic Development Corporation is a public corporation that develops, implements, and administers programs to provide business support and expertise and financial assistance to companies that are investing and creating jobs in Wisconsin and to promote new business start-ups and business expansion and growth in the state. The authority was established in 2011 and assumed many of the functions previously performed by the former Department of Commerce. WEDC is governed by an 18-member board that consists of six appointees of the governor, ten appointees of legislative leaders—four appointees each of the speaker of the assembly and senate majority leader and one appointee each of the minority leaders of both houses—and the secretaries of administration and revenue as nonvoting members. WEDC may issue bonds and incur other debt to achieve its public purposes. WEDC's bonds and other debt do not create a debt of the state.

Wisconsin Health and Educational Facilities Authority

Board of directors chair: James Dietsche
Executive director: Larry D. Wiemer II
Contact: info@whefa.com; 262-792-0466; 18000 West Sarah Lane, Suite 300, Brookfield, WI 53045-5841
Website: www.whefa.com

The Wisconsin Health and Educational Facilities Authority is a public corporation governed by a seven-member board whose members are appointed by the governor with the advice and consent of the senate. No more than four of the members may be of the same political party. The governor appoints the chair annually.

WHEFA issues bonds on behalf of private nonprofit facilities to help them finance their capital costs.

The authority has no taxing power. WHEFA's bonds are not a debt, liability, or obligation of the State of Wisconsin or any of its subdivisions. The authority may issue bonds to finance any qualifying capital project, including new construction, remodeling, and renovation; expansion of current facilities; and purchase of new equipment or furnishings. WHEFA may also issue bonds to refinance outstanding debt.

Wisconsin Housing and Economic Development Authority

Board of directors chair: Ranell Washington
Executive director and CEO: Elmer Moore Jr.
Contact: info@wheda.com; 608-266-7884 or 800-334-6873 (Madison, toll free); 414-227-4039 or 800-628-4833 (Milwaukee, toll free); PO Box 1728, Madison, WI 53701-1728; 908 East Main Street, Suite 501, Madison WI 53703; 611 West National Avenue, Suite 110, Milwaukee, WI 53204 (Milwaukee office)
Website: www.wheda.com

The Wisconsin Housing and Economic Development Authority is a public corporation governed by a 12-member board that includes six appointees of the governor and four legislators representing both parties and both houses. WHEDA administers numerous loan programs and other programs and projects that provide housing and related assistance to Wisconsin residents, including single and multifamily housing for individuals and families of low and moderate income, and that promote and support home ownership. WHEDA also finances loan guarantees and administers other programs to support business and agricultural development in the state. WHEDA issues bonds to support its operations, which, however, do not create a debt of the state.

Nonprofit corporations

Bradley Center Sports and Entertainment Corporation (inactive and dissolved)

The Bradley Center Sports and Entertainment Corporation is a public nonprofit corporation that was created as an instrumentality of the state to receive and operate the Bradley Center, a sports and entertainment facility located in Milwaukee County and donated by the Bradley Center Corporation. The Bradley Center was the home of the Milwaukee Bucks basketball team from 1988 to 2018 and hosted other sporting events as well as numerous entertainment shows and concerts. The Bradley Center has been replaced by a new facility, the Fiserv Forum, which is owned and operated by the Wisconsin Center District, a local governmental entity (see page 251). In 2019, the Bradley Center Sports and Entertainment Corporation submitted its final audited financial statements to state officials, announced completion of its business affairs, and transferred its remaining assets ($4.29 million) to the state.

Wisconsin Artistic Endowment Foundation (inactive)

The Wisconsin Artistic Endowment Foundation is a public nonprofit corporation that was created by the legislature for the purpose of supporting the arts, distributing funds, and facilitating the conversion of donated property into cash to support the arts. The foundation may not be dissolved except by an enactment of the legislature.

Regional planning commissions

Regional planning commissions advise cities, villages, towns, and counties on the planning and delivery of public services to the residents of a defined region, and they prepare and adopt master plans for the physical development of the region they serve.

The commissions may conduct research studies; make and adopt plans for the physical, social, and economic development of the region; provide advisory services to local governmental units and other public and private agencies; and coordinate local programs that relate to their objectives.

Currently, there are nine regional planning commissions serving all but five of the state's 72 counties. Their boundaries are based on factors including common topographical and geographical features; the extent of urban development; the existence of special or acute agricultural, forestry, or other rural problems; and the existence of physical, social, and economic problems of a regional character.

Regional planning commissions have developed and assisted with projects in areas including rail and air transportation, waste disposal and recycling, highways, air and water quality, farmland preservation and zoning, land conservation and reclamation, outdoor recreation, parking and lakefront studies, and land records modernization.

Membership of regional planning commissions varies according to conditions defined by statute. The commissions are funded through state and federal planning grants, contracts with local governments for special planning services, and a statutorily authorized levy of up to 0.003 percent of equalized real estate value charged to each local governmental unit.

Wisconsin's regional planning commissions have established the Association of Wisconsin Regional Planning Commissions. The association's purposes include assisting the study of common problems and serving as an information clearinghouse.

Bay-Lake Regional Planning Commission
Counties in region: Brown, Door, Florence, Kewaunee, Manitowoc, Marinette, Oconto, Sheboygan
Chair: Mike Hotz
Executive director: Cindy J. Wojtczak
Contact: 920-448-2820; 1861 Nimitz Drive, De Pere, WI 54115
Website: www.baylakerpc.org

Capital Area Regional Planning Commission
County in region: Dane
Chair: David Pfeiffer
Agency director: Steve Steinhoff
Contact: info@capitalarearpc.org; 608-474-6017; 100 State Street, Suite 400, Madison, WI 53703
Website: www.capitalarearpc.org

East Central Wisconsin Regional Planning Commission
Counties in region: Calumet, Fond du Lac, Green Lake (not participating), Marquette (not participating), Menominee, Outagamie, Shawano, Waupaca, Waushara, Winnebago
Chair: Jeff Nooyen
Executive director: Melissa Kraemer-Badtke
Contact: 920-751-4770; 400 Ahnaip Street, Suite 100, Menasha, WI 54952
Website: www.ecwrpc.org

Mississippi River Regional Planning Commission
Counties in region: Buffalo, Crawford, Jackson, La Crosse, Monroe, Pepin, Pierce, Trempealeau, Vernon
Chair: James Kuhn
Executive director: Jon Bingol
Contact: plan@mrrpc.com; 608-785-9396; 1707 Main Street, Suite 435, La Crosse, WI 54601
Website: www.mrrpc.com

North Central Wisconsin Regional Planning Commission
Counties in region: Adams, Forest, Juneau, Langlade, Lincoln, Marathon, Oneida, Portage, Vilas, Wood
Chair: Paul Millan

Regional planning commission areas

Map of Wisconsin showing regional planning commission areas: Northwest, West Central Wis., North Central Wis., Bay-Lake, East Central Wis., Mississippi River, no RPC, Capital Area, Southeastern Wis., Southwestern Wis.

Executive director: Dennis L. Lawrence
Contact: info@ncwrpc.org; 715-849-5510; 210 McClellan Street, Suite 210, Wausau, WI 54403
Website: www.ncwrpc.org

Northwest Regional Planning Commission

Counties in region: Ashland, Bayfield, Burnett, Douglas, Iron, Price, Rusk, Sawyer, Taylor, Washburn
Participating tribal nations: Bad River, Lac Courte Oreilles, Lac du Flambeau, Red Cliff, St. Croix
Chair: Tom Mackie
Executive director: Sheldon Johnson
Contact: info@nwrpc.com; 715-635-2197; 1400 South River Street, Spooner, WI 54801
Website: www.nwrpc.com

Southeastern Wisconsin Regional Planning Commission
Counties in region: Kenosha, Milwaukee, Ozaukee, Racine, Walworth, Washington, Waukesha
Chair: Charles L. Colman
Interim executive director: Benjamin McKay
Contact: sewrpc@sewrpc.org; 262-547-6721; W239 N1812 Rockwood Drive, PO Box 1607, Waukesha, WI 53187-1607
Website: www.sewrpc.org

Southwestern Wisconsin Regional Planning Commission
Counties in region: Grant, Green, Iowa, Lafayette, Richland
Chair: Bob Keeney
Executive director: Troy Maggied
Contact: info@swwrpc.org; 608-342-1636; 20 South Court Street, Platteville, WI 53818
Website: www.swwrpc.org

West Central Wisconsin Regional Planning Commission
Counties in region: Barron, Chippewa, Clark, Dunn, Eau Claire, Polk, St. Croix
Chair: Louie Okey
Executive director: Lynn Nelson
Contact: wcwrpc@wcwrpc.org; 715-836-2918; 800 Wisconsin Street, Building D2, Room 401, Mail Box 9, Eau Claire, WI 54703
Website: www.wcwrpc.org

Other regional entities

Professional Football Stadium District
Board of directors chair: Leah Weycker
Executive director: Patrick Webb
Contact: 920-965-6997; 1229 Lombardi Avenue, Green Bay, WI 54304
Website: www.gbbcstadiumdistrict.com

The Professional Football Stadium District is an owner and the landlord of Lambeau Field, the designated home of the Green Bay Packers football team. It is a local governmental unit that may acquire, construct, equip, maintain, improve, operate, and manage football stadium facilities or hire others to do the same. Maintenance and operation of the stadium is governed by provisions of the Lambeau Field Lease Agreement by and among the district; Green Bay Packers, Inc.; and the City of Green Bay. The district board consists of seven members who are appointed by local elected officials.

Southeast Wisconsin Professional Baseball Park District
Board of directors chair: Tim Sheehy
Executive director: Pat Goss
Contact: contact@wibaseballdistrict.com; 414-902-4040; 1 Brewers Way, Milwaukee, WI 53214
Website: www.wibaseballdistrict.com

The Southeast Wisconsin Professional Baseball Park District is the majority owner of American Family Field, the home of the Milwaukee Brewers Baseball Club. It is a local governmental unit that may acquire, construct, maintain, improve, operate, and manage baseball park facilities, which include parking lots, garages, restaurants, parks, concession facilities, entertainment facilities, and other related structures. The district is also authorized to issue bonds for certain purposes related to baseball park facilities. To pay off the bonds, the district may impose a sales tax and a use tax, known as the baseball stadium tax. As of April 1, 2020, however, retailers may no longer collect the baseball stadium tax; the district's board certified in March 2020 that the district's bonds had been paid and other required obligations had been met. A city or county within the district's jurisdiction may make loans or grants to the district, expend funds to subsidize the district, borrow money for baseball park facilities, or grant property to the state dedicated for use by a professional baseball park.

The district includes Milwaukee, Ozaukee, Racine, Washington, and Waukesha counties. The district's governing board consists of 13 members appointed by the governor and elected officials from within its jurisdiction. The governor appoints the chair of the governing board.

Wisconsin Center District
Board of directors chair: James Kanter
President and CEO: Marty Brooks
Contact: 414-908-6000; 400 West Wisconsin Avenue, Milwaukee, WI 53203
Website: https://wcd.org

The Wisconsin Center District operates the University of Wisconsin-Milwaukee Panther Arena, the Miller High Life Theatre, and the Wisconsin Center. It also assists in the development and construction of sports and entertainment facilities, including a new arena for the Milwaukee Bucks, which opened in August 2018. The arena, known as the Fiserv Forum, is owned by the District, but operated, maintained, and managed by the Bucks organization. After the new sports and entertainment facilities were completed, the Wisconsin Center District oversaw the demolition of the Bradley Center, the previous large-event arena for the Milwaukee area. The demolition was completed in 2019.

The Wisconsin Center District is a local governmental unit that may acquire, construct, and operate an exposition center and related facilities; enter into contracts and grant concessions; mortgage district property and issue bonds; and invest funds as the district board considers appropriate. The district is funded by operating revenue and special sales taxes on hotel rooms, restaurant food and beverages, and car rentals within its taxing jurisdiction. The district board has 17 members, including legislative leaders, local government finance officials, and members who are appointed by the governor, Milwaukee County executive, city of Milwaukee mayor, and city of Milwaukee common council president.

Interstate compacts

Wisconsin has entered with other states into various interstate compacts, under which the compacting states agree to coordinate their activities related to a particular matter according to uniform guidelines or procedures. Some of these compacts include provisions creating an interstate entity made up of representatives from the compacting states, while others do not.

Interstate entities created by interstate compacts

EDUCATION COMMISSION OF THE STATES
Wisconsin delegation: Tony Evers (governor); Camille Crary (governor's proxy); Senator Jacque; Zach Madden; Anju Reejhsinghani; Amy Traynor; Jill Underly (state superintendent of public instruction); Dean Haen, *alternate commissioner*
Contact: 303-299-3600; 700 Broadway Street, Suite 810, Denver, CO 80203
Website: www.ecs.org

The Education Commission of the States was established to foster national cooperation among executive, legislative, educational, and lay leaders of the various states concerning education policy and the improvement of state and local education systems. The seven-member Wisconsin delegation includes the governor and the state superintendent of public instruction.

GREAT LAKES COMMISSION
Wisconsin delegation: Todd Ambs, *commission chair*; Melonee Montano; 1 vacancy
Contact: 734-971-9135; 1300 Victors Way, Suite 1350, Ann Arbor, MI 48108
Website: www.glc.org

The Great Lakes Commission was established under the Great Lakes Basin Compact to promote the orderly, integrated, and comprehensive development, use, and conservation of the water and related natural resources of the Great Lakes basin and St. Lawrence River. Its members include the eight Great Lakes states of Illinois, Indiana, Michigan, Minnesota, New York, Ohio, Pennsylvania, and Wisconsin, with associate member status for the Canadian provinces of Ontario and Québec. A three-member delegation, appointed by the governor, represents Wisconsin on the commission. The commission develops and recommends the adoption of policy positions by its members and offers advice on issues such as clean energy, climate change, habitat and coastal management, control of aquatic invasive species, water quality, and water resources.

GREAT LAKES PROTECTION FUND

Wisconsin representatives to the board of directors: Demetria Smith; Erin Deeley
Contact: 847-425-8150; 1560 Sherman Avenue, Suite 1370, Evanston, IL 60201
Website: www.glpf.org

The Great Lakes Protection Fund is a private nonprofit corporation, the members of which are the governors of Illinois, Michigan, Minnesota, New York, Ohio, Pennsylvania, and Wisconsin. The purpose of the corporation is to finance projects for the protection and cleanup of the Great Lakes. The corporation is managed by a board of directors composed of two representatives from each member state. The governor appoints the two Wisconsin representatives.

GREAT LAKES-ST. LAWRENCE RIVER BASIN WATER RESOURCES COUNCIL

Wisconsin members: Tony Evers (governor), *council chair*
Contact: gsgp@gsgp.org; 312-407-0177; 20 North Wacker Drive, Suite 2700, Chicago, IL 60606
Website: www.glslcompactcouncil.org

The Great Lakes-St. Lawrence River Basin Water Resources Council is charged with aiding, promoting, and coordinating the activities and programs of the Great Lakes states concerning water resources management in the Great Lakes-St. Lawrence River basin. The council may promulgate and enforce rules and regulations as may be necessary for the implementation and enforcement of the Great Lakes-St. Lawrence River Basin Water Resources Compact. The legally binding compact governs withdrawals, consumptive uses, conservation and efficient use, and diversions of basin water resources, and the council may initiate legal actions to compel compliance with the compact. In addition, the council must review and approve proposals from certain parties for the withdrawal, diversion, or consumptive use of water from the basin that is subject to the compact.

Under the compact, the governors from the states of Illinois, Indiana, Michigan, Minnesota, New York, Ohio, Pennsylvania, and Wisconsin jointly pursue intergovernmental cooperation and consultation to protect, conserve, restore, improve, and effectively manage the waters and water dependent natural resources of the basin. The governor serves as Wisconsin's representative on the council.

GREAT LAKES-ST. LAWRENCE RIVER WATER RESOURCES REGIONAL BODY

Wisconsin members: Tony Evers (governor)
Contact: gsgp@gsgp.org; 312-407-0177; 20 North Wacker Drive, Suite 2700, Chicago, IL 60606
Website: www.glslregionalbody.org

The Great Lakes-St. Lawrence River Water Resources Regional Body is an entity charged with aiding and promoting the coordination of the activities and programs of the Great Lakes states and provinces concerned with water resources management in the Great Lakes and St. Lawrence River basin. The regional body may develop procedures for the implementation of the Great Lakes-St. Lawrence River Basin Sustainable Water Resources Agreement, which is a good-faith agreement between Great Lakes states and provinces that governs the withdrawal, consumptive use, conservation and efficient use, and diversion of basin water resources. The regional body must review and approve proposals from certain parties for the withdrawal, diversion, or consumptive use of water from the basin that is subject to the agreement. The members of the regional body are the governors from the states of Illinois, Indiana, Michigan, Minnesota, New York, Ohio, Pennsylvania, and Wisconsin, and the premiers of Ontario and Québec. The members of the body jointly pursue intergovernmental cooperation and consultation to protect, conserve, restore, improve, and manage the waters and water dependent natural resources of the basin.

INTERSTATE COMMISSION FOR JUVENILES

Wisconsin member: Casey Gerber (commissioner, Department of Corrections, Division of Juvenile Corrections)
Contact: icjadmin@juvenilecompact.org; 859-721-1061; 836 Euclid Avenue, Suite 322, Lexington, KY 40502
Website: www.juvenilecompact.org

The Interstate Commission for Juveniles was established under the Interstate Compact for Juveniles. The compact is designed to coordinate the supervision of juveniles on probation and parole who move across state lines and assists states in returning youth who run away, escape, or abscond across state lines. The commission has the authority to promulgate rules that have the force of law and enforce compliance with the compact.

INTERSTATE COMMISSION OF NURSE LICENSURE COMPACT ADMINISTRATORS

Wisconsin member: Robert W. Weinman (chairperson, Wisconsin Board of Nursing)
Contact: info@ncsbn.org; 312-525-3600; 111 East Wacker Drive, Suite 2900, Chicago, IL 60601
Website: www.ncsbn.org

The Interstate Commission of Nurse Licensure Compact Administrators was established under the Enhanced Nurse Licensure Compact, now known as the Nurse Licensure Compact. The compact authorizes a nurse licensed in a member state to practice nursing in any other member state without obtaining a license in that state. The commission administers the compact and has the authority to promulgate rules that have the force of law.

INTERSTATE INSURANCE PRODUCT REGULATION COMMISSION
Wisconsin member: Nathan Houdek (commissioner of insurance)
Contact: 202-471-3962; 444 North Capitol Street, NW, Hall of the States, Suite 700, Washington, DC 20001-1509
Website: www.insurancecompact.org

The Interstate Insurance Product Regulation Commission was established under the Interstate Insurance Product Regulation Compact. The compact's purposes are to promote and protect the interest of consumers of, and establish uniform standards for, annuity, life, disability income, and long-term care insurance products; establish a central clearinghouse for the review of those insurance products and related matters, such as advertising; and improve the coordination of regulatory resources and expertise among the various insurance agencies of the member states.

INTERSTATE MEDICAL LICENSURE COMPACT COMMISSION
Wisconsin members: Sheldon Wasserman, Clarence Chou
Contact: inquiry@imlcc.net; 303-997-9842
Website: www.imlcc.org

The Interstate Medical Licensure Compact Commission was established under the Interstate Medical Licensure Compact. The compact provides an expedited process for physicians to become licensed to practice medicine in member states. The commission administers the compact and has the authority to promulgate rules that have the force of law.

INTERSTATE WILDLIFE VIOLATOR COMPACT BOARD OF ADMINISTRATORS
Wisconsin member: Summer Wilson (compact coordinator, Department of Natural Resources)
Contact: Department of Natural Resources; 608-267-0859
Website: www.naclec.org/wvc

The Interstate Wildlife Violator Compact is intended to promote compliance with laws and rules relating to the management of wildlife resources in the member states. The compact establishes a process for handling a wildlife resources law violation by a nonresident in a member state as if the violator were a resident of that state. The compact also requires each member state to recognize the revocation or suspension of an individual's wildlife resources privileges in another member state. The compact board of administrators resolves all matters relating to the operation of the compact.

LOWER ST. CROIX MANAGEMENT COMMISSION
Wisconsin member: Dan Baumann (designated by secretary of natural resources)
Contact: Department of Natural Resources, West Central Region; 715-839-3722; 1300 West Clairemont Avenue, Eau Claire, WI 54701

The Lower St. Croix Management Commission was created to provide a forum for discussion of problems and programs associated with the Lower St. Croix National Scenic Riverway. It coordinates planning, development, protection, and management of the riverway between Wisconsin, Minnesota, and the U.S. government.

MIDWEST INTERSTATE LOW-LEVEL RADIOACTIVE WASTE COMMISSION
Wisconsin member: Mark Paulson (Nuclear Safety Manager, Department of Health Services)
Website: www.midwestcompact.org

The Midwest Interstate Low-Level Radioactive Waste Commission administers the Midwest Interstate Low-Level Radioactive Waste Compact. The compact is an agreement between the states of Indiana, Iowa, Minnesota, Missouri, Ohio, and Wisconsin that provides for the cooperative and safe disposal of commercial low-level radioactive waste.

MIDWEST INTERSTATE PASSENGER RAIL COMMISSION
Wisconsin members: Scott Rogers, Senator Wanggaard, 2 vacancies
Contact: miprc@miprc.org; 630-925-1922; 701 East 22nd Street, Suite 110, Lombard, IL 60148
Website: www.miprc.org

The Midwest Interstate Passenger Rail Commission brings together state leaders from the members of the Midwest Interstate Passenger Rail Compact to advocate for passenger rail improvements. The commission also works to educate government officials and the public with respect to the advantages of passenger rail. The current members of the compact are Illinois, Indiana, Kansas, Michigan, Minnesota, Missouri, North Dakota, and Wisconsin.

MIDWESTERN HIGHER EDUCATION COMMISSION
Wisconsin members: Senator Ballweg, Connie Hutchison, Rebecca Larson, Representative Murphy, Julie Underwood
Contact: 612-677-2777; 105 Fifth Avenue South, Suite 450, Minneapolis, Minnesota 55401
Website: www.mhec.org

The Midwestern Higher Education Commission was organized to further higher educational opportunities for residents of states participating in the Midwestern Higher Education Compact. The commission may enter into agreements with states, universities, and colleges to provide student programs and services. The commission also studies the compact's effects on higher education.

MILITARY INTERSTATE CHILDREN'S COMPACT COMMISSION
Wisconsin commissioner: Shelley Joan Weiss
Contact: mic3info@csg.org; 859-244-8000; 1776 Avenue of The States, Lexington, KY 40511
Website: www.mic3.net

The Military Interstate Children's Compact Commission oversees implementation of the Interstate Compact on Educational Opportunity for Military Children. The compact is intended to facilitate the education of children of military families and remove barriers to educational success due to frequent moves and parent deployment.

The commission is composed of one commissioner from each of the compacting states. In each compacting state, a council or other body in state government administers the compact within that state. In Wisconsin, the compact is administered by the State Council on the Interstate Compact on Educational Opportunity for Military Children.

MISSISSIPPI RIVER PARKWAY COMMISSION
Wisconsin commission chair: Sherry Quamme
Contact: mrpc@pilchbarnet.com; 866-763-8310 (toll free); PO Box 7395, Madison, WI 53707-7395
Website: https://mrpcmembers.com

The Mississippi River Parkway Commission coordinates the development and preservation of Wisconsin's portion of the Great River Road corridor along the Mississippi River. It advises state and local agencies on maintaining and enhancing the scenic, historic, economic, and recreational assets within the corridor and works with similar commissions in other Mississippi River states and the province of Ontario. The 16-member Wisconsin commission includes 12 voting members. Four of these are legislative members who represent the two major political parties in each house, and eight others are appointed by the governor. The four nonvoting members are ex officio, consisting of the secretaries of tourism, natural resources, and transportation and the director of the historical society. The commission selects its own chair to act as Wisconsin's sole voting representative at national meetings of the Mississippi River Parkway Commission.

OCCUPATIONAL THERAPY COMPACT COMMISSION
Wisconsin representative: Teri Black
Website: https://otcompact.org

The Occupational Therapy Compact Commission was established under the Occupational Therapy Licensure Compact, which allows occupational therapists and occupational therapy assistants who are licensed in one state that is party to the compact to practice in other member states. The commission administers the compact and includes delegates from each member state's licensing board.

PHYSICAL THERAPY COMPACT COMMISSION
Wisconsin representative: Kathryn Zalewski
Contact: 703-562-8500; 124 West Street South, Third Floor, Alexandria, VA 22314
Website: http://ptcompact.org

The Physical Therapy Compact Commission was established under the Physical Therapy Licensure Compact, which allows physical therapists and physical therapist assistants that are licensed in one state that is party to the compact to practice in other member states. The commission administers the compact and includes delegates from each member state's licensing board.

PSYCHOLOGY INTERJURISDICTIONAL COMPACT COMMISSION
Wisconsin representative: Daniel Schroeder
Contact: info@psypact.org
Website: https://psypact.site-ym.com

The Psychology Interjurisdictional Compact Commission was established under the Psychology Interjurisdictional Compact (PSYPACT), which was created to authorize telehealth practice and temporary practice outside of the state from which a psychologist is licensed. The commission administers the compact and includes delegates from each member state's licensing board.

UPPER MISSISSIPPI RIVER BASIN ASSOCIATION
Wisconsin representative: Steve G. Galarneau; Jim Fischer, *alternate*
Contact: 651-224-2880; 7831 East Bush Lake Road, Suite 302, Bloomington, MN 55439
Website: www.umrba.org

The Upper Mississippi River Basin Association is a nonprofit regional organization created by Illinois, Iowa, Minnesota, Missouri, and Wisconsin to facilitate cooperative action regarding the basin's water and related land resources. The association consists of one voting member from each state and sponsors studies of river-related issues, cooperative planning for use of the region's resources, and an information exchange. The organization also enables the member states to develop regional positions on resource issues and to advocate for the basin states' collective interests before the U.S. Congress and federal agencies. The association is involved with programs related to commercial navigation, ecosystem restoration, water quality, aquatic nuisance species, hazardous spills, flood risk management, water supply, and other water resource issues. Six federal agencies with major water resources responsibilities serve as advisory members: the Environmental Protection Agency, the U.S. Army Corps of Engineers, and the U.S. departments of Agriculture, Homeland Security, the Interior, and Transportation.

Interstate compacts without interstate entities

EMERGENCY MANAGEMENT ASSISTANCE COMPACT

Authorizes member states to provide mutual assistance to other states in an emergency or disaster declared by the governor of the affected state. Under the compact, member states cooperate in emergency-related training and formulate plans for interstate cooperation in responding to a disaster. The Division of Emergency Management in the Department of Military Affairs administers the compact in Wisconsin.

INTERSTATE COMPACT ON ADOPTION AND MEDICAL ASSISTANCE

Requires each member state to cooperate with other states to ensure that children with special needs who were adopted in or from another member state receive medical and other benefits. The Department of Children and Families administers the compact in Wisconsin.

INTERSTATE COMPACT FOR ADULT OFFENDER SUPERVISION

Creates cooperative procedures for individuals placed on parole, probation, or extended supervision in one state to be supervised in another state if certain conditions are met. The Department of Corrections administers the compact in Wisconsin.

INTERSTATE CORRECTIONS COMPACT

Authorizes Wisconsin to contract with member states for the confinement of Wisconsin inmates in those states and to receive inmates from member states. The Department of Corrections administers the compact in Wisconsin.

INTERSTATE AGREEMENT ON DETAINERS

Allows a member state to obtain temporary custody of an individual incarcerated in another member state to conduct a trial on outstanding charges.

INTERSTATE COMPACT ON MENTAL HEALTH

Facilitates treatment of patients with mental illness and mental disabilities by the cooperative action of the member states, to the benefit of the patients, their families, and society.

NORTHERN EMERGENCY MANAGEMENT ASSISTANCE COMPACT

An international mutual aid agreement created to facilitate the sharing of resources between certain Midwestern states and Canadian provinces during major disasters and to allow for joint planning, exercising, and training for emergencies. The Division of Emergency Management in the Department of Military Affairs administers the compact in Wisconsin.

INTERSTATE COMPACT ON THE PLACEMENT OF CHILDREN

Provides a uniform legal and administrative framework governing the interstate placement of abused, neglected, or dependent children, the interstate placement of children through independent or private adoption, and the interstate placement of any child into residential treatment facilities. The Department of Children and Families administers the compact in Wisconsin.

INTERSTATE AGREEMENT ON QUALIFICATION OF EDUCATIONAL PERSONNEL

Authorizes a state education official designated by each member state to contract with other member states to recognize the credentials of educators from those member states and facilitate the employment of qualified educational personnel. 🆎

THE JUDICIARY

Wisconsin Supreme Court

Justices: Annette Kingsland Ziegler, *chief justice*; Ann Walsh Bradley, Rebecca Grassl Bradley, Rebecca Frank Dallet, Brian Hagedorn, Jill J. Karofsky, Janet C. Protasiewicz
Clerk of the supreme court: Samuel A. Christensen
Supreme court commissioners: Nancy A. Kopp, Timothy M. Barber, Mark A. Neuser, David Runke
Location: Room 16 East, State Capitol, Madison (supreme court); 110 East Main Street, Suite 215, Madison (clerk)
Contact: 608-266-1880 (clerk); 608-266-7442 (commissioners); PO Box 1688, Madison, WI 53701-1688
Website: wicourts.gov/courts/supreme/index.htm
Number of employees: 38.50
Total budget 2021–23: $11,959,800

The Wisconsin Supreme Court is the highest court in Wisconsin's court system. It is the final authority on matters pertaining to the Wisconsin Constitution and the highest tribunal for all actions originating in the state court system, except those involving federal constitutional issues appealable to the U.S. Supreme Court.

Wisconsin's Supreme Court (*from left*): Justice Brian Hagedorn, Justice Rebecca Grassl Bradley, Justice Ann Walsh Bradley, Chief Justice Annette Kingsland Ziegler, former Justice Patience Drake Roggensack, Justice Rebecca Frank Dallet, and Justice Jill J. Karofsky.

In addition, it has regulatory and administrative authority over all courts and the practice of law in the state. In this capacity, it establishes procedural rules and codes of conduct for the courts and for the practice of law, and it regulates and disciplines attorneys, judges, and justices.

The supreme court consists of seven justices elected to 10-year terms. They are chosen in statewide elections on the nonpartisan April ballot and take office on the following August 1. The Wisconsin Constitution provides that only one justice can be elected in any single year. In the event of a vacancy, the governor may appoint a person to serve until an election can be held to fill the seat.

Supreme Court Chief Justice Annette Kingsland Ziegler administers the Oath of Office to Governor Tony Evers during the inauguration ceremony on January 3, 2023.

The justices elect one of themselves to be the chief justice for a term of two years. The chief justice serves as administrative head of the court system. Any four justices constitute a quorum for conducting court business.

The court decides which cases it will hear. The supreme court exercises its appellate jurisdiction to review a decision of a lower court if three or more justices approve a petition for review, if the court decides on its own motion to review a matter that has been appealed to the Wisconsin Court of Appeals, or if the court accepts a petition for bypass or a certification from the court of appeals. The majority of cases advance from the circuit court to the court of appeals before reaching the supreme court, but the supreme court can bypass the court of appeals, either on its own motion or at the request of the parties; in addition, the court of appeals may certify a case to the supreme court, asking the high court to take the case directly from the circuit court. The court accepts cases on bypass or on certification if four or more justices approve. Further, although rarely granted, a person may file a petition requesting the supreme court to exercise its superintending authority over actions and proceedings in the circuit courts and court

Supreme Court Justice Ann Walsh Bradley greets legislators in the assembly chamber before the 2023 State of the State Address. Justices Patience Drake Roggensack and Brian Hagedorn follow behind.

of appeals. The supreme court may also exercise original jurisdiction as the first court to hear a case if four or more justices approve a petition requesting it to do so.

The supreme court does not take testimony. Instead, it decides cases on the basis of written briefs and oral argument. The court is required by statute to deliver its decisions in writing, and it may publish them as it deems appropriate.

Wisconsin Court of Appeals

Chief judge: Maxine A. White
Deputy chief judge: Lisa K. Stark
Clerk of the court of appeals: Samuel A. Christensen
Location: 110 East Main Street, Suite 215, Madison (clerk)
Contact: 608-266-1880; PO Box 1688, Madison, WI 53701-1688
Website: wicourts.gov/courts/appeals/index.htm
Number of employees: 75.50
Total budget 2021–23: $23,830,000

Court of appeals districts

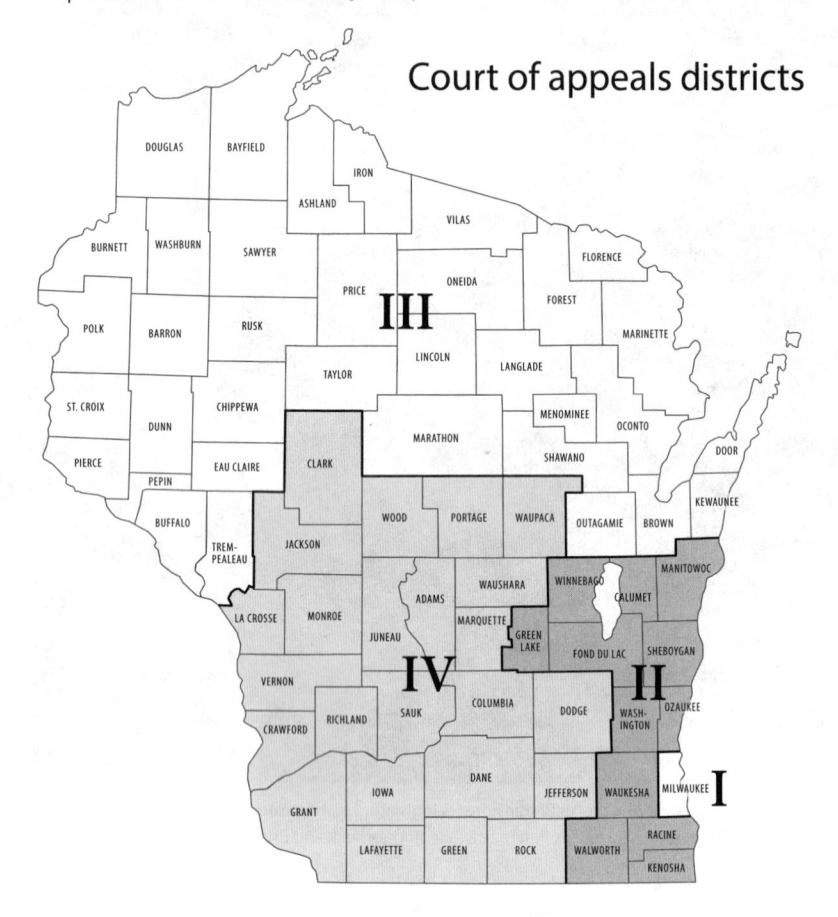

DISTRICT I

M. Joseph Donald, *presiding judge*; Timothy G. Dugan, Sara J. Geenen, Maxine A. White

Contact: 414-227-4680; 330 East Kilbourn Avenue, Suite 1020, Milwaukee, WI 53202-3161

DISTRICT II

Mark D. Gundrum, *presiding judge*; Lisa S. Neubauer, Maria S. Lazar, Shelley A. Grogan

Contact: 262-521-5230; 2727 North Grandview Boulevard, Suite 300, Waukesha, WI 53188-1672

DISTRICT III

Lisa K. Stark, *presiding judge*; Thomas M. Hruz, Gregory B. Gill Jr.

Contact: 715-848-1421; 2100 Stewart Avenue, Suite 310, Wausau, WI 54401

DISTRICT IV

Joanne F. Kloppenburg, *presiding judge*; Brian W. Blanchard, Chris Taylor, Jennifer E. Nashold, Rachel A. Graham

Contact: 608-266-9250; 2921 Landmark Place, Suite 415, Madison, WI 53713-4248

The Wisconsin Court of Appeals consists of 16 judges serving in four districts. The Wisconsin Supreme Court appoints one of these judges to be the chief judge and to serve as administrative head of the court of appeals for a three-year term. The chief judge in turn appoints a presiding judge for each of the districts. The clerk of the supreme court serves as the clerk for the court of appeals. Court of appeals judges are elected to six-year terms in the nonpartisan April election and begin their terms of office on the following August 1. They must reside in the district from which they are elected. Only one court of appeals judge may be elected in a district in any one year. In the event of a vacancy, the governor may appoint a person to serve until an election can be held to fill the seat.

The court of appeals has appellate jurisdiction, as well as original jurisdiction to issue prerogative writs. The primary function of the court of appeals is to correct errors that occur at the circuit court level. The court also has supervisory authority over all actions and proceedings except those of the supreme court. The final judgments and orders of a circuit court may be appealed to the court of appeals as a matter of right. Other judgments or orders may be appealed upon leave of the appellate court.

The court of appeals usually sits as a three-judge panel to dispose of cases on their merits. However, a single judge may decide certain categories of cases, including juvenile cases; small claims actions; municipal ordinance and traffic regulation violations; and mental health, contempt, and misdemeanor cases. No testimony is taken in the appellate court. The court relies on the trial court record and written briefs in deciding a case, and it hears oral argument when the judges determine it is needed. Both oral argument and "briefs only" cases are placed on a regularly issued calendar. When it is possible to do so without undue delay of civil cases, the court gives preference on the calendar to expedited and criminal appeals, as well as to appeals statutorily required to be given scheduling preference.

Decisions of the appellate court are delivered in writing, and the court's publication committee determines which decisions will be published. Published opinions have precedential value and may be cited as controlling law in Wisconsin unless overruled by the Wisconsin Supreme Court.

Circuit Court

Website: https://wicourts.gov/courts/circuit/index.htm
Number of state-funded employees: 543.00
Total budget 2021–23: $222,140,700

DISTRICT 1

Carl Ashley, *chief judge*; Stephanie A. Garbo, *administrator*

Contact: 414-278-5115; Milwaukee County Courthouse, 901 North 9th Street, Room 609, Milwaukee, WI 53233-1425

DISTRICT 2
Jason A. Rossell, *chief judge*; Louis Moore, *administrator*
Contact: 262-636-3133; Racine County Courthouse, 730 Wisconsin Avenue, Racine, WI 53403-1274

DISTRICT 3
Paul Bugenhagen Jr., *chief judge*; Michael Neimon, *administrator*
Contact: 262-548-7209; Waukesha County Courthouse, 515 West Moreland Boulevard, Room C-359, Waukesha, WI 53188-2428

DISTRICT 4
Guy D. Dutcher, *chief judge*; Jon Bellows, *administrator*
Contact: 920-424-0027; District Court Administrator's Office, 201 Main Street, Suite 103, Menasha, WI 54952-3125

DISTRICT 5
Thomas J. Vale, *chief judge*; vacant, *administrator*
Contact: 608-267-8820; Dane County Courthouse, 215 South Hamilton Street, Room 6111, Madison, WI 53703-3290

DISTRICT 6
District 6 was eliminated by supreme court order effective July 31, 2018.

DISTRICT 7
Scott L. Horne, *chief judge*; Patrick Brummond, *administrator*
Contact: 608-785-9546; La Crosse County Law Enforcement Center, 333 Vine Street, Room 3504, La Crosse, WI 54601-3296

DISTRICT 8
Carrie A. Schneider, *chief judge*; Thomas Schappa, *administrator*
Contact: 920-448-4280; District Court Administrator's Office, 414 East Walnut Street, Suite 100, Green Bay, WI 54301-5020

DISTRICT 9
Ann Knox-Bauer, *chief judge*; Susan Byrnes, *administrator*
Contact: 715-842-3872; District Court Administrator's Office, 2100 Stewart Avenue, Suite 310, Wausau, WI 54401

DISTRICT 10
Maureen D. Boyle, *chief judge*; Ross Munns, *administrator*
Contact: 715-245-4104; St. Croix County Government Center, 1101 Carmichael Road, Suite 1260, Hudson, WI 54016

The circuit court is the trial court of general jurisdiction in Wisconsin. It has original jurisdiction in both civil and criminal matters unless exclusive jurisdiction is given to another court. It also reviews state agency decisions and hears appeals from municipal courts. Jury trials are conducted only in circuit courts. The circuit court consists of numerous judges serving in 69 circuits. Each circuit consists of the territory of a single county, except for three two-county circuits (Buffalo-Pepin, Florence-Forest, and Menominee-Shawano). Because of the varying size of their caseloads, some circuits have a single judge, while others have multiple judges. Each judge in a circuit holds court separately—circuit judges do not sit as a panel to hear cases—and each judgeship is called a "branch" of the circuit. As of August 1, 2023, there were a total of 261 circuit court branches in the state.

Circuit judges are elected to six-year terms on a nonpartisan basis in the April election and take office the following August 1. The governor may fill circuit court vacancies by appointment, and the appointees serve until a successor is elected. The state pays the salaries of circuit judges and court reporters. It also covers some of the expenses for interpreters, guardians ad litem, judicial assistants, court-appointed witnesses, and jury per diems. Counties bear the remaining expenses for operating the circuit courts.

The circuit court is divided into nine judicial administrative districts, each

Kewaunee County Circuit Court Judge Jeffrey Wisnicky introduces himself to fellow judges during an orientation event for new judges across the state.

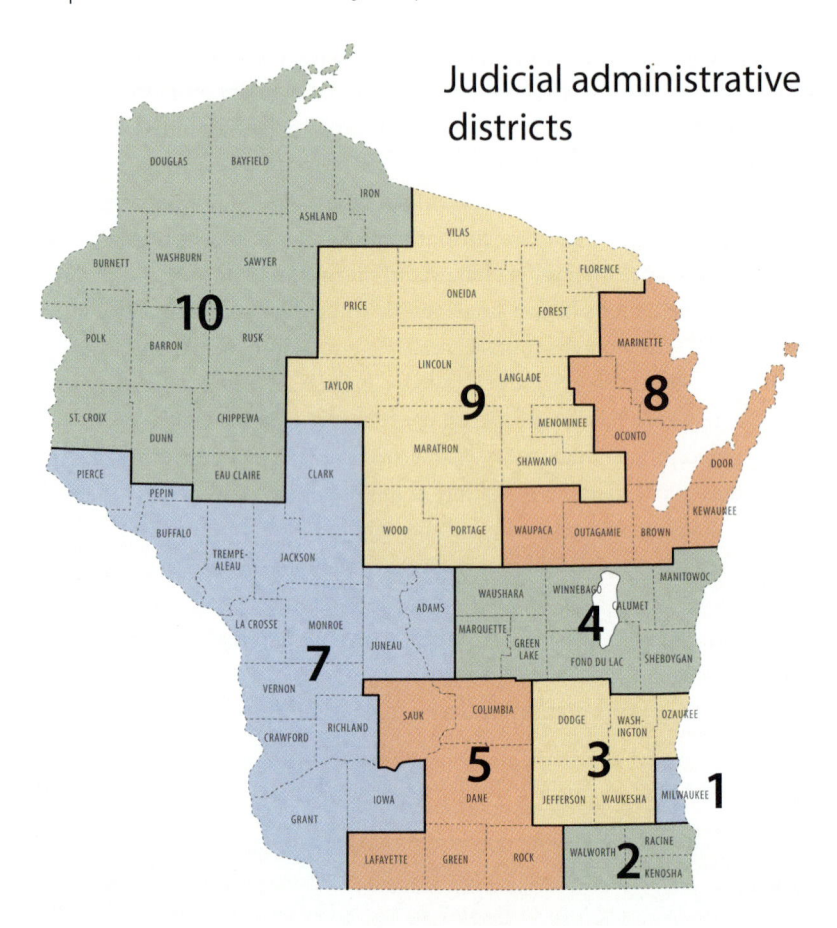

supervised by a chief judge appointed by the supreme court from the district's circuit judges. A judge usually cannot serve more than three successive two-year terms as chief judge. The chief judge has authority to assign judges, manage caseflow, supervise personnel, and conduct financial planning. The chief judge in each district appoints a district court administrator from a list of candidates supplied by the director of state courts. The administrator manages the nonjudicial business of the district at the direction of the chief judge.

Circuit court commissioners are appointed by the circuit court to assist the court, and they must be attorneys licensed to practice law in Wisconsin. They may be authorized by the court to conduct various civil, criminal, family, small claims, juvenile, and probate court proceedings. Their duties include issuing summonses, arrest warrants, or search warrants; conducting initial appearances; setting bail; conducting preliminary examinations and arraignments; imposing monetary penalties in certain traffic cases; conducting certain family, juvenile, and small claims court proceedings; hearing petitions for mental commitments; and conducting uncontested probate proceedings. On their own authority, court commissioners may perform marriages, administer oaths, take depositions, and issue subpoenas and certain writs.

The statutes require the circuit court for Milwaukee County to have full-time family, small claims, and probate court commissioners. In all other counties, the circuit court is required to have a family court commissioner.

Municipal Court

Website: https://wicourts.gov/courts/municipal/index.htm

The legislature has authorized cities, villages, and towns to establish municipal courts to exercise jurisdiction over municipal ordinance violations that have monetary penalties. In addition, municipal courts have the authority to handle first offense Operating While Under the Influence (OWI) cases. Also, municipal courts may rule on the constitutionality of municipal ordinances.

Municipal courts can have multiple branches (judges who hold court separately), and two or more municipalities can form a joint court. As of June 2023, there were 229 municipal courts and 231 municipal judges in Wisconsin. Seventy-three of these courts are joint courts that serve from 2 to 22 municipalities. Milwaukee has the largest municipal court, with three full-time judges.

There are no jury trials in municipal court. All cases are decided by a judge. Upon convicting a defendant, the municipal court may order payment of a forfeiture plus costs, fees, and surcharges, or it may order community service in lieu of a forfeiture. In general, municipal courts may also order restitution up to $10,000. In certain cases, a municipal court may suspend or revoke a driver's license.

If a defendant fails to pay a forfeiture or make restitution, the municipal court may suspend the driver's license or order the defendant to jail. Municipal court decisions may be appealed to the circuit court for the county where the offense occurred.

Municipal judges are elected at the nonpartisan April election and take office on May 1. The term of office is four years, unless the municipality has adopted a charter ordinance designating a different term of at least two years, but less than four years. The governing body determines the judge's salary. There is no state requirement that the office be filled by an attorney, but a municipality may enact such a qualification by ordinance. If a municipal judge is ill, disabled, or temporarily absent, the municipal judge may temporarily designate another municipal judge from any municipality in the state to perform that judge's duties for up to 30 days, subject to an order of the chief judge of the judicial administrative district

The Wisconsin Supreme Court hears oral arguments in two cases at the Waupaca County Courthouse as part of its Justice on Wheels Outreach and Education program. Chief Justice Annette Kingsland Ziegler (*standing*) explains the role of the courts during the opening ceremony.

where the municipality is located. In other circumstances, such as when a judge is disqualified, the chief judge of the judicial administrative district reassigns the matter to another municipal judge. Finally, if a municipal judge is incompetent, is unable to act, or fails to act, the chief justice of the supreme court may assign cases to another municipal judge, a former municipal judge, or a former circuit court judge. If no judge is available, the chief justice may transfer a case from municipal court to circuit court.

Auxiliary entities

Board of Bar Examiners

Chairperson: Daniel Blinka
Director: Jacquelynn B. Rothstein
Location: 110 East Main Street, Suite 715, Madison
Contact: bbe@wicourts.gov; 608-266-9760; PO Box 2748, Madison, WI 53701-2748
Website: wicourts.gov/courts/offices/bbe.htm
Number of employees: 6.00
Total budget 2021–23: $1,432,800

The Board of Bar Examiners administers all bar admissions; it writes and grades the bar examination, reviews motions for admission on proof of practice, and conducts character and fitness investigations of all candidates for admission to the bar, including diploma privilege graduates. The board also administers the Wisconsin mandatory continuing legal education requirement for attorneys.

David T. Prosser Jr. State Law Library

State law librarian: Amy Crowder
Location: 120 Martin Luther King Jr. Blvd., Second Floor, Madison
Contact: wsll.ref@wicourts.gov; 800-322-9755 (toll free); 608-266-1600 (Circulation); 608-267-9696 (reference); PO Box 7881, Madison, WI 53707
Website: http://wilawlibrary.gov

The State Law Library is a public library open to all citizens of Wisconsin. The library supports the information needs of the officers and employees of the state, and of attorneys and the public. The library is administered by the supreme court, which appoints the state law librarian and determines the rules governing library access. The library acts as a consultant and resource for circuit court libraries throughout the state. Milwaukee County and Dane County contract with the State Law Library for management and operation of their courthouse libraries (the Milwaukee County Law Library and the Dane County Law Library).

The library's collection features session laws, statutory codes, case reporters, administrative rules, and legal indexes of the U.S. government, all 50 states, and U.S. territories. It also includes legal and bar periodicals and legal treatises and encyclopedias relevant to all major areas of law. As a federal depository library, it selects federal documents to complement the legal collection. The collection circulates to judges and court staff, attorneys, legislators, and government personnel. The library offers reference, legal research guidance, and document delivery services, as well as training in the use of legal research tools, databases, and websites.

Judicial Commission

Members: Yulonda Anderson, Donald A. Daugherty Jr., Jane Foley, Janet Jenkins, Marci V. Kawski, Mary Beth Keppel, Wynne P. Laufenberg, Judy K. Ziewacz, 1 vacancy
Executive director: Jeremiah C. Van Hecke
Contact: judcmm@wicourts.gov; 608-266-7637; 110 East Main Street, Suite 700, Madison, WI 53703-3328
Website: wicourts.gov/judcom
Number of employees: 2.00
Total budget 2021–23: $690,600

The Judicial Commission conducts investigations regarding allegations that a justice, judge, or court commissioner has committed misconduct or has a permanent disability that substantially impairs his or her judicial performance.

The commission's investigations are confidential. If the commission finds probable cause that a justice, judge, or court commissioner has engaged in misconduct or has a disability that substantially impairs his or her judicial performance, the commission must file a formal complaint of misconduct or a petition regarding disability with the supreme court.

The commission then prosecutes a proceeding against the judge before a three-judge panel or, if the commission so requested when it filed the complaint or petition, before a jury. The panel of judges, or a single judge to preside over a jury proceeding, is selected by the chief judge of the court of appeals. If the proceeding was held before a panel, the supreme court reviews the panel's findings of fact, conclusions of law, and recommended disposition and determines the appropriate discipline in cases of misconduct or appropriate action in cases of permanent disability. If the proceeding was held before a jury, the presiding judge files the jury verdict and his or her recommendations regarding appropriate discipline for misconduct or appropriate action for permanent disability with the supreme court for the court's review.

Judicial Conduct Advisory Committee

Members: Bryan Keberlein, *chair*; M. Joseph Donald, *vice chair*; Cynthia Davis, Dennis Cimpl, Ann Knox-Bauer, Laura Mahan-Schmitz, Christine E. Ohlis, James R. Troupis, 1 vacancy

Contact: 608-266-6828; PO Box 1688, Madison, WI 53701-1688

Website: wicourts.gov/courts/committees/judicialconduct.htm

The Judicial Conduct Advisory Committee gives formal advisory opinions and informal advice to judges and judicial officers regarding whether actions contemplated by the officials comply with the Code of Judicial Conduct. It also makes recommendations to the supreme court about amending of the Code of Judicial Conduct or the rules governing the committee.

Judicial Conference

Website: wicourts.gov/courts/committees/judicialconf.htm

The Judicial Conference is composed of all supreme court justices, court of appeals judges, circuit court judges, and reserve judges; three municipal court judges designated by the Wisconsin Municipal Judges Association; three representatives from the tribal courts; one circuit court commissioner designated by the Family Court Commissioner Association; and one circuit court commissioner designated by the Judicial Court Commissioner Association.

The Judicial Conference meets at least once a year to consider and establish study committees to examine issues relating to the administration of justice and its improvement, consider the reports of such committees, and consider problems pertaining to the administration of justice and make recommendations for improvement; to conduct instructive programs and seminars; to consider and act on reports and recommendations from the committees; to conduct elections; and to consider any other matters and conduct other business included on the agenda.

The Judicial Conference has several standing committees, including committees to prepare model civil, criminal, and juvenile jury instructions. The Judicial Conference may also create additional study committees to examine particular topics. These study committees must report their findings and recommendations to the next annual meeting of the Judicial Conference. The Judicial Conference may also create other committees to perform duties not otherwise covered by the Judicial Conference bylaws.

Judicial Council

Members: William Gleisner, *chair*; Sarah Walkenhorst Barber, Karley Downing, Hon. Eugene Gasiorkiewicz, Lanny Glinberg, Justice Brian Hagedorn, Hon. Thomas Hruz, Steven Kilpatrick, Margo Kirchner, Dennis Myers, Hon. Scott Needham, John Orton, Representative Tusler, Adam Plotkin, Tom Shriner, Hon. Hannah Dugan, Senator Wanggaard, Nick Zales, Sarah Zylstra, 2 vacancies
Contact: 414-651-3182; 19125 Killarney Way, Brookfield, WI 53045
Website: wilawlibrary.gov/judicialcouncil/index.htm

The Judicial Council advises the supreme court, the governor, and the legislature on any matter affecting the administration of justice in Wisconsin, and it may recommend changes in the jurisdiction, organization, operation, or business methods of the courts that would result in a more effective and cost-efficient court system. The council studies the rules of pleading, practice, and procedure and advises the supreme court about changes that will simplify procedure and promote efficiency.

Judicial Education Committee

Members: Justice Rebecca Grassl Bradley, *chair*; Thomas Hammer, Jini Jasti, Randy Koshnick, Lisa K. Stark, Eugene A. Gasiorkiewicz, Thomas R. Hruz, Jason Hanson, Kelly Iselin, Susan Crawford, Gregory Strasser, Jodi Meier, Emily Long, Michael Maxwell, Mark Sanders, Daniel Wood
Director of Office of Judicial Education: Morgan Young
Contact: jed@wicourts.gov; 608-266-7807; Office of Judicial Education, 110 East Main Street, Suite 200, Madison, WI 53703-3328
Website: wicourts.gov/courts/committees/judicialed.htm

The Judicial Education Committee oversees continuing education programs for the judiciary. All supreme court justices and commissioners, appeals court judges and staff attorneys, and circuit court judges and commissioners must earn 60 credit hours of continuing education every six years in approved educational programs. Reserve judges and municipal court judges are subject to similar continuing education requirements. The committee monitors compliance with the continuing education requirements and refers instances of noncompliance to the supreme court. The committee works with the Office of Judicial Education in the Office of the Director of State Courts, which plans and conducts educational seminars for judges and tracks credits earned by judges.

Lawyer Regulation System

Office of Lawyer Regulation: Timothy C. Samuelson, *director*
Preliminary Review Committee: Robert Asti, *chair*
Special Preliminary Review Panel: Bruce A. Schultz, *chair*
Board of Administrative Oversight: Dennis Donohoe, *chair*
Location: 110 East Main Street, Suite 315, Madison
Contact: olr.intake@wicourts.gov; 608-267-7274; 877-315-6941 (toll free); PO Box 1648, Madison, WI 53701-1648
Website: www.wicourts.gov/courts/offices/olr.htm
Number of employees: 27.50
Total budget 2021–23: $6,233,700

The lawyer regulation system consists of several entities that assist the supreme court in supervising the practice of law and protecting the public from professional misconduct by attorneys. The Office of Law Regulation is responsible for screening, investigating, and prosecuting cases involving alleged attorney misconduct or medical incapacity. District Investigative Committees assist in the investigation of certain cases, while the Preliminary Review Committee meets in panels that review investigations and determine whether there is cause to proceed to file a complaint with the court. The Special Investigative Panel investigates allegations of misconduct made against a current participant in the lawyer regulation system, and the Special Preliminary Review Panel receives reports from these panels and determine whether there is cause to proceed. Referees are attorneys or reserve judges appointed by the court to hear discipline cases and make disciplinary recommendations to the court, approve the issuance of certain private and public reprimands, and conduct hearings on petitions for reinstatement of attorney licenses. The Board of Administrative Oversight monitors and assesses the performance of the lawyer regulation system. The supreme court determines appropriate discipline in cases of professional misconduct and appropriate action in cases of medical incapacity.

Office of the Director of State Courts
Director of state courts: Randy R. Koschnick
Deputy director, Office of Court Operations: Holly Szablewski
Deputy director, Office of Management Services: Caitlin M. Frederick
Location: Room 16 East, State Capitol, Madison (director); 110 East Main Street, Madison (staff)
Contact: 608-266-6828 (director); PO Box 1688, Madison, WI 53701-1688 (director); 110 East Main Street, Madison, WI 53703-3356 (staff)
Website: wicourts.gov/courts/offices/director.htm
Number of employees: 160.85
Total budget 2021–23: $47,716,600

The director of state courts is appointed by the supreme court and is the chief nonjudicial officer of the Wisconsin court system. The director is responsible for the management of the court system and advises the supreme court, particularly on matters relating to improvements to the court system. The director supervises most state-level court personnel; develops the court system's budget; and directs the courts' work on legislation, public information, and information systems. This office also controls expenditures; allocates space and equipment; supervises judicial education, interdistrict judicial assignments at the circuit court level, and planning and research; and administers the medical malpractice mediation system.

Planning and Policy Advisory Committee
Chair: Annette Kingsland Ziegler (chief justice of the supreme court)
Contact: 608-266-3121; 110 East Main Street, Suite 410, Madison, WI 53703
Website: wicourts.gov/courts/committees/ppac.htm

The Planning and Policy Advisory Committee advises the Wisconsin Supreme Court and the director of state courts on planning and policy and assists in a continuing evaluation of the administrative structure of the court system. It participates in the budget process of the Wisconsin judiciary and appoints a subcommittee to confer with the supreme court and the director of state courts in the court's review of the budget. The committee meets at least quarterly, and the supreme court meets with the committee annually. The director of state courts participates in committee deliberations, with full floor and advocacy privileges, but is not a member of the committee and does not have a vote.

State Bar of Wisconsin
Board of governors, officer members: Dean R. Dietrich, *president*; Margaret Wrenn Hickey, *past president*; Anna Frances Coyer Munoz, *secretary*; Elizabeth Reeths, *treasurer*; Kristen D. Hardy, *board chair*

Board of governors, district-elected members: Joseph M. Cardamone III, Ryan M. Billings, Elisabeth T. Bridge, Randal J. Brotherhood, Basil J. Buchko, Catarina Anne Colon, Jennifer L. Johnson, Rochelle Johnson-Bent, Lisa M. Lawless, Felicia L. Owen, Thomas J. Pienkos, Mary L. Schanning, Nicholas C. Zales, Renee Ann Read, Julie F. Stodolka, Micabil Diaz Martinez, Alexandra Kathleen Evans, Latrice M. Knighton, AnnMarie M. Sylla, Stephen Walter Sawyer, Gregory James Banchy, Elizabeth A. Fernandez, Marisol Gonzalez Castillo, Alison E. Helland, Kai Hovden, Corey Gayle Lorenz, Mitch, Michael Seung-Hyock Yang, Johanna R. Kirk, Shanna Marie Sanders, Robert G. Barrington, Rachel Eve Maes, Paul P. Dimmer, Lawrence J. Wiesneske

Executive director: Larry J. Martin

Location: 5302 Eastpark Boulevard, Madison

Contact: service@wisbar.org; 608-257-3838 (general); 800-362-9082 (lawyer referral and information service, toll free); PO Box 7158, Madison, WI 53707-7158

Website: www.wisbar.org

The State Bar of Wisconsin is a mandatory professional association of all attorneys who hold a Wisconsin law license. In order to practice law in the state, attorneys must be admitted to practice by the full Wisconsin Supreme Court or by a single justice and must also join the State Bar. The governance and structure of the State Bar are established by the supreme court. The State Bar works to maintain and promote professional standards, improve the administration of justice and the delivery of legal services, and provide continuing legal education to lawyers. The State Bar conducts legal research in substantive law, practice, and procedure and develops related reports and recommendations. It also maintains the roll of attorneys, collects mandatory assessments imposed by the supreme court for supreme court boards and to fund civil legal services for the poor, and performs other administrative services for the judicial system.

3
ABOUT WISCONSIN

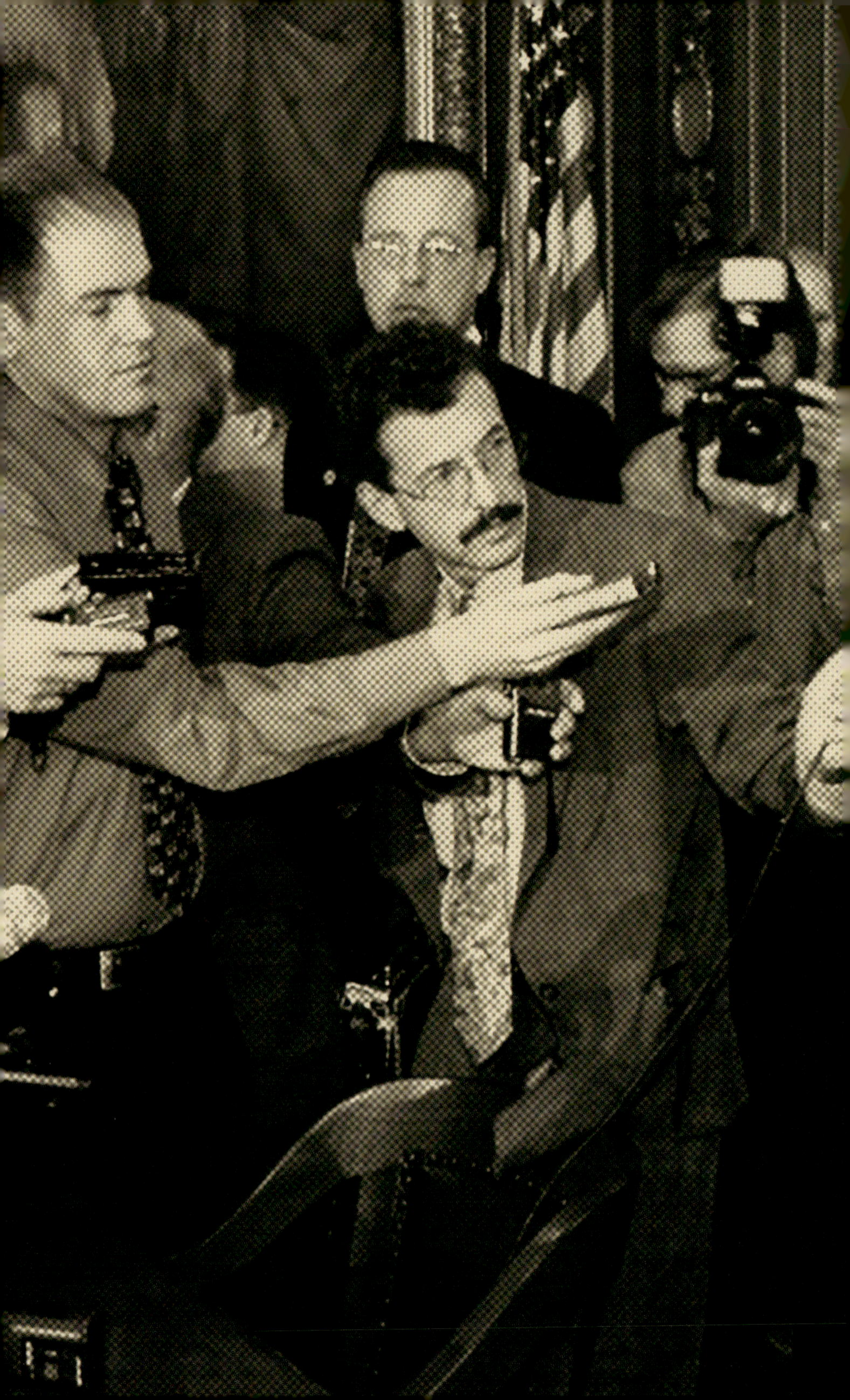

On the Capitol Beat

The scoop on Wisconsin's capitol press corps

by Jillian Slaight

A farmer leafing through the newspaper lingers over an article about agriculture bills before the state senate; a teacher turns up the radio to hear a soundbite of her state representative speaking on a controversial education bill; and a TV segment about a "Hometown Hero" catches the attention of the award recipient's neighbor. For 175 years, Wisconsinites have relied on the capitol press corps to learn what is happening inside the Wisconsin State Legislature. The news coverage these reporters provide may shape whether members of the public approve or disapprove of their elected representatives and, consequently, how they vote. It may also inform legislators' understanding of the issues facing them in committee rooms and on the senate and assembly floors.

The capitol press corps has existed as long as the legislature itself, but many know little about it. Historians draw from newspaper, radio, and television archives to understand and describe key figures in Wisconsin political history, but these sources are silent on the reporters who broke—rather than made—the news. In an effort to illuminate the people behind the bylines, Legislative Reference Bureau staff began conducting long-form audio interviews with past and

Reporters cover remarks from Governor Tommy Thompson in December 2000 at the state capitol in Madison.

present members of the capitol press corps in January 2022. This ongoing oral history project aims to capture the memories of these journalists, whose collective experience spans 50 years, and record stories that might otherwise be lost to history.

This article invites readers to learn more about the role that political reporters play in Wisconsin government. Part I lays out the types of news outlets that have covered the capitol, focusing on how the differences between these outlets shape reporters' experiences. Part II profiles past and present members of the capitol press corps, describing their paths to Wisconsin politics and their efforts to earn reputations for accuracy and trustworthiness. Part III dives into the stories covered by members of the press corps, and Part IV describes the nexus of those stories: the pressroom in 217 SW. Finally, Part V discusses the challenges that capitol reporters face in the course of keeping Wisconsinites informed of the activities of state government—and the rewards that motivate them to pursue this work despite its challenges.

I. The Outlets

Since Wisconsin achieved statehood in 1848, capitol news has been reported by newspaper, wire service, radio, television, and the Internet. The particularities of each type of outlet shape the work of its capitol reporters, dictating their deadlines, word limits, and areas of focus. Each technological development—from the invention of the telegraph wire to the rise of social media—pressures reporters to report political news faster.

"Newspapers in Wisconsin were not far behind the first settlers," writes Donald E. Oehlerts: Albert G. Ellis hauled the first printing press to the territory and began publishing the *Green Bay Intelligencer* in December 1833.[1] Competitors soon sprang up in Green Bay and other emerging settlements. By 1848, most newspapers served as the "political mouthpiece" of a particular person or party; since newspapers reached a wide swathe of voters, they were an efficient way to mobilize political support.[2] Even sparsely populated locales often boasted more than one weekly newspaper: the launch of a Democratic news outlet invariably prompted the launch of a Whig or Republican rival.[3] In this landscape, early statehouse reporters battled to control the narrative around legislative debates and controversies. As a result, competing reports of the same events varied widely.

But over time, neutrality became more profitable than partisanship. As early as the 1840s, newspaper editors began to publish short news dispatches received by telegraph, which broke news from far-flung locales faster than news could travel by train.⁴ Agencies such as the Associated Press (AP) gathered and sold these dispatches to member newspapers across the country. Since these newspapers' party loyalties varied, AP reporters strove for objectivity, and the constraints of wire service reporting—longer copy cost more to transmit—discouraged the inclusion of anything beyond the most essential facts.⁵ By the late nineteenth century, newspaper editors began to follow the AP's lead and emphasized unbiased reporting in order to broaden their readership and attract more advertisers.⁶

Many early capitol reporters covered the state legislature for partisan newspapers, which openly supported specific parties and politicians.

Wire services complemented rather than competed with newspapers, but subsequent technological developments threatened print's dominance. In 1905, the first year the *Wisconsin Blue Book* recorded the names of statehouse reporters, E. R. Petherick of AP was the lone representative of a wire service or national news outlet.⁷ But as radio and television news emerged, reporters from those outlets "scooped" their print competitors by breaking news first and enhancing it with sound and visuals.⁸ Radio news gained ground during World War II by satisfying Americans' demand for a steady stream of information about the conflict.⁹ Television news followed, becoming a substantial force during the turbulent 1960s, when "the political and social turmoil of the decade produced compelling images for television news."¹⁰ Footage of the Dow Riots in 1967, for example, conveyed their intensity to viewers watching hundreds of miles from Madison.

Few sources document the experiences of Wisconsin's early capitol press corps. However, several reporters interviewed for the LRB's oral history project began covering the state legislature in the 1970s and 1980s. Their recollections demonstrate how news outlets shaped the types of stories reporters told and how they told them. Before Internet use became widespread in the late 1990s, the

Women in the press corps

Women reporting on the Wisconsin capitol navigated a male-dominated pressroom for over a century. LRB analyst Isaac Lee identified Alice Krombholz as the first known female member of the press corps, covering the capitol for the *Milwaukee Sentinel* in the mid-1930s. By the early 1940s, an increasing number of women reporters kept Wisconsin updated as the country mobilized for World War II. Betty Pryor reported on the capitol for the United Press during and after the war, when fellow journalists elected her an officer of the newly formed Wisconsin Capitol Correspondents Association.[i] Lucille Bystrom—formerly a society editor for the *Green Bay Press-Gazette*—joined her in the pressroom in 1948 as a capitol correspondent for the *Milwaukee Sentinel*.

Still, the legislature remained something of an "old boys club," and male reporters reaped the benefits of fraternizing with the mostly male legislators. For example, in the 1950s and '60s, politicians and reporters went on alcohol-fueled fishing trips as part of a social club called the Piscatorial and Inside Straight Society (PISS), which boasted members like Governor Warren Knowles.[ii] Male reporters could get tips from adjacent barstools at the Inn on the Park or adjacent bathroom stalls in the men's room between the pressroom and the assembly chamber. By the late twentieth century, the culture began to change. "I never felt like I was being snubbed by the good old boys in the legislature," commented Amy Rinard, who worked the capitol beat in the 1990s. By 2019, nearly half of the capitol press corps members were women. Among this cohort, several interviewees pointed to Gwyn Guenther of The Wheeler Report as a "strong leader" and central figure. In general, Emilee Fannon noted, "women are all there for each other and you can always reach out and talk to someone."

This portrait of Lucille Bystrom, a capitol correspondent during the 1940s, still graces the walls of the pressroom.

PHOTO COURTESY OF THE CAPITOL PRESS CORPS

i. "Capitol Reporters Form Association," *Wisconsin State Journal*, January 17, 1945.
ii. Piscatorial and Inside Straight Society records, 1953–2007, Wisconsin Historical Society Archives, M2010-001 MAD 3/27/A2.

routines and priorities of a reporter for a morning newspaper varied distinctly from those of a wire service reporter or a radio reporter, and even from a reporter for an afternoon paper.

For newspaper reporters, printing schedules dictated deadlines and, consequently, the daily pressures of the job through the 1990s. Reporters not only had to find important stories but also had to race to file them before the newspaper went to press. *Milwaukee Sentinel* reporters, for example, risked missing the widely read state edition of the morning paper if they filed later than six or seven in the evening. Deadlines like these proved problematic during late-night floor sessions, when Steve Walters found himself asking his editors, "Look, if they pass a budget at twelve thirty, do you want to stop the presses and hit, maybe, half the papers for the city of Milwaukee edition? Or do you want to let it pass?" But evening deadlines meant reporters working for the morning papers could start their days later. Tom Still recalled that at the *Wisconsin State Journal* in the 1980s, "nobody was there any earlier than ten." Conversely, reporters for afternoon papers like the *Milwaukee Journal* were expected to file stories before noon. Some reporters viewed these early deadlines as placing the *Journal* at a "competitive disadvantage," especially if news broke in the afternoon.

Opposing deadlines fueled fierce competition, especially between reporters for two Milwaukee papers, the *Milwaukee Journal* and the *Milwaukee Sentinel*, which were bitter rivals before merging in the 1990s. *Sentinel* reporter and later bureau chief Steve Walters noted, "I . . . was judged and scored by how often I beat the *Journal*." His *Sentinel* colleagues considered their paper "the underdog" and focused on undercutting the larger and more amply staffed *Journal* by any means possible, said Amy Rinard. To that end, Rinard and others sought to convince legislators and agency heads to release important information in the afternoon, after the *Journal* deadline had passed. This rivalry also shaped the type of stories each paper published. "The *Sentinel* was very focused on reporting on what happened that day," explained Lee Bergquist. Consequently, shorter stories took precedence over longer, more analytical stories, called "thumb suckers" in reporters' parlance. By contrast, said Dick Jones, the *Journal* compensated for its deadline disadvantage by devoting "more time and more people to . . . explore issues more in-depth." The *Journal* also published a Sunday edition, granting its capitol reporters more space to publish longform articles.

Meanwhile, reporters from other papers carved their own niches. For example, in the 1980s, the *State Journal* differentiated itself from the *Milwaukee Journal* and the *Sentinel* by focusing its attention on executive agencies instead of the internal politics of the legislature. Tom Still described how he devoted several months to pursuing evidence of vulnerabilities in the state computer system, which he and fellow reporter Paul Rix laid bare by hacking into that system.[11] Reporters for local newspapers were more interested in addressing the concerns of their local readership than with scooping the bigger papers. "My job," commented Stan Milam of the *Janesville Gazette*, "[was] to not only cover state government but, more importantly, to cover the local elected representatives and senators on how they worked within those issues." Although these specializations alleviated some of the pressure to scoop other papers, all reporters raced to file stories before their paper's deadline.

In contrast, reporters for wire services like AP and United Press International (UPI) worked against rolling (rather than fixed) deadlines; for these reporters, the pressure to produce stories almost instantaneously predated the rise of the Internet. "If you write for an afternoon newspaper," Dick Jones explained, "you're running throughout the morning until the last absolute deadline, which might be one o'clock in the afternoon. And then you could kick back or catch your breath and work on stories for the next day." But wire service reporters like Jones, who joined UPI in 1974, felt no such relief. Wire service subscribers included various newspapers and broadcasters, which published or aired stories at all hours of the day. Meeting these continuous deadlines was a "migraine-producing experience" akin to "churning out hamburger," reflected Rob Zaleski, who also worked in the UPI's capitol bureau in the 1970s.[12]

Wire service reporters had no fixed deadlines. Instead, they sent news stories to subscriber newspapers and broadcasters via teletype machine, like the one pictured here, at all hours of the day.

Hard limits on story length also continued to distinguish wire service reporting from newspaper reporting, even after reports were no longer carried over telegraph wires. In the 1970s and 1980s, UPI imposed a 300-word limit on most stories. Dick Jones called this limit "a source of frustration" because he "especially enjoyed interviewing people and doing features." Working for AP decades later, in the 2000s, JR Ross also found himself running into word limits. In one instance, he spent months investigating disparities in graduation rates between University of Wisconsin–Madison student athletes and other students, focusing specifically on the 1993 freshman class and members of the Rose Bowl–winning Badger football team. Ultimately, he "crammed everything [that he] could [into] 1,100 words"—the longest story he wrote for AP.

Radio reporting also demands brevity and challenges reporters to communicate complex information in short time frames. "[T]here's only a certain number of facts that you can get across in a one-minute—even a five-minute—radio spot," noted John Powell, who joined the capitol press corps full time in 1975. That same year, John Colbert began covering the capitol for WTSO, where a five-minute newscast contained as many as fifteen stories; none of Colbert's reports could go over forty seconds. Including soundbites from newsmakers, or "actualities," meant losing time to communicate important details about the subject at hand. Jeff Roberts, who ran a capitol news service for subscribing radio stations, filed reports as short as thirty seconds.

Being concise was only half the battle. Radio reporting required technical

Reporter Dick Jones (*center*) interviews Governor Patrick Lucey (*left*) alongside his press secretary, Jeff Smoller (*right*), in the wake of the Menominee Warrior Society's month-long occupation of the Alexian Brothers Novitiate in January 1975.

The art of the interview

John Colbert learned the key to interviewing in 1970, when he was barely 20 years old. His station manager at WCOW Radio in Sparta, Wisconsin, John D. Rice, told him: "Pat Lucey's a Democrat, he's running for governor. Go interview him." With some trepidation, Colbert asked what he should say or ask, to which Rice replied: "Listen. Listen to what he says. Listen to his answers. Pay attention and go from there." That advice guided Colbert throughout his decades-long reporting career. As fellow radio reporter John Powell acknowledged, listening during an interview is no small feat: "[Y]ou have to have some idea of where you're going and what questions you want to ask; [and] at the same time, you have to listen to what the person is saying, and if they say something particularly interesting . . . you have to change gears and follow that up."

In their interviews with the Legislative Reference Bureau, John Colbert (*left*) and John Powell (*right*) said that radio reporting in the 1970s and 1980s required a certain amount of technological expertise and lots of bulky equipment.

expertise and heavy, bulky equipment. In the late 1970s and early 1980s, Colbert recalled, "I had a big leather bag with a Sony tape recorder, a couple of microphones, microphone stand, long cables for the microphone, [and] short cables for plugging into audio systems in the capitol." He carried this bag with him at all times, "because you never know when you might get called up from the radio station at six in the morning to cover a tornado in Barneveld—which I was." Although Powell benefited from a permanent recording space on the third floor of the capitol, he crouched underneath its six-foot ceilings to record stories on a reel-to-reel tape recorder. He produced as many as four stories a day for WHA, which meant not only writing copy but also recording audio and splicing in soundbites for each one.

Reporting to a listening audience, as opposed to a reading audience, also poses distinct challenges. As Powell explained, print not only lets a journalist include more information, but also allows readers to choose whether to skim or absorb each detail, depending on their level of interest. With radio, the audience's attention ebbs and flows: "So many people are in their cars, and you're telling a news story, and the person is cut off in traffic, and they have to mentally divert . . . [and] lose track of what you're saying." These circumstances require radio reporters to think differently about how to capture and retain the audience's attention. To this end, Colbert and Powell both relied on the strength of their voices. Colbert characterized himself as "a reporter who was blessed with having a talent of having a voice," but noted that he never coasted on his natural ability. Instead, he performed frequent "air checks," i.e., recording himself speaking on air, listening back, and critiquing himself. Singing on the drive into work and drinking ice water before a broadcast also helped.

Television reporters, like radio reporters, must pay attention to vocal presentation but have the added complication of visual presentation. While visuals may enhance reporting, incorporating them is time consuming and difficult. Many TV reporters today are multimedia journalists, or MMJs, who are expected not only to report out stories but also to shoot accompanying video and edit the audio and video together. The scope of these responsibilities results in a mad scramble on some busy session days. "I'm trying to gather soundbites on four separate stories," Jessica Arp explained, "but we need sound [and] video for each one of those things." And waiting for the perfect soundbite or video clip, Emilee Fannon noted, often means remaining "stuck behind a camera" in a committee room rather than back in the pressroom, writing her story. A.J. Bayatpour noted that while he enjoys "getting kind of creative with what I'm shooting," juggling information-gathering, shooting, and editing makes for some "very compressed, stressful days."

Moreover, many political stories translate poorly to the TV screen, requiring MMJs to think creatively about visuals. Emilee Fannon explained, "Sometimes politics can be a little black and white. Democrats say this, Republicans say this . . . and here's what the bill will do: X, Y, and Z. But visually telling it can always be a challenge." Both she and Arp alluded to the pitfalls of BOPSA ("bunch of people sitting around") video footage of committee hearings and floor sessions. Arp said she frequently asked herself, "How do we take this story out of the capitol? How do we visualize it to the average person at home?" To this end, TV reporters described relying on stock footage to depict the topic of a bill under debate, such as video of a busy restaurant to accompany a story on a bill about the minimum wage. Selecting the right visual could enliven a story that might otherwise be considered "dry."

Like radio and wire reporters, TV reporters also contend with hard and fast limits on story length. Emilee Fannon's stories used to be capped at one minute and forty-five seconds at ABC 27 and were further reduced when she transferred to CBS 58: "I now get [one minute and fifteen seconds] to tell people everything that happened at a capitol session day." Any time spent explaining backstory to the audience chips away at that limit. Accordingly, Fannon described making difficult decisions about what to cover on air—for example, highlighting the "most compelling" two bills in a package of ten. And as successive hosts of "Capital

Television journalists like Emilee Fannon (*foreground*) have met the challenges of the medium, often communicating complex stories in the span of a minute or less.

Big stories on the small screen

Several interviewees suggested that until recent years, few TV stations devoted resources to meaningful coverage of the capitol; instead, the stations simply sent cameras to key events. The presence of TV cameras, in turn, prompted lawmakers to stage events for better visuals—a source of frustration for reporters in audio and print media. "Too many times, people would bow to the TVs," John Colbert commented. "You'd be [at a] news conference, you'd be there on time at [9 a.m.], and they wouldn't start until twenty after because they were waiting for the cameras to show up." This annoyance prompted disdain towards TV reporters in the pressroom. According to Steve Walters, that began to change with the arrival of Jessica Arp of WISC-TV in 2007. "She really was the first full-time TV reporter that treated it as a serious beat, day in and day out." But Arp and other TV reporters interviewed by the LRB still mentioned feeling they needed to prove themselves to other members of the press corps. Overcoming the perception that TV reporters are "only in it to be on TV," commented A.J. Bayatpour, requires showing up regularly and investing time and energy in understanding the legislative process.

City Sunday" on ABC 27, both Fannon and Bayatpour booked longer interviews with legislators and other state and local officials; Bayatpour explained that these conversations enable him to engage with certain issues in greater depth and build a rapport with legislators.

Finally, in addition to newspaper, wire service, radio, and TV, which are geared toward the general public, subscriber services have delivered news and legislative tracking information for 50 years or more. These services operate much like wire services, providing fast and frequent updates on state government; however, they orient these updates towards an audience of capitol insiders, including legislators and lobbyists. Dick Wheeler cut his teeth as a wire service reporter at UPI before launching The Wheeler Report in 1972, keeping subscribers apprised of everything from floor votes to fiscal estimates and budget motions. By 1998, the service migrated online, with subscribers accessing updates through emails and an accompanying website.[13] Shortly after, in June 2000, Jeff Mayers launched WisPolitics, another Internet-based subscriber news service—or as Mayers called it, "a wire service for political junkies and government junkies."

Although reporters for subscriber services share the same skills as their peers at AP and UPI—the ability to write quickly in a neutral style—their intended audiences differ substantially. As JR Ross explained, "I always said my audience [at AP] was a mile wide and an inch deep. At WisPolitics, my audience is an inch wide and a mile deep." For example, whereas AP does not devote a great deal of attention to changes in legislative leadership beyond the top roles, WisPolitics will analyze the significance of changes in the number four and five leadership spots in a party caucus. Similarly, Gwyn Guenther, who has led The Wheeler Report since her father's death in 2011, has emphasized that the service caters to issues of interest to its subscribers: "We don't write stories on everything the way traditional media do."[14] As

Dick Wheeler earned a reputation as a legend among the capitol press corps. As founder of The Wheeler Report, he created a channel for insider information about the legislature.

the economic models underlying traditional media outlets evolve, it remains to be seen whether the subscription model will expand—whether, as Jeff Mayers put it, everyone would "do like Netflix and [pay] $10 a month for great news."

II. The People

Reporters interviewed by the LRB followed different paths to the capitol pressroom, but their reflections on these paths indicated some key commonalities, including the value of curiosity, discretion, hard work, and help from mentors.

Several interviewees established a connection with the press generally, and newspapers specifically, during childhood. JR Ross's connection developed alongside a Sunday tradition in his household: "My dad got the Sunday paper every week, and we would put a stack of albums on the turntable, and he'd read it from cover to cover. So I was reading the paper from the time I was six or seven—even [when] I couldn't really read it." As an airline mechanic at National Airport in Washington D.C., Tom Still's father brought home newspapers that he found discarded on planes. Still enjoyed paging through the news from disparate places "because . . . as a young person, it gives you a perspective about what's going on elsewhere."

Other interviewees described how specific events sparked their interest in political journalism. John Colbert remembered watching the first televised presidential debate between Richard Nixon and John F. Kennedy as a ten-year-old in 1960 and discussing it with his older brothers around the dinner table. Similarly, Lee Bergquist recalled the excitement he felt upon breaking the news to the

Learning the news business

Before writing for newspapers, several interviewees distributed them. As a kid in Edina, Minnesota, Steve Schultze delivered the *Minneapolis Star* Monday to Saturday. Jeff Smoller was a carrier for the *Milwaukee Sentinel* long before his bylines appeared in the *Milwaukee Journal*. And Patrick Marley spent mornings in Ames, Iowa, delivering the *Des Moines Register*, a paper to which his parents were "religious subscribers." For many, this job was the foundation of their interest in print media—or as Dick Jones explained, "[A]t a very early age, I knew the roar of the pressroom."

> **Renegade broadcaster**
>
> As a high school student, Stan Milam was laser-focused on becoming a disc jockey. Milam and friend Jim Mosher skipped school to secure their third-class FCC permits in Chicago, a prerequisite to working as student engineers at WCLO in Janesville. On the side, the duo installed and operated a radio transmitter in the attic of the Mosher home: "It was only supposed to broadcast in your living room. Well, we souped it up and it covered about a two-or-three-block area. I believe the statute of limitations has run out, so I can admit this—[I] violated federal law." Friends would request songs—by the Beatles, the Rolling Stones, and other "British Invasion" bands—earlier in the day, then park nearby to listen live.
>
> A WIBA disc jockey in the 1950s.

Bergquist household that President Lyndon Johnson would not seek reelection: "He had said it at the end of a telecast from the Oval Office, and my parents had not stayed up to watch him. The next morning, I opened up the paper and it was the top headline. I couldn't wait to tell my parents the news." David Callender recalled the 1972 presidential contest between Richard Nixon and challenger George McGovern, which he followed for a school project, as "the thing that really whetted my interest in government and politics."

For several interviewees, educators encouraged these burgeoning interests by recognizing and fostering their skills as future journalists. For Steve Walters, a fourth grade teacher's affirmation—"Steve, you can write"—set him on a path to newspaper reporting. Likewise, a teacher prompted Emilee Fannon to recognize her potential; after completing a school project that entailed producing a radio broadcast, Fannon's teacher pulled her aside and asked, "Have you ever [thought] of broadcasting? . . . I think you'd be really good at it." John Powell's career had a similar start: when the local radio station in Richland Center called his high school principal looking for temporary on-air talent, the principal volunteered Powell, who had distinguished himself in forensics as an extemporaneous speaker. Initially, the mechanics of a radio control room seemed more daunting to Powell than speaking on air—"My first concern was, now what button to push next?" —but after Powell went on air for the first time, in July 1960, he remained in broadcasting for over 40 years.

Many interviewees worked at their high school newspapers or radio stations, and some cut their teeth at local news outlets. Tom Still's work as an editor for the Mount Vernon High School newspaper won him an opportunity to work as a copy boy at the *Washington Evening Star*, where Still monitored the "wire room," a space filled with machines from the wire services. As printouts of breaking news from AP, UP, and Reuters spat out of these machines, Still tore them off and delivered them to the appropriate copy-editing desks: "That was just such a great experience to be around reporters and editors." JR Ross was actively involved in his high school newspaper while also covering sports part time for the local paper. "That's all I ever wanted to do, is be a journalist," said Ross. Matt Pommer also began as a sports reporter, covering football for the local weekly because his father forbade him from playing football himself.

Following high school, some reporters earned undergraduate or graduate degrees in journalism. But while acknowledging the importance of coursework, most recalled learning the most from hands-on experience. As JR Ross put it, "My real major was the school paper. I spent thirty-plus hours a week there, on top of class, pretty much the entire time I was in school." Likewise, Jessie Opoien described devoting more time to the Iowa State student paper than to her classes, and found that covering faculty senate and board of regents meetings prepared her well for covering the legislature. Opoien even convinced some fellow reporters to drive up to Madison during a snowstorm to cover Act 10 protests in early 2011. A.J. Bayatpour aired stories on a student TV station that also served as the local NBC affiliate for Central Missouri: "If it's bad, somebody forty-five minutes away can see it and call the newsroom and say, 'What was that? What in the world did I just watch?' . . . That pressure forces you to perform."

Several interviewees gained experience in high school through writing their own stories or "ripping and reading" wire service reports from AP or UPI, like this Beloit College student.

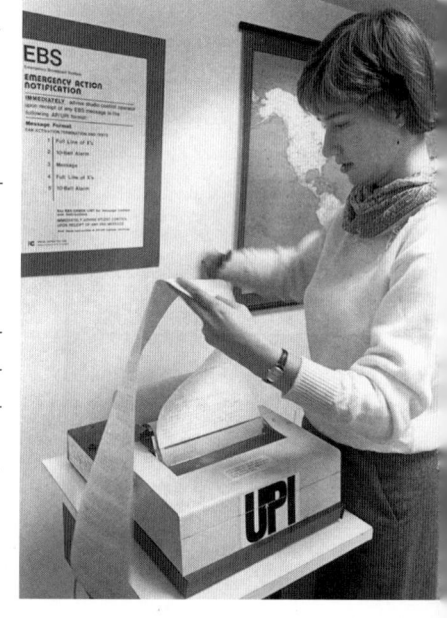

Interviewees leveraged college experiences like these into paying jobs in journalism. In the late 1960s, Jeff Smoller's stories for the *Daily Cardinal*, the University of Wisconsin paper, caught the attention of the *Milwaukee Journal*. The paper offered him work covering the campus—especially protests surrounding the Vietnam War and other issues—as a "stringer," a reporter paid per story. "I became a heck of a stringer. By the second year, I became the head correspondent." Likewise, David Callender joined the *Capital Times* as an intern and subsequently reported for the paper as a suburban stringer, covering local government issues in suburbs such as Middleton, Monona, and Fitchburg.

Many capitol reporters started on the crime beat—the subject area, according to Jessie Opoien, "that every young journalist gets shoved into covering." Working for the City News Bureau, a Chicago wire service, Lee Bergquist scoured police stations for information: "You would go around every couple of hours and check in with [police officers] and say, 'Anything going on?'" Molly Beck covered the same beat for a small daily in southern Minnesota, and while there were fewer crimes to report than in Chicago, it was an active and instructive beat. "It taught me a lot about managing my time and being able to turn around stories really quickly, because we had [a] quota: we had to write three stories a day."

Reporters also honed their skills at smaller newspapers. Amy Rinard gained expertise at the Polk County *Ledger*, for which she covered everything from the circuit court and the county board to deer hunting and snowmobile racing. "You're the only reporter covering your entire community," Patrick Marley explained of his time with the *Brookfield News*, "so you've got to cover the school board. You've got to cover the city council. You've got to do profiles. You've got to write about businesses. So you have to do everything." These broad responsibilities helped clarify for Marley the type of stories he enjoyed covering.

Some reporters covered other state legislatures before coming to Madison, but they acknowledged the limits of prior legislative experience. "The spotlight wasn't so bright," Scott Bauer remarked of his work in the Nebraska Legislature, where he learned political reporting in a smaller state with more predictable politics. "Once I came [to Wisconsin], that was a whole different level of spotlight." Walters put it bluntly: "Nobody in this capitol was impressed that I'd covered the Iowa Legislature. I had to prove my ability to cover this place." Familiarity with the particularities of Wisconsin politics was paramount. Although Steve Schultze became familiar with the legislative process during his time in the Minnesota Legislature, he knew little about the "huge cast of characters" under the capitol dome in Madison. "Yes, you can cover the day-to-day legislation, you can read a bill," Emilee Fannon noted of her transition to Madison from Springfield, Illinois, "but what happened ten years ago?"

Most members of the press corps described "ad hoc" training, often with no formal introductions to legislators and legislative staff. "You're putting out a newspaper every day," Steve Schultze pointed out, "so you don't really have time to do a whole lot of that." Patrick Marley, who arrived at the tail end of the 2003–04 legislative session, observed that "It wasn't the greatest time to show up. . . . But [I] don't think there ever is, because . . . you're dropped in the deep end either way." Unsurprisingly, interviewees described feeling overwhelmed by the sheer volume of information needed to understand the workings of the capitol. Jessie Opoien and JR Ross both compared their attempts to absorb information to "drinking from a firehose." Ross took the *Blue Book* home to cram biographical information about legislators while doing laundry: "I knew how to be a journalist, but I didn't know the ins and outs of the capitol—who the players were." Others relied on The Wheeler Report or trial subscriptions to WisPolitics. And in addition to scrambling to digest these materials, rookies endeavored to identify and establish relationships with sources who could explain or provide context around certain situations. For Molly Beck, that meant "lots of phone calls."

Newcomers in any field inevitably blunder, and interviewees shared tales of their most cringeworthy moments. Emilee Fannon mispronounced "Lodi," which quickly prompted more than a dozen calls to the newsroom: "People were very upset." Embarrassing incidents often stemmed from ignorance about certain unwritten codes of the "tradition-bound" press corps. In the 1970s and 1980s, newbie reporters provoked consternation when they unwittingly occupied choice seats in the assembly and senate chambers that were unofficially assigned to veteran journalists like AP's Art Srb—or occupied undesirable seats customarily reserved for less prestigious news outlets. After two weeks with the *Milwaukee Journal*, Steve Schultze recalled, "Somebody took me aside and said, 'Don't go sitting over on the other side of the chamber. That's where the people from the little Podunk papers who show up twice during the session [sit].'" Schultze described feeling sheepish but also thinking the custom a bit "silly."

Newcomers consequently looked to longstanding members of the press corps as essential mentors. When Dick Jones first covered assembly floor sessions in the 1970s, he sat beside Cliff Behnke of the *Wisconsin State Journal*, who guided him through various confusing customs—"you know, the engrossed votes, the move for reconsideration, and all the parliamentary stuff." Dick Wheeler played a similar role for several generations of reporters, many of whom described him as a font of knowledge about the Wisconsin State Legislature. "There were many, many, many times," recalled Scott Bauer, "where I would just turn to Dick and say, 'Is this important? What does this mean? Can they do that? What is this procedural move?'" Veteran reporters not only demystified legislative maneuvers but also contextualized perennial political issues. Dick Wheeler, Matt Pommer, and Art Srb had "seen it all," commented David Callender. They could unpack complex issues like shared revenue or higher education funding, explaining, "This is how they did it the last time," or "This is why it's in the mess that it's in right now."

Mentors often provided much-needed morale boosts at times when new reporters felt demoralized. The *Milwaukee Journal*'s Gene Harrington buoyed Stan Milam: "Here I am, I'm nothing," Milam recalled. "I'm new at the *Janesville Gazette*, which I think was the smallest paper that had a Madison bureau." Harrington pulled him aside and reassured him, "Kid . . . you're getting a lot of gas from everybody, but you'll do just fine." Milam also described how Neil

Rules of engagement

Until the late twentieth century, the press operated by certain unspoken rules. Among them, any press conference with the governor came to an immediate conclusion when the most senior reporter present said, "Thank you, Governor"—a tradition apparently modeled after White House press corps custom.[i] For many years, John Wyngaard wielded this authority, having covered the capitol for the *Green Bay Press-Gazette* and *Appleton Post-Crescent* from the 1940s onward. How did Wyngaard determine when to utter the magic words? Matt Pommer guessed that Wyngaard interceded after his fellow reporters had questioned the governor on all the major issues of the day and begun to "wander afield into minor things."

On occasion, another party usurped the senior reporter's authority, but more often, breaches of custom were accidental rather than intentional. When Stan Milam began covering the capitol for the *Janesville Gazette*, no one apprised him of the tradition. One day, after Art Srb of AP thanked the governor, other reporters rose to leave, but Milam started to interject: "I'm going, 'Well, I want to—.'" Milam realized that everyone was staring at him. Laughing at the incident in retrospect, he summed up: "You learn those lessons."

Ultimately, the tradition seemed to have died in the 1990s, in large part due to lack of awareness. As press conferences became larger, expanding beyond a handful of pressroom mainstays, reporters unfamiliar with the unspoken protocol increasingly disregarded it. But Pommer also attributed the shift to Governor Tommy Thompson, who "just kept going" if he decided there was more to say.

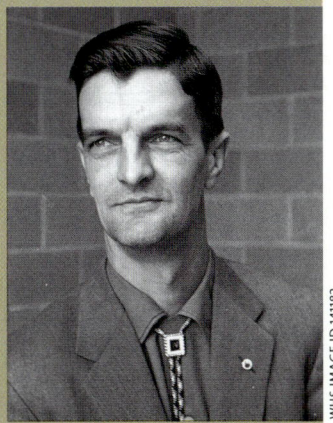

John Wyngaard, whose career spanned four decades, became the unofficial steward of capitol press corps traditions.

i. Donald A. Ritchie, *Reporting from Washington: The History of the Washington Press Corps* (Oxford: Oxford University Press, 2005), 119–20; Merriman Smith, *Thank You, Mr. President* (New York: Harper & Brothers, 1946), 17.

Shively counseled him on how to cover an impossibly broad slate of stories and deadlines: "Calm down. Prioritize." Shively said, "What if one of the stories didn't get published? Which one has to get published? Start there." Those encouragements often meant the difference between soldiering on and bowing out. JR Ross acknowledged that Dick Wheeler kept him afloat during a difficult first year in the capitol, admitting, "I don't know if I'd have made it without him."

Over time, fresh reporters gained their footing and established a name for themselves. In some instances, new reporters might benefit from the standing of their news outlet. "People take your phone calls when you're calling from the AP," Scott Bauer said. But as he noted, reporters must build their own reputations through their work: "You prove that you're going to be fair and you're going to be accurate." To this end, reporters emphasized the importance of building mutual trust. According to Stan Milam, reporters and public officials followed an unwritten rule in the 1980s and 1990s: "I will never intentionally misquote you or blindside you with something. In exchange, you will never lie to me." Jason Stein operated by a similar principle, commenting, "Sometimes it's as simple as just not surprising people." That means keeping the cover of an anonymous source or refraining from quoting a source who agreed only to speak on background. It might also mean calling the subject of a story to provide advance notice and an opportunity to react. Reporters who fail to meet these standards do so at their peril. "In politics, your word is your currency," JR Ross explained. "If people can't trust you, then you don't have any currency in the building."

Keeping that currency also demands adherence to strict standards of nonpartisanship. Interviewees described certain basic rules of nonpartisanship: no yard signs, no petitions, no political contributions, and as Scott Bauer put it, "nothing that would give the appearance either in reality or perception that you're aligned with one side or the other." As an example, Jason Stein mentioned that he could not become a range safety officer at his gun club because the position required joining the National Rifle Association, an active lobbying organization.

Beyond avoiding partisan affiliations and activities, reporters must refrain from disclosing their opinions on political issues. Journalists are not "robots who don't have thoughts and feelings and opinions about things," Jessie Opoien said. The trick is keeping those thoughts, feelings, and opinions private. As an example, a radio interviewer pressed Patrick Marley to share his opinion of Act 10 during the height of the protests around the controversial 2011 legislation. He reacted by saying, "I'm not going to tell you what I think of it. I'm here to tell you that I think it's important enough for people to know about." Similarly, JR Ross explained that he relies on phrases like "I hear," "I understand," and "people tell

In May 1979, members of the capitol press corps engaged in friendly competition with legislators on the baseball field, with Governor Lee Dreyfus acting as umpire. The Yellow Journalists won 7–1, with Assembly Speaker Ed Jackamonis stealing home for the legislators' sole run.

Social connections

Most interviewees described themselves as uninterested in pursuing social relationships with legislators, staffers, or other sources. As Steve Schultze put it, reporters' relationships with newsmakers are "adversarial" by nature. Still, some reporters enjoyed personal relationships while establishing guardrails. Through the 1980s, for example, a rotating group of politicians and reporters gathered for Friday lunches at the Avenue Bar and various other downtown restaurants. Reporters Matt Pommer, Frank Ryan, Tim Wyngaard, Neil Shively, and Cliff Miller were sometimes present, as were Democratic and Republican politicians, such as Bill Kraus, chief of staff to Governor Lee Dreyfus, and Governor Tony Earl. Participants talked politics, but everything was off the record. Social connections—whether sharing a beer or shooting hoops at a nearby basketball court—did not insulate anyone against unfavorable coverage. "You might have a basketball game one day and a scathing exposé the next," Tom Still recalled.

> **Off the record**
>
> Sometimes, working with sources took on a "cloak and dagger" aspect as reporters attempted to honor sources' desire for secrecy. David Callender described an instance in which a source agreed to meet with him to confirm details of a story about alleged rifts among justices of the State Supreme Court: "My source agreed to meet me in the stacks of the [State] Law Library, and I passed across the draft of the story in a brown envelope to my source, who was on the other side of the stacks and who then read the story and confirmed each paragraph." Before he knew it, Callender looked up to an empty space in the stacks: "My source disappeared."

me" to underscore the fact that he is reporting—rather than opining on—the news. Steve Walters prided himself in keeping his political opinions so close to the vest that even his children remained in the dark.

Once reporters establish a reputation, sources—including lawmakers, legislative staff, and state agency officials—may seek them out with tips and information. As Jason Stein explained, someone with a "track record" on a certain subject knows more about that subject and "will be in a better position to do a good story on it." For example, because of her extensive and ongoing coverage of the Brewers stadium issue in the early 1990s, Amy Rinard received a call from a state agency official hinting that she should send an open records request for correspondence between his agency and Bud Selig; the correspondence showed that the Brewers expected taxpayers to cover more costs associated with the new stadium than previously understood. Similarly, Jessie Opoien described a "ripple effect" from her reporting on challenges faced by women in politics. On the basis of those stories, she received tips relating to sexual misconduct within the legislature from sources who trusted her with a "really sensitive issue."

Granted, having a reputation for fairness does not guarantee that legislators will look favorably on a journalist. "You're a journalist covering politics," said JR Ross, "so nobody's ever happy with you 100 percent." A.J. Bayatpour described a "mutual understanding" that permeates his interactions with legislators: "I'm not this caricature of what they think the media is, and . . . they're not a caricature of what people might think a politician is." To maintain that understanding, several reporters said that they welcome legislators to contact them directly with criticism. Patrick Marley said, "I try to take it seriously and see, is there a kernel of truth here? Is there something that I'm not getting at or something I'm missing?" Likewise, Steve Walters described asking himself, "Did I screw this up? Or did I run afoul of somebody's ego?"

Interviewees stressed that legislators rarely react to their reporting with overt hostility. John Colbert recalled approaching Representative Walter Ward in 1977 to ask for a statement on allegations that he had improperly claimed telephone expenses. Rather than say "No comment," Ward kicked Colbert out of his office.[15] Years later, Dick Jones described being "dumbfounded" after Senator Chuck Chvala ran into him on State Street and proceeded to "rip into [him] about some story." (Senator Mike Ellis happened to be nearby and "took delight" in witnessing the confrontation, prompting Jones to laugh about it himself.) Reporters working more recently described legislators and their staff as avoiding direct confrontations like these: instead, someone holding a grudge might simply ignore or turn down a request for an interview because, as Jessie Opoien reasoned, "We're Midwestern, right? . . . We don't ever want to have a fight about it."

III. The Stories

In their interviews, capitol reporters reflected on their coverage of the biennial legislative session, as well as other stories about the operations of state government. Although some said they preferred covering certain parts of the legislative session, most appreciated the variety involved. "It's kind of like the change of the seasons," Scott Bauer explained. And like subzero Wisconsin winters, journalists tolerate "sitting in on the [assembly or senate] floor at three in the morning" only because it is temporary. The months following the passage of the biennial budget are a time to "get your head above water for a second and catch your breath" before returning for fall floor sessions, said A.J. Bayatpour. With the conclusion of the legislative floor period comes the start of election season in the spring of even-numbered years, "and then right around the time when you start getting tired of people trying to get you to write their [opposition] research talking points," said Jessie Opoien, "it's time to go back to the legislature."

Floor sessions are particularly unpredictable. To start, the legislative calendar usually entails frequent delays. David Callender put it this way: "Nine o'clock comes around and nothing happens. And then eleven o'clock, and eleven o'clock becomes one o'clock, and one o'clock becomes three o'clock," and so on until "they've adjourned and nothing has happened." Even when they start on time, floor sessions may extend late into the night. Reporters described having watched, bleary-eyed, as tempers frayed in the early morning hours. JR Ross recalled a heated debate during which one senator wrenched out a piece of the chief clerk's AV equipment and threw it to the ground. "You're trying to describe that," he recalled, but "You haven't had any sleep. You've been in this room for twenty-four

Dick Jones was called up to cover the Menominee Warrior Society's takeover of the Alexian Brothers' Novitiate (Gresham, WI) in January 1975. He expected to be there for a day but stayed for a week. His reporting earned him a banner headline in the *Milwaukee Journal*—and a Marlon Brando sighting.

hours, essentially." As Jessie Opoien joked, the press endure marathon floor sessions under less-than-ideal conditions: "When they do press conferences in the front of the chamber and we get to sit in the legislators' seats, I'm like, 'Well, no wonder you guys can stay here this whole time! This is very comfortable. We have to sit on just wood.'"

Still, journalists conveyed the thrill of watching and reporting on legislative debate. John Colbert said that although his scheduled hours were five in the morning to one in the afternoon, "I found it so interesting, I'd stick around." At the conclusion of a late-night floor session, he would simply shower and return to the radio station at five to deliver that morning's newscast. Colbert once brought his teenage daughter Robin for an all-night floor session: "She got the bug right there" and eventually pursued a career in radio news. For Amy Rinard, late floor sessions meant an early morning commute back home to Jefferson County. But, like magic, her stories appeared in print just hours after her return: "By nine or nine thirty, my newspaper gets delivered at my house in my newspaper tube on my driveway. And there's my story."

Most reporters described press conferences—in contrast to floor sessions—as being fairly uninteresting and limited in their usefulness. For one thing, the communal nature of a press conference prevents any one reporter from scooping another. "You asked a question at a news conference," Tom Still pointed out, "and whatever the answer is, you just shared it with everybody else you're competing with." Reporters often attend press conferences for the sake of not missing something, rather than in hopes of "[having] this great story develop in front of your eyes," Still explained. Nevertheless, reporters try to make the most of press conferences by asking questions intended to derail the speaker. John Colbert shared his delight at "getting people off script," especially during press conferences that involved a long line of speakers before the designated question-and-answer period. After the first speaker, Colbert would interject, "I'm sorry, I have to leave. But I have one question just to clarify what you said." His question would invariably prompt a question from another journalist, and "it would just blow up on them." As Jessie Opoien noted, the "unwritten rule" of press conferences is that for each topic a politician wishes to discuss, reporters will ask about "ten other things."

Several reporters singled out Matt Pommer as being particularly skilled at "flipping" a press conference, i.e., asking a question that turns the event in an unforeseen direction. *Cap Times* colleague David Callender described how Pommer would "ask a series of very probative questions that . . . create a trap unless you really understand where he is going with them." Pommer himself recalled a press conference in the mid-1960s at which legislators touted a system of higher education in which professors would primarily teach in lieu of conducting research.[16] "What about Har Gobind Khorana?" Pommer asked, referring to the Nobel Prize–winning University of Wisconsin biochemist. "Do you want him to teach?" The question placed the speaker in a tight spot, at risk of responding in a way that undermined Dr. Khorana's prestigious work. In another instance, Pommer and Tim Wyngaard of the *Green Bay Press-Gazette* arrived at a meeting of the UW Board of Regents but quickly realized that "there was no news." So they asked UW President Fred Harrington what he thought about hosting a Packers game at Camp Randall. Harrington's response—he approved—made the front page of the *Cap Times*, eclipsing any reporting on the meeting itself.[17]

As an exception to the rule, several interviewees described how Governor Lee Sherman Dreyfus spoke so unpredictably, and with such roundabout wording, that reporters hung on his every word during press conferences. To start, the governor's flexibility on certain issues often caught reporters off guard. "If you left his news conference early to meet a deadline," Dick Jones recalled, "you would run the risk of him perhaps changing his mind later in the news conference and taking a [different position] on what you were writing about." In addition, Dreyfus was far from straightforward. "[Dreyfus] was a funny man, and he was very quotable," John Colbert noted, but "he didn't always say what you thought he said." John

Powell explained that words that had sounded "perfectly good and wonderful" coming out of the governor's mouth prompted some head scratching when Powell transcribed them later. Radio reporters like Colbert and Powell were already accustomed to carrying tape recorders, but print reporters adopted them during the Dreyfus administration to sort out the governor's statements.

Whether covering the legislature or the governor, several interviewees described the importance of doing so in a way that feels relevant to Wisconsinites. "There is always a temptation to get caught up in the intrigue," David Callender explained. "[But] you walk out of the building, a block in any direction, and nobody knows who any of these people are. What they care about is, 'What are you doing, and how is what you're doing affecting me?'" To this end, when interviewing a legislator on a particular bill, Jessica Arp always asked for an introduction to the person who inspired that bill. She reasoned that the person's story could bring the legislation to life for her TV audience. Jessie Opoien also said she took pride in stories that demonstrate how legislation touches people's lives; for example, in the wake of newly enacted laws restricting access to abortion, Opoien spent a day shadowing patients at a Planned Parenthood clinic. "It was eye opening, because you write about these laws in an abstract way of 'This is what it does.' But it was just so different to actually see how those laws work in practice." Although the demands of the job often keep them close to the building, capitol reporters recalled stories like these as highlights.

Interviewees also highlighted stories that exposed problems in state government. David Callender spotlighted his reporting on the Supermax prison in Boscobel, which he pursued through the story of a young car thief who was

Among the press, Governor Lee Dreyfus earned a reputation for being unpredictable, engaging, and accessible, welcoming exchanges with reporters rather than shying away from them.

WHS IMAGE ID 55047

incarcerated under increasingly restrictive conditions there. "We were able to use this kid's story as symptomatic of many of the problems that were occurring in Supermax," said Callender, including "the fact that this was an institution that was not built for de-escalating mental health issues." Reflecting on that story and its aftermath, Callender spoke to the role of journalists in shedding light on the inevitable shortcomings of policy-making. "There's never going to be a perfect policy," he conceded. With that in mind, journalists "[enable] folks to understand what's being done in their name and by their legislators and in their communities, and how those things can be improved or changed."

Steve Walters convinced his editors at the *Milwaukee Sentinel* to let him cover Governor Thompson's annual motorcycle tour through Wisconsin, a tradition that began in 1995. Although initially disappointed not to be riding a Harley himself, Walters was relieved to be sitting behind the wheel of his Volkswagen when a downpour soaked Governor Thompson on the first day of the tour.

Likewise, Patrick Marley's extensive coverage of Lincoln Hills shed light on major problems there. Over the course of several years, Marley spoke with workers, both over the phone and in person at nearby bars, about what they had seen or heard at the juvenile correctional facility. He also took calls from concerned family members who shared details that were otherwise impossible to uncover because juveniles' records are sealed. At the same time, he requested and sifted through pages upon pages of documents from the Department of Corrections. All these sources provided as many dead ends as decent leads—and a fair amount of pushback from sources themselves. "It's not something I enjoyed covering," Marley noted, "but it's something I've felt gratified having covered—that I helped expose some very significant problems."

Interviewees also expressed gratification and pride in reporting that aimed to keep Wisconsinites informed ahead of elections. In her "Reality Check" series, Jessica Arp dug into claims made in candidates' campaign ads and speeches, sometimes at the prompting of TV viewers who ran into her at the grocery store: "People wanted to have information to make informed decisions, but the world doesn't always allow them the time to do that. And they would see these ads on TV and be like, 'All right, is that really true? Does that guy really hate puppies?'" In one instance, Arp pored over all the cases on a judge's docket to debunk his claim to have tried a wide variety of violent crime cases. For her part, Jessie Opoien hosted a podcast called "Wedge Issues" ahead of the November 2018 elections, interviewing candidates for state office on key issues. She found that these interviews humanized candidates in a way that helped listeners feel better informed.

IV. The Place

Although plans for the capitol that were drawn up in 1909 contained a dedicated press space, it appears this room, which was adjacent to the assembly parlor, was never used as intended.[18] Reporters remained nomads in the building they covered daily. That ended in 1947, when Senate Joint Resolution 20 provided that Room 204 S, formerly a men's restroom, be made available "for use as a press room during the 1947 legislative session." The state would provide surplus tables, chairs, and rugs, and reporters would be held responsible for any damages to the room or its furnishings.[19] This space served as the pressroom until 1971, when reporters relocated to 217 SW, a circular room between the senate and assembly chambers. Later renumbered 235 SW, the same room remains their home base today.[20] In their interviews with the LRB, reporters described the pressroom as more than a physical space; it facilitates effective reporting, encourages connections with elected officials, and creates a sense of community among the press.

Until the 1990s, when the pressroom was remodeled as part of the capitol renovation, the space was cramped and chaotic. Lean back too far, and Steve Walters might collide with fellow *Sentinel* reporter Amy Rinard; open the door too hard, and he might hit Joanne Haas of UPI. Workspaces were separated by partitions "piled high with materials that could easily go up in flames," making the room a veritable "fire trap." Reporters' smoking habits—from Stan Milam's cigarettes to Neil Shiveley's cigars and Dick Wheeler's pipe—only exacerbated the problem. "Everybody smoked," Milam recalled. "It was a cloud in there." Ultimately, 1999 Wisconsin Act 72 prohibited smoking in the state capitol building, although most reporters had ceased smoking inside by that time.

Heat posed another significant hazard. Before air conditioning was installed in the early 1990s, the pressroom would become sweltering, especially as the afternoon sun poured in through the tall windows. Amy Rinard would escape to the State Law Library, just above the State Supreme Court chambers, to bask in its air conditioning. Art Srb reportedly tried to beat the heat with a large, loud, and unwieldy oscillating fan nicknamed the Gerald Lorge Memorial Fan after the longtime (and, at the time, still very much alive) state senator. Stan Milam remembered one especially hot day when everyone in the pressroom was struggling to file stories on deadline. "All of a sudden," he recounted, "Art starts screaming . . .

Many interviewees cited Neil Shively as a top-notch reporter, a key mentor, and a source of levity in the pressroom.

Friendly wagers

During Neil Shively's tenure in the capitol press corps, the pressroom hosted an annual election pool. One day, a chart would appear in the pressroom, and journalists and legislative aides would submit a dollar each to join. Participants bet on winners and winning vote percentages in a handful of key legislative districts. WPR's John Powell fondly recalled the year he came out on top with $24 and "bragging rights." Of course, pool participants took some flack for their positions. In 1986, Stan Milam voted against the likelihood of Tommy Thompson winning the governorship and never heard the end of it from Thompson.

[T]he Gerald Lorge Memorial Fan had caught his pant leg! And it was eating up his trousers! And Art is kicking this thing, and he's still typing. He had a deadline. So he's fighting off the Gerald Lorge Memorial Fan and typing at the same time."

A hodgepodge of surplus and scavenged furniture reinforced the pressroom's chaotic atmosphere. "Before the capitol renovation, the furniture looked like what's on the curb at hippie Christmas," John Powell said, referring to the profusion of castoff furniture in Madison every year at the end of student leases. Amy Rinard recalled working on a green metal World War II–era typist's desk, flanked by another colleague's ancient, oversized wooden desk and a TV stand that housed the *Sentinel*'s telephone and answering machine. Over time, reporters developed a knack for "scavenging furniture from the hallways." To Powell, the atmosphere was a point of pride: "Some of us . . . were really proud of it. That we were not feathering our nests . . . [and] that this was basically hand-me-down furniture and a place to work, which is the image that I think most of us wanted to project." Since the capitol renovation, the room now boasts uniform desks and chairs, but retains a lived-in feel: "Reporters are not the neatest," Jason Stein conceded. "It's not like an army barracks in terms of being spick-and-span."

Many reporters told the LRB that the pressroom—rather than their outlet's offices or newsroom—served as their home base. As Jason Stein put it, "I tried to be at the capitol more because I felt that that was where I . . . would be most likely to learn news relating to state government." Long before they became available online, legislative materials—from press releases to service agency reports—would be printed and delivered to pressroom mailboxes. Amy Rinard associated certain sounds with Legislative Fiscal Bureau reports: "They'd go *thunk, thunk, thunk, thunk*. . . . And you'd go, 'Oh, that sounds like news.'"

Working from the pressroom also granted reporters, especially those from the Milwaukee outlets, an opportunity to work independently from their editors. Steve Schultze explained that while *Journal* editors frequently telephoned, "You felt like you were more on your own and didn't have people breathing down your neck." Amy Rinard agreed: at a substantial distance from the *Sentinel* newsroom, "you couldn't be micromanaged."

Autonomy from editors came at the cost of unpredictability because, as Rinard put it, "That room was everybody's room. And whatever was going on in there, we weren't in charge of it." Legislators and cabinet secretaries sometimes appeared in their workspace without warning. One day, Rinard was finishing a story on deadline when Governor Thompson and Department of Administration Secretary Jim Klauser entered the pressroom, armed with "a handful of tiny plastic shot glasses and a bottle of . . . Schnapps or something." She had filed and sent

After months reporting from the capitol basement, Amy Rinard (*left*) and Joanne Haas (*right*) admire a plaque commemorating the 1998 budget provision granting the press future use of their second-floor space.

Safeguarding the pressroom

In 1995, the capitol press corps found itself temporarily relegated to the basement, and some feared they might remain there indefinitely. Dick Wheeler, head of the Capitol Correspondents Association, accused senate leaders of having "no intention of ever providing working facilities for the media on the second floor again" and made it his mission to counter their plans.[i] "He was very, very protective of the pressroom," Stan Milam recalled, noting its strategic location between the senate and assembly chambers. By contrast, the windowless basement offices were difficult to access and left reporters with no sense of whether it was day or night.

Wheeler began to lobby informally for the press's return to 217 SW and found an opening during a chance encounter with Mark Bugher, the secretary of administration under Governor Tommy Thompson. Wheeler and David Callender were eating their lunches outside the capitol when Bugher spotted them and asked if there was anything he could do for them, whereupon Wheeler launched into the predicament with respect to press workspace. His initiative paid off: weeks later, the Department of Administration included the following language among changes requested to the governor's budget repair bill: "The circular room on the 2nd floor of the capitol located between the assembly and senate chambers shall be made available for the use of the capitol press corps." With the enactment of 1997 Wis. Act 237 in June 1998, this language was codified under Wis. Stat. § 16.835. "It wasn't that we were necessarily doing it for ourselves," Callender recalled. Instead, the statutory provision recognized the role of the press in providing Wisconsinites with a direct point of access to their government.

i. Doug Moe, "Press Corps Can't Go Much Lower," *Capital Times*, August 31, 1998.

Governor Tommy Thompson and Senator Chuck Chvala join the festivities at the reopening of the pressroom following capitol renovations in the mid-1990s. Thompson and members of his cabinet visited frequently, creating an atmosphere of spontaneity.

her story when an editor called with a question. Upon hearing "raucous noise" in the background, the editor asked, "Are you in a tavern?" to which she replied: "Well, no . . . I'm in the capitol pressroom."

Still, most interviewees cited that spontaneity as a benefit instead of a downside. For decades, the pressroom has enabled in-person interaction between reporters and policymakers. As Steve Walters put it, "When a cabinet secretary is angry at what just happened at joint finance and she or he walks into the pressroom, it's an instant news conference." Working from the pressroom might also mean running into legislative leaders on the way to or from the restroom—or sampling the spoils of Representative Joel Kleefisch's latest hunting trip.

In addition to access to lawmakers, interviewees cited the pooled expertise of the press corps as another benefit of working from the pressroom. Several recent reporters described their colleagues in the press corps as an essential sounding board. "We kind of have each other's backs," Scott Bauer explained, answering questions like, "Hey, did that ruling say what I thought it did? Am I understanding this correctly?" Sometimes, cooperation might mean putting Legislative Fiscal Bureau Director Bob Lang on speakerphone to gain clarity on a difficult-to-understand budget provision. This kind of collaboration prompts some reporters from different outlets to consider each other as colleagues. "To me," Molly Beck commented, "it feels like a regular newsroom, even though we don't technically work with each other." On session days, reporters even coordinate coffee runs and takeout orders.

Still, this spirit of camaraderie has its limits, as Beck acknowledged, "We're competitors at the end of the day." Or, as Scott Bauer put it, "If I get a hot tip, I'm not going to be like, 'You won't believe what I just heard from [Speaker] Robin Vos.'" And as many interviewees acknowledge, keeping information from competitors poses one of the great challenges of working from the pressroom. "We're in a round room with a high ceiling, and everything bounces," David Callender explained. "You're going to hear each other's phone calls." Callender operated on the principle that a reporter should not act on an overheard scoop—but he and other reporters took no chances that a scoop *could* be overheard. "There used to be a pay phone down on the ground floor of the capitol, and you would go to the pay phone to call the [newsroom] desk and let them know what you had coming." Former *Milwaukee Sentinel* bureau chief Steve Walters agreed that fierce competition necessitated covert phone calls from the first-floor pay phone: "It was a close-knit community. But when I was paid according to how often I beat the *Journal*, you just couldn't share any secrets in there."

Technological advances have eased this problem a bit. Jason Stein spelled out a hypothetical in which a reporter receives a tip about an amendment poised to break a budget impasse: "Now you could send an email, you could call by cell phone in the hall, you could Slack them, whatever. There's a million ways to do it." But efforts to maintain privacy can be unsettling. Jessie Opoien mentioned how hushed conversations between former *Journal Sentinel* reporting partners Jason Stein and Patrick Marley would prompt her gnawing curiosity: "They would just get really quiet. And I'd be like, 'What are they doing? What do they have? . . . What am I going to have to chase later today?'"

V. Challenges and Rewards

Some reporters told the LRB they could not imagine doing anything else, and some now do other work, including public relations and policy research. Although their career trajectories differed, all interviewees emphasized the challenges that come with the job of covering the legislature, including both the practical (e.g., struggling against technology to submit stories) and the personal (e.g., missing out on family events due to long hours at the capitol). But the richness of the capitol beat, interviewees were quick to note, can compensate for these stressors and sacrifices.

Before the rise of the Internet, reporters faced a host of technical challenges in submitting stories to their editors. In the late 1960s, the Badger Bus sometimes shepherded *Milwaukee Journal* stories from Madison to Milwaukee. Jeff Smoller recalled running to the bus station with carbon copies that would be picked up in Milwaukee and set in type overnight. Alternatively, reporters would dictate stories over the phone: "So you would get your information, you'd organize it in your head ... and you'd dictate that to a rewrite person in Milwaukee, who would take down what you were saying and clean it up." In fact, some reporters stockpiled quarters on the off chance they might need to call in a story from a pay phone outside the capitol. Dick Jones recalled receiving an early morning call instructing him to cover the Barneveld tornado in 1984. On top of "getting there and finding out what happened [and] interviewing people," he faced one additional challenge: "to find a pay phone and then to hope to God that [I] had the change for it."

The adoption of Tandy computers during the late 1970s and 1980s introduced new frustrations. Although the Tandy resembled a laptop, its memory was limited and its screen was miniscule. Plus, Lee Bergquist noted, "If you hit the button just wrong, you'd wipe out everything." If a reporter managed to successfully type out a story, sending it to the newsroom required the use of an acoustic coupler, a device that transmitted text over phone lines. These transmissions sent at a glacial pace—and were notoriously unreliable. Steve Schultze pointed out: "You'd send it and sort of pray that it got there intact. And then you had to call your editor immediately and say, 'Did you get it? Did you get the story?' And they'd open it up, and they'd go, 'Oh, it's all garbled. Resend it.'" Technical difficulties like these meant that anyone strolling past the doors of the pressroom might be privy to "a lot of profanity."

By the 1990s, technology became more predictable, but the news industry became less so, and a handful of outlets closed their capitol bureaus, consolidated with rivals, or cut staff. Over the course of the 1980s, UPI struggled against increasing competition from television news outlets and the gradual decline of local newspapers that had been loyal subscribers.[21] The wire service filed for bankruptcy in 1985, by which time its capitol reporters

In the 1970s and 1980s, many reporters wrote and transmitted stories on Tandy computers. Like this model from the same era, the Tandy had a small screen and operated slowly.

were regularly receiving late or bounced paychecks in what one reporter called "an agonizing nightmare."[22] The bureau shuttered in October 1990.[23]

Around the same time, print news also faltered. In response to declining circulation, newspapers across the country consolidated, including two former competitors in the capitol pressroom, the *Milwaukee Journal* and the *Milwaukee Sentinel*. Most reporters the LRB interviewed described this merger, which occurred in 1995, as sudden, unexpected, and seismic. "Maybe we were just in denial," the *Journal*'s Dick Jones reflected. "I can remember [Neil] Shively saying 'There will always be two papers.' Well, the day came when there [weren't]." After years of competing with each other for scoops, capitol reporters from the newspapers found themselves reapplying for jobs as colleagues at the merged *Journal Sentinel*. A pervasive sense of uncertainty and distrust made the merger period particularly stressful.

Newspaper consolidation continued throughout the 1990s and early 2000s, with some outlets downsizing their capitol bureaus and others closing them altogether. The *Janesville Gazette*, for example, closed its one-man capitol bureau following the 1997 legislative session in a decision that "blindsided" Stan Milam, who said he "thought the capitol bureau was an important part of the paper." Other papers, such as the *Journal Sentinel*, retained their capitol bureaus but offered periodic buyouts to their reporters during this period in an effort to cut staff. Since then, the *Journal Sentinel*, like most other papers, has relied on fewer journalists to report on the same volume of news. In consequence, said Patrick Marley, "I have less time. Editors have less time. All my colleagues have less time."

By the early 2000s, the spread of the Internet intensified the existing pressure to report breaking news quickly—now within minutes or even seconds. When Scott Bauer started at AP in the 1990s, deadlines punctuated his day, beginning midmorning with deadlines for the afternoon papers. More than twenty years later, "We don't even think about deadlines anymore because everything just goes out everywhere instantaneously." Posting stories this rapidly requires pre-writing as much background information as possible; then, the moment news breaks, there is a mad scramble to synthesize and incorporate that news. As an example, Patrick Marley described the morning Michael Gableman announced the release of his report on the 2020 presidential election: "I'm trying to listen to what he says, get a sense of what's going on in the room, and also read a 130-page report." Meanwhile, Marley's colleague Molly Beck was off site doing the same, and the pair was in constant communication with their editors.

Although interviewees classified social media as an effective tool, especially as a means to promote their work and that of their peers, many also characterized

The onset of the COVID-19 pandemic prompted reporters to relocate from the capitol pressroom to their homes, creating distinct advantages and disadvantages.

Adapting during the pandemic

The COVID-19 pandemic proved challenging for many capitol reporters because it distanced them from the pressroom and limited their access to public officials. According to Scott Bauer, "[The pandemic] cut down on the personal one-on-one interaction with people." More interactions took place over the phone or via Zoom, making it difficult to build relationships and taking some of the thrill out of reporting. Still, interviewees noted some silver linings. For one thing, politicians' increasing familiarity with Zoom meant TV reporters like Emilee Fannon and A.J. Bayatpour snagged a "wider breadth" of interviewees who might have otherwise been unavailable for an in-person interview. Additionally, reporters conceded the distinct advantages of covering floor sessions from the comfort of home, which met with approval from their household pets.

it as a source of stress. Jessica Arp described Twitter as having "amplified by a thousand times" the pressure for her to be following and reporting on the news on a "wake-up-to-go-to-sleep" basis. In a similar vein, Jason Stein remarked, only half-jokingly, that Twitter had "ruined his brain" by making him less able to focus on real conversations. More concerning, reporters described how social media enables abuse and harassment. Patrick Marley noted, "[People] forget that at the other end of the screen is another human being." As a result, they type things in Twitter messages that "they would be horribly embarrassed if their mother or spouse found out about." Reporters stressed both the virulence and volume of online harassment, which Molly Beck called "jarring." In response, most reporters emphasized the necessity of developing a thick skin—or finding humor in the absurd. "It would just crack me up." A.J. Bayatpour told the LRB that, in response to one segment, "I would literally get an email or a Twitter message . . . saying I'm in Governor Evers's pocket . . . [and another saying] this Bayatpour guy, he's just a Republican."

Paradoxically, while social media has facilitated unrestrained communication between the press and the public, several veteran reporters told the LRB that it had the opposite effect within the capitol; specifically, legislators no longer rely on reporters to reach the public because they can do so directly via Twitter or Facebook. As a result, in-person and telephone interviews with the press are lower priorities than before. "Twenty years ago," JR Ross explained, "we had an interview, and I got a live quote to put in my story. About ten [or] twelve years ago, I called your office, and I [got] a statement from you. Now, either I get a statement or I get a tweet." Steve Walters agreed, commenting that reporters are less likely to break a story from an interview with an elected official and more likely to react to a social media post. The downside of this shift, to Ross, is that quotes pulled from conversation sound substantially different from statements or tweets.

On a practical level, interviewees described political reporting as a career that requires long hours and constant attention, to the detriment of personal relationships. More than one reporter relied on the word "consuming" to characterize not only the time commitment but also the "constant need to know what's happening." On top of demanding fifty-to-sixty-hour workweeks, reporters described even longer hours at the close of a floor session or during major events, such as the protests surrounding Act 10 in early 2011. Some felt that they disappointed loved ones as a result. As Emilee Fannon put it, "Campaign season, I have missed weddings, I have missed friends' birthdays, because I just feel . . . obligated to go to the Trump rally." Similarly, Steve Walters commented, "You cheat your families and people that love you."

In addition to these personal sacrifices, reporters also described the mental and emotional toll of covering certain kinds of stories. As Steve Walters explained, he and other *Journal Sentinel* colleagues reported on certain general assignment stories on a rotating basis. These stories cast their reporting on the legislature in sharp relief. "They make hugely important decisions in that building," Walters said, gesturing to the capitol, "but then you go to the site of a fire where three children

> **Social media**
>
> Although several interviewees told the LRB that Twitter is a source of stress, Jessie Opoien said she appreciates how it creates unexpected connections within the capitol. Soon after she began reporting on the legislature, Opoien tweeted about the television show *The Bachelorette*, prompting Representative Jim Steineke to approach her and commiserate about the contestant's decision: "[He] was like, I can't believe she sent him home last night."

Jessie Opoien of the *Capital Times* has forged connections with legislators through social media.

perished, and . . . it's a heck of a balance, emotionally." Stan Milam also emphasized that most reporters cover "unpleasant" topics, tempting them to become cynical. He recalled how Gene Harrington of the *Milwaukee Journal* cautioned against this tendency, advising colleagues, "Get the facts and report them. But don't go in with . . . a negative attitude." But Milam admitted to the difficulty of following Harrington's advice: "It's so hard to be in this business and not be cynical. It's almost like your job is to make sure that somebody isn't pulling the wool over your eyes."

Still, many interviewees spoke of journalism as a calling—one to which they felt inexorably bound, despite its many challenges. "I was made to be a reporter," said Lee Bergquist. "It just suits who I am." Likewise, although he has since worked in another field, Dick Jones described himself as "a reporter at heart." For Stan Milam, no other career was conceivable: "I can write a 600-word story. That's about it. . . . And if I had to go out and make a living doing something else, I'd probably starve to death." Although offered in jest, Milam's comment underscores the extent to which reporting requires a special combination of skills and interests.

For individuals who possess those skills and interests, the capitol is "the richest beat you can get," remarked John Powell, emphasizing the extent to which capitol reporters engage directly with policymakers. Similarly, Patrick Marley described covering the state legislature as a "dream job" because of this "incredible access" to lawmakers, especially compared to the U.S. Congress. "You can catch them in the hallway. You can stop by their offices. You can really get to the bottom of what's going on and what's on their minds." John Colbert likewise described interactions with legislators as "one of the best parts of the job." Equally motivating is the fact that reporters cover issues that range widely and change constantly. "Just about any subject you can think of will come eventually, in some form, before the state legislature or the courts," Powell explained. And reporters engage their intellectual curiosity by digging into all these subjects. As JR Ross noted, "You become an expert—for at least a day—on so many topics." In the process, reporters regularly interact with legislative staff and agency officials who broaden their understanding of various issues. Jason Stein, for example, described himself as being fortunate to "sit at the feet of very knowledgeable people, like [Legislative Fiscal Bureau Director] Bob Lang."

No two days are the same for a capitol reporter. "That's what makes the job so great and interesting," remarked Scott Bauer. "Even though you're covering the statehouse, all the characters, all the issues . . . are always kind of in flux." Accordingly, the work is never predictable or boring. Molly Beck put it this way: "There's never been a time I've looked up and [said], 'Oh man, it's only one o'clock' you know? I've *never* had that feeling—ever." Jessie Opoien likewise described her job satisfaction as being directly tied to the diversity of issues on the capitol beat, noting wryly, "I'll leave when it stops being interesting."

For these reasons and more, the rewards of covering the capitol soften its challenges. "It gives to you more than it takes away," commented Jason Stein. Amy Rinard shared a similar vantage point: "It was stressful work. We were under the microscope all the time. But that was a great place to work." In large part, the camaraderie of the pressroom motivated Rinard and others to persist in telling important stories about the work of the legislature and its effect on Wisconsinites.

Conclusion

When Senate Majority Leader Ernest Keppler handed over the keys to the new pressroom in 1971, he offered the following words: "A representative form of government, to succeed, is dependent on the members of the press to inform citizens of actions by their representatives." The pressroom, he hoped, would aid the press in its mission.[24] Those who have served in the capitol press corps over the intervening fifty years articulate their mission in similar terms. "You're there as a representative of the people," Dick Jones remarked. "You're there in their stead [and] that is vital in the way government works." Gwyn Guenther agreed: "They call the press the Fourth Estate because the public needs to keep an eye on its

Members of the capitol press corps are formally presented with a key to the pressroom in 1998. Dick Wheeler's struggle for a dedicated pressroom reflected a broader mission to ensure Wisconsinites' access to their elected officials.

PHOTO COURTESY OF THE CAPITOL PRESS CORPS

government."[25] That principle animated her father's fight to keep the pressroom, which was posthumously renamed the Dick Wheeler Press Room in his honor.

And while the challenges of the job can prove wearying, many reporters described covering the capitol as a great privilege. As Scott Bauer put it, "You make a lot of great friends, and you see a lot of things that other people don't get to see, and you have an opportunity to tell the world what is going on." Jessica Arp described feeling a "sense of awe" looking at the capitol illuminated at night, even after a long and exhausting day: "There's this sense of history that . . . I don't think you get in any office setting." 🆎

NOTES

1. Donald E. Oehlerts, ed., *Guide to Wisconsin Newspapers, 1833–1957* (Madison: State Historical Society, 1958), vi. See also George W. Purcell, "A Survey of Early Newspapers in the Middle Western States," *Indiana Magazine of History* 20, no. 4 (Dec. 1924), 347–63.

2. Gerald J. Baldasty, *The Commercialization of News in the Nineteenth Century* (Madison: University of Wisconsin Press, 1992), 3.

3. Oehlerts, *Guide to Wisconsin Newspapers*, vi.

4. See, generally, Richard Schwarzlose, "The Associated Press and United Press International," in Philip S. Cook, *The Future of News: Television, Newspapers, Wire Services, Newsmagazines* (Washington: Woodrow Wilson Center Press, 1992), 145–76.

5. Donald A. Ritchie, *Reporting from Washington: The History of the Washington Press Corps* (Oxford: Oxford University Press, 2005), 111, 114.

6. See, generally, Julia Guarneri, *Newsprint Metropolis: City Papers and the Making of Modern Americans* (Chicago: University of Chicago Press, 2017). See also Baldasty, *The Commercialization of News*.

7. "Reporters," *Wisconsin Blue Book* (Madison: Democrat Printing Co., 1905), 567.

8. Ritchie, *Reporting from Washington*, 46.

9. See, generally, "Radio Voices" in Ritchie, *Reporting from Washington*.

10. Ritchie, *Reporting from Washington*, 202.

11. Paul Rix and Tom Still, "State Computer Tapped: Reporters 'Raid' Shows Lack of Security," *Wisconsin State Journal*, August 23, 1983.

12. Rob Zaleski, "UPI Experience Was Quite an Education," *Capital Times*, May 10, 1985.

13. Jason Stein and Patrick Marley, "Wheeler Knew Ins and Outs of Capitol," *Milwaukee Journal Sentinel*, November 12, 2011; Scott Bauer, "For 40 Years, a State Capitol Fixture," Wisconsin State Journal, November 12, 2011.

14. Jessie Opoien, "Q&A: Gwyn Guenther Covers the Wisconsin Capitol for Political Insiders," *Capital Times*, August 20, 2017.

15. Frank Ryan, "Throw Reporter Out," *Kenosha News*, October 29, 1977.

16. See Matt Pommer, "State Bigwigs Get Briefing on 'Profit-Making' College," *Capital Times*, March 9, 1966.

17. Matt Pommer, "Harrington Favors Packers at Randall," *Capital Times*, September 15, 1967; "Hello Wisconsin," *Capital Times*, October 16, 1970.

18. Untitled, *Wisconsin State Journal*, March 12, 1947.

19. Senate Joint Resolution 20, *Senate Journal* (1947), 209.

20. State of Wisconsin Department of Administration, Kahler Slater, and Joyce Inman Historic Interiors, Inc., *Historic Structure Report: Book 5* (Madison: State of Wisconsin Department of Administration, 1995), 220; State of Wisconsin Department of Administration and East Wing Architects, LLC, *Historic Structure Report: Book 3* (Madison: State of Wisconsin Department of Administration, 2003), 6–10; "Capitol Reporters Given New Facility," *Manitowoc Herald Times*, April 1, 1971.

21. Schwarzlose, "The Associated Press and United Press International."

22. Zaleski, "UPI Experience Was Quite an Education."

23. Pat Simms, "UPI Bureau Falls Silent," *Wisconsin State Journal*, October 19, 1990.

24. "Capitol Reporters Given New Facility," *Manitowoc Herald Times*, April 1, 1971.

25. Opoien, "Q&A: Gwyn Guenther Covers the Wisconsin Capitol for Political Insiders."

ELECTIONS IN WISCONSIN

Purposes and days

Wisconsin holds elections for a variety of purposes and, depending on the purpose, on a variety of days.

FILLING THE STATE'S ELECTIVE OFFICES

To fill its elective offices, Wisconsin holds elections on four regular election days.

The general election. On the Tuesday after the first Monday in November of every even-numbered year, Wisconsin elects individuals to fill its partisan elective offices. The elections held on this day are referred to collectively as the "general election."

The partisan offices in Wisconsin are U.S. senator, U.S. representative, state senator, state representative, governor, lieutenant governor, attorney general, secretary of state, state treasurer, and the county-level offices of district attorney, county clerk, sheriff, clerk of circuit court, register of deeds, treasurer, coroner (in counties that have one), and surveyor (in counties in which the office is elective).

The voters of the entire state elect Wisconsin's U.S. senators, governor, lieutenant governor, attorney general, secretary of state, and state treasurer. The voters of each congressional, senate, and assembly district elect that district's U.S. representative, state senator, or state representative. The voters of each county elect that county's clerk, sheriff, clerk of circuit court, register of deeds, treasurer, coroner, and surveyor and the district attorney for the prosecutorial unit serving the county. (For the prosecutorial unit that serves Menominee and Shawano Counties, the voters of both counties elect the district attorney.)

The terms of office for the partisan offices are not all the same length and do not all expire on the same day or in the same year. Accordingly, only some of the partisan offices will be up for election at any particular general election—those, namely, for which the currently running term of office will expire before the next general election is held.

The ballot at each general election lists the offices that are up for election and, under each office, the candidates for the office who have qualified to be listed. Next to each candidate's name, the ballot lists the name of the political party or, in the case of an independent candidate with no party affiliation, the principle that the candidate represents.

An individual who wishes to be listed as a candidate on the ballot must file, no later than the June 1 preceding the general election, 1) a declaration of candidacy indicating the office that the individual seeks and the political party or the principle that he or she proposes to represent and 2) nomination papers signed by a statutorily required number of voters residing in the governmental jurisdiction or election district that the office serves. In addition, the individual must win a partisan primary election if he or she proposes to represent one of the "recognized" political parties (see below). By contrast, an individual who does not propose to represent a recognized political party will be listed on the general election ballot without participating in a partisan primary election. Such an individual is called an "independent candidate."

The candidate who receives the most votes cast for a particular office at the general election fills that office when the currently running term of office expires.

The partisan primary. Prior to the general election, on the second Tuesday in August of every even-numbered year, Wisconsin holds primary elections to select the individuals who will be listed on the general election ballot as the candidates of the "recognized" political parties. The elections held on this day are referred to collectively as the "partisan primary."

A political party qualifies as a recognized political party in one of three situations:

- A candidate of the political party won at least 1 percent of the votes cast in Wisconsin, either for a statewide office at the last general election at which the office of governor was up for election or for U.S. president at the most recent general election, and the political party was a recognized political party for that election.
- An individual representing the political party as an independent candidate won at least 1 percent of the votes cast in Wisconsin, either for a statewide office at the last general election at which the office of governor was up for election or for U.S. president at the most recent general election, and the political party requests recognized status no later than the April 1 preceding the partisan primary.
- The political party submits, no later than the April 1 preceding the partisan primary, a petition requesting recognized status signed by at least 10,000 Wisconsin voters, including at least 1,000 from each of at least three congressional districts.

The ballot at the partisan primary is divided into sections, one for each recognized political party. Each party's section lists all of the offices that will be filled at the general election and, under each office, the individuals, if any, who have filed to be candidates for the office and have proposed, in their declarations of candidacy, to represent the party. A voter at the partisan primary can mark votes in only one of these ballot sections, but can pick any section for this purpose—voters in Wisconsin are not asked to declare a party affiliation when registering or voting and are not obliged in any other way to pick a particular party's section.

However, if a voter marks votes in more than one of the party sections, none of the voter's votes will be counted.

The individual who receives the most votes cast for a particular office in the ballot section for a particular party becomes that party's candidate for that office at the general election, and his or her name, together with the party's name, will be listed under the office on the general election ballot.

The partisan primary is the exclusive means by which a recognized political party can select a candidate to be listed on the general election ballot. The party must accept as its candidate the individual selected by the voters who vote on its section of the partisan primary ballot. Moreover, if no individual is listed under a particular office in that section (because no one who filed to be a candidate for the office proposed to represent that party), the party will not have a candidate for that office listed on the general election ballot.

The spring election. On the first Tuesday in April of every year, Wisconsin elects individuals to fill its nonpartisan elective offices. The elections held on this day are referred to collectively as the "spring election."

The nonpartisan offices in Wisconsin are state superintendent of public instruction; supreme court justice; court of appeals judge; circuit court judge; county executive (in counties that have one); county supervisor; county comptroller (in Milwaukee); every elective town, village, and city office; and school board member.

The voters of the entire state elect Wisconsin's state superintendent of public instruction and supreme court justices. The voters of each court of appeals district elect that district's judges. The voters of each county elect the county's county executive (if any) and county comptroller (in Milwaukee) and the circuit court judges for the circuit that serves the county. (For circuits that serve two counties, the voters of both counties elect the circuit court judges.) The voters of each county supervisory district elect that district's county supervisor. The voters of each town elect that town's officers. Village trustees and city alders can be elected at large by the voters of the entire village or city or from election districts by the voters residing in each election district. All other village and city officers are elected at large by the voters of the entire village or city. School board members can be elected at large by the voters of the entire school district, from election districts by the voters residing in each election district, or from election districts by the voters of the entire school district.

Just as with the partisan offices, the terms of office for the nonpartisan offices are not all the same length and do not all expire on the same day or in the same year. At each spring election, accordingly, the only nonpartisan offices up for election are those for which the currently running term of office will expire before the next spring election is held.

The ballot at each spring election lists the offices that are up for election and, under each office, the candidates for the office who have qualified to be listed. Ordinarily, no more than two candidates can be listed. The situation is different, however, when multiple, undifferentiated instances of the same office exist in a particular governmental jurisdiction or election district. In many villages, for example, the trustees who make up the village board are elected at large rather than from election districts, and no distinction is made between the "seat" occupied by one trustee and the "seat" occupied by another. In this situation, the ballot can list up to twice as many candidates for an office as the number of seats to be filled. The ballot would also include an instruction to vote for no more of those candidates than the number of seats to be filled.

An individual who wishes to be listed as a candidate on the ballot must file, no later than the first Tuesday in the January preceding the spring election, 1) a declaration of candidacy indicating the office that the individual seeks and 2) nomination papers signed by a required number of voters residing in the governmental jurisdiction or election district that the office serves. In addition, the individual must win a spring primary election (see below) if the total number of individuals who file to be candidates for the office is more than two or, if applicable, is more than twice the number of seats to be filled. By contrast, if the total number of individuals is less than two, or is less than twice the number of seats to be filled, each individual will be listed on the spring election ballot without participating in a spring primary election.[1]

The candidate who receives the most votes cast for a particular office at the spring election fills that office when the currently running term of office expires. If multiple seats are to be filled for a particular office, the candidates equal in number to the number of those seats who receive the most votes fill those seats when the currently running term of office expires.

The spring primary. Prior to the spring election, on the third Tuesday in February of every year, Wisconsin holds primary elections to select, for some of the offices that will be filled at the spring election, the individuals who will be listed as candidates on the spring election ballot. The elections held on this day are referred to collectively as the "spring primary."

The ballot at the spring primary lists only those offices for which more than two individuals or, if applicable, more individuals than twice the number of seats to be filled have filed to be candidates and, under each office, the individuals who have filed to be candidates for the office. The ballot also includes for each office an instruction to vote for not more than one individual or for not more individuals than the number of seats to be filled.

The two individuals, or the individuals equal in number to twice the number of seats to be filled, who receive the most votes cast for an office at a spring primary election will be listed as the candidates for that office on the spring election ballot.

ELECTING THE U.S. PRESIDENT AND VICE PRESIDENT

As part of the process by which the United States elects its president and vice president, Wisconsin holds two elections, each on one of the regular election days just discussed.

At the spring election. On the day of the spring election, in presidential election years, Wisconsin conducts its presidential preference primary.

This primary is advisory, rather than binding. Wisconsin's voters indicate which individual they would like a political party to select as its candidate for U.S. president, but Wisconsin law does not require the party's Wisconsin members to vote for that individual at the party's national convention. Rather, the party conducts its convention according to rules that it determines for itself, and it can select its presidential candidate using any mechanism it chooses.

A political party qualifies to participate in Wisconsin's presidential preference primary only if 1) it was a recognized political party (see above, page 319) at Wisconsin's last general election, 2) it had a candidate for governor at that election, and that candidate won at least 10 percent of the votes cast for that office, and 3) its state chair certifies to the Elections Commission, no later than the second Tuesday in the December preceding the presidential preference primary, that the party will participate.

The spring election ballot includes a separate section for the presidential preference primary of each participating political party. Each party's section lists the individuals who wish to be selected as the party's candidate for president and have qualified to be listed.

An individual can qualify in two ways to be listed on the ballot as a candidate in a party's presidential preference primary. First, the individual can be certified by a special committee that meets in the state capitol on the first Tuesday in the January preceding the presidential preference primary. This committee consists of the state chair, one national committeeman, and one national committeewoman of each participating political party; the speaker and the minority leader of the state assembly; the president and the minority leader of the state senate; and an additional member selected by the rest of the committee to be its chair. The committee identifies, for each of the participating political parties, the individuals who are generally recognized in the national media as the party's candidates for U.S. president and any additional individuals that the committee believes should be included as candidates on the party's ballot list. The committee must certify these candidates to the Elections Commission no later than the Friday following its meeting.

Alternatively, an individual can submit to the Elections Commission, no later than the last Tuesday in January, a petition requesting to be listed as a candidate in a party's presidential preference primary. The petition must be signed by a required number of voters from each of Wisconsin's congressional districts.

A voter at the spring election can cast votes in the presidential preference primary of just one of the participating political parties. As at the partisan primary, the voter can pick any party's section on the ballot to vote on and is not obliged, based on party affiliation or any other criteria, to pick the section of a particular party.

At the general election. In presidential election years, on the day of the general election, Wisconsin elects the slate of presidential electors that will be its delegation to the Electoral College, the nationwide body that actually elects the U.S. president and vice president.

The ballot at the general election does not list slates of would-be presidential electors. Rather, it lists the pairs of candidates who are running together, one for president and one for vice president, and who have qualified to be listed. Each of these candidate pairs has its own slate of would-be presidential electors, and a vote cast for a candidate pair is simultaneously a vote cast for its slate.

A pair of individuals can qualify to be listed on the general election ballot as candidates for U.S. president and vice president in two ways. They can be selected by a recognized political party (see above, page 319) to be its candidates. Each recognized political party selects its candidates at a national convention of party members conducted according to rules that the party determines for itself. The pair of individuals that a recognized political party selects will be listed on the general election ballot if 1) the party's state or national chair certifies to the Elections Commission, no later than the first Tuesday in the September preceding the general election, that the individuals are the party's candidates and 2) each of the individuals files a declaration of candidacy with the Elections Commission by the same deadline.

Alternatively, a pair of individuals can qualify to be listed as independent candidates. To do this, each of the individuals must file with the Elections Commission, no later than the first Tuesday in the August preceding the general election, a declaration of candidacy indicating the office that he or she seeks and the political party or principle that he or she proposes to represent, and the two individuals jointly must file nomination papers, signed by a required number of Wisconsin voters, nominating them as a pair.

The slate of presidential electors for each candidate pair must consist of ten individuals, one from each of Wisconsin's eight congressional districts and two more from anywhere in the state.

A slate can be determined in two ways. For the candidates of the recognized political parties, the slates are determined at a special convention held at the state capitol on the first Tuesday in the October preceding the general election. The convention consists of certain officials holding partisan elective offices in state government—the governor, lieutenant governor, attorney general, secretary of state, state treasurer, and those state senators whose seats are not up for election—together with the individuals who will be listed on the general election ballot as the candidates of the recognized political parties for the offices of state senator and state representative. The convention participants meet separately according to the parties they belong to, and each party designates a slate of presidential electors for its pair of candidates for president and vice president. The state chair of each party then certifies that party's slate to the Elections Commission.

By contrast, each pair of independent candidates for U.S. president and vice president designates its own slate of presidential electors in its nomination papers.

The slate of presidential electors of the candidate pair that wins the most votes at Wisconsin's general election becomes Wisconsin's delegation to the Electoral College. On the Monday after the second Wednesday in the December following the general election, this delegation assembles in the state capitol and casts its votes as members of that body.

FILLING A MIDTERM VACANCY

A "special election" can be held to fill a midterm vacancy in certain elective offices. This kind of election can be held on one of the four regular election days or on a different day.

A vacancy in the office of U.S. senator, U.S. representative, state senator, or state representative can be filled only by a special election called by the governor. A vacancy in the office of attorney general, state superintendent of public instruction, secretary of state, or state treasurer can be filled either by a special election called by the governor, if the vacancy occurs more than six months before the term of office expires, or by appointment by the governor, regardless of when the vacancy occurs. (A vacancy in the office of supreme court justice, court of appeals judge, circuit court judge, district attorney, sheriff, coroner, or register of deeds can be filled only by appointment by the governor.) In some county and municipal offices, a vacancy can be filled either by special election or by appointment, at the discretion of the local governing body.

An individual who wishes to be listed as a candidate on a special election ballot must file a declaration of candidacy and nomination papers and must also win a special primary election if one is required. For a partisan office, a special primary must be held for each of the recognized political parties if it is the case for any one of them that two or more individuals have proposed in their declarations of candidacy to represent it. For a nonpartisan office, a special primary must be held if three or more individuals file to be candidates.

RECALLING AN ELECTED OFFICIAL FROM OFFICE

A "recall election" can be held to decide whether an elected official will be recalled from office before his or her term of office expires and, if so, who will serve in the official's place for the remainder of the term. This kind of election can be held on one of the four regular election days or on a different day. However, a recall election cannot be held before an official has served one year of his or her term. In addition, no more than one recall election can be held for the same official during a single term of office.

A recall election is held only if voters of the governmental jurisdiction or election district that elected an official file a petition to recall the official. The petition must be signed by a number of voters equal to at least 25 percent of the vote cast for governor in the jurisdiction or district at the last election for governor. In addition, if the petition seeks the recall of a city, village, town, or school district official, it must assert a reason that is related to the duties of the office.

Other than the official named in the recall petition, an individual who wishes to be listed as a candidate on a recall election ballot must file a declaration of candidacy and nomination papers and might also have to win a recall primary election if one is required. The official named in the recall petition might similarly have to win a recall primary but otherwise will be listed on the recall election ballot automatically (unless he or she resigns).

For a partisan office, a recall primary must be held for each recognized political party for which it is the case that two or more individuals, who might include the official named in the recall petition, seek to be listed as its candidate on the recall election ballot. If only one individual seeks to be listed as a party's candidate, the individual will be listed as such without a primary being held for that party.

For a nonpartisan office, a recall primary must be held if three or more individuals, who might include the official named in the recall petition, seek to be listed as candidates on the recall election ballot. In contrast to other nonpartisan primaries, if one individual receives over 50 percent of the votes cast at the recall primary, no further election is held, and that individual fills the office for the remaining term.

APPROVING OR REJECTING A PROPOSAL

A "referendum" can be held in Wisconsin to approve or reject a proposal (rather than to choose an individual to fill an office). This kind of election can be held on one of the four regular election days or on a different day.

A referendum can be binding or nonbinding. In the former case, a proposal is implemented automatically if approved by a majority of the voters voting at the referendum; in the latter, the voters' approval or rejection of a proposal is merely advisory.

At the state level, binding referenda can be held on proposals 1) to amend the state constitution, 2) to extend the right to vote, 3) to allow the state to contract public debt in excess of the limit imposed by the state constitution, and 4) to permit an act of the legislature to take effect when the legislature has provided that the act's taking effect is contingent upon voter approval.

A referendum ballot presents the referendum proposal in the form of a yes-or-no question, and the voter votes the ballot by marking "yes" or "no." The question on the ballot summarizes the effect of the proposal. The full text of the proposal along with an explanation of its effect must be posted at the polling place.

Administration

The responsibility for administering elections is distributed across several levels of government.

Elections Commission. The state Elections Commission oversees and facilitates the performance of elections-related functions by officials at lower levels of government. The commission:

- Determines the format that must be used for ballots.
- Certifies all equipment and materials used to record votes at elections.
- Trains and certifies officials at lower levels of government.
- Maintains the electronic statewide voter registration list.

The Elections Commission also performs certain functions related to state and national elections. The commission:

- Determines which candidates for elective state and national offices qualify to be listed on the ballot. Such candidates must file with the commission their declarations of candidacy, nomination papers, and other documents that demonstrate that they are qualified.
- Certifies the tally of the votes cast in the state at each election held to fill a state or national office or to vote on a state referendum.

County clerk. The county clerk performs certain functions related to county, state, and national elections. The county clerk:

- Determines which candidates for elective offices in county government qualify

to be listed on the ballot. Such candidates must file with the county clerk their declarations of candidacy, nomination papers, and other documents that demonstrate that they are qualified.
- Prepares the ballots for elections held to fill county, state, and national offices and to vote on county and state referenda and distributes these ballots to the municipalities (cities, villages, and towns) located within the county.
- Processes voter registrations for county residents who ask to register at the county clerk's office and forwards the information obtained to the municipal clerk of the municipality in which the registrant resides so that the municipal clerk can update the electronic statewide registration list.
- Tabulates the votes cast in the county at each election held to fill a county, state, or national office or to vote on a county or state referendum.
- Reports to the Elections Commission the votes cast in the county related to a state or national election.

In Wisconsin's most populous county, Milwaukee, a special commission performs these functions instead of a clerk.

Municipal clerk. The municipal clerk—i.e., the city, village, or town clerk—performs certain functions related to municipal, county, state, and national elections. The municipal clerk:

- Determines which candidates for elective offices in municipal government qualify to be listed on the ballot. Such candidates must file with the municipal clerk their declarations of candidacy, nomination papers, and other documents that demonstrate that they are qualified.
- Prepares the ballots for elections held to fill municipal offices and to vote on municipal referenda.
- Processes voter registrations for residents of the municipality and updates the electronic statewide registration list to reflect the information obtained. In some cases, a county clerk, by agreement with a municipal clerk, acts in place of the municipal clerk as that clerk's agent for the performance of all registration functions, including updating the statewide registration list.
- Provides the ballots for each election to the voters who desire to vote and receives the ballots back from those voters when they cast them. Only the municipal clerk provides ballots to voters and receives cast ballots back; county clerks and the Elections Commission do not.
- Operates polling places in the municipality on the day of an election. Only the municipal clerk operates polling places; county clerks and the Elections Commission do not.
- Tabulates the votes cast in the municipality at each election held to fill a municipal, county, state, or national office or to vote on a municipal, county, or state referendum.

- Reports to the county clerk of each county in which the municipality is located the votes cast in the municipality related to a county, state, or national election.

The municipal clerk also handles most matters related to elections held by school districts that are located in whole or part within the municipality. However, the school district clerk determines which candidates for school district elective offices qualify to be listed on the ballot, and such candidates must file with the school district clerk their declarations of candidacy, nomination papers, and other documents that demonstrate that they are qualified.

In Wisconsin's most populous city, Milwaukee, a special commission performs these functions instead of a clerk.

Voting

Eligibility. To vote at an election in Wisconsin, an individual must be a U.S. citizen, must be 18 years of age or older, and must reside in the governmental jurisdiction or election district for which the election is held. For example, an individual must reside in a particular county to vote at an election for that county's sheriff and must reside in a particular supervisory district within the county to vote at an election for that district's member of the county board of supervisors.

To establish residence for voting purposes, an individual must reside at the same address for at least 28 consecutive days prior to the election at which the individual wishes to vote.

An individual who moves to a new address in Wisconsin during the 28 days preceding an election is considered, for that election, to reside at his or her former address if the individual had established residence at the former address before the move. The individual can vote at the election only if the former address is located within the governmental jurisdiction or election district for which the election is held.

An individual who has resided in Wisconsin for less than 28 days but who is otherwise eligible to vote can vote for U.S. president and vice president (but no other offices) under a special procedure.

Certain individuals are not eligible to vote at any election:

- An individual who has been convicted of treason, felony, or bribery, unless the individual has been pardoned or has completed his or her sentence—including any parole, probation, or extended supervision—for the crime.
- An individual who has been adjudicated incompetent by a court, unless the court has determined that the individual is competent to exercise the right to vote.

In addition, an individual is not eligible to vote at a particular election if the individual has bet upon the result of the election.

Registration. Registration is the means by which an individual demonstrates that the individual is eligible to vote. With limited exceptions, an individual must register to vote before being allowed to vote.

To register, an individual must fill out, sign, and submit a registration form and present acceptable proof of residence.

On the registration form, the individual must:

- Provide the individual's name and date of birth; current address; previous address; and the number and expiration date of the individual's Wisconsin driver's license or identification card, if any, or the last four digits of the individual's social security number, if any.
- Indicate whether the individual has been convicted of a felony for which the individual has not been pardoned and, if so, whether the individual is incarcerated or on parole, probation, or extended supervision.
- Indicate whether the individual is currently registered to vote at an address other than the current one.
- Certify that the individual is a U.S. citizen, will be 18 years of age or older on the day of the next election, and will have resided at his or her current address for at least 28 consecutive days prior to that day. Registrants are not asked to indicate a political party affiliation.

Documents that qualify as proof of residence include:

- A current and valid Wisconsin driver's license or identification card.
- A student identification card accompanied by a fee receipt dated within the preceding nine months.
- A property tax bill or receipt for the current or previous year.
- A bank statement.
- A utility bill for a period beginning no earlier than 90 days before the date of registration.

Through the third Wednesday preceding an election, an eligible voter can register in person at the office of the municipal clerk or county clerk, by mail with the municipal clerk, or via an electronic registration system maintained by the Elections Commission and accessible at myvote.wi.gov.[2] After that Wednesday and through the Friday preceding the election, an eligible voter can register only in person at the office of the municipal clerk (or of the county clerk, if the county clerk is acting as the municipal clerk's agent for registration purposes). After that Friday, an eligible voter who still has not registered and who wishes to vote at the election must register on the day of the election at his or her polling place.

The Elections Commission maintains an electronic list of all eligible voters who are registered to vote in Wisconsin. Every municipal clerk (or county clerk acting as the agent of a municipal clerk) who processes a registration for an eligible voter must update the list via an interface provided by the Elections Commission to reflect the information obtained. The list updates automatically to reflect registrations submitted via the electronic registration system.

An individual who has registered once does not need to register again, unless the individual changes his or her name or address. However, an individual's registration can be suspended if the individual has not voted for four years and fails to respond to a mailed postcard that asks whether the individual wishes to continue his or her registration. The Elections Commission sends out the postcards to such voters every two years.

Military voters who are residents of Wisconsin, as well as their spouses and dependents who reside with or accompany them, are not required to register as a prerequisite to voting. In addition, an individual who has resided in Wisconsin for less than 28 days, but who is otherwise eligible to vote, can vote for U.S. president and vice president without being registered. Similarly, a former Wisconsin resident who has moved to another state and is not eligible to vote in the new state can, if the individual is otherwise eligible to vote, cast a Wisconsin absentee ballot for U.S. president and vice president without being registered for up to 24 months after the move.

Voter registration information is generally open to public inspection. However, voters who are victims of certain crimes, such as domestic abuse, sexual assault, and stalking, can request confidential voter status. If a voter qualifies for this status, the municipal clerk updates the electronic statewide registration list to indicate that the voter's registration must be kept confidential and issues a confidential voter identification card to the voter.

Photo identification. With few exceptions,[3] a registered voter (or an eligible voter exempt from registration) who wishes to vote at an election in Wisconsin must present acceptable proof of identification in order to obtain a ballot. In most cases, photo identification is required. Acceptable forms of photo identification include:

- A Wisconsin driver's license or identification card issued by the Wisconsin Department of Transportation.
- A U.S. passport.
- A Veterans Affairs identification card.
- An identification card issued by a federally recognized Indian tribe in Wisconsin.
- A photo identification card issued by a Wisconsin university, college, or technical college, if certain conditions are satisfied.

Individuals who have a religious objection to being photographed can obtain and present a Wisconsin driver's license or identification card issued without a photo. In addition, an individual who has had to surrender his or her driver's license to a law enforcement officer within 60 days of the election can present in place of the driver's license the citation or notice that the individual received. A confidential voter can present his or her confidential voter identification card instead of photo identification.

Voting at a polling place. Polling places are operated by the municipal clerk and are open for voting only on the day of an election. Each address in a municipality is served by a designated polling place, and a voter can vote only at the polling place that serves the voter's address. (If a registered voter has moved within Wisconsin during the 28 days preceding an election, the voter is considered to reside at his or her former address for that election and can vote only at the polling place that serves the former address.) Each polling place is staffed by poll workers who have been trained by the municipal clerk. Each polling place is supplied with duplicate "poll lists,"[4] which are generated from the electronic statewide registration list, of all eligible voters served by the polling place who registered before the day of the election. Each polling place is also supplied with ballots that are specific to the elections at which the voters served by the polling place are eligible to vote.

When an individual comes to a polling place to vote, a poll worker asks the individual to state his or her name and address and to present proof of identification. (A confidential voter can present a confidential voter identification card without stating anything or can state his or her name and the serial number of the card without presenting anything.) A poll worker confirms that the individual's name and address are listed in the poll list, that the name on the proof of identification is consistent with the name on the poll list, and that any photograph on the proof of identification reasonably resembles the individual.[5] The individual is then required to sign the poll list, unless the individual cannot sign due to a physical disability.

Following these preliminaries, the poll workers assign the individual a voter number, record the number on both copies of the poll list, and give the individual a paper ballot or a card that will permit the voter to access an electronic ballot on a voting machine.

The voter takes the ballot or card to a voting booth and marks the paper ballot, or marks an electronic ballot via an interface on a voting machine, to indicate the voter's votes. After marking a paper ballot, the voter casts it by depositing it through a slot into a locked ballot box or by feeding it into an optical scanning machine. (An optical scanning machine reads and tabulates electronically the votes marked on a paper ballot and stores the ballot in a locked compartment.)

After marking an electronic ballot, the voter verifies a record of the voter's votes that the voting machine prints on a paper tape. The voter then casts the ballot by giving a direction via the machine's interface. (A voting machine records a voter's votes in its electronic memory, tabulates them electronically, and advances the paper tape so that the paper record of the voter's votes is stored within a locked compartment.)

Voting by absentee ballot. A registered voter (or an eligible voter exempt from registration) who is unwilling or unable to vote at his or her polling place on the day of an election can vote by absentee ballot instead.

To obtain an absentee ballot, the voter must submit a written request to the municipal clerk. This can be done in person at the clerk's office or at an alternate site designated by the clerk. It can also be done by mail, email, or fax. In-person requests must be made prior to the Monday preceding the election; other requests, in most cases, must be made no later than the Thursday preceding the election.

An in-person requester must present acceptable proof of identification to the municipal clerk or an individual designated by the clerk before the requester will be issued a ballot. Most other requesters must submit a copy of their proof of identification with their request for a ballot.[6]

To cast an absentee ballot, the voter must mark his or her votes on the ballot and seal the marked ballot in a special envelope that is provided with the ballot. The voter must take these actions in the presence of a witness. The voter must also show the unmarked ballot to the witness prior to marking it and must make sure that no one, including the witness, sees how the voter marked the ballot. After the ballot is sealed in the special envelope, the voter and the witness must sign a certification that is printed on the special envelope—the voter to attest that the voter is eligible to cast the ballot, will not cast any other ballot at the election, and followed the required procedures in casting the ballot; and the witness to attest that the voter followed the required procedures in casting the ballot. If the voter requested the absentee ballot in person, the voter must return it before leaving the municipal clerk's office or alternate site. In these cases, the municipal clerk or an individual designated by the clerk serves as the witness. If the voter requested the absentee ballot in another way, the voter must seal the special envelope containing the ballot in a second envelope[7] and either mail it or deliver it in person to the municipal clerk so that it is received by the municipal clerk no later than the day of the election.

Campaign finance regulation

Wisconsin regulates campaign finance—the spending of money on campaigning and the giving of money to others to spend on campaigning—in several ways:

- Only a particular kind of entity, called a "committee," is allowed to use money that it has accepted from others to engage in campaign spending and campaign giving. If the amount of money exceeds a specified threshold, a committee must register and file reports of its financial activity.[8]
- Limits are placed on who can give money to a committee and how much money can be given.
- Limits are also placed on some campaign spending, and some campaign spending is subject to special disclosure requirements.

Three kinds of campaigning are covered by the regulations: 1) express advocacy related to a candidate for elective office in state or local government,[9] 2) campaigning related to a state or local referendum question, and 3) campaigning related to the recall of an elected official in state or local government.[10]

COMMITTEES

A "committee" is a group of two or more individuals that comes together, or an organization that is established, specifically for the purpose of accepting money from others and using that money for campaign spending or campaign giving.[11] An entity that is not formed specifically for that purpose—for example, a business or a social club—cannot accept money from others to use for campaign spending or campaign giving, and neither can an individual acting alone. However, such an entity or individual could set up a committee as a separate entity that would be able to undertake those activities.

Registration. A committee must register with a state or local filing officer before it accepts or disburses money above a specified threshold. Wisconsin's regulations distinguish seven types of committee (described below) and specify a threshold for each type. A committee must identify the type of committee it is when it registers. It must also identify a single depository account that it will use to accept and disburse money and an individual who will be in charge of the account.

A "candidate committee" is a committee formed by a candidate to accept contributions and make disbursements to support the candidate's election. A candidate cannot accept or disburse any money except through a candidate committee. In addition, a candidate can have only one candidate committee for any one office that the candidate seeks. However, the candidate can be the individual in charge of the candidate committee depository account. (For that matter, the candidate can be the sole member of the candidate committee—an exception to the rule that a committee consists of two or more individuals.) A candidate committee must register with the appropriate filing officer[12] as soon as the candidate qualifies[13] to be considered a candidate.

A "political party" is a committee that qualifies for a separate section on the partisan primary ballot—in other words, it is a "recognized" political party. (See page 319, above.) Local affiliates of a recognized political party that are authorized to operate under the same name are also considered political parties. A political party must register with the Ethics Commission before it accepts or disburses any money in a calendar year. (An entity that calls itself a political party, but that does not meet the criteria just described, would have to register as a different type of committee.)

A "legislative campaign committee" is a committee that is formed by state senators or state representatives of a particular political party to support candidates for legislative office by engaging in express advocacy on their behalf and by giving money to their candidate committees. A legislative campaign committee must register with the Ethics Commission before it accepts or disburses any money in a calendar year.

A "political action committee," or "PAC," is a committee, other than a candidate committee, political party, or legislative campaign committee, that 1) is formed to engage in express advocacy; 2) might do this independently or in coordination with a candidate, candidate committee, political party, or legislative campaign committee;[14] 3) might also campaign for and against referenda; and 4) might also give money to other committees. A PAC must register with the Ethics Commission if it accepts or disburses more than $2,500 in a calendar year.

An "independent expenditure committee," or "IEC," is a committee, other than a candidate committee, political party, or legislative campaign committee, that 1) is formed to engage in express advocacy; 2) will do this independently only and not in coordination with a candidate, candidate committee, political party, or legislative campaign committee; 3) might also campaign for and against referenda; and 4) might also give money to other committees, but will not give money to a candidate committee or to a committee that is able to give the money subsequently to a candidate committee. An IEC must register with the Ethics Commission if it accepts or disburses more than $2,500 in a calendar year.

A "referendum committee" is a committee that 1) is formed specifically to campaign for or against a referendum and 2) will not attempt to influence how voters vote with respect to a candidate. A referendum committee must register with the appropriate filing officer[15] if it accepts or disburses more than $10,000 in a calendar year.

A "recall committee" is a committee that is formed specifically to campaign for or against the recall of an elected official. A recall committee must register with the appropriate filing officer[16] if it accepts or disburses more than $2,000 in a calendar year. However, if a recall committee intends to gather signatures on a recall petition, it must register beforehand, regardless of whether it has accepted or disbursed any money.

Reporting financial activity. Each registered committee must file with its filing officer regular reports of its financial activity. Reports are due every January 15 and July 15. A report is also due on September 30 of an even-numbered year if a committee accepts or disburses money after July 1 for campaigning related to a partisan office or a referendum that will be held on the day of the partisan primary or general election. Other reports are required in advance of each primary and election with respect to which a committee accepts or disburses money. All of a committee's reports are made public within two days of their filing.

Each report must include, among other things:

- A listing of each gift of money received from an individual, specifying the amount and date of the gift and the name and address of the individual.
- A listing of each gift of money received from a committee, specifying the amount and date of the gift and the name and address of the committee.
- A listing of any other income received from any source, specifying the amount, date, and type of the income and the name and address of the source.
- A listing of each gift of money given to another committee, specifying the amount and date of the gift and the name and address of the committee.
- A listing of each other disbursement of money made to any individual or entity, specifying the amount, date, and purpose of the disbursement and the name and address of the individual or entity.

CAMPAIGN GIVING LIMITS

Campaign giving consists of giving money to a committee (necessarily, since an entity that is not a committee cannot use money given by others for campaigning). Wisconsin's regulations place limits on who can give money to a committee and how much money can be given. The limits apply simultaneously to the giver and the recipient; both are guilty if the latter accepts a gift that violates a limit.

Generally, only individuals and committees are allowed to give money to a committee. However, corporations, labor unions, cooperative associations, and federally recognized American Indian tribes can also give money in certain cases—but not to a candidate committee and not to a committee that is able to give the money subsequently to a candidate committee.

Giving to a candidate committee. An individual can give up to $20,000 to the candidate committee of a candidate for a statewide office (governor, lieutenant governor, attorney general, superintendent of public instruction, secretary of state, state treasurer, or supreme court justice). Other limits apply to other offices, including $2,000 for state senator and $1,000 for state representative.

A candidate committee can give to another candidate committee up to the same amount as an individual can give. However, the candidate committees of candidates who are running together for governor and lieutenant governor can give unlimited amounts to each other. A candidate can give unlimited amounts to his or her own candidate committee.

A political party or legislative campaign committee can give unlimited amounts to a candidate committee.

A PAC can give up to $86,000 to the candidate committee of a candidate for governor. Other limits apply to other offices, including $26,000 for lieutenant governor; $44,000 for attorney general; $18,000 for superintendent of public instruction, secretary of state, state treasurer, or supreme court justice; $2,000 for state senator; and $1,000 for state representative.

No other person may give money to a candidate committee.

Giving to a political party or legislative campaign committee. An individual, candidate committee, political party, or legislative campaign committee can give unlimited amounts to a political party or a legislative campaign committee. A PAC can give up to $12,000 in a calendar year to a political party or legislative campaign committee.

In addition to those amounts, an individual, candidate committee, political party, or legislative campaign committee can give unlimited amounts to a segregated fund established by a political party or legislative campaign committee to be used for purposes other than express advocacy or making contributions to a candidate committee. A PAC can give up to $12,000 in a calendar year to such a fund. A corporation, labor union, cooperative association, or American Indian tribe can also give up to $12,000 in a calendar year to such a fund, even though those entities cannot otherwise give money to a political party or legislative campaign committee.

No other person may give money to a political party or legislative campaign committee.

Giving to a PAC. An individual, candidate committee, political party, legislative campaign committee, or PAC can give unlimited amounts to a PAC. No other person may give money to a PAC.

Giving to an IEC. An individual, candidate committee, political party, legislative campaign committee, PAC, or IEC can give unlimited amounts to an IEC. A corporation, labor union, cooperative association, or American Indian tribe can also give unlimited amounts to an IEC. No other person may give money to an IEC.

Giving to a referendum committee. Individuals and committees can give unlimited amounts to a referendum committee. A corporation, labor union, cooperative association, or American Indian tribe can also give unlimited amounts to a referendum committee. No other person may give money to a referendum committee.

Giving to a recall committee. Individuals and committees other than IECs or referendum committees can give unlimited amounts to a recall committee. No other person may give money to a recall committee.

CAMPAIGN SPENDING LIMITS

Committees, entities that are not committees, and individuals can generally spend unlimited amounts on campaigning that they do themselves. The exception is spending on express advocacy that is coordinated with a candidate, candidate committee, political party, or legislative campaign committee.[17] Spending of this kind is treated as a gift given to the candidate committee of the candidate who benefits from the express advocacy. As such, it is subject to the limits that apply to giving to a candidate committee.

CAMPAIGN SPENDING SPECIAL DISCLOSURE REQUIREMENTS

Special disclosures are required for some kinds of campaign spending. These are the only disclosures that individuals and entities that are not committees must make about their campaign spending.[18] Committees, by contrast, must also report their campaign spending in the regular reports they file covering all of their financial activity.

Specific reporting of certain communications. If an individual, PAC, IEC, or entity that is not a committee spends $2,500 or more to make express advocacy communications during the 60 days preceding a primary or election, the individual, PAC, IEC, or entity must report that spending to the Ethics Commission within 72 hours after the first $2,500 has been spent and within 72 hours after any additional expenditure. Reports must specify the date, amount, recipient, and purpose of each expenditure, as well as the name of and office sought by any candidate who is the subject of the express advocacy. (However, these details are not required for the expenditures made prior to reaching the $2,500 threshold.) The reports are made public within two days of their filing.

Candidate committees, political parties, and legislative campaign committees are not required to report these expenditures other than in their regular financial activity reports.

Information required in certain communications. If an individual, committee, or other entity spends money to make an express advocacy communication or to make a communication to influence the outcome of a recall effort or to support or oppose a referendum, the individual, committee, or entity must include in the communication the phrase, "Paid for by," followed by the name of the individual, committee, or other entity.[19] For individuals and entities that are not committees, this requirement applies only to a communication whose cost exceeds $2,500. [BB]

NOTES

1. An alternative mechanism exists by which an individual can qualify to be listed on the spring election ballot. A town or village (but no other type of governmental jurisdiction) can hold a special meeting called a "caucus" to select the individuals who will be the candidates at the spring election for the offices of the town or village. The caucus must be held on or between the January 2 and the January 21 preceding the spring election. The caucus is open to the public, but only the eligible voters of the town or village can participate. The caucus participants nominate one or more individuals to be the candidates for each office and vote, if the total number of nominated candidates for a particular office is more than two (or is more than twice the number of seats to be filled), to determine which ones will be the candidates. An individual who is selected at a caucus to be a candidate for a town or village office must subsequently file a declaration of candidacy in order to be listed on the spring election ballot.

2. To register via the electronic registration system, an individual must possess a current and valid Wisconsin driver's license or identification card. The system requires the individual to enter his or her name, address, and date of birth together with the number of the driver's license or identification card. If the system confirms that the individual's information matches the records of the state Department of Transportation pertaining to the driver's license or identification card, the system permits the individual to register by 1) filling out and submitting an electronic version of the registration form, 2) "signing" the form by authorizing the use of a copy of the signature that he or she provided when applying for the driver's license or identification card, and 3) using as proof of residence the number of his or her driver's license or identification card.

3. Military voters (members of a uniformed service who are residents of Wisconsin and their spouses and dependents who reside with or accompany them) and overseas voters (former Wisconsin residents who no longer reside in the U.S. but remain U.S. citizens) can obtain and cast a Wisconsin absentee ballot without providing proof of identification. Overseas voters are entitled to vote for offices in national government only (U.S. president, vice president, senator, and representative).

4. Some municipalities use electronic poll books as an alternative to creating paper copies of a poll list.

5. If an individual's name and address are not listed in the poll list or electronic poll book, the poll worker will determine whether the voter is at the wrong polling place or is at the correct polling place but not registered. In the one case, the poll worker will direct the voter to the correct polling place; in the other, the poll worker will tell the voter where to go so that the voter can register.

If an individual's name and address are listed in the poll list or electronic poll book but a poll worker believes that the name on the proof of identification is not consistent with the name on the poll list or electronic poll book, or that a photograph on the proof of identification does not reasonably resemble the individual, the poll worker must challenge the individual as unqualified to vote. The individual must reply to the challenge under oath in order to obtain a ballot. If the poll worker does not withdraw the challenge, the individual must also take an oath that he or she is eligible to cast the ballot, and a poll worker must make a note in the poll list or electronic poll book and on the ballot before issuing it. The individual's votes will be considered valid unless the election officials responsible for counting the votes determine beyond a reasonable doubt, based on evidence presented, that the individual was not eligible to vote or was not properly registered.

If an individual's name and address are listed in the poll list or electronic poll book but the individual is unable or unwilling to present proof of identification, he or she is given an opportunity to cast a provisional ballot, rather than a regular ballot. The voter must sign a certification attesting that he or she is eligible to cast the ballot. The provisional ballot will not be counted unless the voter subsequently presents the proof of identification. The voter can return to the polling place to do this, until 8:00 p.m. when the polls close, or the voter can bring the proof of identification to the municipal clerk's office, until 4:00 p.m. on the Friday following the election.

6. Military and overseas voters are exempt from this requirement. (See note 3.)

7. If the voter requested the ballot by email or fax, the voter must also include in the second envelope a signed, printed copy of the request.

8. Another kind of entity, called a "conduit," is subject to similar requirements. Conduits do not spend money on campaigning themselves, nor do they give money to others to spend on campaigning. Rather, they hold money on behalf of givers and pass it on to a committee at the direction of those givers.

9. Express advocacy is communication that 1) uses words such as "vote for," "elect," "support," "vote against," "defeat," or "oppose" with reference to a clearly identified candidate and 2) unambiguously relates to the election or

defeat of that candidate. Communication that refers to a candidate but that does not qualify as express advocacy would not, by itself, subject the communicator to Wisconsin's regulations, even if the communication was intended to influence voters' opinion of the candidate.

10. Not covered by the regulations is campaigning related to a candidate for elective office in national government. That kind of campaigning is regulated under federal law. There is no national-level referendum or recall process.

11. The money that a committee accepts from others can consist exclusively of money provided by the committee's own members; the committee is an entity distinct from its individual members. A committee is formed, therefore, whenever individuals pool their money to engage in campaign spending or campaign giving, regardless of how informal their decision-making process is or how little campaign spending or giving they actually do.

12. The Ethics Commission, if the candidate is seeking office in state government, or a county, municipal, or school district clerk, if the candidate is seeking office in local government.

13. Based on one of the following criteria: 1) filing nomination papers, 2) being certified as the nominee of a political party or a village or town caucus, 3) accepting or disbursing any money in an effort to win a primary or election, or 4) being an incumbent elective office holder. See note 1 for details regarding village and town caucuses.

14. Under Wisconsin law, coordination exists in only two situations: 1) a candidate, candidate committee, political party, or legislative campaign committee communicates directly with an individual or with an entity other than a political party or legislative campaign committee to specifically request that the individual or entity make an expenditure for express advocacy, and the individual or entity explicitly assents before making the expenditure; or 2) a candidate, candidate committee, political party, or legislative campaign committee exercises control over an expenditure made for express advocacy by an individual or by an entity other than a political party or legislative campaign committee or exercises control over the content, timing, location, form, intended audience, number, or frequency of the express advocacy.

15. The Ethics Commission, for a statewide referendum, or a county, municipal, or school district clerk, for a local one.

16. The Ethics Commission, if the petition pertains to an official in state government, or a county, municipal, or school district clerk, if it pertains to an official in local government.

17. Also, some entities that enjoy tax-exempt status under federal law, based on the fact that they have limited themselves to specific activities, would lose that status if they were to spend money on campaigning. In addition, a registered committee cannot spend money on a kind of campaigning that is inconsistent with the type of committee that it has registered as. See note 14 for the criteria that define coordination.

18. Campaign giving is a different story. For every gift of money that an individual or entity makes to a committee, the individual or entity must disclose to the committee the information (such as name and address) that the committee needs to complete its financial activity reports, and those reports, in turn, are made public soon after they are filed.

19. An additional phrase—"Not authorized by any candidate or candidate's agent or committee"—must be included in an express advocacy communication that is made independently, rather than in coordination with a candidate, candidate committee, political party, or legislative campaign committee.

LOCAL GOVERNMENT IN WISCONSIN

Government in Wisconsin includes not only the state government, but also numerous local governments that exist and operate under the authority of the state government. Some local governments are "general purpose districts," which have broad authority to administer a particular locale, while others are "special purpose districts," whose authority is limited to the performance of a specific function.

General purpose districts

Counties and municipalities—towns, villages, and cities—are Wisconsin's general purpose districts. The territory of the state is divided into counties, and it is also divided into towns, villages, and cities. Towns lie entirely within the boundaries of counties, but villages and cities can lie across county boundaries.

Historically, counties were created to be administrative subdivisions of the state. Towns were created within counties to enable sparsely populated areas to provide basic services for themselves, whereas villages and cities were created to enable population centers, wherever they had formed, to govern their local affairs. Today, counties continue to act as the local arm of state government, and towns continue to be providers of basic services, but all general purpose districts have some authority to make decisions about their local affairs.

General purpose districts determine their own budgets and raise money to pay for their operations by establishing fees, imposing property taxes on real property within their boundaries, and incurring debt.

Counties. Wisconsin has 72 counties. County boundaries are drawn by the legislature and specified in state law. County boundary lines generally run north to south or east to west or follow major physical features like rivers.

The governing body of a county is the county board. The county board is composed of supervisors who are elected from election districts within the county for two-year terms at the nonpartisan spring election. Each county decides for itself how many supervisors it will have (subject to a statutory maximum that is based on a county's population) and whether their terms will be concurrent or staggered. In addition to the county board, counties are required to have a central administrative officer. For this purpose, a county can create the office of county executive or county administrator, or it can designate an individual holding an existing elective or appointive office (other than county supervisor) to serve also as the county's administrative coordinator.

A county executive is elected for a four-year term at the nonpartisan spring election. Twelve counties have a county executive, including Wisconsin's eight most populous counties. The county executive directs all administrative functions; proposes to the county board an annual budget for the county; appoints (subject to approval by the county board) members of boards and commissions and heads of departments; and can veto actions of the county board.

A county administrator is appointed by the county board. About half of Wisconsin counties have county administrator positions. The powers and responsibilities of this office are similar to those of a county executive, but a county administrator has no veto power and can be removed by the county board.

A county administrative coordinator, finally, has only the powers and responsibilities assigned by the county board. These could be as extensive as those of a county administrator but need not be. An individual serving as county administrative coordinator has no veto power, and his or her service in this capacity can be terminated by the county board.

Apart from its supervisors and county executive (if any), the elected officers of a county, including the sheriff, district attorney, clerk, and treasurer, are elected for four-year terms at the partisan general election.

Counties administer state programs in a variety of ways. County district attorneys enforce the state's criminal laws, and county jails incarcerate many violators of those laws; county clerks and registers of deeds maintain state-mandated vital and property records; county clerks oversee elections; and county human services departments administer state family and human service programs. In performing these functions for the state, counties have a limited role in determining policy, because the state sets specific standards that counties must abide by.

At the same time, however, counties have some authority to determine policy on local matters. For example, counties can regulate land use in the county (though not within the territory of a city or village), operate county highway systems, and establish recreational programs and social services programs.

Generally, all counties have the same powers and duties, but the legislature has imposed special requirements on the state's most populous county, Milwaukee. Among other things, that county must utilize a specific budgeting procedure that includes various reports and notices and that limits certain types of expenditures; and it must use a county executive system rather than an appointed central administrative officer.

Towns. Wisconsin has 1,245 towns. Town boundaries can be drawn by a county or a circuit court, according to procedures authorized by the legislature, and also by the legislature directly. Town boundary lines, like those of counties, generally run north to south or east to west or follow major physical features. However, town boundary lines can vary from this pattern when part of a town has been incorporated as, or annexed by, a city or village.

The governing body of a town is the town board. This board is typically composed of three supervisors, but towns that meet certain criteria can opt to have up to five. Supervisors are elected at large for two-year terms at the nonpartisan spring election. In towns that have four or five supervisors, the terms can be staggered. One of the supervisor seats is designated for the town board chair, and the supervisor elected to that seat presides over the board's meetings and acts on behalf of the board in certain matters. Towns do not have a separate elected executive officer, but a town can create the appointive position of town administrator to perform administrative functions. Other town officers include the town clerk, treasurer, surveyor, assessor, and constable. Each town can decide for itself whether these officers will be elected or appointed. If elected, they are elected for two-year terms at the nonpartisan spring election. Towns are also permitted to combine or abolish some of these offices.

A distinctive feature of the town form of government is the annual town meeting. The annual meeting is held either on the third Tuesday of April or on another date set by the voters at the preceding town meeting. During the meeting all eligible voters of the town are entitled to debate and vote on certain matters, including major issues affecting the town, such as establishing the tax levy and authorizing bonding. Determinations of the town meeting are binding on the town board and cannot be overturned by it.

Towns are required to provide certain basic services, in particular fire protection and the maintenance of local roads, and are allowed to provide other basic services, such as law enforcement and garbage collection. Many towns, particularly less populous and more rural ones, do little more than this. However, towns can also make policy on local matters. In particular, a town can opt to exercise village powers (by approving a resolution at a town meeting), which permits it to take any of the actions a village can take, except actions relating to the structure of its government. The village powers that towns most often exercise are those related to land use regulation. (Towns are otherwise subject to county land use regulation.)

Cities and villages. Wisconsin has 190 cities and 415 villages. City and village boundaries do not follow any particular pattern and are determined when the residents of territory lying within one or more towns incorporate the territory as a city or village. Incorporation is authorized by state law, and several procedures are provided. Typically, residents who wish to incorporate territory file a petition with the circuit court. If the circuit court determines that the petition is formally sufficient and that requirements pertaining to size, population, and population density have been met, the petition is forwarded to the state's Incorporation

Review Board. If that board determines that the incorporation is in the public interest, a referendum on the incorporation is held in the territory that is proposed to be incorporated. If the referendum is approved, the city or village is established.

The governing body of a city is the common council, which is composed of alders and, in cities that have one, a mayor. The alders are elected at the nonpartisan spring election. Each city decides for itself how many alders it will have, whether they will be elected at large or from election districts, what the term of office will be, and whether terms will be staggered or concurrent. The mayor is elected at large at the nonpartisan spring election for a term decided by the city. The mayor presides over meetings of the common council but has no vote, except to break a tie.

Cities use two forms of executive organization. In most cities, the mayor is the chief executive officer. The mayor can veto the council's actions and has a general responsibility to ensure that the laws are obeyed and that city officials and employees carry out their duties. Specific responsibilities, however, vary from city to city. In some cities, for example, the mayor proposes an annual budget for the city, but in others, the council develops the budget itself. Similarly, the mayor might have authority to appoint many or few of a city's appointive positions.

In place of a mayor, about a dozen cities have created the position of city manager. A city manager is appointed (and can be removed) by the common council. A city manager can attend, but does not preside or vote at, meetings of the council and cannot veto its actions. The responsibilities of a city manager include proposing an annual budget and appointing department heads, unless the common council defines the position differently.

City officers other than alders and the mayor or city manager can be elected or appointed, as decided by the city. If elected, they are elected at the nonpartisan spring election.

The governing body of a village is the village board, which is composed of trustees and a village president. Trustees are elected at the nonpartisan spring election for staggered terms. Each village decides for itself how many trustees it will have, whether they will be elected at large or from election districts, and what the term of office will be. The village president is elected at large at the nonpartisan spring election, for a term decided by the village. The village president presides over meetings of the village board and votes as a trustee. The president also acts on behalf of the board in certain matters.

Villages do not have a separate elected executive officer, but about a dozen villages have created the position of village manager to perform much the same role as a city manager performs in a city. A village manager is appointed (and can be removed) by the village board.

Village officers other than the trustees, president, and village manager (if any) can be elected or appointed, as decided by the village. If elected, they are elected at the nonpartisan spring election.

Cities and villages, like towns, provide basic services. These include fire protection, road maintenance, and police service. To a greater extent than towns or counties, however, cities and villages have broad authority to make local policy. Some powers are granted expressly in state statutes. Among the most characteristic of these are powers related to land use regulation, including authority to make rules that limit land uses in particular areas and that limit the kinds of structures that can be built or maintained in the city or village and authority to grant exceptions to the rules.

Beyond the authority granted in the statutes, however, cities and villages possess "home rule" powers conferred by the state constitution. The home rule provision states that cities and villages have the authority to "determine their local affairs and government, subject only to this constitution and to such enactments of the legislature of statewide concern as with uniformity shall affect every city or every village." The extent of the powers conferred by the provision and the extent to which those powers may be restricted by the state have varied over time, based on judicial decisions. Typically, however, the provision has been understood to allow cities and villages to take action on local matters without specific authorization from the state. That is, conversely to the situation with towns or counties, cities and villages can take such action unless specifically prohibited from doing so.

An additional power exercised only by cities and villages is the power of annexation: the power to detach territory from a town and attach it to the city or village. There are several different procedures by which an annexation can take place. Usually, all of the owners of property in the territory to be annexed sign on to a petition for annexation that is filed with the annexing city or village. If the petition meets certain statutory requirements and the governing body of the city or village enacts an ordinance approving the annexation, the territory becomes part of the city or village. In most cases, a town has no power to prohibit an annexation of part of its territory, but it can challenge the legality of an annexation in court.

Although cities and villages ordinarily have the same powers and duties, the legislature has imposed special requirements on "1st class" cities, including specific standards for budgeting, public employment, and police and fire department administration. Currently, Milwaukee is Wisconsin's only 1st class city.

Special purpose districts

Wisconsin has over 1,100 special purpose districts. The legislature has created some special purpose districts directly, and it has also authorized general purpose districts to create certain types of special purpose districts. Although a special purpose district exists only to perform a special function, the scope of its authority and its effect on the people who reside within its jurisdiction can be significant. For example, some school districts have jurisdiction over the education of tens of thousands of children, and some metropolitan sewerage districts manage sewage for hundreds of thousands of people. Other special purpose districts, however, such as certain public inland lake protection and rehabilitation districts, have authority over a very small geographic area and directly affect only a very small number of people.

School districts. Wisconsin has 421 school districts, which collectively cover the entire territory of the state. District boundaries can be modified, including by subdividing or consolidating existing districts, so long as no territory of the state is left outside of a district. Boundary modifications are typically initiated by the affected districts and might require ratification by referendum. The governing body of a school district is the school board. School board members are elected at the nonpartisan spring election, usually for staggered three-year terms. The number of members on a school board varies between three and eleven, and school board members can be elected at large or from election districts. School districts operate primary and secondary schools and otherwise provide educational services to the children who reside in the district. School districts are authorized to levy property taxes and to incur debt.

Technical college districts. Wisconsin has 16 technical college districts, which collectively cover the entire territory of the state. The number of districts and their boundaries were originally determined by a predecessor of the state Technical College System Board, which now has the power to reorganize the districts. Technical college districts are governed by boards of nine members who are appointed for staggered three-year terms. Depending on the district, the appointments are made by a committee composed of the county board chairs of the counties that lie within the district or by a committee composed of the school board presidents of the school districts that lie within the district. For the Milwaukee Area Technical College District, the appointing committee is composed of the Milwaukee county executive and the Milwaukee, Ozaukee, and Washington county board chairs. Technical college districts operate technical colleges that provide postsecondary education and occupational training to students who enroll in their programs. Districts are authorized to charge tuition and other fees, levy property taxes, and incur debt.

Metropolitan sewerage districts. Wisconsin has seven metropolitan sewerage districts. The legislature created the Milwaukee Metropolitan Sewerage District (MMSD) in the Milwaukee area. State law authorizes general purpose districts in the rest of the state to create their own metropolitan sewerage districts. Sewerage districts plan, design, construct, maintain, and operate sewerage systems for the collection, transmission, disposal, and treatment of both sewage and storm water. An 11-member commission governs the MMSD, and commissions made up of five or nine members govern other sewerage districts. Commissioners of the MMSD are appointed to staggered three-year terms by officials of the municipalities located in Milwaukee County. Commissioners of the Madison Metropolitan Sewerage District are appointed to staggered three-year terms by officials of the municipalities included in the district. Commissioners of other sewerage districts are generally appointed to staggered five-year terms by the county board of the county in which the district is located. Funds for a district's projects and operations are generated from property taxes assessed against property located in the district, from the issuance of bonds, and from user fees that are paid by the individuals and businesses that use the district's services. A large district, like the MMSD, provides services both to people who live within its jurisdiction and to people whose municipalities have contracted with it for its services.

Professional sports team stadium districts. Wisconsin has three professional sports team stadium districts. The Southeast Wisconsin Professional Baseball Park District was created by the legislature in 1995 and is authorized to issue bonds to acquire, construct, own, and operate a baseball park and related facilities. The district built, and is the majority owner of, American Family Field, the home stadium of the Milwaukee Brewers baseball team. To pay off the debt incurred in constructing the stadium and to pay for stadium maintenance, the district charges fees for the use of its facilities and was authorized to impose a sales tax within the district's jurisdiction, which consists of Milwaukee, Ozaukee, Racine, Waukesha, and Washington Counties. This tax ended on March 31, 2020. The district is governed by a board of 13 members: six appointed by the governor, three for two-year terms and three for four-year terms; two appointed by and serving at the pleasure of the Milwaukee county executive for indefinite terms; and one each appointed by and serving at the pleasure of the Racine county executive, Waukesha county executive, Ozaukee county board chair, Washington county board chair, and Milwaukee mayor.

The Professional Football Stadium District was created by the legislature in 1999 to acquire, renovate, and operate Lambeau Field, the home stadium of the Green Bay Packers football team. The district was authorized to finance the acquisition and renovation of the stadium by issuing bonds and to pay off the bonds by imposing a sales tax within the district's jurisdiction, which is coextensive with the boundaries of Brown County. The sales tax was imposed until September 2015, at which time sufficient money had been collected to repay the bonds and to set aside a required reserve fund. While the renovation of Lambeau Field is complete, the district continues to manage and maintain the stadium by charging fees for use of its facilities and seat fees and by drawing on its reserve fund. The district is governed by a board of seven members who are appointed for concurrent two-year terms by elected local officials, including the mayor of Green Bay and the Brown county executive.

The Wisconsin Center District was created in 1994 by the City of Milwaukee under a state law that permits general purpose districts in the state to create a kind of special purpose district called a "local exposition district." The district was authorized to issue bonds to build, own, and operate certain entertainment facilities in Milwaukee; these facilities are known today as the Miller High Life Theatre, Wisconsin Center, and UW-Milwaukee Panther Arena. To pay off the bonds, the district is authorized to impose special sales taxes in Milwaukee County on hotel rooms, on food and beverages sold in restaurants and taverns, and on car rentals. Operating revenues of the facilities pay for the district's operations. In 2015, the legislature expanded the district's purpose, altered its governance structure, and authorized it to issue bonds to finance the development and construction of the Fiserv Forum, home arena of the Milwaukee Bucks basketball team. The state, the City of Milwaukee, and Milwaukee County are required to provide the district the money that the district will need to pay off the bonds. The district is governed by a board of 17 members, including the state assembly speaker and minority leader, the state senate majority leader and minority leader, and appointees of the governor, the Milwaukee mayor, the Milwaukee common council president, and the Milwaukee county executive.

Other special purpose districts. State law also authorizes the creation of other types of special purpose districts. These include agricultural drainage districts, sanitary districts, public inland lake protection and rehabilitation districts, sewer utility districts, solid waste management systems, long-term care districts, water utility districts, and mosquito control districts. BB

PUBLIC EDUCATION IN WISCONSIN

Article X, section 3 of the Wisconsin Constitution requires the legislature to provide a free uniform basic education to all children in the state. At the same time, the constitution does not prohibit the legislature from creating additional forms of publicly funded education; nor does it require the additional forms, if any, to be available to all children, to be entirely free, or to provide the same basic education as the legislature must make available to all children. This article describes first the general educational system that the legislature has established to meet its obligation under the constitution and then each of the currently existing additional forms of publicly funded education that the legislature has created. The article reflects education law as of July 1, 2022.

The general system

In Wisconsin, every child resides within a school district and is entitled to a free education at a public school operated by that school district. The education provided at the public school must conform to requirements specified in state law.

Wisconsin is organized into 421 school districts. Each school district is governed by a school board whose members are elected by the residents of the district. For the purpose of operating public schools, school districts can, among other things, own and lease property; employ teachers and other personnel; and contract for the provision of services. Funding for school district operations comes primarily from state aid and property taxes levied by each district, but also from federal aid and miscellaneous fees, sales, and interest earnings. The amount of general state aid that each school district receives is based on several factors, including the number of pupils enrolled in the district's schools. State law limits the total amount of revenue that a school district can receive each year from general state aid, computer aid, and property taxes. However, a school district can exceed its revenue limit if it obtains voter approval at a referendum. School districts also receive aid for specified purposes, known as categorical aids, that are not counted toward revenue limits.

State law sets out general educational goals for children attending public schools and requires school districts to provide educational programs that will enable students to attain those goals. State law requires school districts to specify the knowledge and skills that they intend students in each grade to acquire; to maintain curriculum plans; and to define criteria for promoting students to the fifth grade and the ninth grade and for awarding high school diplomas.

It requires school districts to schedule a minimum number of hours of direct student instruction in each grade. It also requires school districts to ensure that every teacher and professional staff member holds a certificate, license, or permit to teach issued by the state Department of Public Instruction (DPI), unless that teacher is a faculty member at an institution of higher education teaching in a high school. Within these parameters, and subject to further requirements, school districts have discretion to determine the specifics of their educational programs and policies.

Additional requirements under both state and federal law apply to how school districts provide education to children with disabilities. Each school district must identify, locate, and evaluate children with disabilities who reside in the district. It must develop an individualized education program (IEP) for each child with a disability that describes the special education and related services that the child needs to make appropriate progress. As long as the child is enrolled in the district, the district must regularly reevaluate the child, review and revise the IEP, and offer the child an educational setting in which it will implement the IEP. In addition, the school district must make special education and related services available to a child with a disability beginning in the year the child turns three years old and continuing through the year in which the child turns 21.

For state oversight purposes, school districts are required to report various kinds of information to DPI and to administer annually certain standardized tests to public school students in specific grades. In addition, DPI is required to publish an annual report, called the school and school district accountability report, which evaluates the performance of every public school and school district. (The individual evaluations in the report are called school or school district "report cards.")

Additional forms of publicly funded education

FULL-TIME OPEN ENROLLMENT PROGRAM

Under the Full-Time Open Enrollment Program (open enrollment), a child can attend a public school in a school district other than the one in which the child resides. For each open enrollment student, the state transfers to the nonresident school district a set amount from the state aid that is allocated for the student's resident school district. This transfer is greater for students with disabilities and may vary based on the actual costs incurred to educate the student.

In most cases, a child must apply to participate in the open enrollment program in the school year preceding the school year for which the application is made. The nonresident school district in which the child wishes to enroll cannot deny the application except for certain reasons, such as that the nonresident school district does not have space for additional students; that the nonresident school district does not provide the special education or related services specified in the IEP of an applicant who is a child with a disability; that the child has been habitually truant from the nonresident school district in a prior school year; or that the child has been expelled from any school district in the previous three years because of specific behaviors. Under special circumstances, a child can apply to participate in the program immediately.

The nonresident school district must afford an open enrollment student the same educational opportunities and programs as it affords a student who resides in the district. If the open enrollment student is a child with a disability, the nonresident school district assumes, in place of the resident school district, the duties under state and federal law that apply to the education of such children. The parent, rather than the school district, is responsible for providing transportation to and from school for an open enrollment student who is not a child with a disability. However, parents can apply to DPI for financial assistance based on need.

PART-TIME OPEN ENROLLMENT PROGRAM

The Part-Time Open Enrollment Program allows a student who is attending a public high school to take up to two courses at one time in a public school in a nonresident school district. If the student has a disability, the student's resident school district may deny the student's application if the school district determines that the course conflicts with the student's IEP. The student's resident district can also deny an application if the cost of the course the student wishes to take would impose an undue financial burden on the district. Lastly, a resident school district can reject an application for a course that does not satisfy graduation requirements in the resident school district.

In general, the resident school district pays the nonresident school district for a course that the student takes under part-time open enrollment. The amount of the payment is based on the total number of hours of instruction provided to the student in the particular course. Parents are responsible for transporting their student to and from the school in the other school district, unless a course is being taken to implement the student's IEP. Parents can apply to DPI for financial aid to offset the cost of transportation based on need.

EARLY COLLEGE CREDIT PROGRAM

The Early College Credit Program (ECCP) allows a student who is attending public or private high school to take college courses at a University of Wisconsin System institution, a tribally controlled college, or a private, nonprofit institution of higher education in Wisconsin. A student can indicate on the application whether he or she wants to take the class for high school credit, college credit, or both. The ECCP does not include courses taken at a public or private high school for college credit, commonly known as dual enrollment.

If the course a student takes is for high school credit, and if the course is not comparable to a course offered by the school district or private school, then the student pays nothing. The Department of Workforce Development and the school district or private school split the cost. The student pays for each course that the student takes for college credit only, although this cost is reduced. The student also pays for each course that the school board or private school governing board finds to be comparable to an existing course at the student's school or that the student does not successfully complete. Parents are responsible for providing transportation to and from courses under the ECCP, but can apply to DPI for financial assistance based on need.

TECHNICAL COLLEGE DUAL CREDIT

Wisconsin allows students who are attending a public school in grade 11 or 12 to take courses at a technical college. If the course is taken for high school credit and if the course is not comparable to a course at the student's high school but is eligible for credit, then the school district will pay for the student's tuition, fees, and books. Parents are responsible for providing transportation to and from courses at the technical college, unless a course is being taken to implement a student's IEP. If a student with a disability applies to the program, he or she may be denied if the cost of their participation would impose an undue burden on the school district.

CHARTER SCHOOLS

A charter school is a type of public school that is operated by an organization that contracts with an entity that the legislature has empowered to authorize charter schools. Currently, all school districts and several other entities have this power. The contract describes the school's educational program and governance structure and specifies the facilities and funds that will be available to it. The authorizing entity can revoke a charter school contract if the charter school operator fails to comply with the terms of the contract. The authorizing entity can also revoke the contract if the children attending the charter school fail to make sufficient progress towards attaining the general educational goals set out in state law for children attending public schools. Like other public schools, charter schools are free to students.

In general, charter schools are largely exempt from state education laws that apply to other public schools. However, charter schools are not exempt from state education laws that pertain to public health and safety or any law that explicitly applies to charter schools. In addition, all professional employees of a charter school who have direct contact with students or involvement with the instructional program must hold a license or permit to teach issued by DPI, with two exceptions: teachers at virtual charter schools and high school grade teachers who are faculty at an institution of higher learning may not need licenses.

Charter school operators must report the same kinds of information to DPI as school districts and administer the same standardized tests to their students as school districts must administer to students in other public schools. In addition, DPI must include performance evaluations of charter schools in the annual school and school district accountability report.

As public schools, charter schools are subject to federal laws pertaining to education, the education of children with disabilities, and civil rights.

School district charter schools. A charter school established by a school district is a public school of that school district, even though the school district does not directly operate the charter school. As a result, a school district charter school is subject to school district policies, except as otherwise negotiated in the charter contract. A student who attends a school district charter school is enrolled in the school district just the same as if the student attended a school that the school district operated directly. The school district receives the same amount of state aid or the same full-time open enrollment transfer payment for the child, and the school district has the same duties to provide special education and related services. However, a school district cannot require a student to attend a charter school and must provide other public school attendance arrangements for a student who does not wish to attend a charter school. A school district that establishes a charter school pays the charter school operator an amount negotiated in the charter contract to operate the charter school.

A school district can also establish a "virtual" charter school, where all or a portion of the instruction is provided on the Internet. A virtual charter school is considered to be located in the school district that establishes it, even if it has no physical presence there. In contrast to a bricks-and-mortar school, it is feasible under the Full-Time Open Enrollment Program for children who reside anywhere in the state to attend a virtual charter school. A teacher for a virtual charter school is not required to have a license from DPI if the teacher is licensed to teach the grade and subject they are teaching in the state from which the online course is provided.

Independent charter schools. Several entities other than school districts can authorize independent charter schools. This includes the chancellors of any institution in the University of Wisconsin System, the City of Milwaukee, any technical college district board, the county executive of Waukesha County, the

College of Menominee Nation, the Lac Courte Oreilles Ojibwe University, and the Office of Educational Opportunity in the University of Wisconsin System.

An independent charter school established by one of these entities is not part of any school district. Accordingly, an independent charter school is not subject to any school district's policies. If a child with a disability attends an independent charter school, the charter school operator is subject to the same federal laws pertaining to the education of such children as a school district would be and must evaluate the child, develop an IEP, offer the child an educational setting in which it will provide the special education and services specified in the IEP, and regularly reevaluate the child and revise the IEP. None of the chartering entities may establish or contract with a virtual charter school.

The state pays an independent charter school operator a set amount for each student attending the independent charter school.

PARENTAL CHOICE PROGRAMS

Under a parental choice program, the state makes a payment (sometimes referred to as the "voucher amount") that pays for a child from an eligible family to attend a private school participating in the parental choice program. There are three parental choice programs in Wisconsin: the Milwaukee Parental Choice Program, which has existed since 1989; the Racine Parental Choice Program, which was created in the 2011–13 biennial budget act; and the Statewide Parental Choice Program, which was created in the 2013–15 biennial budget act.

Each of these programs is available to children whose family income, at the time that the child first participates, is below a specified level (three times the federal poverty level for the Milwaukee and Racine programs and 2.2 times that level for the statewide program). A child must reside in the city of Milwaukee to participate in the Milwaukee program, in the Racine Unified School District to participate in the Racine program, and anywhere else in the state to participate in the statewide program. Except in certain circumstances, a child cannot participate in the Racine or statewide program if the child was attending a private school in the previous school year other than as a participant in one of those programs. In addition, a temporary limit has been imposed on the number of children from each school district who can participate in the statewide program. This limit was 7 percent of a school district's student membership in the 2022–23 school year. The limit will increase by one percentage point each school year until the 2025–26 school year and ceases to apply after that.

A private school that wishes to participate in a parental choice program must report to DPI, by the January 10 preceding each school year of participation, the number of spaces it has for choice students and pay an annual fee. Additional requirements apply to a private school that has been in continuous operation in this state for less than 12 consecutive months or provides education to fewer than 40 students divided into two or fewer grades.

A student who wishes to participate in a parental choice program must apply to a participating private school during specific enrollment periods. The private school may reject an applicant only if the spaces it has for choice students are full. If a private school rejects an application, the applicant can transfer his or her application to another participating private school. A private school must generally accept applicants on a random basis, but may give preference to applicants who participated in a parental choice program in the previous school year, siblings of such applicants, and siblings of applicants whom the private school has accepted for the current school year on a random basis.

A participating private school must satisfy all state health and safety laws and codes that are applicable to public schools and federal laws prohibiting discrimination on the basis of race, color, or national origin. It must satisfy at least one of four achievement standards to continue participating in the program, and it may not require a choice student to participate in any religious activity. The private school must also provide a prescribed minimum number of hours of direct student instruction in each grade. Additionally, all of the private school's teachers and administrators must have a bachelor's or higher degree or a license issued by DPI, with some exceptions for those who teach or administer courses that train rabbinical students.

Participating private schools must report the same kinds of information to DPI as school districts must report, but only with respect to the choice students attending them. They must also administer the same standardized tests to their choice students as school districts must administer to public school students. In addition, DPI must include an evaluation of each participating private school's performance with respect to its choice students in the annual school and school district accountability report.

A private school cannot charge tuition to a choice student unless the student's family income exceeds a set percentage of the federal poverty line. A private school can charge a choice student fees related to certain expenses (such as social and extracurricular activities, musical instruments, meals, and transportation) but cannot take adverse action against a choice student or the student's family if the fees are not paid.

SPECIAL NEEDS SCHOLARSHIP PROGRAM

Under the Special Needs Scholarship Program, the state makes a payment (the scholarship) to a private school, on behalf of the parent of a child with a disability, for the child to attend the private school. In the 2022–23 school year, the scholarship amount was $13,076. Beginning in the 2019–20 school year, if a student has participated in the program for a year, the scholarship amount can be the actual costs incurred by the private school in the previous year, if that is greater than the standard scholarship amount. There is no limit on the amount of additional tuition or fees a private school may charge a child who receives a scholarship under the program. A child with a disability is eligible for a scholarship under the program if three conditions are met. First, the child must have an IEP or services plan in effect. (A services plan outlines the services that a school district has agreed to provide to a child with a disability whose parent has enrolled the child in a private school rather than in the school district.) Second, the child's parent or guardian must consent to make the child available for reevaluation upon request of the child's school district of residence. And third, the private school that the child wishes to attend with the scholarship must be accredited or approved as a private school by DPI and must have notified DPI of its intent to participate in the program.

A private school that wishes to participate in the program must notify DPI of the number of spaces it has available for children who receive a scholarship under the program. A participating private school must accept applications under the program on a first-come, first-served basis, but may give preference to siblings of students who are already attending the private school if it receives more applications than the number of spaces it has available.

A participating private school must implement, for each child that receives a scholarship, either 1) the IEP or services plan that the child's school district of residence developed in its most recent evaluation of the child or 2) a modified version of that IEP or services plan agreed to between the private school and the child's parent. The private school must also provide the child with any related services agreed to between the private school and the child's parent that are not included in the child's IEP or services plan. A child with a disability who attends a private school under the program is not entitled to all the special education and related services to which he or she would be entitled under state and federal law if he or she attended a public school.

A participating private school must comply with all health and safety laws that apply to public schools; must provide each child who applies for a scholarship with a profile of the private school's special education program; and must submit to DPI an annual school financial information report.

Unless it is also participating in a parental choice program, a private school participating in the Special Needs Scholarship Program is not required to report to DPI the kinds of information that school districts must report or to administer to any of its students the standardized tests that school districts must administer to public school students, and no performance evaluation of the private school is included in the annual school and school district accountability report.

Once awarded, a scholarship continues until the child graduates from high school or until the end of the school term in which the child attains the age of 21, whichever comes first, unless, upon reevaluation by the child's school district of residence, it is determined that the child is no longer a child with a disability. In that case, the child can continue to receive a scholarship under the program, but the amount of the scholarship is reduced to the per student amount paid under the parental choice programs.

THE LEGISLATURE AND THE STATE BUDGET

The legislature has the power of the purse. In Wisconsin, the state government may not spend a single dollar without the legislature specifically authorizing the expenditure by law. The legislature controls the expenditure of state funds through its appropriation power, which is a power granted to the legislature under the Wisconsin Constitution. In the 1936 case *Finnegan v. Dammann*, the Wisconsin Supreme Court defined an appropriation as "the setting aside from the public revenue of a certain sum of money for a specified object, in such a manner that the executive officers of the government are authorized to use that money, and no more, for that object, and no other."[1] It is the legislature that directs the governor and the executive branch to spend state moneys and that decides the purposes for which they may be spent.

The most consequential exercise of the legislature's appropriation power is the enactment of the state budget. The biennial budget bill is easily the most significant piece of legislation that is enacted during the entire legislative session. This is the case for two reasons. First, the biennial budget bill appropriates almost all dollars that the state government will spend during the two fiscal years covered by the bill. These dollars mostly consist of state taxes and revenues, program and license fees, and federal moneys allocated to Wisconsin. In 2021 Wisconsin Act 58, the state budget act for the 2021–23 fiscal biennium, the legislature authorized over $87 billion in total state government spending from all revenue sources. The second reason for the significance of the biennial budget bill is that it contains most of the governor's public policy agenda for the entire legislative session. The biennial budget bill is generally considered the one bill that "must pass" in order to sufficiently fund state government operations and programs during the fiscal years covered in the bill. As such, there is a strong incentive for the governor and for legislators to try to incorporate major public policy items that they support into the budget bill. The state budget process is therefore unequaled in its effect on the operations of state government and on the people of Wisconsin.

The state budget process: core principles

There are four core principles to the state budget process in Wisconsin. First, the state budget is a biennial budget, covering two fiscal years of state government operations and programs, with each fiscal year beginning on July 1 and ending on June 30. Many states have a "drop-dead" date by which a new state budget must be enacted in order for state government to continue to operate. Wisconsin does not have such a deadline. In Wisconsin, if a new state budget is not enacted by June 30 of the odd-numbered year, state government continues to operate and its programs are funded, but only at the prior year's appropriation amounts. The governor and the legislature strive to enact the state budget bill before July 1 of the odd-numbered year, but there is little short-term fiscal impact if that deadline is not met.

Second, Wisconsin uses what is known as "program budgeting," which means that executive branch state agencies are assigned to different functional areas and, generally, lump-sum appropriations are made to each agency to fund its programs. The biennial budget bill therefore lists the overall amounts appropriated for agency operations and programs, but does not contain the expenditure details that one might find in a state that uses a "line-item" budget, where each agency expenditure is specifically budgeted by line in the bill. This level of detail is not found in the biennial budget bill in Wisconsin; instead, it appears in accompanying budget documents, which are not law but which do capture the intentions of the governor and the legislature in budget deliberations. Consequently, the portion of the executive budget bill that sets the expenditure levels of state operations and programs is roughly 200 pages in length, which is typically about 10 to 20 percent of the total number of pages of recent biennial budget bills.

Third, the Wisconsin Constitution requires that the legislature "provide for an annual tax sufficient to defray the estimated expenses of the state for each year."[2] What this means in practice is that Wisconsin has a balanced-budget requirement: state expenditures must equal revenues received by the state. Generally speaking, at each stage of the budget process, when different versions of the budget are formulated and considered, each version of the budget must be balanced by having proposed state expenditures in any fiscal year be less than or equal to anticipated state revenues. This is a real constraint on state budgeting, one that is not found at the federal level.

Finally, the Wisconsin Constitution grants the governor partial veto power over appropriation bills. This partial veto power allows the governor to reduce amounts appropriated to state agencies for their operations and programs by writing in a lower amount and allows the governor, with limitations, to veto specific words and digits within newly created statutory text in appropriation bills. The governor can thus significantly alter the legislature's budget actions. While this power has been curtailed in recent years by amendments to the constitution as well as through litigation, the governor still can reduce all state expenditures, or the expenditures of any specific state agency, with the stroke of a pen, subject only to an override of his or her actions by a two-thirds vote of each house of the legislature—an event that last occurred in 1985.

The state budget process: an overview of executive action

The provision for a biennial executive budget bill was created by Chapter 97, Laws of 1929,[3] and it has applied to all legislative sessions since 1931. Prior to that time, the governor was not responsible for submitting an executive budget bill to the legislature; individual bills were introduced for each department. The legislature delegated the biennial budget task to the governor for understandable reasons. As head of the executive branch, the governor can assess and coordinate the expenditure needs of each executive branch agency. In addition, the growth in state government in the twentieth century resulted in a level of public policy and budgetary expertise in the executive branch that is generally not available in the legislative branch, which has a much smaller professional staff. Requiring the governor to produce the budget bill allows the legislature to work from a document that may require modification, because of different legislative public policy or budgetary priorities, but which already contains numerous budgetary matters and details that the legislature need not address. The governor's budget is a solid foundation on which the legislature can build its version of the budget, a process which serves both the governor and the legislature well.

To begin the biennial budget process, in the summer of each even-numbered year, the State Budget Office in the Department of Administration provides budget instructions to executive branch agencies, establishing the manner of submitting budget requests and informing them of any broad fiscal or policy goals that the governor intends the state agencies to achieve. By September 15, state agencies must submit their budget requests to the State Budget Office for review by that office, the state budget director, and the governor. By November 20, the Department of Administration publishes a compilation and summation of the agency budget requests, as well as estimated revenues to the state for the current and forthcoming fiscal biennia. The State Budget Office oversees the preparation of legislation to achieve the governor's budget and policy recommendations. In this endeavor, the State Budget Office works closely with legal counsel at the Legislative Reference Bureau—the legislature's bill-drafting agency—to draft the statutory language that will ultimately be incorporated into the governor's budget bill. Throughout the process, the governor is briefed on individual items in the budget bill, and the bill is complete only when the governor has signed off on the items in the bill. The governor is then required to deliver the budget bill to the legislature no later than the last Tuesday in January of each odd-numbered year, though the legislature regularly moves this deadline back into February to allow the governor to make changes in the bill once more accurate revenue estimates for the current and forthcoming fiscal biennia are available in late January. When the budget bill is delivered to the legislature, the governor addresses the legislature on the proposals contained in the bill, which more often than not are the key public policy goals of the governor's administration for the entire legislative session.

The first thing to note about the production of the executive budget bill is the role of the State Budget Office. The State Budget Office is headed by the state budget director and consists of about 25 budget analysts who serve in classified civil service positions. These analysts serve both Republican and Democratic gubernatorial administrations in a strictly nonpartisan and highly professional manner and are able to provide independent review of state agency funding requirements, as well as fashion fiscal and nonfiscal policies to achieve the governor's political and public policy aims. The State Budget Office translates the governor's public policy goals into workable and funded programs.

The second thing to note about the production of the executive budget bill is that the State Budget Office works directly with nonpartisan legal counsel in the Legislative Reference Bureau to prepare statutory text that achieves the governor's policy goals. The Legislative Reference Bureau has about 20 licensed attorneys, each of whom has specialized legal expertise. Together, their knowledge covers virtually all policy areas. This is significant. The governor's budget bill is drafted in a professional, nonpartisan manner, so that the legislators need only focus on the public policies in the bill and not worry about the bill's legal quality or effectiveness. In addition, when the legislature takes up the governor's budget bill, the Legislative Reference Bureau attorneys who originally drafted the governor's provisions in the bill will be the ones who draft the legislature's alternatives. Consequently, often the same attorneys are working on the same language in the bill throughout the process. The legislature can thus depend on experienced and competent legal counsel to prepare its budget bill in an accurate, high-quality, and nonpartisan manner.

Finally, it is important to note the political uses of the executive budget bill. Given that it must pass, the budget bill is the primary tool by which a governor may advance his or her public policy agenda during the legislative session. Consequently, it is by far the longest and most complex bill before the legislature during the entire biennium. In recent years the bill has grown substantially in length. From 1961 to 1986, executive budget bills averaged 367 pages in length. From 1987 to 2021 in contrast, executive budget bills averaged 1,484 pages in length, roughly a fourfold increase in size. The governor uses the massive bill as a tool to garner public support for various policy changes.

The executive budget bill is now a blueprint for the legislature for taking up the governor's goals for public policy change. When the governor steps up to the assembly podium, usually around early February, to present the budget address to the legislature, an event that is televised throughout the state and broadcast live on the Internet, in many ways the political season commences in Wisconsin.

The state budget process: the role of the legislature

The Wisconsin Legislature is the policymaking body in this state and has the sole power to appropriate all moneys expended by the state. The biennial budget bill is, therefore, every bit as much of a product of legislative deliberation and action as it is a product of the governor's actions. The governor sets the agenda for legislative action on the budget, but the legislature examines, modifies or rejects, and eventually recreates what the governor originally had in the budget bill. In addition, the legislature devises policies of its own, often from whole cloth, and sometimes refashions the governor's policies so differently from their original form that they are barely recognizable. Much of what the governor has proposed in the budget bill will survive the legislative process, but the document that emerges from the legislature is very much a product of the legislature.

When the governor presents the budget bill to the legislature, it is legally required to be introduced by the Joint Committee on Finance and referred to that committee. In 1885, a young congressional scholar by the name of Woodrow Wilson, then a professor at Bryn Mawr College, wrote that "Congress in session is Congress on public exhibition, whilst Congress in its committee rooms is Congress at work."[4] This applies perfectly to the Wisconsin Legislature, and no committee more exemplifies that work ethic than the Joint Committee on Finance.

The Joint Committee on Finance consists of eight senators and eight representatives to the assembly. Any bill that affects revenues, taxes, or expenditures is referred to that committee and must be reported out of that committee before the legislature may take the bill up for consideration and passage. It is fair to say that this committee is the most powerful standing committee in the legislature and is a training ground for legislative leadership. Legislators on this committee work long hours.

The Joint Committee on Finance does not work alone, but is staffed by the Legislative Fiscal Bureau, a nonpartisan legislative service agency. The Legislative Fiscal Bureau has about 25 analysts, each of whom has policy and budgetary expertise in specific areas of state government. The analysts perform their work in a professional, nonpartisan manner, serving both the majority and minority parties in the legislature. After the budget bill is introduced, Legislative Fiscal Bureau analysts prepare a lengthy, detailed summary document that contains an analysis of every single item in the bill. The summary is written in plain English, is precise and exhaustive in its presentation of the governor's policies, and is hundreds of pages in length. The Legislative Fiscal Bureau summary is the document that forms the basis on which the Joint Committee on Finance begins its work on the budget.

The Joint Committee on Finance will often hold hearings at different locations throughout the state to receive testimony from the general public and interest group representatives. Beginning in April and continuing into May, the Legislative Fiscal Bureau prepares papers on the items contained in the budget bill, laying out alternatives to address the same items in the bill. The Legislative Fiscal Bureau derives its policy alternatives from its own public policy expertise and from committee member involvement. Sometimes working groups will form among members of the committee to consider and propose policy alternatives. During this time, the Joint Committee on Finance meets to approve items it will include in its version of the budget. These are lengthy and often contentious meetings that run late into the evening or early morning. It is not uncommon to see Joint Committee on Finance members and Legislative Fiscal Bureau analysts leaving the capitol building in the bright light of early morning. While the executive branch often has six months or more to prepare the governor's budget bill, the Joint Committee on Finance does its work in a much shorter time span, often only six to eight weeks.

In recent sessions, with the cooperation of leadership in both houses, the Joint Committee on Finance has removed many policy items that the governor submitted as part of the budget. For example, the substitute amendment adopted by the Joint Committee on Finance to replace Governor Evers's 2021 budget bill contained 1,446 fewer pages than the original bill. The enacted budget, 2021 Wisconsin Act 58, contained 175 pages; it was the shortest biennial budget in at least two decades.

Once the committee finishes its work, the Legislative Fiscal Bureau oversees the production of a substitute amendment that incorporates the committee's version of the budget to replace the governor's budget bill. To accomplish this, the Legislative Fiscal Bureau gives drafting instructions to attorneys at the Legislative Reference Bureau, who also work around the clock to prepare the substitute amendment.

The committee's substitute amendment is not always the final and complete version of the legislature's budget bill. Each house of the legislature has the option to further amend the substitute amendment to include items of its own design or to modify or reject items included by the Joint Committee on Finance. The extent to which the substitute amendment is modified by the houses depends on a number of factors, such as whether the same political party is the majority party in both houses, whether legislators who do not serve on the Joint Committee on Finance believe that their interests and concerns have been addressed in the substitute amendment, and the likelihood of the convening of a conference committee on the bill to resolve differences between the two houses. These calculations are based on substantive factors, in that members work to include items that benefit them or their constituents, as well as on strategic considerations, in that members want to fortify their own house's position in conference committee negotiations with the other house.

Once the legislature passes its version of the budget bill, the bill is presented to the governor for signing. As mentioned above, the governor has partial veto power over appropriation bills and uses that power to modify what the legislature has passed. The governor can reduce appropriations, as well as modify some statutory text. The extent to which the governor partially vetoes the bill also depends on a number of factors, such as the partisan makeup of the legislature, the degree to which the governor agrees with what the legislature has done, and whether the governor has made agreements in negotiations with the legislature over what can and cannot be vetoed. Once the governor has signed the bill into law, the budget-making process is concluded, as the only other possible step is for the legislature to override one or more of the governor's partial vetoes—an action, as mentioned earlier, that has not happened since 1985.

Concluding considerations

The state budget-making process is truly a year-long event, beginning in the summer of each even-numbered year when the State Budget Office sends budget instructions to the state agencies and concluding the following summer with the enactment of the biennial budget act. The process is characterized both by careful deliberation and by frenzied, all-night sessions and meetings. The budget bill is the work product of the governor, every elected member of the Senate and the Assembly, and numerous professional staff in both the executive and legislative branches. There is never an "easy" budget, as each fiscal biennium presents its own unique budgetary and political challenges. But there is never complete gridlock, as the legislature and the governor do always complete their work. Sometimes the budget is late, especially when the two houses are controlled by different political parties, but in the end Wisconsin will have a state budget. BB

NOTES

1. Finnegan v. Dammann, 220 Wis. 143, 148, 264 N.W. 622 (1936).

2. Wis. Const., art. VIII, § 5.

3. This would have been called Act 97 if it took effect today; before 1983, a bill that was enacted into law was called a "chapter" rather than an "act."

4. Wilson, Woodrow. *Congressional Government: A Study in American Politics* (Boston: Houghton Mifflin and Co., 1900), 79.

SIGNIFICANT ENACTMENTS OF THE 2021 LEGISLATURE

Agriculture

Act 92 (AB-314) requires the Department of Agriculture, Trade and Consumer Protection to establish an agricultural exports program to promote the export of the state's agricultural and agribusiness products and to cooperate with the Wisconsin Economic Development Corporation to increase the value of the state's dairy, meat, and crop exports by at least 25 percent over current values.

Beverages

Act 21 (AB-32) allows certain liquor retailers, such as restaurants and bars, to sell wine and distilled spirits to-go if the retailer seals the container of wine or distilled spirits with a tamper-evident seal before it is removed from the premises.

Act 43 (AB-277) allows the State Fair Park Board to issue retail alcohol beverage permits authorizing the retail sale of alcohol beverages at the state fair park, requires board approval before a brewer or brewpub may sell beer at the state fair park, and allows alcohol beverage suppliers to provide things of value to state fair park vendors.

Business and consumer law

Act 258 (SB-566) adopts, with modifications, the most recent versions of the Uniform Law Commission's Limited Liability Company Act and Limited Partnership Act and makes corresponding changes to this state's partnership law and corporations law. Among its many changes, the act includes provisions relating to LLC and LP formation, LLC operating agreements, LP partnership agreements, LLC members' authority, LP partner liability, creation of limited liability LPs, fiduciary and other duties of LLC members and managers and LP partners, LLC and LP operating requirements, dissociation of LLC members and LP partners, dissolution and winding up of LLCs and LPs, and business mergers involving LLCs or LPs. The act includes phase-in and opt-out provisions.

Children

Act 41 (AB-142) extends immunity from criminal and civil liability to a person who assists in the medical examination of a child or expectant mother and to any person who otherwise, in good faith, provides information, assistance, or consultation in connection with a child abuse or neglect report, investigation, or legal intervention.

Act 58 (AB-68) does the following:
1. Increases by 2.5 percent, beginning on January 1, 2022, the monthly basic maintenance rates paid to foster parents and the monthly kinship care payments made to relatives who provide care for children.
2. Allocates funding to programs and subsidies from federal moneys received under Temporary Assistance for Needy Families.
3. Increases the per-person daily rates that are assessed on counties for state-provided juvenile correctional services.

Act 72 (SB-24) changes the background check requirements for an individual who receives an out-of-home placement of a child under the Children's Code. Prior law prohibited a person from working for or residing with a licensed out-of-home care provider if the person had been convicted of certain crimes. The act adds to the list of crimes that lead to disqualification specified crimes against children and includes persons who pleaded no contest for those crimes or had the charges dropped for those crimes as part of a plea agreement. The act also generally prohibits a court from placing a child with an unlicensed relative other than a parent or temporarily placing a child with another unlicensed person under the Children's Code if the relative or unlicensed person has been convicted of, pleaded no contest to, or been subject to a plea agreement for the crimes against a child that would disqualify that person from receiving a license.

Act 150 (SB-524) provides an avenue for the adult offspring of a person whose birth parents' parental rights have been terminated to access the offspring's parent's original birth certificate and information about the birth parents.

Corrections

Act 53 (SB-299) requires a person to submit a DNA specimen to the state crime laboratories if the person is moving to Wisconsin and will be supervised by the Department of Corrections and the person was placed on probation, extended supervision, or parole in the person's state on or after April 1, 2015, for the commission of any crime. Under prior law, the person had to have been placed on probation, extended supervision, or parole on or after January 1, 2000, for a crime that would have been a felony if committed in Wisconsin or before January 1, 2000, for a crime that would have been comparable to first or second degree sexual assault.

Act 58 (AB-68) provides an additional $5 per hour worked during the 2021–23 biennium to correctional officers and correctional sergeants in correctional facilities when the vacancy rate for those positions is more than 40 percent. This rate continues until the vacancy rate is 40 percent or less for six consecutive months.

Act 186 (AB-825) requires each state correctional institution to make a record of any alleged battery that a prisoner commits against a DOC correctional officer or teacher. Under the act, DOC must forward all such records to the law enforcement agency with jurisdiction over the institution.

Courts and legal process

Act 4 (January 2021 Special Session SB-1) establishes, subject to certain exceptions, an exemption for entities from civil liability for any death, injuries, or damages caused by an act or omission resulting in or relating to exposure to the novel coronavirus identified as SARS-CoV-2 or COVID 19. The entities covered by the exemption include partnerships, corporations, associations, governmental entities, tribal governments and entities, and any other legal entity, such as a school, institution of higher education, or nonprofit organization. The act also exempts from liability any employer or business owner, employee, agent, or independent contractor of an entity.

Act 32 (SB-51) requires that every newspaper publishing legal notices have an Internet site that includes on its home page a prominent link to its legal notices section; place an electronic copy of the notices at no additional charge on its Internet site; and make its legal notices section available for free and include a link to the Wisconsin newspapers legal notices Internet site.

Act 182 (SB-627) provides that when a child under 14 years old has two living parents, one parent's petition to change the legal name of that child may be granted without the parent providing notice to the other parent if that other parent has been convicted of certain homicide or sex offenses. The act further provides that, in such a situation, the petition may be granted regardless of whether the nonpetitioning parent appears at the hearing on the petition.

Act 194 (SB-341) generally limits the time a person has to start a lawsuit for damages against a licensed or certified real estate appraiser to five years from the date the appraiser submits the appraisal report to the client for whom services are performed. Prior law did not provide a specific limitations period for real estate appraisal services.

Act 256 (SB-519) allows a court to issue a permanent restraining order in cases when the person against whom the restraining order is requested has been convicted of the sexual assault of the person requesting the restraining order. Under preexisting law, generally, initial restraining orders were limited to a maximum period of two to four years.

Crime

Act 28 (SB-85) expands the definition of "stalking" in the criminal code to include attempts to contact a victim via text messaging and other electronic means of communication, including sending and posting online content.

Act 54 (SB-99) allows a court to require any criminal defendant who throws or expels blood, semen, vomit, saliva, urine, feces, or another bodily substance at or toward a public safety worker or a prosecutor to be tested for communicable diseases if there is probable cause to believe that there was a potential for transmitting a communicable disease to the public safety worker or prosecutor.

Act 76 (SB-17) provides increased penalties for specified crimes, including sexual assault, when the victim is an elder person (over the age of 60) and creates the crime of physical abuse of an elder person, which is modeled after the current law crime of physical abuse of a child. The act also allows elder persons seeking a restraining order to appear by audiovisual means rather than in person and creates procedures for freezing the assets of a criminal defendant charged with financial exploitation of an elder person.

Act 116 (SB-71) creates statutory procedures for the transmission, processing, and storage of sexual assault kits.

Act 117 (SB-94) requires the Department of Justice to establish a database to provide victims of sexual assault access to information about the status of any sexual assault kit the victim provided and to allow health care professionals, forensic laboratories, law enforcement agencies, prosecutors, and DOJ to update and track the location and status of sexual assault kits.

Act 120 (SB-242) makes it a Class I felony to destroy, handle, store, or treat a vaccine or drug with the intent to render it unsafe, tainted, spoiled, ineffective, or otherwise unusable.

Act 179 (SB-352) increases the penalties associated with the manufacture, distribution, and delivery of, and for the possession with intent to manufacture, distribute, or deliver, fentanyl or fentanyl analogs. Under the act, the penalty increase depends on the amount of the controlled substance involved with the violation.

Act 187 (SB-100) expands the crime of a special circumstances battery so that it is a Class H felony to intentionally harm a family member of a probation, extended supervision, and parole agent or to threaten to harm such an agent or a family member of the agent. Under former law, it was a Class H felony to intentionally harm the agent. The act also expands the definition of the agent so that it includes an agent in a comparable program authorized by a federally recognized American Indian tribe or band.

Act 209 (AB-960) expands the crime of a special circumstances battery by making it a Class H felony to intentionally harm or threaten harm to a health care provider or a family member of a health care provider. Under preexisting law, it is a Class H felony to intentionally harm a nurse or an emergency medical care provider.

Act 263 (AB-251) provides that it is a Class I felony to impersonate or represent oneself to be a public officer, employee, or utility employee with the intent to mislead others into believing that he or she is actually a public officer or employee or the employee of a utility.

Domestic relations

Act 37 (SB-112) requires a court that grants physical placement of a child with one parent for less than 25 percent of the time to enter specific findings of fact as to the reasons the placement is in the best interest of the child. The act also rearranges the statutory factors for consideration of the best interest of the child in a child custody proceeding and removes the factors of the stability in placement and the availability of child care services.

Act 84 (AB-270) makes changes relating to marriage ceremonies and the issuance and validity of marriage licenses. The act allows residents and nonresidents to obtain a marriage license and marry in any county; extends license validity from 30 to 60 days; reduces the license waiting period from five to three days; and allows certain service members to marry with only one witness other than the officiant present. The act allows a county clerk to decide whether documentation required for a license is unobtainable, but if an applicant presents specified documentation in lieu of a birth record, the act requires the clerk to consider it satisfactory for licensing purposes. The act also provides that if a clerk is not satisfied with the documentation presented, the clerk must notify the applicant of the right to judicial review and, upon request, submit the documentation to a judge.

Act 160 (SB-104) changes the Department of Children and Families administrative code definition of "gross income" for purposes of calculating child support to specify that gross income includes veterans disability compensation benefits and military allowances, including basic allowances for subsistence and housing, but not variable housing costs.

Act 161 (SB-108) adopts the Uniform Deployed Parents Custody and Visitation

Act to provide a process and standards for a temporary delegation of custodial responsibilities when a parent is deployed in military or other national service.

Economic development

Act 58 (AB-68) requires WEDC to expend at least $3 million in the 2021–23 fiscal biennium on initiatives that attract talent to Wisconsin or retain talent in Wisconsin.

Education

HIGHER EDUCATION

Act 11 (SB-79) requires the Board of Regents of the UW System to monitor, and to report in the aggregate, the extension and outreach hours of UW System faculty and academic staff who provide extension services in applied agricultural research.

Act 58 (AB-68) does the following:
1. Allows dentists who agree to practice in rural areas under an educational loan repayment assistance program to receive the same amount of financial assistance that physicians may receive under the program. Accordingly, the act allows a dentist who agrees to practice under the conditions of the program to receive up to $100,000 in loan repayment assistance.
2. Provides $5 million for release to the Higher Educational Aids Board upon request and approval by the Joint Committee on Finance to fund a new HEAB nurse educator financial assistance program that provides fellowships, educational loan repayment assistance, and postdoctoral fellowships for nurse educators and certain nursing students. Nurse educators who receive financial assistance under the program must commit to teach for at least three consecutive years in a nursing program in a higher education institution in Wisconsin.

PRIMARY AND SECONDARY EDUCATION

Act 18 (SB-109) allows a pupil, during the 2021–22 school year, to attend a fully virtual option offered by a nonresident school board or a charter school located in a nonresident school district under the full-time open enrollment program.

Act 30 (SB-69) requires the state superintendent to incorporate the study of the Holocaust and other genocides into the model academic standards for social studies and to develop model curricula and instructional materials for pupils on the same subject. The act also requires a school board, independent charter school, or private school participating in a parental choice program to include instruction on the Holocaust and other genocides in its respective curriculum at least once in grades 5 to 8 and once in grades 9 to 12.

Act 58 (AB-68) makes the following changes to the laws governing primary and secondary education:

1. Deletes the general school aids reduction associated with payments to independent charter schools authorized by the city of Milwaukee, UW–Milwaukee, and UW–Parkside, which results in net general school aids received by school districts increasing correspondingly. Under prior law, DPI paid the operators of those charter schools a statutorily determined per pupil amount from a separate, general purpose revenue appropriation.

2. Creates an additional tier of eligibility for sparsity aid. In addition to preexisting sparsity aid in the amount of $400 per pupil that is provided if the school district's membership in the previous school year did not exceed 745 pupils and the number of pupils per square mile in the school district is fewer than 10, the act creates a new tier of eligibility for school districts with fewer than 10 pupils per square mile and whose membership in the previous school year was between 745 and 1,000 pupils. Under prior law and under the act, if funding is insufficient, payments are prorated.

3. Changes the eligibility threshold for a school district to receive high cost transportation aid. Under prior law, one eligibility criterion was that a school district's per pupil transportation cost exceeded 145 percent of the statewide average per pupil transportation cost. The act lowers this criterion to a per pupil transportation cost that exceeds 140 percent of the statewide average per pupil transportation cost.

4. Increases from $365 to $375 per school year the reimbursement rate to school districts and independent charter schools for transporting a pupil who lives more than 12 miles from the school. The act also eliminates a provision that required DPI to prorate summer school transportation payments for pupils who were transported fewer than 30 days for summer classes.

Act 90 (SB-555) requires a school board that provides a human growth and development instructional program to include in the program an explanation of the process under preexisting law by which a parent of a newborn may relinquish custody of the newborn to a law enforcement officer, emergency medical services practitioner, or hospital staff member (commonly referred to as Safe Haven).

Act 219 (AB-420) changes the per pupil amount that DPI pays to an independent charter school authorized by a tribal college from the per pupil academic base funding that the federal Bureau of Indian Education provides to tribal schools to the same amount that DPI pays to other independent charter schools, which is set by state law.

Act 236 (AB-975) requires the state superintendent to grant a substitute teacher permit to an individual who passes a background check; is at least 20 years of age; is enrolled in an approved teacher preparatory program; has achieved junior level status; and has completed at least 15 hours of classroom observation. Under preexisting law, the state superintendent also must grant a substitute teacher permit to an individual who passes a background check, has an associate degree, and completes substitute teacher training.

Elections

Act 34 (SB-102) allows a pupil who is 16 or 17 years of age and enrolled in a home-based private educational program to serve as a poll worker. Preexisting law applied only to students enrolled in a public or private school or in a tribal school.

Act 38 (SB-208) requires the Wisconsin Elections Commission, no later than 48 hours after each meeting, to post on its Internet site the minutes of each meeting conducted by WEC, along with a summary of all actions taken by each member of WEC at the meeting.

Employment

PUBLIC EMPLOYMENT

Act 7 (SB-62) allows the Public Defender Board to provide merit-based pay raises in fiscal year 2021–22 that exceed the 10 percent base pay of an assistant state public defender, which is the statutory limit to that position's pay progression.

Act 58 (AB-68) provides an additional $5 per hour worked during the 2021–23 biennium to correctional officers and correctional sergeants in correctional facilities when the vacancy rate for those positions is more than 40 percent. This rate continues until the vacancy rate is 40 percent or less for six consecutive months.

WORKERS COMPENSATION

Act 29 (SB-11) provides that an employer is not required to make a payment to the work injury supplemental benefit fund in the case of an employee who violates a policy against drug or alcohol use that contributes to an employee's injury that results in the employee's death and when the employee leaves no dependent for support or one or more persons partially dependent for support.

Act 232 (AB-911) does the following:
1. Changes the conditions under which earnings that are based on part-time work are expanded to full-time work, for purposes of benefits paid to an individual under workers' compensation.
2. Increases the amount of permanent partial disability benefits payable under the workers' compensation law.

3. Allows an employee to have an observer present during a medical examination for a workers' compensation claim.

GENERAL EMPLOYMENT

Act 58 (AB-68) does the following:
1. Requires $60 million to be transferred from the general fund to the unemployment trust fund in each of fiscal years 2021–22 and 2022–23.
2. Increases from a maximum of $900 to a maximum of $1,100 the amount of a grant that the Department of Workforce Development may award each youth apprentice in the youth apprenticeship program.

Environment

Act 58 (AB-68) does the following:
1. Increases by $24.7 million the revenue obligation bonding authority for the environmental improvement fund.
2. Provides an additional $10 million in bonding authority for dam safety grants.
3. Provides an additional $6.5 million in bonding authority for rural nonpoint source water pollution abatement grants.
4. Provides an additional $4 million in bonding authority for the urban nonpoint source and storm water management and municipal flood control and riparian restoration programs.
5. Provides an additional $4 million in bonding authority for removing contaminated sediments in Lake Michigan, Lake Superior, and their tributaries.
6. Allows the Department of Natural Resources to request up to $1 million from JCF for collecting and disposing of firefighting foam containing perfluoroalkyl and polyfluoroalkyl substances.
7. Provides an additional $1 million in funding for well compensation and well abandonment grants.

Act 79 (SB-248) makes changes to the state's electronic recycling program, known as E-Cycle. Among other things, the act changes the fees required to be paid to DNR by manufacturers that sell recyclable electronic devices and requires DNR to create a program to provide grants to expand electronics recycling and recovery programs in underserved areas of the state.

Financial institutions

Act 119 (SB-158) requires the Department of Financial Institutions to study and report on establishing a Wisconsin section 529A ABLE account program allowing tax-exempt savings accounts for qualified expenses incurred by individuals with disabilities.

Health and human services

HEALTH

Act 58 (AB-68) does the following:

1. Allows the Department of Health Services to award a onetime grant to support surgical quality activities.
2. Increases the grant that DHS must award each fiscal year for lead screening and outreach activities at a community-based human service agency that provides services to low-income individuals in Milwaukee.

Act 113 (SB-538) generally prohibits discrimination in the receipt of an anatomical gift or related services solely on the basis of an individual's disability. Under the act, a hospital may consider the disability under certain limited circumstances.

Act 122 (SB-395) requires elder-adult-at-risk agencies and adult-at-risk agencies to investigate alleged abuse, financial exploitation, or self-neglect of an adult at risk or elder adult at risk. The act also requires the investigating agency to take at least one action from a specified list of actions.

Act 184 (AB-333) expands an existing grant program that establishes and enhances crisis programs in rural areas to include counties, municipalities, and regions composed of counties and municipalities.

MEDICAL ASSISTANCE

Act 58 (AB-68) makes the following changes related to the Medical Assistance program:

1. Transfers moneys to the Medical Assistance trust fund from the general fund and from the permanent endowment fund, which contains proceeds from the sale of rights to receive payments under the tobacco litigation settlement.
2. Increases reimbursement to nursing facilities and intermediate care facilities for persons with an intellectual disability for staff support, to home health agencies for nursing care, and to agencies that provide personal care services to support staff who perform direct care.
3. Increases payments to hospitals with a disproportionate share of low-income patients.
4. Extends Medical Assistance benefits for certain postpartum women to the last day of the month in which falls the 90th day after pregnancy ends.

Act 225 (AB-765) requires reimbursement of group physical therapy under the Medical Assistance program.

Act 228 (AB-874) requires DHS to provide a supplemental reimbursement under the Medical Assistance program for private ambulance service providers based on an assessment charged to those ambulance service providers. The act also requires DHS to allow for supplemental reimbursements to public ambulance service providers through certified public expenditure.

MENTAL AND BEHAVIORAL HEALTH

Act 57 (AB-374) requires the attorney general to cooperate with local governments that are parties to the multidistrict opioid-related litigation in settling that litigation if JCF approves the proposed settlement and if the settlement agreement includes certain provisions. The act allocates to DHS moneys from the settlement that are payable to the state. Moneys allocated for local governments may be paid directly only to local governments that are parties in the opioid litigation, but the act allows the local governments to sell the rights to those payments.

Housing

Act 221 (AB-607) authorizes the Wisconsin Housing & Economic Development Authority to make low-interest or no-interest loans for the rehabilitation of residential properties if the loan applicant's annual income meets specified requirements and if the rehabilitation consists of structural improvements or the removal of lead paint.

Insurance

Act 111 (SB-482) makes changes to the regulation of travel insurance, including specifying when a person may receive a full refund for cancelling a travel protection plan, requiring disclosures to prospective purchasers of travel insurance policies, and requiring a person who acts as a travel administrator to hold one of three possible licenses.

Law enforcement

Act 48 (SB-121) prohibits a law enforcement agency from authorizing in a use-of-force policy its law enforcement officers to use choke holds unless the officer is acting in a life-threatening situation or in self defense.

Act 49 (SB-122) requires law enforcement agencies to post their use-of-force policies on their websites and to update the online version of the policies as soon as practically possible if the policies are changed.

Act 50 (SB-123) requires DOJ to collect data and publish an annual report on law enforcement use-of-force incidents, which include any incident when a firearm was discharged in the direction of a person (even if there was no injury) and when great bodily harm resulted from the incident. The act requires demographic information to be collected about each use-of-force incident, including any information required to be collected to comply with the reporting standards of the Federal Bureau of Investigation, as well as a description of each incident.

Act 75 (SB-120) provides standards for the use of physical force by law enforcement officers, requires law enforcement officers to intervene in and report any noncompliant use of force by another law enforcement officer, and establishes protections for any law enforcement officer who makes such an intervention or report.

Act 185 (AB-335) requires DOJ to award grants to law enforcement agencies to purchase body cameras. An agency that receives a grant must use body cameras for at least three years on all officers whose primary duties are patrolling and must require each patrol officer to activate the camera when the officer has contact with a member of the public.

Act 188 (SB-199) prohibits sexual contact by a law enforcement officer with a person who is detained or in custody and provides that such conduct constitutes a second degree sexual assault.

Local government

Act 69 (SB-187) allows a member of a village board to receive an hourly wage as a village employee. Prior law prohibited a board member from also being a village employee.

Act 124 (SB-425) allows the Milwaukee Metropolitan Sewerage District, subject to contingencies, to finance and construct a dredged material management facility in the city of Milwaukee by 2032. The act provides that MMSD may reserve space in the facility for the disposal of sediment from flood management projects. Under the act, MMSD must pay for the project through its capital budget and may finance the project by the issuance of bonds or notes that must be made payable within 35 years.

Act 198 (SB-835) modifies restrictions on local land use, including the following:
1. Limiting consolidation, annexation, and boundary agreements by newly incorporated cities and villages during the first five years after their incorporation.
2. Allowing annexation of town territory across county lines if there is unanimous approval from the owners of the annexed land.
3. Limiting municipal extraterritorial land division and zoning powers.
4. Prohibiting municipal use of condemnation powers to acquire certain blighted

properties for the purpose of transferring the property to a third-party developer.
5. Modifying requirements for interim ordinances to freeze extraterritorial zoning.

Natural resources

CONSERVATION

Act 58 (AB-68) does the following:
1. Reauthorizes and funds the Warren Knowles-Gaylord Stewardship 2000 program until June 30, 2026, and grants additional bonding authority. The act allocates an amount to be transferred annually from the forestry account of the conservation fund for DNR land acquisitions and county forest grants under the stewardship program.
2. Provides $3 million in bonding authority from the stewardship program for a project to restore the Pierce County Islands Wildlife Area on the Mississippi River in Pierce County.

Act 173 (SB-664) requires DNR to obligate up to $5.6 million in unobligated moneys under the Warren Knowles-Gaylord Nelson Stewardship 2000 Program to fund state park system water infrastructure projects.

FISH AND GAME

Act 15 (SB-48) eliminates the provision that a person may receive a governor's bear tag only once in his or her lifetime.

NAVIGABLE WATERS AND WETLANDS

Act 47 (SB-46) creates a presumption that an owner of land that abuts a navigable waterway is a riparian owner and is entitled to exercise all rights afforded to a riparian owner, even if the bed of the waterway is owned in whole or in part by another.

Act 77 (SB-91) requires DNR to issue a general permit that authorizes wetland, stream, and floodplain restoration and management activities that will result in a net improvement in hydrologic connections, conditions, and functions.

Act 105 (SB-387) provides that a county shoreland zoning ordinance may not prohibit within a shoreland setback area the construction of a fence that is (1) no taller than 15 feet; (2) located at least two feet landward of the ordinary high-water mark, entirely outside a highway right-of-way, no less than 10 feet from the edge of a roadway, and no more than 40 feet from the edge of a roadway or highway right-of-way, whichever is greater; and (3) generally perpendicular to the shoreline.

PARKS, FORESTRY, AND RECREATION

Act 27 (SB-64) provides that the proceeds from the sale of DNR properties may be used to acquire or develop any land or easement, with no restrictions or limitations on use or location unless the property was originally purchased with federal funds.

Act 58 (AB-68) does the following:
1. Increases from 30 to 63 cents per acre the county forest acreage share payments that DNR makes to counties.
2. Increases the minimum amount that DNR must pay each city, village, or town where DNR owns land. The act provides that the payment may not be less than $3.50 an acre for all such lands. Under preexisting law, the payment for lands that DNR acquired since 1992 was generally determined using the estimated value of the land in the year prior to the acquisition.
3. Authorizes DNR to retain a fee for issuing all-terrain vehicle trail passes and snowmobile trail use stickers and for issuing and renewing registrations for ATVs, utility terrain vehicles, off-highway motorcycles, boats, and snowmobiles that occur through DNR's statewide automated system.

Act 70 (SB-269) raises from 2,000 pounds to 3,000 pounds the maximum weight allowable for a motor-driven device to be classified as a UTV.

Act 103 (SB-364) authorizes the operation of ATVs, UTVs, and snowmobiles adjacent to a highway at night, regardless of the direction of traffic, if operated on a designated and marked ATV or snowmobile trail. The act also requires a person operating a snowmobile during the hours of darkness or adjacent to a roadway to dim his or her head lamp when an oncoming snowmobile, ATV, UTV, or motor vehicle is within 500 feet. The act also lowers the permissible decibel level for snowmobile exhaust and engine noise.

Occupational regulation

Act 3 (AB-4) authorizes pharmacy technicians and first-year and second-year pharmacy students to administer vaccines to people who are age six or older. The act requires pharmacy technicians and first-year and second-year pharmacy students to complete training and to be supervised by a health care provider while administering vaccines.

Act 8 (SB-13) authorizes dentists to administer COVID-19 and flu vaccines. The act requires dentists to complete eight hours of training and have liability insurance to administer those vaccines, and dentists must update DHS's Wisconsin Immunization Registry after administering a vaccine.

Act 22 (AB-63) makes changes to the laws governing the practice of psychology and the Psychology Examining Board, including the following:
1. Revises the definition of the "practice of psychology" and various exemptions to

the practice of psychology and adds new exemptions to the practice of psychology.
2. Discontinues the licensure of private practice school psychologists, but allows those who currently hold this license to continue to renew their licenses and engage in the private practice of school psychology.
3. Changes licensure requirements for psychologists, including changing the required hours of supervised experience, allowing the examining board to promulgate rules requiring an internship, and prohibiting the denial of an applicant's license based on his or her arrest record.

Act 23 (AB-125) makes changes to the licensure, regulation, and practice of physician assistants, including the following:
1. Creates the Physician Assistant Affiliated Credentialing Board attached to the Medical Examining Board and authorizes the board to promulgate rules that regulate the practice of physician assistants.
2. Requires a practicing physician assistant to provide to the board, upon request, evidence either that there is a physician who is primarily responsible for the overall direction and management of the physician assistant's professional activities or that the physician assistant has a written collaborative agreement with a physician that describes the physician assistant's scope of practice.
3. Defines the practice of a physician assistant similarly to the practice of medicine and surgery and provides that a physician assistant may prescribe, dispense, and administer drugs, but requires a physician assistant to limit his or her practice to the scope of his or her experience, education, and training.

Act 60 (AB-121) specifies that a person does not need a barbering or cosmetology license to perform natural hair braiding.

Act 71 (SB-329) repeals provisions requiring a licensed athletic trainer to have a consulting physician.

Act 100 (SB-300) requires pharmacy technicians to be registered by and subject to the authority of the Pharmacy Examining Board. Under the act, no person may engage in the practice of a pharmacy technician without being so registered.

Act 121 (SB-309) requires the Department of Safety and Professional Services and any attached entity to define "telehealth" as it is defined under the Medical Assistance program.

Act 123 (SB-412) enters Wisconsin into the Occupational Therapy Licensure Compact, which allows occupational therapists and occupational therapy assistants who are licensed in one state that is a party to the compact to practice in other member states. The compact provides for the creation of the Occupational Therapy Compact Commission, which is charged with administering the compact and which includes delegates from each member state's licensing board. The act also contains provisions relating to implementation of the compact in Wisconsin.

Act 130 (AB-529) allows the practice of naturopathic medicine by individuals who have met certain educational requirements, passed examinations, and been granted a license by the Naturopathic Medicine Examining Board, which is created by the act. Under former law, naturopathic medicine was not specifically regulated, but individuals were allowed to practice it only to the extent that their activities did not fall within another profession's scope of practice.

Act 131 (AB-537) enters Wisconsin into the Psychology Interjurisdictional Compact, which allows psychologists who are licensed in one state that is a party to the compact to practice in other member states via telespsychology or, temporarily, in person. The compact provides for the creation of the Psychology Interjurisdictional Compact Commission, which is charged with administering the compact and which includes delegates from each member state's licensing board. The act also contains provisions relating to implementation of the compact in Wisconsin.

Act 251 (SB-259) provides for regulation and licensing for the practice of genetic counseling. The act establishes a Genetic Counselors Affiliated Credentialing Board to grant genetic counselor licenses, promulgate rules related to genetic counseling, and discipline genetic counselors and prohibits a person from practicing genetic counseling without a license.

Public utilities

Act 24 (AB-27) makes changes to the statutes administered by the Public Service Commission, including requiring PSC to require investor-owned electric and natural gas public utilities to provide funding to the Citizens Utility Board, a consumer advocate. Under the act, PSC must ensure that the utilities recover the amount they provided to the advocate from their customers.

Real estate

Act 96 (SB-73) changes the process under preexisting law that, among other things, requires a seller of residential real property or vacant land to provide a prospective buyer with a real estate condition report on which the seller discloses conditions of, and other information about, the real property. Specifically, the act (1) specifies that a real estate condition report is complete only if the seller has answered or supplied information for each item on the report; (2) specifies that a prospective buyer that exercises its preexisting statutory right to rescind an offer of sale because the seller does not timely provide a real estate condition report is entitled to the return of any deposits or option fees; and (3) adds to the real estate condition report form a requirement that the owner indicate whether the owner is a foreign person for purposes of federal taxation.

Act 199 (SB-865) creates requirements for and restrictions on the authority of certain homeowners associations. Among other things, the act (1) requires an association to make certain information publicly available; (2) requires an association to give notice of any association meeting; (3) limits the fees an association may charge for providing certain documentation to a member; (4) requires an association to provide notice before suspending certain rights of a member; and (5) requires an association to provide a payoff statement to a member upon request and limits the fees the association may charge for providing the statement.

Shared revenue

Act 61 (AB-56) clarifies that following the termination of a tax incremental district (TID), the state aid payment for tax-exempt personal property that would have been paid to the TID is distributed to other taxing jurisdictions.

State government

STATE BUILDING PROGRAM

Act 58 (AB-68) does all of the following:
1. Authorizes $125 million in general fund–supported borrowing to assist PSC in awarding grants to construct broadband infrastructure in underserved and unserved areas of Wisconsin.
2. Authorizes $40 million in general fund–supported borrowing to assist Historic Haymarket Milwaukee, LLC, in the construction of a museum of nature and culture in the city of Milwaukee.
3. Authorizes $5 million in general fund–supported borrowing for the renovation of a mental health facility in Marathon County to expand the facility's psychiatric bed and behavioral health treatment capacity.
4. Authorizes $5 million in general fund–supported borrowing to assist Beyond Vision in the purchase and renovation of a new facility in Milwaukee County to employ and provide related services to blind and visually impaired individuals.
5. Authorizes the Building Commission to expend up to $4 million for project planning, development, design, site selection, and land and property acquisition for a new Wisconsin History Museum.

6. Allocates $3 million, from an existing authorization of $25 million in general fund–supported borrowing for construction projects having a public purpose, to assist the Incourage Community Foundation, Inc., in redeveloping the former Daily Tribune building in the city of Wisconsin Rapids into an economic and community hub.

Act 252 (SB-520) authorizes an additional $41,791,000 for the construction of a new Type 1 juvenile correctional facility in Milwaukee County.

GENERAL STATE GOVERNMENT

Act 58 (AB-68) increases from $375 to $385 the registration fee for a lobbying principal and from $125 to $135 the lobbyist authorization fee. Under preexisting law, a lobbying principal (any person who hires a lobbyist) pays the fees to the Ethics Commission.

Act 87 (AB-325) adopts the Revised Uniform Unclaimed Property Act, which addresses the disposition of unclaimed property, including gift cards, life insurance benefits, securities, and virtual currencies.

Act 95 (AB-388) creates the Wisconsin Commission for the United States Semiquincentennial Commission, attached to the Department of Veterans Affairs, that will plan, coordinate, and implement a program to commemorate the 250th anniversary of the founding of the United States.

Act 266 (SB-719) makes minor and technical changes to the laws relating to lobbying, as recommended by the Ethics Commission. The act also applies the code of ethics for public officials to a school district administrator. In addition, the act allows an agency official, an elected state public official, or a legislative employee to attend a meeting of a special interest group, political group, or school group to discuss state government processes, proposals, and issues without paying the cost of admission.

Taxation

Act 1 (AB-2) changes laws related to taxation as follows:
1. Provides a property tax exemption for property of a church or religious association leased to an educational association.
2. Excludes from taxable income grants from the federal coronavirus relief fund for economic support, broadband expansion, childcare, and farm support.
3. Adopts for state income tax purposes changes made by the Internal Revenue Code related to the earned income tax credit, the paycheck protection program, the economic injury disaster loan program, payment assistance for certain loan programs, and grants to shuttered venue operators.

Act 40 (AB-18) changes the state individual income tax return due date from April 15 to instead align with the federal due date each year, whatever that date may be in the future.

Act 58 (AB-68) does the following:
1. Reduces from 6.27 percent to 5.30 percent the tax rate in the third individual income tax bracket beginning with the 2021 tax year.
2. Provides an individual income tax credit beginning with the 2022 tax year for household and dependent care expenses equal to 50 percent of the amount an individual may claim on the individual's federal tax return for household and dependent care expenses.
3. Provides an individual income tax exclusion for all basic, special, and incentive pay income received by a member of the U.S. armed forces while serving on active duty.
4. Provides an individual income tax exclusion for income derived from a certified national service educational award.
5. Provides a property tax exemption for any parcel of vacant land owned by a church or religious association that is no more than 0.8 acres, located in the City of Milwaukee near the Lake Michigan shoreline, and adjacent or contiguous to the City of St. Francis.
6. Provides a sales and use tax exemption for sweetened dried fruit.
7. Provides that partnerships, limited liability companies, and tax-option corporations may elect to claim certain refundable economic development tax credits that would otherwise be claimed by the partners, members, or shareholders.

Trade and consumer protection

Act 189 (SB-408) designates a "catalytic converter" as a type of proprietary article for which scrap dealers must follow certain requirements, including record-keeping requirements regarding the people who sell a catalytic converter to the scrap dealer and a requirement that scrap dealers obtain certain evidence establishing that the seller lawfully possessed the catalytic converter before the sale. A scrap dealer who intentionally fails to comply with the requirements may be subject to imprisonment for up to nine months, a fine up to $10,000, or both.

Transportation

DRIVERS AND MOTOR VEHICLES

Act 64 (SB-15) lowers the age of eligibility for an instruction permit from 15 years and 6 months to 15 years, increases the duration of an instruction permit from 12 months to 18 months, and increases the number of behind-the-wheel practice hours required before a person is eligible for an operator's license from 30 to 50.

Act 108 (SB-437) allows a person to operate an unregistered vehicle on a highway in response to an emergency if the operation is necessary to prevent imminent death or imminent great bodily harm or an imminent public disaster. This exception to the prohibition against operating an unregistered motor vehicle replaces the prior law exception that allowed a person to operate an unregistered vehicle on a highway during a state of emergency.

Act 163 (SB-429) requires the Department of Transportation to replace motor vehicle registration plates on a rolling 10-year basis beginning in 2022 and establishes requirements for the construction of plates.

HIGHWAYS AND LOCAL ASSISTANCE

Act 58 (AB-68) does the following:
1. Makes changes relating to alternative highway project delivery methods, including creating a technical review committee to review design-build proposals and providing requirements for requests for qualifications and requests for proposals.
2. Enumerates the I-94 East-West corridor reconstruction project from 70th Street to 16th Street in Milwaukee County as a southeast Wisconsin freeway megaproject and provides $40 million in bonding authority for the project.
3. Provides $100 million in additional funding for local roads improvement discretionary grants.

Act 74 (SB-101) designates the bridge on STH 29 across the Fox River in the city of Green Bay as the "Bart Starr Memorial Bridge."

Veterans and military affairs

Act 31 (AB-154) designates May 14 as Hmong-Lao Veterans Day, the purpose of which is to recognize Southeast Asians, Americans, and their allies who served in the Secret War in Laos during the Vietnam War in support of the U.S. armed forces.

Act 261 (SB-673) provides that the Department of Military Affairs is primarily responsible for the statewide emergency number system known as 911 and adds several requirements to DMA's previous responsibilities relating to the system. The act also requires DMA to award grants to county land information offices for the purpose of preparing geographic information systems data to help enable advanced 911 operations, known as Next Generation 911.

Constitutional amendments

The below proposed amendments to the Wisconsin Constitution were passed by the 2021 legislature on first consideration. With respect to each amendment, to become a part of the constitution, the 2023 legislature must concur in the amendment, and the amendment must then be ratified by the voters at a statewide referendum.

Enrolled Joint Resolution 6 (AJR-107) authorizes the imposition of monetary bail as a condition of release before conviction for a person accused of a violent crime only upon a finding that there is a reasonable basis to believe that it is necessary based on the totality of the circumstances, taking into account certain factors specified in the amendment. For a person accused of a nonviolent crime, monetary bail may be imposed as a condition of release before conviction only upon a finding that there is a reasonable basis to believe that it is necessary to assure the appearance of the accused in court, which is the constitutional standard that currently applies for all crimes.

Enrolled Joint Resolution 13 (SJR-32) provides that only a United States citizen age 18 or older who is a resident of an election district in Wisconsin is qualified to vote in that district in an election for national, state, or local office or at a statewide or local referendum.

Enrolled Joint Resolution 14 (SJR-84) prohibits the legislature from delegating its sole power to determine how moneys may be appropriated and prohibits the governor from allocating any federal moneys that the governor accepts on behalf of the state without the approval of the legislature by joint resolution or as provided by legislative rule.

Enrolled Joint Resolution 17 (SJR-101) prohibits state and local governments from using privately sourced moneys or equipment in connection with the conduct of elections and specifies who may perform tasks related to the conduct of an election. 🆎

SURVEY OF SIGNIFICANT WISCONSIN COURT DECISIONS

JULY 2020–JULY 2022

The *LRB Survey of Significant Wisconsin Court Decisions*, 2019–2020, noted that "[r]arely have so many cases involving the core and essential powers of the state's political institutions been on the court's docket."[1] That statement holds true for recent court activity. Between July 2020 and July 2022, the legislature once again actively participated in litigation to represent the state's interest in the validity of state laws and to protect core legislative powers.[2] Political conflict inevitably made its way onto the court's docket.[3]

Most consequently, the legislature prevailed in convincing the Wisconsin Supreme Court, after remand from the U.S. Supreme Court, to adopt senate and assembly district maps that had passed the legislature, but were vetoed by the governor.[4] Also in the area of elections law, the Wisconsin Supreme Court rendered important decisions involving election administration, guidance, and practices, such as timeliness of challenges to election administration procedures and the legality of drop boxes for the return of absentee ballots. Litigation also centered on the rulemaking authority of executive branch agencies and the power of the governor to replace appointees whose terms of office had expired. The court even decided a case on the legal authority of the legislature to contract for legal services, a long-standing legislative practice.

State and local government responses to the COVID-19 pandemic continued to cause legal controversy, with the court adjudicating cases involving the governor's power to declare successive public health emergencies, local public health officials' power to issue public health orders and to close public and private schools, and the state's power to limit indoor gatherings across the state. While these cases centered on the immediate COVID-19 pandemic, the court's holdings may well extend to state and local government actions in other public policy areas and crises.

Finally, there were a number of other cases that received less attention, but were significant. These court decisions involved employment discrimination on the basis of domestic violence convictions, legal defenses for crimes committed by sex trafficking victims, and the legal right of an individual to change his or her name.

The following survey prepared by LRB attorneys summarizes these critical judicial decisions. The LRB attorneys who prepared these summaries practice law, conduct research, and draft legislation in these issue areas. To be sure, each decision merits a much longer discussion because the issues confronted by the court in these cases touch on competing views of the legal authority of Wisconsin's political institutions and the role of government in society and the economy. The case summaries presented in this article serve as a concise introduction to the court's important activities in the last two years. Please contact us at the LRB offices if you would like a fuller discussion of any of these decisions, as well as the significant issues litigated in these cases.

Richard A. Champagne, Director and General Counsel
Wisconsin Legislative Reference Bureau

Legislative and congressional redistricting

Every 10 years following the U.S. Census, the Wisconsin Legislature must establish new state legislative and congressional districts to accommodate population shifts during the previous decade. State and federal law require that all state legislative districts be substantially equal in population and that all congressional districts be as nearly equal in population as is practicable. In addition, all such plans must comply with state and federal constitutional requirements and the federal Voting Rights Act (VRA). Although the legislature must create new plans, the redistricting process is a lawmaking function: the legislature passes a bill that becomes law only with the governor's approval. If the governor and the legislature cannot agree on state legislative and congressional plans, then the courts must step in to complete the process. Since the 1960s, the federal courts have generally settled redistricting disputes and adopted new plans. In Wisconsin, following the 2020 Census, the state supreme court, for the first time in nearly 60 years, adopted new state legislative and congressional redistricting plans after the governor vetoed plans adopted by the legislature.

In *Johnson v. Wisconsin Elections Commission*, 2021 WI 87, 399 Wis. 2d 623, 967 N.W.2d 469, the supreme court set forth the process it would follow for considering new state legislative and congressional redistricting plans that would ensure "equality of the people's representation in the state legislature and in the United States House of Representatives."

Wis. Const. art IV, § 3, provides the following: "At its first session after each enumeration [census] made by the authority of the United States, the legislature shall apportion and district anew the members of the senate and assembly, according to the number of inhabitants." U.S. Const. Art I, § 2, requires that representatives "be apportioned among the several states which may be included within this Union, according to their respective numbers." Art. I, § 2, also requires that a census occurs once every 10 years to facilitate re-apportionment.

On August 23, 2021, Billie Johnson and three other Wisconsin voters filed a petition with the Wisconsin Supreme Court for leave to commence an original action, claiming that, following the 2020 Census, the state's legislative and congressional districts were malapportioned and no longer met the redistricting requirements of the state constitution. All parties agreed that the state legislative and congressional plans enacted in 2011 violated constitutional requirements ensuring equal representation because of shifts in the state population. The petitioners asked the court to make "only those changes necessary for the maps to comport with the one person, one vote principle while satisfying other constitutional and statutory mandates (a 'least-change' approach)." The court granted the petition, but stayed any further action, other than the consideration of preliminary matters, until the legislature passed congressional and state legislative reapportionment plans or until the legislature failed to pass plans after having a reasonable opportunity to do so. In addition, the court allowed Governor Tony Evers and other parties to intervene. Some of the intervening parties asserted that the plans adopted in 2011 unduly favored one major political party over the other and that the court should provide a remedy for that inequality.

On November 11, 2021, the legislature adopted 2021 Senate Bill 621, establishing new state legislative districts, and 2021 Senate Bill 622, establishing new congressional districts. Governor Evers vetoed both bills seven days later. On November 30, 2021, in an opinion written by Justice R. G. Bradley, the court held that it would act on the petition "only to the extent necessary to remedy the violation of a justiciable and cognizable right" under the Wisconsin and U.S. Constitutions and the VRA, while making only minimal changes to the existing maps. In other words, the court adopted the "least-change" approach, as requested by the petitioners. In addition, the court held that it would not examine the partisan composition of any proposed legislative or congressional districts because such an inquiry would be beyond the purview of the court, consistent with recent U.S. Supreme Court decisions. Chief Justice Ziegler and Justice Roggensack joined the majority in whole, and Justice Hagedorn joined in part.

Justice Hagedorn, in his concurrence, agreed with most of the majority opinion, but disagreed with holding that the court could consider only legal rights and requirements in adopting new maps. Justice Hagedorn asserted that the court could go beyond what federal and state law required and examine "traditional redistricting criteria," such as maintaining communities of interest and minimizing the temporary disenfranchisement of voters that occurs by moving voters between odd- and even-numbered senate districts. Justice Hagedorn also invited all parties to the litigation to submit legislative and congressional plans for the court's consideration.

In her dissent, Justice Dallet took issue with the majority holding that the "least-change" approach provides a neutral, nonpartisan standard by which to judge a proposed redistricting plan. She argued that the court should not adopt an approach that would give undue deference to the policy choices of the legislature that created the legislative and congressional plans in 2011. "It is one thing for the current legislature to entrench a past legislature's partisan choices for another decade. It is another thing entirely for this court to do the same." Justice Dallet asserted a "least-change" approach was not as common as the majority determined it to be and that a truly neutral judicial approach would consider all neutral factors under the state and federal constitutions and the VRA and put greater emphasis on traditional redistricting principles. Justices A. W. Bradley and Karofsky joined Justice Dallet's dissent.

On March 3, 2022, in *Johnson v. Wisconsin Elections Commission*, 2022 WI 14, 400 Wis. 2d 626, 971 N.W.2d 402, the supreme court approved the congressional and state legislative redistricting plans submitted by Governor Evers as the plans that best complied with the court's previously adopted criteria and "least-change" approach.

With regard to congressional maps, the court received proposed maps from four parties, including a group of the state's five Republican Congressmen, whose map the legislature endorsed, and Governor Evers. Justice Hagedorn, writing for the majority, stated that the governor's proposed congressional district maps complied with constitutional requirements and moved the fewest individuals from one district to another, thereby receiving the highest score with regard to core retention. "Core retention represents the percentage of people on average that remain in the same district they were in previously. It is thus a spot-on indicator of least change statewide, aggregating the many district-by-district choices a mapmaker has to make."

With regard to the state legislative maps, the court received proposed maps from six parties, including Governor Evers, the legislature, and Senate Minority Leader Janet Bewley on behalf of the Senate Democratic Caucus. The plan that the legislature submitted was the plan it had adopted under 2021 Senate Bill 621 and that the governor had vetoed. The majority again found that the governor's plan performed the best under the "least-change" approach, moving fewer people from their current districts than any other plan, and resulting in "less overall change than other submissions." The court also found that the governor's plan best satisfied state and federal constitutional requirements and traditional redistricting principles. Finally, the court found that Governor Evers had "good reasons" for creating a seventh majority-black district in the Milwaukee area in order to satisfy the requirements of the VRA. However, the court acknowledged that, based on the record, it was not certain whether compliance with the VRA actually required the creation of an additional majority-black district. By comparison, the legislative redistricting plan that the legislature created in 2011 established six majority-black districts in and around the city of Milwaukee. Generally, majority-minority districts, such as the majority-black districts created in 2011 and under the governor's plan, are districts in which minority group members constitute more than 50 percent of the voting-age population and are established to give the minority group an equal opportunity to elect their preferred candidates.

Justice A. W. Bradley concurred with the majority opinion, agreeing that the governor's plans best complied with the court's "least-change" approach, but objected to using the approach, much as she had in the court's earlier decision establishing the process it would undertake. "Although I disapprove of the 'least change' approach, I am limited by that prior determination and obligated to apply it here." Justices Dallet and Karofsky joined the concurrence.

In her dissent, Chief Justice Ziegler asserted that the court should have adopted the state legislative plan submitted by the legislature and the congressional plan submitted by the Republican Congressmen. The chief justice also suggested that the court could have, as an alternative, adopted maps submitted by the Citizen Mathematicians and Scientists, drawn its own plans, or required the parties to submit new plans. "The maps submitted by the Governor are unconstitutional and fatally flawed." Specifically, the chief justice determined that the governor's legislative plan impermissibly considered race alone as a deciding factor in drawing new districts in the Milwaukee area and that the governor did not sufficiently prove that creating an additional majority-minority district was necessary to remedy a VRA violation. Rather than increase the percentage of the minority voting-age population in the majority-black districts, the governor's plan actually decreased the minority voting-age population and increased the white voting-age population in each district. Chief Justice Ziegler also asserted that the legislature and the Citizen Mathematicians and Scientists were the only parties that submitted race-neutral plans.

The chief justice also noted that the court's opinion from November 30, 2021, establishing the process by which the court would provide a remedy, never mentioned "core retention" as the criteria the parties would need to satisfy when submitting plans. "The core retention analysis in the majority is an invention, made after-the-fact to justify a policy preference." In addition, Chief Justice Ziegler noted that the population deviations under the governor's plans were higher than those under other plans and under the plan enacted in 2011. She also noted that the governor's plans provided less deference to communities of interest. Justices

Roggensack and R. G. Bradley joined Chief Justice Ziegler's dissent, but also wrote separate dissenting opinions.

Justice Roggensack, in her dissent, also took issue with the consideration of race under the governor's legislative plan. "In adopting the governor's map, a majority of this court engages in racial gerrymandering contrary to the Equal Protection Clause of the Fourteenth Amendment of the United States Constitution, which prohibits separating voters into different voting districts based on the race of the voter." Justice Roggensack expressed her hope that at least one of the parties would petition the U.S. Supreme Court to review the state supreme court's decision. Chief Justice Ziegler and Justice R. G. Bradley joined Justice Roggensack's dissent.

In her dissent, Justice R. G. Bradley reiterated the point made by Chief Justice Ziegler that core retention was not a concept that the court mentioned in its previous decision. Furthermore, she concluded that the introduction of that idea by Justice Hagedorn at such a late stage in the litigation, along with his concurrence in the previous decision, created confusion and "derailed the case presentations of several parties." She also determined that the court had impermissibly put core retention above state constitutional requirements such as population equality and respecting county and municipal boundaries. Justice R. G. Bradley noted that the governor's legislative plan had a greater population deviation and split more municipalities and wards than the legislature's plan. Chief Justice Ziegler and Justice Roggensack joined Justice R. G. Bradley's dissent.

On March 7, 2022, the petitioners and the legislature filed an application for a stay and injunctive relief to the U.S. Supreme Court with regard to the legislative plan adopted by the state supreme court. Specifically, the petitioners and the legislature asserted that the state supreme court "selected race-based maps without sufficient justification, in violation of the Equal Protection Clause" of the U.S. Constitution. On March 23, the U.S. Supreme Court issued a per curiam opinion agreeing with the petitioners and the legislature and granting relief.

In *Wisconsin Legislature v. Wisconsin Elections Commission*, 142 S. Ct. 1245 (2022), the U.S. Supreme Court found that the state supreme court misapplied the previous decisions of the higher court regarding the standards for complying with the federal constitution and the VRA. The Court noted that the governor had provided no evidence to support his decision to create a seventh majority-black district other than to indicate that he believed "there is now a sufficiently large and compact population of black residents to fill it." Both the governor and the lower court had failed to analyze the preconditions and circumstances necessary to remedy the potential for diluting the vote of a minority population. In other words, a mapmaker is legally required to have a "strong basis in evidence" in order to move voters from one district to another based on race so that a minority population has a fair opportunity to select its chosen candidates. The Court remanded the case back to the state supreme court to select another state legislative plan or to reconsider the governor's plan upon submission of additional evidence.

Justice Sotomayor, in a dissent joined by Justice Kagan, called the Court's summary reversal of the state court decision unprecedented, especially in light of the fact that she did not find the prior decisions of the Court regarding racial gerrymandering to be clear and settled law. "Despite the fact that summary reversals are generally reserved for decisions in violation of settled law, the Court today faults the State Supreme Court for its failure to comply with an obligation that, under existing precedent, is hazy at best."

The Wisconsin Republican Congressmen had also filed an application for a stay and injunctive relief to the U.S. Supreme Court with regard to the congressional plan adopted by the state supreme court. The U.S. Supreme Court denied that application.

On April 15, 2022, in *Johnson v. Wisconsin Elections Commission*, 2022 WI 19, 401 Wis. 2d 198, 972 N.W.2d 559, on remand from the U.S. Supreme Court, the Wisconsin Supreme Court adopted the state legislative redistricting plan submitted by the legislature—the same plan the legislature adopted in 2021 Senate Bill 621 and that the governor vetoed. In a majority opinion authored by Chief Justice Ziegler, the court found insufficient evidence in the record to support establishing race-based districts under the governor's plan, whereas the court determined that the legislature's plan was race-neutral. In addition, the court held that the legislature's plan complied with all federal and state legal requirements and made "minimal changes to the existing maps, in accordance with the least-change approach." Justices Roggensack, Hagedorn, and R. G. Bradley joined the majority, while Justices R. G. Bradley and Hagedorn wrote separate concurrences.

Justice R. G. Bradley wrote her concurrence, in her own words, "to expound on the primacy of color-blindness in Equal Protection jurisprudence." She also noted that the legislature was the only party to submit a plan that did not consider race as a factor for producing new maps. Chief Justice Ziegler and Justice Roggensack joined her concurrence.

In his concurrence, Justice Hagedorn stated that, in its previous opinion, the majority of the court did not believe that it needed to analyze and adjudicate a possible VRA claim or equal protection violation before selecting a plan. However, Justice Hagedorn wrote, "we anticipated further litigation involving a fully developed Equal Protection or VRA claim could, and likely would, follow." Justice Hagedorn noted that any future consideration of redistricting plans would require a fully developed record and establishment of a baseline by which the court could recognize and adopt a race-neutral district or remedy a violation of equal protection or the VRA.

In her dissent, Justice Karofsky compared the court's process for considering malapportionment and redistricting as "an odyssey—a long wandering marked by many changes in fortune." Essentially, Justice Karofsky objected to the process as a whole, and asserted that a federal court would have been the appropriate forum for adjudicating the claims that arose in the state court as the state court had no recent experience addressing such claims or adopting a legally sufficient state legislative redistricting plan. Justice Karofsky also concluded that the "least-change" approach adopted by the court "served only to entrench the prior—and blatantly partisan—district maps." In addition, Justice Karofsky asserted the court should have taken additional evidence in order to evaluate and address concerns regarding equal protection and the VRA before rejecting the governor's plan and adopting the legislature's plan. Justices A. W. Bradley and Dallet joined the dissent.

Legislature's power to defend state laws in litigation

In *Democratic National Committee v. Bostelmann*, 2020 WI 80, 394 Wis. 2d 33, 949 N.W.2d 423, the supreme court held that the Wisconsin Legislature has the authority to represent the state's interest in the validity of state laws.

The case arose in the context of litigation over state election laws challenged in federal court. In that litigation, the Seventh Circuit Court of Appeals determined that the legislature did not have standing to appeal an adverse ruling by the federal district court. When the legislature challenged that determination, the Seventh Circuit certified the question to the Wisconsin Supreme Court and requested that the court determine the relevant question of state law. Specifically, the Seventh Circuit asked whether the legislature has the authority under Wis. Stat. § 803.09 (2m) to represent the State of Wisconsin's interest in the validity of state laws.

Wis. Stat. § 803.09 (2m) is a rule of civil procedure that gives the legislature the power to intervene in certain types of state and federal litigation. Generally, intervention allows a person that is not an original party to a lawsuit but that has a personal stake in the outcome of the lawsuit to become a party in order to protect its interests.

In a majority opinion written by Justice Hagedorn, the supreme court answered the certified question in the affirmative. The court explained that, by enacting the statute, the legislature adopted a public policy that the legislature has an interest in any litigation that (1) questions the constitutionality of a statute; (2) argues that a statute violates or is preempted by federal law; or (3) otherwise challenges the construction or validity of a statute. Furthermore, the legislature's interest is not only in protecting its own interests as a legislative body—the legislature is empowered to defend the interests of the State of Wisconsin. The court noted that, although defending state law is normally within the province and power of the Wisconsin Attorney General, the legislature has given itself concurrent power to defend the validity of state law.

In short, the supreme court informed the Seventh Circuit that, when the validity of a state statute is at issue in litigation, the legislature has a statutory right to intervene and participate as a party, with all the rights and privileges of any other party, and to defend the state's interest in the validity of its laws.

Justice Dallet dissented in an opinion joined by Justices A. W. Bradley and Karofsky.

Legislative authority to contract for attorney services

In *Waity v. LeMahieu*, 2022 WI 6, 400 Wis. 2d 356, 969 N.W.2d 263, the supreme court upheld the validity of two contracts for legal services entered into by the Wisconsin Legislature while also addressing the appropriate application of the standard for stays pending appeal.

Speaker of the Wisconsin State Assembly Robin Vos and Majority Leader of the Wisconsin State Senate Devin LeMahieu, on behalf of the legislature, entered into contracts for attorney services regarding the decennial redistricting process and any resulting litigation.

Andrew Waity and other taxpayers (collectively, Waity) filed suit in circuit court against Vos and LeMahieu (collectively, the Legislative Leadership), seeking a declaration that the two attorney services agreements were void *ab initio* (from the beginning). Waity argued that no legal authority permitted the Legislative Leadership to sign these contracts on behalf of the senate and assembly. Waity moved for a temporary injunction barring the legislature from issuing payment under the contracts and also prohibiting the Legislative Leadership from seeking legal advice other than from the Department of Justice. The circuit court denied Waity's motion. In April 2021, however, the circuit court issued a decision granting Waity summary judgment, holding that there was no statutory or constitutional authority by which the Legislative Leadership could enter into and perform on the attorney services agreements. The circuit court found that the language of Wis. Stat. § 16.74 (1) would not allow the legislature to contract for stand-alone attorney services.

The circuit court enjoined the Legislative Leadership from issuing payments under the two contracts and declared the contracts void *ab initio*. The Legislative Leadership filed a notice of appeal and an emergency motion for a stay pending appeal. The circuit court denied the motion for a stay. The Legislative Leadership filed a motion for a stay pending appeal at the court of appeals. The court of appeals denied the motion, finding that the circuit court properly analyzed the relevant standard and that its decision was not an erroneous exercise of discretion.

The Legislative Leadership filed a petition to bypass the court of appeals, along with a motion to stay the circuit court's injunction pending appeal. The supreme court granted the petition to bypass and the motion for a stay, concluding that the circuit court had misapplied the relevant standard in its stay analysis.

The majority, in an opinion authored by Chief Justice Ziegler, held that Wis. Stat. § 16.74 "grants the legislature authority to enter into legal contracts to assist in redistricting and related litigation." Wisconsin Stat. § 16.74 (1) provides that "[a]ll supplies, materials, equipment, permanent personal property and contractual services required within the legislative branch shall be purchased by the joint committee on legislative organization or by the house or legislative service agency utilizing the supplies, materials, equipment, property or services." The court held that the statute "explicitly permits each house of the legislature to purchase 'contractual services' that are 'required within the legislative branch'" and does not include any requirement that the purchase of services be tied to other physical purchases, as asserted by the circuit court. The court found that the term "contractual services" in Wis. Stat. § 16.74 is unambiguous and includes attorney services.

Waity argued that Wis. Stat. § 16.74 contains no conferral of purchasing authority and that some other provision supplies the authority for the legislature to make basic purchasing decisions, but the court found that Wis. Stat. § 16.74 "is an independent grant of legal authority by which the legislature can buy the goods and services it needs." The court also rejected Waity's arguments that a more specific statute, Wis. Stat. § 13.124 (relating to legal representation), is in conflict with Wis. Stat. § 16.74, finding rather that these statutes apply in distinct circumstances. The court found that Wis. Stat. § 13.124 provides a "quick, streamlined basis for the legislature's leadership to obtain counsel for the legislature in 'any action.' By contrast, [Wis. Stat.] § 16.74 allows each house of the legislature to obtain counsel as needed, irrespective of whether an 'action' exists." The court also rejected Waity's argument that the legislature did not comply with the procedural requirements of Wis. Stat. § 16.74, finding that the legislature "complied with Wis. Stat. § 16.74 and received the payments it properly approved, validated, and requested."

The court also addressed the standard for stays pending appeal, reiterating its existing test requiring that a court must consider four factors when reviewing a request to stay an order pending appeal: "(1) whether the movant makes a strong showing that it is likely to succeed on the merits of the appeal; (2) whether the movant shows that, unless a stay is granted, it will suffer irreparable injury; (3) whether the movant shows that no substantial harm will come to other interested parties; and (4) whether the movant shows that a stay will do no harm to the public interest." The court went on to explain, however, that when evaluating a party's likelihood of success on the merits of an appeal, a circuit court "cannot simply input its own judgment on the merits of the case and conclude that a stay is not warranted," but instead should "consider[] how other reasonable jurists on appeal may have interpreted the relevant law and whether they may have come to a different conclusion." The supreme court also noted that when considering potential harm, circuit courts "must consider whether the harm can be undone if, on appeal, the circuit court's decision is reversed" and, if not, "that fact must weigh in favor of the movant." After evaluating all of the required factors, the supreme court found that the circuit court had erroneously exercised its discretion by refusing to stay its injunction pending appeal.

Justice Hagedorn joined the majority, but filed a separate concurrence, emphasizing that the supreme court was not setting a new standard for a stay pending appeal, but rather correcting an improper understanding of the existing test.

Justice Dallet wrote a dissent, joined by Justices A. W. Bradley and Karofsky.

Gubernatorial appointment authority

In *State ex rel. Kaul v. Prehn*, 2022 WI 50, 402 Wis. 2d 539, 976 N.W.2d 821, the supreme court considered whether a previously appointed member of the Natural Resources Board (the board) could continue to serve as a member of the board after his term had expired, notwithstanding the fact that a successor had been nominated.

In May 2015, Frederick Prehn was nominated by Governor Scott Walker for a six-year term to the board, a supervisory body that has advisory and policy making powers for the Department of Natural Resources. Prehn's nomination was confirmed by the senate, his term to expire on May 1, 2021. On April 30, 2021, succeeding Governor Tony Evers acted to appoint a successor for Prehn's position on the board. Prehn, however, declined to step down from the office and continued to actively serve on the board. The senate took no action on Evers's nomination of a successor.

In August 2021, the attorney general brought an action in circuit court alleging that Prehn's continued service on the board was unlawful, owing to the fact that a "vacancy" had arisen on the board that must be filled by the governor's provisional appointment. The attorney general therefore asked that Prehn be either removed from office or, alternatively, declared to be subject to removal by the governor. The circuit court dismissed the action, finding that Prehn was not unlawfully holding the office and that the governor did not have the authority to provisionally appoint a successor or to remove Prehn without cause. The attorney general appealed and filed a petition to bypass the court of appeals, which the supreme court granted, while also allowing the Wisconsin Legislature to intervene as a party. In an opinion authored by Chief Justice Ziegler that addressed both statutory and constitutional questions, the majority affirmed the decision of the circuit court to dismiss the case.

The majority first considered whether Prehn was lawfully continuing to hold office. The majority first observed that Wis. Const. art XIII charges the legislature with determining when offices are to be deemed vacant and the manner of filling vacancies, to the extent not otherwise provided in the constitution. The statutes governing the board, which also govern appointments to various other offices in state government, provide for six-year terms on the board, with members appointed by the governor but subject to senate confirmation. Once a term expires, the majority wrote, the governor has the prerogative to make a nomination for the succeeding term. The statutes also provide for the governor to make provisional appointments, not subject to senate confirmation. Provisional appointments, however, can be made only in the case of a statutorily prescribed "vacancy." While the statutes provide for vacancies in public offices to occur in a host of other circumstances, such as the death or resignation of an incumbent, the expiration of a term of an appointive state office is not among the circumstances deemed a vacancy. The majority also affirmed that an incumbent, such as Prehn, could serve as a "holdover" until a successor was properly appointed, a result that was in accord with both the common law and earlier case law. These conclusions, the majority wrote, are consistent with *State ex rel. Thompson v. Gibson*, 22 Wis. 2d 275, 125 N.W.2d 636 (1964), which had addressed substantially the same question.

The majority also addressed whether Prehn had "for cause" protections, in which case he could be removed only for reasons such as misconduct or malfeasance. The majority, citing to the statutes and the fact that Prehn had previously been appointed and confirmed by the senate, concluded that Prehn could still be removed only for cause. This result, the majority said, was also consistent with the common law principle that "lawful holdovers" have the same rights and responsibilities as when they hold office prior to holding over. The majority declined to hold that allowing Prehn to hold over violated constitutional separation of powers principles—it rejected analogies to the federal power of the president of the United States and instead pointed to the history of the state constitution and early state history that suggested that the governor's appointment power was much more limited and not inherent to the office.

Justice Dallet dissented in an opinion joined by Justices A. W. Bradley and

Karofsky, calling the majority's decision a threat to separation of powers principles. While agreeing that, under the common law, an office holder could "hold over" after his or her term had expired, she concluded that the statutes provided for a vacancy that could be filled by the governor as a provisional appointment. Acknowledging that her result was inconsistent with *Thompson*, Justice Dallet called for overruling *Thompson* while also distinguishing it. She also concluded that while appointive officers such as Prehn had "for cause" protections during their terms, those protections expired once their terms ended and they held over, therefore making Prehn subject to removal by the governor.

Ballot drop boxes are illegal

In *Teigen v. Wisconsin Elections Commission*, 2022 WI 64, 403 Wis. 2d 607, 976 N.W.2d 519, the supreme court held that two guidance documents created by the Wisconsin Elections Commission (WEC) pertaining to absentee voting were invalid. The court further held that ballot drop boxes are illegal and an absentee ballot must be returned by mail or personally delivered by the voter to the municipal clerk.

Prior to the 2020 general election, WEC issued two documents. The first stated that ballot drop boxes may be used for voters to return ballots and that a family member or other person may return an absentee ballot on behalf of a voter. The second specified that ballot drop boxes may be unstaffed.

Two Wisconsin voters, Richard Teigen and Richard Thom (collectively, Teigen), challenged the validity of the documents, and the circuit court granted summary judgment in their favor. The court declared that the WEC documents were administrative rules and were invalid because they were not promulgated as rules. The court further found that the guidance provided in the documents was inconsistent with state law, which provides that an elector must personally mail or deliver his or her own absentee ballot by mail or delivery to the municipal clerk. Ballot drop boxes, the court reasoned, would be legal only if staffed by the clerk and located at the clerk's office or a designated alternate site.

The court permanently enjoined WEC and ordered it to withdraw its documents and issue clarifying statements. WEC appealed the decision, and Teigen filed a petition to bypass the court of appeals, which the supreme court granted.

The supreme court, with Justice R. G. Bradley writing for the majority, held that ballot drop boxes are unlawful because Wis. Stat. § 6.87 (4) (b) 1. requires that an absentee ballot be mailed by the elector, or delivered in person, to the municipal clerk issuing the ballot. The court noted that "municipal clerk" is a defined term and does not include a ballot drop box. The court also found that

WEC erred in stating that a person may return another person's absentee ballot, noting that Wis. Stat. § 6.87 (4) (b) 1. requires that an absentee ballot be mailed by the voter or delivered in person to the municipal clerk.[5] The court noted that there is an exception to this requirement, Wis. Stat. § 6.86, which allows a voter to rely on an agent to deliver the absentee ballot, but found that this option applies only to voters who meet the exception provided by that provision.

The court did not address whether WEC's guidance should have been promulgated as administrative rules because the court found the guidance to be invalid, regardless of its origin.

In addition to the lead opinion, portions of which were the opinion of the court, there were separate concurrences filed by Justice Roggensack, Justice Hagedorn, and Justice R. G. Bradley (joined by Chief Justice Ziegler and Justice Roggensack).

There was also one dissenting opinion, filed by Justice A. W. Bradley and joined by Justices Dallet and Karofsky. Justice A. W. Bradley argued as a preliminary matter that Teigen had no standing to challenge the WEC documents because Teigen suffered no "injury in fact." In contrast, Justice R. G. Bradley's opinion found that Teigen had standing, finding that WEC's documents threatened to interfere with Teigen's rights as a voter, but this portion of the opinion was joined only by Justice Roggensack and Chief Justice Ziegler.

On the merits, Justice A. W. Bradley's dissent noted that Wis. Stat. § 6.87 (4) (b) 1. requires that an absentee ballot be returned "to the municipal clerk" and not "to the municipal clerk's office." A ballot drop box, Justice A. W. Bradley argued, that is set up, maintained, and emptied by the municipal clerk or the clerk's designee is an acceptable means of delivering a ballot to the municipal clerk. On the issue of who may return an absentee ballot, Justice A. W. Bradley noted that Wis. Stat. § 6.87 (4) (b) 1. requires that an absentee ballot be "mailed by the elector, or delivered in person" but does not say "delivered in person by the elector."

Wisconsin Elections Commission is not responsible for changing voter status

In *State ex rel. Zignego v. Wisconsin Elections Commission*, 2021 WI 32, 396 Wis. 2d 391, 957 N.W.2d 208, the supreme court held that the law requiring that the registration status of an elector be changed when the elector moves out of a municipality creates a duty of municipal clerks and municipal boards of election commissioners, not of the Wisconsin Elections Commission (WEC).

WEC received a report from the multi-state consortium, the Electronic Registration Information Center, Inc., that identifies registered voters who may no longer be eligible to vote at their registered address because they moved or died. WEC conducted a review of the report and sent notices to approximately 230,000 electors identified in the report, informing them how they could affirm their address. Registered electors and taxpayers Timothy Zignego, David W. Opitz, and Frederick G. Luehrs III (collectively, Zignego) filed a complaint with WEC, pleading that WEC instead change the status of non-responsive electors to ineligible. WEC dismissed the complaint, and Zignego filed suit against WEC, arguing that Wis. Stat. § 6.50 (3) required WEC to change the status of ineligible electors. The circuit court agreed and issued a writ of mandamus order compelling WEC to deactivate the registration of electors who failed to apply for continuation of their registration within 30 days of the date the notice was mailed.

When WEC took no action to comply with the writ, Zignego filed a motion asking the circuit court to hold WEC and several of its commissioners in contempt. The circuit court held a hearing and found WEC and the commissioners who voted to take no action on the writ in contempt and assessed monetary sanctions against both WEC and the commissioners. The same day, WEC filed a notice of appeal with respect to the contempt order. The following day, the court of appeals stayed both the contempt order and the writ of mandamus and subsequently issued an opinion reversing the circuit court. Zignego petitioned the supreme court for review, which the court granted.

The court, with Justice Hagedorn writing for the majority, noted that Wisconsin's decentralized election administration creates duties and responsibilities for WEC, local boards of election commissioners, and municipal clerks. The court further noted that local boards of election commissioners, which are required in counties and cities with a large population, are statutorily required to perform the same elections functions performed by county and municipal clerks throughout the state. Thus, the court noted, the phrase "municipal clerk or board of election commissioners" frequently appears throughout the election statutes and describes local election officials. WEC, the court explained, is repeatedly referred to throughout the elections statutes as simply the "commission," a term defined in Wis. Stat. § 5.025.

The court explained that the statutory provision at issue, Wis. Stat. § 6.50 (3), requires the municipal clerk or board of election commissioners to change an elector's registration status to ineligible upon receipt of reliable information that an elector no longer resides in the municipality. The court explicitly rejected Zignego's argument that WEC is a "board of election commissioners" when the statutes refer to WEC exclusively as the "commission." The court held that surrounding context made it clear that the duties created by Wis. Stat. § 6.50 (3) are duties of municipal clerks and municipal boards of election commissioners, not WEC.

The court subsequently held that the circuit court's writ of mandamus compelling WEC to comply with Wis. Stat. § 6.50 (3) was erroneously granted and must be reversed. The court further held that the circuit court's contempt order must be reversed as well. The court did note, however, that WEC had a duty to comply with the circuit court's writ of mandamus until the request for a stay was granted.

Justice R. G. Bradley, in a dissent joined by Justice Ziegler, agreed that municipal clerks and boards of election commissioners have a statutory obligation to change the status of ineligible voters, but argued that WEC has the same obligation. Justice R. G. Bradley noted that Wis. Stat. § 5.05 (15) makes WEC responsible for maintenance of the official voter registration list and Wis. Stat. § 6.36 (1) (a) requires WEC to compile and maintain an electronic registration list. These requirements, Justice R. G. Bradley argued, must mean more than simply creation of the list, but also ensuring its accuracy.

Justice R. G. Bradley also expressed concern at WEC's refusal to comply with the circuit court's writ of mandamus and criticized the court of appeals for imposing a stay on the circuit court's contempt order before deciding the merits of the order. Justice R. G. Bradley argued that the contempt order should have remained in place until the court of appeals decided the merits of the circuit court decision and the imposed sanctions should have been upheld regardless of the outcome of the appeal.

Timeliness of challenges to election procedure

In *Trump v. Biden*, 2020 WI 91, 394 Wis. 2d 629, 951 N.W.2d 568, the supreme court ruled that the Trump campaign's challenges to four different categories of absentee ballots were meritless or barred by the doctrine of laches.

The initial results of the 2020 presidential election indicated that Joe Biden and Kamala Harris were to be the recipients of Wisconsin's Electoral College votes, having won the state by 20,427 votes. Donald Trump, Mike Pence, and Donald J. Trump for President, Inc., (collectively, the Campaign) sought a recount of the votes in Dane and Milwaukee Counties. The recount was conducted and resulted in an increase in the margin of victory for Biden and Harris. The Campaign appealed the results of the recount to the circuit court, which affirmed the determinations of the Dane County Board of Canvassers and the Milwaukee Elections Commission. The Campaign appealed the circuit court ruling, filing a petition to bypass the court of appeals, which the supreme court granted.

The Campaign challenged four categories of ballots in Dane and Milwaukee

Counties: those cast by voters who declared themselves indefinitely confined, all in-person absentee ballots cast, all absentee ballots containing witness address information added by municipal clerks, and all ballots returned at "Democracy in the Park" events in the city of Madison.

On the issue of indefinitely confined voters, the Campaign objected to votes that had been cast by voters who declared themselves indefinitely confined following guidance provided by the clerks for Dane and Milwaukee Counties. The court, with Justice Hagedorn writing for the majority, noted that Wis. Stat. § 6.86 (2) (a) allows voters to declare themselves indefinitely confined, provided they meet the statutory requirements, and held that the Campaign's request to invalidate the votes of all indefinitely confined voters, without regard to whether any individual voter was in fact indefinitely confined, was without merit.

On the remaining three issues, the court held that the challenges failed under the doctrine of laches. As the court explained, "[l]aches is founded on the notion that equity aids the vigilant," and application of the doctrine is "within the court's discretion upon a showing by the party raising the claim of unreasonable delay, lack of knowledge the claim would be raised, and prejudice." The court noted that laches is of special importance when the challenge involves elections, which require "extreme diligence and promptness."

On the matter of unreasonable delay, the court held that it was unreasonable for the Campaign to wait until after the election to challenge the validity of the form used to obtain an absentee ballot, a form that had been used by municipalities throughout the state for at least a decade. Similarly, the court found it unreasonable that the Campaign waited until after the election to challenge guidance for handling missing witness information, guidance that had been relied on in 11 statewide elections since 2016. Finally, the court found it unreasonable that the Campaign waited until after the election to challenge the legality of "Democracy in the Park" events, at which absentee ballots were collected in reliance on representations made by municipal officials that the events were legal.

On the matter of lack of knowledge, the court held that the record was sufficient to demonstrate that Biden and Harris had no knowledge that the Campaign would challenge numerous election procedures after the election.

On the final matter of prejudice, the court held that voters who would be affected by the Campaign's claims for relief were acting according to long-standing guidance by the Wisconsin Elections Commission (WEC) and local election officials and would be unfairly prejudiced if their votes were deemed invalid.

Finally, the court noted that it is within the court's discretion to apply laches. The court held that application of the doctrine was the only just resolution of the claims, which were not of improper activity by the voters, but technical issues of election administration. The court noted that voters followed procedures and policies communicated to them and local election officials followed the guidance provided by WEC. The court affirmed the judgment of the circuit court.

In addition to the majority opinion, there were separate concurrences filed by Justice Hagedorn and Justice Dallet (joined by Justice Karofsky). There were also three dissenting opinions.

Chief Justice Roggensack dissented in an opinion joined by Justices Ziegler and R. G. Bradley, arguing that officials in Dane and Milwaukee Counties based their decisions on erroneous advice regarding correcting witness addresses and, in Dane County, in approving "Democracy in the Park" locations. Chief Justice Roggensack argued that the court should address these errors rather than barring the claims under the doctrine of laches.

Justice Ziegler, writing separately in a dissent joined by Chief Justice Roggensack and Justice R. G. Bradley, argued that the doctrine of laches did not apply because the Campaign did not unreasonably delay making its claims and because Biden and Harris knew ballots would be challenged and failed to demonstrate that they were prejudiced by the claims.

Justice R. G. Bradley, writing separately in a dissent joined by Chief Justice Roggensack and Justice Ziegler, argued that laches should not have been applied to the claims and the court should have resolved the underlying legal disputes.

Supreme court declines to interfere with ballot for election that is underway

In *Hawkins v. Wisconsin Elections Commission*, 2020 WI 75, 393 Wis. 2d 629, 948 N.W.2d 877, the supreme court entered an order denying Howie Hawkins and Angela Walker their petition for leave to commence an original action and their motion for temporary injunctive relief related to their request to appear on the general election ballot.

On August 4, 2020, Hawkins and Walker filed nomination papers with the Wisconsin Elections Commission (WEC) to be placed on the ballot for the November 3, 2020, general election as the Green Party's candidates for president and vice president of the United States. On August 7, 2020, Wisconsin voter Allen Arntsen filed a complaint with WEC alleging that 2,046 of the signatures appearing on the nomination papers did not list a correct address for Walker. On August 20, 2020, WEC sustained Arntsen's challenge to a portion of the signatures, rejected Arntsen's challenge to another portion of the signatures, and deadlocked on Arntsen's challenge to the remainder of the signatures. On August

21, 2020, WEC notified Hawkins and Walker that WEC had certified a total of 1,789 valid signatures, fewer than the 2,000 required, and Hawkins and Walker would therefore not appear on the ballot.

On August 26, 2020, WEC certified the list of independent candidates for president and vice president who would appear on the ballot. On September 1, 2020, WEC certified the remainder of the list of candidates for president and vice president that would appear on the ballot. Hawkins and Walker did not appear on either list. On September 3, 2020, Hawkins and Walker filed a petition for leave to commence an original action and motion for temporary injunctive relief, asking the supreme court to place them on the ballot.

In its order, the court noted that Wisconsin law establishes various deadlines for production and delivery of absentee ballots in advance of an election. The court further noted that, because of the COVID-19 pandemic, absentee ballot requests were unusually high for the 2020 fall general election, and local election officials were, in turn, distributing absentee ballots earlier than usual. The court argued that, by the time Hawkins and Walker filed their petition and motion, many ballots had already been printed and distributed without Hawkins and Walker listed as candidates.

In declining to grant the petition for leave to commence an original action or the motion for temporary injunctive relief, the court held that ordering the printing of new ballots would be expensive and time-consuming and would not allow local election officials to meet statutory deadlines. The court further held that ordering the printing and mailing of replacement ballots would create confusion among voters who had already received and returned ballots. The court explicitly stated that it was not considering the merits of the issues raised by Hawkins and Walker, but was declining to interfere in an election that, "for all intents and purposes, has already begun."

Chief Justice Roggensack, in a dissent joined by Justices Ziegler and R. G. Bradley, argued that WEC was required by its own administrative rules to presume that the address listed on the nomination papers was valid. Chief Justice Roggensack argued that Wis. Admin. Code EL § 2.07 (3) (a) placed the burden on Arntsen to establish the insufficiency of the address, which he lacked the personal knowledge to do.

Justice Ziegler, in a dissent joined by Chief Justice Roggensack and Justice R. G. Bradley, argued that there was sufficient time for the court to intervene and correct the ballots to include Hawkins and Walker as candidates.

In a separate dissent, Justice R. G. Bradley argued that Wisconsin law "unquestionably requires" that Hawkins and Walker appear on the ballot and expressed concern about the "pandemonium that would ensue" if the United States Supreme

Court ordered Wisconsin to repeat its November election for failure to correct this ballot issue.

COVID-19 public health order authority

In several cases arising in the wake of the COVID-19 pandemic, the supreme court considered issues relating to the scope of the authority of various government officials to act in response to the pandemic.

In *Fabick v. Evers*, 2021 WI 28, 396 Wis. 2d 231, 956 N.W.2d 856, the supreme court held that the governor's successive declarations of a state of emergency during the COVID-19 pandemic were unlawful.

On March 12, 2020, Governor Tony Evers issued an executive order declaring a public health emergency and setting out certain restrictions. Under Wis. Stat. § 323.10, no state of emergency may last longer than 60 days unless extended by the legislature. The original executive order expired on May 11, 2020, 60 days after it was issued. The governor issued subsequent executive orders on July 30 and September 22, 2020, and January 19, 2021, again proclaiming a public health emergency based on the COVID-19 pandemic. The legislature revoked the governor's January order in February 2021, after which the governor immediately issued a new order declaring an emergency.

Jeré Fabick filed an original action, as a Wisconsin taxpayer, directly in the supreme court, challenging the March, July, and September 2020 orders, arguing that the governor lacks authority under the statutes to declare successive states of emergency arising from the same public health emergency.

In a majority opinion authored by Justice Hagedorn, the court held that Wis. Stat. § 323.10 "must be read to forbid the governor from proclaiming repeated states of emergency for the same enabling condition absent legislative approval." The court contrasted the language of Wis. Stat. § 323.10 to the language in Wis. Stat. § 323.11, which outlines similar emergency declaration powers for local governments but, unlike Wis. Stat. § 323.10, provides that the declaration of emergency is limited "to the time during which the emergency conditions exist or are likely to exist." The court also noted that the legislature, in redrafting Wis. Stat. § 323.10 in 2002, borrowed extensively from the Model State Emergency Health Powers Act but did not adopt the model act's proposal to allow the governor to renew a public health emergency declaration every 30 days.

The court therefore agreed with Fabick and held that the governor's July 2020 and September 2020 executive orders were unlawful. The court also invalidated the governor's February 2021 order.

Justice R. G. Bradley joined the majority opinion but also filed a concurring opinion that was joined by Chief Justice Roggensack.

Justice A. W. Bradley dissented, joined by Justices Dallet and Karofsky. The dissent argued that, because Fabick did not personally sustain any losses, the court should not have considered his case in the first place. The dissent further found that, under Wis. Stat. § 323.10 and the definition of "public health emergency" under Wis. Stat. § 323.02 (16), successive declarations of emergencies are allowed when they are based on separate "'occurrences,' even if those occurrences share the same underlying cause." The dissent agreed with the governor that each successive declaration of an emergency was based on new and different on-the-ground conditions related to COVID-19, therefore justifying a new declaration of emergency.

In *James v. Heinrich*, 2021 WI 58, 397 Wis. 2d 516, 960 N.W.2d 350, the supreme court exercised its original jurisdiction to consider three consolidated cases challenging the authority of Janel Heinrich, the local health officer for Public Health of Madison and Dane County (PHMDC), to issue an order closing all schools in Dane County for in-person instruction in grades 3–12 in an effort to limit the spread of a novel strain of coronavirus, COVID-19.

Beginning in May 2020, Heinrich and PHMDC began issuing a series of emergency orders governing Dane County in response to the COVID-19 pandemic. On August 21, 2020, Heinrich issued Emergency Order No. 9, which closed all public and private schools for in-person instruction in grades 3–12. The order exempted students in grades K–2, so long as schools provided an option for virtual learning. The order allowed schools to continue to operate in person as "child care and youth settings" and further allowed higher education institutions to remain open for in-person instruction. The order also allowed many businesses to conduct in-person operations, subject to certain capacity limits and social-distancing guidelines.

Sara Lindsey James, a parent of two students enrolled in Our Redeemer Lutheran School in the city of Madison, the Wisconsin Council of Religious and Independent Schools, along with a group of parents, other associations, individual schools, and St. Ambrose Academy, Inc., a classical Catholic school located in the city of Madison (collectively, the petitioners), filed petitions for original action challenging the lawfulness of the order. The petitioners claimed both that the order exceeded Heinrich's authority under Wis. Stat. § 252.03 and that the order violated the petitioners' fundamental right to the free exercise of religion under Wis. Const. art. I § 18. The supreme court granted the petitions for original action on September 10, 2020, and consolidated the cases. The court also enjoined those provisions of Emergency Order No. 9 "which purport to prohibit schools throughout Dane County from providing in-person instruction to students."

In a majority opinion written by Justice R. G. Bradley, the court held that local health officers do not have the statutory power to close schools under Wis. Stat. § 252.03 and, further, that Heinrich's order infringed on the petitioners' fundamental right to free exercise of religion as guaranteed under Wis. Const. art. I, § 18.

Wis. Stat. § 252.03 sets forth the powers of local health officers regarding communicable diseases, including directing a local health officer to "promptly take all measures necessary to prevent, suppress and control communicable diseases," and allowing a local health officer to "do what is reasonable and necessary for the prevention and suppression of disease," and to "forbid public gatherings when deemed necessary to control outbreaks or epidemics." The court found that "[b]ecause the legislature expressly granted local health officers discrete powers under Wis. Stat. § 252.03 but omitted the power to close schools, local health officers do not possess that power."

With respect to the arguments regarding the right to free exercise of religion under the Wisconsin Constitution, the court noted that when examining alleged violations of the freedom of religious exercise, the court has "generally applied the compelling state interest/least restrictive alternative test." Under that test, the person or organization asserting the violation must prove (1) that it has a sincerely held religious belief, and (2) that such belief is burdened by the application of the law. If the party makes this showing, the burden shifts to the state to prove both that "the law is based upon a compelling state interest" and that the interest "cannot be served by a less restrictive alternative." The court found the petitioners had sincerely held beliefs that were burdened by Heinrich's order. While accepting that the state "certainly has a compelling interest in slowing the spread of COVID-19," the court also found that less restrictive measures in earlier orders and the distinctions among age groups of students in Heinrich's order demonstrated that less restrictive alternatives were available. As such, the court held that Heinrich's order fails the strict scrutiny test, finding that "the application of the Order burdens the Petitioners' sincerely-held religious beliefs, and Heinrich fails to demonstrate why the Order, although based upon a compelling interest, cannot be met by less restrictive alternatives."

Justice Hagedorn joined the court's opinion with the exception of one footnote relating to the court's role in addressing constitutional questions. He filed a concurrence agreeing that it was appropriate to address the religious liberty question in the case, but finding "unprecedented" the assertion in the footnote of the opinion of the court that the court is "duty-bound to address important constitutional questions raised in a case even though it can be resolved on other grounds."

Justice Dallet filed a dissenting opinion, joined by Justices A. W. Bradley and Karofsky, finding that the plain language of Wis. Stat. § 252.03, its history, and related statutes "all confirm that local health officers may close schools, so long as doing so is at least reasonable and necessary to suppress disease." Justice Dallet further found that because the majority resolved the case by striking down the order based on its statutory analysis, the majority should not have proceeded to opine on the constitutional challenge.

In *Becker v. Dane County*, 2022 WI 63, 403 Wis. 2d 424, 977 N.W.2d 390, the supreme court again considered the authority of Janel Heinrich, the local health officer and director of PHMDC, reviewing whether local health officers may lawfully issue public health orders.

Heinrich's COVID-19-related orders included orders requiring face coverings, limiting or forbidding gatherings, requiring sanitation protocols for certain facilities, limiting or forbidding certain sport activities, limiting the permissible indoor capacity for businesses, and requiring physical distancing between individuals. Heinrich issued these orders pursuant to her authority under Wis. Stat. § 252.03 (1) and (2). About the time Heinrich issued a fourth COVID-19-related public health order, Dane County duly enacted Dane County Ordinance § 46.40 relating to the prevention, suppression, and control of communicable diseases. Among other things, the ordinance made it a violation of Dane County Ordinance ch. 46 to "refuse to obey an Order of the Director of Public Health Madison and Dane County entered to prevent, suppress or control communicable disease pursuant to Wis. Stat. s. 252.03." Under Dane County Ordinance § 46.27 (1), a violation of chapter 46 could result in a civil forfeiture of between $50 and $200 for each day that a violation exists.

Jeffrey Becker and Andrea Klein, two Dane County residents, and later, A Leap Above Dance, LLC, (collectively, Becker) sued Dane County, PHMDC, and Heinrich, challenging their legal authority to enforce Heinrich's COVID-19-related orders. The circuit court denied Becker's motion for a temporary injunction preventing enforcement, but also granted Becker's request to enter summary judgment against Becker to allow for appeal. The supreme court granted Becker's petition to bypass the court of appeals to interpret the scope of authority granted under Wis. Stat. § 252.03, whether state law preempts Dane County Ordinance § 46.40, and to "assess both provisions' constitutionality with respect to separation-of-powers principles."

In a majority opinion authored by Justice Karofsky, the court found that Wis. Stat. § 252.03 grants local health officers the authority to issue orders. The court further held that no state law preempts Dane County Ordinance § 46.40 and, finally, that a local health officer's authority to issue enforceable public health orders under Wis. Stat. § 252.03 or Dane County Ordinance § 46.40 does not constitute an unconstitutional delegation of legislative power in violation of the separation of powers.

The court held that, "based on the common and approved meaning of the operative language, the context in which it appears, and the statutory history," the authority granted by Wis. Stat. § 252.03 includes the authority for a local health officer to act via order.

With regard to preemption, the court held that state law preempts a local ordinance when "(1) the state legislature has expressly withdrawn the power of municipalities to act; (2) the ordinance logically conflicts with state legislation; (3) the ordinance defeats the purpose of state legislation; or (4) the ordinance violates the spirit of state legislation." Except in those circumstances, a county "may enact ordinances in the same field and on the same subject as that covered by state legislation." The court found that none of these circumstances exist. Rather, the ordinance at issue was not preempted because it permissibly grants authority redundant to that authorized under state statute, and the enforcement authority presents no conflict with state law.

In a portion of the decision not joined by Justice Hagedorn, and therefore not garnering a majority, the court addressed the separation of powers and whether the grant of authority to the local health officer to issue public health orders is an unconstitutional delegation of legislative power. Justice Karofsky stated in the lead opinion as to this issue that "[s]o long as the legislative grant contains an 'ascertainable' purpose and 'procedural safeguards' exist to ensure conformity with that legislative purpose, the grant of authority is constitutional." The lead opinion further stated that both Wis. Stat. § 252.03 and the Dane County ordinance pass constitutional muster, noting that the provisions "'la[y] down the fundamentals of the law'—the who, what, when, where, why, and how" and that there are substantial state and local procedural safeguards in place, including the state legislature's authority to change the granted authority, and local controls, such as supervisory authority by a local health board and the power of local elected officials to remove the local health officer.

Justice Hagedorn filed a separate concurrence to discuss Becker's request that the court revisit its precedents and "revitalize a more robust, judicially-enforced nondelegation doctrine at both the state and local levels." Justice Hagedorn noted that analysis of these issues requires "a resort to first principles" and an examination of the language as it was originally understood. While noting that he remains open to reconsidering the approach to the nondelegation doctrine in a future case, Justice Hagedorn explained that the delegation of authority under Wis. Stat. § 252.03 is supported by historical evidence. He further explained that the Dane County ordinance does not implicate the delegation doctrine because the ordinance does not separately authorize local health orders, but rather, is limited to penalizing those who violate orders lawfully issued by local health officers under authority granted by the legislature in Wis. Stat. § 252.03.

Justice R. G. Bradley filed a dissent, joined by Chief Justice Ziegler and Justice Roggensack, finding that Dane County Ordinance § 46.40 violates the Wisconsin Constitution because it impermissibly subdelegates to a local health officer the lawmaking power granted to the county board of supervisors under Wis. Const. art. I, § 22.

In *Tavern League of Wisconsin, Inc. v. Palm*, 2021 WI 33, 396 Wis. 2d 434, 957 N.W.2d 261, the supreme court considered a challenge to an order limiting indoor public gatherings issued as a response to the COVID-19 pandemic by Andrea Palm, the secretary-designee of health services.

On October 6, 2020, Secretary-designee Palm issued Emergency Order No. 3, which limited the size of indoor public gatherings to either 25 percent of the total occupancy limits for the room or building, as established by the local municipality or, for indoor spaces without a limit (such as a private residence), to no more than 10 people. Emergency Order No. 3 defined a "public gathering" as "an indoor event, convening, or collection of individuals, whether planned or spontaneous, that is open to the public and brings together people who are not part of the same household in a single room." Under the order, office spaces, manufacturing plants, other facilities that are accessible only by employees or other authorized personnel, invitation-only events that exclude uninvited guests, and private residences were considered to be not open to the public, except that a private residence "is considered open to the public during an event that allows entrance to any individual" and "such public gatherings are limited to 10 people." The order provided that entities such as childcare settings, schools and universities, Tribal nations, places of religious worship, political rallies, and other gatherings protected by the First Amendment were exempt from the limits. The limits under the order were enforceable by civil forfeiture.

The Tavern League of Wisconsin, Inc., and other plaintiffs (collectively, the Tavern League) filed suit in circuit court, seeking a temporary injunction and a declaration that Emergency Order No. 3 was unlawful because the order was a rule and the Department of Health Services (DHS) did not undertake proper rulemaking procedures as required by Wis. Stat. ch. 227 and *Wisconsin Legislature v. Palm*, 2020 WI 42, 391 Wis. 2d 497, 942 N.W.2d 900. The court in *Palm* struck down an earlier COVID-19-related order by Secretary-designee Palm known as a "Safer at Home" order that limited travel and forced closures of businesses not deemed essential.[6] After initially granting an ex parte temporary injunction, the circuit court (by a different judge substituted after the initial ruling) allowed The Mix Up, Inc., and several other individuals and entities to intervene (collectively, The Mix Up), but vacated the initial order and denied the motion for temporary injunctive relief. The circuit court held that the parties seeking injunctive relief did not meet the necessary standards, finding that they did not have a reasonable probability of success on the merits, that enjoining the emergency order would disrupt the status quo, and that there was no proof of irreparable harm by the emergency order, because there was no evidence of compliance with the emergency order. The Mix Up moved for leave to appeal and, when the court of appeals granted the motion, DHS filed a petition for bypass. The supreme court denied that motion, and the case remained with the court of appeals.

The court of appeals summarily reversed the circuit court, finding that under the supreme court's prior ruling in *Palm*, Emergency Order No. 3 was invalid and unenforceable as a matter of law and that, accordingly, the standard for injunctive relief was met. The supreme court granted the DHS petition for review to determine whether Emergency Order No. 3 is a rule.

There was no majority opinion in this case. Chief Justice Roggensack, joined by Justices Ziegler and R. G. Bradley, authored a lead opinion announcing the mandate of the court and affirming the court of appeals. Justice Hagedorn concurred in the mandate, but did not join the lead opinion. The lead opinion first addressed whether the case was moot. The lead opinion noted that, although the emergency order expired, the issue regarding whether the secretary-designee of health services issued an order in violation of the laws of Wisconsin satisfied the great public importance exception to mootness.

On the merits, the lead opinion stated that "agencies must comport with rulemaking procedures set forth in Wis. Stat. ch. 227 when the agency's proffered directive meets the definition of a 'rule.'" The lead opinion explained, as the court did in *Palm*, that "agency action that exhibits all of the following criteria meets the definition of a rule: '(1) a regulation, standard, statement of policy or general order; (2) of general application; (3) having the effect of law; (4) issued by an agency; (5) to implement, interpret or make specific legislation enforced or administered by such agency.'" The lead opinion reiterated the court's conclusion from *Palm* that an order issued by an agency is a general order of general application if "the class of people regulated ... 'is described in general terms and new members can be added to the class.'"

The lead opinion found unpersuasive the DHS argument that Emergency Order No. 3 was not a rule because it was issued under a different subsection of Wis. Stat. § 252.02 than the subsections discussed in *Palm*. The lead opinion noted that such an argument reads Palm too narrowly and that the determination of whether DHS's action meets the definition of a rule depends upon the definitional criteria explained in the *Palm* decision.

The lead opinion stated that Emergency Order No. 3 is a general order generally applied and it therefore meets the facial definition of a rule, as was explained in *Palm*. The lead opinion found Emergency Order No. 3 meets the five definitional criteria of a rule that were set forth in that decision. First, the lead opinion found that the order met the first two criteria of a rule and was a general order of general application because, by its own terms, the order applied broadly and created a class that could include new entities and members. Emergency Order No. 3 met the third definitional criterion because it was enforceable by civil forfeiture and thus had the effect of law. The order met the fourth criterion because it was issued by DHS, an agency. Finally, the lead opinion stated that by both implementing and interpreting Wis. Stat. § 252.02 (3)'s grant of authority to "forbid public gatherings ... to control outbreaks and epidemics," Emergency Order No. 3 satisfies the fifth criterion of a rule. Because the lead opinion found that Emergency Order No. 3 satisfied all five criteria that define a rule and was not promulgated through rulemaking procedures, Emergency Order No. 3 was not valid or enforceable.

In his concurrence, Justice Hagedorn noted the court's previous ruling in *Palm*, which held, "among other things, that a statewide order limiting public gatherings met the statutory definition of an administrative rule and must be promulgated as such." The justice noted his objections to the court's analysis in *Palm* and, by extension, the rationale in the lead opinion, but agreed that the court's ruling in *Palm* controlled the outcome with regard to Emergency Order No. 3. Justice Hagedorn stated that if the doctrine of stare decisis (meaning "to stand by things decided") "is to have any import at all in our legal system, it surely must apply when a court has told a specific party that certain conduct is unlawful, and that party does the very same thing again under the same circumstances."

Justice A. W. Bradley dissented, joined by Justices Dallet and Karofsky, finding that the *Palm* decision was inapplicable to the case and that the plain language of Wis. Stat. § 252.02 (3) provides DHS with the authority to forbid public gatherings without going through rulemaking.

DNR authority after 2011 Wisconsin Act 21

In two cases—*Clean Wisconsin, Inc. v. Wisconsin Department of Natural Resources*, 2021 WI 71, 398 Wis. 2d 386, 961 N.W.2d 346 (hereinafter, *Clean Wisconsin v. Kinnard*) and *Clean Wisconsin, Inc. v. Wisconsin Department of Natural Resources*, 2021 WI 72, 398 Wis. 2d 433, 961 N.W.2d 611 (hereinafter, *Clean Wisconsin v.*

WMC)—the supreme court held that the Department of Natural Resources has the explicit authority under state statutes to impose conditions on one permit and to consider environmental effects before approving another.

At issue in both cases was Wis. Stat. § 227.10 (2m), which was created under 2011 Wisconsin Act 21. That statute provides that "[n]o agency may implement or enforce any standard, requirement, or threshold... unless that standard, requirement, or threshold is explicitly required or explicitly permitted by statute or by a rule." Both cases raised the question of whether "explicit" means "specific" or whether an explicit grant of power to an agency in a statute or rule can be broad and general. In 2016, the then Wisconsin attorney general released an opinion (OAG 01-16) stating that Wis. Stat. § 227.10 (2m) barred DNR from imposing conditions on a permit unless those conditions were specifically laid out verbatim in a statute or administrative rule, and that the statute prevented DNR from relying on broad or general grants of authority.

In *Clean Wisconsin v. Kinnard*, Kinnard Farms, Inc., wanted to expand its existing concentrated animal feeding operation (CAFO) by adding 3,000 dairy cows. When DNR approved Kinnard's application for the necessary Wisconsin Pollution Discharge Elimination System (WPDES) permit, five individuals who lived near Kinnard's CAFO petitioned for a contested case hearing to review DNR's decision. Experts at the contested case hearing testified that a large number of private wells in the area were contaminated and that land features under the CAFO made the land extremely susceptible to groundwater contamination.

The administrative law judge (ALJ) presiding at the hearing ordered DNR to modify Kinnard's WPDES permit to include two conditions: a maximum number of animals allowed in the CAFO and off-site groundwater monitoring. However, the secretary of natural resources reversed the part of the ALJ's decision imposing conditions on the permit, based on OAG 01-16. The five individuals and Clean Wisconsin, Inc., petitioned for judicial review. The circuit court concluded that DNR had the explicit authority to impose the two conditions on Kinnard's WPDES permit. Kinnard appealed, and the court of appeals certified the case to the supreme court. The supreme court granted the Wisconsin Legislature's motion to intervene in the case.

Kinnard and the legislature argued that, under Wis. Stat. § 227.10 (2m), "explicit" means "specific," and any condition imposed in a permit must be included verbatim in a statute or administrative rule. The court, in a majority opinion authored by Justice Karofsky, rejected this argument, noting both that the dictionary definitions of the two words are different, and that the legislature had used the term "specific" in other statutes but had chosen not to do so here. The court instead held that "an agency may rely upon a grant of authority that is explicit but broad when undertaking agency action, and such an explicit but broad grant of authority complies with § 227.10 (2m)."

The court also looked to Wis. Stat. § 283.31 (3), which allows DNR to issue a permit "for the discharge of any pollutant . . . upon condition that such discharges will meet," among other things, effluent limitations (restrictions on the amount of pollutants that may be discharged from a particular source) and groundwater protection standards (health-based standards for groundwater set by DNR). In addition, Wis. Stat. § 283.31 (4) provides that DNR "shall prescribe conditions for permits issued under this section to assure compliance" with effluent limitations and groundwater protection standards. Based on these statutes, the court determined that DNR had the explicit authority to impose the two conditions on Kinnard's WPDES permit.

Justice Dallet filed a concurring opinion, in which Justices A. W. Bradley and Karofsky joined. Justice Roggensack filed a dissenting opinion, in which Justice R. G. Bradley joined; Justice R. G. Bradley also filed a separate dissenting opinion.

In *Clean Wisconsin v. WMC*, DNR reviewed several applications for proposed high capacity wells. A high capacity well is a well capable of pumping more than 100,000 gallons per day. Wis. Stat. § 281.34 (4) (a) requires DNR to evaluate the environmental impacts for some, but not all, high capacity well applications. In this case, DNR was not required under Wis. Stat. § 281.34 (4) (a) to perform such an evaluation but still determined that the proposed wells would negatively affect waters of the state. However, based on the attorney general's 2016 opinion, DNR stopped its practice of reviewing the potential environmental effects of all proposed high capacity wells and approved all of the high capacity well applications at issue here without imposing any conditions to limit the environmental impacts of the wells.

Clean Wisconsin, Inc., and the Pleasant Lake Management District (collectively, Clean Wisconsin) appealed DNR's approval of the wells to the circuit court, and several business associations intervened in the action. The circuit court reversed the approvals. The business associations appealed, and the court of appeals certified the appeal to the supreme court. The supreme court granted the legislature's motion to intervene in the case.

In a majority opinion authored by Justice Dallet, the court first noted that it had addressed the same issue in *Lake Beulah Management District v. State Department of Natural Resources*, 2011 WI 54, 335 Wis. 2d 47, 799 N.W.2d 73. The court explained that, in *Lake Beulah*, the court had unanimously held that "DNR has both a constitutional duty and the statutory authority to consider the environmental effects of all proposed high capacity wells" and that DNR cannot ignore "concrete, scientific evidence of potential harm to waters of the state." The public trust doctrine in Wis. Const. art. IX, § 1, requires the state to protect its navigable waters for the public's benefit. The court noted, as it had in *Lake Beulah*, that the legislature has delegated some of its public trust duties to DNR. Specifically, the legislature charged DNR with the "general supervision and control over the waters of the state" under Wis. Stat. § 281.12 (1); granted to DNR the "necessary powers" to enhance the "quality management and protection of all waters of the state" against "all present and potential sources of water pollution" under Wis. Stat. § 281.11; and required DNR to "carry out the planning, management[,] and regulatory programs necessary for implementing the policy and purpose of [Wis. Stat. ch. 281]" under Wis. Stat. § 281.12 (1). In order to fulfill these duties, the court in *Lake Beulah* found that DNR must be able to consider the environmental effects of a proposed high capacity well. Additionally, the court noted that the legislature also required DNR, under Wis. Stat. §§ 281.34 (5) (e) and 281.35 (5) (d), to impose conditions on approved wells to ensure that the wells will not adversely affect any public water right in navigable waters or have a significant detrimental effect on the waters of the state.

The court then rejected the business associations' and legislature's argument that the enactment of Wis. Stat. § 227.10 (2m) necessarily altered the court's conclusion in *Lake Beulah*. The court held that Wis. Stat. § 227.10 (2m) requires "explicit" grants of authority rather than "implicit" grants, but that this does not mean that an explicit grant of authority cannot be broad and general. The court found that the legislature "granted the DNR the broad but explicit authority to consider the environmental effects of a proposed high capacity well" under the statutes discussed above. In considering a proposed well's potential effect on the environment, then, DNR is carrying out its explicit statutory directives.

In both cases, Justices Roggensack and R. G. Bradley dissented, finding that there is not explicit authority in the statutes or administrative rules that gives DNR the power to either impose the two conditions on Kinnard's WPDES permit or conduct an environmental impact review for proposed high capacity wells when that review is not specifically required.

Justice Hagedorn did not participate in either case.

Employment discrimination on the basis of domestic violence convictions

In *Cree, Inc. v. Labor & Industry Review Commission*, 2022 WI 15, 400 Wis. 2d 827, 970 N.W.2d 837, the supreme court considered whether an employer unlawfully discriminated against a job applicant when the employer rescinded its job offer after learning about the applicant's record of domestic violence convictions.

In June 2015, shortly after his release from prison, Derrick Palmer applied for a job as an applications specialist at the Cree, Inc., facility in Racine, Wisconsin, which manufactured and marketed lighting components. The primary responsibilities of the position included designing and recommending lighting systems to Cree's customers. Cree offered Palmer the job subject to a standard background check but then rescinded the offer after the background check revealed the details of Palmer's convictions in 2013 of multiple crimes involving domestic violence against his live-in girlfriend. Palmer filed a complaint with the Equal Rights Division (ERD) of the Department of Workforce Development, alleging that Cree unlawfully discriminated against him on the basis of his conviction record in violation of the Wisconsin Fair Employment Act (WFEA).

The WFEA generally prohibits employers from discriminating against current and prospective employees on the basis of their criminal conviction records. However, the WFEA contains an exception, known as the "substantial relationship test," that allows an employer to deny employment if the circumstances of the individual's convicted offense substantially relate to the circumstances of the particular job. ERD's administrative law judge agreed with Cree and concluded that Palmer's convictions were substantially related to the circumstances of the job, and that, therefore, Cree did not unlawfully discriminate against Palmer when it rescinded the job offer. Palmer appealed the decision to the Labor and Industry Review Commission (LIRC), which reversed ERD's decision. Cree appealed that determination to the circuit court, which reversed LIRC's decision. Palmer again appealed, and the court of appeals reversed the circuit court's decision. Finally, Cree appealed to the supreme court, which yet again reversed.

In a majority opinion authored by Justice Karofsky, the supreme court explained that the substantial relationship test requires an employer to show that the facts, events, and conditions surrounding the convicted offense "materially relate" to the facts, events, and conditions surrounding the job; however, the test does not require an exact identity between the circumstances of the offense and the circumstances of the job. The relevant circumstances are those "material to fostering criminal activity"; in other words, the circumstances must be material to the likelihood that the individual will reoffend in the workplace.

The court noted that the "seesawing" history of the case demonstrated a need for clarifying how the substantial relationship test applies to domestic violence convictions and explained that the underlying decisions were based on the common, but unsupported, belief that domestic batterers have a tendency to be violent only towards intimate partners. Rather, the court explained, the domestic setting of the offense and the intimate relationship with the victim are circumstances of the offense of domestic violence that are immaterial to determining whether a substantial relationship exists.

Regarding the circumstances of Palmer's convictions, the court analyzed the character traits revealed by the elements of Palmer's offenses and concluded that the elements and particular facts of the offenses showed that Palmer has a "tendency to violently exert his power to control others, and thus Palmer poses a real threat to the safety of others." In addition to character traits, the court also considered other circumstances of the offense, including: (1) the seriousness and number of offenses—the more serious the offense, the less an employer should be expected to carry the risk and liability that the employee will reoffend; (2) how recent the conviction was—a recent conviction may eliminate any favorable inference of rehabilitation; and (3) whether there is a pattern of behavior—the existence of prior convictions with similar elements may increase the risk the employee will reoffend. With respect to those additional circumstances, the court concluded that Palmer's offenses were undeniably serious, the offenses were recent, and the offenses, together with a prior 2001 domestic battery conviction, indicated an emerging pattern of domestic violence convictions.

In evaluating the circumstances of the job, the court noted that the applications specialist works largely independently without regular supervision, travels to customer sites and trade shows, and has access to most of Cree's facility, including secluded areas, extremely loud places that could cover the sounds of a struggle, and portions not covered by security cameras.

In short, the court concluded that Cree had sufficiently proven that the circumstances of Palmer's domestic violence convictions substantially related to the circumstances of the applications specialist job for at least two reasons: (1) Palmer's willingness to use violence to exert power and control over others substantially relates to the independent and interpersonal nature of the job; and (2) the absence of regular supervision creates opportunities for violent encounters. Therefore, the court concluded, Cree did not unlawfully discriminate against Palmer by rescinding its job offer.

The court stressed that its holding was fact-specific and that "[n]othing in this opinion condemns all domestic violence offenders to a life of unemployment."

Justice Dallet dissented in an opinion joined by Justices A. W. Bradley and Hagedorn. In the dissenter's view, the majority focused on generic character traits at a high level of generality and general qualities of Cree's workplace, and, in doing so, undermined the WFEA's policy of reintegration of offenders into the workforce by "concluding that individuals convicted of crimes of domestic violence are unfit to work in close proximity to other people, regardless of the circumstances."

Defense for crimes committed by a victim of sex trafficking

In *State v. Kizer*, 2022 WI 58, 403 Wis. 2d 142, 976 N.W.2d 356, the supreme court

(1) defined the meaning of "direct result" in the context of a defense against prosecution for crimes committed by a victim of sex trafficking and (2) held that such a defense is a complete defense against first-degree intentional homicide.

Chrystul Kizer was charged with, among other crimes, first-degree intentional homicide following an incident in which she allegedly shot and killed a man who she alleged was sex trafficking her. The supreme court's opinion in this case came after a series of pretrial appeals relating to whether Kizer could raise the defense under Wis. Stat. § 939.46 (1m): "A victim of [sex trafficking] has an affirmative defense for any offense committed as a direct result of the [sex trafficking] without regard to whether anyone was prosecuted or convicted for the [sex trafficking]."

The circuit court determined that the defense under Wis. Stat. § 939.46 (1m) is available only to a defendant who is charged with trafficking. Kizer appealed. Both Kizer and the prosecution agreed that the circuit court's interpretation of the availability of the defense was incorrect because the language of the statute specifies that the defense applies to "any offense" and applies "without regard to whether anyone was prosecuted or convicted" for sex trafficking. However, the parties disagreed about what qualifies as an offense committed "as a direct result" of sex trafficking and whether, as a threshold matter, she could raise the defense with regard to her alleged actions. The parties then disagreed about whether the defense would provide the defendant with a complete defense against first-degree intentional homicide or whether the defense would mitigate first-degree intentional homicide to second-degree intentional homicide.

The court of appeals held that "direct result" means that the victim's offense arose relatively immediately from the trafficking violation, is motivated primarily by the trafficking violation, is a logical and reasonably foreseeable consequence of the violation, and is not in significant part caused by events, circumstances, or considerations other than that violation. The court of appeals also concluded that the defense was a complete defense to first-degree intentional homicide. The state appealed.

The supreme court, in a 4–3 opinion authored by Justice Dallet, first considered the question of how to define "direct result" for the purposes of the defense statute. When the court conducts a statutory analysis, it begins with the language of the statute. If the meaning of the statute is plain, the inquiry ends there. Generally, the court gives the words in a statute their common, everyday meaning. If a word or phrase is not defined in the statute, the court consults the dictionary definition. Using this process in this case, the majority determined that an offense is "committed as a direct result" of a trafficking offense if there is a "logical, causal connection between the offense and the trafficking such that the offense is not the result, in significant part, of other events, circumstances, or considerations apart from the trafficking violation." The court declined to adopt the court of appeals' interpretation, which would require the offense to be a foreseeable result of the trafficking violation and to proceed relatively immediately from the trafficking violation.

The supreme court's decision on the question of whether the defense is mitigating or complete involved a more complicated statutory analysis. The state's interpretation of the defense as mitigating rested on the interplay of several statutory provisions, including Wis. Stat. §§ 939.45 (1), 939.46, and 940.01 (2) (d).

Wis. Stat. § 940.01 (2) (d) is part of the first-degree intentional homicide statute. That provision states that when death was caused "in the exercise of a privilege under 939.45 (1)," the defendant has an affirmative defense to prosecution that mitigates the offense from first-degree intentional homicide to second-degree intentional homicide.

Wis. Stat. § 939.45 (1) refers to an actor's conduct that occurs under "circumstances of coercion or necessity so as to be privileged under s. 939.46 or 939.47." Because the defense at issue in this case falls under Wis. Stat. § 939.46, titled "Coercion," the state argued that the defense would serve to mitigate the offense to second-degree intentional homicide.

Kizer, however, argued that the mitigation specified in Wis. Stat. § 940.01 (2) (d) does not apply to the defense under Wis. Stat. § 939.46 (1m) and that instead, the defense under Wis. Stat. § 939.46 (1m) serves as a complete defense to first-degree intentional homicide. Her argument relied on the legislative history of the relevant statutes as well as the mitigation language itself, which is present in every other statute that creates a defense referenced in Wis. Stat. § 940.01 (2), including coercion under Wis. Stat. § 939.46 (1), but which is notably absent from the defense under Wis. Stat. § 939.46 (1m).

The lead opinion authored by Justice Dallet ultimately determined that both readings of the statute are reasonable, rendering the statute ambiguous. Justices Dallet, A. W. Bradley, and Karofsky therefore ruled in Kizer's favor after applying the rule of lenity, which requires a court to resolve an ambiguity in the defendant's favor.

A concurrence and a dissent were both filed on the second issue in the case. Justice R. G. Bradley filed a concurring opinion stating that she disagreed with the lead opinion's process for applying the rule of lenity. The lead opinion stated that the rule of lenity requires the court to first look to the legislative history of a statute to resolve any ambiguity before ruling in the defendant's favor. Justice R. G. Bradley elaborated that she disagreed with this approach because it "elevates legislative history over a rule of statutory construction." This approach, she reasoned, is erroneous because nothing in the legislative history may cause the criminal law to be stricter than the text of the law itself. Therefore, the rule of lenity requires ruling in the defendant's favor regardless of what may or may not be revealed by the legislative history.

The dissent, authored by Justice Roggensack and joined by Chief Justice Ziegler and Justice Hagedorn, disagreed with the lead opinion that the statute was ambiguous. The dissent relied on the statutory structure and context to find that the defense is a "coercion" defense and therefore falls under the definition of mitigating defenses for the purposes of first-degree intentional homicide. The dissent also relied on the common law rule that coercion only serves to mitigate first-degree intentional homicide and opined that if the legislature intended to overrule this common law rule in the context of this defense, the legislature should have clearly expressed its intent to do so in the language of the statute.

Legal name change not protected by the first amendment

In *State v. C. G.* (*In re interest of C. G.*), 2022 WI 60, 403 Wis. 2d 229, 976 N.W.2d 318, the supreme court decided that a legal name change is not a constitutionally protected form of speech.

The petitioner, C. G., was a transgender female who was prevented from legally changing her name because she was subject to the sex offender registry. C. G. entered the juvenile justice system as a male and subsequently realized she was a transgender female. C. G. had a traditionally masculine legal name but chose to go by the name of Ella. Ella believed her legal name was incompatible with her gender identity, but was prohibited from petitioning for a legal name change because of her status as subject to the sex offender registry. Ella was not prohibited from adopting and using an alias of her choosing, which would also be listed in the sex offender registry.

Ella challenged the registration requirement on two grounds: (1) it constitutes cruel and unusual punishment as applied to her in violation of the Eighth Amendment to the U.S. Constitution, and (2) it violates her right to free speech in violation of the First Amendment to the U.S. Constitution. Both arguments are based on her inability to legally change her name to conform to her gender identity as a result of the registration requirement.

In a majority opinion authored by Justice R. G. Bradley and joined by Chief Justice Ziegler and Justices Roggensack and Hagedorn, the court decided that Ella's constitutional right to be free from cruel and unusual punishment was not violated by the registration requirement. The court decided this for two reasons. First, a cruel and unusual punishment analysis may be conducted only as a facial challenge (i.e., the law does not recognize an as-applied analysis to determine whether a punishment is cruel and unusual for the purposes of the Eighth Amendment). Second, it is well-established law that a requirement to register on the sex-offender registry does not constitute "punishment" as a matter of law.

On Ella's First Amendment claim, the majority addressed two theories advanced by Ella: first, that expression of her gender identity through a legal name change is expressive conduct protected by the First Amendment, and second, that registration not only prevents Ella from expressing her gender identity, but also it impermissibly compels speech by forcing Ella to disclose her transgender status.

The court rejected Ella's argument that use of a gender-appropriate name is expressive conduct. The First Amendment protection for expressive conduct is limited to conduct that is "inherently expressive." The court determined that the act of producing identification constitutes conduct that is not inherently expressive, and is therefore not protected by the First Amendment. The court stated that when Ella presents herself to the world as a woman, her conduct is expressive, but it becomes no less or more expressive depending on her legal name. The court opined, "The expressive component of her transgender identity is not created by the legal name printed on her identification but by the various actions she takes to present herself in a specific manner, e.g., dressing in women's clothing, wearing make-up, growing out her hair, and using a feminine alias." The majority then undertook a historical analysis of the law and determined that under the original meaning of the First Amendment, a legal name change does not constitute protected speech. The court based its analysis on the history of statutory provisions for legal name changes and noted that in most states, including Wisconsin, whether to grant a petition for a legal name change is left to the discretion of the court. "The fact that petitions may be denied under this discretionary standard," the court concluded, "suggests a legal name change, as traditionally understood, does not implicate the freedom of speech."

Next, the court turned to an analysis of Ella's argument that registration compels speech by forcing her to reveal her transgender status whenever she is required to produce her legal name. The court also rejected this argument, stating that Ella failed to explain how presenting legal documentation bearing a male-sounding name constitutes compelled speech. The court reiterated its position that identifying oneself is merely an act of providing information, not a mode of expression. The court offered an example to illustrate its point: "When the government requires a person to accurately list her hallmarks of identification on a tax form, the government does not compel her to speak but merely to produce information; Ella's claim is indistinguishable." Finally, the court concluded, "The State did not give Ella her legal name—her parents did . . . and when Ella presents a government-issued identification card, she is free to say nothing at all or to say, 'I go by Ella.'"

Justice Hagedorn filed a concurrence in part.

The dissent in this case, authored by Justice A. W. Bradley and joined by Justices Dallet and Karofsky, argued that the majority's view of expressive conduct is too narrow, and that the proposition that a name is not expressive conduct implicating the First Amendment goes against the tide of relevant case law. Instead, the dissent argued, the name-change ban is a limitation on expressive conduct subject to the First Amendment, and should be analyzed as such under the intermediate scrutiny test. Using intermediate scrutiny, the dissent argued, the court should have analyzed whether the restriction is a reasonable, content-neutral restriction that is narrowly tailored to serve a significant government interest. The dissent offered such an analysis and found that the name-change ban failed this test as applied to Ella. BB

NOTES

1. Wis. Legis. Reference Bureau, "LRB Survey of Significant Wisconsin Court Decisions, 2019–2020," *LRB Reports* 4, no. 17 (Madison, WI: Legislative Reference Bureau, Dec. 2020): 1.

2. This publication's scope of coverage includes supreme court cases released through July 2022 and court of appeals cases released through June 2022.

3. That political conflicts in the United States inevitably become judicial conflicts is a well-known fact of American political life. As Alexis de Tocqueville observed nearly 190 years ago, "There is hardly a political question in the United States which does not sooner or later turn into a judicial one." Alexis de Tocqueville, *Democracy in America, and Two Essays on America*, trans. Gerald E. Bevan, ed. Isaac Kramnick (London: Penguin Books, 2003), 315.

4. 2021 Wis. SB 621.

5. In *Carey v. Wisconsin Elections Commission*, No. 22-cv-402-jdp, 2022 U.S. Dist. LEXIS 156973 (W.D. Wis. Aug. 30, 2022), the U.S. District Court for the Western District of Wisconsin held that this interpretation is preempted by the federal Voting Rights Act "to the extent it prohibits third-party ballot-return assistance to disabled voters who require such assistance."

6. The supreme court's opinion in *Wisconsin Legislature v. Palm* is summarized in the 2021–22 *Wisconsin Blue Book*. Wis. Legis. Reference Bureau, "Survey of Significant Wisconsin Court Decisions, 2019–20," part 3 in *Wisconsin Blue Book: 2021–22* (Madison, WI: Legislative Reference Bureau, 2021), 402–4.

SPECIAL SESSIONS OF THE WISCONSIN LEGISLATURE

BY RICHARD A. CHAMPAGNE AND MADELINE KASPER

The Wisconsin Constitution authorizes the governor to convene the state legislature in "special session." Typically, the governor convenes a special session of the legislature to address one or more matters the governor considers so important that the matters must be addressed promptly and separately from other legislative business. When it is in regular session, the legislature may act on any public policy issue; but in special session, the legislature may consider and act only on those subjects enumerated by the governor in the special session proclamation or call. In addition, there are unique legislative procedures in a special session to speed up the lawmaking process, in recognition of the fact that special session issues may require prompt attention. Since Wisconsin became a state in 1848, the governor has called the legislature into special session 110 times.[1] The most recent special session was the October 2022 Special Session, called by Governor Tony Evers to consider a constitutional amendment that would provide for statewide binding referenda and ballot initiatives. In his special session call, Governor Evers stated that such a process was necessary to overturn Wisconsin's statutory abortion ban.[2]

This article summarizes the Wisconsin governor's authority to call a special session of the legislature, explains how these sessions are convened and conducted, and briefly examines trends in special sessions over time.

Before turning to this discussion, it is helpful to understand the basic contours of Wisconsin's legislative schedule. The Wisconsin Legislature is a full-time, biennial body that convenes for the first time in January of each odd-numbered year. Typically, the legislature meets in regular session throughout the odd-numbered year and then through the early months of the next even-numbered year before adjourning the regular session until the inauguration date of the next succeeding legislature. The regular session consists both of regularly scheduled floorperiods, as well as nonscheduled, extraordinary sessions and special sessions. Extraordinary sessions differ from special sessions in that the legislature convenes extraordinary sessions on its own initiative, while the governor convenes special sessions. The Wisconsin Supreme Court has affirmed that special and extraordinary sessions may be convened at any time throughout the legislative biennium.[3] The purpose of special and extraordinary sessions is typically to focus attention on important public policy matters or, as is sometimes the case with extraordiny sessions, to address unfinished legislative business after the last general-business floorperiod ends. Unlike an extraordinary session, which is initiated by members of the legislature or legislative committees, a special session is called for and directed by the governor. For more information on extraordinary sessions, see page 435.

Authority to call a special session

The authority for the governor to call a special session derives from two constitutional provisions, which were included in the original Wisconsin Constitution. Wis. Const. art. V, § 4, authorizes the governor to "convene the legislature on extraordinary occasions." Wis. Const. art. IV, § 11, provides the following:

> The legislature shall meet at the seat of government at such time as shall be provided by law, unless convened by the governor in special session, and when so convened no business shall be transacted except as shall be necessary to accomplish the special purposes for which it was convened.

The constitution thus authorizes the governor to call a special session and to limit the scope of that session to specific purposes, but it does not prescribe how the session must be convened or conducted. The rules and procedures for holding a special session have evolved over time and are governed by legislative rules and practice, attorney general opinions, and court decisions.[4]

It is important to note that a special session is not part of the legislature's regular session. A special session is a distinct session of the legislature called by the governor. As a separate session, the only legislation that may be enacted in that session is legislation introduced and passed by the assembly and senate in that session. In 1963, Assembly Speaker Robert D. Hasse discussed how a special session is distinct from a regular session:

> A special session of the Wisconsin Legislature is a "new session" in the sense that, when it convenes, it has nothing before it on which it can act. Each proposal, in order to be acted on by the legislature meeting in special session, must be placed before the legislature in the proper form of a bill, joint resolution or resolution, introduced in that special session. [. . .]
>
> A special session of the Wisconsin Legislature is a "new session" in the sense that it is not bound by the action of the legislature in the preceding regular session, but that any action taken by the legislature meeting in special session must be taken from the beginning and, if a law is to be enacted, go through the complete lawmaking cycle.[5]

That said, on two different occasions, in 1977 and in 1983, governors included consideration of partial vetoes of regular session bills in their special session calls. In fact, during the June 1977 Special Session, the legislature successfully overrode several partial vetoes of provisions in 1977 Senate Bill 77 (the biennial budget bill), thereby enacting those provisions into law. These two instances indicate that a regular session bill may be considered during a special session if the special session is called for the purpose of overriding the governor's veto of the regular session bill. This is an exception to the general rule that legislation and other legislative business from the regular session may not be carried over into a special session.

Process for calling a special session

The first formal step in organizing a special session is the issuance of a proclamation or call by the governor setting forth the day and hour for convening the session and the purpose for which the session is to be held. The Wisconsin Constitution does not stipulate how the subjects of the call must be enumerated, or even the manner in which the call must be issued. Over 100 years ago, in an opinion to Governor Emanuel L. Philipp in 1918, Attorney General Spencer Haven described the broad options available to the governor in calling a special session:

> [T]he constitution leaves the matter wholly within your hands. You are hampered by no machinery, and no limitations. The time of issuing the proclamation, the time when the session shall convene, the subjects to be considered thereat, the length of notice to be given to the members, the method of notifying them, all are left entirely to your discretion.[6]

Since 1983, governors have issued special session proclamations via executive order.[7] Between 1983 and 2013, executive orders calling for special sessions typically listed the general topic or topics of the session, sometimes including some or all of the language in a relating clause of legislation the governor would ultimately go on to have introduced as part of the special session.[8] Within the last 10 years, however, these executive orders have regularly identified individual pieces of legislation by Legislative Reference Bureau (LRB) draft number, a practice first used by Governor Scott McCallum in 2001 and regularly used by Governors Scott Walker and Evers since then.[9]

Identifying a special session call by LRB draft numbers can result in some ambiguity in determining the purpose of the special session call. For example, questions arise as to whether the special session call is the relating clause of the LRB draft identified in the executive order or any matter addressed in the LRB draft or drafts. Importantly, whether the special session call includes LRB draft numbers or relating clauses, the legislature is under no legal obligation to act on any of the legislation identified by the governor. Instead, the legislature may consider any legislation that is germane to the special session call, as discussed later in this article.[10] It is also important to note that the legislature is under no constitutional obligation to introduce, consider, or pass any legislation during a special session.

On the date specified in the governor's special session call, each house of the legislature usually convenes the session in "skeletal session," attended only by a few members at most, during which the body convenes and then immediately adjourns to a date certain or adjourns the special session permanently, without engaging in any legislative business. In doing this, each house of the legislature satisfies the constitutional requirement to convene the special session at the time and date set by the governor, but each house can still determine for itself when, if at all, it will act on the special session call. Also, the governor may later supplement the original call by issuing new proclamations and adding topics for the legislature to consider in special session. In January 2011, for example, Governor Walker called the legislature into special session to consider legislation relating to taxes, rule-making authority and procedures, health savings accounts, tort reform, and the creation of the Wisconsin Economic Development Corporation. He went on to supplement that call four times, adding other subjects such as regulation of telecommunication utilities and consideration of a budget repair bill.[11]

Special session legislative procedures

At its first meeting in January of an odd-numbered year, the legislature organizes itself to conduct business during the biennium through adoption of a joint resolution establishing the regular session calendar.[12] The legislative schedule, typically adopted as Senate Joint Resolution 1, is divided into regular session floorperiods interspersed with periods for committee work. A special session can be called at any point in the biennium, and there is a continuity of procedural rules for regular sessions and special sessions. Rules in effect at the conclusion of the preceding regular session are carried forward, which means that when a special session is convened, each house already has a body of rules in force.[13]

However, there are also a number of rules that specifically apply only during special and extraordinary sessions.[14] During a special session, any newly introduced proposals are numbered specifically as special session proposals.[15] In other words, the first special session assembly bill is Special Session Assembly Bill 1 and the first special session senate bill is Special Session Senate Bill 1. Each special session bill is also identified by the month for which the special session is called. For example, for the special session convened by Governor Evers on January 19, 2021, relating to the state's unemployment insurance program, the two introduced bills were January 2021 Special Session Assembly Bill 1 and January 2021 Special Session Senate Bill 1. This rule is in keeping with the idea that a special session is an entirely different legislative session from a regular session, and requires that all legislative proposals to be considered at the special session be introduced in that special session.[16] A special session differs from an extraordinary session in that extraordinary session proposals are introduced and numbered in sequence with regular session proposals, since an extraordinary session is still considered part of a regular session. Also, in an extraordinary session, regular session bills already introduced or acted on may be taken up if included in the extraordinary session call, including bills already passed by one house. This is not the case for a special session.

During a special session, only certain actors may introduce legislation. The joint rules provide that special session proposals may be introduced only by the following committees: the Joint Committee on Legislative Organization (JCLO), the Joint Committee on Employment Relations, the organization committee of either house, or "any other committee of either house authorized to do so by the rules of that house."[17] The senate and assembly rules authorize introduction of proposals by each house's respective committee on finance, as well as the Joint Committee on Finance; the assembly rules also authorize the Assembly Committee on Rules to introduce proposals.[18] Special session legislation is often introduced by these committees "by request of" the governor.[19] However, although the legislature must convene on the date specified in the special session call, the legislature is not required to introduce or consider any special session proposals. Indeed, during the 2019–20 and 2021–22 legislative sessions, the legislature did not introduce any of the proposals identified by LRB number in eight different special session calls issued by Governor Evers.[20]

The senate and assembly rules provided specifically for special sessions serve generally to expedite the legislative process and are the same procedural modifications provided for extraordinary sessions. For example, under the senate rules, notice for special session committee meetings need only be posted on the legislative bulletin board; under the assembly rules, notice need only be posted on the bulletin board and on the legislative website.[21] Further, the senate and assembly rules both provide that, during a special session, proposals may be referred to the day's calendar and taken up immediately and that a calendar does not have to be provided.[22]

Other modifications affect floor debate during special sessions. For example, both houses prohibit motions to postpone proposals.[23] To advance a proposal to a third reading on the day that it is given its second reading or to message it to the other house on the same day that it is passed, both houses require only a simple majority vote of those present and not a suspension of the rules, as is usually the case in regular session.[24] During special session in the assembly, in almost all cases, motions to reconsider must be taken up immediately.[25] In the senate, any point of order must be decided within an hour.[26] Together, these modifications allow bills to be taken up on a legislative day, amended, and passed and messaged to the other house on the same legislative day. This is not possible on a regular session day unless the rules are suspended.

Each house's rules also provide that procedural modifications may be adopted for a specific special or extraordinary session.[27] While this practice has been exceedingly rare in recent decades, note that procedural modifications were adopted when the April 2020 Extraordinary Session was called to address the COVID-19 pandemic. When the organization committees in each house adopted motions to convene the session, the committees also adopted a number of special procedures to account for the fact that the session would be a primarily virtual meeting and to accelerate the usual extraordinary session procedures even further. For example, the rule modifications required that all amendments be introduced by 9 a.m. on the day of the session and also prohibited members from offering privileged resolutions during the session.[28]

Per longstanding legislative custom and practice, special sessions may be held concurrently with regular session floorperiods or extraordinary sessions. In other words, in a single calendar day, the senate or the assembly can, and sometimes will, meet on the floor in special session as well as in regular or extraordinary session, a practice upheld by the Wisconsin supreme court.[29]

The governor has the power to convene a special session but not to adjourn it. The legislature may adjourn a special session at any time, either in skeletal session or when the full body is on the floor.[30] The session schedule adopted at the beginning of the legislature's biennial session typically provides that a motion adopted in each house to adjourn a special session pursuant to the session schedule constitutes final adjournment of the special session.[31] In other words, when the senate and the assembly want to end the special session, the houses adjourn expressly pursuant to Senate Joint Resolution 1. Special session bills die at the adjournment of the session and are no longer available for consideration in regular session. Importantly, however, Senate Joint Resolution 1 provides that a majority of members of JCLO may reconvene a special session after final adjournment, solely for the consideration of full or partial vetoes of bills passed during the special session.[32]

Scope and germaneness

The most significant limitation on the powers of the legislature when it is meeting in special session is set forth in Wis. Const. art. IV, § 11: "[W]hen [the legislature is] so convened no business shall be transacted except as shall be necessary to accomplish the special purposes for which it was convened." In other words, the legislature may only pass legislation relating to the special session call. This germaneness requirement gives the governor the power to set the scope of a special session by detailing the subjects on which the legislature may act, but the legislature retains considerable discretion to shape the substance of legislation, and thus the enactments, of a special session. The extent to which the legislature is constrained in its lawmaking actions during a special session is based partly on the specificity of the governor's call. However, Wisconsin Supreme Court and attorney general opinions have long affirmed the power of the legislature to broadly interpret the purpose of a governor's special session call.

During the March 1922 Special Session, for example, Attorney General William J. Morgan opined that, although a call for a special session of the legislature may specify in minute detail the laws that the governor wishes to be enacted, the legislature has the constitutional authority to enact any law designed to accomplish subjects of legislation suggested in the call.[33] In this respect, the legislature may specify the means or manner by which the subject of a governor's special session call is accomplished.

The most important litigation on this issue occurred a decade later, in response to the November 1931 Special Session. Attorney General John W. Reynolds Sr. was asked his opinion about the germaneness of a bill relating to the governor's call asking the legislature "to make provisions for the relief of unemployed citizens." The bill generally provided for the postponement for six months of the payment of real estate taxes, which applied to both employed and unemployed persons. He responded that the postponement "unquestionably would be 'relief'" of unemployed persons "as this term is generally understood and within the meaning of the governor's call" but that the overall plan was beyond the scope of the call because it would also provide such relief to numerous employed persons, as well as the unemployed.[34] Litigation eventually ensued over the constitutionality of legislation enacted during that special session.

In *State ex rel. Madison v. Industrial Commission* (1932), a case involving the construction and application of the special session laws, the Wisconsin Supreme Court indirectly affirmed the legislature's power to broadly interpret the purpose of a special session call: "The language of a statute must be construed with reference to its context and the purposes sought to be accomplished." The court continued, "[I]t must be presumed that the legislature of the state, being its supreme law-making body, has made careful investigation of the entire situation."[35] The court found that the legislature, during the November 1931 Special Session, was justified in its expansive understanding of the unemployment situation it confronted when responding to the special session call:

> We may take judicial notice of the fact that commencing late in 1929 and continuing down to the present time depression and unemployment have

existed throughout the length and breadth of this land; that during the year 1931 the unemployment situation was particularly acute; that at the time the legislature was in session, the winter of 1931 and 1932 promised no substantial change for the better.[36]

In *Van Dyke v. Wis. Tax Comm'n (In re Van Dyke)*, a 1935 decision in which the legislation enacted during the November 1931 Special Session law was challenged directly as being outside of the special session call, the Wisconsin Supreme Court referred to its decision in *State ex rel. Madison v. Industrial Commission*, and reaffirmed that the legislature, in passing special session legislation, could consider "broadly the purposes which the governor had in mind in convening the Legislature in special session."[37] Put differently, the governor could set the special session agenda by designating the special session call, but the legislature was free to act on that agenda as it determined best.

As mentioned earlier, over the last decade, governors have regularly issued special session calls that do not identify a general purpose, but rather identify LRB drafts and include the relating clauses to those drafts in the call.[38] Presumably, this is done in an effort to require the legislature to consider legislation drafted specifically by the governor to address the purpose of the special session. There are two problems with this approach. First, the legislature is not required to introduce or even to take up any of the LRB drafts identified in the special session. Instead, the legislature may act on any legislative proposal introduced during the special session so long as the proposal is germane to the call. Second, the purpose of a special session is clouded and made ambiguous by a call that refers to LRB drafts rather than a call that clearly states a legislative purpose. A relating clause of a bill draft may capture the general subject of a bill, but a bill may also contain related items or tangentially affect statutory sections or subjects not identified in the relating clause. The question then becomes whether these tangential statutory sections or subjects are also included within the call. Moreover, a related issue concerns whether the LRB drafts identified in the special session call are what constitute the special session call or whether the LRB drafts are instead examples of legislation that may be taken up and that are related to an unstated general purpose or call. For these reasons, a special session call that refers only to LRB drafts, and not a specific purpose, may be ambiguous and, insofar as the call seeks to constrain the legislature in its actions, may actually expand the limits of what the legislature can address and accomplish during a special session.

Concluding comments: special session trends

The governor's power to convene the state legislature in special session was a power contained in Wisconsin's original constitution. Wisconsin's constitution embodies both the separation of powers doctrine and the system of checks and balances in which political power is disbursed among the three branches of government, each with unique and some overlapping powers. The ability of the legislature to convene itself into session is a legislative power, but the governor's ability to convene the legislature in special session provides the governor with a modicum of legislative power. As the Wisconsin Supreme Court put it, "This power of the governor is a part of the checks and balances in our tripartite form of government."[39]

For most of Wisconsin history, the governor's power to convene the legislature in special session was seldom used. Between 1848 and 1970, for instance, the governor called a total of 27 special sessions—which averages out to about one special session every five years. Governors exercised restraint in using the special session power. Importantly, these special sessions shared several characteristics. First, the special sessions were almost always called after the legislature had adjourned its regular session *sine die*.[40] In other words, the legislature had permanently adjourned itself for the legislative session and could only reconvene in special session. Second, the special session calls were often to address major economic and political issues. Special sessions were called to expand state powers during the Civil War; to deal with tornado damage in 1878 and flooding in 1912; to allow for absentee voting for soldiers during World War I; to provide for unemployment relief during the Great Depression; and to address veterans housing after World War II. These issues often demanded immediate legislative action. Finally, in every special session convened, the legislature carried out actions specified in the governor's call, such as to pass laws, adopt joint resolutions, or confirm gubernatorial appointments.

Over the past five decades, however, the governor's use of the special session power and legislative action during a special session have changed. An initiator for this shift was a 1969 Wisconsin Supreme Court decision, holding that the governor could convene the legislature in special session before the legislature had adjourned its regular session.[41] This meant that governors were not constitutionally limited in their use of the special session power to periods after *sine die* adjournment. Whereas the special session power had historically been used to augment and enhance legislative power, by allowing the legislature to reconvene for purposes of enacting legislation, the new use of the special session power was one in which the governor could try to require the legislature to address political and economic issues that the legislature could have chosen to address on its own. The governor's power to convene the legislature in special session was not just to allow the legislature to address emergency situations, but rather to force the legislature to address issues that the governor considered pressing policy matters. In this respect, the governor's special session power became more of an agenda-setting power.

From 1971 through 2022, there were a total of 83 special sessions called by the governor—which averages out to about eight every five years. This was a dramatic increase in the number of special sessions. Moreover, of these 83 special sessions, 53 were called before the legislature had adjourned its last general-business floor-period. In other words, the governor was attempting to require the legislature to act on certain issues during the regular session. Convening a special session became a gubernatorial tool to set the legislative agenda.

Also, in the 1960s, the legislature began the practice of remaining in session throughout the entire duration of the biennium. Soon thereafter, in 1980, the legislature began the practice of reconvening itself in extraordinary session, including after the adjournment of the last general-business floorperiod.[42] The legislature did not need the governor to call a special session in order to reconvene in session and address pressing policy issues; it had the power to do this itself.

During the period between 1971 and 2022, therefore, while special sessions were sometimes convened to have the legislature act expeditiously upon urgent matters, it became more common for governors to call special sessions for ordinary legislative matters. Few special sessions dealt with emergency situations requiring immediate legislative action. This can be seen in the table on page 502, which lists the topics of each special session called in Wisconsin history. The vast majority of special sessions called after 1971 were on ordinary public policy items that could have quickly and easily been addressed in regular session. Instead, special sessions were often called to address key components of the governor's policy agenda. This was a new and innovative use of the governor's special session power.

But just as the governor's use of special sessions evolved to become an agenda-setting tool, so too did the legislative response to convening in special sessions. As previously stated, in every special session convened between 1848 and 1970, the legislature took action related to the governor's call, such as to pass laws, adopt joint resolutions, or confirm gubernatorial appointments. Governors called special sessions and the legislature responded. In contrast, during the period between 1971 and 2022, there were 19 special sessions that did not result in legislative action related to the governor's call. These sessions occurred not just when there was split political-party control of the legislature and the governor's office, but also when the same political party controlled both the executive and legislative branches of government. But this trend has been at its peak during the Evers gubernatorial administration with divided political-party control of state government. As the table on page 502 shows, Governor Evers called 12 special sessions during his first term in office—the second-highest number during a four-year term of office of any Wisconsin governor—and the legislature did not pass any legislation in 11 of these sessions. In fact, for 10 of these sessions, no legislation was even introduced and neither house of the legislature convened as a full body. Prior to Governor Evers's time in office, there were only two special sessions for which only skeletal sessions were held in both houses before adjournment.[43] While the governor may call special sessions, the legislature need not respond. As an agenda-setting tool, the governor's special session power may have lost its vitality.

This article has shown that the governor's power to convene the legislature in special session has evolved over time. For most of Wisconsin history, the governor's special session power enabled the legislature to better exercise its lawmaking powers by allowing the legislature to convene at times when the legislature was constitutionally forbidden to meet. In this way, the governor's power to convene the legislature when it could not convene itself made the legislature stronger and encouraged legislative-gubernatorial cooperation and partnerships. But as the legislature acquired for itself the ability to meet throughout the legislative biennium by extending its regular session in extraordinary session, and as governors increasingly convened special sessions when the legislature was already meeting in regular session, the special session power evolved into one that was more suited to allowing the governor to pursue the governor's public policy agenda. Special sessions were often called on ordinary legislative business and less often on emergencies facing the state. But the evolution of the governor's special session power into an agenda-setting tool may have reached its apogee. Repeatedly, during the Evers administration, the legislature has not responded to gubernatorial attempts to set the legislative agenda in special session. It is unclear if this is simply a function of divided political-party control of state government or a trend that will continue, even when the same political party controls the legislature and the governor's office. Time will tell. 🆒

NOTES

1. This number includes Governor Gaylord Nelson's June 1962 special session call. The legislature went on to convene in regular session to act on items in the governor's special session call as well as other pending legislative business. See *Legislative Journals and Indexes Vol. III*, June 18, 1962–January 9, 1963.

2. 2022 Executive Order No. 175.

3. State *ex rel.* Groppi v. Leslie, 44 Wis. 2d 282, 300 (1969); League of Women Voters v. Evers, 2019 WI 75, 387 Wis. 2d 511, 929 N.W.2d 209.

4. Although there is no statute explicitly governing special sessions, the term does appear in the statutes. For example, Wis. Stat. § 8.50 (4) (d) provides, in part, that "any vacancy in the office of state senator or representative to the assembly occurring after the close of the last regular floorperiod of the legislature held during his or her term shall be filled only if a special session or extraordinary floorperiod of the legislature is called or a veto review period is scheduled during the remainder of the term."

About Wisconsin: Special sessions | 433

5. Wis. Assembly Journal (1963) 14–16.

6. 7 Wis. Op. Att'y Gen. 49, 49–50 (1918).

7. Governor Anthony Earl issued 1983 Executive Order No. 32, calling for a special session focusing on a variety of policy topics.

8. See, for example, 2008 Executive Order No. 246, which called for a special session to "consider and act upon legislation relating to: the Great Lakes-St. Lawrence River Basin Water Resources Compact, withdrawals of water from the Great Lakes Basin, water withdrawal and use, water supply planning, water conservation, granting rule-making authority, and providing a penalty."

9. See 2001 Executive Order No. 7, which called for a special session to consider and act upon LRB-3092/8. LRB numbers are identifiers used by the Wisconsin Legislative Reference Bureau for drafted bills that have not yet been introduced.

10. In a 1987 letter to Governor Tommy Thompson, Assembly Speaker Tom Loftus made clear the legislature's power in addressing a special session: "Calling a special session, a Governor can only limit the purpose for which the special session is called. The means by which and the extent to which the general purposes of the call are to be implemented are policy decisions for the Legislature." Quoted in "The Ground Rules of a Special Session," *LRB Information Bulletin* 96-8, November 1996, 8.

11. See 2011 Executive Order No. 1, the original call, and the four supplemental calls: 2011 Executive Order No. 4, 2011 Executive Order No. 14, 2011 Executive Order No. 25, and 2011 Executive Order No. 33.

12. Wis. Stat. § 13.02. See 2023 Wis. SJR 1.

13. Assembly Rule 92; Senate Rule 92. This was an issue in the past when the legislature regularly adjourned its regular session *sine die* and was required to reconstitute itself as a legislative body when it reconvened in a special session by the governor. Adjournment *sine die* (Latin for "without day") meant that the legislature essentially dissolved.

14. Senate Rule 93; Assembly Rule 93.

15. Joint Rule 79 (3).

16. As noted earlier, there were two special sessions called for the purpose of overriding the governor's partial vetoes of regular session bills. Veto overrides of regular session bills during a special session, if the special session is called for the purpose of overriding regular session bill vetoes, appears to be an exception to the general rule that all legislative proposals considered during a special session must have been introduced during that special session.

17. Joint Rule 81 (2) (c).

18. Senate Rule 93 (1p); Assembly Rule 93 (2). Note that these senate and assembly rules provide that proposals may not be considered unless they are "recommended to be introduced, offered, or considered" by these identified committees, suggesting that individual legislators may introduce special session bills so long as they are "considered" by one of the committees. These rules would seem to contradict the wording of the joint rule, which effectively prohibits individual members from introducing special session proposals. However, this has only happened once in recent decades. During the January 2011 Special Session, Representative Chris Kapenga introduced January 2011 Special Session Assembly Bill 12, which was referred to the Assembly Committee on Labor and Workforce Development.

19. See January 2020 Special Session Assembly Bill 1, "Introduced by Committee on Assembly Organization, by request of Governor Tony Evers."

20. See 2019 Executive Order No. 54, 2020 Executive Order No. 69, 2020 Executive Order No. 84, 2021 Executive Order No. 116, 2021 Executive Order No. 127, 2022 Executive Order No. 156, 2022 Executive Order No. 168, and 2022 Executive Order No. 175.

21. Senate Rule 93 (2); Assembly Rule 93 (3).

22. Senate Rule 93 (3); Assembly Rule 93 (4).

23. Senate Rule 93 (5); Assembly Rule 93 (5).

24. Senate Rule 93 (6); Assembly Rule 93 (7).

25. Assembly Rule 93 (6). In the senate, no such rule is necessary because all actions to advance a proposal are decided by simple majority vote, including messaging the senate's actions to the assembly.

26. Senate Rule 93 (4).

27. Senate Rule 93 (intro.); Assembly Rule 93 (intro.).

28. Wis. Senate Journal (April 2020) 820; Wis. Assembly Journal (April 2020) 746–47.

29. State *ex rel.* Groppi v. Leslie, 44 Wis. 2d 282, 300 (1969).

30. Senate Rule 15, 85 (6); Assembly Rule 30 (3).

31. See, for example, 2023 Wis. SJR 1 § 1 (5) (a).

32. See, for example, 2023 Wis. SJR 1 § 1 (5) (c).

33. 11 Wis. Op. Att'y Gen. 249 (1922).

34. 20 Wis. Op. Att'y Gen. 1241, 1242 (1931).

35. State *ex rel.* Madison v. Industrial Commission, N.W. 207 Wis. 652, 660 (1932).

36. *Madison*, N.W. 207 Wis. 652, 658.

37. Van Dyke v. Wis. Tax Comm'n (In re Van Dyke), 217 Wis. 528, 542 (1935).

38. The most recent example is Governor Evers's special session call for October 4, 2022. See 2022 Executive Order No. 175.

39. *Groppi*, 44 Wis. 2d at 282, 300.

40. The only exception was in June 1962, when the legislature was called into special session, but had yet to formally adjourn the regular session. A 1962 attorney general opinion was issued to argue that the governor could call a special session at this time. 51 Wis. Op. Att'y Gen. 1 (1962). Adjournment *sine die* (Latin for "without a day") means the absolute end of the session; it essentially terminates the sitting and the power of the legislature.

41. *Groppi*, 44 Wis. 2d at 300. This decision was consistent with the 1962 attorney general opinion in 51 Wis. Op. Att'y Gen. 1 (1962).

42. An extraordinary session is simply an unscheduled regular session floorperiod. See League of Women Voters v. Evers, 2019 WI 75, 387 Wis. 2d 511, 929 N.W.2d 209.

43. The June 2009 Special Session and the March 2018 Special Session.

EXTRAORDINARY SESSIONS OF THE WISCONSIN LEGISLATURE

BY MADELINE KASPER

In December 2018, the Wisconsin Legislature convened in extraordinary session, weeks after State Superintendent of Public Instruction Tony Evers defeated incumbent Governor Scott Walker in the general election. The legislation that came out of this post-election, extraordinary session sparked considerable opposition, and several lawsuits were subsequently filed, challenging the manner in which the session was called and the content of the legislation enacted. In one of these cases, *League of Women Voters v. Evers*, the plaintiffs challenged the constitutionality of the December 2018 Extraordinary Session.[1] The plaintiffs argued that the Wisconsin Constitution does not provide the legislature the authority to convene itself into extraordinary session and that, therefore, all gubernatorial appointments confirmed and legislation passed during the December 2018 Extraordinary Session were void. The Wisconsin Supreme Court ultimately ruled that the legislature does indeed have the authority to convene itself in extraordinary session, stating:

> We hold that extraordinary sessions do not violate the Wisconsin Constitution because the text of our constitution directs the Legislature to meet at times as "provided by law," and Wis. Stat. §13.02(3) provides the law giving the Legislature the discretion to construct its work schedule, including preserving times for it to meet in an extraordinary session. The work schedule the Legislature formulated for its 2017–2018 biennial session established the beginning and end dates of the session period and specifically contemplated the convening of an extraordinary session, which occurred within the biennial session.[2]

With this decision, the Wisconsin Supreme Court affirmed for the first time the legislature's power to call itself into extraordinary session throughout the biennial session, something the legislature has done dozens of times over the past four decades, most recently to deal expeditiously with various bills, including the 2021–23 biennial budget bill, and to consider a full veto override. The ruling all but ensures that this powerful tool will continue to be used by the legislature for decades to come.

This article summarizes the Wisconsin Legislature's authority to convene in extraordinary session, explains how these sessions are called and conducted, and briefly examines similar powers in other states. In addition, the article traces the origins of extraordinary sessions and highlights some of the most notable extraordinary sessions that have been held.

Before turning to this discussion, it is helpful to understand the basic contours of Wisconsin's legislative schedule. The Wisconsin Legislature is a full-time, biennial body that convenes for the first time in January of each odd-numbered year. Typically, the legislature meets in regular session throughout the odd-numbered year and through the first few months of the even-numbered year before adjourning the regular session until the inauguration date of the next succeeding legislature. However, the legislature may meet in special or extraordinary session at any time throughout the biennium. The purpose of special and extraordinary sessions is typically to focus attention on important public policy matters or to address unfinished business after the the last general-business floorperiod ends. Unlike a special session, which is called for and guided by the governor, an extraordinary session is initiated by members of the legislature. For more information on special sessions, see page 422.

Authority to convene in extraordinary session

Extraordinary sessions, unlike special sessions, are not explicitly authorized by the constitution or the statutes.[3] However, as the Wisconsin Supreme Court confirmed in *League of Women Voters*, the authority for the legislature to convene in extraordinary session can be traced to Wis. Const. art. IV, § 11. That section provides that "[t]he legislature shall meet at the seat of government *at such time as shall be provided by law*, unless convened by the governor in special session . . . " (emphasis added).[4] The only law relating to meetings of the legislature is Wis. Stat. § 13.02, which requires the legislature to meet annually and to convene on the first Monday of January in each odd-numbered year. The law further requires the Joint Committee on Legislative Organization (JCLO) to meet early in each biennial legislative term to develop a work schedule for the biennium to be submitted to the legislature as a joint resolution.[5] The law requires this work schedule to include at least one meeting in January of each year.

Accordingly, the Wisconsin Legislature adopts a joint resolution at the beginning of each biennium that lays out the session schedule. Typically adopted as Senate Joint Resolution 1, the schedule establishes start and end dates for several "floorperiods,"[6] and specifies that days not scheduled for floorperiods are designated for committee work. Every adopted session schedule (beginning with the first such schedule, adopted for the 1971–72 biennium) has also provided for the legislature to convene "extraordinary" sessions—i.e., meetings other than the scheduled, regular session floorperiods. For example, the 2023 session schedule states:

Unless reserved under this subsection as a day to conduct an organizational meeting or to be part of a scheduled floorperiod of the legislature, every day of the biennial session period is designated as a day for committee activity and is available to extend a scheduled floorperiod, convene an extraordinary session, or take senate action on appointments as permitted by joint rule 81.[7]

This language, along with a clause establishing the end of the biennial session period as the inauguration date of the next succeeding legislature, ensures that an extraordinary session may be convened at any time throughout the biennium.[8]

Since 1977, extraordinary sessions have also been provided for in the joint rules adopted at the beginning of each session. These rules define extraordinary sessions and lay out various procedures for convening them.[9] Additionally, Joint Rule 81 (3) (a) mirrors the language in the session schedule by providing that any day of the biennial session not reserved by the session schedule for an organizational meeting or scheduled floorperiod may be assigned to an extraordinary session. Extraordinary sessions may be held concurrently with regular session floorperiods or special sessions, per longstanding legislative custom and practice. In other words, in a single calendar day, the senate or the assembly can, and often does, meet on the floor in extraordinary session as well as in regular or special session.

Process for convening an extraordinary session

The joint rules, as well as the assembly and senate rules, provide that an extraordinary session may be called at the direction of a majority of the members of the organization committees of each house or by the passage of a joint resolution approved by a majority of the elected membership in each house (not merely those present to vote).[10] The joint rules also permit extraordinary sessions to be called by joint petition of a majority of the members elected to each house. However, virtually all extraordinary sessions held over the last four decades have been called by the organization committees of each house.[11]

The joint rules also provide that action in an extraordinary session is limited to the business "specified in the action by which it is authorized."[12] The extraordinary session call may include broad subjects or specific proposals or amendments, identified by bill or resolution number or even by LRB draft number. During an extraordinary session, new bills may be considered and so may previously introduced bills. In addition, any new bills are numbered in the same sequence as regular session bills. This differs from a special session, in which only new bills, numbered as special session bills, may be considered. For extraordinary sessions called after the adjournment of the last general-business floorperiod,[13] the date on which all regular session bills are adversely disposed of, the call may revive a bill to the same stage of the legislative process it had attained before that date.[14] In other words, a bill that had already been passed by one house during the regular session would not need to be reconsidered by that house in an extraordinary session.

In the following example, the senate's call for the April 2018 Extraordinary Session, the call references an introduced bill and an unintroduced substitute amendment to the bill and also revives the bill to its status at the conclusion of the regular session:

> In accordance with Joint Rule 81 (2) and Senate Rule 93, it is moved that the Committee on Senate Organization authorize the Legislature to meet in Extraordinary Session beginning at 9:00 A.M. on Wednesday, April 4, 2018, solely for the consideration of Assembly Bill 947, and a substitute amendment to Assembly Bill 947: LRBs0436. This bill shall be considered to be at the same stage of the proceedings as it had attained during the regular session.[15]

The legislature may also expand the purpose of an extraordinary session at any time by supplementing the call, using any of the methods permitted for convening an extraordinary session.[16]

Extraordinary session legislative procedures

As previously noted, during an extraordinary session, only bills and amendments germane to the call may be considered, with limited exceptions.[17] The joint rules further state that proposals may be introduced only by the following committees: JCLO, the Joint Committee on Employment Relations, the organization committee of either house, or "any committee of either house authorized to do so by the rules of that house."[18] The senate and assembly rules authorize introduction of proposals by each house's respective committee on finance, as well as the Joint Committee on Finance; the assembly rules also authorize the Assembly Committee on Rules to introduce proposals.[19]

The senate and assembly rules provide that the procedures for regular sessions apply also to extraordinary sessions, subject to a number of modifications.[20] These modifications serve generally to expedite the legislative process during extraordinary sessions and are the same modifications provided for special sessions. For example, under the senate rules, notice for extraordinary session committee meetings need only be posted on the legislative bulletin board; under the assembly rules, notice need only be posted on the bulletin board and on the legislative website.[21] Further, the senate and assembly rules both provide that, during an extraordinary session, proposals may be referred to the day's calendar and taken up immediately and that a calendar does not have to be provided.[22]

Other modifications affect floor debate during extraordinary sessions. Both houses prohibit motions to postpone proposals.[23] To advance a proposal to a third reading or to message it to the other house, both houses require only a simple majority vote of those present.[24] In the assembly, in almost all cases, motions to reconsider must be taken up immediately.[25] In the senate, any point of order must be decided within an hour.[26] Together, these modifications allow bills to be taken up on a legislative day, amended, passed, and messaged to the other house on the same legislative day.

Each house's rules also provide that procedural modifications may be adopted for a specific extraordinary session.[27] This has happened only a few times. Most notably, when the senate and assembly organization committees adopted motions convening the April 2020 Extraordinary Session to address the COVID-19 pandemic, they also adopted a number of special procedures to account for the fact that the session would be a primarily virtual meeting and to accelerate the usual extraordinary session procedures even further.[28] For example, the rule modifications required that all amendments be introduced by 9:00 a.m. on the day of the session and also prohibited members from offering privileged resolutions during the session.

Finally, the session schedule adopted at the beginning of the legislature's biennial session typically provides that a motion adopted in each house to adjourn an extraordinary session pursuant to the session schedule constitutes final adjournment of the extraordinary session.[29] In other words, when the senate and the assembly want to end an extraordinary session, they adjourn pursuant to Senate Joint Resolution 1. Unlike special session bills which die at the adjournment of the session, any bill which does not receive final action in the extraordinary session remains available for consideration, either in a regular session floorperiod or in another extraordinary session.

Other states

The power of the Wisconsin Legislature to convene itself in an unscheduled session is not unique. According to the National Conference of State Legislatures, 36 state legislatures have this power.[30] Comparing this power across legislatures is difficult, as the limitations for convening such a session (called an extraordinary or special session, depending on the state) vary and often depend in part on parliamentary custom and practice as well as case law. However, it is safe to conclude that the Wisconsin Legislature's extraordinary session power is unusually broad and is more frequently used than in other states.

For one, most of the 36 state legislatures that have the power to convene extraordinary or special sessions must do so via a petition, poll, or written request of a specified majority of their members. The Wisconsin Legislature is one of only a handful in which certain legislative leaders can convene the session without such input from all members.[31] Out of the same group of 36 legislatures, the Wisconsin Legislature is one of only eight that operate on a full-time basis.[32] Most of the remaining, part-time legislatures adjourn *sine die* once they have concluded legislative business.[33] In addition, although several state legislatures have the power to convene themselves into session after *sine die* adjournment, they do not typically allow bills to be revived after that time.[34] Finally, some of the legislatures that have the power to convene extraordinary or special sessions have never attempted to hold such a session concurrently with a regular session floorperiod as the Wisconsin Legislature frequently does.[35]

In short, the Wisconsin Legislature maintains a relatively unique power to convene itself by a variety of means at any time throughout the biennial term and exercises this power more frequently than other state legislatures.

Origins of the extraordinary session

Extraordinary sessions have been provided for in the biennial session schedule since the very first such schedule was adopted in 1971. However, the origins of the extraordinary session go back much further. The original Wisconsin Constitution provided for an annual legislature that was authorized to meet once a year "at such times as shall be provided by law" unless it was convened by the governor.[36] The 1849 statutes established that "[t]he regular annual session of the legislature shall commence on the second Wednesday in January each year."[37] For the first four decades of the state's history, the legislature met in regular session for only a few months at the beginning of its term before adjourning *sine die* for the remainder of the year.[38]

In 1881, Wisconsin voters approved a constitutional amendment establishing a biennial instead of an annual session but limiting the biennial legislature to meeting "once in two years, and no oftener," unless convened by the governor.[39] News articles from the time indicate that support for the measure derived primarily from a belief that biennial sessions, and therefore biennial general elections, would be more economical.[40] Following this constitutional change, Chapter 153, Laws of 1882, amended the session language in the statutes to provide that the regular session would commence "on the second Wednesday of January of the year 1883 and biennially thereafter upon the same day and month."[41] Neither the amended constitution nor the statutes limited the length of the regular session, but together, they effectively required that the regular session be continuous once convened.[42]

Unlike Wisconsin, many other states had a constitutional or statutory provision providing for what was known as a bifurcated or split session, which allowed the legislature to adjourn for a long period of time during the regular session and then reconvene.[43] Without this split session option, in the decades following the 1881 constitutional amendment, the Wisconsin Legislature would typically meet in a continuous session from January of the odd-numbered year until early summer of the same year and then adjourn *sine die*. The legislature would remain dissolved until the swearing in of the next succeeding legislature a year and a half later, unless called into special session by the governor.[44]

This schedule resulted in a number of problems for the legislature. First, the legislature had to make decisions on fiscal matters for the entire biennium using estimates of revenue calculated at the very beginning of the biennium. Second, if the governor vetoed a bill after the legislature had adjourned *sine die*, the legislature was unable to review the governor's action and consider veto overrides. Third, the legislature was often unable to enact revisor's correction bills, which would then need to wait until the next session.[45] Finally, the schedule was grueling for legislators. Although most sessions wrapped up by early summer, some continued into the fall.[46] Not only did the legislature remain in a single, continuous session without a long break, but also Wis. Const. art. IV, § 10 prevented either house from adjourning for more than three days without the consent of the other house.[47] As such, the legislature would typically meet in floor sessions every week, sometimes holding skeletal sessions on Mondays and Fridays so legislators could travel home to their districts.[48] The legislature would also regularly adopt joint resolutions recessing for a week or so, further prolonging the length of the session.[49]

Several proposals to remedy these issues were considered throughout the first few decades of the 20th century—including proposals to provide for a split session—but none of them passed.[50] However, beginning in the 1943 session, the Wisconsin Legislature began regularly adjourning for very long periods prior to final adjournment, essentially splitting the session.[51] The 1943 legislature, in a show of animosity to Governor Walter Goodland, adopted a joint resolution in August 1943 adjourning until January 12, 1944.[52] Additionally, the joint resolution provided the legislature flexibility to promptly reconvene before January 12, 1944, if necessary to address the "present war emergency," by a call of a special joint committee of the legislature.[53] Some alleged that in addition to providing for legislative review of the governor's actions, this move would prevent the governor from calling a WWII-related special session in which he alone could determine the subject matter of legislation to be considered.[54] Although no occasion arose prompting the legislature to call itself back into session before January 12, it marked the first time that such an option was agreed to.[55]

This practice of splitting the regular session by adjourning for prolonged periods continued for the remainder of the 1940s and throughout the 1950s.[56] These adjournments were effected by joint resolutions, sometimes referred to as "recess resolutions." These recess resolutions specified the date the legislature would reconvene and for what limited purpose, although the legislature did not always adhere to the recess resolution's scope once reconvened.[57] Typically, the legislature would adopt a recess resolution in early summer of the odd-numbered year and then reconvene in the fall, often for the purpose of considering executive vetoes and appointments as well as revisor's correction bills.[58] These long recesses and later meetings with a limited focus, often called "recessed sessions" or "adjourned sessions," were an attempt to maintain a continuous session to comply with the "once in two years, and no oftener" restriction in article IV, section 11, while allowing for greater legislative flexibility and oversight.[59] Following the final recessed session in the fall, the legislature would adjourn *sine die* until the start of the next legislative session.

During the gubernatorial terms of Democrats Gaylord Nelson (1959–62) and John Reynolds (1963–64), an additional session schedule issue came to the fore. For almost the entire duration of these terms, Republicans held a majority in both houses of the legislature. At that time, gubernatorial appointments requiring the advice and consent of the senate were assumed to not need legislative review once the legislature had adjourned the regular session *sine die*.[60] To prevent the governor from making objectionable interim appointments, the 1961 and 1963 legislatures did not adjourn *sine die* and instead adjourned once the business of the session was complete via a joint resolution permitting the legislature to reconvene on the morning of the final day of the legislative session.[61] By doing so, the legislature sought to retain the senate's ability to reject gubernatorial appointments throughout the entire biennial session.[62] Notably, the 1961 and 1963 recess resolutions contained provisions similar to the 1943 provision that permitted the regular session to resume earlier than the specified reconvening date; now, however, an earlier resumption would be effected by a majority petition of members, rather than by the call of a special joint committee.[63]

In 1964, Governor Reynolds challenged one of the 1963 legislature's prolonged recesses as a violation of article IV, section 11. In particular, the governor alleged that when the legislature adjourned from August 6 to November 4, 1963 (which he claimed was an attempt to block his appointments), it was not a legitimate recess but was instead a *sine die* adjournment.[64] In the resulting *State ex rel. Thompson v. Gibson*, the Wisconsin Supreme Court upheld the power of the legislature to "recess" without violating article IV, section 11, stating that, "one single session may be interrupted by recesses, and validly continue after a recess as long as such recesses can be said to be taken for a proper legislative purpose."[65] With this ruling, the court affirmed that a session could still be continuous in spite of the legislature's well-established practice of interrupting the session with long recesses. However, the court did not address whether a continuous session could stretch into the even-numbered year.

In an effort to codify what was already taking place, the 1965 Wisconsin Legislature adopted on first consideration 1965 Assembly Joint Resolution 5, which proposed amending article IV, section 11, so as to permit the legislature to meet in regular session more than once in two years, leaving regular session schedule requirements to be "provided by law" alone.[66] Those who advocated for the change saw it as the first step in officially permitting the legislature to meet again in the second year of the biennium after adjourning in the first year, something that it was already in the practice of doing. In addition to allowing for more legislative oversight of gubernatorial vetoes and appointments, those in favor of permitting annual meetings of the legislature argued that they would allow for greater flexibility in handling the state's finances.[67] Additionally, the move to annual meetings was in line with the nationwide trend at that time.[68] Those opposed to the change argued that annual meetings would result in higher state spending because legislators would face "prolonged exposure" to "pressure group influences," as well as an increase in legislative salaries, which some feared would serve to attract "professional politicians."[69] The 1967 legislature adopted the proposal on second consideration in a near-unanimous vote as 1967 Assembly Joint Resolution 15, and in April 1968 the amendment was ratified in a decisive 670,757 to 267,997 vote.[70]

During the 1965, 1967, and 1969 sessions, as the constitutional amendment was being considered, the legislature continued the practice of remaining in session throughout the biennium and adjourning for long periods via joint resolutions that also provided for the legislature to convene at an earlier date via majority petition of the members of each house.[71] Notably, the 1969 recess resolution provided for the first time that the organization committees of the two houses could also convene the legislature in advance of the scheduled reconvening date via majority petition of the members of each committee.[72]

The 1969 legislature considered several bills to officially establish an annual meeting schedule under the ratified constitutional amendment, but none of them passed. The following session, the legislature enacted Chapter 15, Laws of 1971, in a bipartisan vote, which provided for annual meetings and created the requirement that JCLO meet early in each biennium to develop a work schedule to be submitted to the legislature as a joint resolution. The session schedule was seen by many legislators to be more significant than the annual meetings provision, as it would bring a higher degree of order and predictability to the legislative process. Rupert H. Theobald, head of the Legislative Reference Bureau at the time, stated that he hoped the work schedule would solve the problem that "once a session starts, no one knows how to end it."[73] The law further stated that any measures introduced in the odd-numbered year of the biennium would carry over into the even-numbered year.

As the legislature was considering this session schedule requirement, it concurrently considered and adopted its first session schedule, 1971 Senate Joint Resolution 21. The session schedule more or less mirrored the pattern that had already been established: three floorperiods in 1971 and one floorperiod followed by a three-day veto review period in 1972. The session schedule also provided that additional floorperiods could be called between the scheduled floorperiods by adoption of a joint resolution or by a majority of the members of each house and that, after the adjournment of the veto review period (on March 10, 1972), additional floorperiods could be called by a majority petition of the members of each house or by a majority petition of the members of the organization committee of each house. The session schedule referred to these extra floorperiods as "extraordinary sessions" and limited them to the issues specified in the action by which they were authorized.[74] This concept of extraordinary sessions was essentially a codification of what recent recess resolutions had already been providing for, and was so unremarkable that news articles describing this first session schedule did not mention the provision at all.[75]

The 1977 Joint Rules, adopted as 1977 Assembly Joint Resolution 23, were the first joint rules to explicitly mention extraordinary sessions. The analysis for Assembly Joint Resolution 23 explained that the rule changes pertaining to extraordinary sessions and the session schedule incorporated "the standard provisions previously adopted every two years as part of the session schedule." The joint rules, since 1977, and every session schedule, from 1971 on, have provided for extraordinary sessions. In 1983, both houses amended their respective rules to establish the same accelerated procedures for extraordinary sessions that they had already established for special sessions.[76]

Extraordinary sessions, 1980–present

The first extraordinary session was convened in January 1980, nine years after extraordinary sessions were first provided for in the session schedule. On January 3, 1980, the senate and assembly organization committees, both with Democratic majorities, voted to convene in extraordinary session at 10 a.m. on January 22 to consider 22 bills related to "crime and energy."[77] On January 15, Republican Governor Lee Dreyfus issued a proclamation to convene a special session at 9:30 a.m. on January 22, 30 minutes before the start of the planned extraordinary session, to consider four additional crime measures he claimed the legislature was trying to bury.[78] Assembly Speaker Edward Jackamonis called the action an "intrusion into the legislative process."[79]

In response, the assembly and senate rules committees blocked the special session bills offered by Governor Dreyfus.[80] When the assembly convened in special session on January 22, Republicans tried to pull the governor's measures from committee but the vote failed. At 10 a.m., Assembly Majority Leader James Wahner rose to the point of order that the hour of 10 a.m. having arrived, the assembly was in extraordinary session.[81] Speaker Jackamonis ruled Majority Leader Wahner's point of order well taken and that a regular session or an extraordinary session called by the legislature takes precedence over a special session called by the governor.[82] By a 59–36 vote, the assembly upheld the decision of the chair, then it recessed the special session and commenced its first extraordinary session. The senate likewise refused to let the governor's bills reach the floor for debate, in a 21–11 party-line vote, and promptly adjourned the special session to convene the extraordinary session.[83] The legislature went on to enact 16 of the bills considered during the January 1980 Extraordinary Session; no special session bills were enacted.[84]

The next six extraordinary sessions were far less dramatic, dealing primarily with ratifying collective bargaining contracts and considering time-sensitive legislation and veto overrides. The next extraordinary session to garner significant media attention was held in June 1988. The legislature, controlled by Democrats, held a one-day extraordinary session primarily for the purpose of adopting 1987 Senate Joint Resolution 71 to limit the governor's partial veto power. Specifically, the measure proposed amending the Wisconsin Constitution to specify that in approving an appropriation bill in part, the governor could not create a new word by striking individual letters in the words of the enrolled bill, a move that had been dubbed the "Vanna White Veto."[85] This extraordinary session convened three weeks after the Wisconsin Supreme Court ruled in *State ex rel. Wisconsin Senate v. Thompson* that such a veto did not violate the constitution.[86]

Ten years and three extraordinary sessions later, the legislature called for an extraordinary session in April 1998, following a special election that gave Republicans control of the senate. Now in control of both houses and the governor's office, Republicans considered 116 bills during the extraordinary session on a variety of topics that they had delayed addressing until after the election.[87] The extraordinary session was held concurrently with a special session called by Governor Tommy Thompson. In total, nearly 100 of the bills considered during the April 1998 Extraordinary Session were ultimately enacted, the most of any session to date.

A total of seven extraordinary sessions were held during the 2003–04 legislative session, the most of any biennial term to date. The Republican-controlled legislature convened extraordinary sessions to address a number of issues about which they were at odds with Democratic Governor Jim Doyle.[88] Most notably, the legislature called an extraordinary session in February 2003 to consider a proposal that would require legislative ratification of Indian gaming compacts between the governor and state tribes.[89] The session was called in response to the announcement that Governor Doyle had reached an agreement with the Potawatomi Nation on a compact with no expiration date.[90] The legislature passed the bill but it was vetoed days later by Governor Doyle.[91] The legislature reconvened the February 2003 Extraordinary Session to consider an override of the governor's veto, but the override failed in the senate.[92]

In December 2010, with just a few weeks remaining before the Republicans would take control of the legislature and the governor's office in the upcoming session, the legislature's Democratic leaders convened an extraordinary session to ratify labor contracts. This was in spite of the fact that Governor-elect Walker had publicly demanded that Governor Doyle's administration stop negotiations on the labor contracts.[93] The assembly narrowly ratified the contracts, but when the contracts arrived in the senate, Senate Majority Leader Russ Decker surprised his fellow Democrats by announcing he would vote against ratification, stating that he believed the incoming Republicans should deal with the contracts.[94] His opposition vote, and that of fellow Democratic Senator Jeff Plale, effectively killed the contracts.

Between 2011 and 2018, with Republicans in control of both houses and the governor's office, nine extraordinary sessions were held, including a February 2015 session to pass right-to-work legislation and the December 2018 Extraordinary Session described at the beginning of this article. During the December 2018 Extraordinary Session, legislators passed three sweeping bills that limited the powers of the governor and the attorney general and included provisions related to early voting, agency guidance documents, online sales tax revenue, and federal transportation funding, among other things.[95]

In April 2020, the legislature convened an extraordinary session to consider a bill to address the COVID-19 pandemic. In order to meet safely, the legislature for the first time in state history met in a virtual session, invoking the emergency virtual session law under Wis. Stat. § 13.42.[96] As previously mentioned, the organization committee of each house, in its motion calling the extraordinary session, also provided for special virtual session rules. In the virtual extraordinary session, in a near-unanimous vote, the legislature passed 2019 Assembly Bill 1038, later enacted as 2019 Wisconsin Act 185. The act made a number of changes to address the pandemic and its economic impacts, including lifting a one-week waiting period for unemployment insurance; prohibiting insurers from charging copays on COVID-19 tests and from discriminating against people who have had the virus; and making it easier for out-of-state or retired health care workers to practice in the state.

The legislature convened two extraordinary sessions during the 2021–22 biennium. First, in February 2021, the legislature met in extraordinary session to pass 2021 Assembly Bill 1, a bill related to state government actions to address the COVID-19 pandemic, and to adopt a joint resolution terminating the COVID-19 public health emergency declared by Governor Evers in Executive Order 104. The second extraordinary session was called in June of 2021 to deal expeditiously with various pieces of legislation, including the biennial budget bill. The call was later expanded to include consideration of the full veto of 2021 Assembly Bill 336. The veto override attempt failed in the assembly in a 59–37 vote.[97]

In total, 40 extraordinary sessions have been called since 1980. Some of these sessions have occurred after the conclusion of the last general-business floorperiod, while others have occurred during interim committee work periods or concurrently with regular session floorperiods or special sessions. Nearly all of these sessions have been called by the committee on organization of each house. Over 300 laws have been enacted that were considered during an extraordinary session. See the table on page 506 for a complete listing of extraordinary sessions.

Conclusion

Extraordinary sessions are an important means for the legislature to conduct its business. They enable the legislature to respond to matters that it considers important or urgent at the time when those matters present themselves, rather than being restricted to previously scheduled floorperiods. In addition, they enable the legislature to conduct the lawmaking process in an expedited manner by permitting a simple majority of members to advance legislation at every stage. In the absence of extraordinary sessions, the lawmaking process would be slower, and the legislature would have to rely on the governor to call special sessions to have the legislature return to Madison after final adjournment. The legislature would be a far weaker institution.

The legislature's ability to call itself into extraordinary session is an aspect of the legislature's core, lawmaking power. The state constitution vests the lawmaking power in the legislature and provides that it may determine by law when it shall meet, the one exception to this self-determination being that the legislature must also convene when called into special session by the governor. If the legislature did not have the power to meet at any time of its choosing (provided that it determined the meeting time in a manner provided by law), it would not truly possess its core, lawmaking power. Instead, its ability to exercise that power would sometimes depend on a decision of the governor as to whether to convene the legislature.

An extraordinary session is one way for the legislature to maintain its independence from the governor. As former Assembly Speaker Tom Loftus noted in an op-ed while the supreme court was considering *League of Women Voters*, extraordinary sessions were established to "bring some parity with the governor and exercise the right of the legislature to govern itself."[98] The legislature's power to convene itself in extraordinary sessions leveled the playing field, as it were. If the governor could call the legislature into session at any time, why could not the legislature do the same?

For over 40 years, the legislature has used extraordinary sessions to enact legislation, including innovative and sometimes urgent measures and even biennial state budgets, as well as to propose amendments to the constitution. Over this period, extraordinary sessions have sometimes been convened along party lines, both by Republicans and by Democrats, and sometimes on a bipartisan basis. This article has documented the importance of extraordinary sessions and described the legislative procedures and practices unique to extraordinary sessions. Clearly, extraordinary sessions are now an engrained and vital part of the Wisconsin lawmaking process. ☒

NOTES

1. League of Women Voters v. Evers, 2019 WI 75, 387 Wis. 2d 511, 929 N.W.2d 209.

2. *Id.* ¶ 2.

3. Although there is no law explicitly providing for extraordinary sessions, the term does appear in the statutes. For example, see Wis. Stat. § 13.625 (1m) (b) 1., which states: "A contribution to a candidate for legislative office may be made during that period only if the legislature has concluded its final floorperiod, and is not in special or extraordinary session."

4. In *League of Women Voters*, the supreme court reasoned that this provision authorizes the legislature to lawfully meet "when a statute so provides." 2019 WI 75, ¶ 17, 387 Wis. 2d 511, 929 N.W.2d 209.

5. Wis. Stat. § 13.02 (3). In *League of Women Voters*, the plaintiffs argued in part that Wis. Stat. § 13.02 limits the legislature's meeting to the regular session only, because the statute does not explicitly include the term "extraordinary session." However, the court ruled that the absence of the word "extraordinary" in Wis. Stat. § 13.02 "does not make an extraordinary session unconstitutional, just as the absence of the words 'floorperiods,' and 'committee work periods' from the statute doesn't make those meetings unconstitutional either." 2019 WI 75, ¶ 22, 387 Wis. 2d 511, 929 N.W.2d 209. The court further stated: "The terminology the Legislature chooses to accomplish the legislative process is squarely the prerogative of the Legislature." *Id.* ¶ 42. In addition to confirming the authority under Wis. Const. art. IV, § 11, the court also recognized that the session schedule requirement under Wis. Stat. § 13.02 is expressly authorized under Wis. Const. art. IV, § 8, which provides that "each house may determine the rules of its own proceedings." *Id.* ¶ 28. For more information about the latter clause, see Richard A. Champagne, "The Rules of Proceedings Clause," *Reading the Constitution* 1, no. 1 (Madison, WI: Legislative Reference Bureau, October 2016).

6. Floorperiods are periods of time available for consideration of proposals by the full assembly and senate.

7. 2023 Wis. SJR 1 § 1 (3) (a).

About Wisconsin: Extraordinary sessions | 449

8. The plaintiffs in *League of Women Voters* argued that the conclusion of the final scheduled floorperiod on March 22, 2018, constituted a *sine die* adjournment, meaning that the legislature had terminated the session, thereby preventing the legislature from reconvening unless the governor called a special session. The court disagreed, stating: "Characterizing the March 22, 2018 adjournment as a *sine die* adjournment conflicts with both the work schedule adopted in JR1, as well as cases defining *sine die* adjournment." 2019 WI 75, ¶ 25, 387 Wis. 2d 511, 929 N.W.2d 209.

9. See Joint Rules 99 (27m) and 81.

10. Joint Rule 81 (2) (a); Senate Rule 93 (intro.); Assembly Rule 93 (intro.).

11. One exception was the February 1987 Extraordinary Session, convened by 1987 Wis. SJR 7 for the purposes of introduction and reference of the governor's budget bill and holding a joint convention to receive the governor's budget message. See Wis. Senate Journal (1987) 52. The other exception was the June 1994 Extraordinary Session, convened to consider a joint resolution amending the constitution to authorize a sports lottery. That session was initially called for by the senate and assembly organization committees, but the full legislature later revised the call by adopting 1993 Wis. AJR 145. See Wis. Senate Journal (1993) 1052–3.

12. Joint Rule 81 (2) (b).

13. The session schedule lays out a series of scheduled floorperiods, including the "last general-businesses floorperiod," in spring of the even-numbered year. After the last general-business floorperiod, there is only a "limited-business floorperiod," which is limited to matters allowed under Joint Rule 81m (2) and extraordinary sessions, as well as a "veto review floorperiod," limited to matters allowed under Joint Rule 82 (1m). See 2023 Wis. SJR 1 § 1 (3) (u), (v), and (x), for example. At the adjournment of the last general-businesses floorperiod, any bill not yet agreed to by both houses is adversely disposed of for the biennial session and recorded as "failed to pass," "failed to adopt," or "failed to concur." See Joint Rule 83 (4).

14. See Senate Rule 93 (1): "Notwithstanding rule 46 (6), any proposal that is adversely and finally disposed of for the biennial session may be revived by specific inclusion in the action authorizing an extraordinary session, provided that the proposal had not failed a vote of concurrence or passage in the senate. Any proposal revived under this subsection is considered to be at the same stage of the proceedings as it had attained upon being adversely and finally disposed of." Although there is no comparable assembly rule, the assembly practice is to allow bills to be revived in the same way. See, for example, the Committee on Assembly Organization's call for the November 2018 Extraordinary Session, which revived 2017 Wis. AB 963. Wis. Assembly Journal (2017) 958.

15. Wis. Senate Journal (2017) 890.

16. For example, see Wis. Senate Journal (2003) 896.

17. Joint Rule 81 (2) (b) allows for advice and consent on nominations for appointment; Senate Rule 93 (1) and (1d) allows the senate to consider certain resolutions, including those offering commendations, memorializing Congress, or affecting senate or legislative rules or proceedings, and also allows the senate to consider nominations for appointments; Assembly Rule 93 (1) allows the assembly to consider proposals or amendments pertaining to the organization of the legislature.

18. Joint Rule 81 (2) (c).

19. Senate Rule 93 (1p); Assembly Rule 93 (2).

20. Senate Rule 93 (intro.); Assembly Rule 93 (intro.).

21. Senate Rule 93 (2); Assembly Rule 93 (3).

22. Senate Rule 93 (3); Assembly Rule 93 (4).

23. Senate Rule 93 (5); Assembly Rule 93 (5).

24. Senate Rule 93 (6); Assembly Rule 93 (7).

25. Assembly Rule 93 (6). In the senate, no such rule is necessary because all actions to advance a proposal are decided by simple majority vote, including messaging the senate's actions to the assembly.

26. Senate Rule 93 (4).

27. Senate Rule 93 (intro.); Assembly Rule 93 (intro.).

28. Wis. Senate Journal (2019) 820; Wis. Assembly Journal (2019) 746–47. For a summary of this virtual extraordinary session, see Richard A. Champagne and Alex Rosenberg, "The First Virtual Meeting of the Wisconsin State Legislature," *LRB Reports* 4, no. 10 (Madison, WI: Legislative Reference Bureau, June 2020).

29. See, for example, 2023 Wis. SJR 1 § 1 (5) (a).

30. In all of those states, the governor can also call such a session. In the 14 remaining states, only the governor can call such a session: Alabama, Arkansas, California, Idaho, Indiana, Kentucky, Michigan, Minnesota, Mississippi, North Dakota, Rhode Island, South Carolina, Texas, and Vermont. "Special Sessions," National Conference of State Legislatures, accessed July 18, 2022, https://ncsl.org.

31. In Wisconsin, these leaders are the members of the houses' committees on organization. Connecticut, Delaware, Florida, Illinois, and Ohio also allow legislative leaders to convene a special or extraordinary session. "Special Sessions," National Conference of State Legislatures.

32. The other states are Alaska, Hawaii, Illinois, Massachusetts, New York, Ohio, and Pennsylvania. "Full- and Part-Time Legislatures," National Conference of State Legislatures, accessed July 18, 2022, https://ncsl.org.

33. National Conference of State Legislatures, "Provisions Relating to Regular Legislative Sessions" (unpublished manuscript, May 2017). National Conference of State Legislatures, "Special or Extraordinary Legislative Sessions" (unpublished manuscript, January 10, 2013).

34. Adjournment *sine die* (Latin for "without a day") means the absolute end of the session; it essentially terminates the sitting and the power of the legislature. National Conference of State Legislatures, "Reconvening Special Session after Adjournment *Sine Die*" (unpublished manuscript compiling results of an NCSL listserv survey of the American Society of Legislative Clerks and Secretaries, September 2008).

35. National Conference of State Legislatures, "Nesting Regular and Special Sessions" (unpublished manuscript compiling results of an NCSL listserv survey of the American Society of Legislative Clerks and Secretaries, March 2006).

36. Art. IV, § 11, of the original Wisconsin Constitution specifically stated: "The legislature shall meet at the seat of government at such time as shall be provided by law, once in each year and not oftener, unless convened by the governor."

37. 1849 Wis. Rev. Stat. § 8.1 (1849). The section was later renumbered as 1858 Wis. Rev. Stat. § 9.1 (1858) and later still as 1878 Wis. Rev. Stat § 10.99 (1878).

38. Adjournment *sine die* meant that the legislature essentially dissolved. As such, if called into special session by the governor, the legislature would need to reorganize and elect new leaders.

39. Wis. Const. art. IV, § 11, was amended to read: "The legislature shall meet at the seat of government, at such time as shall be provided by law, once in two years and no oftener, unless convened by the governor in special session, and when so convened no business shall be transacted except as shall be necessary to accomplish the special purposes for which it was convened." 1880 Wis. SJR 9; 1881 Wis. AJR 7; ratified in November 1881 in a 53,532–13,936 vote.

40. "Against Biennial Sessions," *Janesville Daily Gazette*, February 18, 1880; "The Biennial Business," *Janesville Daily Gazette*, March 26, 1881; "Biennial Sessions: What the Milwaukee Press Say of 'a Barren Ideality,'" *Wisconsin State Journal*, February 24, 1879.

41. Wis. Stat. § 10.99 (1882). Section 4 of Chapter 634, Laws of 1917, renumbered the statutory section to its present location of Wis. Stat. § 13.02 and simplified the language to say that biennial sessions would begin in each odd-numbered year. It also added the "Regular Sessions" section title that still appears in the statutes today.

42. The Wisconsin Supreme Court affirmed this in *State ex rel. Sullivan v. Dammann*: "Here in Wisconsin the legislature generally adjourns each week from Friday until the following Tuesday, and occasionally recesses or temporarily adjourns for a week or two. We have but one biennial session." 221 Wis. 551, 562, 267 N.W. 433 (1936). In *League of Women Voters*, the supreme court affirmed this once again, stating: "The Legislature is 'in session' continually during the biennial session until a *sine die* adjournment." 2019 WI 75, ¶ 26, 387 Wis. 2d 511, 929 N.W.2d 209.

43. Kathleen Kepner, "The Adjourned Legislative Session in Wisconsin," *LRL Brief* no. 42, (Madison, WI: Legislative Reference Library, May 1956), 2.

44. For the first 120 years of Wisconsin's history, the vast majority of special sessions were convened after the final adjournment of the regular session. See Richard A. Champagne and Madeline Kasper, "Special Sessions of the Wisconsin Legislature," *Reading the Constitution* 7, no. 2 (Madison, WI: Legislative Reference Bureau, 2023): 10–12.

45. Kepner, "The Adjourned Session," 4.

46. For example, the 1935 session continued for 262 calendar days, from January 7 to September 27. Unlike other states, Wisconsin did not limit the length of regular sessions.

47. Specifically, Wis. Const. art. IV, § 10, provided that "neither house shall, without the consent of the other, adjourn for more than three days."

48. Kepner, "The Adjourned Session," 2.

49. See for example 1929 Wis. SJR 135, adjourning the legislature from August 31, 1929, until September 5, 1929.

50. For example, 1941 Wis. SB 95 proposed a split session, divided into three parts: the first five weeks would be for the introduction of bills, then the legislature would recess for a period to hold committee hearings, then the legislature would reconvene to act upon bills that the committees had considered. Other proposals sought to

require the legislature to remain on the floor five days a week to speed up the session (e.g., 1935 Wis. AJR 71) or to limit the length of the session (e.g., 1935 Wis. AJR 40).

51. Although the legislature began regularly adjourning for long periods in 1943, it had done so at least five times prior. According to Kepner, "The Adjourned Session," 2: "In 1853 the legislature adjourned to sit as a Court of Impeachment in a case of a circuit judge charged with corruption and malfeasance in office. The 1856 and 1858 legislatures recessed so that joint committees of the legislature could investigate charges of fraud and the conduct of affairs in various state agencies. Adjournment in 1862 was to enable legislative committees to work on reassessment of taxes and in 1897 to consider revisor's bills and executive messages." See 1853 Wis. JR of March 25, 1853 (Wis. Senate Journal (1853) 601); 1856 Wis. JR March 28, 1856 (Wis. Senate Journal (1856) 800); 1858 Wis. AJR 46 (Wis. Assembly Journal (1858) 1178); 1862 Wis. SJR 40 (Wis. Senate Journal (1862) 659); and 1897 Wis. SJR 76 (Wis. Senate Journal (1897) 881).

52. 1943 Wis. AJR 107; Kepner, "The Adjourned Session," 3. The legislature had already adjourned for relatively long periods over the summer via 1943 Wis. AJR 95 and AJR 99, with the stated purpose of reconvening for the "completion of legislative business."

53. See 1943 Wis. AJR 107.

54. Kepner, "The Adjourned Session," 3.

55. Wisconsin Legislative Reference Library, "Recalling the Legislature During an Adjournment Prior to Sine Die Adjournment," *LRL Brief* no. 102 (Madison, WI: Legislative Reference Library, September 1961), 2.

56. See 1945 Wis. SJR 93; 1947 Wis. SJR 79; 1949 Wis. SJR 64; 1953 Wis. SJR 58; 1955 Wis. AJR 117; 1957 Wis. AJR 116; 1959 Wis. AJR 107. The 1951 legislature did not split the session and adjourned *sine die* on June 14, 1951.

57. Wisconsin Legislative Reference Library, "The Mechanics of Disposal of All Measures prior to Sine Die Adjournment or Adjournment for an Extended Period by the Wisconsin Legislature and the Nature of the Joint Resolution Adjourning the Legislature for an Extended Period," *LRL Brief* no. 74 (Madison, WI: Legislative Reference Library, June 1959), 4; Kepner, "The Adjourned Session," 1.

58. Kepner, "The Adjourned Session," 4.

59. "Constitutional Referendums ...," *Green Bay Press Gazette*, March 24, 1968.

60. H. Rupert Theobald, "Rules and Rulings: Parliamentary Procedure from the Wisconsin Perspective," in *State of Wisconsin 1985–1986 Blue Book*, ed. Wisconsin Legislative Reference Bureau (Madison, WI: Legislative Reference Bureau, 1985), 131–32.

61. 1961 Wis. AJR 167; Wis. Senate Journal (June 8, 1962–January 9, 1963) 156–57; Wis. Assembly Journal (June 8, 1962– January 9, 1963) 159; 1963 Wis. AJR 128; Wis. Senate Journal (1963) 2475; Wis. Assembly Journal (1963) 2881. Theobald, "Rules and Rulings," 131–32.

62. Theobald, "Rules and Rulings," 131–32.

63. 1961 Wis. AJR 167; 1963 Wis. AJR 128.

64. Aldric Revell, "Fight Seen by Governor," *Capital Times*, April 27, 1964.

65. State *ex rel.* Thompson v. Gibson, 22 Wis. 2d 275, 290 (1964). The court also distinguished between the legislature being no longer in session, "i.e. where there has been termination or dissolution of a session," and the legislature being in a recess, "i.e. a temporary adjournment during the biennial session." It also provided that "The ordinary form of termination of a session is by sine die adjournment, although we do not here decide that there could be no other form of adjournment which would terminate the session." *Id.*

66. Specifically, 1965 Wis. AJR 5 proposed deleting the words "once in two years and no oftener" from Wis. Const. art. IV, § 11, so that it would simply read: "The legislature shall meet at the seat of government at such time as shall be provided by law...."

67. William Brissee, "Proposal for Annual Session of Legislature Wins Support," *Wisconsin State Journal*, August 6, 1964.

68. John Wyngaard, "Legislators Talking More about Sessions Each Year," *Green Bay Press Gazette*, October 1965.

69. Wyngaard, "Legislators Talking More About Sessions Each Year"; "Annual Sessions Needed," *The Paper* (Oshkosh), March 21, 1968; Arthur L. Srb, "Should State Lawmakers Meet in Annual Session," *Waukesha Daily Freeman*, March 21, 1968; "Final OK for Annual Session Bill," *Milwaukee Journal*, March 19, 1971.

70. The April 1968 ballot question read: "Shall article IV, section 11 of the constitution be amended to permit the legislature to meet in regular session oftener than once in two years?" The language in Wis. Const. art. IV, § 11 has not been amended since.

71. 1965 Wis. AJR 163; 1967 Wis. AJR 97.

72. 1969 Wis. SJR 105.

73. Charles E. Friederich, "Annual Session Bill May bring New Order to Legislature," *Milwaukee Journal*, January 31, 1971.

74. Note that prior to this time, the term "extraordinary session" was often used interchangeably with "special session" in the press. See, for example, John Wyngaard, "Is Crash Highway Program True Legislative Emergency," *Wisconsin Rapids Daily Tribune*, December 9, 1963. The article refers to the 1958 special session convened by Governor Vernon Thompson as an extraordinary session.

75. "Annual Sessions Approved," *Wisconsin State Journal*, March 11, 1971; H. Carl Mueller, "Senate OKs Measure for Annual Sessions," *Milwaukee Sentinel*, March 12, 1971.

76. 1983 Wis. AR 12; 1983 Wis. SR 4.

77. Wis. Senate Journal (1979) 1106.

78. Wis. Senate Journal (1979) 1100–1101. Patricia Simms, "Legislators Vent Anger at Dreyfus," *Wisconsin State Journal*, January 16, 1980.

79. Simms, "Legislators Vent Anger."

80. Patricia Simms, "Rules Panel Won't Introduce 3 of Governor's Crime Bills," *Wisconsin State Journal*, January 18, 1980; "Crime Session Under Way," *Kenosha News*, January 22, 1980.

81. Wis. Assembly Journal (1979) 1848.

82. In issuing this ruling, Speaker Jackamonis relied on precedent set in 1962 and 1963 when Republicans controlled the legislature, which held that when the legislature was in session anyway, it had no special obligation to consider a governor's bills ahead of its own business.

83. Wis. Senate Journal (1979) 1103.

84. Chapters 111, 112, 113, 114, 115, 116, 117, 118, 119, 189, 219, 238, 295, 329, 349, and 350, Laws of 1979.

85. For a recent discussion of the partial veto power, see Richard A. Champagne, Staci Duros, and Madeline Kasper, "The Wisconsin Governor's Partial Veto Power after *Bartlett v. Evers*," *Reading the Constitution* 5, no. 3 (Madison, WI: Legislative Reference Bureau, July 2020).

86. State *ex rel.* Wisconsin Senate v. Thompson, 144 Wis. 2d 429, 437 (1988).

87. David Callender, "GOP puts 116 Bills on Agenda," *Capital Times*, April 17, 1998.

88. "Legislature Finishes Session," *Janesville Gazette*, March 17, 2004.

89. 2003 Wis. SB 41.

90. "Do Odds Improve for Casino?" *Janesville Gazette*, February 21, 2003; Gordon Govier, "Doyle's Gaming Stance Dismays Clerics," *Capital Times*, March 3, 2003.

91. Wis. Senate Journal (2003) 102.

92. The vote was 20 for and 11 against, one vote short of the two-thirds majority required for a veto override. Wis. Senate Journal (2003) 104.

93. "Dems End Lame Duck Session After Failure to Pass Union Contracts," *Associated Press*, December 16, 2010.

94. "Union Contracts Stall in Senate," *Wisconsin State Journal*, December 16, 2010.

95. 2017 Wis. Act 368, 2017 Wis. Act 369, 2017 Wis. Act 370.

96. For a summary of this virtual session, see Champagne and Rosenberg, "First Virtual Meeting."

97. Wis. Assembly Journal (2021), 431.

98. Tom Loftus, "Tom Loftus: Wisconsin Legislature Alone Controls 'Extraordinary' Sessions," *Cap Times*, April 26, 2019, https://madison.com.

4
STATISTICS AND REFERENCE

WISCONSIN STATE SYMBOLS

Over the years, the Wisconsin Legislature has officially recognized a wide variety of state symbols. In order of adoption, Wisconsin has designated an official seal, coat of arms, flag, song, flower, bird, tree, fish, state animal, wildlife animal, domestic animal, mineral, rock, symbol of peace, insect, soil, fossil, dog, beverage, grain, dance, ballad, waltz, fruit, tartan, pastry, dairy product, and herb. These symbols provide a focus for expanding public awareness of Wisconsin's history and diversity. They are listed and described in Section 1.10 of the Wisconsin Statutes.

COAT OF ARMS The large shield at the center of the coat of arms is divided into quarters on which appear symbols for agriculture (plow), mining (pick and shovel), manufacturing (arm and hammer), and navigation (anchor). At the center of the large shield, a small shield and the band that encircles it represent the United States coat of arms and symbolize Wisconsin's membership in and loyalty to the United States. Supporting the large shield from the sides are a sailor holding a coil of rope and a yeoman resting on a pick. These figures represent labor on water and land. At the base of the large shield, a horn of plenty represents prosperity and abundance, and a pyramid of 13 lead ingots represents mineral wealth and the 13 original states of the United States. Above the large shield appears a badger, the state animal, and above the badger appears the state motto, "Forward."

GREAT SEAL The great seal consists of the state coat of arms; the words "Great Seal of the State of Wisconsin" in a curve above; and a line of 13 stars, representing the 13 original states of the United States, in a curve below, all enclosed within an ornamental border. The great seal is used to authenticate the official acts of the governor other than the governor's approval of laws.

FLAG The state flag consists of the state coat of arms; the word "Wisconsin" in white letters above; and the statehood date "1848" in white numbers below, all centered on a royal blue field.

SONG "On, Wisconsin," music by William T. Purdy, words by Joseph S. Hubbard and Charles D. Rosa.

On, Wisconsin! On, Wisconsin! Grand old badger state! We, thy loyal sons and daughters, Hail thee, good and great. ▪ On, Wisconsin! On, Wisconsin! Champion of the right, "Forward", our motto—God will give thee might!

BALLAD "Oh Wisconsin, Land of My Dreams," words by Erma Barrett, music by Shari A. Sarazin.

Oh Wisconsin, land of beauty, with your hillsides and your plains, with your jackpine and your birch tree, and your oak of mighty frame. ▪ Land of rivers, lakes and valleys, land of warmth and winter snows, land of birds and beasts and humanity, oh Wisconsin, I love you so. ▪ Oh Wisconsin, land of my dreams. Oh Wisconsin, you're all I'll ever need. A little heaven here on earth could you be? Oh Wisconsin, land of my dreams. ▪ In the summer, golden grain fields; in the winter, drift of white snow; in the springtime, robins singing; in the autumn, flaming colors show. ▪ Oh I wonder who could wander, or who could want to drift for long, away from all your beauty, all your sunshine, all your sweet song? ▪ Oh Wisconsin, land of my dreams. Oh Wisconsin, you're all I'll ever need. A little heaven here on earth could you be? Oh Wisconsin, land of my dreams. ▪ And when it's time, let my spirit run free in Wisconsin, land of my dreams.

WALTZ "The Wisconsin Waltz," words and music by Eddie Hansen.

Music from heaven throughout the years; the beautiful Wisconsin Waltz. Favorite song of the pioneers; the beautiful Wisconsin Waltz. ▪ Song of my heart on that last final day, when it is time to lay me away. One thing I ask is to let them play the beautiful Wisconsin Waltz. ▪ My sweetheart, my complete heart, it's for you when we dance together; the beautiful Wisconsin Waltz. I remember that September, before love turned into an ember, we danced to the Wisconsin Waltz. ▪ Summer ended, we intended that our lives then would both be blended, but somehow our planning got lost. ▪ Memory now sings a dream song, a faded love theme song; the beautiful Wisconsin Waltz.

TARTAN The thread count of the state tartan is 44 threads muted blue; 6 threads scarlet; 4 threads muted blue; 6 threads gray; 28 threads black; 40 threads dark green; 4 threads dark yellow; 40 threads dark green; 28 threads black; 22 threads muted blue; and 12 threads dark brown (half sett with full count at the pivots).

FLOWER
Wood violet *(Viola papilionacea)*

BIRD Robin *(Turdus migratorius)*

TREE
Sugar maple
(Acer saccharum)

FISH Muskellunge
(Esox masquinongy masquinongy Mitchell)

ANIMAL Badger *(Taxidea taxus)*

Statistics and Reference: Symbols | 457

DOMESTIC ANIMAL
Dairy cow *(Bos taurus)*

INSECT Honey bee *(Apis mellifera)*

DOG American water spaniel

WILDLIFE ANIMAL
White-tailed deer *(Odocoileus virginianus)*

458 | Wisconsin Blue Book 2023–2024

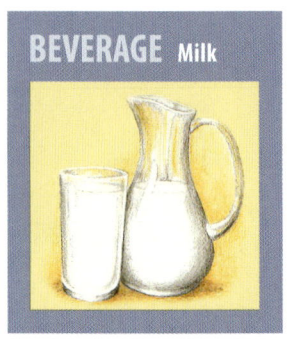

BEVERAGE Milk

SYMBOL OF PEACE
Mourning dove
(Zenaidura macroura carolinensis Linnaeus)

SOIL Antigo silt loam
(Typic glossoboralf)

ROCK Red granite

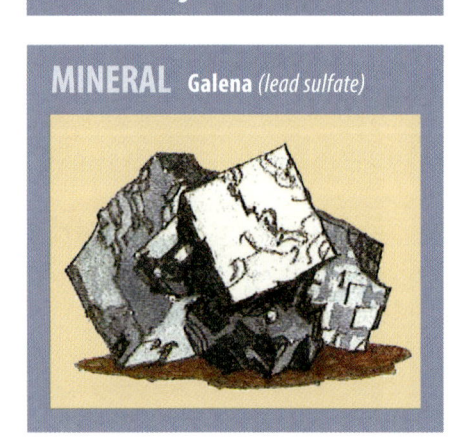

MINERAL Galena (lead sulfate)

GRAIN Corn (Zea mays)

Statistics and Reference: Symbols | 459

FRUIT Cranberry *(Vaccinium macrocarpon)*

FOSSIL Trilobite *(Calymene celebra)*

PASTRY Kringle

HERB Ginseng *(Panax quinquefolius)*

DANCE Polka

DAIRY PRODUCT Cheese

SIGNIFICANT EVENTS IN WISCONSIN HISTORY

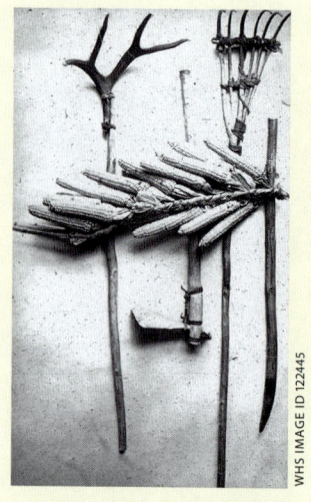

First nations

Wisconsin's original residents were Native American hunters who arrived here about 14,000 years ago. The area's first farmers appear to have been the Hopewell people, who raised corn, squash, and pumpkins around 2,000 years ago. They were also hunters and fishers, and their trade routes stretched to the Atlantic Coast and the Gulf of Mexico. Later arrivals included the Chippewa, Ho-Chunk (Winnebago), Mohican/Munsee, Menominee, Oneida, Potawatomi, and Sioux.

Indian agricultural implements.

Under the flag of France

The written history of the state began with the accounts of French explorers. The French explored areas of Wisconsin, named places, and established trading posts; however, they were interested in the fur trade, rather than agricultural settlement, and were never present in large numbers.

1600s

1634. Jean Nicolet became the first known European to reach Wisconsin.

1654–59. Pierre-Esprit Radisson and Médart Chouart des Groseilliers became the first known fur traders in Wisconsin.

1661. Father René Médard became the first missionary to set foot in Wisconsin.

1665. Father Claude Allouez founded a mission at La Pointe.

1668. Nicolas Perrot opened fur trade with Wisconsin Indians near Green Bay.

1672. Father Allouez and Father Louis André built the St. François Xavier mission at De Pere.

1673. Louis Jolliet and Father Jacques Marquette traveled the length of the Mississippi River.

1679. Daniel Greysolon Sieur du Lhut (Duluth) explored the western end of Lake Superior.

1689. Perrot asserted the sovereignty of France over various Wisconsin Indian tribes.

1690. Lead mines were discovered in Wisconsin and Iowa.

1700s

1701–38. The Fox Indian Wars occurred.

1755. Wisconsin Indians, under Charles Langlade, helped defeat British General Braddock during the French and Indian War.

1763. The Treaty of Paris was signed, making Wisconsin part of British colonial territory. ▪ Wisconsin Indians staged a revolt against the new and comparatively more hostile British regime.

1764. Charles Langlade—later known as the "Father of Wisconsin"—settled at Green Bay.

1766. Jonathan Carver explored various sites along the Mississippi River, including a Fox Indian settlement at Prairie du Chien.

1774. The Quebec Act made Wisconsin a part of the Province of Quebec.

1783. The second Treaty of Paris was signed, making Wisconsin a U.S. territory.

1787. Under the Northwest Ordinance of 1787, Wisconsin was made part of the Northwest Territory. The governing units for the Wisconsin area prior to statehood were:

1787–1800	Northwest Territory.
1800–1809	Indiana Territory.
1809–1818	Illinois Territory.
1818–1836	Michigan Territory.
1836–1848	Wisconsin Territory.

1795. Jacques Vieau established a trading post at Milwaukee and outposts at Kewaunee, Manitowoc, and Sheboygan.

Under the flag of Great Britain

Wisconsin experienced few changes under British control. It remained the western edge of European penetration into the American continent, important only as a source of valuable furs for export. French traders plied their trade, and British and colonial traders began to appear, but Europeans continued to be visitors rather than settlers.

Achieving territorial status

In spite of the second Treaty of Paris, Wisconsin remained British in all but title until after the War of 1812. In 1815, the American army established control. Gradually, the British extinguished Indian title to the southeastern half of the state. Lead mining brought the first heavy influx of settlers and ended the dominance of the fur trade in the economy of the area. The lead mining period ran from about 1824 to 1861. Almost half of the 11,683 people who lived in the territory in 1836 were residents of the lead mining district in the southwestern corner of the state.

1800s

1804. William Henry Harrison's treaty with Indians at St. Louis extinguished Indian title to land in the lead region, which eventually became a contributing cause of the Black Hawk War.

1815. The War of 1812 concluded, leading to the abandonment of Fort McKay (formerly Fort Shelby) by the British.

Fort Shelby, renamed Fort McKay.

1816. Astor's American Fur Company began operations in Wisconsin.

1819. Solomon Juneau bought Jacques Vieau's Milwaukee trading post.

1820. Rev. Jedediah Morse traveled to the Green Bay area to report on Indian tribes to the U.S. secretary of war. ▪ Lewis Cass, James Duane Doty, and Henry Schoolcraft made an exploratory trip through Wisconsin.

1821. Oneida, Stockbridge, Munsee, and Brothertown tribes began migrating to Wisconsin from the New York area.

1822. The first mining leases in southwest Wisconsin were issued.

1825. A treaty concluded at Prairie du Chien established tribal boundaries.

1827. The Winnebago War began and quickly ended with the surrender of Chief Red Bird to the United States.

1832. The Black Hawk War occurred.

1833. The second Treaty of Chicago between the United States and the Potawatomi granted the U.S. government the land between Lake Michigan and Lake Winnebago. ▪ The first Wisconsin newspaper, the *Green Bay Intelligencer*, was established.

1834. Land offices were established in Green Bay and Mineral Point. ▪ The first public road was laid.

1835. The first steamboat arrived in

Wisconsin territory

Wisconsin's population had reached 305,000 by 1850. Newcomers were primarily migrants from New York and New England, or immigrants from England, Scotland, Ireland, Germany, and Scandinavia. New York's Erie Canal gave Wisconsin a water outlet to the Atlantic Ocean and a route for new settlers. Wheat was the primary cash crop for most of the newcomers.

State politics revolved around factions headed by James Doty and Henry Dodge. As political parties developed, the Democrats proved dominant throughout the period.

Early statehood

Heavy immigration continued, and the state remained largely agricultural. Slavery, banking laws, and temperance were the major political issues of the period. Despite the number of foreign immigrants, most political leaders continued to have ties to the northeastern United States, and New York state laws and institutions provided models for much of the activity of the early legislative sessions. Control shifted from the Democrats to the Republicans during this period.

Milwaukee. ▪ The first bank in Wisconsin obtained its charter and later opened in Green Bay.

1836. President Andrew Jackson signed the act creating the Territory of Wisconsin on April 20. (Provisions of the Ordinance of 1787 were made part of the act.) ▪ Henry Dodge was appointed governor by President Andrew Jackson. ▪ The first session of the legislature was held, and Madison was chosen as the permanent capital. (The capital had initially been located in Belmont.) ▪ Madison was surveyed and platted.

1837. Construction on the first capitol building began. ▪ The Panic of 1837 drove territorial banks to failure and initiated a five-year economic depression. ▪ The Winnebago Indians ceded all claims to land in Wisconsin. ▪ Imprisonment for debt was abolished.

1838. The territorial legislature met in Madison. ▪ The Milwaukee & Rock River Canal Company was chartered to create a canal connecting Lake Michigan to the Rock River and, accordingly, a waterway to the Mississippi River.

1841. James D. Doty was appointed governor by President John Tyler.

Yellow Thunder of the Winnebago tribe.

1842. Legislator James Vineyard shot and killed fellow legislator Charles Arndt in the capitol.

1844. Nathaniel P. Tallmadge was appointed governor by President Tyler. ▪ The Wisconsin Phalanx, a utopian commune, was established in Ceresco (later annexed by Ripon).

1845. Dodge was reappointed governor by President James Polk. ▪ Mormons settled in Voree (near Burlington). ▪ Swiss immigrants founded New Glarus.

1846. Congress passed the enabling act for the admission of Wisconsin as state. ▪ The first constitutional convention met in Madison.

1847. The first proposed state constitution was rejected by the people. A second constitutional convention was held.

1848. The second proposed state constitution was adopted. ▪ President Polk signed a bill on May 29 making Wisconsin a state. ▪ The legislature met on June 5, and Governor Nelson Dewey was inaugurated June 7. ▪ The University of Wisconsin was founded. ▪ Large-scale German immigration began.

1849. A school code was adopted, and the first free, tax-supported, graded school with a high school was established in Kenosha. ▪ The first telegram reached Milwaukee.

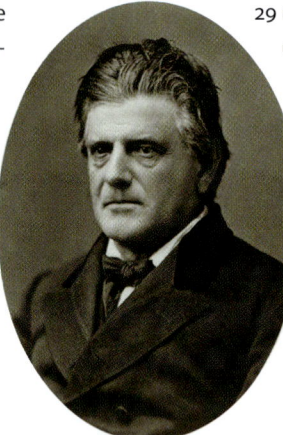

Governor Nelson Dewey.
WHS IMAGE ID 117519

The maturing commonwealth

After the Civil War, Wisconsin matured into a modern political and economic entity. Heavy immigration continued, with composition remaining similar to the antebellum period until the end of the century, when Poles arrived in larger numbers.

The Republican Party remained in control of state government throughout the period, but was challenged by Grangers, Populists, Socialists, and Temperance candidates in addition to the Democratic Party and dissidents within the Republican Party. Temperance, the use of foreign languages in schools, railroad regulation, and currency reform were major political issues in the state.

In the 1880s and 1890s, dairying surpassed wheat culture to become the state's primary agricultural activity, with the University of Wisconsin's agricultural school becoming a national leader in the field of dairy science. From the 1870s to the 1890s, lumbering prospered in the north, accounting for one-fourth of all wages paid in the state at its peak. During the same period, Milwaukee developed a thriving heavy machinery industry, and the paper industry emerged in the Fox River Valley. The tanning and the brewing industries were also prominent.

1850. The state opened the Wisconsin Institute for Education of the Blind at Janesville.

1851. The first railroad train ran from Milwaukee to Waukesha. ▪ The first state fair was held in Janesville.

1852. The Wisconsin School for the Deaf opened in Delavan. ▪ Prison construction begun at Waupun.

Art class at the State School for the Deaf.

1853. Capital punishment was abolished following the controversial execution of John McCaffary in 1851.

1854. The Republican Party formed in Ripon. ▪ The first class graduated from the University of Wisconsin. ▪ Joshua Glover, a fugitive slave, was arrested in Racine, and the Wisconsin Supreme Court, in a related matter, declared the Fugitive Slave Law of 1850 unconstitutional. ▪ The Milwaukee and Mississippi Railroad reached Madison.

1856. Two candidates claimed themselves winners of a contested gubernatorial race. Coles Bashford took office only after acting Governor William Barstow was found to have committed election fraud.

1857. The first passenger train reached Prairie du Chien, connecting Milwaukee with the Mississippi River.

1858. Legislators uncovered bribery by former Governor Bashford and other members of the 1856 Legislature.

1859. Abraham Lincoln spoke at the state fair in Milwaukee.

1861. The U.S. Civil War began. ▪ A bank riot occurred in Milwaukee. ▪ The office of county superintendent of schools was created.

1862. Governor Louis P. Harvey drowned. ▪ Draft riots occurred.

1864. Chester Hazen founded the state's first cheese factory in Ladoga.

1865. The U.S. Civil War ends. Approximately 96,000 Wisconsin soldiers served in the war, and 12,216 died.

1866. The Platteville Normal School (University of Wisconsin-Platteville) opened as the first teacher preparation institution in the state. ▪ The legislature formally named the University of Wisconsin a land-grant institution and incorporated an agricultural department.

1871. The Peshtigo fire resulted in over 1,000 deaths—the most fatalities by fire in U.S. history.

1872. The Wisconsin Dairymen's Association organized in Watertown.

1873. Milwaukee newspaper publisher and Wisconsin legislator Christopher

The progressive era

The state's prominent role in the reform movements that swept the country at the beginning of the century gave Wisconsin national fame and its first presidential candidate. Republicans controlled the state legislature, but the Progressive and Stalwart factions fought continually for control of the party. Milwaukee consistently sent a strong Socialist contingent to the legislature.

Large-scale European immigration ended during this period, but ethnic groups retained strong individual identities and remained a significant force in the politics and culture of the state. Of those groups, Germans faced disproportionate suspicion and hostility during the two world wars.

Heavy machinery manufacturing, paper products, and dairying continued to drive the state economy. Meanwhile, lumbering faded in importance and brewing ground to a halt with the onset of Prohibition.

Latham Sholes invented the typewriter. ▪ The Patrons of Husbandry, an agricultural organization nicknamed the Grangers, helped elect William R. Taylor as governor.

1874. The Potter Law, which limited railroad rates, was enacted—only to be repealed two years later.

1875. A free high school law was enacted. ▪ The State Industrial School for Girls was established in Milwaukee. ▪ Republican Harrison Ludington defeated Governor Taylor. ▪ Oshkosh, a leader in the lumber trade, was almost destroyed by fire.

1876. The community of Hazel Green was destroyed by a tornado.

1877. John Appleby developed and later patented a device to bind bundles of grain with twine, a significant contribution to automating agricultural production.

1882. The Wisconsin Constitution was amended to make legislative sessions biennial. ▪ The world's first hydroelectric plant was built in Appleton.

World's first hydroelectric plant in Appleton.

1883. Fire at the Newhall House in Milwaukee killed 71—the country's most lethal hotel fire. ▪ The south wing of the capitol extension collapsed; seven were killed. ▪ The legislature established the Agricultural Experiment Station at the

University of Wisconsin. ▪ Wisconsin first observed Arbor Day.

1885. Gogebic iron range discoveries made Ashland a major shipping port.

1886. Strikes related to the eight-hour work day movement in Milwaukee culminated in confrontation with the militia at Bay View; five were killed. ▪ The University of Wisconsin established an agricultural short course.

1887. Marshfield was almost destroyed by fire.

1889. The Bennett Law, requiring classroom instruction in English, passed but was repealed two years later after bitter opposition from German Protestants and Catholics. ▪ In the "Edgerton Bible case," the Wisconsin Supreme Court prohibited reading and prayers from the King James Bible in public schools. ▪ Former Governor Jeremiah Rusk became the first U.S. secretary of agriculture.

1890. Stephen M. Babcock invented an easy and accurate test for milk butterfat content.

1893. The Wisconsin Supreme Court ordered the state treasurer to refund to the state interest on state deposits, which had customarily been retained by treasurers.

1897. Corrupt practices legislation was enacted to regulate caucuses and prohibit bribery of voters. ▪ The Wisconsin Tax Commission was created.

1898. Wisconsin sent 5,469 men to fight in the Spanish-American War, suffering 134 losses.

Dr. Stephen Babcock with butterfat tester.

1899. A new law prohibited railroads from giving public officials free rides. ▪ The New Richmond Tornado, the deadliest ever recorded in Wisconsin, killed 117 people.

1900s

1900. Interstate Park, Wisconsin's first state park, was established near St. Croix Falls.

1901. The first Wisconsin-born governor, Robert M. La Follette, was inaugurated. ▪ Agricultural education was introduced into rural schools. ▪ The Legislative Reference Library, which served as a model for other states and for the Library of Congress, was established and later renamed the Legislative Reference Bureau.

1904. A referendum vote approved popular election of primary candidates for state-level offices (in place of selection by party leaders). ▪ The state capitol burned down, destroying many records and state artifacts.

Wisconsin's first state park.

1905. The state civil service was established. ▪ An auto license law that required residents to register their automobiles and display license plates was enacted. ▪ A law was enacted that authorized the establishment of a state-owned sanitarium for tuberculosis patients. ▪ The Forestry Board and Railroad Commission were created.

1907. Construction on the current capitol building began.

1908. A referendum amended the Wisconsin Constitution to permit taxing the income of individuals and corporations.

1910. Milwaukee elected Emil Seidel as the first Socialist mayor of a major city in the United States. ▪ Eau Claire became the first Wisconsin city to adopt a commission form of government.

1911. The legislature enacted a bill to establish the state income tax. ▪ The Workmen's Compensation Act required employer compensation for on-the-job injuries. ▪ The legislature created a pension plan for public school teachers statewide. It also required every town, city, or village with a population of over 5,000 to establish an industrial school. ▪ The State Highway Commission was created to regulate the construction and inspection of highways and bridges and to ensure highways would form continuous routes. ▪ The State Industrial Commission was formed to investigate and create administrative rules relating to industrial safety.

1913. Wisconsin ratified the Seventeenth Amendment, which provided that the people, rather than the state legislature, would directly elect U.S. senators.

1915. The Conservation Commission, the State Board of Agriculture, and the State Board of Education were created.

1917. The new capitol building was completed at a final cost of over $7 million. ▪ Wisconsin sent approximately 120,000 soldiers to serve during World War I, of which nearly 4,000 died. ▪ Wisconsin was the first state to meet national draft requirements.

1919. Wisconsin ratified the Eighteenth Amendment, which established Prohibition, and was the first state to deliver the ratification of the Nineteenth Amendment, which granted American women the right to vote.

1921. Laws establishing Prohibition and equal rights for women were enacted.

1923. Military training at the University of Wisconsin was made optional, rather than compulsory.

The middle years of the twentieth century

After the demise of the Progressives, the Democratic Party began a gradual resurgence and, by the late 1950s, became strongly competitive for the first time in over a century. As the black population grew in urban areas of the state, discrimination in housing and employment became matters of increasing concern. Other issues included the growth in the size of state government, radicalism on the university campuses, welfare programs, and environmental questions. Tourism emerged as a major industry during this period.

1924. Robert M. La Follette, Sr., ran for president as the Progressive Party candidate and won the state of Wisconsin.

1925. Professor Harry Steenbock developed a way to increase vitamin D in certain foods and prompted the formation of the Wisconsin Alumni Research Foundation to ensure that his patent would benefit the University of Wisconsin.

1929. The legislature repealed all Wisconsin laws enforcing Prohibition.

1933. Dairy farmers orchestrated strikes to protest low milk prices. ▪ Wisconsin voted for the repeal of the Eighteenth Amendment (Prohibition).

1935. A researcher from the Forest Products Laboratory in Madison helped convict the kidnapper and murderer of Charles Lindbergh's son in 1932.

1942. Governor-elect Orland Loomis died; the Wisconsin Supreme Court decided that Lieutenant Governor Walter Goodland would serve as acting governor.

1941–45. Wisconsin sent over 330,000 to serve in World War II (including approximately 9,000 enlisted women), of whom about 8,000 died.

1946. The Wisconsin Progressive Party dissolved and rejoined the Republican Party.

1948. Wisconsin's Centennial Year.

1949. The legislature enacted a new formula for the distribution of state educational aids and classified school districts for this purpose.

1950. Approximately 132,000 Wisconsinites served during the Korean Conflict, and 747 died.

Wisconsin Centennial postage stamp.

Korean War Veteran Corporal Albert Griffin.

1951. Legislative districts were reapportioned to reflect the rapid growth of urban populations.

1957. A new law prohibited lobbyists from giving anything of value to a state employee.

1958. Professor Joshua Lederberg, a geneticist at the University of Wisconsin, won the Nobel Prize in Physiology or Medicine.

1959. Gaylord Nelson, the first Democratic governor since 1933, was inaugurated. ▪ The Circus World Museum was established in Baraboo. ▪ Famous Wisconsin architect Frank Lloyd Wright died.

1960. Dena Smith was elected state treasurer, becoming the first woman elected to statewide office in Wisconsin.

1961. The legislature initiated a long-range program of acquisition and improvement of state recreation facilities (the ORAP program). ▪ Menominee became Wisconsin's 72nd county when federal supervision of the Indian tribe terminated.

1962. Selective sales tax and income tax withholding were enacted. ▪ The Kohler Company recognized its workers' union after a record-long strike that began in 1954.

1963. John Gronouski, the state tax commissioner, was appointed U.S. postmaster general. ▪ State expenditures from all funds for the 1963–64 fiscal year topped $1 billion for the first time.

1964. The Wisconsin Supreme Court redistricted the legislative districts after the legislature and the governor failed to agree on a plan. ▪ Two National Farmers Organization members were killed in a demonstration at a Bonduel stockyard. ▪ The legislature enacted property tax relief for the elderly. ▪ The office of county superintendent of schools was abolished, but Cooperative Educational Service Agencies (CESAs) were created to provide regional services.

1965. The school compulsory attendance age was raised to 18. ▪ All parts of the state were placed into vocational school districts. ▪ County boards were reapportioned on the basis of population. ▪ A new state law prohibited discrimination in housing. ▪ The capitol building, in use since 1917, was officially dedicated after extensive remodeling and cleaning.

1966. The 1965 Legislature held the first full even-year regular session since 1882. ▪ Governor Warren P. Knowles called the National Guard to keep order during civil rights demonstrations in Wauwatosa. ▪ The Wisconsin Supreme Court upheld the Milwaukee Braves baseball team's move to Atlanta. ▪ A grand jury investigation of illegal lobbying activities in the legislature resulted in 13 indictments.

State Treasurer Dena Smith.

1967. The executive branch was reorganized. ▪ Legislators repealed a ban on colored oleomargarine. ▪ Civil disturbances broke out in Milwaukee in late July. ▪ Activists advocated for a Milwaukee open housing ordinance. ▪ Anti-war protests at the University of Wisconsin-Madison culminated in violence.

1968. A constitutional amendment permitted the legislature to meet as provided by law rather than once per biennium. ▪ The State University of Wisconsin at Oshkosh expelled 94 black students who confronted administrators about civil rights issues. ▪ Doctors performed Wisconsin's first heart transplant at St. Luke's Hospital in Milwaukee. ▪ The first successful bone marrow transplant that was not between identical twins was performed by a team of scientists and surgeons at UW-Madison.

1969. Wisconsin implemented a general sales tax in place of elective sales taxes. ▪ Father James Groppi led protests at the capitol on the opening day of a special legislative session on welfare and urban aids. The National Guard was called, and Groppi was cited for contempt and jailed. ▪ Student strikes at UW-Madison demanded a black studies department, and the National Guard was again

The late twentieth century

Democrats lost control of the senate in 1993 for the first time since 1974, and in 1995 they lost control of the assembly for the first time since 1970. Women began to be widely represented in the legislature for the first time in the 1990s.

Health care reform, welfare, the state's business climate, taxation, education, and prisons were the chief concerns of policymakers in the 1990s.

California challenged Wisconsin's dominance of the dairy industry. After an economic downturn in the 1980s, the 1990s saw a robust economy throughout most of the state, with Madison leading the entire country in employment for several months. The farm sector and brewing industry continued to experience difficulties.

Litigation and demonstrations over off-reservation resource rights of the Chippewa Indians continued throughout the 1980s, to be replaced by controversy over Indian gaming in the 1990s and into the new century.

Father Groppi with civil rights activists.

activated. ▪ Wisconsin Congressional Representative Melvin R. Laird was appointed U.S. secretary of defense. ▪ Wisconsin's portion of the Interstate Highway System was completed.

1970. Anti-war protestors bombed the Army Mathematics Research Building at UW-Madison, resulting in one death. ▪ "Old Main" at Wisconsin State University-Whitewater burned down in an apparent arson. ▪ State constitutional officers were elected to four-year terms for the first time in Wisconsin history following a constitutional amendment ratified in 1967. ▪ University of Wisconsin scientists, headed by Dr. Har Gobind Khorana, succeeded in the first total synthesis of a gene.

1971. The legislature enacted major shared tax redistribution, the merger of the University of Wisconsin and State University systems, and a revision of municipal employee relations laws.

1972. The legislature enacted comprehensive consumer protection, lowered the age of majority from 21 to 18, required an environmental impact statement for all legislation affecting the environment, repealed the railroad full crew law, and ratified the unsuccessful "equal rights" amendment to the U.S. Constitution.

1973. A state constitutional amendment permitting bingo was adopted. ▪ Barbara Thompson became the first woman to hold the elective office of state superintendent of public instruction. ▪ The 1954 Menominee Termination Act was repealed by the U.S. Congress. ▪ The legislature enacted a state ethics code, repealed an oleomargarine tax, funded programs for the education of all children with disabilities, and established procedures for the informal probate of simple estates.

1974. The legislature enacted a comprehensive campaign finance act and strengthened the open meetings law. ▪ Democrats swept all constitutional offices and gained control of both houses of the 1975 Legislature for the first time since 1893. ▪ Kathryn Morrison became the first woman elected to the state senate. ▪ The Hortonville School District fired striking teachers.

1964–75. 165,400 Wisconsinites served in Vietnam; at least 1,161 were killed.

1975. Menominee Indians occupied the Alexian Brothers Novitiate. ▪ The legislature made voter registration easier, established property tax levy limits on local governments, and eliminated statutory distinctions based on sex.

Statistics and Reference: History | 473

- UW-Madison scientist Dr. Howard Temin won the 1975 Nobel Prize in Physiology or Medicine. - Exxon discovered sulfide zinc and copper deposits near Crandon.

1976. A U.S. district court judge ordered the integration of Milwaukee public schools. - Ice storms caused $50.4 million in damages. - The legislature established a system for compensating crime victims. - Shirley S. Abrahamson was appointed the first woman on the Wisconsin Supreme Court.

1977. Governor Patrick Lucey was appointed as the ambassador to Mexico, and Lieutenant Governor Martin Schreiber became the acting governor. - The first state employees' union strike lasted 15 days, leaving the National Guard to run Wisconsin prisons. - Constitutional amendments authorized raffle games and revised the structure of the court system by creating a court of appeals. - Legislation enacted included public support of elections campaigns, no-fault divorce, and an implied consent law for drunk driving.

1978. Vel Phillips, elected as secretary of state, became Wisconsin's first black constitutional officer. - The legislature enacted a hazardous waste management program.

1979. The Wisconsin Supreme Court allowed cameras in state courtrooms. - A constitutional amendment removed the lieutenant governor from serving as the president of the senate. - A moratorium on tax collections gave state taxpayers a three-month "vacation" from taxes. - Shirley Abrahamson became the first woman elected to the Wisconsin Supreme Court after having served by appointment for three years. - The legislature established a school of veterinary medicine at UW-Madison.

1980. Eric Heiden of Madison broke several Olympic records when he won five gold medals for ice speed skating. - Fort McCoy housed 14,250 Cuban refugees following the Mariel boatlift. - Former Governor Patrick Lucey ran as an independent candidate for U.S. vice president. - A state revenue shortfall led to a 4.4 percent cut in state spending.

1981. The U.S. Supreme Court ruled against Wisconsin's historic open primary. - The legislature enacted stronger penalties for drunk driving and changes in mining taxes.

1982. State unemployment hit the highest levels since the Great Depression. - Voters endorsed the first statewide referendum in the nation calling for a freeze on nuclear weapons. - Stroh

Shirley Abrahamson takes her oath of office.

WHS IMAGE ID 98857

Brewery Company of Detroit acquired the Schlitz Brewing Company and closed all Milwaukee operations.

Schlitz Brewing Company.

1983. The continued recession resulted in a budget including a 10 percent tax surcharge and a pay freeze for state employees. ▪ A law raising the minimum drinking age to 19 passed (to become effective in 1985). ▪ Inmates at Waupun State Prison took 15 hostages but released them uninjured the same day. ▪ Laws enacted included a "lemon law" on motor vehicle warranties and changes in child support collection procedures. ▪ The UW-Madison School of Veterinary Medicine enrolled its first class.

1984. The most powerful U.S. tornado of 1984 destroyed Barneveld, killing nine residents. ▪ The Democratic Party chose presidential convention delegates in caucuses rather than by a presidential preference primary because of new Democratic National Committee rules. ▪ Economic conditions began to improve from the low point of the previous two years.

1985. A Milwaukee plane crash killed 31. ▪ A major consolidation of state banks by large holding companies occurred.

▪ A state tax amnesty program was implemented for the first time.

1986. Farm land values fell across the state. ▪ Exxon dropped plans to develop a copper mine near Crandon. ▪ Legislation raised the drinking age to 21 and limited damages payable in malpractice actions. ▪ Protests against Ojibwa spearfishing intensified, and some lawmakers proposed suspending or eliminating Indian hunting and fishing rights.

1987. Voters approved a constitutional amendment allowing pari-mutuel betting and a state lottery. ▪ Laws enacted included a mandatory seatbelt law, antitakeover legislation, a gradual end to the inheritance and gift taxes, and a "learnfare" program designed to keep children of families on welfare in school.

1988. The first state lottery games began. ▪ Chrysler Corporation's automobile assembly plant in Kenosha, the nation's oldest car plant, closed. ▪ Mandatory family leave for employees was enacted.

1989. The legislature created the Department of Corrections, the Lower Wisconsin State Riverway, and a statewide land stewardship program.

1990. More than 1,400 Wisconsin National Guard and Reserve soldiers were called to active duty in the Persian Gulf crisis, and 10 died. ▪ Milwaukee's homicide rate broke records, raising concerns about drugs and crime. ▪ Laws enacted included a major recycling law and a Milwaukee Parental Choice voucher program for public and nonsectarian private schools.

1991. The price of milk hit its lowest point since 1978. ▪ The first state-tribal gambling compacts were signed. ▪ Governor Tommy G. Thompson vetoed a record 457 items in the state budget.

1992. A train derailed, spilling toxic chemicals and forcing the evacuation of over 22,000 people in Superior. ▪ Protests at six abortion clinics in Milwaukee led to hundreds of arrests. ▪ Laws enacted included parental consent requirements for abortion, health care reform, and the creation of a three-member Gaming Commission.

1993. President Bill Clinton appointed Wisconsin Congressman Les Aspin as secretary of defense and UW-Madison Chancellor Donna Shalala as secretary of health and human services. ▪ Thousands in Milwaukee became ill as a result of cryptosporidium in the water supply. ▪ California passed Wisconsin in milk production. ▪ Republicans won control of the state senate for the first time since 1974. ▪ Laws enacted included a 1999 sunset for traditional welfare programs, a cap on school spending, and permission to organize limited liability companies.

1994. Laws enacted include the removal of about $1 billion in public school operating taxes from property taxes, to take effect by 1997; a new framework for the Public Service Commission's regulation of telecommunication utilities; and granting towns most of the same powers exercised by cities and villages.

1995. Republicans won control of the state assembly for the first time since 1970. ▪ Elk were reintroduced in northern Wisconsin. ▪ A July heat wave contributed to 152 deaths.

1996. Governor Thompson's welfare reform plan, known as Wisconsin Works (W-2), received national attention. ▪ A train derailment forced the evacuation of Weyauwega. ▪ Pabst Brewing closed its 152-year-old brewery in Milwaukee. ▪ Following his tie-breaking vote in favor of the new Brewers stadium, State Senator George Petak was removed from office in the first successful legislative recall election in state history.

1997. Workers broke ground on Miller Park, the future home of the Milwaukee Brewers.

1998. Tammy Baldwin became the first Wisconsin woman and first openly gay woman elected to U.S. Congress. ▪ The U.S. Supreme Court upheld the constitutionality of the extension of Milwaukee Parental Choice school vouchers to religious schools. ▪ Laws enacted included a mining moratorium, new

Artist's rendering of Miller Park Stadium.

WHS IMAGE ID 66988

penalties for failure to pay child support, truth-in-sentencing, and penalties for substance abuse by expectant mothers.

1999. Laws enacted included requirements for local comprehensive plans, graduated drivers licensing, and a sales tax rebate. ▪ Supermax, the state's high security prison, opened at Boscobel. ▪ State unemployment reached a record low. ▪ The Department of Natural Resources began monitoring chronic wasting disease in the state's deer herd.

2000s

2000. The legislature approved a local sales tax and revenue bonds for the renovation of Lambeau Field, home of the Green Bay Packers.

2001. Governor Thompson ended a record 14 years in office and became U.S. secretary of health and human services. ▪ Lieutenant Governor Scott McCallum became governor and appointed State Senator Margaret Farrow as the first woman to serve as lieutenant governor. ▪ Extensive Mississippi River flooding occurred. ▪ Miller Park opened. ▪ Laws enacted included establishing a telemarketing "no call" list, wetland protection, and the "SeniorCare" prescription drug assistance plan.

2002. Barbara Lawton became the first woman elected lieutenant governor, and Peggy Lautenschlager became the first woman elected attorney general. ▪ The deadliest single traffic accident in state history killed 10 and injured almost 40 near Sheboygan. ▪ Several state legislators faced criminal charges following an investigation into legislative caucus staffs. ▪ Milwaukee County Board members resigned or were recalled over a pension scandal.

2003. Jim Doyle became the first Democratic governor in 16 years. ▪ Controversy over the Crandon mine ended when local Indian tribes purchased land and mining rights. ▪ The renovated Lambeau Field opened. ▪ State Senator Gary George became the second legislator in Wisconsin history to be recalled. ▪ Wisconsin National Guard and Reserve units were activated for service in the Iraq War. ▪ Wisconsin held its first mourning dove hunt.

2004. Louis Butler Jr., became the first black justice of the Wisconsin Supreme Court. ▪ The state government reduced its automobile fleet after allegations of misuse. ▪ Significant legislation included a livestock facility siting law and a revision to clean air and water laws intended to spur job creation. ▪ Voter turnout in the fall election was 73 percent, the highest in many years.

2005. The state minimum wage was increased. ▪ Wisconsin experienced a record 62 tornadoes during the year, including a record 27 on August 18. ▪ Several current and former members of the legislature were convicted of illegal campaign activities.

2006. The legislature limited the use of condemnation power for the benefit of private individuals. ▪ Voters approved a constitutional amendment limiting marriage to persons of the opposite sex. ▪ An advisory referendum in favor of the death penalty was also approved by the voters.

2007. The legislature modified ethics laws and elections regulations. ■ Milwaukee-based Miller Brewing Company merged with Denver's Coors Brewing Company. ■ The state budget passed in late October as one of the latest budgets in state history.

2008. A sharp economic downturn led to rising unemployment and the closing of the General Motors plant in Janesville. ■ Louis Butler Jr., became the first sitting Wisconsin Supreme Court justice to be defeated at the polls in 40 years, losing to Michael Gableman. ■ The Great Lakes Compact received state and federal approval, regulating the use of Great Lakes water outside its watershed.

2009. Democrats controlled the governor's office and both houses of the legislature for the first time since the 1985 session. ■ The ongoing economic crisis resulted in a projected budget deficit of $6 billion for the next biennium. ■ More than 3,000 members of the Wisconsin National Guard prepared for mobilization to Iraq. ■ A severe influenza outbreak resulted in 47 deaths.

2010. Several powerful tornadoes hit southern Wisconsin, severely damaging the Old World Wisconsin historic site. ■ Republicans swept the November elections, capturing the governor's office and both houses of the legislature—the first time in over 70 years that partisan control of all three switched in the same election. ■ Governor-elect Scott Walker declined $810 million in federal funds to build a high speed rail line between Madison and Milwaukee.

2011. Governor Walker's proposal to curtail collective bargaining rights for public workers led 14 Democrats to leave the state to deny the senate a quorum. Thousands of protesters surrounded the capitol to oppose the legislation, which was ultimately enacted. Wisconsin remained in a state of political agitation into the summer as nine senators were the subject of recall elections; two senators were recalled. ■ The legislature enacted a legislative redistricting plan for the first time in three decades, revamped the state's economic development efforts, and expanded the parental school choice program.

2012. Governor Walker, Lieutenant Governor Rebecca Kleefisch, and four senators were the subject of recall elections. Walker, Kleefisch, and two senators were retained; one senator resigned; and one senator was defeated, giving the Democrats control of the senate. ■ A period of severe heat and drought occurred in June and July. ■ U.S. Rep. Paul Ryan was nominated for U.S. vice president. ■ In November elections, Republicans regained control of the state senate, and Tammy Baldwin became the first Wisconsin woman and first openly gay woman elected to the U.S. Senate.

2013. The legislature revised regulations for the mining of metallic ferrous minerals, easing the way for the construction of an iron mine in northern Wisconsin's Gogebic Range. ■ Wisconsin's role as a major source of sand used in the "fracking" method of natural gas extraction presented questions for state and local quarry regulators.

2014. Voters passed a constitutional amendment requiring that transportation fund resources be used only for transportation. ▪ Court rulings legalized same-sex marriage in Wisconsin. ▪ The deer harvest was the lowest in 30 years. ▪ Governor Walker denied the Menominee Nation permission to operate a casino in Kenosha.

Vice Presidential candidate Paul Ryan.

2015. Senator Mary Lazich was elected president of the senate, becoming the first woman to be elected presiding officer of either house of the legislature. ▪ Efforts to open an iron mine in the Gogebic Range were abandoned. ▪ The legislature enacted "Right to Work" legislation, raised the speed limit to 70 miles per hour on certain highways, and approved funding for a new Milwaukee Bucks arena. ▪ Voters approved a constitutional amendment requiring the Wisconsin Supreme Court to elect its chief justice by majority vote. ▪ Governor Walker announced his candidacy for U.S. president in July but dropped out of the race in September. ▪ U.S. Rep. Paul Ryan was elected Speaker of the House.

2016. The Wisconsin Elections Commission and the Wisconsin Ethics Commission replaced the Wisconsin Government Accountability Board. ▪ An outbreak of Elizabethkingia meningoseptica killed 18 people. ▪ Donald Trump became the first Republican presidential candidate to win Wisconsin since President Reagan in 1984.

2017. A special session of the legislature was held to consider and pass legislation to address the opioid epidemic. ▪ The legislature voted to eliminate the forestry mill tax, Wisconsin's only state property tax. ▪ The legislature passed a $3 billion incentive package for Foxconn, a Taiwanese tech company that agreed to establish a large manufacturing facility in Mount Pleasant.

2018. Voters rejected a constitutional amendment eliminating the office of the state treasurer. ▪ After hearing oral arguments, the U.S. Supreme Court handed *Gill v. Whitford*—a case asking whether Wisconsin district lines were an unconstitutional partisan gerrymander—back to the lower courts. ▪ Wisconsin's unemployment rate reached a record low. ▪ Several areas of the state saw severe flooding following heavy storms. ▪ The legislature met in extraordinary session to enact legislation curbing the powers of the governor and attorney general. ▪ Tony Evers was elected governor, defeating two-term incumbent Scott Walker.

2019. Mandela Barnes became the state's first black lieutenant governor. ▪ Milwaukee was chosen to host the 2020 Democratic National Convention.

- Heavy rainfall caused record-breaking water levels in the Great Lakes.
- A rainbow flag flew above the Wisconsin Capitol to commemorate LGBT Pride Month for the first time in state history.
- Dairy farmers struggled due to low milk prices and a continued trade war with China.
- The Wisconsin Institute for Law & Liberty launched a legal challenge to Governor Evers's use of the partial veto power.
- The state first observed Indigenous Peoples' Day on the second Monday of October.

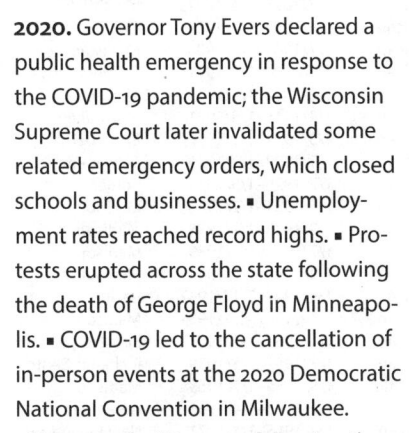

A rainbow flag at the Capitol.

2020. Governor Tony Evers declared a public health emergency in response to the COVID-19 pandemic; the Wisconsin Supreme Court later invalidated some related emergency orders, which closed schools and businesses.
- Unemployment rates reached record highs.
- Protests erupted across the state following the death of George Floyd in Minneapolis.
- COVID-19 led to the cancellation of in-person events at the 2020 Democratic National Convention in Milwaukee.
- Unrest rocked Kenosha following the shooting of Jacob Blake by police.
- The Wisconsin Supreme Court denied an attempt by the presidential campaign of Donald Trump to invalidate over 220,000 ballots cast in Wisconsin in the presidential election.

2021. Fred Risser retired after serving 64 years in the legislature, the longest tenure of any legislator in state history.
- The COVID-19 vaccine became available in Wisconsin.
- Giannis Antetokounmpo led the Milwaukee Bucks to their first NBA Championship in 50 years.
- Afghan refugees arrived at Fort McCoy following the U.S. military's withdrawal from Afghanistan.
- Six were killed and dozens injured when a driver tore through the Waukesha Christmas Parade.
- Wisconsin deaths attributed to COVID-19 surpassed 10,000.

2022. The Wisconsin Supreme Court adopted a state legislative redistricting plan submitted by the legislature and previously vetoed by Governor Evers. The court also declared ballot drop boxes illegal.
- The U.S Supreme Court overturned *Roe v. Wade*, prompting the cessation of most abortion services in Wisconsin.
- Former state supreme court justice Michael Gableman concluded a controversial investigation into alleged fraud during the 2020 presidential election.
- A 3,000 year-old canoe was recovered from Lake Mendota.

HISTORICAL LISTS

Wisconsin governors since 1848

	Party	Service	Residence[1]
Nelson Dewey.	Democratic	6/7/1848–1/5/1852	Lancaster
Leonard James Farwell	Whig	1/5/1852–1/2/1854	Madison
William Augustus Barstow	Democratic	1/2/1854–3/21/1856	Waukesha
Arthur McArthur[2]	Democratic	3/21/1856–3/25/1856	Milwaukee
Coles Bashford	Republican	3/25/1856–1/4/1858	Oshkosh
Alexander William Randall	Republican	1/4/1858–1/6/1862	Waukesha
Louis Powell Harvey[3]	Republican	1/6/1862–4/19/1862	Shopiere
Edward Salomon	Republican	4/19/1862–1/4/1864	Milwaukee
James Taylor Lewis	Republican	1/4/1864–1/1/1866	Columbus
Lucius Fairchild	Republican	1/1/1866–1/1/1872	Madison
Cadwallader Colden Washburn	Republican	1/1/1872–1/5/1874	La Crosse
William Robert Taylor	Democratic	1/5/1874–1/3/1876	Cottage Grove
Harrison Ludington	Republican	1/3/1876–1/7/1878	Milwaukee
William E. Smith.	Republican	1/7/1878–1/2/1882	Milwaukee
Jeremiah McLain Rusk.	Republican	1/2/1882–1/7/1889	Viroqua
William Dempster Hoard	Republican	1/7/1889–1/5/1891	Fort Atkinson
George Wilbur Peck	Democratic	1/5/1891–1/7/1895	Milwaukee
William Henry Upham.	Republican	1/7/1895–1/4/1897	Marshfield
Edward Scofield.	Republican	1/4/1897–1/7/1901	Oconto
Robert Marion La Follette, Sr.[4].	Republican	1/7/1901–1/1/1906	Madison
James O. Davidson	Republican	1/1/1906–1/2/1911	Soldiers Grove
Francis Edward McGovern	Republican	1/2/1911–1/4/1915	Milwaukee
Emanuel Lorenz Philipp.	Republican	1/4/1915–1/3/1921	Milwaukee
John James Blaine	Republican	1/3/1921–1/3/1927	Boscobel
Fred R. Zimmerman	Republican	1/3/1927–1/7/1929	Milwaukee
Walter Jodok Kohler, Sr.	Republican	1/7/1929–1/5/1931	Kohler
Philip Fox La Follette.	Republican	1/5/1931–1/2/1933	Madison
Albert George Schmedeman.	Democratic	1/2/1933–1/7/1935	Madison
Philip Fox La Follette.	Progressive	1/7/1935–1/2/1939	Madison
Julius Peter Heil.	Republican	1/2/1939–1/4/1943	Milwaukee
Walter Samuel Goodland[3, 5]	Republican	1/4/1943–3/12/1947	Racine
Oscar Rennebohm	Republican	3/12/1947–1/1/1951	Madison
Walter Jodok Kohler Jr.	Republican	1/1/1951–1/7/1957	Kohler
Vernon Wallace Thomson.	Republican	1/7/1957–1/5/1959	Richland Center
Gaylord Anton Nelson.	Democratic	1/5/1959–1/7/1963	Madison
John W. Reynolds.	Democratic	1/7/1963–1/4/1965	Green Bay
Warren Perley Knowles	Republican	1/4/1965–1/4/1971	New Richmond
Patrick Joseph Lucey[4]	Democratic	1/4/1971–7/6/1977	Madison
Martin James Schreiber	Democratic	7/6/1977–1/1/1979	Milwaukee
Lee Sherman Dreyfus	Republican	1/1/1979–1/3/1983	Stevens Point
Anthony Scully Earl	Democratic	1/3/1983–1/5/1987	Madison
Tommy George Thompson[4]	Republican	1/5/1987–2/1/2001	Elroy
Scott McCallum	Republican	2/1/2001–1/6/2003	Fond du Lac
James Edward Doyle Jr.	Democratic	1/6/2003–1/3/2011	Madison
Scott Kevin Walker	Republican	1/3/2011–1/7/2019	Wauwatosa
Tony Evers	Democratic	1/7/2019–	Madison

Note: Prior to 1971, the term of office was two years rather than four. Prior to 1885, the term of office began in January in even-numbered years rather than in odd-numbered years.

1. Residence at the time of election.   2. Served as acting governor during dispute over outcome of gubernatorial election.   3. Died in office.   4. Resigned.   5. Served as acting governor for the 1943–44 term following the death of Governor-elect Orland Loomis.

Sources: "Wisconsin's Former Governors," 1960 *Wisconsin Blue Book*, pp. 69–206; *Blue Book* biographies.

Vote for Wisconsin governor in general elections since 1848

1848
Nelson Dewey[1]—D 19,875
John H. Tweedy[1]—W 14,621
Charles Durkee[1]—I 1,134
Total. 35,309

1849
Nelson Dewey—D 16,649
Alexander L. Collins—W . . 11,317
Warren Chase—I 3,761
Total. 31,759

1851
Leonard J. Farwell—W . . . 22,319
Don A. J. Upham—D 21,812
Total. 44,190

1853
William A. Barstow—D . . . 30,405
Edward D. Holton—FS . . . 21,886
Henry S. Baird—W 3,304
Total. 55,683

1855
William A. Barstow[2]—D . . 36,355
Coles Bashford—R 36,198
Total. 72,598

1857
Alexander W. Randall—R . 44,693
James B. Cross—D 44,239
Total. 90,058

1859
Alexander W. Randall—R . 59,999
Harrison C. Hobart—D . . . 52,539
Total. 112,755

1861
Louis P. Harvey—R 53,777
Benjamin Ferguson—D . . 45,456
Total. 99,258

1863
James T. Lewis—R 72,717
Henry L. Palmer—D 49,053
Total. 122,029

1865
Lucius Fairchild—R 58,332
Harrison C. Hobart—D . . . 48,330
Total. 106,674

1867
Lucius Fairchild—R 73,637
John J. Tallmadge—D . . . 68,873
Total. 142,522

1869
Lucius Fairchild—R 69,502
Charles D. Robinson—D . . 61,239
Total. 130,781

1871
Cadwallader C. Washburn—R
. . . . 78,301
James R. Doolittle—D . . . 68,910
Total. 147,274

1873
William R. Taylor—D 81,599
Cadwallader C. Washburn—R
. . . . 66,224
Total. 147,856

1875
Harrison Ludington—R . . 85,155
William R. Taylor—D 84,314
Total. 170,070

1877
William E. Smith—R 78,759
James A. Mallory—D 70,486
Edward P. Allis—G 26,216
Collin M. Campbell—S . . . 2,176
Total. 178,122

1879
William E. Smith—R . . . 100,535
James G. Jenkins—D 75,030
Reuben May—G 12,996
Total. 189,005

1881
Jeremiah M. Rusk—R 81,754
N.D. Fratt—D 69,797
T.D. Kanouse—Pro 13,225
Edward P. Allis—G 7,002
Total. 171,856

1884
Jeremiah M. Rusk—R . . . 163,214
N.D. Fratt—D 143,945
Samuel D. Hastings—Pro . . 8,545
William L. Utley—G 4,274
Total. 319,997

1886
Jeremiah M. Rusk—R . . . 133,247
Gilbert M. Woodward—D 114,529
John Cochrane—PPop . . . 21,467
John Myers Olin—Pro . . . 17,089
Total. 286,368

1888
William D. Hoard—R . . . 175,696
James Morgan—D 155,423
E.G. Durant—Pro 14,373
D. Frank Powell—L 9,196
Total. 354,714

1890
George W. Peck—D 160,388
William D. Hoard—R . . . 132,068
Charles Alexander—Pro . . 11,246
Reuben May—UL 5,447
Total. 309,254

1892
George W. Peck—D 178,095
John C. Spooner—R . . . 170,497
Thomas C. Richmond—Pro 13,185
C.M. Butt—PPop 9,638
Total. 371,559

1894
William H. Upham—R . . 196,150
George W. Peck—D 142,250
D. Frank Powell—PPop . . . 25,604
John F. Cleghorn—Pro . . . 11,240
Total. 375,449

1896
Edward Scofield—R 264,981
Willis C. Silverthorn—D . 169,257
Joshua H. Berkey—Pro 8,140
Christ Tuttrop—SL 1,306
Robert Henderson—Nat . . . 407
Total. 444,110

1898
Edward Scofield—R 173,137
Hiram W. Sawyer—D . . . 135,353
Albinus A. Worsley—PPop . . 8,518
Eugene W. Chafin—Pro . . . 8,078
Howard Tuttle—SDA 2,544
Henry Riese—SL 1,473
Total. 329,430

1900
Robert M. La Follette—R. 264,419
Louis G. Bomrich—D . . . 160,674
J. Burritt Smith—Pro 9,707
Howard Tuttle—SD 6,590
Frank R. Wilke—SL 509
Total. 441,900

1902
Robert M. La Follette—R. 193,417
David S. Rose—D 145,818
Emil Seidel—SD 15,970
Edwin W. Drake—Pro 9,647
Henry E.D. Puck—SL 791
Total. 365,676

Vote for Wisconsin governor in general elections since 1848, continued

1904
Robert M. La Follette—R . 227,253
George W. Peck—D 176,301
William A. Arnold—SD . . . 24,857
Edward Scofield—NR. . . . 12,136
William H. Clark—Pro. 8,764
Charles M. Minkley—SL . . . 249
Total. 449,570

1906
James O. Davidson—R . . 183,558
John A. Aylward—D . . . 103,311
Winfield R. Gaylord—SD. . 24,437
Ephraim L. Eaton—Pro. . . . 8,211
Ole T. Rosaas—SL 455
Total. 320,003

1908
James O. Davidson—R . . 242,935
John A. Aylward—D . . . 165,977
H.D. Brown—SD 28,583
Winfred D. Cox—Pro 11,760
Herman Bottema—SL 393
Total. 449,656

1910
Francis E. McGovern—R . 161,619
Adolph H. Schmitz—D . . 110,442
William A. Jacobs—SD . . . 39,547
Byron E. Van Keuren—Pro . . 7,450
Fred G. Kremer—SL. 430
Total. 319,522

1912
Francis E. McGovern—R . 179,360
John C. Karel—D 167,316
Carl D. Thompson—SD. . . 34,468
Charles L. Hill—Pro 9,433
William H. Curtis—SL. 3,253
Total. 393,849

1914
Emanuel L. Philipp—R . . 140,787
John C. Karel—D 119,509
John J. Blaine—I. 32,560
Oscar Ameringer—SD . . . 25,917
David W. Emerson—Pro . . . 6,279
John Vierthaler—I. 352
Total. 325,430

1916
Emanuel L. Philipp—R . . 229,889
Burt Williams—D 164,555
Rae Weaver—Soc 30,649
George McKerrow—Pro . . . 9,193
Total. 434,340

1918
Emanuel L. Philipp—R . . 155,799
Henry A. Moehlenpah—D 112,576
Emil Seidel—SD 57,523
William C. Dean—Pro. 5,296
Total. 331,582

1920
John J. Blaine—R 366,247
Robert McCoy—D. 247,746
William Coleman—S 71,126
Henry H. Tubbs—Pro 6,047
Total. 691,294

1922
John J. Blaine—R 367,929
Arthur A. Bentley—ID . . . 51,061
Louis A. Arnold—S 39,570
M.L. Welles—Pro. 21,438
Arthur A. Dietrich—ISL. . . . 1,444
Total. 481,828

1924
John J. Blaine—R 412,255
Martin L. Lueck—D 317,550
William F. Quick—S 45,268
Adolph R. Bucknam—Pro . 11,516
Severi Alanne—IW 4,107
Farrand K. Shuttleworth—IPR 4,079
Jose Snover—SL. 1,452
Total. 796,432

1926
Fred R. Zimmerman—R . 350,927
Charles Perry—I 76,507
Virgil H. Cady—D 72,627
Herman O. Kent—S. 40,293
David W. Emerson—Pro . . . 7,333
Alex Gorden—SL 4,593
Total. 552,912

1928
Walter J. Kohler, Sr—R . . 547,738
Albert G. Schmedeman—D 394,368
Otto R. Hauser—S. 36,924
Adolph R. Bucknam—Pro . . 6,477
Joseph Ehrhardt—IL 1,938
Alvar J. Hayes—IW 1,420
Total. 989,143

1930
Philip F. La Follette—R . . 392,958
Charles E. Hammersley—D 170,020
Frank B. Metcalfe—S 25,607
Alfred B. Taynton—Pro. . . 14,818
Fred B. Blair—IC 2,998
Total. 606,825

1932
Albert G. Schmedeman—D
. . . . 590,114
Walter J. Kohler, Sr—R . . 470,805
Frank B. Metcalfe—S 56,965
William C. Dean—Pro. 3,148
Fred B. Blair—Com 2,926
Joe Ehrhardt—SL 398
Total. 1,124,502

1934
Philip F. La Follette—P . . 373,093
Albert G. Schmedeman—D
. . . . 359,467
Howard Greene—R. . . . 172,980
George A. Nelson—S. . . . 44,589
Morris Childs—IC 2,454
Thomas W. North—IPro 857
Joe Ehrhardt—ISL. 332
Total. 953,797

1936
Philip F. La Follette—P . . 573,724
Alexander Wiley—R. . . . 363,973
Arthur W. Lueck—D. . . . 268,530
Joseph F. Walsh—U 27,934
Joseph Ehrhardt—ISL. 1,738
August F. Fehlandt—Pro. . . 1,008
Total. 1,237,095

1938
Julius P. Heil—R 543,675
Philip F. La Follette—P . . 353,381
Harry W. Bolens—D. 78,446
Frank W. Smith—U 4,564
John Schleier, Jr—ISL. 1,459
Total. 981,560

1940
Julius P. Heil—R 558,678
Orland S. Loomis—P . . . 546,436
Francis E. McGovern—D . 264,985
Fred B. Blair—Com 2,340
Louis Fisher—SL. 1,158
Total. 1,373,754

1942
Orland S. Loomis—P . . . 397,664
Julius P. Heil—R 291,945
William C. Sullivan—D . . . 98,153
Frank P. Zeidler—P 11,295
Fred Bassett Blair—IC 1,092
Georgia Cozzini—ISL. 490
Total. 800,985

Vote for Wisconsin governor in general elections since 1848, continued

1944
Walter S. Goodland—R. . 697,740
Daniel W. Hoan—D 536,357
Alexander O. Benz—P . . . 76,028
George A. Nelson—S 9,183
Georgia Cozzini—I (ISL) . . . 1,122
Total. 1,320,483

1946
Walter S. Goodland—R. . 621,970
Daniel W. Hoan—D 406,499
Walter H. Uphoff—S 8,996
Sigmund G. Eisenscher—IC 1,857
Jerry R. Kenyon—ISL 959
Total. 1,040,444

1948
Oscar Rennebohm—R . . 684,839
Carl W. Thompson—D . . 558,497
Henry J. Berquist—PP . . . 12,928
Walter H. Uphoff—S 9,149
James E. Boulton—ISW 356
Georgia Cozzini—ISL 328
Total. 1,266,139

1950
Walter J. Kohler, Jr—R . . 605,649
Carl W. Thompson—D . . 525,319
M. Michael Essin—PP. 3,735
William O. Hart—S 3,384
Total. 1,138,148

1952
Walter J. Kohler, Jr—R . 1,009,171
William Proxmire—D . . . 601,844
M. Michael Essin—I 3,706
Total. 1,615,214

1954
Walter J. Kohler, Jr—R . . 596,158
William Proxmire—D . . . 560,747
Arthur Wepfer—I 1,722
Total. 1,158,666

1956
Vernon W. Thomson—R . 808,273
William Proxmire—D . . . 749,421
Total. 1,557,788

1958
Gaylord A. Nelson—D . . 644,296
Vernon W. Thomson—R . 556,391
Wayne Leverenz—I 1,485
Total. 1,202,219

1960
Gaylord A. Nelson—D . . 890,868
Philip G. Kuehn—R 837,123
Total. 1,728,009

1962
John W. Reynolds—D. . . 637,491
Philip G. Kuehn—R 625,536
Adolf Wiggert—I 2,477
Total. 1,265,900

1964
Warren P. Knowles—R . . 856,779
John W. Reynolds—D. . . 837,901
Total. 1,694,887

1966
Warren P. Knowles—R . . 626,041
Patrick J. Lucey—D 539,258
Adolf Wiggert—I 4,745
Total. 1,170,173

1968
Warren P. Knowles—R . . 893,463
Bronson C. La Follette—D 791,100
Adolf Wiggert—I 3,225
Robert Wilkinson—I 1,813
Total. 1,689,738

1970
Patrick J. Lucey—D 728,403
Jack B. Olson—R. 602,617
Leo J. McDonald—A 9,035
Georgia Cozzini—I (SL). . . . 1,287
Samuel K. Hunt—I (SW) 888
Myrtle Kastner—I (PLS) 628
Total. 1,343,160

1974
Patrick J. Lucey—D 628,639
William D. Dyke—R 497,189
William H. Upham—A . . . 33,528
Crazy Jim[3]—I. 12,107
William Hart—I (DS) 5,113
Fred Blair—I (C) 3,617
Georgia Cozzini—I (SL). . . . 1,492
Total. 1,181,685

1978
Lee S. Dreyfus—R 816,056
Martin J. Schreiber—D. . 673,813
Eugene R. Zimmerman—C . 6,355
John C. Doherty—I 2,183
Adrienne Kaplan—I (SW) . . 1,548
Henry A. Ochsner—I (SL) . . . 849
Total. 1,500,996

1982
Anthony S. Earl—D 896,872
Terry J. Kohler—R 662,738
Larry Smiley—Lib 9,734
James P. Wickstrom—Con . . 7,721
Peter Seidman—I (SW). . . . 3,025
Total. 1,580,344

1986
Tommy G. Thompson—R
. . . . 805,090
Anthony S. Earl—D 705,578
Kathryn A. Christensen—LF 10,323
Darold E. Wall—I. 3,913
Sanford Knapp—I. 1,668
Total. 1,526,573

1990
Tommy G. Thompson—R
. . . . 802,321
Thomas A. Loftus—D. . . 576,280
Total. 1,379,727

1994
Tommy G. Thompson—R 1,051,326
Charles J.Chvala—D . . . 482,850
David S. Harmon—Lib . . . 11,639
Edward J. Frami—Tax. 9,188
Michael J. Mangan—I 8,150
Total. 1,563,835

1998
Tommy G. Thompson—R
. . . . 1,047,716
Ed Garvey—D 679,553
Jim Mueller—Lib 11,071
Edward J. Frami—Tax. . . . 10,269
Mike Mangan—I. 4,985
A-Ja-mu Muhammad—I . . 1,604
Jeffrey L. Smith—WG. 14
Total. 1,756,014

2002
Jim Doyle—D 800,515
Scott McCallum—R 734,779
Ed Thompson—Lib 185,455
Jim Young—WG 44,111
Alan D. Eisenberg—I 2,847
Ty A. Bollerud—I. 2,637
Mike Mangan—I. 1,710
Aneb Jah Rasta Sensas-Utcha
Nefer-I—I 929
Total. 1,775,349

2006
Jim Doyle—D 1,139,115
Mark Green—R 979,427
Nelson Eisman—WG 40,709
Total. 2,161,700

2010
Scott Walker—R 1,128,941
Tom Barrett—D 1,004,303
Jim Langer—I 10,608
James James—I 8,273
Total[4] 2,160,832

Vote for Wisconsin governor in general elections since 1848, continued

June 5, 2012 recall election	Robert Burke—I (Lib). . . . 18,720	Michael J. White—WG . . . 11,087
Scott Walker—R 1,335,585	Dennis Fehr—I (Peo) 7,530	Arnie Enz—I (Wis) 2,745
Tom Barrett—D 1,164,480	Total. 2,410,314	Total. 2,673,308
Hari Trivedi—I 14,463		
Total. 2,516,065	**2018**	**2022**
	Tony Evers—D 1,324,307	Tony Evers—D. 1,358,774
2014	Scott Walker—R 1,295,080	Tim Michels—R 1,268,535
Scott Walker—R 1,259,706	Phillip Anderson—Lib . . . 20,225	Joan Ellis Beglinger—I . . . 27,198
Mary Burke—D 1,122,913	Maggie Turnbull—I 18,884	Total. 2,656,490

Note: A candidate whose party did not receive 1% of the vote for a statewide office in the previous election or who failed to meet the alternative requirement of Wis. Stat. § 5.62 is listed on the Wisconsin ballot as "independent." When a candidate's party affiliation is listed as "I," followed by a party designation in parentheses, "independent" was the official ballot listing, but a party designation was found by the Wisconsin Legislative Reference Bureau in newspaper reports.

Totals include scattered votes for other candidates.

A—American
C—Conservative
Com—Communist
Con—Constitution
D—Democrat
DS—Democratic Socialist
FS—Free Soil
G—Greenback
I—Independent
IC—Independent Communist
ID—Independent Democrat
IL—Independent Labor
IPR—Independent Prohibition Republic

IPro—Independent Prohibition
ISL—Independent Socialist Labor
ISW—Independent Socialist Worker
IW—Independent Worker
L—Labor
LF—Labor-Farm/Laborista-Agrario
Lib—Libertarian
Nat—National
NR—National Republic
P—Progressive
Peo—People's
PLS—Progressive Labor Socialist
PP—People's Progressive
PPop—People's (Populist)

Pro—Prohibition
R—Republican
S—Socialist
SD—Social Democrat
SDA—Social Democrat of America
SL—Socialist Labor
SW—Socialist Worker
Tax—U.S. Taxpayers
U—Union
UL—Union Labor
W—Whig
WG—Wisconsin Green
Wis—Wisconsin Party

1. Votes for Dewey and Tweedy are from 1874 *Blue Book*; Durkee vote is based on county returns, as filed in the Office of the Secretary of State, but returns from Manitowoc and Winnebago Counties were missing. Without these two counties, Dewey had 19,605 votes and Tweedy had 14,514 votes. 2. Barstow's plurality was set aside in *Atty. Gen. ex rel. Bashford v. Barstow*, 4 Wis. 567 (1855), because of irregularities in the election returns. 3. Legal name. 4. Total includes 6,780 votes for the Libertarian ticket, which had a candidate for lieutenant governor, but no candidate for governor.

Source: Canvass reports and Wisconsin Elections Commission records.

Wisconsin lieutenant governors since 1848

	Party	Service	Residence[1]
John E. Holmes	Democratic	1848–1850	Jefferson
Samuel W. Beall	Democratic	1850–1852	Taycheedah
Timothy Burns	Democratic	1852–1854	La Crosse
James T. Lewis	Republican	1854–1856	Columbus
Arthur McArthur[2]	Democratic	1856–1858	Milwaukee
Erasmus D. Campbell	Democratic	1858–1860	La Crosse
Butler G. Noble	Republican	1860–1862	Whitewater
Edward Salomon[3]	Republican	1862–1864	Milwaukee
Wyman Spooner	Republican	1864–1870	Elkhorn
Thaddeus C. Pound	Republican	1870–1872	Chippewa Falls
Milton H. Pettit[4]	Republican	1872–3/23/73	Kenosha
Charles D. Parker	Democratic	1874–1878	Pleasant Valley
James M. Bingham	Republican	1878–1882	Chippewa Falls
Sam S. Fifield	Republican	1882–1887	Ashland
George W. Ryland.	Republican	1887–1891	Lancaster
Charles Jonas	Democratic	1891–1895	Racine
Emil Baensch	Republican	1895–1899	Manitowoc
Jesse Stone	Republican	1899–1903	Watertown
James O. Davidson[5]	Republican	1903–1907	Soldiers Grove

Statistics and Reference: Historical lists | 485

Wisconsin lieutenant governors since 1848, continued

	Party	Service	Residence[1]
William D. Connor	Republican	1907–1909	Marshfield
John Strange	Republican	1909–1911	Oshkosh
Thomas Morris	Republican	1911–1915	La Crosse
Edward F. Dithmar	Republican	1915–1921	Baraboo
George F. Comings	Republican	1921–1925	Eau Claire
Henry A. Huber	Republican	1925–1933	Stoughton
Thomas J. O'Malley	Democratic	1933–1937	Milwaukee
Henry A. Gunderson[6]	Progressive	1937–10/16/37	Portage
Herman L. Ekern[7]	Progressive	5/16/38–1939	Madison
Walter S. Goodland[8]	Republican	1939–1945	Racine
Oscar Rennebohm[9]	Republican	1945–1949	Madison
George M. Smith	Republican	1949–1955	Milwaukee
Warren P. Knowles	Republican	1955–1959	New Richmond
Philleo Nash	Democratic	1959–1961	Wisconsin Rapids
Warren P. Knowles	Republican	1961–1963	New Richmond
Jack Olson	Republican	1963–1965	Wisconsin Dells
Patrick J. Lucey	Democratic	1965–1967	Madison
Jack Olson	Republican	1967–1971	Wisconsin Dells
Martin J. Schreiber[10]	Democratic	1971–1979	Milwaukee
Russell A. Olson	Republican	1979–1983	Randall
James T. Flynn	Democratic	1983–1987	West Allis
Scott McCallum[11]	Republican	1987–2/1/01	Fond du Lac
Margaret A. Farrow[12]	Republican	5/9/01–2003	Pewaukee
Barbara Lawton	Democratic	2003–2011	Green Bay
Rebecca Kleefisch	Republican	2011–2019	Oconomowoc
Mandela Barnes	Democratic	2019–2023	Milwaukee
Sara Rodriguez	Democratic	2023–	Brookfield

Note: Prior to 1971, the term of office was two years rather than four. Prior to 1885, the term of office began in January in even-numbered years rather than in odd-numbered years.. Prior to 1979, lieutenant governors did not cease to hold the office of lieutenant governor while acting in place of a governor who had died or resigned.

1. Residence at the time of election. 2. Served as acting governor 3/21/1856 to 3/25/1856 during dispute over outcome of gubernatorial election. 3. Became acting governor on the death of Governor Harvey, 4/19/1862. 4. Died in office. 5. Became acting governor when Governor La Follette resigned, 1/1/1906. 6. Resigned. 7. Appointed to serve the rest of Gunderson's term. 8. Became acting governor on the death of Governor-elect Orland Loomis, 1/1/1943. 9. Became acting governor on the death of Governor Goodland, 3/12/1947. 10. Became acting governor when Governor Lucey resigned, 7/6/1977. 11. Became governor when Governor Thompson resigned, 2/1/2001. 12. Appointed to serve the rest of McCallum's term.

Source: Wisconsin Legislative Reference Bureau, *Wisconsin Blue Book*, various editions, and bureau records.

Wisconsin attorneys general since 1848

	Party	Service	Residence[1]
James S. Brown	Democratic	1848–1850	Milwaukee
S. Park Coon	Democratic	1850–1852	Milwaukee
Experience Estabrook	Democratic	1852–1854	Geneva
George B. Smith	Democratic	1854–1856	Madison
William R. Smith	Democratic	1856–1858	Mineral Point
Gabriel Bouck	Democratic	1858–1860	Oshkosh
James H. Howe[2]	Republican	1860–10/7/62	Green Bay
Winfield Smith[3]	Republican	10/7/62–1866	Milwaukee
Charles R. Gill	Republican	1866–1870	Watertown
Stephen Steele Barlow	Republican	1870–1874	Dellona
Andrew Scott Sloan	Republican	1874–1878	Beaver Dam
Alexander Wilson	Republican	1878–1882	Mineral Point
Leander F. Frisby	Republican	1882–1887	West Bend
Charles E. Estabrook	Republican	1887–1891	Manitowoc

Wisconsin attorneys general since 1848, continued

	Party	Service	Residence[1]
James L. O'Connor	Democratic	1891–1895	Madison
William H. Mylrea	Republican	1895–1899	Wausau
Emmett R. Hicks	Republican	1899–1903	Oshkosh
Lafayette M. Sturdevant	Republican	1903–1907	Neillsville
Frank L. Gilbert	Republican	1907–1911	Madison
Levi H. Bancroft	Republican	1911–1913	Richland Center
Walter C. Owen[2]	Republican	1913–1/7/18	Maiden Rock
Spencer Haven[3]	Republican	1/7/18–1919	Hudson
John J. Blaine	Republican	1919–1921	Boscobel
William J. Morgan	Republican	1921–1923	Milwaukee
Herman L. Ekern	Republican	1923–1927	Madison
John W. Reynolds	Republican	1927–1933	Green Bay
James E. Finnegan	Democratic	1933–1937	Milwaukee
Orlando S. Loomis	Progressive	1937–1939	Mauston
John E. Martin[2]	Republican	1939–6/1/48	Madison
Grover L. Broadfoot[4]	Republican	6/5/48–11/12/48	Mondovi
Thomas E. Fairchild[5]	Democratic	11/12/48–1951	Verona
Vernon W. Thomson	Republican	1951–1957	Richland Center
Stewart G. Honeck	Republican	1957–1959	Madison
John W. Reynolds	Democratic	1959–1963	Green Bay
George Thompson	Republican	1963–1965	Madison
Bronson C. La Follette	Democratic	1965–1969	Madison
Robert W. Warren[2]	Republican	1969–10/8/74	Green Bay
Victor A. Miller[6]	Democratic	10/8/74–11/25/74	St. Nazianz
Bronson C. La Follette[7]	Democratic	11/25/74–1987	Madison
Donald J. Hanaway	Republican	1987–1991	Green Bay
James E. Doyle	Democratic	1991–2003	Madison
Peggy A. Lautenschlager	Democratic	2003–2007	Fond du Lac
J.B. Van Hollen	Republican	2007–2015	Waunakee
Brad D. Schimel	Republican	2015–2019	Waukesha
Josh Kaul	Democratic	2019–	Madison

Note: Prior to 1971, the term of office was two years rather than four. Prior to 1885, the term of office began in January in even-numbered years rather than in odd-numbered years.

1. Residence at the time of election. 2. Resigned. 3. Appointed to serve the rest of the unfinished term. 4. Appointed to serve the rest of Martin's term. Resigned. 5. Attorney General-elect Fairchild appointed to serve the rest of Martin's term after Broadfoot's resignation. 6. Appointed to serve the rest of Warren's term. Resigned. 7. Attorney General-elect La Follette appointed to serve the rest of Warren's term after Miller's resignation.

Source: Wisconsin Legislative Reference Bureau, *Wisconsin Blue Book*, various editions, and bureau records.

Wisconsin superintendents of public instruction since 1849

	Service	Residence[1]
Eleazer Root	1849–1852	Waukesha
Azel P. Ladd	1852–1854	Shullsburg
Hiram A. Wright[2]	1854–5/29/55	Prairie du Chien
A. Constantine Barry[3]	6/26/55–1858	Racine
Lyman C. Draper	1858–1860	Madison
Josiah L. Pickard[4]	1860–9/30/64	Platteville
John G. McMynn[3]	10/1/64–1868	Racine
Alexander J. Craig[2]	1868–7/6/70	Madison
Samuel Fallows[3]	7/6/70–1874	Milwaukee
Edward Searing	1874–1878	Milton
William Clarke Whitford	1878–1882	Milton
Robert Graham	1882–1887	Oshkosh
Jesse B. Thayer	1887–1891	River Falls
Oliver Elwin Wells	1891–1895	Appleton

Wisconsin superintendents of public instruction since 1849, continued

	Service	Residence[1]
John Q. Emery	1895–1899	Albion
Lorenzo D. Harvey	1899–1903	Milwaukee
Charles P. Cary	1903–1921	Delavan
John Callahan	1921–1949	Madison
George Earl Watson	1949–1961	Wauwatosa
Angus B. Rothwell[4]	1961–7/1/66	Manitowoc
William C. Kahl[3]	7/1/66–1973	Madison
Barbara Thompson	1973–1981	Madison
Herbert J. Grover[5]	1981–4/9/93	Cottage Grove
John T. Benson	1993–2001	Marshall
Elizabeth Burmaster	2001–2009	Madison
Tony Evers[4]	2009–1/7/19	Madison
Carolyn Stanford Taylor[6]	1/7/19–2021	Madison
Jill Underly	2021–	Hollandale

Note: Prior to 1885, the term of office began in January of even-numbered years rather than odd-numbered years and lasted for two years. Beginning in 1885, the two-year term began in January of the odd-numbered year. From 1905 onward, the term of office was extended to four years and began in July rather than January, with the election being held at the nonpartisan spring election rather than at the November general election.

1. Residence at the time of election. 2. Died in office. 3. Appointed to serve the rest of the unfinished term. 4. Resigned. 5. Resigned. Lee Sherman Dreyfus was appointed to serve as "interim superintendent" for the rest of Grover's term but did not officially become superintendent. 6. Appointed by Governor Tony Evers to serve the rest of his unfinished term.

Source: Wisconsin Legislative Reference Bureau, *Wisconsin Blue Book*, various editions, and bureau records.

Wisconsin secretaries of state since 1848

	Party	Service	Residence[1]
Thomas McHugh	Democratic	1848–1850	Delavan
William A. Barstow	Democratic	1850–1852	Waukesha
Charles D. Robinson	Democratic	1852–1854	Green Bay
Alexander T. Gray	Democratic	1854–1856	Janesville
David W. Jones	Democratic	1856–1860	Belmont
Lewis P. Harvey	Republican	1860–1862	Shopiere
James T. Lewis	Republican	1862–1864	Columbus
Lucius Fairchild	Republican	1864–1866	Madison
Thomas S. Allen	Republican	1866–1870	Mineral Point
Llywelyn Breese	Republican	1870–1874	Portage
Peter Doyle	Democratic	1874–1878	Prairie du Chien
Hans B. Warner	Republican	1878–1882	Ellsworth
Ernst G. Timme	Republican	1882–1891	Kenosha
Thomas J. Cunningham	Democratic	1891–1895	Chippewa Falls
Henry Casson	Republican	1895–1899	Viroqua
William H. Froehlich	Republican	1899–1903	Jackson
Walter L. Houser	Republican	1903–1907	Mondovi
James A. Frear	Republican	1907–1913	Hudson
John S. Donald	Republican	1913–1917	Mt. Horeb
Merlin Hull	Republican	1917–1921	Black River Falls
Elmer S. Hall	Republican	1921–1923	Green Bay
Fred R. Zimmerman	Republican	1923–1927	Milwaukee
Theodore Dammann	Republican	1927–1935	Milwaukee
Theodore Dammann	Progressive	1935–1939	Milwaukee
Fred R. Zimmerman[2]	Republican	1939–12/14/54	Milwaukee
Louis Allis[3]	Republican	12/16/54–1955	Milwaukee
Glenn M. Wise[4]	Republican	1955–1957	Madison
Robert C. Zimmerman	Republican	1957–1975	Madison
Doug La Follette	Democratic	1975–1979	Kenosha
Vel R. Phillips	Democratic	1979–1983	Milwaukee

Wisconsin secretaries of state since 1848, continued

	Party	Service	Residence[1]
Doug La Follette[5]	Democratic	1983– 3/17/23	Madison
Sarah Godlewski[6]	Democratic	3/17/23–	Madison

Note: Prior to 1971, the term of office was two years rather than four. Prior to 1885, the term of office began in January in even-numbered years rather than in odd-numbered years.

1. Residence at the time of election. 2. Died after being reelected for a new term but before the new term began. 3. Appointed to serve the rest of Zimmerman's unfinished term. 4. Appointed to serve Zimmerman's new term. 5. Resigned. 6. Appointed to serve the rest of La Follette's term.

Source: Wisconsin Legislative Reference Bureau, *Wisconsin Blue Book*, various editions, and bureau records.

Wisconsin state treasurers since 1848

	Party	Service	Residence[1]
Jarius C. Fairchild	Democratic	1848–1852	Madison
Edward H. Janssen	Democratic	1852–1856	Cedarburg
Charles Kuehn	Democratic	1856–1858	Manitowoc
Samuel D. Hastings	Republican	1858–1866	Trempealeau
William E. Smith	Republican	1866–1870	Fox Lake
Henry Baetz	Republican	1870–1874	Manitowoc
Ferdinand Kuehn	Democratic	1874–1878	Milwaukee
Richard Guenther	Republican	1878–1882	Oshkosh
Edward C. McFetridge	Republican	1882–1887	Beaver Dam
Henry B. Harshaw	Republican	1887–1891	Oshkosh
John Hunner	Democratic	1891–1895	Eau Claire
Sewell A. Peterson	Republican	1895–1899	Rice Lake
James O. Davidson	Republican	1899–1903	Soldiers Grove
John J. Kempf[2]	Republican	1903–7/30/04	Milwaukee
Thomas M. Purtell[3]	Republican	7/30/04–1905	Cumberland
John J. Kempf	Republican	1905–1907	Milwaukee
Andrew H. Dahl	Republican	1907–1913	Westby
Henry Johnson	Republican	1913–1923	Suring
Solomon Levitan	Republican	1923–1933	Madison
Robert K. Henry	Democratic	1933–1937	Jefferson
Solomon Levitan	Progressive	1937–1939	Madison
John M. Smith[4]	Republican	1939–8/17/47	Shell Lake
John L. Sonderegger[5]	Republican	8/19/47–9/30/47	Madison
Clyde M. Johnston (appointed from staff)[3]	X	10/1/48–1949	Madison
Warren R. Smith[4]	Republican	1949–12/4/57	Milwaukee
Dena A. Smith[3]	Republican	12/5/57–1959	Milwaukee
Eugene M. Lamb	Democratic	1959–1961	Milwaukee
Dena A. Smith[4]	Republican	1961–2/20/68	Milwaukee
Harold W. Clemens[3]	Republican	2/21/68–1971	Oconomowoc
Charles P. Smith	Democratic	1971–1991	Madison
Cathy S. Zeuske	Republican	1991–1995	Shawano
Jack C. Voight	Republican	1995–2007	Appleton
Dawn Marie Sass	Democratic	2007–2011	Milwaukee
Kurt W. Schuller	Republican	2011–2015	Eden
Matt Adamczyk	Republican	2015–2019	Wauwatosa
Sarah Godlewski	Democratic	2019–2023	Madison
John S. Leiber	Republican	2023–	Cottage Grove

Note: Prior to 1971, the term of office was two years rather than four. Prior to 1885, the term of office began in January in even-numbered years rather than in odd-numbered years.

X—Not applicable.

1. Residence at the time of election. 2. Vacated office by failure to give the required bond. 3. Appointed to serve the rest of the unfinished term. 4. Died in office. 5. Appointed to serve the rest of Smith's term. Resigned.

Source: Wisconsin Legislative Reference Bureau, *Wisconsin Blue Book*, various editions, and bureau records.

Wisconsin Supreme Court justices since 1836

	Service	Residence[1]
Judges during the territorial period		
Charles Dunn (Chief Justice)[2]	1836–1848	NA
William C. Frazier	1836–1838	NA
David Irvin	1836–1838	NA
Andrew G. Miller	1836–1848	NA
Circuit judges who served as justices 1848–1853[3]		
Alexander W. Stow	1848–1851 (C.J.)	Fond du Lac
Levi Hubbell	1848–1853 (C.J. 1851)	Milwaukee
Edward V. Whiton	1848–1853 (C.J. 1852–53)	Janesville
Charles H. Larrabee	1848–1853	Horicon
Mortimer M. Jackson	1848–1853	Mineral Point
Wiram Knowlton	1850–1853	Prairie du Chien
Timothy O. Howe	1851–1853	Green Bay
Justices since 1853		
Edward V. Whiton	1853–1859 (C.J.)	Janesville
Samuel Crawford	1853–1855	New Diggings
Abram D. Smith	1853–1859	Milwaukee
Orsamus Cole	1855–1892 (C.J. 1880–92)	Potosi
Luther S. Dixon[4]	1859–1874 (C.J.)	Portage
Byron Paine[4]	1859–1864, 1867–71	Milwaukee
Jason Downer[4]	1864–1867	Milwaukee
William P. Lyon[4]	1871–1894 (C.J. 1892–94)	Racine
Edward G. Ryan[4]	1874–1880 (C.J.)	Racine
David Taylor	1878–1891	Sheboygan
Harlow S. Orton	1878–1895 (C.J. 1894–95)	Madison
John B. Cassoday[4]	1880–1907 (C.J. 1895–07)	Janesville
John B. Winslow[4]	1891–1920 (C.J. 1907–20)	Racine
Silas U. Pinney	1892–1898	Madison
Alfred W. Newman	1894–1898	Trempealeau
Roujet D. Marshall[4]	1895–1918	Chippewa Falls
Charles V. Bardeen[4]	1898–1903	Wausau
Joshua Eric Dodge[4]	1898–1910	Milwaukee
Robert G. Siebecker[5]	1903–1922 (C.J. 1920–22)	Madison
James C. Kerwin	1905–1921	Neenah
William H. Timlin	1907–1916	Milwaukee
Robert M. Bashford[4]	Jan.–June 1908	Madison
John Barnes	1908–1916	Rhinelander
Aad J. Vinje[4]	1910–1929 (C.J. 1922–29)	Superior
Marvin B. Rosenberry[4]	1916–1950 (C.J. 1929–50)	Wausau
Franz C. Eschweiler[4]	1916–1929	Milwaukee
Walter C. Owen	1918–1934	Maiden Rock
Burr W. Jones[4]	1920–1926	Madison
Christian Doerfler[4]	1921–1929	Milwaukee
Charles H. Crownhart[4]	1922–1930	Madison
E. Ray Stevens	1926–1930	Madison
Chester A. Fowler[4]	1929–1948	Fond du Lac
Oscar M. Fritz[4]	1929–1954 (C.J. 1950–54)	Milwaukee
Edward T. Fairchild[4]	1929–1957 (C.J. 1954–57)	Milwaukee
John D. Wickhem[4]	1930–1949	Madison
George B. Nelson[4]	1930–1942	Stevens Point
Theodore G. Lewis[4]	Nov. 15–Dec. 5, 1934	Madison
Joseph Martin[4]	1934–1946	Green Bay
Elmer E. Barlow[4]	1942–1948	Arcadia
James Ward Rector[4]	1946–1947	Madison
Henry P. Hughes	1948–1951	Oshkosh
John E. Martin[4]	1948–1962 (C.J. 1957–62)	Green Bay
Grover L. Broadfoot[4]	1948–1962 (C.J. Jan.–May 1962)	Mondovi
Timothy Brown[4]	1949–1964 (C.J. 1962–64)	Madison

Wisconsin Supreme Court justices since 1836, continued

	Service	Residence[1]
Edward J. Gehl	1950–1956	Hartford
George R. Currie[4]	1951–1968 (C.J. 1964–68)	Sheboygan
Roland J. Steinle[4]	1954–1958	Milwaukee
Emmert L. Wingert[4]	1956–1959	Madison
Thomas E. Fairchild	1957–1966	Verona
E. Harold Hallows[4]	1958–1974 (C.J. 1968–74)	Milwaukee
William H. Dieterich	1959–1964	Milwaukee
Myron L. Gordon	1962–1967	Milwaukee
Horace W. Wilkie[4]	1962–1976 (C.J. 1974–76)	Madison
Bruce F. Beilfuss	1964–1983 (C.J. 1976–83)	Neillsville
Nathan S. Heffernan[4]	1964–1995 (C.J. 1983–95)	Sheboygan
Leo B. Hanley[4]	1966–1978	Milwaukee
Connor T. Hansen[4]	1967–1980	Eau Claire
Robert W. Hansen	1968–1978	Milwaukee
Roland B. Day[4]	1974–1996 (C.J. 1995–96)	Madison
Shirley S. Abrahamson[4]	1976–2019 (C.J. 1996–2015)	Madison
William G. Callow	1978–1992	Waukesha
John L. Coffey	1978–1982	Milwaukee
Donald W. Steinmetz	1980–1999	Milwaukee
Louis J. Ceci[4]	1982–1993	Milwaukee
William A. Bablitch	1983–2003	Stevens Point
Jon P. Wilcox[4]	1992–2007	Wautoma
Janine P. Geske[4]	1993–1998	Milwaukee
Ann Walsh Bradley	1995–	Wausau
N. Patrick Crooks	1996–2015	Green Bay
David T. Prosser Jr.[4]	1998–2016	Appleton
Diane S. Sykes[4]	1999–2004	Milwaukee
Patience D. Roggensack	2003–2023 (C.J. 2015–2021)	Madison
Louis B. Butler Jr.[4]	2004–2008	Milwaukee
Annette K. Ziegler	2007– (C.J. 2021–)	West Bend
Michael J. Gableman	2008–2018	Webster
Rebecca Grassl Bradley[4]	2015–	Milwaukee
Daniel Kelly[4]	2016–2020	North Prairie
Rebecca Frank Dallet	2018–	Whitefish Bay
Brian Hagedorn	2019–	Oconomowoc
Jill Karofsky	2020–	Madison
Janet C. Protasiewicz	2023–	Franklin

Note: The structure of the Wisconsin Supreme Court has varied. There were three justices during the territorial period. From 1848 to 1853, circuit judges acted as supreme court justices—five from 1848 to 1850 and six from 1850 to 1853. From 1853 to 1877, there were three elected justices. The number was increased to five in 1877, and to seven in 1903.

C.J.—Chief justice; NA—Not available.

1. Residence at the time of election or appointment. 2. Before 1889, the chief justice was elected or appointed to the position. From 1889 to 2015, the most senior justice seved as chief justice. From 2015 onward, the justices have elected one of themselves to be chief justice for a two-year term. 3. Circuit judges acted as supreme court justices from 1848 to 1853. 4. Initially appointed to the court. 5. Siebecker was elected April 7, 1903, but prior to inauguration for his elected term was appointed April 9, 1903, to fill the vacancy caused by the death of Justice Bardeen.

Sources: Wisconsin Legislative Reference Bureau, *Wisconsin Blue Book*, 1935, 1944, 1977; Wisconsin Elections Commission; Wisconsin Supreme Court, *Wisconsin Reports*, various volumes.

Wisconsin senate presidents, or presidents pro tempore, and assembly speakers since 1848

Session	Senate presidents or presidents pro tempore[1]	Residence[2]	Assembly speakers	Residence[2]
1848	X	X	Ninian E. Whiteside—D	Lafayette County
1849	X	X	Harrison C. Hobart—D	Sheboygan

Wisconsin senate presidents, or presidents pro tempore, and assembly speakers since 1848, continued

Session	Senate presidents or presidents pro tempore[1]	Residence[2]	Assembly speakers	Residence[2]
1850	NA	NA	Moses M. Strong—D	Mineral Point
1851	NA	NA	Frederick W. Horn—D	Cedarburg
1852	E.B. Dean Jr.—D	Madison	James M. Shafter—W	Sheboygan
1853	Duncan C. Reed—D	Milwaukee	Henry L. Palmer—D	Milwaukee
1854	Benjamin Allen—D	Hudson	Frederick W. Horn—D	Cedarburg
1855	Eleazor Wakeley—D	Whitewater	Charles C. Sholes—R	Kenosha
1856	Louis Powell Harvey—R	Shopiere	William Hull—D	Grant County
1857	X	X	Wyman Spooner—R	Elkhorn
1858	Hiram H. Giles—R	Stoughton	Frederick S. Lovell—R	Kenosha County
1859	Dennison Worthington—R	Summit	William P. Lyon—R	Racine
1860	Moses M. Davis—R	Portage	William P. Lyon—R	Racine
1861	Alden I. Bennett—R	Beloit	Amasa Cobb—R	Mineral Point
1862	Frederick O. Thorp—D	West Bend	James W. Beardsley—UD	Prescott
1863	Wyman Spooner—R	Elkhorn	J. Allen Barber—R	Lancaster
1864	Smith S. Wilkinson—R	Prairie du Sac	William W. Field—U	Fennimore
1865	Willard H. Chandler—U	Windsor	William W. Field—U	Fennimore
1866	Willard H. Chandler—U	Windsor	Henry D. Barron—U	St. Croix Falls
1867	George F. Wheeler—U	Nanuapa	Angus Cameron—U	La Crosse
1868	Newton M. Littlejohn—R	Whitewater	Alexander M. Thomson—R	Janesville
1869	George C. Hazelton—R	Boscobel	Alexander M. Thomson—R	Janesville
1870	David Taylor—R	Sheboygan	James M. Bingham—R	Palmyra
1871	Charles G. Williams—R	Janesville	William E. Smith—R	Fox Lake
1872	Charles G. Williams—R	Janesville	Daniel Hall—R	Watertown
1873	Henry L. Eaton—R	Lone Rock	Henry D. Barron—R	St. Croix Falls
1874	John C. Holloway—R	Lancaster	Gabriel Bouck—D	Oshkosh
1875	Henry D. Barron—R	St. Croix Falls	Frederick W. Horn—R	Cedarburg
1876	Robert L. D. Potter—R	Wautoma	Sam S. Fifield—R	Ashland
1877	William H. Hiner—R	Fond du Lac	John B. Cassoday—R	Janesville
1878	Levi W. Barden—R	Portage	Augustus R. Barrows—GB	Chippewa Falls
1879	William T. Price—R	Black River Falls	David M. Kelly—R	Green Bay
1880	Thomas B. Scott—R	Grand Rapids	Alexander A. Arnold—R	Galesville
1881	Thomas B. Scott—R	Grand Rapids	Ira B. Bradford—R	Augusta
1882	George B. Burrows—R	Madison	Franklin L. Gilson—R	Ellsworth
1883	George W. Ryland—R	Lancaster	Earl P. Finch—D	Oshkosh
1885	Edward S. Minor—R	Sturgeon Bay	Hiram O. Fairchild—R	Marinette
1887	Charles K. Erwin—R	Tomah	Thomas B. Mills—R)	Millston
1889	Thomas A. Dyson—R	La Crosse	Thomas B. Mills—R	Millston
1891	Frederick W. Horn—D	Cedarburg	James J. Hogan—D	La Crosse
1893	Robert J. MacBride—D	Neillsville	Edward Keogh—D	Milwaukee
1895	Thompson D. Weeks—R	Whitewater	George B. Burrows—R	Madison
1897	Lyman W. Thayer—R	Ripon	George A. Buckstaff—R	Oshkosh
1899	Lyman W. Thayer—R	Ripon	George H. Ray—R	La Crosse
1901	James J. McGillivray—R	Black River Falls	George H. Ray—R	La Crosse
1903–05	James J. McGillivray—R	Black River Falls	Irvine L. Lenroot—R	West Superior
1907	James H. Stout—R	Menomonie	Herman L. Ekern—R	Whitehall
1909	James H. Stout—R	Menomonie	Levi H. Bancroft—R	Richland Center
1911	Harry C. Martin—R	Darlington	C.A. Ingram—R	Durand
1913	Harry C. Martin—R	Darlington	Merlin Hull—R	Black River Falls
1915	Edward T. Fairchild—R	Milwaukee	Lawrence C. Whittet—R	Edgerton
1917	Timothy Burke—R	Green Bay	Lawrence C. Whittet—R	Edgerton
1919	Willard T. Stevens—R	Rhinelander	Riley S. Young—R	Darien
1921	Timothy Burke—R	Green Bay	Riley S. Young—R	Darien
1923	Henry A. Huber—R	Stoughton	John L. Dahl—R	Rice Lake
1925	Howard Teasdale—R	Sparta	Herman Sachtjen[3]—R	Madison
			George A. Nelson[3]—R	Milltown
1927	William L. Smith—R	Neillsville	John W. Eber—R	Milwaukee
1929	Oscar H. Morris—R	Milwaukee	Charles B. Perry—R	Wauwatosa

Wisconsin senate presidents, or presidents pro tempore, and assembly speakers since 1848, continued

Session	Senate presidents or presidents pro tempore[1]	Residence[2]	Assembly speakers	Residence[2]
1931.....	Herman J. Severson—P	Iola	Charles B. Perry—R	Wauwatosa
1933.....	Orland S. Loomis—R	Mauston	Cornelius T. Young—D	Milwaukee
1935.....	Harry W. Bolens—D	Port Washington	Jorge W. Carow—P	Ladysmith
1937.....	Walter J. Rush—P	Neillville	Paul R. Alfonsi—P	Pence
1939.....	Edward J. Roethe—R	Fennimore	Vernon W. Thomson—R	Richland Center
1941–43 ..	Conrad Shearer—R	Kenosha	Vernon W. Thomson—R	Richland Center
1945.....	Conrad Shearer—R	Kenosha	Donald C. McDowell—R	Soldiers Grove
1947.....	Frank E. Panzer—R	Brownsville	Donald C. McDowell—R	Soldiers Grove
1949.....	Frank E. Panzer—R	Brownsville	Alex L. Nicol—R	Sparta
1951–53 ..	Frank E. Panzer—R	Brownsville	Ora R. Rice—R	Delavan
1955.....	Frank E. Panzer—R	Brownsville	Mark Catlin Jr.—R	Appleton
1957.....	Frank E. Panzer—R	Brownsville	Robert G. Marotz—R	Shawano
1959.....	Frank E. Panzer—R	Brownsville	George Molinaro—D	Kenosha
1961.....	Frank E. Panzer—R	Brownsville	David J. Blanchard—R	Edgerton
1963.....	Frank E. Panzer—R	Brownsville	Robert D. Haase—R	Marinette
1965.....	Frank E. Panzer—R	Brownsville	Robert T. Huber—D	West Allis
1967–69 ..	Robert P. Knowles—R	New Richmond	Harold V. Froehlich—R	Appleton
1971.....	Robert P. Knowles—R	New Richmond	Robert T. Huber[4]—D	West Allis
			Norman C. Anderson[4]—D	Madison
1973.....	Robert P. Knowles—R	New Richmond	Norman C. Anderson—D	Madison
1975.....	Fred A. Risser—D	Madison	Norman C. Anderson—D	Madison
1977–81 ..	Fred A. Risser—D	Madison	Edward G. Jackamonis—D	Waukesha
1983–89 ..	Fred A. Risser—D	Madison	Thomas A. Loftus—D	Sun Prairie
1991.....	Fred A. Risser—D	Madison	Walter J. Kunicki—D	Milwaukee
1993.....	Fred A. Risser[5]—D	Madison	Walter J. Kunicki—D	Milwaukee
	Brian D. Rude[5]—R	Coon Valley		
1995.....	Brian D. Rude[6]—R	Coon Valley	David T. Prosser Jr.—R	Appleton
	Fred A. Risser[6]—D	Madison		
1997.....	Fred A. Risser[7]—D	Madison	Ben Brancel[8]—R	Endeavor
	Brian D. Rude[7]—R	Coon Valley	Scott R. Jensen[8]—R	Waukesha
1999.....	Fred A. Risser—D	Madison	Scott R. Jensen—R	Waukesha
2001.....	Fred A. Risser—D	Madison	Scott R. Jensen—R	Waukesha
2003–05 ..	Alan J. Lasee—R	De Pere	John Gard—R	Peshtigo
2007.....	Fred A. Risser—D	Madison	Michael D. Huebsch—R	West Salem
2009.....	Fred A. Risser—D	Madison	Michael J. Sheridan—D	Janesville
2011.....	Michael G. Ellis[9]—R	Neenah	Jeff Fitzgerald—R	Horicon
	Fred A. Risser[9]—D	Madison		
2013.....	Michael G. Ellis—R	Neenah	Robin J. Vos—R	Burlington
2015.....	Mary A. Lazich—R	New Berlin	Robin J. Vos—R	Burlington
2017–19 ..	Roger Roth—R	Appleton	Robin J. Vos—R	Burlington
2021–23 ..	Chris Kapenga—R	Delafield	Robin J. Vos—R	Burlington

Note: Political party indicated is for session elected and is obtained from newspaper accounts for some early legislators.

X–Not applicable. No permanent president pro tempore; NA–Not available; D–Democrat; GB–Greenback; P–Progressive; R–Republican; U–Union; UD–Union Democrat; W–Whig.

1. Prior to May 1, 1979, the president pro tempore is listed because the lieutenant governor, rather than a legislator, was the president of the senate under the constitution until that time. 2. Residence at the time of election. 3. Nelson was elected to serve at special session, 4/15/76 to 4/16/26, as Sachtjen had resigned. 4. Anderson was elected speaker 1/18/72 after Huber resigned 5. A new president was elected on 4/20/93 after a change in party control following two special elections. 6. A new president was elected on 7/9/96 after a change in party control following a recall election. 7. A new president was elected on 4/21/98 after a change in party control following a special election. 8. Jensen was elected speaker 11/4/97 after Brancel resigned. 9. A new president was elected on 7/17/12 after a change in party control following a recall election.

Sources: Senate and Assembly Journals; Wisconsin Legislative Reference Bureau records.

Majority and minority leaders of the Wisconsin legislature since 1937

Session	Senate majority	Senate minority	Assembly majority	Assembly minority
1937...	Maurice Coakley—R	NA	NA	NA
1939...	Maurice Coakley—R	Philip Nelson—P	NA	Paul Alfonsi—P
1941...	Maurice Coakley—R	Cornelius Young—D	Mark Catlin Jr.—R	Andrew Biemiller—P
				Robert Tehan—D
1943...	Warren Knowles[1]—R	NA	Mark Catlin Jr.—R	Elmer Genzmer—D
	John Byrnes[1]—R			Lyall Beggs—P
1945...	Warren Knowles—R	Anthony Gawronski—D	Vernon Thomson—R	Lyall Beggs—P
				Leland McParland—D
1947...	Warren Knowles—R	Robert Tehan—D	Vernon Thomson—R	Leland McParland—D
1949...	Warren Knowles—R	NA	Vernon Thomson—R	Leland McParland—D
1951...	Warren Knowles—R	Gaylord Nelson—D	Arthur Mockrud—R	George Molinaro—D
1953...	Warren Knowles—R	Henry Maier—D	Mark Catlin Jr.—R	George Molinaro—D
1955...	Paul Rogan[2]—R	Henry Maier—D	Robert Marotz—R	Robert Huber—D
1957...	Robert Travis—R	Henry Maier—D	Warren Grady—R	Robert Huber—D
1959...	Robert Travis—R	Henry Maier—D	Keith Hardie—D	David Blanchard—R
1961...	Robert Travis—R	William Moser[3]—D	Robert Haase—R	Robert Huber—D
1963...	Robert Knowles—R	Richard Zaborski—D	Paul Alfonsi—R	Robert Huber—D
1965...	Robert Knowles—R	Richard Zaborski—D	Frank Nikolay—D	Robert Haase[4]—R
				Paul Alfonsi[4]—R
1967...	Jerris Leonard—R	Fred Risser—D	J. Curtis McKay—R	Robert Huber—D
1969...	Ernest Keppler—R	Fred Risser—D	Paul Alfonsi—R	Robert Huber—D
1971...	Ernest Keppler—R	Fred Risser—D	Norman Anderson[5]—D	Harold Froehlich—R
			Anthony Earl[5]—D	
1973...	Raymond Johnson—R	Fred Risser—D	Anthony Earl—D	John Shabaz—R
1975...	Wayne Whittow[6]—D	Clifford Krueger—R	Terry Willkom—D	John Shabaz—R
	William Bablitch[6]—D			
1977...	William Bablitch—D	Clifford Krueger—R	James Wahner—D	John Shabaz—R
1979...	William Bablitch—D	Clifford Krueger—R	James Wahner[7]—D	John Shabaz—R
			Gary Johnson[7]—D	
1981...	William Bablitch[9]—D	Walter Chilsen—R	Thomas Loftus—D	John Shabaz[8]—R
	Timothy Cullen[9]—D			Tommy Thompson[8]—R
1983...	Timothy Cullen—D	James Harsdorf—R	Gary Johnson—D	Tommy Thompson—R
1985...	Timothy Cullen—D	Susan Engeleiter—R	Dismas Becker—D	Tommy Thompson—R
1987...	Joseph Strohl—D	Susan Engeleiter—R	Thomas Hauke—D	Betty Jo Nelsen—R
1989...	Joseph Strohl—D	Michael Ellis—R	Thomas Hauke—D	David Prosser—R
1991...	David Helbach—D	Michael Ellis—R	David Travis—D	David Prosser—R
1993...	David Helbach[10]—D	Michael Ellis[10]—R	David Travis—D	David Prosser—R
	Michael Ellis[10]—R	David Helbach[10,11]—D		
		Robert Jauch[11]—D		
1995...	Michael Ellis[13]—R	Robert Jauch[12]—D	Scott Jensen—R	Walter Kunicki—D
		Charles Chvala[12,13]—D		
	Charles Chvala[13]—D	Michael Ellis[13]—R		
1997...	Charles Chvala[14]—D	Michael Ellis[14]—R	Steven Foti—R	Walter Kunicki[15]—D
	Michael Ellis[14]—R	Charles Chvala[14]—D		Shirley Krug[15]—D
1999...	Charles Chvala—D	Michael Ellis[16]—R	Steven Foti—R	Shirley Krug—D
		Mary Panzer[16]—R		
2001...	Charles Chvala—D	Mary Panzer—R	Steven Foti—R	Shirley Krug—D
	Russell Decker[17]—D			Spencer Black[18]—D
	Fred Risser[17]—D			
	Jon Erpenbach[17]—D			
2003...	Mary Panzer[19]—R	Jon Erpenbach—D	Steven Foti—R	James Kreuser—D
	Scott Fitzgerald[19]—R			
	Dale Schultz[20]—R	Judith Robson[20]—D		
2005...	Dale Schultz—R	Judith Robson—D	Michael Huebsch—R	James Kreuser—D
2007...	Judith Robson—D	Scott Fitzgerald—R	Jeff Fitzgerald—R	James Kreuser—D
	Russell Decker[21]—D			
2009...	Russell Decker[22]—D	Scott Fitzgerald—R	Thomas Nelson—D	Jeff Fitzgerald—R
	Dave Hansen[22]—D			
2011...	Scott Fitzgerald—R	Mark Miller—D	Scott Suder—R	Peter Barca—D

Majority and minority leaders of the Wisconsin legislature since 1937, continued

Session	Senate majority	Senate minority	Assembly majority	Assembly minority
2013...	Mark Miller[23]—D Scott Fitzgerald—R	Scott Fitzgerald[23]—R Chris Larson—D	Scott Suder[24]—R Bill Kramer[25]—R Pat Strachota—R	Peter Barca—D
2015...	Scott Fitzgerald—R	Jennifer Shilling—D	Jim Steineke—R	Peter Barca—D
2017...	Scott Fitzgerald—R	Jennifer Shilling—D	Jim Steineke—R	Peter Barca[26]—D Gordon Hintz[26]—D
2019...	Scott Fitzgerald—R	Jennifer Shilling[27]—D Janet Bewley[27]—D	Jim Steineke—R	Gordon Hintz—D
2021...	Devin LeMahieu—R	Janet Bewley[28]—D Melissa Agard[28]—D	Jim Steineke[29]—R Tyler August[29]—R	Gordon Hintz[30]—D Greta Neubauer[30]—D
2023...	Devin LeMahieu—R	Melissa Agard—D	Tyler August—R	Greta Neubauer—D

Note: Majority and minority leaders, who are chosen by the party caucuses in each house, were first recognized officially in the senate and assembly rules in 1963. Prior to the 1977 session, these positions were also referred to as "floor leader."

NA–Not available; D–Democrat; P–Progressive; R–Republican.

1. Knowles granted leave of absence to return to active duty in U.S. Navy; Byrnes chosen to succeed him on 4/30/1943. 2. Resigned after sine die adjournment. 3. Resigned 1/30/1962. 4. Haase resigned 9/15/1965; Alfonsi elected 10/4/1965. 5. Earl elected 1/18/1972 to succeed Anderson who became assembly speaker. 6. Whittow resigned 4/30/1976; Bablitch elected 5/17/1976. 7. Wahner resigned 1/28/1980; Johnson elected 1/28/1980. 8. Shabaz resigned 12/18/1981; Thompson elected 12/21/1981. 9. Bablitch resigned 5/26/1982; Cullen elected 5/26/1982. 10. Democrats controlled senate from 1/4/1993 to 4/20/1993 when Republicans assumed control after a special election. 11. Helbach resigned 5/12/1993; Jauch elected 5/12/1993. 12. Jauch resigned 10/17/1995; Chvala elected 10/24/1995. 13. Republicans controlled senate from 1/5/1995 to 6/13/1996 when Democrats assumed control after a recall election. 14. Democrats controlled the senate from 1/6/1997 to 4/21/1998 when Republicans assumed control after a special election. 15. Kunicki resigned 6/3/1998; Krug elected 6/3/1998. 16. Ellis resigned 1/25/2000; Panzer elected 1/25/2000. 17. Decker and Risser elected co-leaders 10/22/2002. Erpenbach elected leader 12/4/2002. 18. Black elected 5/1/2001. 19. Panzer resigned 9/17/2004; Fitzgerald elected 9/17/2004. 20. Schultz elected 11/9/2004; Robson elected 11/9/2004. 21. Decker elected 10/24/2007. 22. Hansen replaced Decker as leader, 12/15/2010. 23. After a resignation on 3/16/2012 resulted in a 16–16 split, Fitzgerald and Miller served as co-leaders. A recall election gave Democrats control of the senate as of 7/17/2012. 24. Suder resigned 9/3/2013; Kramer elected 9/4/2013. 25. Kramer removed 3/4/2014; Strachota elected 3/4/2014. 26. Barca resigned effective 9/30/2017; Hintz became minority leader 10/1/2017. 27. Shilling resigned 4/24/2020; Bewley elected 4/24/2020. 28. Agard elected to replace Bewley on 11/15/2022. 29. Steineke resigned 7/27/2022; Tyler August elected 11/10/2022. 30. Hintz resigned and replaced by Neubauer effective 1/10/2022.

Sources: *Wisconsin Blue Book*, various editions; Senate and Assembly Journals; newspaper accounts.

Chief clerks and sergeants at arms of the Wisconsin legislature since 1848

	Senate		Assembly	
Session	Chief clerk	Sergeant at arms	Chief clerk	Sergeant at arms
1848......	Henry G. Abbey	Lyman H. Seaver	Daniel N. Johnson	John Mullanphy
1849......	William R. Smith	F. W. Shollner	Robert L. Ream	Felix McLinden
1850......	William R. Smith	James Hanrahan	Alex T. Gray	E. R. Hugunin
1851......	William Hull	E. D. Masters	Alex T. Gray	C. M. Kingsbury
1852......	John K. Williams	Patrick Cosgrove	Alex T. Gray	Elisha Starr
1853......	John K. Williams	Thomas Hood	Thomas McHugh	Richard F. Wilson
1854......	Samuel G. Bugh	J. M. Sherwood	Thomas McHugh	William H. Gleason
1855......	Samuel G. Bugh	William H. Gleason	David Atwood	William Blake
1856......	Byron Paine	Joseph Baker	James Armstrong	Egbert Mosely
1857......	William H. Brisbane	Alanson Filer	William C. Webb	William C. Rogers
1858......	John L. V. Thomas	Nathaniel L. Stout	L. H. D. Crane	Francis Massing
1859......	Hiram Bowen	Asa Kinney	L. H. D. Crane	Emmanuel Munk
1860......	J. H. Warren	Asa Kinney	L. H. D. Crane	Joseph Gates
1861......	J. H. Warren	J. A. Hadley	L. H. D. Crane	Craig B. Peebe
1862......	J. H. Warren	B. U. Caswell	John S. Dean	A. A. Huntington
1863......	Frank M. Stewart	Luther Bashford	John S. Dean	A. M. Thompson

Chief clerks and sergeants at arms of the Wisconsin legislature since 1848, continued

	Senate		Assembly	
Session	Chief clerk	Sergeant at arms	Chief clerk	Sergeant at arms
1864......	Frank M. Stewart	Nelson Williams	John S. Dean	A. M. Thompson
1865......	Frank M. Stewart	Nelson Williams	John S. Dean	Alonzo Wilcox
1866......	Frank M. Stewart	Nelson Williams	E. W. Young	L. M. Hammond
1867......	Leander B. Hills	Asa Kinney	E. W. Young	Daniel Webster
1868......	Leander B. Hills	W. H. Hamilton	E. W. Young	C. L. Harris
1869......	Leander B. Hills	W. H. Hamilton	E. W. Young	Rolin C. Kelly
1870......	Leander B. Hills	E. M. Rogers	E. W. Young	Ole C. Johnson
1871......	O. R. Smith	W. W. Baker	E. W. Young	Sam S. Fifield
1872......	J. H. Waggoner	W. D. Hoard	E. W. Young	Sam S. Fifield
1873......	J. H. Waggoner	Albert Emonson	E. W. Young	O. C. Bissel
1874......	J. H. Waggoner	O. U. Aiken	George W. Peck	Joseph Deuster
1875......	Fred A. Dennett	O. U. Aiken	R. M. Strong	J. W. Brackett
1876......	A. J. Turner	E. T. Gardner	R. M. Strong	Elisha Starr
1877......	A. J. Turner	C. E. Bullard	W. A. Nowell	Thomas B. Reid
1878......	A. J. Turner[1] Charles E. Bross[1]	L. J. Brayton	Jabez R. Hunter	Anton Klaus
1879......	Charles E. Bross	Chalmers Ingersoll	John E. Eldred	Miletus Knight
1880......	Charles E. Bross	Chalmers Ingersoll	John E. Eldred	D. H. Pulcifer
1881......	Charles E. Bross	W. W. Baker	John E. Eldred	G. W. Church
1882......	Charles E. Bross	A. T. Glaze	E. D. Coe	D. E. Welch
1883......	Charles E. Bross	A. D. Thorp	I. T. Carr	Thomas Kennedy
1885......	Charles E. Bross	Hubert Wolcott	E. D. Coe	John M. Ewing
1887......	Charles E. Bross	T. J. George	E. D. Coe	William A. Adamson
1889......	Charles E. Bross	T. J. George	E. D. Coe	F. E. Parsons
1891......	J. P. Hume	John A. Barney	George W. Porth	Patrick Whelan
1893......	Sam J. Shafer	John B. Becker	George W. Porth	Theodore Knapstein
1895......	Walter L. Houser	Charles Pettibone	W. A. Nowell	B. F. Millard
1897......	Walter L. Houser	Charles Pettibone	W. A. Nowell	C. M. Hambright
1899......	Walter L. Houser	Charles Pettibone	W. A. Nowell	James H. Agen
1901......	Walter L. Houser	Charles Pettibone	W. A. Nowell	A. M. Anderson
1903......	Theodore W. Goldin	Sanfield McDonald	C. O. Marsh	A. M. Anderson
1905......	L.K. Eaton	R. C. Falconer	C. O. Marsh	Nicholas Streveler
1907......	A. R. Emerson	R. C. Falconer	C. E. Shaffer	W. S. Irvine
1909......	F. E. Andrews	R. C. Falconer	C. E. Shaffer	W. S. Irvine
1911–13 ...	F. M. Wylie	C. A. Leicht	C. E. Shaffer	W. S. Irvine
1915......	O. G. Munson	F. E. Andrews	C. E. Shaffer	W. S. Irvine
1917......	O. G. Munson	F. E. Andrews	C. E. Shaffer	T. G. Cretney
1919......	O. G. Munson	John Turner	C. E. Shaffer	T. G. Cretney
1921......	O. G. Munson	Vincent Kielpinski	C. E. Shaffer	T. G. Cretney
1923......	F. W. Schoenfeld	C. A. Leicht	C. E. Shaffer	T. W. Bartingale
1925......	F. W. Schoenfeld	C. A. Leicht	C. E. Shaffer	C. E. Hanson
1927–29 ...	O. G. Munson	George W. Rickeman	C. E. Shaffer	C. F. Moulton
1931......	R. A. Cobban	Emil A. Hartman	C. E. Shaffer	Gustave Rheingans
1933......	R. A. Cobban	Emil A. Hartman	John J. Slocum	George C. Faust
1935–37 ...	Lawrence R. Larsen	Emil A. Hartman	Lester R. Johnson	Gustave Rheingans
1939......	Lawrence R. Larsen	Emil A. Hartman	John J. Slocum	Robert A. Merrill
1941–43 ...	Lawrence R. Larsen	Emil A. Hartman	Arthur L. May	Norris J. Kellman
1945......	Lawrence R. Larsen	Harold E. Damon	Arthur L. May	Norris J. Kellman
1947–53 ...	Thomas M. Donahue	Harold E. Damon	Arthur L. May	Norris J. Kellman
1955–57 ...	Lawrence R. Larsen	Harold E. Damon	Arthur L. May	Norris J. Kellman
1959......	Lawrence R. Larsen	Harold E. Damon	Norman C. Anderson	Thomas H. Browne
1961......	Lawrence R. Larsen	Harold E. Damon	Robert G. Marotz	Norris J. Kellman
1963......	Lawrence R. Larsen	Harold E. Damon	Kenneth E. Priebe	Norris J. Kellman
1965......	Lawrence R. Larsen[2] William P. Nugent[2]	Harold E. Damon	James P. Buckley	Thomas H. Browne
1967......	William P. Nugent	Harry O. Levander	Arnold W. F. Langner[3] Wilmer H. Struebing[3]	Louis C. Romell

Chief clerks and sergeants at arms of the Wisconsin legislature since 1848, continued

Session	Senate Chief clerk	Senate Sergeant at arms	Assembly Chief clerk	Assembly Sergeant at arms
1969	William P. Nugent	Kenneth Nicholson	Wilmer H. Struebing	Louis C. Romell
1971	William P. Nugent	Kenneth Nicholson	Thomas P. Fox	William F. Quick
1973	William P. Nugent	Kenneth Nicholson	Thomas S. Hanson	William F. Quick
1975	Glenn E. Bultman	Robert M. Thompson	Everett E. Bolle	Raymond J. Tobiasz
1977	Donald J. Schneider	Robert M. Thompson	Everett E. Bolle	Joseph E. Jones
1979	Donald J. Schneider	Daniel B. Fields	Marcel Dandeneau	Joseph E. Jones
1981	Donald J. Schneider	Daniel B. Fields	David R. Kedrowski	Lewis T. Mittness
1983	Donald J. Schneider	Daniel B. Fields	Joanne M. Duren	Lewis T. Mittness
1985	Donald J. Schneider	Daniel B. Fields	Joanne M. Duren	Patrick Essie
1987	Donald J. Schneider	Daniel B. Fields	Thomas T. Melvin	Patrick Essie
1989–91	Donald J. Schneider	Daniel B. Fields	Thomas T. Melvin	Robert G. Johnston
1993	Donald J. Schneider	Daniel B. Fields[4] Jon H. Hochkammer[4]	Thomas T. Melvin	Robert G. Johnston
1995	Donald J. Schneider	Jon H. Hochkammer	Thomas T. Melvin [5] Charles R. Sanders [5]	John A. Scocos
1997	Donald J. Schneider	Jon H. Hochkammer	Charles R. Sanders	John A. Scocos[6] Denise L. Solie[6]
1999	Donald J. Schneider	Jon H. Hochkammer	Charles R. Sanders	Denise L. Solie
2001	Donald J. Schneider	Jon H. Hochkammer[7]	John A. Scocos[7]	Denise L. Solie
2003	Donald J. Schneider[8] Robert J. Marchant[8]	Edward A. Blazel	Patrick E. Fuller	Richard A. Skindrud
2005–07	Robert J. Marchant	Edward A. Blazel	Patrick E. Fuller	Richard A. Skindrud
2009	Robert J. Marchant	Edward A. Blazel	Patrick E. Fuller	William M. Nagy
2011	Robert J. Marchant[9]	Edward A. Blazel	Patrick E. Fuller	Anne Tonnon Byers
2013–19	Jeffrey Renk	Edward A. Blazel	Patrick E. Fuller	Anne Tonnon Byers
2021–23	Michael Queensland	Tom Engels	Edward A. Blazel	Anne Tonnon Byers

1. Bross elected 2/6/1878; Turner resigned 2/7/1878. 2. Larsen died 3/2/1965; Nugent elected 3/31/1965. 3. Langner resigned 5/2/1967; Struebing elected 5/16/1967. 4. Fields served until 8/2/1993. Randall Radtke served as acting sergeant from 8/3/1993 to 11/3/1993. Hochkammer elected 1/25/1994. 5. Melvin retired 1/31/1995; Sanders elected 5/24/1995. 6. Scocos resigned 9/25/1997; Solie elected 1/15/1998. 7. Scocos resigned 2/25/2002. Hochkammer resigned 9/2002. No replacement was elected for either. 8. Schneider resigned 7/4/2003; Marchant elected 1/20/2004. 9. Marchant resigned 1/2/2012.

Sources: Wisconsin Legislative Reference Bureau, *Wisconsin Blue Book*, various editions; journals and organizing resolutions of each house.

Political composition of the Wisconsin legislature since 1885

Session[1]	Senate[2] Dem.	Senate[2] Rep.	Senate[2] Prog.	Senate[2] Soc.	Senate[2] Soc. Dem.	Assembly[3] Dem.	Assembly[3] Rep.	Assembly[3] Prog.	Assembly[3] Soc.	Assembly[3] Soc. Dem.
1885	13	20	—	—	—	39	61	—	—	—
1887	6	25	—	—	—	30	57	—	—	—
1889	6	24	—	—	—	29	71	—	—	—
1891	19	14	—	—	—	66	33	—	—	—
1893	26	7	—	—	—	56	44	—	—	—
1895	13	20	—	—	—	19	81	—	—	—
1897	4	29	—	—	—	8	91	—	—	—
1899	2	31	—	—	—	19	81	—	—	—
1901	2	31	—	—	—	18	82	—	—	—
1903	3	30	—	—	—	25	75	—	—	—
1905	4	28	—	—	1	11	85	—	—	4
1907	5	27	—	—	1	19	76	—	—	5

Political composition of the Wisconsin legislature since 1885, continued

Session[1]	Senate[2] Dem.	Rep.	Prog.	Soc.	Soc. Dem.	Assembly[3] Dem.	Rep.	Prog.	Soc.	Soc. Dem.
1909	4	28	—	—	1	17	80	—	—	3
1911	4	27	—	—	2	29	59	—	—	12
1913	9	23	—	—	1	37	57	—	—	6
1915	11	21	—	—	1	29	63	—	—	8
1917	6	24	—	3	—	14	79	—	7	—
1919	2	27	—	4	—	5	79	—	16	—
1921	2	27	—	4	—	2	92	—	6	—
1923	—	30	—	3	—	1	89	—	10	—
1925	—	30	—	3	—	1	92	—	7	—
1927	—	31	—	2	—	3	89	—	8	—
1929	—	31	—	2	—	6	90	—	3	—
1931	1	30	—	2	—	2	89	—	9	—
1933	9	23	—	1	—	59	13	24	3	—
1935	13	6	14	—	—	35	17	45	3	—
1937	9	8	16	—	—	31	21	48	—	—
1939	6	16	11	—	—	15	53	32	—	—
1941	3	24	6	—	—	15	60	25	—	—
1943	4	23	6	—	—	14	73	13	—	—
1945	6	22	5	—	—	19	75	6	—	—
1947	5	27	1	—	—	11	88	—	—	—
1949	3	27	—	—	—	26	74	—	—	—
1951	7	26	—	—	—	24	75	—	—	—
1953	7	26	—	—	—	25	75	—	—	—
1955	8	24	—	—	—	36	64	—	—	—
1957	10	23	—	—	—	33	67	—	—	—
1959	12	20	—	—	—	55	45	—	—	—
1961	13	20	—	—	—	45	55	—	—	—
1963	11	22	—	—	—	46	53	—	—	—
1965	12	20	—	—	—	52	48	—	—	—
1967	12	21	—	—	—	47	53	—	—	—
1969	10	23	—	—	—	48	52	—	—	—
1971	12	20	—	—	—	67	33	—	—	—
1973	15	18	—	—	—	62	37	—	—	—
1975	18	13	—	—	—	63	36	—	—	—
1977	23	10	—	—	—	66	33	—	—	—
1979	21	10	—	—	—	60	39	—	—	—
1981	19	14	—	—	—	59	39	—	—	—
1983	17	14	—	—	—	59	40	—	—	—
1985	19	14	—	—	—	52	47	—	—	—
1987	19	11	—	—	—	54	45	—	—	—
1989	20	13	—	—	—	56	43	—	—	—
1991	19	14	—	—	—	58	41	—	—	—
1993[4]	15	15	—	—	—	52	47	—	—	—
1995[4]	16	17	—	—	—	48	51	—	—	—
1997[4]	17	16	—	—	—	47	52	—	—	—
1999	17	16	—	—	—	44	55	—	—	—
2001	18	15	—	—	—	43	56	—	—	—
2003	15	18	—	—	—	41	58	—	—	—
2005	14	19	—	—	—	39	60	—	—	—
2007	18	15	—	—	—	47	52	—	—	—
2009	18	15	—	—	—	52	46	—	—	—
2011[5]	14	19	—	—	—	38	60	—	—	—
2013	15	18	—	—	—	39	59	—	—	—
2015	14	18	—	—	—	36	63	—	—	—
2017	13	20	—	—	—	35	64	—	—	—

Political composition of the Wisconsin legislature since 1885, continued

Session[1]	Senate[2] Dem.	Rep.	Prog.	Soc.	Soc. Dem.	Assembly[3] Dem.	Rep.	Prog.	Soc.	Soc. Dem.
2019	14	19	—	—	—	36	63	—	—	—
2021	12	20	—	—	—	38	60	—	—	—
2023	11	21	—	—	—	35	64	—	—	—

Note: The number of assembly districts was reduced from 100 to 99 beginning in 1973. There have been 33 senate districts since 1862. Any deviation of a session's total from these numbers indicates vacant seats or miscellaneous affiliations (described in notes 2 and 3 below).

— Represents zero; Dem.–Democrat; Prog.–Progressive; Rep.–Republican; Soc.–Socialist; Soc. Dem.–Social Democrat.

1. Political composition at inauguration. 2. Miscellaneous affiliations for senate seats not shown in the table are: one Independent and one People's (1887); one Independent and two Union Labor (1889). 3. Miscellaneous affiliations for assembly seats not shown: three Independent, four Independent Democrat, and six People's (1887); one Union Labor (1891); one Fusion (1897); one Independent (1929, 2009, 2011); one Independent Republican (1933). 4. In the 1993, 1995, and 1997 Legislatures, majority control of the senate shifted during the session. On 4/20/1993, vacancies were filled resulting in a total of 16 Democrats and 17 Republicans; on 6/16/1996, there were 17 Democrats and 16 Republicans; on 4/19/1998, there were 16 Democrats and 17 Republicans. 5. A series of recall elections during the session resulted in a switch in majority control of the senate, with 17 Democrats and 16 Republicans as of 7/16/2012.

Sources: Pre-1943 data compiled from the Secretary of State, *Officers of Wisconsin: U.S., State, Judicial, Congressional, Legislative and County Officers*, 1943 and prior editions, and the *Wisconsin Blue Book*, various editions. Later data compiled from Wisconsin Legislative Reference Bureau records.

Wisconsin legislative sessions since 1848

	Opening/final adjournment	Calendar days[1]	Bills	Joint res.	Res.	Bills vetoed[2] (overridden)	Laws enacted
1848	6/5–8/21	78	217	—	—	—	155
1849	1/10–4/2	83	428	—	—	2 (1)	220
1850	1/9–2/11	34	438	—	—	1	284
1851	1/8–3/17	69	707	—	—	9	407
1852	1/14–4/19	97	813	—	—	3 (1)	504
1853	1/12–7/13	183	1,145	—	—	6	521
1854	1/11–4/3	83	880	—	—	2	437
1855	1/10–4/2	83	955	—	—	6	500
1856	1/9–10/14	288	1,242	—	—	1	688
1857	1/14–3/9	55	895	—	—	—	517
1858	1/13–5/17	125	1,364	157	342	28	436
1859	1/12–3/21	69	986	113	143	9	680
1860	1/11–4/2	83	1,024	69	246	2	489
1861	1/9–4/17	99	857	100	235	2	387
1861 SS	5/15–5/27	13	28	24	34	—	15
1862	1/8–6/17	161	1,008	125	207	36[3] (8)	514
1862 SS	9/10–9/26	17	43	25	37	—	17
1863	1/14–4/2	79	895	101	157	10 (1)	383
1864	1/13–4/4	83	835	66	141	—	509
1865	1/11–4/10	90	1,132	82	190	2	565
1866	1/10–4/12	93	1,107	64	208	5	733
1867	1/9–4/11	93	1,161	97	161	2	790
1868	1/8–3/6	59	987	73	119	2 (2)	692
1869	1/13–3/11	58	887	52	81	14 (1)	657
1870	1/12–3/17	65	1,043	54	89	2	666
1871	1/11–3/25	74	1,066	55	82	4	671
1872	1/10–3/26	77	709	79	124	2	322
1873	1/8–3/20	72	611	62	122	4	308
1874	1/14–3/12	58	688	91	111	2	349

Wisconsin legislative sessions since 1848, continued

	Opening/final adjournment	Calendar days[1]	Measures introduced Bills	Joint res.	Res.	Bills vetoed[2] (overridden)	Laws enacted
1875	1/13–3/6	53	637	39	93	2	344
1876	1/12–3/14	63	715	57	115	2	415
1877	1/10–3/8	58	720	59	95	4	384
1878	1/9–3/21	72	735	79	134	2	342
1878 SS	6/4–6/7	4	6	14	10	—	5
1879	1/8–3/5	57	610	49	105	—	256
1880	1/14–3/17	64	669	58	93	3	323
1881	1/12–4/4	83	780	104	100	6	334
1882	1/11–3/31	80	728	57	90	6	330
1883	1/10–4/4	85	705	75	100	2	360
1885	1/14–4/13	90	963	97	108	8	471
1887	1/12–4/15	94	1,293	114	60	10	553
1889	1/9–4/19	101	1,355	136	82	6 (1)	529
1891	1/14–4/25	102	1,216	137	91	10 (1)	483
1892 SS	6/28–7/1	4	4	7	16	—	1
1892 SS	10/17–10/27	11	8	6	14	—	2
1893	1/11–4/21	101	1,124	135	86	6	312
1895	1/9–4/20	102	1,154	139	88	—	387
1896 SS	2/18–2/28	11	3	11	15	—	1
1897	1/13–8/20	220	1,077	155	39	19 (1)	381
1899	1/11–5/4	114	910	113	40	3	357
1901	1/9–5/15	127	1,091	81	39	24	470
1903	1/14–5/23	130	1,115	65	81	23	451
1905	1/11–6/21	162	1,357	134	101	22	523
1905 SS	12/4–12/19	16	24	15	26	—	17
1907	1/9–7/16	189	1,685	205	84	28 (1)	677
1909	1/13–6/18	157	1,567	213	49	22	550
1911	1/11–7/15	186	1,710	267	37	15	665
1912 SS	4/30–5/6	7	41	7	6	—	22
1913	1/8–8/9	214	1,847	175	79	24	778
1915	1/13–8/24	224	1,560	220	79	15	637
1916 SS	10/10–10/11	2	2	8	4	—	2
1917	1/10–7/16	188	1,439	229	115	18	679
1918 SS	2/19–3/9	19	27	22	28	2	16
1918 SS	9/24–9/25	2	2	6	9	—	2
1919	1/8–7/30	204	1,350	268	100	39	703
1919 SS	9/4–9/8	5	7	4	6	—	7
1920 SS	5/25–6/4	11	46	10	22	2	32
1921	1/12–7/14	184	1,199	207	93	41 (1)	591
1922 SS	3/22–3/28	7	10	7	12	1	4
1923	1/10–7/14	186	1,247	215	93	52	449
1925	1/14–6/29	167	1,144	200	115	73	454
1926 SS	4/15–4/16	2	1	8	12	—	1
1927	1/12–8/13	214	1,341	235	167	90 (2)	542
1928 SS	1/24–2/4	12	20	35	23	—	5
1928 SS	3/6–3/13	8	13	9	17	—	2
1929	1/9–9/20	255	1,366	278	185	44	530
1931	1/14–6/27	165	1,429	291	160	56	487
1931 SS	11/24/31–2/5/32	74	99	93	83	2	31
1933	1/11–7/25	196	1,411	324	157	15	496
1933 SS	12/11/33–2/3/34	55	45	160	53	—	20
1935	1/9–9/27	262	1,662	346	190	27	556
1937	1/13–7/2	171	1,404	228	127	10	432
1937 SS	9/15–10/16	32	28	18	23	—	15
1939	1/11–10/6	269	1,559	268	133	22	535
1941	1/8–6/6	150	1,368	160	109	17	333
1943	1/13/43–1/22/44	375	1,153	202	136	39 (20)	577
1945	1/10–9/6	240	1,156	208	109	30 (5)	590

Wisconsin legislative sessions since 1848, continued

	Opening/final adjournment	Calendar days[1]	Measures introduced Bills	Joint res.	Res.	Bills vetoed[2] (overridden)	Laws enacted
1946 SS	7/29–7/30	2	2	6	14	—	2
1947	1/8–9/11	247	1,220	195	97	10 (1)	615
1948 SS	7/19–7/20	2	—	5	11	—	—
1949	1/12–9/13	245	1,432	188	86	17 (2)	643
1951	1/10–6/14	156	1,559	157	73	18	735
1953	1/14–11/6	297	1,593	175	70	31 (3)	687
1955	1/12–10/21	283	1,503	256	74	38	696
1957	1/9–9/27	262	1,512	246	71	35 (1)	706
1958 SS	6/11–6/13	3	3	7	13	—	3
1959	1/14/59–5/27/60	500	1,769	272	84	36 (4)	696
1961	1/11/61–1/9/63	729	1,592	295	68	70 (2)	689
1963	1/9/63–1/13/65	736	1,619	241	110	72 (4)	580
1963 SS	12/10–12/12	3	8	10	10	—	3
1965[4]	1/13/65–1/2/67	720	1,818	293	86	24 (1)	666
1967	1/11/67–1/6/69	727	1,700	215	61	18	355
1969	1/6/69–1/4/71	729	2,014	232	101	34 (1)	501
1969 SS[5]	9/29/69–1/17/70	111	5	5	8	—	1
1970 SS	12/22	1	—	1	5	—	—
1971	1/4/71–1/1/73	729	2,568	291	121	32 (3)	336
1972 SS	4/19–4/28	10	9	4	4	—	6
1973	1/1/73–1/6/75	736	2,501	277	126	13	332
1973 SS	12/17–12/21	5	3	2	6	—	2
1974 SS	4/29–6/13	46	12	1	4	—	6
1974 SS	11/19–11/20	2	2	—	—	—	1
1975	1/6/75–1/3/77	729	2,325	169	88	36 (6)	414
1975 SS	12/9–12/11	3	13	1	2	1	6
1976 SS	5/18	1	2	2	3	—	1
1976 SS	6/15–6/17	3	13	4	3	—	9
1976 SS	9/8	1	4	1	4	—	2
1977	1/3/77–1/3/79	730	2,053	182	48	21 (4)	442
1977 SS	6/30	1	—	1	2	—	—
1977 SS	11/7–11/11	5	6	4	2	—	5
1978 SS	6/13–6/15	3	2	5	2	—	2
1978 SS	12/20	1	2	4	2	—	2
1979[6]	1/3/79–1/5/81	734	1,920	203	40	19 (3)	350
1979 SS	9/5	1	10	3	2	—	5
1980 SS	1/22–1/25	4	8	3	2	—	—
1980 SS	6/3– 7/3	31	20	14	2	—	7
1981[7]	1/5/81–1/3/83	729	1,987	176	70	10 (2)	381
1981 SS	11/4–11/17	14	6	3	2	—	3
1982 SS	4/6–5/20	45	4	2	2	1	1
1982 SS	5/26–5/28	3	13	7	2	—	9
1983	1/3/83–1/7/85	736	1,902	173	50	3	521
1983 SS	1/4–1/6	3	2	2	1	—	2
1983 SS	4/12–4/14	3	1	1	—	—	1
1983 SS	7/11–7/14	4	5	3	1	—	4
1983 SS	10/18–10/28	11	12	1	—	—	11
1984 SS	2/2–4/4	63	2	1	—	—	—
1984 SS	5/22–5/24	3	12	5	1	—	11
1985	1/7/85–1/5/87	729	1,624	171	41	7	293
1985 SS	3/19–3/21	3	6	1	—	—	3
1985 SS	9/24–10/19	26	22	1	—	—	17
1985 SS	10/31	1	1	3	—	—	1
1985 SS	11/20	1	24	2	—	—	12
1986 SS	1/27–5/30	124	1	4	—	—	1
1986 SS	3/24–3/26	3	1	1	—	—	1
1986 SS	5/20–5/29	10	44	3	—	—	12
1986 SS	7/15	1	3	1	—	—	2

Wisconsin legislative sessions since 1848, continued

	Opening/final adjournment	Calendar days[1]	Measures introduced Bills	Joint res.	Res.	Bills vetoed[2] (overridden)	Laws enacted
1987[8]	1/5/87–1/3/89	730	1,631	196	21	35	413
1987 SS	9/15–9/16	2	2	1	—	—	2
1987 SS	11/18/87–6/7/88	203	19	3	—	3	5
1988 SS	6/30	1	4	1	3	—	2
1989[9]	1/3/89–1/7/91	735	1,557	244	45	35	361
1989 SS	10/10/89–3/22/90	164	52	6	—	—	7
1990 SS	5/15/90	1	7	1	—	—	—
1991[10]	1/7/91–1/4/93	729	1,676	244	32	33	318
1991 SS	1/29/–7/4	157	16	1	—	—	2
1991 SS	10/15/91–5/21/92	220	9	2	—	—	1
1992 SS	4/14–6/4	52	7	1	2	—	2
1992 SS	6/1	1	—	2	—	—	—
1992 SS	8/25–9/15	22	1	1	2	—	1
1993[11]	1/4/93–1/3/95	730	2,147	207	47	8	491
1994 SS	5/18–5/19	2	6	1	—	—	3
1994 SS	6/7–6/23	17	3	4	—	—	3
1995	1/3/95–1/6/97	735	1,780	163	38	4	467
1995 SS	1/4	1	1	1	—	—	1
1995 SS	9/5–10/12	36	1	1	—	—	1
1997[12]	1/6/97–1/4/99	729	1,508	183	30	3	333
1998 SS	4/21–5/21	31	13	2	2	—	5
1999[13]	1/4/99–1/3/01	731	1,498	168	52	5	196
1999 SS	10/27–11/11	16	3	1	—	—	1
2000 SS	5/4–5/9	8	2	2	1	—	1
2001	1/3/01–1/6/03	734	1,436	174	75	—	106
2001 SS	5/1–5/3	3	1	—	—	—	1
2002 SS	1/22–7/8	168	1	2	7	—	1
2002 SS	5/13–5/15	3	2	—	—	—	1
2003[14]	1/6/03–1/3/05	729	1,567	164	78	54	326
2003 SS	1/30–2/20	22	1	—	—	—	1
2005[15]	1/3/05–1/3/07	731	1,967	196	76	47	489
2005 SS	1/12–1/20	9	2	—	—	—	1
2006 SS	2/14–3/7	22	2	—	—	—	1
2007	1/3/07–1/5/09	733	1,574	230	50	1	239
2007 SS	1/11–2/1	22	2	1	—	—	1
2007 SS	10/15–10/23	9	2	—	—	—	—
2007 SS	12/11/07–5/14/08	156	1	1	—	—	—
2008 SS	3/12–5/14	65	1	4	2	—	1
2008 SS	4/17–5/15	29	1	4	2	—	1
2009[16]	1/5/09–1/3/11	729	1,720	221	44	6	406
2009 SS	6/24–6/27	4	1	—	—	—	—
2009 SS	12/16–3/4/10	79	2	—	—	—	—
2011[17]	1/3/11–1/7/13	735	1,325	211	48	—	267
2011 SS	1/4–9/27	267	27	1	3	—	12
2011 SS	9/29–12/8	71	48	—	—	—	7
2013	1/7/13–1/5/15	730	1,627	214	37	1	373
2013 SS	10/10–11/12	34	8	—	—	—	4
2013 SS	12/2–12/19	18	2	—	—	—	1
2014 SS	1/23–3/20	57	4	—	—	—	2
2015[18]	1/5/15–1/3/17	730	1,830	236	45	2	392
2017[19]	1/3/17–1/7/19	735	1,960	237	39	—	349
2017 SS	1/5–6/14	161	22	—	—	—	11
2017 SS	8/1–9/15	46	2	—	1	—	1
2018 SS	1/18–2/27	41	20	—	—	—	9
2018 SS	3/15–3/29	15	6	—	—	—	—
2019[20]	1/7/19–1/4/21	729	1,970	264	29	20	186
2019 SS	11/7	1	—	—	—	—	—
2020 SS	1/28–4/14	78	16	—	—	—	—

Wisconsin legislative sessions since 1848, continued

	Opening/final adjournment	Calendar days[1]	Measures introduced Bills	Joint res.	Res.	Bills vetoed[2] (overridden)	Laws enacted
2020 SS	2/11–2/25	15	—	—	—	—	—
2020 SS	4/4–4/8	5	—	—	—	—	—
2020 SS	4/7–4/8	2	—	—	—	—	—
2020 SS	8/31–12/22	114	—	—	—	—	—
2021[21]	1/4/21–1/3/23	730	2,305	266	46	126	266
2021 SS	1/19–2/23	36	2	—	—	—	1
2021 SS	5/25	1	—	—	—	—	—
2021 SS	7/27	1	—	—	—	—	—
2022 SS	3/8	1	—	—	—	—	—
2022 SS	6/22	1	—	—	—	—	—
2022 SS	10/4	1	—	—	—	—	—

— Represents zero; Res.–Resolution; SS–Special session.

1. Number of calendar days from opening date of the session to final adjournment. 2. Partial vetoes not included. See executive vetoes table. 3. Does not include 18 bills that the lieutenant governor asserted had been vetoed by pocket veto when the governor, to whom they had been sent, died without signing them. 4. Although 1965 Legislature adjourned to 1/11/67, terms automatically expired on 1/2/67. 5. Senate adjourned the special session 11/15/69; assembly, 1/17/70. 6. Extraordinary session held in January 1980. 7. Extraordinary session held in December 1981. 8. Extraordinary sessions held in February, September, and November 1987 and April, May, and June 1988. 9. Extraordinary session held in May 1990. 10. Extraordinary session held in April 1992. 11. Extraordinary session held in June 1994. 12. Extraordinary session held in April 1998. 13. Extraordinary session held in May 2000. 14. Extraordinary sessions held in February, July, August, and December 2003 and March, May, and July 2004. 15. Extraordinary sessions held in July 2005 and April 2006. 16. Extraordinary sessions held in February, May, June, and December 2009 and December 2010. 17. Extraordinary sessions held in June and July 2011. 18. Extraordinary sessions held in February, July, and November 2015. 19. Extraordinary sessions held in March, April, November, and December 2018. 20. Extraordinary sessions held in February 2019 and April 2020. 21. Extraordinary sessions held in February and June 2021.

Sources: *Bulletin of the Proceedings of the Wisconsin Legislature*, various editions; Senate and Assembly Journals.

Wisconsin special session calls since 1848

	Main purpose
1861 May	Civil War powers.
1862 September	Militia organization; soldiers' right to vote; Indian uprising; payment to military office employees.
1878 June	Revision of general statutes; tornado damage.
1892 June	Legislative apportionment.
1892 October	Legislative apportionment.
1896 February	Legislative apportionment.
1905 December	Railroad regulation; primary election law.
1912 April	Black River Falls flooding.
1916 October	Absentee voting by soldiers.
1918 February	War economy.
1918 September	Reserve officers training facilities.
1919 September	Soldiers rehabilitation funds.
1920 May	Cost of living; medical education; educational standards.
1922 March	Income tax administration.
1926 April	Indemnities for cattle with tuberculosis.
1928 January	Appropriations for state colleges and public welfare.
1928 March	Appropriations for charitable and penal institutions.
1931 November	Unemployment; apportionment.
1933 December	Prohibition repeal.
supplementary	Operation of banks.

Statistics and Reference: Historical lists | 503

Wisconsin special session calls since 1848, continued

	Main purpose
supplementary . .	Extension of property tax payment deadline; Milwaukee County circuit court; drainage districts; reimbursement of Firemen's Association; student loans.
supplementary . .	Banking operations.
supplementary . .	School districts; public deposits; delinquent banks.
1937 September . .	Economic emergency relief; tax revisions; highway safety.
supplementary . .	Agricultural marketing; creation of a Department of Commerce; old-age assistance; chain stores; unfair trade practices; housing programs.
supplementary . .	Government reorganization; Milwaukee school tax levy; employment of minors.
1946 July	Rent control; veterans housing; state personnel salaries and state government operation.
1948 July	Veterans housing.
1958 June	Unemployment compensation; general relief for poor; state residency; urban renewal.
1962 June	Legislative and congressional apportionment.
1963 December . . .	Accelerated construction of state freeway system.
supplementary . .	Additional courts; state purchase of Menominee Enterprise securities; constitutional amendment procedure.
1969 September . .	Urban problems; public welfare; state assistance to Marquette Medical School; revenues.
1970 December . . .	Confirmation of appointments.
1972 April	Legislative apportionment.
supplementary . .	Full train crew law; ratification of U.S. equal rights amendment; charge account usury; revisor's bills.
1973 December . . .	Emergency energy regulations; shared tax distribution.
1974 April	Budget review bill; merger of the University of Wisconsin and the state universities; campaign finance reform; power plant siting; supplemental retirement benefits for teachers; youthful offenders program; reorganization of Department of Transportation; cable television; studded tires.
supplementary . .	Supplemental retirement benefits for teachers.
1974 November . . .	Collective bargaining agreements for state employees.
1975 December . . .	Reorganization of Department of Transportation; presidential primary; power of condemnation for VTAE districts; collective bargaining agreements for state employees.
1976 May	Unemployment compensation.
1976 June	Open meetings law; influenza immunization; recodification of mental health laws; taxpayer funding of election campaigns.
supplementary . .	Creation of council on migrant labor; clean election campaign fund.
1976 September . .	Collective bargaining agreements for state employees.
supplementary . .	Agricultural water diversion permits.
1977 June	Partial vetoes.
1977 November . . .	State personnel procedures; driving under the influence of intoxicants.
supplementary . .	Confirmation of appointments.
1978 June	Various changes concerning the courts.
supplementary . .	Veterans home loan program.
1978 December . . .	Confirmation of appointments.
supplementary . .	Special election laws.
1979 September . .	Collective bargaining agreements for state employees; salary adjustments for elected state officials.
supplementary . .	Open presidential primary.
1980 January	Felonies committed with a dangerous weapon; constitutional amendment to deny release on bail; mandatory minimum sentences; restricting probation and parole.
1980 June	Denying bail; executive branch reorganization; low and moderate income neighborhood investment and home ownership program.
1981 November . . .	Soil and water conservation; school cost controls; gift and estate taxes; property tax credit; veterans trust fund.
supplementary . .	Usury laws.

Wisconsin special session calls since 1848, continued

	Main purpose
1982 April	State finances; constitutional amendment to earmark sales tax for educational property tax relief.
supplementary	Unemployment compensation.
supplementary	Legislative apportionment.
1982 May	Judicial salaries; relief for needy Indian persons; early retirement for state employees.
supplementary	Milwaukee prison site.
1983 January	Sales and cigarette taxes; special elections.
supplementary	Extension of budget introduction submission.
1983 April	Unemployment compensation.
1983 July	Legislative apportionment; tax incremental finance joint review board.
supplementary	Confirmation of appointments; consideration of vetoes.
supplementary	Nonrepresented classified state employee compensation plan.
1983 October	Wisconsin Housing Finance Authority; trade office; permit Information Center; rulemaking for small businesses; utility holding companies.
1984 February	State property tax relief; reducing surtaxes.
1984 May	Group deer hunting; domestic abuse; nursing home payroll record inspection.
supplementary	Financial assistance for septic systems.
1985 March	Emergency loan processing centers; animal waste pollution; Wisconsin Housing and Economic Development Authority agricultural production loans.
1985 September	Strategic planning council; water diversion; funding for business development; UW tuition and fall start date; education and employment projects; utility diversification.
1985 October	Alcohol beverage laws.
1985 November	Collective bargaining agreements for state employees; Martin Luther King Jr. holiday.
1986 January	Appropriations; Homestead Tax relief.
1986 March	Higher Educational Aids Board; alcohol fuels; farm credit mediation and arbitration; Wisconsin Housing and Economic Development Authority agricultural loans; specialty crop cultivation.
1986 May	Raising legal drinking age to 21; UW–Madison indoor athletic practice facility; patients compensation fund; cocaine penalties; mandatory vehicle insurance; intoxicated driving penalties.
1986 July	Labor training program.
supplementary	Highway improvements.
1987 September	Corporate hostile takeovers.
supplementary	Corporate hostile takeovers.
1987 November	Homestead tax credit and farmland preservation credit; AFDC employment and training programs.
supplementary	Obscenity; parole and probation for crimes punishable by life imprisonment; spearfishing law enforcement aids; school tax credit.
supplementary	Wisconsin Retirement System; local property tax limits; local government dispute settlement procedure.
supplementary	Wisconsin Retirement System; limiting property tax levies and state and local expenditures; local government dispute settlement procedures.
1988 June	Drought relief; water diversion for agricultural purposes.
1989 October	Illicit drug use and alcohol abuse.
supplementary	Controlled substances and drug paraphernalia, drug courts, judge substitution in criminal drug violations; correctional institutions, probation, parole; alcohol and drug abuse prevention and treatment.
supplementary	Expansion of farmland tax credit.
supplementary	Vaccinations; ratification of union contract.
supplementary	State employee health insurance program; state employee reimbursement for damaged personal articles.
supplementary	Controlled substances; lottery proceeds and school property tax credits; levy restraint payment to municipalities and counties; tort reform; lobbying and the ethics code; economic development for 18 northern counties and Indian tribes; mutual aid law enforcement services; juvenile detention.

Wisconsin special session calls since 1848, continued

	Main purpose
supplementary . .	Business improvement loan guarantee program; technical assistance and grants to municipalities and tribal governing bodies; tourism promotion; spearfishing law enforcement aid.
1990 May	Ratification of state employee contracts.
1991 January	Crime control: Minimum sentences for crimes involving dangerous weapons and controlled substance offenses; gun-free school zones; concealed weapon penalties; drug paraphernalia.
1991 October	Education reform: Recommendations of the Commission on Schools for the 21st Century; statewide pupil achievement tests and minimum competency program; compliance with state education standards; children-at-risk services; a statewide pupil database.
supplementary . .	Education reform: Extending the school year; staff development; school management restructuring; grants for science and mathematics programs; postsecondary enrollment options program; community service work as part of the high school curriculum; school district consolidation incentives; teacher exchange programs; truancy abatement and suppression; suspension and expulsion; pupil evaluation of teachers; pupil assessment.
1992 April	Restricting gambling conducted by the state; wagering on out-of-state simulcasts at pari-mutuel racetracks; grants for research on or the treatment of compulsive gambling.
1992 June	Consider a constitutional amendment to distinguish the state lottery from prohibited gambling, to limit "lottery," and to prohibit lottery expansion to other games.
1992 August	Confirmation of appointments.
supplementary . .	Refinancing existing public debt.
1994 May	Controlled substance violations; paternity and child support; civil commitment of sexually violent persons; sex offender registration and notice of release.
1994 June	Testing criminal defendants for HIV infection; regulation of the telecommunications industry.
supplementary . .	County and district fair aids.
supplementary . .	Confirmation of an appointment.
1995 January	Ratification of state employee labor contract.
1995 September . .	Local professional baseball park districts.
supplementary . .	Financing for local professional baseball park districts and sports and entertainment home stadia; funding for state highway rehabilitation.
1998 April	Criminal code and sentences; Milwaukee Public Schools governance and administration; election law.
supplementary . .	Excluding agricultural transactions from provisions of the Wisconsin Consumer Act; DNR legislation; tax credits for sales paid on fuel and electricity used in manufacturing; food stamps for qualified aliens; changing requirements for organ donation requirements.
supplementary . .	Additional legislation related to Milwaukee Public Schools.
1999 October	Tax rebate; school property tax credit.
2001 May	Property tax relief.
2002 May	Wetlands water quality.
2002 January	Budget reform legislation to adress economic downturn.
2002 May	Chronic Wasting Disease in Wisconsin deer.
supplementary . .	Hunting regulations.
2003 January	Decreasing appropriations; lapsing monies from certain program revenue accounts to the general fund; transferring monies from segregated accounts to the general fund; increasing funding for out-of-state inmate contracts and for health care of state prison inmates; increasing funding for Medical Assistance and BadgerCare; increasing funding for land acquisition and development under the stewardship program; restricting distribution of funds by the Tobacco Control Board; lapsing or reestimating expenditures from certain general purpose revenue appropriations; exempting legislative actions from the required general fund structural balance and statutory balance.
2005 January	Public debt to finance tax-supported or self-amortizing facilities.

Wisconsin special session calls since 1848, continued

	Main purpose
2006 February....	Low-income energy assistance.
2007 January	Creating a Government Accountability Board; laws relating to elections, ethics, and lobbying regulations.
2007 October	State finances and appropriations relating to the 2007 budget act.
2007 December...	Campaign financing and various election-related laws.
2008 March	State finances and appropriations.
2008 April	Great Lakes-St. Lawrence River Basin water issues.
2009 June	Hospital assessment and medical assistance.
2009 December...	General public school district curriculum and administration and governance and administration of Milwaukee Public School District.
2011 January	Creation of Wisconsin Economic Development Corporation; various tax and business development-related matters; administrative rules issues; limiting noneconomic damages awards in certain lawsuits; and health savings accounts.
supplementary ..	Increasing the amount of credits under the economic development tax credit program.
supplementary ..	The Budget Repair Bill.
supplementary ..	Regulation of telecommunications utilities.
supplementary ..	LRB 2035/3 and LRB 2181/1.
2011 September ..	Early stage seed and angel investment tax credits and other business, agricultural, and community development and taxation matters; multi-jurisdictional tax incremental financing districts; wetlands, habitat, and navigable waterways matters; Department of Revenue duties; vocational and technical skills education; individual income taxes relating to medical care and mass transit expenses; seasonal vehicle weight limits for transporting agricultural crops and other laws relating to overweight and overlength vehicles; attorney fees; immunity from liability for certain drug and device manufacturers; trespassing; interest rates on judgment in certain civil actions.
2013 October	Property tax relief to certain school districts; municipal tax incremental financing districts; historic preservation tax credits.
2013 December...	Delaying effective dates of BadgerCare and the Health Insurance Risk-Sharing Plan.
2014 January	Various employment-related technical training and workforce education.
2017 January	Legislation related to opioid abuse.
2017 August.....	Promotion of economic development and job retention.
2018 January	Legislation related to welfare reform.
2018 March	Legislation related to school security and safety.
2019 November...	Legislation related to gun violence.
2020 January	Legislation related to farm relief.
2020 February....	Legislation related to school aids.
2020 April	Provide for an all-mail spring election and special election due to COVID-19.
2020 April II	Set a new in-person voting date for the 2020 spring election due to COVID-19.
2020 August.....	Use of force by law enforcement.
2021 January	Legislation related to unemployment insurance modernization.
2021 May	Legislation to expand BadgerCare and fund various initiatives.
2021 July........	Legislation related to funding for education.
2022 March	Legislation to spend surplus dollars for various social programs.
2022 June	Legislation to eliminate abortion prohibitions.
2022 October.....	Constitutional amendment to provide for binding referenda and ballot initiatives

Source: Assembly and Senate Journals, Governor's Proclamations and Executive Orders.

Wisconsin extraordinary session calls since 1980

	Month	Principal subject of original and expanded calls
1979–80...	Jan. 1980	Various bills related to: crime and crime victims; energy conservation; firearms.
1981–82...	Dec. 1981	Redistricting; collective bargaining contracts; compensation of elected officials.

Wisconsin extraordinary session calls since 1980, continued

	Month	Principal subject of original and expanded calls
1987–88. . .	Feb. 1987	Gov. Thompson's budget address.
	Sept. 1987	Partial vetoes of budget bill (SB 100).
	Nov. 1987	Full vetoes of two bills (AB 462 & AB 677).
	Apr. 1988	Budget; retirement; taxes and property tax relief; local government.
	May 1988	Local government; property tax relief; retirement.
	June 1988	Limiting governor's partial veto powers; drought relief.
1989–90. . .	May 1990	Collective bargaining contracts; property tax relief; state compensation plan; general relief.
1991–92. . .	Apr. 1992	Congressional and legislative redistricting; lottery and gambling; lottery tax credit; collective bargaining contracts; juvenile detention; open records law.
1993–94. . .	June 1994	Sports lottery.
1997–98. . .	Apr. 1998	Election of officers; ratification of state employee contracts; budget review legislation; revival of regular session proposals; gubernatorial nominations for appointment.
1999–2000 .	May 2000	Collective bargaining contracts; revisor's correction bills; reconciliation bill relating to public debt limit for housing state departments and agencies.
2003–04 . .	Feb. 2003	Legislative approval of Indian gaming compacts (SB 41).
	July 2003	Lowering prohibited alcohol concentration in drunk driving to 0.08 (AB 88); promissory notes issued by the city of Milwaukee to pay for unfunded prior service liability contributions under the Wisconsin Retirement System (SB 77).
	Aug. 2003	Partial veto of budget bill (SB 44); school district revenue limits and levy limits for cities, villages, towns, counties, and technical college districts (AB 466).
	Dec. 2003	Zoning; navigable waters; public utilities.
	Mar. 2004	Consideration of various bills.
	May 2004	Adopting federal law as it relates to health savings accounts for state income tax purposes; Medical Assistance Program and Community Aids Program funding; legislative approval of Indian gaming compacts.
	July 2004	School and local government funding and spending.
2005–06 . .	July 2005	Ratification of state employee collective bargaining contracts; paid vacation leave for certain nonrepresented state employees.
	Apr. 2006	Consideration of several bills.
2009–10 . .	Feb. 2009	State finances and appropriations; diverse changes in the statutes.
	May 2009	Unemployment insurance benefits; confidentiality of pupil records; residential energy improvement programs (AB 255 & SB 189).
	June 2009	Payment of state school aid (SB 232).
	Dec. 2009	Operation of a motor vehicle while under the influence of an intoxicant (SB 66).
	Dec. 2010	State employee collective bargaining contracts.
2011–12 . .	June 2011	Biennial budget bill (SB 40 & AB 27).
	July 2011	Consideration of various bills.
2015–16 . .	Feb. 2015	Right to work (SB 44 & AB 61).
	July 2015	Consideration of various bills.
	Nov. 2015	Consideration of various bills.
2017–18 . .	Mar. 2018	Consideration of various bills.
	Apr. 2018	Absentee ballots cast by overseas and military voters (AB 947).
	Nov. 2018	Tax credits for Kimberly-Clark paper products manufacturing plant (AB 963).
	Dec. 2018	Consideration of various bills.
2019–20 . .	Feb. 2019	Gov. Evers's budget address.
	Apr. 2020	COVID-19 bill (AB 1038).
2021–22 . .	Feb. 2021	COVID-19 bill (AB 1) and termination of the COVID-19 public health emergency (AJR 4 & SJR 3).
	June 2021	Consideration of various bills and a full veto of one bill (AB 336).

Source: Assembly and Senate Journals.

Executive vetoes in Wisconsin since 1931

Session	Bills vetoed (overridden)	Bills partially vetoed (overridden)	Biennial budget bill partial vetoes[1] (overridden)
1931.	58	2	12
1933.	15	1	12
1935.	27	4	—
1937.	10	1	—
1939[2].	22	4	1
1941.	17	1	1
1943.	39 (20)	1 (1)	—
1945.	30 (5)	2 (1)	1
1947.	10 (1)	1	1
1949.	17 (2)	2 (1)	—
1951.	18	—	—
1953[3].	31 (3)	4	2
1955.	38	—	—
1957.	35 (1)	3	2
1959.	36 (4)	1	—
1961.	70 (2)	3	2
1963.	72 (4)	1	—
1965.	24 (1)	4	1
1967.	18	5	—
1969.	34 (1)	11	27
1971.	32 (3)	8	12
1973.	13	18 (3)	38 (2)
1975.	37 (6)	22 (4)	42 (5)
1977.	21 (4)	16 (3)	67 (21)
1979.	19 (3)	9 (2)	45 (1)
1981[4].	11 (2)	11 (1)	121
1983.	3	11 (1)	70 (6)
1985.	7	7 (1)	78 (2)
1987.	38	20	290
1989.	35	28	208
1991.	33	13	457
1993.	8	24	78
1995.	4	21	112
1997.	3	8	152
1999.	5	10	255
2001.	—	3	315
2003.	54	10	131
2005.	47	2	139
2007.	1	4	33
2009.	6	5	81
2011.	—	3	50
2013.	1	4	57
2015.	2	5	104
2017.	—	4	98
2019.	20	2	78
2021.	126	1	50

— Represents zero.

1. The number of individual veto statements in the governor's veto message. 2. Attorney general ruled veto of 1939 SB-43 was void and it became law (see Vol. 28, *Opinions of the Attorney General*, p. 423). 3. 1953 AB-141, partially vetoed in two separate sections by separate veto messages, is counted as one. 4. Attorney general ruled several vetoes "ineffective" because the governor failed to express his objections (see Vol. 70, *Opinions of the Attorney General*, p. 189).

Source: *Bulletin of the Proceedings of the Wisconsin Legislature*, various editions; Senate and Assembly Journals.

Proposed Wisconsin constitutional amendments since 1854

Article	Section	Subject	Election result	Vote totals	Date	Proposed amendment
IV	4	Assemblymen, 2-year terms	rejected	6,549–11,580	Nov. 1854	1854 Ch. 89
IV	5	Senators, 4-year terms	rejected	6,348–11,885	Nov. 1854	1854 Ch. 89
IV	11	Biennial legislative sessions	rejected	6,752–11,589	Nov. 1854	1854 Ch. 89
IV	5	Governor's salary, changed from $1,250 to $2,500 a year	rejected	14,519–32,612	Nov. 1862	1862 JR 6
IV	21	Change legislators' pay to $350 a year	ratified	58,363–24,418	Nov. 1867	1866 JR 3
V	5	Change governor's salary from $1,250 to $5,000 a year	ratified	47,353–41,764	Nov. 1869	1869 JR 2
V	9	Change lieutenant governor's salary to $1,000 a year	ratified	47,353–41,764	Nov. 1869	1869 JR 2
I	8	Grand jury system modified	ratified	48,894–18,606	Nov. 1870	1870 JR 3
IV	31, 32	Private and local laws, prohibited on 9 subjects	ratified	54,087–3,675	Nov. 1871	1871 JR 1
VII	4	Supreme court, 1 chief and 4 associate justices	rejected	16,272–29,755	Nov. 1872	1872 JR 8
XI	3	Indebtedness of municipalities limited to 5%	ratified	66,061–1,509	Nov. 1874	1873 JR 4
VII	4	Supreme court, 1 chief and 4 associate justices	ratified	79,140–16,763	Nov. 1877	1877 JR 1
VIII	2	Claims against state, 6-year limit	ratified	33,046–3,371	Nov. 1877	1877 JR 4
IV	4, 5, 11	Biennial sessions; assemblymen 2-year, senators 4-year terms	ratified	53,532–13,936	Nov. 1881	1881 AJR 7[1]
IV	21	Change legislators' pay to $500 a year	ratified	53,532–13,936	Nov. 1881	1881 AJR 7[1]
III	1	Voting residence 30 days; in municipalities voter registration	ratified	36,223–5,347	Nov. 1882	1882 JR 5
VI	4	County officers except judicial, vacancies filled by appointment	ratified	60,091–8,089	Nov. 1882	1882 JR 3
VII	12	Clerk of court, full term election	ratified	60,091–8,089	Nov. 1882	1882 JR 3
XIII	1	Political year; biennial elections	ratified	60,091–8,089	Nov. 1882	1882 JR 3
X	1	State superintendent, qualifications and pay fixed by legislature	rejected	12,967–18,342	Nov. 1888	1887 JR 4
VII	4	Supreme court, composed of 5 justices of supreme court	ratified	125,759–14,712	Apr. 1889	1889 JR 3
IV	31	Cities incorporated by general law	ratified	15,718–9,015	Nov. 1892	1891 JR 4
X	1	State superintendent, pay fixed by law	rejected	38,752–56,506	Nov. 1896	1895 JR 2
VII	7	Circuit judges, additional in populous counties	ratified	45,823–41,513	Apr. 1897	1897 JR 9
X	1	State superintendent, nonpartisan 4-year term, pay fixed by law	ratified	71,550–57,411	Nov. 1902	1901 JR 3
XI	4	General banking law authorized	ratified	64,836–44,620	Nov. 1902	1901 JR 2
XI	5	Banking law referenda requirement repealed	ratified	64,836–44,620	Nov. 1902	1901 JR 2
XIII	11	Free passes prohibited	ratified	67,781–40,697	Nov. 1902	1901 JR 9
VII	4	Supreme court, 7 justices, 10-year terms	ratified	51,377–39,857	Apr. 1903	1903 JR 7
III	1	Suffrage for full citizens only	ratified	85,838–36,733	Nov. 1908	1907 JR 25
V	10	Governor's approval of bills in 6 days	ratified	85,958–27,270	Nov. 1908	1907 JR 13
VIII	1	Income tax	ratified	85,696–37,729	Nov. 1908	1907 JR 29
VIII	10	Highways, appropriations for	ratified	116,421–46,739	Nov. 1908	1907 JR 18
IV	3	Apportionment after each federal census	ratified	54,932–52,634	Nov. 1910	1909 JR 55
IV	21	Change legislators' pay to $1,000 a year	rejected	44,153–76,278	Nov. 1910	1909 JR 7

Proposed Wisconsin constitutional amendments since 1854, continued

Article	Section	Subject	Election result	Vote totals	Date	Proposed amendment
VIII	10	Water power and forests, appropriations for [2]	rejected	62,468-45,924 [2]	Nov. 1910	1909 Ch. 514
VII	10	Judges' salaries, time of payment	ratified	44,855-34,865	Nov. 1912	1911 JR 24
XI	3	City or county debt for lands, discharge within 50 years	ratified	46,369-34,975	Nov. 1912	1911 JR 42
XI	3a	Public parks, playgrounds, etc.	ratified	48,424-33,931	Nov. 1912	1911 JR 48
IV	1	Initiative and referendum	rejected	84,934-148,536	Nov. 1914	1913 JR 22
IV	21	Change legislators' pay to $600 a year, 2 cents a mile for additional round trips	rejected	68,907-157,202	Nov. 1914	1913 JR 24
VII	6,7	Judicial circuits, decreased number, additional judges	rejected	63,311-154,827	Nov. 1914	1913 JR 26
VIII	—	State annuity insurance	rejected	59,909-170,338	Nov. 1914	1913 JR 35
VIII	—	State insurance	rejected	58,490-165,966	Nov. 1914	1913 JR 12
XI	—	Home rule of cities and villages	rejected	86,020-141,472	Nov. 1914	1913 JR 21
XI	—	Municipal power of condemnation	rejected	61,122-154,945	Nov. 1914	1913 JR 25
XII	1	Constitutional amendments, submission after 3/5 approval by one legislature	rejected	71,734-160,761	Nov. 1914	1913 JR 17
XII	—	Constitution amended upon petition	rejected	68,435-150,215	Nov. 1914	1913 JR 22
XIII	—	Recall of civil officers	rejected	81,628-144,386	Nov. 1914	1913 JR 15
IV	21	Legislators' pay fixed by law	rejected	126,243-132,258	Apr. 1920	1919 JR 37
VII	6,7	Judicial circuits, decreased number, additional judges	rejected	113,786-116,436	Apr. 1920	1919 JR 92
I	5	Jury verdict, 5/6 in civil cases	ratified	171,433-156,820	Nov. 1922	1921 JR 17
VI	4	Sheriffs, no limit on successive terms	rejected	161,832-207,594	Nov. 1922	1921 JR 36
XI	—	Municipal indebtedness for public utilities	rejected	105,234-219,639	Nov. 1922	1921 JR 37
IV	21	Change legislators' pay to $750 a year	rejected	189,635-250,236	Apr. 1924	1923 JR 18
VII	7	Circuit judges, additional in populous counties	ratified	240,207-226,562	Nov. 1924	1923 JR 64
VIII	10	Forestry, appropriations for	ratified	336,360-173,563	Nov. 1924	1923 JR 57
XI	3	Home rule for cities and villages	ratified	299,792-190,165	Nov. 1924	1923 JR 34
V	5	Governor's salary fixed by law	ratified	202,156-188,302	Nov. 1926	1925 JR 52
XIII	12	Recall of elective officials	ratified	205,868-201,125	Nov. 1926	1925 JR 16
IV	21	Change legislators' pay to $1,000 for session	rejected	151,786-199,260	Apr. 1927	1927 JR 12
VIII	1	Severance tax: forests, minerals	ratified	179,217-141,888	Apr. 1927	1927 JR 13
IV	21	Legislators' salary repealed; to be fixed by law	ratified	237,250-212,846	Apr. 1929	1929 JR 6
VI	4	Sheriffs succeeding themselves for 2 terms	ratified	259,881-210,964	Apr. 1929	1929 JR 13
V	10	Item veto on appropriation bills	ratified	252,655-153,703	Nov. 1930	1929 JR 43
V	5	Governor's salary provision repealed; fixed by law	ratified	452,605-275,175	Nov. 1932	1931 JR 52
V	9	Lieutenant governor's salary repealed; fixed by law	ratified	427,768-267,120	Nov. 1932	1931 JR 53
VII	1	Wording of section corrected	ratified	436,113-221,563	Nov. 1932	1931 JR 58
XI	3	Municipal indebtedness for public utilities	ratified	401,194-279,631	Nov. 1932	1931 JR 71

Statistics and Reference: Historical lists | 511

Art	Sec	Subject	Outcome	Vote	Submitted	Source
III	1	Women's suffrage	ratified	411,088–166,745	Nov. 1934	1933 JR 76
XIII	11	Free passes, permitted as specified	ratified	365,971–361,799	Nov. 1936	1935 JR 98
VIII	1	Installment payment of real estate taxes	ratified	330,971–134,808	Apr. 1941	1941 JR 18
VII	15	Justice of peace, abolish office in first class cities	ratified	160,965–113,408	Apr. 1945	1945 JR 2
VIII	10	Aeronautical program	ratified	187,111–101,169	Apr. 1945	1945 JR 3
VI	4	Sheriffs, no limit on successive terms	rejected	121,144–170,131	Apr. 1946	1945 JR 47
IV	33	Auditing of state accounts	ratified	480,938–308,072	Nov. 1946	1945 JR 73
VI	2	Auditing (part of same proposal)	ratified	480,938–308,072	Nov. 1946	1945 JR 73
X	3	Public transportation of school children to any school	rejected	437,817–545,475	Nov. 1946	1945 JR 78
XI	2	Repeal; relating to exercise of eminent domain by municipalities	rejected	210,086–807,318	Nov. 1948	1947 JR 48
II	2	Prohibition on taxing federal lands repealed	rejected	245,412–297,237	Apr. 1949	1949 JR 2
VIII	10	Allow internal improvement debt for veterans' housing	ratified	311,576–290,736	Apr. 1949	1949 JR 1
II	2	Prohibition on taxing federal lands repealed	ratified	305,612–186,284	Apr. 1951	1951 JR 7
XI	3	City debt limit 8% for combined city and school purposes	ratified	313,739–191,897	Apr. 1951	1951 JR 6
IV	3, 4, 5	Apportionment based on area and population[3]	rejected	433,043–406,133 [3]	Apr. 1953	1953 JR 9
VII	9	Judicial elections to full terms	ratified	386,972–345,094	Apr. 1953	1953 JR 12
VII	24	Judges: qualifications, retirement	ratified	380,214–177,929	Apr. 1955	1953 JR 14
XI	3	School debt limit, equalized value	ratified	320,376–228,641	Apr. 1955	1955 JR 12
IV	26	Teachers' retirement benefits	ratified	365,560–255,284	Apr. 1956	1955 JR 17
VI	4	Sheriffs, no limit on successive terms	rejected	269,722–328,603	Apr. 1956	1955 JR 53
XI	3a	Municipal acquisition of land for public purposes	ratified	376,692–193,544	Apr. 1956	1955 JR 36
XIII	11	Free passes, not for public use	ratified	188,715–380,207	Apr. 1956	1955 JR 54
VIII	10	Port development	ratified	472,177–451,045	Apr. 1960	1959 JR 15
XI	3	Debt limit in populous counties, 5% of equalized valuation	ratified	686,104–529,467	Nov. 1960	1959 JR 32
IV	26	Salary increases during term for various public officers	rejected	297,066–307,575	Apr. 1961	1961 JR 11
IV	34	Continuity of civil government	ratified	498,869–132,728	Apr. 1961	1961 JR 10
VI	4	Sheriffs, no limit on successive terms	rejected	283,495–388,238	Apr. 1961	1961 JR 9
VIII	1	Personal property classified for tax purposes	ratified	381,881–220,434	Apr. 1961	1961 JR 13
XI	2	Municipal eminent domain, abolished jury verdict of necessity	ratified	348,406–259,566	Apr. 1961	1961 JR 12
IV	3	Debt limit 10% of equalized valuation for integrated aid school district	ratified	409,963–224,783	Apr. 1961	1961 JR 8
IV	3	"Indians not taxed" exclusion removed from apportionment formula	ratified	631,296–259,577	Nov. 1962	1961 JR 32
VI	23	County executive: 4-year term	ratified	527,075–331,393	Nov. 1962	1961 JR 64
VI	4	County executive: 2-year terms	ratified	527,075–331,393	Nov. 1962	1961 JR 64
IV	23a	County executive veto power	ratified	524,240–319,378	Nov. 1962	1961 JR 64
IV	3	Time for apportionment of seats in the state legislature	rejected	232,851–277,014	Apr. 1963	1963 JR 9
IV	26	Salary increases during term for justices and judges	rejected	216,205–335,774	Apr. 1963	1963 JR 7
XI	3	Equalized value debt limit	ratified	285,296–231,702	Apr. 1963	1963 JR 8
VIII	10	Maximum state appropriation for forestry increased	rejected	440,978–536,724	Apr. 1964	1963 JR 32
XII	3	Property valuation for debt limit adjusted	rejected	336,994–572,276	Apr. 1964	1963 JR 33
XII	1	Constitutional amendments, submission of related items in a single proposition	rejected	317,676–582,045	Apr. 1964	SS 1963 JR 1[4]

Proposed Wisconsin constitutional amendments since 1854, continued

Article	Section	Subject	Election result	Vote totals	Date	Proposed amendment
VI	4	Coroner and surveyor abolished in counties of 500,000	ratified	380,059–215,169	Apr. 1965	1965 JR 5
IV	24	Lotteries, definition revised	ratified	454,390–194,327	Apr. 1965	1965 JR 2
IV	13	Legislators on active duty in armed forces	ratified	362,935–189,641	Apr. 1966	1965 JR 14
VII	2	Establishment of inferior courts	ratified	321,434–216,341	Apr. 1966	1965 JR 50
VII	15	Justices of the peace abolished	ratified	321,434–216,341	Apr. 1966	1965 JR 51
XI	3	Special district public utility debt limit	ratified	307,502–199,919	Apr. 1966	1965 JR 58
I	23	Transportation of children to private schools	ratified	494,236–377,107	Apr. 1967	1967 JR 13
IV	26	Judicial salary increased during term	ratified	489,989–328,292	Apr. 1967	1967 JR 17
V	1m, 1n	4-year term for governor and lieutenant governor	ratified	534,368–310,478	Apr. 1967	1967 JR 10
V	3	Joint election of governor and lieutenant governor	ratified	507,339–312,267	Apr. 1967	1967 JR 11
VI	1m	4-year term for secretary of state	ratified	520,326–311,974	Apr. 1967	1967 JR 14
VI	1n	4-year term for state treasurer	ratified	514,280–314,873	Apr. 1967	1967 JR 10
VI	1p	4-year term for attorney general	ratified	515,962–311,603	Apr. 1967	1967 JR 10
VI	4	Sheriffs, no limit on successive terms	ratified	508,242–324,544	Apr. 1967	1967 JR 12
IV	11	Legislative sessions, more than one permitted in biennium	ratified	670,757–267,997	Apr. 1968	1967 JR 48
VII	24	Uniform retirement date for justices and circuit judges	ratified	734,046–215,455	Apr. 1968	1967 JR 56
VII	24	Temporary appointment of justices and circuit judges	ratified	678,249–245,807	Apr. 1968	1967 JR 56
VIII	10	Forestry appropriation from sources other than property tax	ratified	652,705–286,512	Apr. 1969	1967 JR 25
IV	23	Uniform county government modified	ratified	326,445–321,851	Apr. 1969	1969 JR 2
IV	23a	County executive to have veto power	ratified	326,445–321,851	Apr. 1969	1969 JR 3
VIII	7	State public debt for specified purposes allowed	ratified	411,062–258,366	Apr. 1969	1969 JR 27
I	24	Private use of school buildings	ratified	871,707–298,016	Apr. 1972	1971 JR 27
IV	23	County government systems authorized	ratified	571,285–515,255	Apr. 1972	1971 JR 13
VI	4	Coroner/medical examiner option	ratified	795,497–323,930	Apr. 1972	1971 JR 21
X	3	Released time for religious instruction	ratified	595,075–585,511	Apr. 1972	1971 JR 28
I	25	Equality of the sexes	rejected	447,240–520,936	Apr. 1973	1973 JR 5
IV	24	Charitable bingo authorized	ratified	645,544–391,499	Apr. 1973	1973 JR 3
IV	26	Increased benefits for retired public employees	ratified	396,051–315,545	Apr. 1974	1973 JR 15
VI	13	Removal of judges by 2/3 vote of legislature for cause	ratified	493,496–193,867	Apr. 1974	1973 JR 25
VIII	1	Taxation of agricultural lands	ratified	353,377–340,518	Apr. 1974	1973 JR 29
VIII	3, 7	Public debt for veterans' housing	ratified	385,915–300,232	Apr. 1975	1975 JR 3
VIII	7, 10	Internal improvements for transportation facilities[5]	rejected	342,396–341,291[5]	Apr. 1975	1975 JR 2

Statistics and Reference: Historical lists | 513

Art.	Sec.	Description	Result	Vote	Date	Source
XI	3	Exclusion of certain debt from municipal debt limit	rejected	310,434–337,925	Apr. 1975	1973 JR 133
XIII	2	Dueling: repeal of disenfranchisement	ratified	395,616–282,726	Apr. 1975	1975 JR 4
XI	3	Municipal indebtedness increased up to 10% of equalized valuation	rejected	328,097–715,420	Apr. 1976	1975 JR 6
VIII	7(2)(a), 10	Internal improvements for transportation facilities [5]	rejected	722,658–935,152	Nov. 1976 [5]	1975 JR 2
IV	24	Charitable raffle games authorized	ratified	483,518–300,473	Apr. 1977	1977 JR 6
VII	2	Unified court system [also affected I 21; IV 17, 26; VII 3–11, 14, 16–23; XIV 16(1)–(4)]	ratified	490,437–215,939	Apr. 1977	1977 JR 7
VII	5	Court of appeals created [also affected I 21(1); VII 2, 3(3); XIV 16(5)]	ratified	455,350–229,316	Apr. 1977	1977 JR 7
VII	11, 13	Court system disciplinary proceedings	ratified	565,087–151,418	Apr. 1977	1977 JR 7
VII	24	Retirement age for justices and judges set by law	ratified	506,207–244,170	Apr. 1977	1977 JR 7
IV	23	Town government uniformity	rejected	179,011–383,395	Apr. 1978	1977 JR 18
V	7, 8	Gubernatorial succession	ratified	538,959–187,440	Apr. 1979	1979 JR 3
XIII	10	Lieutenant governor vacancy	ratified	540,186–181,497	Apr. 1979	1979 JR 3
IV	9	Senate presiding officer	ratified	372,734–327,008	Apr. 1979	1979 JR 3
V	1	4-year constitutional officer terms (improved wording) [also affected V 1m, 1n; VI 1, 1m, 1n, 1p]	ratified	533,620–164,768	Apr. 1979	1979 JR 3
I	8	Right to bail [6]	ratified	505,092–185,405 [6]	Apr. 1981	1981 JR 8
XI	1, 4	Obsolete corporation and banking provisions	ratified	418,997–186,898	Apr. 1981	1981 JR 9
XI	3	Indebtedness period for sewage collection or treatment systems	ratified	386,792–250,866	Apr. 1981	1981 JR 7
XIII	12	Obsolete 1881 amendment reference	ratified	366,635–259,820	Apr. 1981	1981 JR 6
VI	4	Counties responsible for acts of sheriff	ratified	316,156–219,752	Apr. 1982	1981 JR 15
I	1, 18	Gender-neutral wording [also affected X 1, 2]	ratified	771,267–479,053	Nov. 1982	1981 JR 29
XI	3	Military personnel treatment in redistricting	ratified	834,188–321,331	Nov. 1982	1981 JR 29
IV	4, 5	Primaries in recall elections	ratified	919,349–238,884	Nov. 1982	1981 JR 29
IV	30	Elections by legislature	ratified	977,438–193,679	Nov. 1982	1981 JR 29
X	1	Obsolete reference to election and term of superintendent of public instruction	ratified	934,236–215,961	Nov. 1982	1981 JR 29
X	2	Obsolete reference to military draft exemption purchase; school fund	ratified	887,488–295,693	Nov. 1982	1981 JR 29
XIV	16(1)	Obsolete transition from territory to statehood [also affected XIV 4–12; XIV 14, 15]	ratified	926,875–223,213	Nov. 1982	1981 JR 29
XIV	16(4)	Obsolete transitional provisions of 1977 court reorganization [also affected XIV 16(2), (3), (5)]	ratified	882,091–237,698	Nov. 1982	1981 JR 29
XIV	1	Terms on supreme court effective date provision	ratified	960,540–190,366	Nov. 1982	1981 JR 29
I	1	Rewording to parallel Declaration of Independence	ratified	419,699–65,418	Apr. 1986	1985 JR 21
III	1–6	Revision of suffrage defined by general law	ratified	401,911–83,183	Apr. 1986	1985 JR 14
XIII	1	Modernizing constitutional text	ratified	404,273–82,512	Apr. 1986	1985 JR 14
XIII	5	Obsolete suffrage right on Indian land	ratified	381,339–102,090	Apr. 1986	1985 JR 14
IV	24(5)	Permitting pari-mutuel on-track betting	ratified	580,089–529,729	Apr. 1987	1987 JR 3
IV	24(6)	Authorizing the creation of a state lottery	ratified	739,181–391,942	Apr. 1987	1987 JR 4
VIII	1	Authorizing income tax credits or refunds for property or sales taxes	rejected	405,765–406,863	Apr. 1989	1989 JR 2
V	10	Redefining the partial veto power of the governor	ratified	387,068–252,481	Apr. 1990	1989 JR 39
V	10	Providing housing for persons of low or moderate income	rejected	295,823–402,921	Apr. 1991	1991 JR 2
VIII	7(2)(a)1	Railways and other railroad facilities [also created VIII 10]	ratified	650,592–457,690	Apr. 1992	1991 JR 9
IV	26	Legislative and judiciary compensation, effective date	ratified	736,832–348,645	Apr. 1992	1991 JR 13

Proposed Wisconsin constitutional amendments since 1854, continued

Article	Section	Subject	Election result	Vote totals	Date	Proposed amendment
VIII	1	Residential property tax reduction	rejected	675,876–1,536,975	Nov. 1992	1991 JR 14
I	9m	Crime victims	ratified	861,405–163,087	Apr. 1993	1993 JR 2
IV	24	Gambling, limiting "lottery"; divorce under general law [also affected IV 31, 32]	ratified	623,987–435,180	Apr. 1993	1993 JR 3
I	3	Removal of unnecessary references to masculine gender [also affected I 3, 7, 9, 19, 21(2); IV 6, 12, 13, 23a; V 4, 6; VI 2; VII 1, 12; XI 3a; XIII 4, 11, 12(6)]	rejected	412,032–498,801	Apr. 1995	1995 JR 3
IV	24(6)(a)	Authorizing sports lottery dedicated to athletic facilities	rejected	348,818–618,377	Apr. 1995	1995 JR 2
VII	10(1)	Removal of restriction on judges holding nonjudicial public office after resignation during the judicial term	rejected	390,744–503,239	Apr. 1995	1995 JR 4
XIII	3	Eligibility to seek or hold public office if convicted of a felony or a misdemeanor involving violation of a public trust	ratified	1,292,934–543,516	Nov. 1996	1995 JR 28
I	25	Guaranteeing the right to keep and bear arms	ratified	1,205,873–425,052	Nov. 1998	1997 JR 21
VI	4(1), (3), (5), (6)	4-year term for sheriff; sheriffs permitted to hold nonpartisan office; allowed legislature to provide for election to fill vacancy during term	ratified	1,161,942–412,508	Nov. 1998	1997 JR 18
IV	24(3), (5), (6)	Distributing state lottery, bingo and pari-mutuel proceeds for property tax	ratified	648,903–105,976	Apr. 1999	1999 JR 2
I	26	Right to fish, hunt, trap, and take game	ratified	668,459–146,182	Apr. 2003	2003 JR 8
VI	4(1), (3), (4)	4-year term for county clerks, treasurers, clerks of circuit court, district attorneys, coroners, elected surveyors, and registers of deeds [also affected VII 12]	ratified	534,742–177,037	Apr. 2005	2005 JR 2
XIII	13	Marriage between one man and one woman	ratified	1,264,310–862,924	Nov. 2006	2005 JR 30
V	10(1)(c)	Gubernatorial partial veto power	ratified	575,582–239,613	Apr. 2008	2007 JR 26
IV	9(2)	Department of transportation and transportation fund [also created VIII 11]	ratified	1,733,101–434,806	Nov. 2014	2013 JR 1
VIII	1	Election of chief justice of the supreme court	ratified	433,533–384,503	Apr. 2015	2015 JR 2
VI	1,3	Elimination of state treasurer [also affected X 7, 8 and XIV 17]	rejected	363,562–586,134	Apr. 2018	2017 JR 7
I	9m	Additional rights of crime victims	ratified	1,107,067–371,013	Apr. 2020	2019 JR 3
I	8(2)	Conditions of release before conviction	ratified	1,163,303–584,624	Apr. 2023	2023 JR 2
I	8(2)	Cash bail before conviction	ratified	1,186,025–569,286	Apr. 2023	2023 JR 2

Note: To amend the Wisconsin Constitution, two consecutive legislatures must adopt an identical amendment (known as "first consideration" and "second consideration") and a majority of the electorate must ratify the amendment at a subsequent election. See Art. XII, Sec. 1. Since the adoption of the Wisconsin Constitution in 1848, the electorate has voted 200 times on whether to amend the constitution, including one vote that was later resubmitted by the legislature and two votes that were declared invalid by the courts. 148 of these proposed amendments have been ratified.

AJR–Assembly Joint Resolution; Ch.–Chapter; JR–Joint resolution; SS–Special session.

1. No other number was assigned to this joint resolution. 2. Ratified but declared invalid by Supreme Court in *State v. Donald*, 160 Wis. 21 (1915). 3. Ratified but declared invalid by Supreme Court in *State ex rel. Thomson v. Zimmerman*, 264 Wis. 644 (1953). 4. Special session December 1964. 5. Recount resulted in rejection (342,132 to 342,309). However, the Dane County Circuit Court ruled the recount invalid due to election irregularities and required that the referendum be resubmitted to the electorate. Resubmitted November 1976 by the 1975 Wisconsin Legislature through Ch. 224, s.145r, Laws of 1975. 6. As a result of a Dane County Circuit Court injunction, vote totals were certified April 7, 1982, by the Board of State Canvassers.

Sources: Official records of the Wisconsin Elections Commission; *Laws of Wisconsin*, 2021 and prior volumes.

Wisconsin statewide referenda other than constitutional amendments since 1849

Subject	Election result	Vote totals	Date	Submitting legislation
Extend suffrage to colored persons [1]	Approved	5,265–4,075	Nov. 1849	1849 Ch. 137
State banks; advisory	Approved	31,289–9,126	Nov. 1851	1851 Ch. 143
General banking law	Approved	32,826–8,711	Nov. 1852	1852 Ch. 479
Liquor prohibition; advisory	Approved	27,519–24,109	Nov. 1853	1853 Ch. 101
Extend suffrage to colored persons	Rejected	28,235–41,345	Nov. 1857	1857 Ch. 44
Amend general banking law; redemption of bank notes	Approved	27,267–2,837	Nov. 1858	1858 Ch. 98
Amend general banking law; circulation of bank notes	Approved	57,646–2,515	Nov. 1861	1861 Ch. 242
Amend general banking law; interest rate 7% per year	Approved	46,269–7,794	Nov. 1862	1862 Ch. 203
Extend suffrage to colored persons [1]	Rejected	46,588–55,591	Nov. 1865	1865 Ch. 414
Amend general banking law; taxing shareholders	Approved	49,714–19,151	Nov. 1866	1866 Ch. 102
Amend general banking law; winding up circulation	Approved	45,796–11,842	Nov. 1867	1866 Ch. 143; 1867 Ch. 12
Abolish office of bank comptroller	Approved	15,499–1,948	Nov. 1868	1868 Ch. 28
Incorporation of savings banks and savings societies	Approved	4,029–3,069	Nov. 1876	1876 Ch. 384
Women's suffrage upon school matters	Approved	43,581–38,998	Nov. 1886	1885 Ch. 211
Revise 1897 banking law; banking department under commission	Rejected	86,872–92,607	Nov. 1898	1897 Ch. 303
Primary election law	Approved	130,366–80,102	Nov. 1904	1903 Ch. 451
Pocket ballots and coupon voting systems	Approved	45,958–111,139	Apr. 1906	1905 Ch. 522
Women's suffrage	Rejected	135,545–227,024	Nov. 1912	1911 Ch. 227
Soldiers' bonus financed by 3-mill property tax and income tax	Approved	165,762–57,324	Sept. 1919	1919 Ch. 667
Wisconsin prohibition enforcement act	Approved	419,309–199,876	Nov. 1920	1919 Ch. 556
U.S. prohibition act (Volstead Act); memorializing Congress to amend	Approved	349,443–177,603	Nov. 1926	1925 JR 47
Repeal of Wisconsin prohibition enforcement act; advisory	Approved	350,337–196,402	Nov. 1926	1925 JR 47
Modification of Wisconsin prohibition enforcement act; advisory	Approved	321,688–200,545	Apr. 1929	1929 JR 16
County distribution of auto licenses; advisory	Rejected	183,716–368,674	Apr. 1931	1931 JR 11
Sunday blue law repeal; advisory	Approved	396,436–271,786	Apr. 1932	1931 JR 114
Old-age pensions; advisory	Approved	531,915–154,729	Apr. 1934	SS 1933 JR 64
Teacher tenure law repeal; advisory	Approved	403,782–372,524	Apr. 1940	1939 JR 100
Property tax levy for high school aid; 2 mills of assessed valuation	Rejected	131,004–410,315	Apr. 1944	1943 Ch. 525
Daylight saving time; advisory	Rejected	313,091–379,740	Apr. 1947	1947 JR 4
3% retail sales tax for veterans bonus; advisory	Rejected	258,497–825,990	Nov. 1948	1947 JR 62
4-year term for constitutional officers; advisory	Rejected	210,821–328,613	Apr. 1951	1951 JR 13
Apportionment of legislature by area and population; advisory	Rejected	689,615–753,092	Nov. 1952	1951 Ch. 728

Wisconsin statewide referenda other than constitutional amendments since 1849, continued

Subject	Election result	Vote totals	Date	Submitting legislation
New residents entitled to vote for president and vice president.	Approved	550,056–414,680	Nov. 1954	1953 Ch. 76
Statewide educational television tax-supported; advisory	Rejected	308,385–697,262	Nov. 1954	1953 JR 66
Daylight saving time.	Approved	578,661–480,656	Apr. 1957	1957 Ch. 6
Ex-residents entitled to vote for president and vice president	Approved	627,279–229,375	Nov. 1962	1961 Ch. 512
Gasoline tax increase for highway construction; advisory.	Rejected	150,769–889,364	Apr. 1964	SS 1963 JR 3
New residents entitled to vote after 6 months.	Approved	582,389–256,246	Nov. 1966	1965 Chs. 88,89
State control and funding of vocational education; advisory.	Rejected	292,560–409,789	Apr. 1969	1969 JR 4
Recreational lands bonding; advisory.	Approved	361,630–322,882	Apr. 1969	1969 JR 5
Water pollution abatement bonding; advisory	Approved	446,763–246,968	Apr. 1969	1969 JR 5
New residents entitled to vote after 10 days	Approved	1,017,887–660,875	Nov. 1976	1975 Ch. 85
Presidential voting revised.	Approved	782,181–424,386	Nov. 1978	1977 Ch. 394
Overseas voting revised.	Approved	658,289–524,029	Nov. 1978	1977 Ch. 394
Public inland lake protection and rehabilitation districts	Approved	1,210,452–355,024	Nov. 1980	1979 Ch. 299
Nuclear weapons moratorium and reduction; advisory.	Approved	641,514–205,018	Sept. 1982	1981 JR 38
Nuclear waste site locating; advisory	Rejected	78,327–628,414	Apr. 1983	1983 JR 5
Gambling casinos on excursion vessels; advisory	Rejected	465,432–604,289	Apr. 1993	1991 WisAct 321
Gambling casino restrictions; advisory.	Approved	646,827–416,722	Apr. 1993	1991 WisAct 321
Video poker and other forms of video gambling allowed; advisory.	Rejected	358,045–702,864	Apr. 1993	1991 WisAct 321
Pari-mutuel on-track betting continuation; advisory.	Approved	548,580–507,403	Apr. 1993	1991 WisAct 321
State-operated lottery continuation; advisory.	Approved	773,306–287,585	Apr. 1993	1991 WisAct 321
Extended suffrage in federal elections to adult children of U.S. citizens living abroad	Approved	1,293,458–792,975	Nov. 2000	1999 WisAct 182
Death penalty; advisory.	Approved	1,166,571–934,508	Nov. 2006	2005 JR 58
Welfare benefits; advisory	Approved	1,417,035–363,941	Apr. 2023	2023 JR 3

Note: Statewide referendum questions are submitted to the electorate by the Wisconsin Legislature: 1) to ratify a law extending the right of suffrage (as required by the state constitution); 2) to ratify a law that has been passed contingent on voter approval; or 3) to seek voter opinion through an advisory referendum. Since 1848, the Wisconsin Legislature has presented 55 referendum questions to the Wisconsin electorate through the passage of acts or joint resolutions; 38 have been approved. Prior to statehood, the territorial legislature sent four questions to the electorate, as follows: Formation of a state government, submitted by Territorial Laws 1846, page 5 (Jan.31), approved April 1846, 12,334 votes for, 2,487 against; Ratification of first constitution, submitted by Art. XIX, Sec. 9 of 1846 Constitution, rejected April 1847, 14,119 votes for, 20,231 against; Extend suffrage to colored persons, submitted by supplemental resolution to 1846 Constitution, rejected April 1847, 7,664 votes for, 14,615 against; Ratification of second constitution, submitted by Art. XIV, Sec. 9 of 1848 Constitution, approved March 1848, 16,799 votes for, 6,384 against.

Ch.—Chapter; JR—Joint resolution; SS—Special session.

1. In *Gillespie v. Palmer*, 20 Wis. 544 (1866), the Wisconsin Supreme Court ruled that Chapter 137, Laws of 1849, extending suffrage to colored persons, was ratified November 6, 1849.

Sources: Official records of the Wisconsin Elections Commission; *Laws of Wisconsin*, 2021 and prior volumes.

Wisconsin vote in presidential elections since 1848

1848—4 electoral votes
Lewis Cass—D 15,001
Zachary Taylor—W 13,747
Martin Van Buren—FS . . . 10,418
Total. 39,166

1852—5 electoral votes
Franklin Pierce—D 33,658
Winfield Scott—W 22,210
John P. Hale—FS. 8,814
Total. 64,682

1856—5 electoral votes
John C. Fremont—R 66,090
James Buchanan—D 52,843
Millard Fillmore—A. 579
Total. 119,512

1860—5 electoral votes
Abraham Lincoln—R 86,113
Stephen A. Douglas—D . . 65,021
John C. Breckinridge—SoD . . 888
John Bell—CU 161
Total. 152,183

1864—8 electoral votes
Abraham Lincoln—R 83,458
George B. McClellan—D . . 65,884
Total. 149,342

1868—8 electoral votes
Ulysses S. Grant—R. . . . 108,857
Horatio Seymour—D 84,707
Total. 193,564

1872—10 electoral votes
Ulysses S. Grant—R. . . . 104,994
Horace Greeley—D & LR . . 86,477
Charles O'Conor—D 834
Total. 192,305

1876—10 electoral votes
Rutherford B. Hayes—R . 130,668
Samuel J. Tilden—D . . . 123,927
Peter Cooper—G 1,509
Green Clay Smith—Pro. 27
Total. 256,131

1880—10 electoral votes
James A. Garfield—R . . . 144,398
Winfield S. Hancock—D . . 114,644
James B. Weaver—G 7,986
John W. Phelps—A 91
Neal Dow—Pro 68
Total. 267,317

1884—11 electoral votes
James G. Blaine—R 161,157
Grover Cleveland—D. . . 146,477
John P. St. John—Pro. 7,656
Benjamin F. Butler—G 4,598
Total. 319,888

1888—11 electoral votes
Benjamin Harrison—R   176,553
Grover Cleveland—D. . . 155,232
Clinton B. Fisk—Pro. 14,277
Alson J. Streeter—UL. 8,552
Total. 354,614

1892—12 electoral votes
Grover Cleveland—D. . . 177,325
Benjamin Harrison—R . . 171,101
John Bidwell—Pro 13,136
James B. Weaver—PPop . . 10,019
Total. 371,581

1896—12 electoral votes
William McKinley—R . . . 268,135
William J. Bryan—D. . . . 165,523
Joshua Levering—Pro 7,507
John M. Palmer—ND 4,584
Charles H. Matchett—SL. . .1,314
Charles E. Bentley—Nat . . . 346
Total. 447,409

1900—12 electoral votes
William McKinley—R . . . 265,760
William J. Bryan—D. . . . 159,163
John G. Wooley—Pro. . . . 10,027
Eugene V. Debs—SD 7,048
Joseph F. Malloney—SL 503
Total. 442,501

1904—13 electoral votes
Theodore Roosevelt—R . 280,164
Alton B. Parker—D 124,107
Eugene V. Debs—SD 28,220
Silas C. Swallow—Pro 9,770
Thomas E. Watson—PPop . . . 530
Charles H. Corregan—SL . . . 223
Total. 443,014

1908—13 electoral votes
William H. Taft—R. 247,747
William J. Bryan—D. . . . 166,632
Eugene V. Debs—SD 28,164
Eugene W. Chafin—Pro . . 11,564
August Gillhaus—SL 314
Total. 454,421

1912—13 electoral votes
Woodrow Wilson—D . . . 164,230
William H. Taft—R. 130,596
Theodore Roosevelt—P . . 62,448
Eugene V. Debs—SD 33,476
Eugene W. Chafin—Pro . . . 8,584
Arthur E. Reimer—SL. 632
Total. 399,966

1916—13 electoral votes
Charles E. Hughes—R . . 220,822
Woodrow Wilson—D . . . 191,363
Allan Benson—S. 27,631
J. Frank Hanly—Pro. 7,318
Total. 447,134

1920—13 electoral votes
Warren G. Harding—R . . 498,576
James M. Cox—D 113,422
Eugene V. Debs—S 80,635
Aaron S. Watkins—Pro 8,647
Total. 701,280

1924—13 electoral votes
Robert M. La Follette—P . 453,678
Calvin Coolidge—R. . . . 311,614
John W. Davis—D 68,096
William Z. Foster—Wrk. . . .3,834
Herman P. Faris—Pro. 2,918
Total. 840,140

1928—13 electoral votes
Herbert Hoover—R 544,205
Alfred E. Smith—D 450,259
Norman Thomas—S 18,213
William F. Varney—Pro 2,245
William Z. Foster—Wrk. . . .1,528
Verne L. Reynolds—SL 381
Total. 1,016,831

1932—12 electoral votes
Franklin D. Roosevelt—D 707,410
Herbert Hoover—R 347,741
Norman Thomas—S 53,379
William Z. Foster—Com . . .3,112
William D. Upshaw—Pro. . .2,672
Verne L. Reynolds—SL. 494
Total. 1,114,808

1936—12 electoral votes
Franklin D. Roosevelt—D 802,984
Alfred M. Landon—R . . . 380,828
William Lemke—U 60,297
Norman Thomas—S 10,626
Earl Browder—Com. 2,197
David L. Calvin—Pro 1,071
John W. Aiken—SL 557
Total. 1,258,560

Wisconsin vote in presidential elections since 1848, continued

1940—12 electoral votes
Franklin D. Roosevelt—D 704,821
Wendell Willkie—R 679,206
Norman Thomas—S 15,071
Earl Browder—Com. 2,394
Roger Babson—Pro. 2,148
John W. Aiken—SL 1,882
Total. 1,405,522

1944—12 electoral votes
Thomas Dewey—R 674,532
Franklin D. Roosevelt—D 650,413
Norman Thomas—S 13,205
Edward Teichert—I 1,002
Total. 1,339,152

1948—12 electoral votes
Harry S Truman—D 647,310
Thomas Dewey—R 590,959
Henry Wallace—PP 25,282
Norman Thomas—S 12,547
Edward Teichert—I 399
Farrell Dobbs—ISW 303
Total. 1,276,800

1952—12 electoral votes
Dwight D. Eisenhower—R 979,744
Adlai E. Stevenson—D . . 622,175
Vincent Hallinan—IP 2,174
Farrell Dobbs—ISW 1,350
Darlington Hoopes—IS . . . 1,157
Eric Hass—ISL 770
Total. 1,607,370

1956—12 electoral votes
Dwight D. Eisenhower—R 954,844
Adlai E. Stevenson—D . . 586,768
T. Coleman Andrews—I (Con)
. . . . 6,918
Darlington Hoopes—I (S) . . . 754
Eric Hass—I (SL) 710
Farrell Dobbs—I (SW) 564
Total. 1,550,558

1960—12 electoral votes
Richard M. Nixon—R . . . 895,175
John F. Kennedy—D . . . 830,805
Farrell Dobbs—I (SW) 1,792
Eric Hass—I (SL) 1,310
Total. 1,729,082

1964—12 electoral votes
Lyndon B. Johnson—D 1,050,424
Barry M. Goldwater—R. . 638,495
Clifton DeBerry—I (SW) . . 1,692
Eric Hass—I (SL) 1,204
Total. 1,691,815

1968—12 electoral votes
Richard M. Nixon—R . . . 809,997
Hubert H. Humphrey—D 748,804
George C. Wallace—I (A) . 127,835
Henning A. Blomen—I (SL) . 1,338
Frederick W. Halstead
—I (SW) 1,222
Total. 1,689,196

1972—11 electoral votes
Richard M. Nixon—R . . . 989,430
George S. McGovern—D. 810,174
John G. Schmitz—A. 47,525
Benjamin M. Spock—I (Pop)
. . . . 2,701
Louis Fisher—I (SL) 998
Gus Hall—I (Com) 663
Evelyn Reed—I (SW) 506
Total. 1,851,997

1976—11 electoral votes
Jimmy Carter—D 1,040,232
Gerald R. Ford—R 1,004,987
Eugene J. McCarthy—I . . . 34,943
Lester Maddox—A 8,552
Frank P. Zeidler—I (S) 4,298
Roger L. MacBride—I (Lib). . 3,814
Peter Camejo—I (SW) 1,691
Margaret Wright—I (Pop) . . . 943
Gus Hall—I (Com) 749
Lyndon H. LaRouche, Jr—
I (USL). 738
Jules Levin—I (SL). 389
Total. 2,104,175

1980—11 electoral votes
Ronald Reagan—R . . . 1,088,845
Jimmy Carter—D 981,584
John Anderson—I. 160,657
Ed Clark—I (Lib) 29,135
Barry Commoner—I (Cit) . . 7,767
John Rarick—I (Con) 1,519
David McReynolds—I (S) . . . 808
Gus Hall—I (Com) 772
Deidre Griswold—I (WW) . . . 414
Clifton DeBerry—I (SW) 383
Total. 2,273,221

1984—11 electoral votes
Ronald Reagan—R . . . 1,198,800
Walter F. Mondale—D . . 995,847
David Bergland—Lib 4,884
Bob Richards—Con 3,864
Lyndon H. LaRouche, Jr—I 3,791
Sonia Johnson—I (Cit) 1,456
Dennis L. Serrette—I (WIA) . 1,007
Larry Holmes—I (WW) 619
Gus Hall—I (Com) 597
Melvin T. Mason—I (SW) . . . 445
Total. 2,212,018

1988—11 electoral votes
Michael S. Dukakis—D
. . . . 1,126,794
George Bush—R. 1,047,499
Ronald Paul—I (Lib). 5,157
David E. Duke—I (Pop) 3,056
James Warren—I (SW) 2,574
Lyndon H. LaRouche, Jr—I (NER)
. . . . 2,302
Lenora B. Fulani—I (NA) . . 1,953
Total. 2,191,612

1992—11 electoral votes
Bill Clinton—D. 1,041,066
George Bush—R. 930,855
Ross Perot—I. 544,479
Andre Marrou—Lib 2,877
James Gritz—I (AFC) 2,311
Ron Daniels—LF. 1,883
Howard Phillips—I (Tax) . . . 1,772
J. Quinn Brisben—I (S) 1,211
John Hagelin—NL. 1,070
Lenora B. Fulani—I (NA) 654
Lyndon H. LaRouche, Jr—I (ER)
. . . . 633
Jack Herer—I (Gr) 547
Eugene A. Hem—3rd. 405
James Warren—I (SW) 390
Total. 2,531,114

1996—11 electoral votes
Bill Clinton—D. 1,071,971
Bob Dole—R 845,029
Ross Perot—Rfm 227,339
Ralph Nader—I (WG). . . . 28,723
Howard Phillips—Tax. 8,811
Harry Browne—Lib 7,929
John Hagelin—I (NL) 1,379
Monica Moorehead—I (WW)
. . . . 1,333
Mary Cal Hollis—I (S) 848
James E. Harris—I (SW) 483
Total. 2,196,169

2000—11 electoral votes
Al Gore—D 1,242,987
George W. Bush—R . . . 1,237,279
Ralph Nader—WG 94,070
Pat Buchanan—I (Rfm) . . . 11,446
Harry Browne—Lib 6,640
Howard Phillips—Con 2,042
Monica G. Moorehead—I (WW)
. . . . 1,063
John Hagelin—I (Rfm) 878
James Harris—I (SW) 306
Total. 2,598,607

Wisconsin vote in presidential elections since 1848, continued

2004—10 electoral votes
John F. Kerry—D 1,489,504
George W. Bush—R . . . 1,478,120
Ralph Nader—I (TBL) 16,390
Michael Badnarik—Lib 6,464
David Cobb—WG 2,661
Walter F. Brown—I (SPW) . . . 471
James Harris—I (SW) 411
Total 2,997,007

2008—10 electoral votes
Barack Obama—D . . . 1,677,211
John McCain—R 1,262,393
Ralph Nader—I 17,605
Bob Barr—Lib 8,858
Chuck Baldwin—I (Con) . . . 5,072
Cynthia McKinney—WG . . . 4,216

Jeffrey J. Wamboldt—I (WtP) . 764
Brian Moore—I (SocUSA) . . . 540
Gloria La Riva—I (S&L) 237
Total 2,983,417

2012—10 electoral votes
Barack Obama—D . . . 1,620,985
Mitt Romney—R 1,407,966
Gary Johnson—I (Lib) . . . 20,439
Jill Stein—I (Grn) 7,665
Virgil Goode—Con 4,930
Jerry White—I (SE) 553
Gloria La Riva—I (S&L) 526
Total 3,068,434

2016—10 electoral votes
Donald J. Trump—R . . 1,405,284

Hillary Clinton—D 1,382,536
Gary Johnson—Lib 106,674
Jill Stein—WG 31,072
Darrell L. Castle—Con . . . 12,162
Monica Moorehead—I (WW)
. . . . 1,770
Rocky Roque De La Fuente—I (AD)
. . . . 1,502
Total 2,976,150

2020—10 electoral votes
Joseph R. Biden—D . . 1,630,866
Donald J. Trump—R . . 1,610,184
Jo Jorgensen—I (Lib) . . . 38,491
Brian Carroll—I (ASP) 5,259
Don Blankenship—Con . . . 5,146
Total 3,298,041

Note: The party designation listed for a candidate is taken from the Congressional Quarterly, *Guide to U.S. Elections*. A candidate whose party did not receive 1% of the vote for a statewide office in the previous election or who failed to meet the alternative requirement of Wis. Stat. § 5.62 must be listed on the Wisconsin ballot as "independent." In this listing, candidates whose party affiliations appear as "I," followed by a party designation in parentheses, were identified on the ballot simply as "independent" although they also provided a party designation or statement of principle.

Under the Electoral College system, each state is entitled to electoral votes equal in number to its total congressional delegation of U.S. Senators and U.S. Representatives.

Some totals include scattered votes for other candidates.

A—American (Know Nothing)
AD—American Delta
AFC—America First Coalition
ASP—American Solidarity Party
Cit—Citizens
Com—Communist
Con—Constitution
CU—Constitutional Union
D—Democrat
ER—Independents for Economic Recovery
FS—Free Soil
G—Greenback
Gr—Grassroots
Grn—Green
I—Independent
IP—Independent Progressive
IS—Independent Socialist
ISL—Independent Socialist Labor
ISW—Independent Socialist Worker

LF—Labor-Farm/Laborista-Agrario
Lib—Libertarian
LR—Liberal Republican
NA—New Alliance
Nat—National
ND—National Democrat
NER—National Economic Recovery
NL—Natural Law
P—Progressive
Pop—Populist
PP—People's Progressive
PPop—People's (Populist)
Pro—Prohibition
R—Republican
Rfm—Reform
S—Socialist
SD—Social Democrat
SE—Socialist Equality
SL—Socialist Labor

S&L—Party for Socialism and Liberation
SocUSA—Socialist Party USA
SoD—Southern Democrat
SPW—Socialist Party of Wis.
SW—Socialist Worker
Tax—U.S. Taxpayers
TBL—The Better Life
3rd—Third Party
U—Union
UL—Union Labor
USL—U.S. Labor
W—Whig
WG—Wisconsin Green
WIA—Wis. Independent Alliance
Wrk—Workers
WtP—We, the People
WW—Worker's World

Sources: Official records of the Wisconsin Elections Commission and Congressional Quarterly, *Guide to U.S. Elections*, 1994.

Wisconsin members of the U.S. Senate since 1848

Class 1	Term
Henry Dodge—D	1848–1857
James R. Doolittle—R	1857–1869
Matthew H. Carpenter—R	1869–1875
Angus Cameron[1]—R	1875–1881

Class 3	Term
Isaac P. Walker—D	1848–1855
Charles Durkee—UR	1855–1861
Timothy O. Howe—UR	1861–1879
Matthew H. Carpenter—R	1879–1881

Wisconsin members of the U.S. Senate since 1848

Class 1		Class 3	
	Term		Term
Philetus Sawyer—R.	1881–1893	Angus Cameron[1]—R.	1881–1885
John Lendrum Mitchell—D.	1893–1899	John C. Spooner—R	1885–1891
Joseph Very Quarles—R.	1899–1905	William F. Vilas—D	1891–1897
Robert M. La Follette, Sr.[2]—R.	1906–1925	John C. Spooner—R	1897–1907
Robert M. La Follette Jr.[3]—R.	1925–1935	Isaac Stephenson[5]—R	1907–1915
Robert M. La Follette Jr.—P	1935–1947	Paul O. Husting—D.	1915–1917
Joseph R. McCarthy—R	1947–1957	Irvine L. Lenroot[6]—R.	1918–1927
William Proxmire[4]—D	1957–1989	John J. Blaine—R	1927–1933
Herbert H. Kohl—D.	1989–2013	F. Ryan Duffy—D	1933–1939
Tammy Baldwin—D.	2013–	Alexander Wiley—R.	1939–1963
		Gaylord A. Nelson—D	1963–1981
		Robert W. Kasten Jr.—R	1981–1993
		Russell D. Feingold—D.	1993–2011
		Ron Johnson—R.	2011–

Note: Each state has two U.S. Senators, and each serves a six-year term. They were elected by their respective state legislatures until passage of the 17th Amendment to the U.S. Constitution on April 8, 1913, which provided for popular election. Article I, Section 3, Clause 2, of the U.S. Constitution divides senators into three classes so that one-third of the senate is elected every two years. Wisconsin's seats were assigned to Class 1 and Class 3 at statehood.

D–Democrat; P–Progressive; R–Republican; UR–Union Republican.

1. Not a candidate for reelection to Class 1 seat, but elected 3/10/1881 to fill vacancy caused by death of Class 3 Senator Carpenter on 2/24/1881. 2. Elected 1/25/1905 but continued to serve as governor until 1/1/1906. 3. Elected 9/29/1925 to fill vacancy caused by death of Robert La Follette Sr. on 6/18/1925. 4. Elected 8/27/1957 to fill vacancy caused by death of McCarthy on 5/2/1957. 5. Elected 5/17/1907 to fill vacancy caused by resignation of Spooner on 4/30/1907. 6. Elected 5/2/1918 to fill vacancy caused by death of Husting on 10/21/1917.

Source: Wisconsin Legislative Reference Bureau records.

Wisconsin members of the U.S. House of Representatives since 1848

	Party	District	Term	Residence
Adams, Henry C.	Rep.	2	1903–1906	Madison
Amlie, Thomas R	Rep., Prog.	1	1931–1933; 1935–1939	Elkhorn
Aspin, Les	Dem.	1	1971–1993	East Troy
Atwood, David	Rep.	2	1870–1871	Madison
Babbitt, Clinton.	Dem.	1	1891–1893	Beloit
Babcock, Joseph W.	Rep.	3	1893–1907	Necedah
Baldus, Alvin.	Dem.	3	1975–1981	Menomonie
Baldwin, Tammy	Dem.	2	1999–2013	Madison
Barber, J. Allen	Rep.	3	1871–1875	Lancaster
Barca, Peter W.	Dem.	1	1993–1995	Kenosha
Barnes, Lyman E	Dem.	8	1893–1895	Appleton
Barney, Samuel S.	Rep.	5	1895–1903	West Bend
Barrett, Thomas M	Dem.	5	1993–2003	Milwaukee
Barwig, Charles	Dem.	2	1889–1895	Mayville
Beck, Joseph D	Rep.	7	1921–1929	Viroqua
Berger, Victor L	Soc.	5	1911–1913; 1919; 1923–1929	Milwaukee
Biemiller, Andrew J.	Dem.	5	1945–1947; 1949–1951	Milwaukee
Billinghurst, Charles	Rep.	3	1855–1859	Juneau
Blanchard, George W	Rep.	1	1933–1935	Edgerton
Boileau, Gerald J	Rep., Prog.	8, 7	1931–1939	Wausau
Bolles, Stephen	Rep.	1	1939–1941	Janesville

Wisconsin members of the U.S. House of Representatives since 1848, continued

	Party	District	Term	Residence
Bouck, Gabriel.	Dem.	6	1877–1881	Oshkosh
Bragg, Edward S	Dem.	5, 2	1877–1883; 1885–1887	Fond du Lac
Brickner, George H	Dem.	5	1889–1895	Sheboygan Falls
Brophy, John C	Rep.	4	1947–1949	Milwaukee
Brown, James S	Dem.	1	1863–1865	Milwaukee
Brown, Webster E.	Rep.	9, 10	1901–1907	Rhinelander
Browne, Edward E	Rep.	8	1913–1931	Waupaca
Burchard, Samuel D	Dem.	5	1875–1877	Beaver Dam
Burke, Michael E	Dem.	6, 2	1911–1917	Beaver Dam
Bushnell, Allen R	Dem.	3	1891–1893	Madison
Byrnes, John W	Rep.	8	1945–1973	Green Bay
Cannon, Raymond J	Dem.	4	1933–1939	Milwaukee
Cary, William J.	Rep.	4	1907–1919	Milwaukee
Caswell, Lucien B	Rep.	2, 1	1875–1883; 1885–1891	Fort Atkinson
Cate, George W	Reform	8	1875–1877	Stevens Point
Clark, Charles B	Rep.	6	1887–1891	Neenah
Classon, David G	Rep.	9	1917–1923	Oconto
Cobb, Amasa	Rep.	3	1863–1871	Mineral Point
Coburn, Frank P.	Dem.	7	1891–1893	West Salem
Cole, Orasmus.	Whig	2	1849–1851	Potosi
Cook, Samuel A.	Rep.	6	1895–1897	Neenah
Cooper, Henry Allen	Rep.	1	1893–1919; 1921–1931	Racine
Cornell, Robert J	Dem.	8	1975–1979	De Pere
Dahle, Herman B	Rep.	2	1899–1903	Mount Horeb
Darling, Mason C	Dem.	2	1848–1849	Fond du Lac
Davidson, James H.	Rep.	6, 8	1897–1913; 1917–1918	Oshkosh
Davis, Glenn R.	Rep.	2, 9	1947–1957; 1965–1975	Waukesha
Deuster, Peter V.	Dem.	4	1879–1885	Milwaukee
Dilweg, La Vern R.	Dem.	8	1943–1945	Green Bay
Doty, James D.	Dem.	3	1849–1853	Neenah
Duffy, Sean P.	Rep.	7	2011–2019	Wausau
Durkee, Charles.	Free Soil	1	1849–1853	Kenosha
Eastman, Ben C	Dem.	2	1851–1855	Platteville
Eldredge, Charles A	Dem.	4, 5	1863–1875	Fond du Lac
Esch, John Jacob	Rep.	7	1899–1921	La Crosse
Fitzgerald, Scott	Rep.	5	2021–	Juneau
Flynn, Gerald T	Dem.	1	1959–1961	Racine
Frear, James A.	Rep.	10, 9	1913–1935	Hudson
Froehlich, Harold V.	Rep.	8	1973–1975	Appleton
Gallagher, Mike	Rep.	8	2017–	Allouez
Gehrmann, Bernard J	Prog.	10	1935–1943	Mellen
Green, Mark A.	Rep.	8	1999–2007	Green Bay
Griffin, Michael	Rep.	7	1894–1899	Eau Claire
Griswold, Harry W	Rep.	3	1939–1941	West Salem
Grothman, Glenn.	Rep.	6	2015–	Glenbeulah
Guenther, Richard W.	Rep.	6, 2	1881–1889	Oshkosh
Gunderson, Steven.	Rep.	3	1981–1997	Osseo
Hanchett, Luther	Rep.	2	1861–1862	Plover
Haugen, Nils P.	Rep.	8, 10	1887–1895	Black River Falls
Hawkes, Charles, Jr.	Rep.	2	1939–1941	Horicon
Hazelton, George C	Rep.	3	1877–1883	Boscobel
Hazelton, Gerry W	Rep.	2	1871–1875	Columbus
Henney, Charles W	Dem.	2	1933–1935	Portage
Henry, Robert K.	Rep.	2	1945–1947	Jefferson
Hopkins, Benjamin F.	Rep.	2	1867–1870	Madison
Hudd, Thomas R	Dem.	5	1886–1889	Green Bay
Hughes, James	Dem.	8	1933–1935	De Pere

Wisconsin members of the U.S. House of Representatives since 1848, continued

	Party	District	Term	Residence
Hull, Merlin	Prog.	7, 9	1929–1931; 1935–1953	Black River Falls
Humphrey, Herman L	Rep.	7	1877–1883	Hudson
Jenkins, John J	Rep.	10, 11	1895–1909	Chippewa Falls
Johns, Joshua L	Rep.	8	1939–1943	Appleton
Johnson, Jay	Dem.	8	1997–1999	New Franken
Johnson, Lester R.	Dem.	9	1953–1965	Black River Falls
Jones, Burr W	Dem.	3	1883–1885	Madison
Kading, Charles A.	Rep.	2	1927–1933	Watertown
Kagen, Steve.	Dem.	8	2007–2011	Appleton
Kasten, Robert W., Jr.	Rep.	9	1975–1979	Waukesha
Kastenmeier, Robert W	Dem.	2	1959–1991	Sun Prairie
Keefe, Frank B	Rep.	6	1939–1951	Oshkosh
Kersten, Charles J.	Rep.	5	1947–1949; 1951–1955	Whitefish Bay
Kimball, Alanson M.	Rep.	6	1875–1877	Waushara
Kind, Ron.	Dem.	3	1997–2023	La Crosse
Kleczka, Gerald D.	Dem.	4	1984–2005	Milwaukee
Kleczka, John C	Rep.	4	1919–1923	Milwaukee
Klug, Scott L	Rep.	2	1991–1999	Madison
Konop, Thomas F	Dem.	9	1911–1917	Kewaunee
Kopp, Arthur W	Rep.	3	1909–1913	Platteville
Kustermann, Gustav	Rep.	9	1907–1911	Green Bay
La Follette, Robert M., Sr	Rep.	3	1885–1891	Madison
Laird, Melvin R	Rep.	7	1953–1969	Marshfield
Lampert, Florian	Rep.	6	1918–1930	Oshkosh
Larrabee, Charles H	Dem.	3	1859–1861	Horicon
Lenroot, Irvine L	Rep.	11	1909–1918	Superior
Lynch, Thomas	Dem.	9	1891–1895	Antigo
Lynde, William Pitt	Dem.	1, 4	1848–1849; 1875–1879	Milwaukee
Macy, John B.	Dem.	3	1853–1855	Fond du Lac
Magoon, Henry S	Rep.	3	1875–1877	Darlington
McCord, Myron H.	Rep.	9	1889–1891	Merrill
McDill, Alexander S	Rep.	8	1873–1875	Plover
McIndoe, Walter D	Rep.	6	1863–1867	Wausau
McMurray, Howard J.	Dem.	5	1943–1945	Milwaukee
Miller, Lucas M	Dem.	6	1891–1893	Oshkosh
Minor, Edward S	Rep.	8, 9	1895–1907	Sturgeon Bay
Mitchell, Alexander	Dem.	1, 4	1871–1875	Milwaukee
Mitchell, John L	Dem.	4	1891–1893	Milwaukee
Monahan, James G.	Rep.	3	1919–1921	Darlington
Moody, James P.	Dem.	5	1983–1993	Milwaukee
Moore, Gwen	Dem.	4	2005–	Milwaukee
Morse, Elmer A	Rep.	10	1907–1913	Antigo
Murphy, James W.	Dem.	3	1907–1909	Platteville
Murray, Reid F.	Rep.	7	1939–1953	Ogdensburg
Nelson, Adolphus P	Rep.	11	1918–1923	Grantsburg
Nelson, John Mandt	Rep.	2, 3	1906–1919; 1921–1933	Madison
Neumann, Mark W	Rep.	1	1995–1999	Janesville
Obey, David R	Dem.	7	1969–2011	Wausau
O'Konski, Alvin E	Rep.	10	1943–1973	Mercer
O'Malley, Thomas D. P.	Dem.	5	1933–1939	Milwaukee
Otjen, Theobald.	Rep.	4	1895–1907	Milwaukee
Paine, Halbert E.	Rep.	1	1865–1871	Milwaukee
Peavey, Hubert H.	Rep.	11, 10	1923–1935	Washburn
Petri, Thomas E	Rep.	6	1979–2015	Fond du Lac
Pocan, Mark	Dem.	2	2013–	Black Earth
Potter, John F	Rep.	1	1857–1863	East Troy
Pound, Thaddeus C.	Rep.	8	1877–1883	Chippewa Falls
Price, Hugh H	Rep.	8	1887	Black River Falls

Wisconsin members of the U.S. House of Representatives since 1848, continued

	Party	District	Term	Residence
Price, William T.	Rep.	8	1883–1886	Black River Falls
Race, John A.	Dem.	6	1965–1967	Fond du Lac
Randall, Clifford E.	Rep.	1	1919–1921	Kenosha
Rankin, Joseph	Dem.	5	1883–1886	Manitowoc
Reilly, Michael K.	Dem.	6	1913–1917; 1930–1939	Fond du Lac
Reuss, Henry S.	Dem.	5	1955–1983	Milwaukee
Ribble, Reid J.	Rep.	8	2011–2017	Appleton
Roth, Toby	Rep.	8	1979–1997	Appleton
Rusk, Jeremiah M.	Rep.	6, 7	1871–1877	Viroqua
Ryan, Paul	Rep.	1	1999–2019	Janesville
Sauerhering, Edward	Rep.	2	1895–1899	Mayville
Sauthoff, Harry	Prog.	2	1935–1939; 1941–1945	Madison
Sawyer, Philetus	Rep.	5, 6	1865–1875	Oshkosh
Schadeberg, Henry C.	Rep.	1	1961–1965; 1967–1971	Burlington
Schafer, John C.	Rep.	4	1923–1933; 1939–1941	Milwaukee
Schneider, George J.	Rep., Prog.	9, 8	1923–1933; 1935–1939	Appleton
Sensenbrenner, F. James, Jr.	Rep.	9, 5	1979–2021	Menomonee Falls
Shaw, George B.	Rep.	7	1893–1894	Eau Claire
Sloan, A. Scott.	Rep.	3	1861–1863	Beaver Dam
Sloan, Ithamar C.	Rep.	2	1863–1867	Janesville
Smith, Henry.	Union Labor	4	1887–1889	Milwaukee
Smith, Lawrence H.	Rep.	1	1941–1959	Racine
Somers, Peter J.	Dem.	4	1893–1895	Milwaukee
Stafford, William H.	Rep.	5	1903–1911; 1913–1919; 1921–1923; 1929–1933	Milwaukee
Stalbaum, Lynn E.	Dem.	1	1965–1967	Racine
Steiger, William A.	Rep.	6	1967–1978	Oshkosh
Steil, Bryan.	Rep.	1	2019–	Janesville
Stephenson, Isaac	Rep.	9	1883–1889	Marinette
Stevenson, William H.	Rep.	3	1941–1949	La Crosse
Stewart, Alexander.	Rep.	9	1895–1901	Wausau
Sumner, Daniel H.	Dem.	2	1883–1885	Waukesha
Tewes, Donald E.	Rep.	2	1957–1959	Waukesha
Thill, Lewis D.	Rep.	5	1939–1943	Milwaukee
Thomas, Ormsby B.	Rep.	7	1885–1891	Prairie du Chien
Thomson, Vernon W.	Rep.	3	1961–1975	Richland Center
Tiffany, Tom	Rep.	7	2020–	Minocqua
Van Orden, Derrick.	Rep.	3	2023–	Prairie du Chien
Van Pelt, William K.	Rep.	6	1951–1963	Fond du Lac
Van Schaick, Isaac W.	Rep.	4	1885–1887; 1889–1891	Milwaukee
Voigt, Edward	Rep.	2	1917–1927	Sheboygan
Washburn, Cadwallader C.	Rep.	2, 6	1855–1861; 1867–1871	Mineral Point, La Crosse
Wasielewski, Thaddeus F.	Dem.	4	1941–1947	Milwaukee
Weisse, Charles H.	Dem.	6	1903–1911	Sheboygan Falls
Wells, Daniel, Jr.	Dem.	1	1853–1857	Milwaukee
Wells, Owen A.	Dem.	6	1893–1895	Fond du Lac
Wheeler, Ezra	Dem.	5	1863–1865	Berlin
Williams, Charles G.	Rep.	1	1873–1883	Janesville
Winans, John	Dem.	1	1883–1885	Janesville
Withrow, Gardner R.	Rep., Prog.	7, 3	1931–1939; 1949–1961	La Crosse
Woodward, Gilbert M.	Dem.	7	1883–1885	La Crosse
Zablocki, Clement J.	Dem.	4	1949–1983	Milwaukee

Dem.–Democrat; Prog.–Progressive; Rep.–Republican; Soc.–Socialist.
Sources: Wisconsin Legislative Reference Bureau, *Wisconsin Blue Book*, various editions; *Congressional Quarterly's Guide to U.S. Elections* (Washington: CQ, 1985); and official election records.

Wisconsin members of the U.S. House of Representatives since 1941, by district

District		Party	Term	Residence
1	Lawrence H. Smith	Rep.	1941–1959	Racine
	Gerald T. Flynn	Dem.	1959–1961	Racine
	Henry C. Schadeberg	Rep.	1961–1965; 1967–1971	Burlington
	Lynn E. Stalbaum	Dem.	1965–1967	Racine
	Les Aspin[1]	Dem.	1971–1993	East Troy
	Peter W. Barca[1]	Dem.	1993–1995	Kenosha
	Mark W. Neumann	Rep.	1995–1999	Janesville
	Paul Ryan	Rep.	1999–2019	Janesville
	Bryan Steil	Rep.	2019–	Janesville
2	Harry Sauthoff	Prog.	1941–1945	Madison
	Robert K. Henry	Rep.	1945–1947	Jefferson
	Glenn R. Davis	Rep.	1947–1957	Waukesha
	Donald E. Tewes	Rep.	1957–1959	Waukesha
	Robert W. Kastenmeier	Dem.	1959–1991	Sun Prairie
	Scott L. Klug	Rep.	1991–1999	Madison
	Tammy Baldwin	Dem.	1999–2013	Madison
	Mark Pocan	Dem.	2013–	Black Earth
3	William H. Stevenson	Rep.	1941–1949	La Crosse
	Gardner R. Withrow	Rep.	1949–1961	La Crosse
	Vernon W. Thomson	Rep.	1961–1975	Richland Center
	Alvin Baldus	Dem.	1975–1981	Menomonie
	Steven Gunderson	Rep.	1981–1997	Osseo
	Ron Kind	Dem.	1997–2023	La Crosse
	Derrick Van Orden	Rep.	2023–	Prairie du Chien
4[3]	Thaddeus F. Wasielewski	Dem.	1941–1947	Milwaukee
	John C. Brophy	Rep.	1947–1949	Milwaukee
	Clement J. Zablocki[2]	Dem.	1949–1983	Milwaukee
	Gerald D. Kleczka[2]	Dem.	1984–2005	Milwaukee
	Gwen Moore	Dem.	2005–	Milwaukee
5[3]	Howard J. McMurray	Dem.	1943–1945	Milwaukee
	Andrew J. Biemiller	Dem.	1945–1947; 1949–1951	Milwaukee
	Charles J. Kersten	Rep.	1947–1949; 1951–1955	Whitefish Bay
	Henry S. Reuss	Dem.	1955–1983	Milwaukee
	James P. Moody	Dem.	1983–1993	Milwaukee
	Thomas M. Barrett	Dem.	1993–2003	Milwaukee
	F. James Sensenbrenner Jr.	Rep.	2003–2021	Menomonee Falls
	Scott Fitzgerald	Rep.	2021–	Juneau
6	Frank B. Keefe	Rep.	1939–1951	Oshkosh
	William K. Van Pelt	Rep.	1951–1965	Fond du Lac
	John A. Race	Dem.	1965–1967	Fond du Lac
	William A. Steiger[4]	Rep.	1967–1978	Oshkosh
	Thomas E. Petri[4]	Rep.	1979–2015	Fond du Lac
	Glenn Grothman	Rep.	2015–	Glenbeulah
7	Reid F. Murray	Rep.	1939–1953	Ogdensburg
	Melvin R. Laird[5]	Rep.	1953–1969	Marshfield
	David R. Obey[5]	Dem.	1969–2011	Wausau
	Sean P. Duffy[6]	Rep.	2011–2019	Wausau
	Tom Tiffany[6]	Rep.	2020–	Minocqua
8	La Vern R. Dilweg	Dem.	1943–1945	Green Bay
	John R. Byrnes	Rep.	1945–1973	Green Bay
	Harold V. Froehlich	Rep.	1973–1975	Appleton
	Robert J. Cornell	Dem.	1975–1979	De Pere
	Toby Roth	Rep.	1979–1997	Appleton
	Jay Johnson	Dem.	1997–1999	New Franken

Wisconsin members of the U.S. House of Representatives since 1941, by district, continued

District		Party	Term	Residence
	Mark A. Green...............	Rep.	1999–2007	Green Bay
	Steve Kagen................	Dem.	2007–2011	Appleton
	Reid J. Ribble...............	Rep.	2011–2017	Appleton
	Mike Gallagher..............	Rep.	2017–	Allouez
9[3,7]	Merlin Hull..................	Prog.	1935–1953	Black River Falls
	Lester R. Johnson............	Dem.	1953–1965	Black River Falls
	Glenn R. Davis...............	Rep.	1965–1975	Waukesha
	Robert W. Kasten............	Rep.	1975–1979	Thiensville
	F. James Sensenbrenner Jr........	Rep.	1979–2003	Menomonee Falls
10[8]	Alvin E. O'Konski.............	Rep.	1943–1973	Rhinelander

Dem.–Democrat; Prog.–Progressive; Rep.–Republican.
1. Aspin resigned 1/20/1993, to become U.S. Secretary of Defense. Barca was elected in a special election, 5/4/1993. 2. Zablocki died 12/3/1983. Kleczka was elected in a special election, 4/3/1984. 3. In the congressional reapportionment following the 2000 census, Wisconsin's delegation was reduced from nine to eight members. The previous 4th, 5th, and 9th districts were reconfigured into the new 4th and 5th districts. 4. Steiger died 12/4/1978, following his November 1978 election. Petri was elected in a special election, 4/3/1979. 5. Laird resigned 1/21/1969, to become U.S. Secretary of Defense. Obey was elected in a special election, 4/1/1969. 6. Duffy resigned 9/23/2019. Tiffany was elected in a special election, 5/12/2020. 7. In the congressional redistricting following the 1960 census, the previous 9th District in western Wisconsin ceased to exist and a new 9th District was created in the Waukesha-Milwaukee metropolitan area. 8. In the congressional reapportionment following the 1970 census, Wisconsin's delegation was reduced from ten members to nine members.
Sources: 1944 *Wisconsin Blue Book* and Wisconsin Legislative Reference Bureau records.

■ ■ ■

POPULATION AND POLITICAL SUBDIVISIONS

Wisconsin population since 1840

Year	Population	% increase	Rural	Urban (%)[1]	Density[2]
1840	30,945	X	30,945	—	0.6
1850	305,391	886.9	276,768	28,623 (9.4)	5.6
1860	775,881	154.1	664,007	111,874 (14.4)	14.1
1870	1,054,670	35.9	847,571	207,099 (19.6)	19.2
1880	1,315,497	24.7	998,293	317,204 (24.1)	24.0
1890	1,693,330	28.7	1,131,044	562,286 (33.2)	30.9
1900	2,069,042	22.2	1,278,829	790,213 (38.2)	37.4
1910	2,333,860	12.8	1,329,540	1,004,320 (43.0)	43.1
1920	2,632,067	12.8	1,387,209	1,244,858 (47.3)	48.6
1930	2,939,006	11.7	1,385,163	1,553,843 (52.9)	54.3
1940	3,137,587	6.8	1,458,443	1,679,144 (53.5)	57.9
1950	3,434,575	9.5	1,446,687	1,987,888 (57.9)	63.4
1960	3,951,777	15.1	1,429,598	2,522,179 (63.8)	73.0
1970	4,417,731	11.8	1,507,313	2,910,418 (65.9)	81.6
1980	4,705,767	6.5	1,685,035	3,020,732 (64.2)	86.9
1990	4,891,769	4.0	1,679,813	3,211,956 (65.7)	90.3
2000	5,363,675	9.6	1,700,032	3,663,643 (68.3)	99.0
2010	5,686,986	6.0	1,697,348	3,989,638 (70.2)	105.0
2020	5,893,718	3.6	1,940,027	3,953,691 (67.1)	108.8

—Represents zero; X–Not applicable.
1. The defintion of "urban" has changed over time. 2. Population per square mile of land area.
Source: U.S. Census Bureau, decennial census data and *Historical Population Change Data (1910–2020)* and *Historical Population Density Data (1910–2020)*.

Wisconsin population by race since 1890

Year	Total	White (%)	Black (%)	American Indian[1] (%)	Asian[2] (%)	Some other race (%)	Two or more races[3] (%)
1890	1,693,330	1,680,828 (99.3)	2,444 (0.1)	9,930 (0.6)	128 (Z)	—	X
1900	2,069,042	2,057,911 (99.5)	2,542 (0.1)	8,372 (0.4)	217 (Z)	—	X
1910	2,333,860	2,320,555 (99.4)	2,900 (0.1)	10,142 (0.4)	260 (Z)	3 (Z)	X
1920	2,632,067	2,616,938 (99.4)	5,201 (0.2)	9,611 (0.4)	314 (Z)	3 (Z)	X
1930	2,939,006	2,916,255 (99.2)	10,739 (0.4)	11,548 (0.4)	451 (Z)	13 (Z)	X
1940	3,137,587	3,112,752 (99.2)	12,158 (0.4)	12,265 (0.4)	388 (Z)	24 (Z)	X
1950	3,434,575	3,392,690 (98.8)	28,182 (0.8)	12,196 (0.4)	1,119 (Z)	388 (Z)	X
1960	3,951,777	3,858,903 (97.6)	74,546 (1.9)	14,297 (0.4)	2,836 (0.1)	1,195 (Z)	X
1970[4]	4,417,933	4,258,959 (96.4)	128,224 (2.9)	18,924 (0.4)	6,557 (0.2)	5,067 (0.1)	X
1980[4]	4,705,642	4,443,035 (94.4)	182,592 (3.9)	29,320 (0.6)	22,043 (0.3)	41,788 (0.9)	X
1990	4,891,769	4,512,523 (92.2)	244,539 (5.0)	39,387 (0.8)	53,583 (1.2)	42,538 (0.9)	X
2000	5,363,675	4,769,857 (88.9)	304,460 (5.7)	47,228 (0.9)	90,393 (1.7)	84,842 (1.6)	66,895 (1.2)
2010	5,686,986	4,902,067 (86.2)	359,148 (6.3)	54,526 (1.0)	131,061 (2.3)	135,867 (2.4)	104,317 (1.8)
2020	5,893,718	4,737,545 (80.4)	376,256 (6.4)	60,428 (1.0)	177,901 (3.0)	182,054 (3.1)	359,534 (6.1)

Note: Wisconsin's total population (census data by year) of people of Hispanic or Latino origin is as follows: 1970–62,875; 1980–62,782; 1990–93,194; 2000–192,921; 2010–336,056; 2020–447,290. Starting in the 2000 Census, "Hispanic or Latino Origin" represents ethnicity and includes people of Cuban, Mexican, Puerto Rican, South or Central American, or other Spanish culture or origin, regardless of race. For information about how this census category evolved prior to the 2000 census, see "We, the American Hispanics" at https://www.census.gov/library/publications/1993/dec/we-02.html.

Z–Less than 0.1%; —Represents zero; X–Not applicable.

1. Aleut and Eskimo populations included beginning in 1960. 2. Includes Native Hawaiian and other Pacific Islanders. 3. Beginning with the 2000 Census, individuals were allowed to select more than one race. 4. Total has been corrected by the U.S. Census Bureau. Details not adjusted to match revised total.

Sources: U.S. Census Bureau, decennial census data.

Wisconsin population by race, 2021

	Total	Percent
One race	5,458,553	92.6
White	4,732,002	80.3
Black or African American	364,138	6.2
American Indian and Alaska Native	42,107	0.7
Asian	175,743	3.0
Asian Indian	36,438	0.6
Chinese	23,018	0.4
Filipino	13,991	0.2
Japanese	2,004	Z
Korean	6,252	0.1
Vietnamese	5,418	0.1
Other Asian[1]	88,622	1.5
Native Hawaiian and other Pacific Islander	752	Z
Native Hawaiian	N	N
Guamanian or Chamorro	N	N
Samoan	N	N
Other Pacific Islander[2]	N	N
Some other race	143,811	2.4
Two or more races	437,355	7.4

Note: Totals are provided by the U.S. Census Bureau and may not equal the sum of columns or rows.

Z–Less than 0.1%; N– Insufficient number of sample cases to calculate estimate.

1. Other Asian alone, or two or more Asian categories. 2. Other Pacific Islander alone, or two or more Native Hawaiian and Other Pacific Islander categories.

Source: U.S. Census Bureau, *2021 American Community Survey 1-Year Estimates, ACS Demographic and Housing Estimates*, September 2022.

Wisconsin population by Hispanic and non-Hispanic origin, 2021

	Total	Percent
Not Hispanic or Latino[1]	5,454,585	92.5
One race	5,241,213	88.9
White	4,656,345	79.0
Black or African American	357,639	6.1
American Indian and Alaska Native	30,853	0.5
Asian	173,879	2.9
Native Hawaiian and other Pacific Islander	752	Z
Some other race	21,745	0.4
Two or more races	213,372	3.6
Hispanic or Latino[1] **(of any race)**	441,323	7.5
Mexican	298,280	5.1
Puerto Rican	69,917	1.2
Cuban	6,923	0.1
Other Hispanic or Latino	66,203	1.1

Z–Less than 0.1%.

1. "Hispanic or Latino" refers to a person of Cuban, Mexican, Puerto Rican, South or Central American, or other Spanish culture or origin regardless of race.

Source: U.S. Census Bureau, *2021 American Community Survey 1-Year Estimates, ACS Demographic and Housing Estimates*, September 2022.

Wisconsin 2020 census by sex, race, and Hispanic origin

County	Total population	White	Black or African American	American Indian/ Alaska Native	Asian or Pacific Islander	Some other race	Two or more races	Hispanic origin (any race)
Adams . . .	20,654	18,734	603	198	95	220	804	797
Ashland. . .	16,027	12,791	112	2,084	93	52	895	383
Barron. . . .	46,711	42,567	819	472	351	542	1,960	1,277
Bayfield. . .	16,220	13,493	59	1,696	38	94	840	279
Brown. . . .	268,740	212,929	8,404	7,581	8,640	11,793	19,393	26,216
Buffalo . . .	13,317	12,651	43	41	35	147	400	327
Burnett . . .	16,526	14,756	65	721	63	81	840	254
Calumet . .	52,442	46,499	444	252	1,319	1,505	2,423	2,857
Chippewa .	66,297	60,865	1,075	361	994	373	2,629	1,257
Clark.	34,659	31,972	119	172	112	1,189	1,095	2,098
Columbia. .	58,490	53,739	905	320	392	736	2,398	2,139
Crawford . .	16,113	15,107	269	52	73	70	542	260
Dane	561,504	435,458	30,473	2,397	35,999	18,203	38,974	41,954
Dodge . . .	89,396	79,395	2,766	438	528	2,179	4,090	5,490
Door.	30,066	27,754	145	144	148	482	1,393	1,138
Douglas. . .	44,295	39,733	583	801	304	256	2,618	768
Dunn	45,440	41,198	404	207	1,471	433	1,727	1,035
Eau Claire. .	105,710	93,277	1,255	527	4,484	1,158	5,009	3,118
Florence . .	4,558	4,312	9	30	16	15	176	66
Fond du Lac	104,154	91,630	2,416	506	1,291	3,152	5,159	6,717
Forest	9,179	7,407	32	1,228	28	20	464	155
Grant	51,938	48,710	684	129	421	544	1,450	1,236
Green	37,093	34,318	212	105	177	700	1,581	1,500
Green Lake	19,018	17,505	117	68	115	407	806	979
Iowa	23,709	22,326	114	39	192	207	831	455
Iron	6,137	5,831	16	66	13	42	169	72
Jackson . . .	21,145	18,142	442	1,378	77	244	862	678
Jefferson . .	84,900	75,145	888	365	699	2,858	4,945	7,068
Juneau . . .	26,718	24,299	560	381	149	229	1,100	727
Kenosha . .	169,151	128,417	12,082	730	2,962	8,864	16,096	24,546
Kewaunee .	20,563	19,149	60	89	70	484	711	834
La Crosse. .	120,784	106,317	1,994	508	5,634	1,052	5,279	3,051
Lafayette . .	16,611	15,231	28	48	44	615	645	1,089
Langlade . .	19,491	18,125	105	250	74	143	794	459
Lincoln . . .	28,415	26,909	158	120	120	176	932	529
Manitowoc	81,359	72,034	1,070	464	2,268	1,496	4,027	4,050
Marathon. .	138,013	119,902	1,192	648	8,532	1,853	5,886	4,453
Marinette. .	41,872	39,100	201	255	195	450	1,671	1,079
Marquette .	15,592	14,688	46	68	56	164	570	488
Menominee	4,255	500	2	3,643	5	4	101	136
Milwaukee .	939,489	488,198	245,863	7,507	46,815	63,932	87,174	153,017
Monroe . . .	46,274	41,293	649	585	428	985	2,334	2,560
Oconto . . .	38,965	36,432	92	510	121	316	1,494	848
Oneida . . .	37,845	35,468	213	473	223	214	1,254	575
Outagamie	190,705	164,009	3,053	3,143	6,730	3,731	10,039	9,423
Ozaukee . .	91,503	82,306	1,524	241	2,306	961	4,165	3,098
Pepin	7,318	6,899	24	38	26	73	258	157
Pierce	42,212	38,964	406	228	309	473	1,832	1,220
Polk	44,977	42,075	182	390	213	356	1,761	947
Portage . . .	70,377	62,967	945	298	2,279	932	2,956	2,620
Price	14,054	13,236	33	87	193	64	441	180
Racine. . . .	197,727	142,438	23,303	1,061	2,375	10,690	17,860	27,911
Richland . .	17,304	16,157	96	54	96	216	685	526
Rock.	163,687	133,107	8,311	878	2,131	7,457	11,803	15,800
Rusk.	14,188	13,371	45	73	58	83	558	250
St. Croix. . .	93,536	86,227	653	324	1,017	1,073	4,242	2,679
Sauk.	65,763	58,602	622	863	416	2,012	3,248	4,050
Sawyer . . .	18,074	13,920	101	2,940	65	107	941	358

Wisconsin 2010 census by sex, race, and Hispanic origin, continued

County	Total population	White	Black or African American	American Indian/ Alaska Native	Asian or Pacific Islander	Some other race	Two or more races	Hispanic origin (any race)
Shawano . .	40,881	34,679	126	3,455	171	487	1,963	1,176
Sheboygan	118,034	98,204	2,539	540	6,934	3,400	6,417	8,662
Taylor	19,913	18,878	67	42	68	266	592	567
Trempealeau	30,760	26,301	105	377	109	2,428	1,440	3,957
Vernon . . .	30,714	29,315	127	49	106	231	886	464
Vilas	23,047	19,701	58	2,252	58	114	864	459
Walworth. .	106,478	90,957	1,223	479	1,031	4,948	7,840	12,550
Washburn .	16,623	15,442	34	193	73	89	792	299
Washington	136,761	125,351	1,753	371	1,981	1,511	5,794	4,827
Waukesha .	406,978	353,946	6,852	1,202	15,828	6,102	23,048	21,835
Waupaca . .	51,812	48,284	211	308	271	813	1,925	1,864
Waushara. .	24,520	22,048	397	140	113	697	1,125	1,693
Winnebago	171,730	148,041	5,099	1,125	5,654	3,130	8,681	8,328
Wood	74,207	67,814	579	620	1,426	931	2,837	2,376
Total.	5,893,718	4,737,545	376,256	60,428	177,901	182,054	359,534	447,290

Source: U.S. Department of Commerce, U.S. Census Bureau, P.L. 94-171 Redistricting File, August 2021.

Wisconsin American Indian population since 1990

Year	Total	Male	Female
1900.	8,372	4,321	4,051
1910.	10,142	5,231	4,911
1920.	9,611	4,950	4,661
1930.	11,548	5,951	5,597
1940.	12,265	6,354	5,911
1950.	12,196	6,274	5,922
1960.	14,297	7,195	7,102
1970.	18,924	9,251	9,673
1980.	29,320	14,489	14,831
1990.	38,986	19,240	19,746
2000[1].	47,228	23,462	23,766
2010.	54,526	27,212	27,314
2020.	60,428	NA	NA

NA–Not available.
1. Starting in the 2000 census, when individuals were allowed to select more than one race, total includes only those who selected "American Indian" or "American Indian and Alaska Native" alone.
Source: U.S. Census Bureau, P.L. 94-171 Redistricting File, "P1: Race."

Wisconsin voting age population

			2020 not Hispanic or Latino,[1] by race						
County	2022 estimate	2020 census	White	Black/ African Amer- ican	American Indian/ Alaska Native	Asian	Pacific Islander	Some other	Two or more	2020 Hispanic or Latino
Adams . . .	17,892	17,644	15,843	561	158	78	8	38	405	553
Ashland. . .	12,569	12,586	10,311	82	1,397	71	9	18	479	219
Barron. . . .	37,181	36,847	33,880	535	309	281	5	70	985	782

Wisconsin voting age population, continued

County	2022 estimate	2020 census	White	Black/ African American	American Indian/ Alaska Native	Asian	Pacific Islander	Some other	Two or more	2020 Hispanic or Latino
Bayfield...	13,490	13,450	11,528	30	1,151	33	—	54	490	164
Brown....	210,452	206,130	168,143	5,633	4,595	5,687	92	424	5,549	16,007
Buffalo ..	10,590	10,554	10,069	29	24	19	12	5	201	195
Burnett...	13,754	13,642	12,405	52	484	47	9	25	466	154
Calumet ..	41,752	39,712	35,858	260	145	856	24	74	820	1,675
Chippewa .	52,374	51,536	47,552	895	255	622	13	99	1,277	823
Clark.....	24,895	24,688	22,835	56	98	81	4	56	344	1,214
Columbia..	46,449	46,137	42,415	751	202	297	11	90	1,020	1,351
Crawford ..	12,885	12,817	11,959	252	40	40	1	29	293	203
Dane	466,819	448,406	354,403	20,784	1,051	28,477	179	1,546	14,179	27,787
Dodge ...	71,416	71,608	63,352	2,468	321	422	5	140	1,395	3,505
Door.....	25,648	25,305	23,646	93	98	109	—	58	589	712
Douglas...	36,003	35,640	32,375	409	598	229	10	99	1,453	467
Dunn	36,345	36,191	33,115	295	121	1,016	10	70	899	665
Eau Claire..	86,004	83,793	75,086	879	344	3,045	57	177	2,254	1,951
Florence ..	3,881	3,848	3,699	7	22	5	—	5	74	36
Fond du Lac	82,436	82,059	73,084	1,543	310	883	22	138	1,849	4,230
Forest....	7,345	7,302	6,214	25	752	11	7	—	220	73
Grant	40,369	40,847	38,321	529	79	319	5	44	694	856
Green	29,270	28,864	26,934	126	44	139	3	52	688	878
Green Lake	15,139	15,013	13,907	78	37	75	—	32	298	586
Iowa.....	18,700	18,441	17,456	73	21	138	12	36	403	302
Iron	5,270	5,255	5,023	8	54	11	—	22	97	40
Jackson...	16,467	16,416	14,205	396	861	71	—	36	401	446
Jefferson..	68,194	66,349	58,966	602	164	512	15	143	1,624	4,323
Juneau ...	21,594	21,387	19,436	504	278	116	1	44	548	460
Kenosha ..	132,942	131,452	100,231	8,102	316	2,257	54	352	4,419	15,721
Kewaunee .	16,230	16,111	15,158	43	49	44	2	33	294	490
La Crosse..	98,007	96,611	86,478	1,363	333	3,759	12	271	2,306	2,089
Lafayette..	12,574	12,491	11,531	21	11	35	4	13	219	657
Langlade ..	15,692	15,647	14,702	50	169	53	4	33	385	251
Lincoln ...	23,148	23,017	21,995	50	79	95	2	27	448	321
Manitowoc	64,950	64,596	58,192	667	285	1,456	10	138	1,468	2,380
Marathon..	108,296	106,877	95,169	780	415	5,260	28	238	2,403	2,584
Marinette..	34,111	33,918	31,783	133	177	145	7	69	904	700
Marquette .	12,638	12,550	11,832	32	53	42	4	30	280	277
Menominee	2,914	2,893	465	2	2,284	2	—	—	59	81
Milwaukee..	723,717	720,446	391,811	168,815	3,065	32,576	219	3,093	21,043	99,824
Monroe...	35,139	34,674	31,232	434	339	280	44	68	832	1,445
Oconto ...	31,416	31,009	29,185	68	344	90	—	47	784	491
Oneida ...	31,676	31,461	29,697	152	317	157	5	90	678	365
Outagamie	148,542	146,186	128,030	1,990	2,031	4,390	77	285	3,643	5,740
Ozaukee ..	73,046	71,843	65,264	1,092	135	1,695	4	295	1,491	1,867
Pepin	5,761	5,705	5,388	18	26	16	—	6	155	96
Pierce	33,676	33,381	30,818	313	173	248	10	92	895	832
Polk	36,025	35,567	33,511	101	262	152	7	91	852	591
Portage...	57,411	56,525	50,992	672	214	1,633	16	114	1,169	1,715
Price	11,598	11,566	10,957	19	59	59	64	28	275	105
Racine....	154,090	153,051	112,107	16,059	473	1,810	41	524	4,581	17,456
Richland ..	13,413	13,369	12,576	43	33	70	—	16	319	312
Rock.....	127,840	126,282	104,869	5,629	316	1,612	49	378	3,885	9,544
Rusk.....	11,380	11,302	10,668	34	45	39	—	27	325	164
St. Croix...	72,732	70,347	65,189	447	190	744	25	201	1,915	1,636
Sauk.....	51,977	51,197	46,069	420	514	300	15	95	1,195	2,589
Sawyer ...	14,806	14,724	11,857	67	1,960	49	—	39	529	223

Wisconsin voting age population, continued

County	2022 estimate	2020 census	White	Black/ African American	American Indian/ Alaska Native	Asian	Pacific Islander	Some other	Two or more	2020 Hispanic or Latino
Shawano . .	32,540	32,157	27,903	77	2,332	122	6	44	980	693
Sheboygan	93,437	92,434	78,432	1,759	300	4,373	13	259	1,943	5,355
Taylor	15,243	15,126	14,401	38	27	54	3	11	261	331
Trempealeau	23,350	23,150	20,420	57	53	70	—	39	353	2,158
Vernon . . .	23,008	22,734	21,720	87	41	68	2	70	446	300
Vilas	19,623	19,453	17,166	47	1,405	48	—	52	471	264
Walworth. .	84,800	84,970	72,748	883	182	831	10	198	2,011	8,107
Washburn .	13,701	13,612	12,768	19	137	53	4	28	424	179
Washington	108,664	107,030	98,923	1,108	213	1,398	24	268	2,130	2,966
Waukesha .	322,562	318,193	280,196	4,582	649	11,066	92	760	7,218	13,630
Waupaca . .	41,951	41,368	38,720	157	190	201	4	85	871	1,140
Waushara. .	20,124	20,060	17,938	367	107	87	10	48	418	1,085
Winnebago	137,449	136,202	118,978	3,591	757	3,927	42	260	3,382	5,265
Wood	58,801	58,544	54,137	361	386	963	19	123	1,162	1,393
Total.	4,676,183	4,612,300	3,774,226	258,704	35,459	126,019	1,446	12,562	119,815	284,069

Note: The voting age population is 18 and older.
—Represents zero.
1. "Hispanic or Latino" represents ethnicity and includes people of Cuban, Mexican, Puerto Rican, South or Central American, or other Spanish culture or origin, regardless of race.
Sources: U.S. Census Bureau, P.L. 94–171 Redistricting File, "P4: Hispanic or Latino, and Not Hispanic or Latino by Race for the Population 18 Years and Over"; Wisconsin Department of Administration, Demographic Services Center, *Official Final Population Estimates, 1/1/2022, Wisconsin Counties, with Comparison to Census 2020*, October 2022.

Wisconsin population by age group

	Male		Female		Total	
Age (years)	2020 census	2021 estimate	2020 census	2021 estimate	2020 census	2021 estimate
Under 5	183,391	163,690	175,052	156,555	358,443	320,245
5–9	188,286	177,513	180,331	169,311	368,617	346,824
10–14	192,232	193,450	183,695	183,101	375,927	376,551
15–19	204,803	197,968	194,406	189,414	399,209	387,382
20–24	196,897	199,666	189,655	193,825	386,552	393,491
25–29	189,349	191,717	182,998	181,232	372,347	372,949
30–34	178,120	186,579	171,227	178,029	349,347	364,608
35–39	174,619	193,304	170,709	186,860	345,328	380,164
40–44	191,738	186,737	188,600	178,981	380,338	365,718
45–49	218,539	168,981	219,088	162,841	437,627	331,822
50–54	218,303	187,690	217,823	181,650	436,126	369,340
55–59	192,952	205,781	193,034	205,454	385,986	411,235
60–64	155,756	208,494	158,069	209,842	313,825	418,336
65–69	109,168	177,995	117,861	182,372	227,029	360,367
70–74	81,067	139,994	92,400	148,784	173,467	288,778
75–79	62,181	83,461	79,071	95,974	141,252	179,435
80–84	47,549	50,444	69,512	65,710	117,061	116,154
85 and over	37,450	40,410	81,055	72,099	118,505	112,509
All ages	2,822,400	2,953,874	2,864,586	2,942,034	5,686,986	5,895,908

Note: The median age was 38.5 in 2010 and 40.1 in 2021. The median age for males was 37.3 in 2010 and 39.3 in 2021. The median age for females was 39.6 in 2010 and 40.9 in 2021.
Source: U.S. Census Bureau, *Annual Estimates of the Resident Population for Selected Age Groups by Sex for Wisconsin: April 1, 2020 to July 1, 2021*, April 2023.

Wisconsin births and birth rates, 2020

County	Births[1]	Rate[2]	County	Births[1]	Rate[2]	County	Births[1]	Rate[2]
Adams	140	67.1	Iron	37	59.9	Price	94	66.9
Ashland. . . .	156	96.9	Jackson	239	113.2	Racine	2,233	113.4
Barron	454	97.2	Jefferson . . .	805	94.8	Richland . . .	188	109.2
Bayfield	108	66.2	Juneau	222	82.8	Rock	1,773	107.9
Brown	3,060	113.5	Kenosha . . .	1,729	102.5	Rusk	116	82.1
Buffalo	124	93.2	Kewaunee . .	203	98.8	St. Croix	1,009	106.2
Burnett	96	57.3	La Crosse . . .	1,150	95.5	Sauk	687	104.6
Calumet . . .	468	89.1	Lafayette . . .	247	147.2	Sawyer	132	72.2
Chippewa . .	669	100.1	Langlade . . .	181	92.8	Shawano . . .	450	110.1
Clark	599	172.4	Lincoln	267	93.5	Sheboygan . .	1,128	95.8
Columbia . . .	581	99.3	Manitowoc . .	770	94.5	Taylor	214	107.4
Crawford . . .	163	101.4	Marathon . . .	1,420	103.2	Trempealeau	399	129.9
Dane	5,697	101.0	Marinette . . .	345	82.4	Vernon	435	140.7
Dodge	779	87.2	Marquette . .	136	86.1	Vilas	160	68.0
Door	240	79.0	Menominee .	69	160.9	Walworth . . .	916	85.8
Douglas	384	86.9	Milwaukee . .	11,989	129.2	Washburn . .	135	80.6
Dunn	473	103.8	Monroe	600	129.9	Washington .	1,294	94.3
Eau Claire . . .	1,065	100.0	Oconto	339	86.1	Waukesha . .	3,915	95.8
Florence . . .	31	67.5	Oneida	284	74.2	Waupaca . . .	475	92.1
Fond du Lac .	1,038	99.5	Outagamie . .	2,183	114.0	Waushara . . .	171	68.9
Forest	90	97.2	Ozaukee . . .	829	89.6	Winnebago .	1,755	102.3
Grant	570	109.4	Pepin	73	99.1	Wood	714	96.4
Green	359	97.1	Pierce	402	94.4	Total[3]	61,814	104.8
Green Lake . .	199	103.5	Polk	422	92.9			
Iowa	284	119.5	Portage	652	92.5			

1. Wisconsin resident births are reported by mother's county of residence. 2. Birth rates are the number of births per 10,000 population. 3. Total includes 1 birth in an unspecified county.

Source: Wisconsin Department of Health Services, Division of Public Health, Office of Health Informatics, departmental data, April 2023.

Wisconsin deaths and mortality rates, 2020

County	Deaths	Rate[1]	County	Deaths	Rate[1]	County	Deaths	Rate[1]
Adams	321	153.8	Green	397	107.3	Outagamie . .	1,673	87.3
Ashland	207	128.5	Green Lake . .	285	148.2	Ozaukee . . .	905	97.8
Barron	618	132.3	Iowa	212	89.2	Pepin	81	110.0
Bayfield	190	116.4	Iron	108	174.8	Pierce	371	87.1
Brown	2,374	88.1	Jackson	234	110.8	Polk	582	128.1
Buffalo	143	107.5	Jefferson . . .	892	105.0	Portage	718	101.9
Burnett	230	137.4	Juneau	383	142.9	Price	213	151.6
Calumet . . .	404	76.9	Kenosha . . .	1,708	101.2	Racine	2,233	113.4
Chippewa . .	674	100.8	Kewaunee . .	206	100.3	Richland . . .	228	132.5
Clark	389	112.0	La Crosse . . .	1,140	94.7	Rock	1,772	107.8
Columbia . . .	632	108.1	Lafayette . . .	164	97.7	Rusk	234	165.7
Crawford . . .	197	122.6	Langlade . . .	306	156.9	St. Croix	810	85.2
Dane	3,770	66.8	Lincoln	437	153.1	Sauk	751	114.3
Dodge	1,111	124.4	Manitowoc . .	949	116.4	Sawyer	277	151.4
Door	380	125.1	Marathon . . .	1,444	104.9	Shawano . . .	505	123.6
Douglas	499	112.9	Marinette . . .	615	146.9	Sheboygan . .	1,251	106.2
Dunn	414	90.9	Marquette . .	251	158.9	Taylor	226	113.4
Eau Claire . . .	999	93.8	Menominee .	65	151.6	Trempealeau	303	98.6
Florence . . .	66	143.7	Milwaukee . .	9,502	102.4	Vernon	355	114.8
Fond du Lac .	1,183	113.4	Monroe	547	118.4	Vilas	366	155.6
Forest	153	165.3	Oconto	413	104.9	Walworth . . .	1,095	102.5
Grant	578	110.9	Oneida	530	138.5	Washburn . .	279	166.5

Wisconsin deaths and mortality rates, 2020, continued

County	Deaths	Rate[1]	County	Deaths	Rate[1]	County	Deaths	Rate[1]
Washington	1,390	101.3	Waushara	331	133.3	Total[2]	60,972	103.4
Waukesha	4,150	101.5	Winnebago	1,730	100.8			
Waupaca	759	147.2	Wood	1,052	142.0			

1. Death rate is the number of deaths per 10,000 population. 2. Total includes 12 deaths in unspecified counties.
Source: Wisconsin Department of Health Services, Division of Public Health, Office of Health Informatics, departmental data, April 2023.

Wisconsin deaths and mortality rates by age group, 2020

	Total		Male		Female	
Age (years)	Deaths	Rate[1]	Deaths	Rate[1]	Deaths	Rate[1]
0	361	575.8	198	618.1	162	528.4
1–4	52	19.4	28	20.4	24	18.3
5–9	39	11.2	20	11.2	19	11.2
10–14	58	15.8	36	19.1	22	12.2
15–17	93	41.1	70	60.6	23	20.8
18–19	92	60.2	66	84.7	26	34.6
20–24	379	96.7	268	134.4	111	57.7
25–29	476	124.8	320	163.0	156	84.3
30–34	681	187.7	478	257.7	203	114.5
35–39	723	193.1	494	261.1	229	123.6
40–44	789	231.7	508	294.3	281	167.3
45–49	1,071	311.6	677	391.3	394	230.9
50–54	1,802	483.3	1,111	595.9	691	370.7
55–59	2,989	706.4	1,845	882.7	1,144	534.3
60–64	4,329	1,078.0	2,667	1,345.4	1,662	817.3
65–69	5,276	1,554.5	3,242	1,954.0	2,034	1,172.5
70–74	6,597	2,570.5	3,842	3,114.2	2,755	2,067.1
75–79	7,111	4,060.2	3,925	4,899.3	3,186	3,352.8
80–84	8,088	6,818.5	4,129	8,057.1	3,959	5,876.3
85+	21,698	17,070.9	8,518	18,979.1	13,180	16,029.4
All ages	62,704	1,074.5	32,442	1,117.0	30,261	1,032.3

1. Per 100,000 population.
Source: Wisconsin Department of Health Services, Division of Public Health, Office of Health Informatics, departmental data, April 2023.

Basic data on Wisconsin counties

County (year created)[1]	County seat	Full value 2021 assessment ($1,000)[2]	Population 2022 estimate	% change[3]	2022 rank	Land area in sq. miles[4]	2022 population/ sq. mile
Adams (1848)	Friendship	3,045,425	20,836	0.88	51	645.6	32.3
Ashland (1860)	Ashland	1,294,573	15,937	-0.56	63	1,045.0	15.3
Barron (1859)	Barron	5,008,571	46,919	0.45	30	863.0	54.4
Bayfield (1845)	Washburn	2,922,294	16,194	-0.16	61	1,477.9	11.0
Brown (1818)	Green Bay	26,708,663	273,160	1.64	4	530.1	515.3
Buffalo (1853)	Alma	1,315,831	13,301	-0.12	67	675.8	19.7
Burnett (1856)	Meenon	3,095,749	16,585	0.36	60	821.6	20.2
Calumet (1836)	Chilton	5,083,636	54,997	4.87	27	318.3	172.8
Chippewa (1845)	Chippewa Falls	7,010,536	67,082	1.18	24	1,008.4	66.5

Basic data on Wisconsin counties, continued

County (year created)[1]	County seat	Full value 2021 assessment ($1,000)[2]	Population 2022 estimate	% change[3]	2022 rank	Land area in sq. miles[4]	2022 population/ sq. mile
Clark (1853)	Neillsville	2,434,707	34,801	0.41	41	1,209.7	28.8
Columbia (1846)	Portage	6,540,619	58,627	0.23	26	765.5	76.6
Crawford (1818)	Prairie du Chien	1,407,876	16,129	0.10	62	570.6	28.3
Dane (1836)	Madison	76,889,801	582,165	3.68	2	1,196.5	486.6
Dodge (1836)	Juneau	7,690,531	88,822	-0.64	19	875.7	101.4
Door (1851)	Sturgeon Bay	8,556,995	30,328	0.87	44	482.0	62.9
Douglas (1854)	Superior	4,144,023	44,547	0.57	34	1,304.3	34.2
Dunn (1854)	Menomonie	3,836,605	45,454	0.03	32	850.2	53.5
Eau Claire (1856)	Eau Claire	10,591,905	108,019	2.18	14	637.9	169.3
Florence (1881)	Florence	736,947	4,575	0.37	71	488.1	9.4
Fond du Lac (1836)	Fond du Lac	8,904,213	104,162	0.01	16	719.6	144.8
Forest (1885)	Crandon	1,259,268	9,190	0.12	68	1,014.2	9.1
Grant (1836)	Lancaster	3,865,162	51,171	-1.48	29	1,146.9	44.6
Green (1836)	Monroe	3,691,418	37,445	0.95	40	584.0	64.1
Green Lake (1858)	Green Lake	2,577,954	19,091	0.38	55	349.5	54.6
Iowa (1829)	Dodgeville	2,506,857	23,936	0.96	48	762.7	31.4
Iron (1893)	Hurley	1,031,764	6,125	-0.20	70	758.2	8.1
Jackson (1853)	Black River Falls	1,849,554	21,118	-0.13	50	987.9	21.4
Jefferson (1836)	Jefferson	8,726,941	86,576	0.50	20	556.5	155.6
Juneau (1856)	Mauston	2,597,846	26,848	0.49	46	767.1	35.0
Kenosha (1850)	Kenosha	19,742,922	170,272	0.66	8	271.8	626.4
Kewaunee (1852)	Kewaunee	1,929,834	20,621	0.28	52	342.5	60.2
La Crosse (1851)	La Crosse	12,238,689	122,126	1.11	12	451.8	270.3
Lafayette (1846)	Darlington	1,364,211	16,650	0.23	59	633.6	26.3
Langlade (1879)	Antigo	1,866,139	19,457	-0.17	54	870.7	22.3
Lincoln (1874)	Merrill	2,834,274	28,431	0.06	45	878.7	32.4
Manitowoc (1836)	Manitowoc	6,385,054	81,442	0.10	21	589.3	138.2
Marathon (1850)	Wausau	12,764,789	139,205	0.86	10	1,545.2	90.1
Marinette (1879)	Marinette	4,365,485	41,912	0.10	36	1,399.5	29.9
Marquette (1836)	Montello	1,869,463	15,633	0.26	64	455.7	34.3
Menominee (1961)	Keshena	395,192	4,266	0.26	72	357.6	11.9
Milwaukee (1834)	Milwaukee	77,290,319	939,487	0.00	1	241.5	3,890.5
Monroe (1854)	Sparta	3,934,665	46,697	0.91	31	900.9	51.8
Oconto (1851)	Oconto	4,543,648	39,307	0.88	38	997.5	39.4
Oneida (1885)	Rhinelander	7,797,474	37,935	0.24	39	1,113.9	34.1
Outagamie (1851)	Appleton	19,041,095	192,938	1.17	6	637.6	302.6
Ozaukee (1853)	Port Washington	14,289,621	92,623	1.22	18	233.0	397.5
Pepin (1858)	Durand	721,545	7,356	0.52	69	232.0	31.7
Pierce (1853)	Ellsworth	4,148,445	42,408	0.46	35	574.0	73.9
Polk (1853)	Balsam Lake	5,891,358	45,348	0.82	33	914.3	49.6
Portage (1836)	Stevens Point	7,098,581	71,158	1.11	23	800.9	88.9
Price (1879)	Phillips	1,503,797	14,026	-0.20	66	1,254.1	11.2
Racine (1836)	Racine	19,576,633	198,138	0.21	5	332.6	595.7
Richland (1842)	Richland Center	1,348,098	17,282	-0.13	57	586.1	29.5
Rock (1836)	Janesville	14,617,256	164,959	0.78	9	718.1	229.7
Rusk (1901)	Ladysmith	1,342,062	14,223	0.25	65	913.6	15.6
St. Croix (1840)	Hudson	12,439,288	96,269	2.92	17	722.5	133.3
Sauk (1840)	Baraboo	8,639,096	66,497	1.12	25	831.5	80.0
Sawyer (1883)	Hayward	3,995,635	18,093	0.11	56	1,257.6	14.4
Shawano (1853)	Shawano	3,667,700	41,190	0.76	37	893.2	46.1
Sheboygan (1836)	Sheboygan	11,530,755	118,776	0.63	13	511.5	232.2
Taylor (1875)	Medford	1,585,641	19,976	0.32	53	975.1	20.5
Trempealeau (1854)	Whitehall	2,673,075	30,884	0.40	43	733.0	42.1
Vernon (1851)	Viroqua	2,373,697	30,965	0.82	42	791.6	39.1
Vilas (1893)	Eagle River	7,883,731	23,140	0.40	49	857.7	27.0
Walworth (1836)	Elkhorn	18,146,880	106,129	0.85	15	555.4	191.1
Washburn (1883)	Shell Lake	3,002,428	16,655	0.19	58	797.1	20.9

Statistics and Reference: Population | 535

Basic data on Wisconsin counties, continued

County (year created)[1]	County seat	Full value 2021 assessment ($1,000)[2]	Population 2022 estimate	% change[3]	2022 rank	Land area in sq. miles[4]	2022 population/ sq. mile
Washington (1836)	West Bend	18,282,260	138,229	1.07	11	430.6	321.0
Waukesha (1846)	Waukesha	66,686,338	410,769	0.93	3	549.7	747.2
Waupaca (1851)	Waupaca	4,807,805	52,309	0.96	28	747.7	70.0
Waushara (1851)	Wautoma	3,028,687	24,492	-0.11	47	626.2	39.1
Winnebago (1840)	Oshkosh	15,795,068	172,542	0.47	7	434.7	396.9
Wood (1856)	Wisconsin Rapids	6,055,382	74,200	-0.01	22	793.0	93.6
Total		654,820,376	5,949,155	0.94		54,167.4	109.8

1. Counties are created by legislative act. Depending on the date, Wisconsin counties were created by the Michigan Territorial Legislature (1818–1836), the Wisconsin Territorial Legislature (1836–1848), or the Wisconsin State Legislature (after 1848). 2. Reflects actual market value of all taxable general property, including personal property and real estate, as determined by the Wisconsin Department of Revenue. 3. Change from 2020 U.S. census. 4. Detemined by U.S. Census Bureau, 2019.

Sources: Wisconsin Department of Revenue, Division of State and Local Finance, *Town, Village, and City Taxes Levied 2021—Collected 2022*; Wisconsin Department of Administration, Demographic Services Center, *County Final Population Estimates, October 2022*; U.S. Census Bureau, 2019 Census TIGER/Line Data, https://www.census.gov/geo/maps-data/data/tiger-line.html.

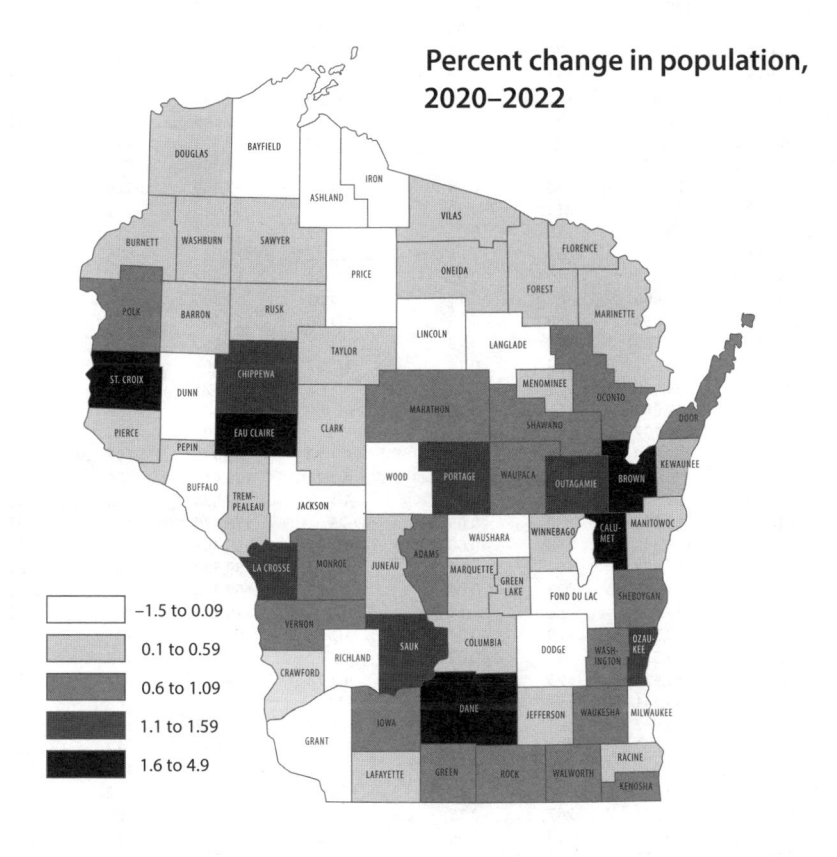

Percent change in population, 2020–2022

- −1.5 to 0.09
- 0.1 to 0.59
- 0.6 to 1.09
- 1.1 to 1.59
- 1.6 to 4.9

Source: Wisconsin Department of Administration, Demographic Services Center, *Official Final Estimate, 1/1/2022, Wisconsin Counties, with Comparison to Census 2020*, October 2022.

Population of Wisconsin legislative districts

District	2020 Population	Deviation from ideal[2] Total	Deviation from ideal[2] Percent	District	2020 Population	Deviation from ideal[2] Total	Deviation from ideal[2] Percent
SD-1.....	178,936	338	0.19	AD-43 ..	59,685	152	0.26
AD-1 ...	59,444	−89	−0.15	AD-44 ..	59,741	208	0.35
AD-2 ...	59,764	231	0.39	AD-45 ..	59,692	159	0.27
AD-3 ...	59,728	195	0.33	SD-16....	178,608	10	0.01
SD-2.....	178,464	−134	−0.08	AD-46 ..	59,320	−213	−0.36
AD-4 ...	59,636	103	0.17	AD-47 ..	59,591	58	0.1
AD-5 ...	59,374	−159	−0.27	AD-48 ..	59,697	164	0.28
AD-6 ...	59,454	−79	−0.13	SD-17....	178,829	231	0.13
SD-3.....	178,536	−62	−0.03	AD-49 ..	59,708	175	0.29
AD-7 ...	59,603	70	0.12	AD-50 ..	59,456	−77	−0.13
AD-8[1] ..	59,362	−171	−0.29	AD-51 ..	59,665	132	0.22
AD-9[1] ..	59,571	38	0.06	SD-18....	178,812	214	0.12
SD-4.....	178,419	−179	−0.10	AD-52 ..	59,579	46	0.08
AD-10 ..	59,503	−30	−0.05	AD-53 ..	59,625	92	0.15
AD-11 ..	59,565	32	0.05	AD-54 ..	59,608	75	0.13
AD-12 ..	59,351	−182	−0.31	SD-19....	178,550	−48	−0.03
SD-5.....	178,536	−62	−0.03	AD-55 ..	59,537	4	0.01
AD-13 ..	59,551	18	0.03	AD-56 ..	59,596	63	0.11
AD-14 ..	59,609	76	0.13	AD-57 ..	59,417	−116	−0.19
AD-15 ..	59,376	−157	−0.26	SD-20....	178,690	92	0.05
SD-6.....	178,495	−103	−0.06	AD-58 ..	59,607	74	0.12
AD-16 ..	59,714	181	0.3	AD-59 ..	59,749	216	0.36
AD-17 ..	59,435	−98	−0.16	AD-60 ..	59,334	−199	−0.33
AD-18 ..	59,346	−187	−0.31	SD-21....	178,368	−230	−0.13
SD-7.....	178,460	−138	−0.08	AD-61 ..	59,409	−124	−0.21
AD-19 ..	59,320	−213	−0.36	AD-62 ..	59,425	−108	−0.18
AD-20 ..	59,548	15	0.03	AD-63 ..	59,534	1	0
AD-21 ..	59,592	59	0.1	SD-22....	178,092	−506	−0.28
SD-8.....	178,552	−46	−0.03	AD-64 ..	59,362	−171	−0.29
AD-22 ..	59,466	−67	−0.11	AD-65 ..	59,365	−168	−0.28
AD-23 ..	59,383	−150	−0.25	AD-66 ..	59,365	−168	−0.28
AD-24 ..	59,703	170	0.29	SD-23....	178,360	−238	−0.13
SD-9.....	178,827	229	0.13	AD-67 ..	59,591	58	0.1
AD-25 ..	59,460	−73	−0.12	AD-68 ..	59,422	−111	−0.19
AD-26 ..	59,640	107	0.18	AD-69 ..	59,347	−186	−0.31
AD-27 ..	59,727	194	0.33	SD-24....	178,407	−191	−0.11
SD-10	178,810	212	0.12	AD-70 ..	59,436	−97	−0.16
AD-28 ..	59,743	210	0.35	AD-71 ..	59,447	−86	−0.14
AD-29 ..	59,504	−29	−0.05	AD-72 ..	59,524	−9	−0.02
AD-30 ..	59,563	30	0.05	SD-25....	178,470	−128	−0.07
SD-11	178,741	143	0.08	AD-73 ..	59,467	−66	−0.11
AD-31 ..	59,594	61	0.1	AD-74 ..	59,587	54	0.09
AD-32 ..	59,556	23	0.04	AD-75 ..	59,416	−117	−0.20
AD-33 ..	59,591	58	0.1	SD-26....	178,749	151	0.08
SD-12	178,519	−79	−0.04	AD-76 ..	59,664	131	0.22
AD-34 ..	59,520	−13	−0.02	AD-77 ..	59,361	−172	−0.29
AD-35 ..	59,558	25	0.04	AD-78 ..	59,724	191	0.32
AD-36 ..	59,441	−92	−0.15	SD-27....	178,960	362	0.2
SD-13	178,437	−161	−0.09	AD-79 ..	59,687	154	0.26
AD-37 ..	59,382	−151	−0.25	AD-80 ..	59,555	22	0.04
AD-38 ..	59,618	85	0.14	AD-81 ..	59,718	185	0.31
AD-39 ..	59,437	−96	−0.16	SD-28....	178,506	−92	−0.05
SD-14	178,331	−267	−0.15	AD-82 ..	59,364	−169	−0.28
AD-40 ..	59,318	−215	−0.36	AD-83 ..	59,606	73	0.12
AD-41 ..	59,431	−102	−0.17	AD-84 ..	59,536	3	0.01
AD-42 ..	59,582	49	0.08	SD-29....	178,791	193	0.11
SD-15	179,118	520	0.29	AD-85 ..	59,672	139	0.23

Population of Wisconsin legislative districts, continued

District	2020 Population	Deviation from ideal[2] Total	Deviation from ideal[2] Percent	District	2020 Population	Deviation from ideal[2] Total	Deviation from ideal[2] Percent
AD-86 . .	59,708	175	0.29	AD-93 . .	59,693	160	0.27
AD-87 . .	59,411	−122	−0.20	SD-32	178,385	−213	−0.12
SD-30	178,583	−15	−0.01	AD-94 . .	59,594	61	0.1
AD-88 . .	59,542	9	0.02	AD-95 . .	59,479	−54	−0.09
AD-89 . .	59,328	−205	−0.34	AD-96 . .	59,312	−221	−0.37
AD-90 . .	59,713	180	0.3	SD-33	178,747	149	0.08
SD-31	178,630	32	0.02	AD-97 . .	59,664	131	0.22
AD-91 . .	59,413	−120	−0.20	AD-98 . .	59,406	−127	−0.21
AD-92 . .	59,524	−9	−0.02	AD-99 . .	59,677	144	0.24

Note: Legislative maps were selected by the Wisconsin Supreme Court in *Johnson v. Wis. Elections Comm'n*, 2022 WI 19 (Wis. 2022).
1. Ideal senate district: 178,598. Ideal assembly district: 59,533.
Source: Wis. Legis. Technology Services Bureau, *Wisconsin Assembly Districts (2022)*, ArcGIS Map, last modified October 21, 2022, https://data-ltsb.opendata.arcgis.com.

Wisconsin population by county and municipality

	2020 census	2022 estimate	% change		2020 census	2022 estimate	% change
Adams	20,654	20,836	0.88	Morse, town	499	499	0.00
Adams, city	1,761	1,755	−0.34	Peeksville, town.	137	137	0.00
Adams, town	1,378	1,387	0.65	Sanborn, town	1,381	1,377	−0.29
Big Flats, town.	948	951	0.32	Shanagolden, town . . .	131	131	0.00
Colburn, town.	215	214	−0.47	White River, town.	1,067	1,072	0.47
Dell Prairie, town	1,631	1,633	0.12	**Barron**	46,711	46,919	0.45
Easton, town.	1,062	1,063	0.09	Almena, town	887	898	1.24
Friendship, village	648	606	−6.48	Almena, village	705	742	5.25
Jackson, town	1,141	1,144	0.26	Arland, town.	712	713	0.14
Leola, town	287	288	0.35	Barron, city.	3,733	3,685	−1.29
Lincoln, town	320	323	0.94	Barron, town.	813	811	−0.25
Monroe, town	391	395	1.02	Bear Lake, town	670	683	1.94
New Chester, town. . . .	1,960	2,071	5.66	Cameron, village	1,872	1,871	−0.05
New Haven, town.	680	680	0.00	Cedar Lake, town	1,076	1,095	1.77
Preston, town	1,377	1,381	0.29	Chetek, city	2,172	2,166	−0.28
Quincy, town	1,159	1,159	0.00	Chetek, town	1,726	1,751	1.45
Richfield, town	138	140	1.45	Clinton, town	870	874	0.46
Rome, town	3,025	3,111	2.84	Crystal Lake, town	743	745	0.27
Springville, town	1,283	1,271	−0.94	Cumberland, city	2,274	2,267	−0.31
Strongs Prairie, town. . .	1,145	1,158	1.14	Cumberland, town	818	817	−0.12
Wisconsin Dells, city (part)	105	106	0.95	Dallas, town	570	572	0.35
Ashland	16,027	15,937	−0.56	Dallas, village	359	358	−0.28
Agenda, town	370	369	−0.27	Dovre, town	825	825	0.00
Ashland, city (part)	7,905	7,816	−1.13	Doyle, town	490	489	−0.20
Ashland, town.	589	586	−0.51	Haugen, village	266	266	0.00
Butternut, village	366	362	−1.09	Lakeland, town	938	939	0.11
Chippewa, town	349	348	−0.29	Maple Grove, town. . . .	877	874	−0.34
Gingles, town	738	744	0.81	Maple Plain, town	844	852	0.95
Gordon, town	261	262	0.38	New Auburn, village (part)	25	25	0.00
Jacobs, town.	648	646	−0.31	Oak Grove, town	960	969	0.94
La Pointe, town	428	430	0.47	Prairie Farm, town	566	575	1.59
Marengo, town	460	464	0.87	Prairie Farm, village . . .	494	498	0.81
Mellen, city	698	694	−0.57	Prairie Lake, town.	1,648	1,674	1.58

Wisconsin population by county and municipality, continued

	2020 census	2022 estimate	% change		2020 census	2022 estimate	% change
Rice Lake, city	9,040	9,080	0.44	Pittsfield, town	2,791	2,811	0.72
Rice Lake, town	2,813	2,833	0.71	Pulaski, village (part)	3,650	3,818	4.60
Sioux Creek, town	667	681	2.10	Rockland, town	1,775	1,779	0.23
Stanfold, town	701	709	1.14	Scott, town	3,636	3,660	0.66
Stanley, town	2,570	2,575	0.19	Suamico, village	12,820	13,230	3.20
Sumner, town	699	701	0.29	Wrightstown, town	2,578	2,637	2.29
Turtle Lake, town	640	649	1.41	Wrightstown, village (part)	2,895	2,921	0.90
Turtle Lake, village (part)	959	962	0.31				
Vance Creek, town	689	695	0.87	**Buffalo**	**13,317**	**13,301**	**-0.12**
				Alma, city	716	717	0.14
Bayfield	**16,220**	**16,194**	**-0.16**	Alma, town	254	255	0.39
Ashland, city (part)	3	3	0.00	Belvidere, town	403	386	-4.22
Barksdale, town	745	742	-0.40	Buffalo, town	746	743	-0.40
Barnes, town	823	820	-0.36	Buffalo City, city	1,007	1,009	0.20
Bayfield, city	584	586	0.34	Canton, town	245	246	0.41
Bayfield, town	787	792	0.64	Cochrane, village	423	421	-0.47
Bayview, town	512	513	0.20	Cross, town	368	369	0.27
Bell, town	355	359	1.13	Dover, town	515	520	0.97
Cable, town	853	859	0.70	Fountain City, city	806	803	-0.37
Clover, town	261	261	0.00	Gilmanton, town	425	423	-0.47
Delta, town	315	316	0.32	Glencoe, town	402	406	1.00
Drummond, town	544	543	-0.18	Lincoln, town	167	166	-0.60
Eileen, town	722	719	-0.42	Maxville, town	321	320	-0.31
Grand View, town	508	507	-0.20	Milton, town	541	540	-0.18
Hughes, town	471	472	0.21	Modena, town	313	310	-0.96
Iron River, town	1,240	1,235	-0.40	Mondovi, city	2,845	2,852	0.25
Kelly, town	436	435	-0.23	Mondovi, town	451	450	-0.22
Keystone, town	373	372	-0.27	Montana, town	268	267	-0.37
Lincoln, town	251	250	-0.40	Naples, town	697	697	0.00
Mason, town	289	287	-0.69	Nelson, town	574	576	0.35
Mason, village	101	101	0.00	Nelson, village	322	322	0.00
Namakagon, town	316	316	0.00	Waumandee, town	508	503	-0.98
Orienta, town	164	164	0.00				
Oulu, town	560	563	0.54	**Burnett**	**16,526**	**16,585**	**0.36**
Pilsen, town	216	223	3.24	Anderson, town	408	409	0.25
Port Wing, town	389	389	0.00	Blaine, town	206	205	-0.49
Russell, town	1,553	1,560	0.45	Daniels, town	676	681	0.74
Tripp, town	244	248	1.64	Dewey, town	545	547	0.37
Washburn, city	2,051	2,004	-2.29	Grantsburg, town	1,174	1,182	0.68
Washburn, town	554	555	0.18	Grantsburg, village	1,330	1,318	-0.90
Brown	**268,740**	**273,160**	**1.64**	Jackson, town	935	943	0.86
Allouez, village	14,156	14,014	-1.00	La Follette, town	559	562	0.54
Ashwaubenon, village	16,991	17,757	4.51	Lincoln, town	367	372	1.36
Bellevue, village	15,935	16,568	3.97	Meenon, town	1,212	1,212	0.00
De Pere, city	25,410	25,525	0.45	Oakland, town	980	986	0.61
Denmark, village	2,408	2,446	1.58	Roosevelt, town	197	198	0.51
Eaton, town	1,662	1,690	1.68	Rusk, town	470	469	-0.21
Glenmore, town	1,045	1,054	0.86	Sand Lake, town	576	579	0.52
Green Bay, city	107,395	107,369	-0.02	Scott, town	583	586	0.51
Green Bay, town	2,197	2,214	0.77	Siren, town	1,004	1,006	0.20
Hobart, village	10,211	10,486	2.69	Siren, village	824	823	-0.12
Holland, town	1,559	1,568	0.58	Swiss, town	807	806	-0.12
Howard, village (part)	19,950	20,952	5.02	Trade Lake, town	904	911	0.77
Humboldt, town	1,299	1,309	0.77	Union, town	345	350	1.45
Lawrence, town	6,306	6,724	6.63	Webb Lake, town	432	437	1.16
Ledgeview, town	8,820	9,373	6.27	Webster, village	694	697	0.43
Morrison, town	1,689	1,698	0.53	West Marshland, town	400	401	0.25
New Denmark, town	1,562	1,557	-0.32	Wood River, town	898	905	0.78

Wisconsin population by county and municipality, continued

	2020 census	2022 estimate	% change		2020 census	2022 estimate	% change
Calumet	52,442	54,997	4.87	Beaver, town.	826	823	-0.36
Appleton, city (part) . . .	11,304	11,276	-0.25	Butler, town	112	116	3.57
Brillion, city	3,262	3,487	6.90	Colby, city (part)	1,275	1,257	-1.41
Brillion, town	1,650	1,682	1.94	Colby, town	922	924	0.22
Brothertown, town. . . .	1,328	1,325	-0.23	Curtiss, village.	292	299	2.40
Charlestown, town. . . .	774	771	-0.39	Dewhurst, town.	349	354	1.43
Chilton, city	4,080	4,064	-0.39	Dorchester, village (part)	846	850	0.47
Chilton, town	1,059	1,055	-0.38	Eaton, town	718	718	0.00
Harrison, town	0	0	0.00	Foster, town	118	119	0.85
Harrison, village (part). .	12,418	14,424	16.15	Fremont, town	1,312	1,326	1.07
Hilbert, village	1,248	1,271	1.84	Grant, town	858	861	0.35
Kaukauna, city (part). . .	0	0	0.00	Granton, village.	381	377	-1.05
Kiel, city (part).	347	367	5.76	Green Grove, town	748	753	0.67
Menasha, city (part) . . .	3,007	3,243	7.85	Greenwood, city	1,058	1,054	-0.38
New Holstein, city	3,195	3,177	-0.56	Hendren, town	433	436	0.69
New Holstein, town . . .	1,534	1,527	-0.46	Hewett, town	295	294	-0.34
Potter, village	244	243	-0.41	Hixon, town	902	899	-0.33
Rantoul, town	740	747	0.95	Hoard, town	787	792	0.64
Sherwood, village	3,271	3,352	2.48	Levis, town.	437	436	-0.23
Stockbridge, town	1,453	1,446	-0.48	Longwood, town	877	871	-0.68
Stockbridge, village . . .	678	685	1.03	Loyal, city.	1,203	1,201	-0.17
Woodville, town	850	855	0.59	Loyal, town.	790	793	0.38
				Lynn, town.	834	850	1.92
Chippewa	66,297	67,082	1.18	Mayville, town.	963	967	0.42
Anson, town	2,297	2,341	1.92	Mead, town	357	363	1.68
Arthur, town.	771	781	1.30	Mentor, town	546	548	0.37
Auburn, town	776	787	1.42	Neillsville, city	2,384	2,320	-2.68
Birch Creek, town.	495	504	1.82	Owen, city	916	917	0.11
Bloomer, city	3,683	3,719	0.98	Pine Valley, town	1,175	1,189	1.19
Bloomer, town	1,090	1,101	1.01	Reseburg, town.	793	808	1.89
Boyd, village.	605	608	0.50	Seif, town.	188	190	1.06
Cadott, village.	1,498	1,498	0.00	Sherman, town	831	831	0.00
Chippewa Falls, city . . .	14,731	14,724	-0.05	Sherwood, town	230	233	1.30
Cleveland, town.	889	895	0.67	Stanley, city (part)	0	0	0.00
Colburn, town.	892	899	0.78	Thorp, city	1,795	1,781	-0.78
Cooks Valley, town	757	758	0.13	Thorp, town	840	857	2.02
Cornell, city	1,453	1,437	-1.10	Unity, town	751	749	-0.27
Delmar, town	1,013	1,020	0.69	Unity, village (part). . . .	151	150	-0.66
Eagle Point, town.	3,237	3,284	1.45	Warner, town	635	636	0.16
Eau Claire, city (part). . .	2,183	2,255	3.30	Washburn, town	289	292	1.04
Edson, town	1,141	1,164	2.02	Weston, town	686	702	2.33
Estella, town.	476	480	0.84	Withee, town	1,033	1,037	0.39
Goetz, town	813	816	0.37	Withee, village	506	505	-0.20
Hallie, town	153	166	8.50	Worden, town	708	711	0.42
Howard, town	777	792	1.93	York, town	844	838	-0.71
Lafayette, town	6,197	6,454	4.15				
Lake Hallie, village (part)	7,170	7,307	1.91	Columbia	58,490	58,627	0.23
Lake Holcombe, town . .	1,011	1,016	0.49	Arlington, town.	803	818	1.87
New Auburn, village (part)	537	537	0.00	Arlington, village	844	846	0.24
Ruby, town.	465	468	0.65	Caledonia, town	1,495	1,504	0.60
Sampson, town	972	985	1.34	Cambria, village.	777	781	0.51
Sigel, town.	1,132	1,164	2.83	Columbus, city (part) . .	5,540	5,530	-0.18
Stanley, city (part)	3,804	3,748	-1.47	Columbus, town	626	631	0.80
Tilden, town	1,516	1,548	2.11	Courtland, town	491	492	0.20
Wheaton, town	2,759	2,818	2.14	Dekorra, town	2,500	2,519	0.76
Woodmohr, town.	1,004	1,008	0.40	Doylestown, village . . .	280	278	-0.71
				Fall River, village	1,801	1,815	0.78
Clark	34,659	34,801	0.41	Fort Winnebago, town. .	812	817	0.62
Abbotsford, city (part). .	1,665	1,774	6.55				

Wisconsin population by county and municipality, continued

	2020 census	2022 estimate	% change		2020 census	2022 estimate	% change
Fountain Prairie, town	938	943	0.53	Bristol, town	4,447	4,499	1.17
Friesland, village	320	322	0.63	Brooklyn, village (part)	1,026	1,028	0.19
Hampden, town	581	587	1.03	Burke, town	3,265	3,264	-0.03
Leeds, town	755	752	-0.40	Cambridge, village (part)	1,539	1,609	4.55
Lewiston, town	1,262	1,260	-0.16	Christiana, town	1,235	1,238	0.24
Lodi, city	3,189	3,226	1.16	Cottage Grove, town	3,791	3,825	0.90
Lodi, town	3,282	3,296	0.43	Cottage Grove, village	7,303	8,854	21.24
Lowville, town	1,017	1,024	0.69	Cross Plains, town	1,494	1,503	0.60
Marcellon, town	1,140	1,145	0.44	Cross Plains, village	4,104	4,123	0.46
Newport, town	607	604	-0.49	Dane, town	934	939	0.54
Otsego, town	670	670	0.00	Dane, village	1,117	1,116	-0.09
Pacific, town	2,791	2,811	0.72	DeForest, village	1,684	1,693	0.53
Pardeeville, village	2,074	2,068	-0.29	Deerfield, town	2,507	2,531	0.96
Portage, city	10,581	10,325	-2.42	Deerfield, village	10,811	11,388	5.34
Poynette, village	2,590	2,594	0.15	Dunkirk, town	1,881	1,872	-0.48
Randolph, town	762	767	0.66	Dunn, town	4,880	4,874	-0.12
Randolph, village (part)	458	456	-0.44	Edgerton, city (part)	146	148	1.37
Rio, village	1,119	1,144	2.23	Fitchburg, city	29,609	31,817	7.46
Scott, town	857	874	1.98	Madison, city	269,840	279,012	3.40
Springvale, town	539	539	0.00	Madison, town[1]	6,236	6,212	-0.38
West Point, town	2,028	2,068	1.97	Maple Bluff, village	1,368	1,433	4.75
Wisconsin Dells, city (part)	2,449	2,571	4.98	Marshall, village	3,787	3,909	3.22
Wyocena, town	1,756	1,798	2.39	Mazomanie, town	1,074	1,087	1.21
Wyocena, village	756	752	-0.53	Mazomanie, village	1,768	1,790	1.24
				McFarland, village	8,991	9,537	6.07
Crawford	**16,113**	**16,129**	**0.10**	Medina, town	1,344	1,353	0.67
Bell Center, village	108	108	0.00	Middleton, city	21,827	23,031	5.52
Bridgeport, town	988	1,004	1.62	Middleton, town	6,792	6,977	2.72
Clayton, town	1,052	1,055	0.29	Monona, city	8,624	8,869	2.84
De Soto, village (part)	83	85	2.41	Montrose, town	1,064	1,064	0.00
Eastman, town	731	739	1.09	Mount Horeb, village	7,754	7,871	1.51
Eastman, village	350	349	-0.29	Oregon, town	3,125	3,136	0.35
Ferryville, village	191	193	1.05	Oregon, village	11,179	11,815	5.69
Freeman, town	727	735	1.10	Perry, town	737	740	0.41
Gays Mills, village	523	522	-0.19	Pleasant Springs, town	3,078	3,101	0.75
Haney, town	317	319	0.63	Primrose, town	750	761	1.47
Lynxville, village	132	133	0.76	Rockdale, village	207	206	-0.48
Marietta, town	507	509	0.39	Roxbury, town	1,871	1,867	-0.21
Mount Sterling, village	189	189	0.00	Rutland, town	1,977	1,984	0.35
Prairie du Chien, city	5,506	5,446	-1.09	Shorewood Hills, village	2,169	2,168	-0.05
Prairie du Chien, town	957	954	-0.31	Springdale, town	2,056	2,085	1.41
Scott, town	519	542	4.43	Springfield, town	2,929	2,936	0.24
Seneca, town	932	941	0.97	Stoughton, city	13,173	13,204	0.24
Soldiers Grove, village	552	558	1.09	Sun Prairie, city	35,967	37,304	3.72
Steuben, village	122	120	-1.64	Sun Prairie, town	2,391	2,389	-0.08
Utica, town	623	627	0.64	Vermont, town	871	883	1.38
Wauzeka, town	376	377	0.27	Verona, city	14,030	14,889	6.12
Wauzeka, village	628	624	-0.64	Verona, town	1,947	2,008	3.13
				Vienna, town	1,666	1,678	0.72
Dane	**561,504**	**582,165**	**3.68**	Waunakee, village	14,879	15,426	3.68
Albion, town	2,069	2,069	0.00	Westport, town	4,191	4,302	2.65
Belleville, village (part)	1,909	2,078	8.85	Windsor, village	8,754	9,305	6.29
Berry, town	1,168	1,177	0.77	York, town	697	699	0.29
Black Earth, town	510	517	1.37				
Black Earth, village	1,493	1,551	3.88	**Dodge**	**89,396**	**88,822**	**-0.64**
Blooming Grove, town	1,622	1,568	-3.33	Ashippun, town	2,663	2,677	0.53
Blue Mounds, town	899	900	0.11	Beaver Dam, city	16,708	16,727	0.11
Blue Mounds, village	948	953	0.53	Beaver Dam, town	4,062	4,069	0.17

Wisconsin population by county and municipality, continued

	2020 census	2022 estimate	% change		2020 census	2022 estimate	% change
Brownsville, village	598	630	5.35	Sturgeon Bay, city	9,646	9,656	0.10
Burnett, town	831	828	-0.36	Sturgeon Bay, town	821	826	0.61
Calamus, town	1,043	1,046	0.29	Union, town	1,005	1,011	0.60
Chester, town	676	676	0.00	Washington, town	777	783	0.77
Clyman, town	712	716	0.56				
Clyman, village	397	398	0.25	**Douglas**	**44,295**	**44,547**	**0.57**
Columbus, city (part)	0	0	0.00	Amnicon, town	1,224	1,223	-0.08
Elba, town	1,041	1,040	-0.10	Bennett, town	632	631	-0.16
Emmet, town	1,310	1,317	0.53	Brule, town	607	609	0.33
Fox Lake, city	1,604	1,640	2.24	Cloverland, town	249	249	0.00
Fox Lake, town	2,588	2,413	-6.76	Dairyland, town	211	211	0.00
Hartford, city (part)	9	9	0.00	Gordon, town	757	755	-0.26
Herman, town	1,135	1,140	0.44	Hawthorne, town	1,058	1,033	-2.36
Horicon, city	3,767	3,797	0.80	Highland, town	340	341	0.29
Hubbard, town	1,772	1,773	0.06	Lake Nebagamon, village	1,123	1,130	0.62
Hustisford, town	1,357	1,361	0.29	Lakeside, town	681	682	0.15
Hustisford, village	1,101	1,099	-0.18	Maple, town	700	710	1.43
Iron Ridge, village	904	910	0.66	Oakland, town	1,170	1,186	1.37
Juneau, city	2,658	2,576	-3.09	Oliver, village	423	423	0.00
Kekoskee, village	896	832	-7.14	Parkland, town	1,231	1,242	0.89
Lebanon, town	1,587	1,583	-0.25	Poplar, village	629	635	0.95
Leroy, town	956	957	0.10	Solon Springs, town	970	976	0.62
Lomira, town	1,099	1,104	0.45	Solon Springs, village	656	663	1.07
Lomira, village	2,678	2,688	0.37	Summit, town	1,030	1,041	1.07
Lowell, town	1,166	1,164	-0.17	Superior, city	26,751	26,943	0.72
Lowell, village	309	306	-0.97	Superior, town	2,264	2,285	0.93
Mayville, city	5,196	5,211	0.29	Superior, village	677	674	-0.44
Neosho, village	591	590	-0.17	Wascott, town	912	905	-0.77
Oak Grove, town	1,028	1,028	0.00				
Portland, town	1,091	1,087	-0.37	**Dunn**	**45,440**	**45,454**	**0.03**
Randolph, village (part)	1,338	1,331	-0.52	Boyceville, village	1,100	1,096	-0.36
Reeseville, village	763	770	0.92	Colfax, town	1,230	1,246	1.30
Rubicon, town	2,117	2,139	1.04	Colfax, village	1,182	1,191	0.76
Shields, town	503	510	1.39	Downing, village	234	233	-0.43
Theresa, town	1,089	1,088	-0.09	Dunn, town	1,473	1,480	0.48
Theresa, village	1,255	1,260	0.40	Eau Galle, town	765	772	0.92
Trenton, town	1,219	1,220	0.08	Elk Mound, town	1,897	1,904	0.37
Watertown, city (part)	8,252	8,260	0.10	Elk Mound, village	985	982	-0.30
Waupun, city (part)	8,014	7,534	-5.99	Grant, town	395	392	-0.76
Westford, town	1,313	1,318	0.38	Hay River, town	627	638	1.75
Williamstown, town	0	0	0.00	Knapp, village	478	485	1.46
				Lucas, town	698	700	0.29
Door	**30,066**	**30,328**	**0.87**	Menomonie, city	16,843	16,616	-1.35
Baileys Harbor, town	1,223	1,238	1.23	Menomonie, town	3,415	3,438	0.67
Brussels, town	1,125	1,125	0.00	New Haven, town	673	675	0.30
Clay Banks, town	385	386	0.26	Otter Creek, town	498	521	4.62
Egg Harbor, town	1,458	1,495	2.54	Peru, town	233	235	0.86
Egg Harbor, village	358	369	3.07	Red Cedar, town	2,359	2,401	1.78
Ephraim, village	345	348	0.87	Ridgeland, village	258	258	0.00
Forestville, town	1,063	1,063	0.00	Rock Creek, town	1,003	1,002	-0.10
Forestville, village	482	479	-0.62	Sand Creek, town	603	607	0.66
Gardner, town	1,218	1,228	0.82	Sheridan, town	460	466	1.30
Gibraltar, town	1,228	1,266	3.09	Sherman, town	922	960	4.12
Jacksonport, town	878	886	0.91	Spring Brook, town	1,687	1,708	1.24
Liberty Grove, town	2,096	2,125	1.38	Stanton, town	758	761	0.40
Nasewaupee, town	1,984	2,002	0.91	Tainter, town	2,643	2,659	0.61
Sevastopol, town	2,826	2,858	1.13	Tiffany, town	617	618	0.16
Sister Bay, village	1,148	1,184	3.14	Weston, town	574	573	-0.17

Wisconsin population by county and municipality, continued

	2020 census	2022 estimate	% change		2020 census	2022 estimate	% change
Wheeler, village	326	329	0.92	Osceola, town	1,836	1,837	0.05
Wilson, town	504	508	0.79	Ripon, city	7,863	7,811	-0.66
Eau Claire	**105,710**	**108,019**	**2.18**	Ripon, town	1,314	1,309	-0.38
Altoona, city	8,293	9,149	10.32	Rosendale, town	738	736	-0.27
Augusta, city	1,567	1,549	-1.15	Rosendale, village	1,039	1,039	0.00
Bridge Creek, town	2,214	2,235	0.95	Springvale, town	675	677	0.30
Brunswick, town	1,958	1,984	1.33	St. Cloud, village	489	496	1.43
Clear Creek, town	778	777	-0.13	Taycheedah, town	4,554	4,598	0.97
Drammen, town	792	795	0.38	Waupun, city (part)	3,549	3,583	0.96
Eau Claire, city (part)	67,238	68,332	1.63	Waupun, town	1,373	1,386	0.95
Fairchild, town	450	456	1.33				
Fairchild, village	451	446	-1.11	**Forest**	**9,179**	**9,190**	**0.12**
Fall Creek, village	1,422	1,428	0.42	Alvin, town	173	173	0.00
Lake Hallie, village (part)	0	0	0.00	Argonne, town	546	548	0.37
Lincoln, town	1,125	1,136	0.98	Armstrong Creek, town	422	420	-0.47
Ludington, town	1,067	1,072	0.47	Blackwell, town	152	168	10.53
Otter Creek, town	427	425	-0.47	Caswell, town	72	72	0.00
Pleasant Valley, town	3,791	3,939	3.90	Crandon, city	1,713	1,688	-1.46
Seymour, town	3,352	3,380	0.84	Crandon, town	606	609	0.50
Union, town	2,696	2,695	-0.04	Freedom, town	324	323	-0.31
Washington, town	7,662	7,780	1.54	Hiles, town	359	360	0.28
Wilson, town	427	441	3.28	Laona, town	1,215	1,214	-0.08
				Lincoln, town	1,133	1,136	0.26
Florence	**4,558**	**4,575**	**0.37**	Nashville, town	1,215	1,233	1.48
Aurora, town	987	988	0.10	Popple River, town	43	43	0.00
Commonwealth, town	390	398	2.05	Ross, town	132	132	0.00
Fence, town	183	183	0.00	Wabeno, town	1,074	1,071	-0.28
Fern, town	181	185	2.21				
Florence, town	2,096	2,098	0.10	**Grant**	**51,938**	**51,171**	**-1.48**
Homestead, town	383	386	0.78	Bagley, village	356	355	-0.28
Long Lake, town	178	178	0.00	Beetown, town	723	722	-0.14
Tipler, town	160	159	-0.63	Bloomington, town	331	333	0.60
				Bloomington, village	741	743	0.27
Fond du Lac	**104,154**	**104,162**	**0.01**	Blue River, village	457	457	0.00
Alto, town	1,055	1,056	0.09	Boscobel, city	3,286	3,130	-4.75
Ashford, town	1,722	1,734	0.70	Boscobel, town	379	378	-0.26
Auburn, town	2,360	2,387	1.14	Cassville, town	402	400	-0.50
Brandon, village	882	879	-0.34	Cassville, village	777	774	-0.39
Byron, town	1,677	1,679	0.12	Castle Rock, town	240	241	0.42
Calumet, town	1,412	1,418	0.42	Clifton, town	380	388	2.11
Campbellsport, village	1,907	1,924	0.89	Cuba City, city (part)	1,890	1,870	-1.06
Eden, town	1,000	1,032	3.20	Dickeyville, village	1,015	1,067	5.12
Eden, village	884	904	2.26	Ellenboro, town	580	588	1.38
Eldorado, town	1,399	1,396	-0.21	Fennimore, city	2,764	2,733	-1.12
Empire, town	2,774	2,769	-0.18	Fennimore, town	594	589	-0.84
Fairwater, village	346	345	-0.29	Glen Haven, town	363	366	0.83
Fond du Lac, city	44,678	44,470	-0.47	Harrison, town	529	528	-0.19
Fond du Lac, town	3,687	3,721	0.92	Hazel Green, town	1,084	1,099	1.38
Forest, town	975	977	0.21	Hazel Green, village (part)	1,151	1,151	0.00
Friendship, town	2,748	2,756	0.29	Hickory Grove, town	568	585	2.99
Kewaskum, village (part)	0	0	0.00	Jamestown, town	2,181	2,210	1.33
Lamartine, town	1,747	1,765	1.03	Lancaster, city	3,907	3,914	0.18
Marshfield, town	1,123	1,114	-0.80	Liberty, town	543	544	0.18
Metomen, town	689	691	0.29	Lima, town	771	771	0.00
Mount Calvary, village	548	549	0.18	Little Grant, town	314	315	0.32
North Fond du Lac, village	5,378	5,385	0.13	Livingston, village (part)	625	626	0.16
Oakfield, town	681	678	-0.44	Marion, town	629	627	-0.32
Oakfield, village	1,052	1,061	0.86	Millville, town	127	127	0.00

Wisconsin population by county and municipality, continued

	2020 census	2022 estimate	% change		2020 census	2022 estimate	% change
Montfort, village (part)	633	629	-0.63	Mackford, town	495	493	-0.40
Mount Hope, town	282	281	-0.35	Manchester, town	1,057	1,069	1.14
Mount Hope, village	215	213	-0.93	Markesan, city	1,377	1,365	-0.87
Mount Ida, town	561	560	-0.18	Marquette, town	523	530	1.34
Muscoda, town	754	762	1.06	Marquette, village	172	170	-1.16
Muscoda, village (part)	1,245	1,252	0.56	Princeton, city	1,267	1,263	-0.32
North Lancaster, town	581	587	1.03	Princeton, town	1,519	1,530	0.72
Paris, town	655	660	0.76	Seneca, town	387	385	-0.52
Patch Grove, town	364	365	0.27	St. Marie, town	352	357	1.42
Patch Grove, village	201	198	-1.49	**Iowa**	**23,709**	**23,936**	**0.96**
Platteville, city	11,836	11,154	-5.76	Arena, town	1,486	1,495	0.61
Platteville, town	1,513	1,518	0.33	Arena, village	844	877	3.91
Potosi, town	813	811	-0.25	Avoca, village	553	551	-0.36
Potosi, village	646	641	-0.77	Barneveld, village	1,331	1,338	0.53
Smelser, town	786	789	0.38	Blanchardville, village (part)	194	206	6.19
South Lancaster, town	884	857	-3.05	Brigham, town	1,037	1,063	2.51
Tennyson, village	348	347	-0.29	Clyde, town	292	300	2.74
Waterloo, town	552	553	0.18	Cobb, village	480	484	0.83
Watterstown, town	372	373	0.27	Dodgeville, city	4,984	5,038	1.08
Wingville, town	378	378	0.00	Dodgeville, town	1,586	1,598	0.76
Woodman, town	158	158	0.00	Eden, town	339	342	0.88
Woodman, village	118	118	0.00	Highland, town	724	738	1.93
Wyalusing, town	336	336	0.00	Highland, village	874	874	0.00
Green	**37,093**	**37,445**	**0.95**	Hollandale, village	306	305	-0.33
Adams, town	540	542	0.37	Linden, town	755	740	-1.99
Albany, town	1,189	1,199	0.84	Linden, village	504	505	0.20
Albany, village	1,096	1,093	-0.27	Livingston, village (part)	12	12	0.00
Belleville, village (part)	582	581	-0.17	Mifflin, town	558	565	1.25
Brodhead, city (part)	3,189	3,189	0.00	Mineral Point, city	2,581	2,583	0.08
Brooklyn, town	1,108	1,115	0.63	Mineral Point, town	974	993	1.95
Brooklyn, village (part)	498	497	-0.20	Montfort, village (part)	72	72	0.00
Browntown, village	245	246	0.41	Moscow, town	582	592	1.72
Cadiz, town	747	748	0.13	Muscoda, village (part)	62	62	0.00
Clarno, town	1,133	1,138	0.44	Pulaski, town	357	357	0.00
Decatur, town	1,685	1,771	5.10	Rewey, village	258	257	-0.39
Exeter, town	2,156	2,206	2.32	Ridgeway, town	563	568	0.89
Jefferson, town	1,170	1,172	0.17	Ridgeway, village	624	644	3.21
Jordan, town	602	602	0.00	Waldwick, town	460	458	-0.43
Monroe, city	10,661	10,691	0.28	Wyoming, town	317	319	0.63
Monroe, town	1,291	1,281	-0.77	**Iron**	**6,137**	**6,125**	**-0.20**
Monticello, village	1,192	1,195	0.25	Anderson, town	54	54	0.00
Mount Pleasant, town	619	625	0.97	Carey, town	172	171	-0.58
New Glarus, town	1,393	1,409	1.15	Gurney, town	145	145	0.00
New Glarus, village	2,266	2,360	4.15	Hurley, city	1,558	1,535	-1.48
Spring Grove, town	919	936	1.85	Kimball, town	490	494	0.82
Sylvester, town	1,001	999	-0.20	Knight, town	212	211	-0.47
Washington, town	842	844	0.24	Mercer, town	1,649	1,656	0.42
York, town	969	1,006	3.82	Montreal, city	801	799	-0.25
Green Lake	**19,018**	**19,091**	**0.38**	Oma, town	320	326	1.88
Berlin, city (part)	5,484	5,483	-0.02	Pence, town	160	159	-0.63
Berlin, town	1,068	1,082	1.31	Saxon, town	290	288	-0.69
Brooklyn, town	1,787	1,811	1.34	Sherman, town	286	287	0.35
Green Lake, city	1,001	998	-0.30	**Jackson**	**21,145**	**21,118**	**-0.13**
Green Lake, town	1,169	1,181	1.03	Adams, town	1,389	1,406	1.22
Kingston, town	1,079	1,093	1.30	Albion, town	1,197	1,200	0.25
Kingston, village	281	281	0.00				

Wisconsin population by county and municipality, continued

	2020 census	2022 estimate	% change		2020 census	2022 estimate	% change
Alma, town.	1,033	1,045	1.16	Clearfield, town.	702	705	0.43
Alma Center, village . . .	487	484	-0.62	Cutler, town	300	304	1.33
Bear Bluff, town.	155	155	0.00	Elroy, city.	1,356	1,319	-2.73
Black River Falls, city . . .	3,523	3,519	-0.11	Finley, town	88	88	0.00
Brockway, town.	3,035	2,991	-1.45	Fountain, town	592	593	0.17
City Point, town.	177	178	0.56	Germantown, town . . .	1,628	1,751	7.56
Cleveland, town.	530	529	-0.19	Hustler, village	162	161	-0.62
Curran, town.	301	310	2.99	Kildare, town	690	698	1.16
Franklin, town.	519	540	4.05	Kingston, town	57	57	0.00
Garden Valley, town . . .	395	397	0.51	Lemonweir, town.	1,658	1,668	0.60
Garfield, town.	756	761	0.66	Lindina, town	685	683	-0.29
Hixton, town.	620	620	0.00	Lisbon, town.	939	944	0.53
Hixton, village.	456	453	-0.66	Lyndon, town	1,493	1,494	0.07
Irving, town	853	861	0.94	Lyndon Station, village .	498	496	-0.40
Knapp, town.	303	307	1.32	Marion, town	444	445	0.23
Komensky, town	505	451	-10.69	Mauston, city	4,347	4,286	-1.40
Manchester, town	825	822	-0.36	Necedah, town	2,448	2,488	1.63
Melrose, town.	470	474	0.85	Necedah, village	924	948	2.60
Melrose, village	544	539	-0.92	New Lisbon, city	2,559	2,526	-1.29
Merrillan, village	562	561	-0.18	Orange, town	540	542	0.37
Millston, town.	168	168	0.00	Plymouth, town.	578	586	1.38
North Bend, town	491	491	0.00	Seven Mile Creek, town .	348	347	-0.29
Northfield, town	674	683	1.34	Summit, town	666	679	1.95
Springfield, town.	693	698	0.72	Union Center, village . .	225	226	0.44
Taylor, village	484	475	-1.86	Wisconsin Dells, city (part)	4	4	0.00
				Wonewoc, town.	677	684	1.03
Jefferson	**86,148**	**86,576**	**0.50**	Wonewoc, village.	758	754	-0.53
Aztalan, town	1,382	1,381	-0.07				
Cambridge, village (part)	99	99	0.00	**Kenosha**	**169,151**	**170,272**	**0.66**
Cold Spring, town	737	730	-0.95	Brighton, town	1,422	1,442	1.41
Concord, town	1,981	1,979	-0.10	Bristol, village	5,192	5,209	0.33
Farmington, town	1,407	1,411	0.28	Genoa City, village (part).	5	5	0.00
Fort Atkinson, city	12,579	12,583	0.03	Kenosha, city	99,986	100,051	0.07
Hebron, town	1,043	1,047	0.38	Paddock Lake, village . .	2,919	2,995	2.60
Ixonia, town	5,120	5,135	0.29	Paris, town	1,397	1,398	0.07
Jefferson, city	7,793	7,747	-0.59	Pleasant Prairie, village .	21,250	21,948	3.28
Jefferson, town	2,067	2,076	0.44	Randall, town	3,285	3,315	0.91
Johnson Creek, village. .	3,318	3,402	2.53	Salem Lakes, village . . .	14,601	14,605	0.03
Koshkonong, town. . . .	3,763	3,790	0.72	Somers, town	992	980	-1.21
Lac La Belle, village (part)	2	2	0.00	Somers, village	8,402	8,501	1.18
Lake Mills, city.	6,211	6,452	3.88	Twin Lakes, village	6,309	6,429	1.90
Lake Mills, town.	2,196	2,217	0.96	Wheatland, town	3,391	3,394	0.09
Milford, town	1,106	1,115	0.81				
Oakland, town	3,231	3,241	0.31	**Kewaunee**	**20,563**	**20,621**	**0.28**
Palmyra, town.	1,220	1,226	0.49	Ahnapee, town	870	883	1.49
Palmyra, village.	1,719	1,721	0.12	Algoma, city.	3,243	3,221	-0.68
Sullivan, town	2,295	2,321	1.13	Carlton, town	1,008	1,008	0.00
Sullivan, village	651	649	-0.31	Casco, town	1,150	1,156	0.52
Sumner, town	846	841	-0.59	Casco, village	630	644	2.22
Waterloo, city	3,492	3,631	3.98	Franklin, town.	964	965	0.10
Waterloo, town	867	874	0.81	Kewaunee, city	2,837	2,822	-0.53
Watertown, city (part). .	14,674	14,758	0.57	Lincoln, town	932	931	-0.11
Watertown, town.	1,933	1,948	0.78	Luxemburg, town.	1,458	1,460	0.14
Whitewater, city (part). .	4,416	4,200	-4.89	Luxemburg, village. . . .	2,685	2,730	1.68
				Montpelier, town.	1,362	1,360	-0.15
Juneau	**26,718**	**26,848**	**0.49**	Pierce, town	772	773	0.13
Armenia, town	705	727	3.12	Red River, town	1,374	1,379	0.36
Camp Douglas, village. .	647	645	-0.31	West Kewaunee, town. .	1,278	1,289	0.86

Wisconsin population by county and municipality, continued

	2020 census	2022 estimate	% change		2020 census	2022 estimate	% change
La Crosse............	120,784	122,126	1.11	Langlade, town......	469	475	1.28
Bangor, town........	617	626	1.46	Neva, town..........	846	845	-0.12
Bangor, village......	1,437	1,568	9.12	Norwood, town......	907	911	0.44
Barre, town..........	1,267	1,296	2.29	Parrish, town........	91	92	1.10
Burns, town.........	946	959	1.37	Peck, town..........	324	326	0.62
Campbell, town......	4,284	4,276	-0.19	Polar, town..........	1,018	1,009	-0.88
Farmington, town....	2,140	2,153	0.61	Price, town..........	221	220	-0.45
Greenfield, town.....	2,187	2,202	0.69	Rolling, town........	1,432	1,431	-0.07
Hamilton, town......	2,428	2,431	0.12	Summit, town........	143	142	-0.70
Holland, town........	4,530	4,603	1.61	Upham, town........	726	729	0.41
Holmen, village......	10,661	11,560	8.43	Vilas, town...........	226	225	-0.44
La Crosse, city.......	52,680	52,160	-0.99	White Lake, village....	262	260	-0.76
Medary, town........	1,604	1,613	0.56	Wolf River, town.....	783	793	1.28
Onalaska, city.......	18,803	19,276	2.52				
Onalaska, town......	5,835	5,875	0.69	Lincoln............	28,415	28,431	0.06
Rockland, village (part).	765	782	2.22	Birch, town..........	570	512	-10.18
Shelby, town.........	4,804	4,810	0.12	Bradley, town........	2,382	2,417	1.47
Washington, town....	519	520	0.19	Corning, town........	825	830	0.61
West Salem, village....	5,277	5,416	2.63	Harding, town........	364	369	1.37
				Harrison, town.......	828	830	0.24
Lafayette...........	**16,611**	**16,650**	**0.23**	King, town...........	964	984	2.07
Argyle, town.........	449	452	0.67	Merrill, city..........	9,347	9,312	-0.37
Argyle, village.......	783	780	-0.38	Merrill, town.........	2,881	2,882	0.03
Belmont, town.......	794	801	0.88	Pine River, town......	1,874	1,886	0.64
Belmont, village.....	989	990	0.10	Rock Falls, town......	635	639	0.63
Benton, town........	474	482	1.69	Russell, town........	693	698	0.72
Benton, village......	946	960	1.48	Schley, town.........	950	969	2.00
Blanchard, town.....	300	308	2.67	Scott, town..........	1,377	1,374	-0.22
Blanchardville, village				Skanawan, town.....	386	387	0.26
(part).............	613	611	-0.33	Somo, town.........	123	124	0.81
Cuba City, city (part)...	248	250	0.81	Tomahawk, city......	3,441	3,436	-0.15
Darlington, city......	2,462	2,432	-1.22	Tomahawk, town.....	458	461	0.66
Darlington, town.....	923	923	0.00	Wilson, town.........	317	321	1.26
Elk Grove, town......	566	567	0.18				
Fayette, town........	381	386	1.31	**Manitowoc**.........	**81,359**	**81,442**	**0.10**
Gratiot, town........	575	575	0.00	Cato, town...........	1,621	1,637	0.99
Gratiot, village......	224	223	-0.45	Centerville, town.....	631	633	0.32
Hazel Green, village (part)	22	22	0.00	Cleveland, village.....	1,579	1,576	-0.19
Kendall, town........	402	409	1.74	Cooperstown, town...	1,300	1,297	-0.23
Lamont, town........	313	312	-0.32	Eaton, town.........	814	819	0.61
Monticello, town.....	138	137	-0.72	Francis Creek, village..	659	661	0.30
New Diggings, town...	486	486	0.00	Franklin, town........	1,250	1,249	-0.08
Seymour, town.......	392	395	0.77	Gibson, town........	1,315	1,304	-0.84
Shullsburg, city......	1,173	1,176	0.26	Kellnersville, village...	307	303	-1.30
Shullsburg, town.....	312	309	-0.96	Kiel, city (part)........	3,585	3,608	0.64
South Wayne, village...	444	437	-1.58	Kossuth, town........	1,969	1,969	0.00
Wayne, town.........	474	479	1.05	Liberty, town........	1,245	1,246	0.08
White Oak Springs, town	109	109	0.00	Manitowoc, city......	34,626	34,722	0.28
Willow Springs, town..	789	800	1.39	Manitowoc, town.....	1,076	1,074	-0.19
Wiota, town.........	830	839	1.08	Manitowoc Rapids, town	2,114	2,100	-0.66
				Maple Grove, town....	773	764	-1.16
Langlade...........	**19,491**	**19,457**	**-0.17**	Maribel, village.......	336	335	-0.30
Ackley, town.........	467	467	0.00	Meeme, town........	1,440	1,444	0.28
Ainsworth, town.....	477	477	0.00	Mishicot, town.......	1,327	1,326	-0.08
Antigo, city..........	8,100	8,053	-0.58	Mishicot, village......	1,432	1,432	0.00
Antigo, town.........	1,369	1,369	0.00	Newton, town........	2,122	2,122	0.00
Elcho, town..........	1,168	1,170	0.17	Reedsville, village....	1,195	1,193	-0.17
Evergreen, town.....	462	463	0.22	Rockland, town......	995	999	0.40

Wisconsin population by county and municipality, continued

	2020 census	2022 estimate	% change		2020 census	2022 estimate	% change
Schleswig, town	1,912	1,916	0.21	Rothschild, village	5,567	5,581	0.25
St. Nazianz, village	714	711	-0.42	Schofield, city	2,157	2,262	4.87
Two Creeks, town	390	389	-0.26	Spencer, town	1,586	1,593	0.44
Two Rivers, city	11,271	11,243	-0.25	Spencer, village	1,818	1,821	0.17
Two Rivers, town	1,672	1,670	-0.12	Stettin, town	2,580	2,595	0.58
Valders, village	952	961	0.95	Stratford, village	1,581	1,633	3.29
Whitelaw, village	737	739	0.27	Texas, town	1,611	1,625	0.87
				Unity, village (part)	233	233	0.00
Marathon	**138,013**	**139,205**	**0.86**	Wausau, city	39,994	40,199	0.51
Abbotsford, city (part)	610	613	0.49	Wausau, town	2,161	2,187	1.20
Athens, village	1,059	1,065	0.57	Weston, town	657	666	1.37
Bergen, town	740	744	0.54	Weston, village	15,723	15,809	0.55
Berlin, town	949	948	-0.11	Wien, town	885	886	0.11
Bern, town	614	622	1.30				
Bevent, town	1,049	1,053	0.38	**Marinette**	**41,872**	**41,912**	**0.10**
Birnamwood, village (part)	14	16	14.29	Amberg, town	693	701	1.15
Brighton, town	620	620	0.00	Athelstane, town	554	556	0.36
Cassel, town	934	947	1.39	Beaver, town	1,153	1,163	0.87
Cleveland, town	1,486	1,496	0.67	Beecher, town	786	786	0.00
Colby, city (part)	677	679	0.30	Coleman, village	726	725	-0.14
Day, town	1,063	1,063	0.00	Crivitz, village	1,093	1,096	0.27
Dorchester, village (part)	3	3	0.00	Dunbar, town	605	606	0.17
Easton, town	1,148	1,166	1.57	Goodman, town	607	608	0.16
Eau Pleine, town	769	772	0.39	Grover, town	1,731	1,731	0.00
Edgar, village	1,439	1,450	0.76	Lake, town	1,186	1,198	1.01
Elderon, town	644	642	-0.31	Marinette, city	11,119	11,129	0.09
Elderon, village	161	160	-0.62	Middle Inlet, town	851	861	1.18
Emmet, town	905	904	-0.11	Niagara, city	1,602	1,580	-1.37
Fenwood, village	141	142	0.71	Niagara, town	852	859	0.82
Frankfort, town	635	638	0.47	Pembine, town	877	880	0.34
Franzen, town	553	561	1.45	Peshtigo, city	3,420	3,361	-1.73
Green Valley, town	515	518	0.58	Peshtigo, town	4,006	4,001	-0.12
Guenther, town	358	357	-0.28	Porterfield, town	1,888	1,894	0.32
Halsey, town	634	643	1.42	Pound, town	1,412	1,412	0.00
Hamburg, town	827	820	-0.85	Pound, village	357	353	-1.12
Harrison, town	312	318	1.92	Silver Cliff, town	514	520	1.17
Hatley, village	648	677	4.48	Stephenson, town	3,494	3,530	1.03
Hewitt, town	636	650	2.20	Wagner, town	653	664	1.68
Holton, town	859	858	-0.12	Wausaukee, town	1,097	1,105	0.73
Hull, town	756	767	1.46	Wausaukee, village	596	593	-0.50
Johnson, town	873	875	0.23				
Knowlton, town	1,984	2,011	1.36	**Marquette**	**15,592**	**15,633**	**0.26**
Kronenwetter, village	8,353	8,561	2.49	Buffalo, town	1,389	1,411	1.58
Maine, village	2,613	2,621	0.31	Crystal Lake, town	452	451	-0.22
Marathon, town	995	991	-0.40	Douglas, town	784	784	0.00
Marathon City, village	1,576	1,565	-0.70	Endeavor, village	432	433	0.23
Marshfield, city (part)	810	916	13.09	Harris, town	748	749	0.13
McMillan, town	2,074	2,086	0.58	Mecan, town	752	756	0.53
Mosinee, city	4,452	4,495	0.97	Montello, city	1,448	1,441	-0.48
Mosinee, town	2,216	2,268	2.35	Montello, town	1,132	1,135	0.27
Norrie, town	1,010	1,018	0.79	Moundville, town	526	534	1.52
Plover, town	683	685	0.29	Neshkoro, town	565	564	-0.18
Reid, town	1,186	1,188	0.17	Neshkoro, village	412	410	-0.49
Rib Falls, town	947	945	-0.21	Newton, town	529	533	0.76
Rib Mountain, town	7,313	7,346	0.45	Oxford, town	930	935	0.54
Rietbrock, town	874	876	0.23	Oxford, village	537	535	-0.37
Ringle, town	1,743	1,756	0.75	Packwaukee, town	1,469	1,475	0.41
				Shields, town	585	585	0.00

Wisconsin population by county and municipality, continued

	2020 census	2022 estimate	% change		2020 census	2022 estimate	% change
Springfield, town	811	814	0.37	Tomah, town	1,488	1,488	0.00
Westfield, town	789	791	0.25	Warrens, village	544	546	0.37
Westfield, village	1,302	1,297	-0.38	Wellington, town	666	676	1.50
				Wells, town	562	571	1.60
Menominee	**4,255**	**4,266**	**0.26**	Wilton, town	963	995	3.32
Menominee, town	4,255	4,266	0.26	Wilton, village	532	530	-0.38
Milwaukee	**939,489**	**939,487**	**0.00**	Wyeville, village	121	118	-2.48
Bayside, village (part)	4,378	4,359	-0.43	**Oconto**	**38,965**	**39,307**	**0.88**
Brown Deer, village	12,507	13,023	4.13	Abrams, town	1,960	2,028	3.47
Cudahy, city	18,204	18,134	-0.38	Bagley, town	275	280	1.82
Fox Point, village	6,934	6,770	-2.37	Brazeau, town	1,340	1,342	0.15
Franklin, city	36,116	35,895	-0.61	Breed, town	698	700	0.29
Glendale, city	13,357	13,472	0.86	Chase, town	3,178	3,244	2.08
Greendale, village	14,854	14,815	-0.26	Doty, town	309	306	-0.97
Greenfield, city	37,803	37,709	-0.25	Gillett, city	1,289	1,284	-0.39
Hales Corners, village	7,720	7,658	-0.80	Gillett, town	989	986	-0.30
Milwaukee, city (part)	577,922	577,309	-0.11	How, town	527	525	-0.38
Oak Creek, city	36,497	37,374	2.40	Lakewood, town	831	838	0.84
River Hills, village	1,602	1,595	-0.44	Lena, town	743	741	-0.27
Shorewood, village	13,859	13,807	-0.38	Lena, village	537	535	-0.37
South Milwaukee, city	20,795	20,703	-0.44	Little River, town	1,092	1,099	0.64
St. Francis, city	9,161	9,156	-0.05	Little Suamico, town	5,536	5,633	1.75
Wauwatosa, city	48,387	48,638	0.52	Maple Valley, town	647	653	0.93
West Allis, city	60,325	60,068	-0.43	Morgan, town	985	1,000	1.52
West Milwaukee, village	4,114	4,097	-0.41	Mountain, town	832	837	0.60
Whitefish Bay, village	14,954	14,905	-0.33	Oconto, city	4,609	4,600	-0.20
				Oconto, town	1,340	1,359	1.42
Monroe	**46,274**	**46,697**	**0.91**	Oconto Falls, city	2,957	2,991	1.15
Adrian, town	733	753	2.73	Oconto Falls, town	1,259	1,266	0.56
Angelo, town	1,697	1,804	6.31	Pensaukee, town	1,352	1,355	0.22
Byron, town	1,234	1,233	-0.08	Pulaski, village (part)	0	0	0.00
Cashton, village	1,158	1,167	0.78	Riverview, town	819	824	0.61
Clifton, town	733	727	-0.82	Spruce, town	918	923	0.54
Glendale, town	663	673	1.51	Stiles, town	1,518	1,517	-0.07
Grant, town	469	480	2.35	Suring, village	517	518	0.19
Greenfield, town	677	685	1.18	Townsend, town	1,044	1,057	1.25
Jefferson, town	841	870	3.45	Underhill, town	864	866	0.23
Kendall, village	484	481	-0.62				
Lafayette, town	447	448	0.22	**Oneida**	**37,845**	**37,935**	**0.24**
LaGrange, town	1,948	1,948	0.00	Cassian, town	1,069	1,075	0.56
Leon, town	1,144	1,154	0.87	Crescent, town	1,984	1,984	0.00
Lincoln, town	793	800	0.88	Enterprise, town	353	353	0.00
Little Falls, town	1,509	1,541	2.12	Hazelhurst, town	1,299	1,308	0.69
Melvina, village	93	94	1.08	Lake Tomahawk, town	1,155	1,140	-1.30
New Lyme, town	193	197	2.07	Little Rice, town	388	392	1.03
Norwalk, village	611	609	-0.33	Lynne, town	139	138	-0.72
Oakdale, town	754	756	0.27	Minocqua, town	5,062	5,068	0.12
Oakdale, village	302	301	-0.33	Monico, town	260	261	0.38
Ontario, village (part)	0	0	0.00	Newbold, town	2,831	2,848	0.60
Portland, town	833	843	1.20	Nokomis, town	1,372	1,394	1.60
Ridgeville, town	479	483	0.84	Pelican, town	2,809	2,813	0.14
Rockland, village (part)	0	0	0.00	Piehl, town	74	74	0.00
Scott, town	106	104	-1.89	Pine Lake, town	2,724	2,724	0.00
Sheldon, town	649	658	1.39	Rhinelander, city	8,285	8,283	-0.02
Sparta, city	10,025	10,075	0.50	Schoepke, town	388	385	-0.77
Sparta, town	3,253	3,258	0.15	Stella, town	569	568	-0.18
Tomah, city	9,570	9,631	0.64	Sugar Camp, town	1,819	1,828	0.49

Wisconsin population by county and municipality, continued

	2020 census	2022 estimate	% change		2020 census	2022 estimate	% change
Three Lakes, town	2,413	2,430	0.70	Pepin	7,318	7,356	0.52
Woodboro, town	808	813	0.62	Albany, town	716	726	1.40
Woodruff, town	2,044	2,056	0.59	Durand, city	1,854	1,848	-0.32
Outagamie	**190,705**	**192,938**	**1.17**	Durand, town	710	712	0.28
Appleton, city (part)	62,899	62,892	-0.01	Frankfort, town	325	328	0.92
Bear Creek, village	427	422	-1.17	Lima, town	693	690	-0.43
Black Creek, town	1,251	1,258	0.56	Pepin, town	741	747	0.81
Black Creek, village	1,357	1,353	-0.29	Pepin, village	731	742	1.50
Bovina, town	1,153	1,178	2.17	Stockholm, town	218	222	1.83
Buchanan, town	6,857	6,865	0.12	Stockholm, village	78	79	1.28
Center, town	3,622	3,675	1.46	Waterville, town	829	838	1.09
Cicero, town	1,008	1,022	1.39	Waubeek, town	423	424	0.24
Combined Locks, village	3,634	3,641	0.19	**Pierce**	**42,212**	**42,408**	**0.46**
Dale, town	2,869	2,899	1.05	Bay City, village	441	447	1.36
Deer Creek, town	630	630	0.00	Clifton, town	2,177	2,237	2.76
Ellington, town	3,174	3,251	2.43	Diamond Bluff, town	478	482	0.84
Fox Crossing, village (part)	0	0	0.00	El Paso, town	724	733	1.24
Freedom, town	6,216	6,225	0.14	Ellsworth, town	1,121	1,121	0.00
Grand Chute, town	23,831	23,964	0.56	Ellsworth, village	3,348	3,332	-0.48
Greenville, village	12,687	13,067	3.00	Elmwood, village	820	817	-0.37
Harrison, village (part)	0	0	0.00	Gilman, town	1,006	1,025	1.89
Hortonia, town	1,052	1,053	0.10	Hartland, town	830	833	0.36
Hortonville, village	3,028	3,292	8.72	Isabelle, town	261	263	0.77
Howard, village (part)	0	0	0.00	Maiden Rock, town	591	605	2.37
Kaukauna, city (part)	17,089	17,441	2.06	Maiden Rock, village	115	115	0.00
Kaukauna, town	1,306	1,323	1.30	Martell, town	1,147	1,164	1.48
Kimberly, village	7,320	7,526	2.81	Oak Grove, town	2,361	2,441	3.39
Liberty, town	826	826	0.00	Plum City, village	596	587	-1.51
Little Chute, village	11,619	12,213	5.11	Prescott, city	4,333	4,408	1.73
Maine, town	851	854	0.35	River Falls, city (part)	12,546	12,451	-0.76
Maple Creek, town	591	590	-0.17	River Falls, town	2,215	2,226	0.50
New London, city (part)	1,752	1,777	1.43	Rock Elm, town	447	442	-1.12
Nichols, village	290	289	-0.34	Salem, town	475	473	-0.42
Oneida, town	4,579	4,555	-0.52	Spring Lake, town	598	598	0.00
Osborn, town	1,200	1,213	1.08	Spring Valley, village (part)	1,390	1,409	1.37
Seymour, city	3,546	3,523	-0.65	Trenton, town	1,911	1,914	0.16
Seymour, town	1,191	1,194	0.25	Trimbelle, town	1,679	1,682	0.18
Shiocton, village	939	931	-0.85	Union, town	602	603	0.17
Vandenbroek, town	1,627	1,667	2.46	**Polk**	**44,977**	**45,348**	**0.82**
Wrightstown, village (part)	284	329	15.85	Alden, town	2,918	2,980	2.12
Ozaukee	**91,503**	**92,623**	**1.22**	Amery, city	2,962	2,952	-0.34
Bayside, village (part)	104	104	0.00	Apple River, town	1,173	1,189	1.36
Belgium, town	1,450	1,461	0.76	Balsam Lake, town	1,416	1,422	0.42
Belgium, village	2,421	2,473	2.15	Balsam Lake, village	934	914	-2.14
Cedarburg, city	12,121	12,446	2.68	Beaver, town	798	804	0.75
Cedarburg, town	6,162	6,180	0.29	Black Brook, town	1,425	1,435	0.70
Fredonia, town	2,078	2,081	0.14	Bone Lake, town	686	692	0.87
Fredonia, village	2,279	2,280	0.04	Centuria, village	891	888	-0.34
Grafton, town	4,355	4,372	0.39	Clam Falls, town	554	558	0.72
Grafton, village	12,094	12,269	1.45	Clayton, town	958	964	0.63
Mequon, city	25,142	25,141	0.00	Clayton, village	550	549	-0.18
Newburg, village (part)	93	93	0.00	Clear Lake, town	888	886	-0.23
Port Washington, city	12,353	12,853	4.05	Clear Lake, village	1,099	1,107	0.73
Port Washington, town	1,538	1,568	1.95	Dresser, village	935	940	0.53
Saukville, town	1,765	1,767	0.11	Eureka, town	1,737	1,749	0.69
Saukville, village	4,258	4,247	-0.26	Farmington, town	1,904	1,959	2.89
Thiensville, village	3,290	3,288	-0.06	Frederic, village	1,154	1,147	-0.61

Wisconsin population by county and municipality, continued

	2020 census	2022 estimate	% change		2020 census	2022 estimate	% change
Garfield, town	1,744	1,760	0.92	Harmony, town	220	219	-0.45
Georgetown, town	1,036	1,047	1.06	Hill, town	366	368	0.55
Johnstown, town	499	501	0.40	Kennan, town	365	364	-0.27
Laketown, town	1,024	1,027	0.29	Kennan, village	143	142	-0.70
Lincoln, town	2,099	2,112	0.62	Knox, town	311	314	0.96
Lorain, town	308	311	0.97	Lake, town	1,106	1,111	0.45
Luck, town	979	980	0.10	Ogema, town	727	727	0.00
Luck, village	1,093	1,089	-0.37	Park Falls, city	2,410	2,378	-1.33
McKinley, town	340	343	0.88	Phillips, city	1,533	1,525	-0.52
Milltown, town	1,219	1,226	0.57	Prentice, town	440	438	-0.45
Milltown, village	948	952	0.42	Prentice, village	563	562	-0.18
Osceola, town	3,023	3,085	2.05	Spirit, town	292	294	0.68
Osceola, village	2,765	2,824	2.13	Worcester, town	1,543	1,546	0.19
St. Croix Falls, city	2,208	2,222	0.63	**Racine**	**197,727**	**198,138**	**0.21**
St. Croix Falls, town	1,164	1,178	1.20	Burlington, city (part)	11,047	11,166	1.08
Sterling, town	724	729	0.69	Burlington, town	6,465	6,493	0.43
Turtle Lake, village (part)	78	78	0.00	Caledonia, village	25,361	25,478	0.46
West Sweden, town	744	749	0.67	Dover, town	4,282	4,134	-3.46
Portage	**70,377**	**71,158**	**1.11**	Elmwood Park, village	510	508	-0.39
Alban, town	863	867	0.46	Mount Pleasant, village	27,732	28,191	1.66
Almond, town	625	623	-0.32	North Bay, village	209	208	-0.48
Almond, village	424	420	-0.94	Norway, town	7,916	7,944	0.35
Amherst, town	1,402	1,418	1.14	Racine, city	77,816	77,240	-0.74
Amherst, village	1,117	1,121	0.36	Raymond, village	3,926	3,948	0.56
Amherst Junction, village	383	382	-0.26	Rochester, village	3,785	3,822	0.98
Belmont, town	623	622	-0.16	Sturtevant, village	6,919	6,804	-1.66
Buena Vista, town	1,145	1,148	0.26	Union Grove, village	4,806	5,040	4.87
Carson, town	1,374	1,385	0.80	Waterford, town	6,514	6,555	0.63
Dewey, town	962	970	0.83	Waterford, village	5,542	5,690	2.67
Eau Pleine, town	1,063	1,068	0.47	Wind Point, village	1,651	1,644	-0.42
Grant, town	1,842	1,853	0.60	Yorkville, village	3,246	3,273	0.83
Hull, town	5,287	5,305	0.34				
Junction City, village	420	419	-0.24	**Richland**	**17,304**	**17,282**	**-0.13**
Lanark, town	1,535	1,551	1.04	Akan, town	391	390	-0.26
Linwood, town	1,070	1,089	1.78	Bloom, town	538	537	-0.19
Milladore, village (part)	0	0	0.00	Boaz, village	129	129	0.00
Nelsonville, village	158	157	-0.63	Buena Vista, town	1,807	1,818	0.61
New Hope, town	711	718	0.98	Cazenovia, village (part)	343	342	-0.29
Park Ridge, village	530	535	0.94	Dayton, town	763	774	1.44
Pine Grove, town	873	873	0.00	Eagle, town	492	492	0.00
Plover, town	1,565	1,563	-0.13	Forest, town	333	338	1.50
Plover, village	13,519	13,872	2.61	Henrietta, town	435	437	0.46
Rosholt, village	478	476	-0.42	Ithaca, town	633	637	0.63
Sharon, town	2,123	2,135	0.57	Lone Rock, village	829	830	0.12
Stevens Point, city	25,666	25,954	1.12	Marshall, town	540	537	-0.56
Stockton, town	3,018	3,036	0.60	Orion, town	541	543	0.37
Whiting, village	1,601	1,598	-0.19	Richland, town	1,175	1,177	0.17
				Richland Center, city	5,114	5,043	-1.39
Price	**14,054**	**14,026**	**-0.20**	Richwood, town	527	528	0.19
Catawba, town	247	252	2.02	Rockbridge, town	697	698	0.14
Catawba, village	141	140	-0.71	Sylvan, town	516	526	1.94
Eisenstein, town	625	624	-0.16	Viola, village (part)	436	434	-0.46
Elk, town	960	965	0.52	Westford, town	516	516	0.00
Emery, town	308	308	0.00	Willow, town	496	503	1.41
Fifield, town	905	902	-0.33	Yuba, village	53	53	0.00
Flambeau, town	488	489	0.20				
Georgetown, town	172	171	-0.58	**Rock**	**163,687**	**164,959**	**0.78**
Hackett, town	189	187	-1.06	Avon, town	570	569	-0.18

Wisconsin population by county and municipality, continued

	2020 census	2022 estimate	% change		2020 census	2022 estimate	% change
Beloit, city	36,657	36,760	0.28	Washington, town	360	362	0.56
Beloit, town	7,721	7,850	1.67	Weyerhaeuser, village	232	233	0.43
Bradford, town	1,013	1,015	0.20	Wilkinson, town	51	50	-1.96
Brodhead, city (part)	85	79	-7.06	Willard, town	525	527	0.38
Center, town	1,046	1,049	0.29	Wilson, town	116	116	0.00
Clinton, town	889	893	0.45				
Clinton, village	2,221	2,235	0.63	**Sauk**	**65,763**	**66,497**	**1.12**
Edgerton, city (part)	5,799	5,849	0.86	Baraboo, city	12,556	12,703	1.17
Evansville, city	5,703	5,821	2.07	Baraboo, town	1,816	1,813	-0.17
Footville, village	772	831	7.64	Bear Creek, town	641	643	0.31
Fulton, town	3,580	3,691	3.10	Cazenovia, village (part)	20	20	0.00
Harmony, town	2,569	2,568	-0.04	Dellona, town	1,901	1,925	1.26
Janesville, city	65,615	66,206	0.90	Delton, town	2,460	2,490	1.22
Janesville, town	3,665	3,692	0.74	Excelsior, town	1,603	1,613	0.62
Johnstown, town	766	763	-0.39	Fairfield, town	1,078	1,082	0.37
La Prairie, town	784	781	-0.38	Franklin, town	668	663	-0.75
Lima, town	1,271	1,274	0.24	Freedom, town	449	449	0.00
Magnolia, town	742	745	0.40	Greenfield, town	909	910	0.11
Milton, city	5,716	5,710	-0.10	Honey Creek, town	749	752	0.40
Milton, town	3,100	3,111	0.35	Ironton, town	662	667	0.76
Newark, town	1,510	1,513	0.20	Ironton, village	274	268	-2.19
Orfordville, village	1,473	1,494	1.43	La Valle, town	1,420	1,441	1.48
Plymouth, town	1,245	1,243	-0.16	La Valle, village	388	375	-3.35
Porter, town	969	977	0.83	Lake Delton, village	3,501	3,515	0.40
Rock, town	2,981	2,990	0.30	Lime Ridge, village	158	157	-0.63
Spring Valley, town	728	725	-0.41	Loganville, village	301	300	-0.33
Turtle, town	2,393	2,411	0.75	Merrimac, town	1,247	1,271	1.92
Union, town	2,104	2,114	0.48	Merrimac, village	527	533	1.14
				North Freedom, village	603	598	-0.83
Rusk	**14,188**	**14,223**	**0.25**	Plain, village	749	748	-0.13
Atlanta, town	560	559	-0.18	Prairie du Sac, town	1,076	1,079	0.28
Big Bend, town	401	408	1.75	Prairie du Sac, village	4,420	4,458	0.86
Big Falls, town	115	116	0.87	Reedsburg, city	9,984	10,181	1.97
Bruce, village	781	775	-0.77	Reedsburg, town	1,185	1,147	-3.21
Cedar Rapids, town	36	36	0.00	Rock Springs, village	327	328	0.31
Conrath, village	88	88	0.00	Sauk City, village	3,518	3,527	0.26
Dewey, town	542	546	0.74	Spring Green, town	1,828	1,835	0.38
Flambeau, town	987	986	-0.10	Spring Green, village	1,566	1,597	1.98
Glen Flora, village	100	100	0.00	Sumpter, town	1,055	1,063	0.76
Grant, town	732	730	-0.27	Troy, town	781	785	0.51
Grow, town	443	443	0.00	Washington, town	1,021	1,037	1.57
Hawkins, town	122	123	0.82	West Baraboo, village	1,627	1,630	0.18
Hawkins, village	331	334	0.91	Westfield, town	582	592	1.72
Hubbard, town	178	179	0.56	Winfield, town	890	898	0.90
Ingram, village	70	70	0.00	Wisconsin Dells, city (part)	384	555	44.53
Ladysmith, city	3,216	3,216	0.00	Woodland, town	839	849	1.19
Lawrence, town	301	305	1.33				
Marshall, town	664	656	-1.20	**Sawyer**	**18,074**	**18,093**	**0.11**
Murry, town	247	253	2.43	Bass Lake, town	2,731	2,755	0.88
Richland, town	197	197	0.00	Couderay, town	393	399	1.53
Rusk, town	551	559	1.45	Couderay, village	81	81	0.00
Sheldon, village	261	263	0.77	Draper, town	241	242	0.41
South Fork, town	115	115	0.00	Edgewater, town	565	576	1.95
Strickland, town	280	282	0.71	Exeland, village	229	229	0.00
Stubbs, town	523	524	0.19	Hayward, city	2,533	2,503	-1.18
Thornapple, town	721	729	1.11	Hayward, town	3,765	3,758	-0.19
Tony, village	105	105	0.00	Hunter, town	779	790	1.41
True, town	237	238	0.42	Lenroot, town	1,337	1,352	1.12

Wisconsin population by county and municipality, continued

	2020 census	2022 estimate	% change		2020 census	2022 estimate	% change
Meadowbrook, town	134	135	0.75	Greenbush, town	1,903	1,862	-2.15
Meteor, town	156	167	7.05	Herman, town	2,162	2,149	-0.60
Ojibwa, town	307	310	0.98	Holland, town	2,273	2,277	0.18
Radisson, town	445	444	-0.22	Howards Grove, village	3,237	3,271	1.05
Radisson, village	273	273	0.00	Kohler, village	2,195	2,208	0.59
Round Lake, town	1,081	1,095	1.30	Lima, town	2,956	2,965	0.30
Sand Lake, town	901	908	0.78	Lyndon, town	1,526	1,539	0.85
Spider Lake, town	487	490	0.62	Mitchell, town	1,900	1,833	-3.53
Weirgor, town	311	311	0.00	Mosel, town	748	753	0.67
Winter, town	1,000	951	-4.90	Oostburg, village	3,056	3,093	1.21
Winter, village	325	324	-0.31	Plymouth, city	8,932	8,964	0.36
				Plymouth, town	3,083	3,066	-0.55
Shawano	**40,881**	**41,190**	**0.76**	Random Lake, village	1,561	1,565	0.26
Almon, town	575	576	0.17	Rhine, town	2,139	2,157	0.84
Angelica, town	1,822	1,840	0.99	Russell, town	384	383	-0.26
Aniwa, town	517	517	0.00	Scott, town	1,764	1,762	-0.11
Aniwa, village	243	238	-2.06	Sheboygan, city	49,929	50,139	0.42
Bartelme, town	810	809	-0.12	Sheboygan, town	8,136	8,175	0.48
Belle Plaine, town	1,800	1,763	-2.06	Sheboygan Falls, city	8,210	8,586	4.58
Birnamwood, town	682	691	1.32	Sheboygan Falls, town	1,824	1,831	0.38
Birnamwood, village (part)	716	716	0.00	Sherman, town	1,452	1,465	0.90
Bonduel, village	1,417	1,411	-0.42	Waldo, village	467	477	2.14
Bowler, village	320	319	-0.31	Wilson, town	3,484	3,486	0.06
Cecil, village	529	531	0.38				
Eland, village	199	196	-1.51	**St. Croix**	**93,536**	**96,269**	**2.92**
Fairbanks, town	538	536	-0.37	Baldwin, town	1,047	1,061	1.34
Germania, town	343	349	1.75	Baldwin, village	4,291	4,356	1.51
Grant, town	976	973	-0.31	Cady, town	880	889	1.02
Green Valley, town	1,026	1,034	0.78	Cylon, town	708	715	0.99
Gresham, village	530	532	0.38	Deer Park, village	249	248	-0.40
Hartland, town	824	834	1.21	Eau Galle, town	1,253	1,274	1.68
Herman, town	739	741	0.27	Emerald, town	831	847	1.93
Hutchins, town	500	504	0.80	Erin Prairie, town	673	670	-0.45
Lessor, town	1,226	1,238	0.98	Forest, town	638	643	0.78
Maple Grove, town	939	936	-0.32	Glenwood, town	747	750	0.40
Marion, city (part)	14	14	0.00	Glenwood City, city	1,306	1,288	-1.38
Mattoon, village	357	356	-0.28	Hammond, town	2,565	2,692	4.95
Morris, town	374	375	0.27	Hammond, village	1,873	1,864	-0.48
Navarino, town	413	414	0.24	Hudson, city	14,755	15,140	2.61
Pella, town	899	908	1.00	Hudson, town	8,671	8,859	2.17
Pulaski, village (part)	220	220	0.00	Kinnickinnic, town	1,815	1,840	1.38
Red Springs, town	993	999	0.60	New Richmond, city	10,079	10,541	4.58
Richmond, town	1,832	1,839	0.38	North Hudson, village	3,803	3,888	2.24
Seneca, town	495	496	0.20	Pleasant Valley, town	567	572	0.88
Shawano, city	9,243	9,515	2.94	Richmond, town	4,074	4,272	4.86
Tigerton, village	708	707	-0.14	River Falls, city (part)	3,636	4,064	11.77
Washington, town	1,965	1,973	0.41	Roberts, village	1,919	2,026	5.58
Waukechon, town	1,002	1,007	0.50	Rush River, town	500	503	0.60
Wescott, town	3,257	3,265	0.25	Somerset, town	4,291	4,421	3.03
Wittenberg, town	823	819	-0.49	Somerset, village	3,019	3,168	4.94
Wittenberg, village	1,015	999	-1.58	Spring Valley, village (part)	11	11	0.00
				Springfield, town	993	1,004	1.11
Sheboygan	**118,034**	**118,776**	**0.63**	St. Joseph, town	4,178	4,322	3.45
Adell, village	498	497	-0.20	Stanton, town	907	908	0.11
Cascade, village	722	726	0.55	Star Prairie, town	3,733	3,779	1.23
Cedar Grove, village	2,101	2,125	1.14	Star Prairie, village	678	675	-0.44
Elkhart Lake, village	941	960	2.02	Troy, town	5,518	5,558	0.72
Glenbeulah, village	451	462	2.44	Warren, town	1,733	1,787	3.12

Wisconsin population by county and municipality, continued

	2020 census	2022 estimate	% change		2020 census	2022 estimate	% change
Wilson, village	209	208	-0.48	**Vernon**	**30,714**	**30,965**	**0.82**
Woodville, village	1,386	1,426	2.89	Bergen, town	1,365	1,365	0.00
Taylor	**19,913**	**19,976**	**0.32**	Chaseburg, village	241	242	0.41
Aurora, town	459	457	-0.44	Christiana, town	993	1,013	2.01
Browning, town	910	917	0.77	Clinton, town	1,374	1,436	4.51
Chelsea, town	710	709	-0.14	Coon, town	729	743	1.92
Cleveland, town	216	229	6.02	Coon Valley, village	758	755	-0.40
Deer Creek, town	677	675	-0.30	De Soto, village (part)	226	230	1.77
Ford, town	265	265	0.00	Forest, town	617	624	1.13
Gilman, village	378	381	0.79	Franklin, town	1,106	1,105	-0.09
Goodrich, town	460	461	0.22	Genoa, town	753	755	0.27
Greenwood, town	621	628	1.13	Genoa, village	232	231	-0.43
Grover, town	208	207	-0.48	Greenwood, town	923	932	0.98
Hammel, town	703	713	1.42	Hamburg, town	956	953	-0.31
Holway, town	930	944	1.51	Harmony, town	882	903	2.38
Jump River, town	275	276	0.36	Hillsboro, city	1,397	1,427	2.15
Little Black, town	1,156	1,169	1.12	Hillsboro, town	787	788	0.13
Lublin, village	117	117	0.00	Jefferson, town	1,270	1,281	0.87
Maplehurst, town	338	343	1.48	Kickapoo, town	722	739	2.35
McKinley, town	408	410	0.49	La Farge, village	730	726	-0.55
Medford, city	4,349	4,305	-1.01	Liberty, town	341	347	1.76
Medford, town	2,482	2,519	1.49	Ontario, village (part)	534	528	-1.12
Molitor, town	308	307	-0.32	Readstown, village	376	372	-1.06
Pershing, town	201	203	1.00	Stark, town	351	352	0.28
Rib Lake, town	763	764	0.13	Sterling, town	550	547	-0.55
Rib Lake, village	935	921	-1.50	Stoddard, village	840	896	6.67
Roosevelt, town	478	478	0.00	Union, town	809	817	0.99
Stetsonville, village	563	564	0.18	Viola, village (part)	240	241	0.42
Taft, town	310	312	0.65	Viroqua, city	4,504	4,444	-1.33
Westboro, town	693	702	1.30	Viroqua, town	1,744	1,778	1.95
				Webster, town	821	826	0.61
Trempealeau	**30,760**	**30,884**	**0.40**	Westby, city	2,332	2,342	0.43
Albion, town	694	696	0.29	Wheatland, town	588	588	0.00
Arcadia, city	3,737	3,749	0.32	Whitestown, town	623	639	2.57
Arcadia, town	1,696	1,702	0.35	**Vilas**	**23,047**	**23,140**	**0.40**
Blair, city	1,325	1,293	-2.42	Arbor Vitae, town	3,403	3,411	0.24
Burnside, town	507	515	1.58	Boulder Junction, town	1,057	1,075	1.70
Caledonia, town	928	933	0.54	Cloverland, town	1,068	1,069	0.09
Chimney Rock, town	258	259	0.39	Conover, town	1,318	1,329	0.83
Dodge, town	394	397	0.76	Eagle River, city	1,628	1,614	-0.86
Eleva, village	685	698	1.90	Lac du Flambeau, town	3,552	3,565	0.37
Ettrick, town	1,285	1,286	0.08	Land O'Lakes, town	944	955	1.17
Ettrick, village	525	526	0.19	Lincoln, town	2,659	2,660	0.04
Gale, town	1,708	1,722	0.82	Manitowish Waters, town	624	628	0.64
Galesville, city	1,662	1,672	0.60	Phelps, town	1,238	1,242	0.32
Hale, town	1,061	1,068	0.66	Plum Lake, town	553	555	0.36
Independence, city	1,498	1,509	0.73	Presque Isle, town	805	808	0.37
Lincoln, town	779	776	-0.39	St. Germain, town	2,083	2,099	0.77
Osseo, city	1,811	1,811	0.00	Washington, town	1,587	1,600	0.82
Pigeon, town	1,018	1,025	0.69	Winchester, town	528	530	0.38
Pigeon Falls, village	381	380	-0.26				
Preston, town	942	946	0.42	**Walworth**	**105,230**	**106,129**	**0.85**
Strum, village	1,076	1,079	0.28	Bloomfield, town	1,778	1,790	0.67
Sumner, town	840	850	1.19	Bloomfield, village	4,781	4,821	0.84
Trempealeau, town	1,951	1,965	0.72	Burlington, city (part)	0	0	0.00
Trempealeau, village	1,843	1,888	2.44	Darien, town	1,651	1,650	-0.06
Unity, town	511	513	0.39	Darien, village	1,573	1,576	0.19
Whitehall, city	1,645	1,626	-1.16	Delavan, city	8,505	8,527	0.26

Wisconsin population by county and municipality, continued

	2020 census	2022 estimate	% change		2020 census	2022 estimate	% change
Delavan, town	5,273	5,265	-0.15	Germantown, village	20,917	21,040	0.59
East Troy, town	3,992	4,020	0.70	Hartford, city (part)	15,617	15,796	1.15
East Troy, village	4,687	4,989	6.44	Hartford, town	3,400	3,381	-0.56
Elkhorn, city	10,247	10,317	0.68	Jackson, town	4,629	4,064	-12.21
Fontana-on-Geneva Lake, village	1,872	1,888	0.85	Jackson, village	7,185	7,844	9.17
Geneva, town	5,390	5,476	1.60	Kewaskum, town	1,118	1,134	1.43
Genoa City, village (part)	2,977	2,962	-0.50	Kewaskum, village (part)	4,309	4,371	1.44
La Grange, town	2,472	2,495	0.93	Milwaukee, city (part)	0	0	0.00
Lafayette, town	2,039	2,081	2.06	Newburg, village (part)	1,049	1,051	0.19
Lake Geneva, city	8,277	8,542	3.20	Polk, town	3,988	4,005	0.43
Linn, town	2,687	2,717	1.12	Richfield, village	11,739	11,866	1.08
Lyons, town	3,648	3,667	0.52	Slinger, village	5,992	6,401	6.83
Mukwonago, village (part)	222	227	2.25	Trenton, town	4,525	4,572	1.04
Richmond, town	1,901	1,919	0.95	Wayne, town	2,182	2,232	2.29
Sharon, town	861	859	-0.23	West Bend, city	31,752	32,067	0.99
Sharon, village	1,586	1,581	-0.32	West Bend, town	4,441	4,415	-0.59
Spring Prairie, town	2,123	2,130	0.33	**Waukesha**	**406,978**	**410,769**	**0.93**
Sugar Creek, town	3,902	3,921	0.49	Big Bend, village	1,483	1,491	0.54
Troy, town	2,355	2,363	0.34	Brookfield, city	41,464	41,430	-0.08
Walworth, town	1,565	1,575	0.64	Brookfield, town	6,477	6,480	0.05
Walworth, village	2,759	2,768	0.33	Butler, village	1,787	1,780	-0.39
Whitewater, city (part)	11,721	11,573	-1.26	Chenequa, village	526	530	0.76
Whitewater, town	1,433	1,437	0.28	Delafield, city	7,185	7,172	-0.18
Williams Bay, village	2,953	2,993	1.35	Delafield, town	8,095	8,148	0.65
Washburn	**16,623**	**16,655**	**0.19**	Dousman, village	2,419	2,426	0.29
Barronett, town	461	456	-1.08	Eagle, town	3,478	3,521	1.24
Bashaw, town	1,079	1,085	0.56	Eagle, village	2,071	2,123	2.51
Bass Lake, town	566	565	-0.18	Elm Grove, village	6,513	6,676	2.50
Beaver Brook, town	795	805	1.26	Genesee, town	7,171	7,187	0.22
Birchwood, town	605	613	1.32	Hartland, village	9,501	9,946	4.68
Birchwood, village	402	402	0.00	Lac La Belle, village (part)	279	283	1.43
Brooklyn, town	311	310	-0.32	Lannon, village	1,355	1,810	33.58
Casey, town	396	394	-0.51	Lisbon, village[2]	10,477	10,735	2.46
Chicog, town	292	293	0.34	Menomonee Falls, village	38,527	39,213	1.78
Crystal, town	280	284	1.43	Merton, town	8,277	8,308	0.37
Evergreen, town	1,191	1,201	0.84	Merton, village	3,441	3,482	1.19
Frog Creek, town	127	127	0.00	Milwaukee, city (part)	0	0	0.00
Gull Lake, town	198	198	0.00	Mukwonago, town	7,781	7,807	0.33
Long Lake, town	628	630	0.32	Mukwonago, village (part)	8,040	8,157	1.46
Madge, town	532	532	0.00	Muskego, city	25,032	25,343	1.24
Minong, town	984	992	0.81	Nashotah, village	1,321	1,319	-0.15
Minong, village	548	550	0.36	New Berlin, city	40,451	40,426	-0.06
Sarona, town	419	417	-0.48	North Prairie, village	2,202	2,208	0.27
Shell Lake, city	1,371	1,369	-0.15	Oconomowoc, city	18,203	18,485	1.55
Spooner, city	2,477	2,453	-0.97	Oconomowoc, town	8,836	8,861	0.28
Spooner, town	827	833	0.73	Oconomowoc Lake, village	566	572	1.06
Springbrook, town	504	508	0.79	Ottawa, town	3,646	3,659	0.36
Stinnett, town	207	208	0.48	Pewaukee, city	15,914	16,127	1.34
Stone Lake, town	515	515	0.00	Pewaukee, village	8,238	8,215	-0.28
Trego, town	908	915	0.77	Summit, village	4,784	5,061	5.79
Washington	**136,761**	**138,229**	**1.07**	Sussex, village	11,487	11,750	2.29
Addison, town	3,464	3,449	-0.43	Vernon, village	7,474	7,486	0.16
Barton, town	2,743	2,795	1.90	Wales, village	2,862	2,917	1.92
Erin, town	3,825	3,842	0.44	Waukesha, city	71,158	71,146	-0.02
Farmington, town	3,645	3,662	0.47	Waukesha, town	8,457	8,489	0.38
Germantown, town	241	242	0.41	**Waupaca**	**51,812**	**52,309**	**0.96**
				Bear Creek, town	748	749	0.13

Wisconsin population by county and municipality, continued

	2020 census	2022 estimate	% change		2020 census	2022 estimate	% change
Big Falls, village	60	60	0.00	Warren, town	656	667	1.68
Caledonia, town	1,712	1,738	1.52	Wautoma, city	2,209	2,216	0.32
Clintonville, city	4,591	4,686	2.07	Wautoma, town	1,270	1,270	0.00
Dayton, town	2,644	2,661	0.64	Wild Rose, village	780	781	0.13
Dupont, town	746	748	0.27				
Embarrass, village	353	353	0.00	**Winnebago**	**171,730**	**172,542**	**0.47**
Farmington, town	3,712	3,757	1.21	Algoma, town	6,866	6,927	0.89
Fremont, town	627	624	-0.48	Appleton, city (part)	1,441	1,437	-0.28
Fremont, village	689	688	-0.15	Black Wolf, town	2,429	2,431	0.08
Harrison, town	459	465	1.31	Clayton, town	4,329	4,375	1.06
Helvetia, town	701	704	0.43	Fox Crossing, village	18,974	19,011	0.20
Iola, town	938	939	0.11	Menasha, city (part)	15,261	15,247	-0.09
Iola, village	1,249	1,245	-0.32	Neenah, city	27,319	27,726	1.49
Larrabee, town	1,286	1,283	-0.23	Neenah, town	3,702	3,701	-0.03
Lebanon, town	1,619	1,623	0.25	Nekimi, town	1,337	1,334	-0.22
Lind, town	1,571	1,580	0.57	Nepeuskun, town	724	724	0.00
Little Wolf, town	1,400	1,398	-0.14	Omro, city	3,652	3,644	-0.22
Manawa, city	1,441	1,441	0.00	Omro, town	2,293	2,356	2.75
Marion, city (part)	1,310	1,306	-0.31	Oshkosh, city	66,816	66,929	0.17
Matteson, town	914	915	0.11	Oshkosh, town	2,439	2,449	0.41
Mukwa, town	2,830	2,831	0.04	Poygan, town	1,261	1,287	2.06
New London, city (part)	5,596	5,714	2.11	Rushford, town	1,623	1,654	1.91
Ogdensburg, village	188	188	0.00	Utica, town	1,364	1,360	-0.29
Royalton, town	1,359	1,365	0.44	Vinland, town	1,769	1,773	0.23
Scandinavia, town	1,049	1,052	0.29	Winchester, town	1,794	1,796	0.11
Scandinavia, village	371	371	0.00	Winneconne, town	2,590	2,627	1.43
St. Lawrence, town	714	712	-0.28	Winneconne, village	2,544	2,542	-0.08
Union, town	778	780	0.26	Wolf River, town	1,203	1,212	0.75
Waupaca, city	6,282	6,422	2.23				
Waupaca, town	1,194	1,199	0.42	**Wood**	**74,207**	**74,200**	**-0.01**
Weyauwega, city	1,796	1,824	1.56	Arpin, town	942	946	0.42
Weyauwega, town	567	571	0.71	Arpin, village	305	304	-0.33
Wyoming, town	318	317	-0.31	Auburndale, town	790	789	-0.13
				Auburndale, village	702	710	1.14
Waushara	**24,520**	**24,492**	**-0.11**	Biron, village	839	849	1.19
Aurora, town	1,006	1,001	-0.50	Cameron, town	539	539	0.00
Berlin, city (part)	87	87	0.00	Cary, town	406	409	0.74
Bloomfield, town	1,054	1,052	-0.19	Cranmoor, town	181	180	-0.55
Coloma, town	730	732	0.27	Dexter, town	350	350	0.00
Coloma, village	448	448	0.00	Grand Rapids, town	7,576	7,611	0.46
Dakota, town	1,143	1,138	-0.44	Hansen, town	747	753	0.80
Deerfield, town	667	668	0.15	Hewitt, village	796	803	0.88
Hancock, town	558	564	1.08	Hiles, town	152	151	-0.66
Hancock, village	393	392	-0.25	Lincoln, town	1,593	1,598	0.31
Leon, town	1,534	1,536	0.13	Marshfield, city (part)	18,119	18,053	-0.36
Lohrville, village	434	432	-0.46	Marshfield, town	763	771	1.05
Marion, town	2,020	2,030	0.50	Milladore, town	668	662	-0.90
Mount Morris, town	1,096	1,107	1.00	Milladore, village (part)	268	268	0.00
Oasis, town	384	381	-0.78	Nekoosa, city	2,449	2,439	-0.41
Plainfield, town	496	495	-0.20	Pittsville, city	813	827	1.72
Plainfield, village	924	920	-0.43	Port Edwards, town	1,356	1,357	0.07
Poy Sippi, town	919	915	-0.44	Port Edwards, village	1,762	1,754	-0.45
Redgranite, village	2,061	1,997	-3.11	Remington, town	230	229	-0.43
Richford, town	737	740	0.41	Richfield, town	1,596	1,610	0.88
Rose, town	661	675	2.12	Rock, town	787	790	0.38
Saxeville, town	996	997	0.10	Rudolph, town	1,027	1,028	0.10
Springwater, town	1,257	1,251	-0.48	Rudolph, village	433	433	0.00

Wisconsin population by county and municipality, continued

	2020 census	2022 estimate	% change		2020 census	2022 estimate	% change
Saratoga, town	5,060	5,092	0.63	Vesper, village	513	512	-0.19
Seneca, town	1,039	1,038	-0.10	Wisconsin Rapids, city	18,877	18,809	-0.36
Sherry, town	755	760	0.66	Wood, town	757	758	0.13
Sigel, town	1,017	1,018	0.10				

1. On October 31, 2022, the town of Madison attached to the cities of Madison and Fitchburg. 2. On February 13, 2023, the entire town of Lisbon became the village of Lisbon.

Sources: Wisconsin Department of Administration, Demographic Services Center, *Official Final Estimates, 1/1/2022, Wisconsin Municipalities, with Comparison to Census 2020, Official Final Estimates, 1/1/2022, Wisconsin Counties, with Comparison to Census 2020,* and *Official Final Estimates, 1/1/2022, Wisconsin Municipalities with Territory in Multiple Counties,* October 2022; Wisconsin Department of Administration, Division of Intergovernmental Relations, *Municipality changes since January 2000,* February 2023.

Wisconsin cities, January 1, 2022

City[1]	Year incorporated	County	2020 census	2022 estimate	% change
First class cities (150,000 or more)—one					
Milwaukee	1846	Milwaukee, Washington, Waukesha	577,922	577,309	-0.11
Second class cities (39,000–149,999)—16					
Appleton	1857	Calumet, Outagamie, Winnebago	75,644	75,605	-0.05
Eau Claire[2]	1872	Chippewa, Eau Claire	69,421	70,587	1.68
Fond du Lac[2]	1852	Fond du Lac	44,678	44,470	-0.47
Green Bay	1854	Brown	107,395	107,369	-0.02
Janesville[2]	1853	Rock	65,615	66,206	0.90
Kenosha	1850	Kenosha	99,986	100,051	0.07
La Crosse	1856	La Crosse	52,680	52,160	-0.99
Madison	1856	Dane	269,840	279,012	3.40
Oshkosh[2]	1853	Winnebago	66,816	66,929	0.17
Racine	1848	Racine	77,816	77,240	-0.74
Sheboygan	1853	Sheboygan	49,929	50,139	0.42
Superior	1858	Douglas	26,751	26,943	0.72
Waukesha	1895	Waukesha	71,158	71,146	-0.02
Wausau	1872	Marathon	39,994	40,199	0.51
Wauwatosa	1897	Milwaukee	48,387	48,638	0.52
West Allis	1906	Milwaukee	60,325	60,068	-0.43
Third class cities (10,000–38,999)—33					
Baraboo	1882	Sauk	12,556	12,703	1.17
Beaver Dam	1856	Dodge	16,708	16,727	0.11
Beloit[2]	1857	Rock	36,657	36,760	0.28
Brookfield	1954	Waukesha	41,464	41,430	-0.08
Chippewa Falls	1869	Chippewa	14,731	14,724	-0.05
Cudahy	1906	Milwaukee	18,204	18,134	-0.38
De Pere	1883	Brown	25,410	25,525	0.45
Fort Atkinson[2]	1878	Jefferson	12,579	12,583	0.03
Franklin	1956	Milwaukee	36,116	35,895	-0.61
Glendale	1950	Milwaukee	13,357	13,472	0.86
Greenfield	1957	Milwaukee	37,803	37,709	-0.25
Hartford	1883	Dodge, Washington	15,626	15,805	1.15
Hudson	1857	St. Croix	14,755	15,140	2.61
Kaukauna	1885	Calumet, Outagamie	17,089	17,441	2.06
Manitowoc	1870	Manitowoc	34,626	34,722	0.28

Wisconsin cities, January 1, 2022, continued

City[1]	Year incorporated	County	2020 census	2022 estimate	% change
Marinette	1887	Marinette	11,119	11,129	0.09
Marshfield	1883	Marathon, Wood	18,929	18,969	0.21
Menasha	1874	Calumet, Winnebago	18,268	18,490	1.22
Middleton	1963	Dane	21,827	23,031	5.52
Muskego	1964	Waukesha	25,032	25,343	1.24
Neenah	1873	Winnebago	27,319	27,726	1.49
New Berlin	1959	Waukesha	40,451	40,426	-0.06
New Richmond	1885	St. Croix	10,079	10,541	4.58
Oak Creek	1955	Milwaukee	36,497	37,374	2.40
Oconomowoc	1875	Waukesha	18,203	18,485	1.55
Pewaukee	1999	Waukesha	15,914	16,127	1.34
River Falls	1875	Pierce, St. Croix	16,182	16,515	2.06
Stevens Point	1858	Portage	25,666	25,954	1.12
Sun Prairie	1958	Dane	35,967	37,304	3.72
Two Rivers[2]	1878	Manitowoc	11,271	11,243	-0.25
Watertown	1853	Dodge, Jefferson	22,926	23,018	0.40
West Bend	1885	Washington	31,752	32,067	0.99
Wisconsin Rapids	1869	Wood	18,877	18,809	-0.36
Fourth class cities (Under 10,000)—140					
Abbotsford	1965	Clark, Marathon	2,275	2,387	4.92
Adams	1926	Adams	1,761	1,755	-0.34
Algoma	1879	Kewaunee	3,243	3,221	-0.68
Alma	1885	Buffalo	716	717	0.14
Altoona	1887	Eau Claire	8,293	9,149	10.32
Amery	1919	Polk	2,962	2,952	-0.34
Antigo	1885	Langlade	8,100	8,053	-0.58
Arcadia	1925	Trempealeau	3,737	3,749	0.32
Ashland	1887	Ashland, Bayfield	7,908	7,819	-1.13
Augusta	1885	Eau Claire	1,567	1,549	-1.15
Barron	1887	Barron	3,733	3,685	-1.29
Bayfield	1913	Bayfield	584	586	0.34
Berlin	1857	Green Lake, Waushara	5,571	5,570	-0.02
Black River Falls	1883	Jackson	3,523	3,519	-0.11
Blair	1949	Trempealeau	1,325	1,293	-2.42
Bloomer	1920	Chippewa	3,683	3,719	0.98
Boscobel	1873	Grant	3,286	3,130	-4.75
Brillion	1944	Calumet	3,262	3,487	6.90
Brodhead	1891	Green, Rock	3,274	3,268	-0.18
Buffalo City	1859	Buffalo	1,007	1,009	0.20
Burlington	1900	Racine, Walworth	11,047	11,166	1.08
Cedarburg	1885	Ozaukee	12,121	12,446	2.68
Chetek	1891	Barron	2,172	2,166	-0.28
Chilton	1877	Calumet	4,080	4,064	-0.39
Clintonville	1887	Waupaca	4,591	4,686	2.07
Colby	1891	Clark, Marathon	1,952	1,936	-0.82
Columbus	1874	Columbia, Dodge	5,540	5,530	-0.18
Cornell	1956	Chippewa	1,453	1,437	-1.10
Crandon	1898	Forest	1,713	1,688	-1.46
Cuba City	1925	Grant, Lafayette	2,138	2,120	-0.84
Cumberland	1885	Barron	2,274	2,267	-0.31
Darlington	1877	Lafayette	2,462	2,432	-1.22
Delafield	1959	Waukesha	7,185	7,172	-0.18
Delavan	1897	Walworth	8,505	8,527	0.26
Dodgeville	1889	Iowa	4,984	5,038	1.08
Durand	1887	Pepin	1,854	1,848	-0.32
Eagle River	1937	Vilas	1,628	1,614	-0.86

Wisconsin cities, January 1, 2022, continued

City[1]	Year incorporated	County	2020 census	2022 estimate	% change
Edgerton	1883	Dane, Rock	5,945	5,997	0.87
Elkhorn	1897	Walworth	10,247	10,317	0.68
Elroy	1885	Juneau	1,356	1,319	-2.73
Evansville	1896	Rock	5,703	5,821	2.07
Fennimore	1919	Grant	2,764	2,733	-1.12
Fitchburg	1983	Dane	29,609	31,817	7.46
Fountain City	1889	Buffalo	806	803	-0.37
Fox Lake	1938	Dodge	1,604	1,640	2.24
Galesville	1942	Trempealeau	1,662	1,672	0.60
Gillett	1944	Oconto	1,289	1,284	-0.39
Glenwood City	1895	St. Croix	1,306	1,288	-1.38
Green Lake	1962	Green Lake	1,001	998	-0.30
Greenwood	1891	Clark	1,058	1,054	-0.38
Hayward	1915	Sawyer	2,533	2,503	-1.18
Hillsboro	1885	Vernon	1,397	1,427	2.15
Horicon	1897	Dodge	3,767	3,797	0.80
Hurley	1918	Iron	1,558	1,535	-1.48
Independence	1942	Trempealeau	1,498	1,509	0.73
Jefferson	1878	Jefferson	7,793	7,747	-0.59
Juneau	1887	Dodge	2,658	2,576	-3.09
Kewaunee	1883	Kewaunee	2,837	2,822	-0.53
Kiel	1920	Calumet, Manitowoc	3,932	3,975	1.09
Ladysmith	1905	Rusk	3,216	3,216	0.00
Lake Geneva	1883	Walworth	8,277	8,542	3.20
Lake Mills[2]	1905	Jefferson	6,211	6,452	3.88
Lancaster	1878	Grant	3,907	3,914	0.18
Lodi	1941	Columbia	3,189	3,226	1.16
Loyal	1948	Clark	1,203	1,201	-0.17
Manawa	1954	Waupaca	1,441	1,441	0.00
Marion	1898	Shawano, Waupaca	1,324	1,320	-0.30
Markesan	1959	Green Lake	1,377	1,365	-0.87
Mauston	1883	Juneau	4,347	4,286	-1.40
Mayville	1885	Dodge	5,196	5,211	0.29
Medford	1889	Taylor	4,349	4,305	-1.01
Mellen	1907	Ashland	698	694	-0.57
Menomonie	1882	Dunn	16,843	16,616	-1.35
Mequon	1957	Ozaukee	25,142	25,141	0.00
Merrill	1883	Lincoln	9,347	9,312	-0.37
Milton	1969	Rock	5,716	5,710	-0.10
Mineral Point	1857	Iowa	2,581	2,583	0.08
Mondovi	1889	Buffalo	2,845	2,852	0.25
Monona	1969	Dane	8,624	8,869	2.84
Monroe	1882	Green	10,661	10,691	0.28
Montello	1938	Marquette	1,448	1,441	-0.48
Montreal	1924	Iron	801	799	-0.25
Mosinee	1931	Marathon	4,452	4,495	0.97
Neillsville	1882	Clark	2,384	2,320	-2.68
Nekoosa	1926	Wood	2,449	2,439	-0.41
New Holstein	1926	Calumet	3,195	3,177	-0.56
New Lisbon	1889	Juneau	2,559	2,526	-1.29
New London	1877	Outagamie, Waupaca	7,348	7,491	1.95
Niagara	1992	Marinette	1,602	1,580	-1.37
Oconto	1869	Oconto	4,609	4,600	-0.20

Wisconsin cities, January 1, 2022, continued

City[1]	Year incorporated	County	2020 census	2022 estimate	% change
Oconto Falls	1919	Oconto	2,957	2,991	1.15
Omro	1944	Winnebago	3,652	3,644	-0.22
Onalaska	1887	La Crosse	18,803	19,276	2.52
Osseo	1941	Trempealeau	1,811	1,811	0.00
Owen	1925	Clark	916	917	0.11
Park Falls	1912	Price	2,410	2,378	-1.33
Peshtigo	1903	Marinette	3,420	3,361	-1.73
Phillips	1891	Price	1,533	1,525	-0.52
Pittsville	1887	Wood	813	827	1.72
Platteville[2]	1876	Grant	11,836	11,154	-5.76
Plymouth	1877	Sheboygan	8,932	8,964	0.36
Port Washington	1882	Ozaukee	12,353	12,853	4.05
Portage	1854	Columbia	10,581	10,325	-2.42
Prairie du Chien	1872	Crawford	5,506	5,446	-1.09
Prescott	1857	Pierce	4,333	4,408	1.73
Princeton	1920	Green Lake	1,267	1,263	-0.32
Reedsburg	1887	Sauk	9,984	10,181	1.97
Rhinelander	1894	Oneida	8,285	8,283	-0.02
Rice Lake	1887	Barron	9,040	9,080	0.44
Richland Center	1887	Richland	5,114	5,043	-1.39
Ripon	1858	Fond du Lac	7,863	7,811	-0.66
St. Croix Falls	1958	Polk	2,208	2,222	0.63
St. Francis	1951	Milwaukee	9,161	9,156	-0.05
Schofield	1951	Marathon	2,157	2,262	4.87
Seymour	1879	Outagamie	3,546	3,523	-0.65
Shawano	1874	Shawano	9,243	9,515	2.94
Sheboygan Falls	1913	Sheboygan	8,210	8,586	4.58
Shell Lake	1961	Washburn	1,371	1,369	-0.15
Shullsburg	1889	Lafayette	1,173	1,176	0.26
South Milwaukee	1897	Milwaukee	20,795	20,703	-0.44
Sparta	1883	Monroe	10,025	10,075	0.50
Spooner	1909	Washburn	2,477	2,453	-0.97
Stanley	1898	Chippewa, Clark	3,804	3,748	-1.47
Stoughton	1882	Dane	13,173	13,204	0.24
Sturgeon Bay	1883	Door	9,646	9,656	0.10
Thorp	1948	Clark	1,795	1,781	-0.78
Tomah	1883	Monroe	9,570	9,631	0.64
Tomahawk	1891	Lincoln	3,441	3,436	-0.15
Verona	1977	Dane	14,030	14,889	6.12
Viroqua	1885	Vernon	4,504	4,444	-1.33
Washburn	1904	Bayfield	2,051	2,004	-2.29
Waterloo	1962	Jefferson	3,492	3,631	3.98
Waupaca	1875	Waupaca	6,282	6,422	2.23
Waupun	1878	Dodge, Fond du Lac	11,563	11,117	-3.86
Wautoma	1901	Waushara	2,209	2,216	0.32
Westby	1920	Vernon	2,332	2,342	0.43
Weyauwega	1939	Waupaca	1,796	1,824	1.56
Whitehall	1941	Trempealeau	1,645	1,626	-1.16
Whitewater[2]	1885	Jefferson, Walworth	16,137	15,773	-2.26
Wisconsin Dells	1925	Adams, Columbia, Juneau, Sauk	2,942	3,236	9.99

1. A city is initially classified according to its population when it incorporates. If its population changes, a city can take action to change its classification, but if it does not take such action, its population remains unchanged.   2. One of ten cities with a city manager.

Sources: Wisconsin Department of Administration, Demographic Services Center, *Official Final Estimates, 1/1/2022, Wisconsin Municipalities, with Comparison to Census 2020*, October 2022; League of Wisconsin Municipalities, *2022 Directory of Wisconsin City and Village Officials* at http://lwm-info.org/1236/Directory-of-Cities-Villages; and data compiled by Wisconsin Legislative Reference Bureau.

Wisconsin villages, January 1, 2022

Village	Year incorporated	County	2020 census	2022 estimate	% change
Adell	1918	Sheboygan	498	497	-0.20
Albany	1918	Green	1,096	1,093	-0.27
Allouez	1986	Brown	14,156	14,014	-1.00
Alma Center	1902	Jackson	487	484	-0.62
Almena	1945	Barron	705	742	5.25
Almond	1905	Portage	424	420	-0.94
Amherst	1899	Portage	1,117	1,121	0.36
Amherst Junction	1912	Portage	383	382	-0.26
Aniwa	1899	Shawano	243	238	-2.06
Arena	1923	Iowa	844	877	3.91
Argyle	1903	Lafayette	783	780	-0.38
Arlington	1945	Columbia	844	846	0.24
Arpin	1978	Wood	305	304	-0.33
Ashwaubenon[1]	1977	Brown	16,991	17,757	4.51
Athens	1901	Marathon	1,059	1,065	0.57
Auburndale	1881	Wood	702	710	1.14
Avoca	1870	Iowa	553	551	-0.36
Bagley	1919	Grant	356	355	-0.28
Baldwin	1875	St. Croix	4,291	4,356	1.51
Balsam Lake	1905	Polk	934	914	-2.14
Bangor	1899	La Crosse	1,437	1,568	9.12
Barneveld	1906	Iowa	1,331	1,338	0.53
Bay City	1909	Pierce	441	447	1.36
Bayside[1]	1953	Milwaukee, Ozaukee	4,482	4,463	-0.42
Bear Creek	1902	Outagamie	427	422	-1.17
Belgium	1922	Ozaukee	2,421	2,473	2.15
Bell Center	1901	Crawford	108	108	0.00
Belleville	1892	Dane, Green	2,491	2,659	6.74
Bellevue	2003	Brown	15,935	16,568	3.97
Belmont	1894	Lafayette	989	990	0.10
Benton	1892	Lafayette	946	960	1.48
Big Bend	1928	Waukesha	1,483	1,491	0.54
Big Falls	1925	Waupaca	60	60	0.00
Birchwood	1921	Washburn	402	402	0.00
Birnamwood	1895	Marathon, Shawano	730	732	0.27
Biron	1910	Wood	839	849	1.19
Black Creek	1904	Outagamie	1,357	1,353	-0.29
Black Earth	1901	Dane	1,493	1,551	3.88
Blanchardville	1890	Iowa, Lafayette	807	817	1.24
Bloomfield	2011	Walworth	4,781	4,821	0.84
Bloomington	1880	Grant	741	743	0.27
Blue Mounds	1912	Dane	948	953	0.53
Blue River	1916	Grant	457	457	0.00
Boaz	1939	Richland	129	129	0.00
Bonduel	1916	Shawano	1,417	1,411	-0.42
Bowler	1923	Shawano	320	319	-0.31
Boyceville	1922	Dunn	1,100	1,096	-0.36
Boyd	1891	Chippewa	605	608	0.50
Brandon	1881	Fond du Lac	882	879	-0.34
Bristol	2009	Kenosha	5,192	5,209	0.33
Brooklyn	1905	Dane, Green	1,524	1,525	0.07
Brown Deer[1]	1955	Milwaukee	12,507	13,023	4.13
Brownsville	1952	Dodge	598	630	5.35
Browntown	1890	Green	245	246	0.41
Bruce	1901	Rusk	781	775	-0.77
Butler	1913	Waukesha	1,787	1,780	-0.39
Butternut	1903	Ashland	366	362	-1.09
Cadott	1895	Chippewa	1,498	1,498	0.00
Caledonia	2005	Racine	25,361	25,478	0.46

Wisconsin villages, January 1, 2022, continued

Village	Year incorporated	County	2020 census	2022 estimate	% change
Cambria	1866	Columbia	777	781	0.51
Cambridge	1891	Dane, Jefferson	1,638	1,708	4.27
Cameron	1894	Barron	1,872	1,871	-0.05
Camp Douglas	1893	Juneau	647	645	-0.31
Campbellsport	1902	Fond du Lac	1,907	1,924	0.89
Cascade	1914	Sheboygan	722	726	0.55
Casco	1920	Kewaunee	630	644	2.22
Cashton	1901	Monroe	1,158	1,167	0.78
Cassville	1882	Grant	777	774	-0.39
Catawba	1922	Price	141	140	-0.71
Cazenovia	1902	Richland, Sauk	363	362	-0.28
Cecil	1905	Shawano	529	531	0.38
Cedar Grove	1899	Sheboygan	2,101	2,125	1.14
Centuria	1904	Polk	891	888	-0.34
Chaseburg	1922	Vernon	241	242	0.41
Chenequa	1928	Waukesha	526	530	0.76
Clayton	1909	Polk	550	549	-0.18
Clear Lake	1894	Polk	1,099	1,107	0.73
Cleveland	1958	Manitowoc	1,579	1,576	-0.19
Clinton	1882	Rock	2,221	2,235	0.63
Clyman	1924	Dodge	397	398	0.25
Cobb	1902	Iowa	480	484	0.83
Cochrane	1910	Buffalo	423	421	-0.47
Coleman	1903	Marinette	726	725	-0.14
Colfax	1904	Dunn	1,182	1,191	0.76
Coloma	1939	Waushara	448	448	0.00
Combined Locks	1920	Outagamie	3,634	3,641	0.19
Conrath	1915	Rusk	88	88	0.00
Coon Valley	1907	Vernon	758	755	-0.40
Cottage Grove	1924	Dane	7,303	8,854	21.24
Couderay	1922	Sawyer	81	81	0.00
Crivitz	1974	Marinette	1,093	1,096	0.27
Cross Plains	1920	Dane	4,104	4,123	0.46
Curtiss	1917	Clark	292	299	2.40
Dallas	1903	Barron	359	358	-0.28
Dane	1899	Dane	1,117	1,116	-0.09
Darien	1951	Walworth	1,573	1,576	0.19
De Soto	1886	Crawford, Vernon	309	315	1.94
Deer Park	1913	St. Croix	249	248	-0.40
Deerfield	1891	Dane	2,507	2,531	0.96
DeForest	1891	Dane	10,811	11,388	5.34
Denmark	1915	Brown	2,408	2,446	1.58
Dickeyville	1947	Grant	1,015	1,067	5.12
Dorchester	1901	Clark, Marathon	849	853	0.47
Dousman	1917	Waukesha	2,419	2,426	0.29
Downing	1909	Dunn	234	233	-0.43
Doylestown	1907	Columbia	280	278	-0.71
Dresser	1919	Polk	935	940	0.53
Eagle	1899	Waukesha	2,071	2,123	2.51
East Troy	1900	Walworth	4,687	4,989	6.44
Eastman	1909	Crawford	350	349	-0.29
Eden	1912	Fond du Lac	884	904	2.26
Edgar	1898	Marathon	1,439	1,450	0.76
Egg Harbor	1964	Door	358	369	3.07
Eland	1905	Shawano	199	196	-1.51
Elderon	1917	Marathon	161	160	-0.62
Eleva	1902	Trempealeau	685	698	1.90

Wisconsin villages, January 1, 2022, continued

Village	Year incorporated	County	2020 census	2022 estimate	% change
Elk Mound	1909	Dunn	985	982	-0.30
Elkhart Lake	1894	Sheboygan	941	960	2.02
Ellsworth	1887	Pierce	3,348	3,332	-0.48
Elm Grove[1]	1955	Waukesha	6,513	6,676	2.50
Elmwood	1905	Pierce	820	817	-0.37
Elmwood Park	1960	Racine	510	508	-0.39
Embarrass	1895	Waupaca	353	353	0.00
Endeavor	1946	Marquette	432	433	0.23
Ephraim	1919	Door	345	348	0.87
Ettrick	1948	Trempealeau	525	526	0.19
Exeland	1920	Sawyer	229	229	0.00
Fairchild	1880	Eau Claire	451	446	-1.11
Fairwater	1921	Fond du Lac	346	345	-0.29
Fall Creek	1906	Eau Claire	1,422	1,428	0.42
Fall River	1903	Columbia	1,801	1,815	0.78
Fenwood	1904	Marathon	141	142	0.71
Ferryville	1912	Crawford	191	193	1.05
Fontana-on-Geneva Lake	1924	Walworth	1,872	1,888	0.85
Footville	1918	Rock	772	831	7.64
Forestville	1960	Door	482	479	-0.62
Fox Crossing[1]	2016	Winnebago, Outagamie	18,974	19,011	0.20
Fox Point[1]	1926	Milwaukee	6,934	6,770	-2.37
Francis Creek	1960	Manitowoc	659	661	0.30
Frederic	1903	Polk	1,154	1,147	-0.61
Fredonia	1922	Ozaukee	2,279	2,280	0.04
Fremont	1882	Waupaca	689	688	-0.15
Friendship	1907	Adams	648	606	-6.48
Friesland	1946	Columbia	320	322	0.63
Gays Mills	1900	Crawford	523	522	-0.19
Genoa	1935	Vernon	232	231	-0.43
Genoa City	1901	Kenosha, Walworth	2,982	2,967	-0.50
Germantown	1927	Washington	20,917	21,040	0.59
Gilman	1914	Taylor	378	381	0.79
Glen Flora	1915	Rusk	100	100	0.00
Glenbeulah	1913	Sheboygan	451	462	2.44
Grafton	1896	Ozaukee	12,094	12,269	1.45
Granton	1916	Clark	381	377	-1.05
Grantsburg	1887	Burnett	1,330	1,318	-0.90
Gratiot	1891	Lafayette	224	223	-0.45
Greendale[1]	1939	Milwaukee	14,854	14,815	-0.26
Greenville	2021	Outagamie	12,687	13,067	3.00
Gresham	1908	Shawano	530	532	0.38
Hales Corners	1952	Milwaukee	7,720	7,658	-0.80
Hammond	1880	St. Croix	1,873	1,864	-0.48
Hancock	1902	Waushara	393	392	-0.25
Harrison	2013	Calumet, Outagamie	12,418	14,424	16.15
Hartland	1891	Waukesha	9,501	9,946	4.68
Hatley	1912	Marathon	648	677	4.48
Haugen	1918	Barron	266	266	0.00
Hawkins	1922	Rusk	331	334	0.91
Hazel Green	1867	Grant, Lafayette	1,173	1,173	0.00
Hewitt	1973	Wood	796	803	0.88
Highland	1873	Iowa	874	874	0.00
Hilbert	1898	Calumet	1,248	1,271	1.84
Hixton	1920	Jackson	456	453	-0.66
Hobart	2003	Brown	10,211	10,486	2.69
Hollandale	1910	Iowa	306	305	-0.33

Wisconsin villages, January 1, 2022, continued

Village	Year incorporated	County	2020 census	2022 estimate	% change
Holmen	1946	La Crosse	10,661	11,560	8.43
Hortonville	1894	Outagamie	3,028	3,292	8.72
Howard	1959	Brown, Outagamie	19,950	20,952	5.02
Howards Grove	1967	Sheboygan	3,237	3,271	1.05
Hustisford	1870	Dodge	1,101	1,099	-0.18
Hustler	1914	Juneau	162	161	-0.62
Ingram	1907	Rusk	70	70	0.00
Iola	1892	Waupaca	1,249	1,245	-0.32
Iron Ridge	1913	Dodge	904	910	0.66
Ironton	1914	Sauk	274	268	-2.19
Jackson	1912	Washington	7,185	7,844	9.17
Johnson Creek	1903	Jefferson	3,318	3,402	2.53
Junction City	1911	Portage	420	419	-0.24
Kekoskee	1958	Dodge	896	832	-7.14
Kellnersville	1971	Manitowoc	307	303	-1.30
Kendall	1894	Monroe	484	481	-0.62
Kennan	1903	Price	143	142	-0.70
Kewaskum	1895	Fond du Lac, Washington	4,309	4,371	1.44
Kimberly	1910	Outagamie	7,320	7,526	2.81
Kingston	1923	Green Lake	281	281	0.00
Knapp	1905	Dunn	478	485	1.46
Kohler	1912	Sheboygan	2,195	2,208	0.59
Kronenwetter	2002	Marathon	8,353	8,561	2.49
La Farge	1899	Vernon	730	726	-0.55
La Valle	1883	Sauk	388	375	-3.35
Lac La Belle	1931	Jefferson, Waukesha	281	285	1.42
Lake Delton	1954	Sauk	3,501	3,515	0.40
Lake Hallie	2003	Chippewa	7,170	7,307	1.91
Lake Nebagamon	1907	Douglas	1,123	1,130	0.62
Lannon	1930	Waukesha	1,355	1,810	33.58
Lena	1921	Oconto	537	535	-0.37
Lime Ridge	1910	Sauk	158	157	-0.63
Linden	1900	Iowa	504	505	0.20
Lisbon[2]	2023	Waukesha	10,477	10,735	2.46
Little Chute	1899	Outagamie	11,619	12,213	5.11
Livingston	1914	Grant, Iowa	637	638	0.16
Loganville	1917	Sauk	301	300	-0.33
Lohrville	1910	Waushara	434	432	-0.46
Lomira	1899	Dodge	2,678	2,688	0.37
Lone Rock	1886	Richland	829	830	0.12
Lowell	1894	Dodge	309	306	-0.97
Lublin	1915	Taylor	117	117	0.00
Luck	1905	Polk	1,093	1,089	-0.37
Luxemburg	1908	Kewaunee	2,685	2,730	1.68
Lyndon Station	1903	Juneau	498	496	-0.40
Lynxville	1899	Crawford	132	133	0.76
Maiden Rock	1887	Pierce	115	115	0.00
Maine	2015	Marathon	2,613	2,621	0.31
Maple Bluff	1930	Dane	1,368	1,433	4.75
Marathon City	1884	Marathon	1,576	1,565	-0.70
Maribel	1963	Manitowoc	336	335	-0.30
Marquette	1958	Green Lake	172	170	-1.16
Marshall	1905	Dane	3,787	3,909	3.22
Mason	1925	Bayfield	101	101	0.00
Mattoon	1901	Shawano	357	356	-0.28
Mazomanie	1885	Dane	1,768	1,790	1.24

Wisconsin villages, January 1, 2022, continued

Village	Year incorporated	County	2020 census	2022 estimate	% change
McFarland	1920	Dane	8,991	9,537	6.07
Melrose	1914	Jackson	544	539	-0.92
Melvina	1922	Monroe	93	94	1.08
Menomonee Falls[1]	1892	Waukesha	38,527	39,213	1.78
Merrillan	1881	Jackson	562	561	-0.18
Merrimac	1899	Sauk	527	533	1.14
Merton	1922	Waukesha	3,441	3,482	1.19
Milladore	1933	Portage, Wood	268	268	0.00
Milltown	1910	Polk	948	952	0.42
Minong	1915	Washburn	548	550	0.36
Mishicot	1950	Manitowoc	1,432	1,432	0.00
Montfort	1893	Grant, Iowa	705	701	-0.57
Monticello	1891	Green	1,192	1,195	0.25
Mount Calvary	1962	Fond du Lac	548	549	0.18
Mount Hope	1919	Grant	215	213	-0.93
Mount Horeb	1899	Dane	7,754	7,871	1.51
Mount Pleasant	2003	Racine	27,732	28,191	1.66
Mount Sterling	1936	Crawford	189	189	0.00
Mukwonago	1905	Walworth, Waukesha	8,262	8,384	1.48
Muscoda	1894	Grant, Iowa	1,307	1,314	0.54
Nashotah	1957	Waukesha	1,321	1,319	-0.15
Necedah	1870	Juneau	924	948	2.60
Nelson	1978	Buffalo	322	322	0.00
Nelsonville	1913	Portage	158	157	-0.63
Neosho	1902	Dodge	591	590	-0.17
Neshkoro	1906	Marquette	412	410	-0.49
New Auburn	1902	Barron, Chippewa	562	562	0.00
New Glarus	1901	Green	2,266	2,360	4.15
Newburg	1973	Ozaukee, Washington	1,142	1,144	0.18
Nichols	1967	Outagamie	290	289	-0.34
North Bay	1951	Racine	209	208	-0.48
North Fond du Lac	1903	Fond du Lac	5,378	5,385	0.13
North Freedom	1893	Sauk	603	598	-0.83
North Hudson	1912	St. Croix	3,803	3,888	2.24
North Prairie	1919	Waukesha	2,202	2,208	0.27
Norwalk	1894	Monroe	611	609	-0.33
Oakdale	1988	Monroe	302	301	-0.33
Oakfield	1903	Fond du Lac	1,052	1,061	0.86
Oconomowoc Lake	1959	Waukesha	566	572	1.06
Ogdensburg	1912	Waupaca	188	188	0.00
Oliver	1917	Douglas	423	423	0.00
Ontario	1890	Vernon, Monroe	534	528	-1.12
Oostburg	1909	Sheboygan	3,056	3,093	1.21
Oregon	1883	Dane	11,179	11,815	5.69
Orfordville	1900	Rock	1,473	1,494	1.43
Osceola	1886	Polk	2,765	2,824	2.13
Oxford	1912	Marquette	537	535	-0.37
Paddock Lake	1960	Kenosha	2,919	2,995	2.60
Palmyra	1866	Jefferson	1,719	1,721	0.12
Pardeeville	1894	Columbia	2,074	2,068	-0.29
Park Ridge	1938	Portage	530	535	0.94
Patch Grove	1921	Grant	201	198	-1.49
Pepin	1860	Pepin	731	742	1.50
Pewaukee	1876	Waukesha	8,238	8,215	-0.28
Pigeon Falls	1956	Trempealeau	381	380	-0.26
Plain	1912	Sauk	749	748	-0.13
Plainfield	1882	Waushara	924	920	-0.43

Wisconsin villages, January 1, 2022, continued

Village	Year incorporated	County	2020 census	2022 estimate	% change
Pleasant Prairie	1989	Kenosha	21,250	21,948	3.28
Plover	1971	Portage	13,519	13,872	2.61
Plum City	1909	Pierce	596	587	-1.51
Poplar	1917	Douglas	629	635	0.95
Port Edwards	1902	Wood	1,762	1,754	-0.45
Potosi	1887	Grant	646	641	-0.77
Potter	1980	Calumet	244	243	-0.41
Pound	1914	Marinette	357	353	-1.12
Poynette	1892	Columbia	2,590	2,594	0.15
Prairie du Sac	1885	Sauk	4,420	4,458	0.86
Prairie Farm	1901	Barron	494	498	0.81
Prentice	1899	Price	563	562	-0.18
Pulaski	1910	Brown, Oconto, Shawano	3,870	4,038	4.34
Radisson	1953	Sawyer	273	273	0.00
Randolph	1870	Columbia, Dodge	1,796	1,787	-0.50
Random Lake	1907	Sheboygan	1,561	1,565	0.26
Raymond	2019	Racine	3,926	3,948	0.56
Readstown	1898	Vernon	376	372	-1.06
Redgranite	1904	Waushara	2,061	1,997	-3.11
Reedsville	1892	Manitowoc	1,195	1,193	-0.17
Reeseville	1899	Dodge	763	770	0.92
Rewey	1902	Iowa	258	257	-0.39
Rib Lake	1902	Taylor	935	921	-1.50
Richfield	2008	Washington	11,739	11,866	1.08
Ridgeland	1921	Dunn	258	258	0.00
Ridgeway	1902	Iowa	624	644	3.21
Rio	1887	Columbia	1,119	1,144	2.23
River Hills[1]	1930	Milwaukee	1,602	1,595	-0.44
Roberts	1945	St. Croix	1,919	2,026	5.58
Rochester	1912	Racine	3,785	3,822	0.98
Rock Springs	1894	Sauk	327	328	0.31
Rockdale	1914	Dane	207	206	-0.48
Rockland	1919	La Crosse, Monroe	765	782	2.22
Rosendale	1915	Fond du Lac	1,039	1,039	0.00
Rosholt	1907	Portage	478	476	-0.42
Rothschild	1917	Marathon	5,567	5,581	0.25
Rudolph	1960	Wood	433	433	0.00
Salem Lakes	2017	Kenosha	14,601	14,605	0.03
Sauk City	1854	Sauk	3,518	3,527	0.26
Saukville	1915	Ozaukee	4,258	4,247	-0.26
Scandinavia	1894	Waupaca	371	371	0.00
Sharon	1892	Walworth	1,586	1,581	-0.32
Sheldon	1917	Rusk	261	263	0.77
Sherwood	1968	Calumet	3,271	3,352	2.48
Shiocton	1903	Outagamie	939	931	-0.85
Shorewood[1]	1900	Milwaukee	13,859	13,807	-0.38
Shorewood Hills	1927	Dane	2,169	2,168	-0.05
Siren	1948	Burnett	824	823	-0.12
Sister Bay	1912	Door	1,148	1,184	3.14
Slinger	1869	Washington	5,992	6,401	6.83
Soldiers Grove	1888	Crawford	552	558	1.09
Solon Springs	1920	Douglas	656	663	1.07
Somers	2015	Kenosha	8,402	8,501	1.18
Somerset	1915	St. Croix	3,019	3,168	4.94
South Wayne	1911	Lafayette	444	437	-1.58
Spencer	1902	Marathon	1,818	1,821	0.17
Spring Green	1869	Sauk	1,566	1,597	1.98

Wisconsin villages, January 1, 2022, continued

Village	Year incorporated	County	2020 census	2022 estimate	% change
Spring Valley	1895	Pierce, St. Croix	1,401	1,420	1.36
St. Cloud	1909	Fond du Lac	489	496	1.43
St. Nazianz	1956	Manitowoc	714	711	-0.42
Star Prairie	1900	St. Croix	678	675	-0.44
Stetsonville	1949	Taylor	563	564	0.18
Steuben	1900	Crawford	122	120	-1.64
Stockbridge	1908	Calumet	678	685	1.03
Stockholm	1903	Pepin	78	79	1.28
Stoddard	1911	Vernon	840	896	6.67
Stratford	1910	Marathon	1,581	1,633	3.29
Strum	1948	Trempealeau	1,076	1,079	0.28
Sturtevant	1907	Racine	6,919	6,804	-1.66
Suamico	2003	Brown	12,820	13,230	3.20
Sullivan	1915	Jefferson	651	649	-0.31
Summit	2010	Waukesha	4,784	5,061	5.79
Superior	1949	Douglas	677	674	-0.44
Suring	1914	Oconto	517	518	0.19
Sussex	1924	Waukesha	11,487	11,750	2.29
Taylor	1919	Jackson	484	475	-1.86
Tennyson	1940	Grant	348	347	-0.29
Theresa	1898	Dodge	1,255	1,260	0.40
Thiensville	1910	Ozaukee	3,290	3,288	-0.06
Tigerton	1896	Shawano	708	707	-0.14
Tony	1911	Rusk	105	105	0.00
Trempealeau	1867	Trempealeau	1,843	1,888	2.44
Turtle Lake	1898	Barron, Polk	1,037	1,040	0.29
Twin Lakes	1937	Kenosha	6,309	6,429	1.90
Union Center	1913	Juneau	225	226	0.44
Union Grove	1893	Racine	4,806	5,040	4.87
Unity	1903	Clark, Marathon	384	383	-0.26
Valders	1919	Manitowoc	952	961	0.95
Vernon	2020	Waukesha	7,474	7,486	0.16
Vesper	1948	Wood	513	512	-0.19
Viola	1899	Richland, Vernon	676	675	-0.15
Waldo	1922	Sheboygan	467	477	2.14
Wales	1922	Waukesha	2,862	2,917	1.92
Walworth	1901	Walworth	2,759	2,768	0.33
Warrens	1973	Monroe	544	546	0.37
Waterford	1906	Racine	5,542	5,690	2.67
Waukesha	2020	Waukesha	8,457	8,489	0.38
Waunakee	1893	Dane	14,879	15,426	3.68
Wausaukee	1924	Marinette	596	593	-0.50
Wauzeka	1890	Crawford	628	624	-0.64
Webster	1916	Burnett	694	697	0.43
West Baraboo	1956	Sauk	1,627	1,630	0.18
West Milwaukee	1906	Milwaukee	4,114	4,097	-0.41
West Salem	1893	La Crosse	5,277	5,416	2.63
Westfield	1902	Marquette	1,302	1,297	-0.38
Weston	1996	Marathon	15,723	15,809	0.55
Weyerhaeuser	1906	Rusk	232	233	0.43
Wheeler	1922	Dunn	326	329	0.92
White Lake	1926	Langlade	262	260	-0.76
Whitefish Bay[1]	1892	Milwaukee	14,954	14,905	-0.33
Whitelaw	1958	Manitowoc	737	739	0.27
Whiting	1947	Portage	1,601	1,598	-0.19
Wild Rose	1904	Waushara	780	781	0.13

Wisconsin villages, January 1, 2022, continued

Village	Year incorporated	County	2020 census	2022 estimate	% change
Williams Bay	1919	Walworth	2,953	2,993	1.35
Wilson	1911	St. Croix	209	208	-0.48
Wilton	1890	Monroe	532	530	-0.38
Wind Point	1954	Racine	1,651	1,644	-0.42
Windsor	2015	Dane	8,754	9,305	6.29
Winneconne	1887	Winnebago	2,544	2,542	-0.08
Winter	1973	Sawyer	325	324	-0.31
Withee	1901	Clark	506	505	-0.20
Wittenberg	1893	Shawano	1,015	999	-1.58
Wonewoc	1878	Juneau	758	754	-0.53
Woodman	1917	Grant	118	118	0.00
Woodville	1911	St. Croix	1,386	1,426	2.89
Wrightstown	1901	Brown, Outagamie	3,179	3,250	2.23
Wyeville	1923	Monroe	121	118	-2.48
Wyocena	1909	Columbia	756	752	-0.53
Yorkville	2018	Racine	3,246	3,273	0.83
Yuba	1935	Richland	53	53	0.00

Note: There are 416 villages in Wisconsin as of February, 2023.
1. One of 11 villages with a village manager. 2. On February 13, 2023, the entire town of Lisbon became the village of Lisbon.
Sources: Wisconsin Department of Administration, Demographic Services Center, *Official Final Estimates, 1/1/2022, Wisconsin Municipalities, with Comparison to Census 2020*, October 2022; Wisconsin Department of Administration, Division of Intergovernmental Relations, *Municipality changes since January 2000*, February 2023; League of Wisconsin Municipalities, *2022 Directory of Wisconsin City and Village Officials* at http://lwm-info.org/1236/Directory-of-Cities-Villages; and data compiled by Wisconsin Legislative Reference Bureau.

Wisconsin cities and villages over 10,000 population, January 1, 2022

City or village (county)	2020 census	2022 etimate	% change	2020 rank
Cities				
Milwaukee (Milwaukee, Washington, Waukesha)	577,922	577,309	-0.11	1
Madison (Dane)	269,840	279,012	3.40	2
Green Bay (Brown)	107,395	107,369	-0.02	3
Kenosha (Kenosha)	99,986	100,051	0.07	4
Racine (Racine)	77,816	77,240	-0.74	5
Appleton (Calumet, Outagamie, Winnebago)	75,644	75,605	-0.05	6
Waukesha (Waukesha)	71,158	71,146	-0.02	7
Eau Claire (Chippewa, Eau Claire)	69,421	70,587	1.68	8
Oshkosh (Winnebago)	66,816	66,929	0.17	9
Janesville (Rock)	65,615	66,206	0.90	10
West Allis (Milwaukee)	60,325	60,068	-0.43	11
La Crosse (La Crosse)	52,680	52,160	-0.99	12
Sheboygan (Sheboygan)	49,929	50,139	0.42	13
Wauwatosa (Milwaukee)	48,387	48,638	0.52	14
Fond du Lac (Fond du Lac)	44,678	44,470	-0.47	15
Brookfield (Waukesha)	41,464	41,430	-0.08	16
New Berlin (Waukesha)	40,451	40,426	-0.06	17
Wausau (Marathon)	39,994	40,199	0.51	18
Greenfield (Milwaukee)	37,803	37,709	-0.25	20
Oak Creek (Milwaukee)	36,497	37,374	2.40	21
Sun Prairie (Dane)	35,967	37,304	3.72	22
Beloit (Rock)	36,657	36,760	0.28	23

Wisconsin cities and villages over 10,000 population, January 1, 2020, continued

City or village (county)	2020 census	2022 etimate	% change	2020 rank
Franklin (Milwaukee)	36,116	35,895	-0.61	24
Manitowoc (Manitowoc)	34,626	34,722	0.28	25
West Bend (Washington)	31,752	32,067	0.99	26
Fitchburg (Dane)	29,609	31,817	7.46	27
Neenah (Winnebago)	27,319	27,726	1.49	29
Superior (Douglas)	26,751	26,943	0.72	30
Stevens Point (Portage)	25,666	25,954	1.12	31
De Pere (Brown)	25,410	25,525	0.45	32
Muskego (Waukesha)	25,032	25,343	1.24	34
Mequon (Ozaukee)	25,142	25,141	0.00	35
Middleton (Dane)	21,827	23,031	5.52	36
Watertown (Dodge, Jefferson)	22,926	23,018	0.40	37
South Milwaukee (Milwaukee)	20,795	20,703	-0.44	41
Onalaska (La Crosse)	18,803	19,276	2.52	42
Marshfield (Marathon, Wood)	18,929	18,969	0.21	44
Wisconsin Rapids (Wood)	18,877	18,809	-0.36	45
Menasha (Calumet, Winnebago)	18,268	18,490	1.22	46
Oconomowoc (Waukesha)	18,203	18,485	1.55	47
Cudahy (Milwaukee)	18,204	18,134	-0.38	48
Kaukauna (Calumet, Outagamie)	17,089	17,441	2.06	50
Beaver Dam (Dodge)	16,708	16,727	0.11	51
Menomonie (Dunn)	16,843	16,616	-1.35	52
River Falls (Pierce, St. Croix)	16,182	16,515	2.06	54
Pewaukee (Waukesha)	15,914	16,127	1.34	55
Hartford (Dodge, Washington)	15,626	15,805	1.15	57
Whitewater (Jefferson, Walworth)	16,137	15,773	-2.26	58
Hudson (St. Croix)	14,755	15,140	2.61	60
Verona (Dane)	14,030	14,889	6.12	62
Chippewa Falls (Chippewa)	14,731	14,724	-0.05	64
Glendale (Milwaukee)	13,357	13,472	0.86	70
Stoughton (Dane)	13,173	13,204	0.24	72
Port Washington (Ozaukee)	12,353	12,853	4.05	75
Baraboo (Sauk)	12,556	12,703	1.17	76
Fort Atkinson (Jefferson)	12,579	12,583	0.03	77
Cedarburg (Ozaukee)	12,121	12,446	2.68	78
Two Rivers (Manitowoc)	11,271	11,243	-0.25	86
Burlington (Racine, Walworth)	11,047	11,166	1.08	87
Platteville (Grant)	11,836	11,154	-5.76	88
Marinette (Marinette)	11,119	11,129	0.09	89
Waupun (Dodge, Fond du Lac)	11,563	11,117	-3.86	90
Monroe (Green)	10,661	10,691	0.28	92
New Richmond (St. Croix)	10,079	10,541	4.58	93
Portage (Columbia)	10,581	10,325	-2.42	95
Elkhorn (Walworth)	10,247	10,317	0.68	96
Reedsburg (Sauk)	9,984	10,181	1.97	97
Sparta (Monroe)	10,025	10,075	0.50	98
Villages				
Menomonee Falls (Waukesha)	38,527	39,213	1.78	19
Mount Pleasant (Racine)	27,732	28,191	1.66	28
Caledonia (Racine)	25,361	25,478	0.46	33
Pleasant Prairie (Kenosha)	21,250	21,948	3.28	38
Germantown (Washington)	20,917	21,040	0.59	39
Howard (Brown, Outagamie)	19,950	20,952	5.02	40
Fox Crossing (Outagamie, Winnebago)	18,974	19,011	0.20	43
Ashwaubenon (Brown)	16,991	17,757	4.51	49
Bellevue (Brown)	15,935	16,568	3.97	53
Weston (Marathon)	15,723	15,809	0.55	56

Wisconsin cities and villages over 10,000 population, January 1, 2020, continued

City or village (county)	2020 census	2022 estimate	% change	2020 rank
Waunakee (Dane).	14,879	15,426	3.68	59
Whitefish Bay (Milwaukee)	14,954	14,905	-0.33	61
Greendale (Milwaukee)	14,854	14,815	-0.26	63
Salem Lakes (Kenosha)	14,601	14,605	0.03	65
Harrison (Calumet, Outagamie)	12,418	14,424	16.15	66
Allouez (Brown)	14,156	14,014	-1.00	67
Plover (Portage)	13,519	13,872	2.61	68
Shorewood (Milwaukee)	13,859	13,807	-0.38	69
Suamico (Brown)	12,820	13,230	3.20	71
Greenville (Outagamie)	12,687	13,067	3.00	73
Brown Deer (Milwaukee)	12,507	13,023	4.13	74
Grafton (Ozaukee)	12,094	12,269	1.45	79
Little Chute (Outagamie)	11,619	12,213	5.11	80
Richfield (Washington)	11,739	11,866	1.08	81
Oregon (Dane)	11,179	11,815	5.69	82
Sussex (Waukesha)	11,487	11,750	2.29	83
Holmen (La Crosse)	10,661	11,560	8.43	84
DeForest (Dane)	10,811	11,388	5.34	85
Lisbon (Waukesha)[1]	10,477	10,735	2.46	91
Hobart (Brown)	10,211	10,486	2.69	94

1. On February 13, 2023, the entire town of Lisbon became the village of Lisbon.

Sources: Wisconsin Department of Administration, Demographic Services Center, *Official Final Estimates, 1/1/2022, Wisconsin Municipalities, with Comparison to Census 2020*, October 2022; and Wisconsin Department of Administration, Division of Intergovernmental Relations, *Municipality changes since January 2000*, February 2023.

Wisconsin towns over 2,500 population, January 1, 2022

Town (county)	2020 census	2022 estimate	% change	Town (county)	2020 census	2022 estimate	% change
Addison (Washington)	3,464	3,449	-0.43	Delafield (Waukesha)	8,095	8,148	0.65
Alden (Polk)	2,918	2,980	2.12	Delavan (Walworth)	5,273	5,265	-0.15
Algoma (Winnebago)	6,866	6,927	0.89	Dover (Racine)	4,282	4,134	-3.46
Arbor Vitae (Vilas)	3,403	3,411	0.24	Dunn (Dane)	4,880	4,874	-0.12
Ashippun (Dodge)	2,663	2,677	0.53	Eagle (Waukesha)	3,478	3,521	1.24
Barton (Washington)	2,743	2,795	1.90	Eagle Point (Chippewa)	3,237	3,284	1.45
Bass Lake (Sawyer)	2,731	2,755	0.88	East Troy (Walworth)	3,992	4,020	0.70
Beaver Dam (Dodge)	4,062	4,069	0.17	Ellington (Outagamie)	3,174	3,251	2.43
Beloit (Rock)	7,721	7,850	1.67	Empire (Fond du Lac)	2,774	2,769	-0.18
Bristol (Dane)	4,447	4,499	1.17	Erin (Washington)	3,825	3,842	0.44
Brockway (Jackson)	3,035	2,991	-1.45	Farmington (Washington)	3,712	3,757	1.21
Brookfield (Waukesha)	6,477	6,480	0.05	Farmington (Waupaca)	3,645	3,662	0.47
Buchanan (Outagamie)	6,857	6,865	0.12	Fond du Lac (Fond du Lac)	3,687	3,721	0.92
Burke (Dane)	3,265	3,264	-0.03	Freedom (Outagamie)	6,216	6,225	0.14
Burlington (Racine)	6,465	6,493	0.43	Friendship (Fond du Lac)	2,748	2,756	0.29
Campbell (La Crosse)	4,284	4,276	-0.19	Fulton (Rock)	3,580	3,691	3.10
Cedarburg (Ozaukee)	6,162	6,180	0.29	Genesee (Waukesha)	7,171	7,187	0.22
Center (Outagamie)	3,622	3,675	1.46	Geneva (Walworth)	5,390	5,476	1.60
Chase (Oconto)	3,178	3,244	2.08	Grafton (Ozaukee)	4,355	4,372	0.39
Clayton (Winnebago)	4,329	4,375	1.06	Grand Chute (Outagamie)	23,831	23,964	0.56
Cottage Grove (Dane)	3,791	3,825	0.90	Grand Rapids (Wood)	7,576	7,611	0.46
Dale (Outagamie)	2,869	2,899	1.05	Hammond (St. Croix)	2,565	2,692	4.95
Dayton (Waupaca)	2,644	2,661	0.64	Harmony (Rock)	2,569	2,568	-0.04
Dekorra (Columbia)	2,500	2,519	0.76	Hartford (Washington)	3,400	3,381	-0.56

Wisconsin towns over 2,500 population, January 1, 2022, continued

Town (county)	2020 census	2022 estimate	% change	Town (county)	2020 census	2022 estimate	% change
Hayward (Sawyer)	3,765	3,758	-0.19	Pine Lake (Oneida)	2,724	2,724	0.00
Holland (La Crosse)	4,530	4,603	1.61	Pittsfield (Brown)	2,791	2,811	0.72
Hudson (St. Croix)	8,671	8,859	2.17	Pleasant Springs (Dane)	3,078	3,101	0.75
Hull (Portage)	5,287	5,305	0.34	Pleasant Valley (Eau Claire)	3,791	3,939	3.90
Ixonia (Jefferson)	5,120	5,135	0.29	Plymouth (Sheboygan)	3,083	3,066	-0.55
Jackson (Washington)	4,629	4,064	-12.21	Polk (Washington)	3,988	4,005	0.43
Janesville (Rock)	3,665	3,692	0.74	Randall (Kenosha)	3,285	3,315	0.91
Koshkonong (Jefferson)	3,763	3,790	0.72	Rib Mountain (Marathon)	7,313	7,346	0.45
Lac du Flambeau (Vilas)	3,552	3,565	0.37	Rice Lake (Barron)	2,813	2,833	0.71
Lafayette (Chippewa)	6,197	6,454	4.15	Richmond (St. Croix)	4,074	4,272	4.86
Lawrence (Brown)	6,306	6,724	6.63	Rock (Rock)	2,981	2,990	0.30
Ledgeview (Brown)	8,820	9,373	6.27	Rome (Adams)	3,025	3,111	2.84
Lima (Sheboygan)	2,956	2,965	0.30	Saratoga (Wood)	5,060	5,092	0.63
Lincoln (Vilas)	2,659	2,660	0.04	Scott (Brown)	3,636	3,660	0.66
Linn (Walworth)	2,687	2,717	1.12	Sevastopol (Door)	2,826	2,858	1.13
Lisbon (Waukesha)[1]	10,477	10,735	2.46	Seymour (Eau Claire)	3,352	3,380	0.84
Little Suamico (Oconto)	5,536	5,633	1.75	Sheboygan (Sheboygan)	8,136	8,175	0.48
Lodi (Columbia)	3,282	3,296	0.43	Shelby (La Crosse)	4,804	4,810	0.12
Lyons (Walworth)	3,648	3,667	0.52	Somerset (St. Croix)	4,291	4,421	3.03
Madison (Dane)[2]	6,236	6,212	-0.38	Sparta (Monroe)	3,253	3,258	0.15
Medford (Taylor)	2,482	2,519	1.49	Springfield (Dane)	2,929	2,936	0.24
Menominee (Menominee)	4,255	4,266	0.26	St. Joseph (St. Croix)	4,178	4,322	3.45
Menomonie (Dunn)	3,415	3,438	0.67	Stanley (Barron)	2,570	2,575	0.19
Merrill (Lincoln)	2,881	2,882	0.03	Star Prairie (St. Croix)	3,733	3,779	1.23
Merton (Waukesha)	8,277	8,308	0.37	Stephenson (Marinette)	3,494	3,530	1.03
Middleton (Dane)	6,792	6,977	2.72	Stettin (Marathon)	2,580	2,595	0.58
Milton (Rock)	3,100	3,111	0.35	Stockton (Portage)	3,018	3,036	0.60
Minocqua (Oneida)	5,062	5,068	0.12	Sugar Creek (Walworth)	3,902	3,921	0.49
Mukwa (Waupaca)	2,830	2,831	0.04	Tainter (Dunn)	2,643	2,659	0.61
Mukwonago (Waukesha)	7,781	7,807	0.33	Taycheedah (Fond du Lac)	4,554	4,598	0.97
Neenah (Winnebago)	3,702	3,701	-0.03	Trenton (Washington)	4,525	4,572	1.04
Newbold (Oneida)	2,831	2,848	0.60	Troy (St. Croix)	5,518	5,558	0.72
Norway (Racine)	7,916	7,944	0.35	Union (Eau Claire)	2,696	2,695	-0.04
Oakland (Jefferson)	3,231	3,241	0.31	Washington (Eau Claire)	7,662	7,780	1.54
Oconomowoc (Waukesha)	8,836	8,861	0.28	Waterford (Racine)	6,514	6,555	0.63
Onalaska (La Crosse)	5,835	5,875	0.69	Wescott (Shawano)	3,257	3,265	0.25
Oneida (Outagamie)	4,579	4,555	-0.52	West Bend (Washington)	4,441	4,415	-0.59
Oregon (Dane)	3,125	3,136	0.35	Westport (Dane)	4,191	4,302	2.65
Osceola (Polk)	3,023	3,085	2.05	Wheatland (Kenosha)	3,391	3,394	0.09
Ottawa (Waukesha)	3,646	3,659	0.36	Wheaton (Chippewa)	2,759	2,818	2.14
Pacific (Columbia)	2,791	2,811	0.72	Wilson (Sheboygan)	3,484	3,486	0.06
Pelican (Oneida)	2,809	2,813	0.14	Winneconne (Winnebago)	2,590	2,627	1.43
Peshtigo (Marinette)	4,006	4,001	-0.12	Wrightstown (Brown)	2,578	2,637	2.29

1. On February 13, 2023, the entire town of Lisbon became the village of Lisbon. 2. On October 31, 2022, the town of Madison attached to the cities of Madison and Fitchburg.

Sources: Wisconsin Department of Administration, Demographic Services Center, *Official Final Estimates, 1/1/2022, Wisconsin Municipalities, with Comparison to Census 2020*, October 2022; and Wisconsin Department of Administration, Division of Intergovernmental Relations, *Municipality changes since January 2000*, February 2023.

ELECTIONS

County vote for U.S. senator from Wisconsin, August 9, 2022 partisan primary

	Democrat							Republican		
	Mandela Barnes	Sarah Godlewski	Alex Lasry	Kou C. Lee	Tom Nelson	Steven Olikara	Peter Peckarsky	Darrell Williams	Ron Johnson*	David Schroeder	Total
Adams	1,105	144	147	5	36	12	12	12	2,543	488	4,505
Ashland	1,264	155	138	20	97	31	22	35	968	156	2,893
Barron	1,600	277	279	21	110	20	28	23	4,388	713	7,463
Bayfield	2,125	267	113	19	137	25	18	55	1,706	290	4,762
Brown	13,007	1,643	2,269	171	846	220	78	111	24,357	4,167	46,916
Buffalo	558	97	82	4	27	6	8	10	1,890	612	3,299
Burnett	637	143	61	13	82	15	14	21	1,866	301	3,153
Calumet	2,366	237	385	18	192	28	18	18	6,671	1,173	11,112
Chippewa	3,008	586	561	38	112	33	25	34	7,146	1,520	13,077
Clark	853	129	170	3	44	4	14	17	3,257	712	5,204
Columbia	3,555	391	461	18	44	42	29	30	5,565	1,518	11,661
Crawford	1,136	154	164	10	94	9	7	22	1,218	242	3,056
Dane	79,052	7,328	5,666	573	1,178	1,478	344	344	24,885	8,357	129,368
Dodge	3,176	340	373	17	79	46	23	25	12,868	3,028	19,976
Door	3,008	273	264	21	89	27	21	16	3,733	713	8,173
Douglas	3,148	900	379	59	392	51	86	107	2,800	449	8,390
Dunn	2,274	383	294	40	102	47	19	36	3,292	537	7,024
Eau Claire	7,964	1,472	1,043	131	183	100	45	58	7,538	1,313	19,865
Florence	151	26	13	1	7	0	2	4	697	114	1,015
Fond du Lac	3,570	443	670	35	166	47	28	31	14,113	2,761	21,870
Forest	265	47	69	2	20	0	3	2	1,132	187	1,728
Grant	2,213	229	244	19	79	23	15	21	3,629	980	7,454
Green	2,877	263	287	11	60	37	11	17	3,067	809	7,453
Green Lake	678	71	91	3	26	8	5	1	2,605	471	3,963
Iowa	1,850	170	165	4	28	19	8	14	1,760	645	4,666
Iron	324	82	37	4	16	5	6	7	757	126	1,365
Jackson	1,093	129	188	15	33	20	9	7	1,609	323	3,428
Jefferson	4,498	409	473	26	75	40	25	27	9,736	1,900	17,225
Juneau	1,070	104	127	3	28	8	9	11	3,063	882	5,309
Kenosha	9,332	1,095	1,273	63	184	114	59	108	15,054	3,316	30,657

County vote for U.S. senator from Wisconsin, August 9, 2022 partisan primary, continued

	Democrat							Republican		
	Mandela Barnes	Sarah Godlewski	Alex Lasry	Kou C. Lee	Tom Nelson	Steven Olikara	Peter Peckarsky	Darrell Williams	Ron Johnson*	David Schroeder	Total
Kewaunee	817	114	137	10	48	11	11	11	2,685	516	4,364
La Crosse	9,705	1,267	1,381	170	233	114	64	80	8,089	1,632	22,754
Lafayette	718	55	84	1	23	10	0	3	1,312	383	2,589
Langlade	687	106	140	5	25	8	7	12	2,603	431	4,024
Lincoln	1,113	203	260	6	38	16	11	16	3,504	892	6,062
Manitowoc	3,466	378	606	42	224	34	25	27	9,257	1,743	15,813
Marathon	6,046	885	1,140	146	193	62	67	55	15,695	2,780	27,087
Marinette	1,316	225	274	9	114	10	14	10	5,851	1,421	9,250
Marquette	714	88	86	4	16	5	5	9	2,147	439	3,518
Menominee	120	11	16	3	11	0	0	3	117	27	308
Milwaukee	81,047	4,675	6,986	483	871	1,062	340	962	43,710	8,520	148,814
Monroe	1,963	281	299	19	61	15	19	27	3,751	745	7,187
Oconto	1,391	157	250	14	100	19	9	11	5,619	982	8,555
Oneida	2,072	345	371	9	74	20	23	19	4,806	969	8,718
Outagamie	9,142	904	1,213	116	1,026	159	42	76	18,455	3,520	34,653
Ozaukee	6,571	581	766	37	91	94	39	42	14,647	2,486	25,378
Pepin	302	44	46	4	25	6	3	6	700	114	1,252
Pierce	1,809	428	162	38	138	35	32	37	2,703	490	5,880
Polk	1,596	342	170	27	153	27	27	44	4,180	674	7,240
Portage	6,367	805	942	116	222	77	75	67	6,993	1,149	16,827
Price	679	121	133	2	29	5	10	15	2,008	390	3,392
Racine	11,093	879	1,230	63	166	107	46	100	20,998	3,698	38,429
Richland	973	69	112	5	15	6	9	8	1,557	532	3,291
Rock	10,199	1,148	1,530	78	225	92	72	141	10,266	2,454	26,226
Rusk	578	98	75	2	22	4	16	11	1,993	396	3,198
Sauk	4,220	464	482	19	88	36	20	37	5,493	1,503	12,362
Sawyer	780	163	100	7	53	8	13	16	2,417	593	4,155
Shawano	1,178	158	246	8	89	12	10	11	5,954	1,426	9,092
Sheboygan	5,931	599	884	114	150	66	31	54	14,823	2,571	25,242
St. Croix	3,545	772	419	68	279	54	47	86	7,129	1,170	13,581

County vote for U.S. senator from Wisconsin, August 9, 2022 partisan primary, continued

	Democrat								Republican		
	Mandela Barnes	Sarah Godlewski	Alex Lasry	Kou C. Lee	Tom Nelson	Steven Olikara	Peter Peckarsky	Darrell Williams	Ron Johnson*	David Schroeder	Total
Taylor	468	80	104	5	20	4	4	9	2,796	634	4,124
Trempealeau	1,427	226	199	12	63	11	16	17	2,663	699	5,339
Vernon	2,084	231	224	16	50	17	12	16	3,252	878	6,791
Vilas	1,353	180	140	9	54	7	10	12	3,958	792	6,518
Walworth	4,773	582	538	25	116	54	32	44	13,520	2,881	22,601
Washburn	703	121	82	12	55	14	20	14	2,099	531	3,654
Washington	5,908	597	769	34	105	69	38	49	26,286	3,394	37,252
Waukesha	24,936	2,218	3,034	133	356	585	137	131	71,800	9,653	113,116
Waupaca	1,726	216	263	9	128	21	8	19	7,002	1,814	11,216
Waushara	949	109	149	4	31	15	8	8	3,351	579	5,204
Winnebago	8,554	1,095	1,395	137	512	99	49	60	15,542	3,045	30,517
Wood	3,503	548	686	46	137	34	34	47	8,227	1,568	14,839
Total	390,279	40,555	44,609	3,434	10,995	5,619	2,446	3,646	563,871	109,917	1,176,442

Note: County totals include scattered votes in the following partisan primaries: Constitution, Democratic, Libertarian, and Republican.
*Incumbent.
Source: Official records of the Wisconsin Elections Commission.

County vote for U.S. senator from Wisconsin, November 8, 2022 general election

	Mandela Barnes (Democrat)	Ron Johnson* (Republican)	Total
Adams	3,644	6,202	9,884
Ashland	3,903	3,074	6,986
Barron	7,121	12,928	20,079
Bayfield	5,183	4,082	9,280
Brown	51,421	62,221	113,879
Buffalo	2,201	3,907	6,118
Burnett	2,834	5,362	8,196
Calumet	9,444	15,466	24,951
Chippewa	11,069	17,694	28,823
Clark	3,451	8,181	11,654
Columbia	13,410	13,899	27,373
Crawford	3,179	3,797	6,989
Dane	231,818	68,228	300,728
Dodge	12,830	25,914	38,744
Door	8,611	8,685	17,322
Douglas	10,270	8,373	18,665
Dunn	7,876	10,544	18,420
Eau Claire	26,529	21,208	47,852
Florence	620	1,898	2,518
Fond du Lac	15,982	30,584	46,604
Forest	1,371	2,785	4,163
Grant	8,671	11,397	20,109
Green	9,097	8,350	17,480
Green Lake	2,626	6,061	8,692
Iowa	6,514	5,082	11,621
Iron	1,197	2,064	3,265
Jackson	3,288	4,700	7,988
Jefferson	16,141	22,402	38,607
Juneau	3,782	6,944	10,746
Kenosha	31,371	34,393	65,923
Kewaunee	3,273	6,627	9,920
La Crosse	30,695	24,413	55,223
Lafayette	2,787	3,779	6,566
Langlade	2,818	6,190	9,008
Lincoln	4,920	8,541	13,490
Manitowoc	13,288	22,561	35,918
Marathon	23,912	37,527	61,542
Marinette	5,816	12,677	18,535
Marquette	2,589	4,753	7,353
Menominee	962	264	1,226
Milwaukee	243,638	103,666	348,059
Monroe	6,461	10,801	17,311
Oconto	5,527	13,961	19,535
Oneida	8,279	11,866	20,186
Outagamie	37,922	47,805	85,727
Ozaukee	21,954	30,209	52,293
Pepin	1,177	2,122	3,300
Pierce	7,709	10,313	18,037
Polk	7,313	13,132	20,447
Portage	17,186	16,339	33,575
Price	2,459	4,584	7,047
Racine	37,252	44,221	81,691
Richland	3,173	3,827	7,012
Rock	36,024	28,758	64,942
Rusk	2,056	4,326	6,384
Sauk	14,618	14,289	28,907
Sawyer	3,597	4,949	8,559

County vote for U.S. senator from Wisconsin, November 8, 2022 general election, continued

	Mandela Barnes (Democrat)	Ron Johnson* (Republican)	Total
Shawano	5,495	12,415	17,912
Sheboygan	21,350	32,058	53,537
St. Croix	17,827	26,143	44,022
Taylor	2,130	6,527	8,657
Trempealeau	4,920	7,322	12,255
Vernon	6,206	6,950	13,174
Vilas	4,803	8,350	13,177
Walworth	17,824	27,995	45,931
Washburn	3,074	5,277	8,355
Washington	21,566	52,401	73,967
Waukesha	83,408	140,156	224,073
Waupaca	7,653	15,525	23,220
Waushara	3,567	7,765	11,335
Winnebago	34,860	39,372	74,417
Wood	12,925	20,004	32,993
Total	1,310,467	1,337,185	2,652,477
% of total vote	49.41	50.41	

Note: County totals include scattered and write-in votes. Write-in candidate Adam Paul received 67 votes.
*Incumbent.
Source: Official records of the Wisconsin Elections Commission.

District vote for U.S. representatives from Wisconsin, August 9, 2022 partisan primary

First congressional district

County	Ann Roe (Dem.)	Bryan Steil* (Rep.)
Kenosha	11,134	16,494
Milwaukee (part)	10,893	13,432
Racine	11,705	22,247
Rock (part)	9,332	8,105
Walworth (part)	5,084	12,913
Total	48,148	73,191

Second congressional district

County	Mark Pocan* (Dem.)	Charity Barry (Rep.)	Erik Olsen (Rep.)
Dane	91,970	13,487	14,219
Green	3,385	1,953	1,505
Iowa	2,174	1,114	1,010
Lafayette	842	857	586
Rock (part)	3,365	1,278	1,808
Sauk	4,859	3,022	2,646
Total	106,595	21,711	21,774

Third congressional district

County	Rebecca Cooke (Dem.)	Deb Baldus McGrath (Dem.)	Mark Neumann (Dem.)	Brad Pfaff (Dem.)	Derrick Van Orden (Rep.)
Adams	637	182	320	294	2,735

District vote for U.S. representatives from Wisconsin, August 9, 2022 partisan primary, continued

Third congressional district, continued

County	Rebecca Cooke (Dem.)	Deb Baldus McGrath (Dem.)	Mark Neumann (Dem.)	Brad Pfaff (Dem.)	Derrick Van Orden (Rep.)
Buffalo	258	149	63	340	2,259
Chippewa (part)	1,107	531	268	879	3,521
Crawford	226	208	128	1,048	1,334
Dunn	1,053	1,407	206	556	3,458
Eau Claire	4,327	2,967	869	2,763	7,789
Grant	1,112	425	578	608	3,882
Jackson (part)	287	242	75	778	1,438
Juneau (part)	365	118	238	269	2,531
La Crosse	1,814	1,839	1,041	8,384	8,713
Monroe (part)	438	313	185	1,518	3,516
Pepin	146	114	29	143	758
Pierce	1,435	549	240	452	3,005
Portage	3,141	1,557	1,319	2,242	6,331
Richland	595	104	208	258	1,758
Sauk (part)	111	27	57	52	446
Trempealeau	484	261	163	1,069	3,011
Vernon	531	310	203	1,600	3,656
Wood (part)	1,154	467	482	788	5,023
Total	19,221	11,770	6,672	24,041	65,164

Fourth congressional district

County	Gwen S. Moore* (Dem.)	Travis Clark (Rep.)	Tim Rogers (Rep.)
Milwaukee (part)	72,845	5,583	16,528
Total	72,845	5,583	16,528

Fifth congressional district

County	Mike Van Someren (Dem.)	Scott Fitzgerald* (Rep.)
Dodge (part)	1,685	7,522
Jefferson	4,822	10,254
Milwaukee (part)	4,281	4,834
Walworth (part)	455	1,567
Washington	6,507	26,251
Waukesha	26,555	67,983
Total	44,305	118,411

Sixth congressional district

County	Glenn Grothman* (Rep.)	Douglas H. Mullenix (Rep.)
Calumet (part)	876	197
Columbia	5,152	1,491
Dodge (part)	5,516	1,551
Fond du Lac	13,735	2,733
Green Lake	2,484	489
Manitowoc	9,010	1,569
Marquette	2,019	480
Ozaukee	13,982	2,586
Sheboygan	14,314	2,659
Waushara	3,100	713

District vote for U.S. representatives from Wisconsin, August 9, 2022 partisan primary, continued

Sixth congressional district, continued

County	Glenn Grothman* (Rep.)	Douglas H. Mullenix (Rep.)
Winnebago (part)	13,868	3,305
Total	**84,056**	**17,773**

Seventh congressional district

County	Richard Dick Ausman (Dem.)	David W. Kunelius II (Rep.)	Tom Tiffany* (Rep.)
Ashland	1,566	134	967
Barron	2,246	532	4,522
Bayfield	2,501	232	1,744
Burnett	930	204	1,935
Chippewa (part)	1,411	587	3,808
Clark	1,087	481	3,417
Douglas	4,674	383	2,831
Florence	186	103	684
Forest	355	165	1,140
Iron	465	97	781
Jackson (part)	111	55	239
Juneau (part)	315	171	847
Langlade	856	395	2,588
Lincoln	1,425	751	3,501
Marathon	7,690	2,353	15,736
Monroe (part)	198	83	518
Oneida	2,583	934	4,800
Polk	2,240	479	4,309
Price	849	340	2,008
Rusk	741	316	2,022
Sawyer	1,051	472	2,589
St. Croix	4,909	949	7,173
Taylor	623	488	2,914
Vilas	1,524	727	3,981
Washburn	968	395	2,225
Wood (part)	1,761	630	3,396
Total	**43,265**	**12,456**	**80,675**

Eighth congressional district[1]

County	Shaun Clarmont (Rep.)	Mike Gallagher* (Rep.)
Brown	4,803	23,203
Calumet (part)	810	5,731
Door	512	3,865
Kewaunee	503	2,610
Marinette	937	6,240
Menominee	19	124
Oconto	1,056	5,471
Outagamie	3,134	18,113
Shawano	1,038	6,235
Waupaca	1,501	7,072
Winnebago (part)	64	432
Total	**14,377**	**79,096**

*Incumbent. Dem.–Democrat; Rep.–Republican.

1. Write-in candidate Julie Hancock (Dem.) received 4,120 votes.

Source: Official records of the Wisconsin Elections Commission.

District vote for U.S. representatives from Wisconsin, November 8, 2022 general election

First congressional district

County	Ann Roe (Dem.)	Bryan Steil* (Rep.)	Charles E. Barman (Ind.)
Kenosha	29,592	35,698	436
Milwaukee (part)	30,468	34,132	426
Racine	34,910	45,833	534
Rock (part)	25,678	21,410	400
Walworth (part)	15,177	25,537	451
Total	135,825	162,610	2,247
% of total vote[1]	45.14	54.05	0.75

Second congressional district

County	Mark Pocan* (Dem.)	Erik Olsen (Rep.)	Douglas Alexander (Ind.)
Dane	227,298	65,432	5,770
Green	9,006	7,939	460
Iowa	6,507	4,762	294
Lafayette	2,903	3,494	142
Rock (part)	9,098	7,679	427
Sauk (part)	13,928	12,584	596
Total	268,740	101,890	7,689
% of total vote[1]	70.99	26.92	2.03

Third congressional district

County	Brad Pfaff (Dem.)	Derrick Van Orden (Rep.)
Adams	3,601	6,266
Buffalo	2,301	3,812
Chippewa (part)	7,011	8,306
Crawford	3,334	3,667
Dunn	8,037	10,363
Eau Claire	27,216	20,842
Grant	8,534	11,353
Jackson (part)	3,163	3,936
Juneau (part)	2,984	4,873
La Crosse	31,878	23,234
Monroe (part)	6,082	9,170
Pepin	1,218	2,079
Pierce	7,756	10,232
Portage	17,077	16,120
Richland	3,172	3,790
Sauk (part)	656	1,065
Trempealeau	5,090	7,175
Vernon	6,450	6,705
Wood (part)	7,417	11,755
Total	152,977	164,743
% of total vote[1]	48.12	51.82

Fourth congressional district

County	Gwen S. Moore* (Dem.)	Tim Rogers (Rep.)	Robert R. Raymond (Ind.)
Milwaukee (part)	191,955	57,600	5,164
Total	191,955	57,660	5,164
% of total vote[1]	75.27	22.61	2.03

District vote for U.S. representatives from Wisconsin, November 8, 2022 general election, continued

Fifth congressional district

County	Mike Van Someren (Dem.)	Scott Fitzgerald (Rep.)
Dodge (part)	5,732	14,162
Jefferson	15,557	22,642
Milwaukee (part)	12,346	11,843
Walworth (part)	1,428	3,181
Washington	20,735	52,675
Waukesha	78,783	139,238
Total	134,581	243,741
% of total vote[1]	35.55	64.39

Sixth congressional district

County	Glenn Grothman* (Rep.)
Calumet (part)	2,476
Columbia	18,115
Dodge (part)	13,841
Fond du Lac	35,793
Green Lake	6,977
Manitowoc	27,022
Marquette	5,695
Ozaukee	35,232
Sheboygan	37,384
Waushara	8,965
Winnebago (part)	47,731
Total[2]	239,231
% of total vote[1]	94.93

Seventh congressional district

County	Richard "Dick" Ausman (Dem.)	Tom Tiffany* (Rep.)
Ashland	3,830	3,100
Barron	7,108	12,976
Bayfield	5,161	4,083
Burnett	2,835	5,370
Chippewa (part)	4,287	9,349
Clark	3,367	8,269
Douglas	10,147	8,440
Florence	594	1,916
Forest	1,340	2,826
Iron	1,208	2,066
Jackson (part)	246	645
Juneau (part)	815	1,990
Langlade	2,744	6,292
Lincoln	4,987	8,490
Marathon	23,287	37,969
Monroe (part)	630	1,430
Oneida	8,235	11,954
Polk	7,216	13,238
Price	2,429	4,639
Rusk	2,039	4,345
Sawyer	3,526	4,927
St. Croix	17,623	26,215
Taylor	2,114	6,557

Statistics and Reference: Elections | 579

District vote for U.S. representatives from Wisconsin, November 8, 2022 general election, continued

Seventh congressional district, continued

County	Tom Tiffany* (Rep.)	
Vilas	4,766	8,405
Washburn	3,038	5,313
Wood (part)	5,305	8,420
Total	128,877	209,224
% of total vote[1]	38.10	61.85

Eighth congressional district

County	Mike Gallagher* (Rep.)	Jacob J. VandenPlas (Lib.)	Paul David Boucher (Ind.)
Brown	87,044	13,461	16,975
Calumet (part)	20,138	1,786	3,041
Door	11,255	1,790	3,336
Kewaunee	8,614	929	1,128
Marinette	16,514	1,053	2,318
Menominee	411	131	365
Oconto	17,375	1,721	2,027
Outagamie	64,985	8,396	13,989
Shawano	15,970	1,160	2,253
Waupaca	20,252	1,513	3,247
Winnebago (part)	5,615	117	217
Total[3]	268,173	32,057	48,896
% of total vote[1]	64.18	10.33	15.76

*Incumbent. Dem.–Democrat; Rep.–Republican; Ind.–Independent; Lib.–Libertarian.

1. Percentages do not add up to 100, as scattered and write-in votes have been omitted. 2. Write-in candidate Tom Powell received 340 votes. 3. Write-in candidate Julie Hancock received 3,160 votes; write-in candidate Robbie Hoffman received 135 votes.

Source: Official records of the Wisconsin Elections Commission.

County vote for Wisconsin governor, August 9, 2022 partisan primary

	Tony Evers* (Democrat)	Republican					Total
		Adam J. Fischer	Rebecca Kleefisch	Tim Michels	Kevin Nicholson	Timothy Ramthun	
Adams	1,443	50	1,156	1,564	124	180	4,531
Ashland	1,759	16	260	778	60	48	2,929
Barron	2,359	73	1,341	2,757	252	735	7,522
Bayfield	2,766	54	518	1,232	115	96	4,799
Brown	18,096	279	12,663	11,550	1,013	3,155	46,816
Buffalo	804	79	748	1,354	207	157	3,357
Burnett	983	72	761	933	113	309	3,171
Calumet	3,224	56	3,114	3,857	213	706	11,177
Chippewa	4,324	140	2,574	5,098	411	690	13,255
Clark	1,230	74	1,196	2,363	181	258	5,307
Columbia	4,403	64	2,939	3,728	245	425	11,822
Crawford	1,564	25	376	906	77	151	3,107
Dane	94,593	494	17,011	14,455	1,350	1,420	129,577
Dodge	3,967	121	5,755	9,441	326	711	20,323

County vote for Wisconsin governor, August 9, 2022 partisan primary, continued

	Tony Evers* (Democrat)	Republican Adam J. Fischer	Rebecca Kleefisch	Tim Michels	Kevin Nicholson	Timothy Ramthun	Total
Door	3,691	57	2,015	2,064	129	195	8,160
Douglas	5,134	118	986	1,796	201	177	8,454
Dunn	3,162	76	1,066	2,151	164	459	7,078
Eau Claire	10,826	137	3,159	4,613	356	563	19,688
Florence	194	18	236	496	46	35	1,025
Fond du Lac	4,834	127	5,068	11,417	272	962	22,688
Forest	407	14	366	872	49	49	1,758
Grant	2,787	70	1,763	2,513	188	269	7,597
Green	3,470	51	1,696	1,949	149	266	7,595
Green Lake	839	35	1,088	1,920	74	112	4,068
Iowa	2,214	32	1,034	1,189	93	160	4,728
Iron	501	18	251	556	42	45	1,416
Jackson	1,458	46	491	1,179	133	133	3,440
Jefferson	5,435	102	5,631	5,192	350	732	17,463
Juneau	1,326	184	1,403	1,972	204	308	5,406
Kenosha	11,911	292	7,986	9,041	834	764	30,918
Kewaunee	1,119	28	1,381	1,438	150	351	4,470
La Crosse	12,970	166	4,180	4,685	475	402	22,909
Lafayette	867	16	654	925	75	102	2,640
Langlade	960	41	1,143	1,624	112	205	4,085
Lincoln	1,646	80	1,920	1,988	213	321	6,172
Manitowoc	4,686	109	4,773	5,125	391	974	16,082
Marathon	8,551	217	9,037	7,346	754	1,214	27,158
Marinette	1,918	153	2,289	4,159	394	409	9,338
Marquette	906	30	911	1,568	77	113	3,611
Menominee	161	0	68	67	3	8	307
Milwaukee	92,652	452	26,641	24,055	1,805	1,637	147,586
Monroe	2,632	93	1,433	2,471	295	297	7,231
Oconto	1,883	65	2,280	3,477	262	818	8,790
Oneida	2,878	67	2,329	3,043	272	363	8,961
Outagamie	12,437	231	9,791	9,798	728	1,989	34,976
Ozaukee	8,068	115	8,614	7,772	425	550	25,581
Pepin	439	12	233	492	44	41	1,262
Pierce	2,692	88	1,129	1,266	195	524	5,906
Polk	2,361	211	1,478	1,950	301	1,031	7,332
Portage	8,565	93	4,047	3,214	380	677	17,014
Price	981	37	732	1,445	129	154	3,478
Racine	13,281	221	11,043	12,223	862	1,203	38,905
Richland	1,172	53	823	1,068	102	129	3,353
Rock	13,297	145	5,275	6,433	468	727	26,407
Rusk	792	45	589	1,434	141	202	3,204
Sauk	5,258	100	2,827	3,684	275	392	12,536
Sawyer	1,161	104	1,007	1,392	194	349	4,220
Shawano	1,695	116	3,053	3,443	335	569	9,211
St. Croix	7,671	150	7,591	8,322	624	1,411	25,796
Sheboygan	5,314	255	3,036	3,417	415	1,258	13,720
Taylor	683	42	1,133	1,970	136	211	4,175
Trempealeau	1,954	61	1,089	1,826	192	282	5,411
Vernon	2,608	110	1,414	2,130	287	282	6,842
Vilas	1,767	73	1,787	2,443	215	202	6,493
Walworth	6,096	179	7,640	7,301	548	855	22,664
Washburn	1,030	101	712	1,294	171	367	3,684
Washington	7,410	116	12,742	15,468	613	1,340	37,694
Waukesha	31,061	418	42,405	37,105	2,153	2,514	115,790
Waupaca	2,359	153	3,738	3,899	471	744	11,380

Statistics and Reference: Elections | 581

County vote for Wisconsin governor, August 9, 2022 partisan primary, continued

	Tony Evers* (Democrat)	Republican Adam J. Fischer	Rebecca Kleefisch	Tim Michels	Kevin Nicholson	Timothy Ramthun	Total
Waushara	1,226	50	1,684	2,011	135	267	5,374
Winnebago	11,798	218	7,837	8,888	625	1,113	30,529
Wood	4,947	151	4,245	4,374	471	772	14,984
Total	491,656	8,139	291,384	326,969	24,884	41,639	1,186,436

Note: County totals include scattered votes.
*Incumbent.
Source: Official records of the Wisconsin Elections Commission.

WHS IMAGE ID 96515

County vote for Wisconsin lieutenant governor, August 9, 2022 partisan primary

	Democrat					Republican					Total
	Peng Her	Sara Rodriguez	David D. King	Will Martin	Roger Roth	Patrick Testin	David C. Varnam	Cindy Werner	Jonathan Wichmann	Kyle Yudes	
Adams	269	1,113	98	182	326	1,252	118	547	254	80	4,253
Ashland	314	1,289	67	93	155	170	47	152	137	67	2,499
Barron	423	1,835	329	535	677	866	368	646	927	284	6,902
Bayfield	429	2,153	97	203	310	334	108	275	255	83	4,264
Brown	3,785	13,218	851	1,672	10,913	2,565	807	2,453	3,502	2,758	42,612
Buffalo	148	608	134	164	279	366	154	594	294	143	2,889
Burnett	186	770	118	169	345	307	96	542	276	98	2,907
Calumet	801	2,183	294	372	3,512	779	200	593	916	520	10,187
Chippewa	876	3,218	577	686	1,079	1,137	569	1,148	1,301	956	11,583
Clark	204	948	189	283	700	861	222	529	537	252	4,729
Columbia	992	3,111	386	598	1,296	1,065	402	1,075	910	317	10,177
Crawford	239	1,213	61	131	261	228	190	205	190	42	2,764
Dane	26,275	63,437	1,881	3,527	5,876	4,504	1,714	5,120	3,301	1,305	117,276
Dodge	813	2,941	801	988	4,356	2,052	726	1,858	2,494	603	17,633
Door	642	2,700	163	276	1,586	485	189	531	381	156	7,121
Douglas	892	3,954	208	298	518	521	164	479	350	165	7,576
Dunn	785	2,200	181	302	463	602	264	594	587	439	6,417
Eau Claire	2,486	7,740	510	657	1,021	1,735	538	1,110	1,088	978	17,906
Florence	23	159	84	41	204	99	44	80	112	53	899
Fond du Lac	988	3,429	1,145	975	5,852	1,691	677	1,780	2,102	696	19,360
Forest	47	321	39	76	305	289	45	123	162	43	1,452
Grant	545	2,015	171	339	520	406	1,674	408	440	151	6,681
Green	716	2,490	207	342	735	530	306	587	448	145	6,521
Green Lake	164	610	154	171	1,054	375	108	405	375	136	3,555
Iowa	441	1,640	125	249	363	320	199	415	262	88	4,113
Iron	78	395	26	81	179	152	39	109	115	44	1,219
Jackson	328	1,060	134	151	182	575	152	241	197	83	3,104
Jefferson	1,140	3,980	422	1,062	2,700	1,545	677	1,453	1,869	352	15,250
Juneau	294	942	194	286	510	790	252	728	502	188	4,699
Kenosha	2,599	8,780	799	1,684	4,198	2,759	787	2,892	2,113	745	27,462

County vote for Wisconsin lieutenant governor, August 9, 2022 partisan primary, continued

	Democrat		Republican							Total
	Peng Her	Sara Rodriguez	David D. King	Will Martin	Roger Roth	Patrick Testin	David C. Varnam	Cindy Werner	Jonathan Wichmann	Kyle Yudes	
Kewaunee	175	863	69	176	1,320	289	96	427	395	204	4,024
La Crosse	3,027	9,127	472	812	1,279	2,186	731	1,468	933	367	20,436
Lafayette	160	650	104	157	235	221	268	180	206	50	2,233
Langlade	155	743	139	195	553	894	129	288	331	210	3,637
Lincoln	296	1,203	188	367	538	1,322	189	515	547	196	5,366
Manitowoc	1,094	3,336	658	685	4,270	1,164	344	1,084	1,258	522	14,445
Marathon	2,059	5,988	572	1,457	2,455	7,391	718	1,695	1,767	851	24,998
Marinette	300	1,434	237	349	2,243	936	183	892	1,263	346	8,197
Marquette	180	672	124	167	438	524	126	484	378	93	3,189
Menominee	34	107	3	7	51	21	6	23	10	5	268
Milwaukee	19,340	68,269	1,957	4,637	15,269	5,940	1,879	6,889	6,238	1,399	132,312
Monroe	485	1,976	156	219	326	2,305	367	445	367	145	6,801
Oconto	352	1,386	140	309	2,277	547	161	485	869	1,428	7,963
Oneida	514	2,119	209	401	980	1,760	239	664	597	279	7,775
Outagamie	3,393	8,177	517	1,046	11,262	1,571	488	1,653	2,424	1,582	32,115
Ozaukee	1,593	5,987	581	1,439	5,965	2,011	633	1,917	1,756	420	22,378
Pepin	75	340	51	52	83	146	50	162	110	55	1,125
Pierce	576	2,017	132	288	509	688	168	417	560	202	5,563
Polk	517	1,753	371	428	671	853	250	792	859	311	6,805
Portage	1,917	5,878	135	254	585	5,680	141	356	483	286	15,735
Price	204	706	101	167	304	704	88	314	270	130	2,990
Racine	2,791	9,553	798	3,265	6,392	2,721	877	3,983	3,117	727	34,320
Richland	239	855	112	185	272	353	161	362	243	70	2,860
Rock	2,515	10,128	672	1,066	2,724	1,716	707	1,959	1,530	496	23,579
Rusk	146	612	114	192	277	319	148	277	305	456	2,850
Sauk	1,043	3,897	400	600	1,026	1,197	467	1,224	817	267	10,938
Sawyer	231	848	154	428	326	434	130	402	358	422	3,744
Shawano	302	1,262	231	496	2,637	888	245	576	1,184	399	8,221
Sheboygan	2,039	5,251	762	1,248	5,494	1,902	883	1,898	2,051	1,056	22,632

County vote for Wisconsin lieutenant governor, August 9, 2022 partisan primary, continued

	Democrat					Republican					
	Peng Her	Sara Rodriguez	David D. King	Will Martin	Roger Roth	Patrick Testin	David C. Varnam	Cindy Werner	Jonathan Wichmann	Kyle Yudes	Total
St. Croix.	1,061	4,051	357	724	1,097	1,751	420	1,262	1,403	583	12,741
Taylor	111	530	181	277	387	1,034	211	377	431	170	3,710
Trempealeau	430	1,402	164	259	422	555	265	608	423	248	4,783
Vernon	495	1,942	257	314	421	1,001	252	1,031	302	129	6,154
Vilas	341	1,268	155	340	835	1,398	183	512	378	172	5,598
Walworth	1,340	4,418	850	1,390	4,270	2,352	704	2,075	2,029	644	20,136
Washburn	179	783	308	338	295	328	147	323	396	145	3,252
Washington	1,393	5,642	998	2,874	9,607	3,643	1,251	2,959	3,779	940	33,089
Waukesha	5,208	24,171	2,230	8,554	27,037	10,962	3,272	8,665	8,124	2,349	100,862
Waupaca	442	1,751	238	510	2,947	1,420	226	1,031	1,235	394	10,220
Waushara	237	892	118	189	1,015	1,577	117	364	361	115	4,986
Winnebago	2,874	8,167	696	876	8,672	1,528	603	1,558	1,983	890	27,905
Wood	981	3,654	287	460	731	5,782	281	685	699	328	13,911
Total.	**108,766**	**354,260**	**27,443**	**54,790**	**178,972**	**109,374**	**30,640**	**80,953**	**79,166**	**32,051**	**1,058,856**

Note: County totals include scattered votes. Write-in candidate Angela Kennedy (Dem.) received 39 votes.
Source: Official records of the Wisconsin Elections Commission.

County vote for Wisconsin governor and lieutenant governor, November 8, 2022 general election

	Tony Evers*/ Sara Rodriguez (Dem.)	Tim Michels/ Roger Roth (Rep.)	Joan Ellis Beglinger (Ind.)	Total
Adams	3,860	5,856	184	9,908
Ashland	4,034	2,905	66	7,015
Barron	7,552	12,246	314	20,133
Bayfield	5,367	3,843	73	9,291
Brown	53,887	58,986	1,227	114,205
Buffalo	2,391	3,638	106	6,138
Burnett	2,964	5,061	117	8,142
Calumet	9,935	14,828	248	25,025
Chippewa	11,994	16,792	396	29,201
Clark	3,797	7,690	197	11,692
Columbia	14,168	13,008	276	27,476
Crawford	3,429	3,486	87	7,006
Dane	236,577	62,300	1,946	301,033
Dodge	13,240	25,428	414	39,082
Door	8,984	8,145	166	17,305
Douglas	10,606	7,823	200	18,639
Dunn	8,299	9,899	236	18,435
Eau Claire	28,063	19,856	506	48,461
Florence	655	1,838	24	2,517
Fond du Lac	16,598	29,642	457	46,718
Forest	1,452	2,670	68	4,190
Grant	9,234	10,594	256	20,094
Green	9,603	7,681	234	17,532
Green Lake	2,746	5,864	100	8,714
Iowa	6,837	4,717	119	11,678
Iron	1,259	1,964	36	3,260
Jackson	3,505	4,375	119	7,999
Jefferson	16,765	21,488	425	38,732
Juneau	4,048	6,516	160	10,738
Kenosha	32,176	33,068	752	66,073
Kewaunee	3,529	6,229	129	9,893
La Crosse	32,119	22,325	683	55,169
Lafayette	3,005	3,498	66	6,569
Langlade	2,958	5,966	110	9,035
Lincoln	5,226	8,084	238	13,552
Manitowoc	13,937	21,573	493	36,038
Marathon	25,163	35,860	719	61,770
Marinette	6,110	12,164	259	18,541
Marquette	2,697	4,549	90	7,338
Menominee	979	254	11	1,245
Milwaukee	246,073	97,471	2,980	346,889
Monroe	6,931	10,153	247	17,341
Oconto	5,910	13,363	253	19,537
Oneida	8,667	11,297	252	20,230
Outagamie	39,572	45,601	926	86,102
Ozaukee	23,104	28,827	370	52,367
Pepin	1,280	1,990	41	3,311
Pierce	7,967	9,779	270	18,029
Polk	7,587	12,548	289	20,445
Portage	17,947	15,361	350	33,681
Price	2,596	4,369	97	7,062
Racine	38,241	42,359	853	81,528
Richland	3,354	3,562	87	7,008
Rock	37,755	26,722	759	65,276
Rusk	2,180	4,120	85	6,387
Sauk	15,285	13,348	327	28,960
Sawyer	3,734	4,735	91	8,566

County vote for Wisconsin governor and lieutenant governor, November 8, 2022 general election, continued

	Tony Evers*/ Sara Rodriguez (Dem.)	Tim Michels/ Roger Roth (Rep.)	Joan Ellis Beglinger (Ind.)	Total
Shawano	5,853	11,875	209	17,937
Sheboygan	22,325	30,679	602	53,661
St. Croix	18,516	24,968	532	44,039
Taylor	2,262	6,296	142	8,702
Trempealeau	5,281	6,813	151	12,249
Vernon	6,597	6,409	187	13,201
Vilas	5,088	7,983	143	13,220
Walworth	18,569	26,700	604	45,926
Washburn	3,198	5,032	119	8,351
Washington	22,698	50,749	582	74,029
Waukesha	88,564	134,212	1,566	224,603
Waupaca	7,990	14,939	290	23,227
Waushara	3,766	7,459	112	11,340
Winnebago	36,512	37,242	898	74,712
Wood	13,624	18,865	477	32,992
Total	**1,358,774**	**1,268,535**	**27,198**	**2,654,507**

Note: County totals include scattered votes. Write-in candidate for governor Seth Haskin (Ind.) received 104 votes.
*Incumbent. Dem.–Democrat; Rep.–Republican; Ind.–Independent.
Source: Official records of the Wisconsin Elections Commission.

Wisconsin gubernatorial vote by county and municipality, November 8, 2022 general election

	Tony Evers*/ Sara Rodriguez (Dem.)	Tim Michels/ Roger Roth (Rep.)		Tony Evers*/ Sara Rodriguez (Dem.)	Tim Michels/ Roger Roth (Rep.)
Adams	**3,860**	**5,856**	Butternut, village	73	78
Adams, city	255	320	Chippewa, town	57	125
Adams, town	246	352	Gingles, town	211	191
Big Flats, town	164	295	Gordon, town	57	104
Colburn, town	42	108	Jacobs, town	91	202
Dell Prairie, town	331	460	La Pointe, town	225	48
Easton, town	159	302	Marengo, town	88	93
Friendship, village	97	118	Mellen, city	134	129
Jackson, town	254	346	Morse, town	117	138
Leola, town	33	109	Peeksville, town	21	65
Lincoln, town	58	108	Sanborn, town	330	57
Monroe, town	101	142	Shanagolden, town	24	44
New Chester, town	159	237	White River, town	128	273
New Haven, town	124	181	**Barron**	**7,552**	**12,246**
Preston, town	254	379	Almena, town	136	325
Quincy, town	263	360	Almena, village	69	181
Richfield, town	22	64	Arland, town	111	167
Rome, town	828	1,264	Barron, city	506	552
Springville, town	233	344	Barron, town	92	247
Strongs Prairie, town	231	355	Bear Lake, town	131	230
Wisconsin Dells, city (part)	6	12	Cameron, village	239	442
Ashland	**4,034**	**2,905**	Cedar Lake, town	229	454
Agenda, town	60	153	Chetek, city	374	500
Ashland, city (part)	2,276	1,065	Chetek, town	376	576
Ashland, town	142	140	Clinton, town	99	217

Wisconsin gubernatorial vote by county and municipality, November 8, 2022 general election, continued

	Tony Evers*/ Sara Rodriguez (Dem.)	Tim Michels/ Roger Roth (Rep.)		Tony Evers*/ Sara Rodriguez (Dem.)	Tim Michels/ Roger Roth (Rep.)
Crystal Lake, town	123	237	**Brown**	**53,887**	**58,986**
Cumberland, city	436	494	Allouez, village	3,826	2,906
Cumberland, town	153	258	Ashwaubenon, village	3,860	4,163
Dallas, town	64	192	Bellevue, village	3,348	3,758
Dallas, village	34	110	De Pere, city	5,948	5,302
Dovre, town	138	243	Denmark, village	374	604
Doyle, town	79	186	Eaton, town	284	627
Haugen, village	47	72	Glenmore, town	157	418
Lakeland, town	187	312	Green Bay, city	19,561	15,215
Maple Grove, town	92	299	Green Bay, town	350	864
Maple Plain, town	186	254	Hobart, village	2,073	2,672
New Auburn, village (part)	2	5	Holland, town	242	586
Oak Grove, town	148	288	Howard, village (part)	4,278	5,514
Prairie Farm, town	74	169	Humboldt, town	186	523
Prairie Farm, village	54	99	Lawrence, town	1,392	2,145
Prairie Lake, town	258	554	Ledgeview, town	1,989	2,464
Rice Lake, city	1,571	1,682	Morrison, town	183	617
Rice Lake, town	548	828	New Denmark, town	288	579
Sioux Creek, town	97	218	Pittsfield, town	477	1085
Stanfold, town	106	211	Pulaski, village (part)	558	937
Stanley, town	372	802	Rockland, town	365	694
Sumner, town	111	251	Scott, town	820	1170
Turtle Lake, town	97	205	Suamico, village	2,490	4,410
Turtle Lake, village (part)	110	186	Wrightstown, town	371	886
Vance Creek, town	103	200	Wrightstown, village (part)	467	847
Bayfield	**5,367**	**3,843**	**Buffalo**	**2,391**	**3,638**
Ashland, city (part)	0	0	Alma, city	198	174
Barksdale, town	263	194	Alma, town	67	72
Barnes, town	268	314	Belvidere, town	84	157
Bayfield, city	281	46	Buffalo, town	165	218
Bayfield, town	362	138	Buffalo City, city	216	263
Bayview, town	204	123	Canton, town	54	91
Bell, town	176	76	Cochrane, village	65	98
Cable, town	245	299	Cross, town	57	125
Clover, town	113	74	Dover, town	83	99
Delta, town	110	119	Fountain City, city	177	179
Drummond, town	173	135	Gilmanton, town	75	122
Eileen, town	173	215	Glencoe, town	58	134
Grand View, town	156	157	Lincoln, town	41	57
Hughes, town	128	139	Maxville, town	42	122
Iron River, town	331	328	Milton, town	104	189
Kelly, town	79	136	Modena, town	58	78
Keystone, town	84	120	Mondovi, city	369	576
Lincoln, town	72	98	Mondovi, town	72	140
Mason, town	64	84	Montana, town	38	76
Mason, village	15	24	Naples, town	113	231
Namakagon, town	112	153	Nelson, town	95	191
Orienta, town	43	49	Nelson, village	62	65
Oulu, town	158	178	Waumandee, town	98	181
Pilsen, town	76	56			
Port Wing, town	153	102	**Burnett**	**2,964**	**5,061**
Russell, town	404	62	Anderson, town	54	142
Tripp, town	64	55	Blaine, town	36	95
Washburn, city	815	263	Daniels, town	101	238
Washburn, town	245	106	Dewey, town	73	161

Wisconsin gubernatorial vote by county and municipality, November 8, 2022 general election, continued

	Tony Evers*/ Sara Rodriguez (Dem.)	Tim Michels/ Roger Roth (Rep.)		Tony Evers*/ Sara Rodriguez (Dem.)	Tim Michels/ Roger Roth (Rep.)
Grantsburg, town	159	341	Cornell, city	208	346
Grantsburg, village	181	326	Delmar, town	141	276
Jackson, town	243	346	Eagle Point, town	704	1,046
La Follette, town	127	145	Eau Claire, city (part)	499	388
Lincoln, town	34	132	Edson, town	126	265
Meenon, town	165	363	Estella, town	50	161
Oakland, town	269	326	Goetz, town	140	216
Roosevelt, town	34	66	Hallie, town	51	52
Rusk, town	83	130	Howard, town	143	251
Sand Lake, town	119	150	Lafayette, town	1,484	1,890
Scott, town	166	220	Lake Hallie, village (part)	1,364	1,670
Siren, town	170	305	Lake Holcombe, town	141	414
Siren, village	128	183	New Auburn, village (part)	50	140
Swiss, town	169	205	Ruby, town	51	154
Trade Lake, town	186	295	Sampson, town	152	338
Union, town	85	129	Sigel, town	182	321
Webb Lake, town	111	163	Stanley, city (part)	289	448
Webster, village	98	129	Tilden, town	312	511
West Marshland, town	43	138	Wheaton, town	590	854
Wood River, town	130	333	Woodmohr, town	164	359
Calumet	**9,935**	**14,828**	**Clark**	**3,797**	**7,690**
Appleton, city (part)	2,588	2,138	Abbotsford, city (part)	179	284
Brillion, city	461	863	Beaver, town	66	164
Brillion, town	202	570	Butler, town	15	33
Brothertown, town	170	586	Colby, city (part)	136	265
Charlestown, town	108	308	Colby, town	61	177
Chilton, city	550	1,014	Curtiss, village	15	24
Chilton, town	140	486	Dewhurst, town	69	127
Harrison, village (part)	2,682	3,436	Dorchester, village (part)	57	184
Hilbert, village	124	352	Eaton, town	70	149
Kaukauna, city (part)	0	0	Foster, town	19	37
Kiel, city (part)	55	96	Fremont, town	99	310
Menasha, city (part)	783	827	Grant, town	112	230
New Holstein, city	563	829	Granton, village	55	79
New Holstein, town	192	557	Green Grove, town	50	121
Potter, village	26	94	Greenwood, city	169	231
Rantoul, town	74	327	Hendren, town	70	112
Sherwood, village	747	1097	Hewett, town	60	109
Stockbridge, town	241	627	Hixon, town	60	127
Stockbridge, village	121	255	Hoard, town	60	140
Woodville, town	108	366	Levis, town	68	162
Chippewa	**11,994**	**16,792**	Longwood, town	59	133
Anson, town	489	777	Loyal, city	161	313
Arthur, town	93	241	Loyal, town	56	186
Auburn, town	107	252	Lynn, town	73	169
Birch Creek, town	104	183	Mayville, town	91	224
Bloomer, city	559	1,056	Mead, town	30	88
Bloomer, town	148	342	Mentor, town	67	151
Boyd, village	87	142	Neillsville, city	382	507
Cadott, village	228	285	Owen, city	154	207
Chippewa Falls, city	2,986	2,590	Pine Valley, town	181	370
Cleveland, town	154	298	Reseburg, town	53	89
Colburn, town	100	273	Seif, town	32	78
Cooks Valley, town	98	253	Sherman, town	59	203

Wisconsin gubernatorial vote by county and municipality, November 8, 2022 general election, continued

	Tony Evers*/ Sara Rodriguez (Dem.)	Tim Michels/ Roger Roth (Rep.)		Tony Evers*/ Sara Rodriguez (Dem.)	Tim Michels/ Roger Roth (Rep.)
Sherwood, town	59	74	Eastman, town	134	228
Stanley, city (part)	6	6	Eastman, village	41	109
Thorp, city	208	364	Ferryville, village	56	70
Thorp, town	68	189	Freeman, town	214	186
Unity, town	75	184	Gays Mills, village	117	114
Unity, village (part)	12	34	Haney, town	62	79
Warner, town	64	138	Lynxville, village	32	31
Washburn, town	29	101	Marietta, town	91	154
Weston, town	90	199	Mount Sterling, village	45	29
Withee, town	66	173	Prairie du Chien, city	1,109	844
Withee, village	68	125	Prairie du Chien, town	184	243
Worden, town	64	140	Scott, town	115	105
York, town	100	180	Seneca, town	222	232
			Soldiers Grove, village	115	116
Columbia	**14,168**	**13,008**	Steuben, village	17	34
Arlington, town	219	243	Utica, town	185	135
Arlington, village	219	197	Wauzeka, town	73	121
Caledonia, town	489	353	Wauzeka, village	130	135
Cambria, village	139	145			
Columbus, city (part)	1,412	959	**Dane**	**236,577**	**62,300**
Columbus, town	137	212	Albion, town	558	451
Courtland, town	69	174	Belleville, village (part)	814	343
Dekorra, town	733	744	Berry, town	436	295
Doylestown, village	56	65	Black Earth, town	193	145
Fall River, village	380	359	Black Earth, village	545	261
Fort Winnebago, town	209	265	Blooming Grove, town	675	163
Fountain Prairie, town	230	259	Blue Mounds, town	378	210
Friesland, village	47	111	Blue Mounds, village	364	143
Hampden, town	153	181	Bristol, town	1,378	1,075
Leeds, town	208	243	Brooklyn, village (part)	347	154
Lewiston, town	300	327	Burke, town	1,120	636
Lodi, city	1,069	610	Cambridge, village (part)	630	292
Lodi, town	966	977	Christiana, town	362	297
Lowville, town	271	340	Cottage Grove, town	1,422	847
Marcellon, town	195	276	Cottage Grove, village	2,833	1,179
Newport, town	150	201	Cross Plains, town	589	405
Otsego, town	163	204	Cross Plains, village	1,583	642
Pacific, town	770	775	Dane, town	209	296
Pardeeville, village	437	438	Dane, village	264	249
Portage, city	2,013	1,177	Deerfield, town	508	383
Poynette, village	642	496	Deerfield, village	788	447
Randolph, town	88	325	DeForest, village	3,726	1,790
Randolph, village (part)	61	139	Dunkirk, town	688	445
Rio, village	273	212	Dunn, town	2,080	1,016
Scott, town	130	212	Edgerton, city (part)	25	33
Springvale, town	130	160	Fitchburg, city	11,887	2,560
West Point, town	710	559	Madison, city	126,092	17,965
Wisconsin Dells, city (part)	516	473	Maple Bluff, village	719	290
Wyocena, town	442	462	Marshall, village	940	662
Wyocena, village	142	135	Mazomanie, town	340	261
			Mazomanie, village	610	292
Crawford	**3,429**	**3,486**	McFarland, village	3,882	1,366
Bell Center, village	22	19	Medina, town	357	381
Bridgeport, town	196	282	Middleton, city	9,985	2,038
Clayton, town	252	209	Middleton, town	2,595	1,206
De Soto, village (part)	17	11			

Wisconsin gubernatorial vote by county and municipality, November 8, 2022 general election, continued

	Tony Evers*/ Sara Rodriguez (Dem.)	Tim Michels/ Roger Roth (Rep.)		Tony Evers*/ Sara Rodriguez (Dem.)	Tim Michels/ Roger Roth (Rep.)
Monona, city	4,492	816	Mayville, city	787	1,507
Montrose, town	449	213	Neosho, village	65	232
Mount Horeb, village	2,997	1,198	Oak Grove, town	163	373
Oregon, town	1,357	654	Portland, town	205	358
Oregon, village	4,574	1,650	Randolph, village (part)	175	341
Perry, town	283	161	Reeseville, village	103	172
Pleasant Springs, town	1,201	790	Rubicon, town	239	1,059
Primrose, town	303	147	Shields, town	88	217
Rockdale, village	71	30	Theresa, town	109	487
Roxbury, town	591	452	Theresa, village	162	505
Rutland, town	771	426	Trenton, town	176	473
Shorewood Hills, village	1,334	112	Watertown, city (part)	1,361	2,341
Springdale, town	798	480	Waupun, city (part)	707	1,179
Springfield, town	916	704	Westford, town	265	412
Stoughton, city	5,030	1,764	**Door**	**8,984**	**8,145**
Sun Prairie, city	12,513	4,390	Baileys Harbor, town	509	314
Sun Prairie, town	791	529	Brussels, town	182	389
Vermont, town	397	187	Clay Banks, town	113	121
Verona, city	5,941	1,784	Egg Harbor, town	509	459
Verona, town	880	420	Egg Harbor, village	158	95
Vienna, town	467	396	Ephraim, village	139	104
Waunakee, village	5,544	2,839	Forestville, town	203	338
Westport, town	1,842	966	Forestville, village	91	134
Windsor, village	2,910	1,775	Gardner, town	261	439
York, town	203	199	Gibraltar, town	513	359
Dodge	**13,240**	**25,428**	Jacksonport, town	283	286
Ashippun, town	362	1,183	Liberty Grove, town	841	557
Beaver Dam, city	3,233	2,814	Nasewaupee, town	507	628
Beaver Dam, town	875	1,134	Sevastopol, town	896	924
Brownsville, village	92	284	Sister Bay, village	455	248
Burnett, town	132	315	Sturgeon Bay, city	2,630	1,824
Calamus, town	185	309	Sturgeon Bay, town	204	259
Chester, town	82	231	Union, town	210	393
Clyman, town	89	318	Washington, town	280	274
Clyman, village	39	82			
Columbus, city (part)	0	0	**Douglas**	**10,606**	**7,823**
Elba, town	228	317	Amnicon, town	284	280
Emmet, town	168	565	Bennett, town	163	204
Fox Lake, city	240	390	Brule, town	202	136
Fox Lake, town	200	483	Cloverland, town	48	55
Hartford, city (part)	1	5	Dairyland, town	21	86
Herman, town	114	584	Gordon, town	168	232
Horicon, city	582	948	Hawthorne, town	190	277
Hubbard, town	311	668	Highland, town	104	87
Hustisford, town	160	629	Lake Nebagamon, village	299	341
Hustisford, village	130	391	Lakeside, town	173	181
Iron Ridge, village	115	322	Maple, town	200	150
Juneau, city	319	536	Oakland, town	308	265
Kekoskee, village	105	402	Oliver, village	116	80
Lebanon, town	200	625	Parkland, town	277	224
Leroy, town	95	427	Poplar, village	117	199
Lomira, town	100	528	Solon Springs, town	216	321
Lomira, village	292	816	Solon Springs, village	151	145
Lowell, town	144	380	Summit, town	276	213
Lowell, village	42	86	Superior, city	6,282	3,404

Wisconsin gubernatorial vote by county and municipality, November 8, 2022 general election, continued

	Tony Evers*/ Sara Rodriguez (Dem.)	Tim Michels/ Roger Roth (Rep.)		Tony Evers*/ Sara Rodriguez (Dem.)	Tim Michels/ Roger Roth (Rep.)
Superior, town	559	525	**Florence**	**655**	**1,838**
Superior, village	207	141	Aurora, town	126	364
Wascott, town	245	277	Commonwealth, town	56	157
			Fence, town	19	93
Dunn	**8,299**	**9,899**	Fern, town	21	97
Boyceville, village	140	226	Florence, town	335	795
Colfax, town	215	352	Homestead, town	55	169
Colfax, village	207	208	Long Lake, town	30	83
Downing, village	26	71	Tipler, town	13	80
Dunn, town	298	397			
Eau Galle, town	123	266	**Fond du Lac**	**16,598**	**29,642**
Elk Mound, town	299	519	Alto, town	81	496
Elk Mound, village	148	180	Ashford, town	199	786
Grant, town	79	140	Auburn, town	258	1,166
Hay River, town	104	167	Brandon, village	123	295
Knapp, village	46	133	Byron, town	227	724
Lucas, town	117	236	Calumet, town	207	596
Menomonie, city	3,250	2,025	Campbellsport, village	249	638
Menomonie, town	676	863	Eden, town	121	486
New Haven, town	91	198	Eden, village	81	264
Otter Creek, town	87	162	Eldorado, town	199	600
Peru, town	34	73	Empire, town	554	1,120
Red Cedar, town	448	704	Fairwater, village	41	121
Ridgeland, village	41	53	Fond du Lac, city	7,489	8,654
Rock Creek, town	184	271	Fond du Lac, town	715	1,294
Sand Creek, town	96	155	Forest, town	114	477
Sheridan, town	69	152	Friendship, town	360	825
Sherman, town	161	307	Kewaskum, village (part)	0	0
Spring Brook, town	304	508	Lamartine, town	258	725
Stanton, town	143	251	Marshfield, town	147	484
Tainter, town	611	733	Metomen, town	98	270
Tiffany, town	75	203	Mount Calvary, village	68	212
Weston, town	99	156	North Fond du Lac, village	910	1,014
Wheeler, village	30	47	Oakfield, town	92	282
Wilson, town	98	143	Oakfield, village	168	364
			Osceola, town	223	866
Eau Claire	**28,063**	**19,856**	Ripon, city	1,462	1,637
Altoona, city	2,217	1,616	Ripon, town	246	478
Augusta, city	211	312	Rosendale, town	107	273
Bridge Creek, town	213	360	Rosendale, village	141	365
Brunswick, town	484	553	St. Cloud, village	70	197
Clear Creek, town	138	257	Springvale, town	86	293
Drammen, town	149	253	Taycheedah, town	870	1,891
Eau Claire, city (part)	19,251	10,142	Waupun, city (part)	461	1,140
Fairchild, town	39	88	Waupun, town	173	609
Fairchild, village	55	85			
Fall Creek, village	304	350	**Forest**	**1,452**	**2,670**
Lake Hallie, village (part)	0	0	Alvin, town	21	72
Lincoln, town	201	373	Argonne, town	72	179
Ludington, town	207	337	Armstrong Creek, town	63	161
Otter Creek, town	71	133	Blackwell, town	13	41
Pleasant Valley, town	993	1243	Caswell, town	10	38
Seymour, town	831	972	Crandon, city	223	441
Union, town	646	674	Crandon, town	91	190
Washington, town	2,007	1,983	Freedom, town	76	157
Wilson, town	46	125	Hiles, town	76	152

Wisconsin gubernatorial vote by county and municipality, November 8, 2022 general election, continued

	Tony Evers*/ Sara Rodriguez (Dem.)	Tim Michels/ Roger Roth (Rep.)		Tony Evers*/ Sara Rodriguez (Dem.)	Tim Michels/ Roger Roth (Rep.)
Laona, town	194	347	Wingville, town	75	77
Lincoln, town	209	257	Woodman, town	25	55
Nashville, town	234	318	Woodman, village	13	20
Popple River, town	8	17	Wyalusing, town	74	99
Ross, town	9	67			
Wabeno, town	153	233	**Green**	**9,603**	**7,681**
			Adams, town	152	128
Grant	**9,234**	**10,594**	Albany, town	319	293
Bagley, village	70	82	Albany, village	245	148
Beetown, town	68	203	Belleville, village (part)	192	84
Bloomington, town	57	112	Brodhead, city (part)	598	489
Bloomington, village	112	174	Brooklyn, town	403	296
Blue River, village	80	85	Brooklyn, village (part)	136	58
Boscobel, city	526	480	Browntown, village	40	58
Boscobel, town	76	90	Cadiz, town	164	241
Cassville, town	43	128	Clarno, town	237	360
Cassville, village	157	204	Decatur, town	418	449
Castle Rock, town	51	78	Exeter, town	727	436
Clifton, town	52	55	Jefferson, town	209	346
Cuba City, city (part)	439	339	Jordan, town	149	155
Dickeyville, village	203	267	Monroe, city	2,532	1,726
Ellenboro, town	81	187	Monroe, town	287	358
Fennimore, city	448	471	Monticello, village	318	185
Fennimore, town	87	115	Mount Pleasant, town	192	167
Glen Haven, town	41	125	New Glarus, town	486	345
Harrison, town	92	169	New Glarus, village	824	307
Hazel Green, town	236	248	Spring Grove, town	150	278
Hazel Green, village (part)	219	229	Sylvester, town	247	330
Hickory Grove, town	57	85	Washington, town	220	208
Jamestown, town	374	632	York, town	358	236
Lancaster, city	683	804			
Liberty, town	51	144	**Green Lake**	**2,746**	**5,864**
Lima, town	142	191	Berlin, city (part)	699	1,109
Little Grant, town	39	91	Berlin, town	152	481
Livingston, village (part)	139	132	Brooklyn, town	431	734
Marion, town	70	132	Green Lake, city	210	306
Millville, town	33	42	Green Lake, town	186	535
Montfort, village (part)	120	110	Kingston, town	63	197
Mount Hope, town	25	56	Kingston, village	47	110
Mount Hope, village	29	33	Mackford, town	43	218
Mount Ida, town	72	142	Manchester, town	85	262
Muscoda, town	103	169	Markesan, city	155	414
Muscoda, village (part)	207	215	Marquette, town	70	190
North Lancaster, town	90	162	Marquette, village	30	76
Paris, town	125	232	Princeton, city	180	344
Patch Grove, town	54	63	Princeton, town	296	594
Patch Grove, village	26	33	St. Marie, town	52	153
Platteville, city	2,329	1,435	Seneca, town	47	141
Platteville, town	390	346			
Potosi, town	152	252	**Iowa**	**6,837**	**4,717**
Potosi, village	106	186	Arena, town	458	317
Smelser, town	177	238	Arena, village	205	172
South Lancaster, town	117	197	Avoca, village	91	98
Tennyson, village	55	93	Barneveld, village	358	259
Waterloo, town	82	182	Blanchardville, village (part)	62	39
Watterstown, town	62	105			

Wisconsin gubernatorial vote by county and municipality, November 8, 2022 general election, continued

	Tony Evers*/ Sara Rodriguez (Dem.)	Tim Michels/ Roger Roth (Rep.)		Tony Evers*/ Sara Rodriguez (Dem.)	Tim Michels/ Roger Roth (Rep.)
Brigham, town	414	228	Knapp, town	47	108
Clyde, town	113	78	Komensky, town	101	27
Cobb, village	132	86	Manchester, town	124	230
Dodgeville, city	1,417	741	Melrose, town	64	123
Dodgeville, town	554	358	Melrose, village	105	104
Eden, town	98	103	Merrillan, village	78	87
Highland, town	180	191	Millston, town	35	70
Highland, village	188	173	North Bend, town	91	122
Hollandale, village	85	37	Northfield, town	105	181
Linden, town	147	203	Springfield, town	88	113
Linden, village	102	76	Taylor, village	60	70
Livingston, village (part)	0	2	**Jefferson**	**16,765**	**21,488**
Mifflin, town	106	140	Aztalan, town	315	444
Mineral Point, city	860	399	Cambridge, village (part)	27	17
Mineral Point, town	242	268	Cold Spring, town	172	238
Montfort, village (part)	30	19	Concord, town	347	750
Moscow, town	185	152	Farmington, town	239	581
Muscoda, village (part)	4	5	Fort Atkinson, city	2,842	2,130
Pulaski, town	67	89	Hebron, town	198	399
Rewey, village	55	41	Ixonia, town	703	1,854
Ridgeway, town	221	121	Jefferson, city	1,525	1,544
Ridgeway, village	176	124	Jefferson, town	364	679
Waldwick, town	129	115	Johnson Creek, village	583	765
Wyoming, town	158	83	Koshkonong, town	777	1,137
			Lac La Belle, village (part)	0	0
Iron	**1,259**	**1,964**	Lake Mills, city	1,794	1,363
Anderson, town	19	18	Lake Mills, town	671	585
Carey, town	25	64	Milford, town	237	360
Gurney, town	39	51	Oakland, town	1,032	839
Hurley, city	250	333	Palmyra, town	220	484
Kimball, town	111	167	Palmyra, village	233	518
Knight, town	39	64	Sullivan, town	348	846
Mercer, town	348	624	Sullivan, village	98	206
Montreal, city	167	196	Sumner, town	200	286
Oma, town	86	140	Waterloo, city	725	721
Pence, town	40	55	Waterloo, town	220	286
Saxon, town	61	124	Watertown, city (part)	2,096	3,344
Sherman, town	74	128	Watertown, town	308	822
			Whitewater, city (part)	491	290
Jackson	**3,505**	**4,375**			
Adams, town	299	408	**Juneau**	**4,048**	**6,516**
Albion, town	245	319	Armenia, town	120	232
Alma, town	150	271	Camp Douglas, village	85	138
Alma Center, village	108	79	Clearfield, town	116	252
Bear Bluff, town	8	66	Cutler, town	51	134
Black River Falls, city	709	574	Elroy, city	235	209
Brockway, town	394	271	Finley, town	9	36
City Point, town	40	58	Fountain, town	99	181
Cleveland, town	64	148	Germantown, town	288	599
Curran, town	65	79	Hustler, village	39	40
Franklin, town	63	69	Kildare, town	114	193
Garden Valley, town	59	140	Kingston, town	1	13
Garfield, town	108	205	Lemonweir, town	270	416
Hixton, town	96	172	Lindina, town	169	211
Hixton, village	69	99	Lisbon, town	161	267
Irving, town	130	182			

Wisconsin gubernatorial vote by county and municipality, November 8, 2022 general election, continued

	Tony Evers*/ Sara Rodriguez (Dem.)	Tim Michels/ Roger Roth (Rep.)		Tony Evers*/ Sara Rodriguez (Dem.)	Tim Michels/ Roger Roth (Rep.)
Lyndon, town	277	316	Holland, town	1,091	1,258
Lyndon Station, village	86	96	Holmen, village	2,817	1,944
Marion, town	53	140	La Crosse, city	14,875	6,792
Mauston, city	673	678	Medary, town	522	442
Necedah, town	304	797	Onalaska, city	4,896	3,931
Necedah, village	150	191	Onalaska, town	1,424	1,463
New Lisbon, city	169	304	Rockland, village (part)	158	168
Orange, town	69	164	Shelby, town	1,644	1,114
Plymouth, town	106	186	Washington, town	121	137
Seven Mile Creek, town	60	103	West Salem, village	1,164	1,115
Summit, town	99	215	**Lafayette**	**3,005**	**3,498**
Union Center, village	24	72	Argyle, town	107	122
Wisconsin Dells, city (part)	0	0	Argyle, village	175	129
Wonewoc, town	118	189	Belmont, town	117	146
Wonewoc, village	103	144	Belmont, village	169	191
Kenosha	**32,176**	**33,068**	Benton, town	66	164
Brighton, town	239	608	Benton, village	213	153
Bristol, village	885	1,646	Blanchard, town	78	80
Genoa City, village (part)	0	0	Blanchardville, village (part)	178	98
Kenosha, city	19,339	13,598	Cuba City, city (part)	65	60
Paddock Lake, village	464	815	Darlington, city	440	316
Paris, town	268	579	Darlington, town	168	248
Pleasant Prairie, village	4,584	5,593	Elk Grove, town	70	108
Randall, town	517	1,041	Fayette, town	71	102
Salem Lakes, village	2,241	4,147	Gratiot, town	90	141
Somers, town	203	244	Gratiot, village	43	47
Somers, village	1,911	2,072	Hazel Green, village (part)	6	2
Twin Lakes, village	945	1,643	Kendall, town	50	98
Wheatland, town	580	1,082	Lamont, town	57	76
Kewaunee	**3,529**	**6,229**	Monticello, town	11	39
Ahnapee, town	173	239	New Diggings, town	83	123
Algoma, city	739	644	Seymour, town	38	97
Carlton, town	159	366	Shullsburg, city	253	191
Casco, town	172	438	Shullsburg, town	52	88
Casco, village	92	182	South Wayne, village	43	95
Franklin, town	156	349	Wayne, town	52	145
Kewaunee, city	536	690	White Oak Springs, town	16	41
Lincoln, town	137	252	Willow Springs, town	119	200
Luxemburg, town	187	583	Wiota, town	175	198
Luxemburg, village	408	720	**Langlade**	**2,958**	**5,966**
Montpelier, town	217	542	Ackley, town	86	177
Pierce, town	166	227	Ainsworth, town	63	228
Red River, town	232	495	Antigo, city	1,111	1,591
West Kewaunee, town	155	502	Antigo, town	212	470
La Crosse	**32,119**	**22,325**	Elcho, town	242	485
Bangor, town	133	160	Evergreen, town	70	171
Bangor, village	340	331	Langlade, town	83	178
Barre, town	251	440	Neva, town	135	288
Burns, town	180	303	Norwood, town	125	340
Campbell, town	1,232	866	Parrish, town	20	46
Farmington, town	403	584	Peck, town	37	145
Greenfield, town	563	559	Polar, town	162	401
Hamilton, town	505	718	Price, town	34	72

Wisconsin gubernatorial vote by county and municipality, November 8, 2022 general election, continued

	Tony Evers*/ Sara Rodriguez (Dem.)	Tim Michels/ Roger Roth (Rep.)		Tony Evers*/ Sara Rodriguez (Dem.)	Tim Michels/ Roger Roth (Rep.)
Rolling, town	219	519	Valders, village	113	301
Summit, town	21	56	Whitelaw, village	123	260
Upham, town	133	329			
Vilas, town	18	88	**Marathon**	**25,163**	**35,860**
White Lake, village	49	77	Abbotsford, city (part)	36	61
Wolf River, town	138	305	Athens, village	196	336
			Bergen, town	166	271
Lincoln	**5,226**	**8,084**	Berlin, town	143	390
Birch, town	71	155	Bern, town	55	166
Bradley, town	537	852	Bevent, town	204	351
Corning, town	116	318	Birnamwood, village (part)	4	9
Harding, town	68	139	Brighton, town	48	170
Harrison, town	180	347	Cassel, town	159	337
King, town	244	353	Cleveland, town	193	586
Merrill, city	1,672	1,797	Colby, city (part)	84	115
Merrill, town	505	953	Day, town	169	378
Pine River, town	326	678	Dorchester, village (part)	0	0
Rock Falls, town	114	256	Easton, town	185	477
Russell, town	105	177	Eau Pleine, town	103	252
Schley, town	116	320	Edgar, village	253	407
Scott, town	227	475	Elderon, town	88	246
Skanawan, town	106	142	Elderon, village	22	41
Somo, town	20	39	Emmet, town	162	312
Tomahawk, city	645	764	Fenwood, village	15	55
Tomahawk, town	98	179	Frankfort, town	74	201
Wilson, town	76	140	Franzen, town	72	211
			Green Valley, town	97	215
Manitowoc	**13,937**	**21,573**	Guenther, town	55	149
Cato, town	253	586	Halsey, town	57	205
Centerville, town	119	235	Hamburg, town	109	300
Cleveland, village	254	439	Harrison, town	41	117
Cooperstown, town	193	496	Hatley, village	97	209
Eaton, town	116	344	Hewitt, town	81	250
Francis Creek, village	106	213	Holton, town	71	278
Franklin, town	173	477	Hull, town	66	218
Gibson, town	234	461	Johnson, town	89	233
Kellnersville, village	49	80	Knowlton, town	387	717
Kiel, city (part)	665	996	Kronenwetter, village	1,587	2,285
Kossuth, town	344	704	Maine, village	545	932
Liberty, town	182	508	Marathon, town	141	422
Manitowoc, city	6,108	6,688	Marathon City, village	258	479
Manitowoc, town	195	368	Marshfield, city (part)	226	190
Manitowoc Rapids, town	444	876	McMillan, town	430	653
Maple Grove, town	70	325	Mosinee, city	765	1172
Maribel, village	44	95	Mosinee, town	357	782
Meeme, town	243	572	Norrie, town	157	350
Mishicot, town	194	446	Plover, town	94	222
Mishicot, village	231	411	Reid, town	221	443
Newton, town	322	842	Rib Falls, town	128	396
Reedsville, village	145	327	Rib Mountain, town	1,700	2,297
Rockland, town	117	383	Rietbrock, town	106	324
St. Nazianz, village	82	216	Ringle, town	334	623
Schleswig, town	351	749	Rothschild, village	1,193	1,312
Two Creeks, town	73	154	Schofield, city	410	425
Two Rivers, city	2,084	2,446	Spencer, town	221	505
Two Rivers, town	310	575			

Wisconsin gubernatorial vote by county and municipality, November 8, 2022 general election, continued

	Tony Evers*/ Sara Rodriguez (Dem.)	Tim Michels/ Roger Roth (Rep.)		Tony Evers*/ Sara Rodriguez (Dem.)	Tim Michels/ Roger Roth (Rep.)
Spencer, village	239	441	Springfield, town	163	282
Stettin, town	457	936	Westfield, town	158	265
Stratford, village	227	463	Westfield, village	177	225
Texas, town	294	622	**Menominee**	**979**	**254**
Unity, village (part)	19	57	Menominee, town	979	254
Wausau, city	8,090	6,500			
Wausau, town	411	794	**Milwaukee**	**246,073**	**97,471**
Weston, town	99	238	Bayside, village (part)	1915	661
Weston, village	2,756	3,458	Brown Deer, village	4,271	1,497
Wien, town	117	276	Cudahy, city	4,228	2,958
			Fox Point, village	3,070	1,268
Marinette	**6,110**	**12,164**	Franklin, city	8,387	9,453
Amberg, town	117	281	Glendale, city	5,453	1,845
Athelstane, town	84	225	Greendale, village	4,053	3,558
Beaver, town	134	453	Greenfield, city	8,886	7,390
Beecher, town	114	301	Hales Corners, village	1,831	1,949
Coleman, village	79	230	Milwaukee, city (part)	143,023	31,903
Crivitz, village	145	232	Oak Creek, city	7,853	8,068
Dunbar, town	74	235	River Hills, village	601	447
Goodman, town	116	187	St. Francis, city	2,955	1,660
Grover, town	193	631	Shorewood, village	6,755	1,080
Lake, town	183	431	South Milwaukee, city	4,482	3,869
Marinette, city	1,539	1,874	Wauwatosa, city	18,548	7,838
Middle Inlet, town	144	328	West Allis, city	12,747	9,283
Niagara, city	208	369	West Milwaukee, village	814	319
Niagara, town	118	331	Whitefish Bay, village	6,201	2,425
Pembine, town	120	308			
Peshtigo, city	455	775	**Monroe**	**6,931**	**10,153**
Peshtigo, town	811	1,331	Adrian, town	113	272
Porterfield, town	286	602	Angelo, town	190	384
Pound, town	143	481	Byron, town	178	300
Pound, village	19	113	Cashton, village	155	235
Silver Cliff, town	110	251	Clifton, town	75	111
Stephenson, town	550	1,368	Glendale, town	103	198
Wagner, town	116	238	Grant, town	52	165
Wausaukee, town	192	463	Greenfield, town	104	223
Wausaukee, village	60	126	Jefferson, town	99	169
			Kendall, village	69	92
Marquette	**2,697**	**4,549**	La Grange, town	333	617
Buffalo, town	205	313	Lafayette, town	52	117
Crystal Lake, town	103	196	Leon, town	167	366
Douglas, town	158	255	Lincoln, town	104	277
Endeavor, village	63	97	Little Falls, town	240	414
Harris, town	154	251	Melvina, village	11	24
Mecan, town	157	243	New Lyme, town	29	66
Montello, city	258	310	Norwalk, village	65	93
Montello, town	209	379	Oakdale, town	107	251
Moundville, town	97	139	Oakdale, village	37	73
Neshkoro, town	81	248	Ontario, village (part)	0	0
Neshkoro, village	54	112	Portland, town	149	257
Newton, town	58	159	Ridgeville, town	89	133
Oxford, town	157	304	Rockland, village (part)	0	0
Oxford, village	93	126	Scott, town	13	22
Packwaukee, town	245	445	Sheldon, town	50	163
Shields, town	107	200	Sparta, city	1,662	1,602

Wisconsin gubernatorial vote by county and municipality, November 8, 2022 general election, continued

	Tony Evers*/ Sara Rodriguez (Dem.)	Tim Michels/ Roger Roth (Rep.)		Tony Evers*/ Sara Rodriguez (Dem.)	Tim Michels/ Roger Roth (Rep.)
Sparta, town	582	808	Pine Lake, town	650	755
Tomah, city	1,406	1,586	Rhinelander, city	1,621	1,196
Tomah, town	244	445	Schoepke, town	104	157
Warrens, village	69	109	Stella, town	159	173
Wellington, town	108	126	Sugar Camp, town	386	717
Wells, town	83	182	Three Lakes, town	547	922
Wilton, town	68	151	Woodboro, town	193	305
Wilton, village	100	91	Woodruff, town	493	646
Wyeville, village	25	31	**Outagamie**	**39,572**	**45,601**
			Appleton, city (part)	15,688	10,976
Oconto	**5,910**	**13,363**	Bear Creek, village	35	72
Abrams, town	346	775	Black Creek, town	164	499
Bagley, town	27	145	Black Creek, village	195	361
Brazeau, town	211	600	Bovina, town	142	432
Breed, town	98	261	Buchanan, town	1,502	1,946
Chase, town	462	1,113	Center, town	644	1,476
Doty, town	73	143	Cicero, town	176	338
Gillett, city	173	303	Combined Locks, village	840	1,036
Gillett, town	113	429	Dale, town	429	1,114
How, town	68	208	Deer Creek, town	59	204
Lakewood, town	170	366	Ellington, town	432	1,260
Lena, town	83	256	Freedom, town	883	1,994
Lena, village	75	150	Fox Crossing, village	0	0
Little River, town	130	380	Grand Chute, town	5,268	5,410
Little Suamico, town	827	2,028	Greenville, village	2,397	4,075
Maple Valley, town	78	243	Harrison, village (part)	0	0
Morgan, town	143	404	Hortonia, town	171	408
Mountain, town	200	316	Hortonville, village	525	898
Oconto, city	665	983	Howard, village (part)	0	0
Oconto, town	191	494	Kaukauna, city (part)	3,326	3,415
Oconto Falls, city	425	710	Kaukauna, town	189	549
Oconto Falls, town	198	468	Kimberly, village	1,657	1,606
Pensaukee, town	226	522	Liberty, town	106	322
Pulaski, village (part)	0	0	Little Chute, village	2,253	2,551
Riverview, town	190	311	Maine, town	129	272
Spruce, town	117	322	Maple Creek, town	63	202
Stiles, town	232	553	New London, city (part)	193	383
Suring, village	41	136	Nichols, village	16	68
Townsend, town	231	468	Oneida, town	749	897
Underhill, town	117	276	Osborn, town	201	480
			Seymour, city	599	910
Oneida	**8,667**	**11,297**	Seymour, town	142	444
Cassian, town	274	404	Shiocton, village	90	242
Crescent, town	510	653	Vandenbroek, town	245	646
Enterprise, town	67	151	Wrightstown, village (part)	64	115
Hazelhurst, town	342	456			
Lake Tomahawk, town	240	405	**Ozaukee**	**23,104**	**28,827**
Little Rice, town	67	144	Bayside, village (part)	45	27
Lynne, town	23	58	Belgium, town	276	576
Minocqua, town	1,199	1,817	Belgium, village	363	833
Monico, town	35	116	Cedarburg, city	3,564	3,585
Newbold, town	752	898	Cedarburg, town	1,425	2,483
Nokomis, town	339	517	Fredonia, town	257	942
Pelican, town	653	784	Fredonia, village	300	789
Piehl, town	13	23	Grafton, town	1,019	1,716

Wisconsin gubernatorial vote by county and municipality, November 8, 2022 general election, continued

	Tony Evers*/ Sara Rodriguez (Dem.)	Tim Michels/ Roger Roth (Rep.)		Tony Evers*/ Sara Rodriguez (Dem.)	Tim Michels/ Roger Roth (Rep.)
Grafton, village	3,015	3,630	Black Brook, town	226	429
Mequon, city	7,372	7,486	Bone Lake, town	144	223
Newburg, village (part)	7	30	Centuria, village	82	151
Port Washington, city	3,152	3,147	Clam Falls, town	107	137
Port Washington, town	306	625	Clayton, town	176	301
Saukville, town	287	813	Clayton, village	54	133
Saukville, village	743	1,210	Clear Lake, town	88	308
Thiensville, village	973	935	Clear Lake, village	136	311
Pepin	**1,280**	**1,990**	Dresser, village	115	211
Albany, town	109	163	Eureka, town	268	593
Durand, city	301	456	Farmington, town	298	670
Durand, town	90	233	Frederic, village	183	219
Frankfort, town	59	89	Garfield, town	283	485
Lima, town	84	179	Georgetown, town	212	281
Pepin, town	165	203	Johnstown, town	112	116
Pepin, village	178	164	Laketown, town	169	296
Stockholm, town	73	58	Lincoln, town	415	731
Stockholm, village	40	28	Lorain, town	49	96
Waterville, town	105	264	Luck, town	163	304
Waubeek, town	76	153	Luck, village	184	231
Pierce	**7,967**	**9,779**	McKinley, town	58	135
Bay City, village	50	97	Milltown, town	213	329
Clifton, town	574	706	Milltown, village	112	192
Diamond Bluff, town	85	148	Osceola, town	543	928
El Paso, town	126	189	Osceola, village	513	604
Ellsworth, town	199	359	St. Croix Falls, city	483	489
Ellsworth, village	456	658	St. Croix Falls, town	199	368
Elmwood, village	107	177	Sterling, town	104	207
Gilman, town	213	285	Turtle Lake, village (part)	4	14
Hartland, town	114	291	West Sweden, town	122	217
Isabelle, town	42	99	**Portage**	**17,947**	**15,361**
Maiden Rock, town	116	197	Alban, town	180	282
Maiden Rock, village	26	33	Almond, town	111	250
Martell, town	260	336	Almond, village	51	108
Oak Grove, town	387	758	Amherst, town	373	432
Plum City, village	82	133	Amherst, village	291	255
Prescott, city	838	995	Amherst Junction, village	83	120
River Falls, city (part)	2,549	1,671	Belmont, town	109	212
River Falls, town	613	643	Buena Vista, town	222	419
Rock Elm, town	76	135	Carson, town	268	457
Salem, town	76	146	Dewey, town	245	308
Spring Lake, town	102	198	Eau Pleine, town	217	351
Spring Valley, village (part)	253	308	Grant, town	347	622
Trenton, town	292	493	Hull, town	1,500	1,372
Trimbelle, town	252	515	Junction City, village	55	88
Union, town	79	209	Lanark, town	345	487
Polk	**7,587**	**12,548**	Linwood, town	277	352
Alden, town	525	941	Milladore, village (part)	3	1
Amery, city	541	622	Nelsonville, village	65	33
Apple River, town	181	342	New Hope, town	240	181
Balsam Lake, town	236	475	Park Ridge, village	239	114
Balsam Lake, village	148	209	Pine Grove, town	103	188
Beaver, town	141	250	Plover, town	291	453
			Plover, village	3,343	2,758

Wisconsin gubernatorial vote by county and municipality, November 8, 2022 general election, continued

	Tony Evers*/ Sara Rodriguez (Dem.)	Tim Michels/ Roger Roth (Rep.)		Tony Evers*/ Sara Rodriguez (Dem.)	Tim Michels/ Roger Roth (Rep.)
Rosholt, village	73	122	Eagle, town	71	137
Sharon, town	458	731	Forest, town	83	80
Stevens Point, city	7,246	3,394	Henrietta, town	122	87
Stockton, town	691	918	Ithaca, town	116	146
Whiting, village	521	353	Lone Rock, village	151	159
			Marshall, town	112	143
Price	**2,596**	**4,369**	Orion, town	120	112
Catawba, town	46	96	Richland, town	230	334
Catawba, village	25	34	Richland Center, city	1,003	803
Eisenstein, town	140	204	Richwood, town	112	104
Elk, town	223	352	Rockbridge, town	161	152
Emery, town	60	111	Sylvan, town	72	133
Fifield, town	202	346	Viola, village (part)	101	68
Flambeau, town	97	211	Westford, town	105	125
Georgetown, town	25	46	Willow, town	82	123
Hackett, town	29	64	Yuba, village	17	11
Harmony, town	44	74			
Hill, town	59	143	**Rock**	**37,755**	**26,722**
Kennan, town	38	110	Avon, town	108	188
Kennan, village	29	40	Beloit, city	5,820	3,543
Knox, town	65	119	Beloit, town	1,724	1,707
Lake, town	286	344	Bradford, town	186	298
Ogema, town	97	254	Brodhead, city (part)	30	10
Park Falls, city	396	486	Center, town	297	261
Phillips, city	226	284	Clinton, town	147	289
Prentice, town	71	151	Clinton, village	315	467
Prentice, village	89	168	Edgerton, city (part)	1,681	796
Spirit, town	59	124	Evansville, city	1,822	769
Worcester, town	290	608	Footville, village	213	192
			Fulton, town	1,052	919
Racine	**38,241**	**42,359**	Harmony, town	794	622
Burlington, city (part)	2,131	2,507	Janesville, city	16,137	9,656
Burlington, town	1,047	2,101	Janesville, town	1,045	1,010
Caledonia, village	5,545	7,431	Johnstown, town	160	214
Dover, town	528	1,240	La Prairie, town	171	238
Elmwood Park, village	151	124	Lima, town	274	277
Mount Pleasant, village	6,749	6,829	Magnolia, town	179	180
North Bay, village	77	70	Milton, city	1,540	1,019
Norway, town	1,164	3,365	Milton, town	804	815
Racine, city	14,705	6,950	Newark, town	321	501
Raymond, village	660	1,609	Orfordville, village	331	272
Rochester, village	600	1,484	Plymouth, town	267	350
Sturtevant, village	992	1,142	Porter, town	348	229
Union Grove, village	713	1,370	Rock, town	617	543
Waterford, town	1,012	2,606	Spring Valley, town	146	201
Waterford, village	1,036	1,828	Turtle, town	563	723
Wind Point, village	613	491	Union, town	663	433
Yorkville, village	518	1,212			
			Rusk	**2,180**	**4,120**
Richland	**3,354**	**3,562**	Atlanta, town	78	223
Akan, town	89	112	Big Bend, town	94	187
Bloom, town	90	111	Big Falls, town	29	56
Boaz, village	25	28	Bruce, village	116	179
Buena Vista, town	295	363	Cedar Rapids, town	7	18
Cazenovia, village (part)	59	48	Conrath, village	17	15
Dayton, town	138	183	Dewey, town	111	191

Statistics and Reference: Elections | 599

Wisconsin gubernatorial vote by county and municipality, November 8, 2022 general election, continued

	Tony Evers*/ Sara Rodriguez (Dem.)	Tim Michels/ Roger Roth (Rep.)		Tony Evers*/ Sara Rodriguez (Dem.)	Tim Michels/ Roger Roth (Rep.)
Flambeau, town	153	331	Springfield, town	147	280
Glen Flora, village	9	20	Stanton, town	164	277
Grant, town	110	214	Star Prairie, town	566	1209
Grow, town	28	157	Star Prairie, village	92	159
Hawkins, town	25	34	Troy, town	1,301	1,693
Hawkins, village	58	69	Warren, town	333	520
Hubbard, town	27	68	Wilson, village	23	56
Ingram, village	10	17	Woodville, village	184	287
Ladysmith, city	446	579			
Lawrence, town	34	102	**Sauk**	**15,285**	**13,348**
Marshall, town	35	154	Baraboo, city	3,023	1,867
Murry, town	42	65	Baraboo, town	506	468
Richland, town	34	59	Bear Creek, town	147	168
Rusk, town	126	196	Cazenovia, village (part)	3	3
Sheldon, village	31	65	Dellona, town	380	504
South Fork, town	18	35	Delton, town	533	527
Strickland, town	55	89	Excelsior, town	389	462
Stubbs, town	112	178	Fairfield, town	305	314
Thornapple, town	97	280	Franklin, town	155	190
Tony, village	11	35	Freedom, town	99	149
True, town	49	82	Greenfield, town	284	267
Washington, town	82	128	Honey Creek, town	205	188
Weyerhaeuser, village	27	61	Ironton, town	98	160
Wilkinson, town	8	23	Ironton, village	27	59
Willard, town	83	160	La Valle, town	337	508
Wilson, town	18	50	La Valle, village	43	79
			Lake Delton, village	526	558
St. Croix	**18,516**	**24,968**	Lime Ridge, village	40	34
Baldwin, town	133	355	Loganville, village	55	74
Baldwin, village	643	961	Merrimac, town	397	330
Cady, town	120	282	Merrimac, village	159	109
Cylon, town	97	215	North Freedom, village	104	116
Deer Park, village	21	71	Plain, village	172	205
Eau Galle, town	186	406	Prairie du Sac, town	291	273
Emerald, town	102	247	Prairie du Sac, village	1,395	792
Erin Prairie, town	122	223	Reedsburg, city	1,804	1,714
Forest, town	65	237	Reedsburg, town	231	335
Glenwood, town	106	236	Rock Springs, village	46	80
Glenwood City, city	150	292	Sauk City, village	1,091	577
Hammond, town	373	845	Spring Green, town	523	433
Hammond, village	372	387	Spring Green, village	636	236
Hudson, city	3,650	3,148	Sumpter, town	175	157
Hudson, town	1,916	2,576	Troy, town	184	238
Kinnickinnic, town	411	562	Washington, town	124	192
New Richmond, city	1,817	2,048	West Baraboo, village	334	253
North Hudson, village	989	1,037	Westfield, town	77	174
Pleasant Valley, town	101	195	Winfield, town	180	274
Richmond, town	627	1,172	Wisconsin Dells, city (part)	52	58
River Falls, city (part)	1,094	815	Woodland, town	155	223
Roberts, village	336	432	**Sawyer**	**3,734**	**4,735**
Rush River, town	86	182	Bass Lake, town	605	470
St. Joseph, town	986	1,330	Couderay, town	72	62
Somerset, town	802	1,569	Couderay, village	14	25
Somerset, village	401	661	Draper, town	70	67
Spring Valley, village (part)	0	3	Edgewater, town	111	236

Wisconsin gubernatorial vote by county and municipality, November 8, 2022 general election, continued

	Tony Evers*/ Sara Rodriguez (Dem.)	Tim Michels/ Roger Roth (Rep.)		Tony Evers*/ Sara Rodriguez (Dem.)	Tim Michels/ Roger Roth (Rep.)
Exeland, village	32	46	**Sheboygan**	**22,325**	**30,679**
Hayward, city	401	490	Adell, village	54	184
Hayward, town	746	879	Cascade, village	96	254
Hunter, town	166	200	Cedar Grove, village	253	863
Lenroot, town	356	420	Elkhart Lake, village	341	320
Meadowbrook, town	16	62	Glenbeulah, village	97	137
Meteor, town	31	65	Greenbush, town	283	573
Ojibwa, town	66	113	Herman, town	245	680
Radisson, town	78	140	Holland, town	320	1,046
Radisson, village	26	39	Howards Grove, village	680	1,107
Round Lake, town	295	419	Kohler, village	567	666
Sand Lake, town	215	283	Lima, town	410	1,222
Spider Lake, town	128	174	Lyndon, town	258	606
Weirgor, town	52	140	Mitchell, town	199	494
Winter, town	204	335	Mosel, town	141	284
Winter, village	50	70	Oostburg, village	297	1,439
			Plymouth, city	1,848	2,241
Shawano	**5,853**	**11,875**	Plymouth, town	588	1,194
Almon, town	63	208	Random Lake, village	249	550
Angelica, town	245	647	Rhine, town	498	846
Aniwa, town	59	194	Russell, town	41	153
Aniwa, village	29	55	Scott, town	222	821
Bartelme, town	203	65	Sheboygan, city	9,513	7,548
Belle Plaine, town	282	627	Sheboygan, town	1,935	2,430
Birnamwood, town	107	216	Sheboygan Falls, city	1,741	2,236
Birnamwood, village (part)	103	171	Sheboygan Falls, town	305	688
Bonduel, village	162	435	Sherman, town	182	678
Bowler, village	42	58	Waldo, village	72	165
Cecil, village	82	194	Wilson, town	890	1,254
Eland, village	46	54			
Fairbanks, town	51	218	**Taylor**	**2,262**	**6,296**
Germania, town	44	108	Aurora, town	20	129
Grant, town	79	331	Browning, town	74	323
Green Valley, town	126	389	Chelsea, town	79	275
Gresham, village	87	122	Cleveland, town	28	94
Hartland, town	74	287	Deer Creek, town	50	240
Herman, town	91	244	Ford, town	23	90
Hutchins, town	59	194	Gilman, village	56	96
Lessor, town	137	506	Goodrich, town	46	202
Maple Grove, town	141	337	Greenwood, town	66	260
Marion, city (part)	3	6	Grover, town	21	103
Mattoon, village	41	91	Hammel, town	77	291
Morris, town	64	136	Holway, town	44	205
Navarino, town	53	163	Jump River, town	35	107
Pella, town	111	356	Little Black, town	132	365
Pulaski, village (part)	24	39	Lublin, village	12	34
Red Springs, town	225	177	Maplehurst, town	33	113
Richmond, town	259	709	McKinley, town	25	147
Seneca, town	78	177	Medford, city	671	949
Shawano, city	1,343	1,653	Medford, town	299	955
Tigerton, village	99	188	Molitor, town	54	129
Washington, town	295	657	Pershing, town	26	49
Waukechon, town	131	374	Rib Lake, town	94	287
Wescott, town	567	1,022	Rib Lake, village	75	216
Wittenberg, town	127	273	Roosevelt, town	47	108
Wittenberg, village	121	194	Stetsonville, village	62	151

Wisconsin gubernatorial vote by county and municipality, November 8, 2022 general election, continued

	Tony Evers*/ Sara Rodriguez (Dem.)	Tim Michels/ Roger Roth (Rep.)		Tony Evers*/ Sara Rodriguez (Dem.)	Tim Michels/ Roger Roth (Rep.)
Taft, town	38	93	Union, town	102	91
Westboro, town	75	285	Viola, village (part)	37	30
Trempealeau	**5,281**	**6,813**	Viroqua, city	1,345	746
Albion, town	104	211	Viroqua, town	470	467
Arcadia, city	240	338	Webster, town	179	119
Arcadia, town	273	522	Westby, city	556	417
Blair, city	193	198	Wheatland, town	144	165
Burnside, town	77	96	Whitestown, town	99	126
Caledonia, town	182	261	**Vilas**	**5,088**	**7,983**
Chimney Rock, town	54	85	Arbor Vitae, town	757	1,107
Dodge, town	84	134	Boulder Junction, town	295	452
Eleva, village	118	150	Cloverland, town	251	478
Ettrick, town	275	365	Conover, town	296	533
Ettrick, village	94	132	Eagle River, city	292	398
Gale, town	368	500	Lac du Flambeau, town	776	569
Galesville, city	347	353	Land O'Lakes, town	183	379
Hale, town	203	328	Lincoln, town	517	954
Independence, city	152	215	Manitowish Waters, town	170	343
Lincoln, town	116	170	Phelps, town	245	534
Osseo, city	370	348	Plum Lake, town	149	240
Pigeon, town	136	174	Presque Isle, town	232	313
Pigeon Falls, village	87	80	St. Germain, town	443	800
Preston, town	146	241	Washington, town	360	674
Strum, village	216	220	Winchester, town	122	209
Sumner, town	172	243			
Trempealeau, town	423	548	**Walworth**	**18,569**	**26,700**
Trempealeau, village	434	457	Bloomfield, town	253	358
Unity, town	107	165	Bloomfield, village	501	1,143
Whitehall, city	310	279	Burlington, city (part)	1	0
Vernon	**6,597**	**6,409**	Darien, town	215	495
Bergen, town	362	354	Darien, village	213	330
Chaseburg, village	61	68	Delavan, city	1,360	1,381
Christiana, town	192	282	Delavan, town	973	1,479
Clinton, town	102	111	East Troy, town	703	1,660
Coon, town	204	207	East Troy, village	829	1,395
Coon Valley, village	199	168	Elkhorn, city	1,622	2,116
De Soto, village (part)	59	47	Fontana-on-Geneva Lake, village	459	607
Forest, town	94	139	Geneva, town	1,093	1,637
Franklin, town	224	300	Genoa City, village (part)	365	642
Genoa, town	178	185	Lafayette, town	367	747
Genoa, village	59	49	La Grange, town	496	861
Greenwood, town	73	105	Lake Geneva, city	1,676	1,751
Hamburg, town	224	284	Linn, town	497	839
Harmony, town	134	179	Lyons, town	596	1,112
Hillsboro, city	234	263	Mukwonago, village (part)	38	56
Hillsboro, town	114	189	Richmond, town	396	578
Jefferson, town	280	293	Sharon, town	152	303
Kickapoo, town	126	121	Sharon, village	202	338
La Farge, village	148	157	Spring Prairie, town	339	923
Liberty, town	102	87	Sugar Creek, town	701	1,299
Ontario, village (part)	58	108	Troy, town	459	931
Readstown, village	55	81	Walworth, town	250	573
Stark, town	107	97	Walworth, village	500	594
Sterling, town	98	185	Whitewater, city (part)	2,211	1,214
Stoddard, village	178	189			

Wisconsin gubernatorial vote by county and municipality, November 8, 2022 general election, continued

	Tony Evers*/ Sara Rodriguez (Dem.)	Tim Michels/ Roger Roth (Rep.)		Tony Evers*/ Sara Rodriguez (Dem.)	Tim Michels/ Roger Roth (Rep.)
Whitewater, town	347	468	Chenequa, village	95	254
Williams Bay, village	755	870	Delafield, city	1,696	2,467
Washburn	**3,198**	**5,032**	Delafield, town	1,788	3,449
Barronett, town	72	141	Dousman, village	451	770
Bashaw, town	148	410	Eagle, town	640	1,518
Bass Lake, town	91	180	Eagle, village	292	841
Beaver Brook, town	147	225	Elm Grove, village	1,869	2,058
Birchwood, town	106	275	Genesee, town	1,443	3,096
Birchwood, village	67	107	Hartland, village	1,942	3,033
Brooklyn, town	73	107	Lac La Belle, village (part)	66	147
Casey, town	113	159	Lannon, village	370	575
Chicog, town	77	112	Lisbon, town	1,945	4,316
Crystal, town	47	102	Menomonee Falls, village	9,688	11,495
Evergreen, town	240	378	Merton, town	1,497	3,700
Frog Creek, town	18	46	Merton, village	567	1,380
Gull Lake, town	49	70	Milwaukee, city (part)	0	0
Long Lake, town	162	239	Mukwonago, town	1,300	3,267
Madge, town	149	182	Mukwonago, village (part)	1,405	2,637
Minong, town	242	311	Muskego, city	4,738	9,582
Minong, village	74	113	Nashotah, village	272	530
Sarona, town	72	157	New Berlin, city	9,617	13,473
Shell Lake, city	321	301	North Prairie, village	355	897
Spooner, city	392	448	Oconomowoc, city	4,095	5,911
Spooner, town	138	255	Oconomowoc, town	1,679	3,638
Springbrook, town	73	150	Oconomowoc Lake, village	86	279
Stinnett, town	32	84	Ottawa, town	761	1,596
Stone Lake, town	81	171	Pewaukee, city	3,383	5,803
Trego, town	214	309	Pewaukee, village	1,705	2,316
Washington	**22,698**	**50,749**	Summit, village	1,106	2,105
Addison, town	419	1,515	Sussex, village	2,417	3,756
Barton, town	438	1,247	Vernon, village	1,287	3,345
Erin, town	621	1,860	Wales, village	631	994
Farmington, town	452	1,743	Waukesha, city	14,626	15,786
Germantown, town	58	95	Waukesha, village	1,733	3,375
Germantown, village	4,507	6,929	**Waupaca**	**7,990**	**14,939**
Hartford, city (part)	2,409	4,628	Bear Creek, town	63	315
Hartford, town	482	1,624	Big Falls, village	8	25
Jackson, town	516	1,951	Caledonia, town	282	674
Jackson, village	1,271	2,791	Clintonville, city	627	867
Kewaskum, town	132	559	Dayton, town	538	908
Kewaskum, village (part)	564	1,554	Dupont, town	69	222
Milwaukee, city (part)	0	0	Embarrass, village	40	107
Newburg, village (part)	117	397	Farmington, town	766	1,001
Polk, town	558	1,863	Fremont, town	96	280
Richfield, village	2,075	5,527	Fremont, village	103	278
Slinger, village	884	2,181	Harrison, town	71	171
Trenton, town	630	2,131	Helvetia, town	101	276
Wayne, town	244	1,088	Iola, town	178	348
West Bend, city	5,516	8,953	Iola, village	221	322
West Bend, town	805	2,113	Larrabee, town	183	411
Waukesha	**88,564**	**134,212**	Lebanon, town	226	565
Big Bend, village	228	539	Lind, town	207	535
Brookfield, city	10,794	12,651	Little Wolf, town	148	533
Brookfield, town	1,646	2,160	Manawa, city	134	324
Butler, village	351	473	Marion, city (part)	139	333

Wisconsin gubernatorial vote by county and municipality, November 8, 2022 general election, continued

	Tony Evers*/ Sara Rodriguez (Dem.)	Tim Michels/ Roger Roth (Rep.)		Tony Evers*/ Sara Rodriguez (Dem.)	Tim Michels/ Roger Roth (Rep.)
Matteson, town	128	349	Nekimi, town	230	557
Mukwa, town	500	990	Nepeuskun, town	123	288
New London, city (part)	816	1,206	Omro, city	621	892
Ogdensburg, village	14	56	Omro, town	484	893
Royalton, town	174	516	Oshkosh, city	13,724	10,386
St. Lawrence, town	116	234	Oshkosh, town	634	867
Scandinavia, town	244	340	Poygan, town	214	527
Scandinavia, village	70	87	Rushford, town	227	645
Union, town	99	274	Utica, town	228	513
Waupaca, city	1,114	1,256	Vinland, town	438	672
Waupaca, town	213	396	Winchester, town	347	720
Weyauwega, city	200	402	Winneconne, town	523	1,039
Weyauwega, town	66	212	Winneconne, village	457	815
Wyoming, town	36	126	Wolf River, town	217	562
Waushara	**3,766**	**7,459**	**Wood**	**36,512**	**37,242**
Aurora, town	147	375	Arpin, town	1,817	2,043
Berlin, city (part)	20	30	Arpin, village	188	105
Bloomfield, town	132	406	Auburndale, town	565	910
Coloma, town	133	232	Auburndale, village	858	1,536
Coloma, village	55	127	Biron, village	4,124	4,335
Dakota, town	161	359	Cameron, town	3,042	2,490
Deerfield, town	175	241	Cary, town	6,533	5,366
Hancock, town	82	198	Cranmoor, town	918	1,081
Hancock, village	68	103	Dexter, town	230	557
Leon, town	253	561	Grand Rapids, town	123	288
Lohrville, village	48	124	Hansen, town	621	892
Marion, town	368	731	Hewitt, village	484	893
Mount Morris, town	221	460	Hiles, town	13,724	10,386
Oasis, town	58	155	Lincoln, town	634	867
Plainfield, town	59	165	Marshfield, city (part)	214	527
Plainfield, village	115	181	Marshfield, town	227	645
Poy Sippi, town	103	326	Milladore, town	228	513
Redgranite, village	123	247	Milladore, village (part)	438	672
Richford, town	53	179	Nekoosa, city	347	720
Rose, town	135	222	Pittsville, city	523	1,039
Saxeville, town	188	377	Port Edwards, town	457	815
Springwater, town	303	487	Port Edwards, village	217	562
Warren, town	115	200	Remington, town	42	87
Wautoma, city	261	346	Richfield, town	251	500
Wautoma, town	253	452	Rock, town	140	334
Wild Rose, village	137	175	Rudolph, town	184	365
Winnebago	**36,512**	**37,242**	Rudolph, village	86	122
Algoma, town	1,817	2,043	Saratoga, town	846	1,619
Appleton, city (part)	188	105	Seneca, town	226	324
Black Wolf, town	565	910	Sherry, town	112	270
Clayton, town	858	1,536	Sigel, town	191	359
Fox Crossing, village	4,124	4,335	Vesper, village	74	167
Menasha, city (part)	3,042	2,490	Wisconsin Rapids, city	3,232	3,411
Neenah, city	6,533	5,366	Wood, town	127	272
Neenah, town	918	1,081	**State totals**	**1,358,774**	**1,268,535**

Note: Independent and write-in candidates for governor received the following votes: Joan Ellis Beglinger (Ind.)–27,198; Seth Haskin (Ind.)–104.

*Incumbent. Dem.–Democrat; Rep.–Republican; Ind.–Independent

Source: Official records of the Wisconsin Elections Commission.

County vote for Wisconsin attorney general, August 9, 2022 partisan primary

	Josh Kaul* (Democrat)	Republican Adam Jarchow	Karen Mueller	Eric Toney	Total
Adams	1,409	1,079	783	928	4,211
Ashland	1,587	334	252	316	2,497
Barron	2,272	2,323	1,399	1,096	7,101
Bayfield	2,559	694	413	623	4,305
Brown	17,031	7,527	6,935	10,424	42,008
Buffalo	767	785	757	645	2,959
Burnett	947	1,308	464	342	3,061
Calumet	3,002	2,317	1,699	2,998	10,029
Chippewa	4,075	2,335	3,775	1,747	11,948
Clark	1,179	1,434	1,128	1,068	4,812
Columbia	4,146	2,062	1,895	2,250	10,368
Crawford	1,473	455	410	471	2,811
Dane	90,500	8,925	7,537	11,681	118,996
Dodge	3,712	5,497	3,666	4,997	17,873
Door	3,427	1,119	973	1,591	7,125
Douglas	4,697	1,090	721	928	7,463
Dunn	2,962	1,457	1,195	878	6,492
Eau Claire	10,331	2,922	2,783	2,138	18,206
Florence	176	267	174	277	894
Fond du Lac	4,766	3,190	2,343	10,670	20,970
Forest	382	394	298	384	1,459
Grant	2,614	1,368	1,155	1,465	6,611
Green	3,281	937	1,083	1,317	6,633
Green Lake	784	842	559	1,395	3,581
Iowa	2,124	535	717	815	4,203
Iron	472	254	198	299	1,223
Jackson	1,380	592	530	602	3,105
Jefferson	5,153	3,596	3,305	3,367	15,466
Juneau	1,260	1,127	1,315	1,113	4,826
Kenosha	11,355	5,934	4,105	6,048	27,543
Kewaunee	1,062	949	904	1,073	3,996
La Crosse	12,349	2,688	2,630	3,027	20,737
Lafayette	835	386	497	560	2,278
Langlade	903	1,142	637	938	3,620
Lincoln	1,513	1,356	1,185	1,255	5,312
Manitowoc	4,367	3,248	2,691	3,926	14,264
Marathon	8,161	6,155	4,410	5,908	24,678
Marinette	1,771	1,972	1,850	2,447	8,057
Marquette	853	877	686	805	3,227
Menominee	43	25	47	56	173
Milwaukee	84,313	17,605	9,665	17,184	129,268
Monroe	2,479	1,224	1,320	1,636	6,673
Oconto	1,741	1,824	1,714	2,431	7,719
Oneida	2,703	2,068	1,368	1,697	7,846
Outagamie	11,699	6,861	4,928	7,625	31,113
Ozaukee	7,563	6,151	3,255	5,604	22,622
Pepin	417	258	279	199	1,153
Pierce	2,567	1,303	1,002	724	5,604
Polk	2,239	3,417	839	649	7,144
Portage	7,883	2,198	2,081	2,627	14,816
Price	915	860	592	651	3,018
Racine	12,237	8,476	5,411	8,043	34,253
Richland	1,132	542	598	675	2,950
Rock	12,786	3,398	3,763	3,811	23,815
Rusk	749	871	699	572	2,895
Sauk	5,000	1,823	1,978	2,315	11,116

County vote for Wisconsin attorney general, August 9, 2022 partisan primary, continued

	Josh Kaul* (Democrat)	Republican Adam Jarchow	Karen Mueller	Eric Toney	Total
Sawyer	1,069	960	943	806	3,785
Shawano	1,580	2,346	1,513	2,719	8,158
Sheboygan	7,104	6,327	3,487	5,681	22,641
St. Croix	5,001	3,951	2,155	1,802	12,933
Taylor	653	1467	729	899	3,749
Trempealeau	1,843	964	1,118	885	4,817
Vernon	2,411	1,009	1,148	1,496	6,075
Vilas	1,642	1,485	1,094	1,377	5,612
Walworth	5,701	5,515	4,195	4,725	20,195
Washburn	980	1,187	626	573	3,370
Washington	6,998	11,618	5,050	9,867	33,536
Waukesha	28,789	30,502	13,506	28,177	101,178
Waupaca	2,214	2,788	1,798	3,302	10,126
Waushara	1,151	1,292	944	1,457	4,844
Winnebago	11,122	5,321	4,065	6,700	27,276
Wood	4,663	2,937	2,614	3,125	13,362
Total	461,024	220,045	152,581	222,902	1,058,783

Note: County totals include scattered votes.
*Incumbent.
Source: Official records of the Wisconsin Elections Commission.

County vote for Wisconsin attorney general, November 8, 2022 general election

	Josh Kaul* (Dem.)	Eric Toney (Rep.)	Total
Adams	3,820	6,004	9,832
Ashland	3,934	2,961	6,900
Barron	7,490	12,578	20,077
Bayfield	5,238	3,974	9,216
Brown	53,165	59,968	113,213
Buffalo	2,432	3,653	6,086
Burnett	2,877	5,291	8,168
Calumet	9,953	14,834	24,796
Chippewa	12,252	16,709	28,973
Clark	3,927	7,649	11,581
Columbia	13,381	13,655	27,055
Crawford	3,461	3,500	6,962
Dane	229,828	68,665	298,721
Dodge	13,214	25,464	38,678
Door	8,920	8,286	17,213
Douglas	10,324	8,138	18,474
Dunn	8,245	10,107	18,352
Eau Claire	27,853	20,196	48,081
Florence	643	1,865	2,508
Fond du Lac	16,159	29,998	46,161
Forest	1,539	2,608	4,147
Grant	8,675	11,202	19,892

County vote for Wisconsin attorney general, November 8, 2022 general election, continued

	Josh Kaul (Dem.)	Eric Toney (Rep.)	Total
Green	9,000	8,354	17,359
Green Lake	2,796	5,850	8,651
Iowa	6,621	4,935	11,560
Iron	1,252	1,989	3,241
Jackson	3,589	4,377	7,966
Jefferson	16,306	22,015	38,340
Juneau	3,867	6,829	10,703
Kenosha	31,808	33,553	65,406
Kewaunee	3,602	6,259	9,862
La Crosse	31,849	22,789	54,670
Lafayette	2,818	3,710	6,528
Langlade	3,055	5,920	8,975
Lincoln	5,360	7,986	13,350
Manitowoc	14,294	21,282	35,602
Marathon	25,339	35,958	61,315
Marinette	6,219	12,206	18,440
Marquette	2,595	4,690	7,288
Menominee	938	267	1,205
Milwaukee	241,620	101,577	343,569
Monroe	7,016	10,244	17,271
Oconto	6,038	13,361	19,406
Oneida	8,771	11,347	20,131
Outagamie	39,217	45,975	85,192
Ozaukee	22,278	29,727	52,039
Pepin	1,275	2,020	3,295
Pierce	7,787	10,184	17,980
Polk	7,406	13,021	20,427
Portage	17,859	15,430	33,306
Price	2,678	4,345	7,023
Racine	37,788	43,145	81,014
Richland	3,245	3,724	6,975
Rock	35,901	28,450	64,398
Rusk	2,280	4,084	6,367
Sauk	14,705	13,981	28,686
Sawyer	3,634	4,884	8,525
Shawano	5,933	11,909	17,842
Sheboygan	21,987	30,937	52,960
St. Croix	17,910	25,815	43,745
Taylor	2,460	6,183	8,643
Trempealeau	5,259	6,928	12,195
Vernon	6,622	6,460	13,091
Vilas	5,098	8,053	13,151
Walworth	17,989	27,623	45,638
Washburn	3,144	5,172	8,319
Washington	22,205	51,344	73,549
Waukesha	84,882	137,012	222,013
Waupaca	8,076	15,009	23,093
Waushara	3,775	7,480	11,255
Winnebago	36,119	37,718	73,894
Wood	13,774	18,953	32,738
Total	**1,333,369**	**1,298,369**	**2,633,277**

Note: County totals include scattered votes.
*Incumbent. Dem.–Democrat; Rep.–Republican.
Source: Official records of the Wisconsin Elections Commission.

County vote for Wisconsin state treasurer, August 9, 2022 partisan primary

	Democrat			Republican		Constitution	
	Gillian M. Battino	Aaron Richardson	Angelito Tenorio	John S. Leiber	Orlando Owens	Andrew Zuelke	Total
Adams	432	668	252	1,754	921	1	4,041
Ashland	461	703	365	556	257	—	2,350
Barron	632	1,011	553	2,577	2,004	1	6,788
Bayfield	851	939	610	1,021	580	—	4,015
Brown	5,234	6,964	4,060	14,648	8,343	6	39,353
Buffalo	208	358	159	1,413	676	—	2,816
Burnett	332	393	191	1,077	785	1	2,780
Calumet	934	1,235	698	4,193	2,356	1	9,441
Chippewa	1,155	1,841	887	4,515	2,586	2	11,014
Clark	285	584	237	2,089	1,299	3	4,501
Columbia	1,606	1,542	789	3,681	1,983	1	9,620
Crawford	380	704	291	762	495	—	2,634
Dane	35,160	26,644	22,514	15,892	9,386	19	110,002
Dodge	1,361	1,526	766	9,035	3,863	5	16,557
Door	1,208	1,246	699	2,324	1,037	—	6,526
Douglas	1,557	2,103	1,020	1,599	926	3	7,233
Dunn	944	1,141	754	1,775	1,518	—	6,132
Eau Claire	3,085	3,795	2,630	4,038	3,163	3	16,756
Florence	64	79	41	428	239	—	851
Fond du Lac	1,336	2,017	1,049	9,364	4,486	9	18,277
Forest	87	197	74	735	278	1	1,373
Grant	908	1,052	509	2,527	1,221	3	6,233
Green	1,163	1,278	660	2,009	1,116	1	6,247
Green Lake	259	334	174	1,823	808	—	3,402
Iowa	803	768	425	1,218	720	—	3,940
Iron	176	197	73	470	243	—	1,161
Jackson	372	683	294	1,032	567	3	2,951
Jefferson	1,990	1,790	1,151	6,355	3,004	4	14,340
Juneau	418	564	260	2,142	1,199	2	4,591
Kenosha	4,127	4,186	2,775	9,386	5,592	3	26,156
Kewaunee	290	541	198	1,876	860	3	3,777
La Crosse	3,879	4,548	2,846	5,062	2,632	6	19,014
Lafayette	269	371	152	880	457	2	2,131
Langlade	255	440	178	1,733	791	—	3,397
Lincoln	446	735	269	2,355	1,175	1	4,988
Manitowoc	1,206	2,141	909	6,376	2,844	3	13,509
Marathon	3,059	3,153	1,618	9,607	5,723	8	23,208
Marinette	492	917	329	3,803	2,130	3	7,689
Marquette	346	326	171	1,553	691	1	3,091
Menominee	38	60	44	81	38	—	263
Milwaukee	28,666	29,198	24,450	26,532	12,865	36	122,202
Monroe	767	1,159	463	2,482	1,536	5	6,422
Oconto	467	890	372	3,863	1,810	3	7,414
Oneida	883	1,153	505	3,177	1,584	2	7,318
Outagamie	3,604	4,564	2,879	11,773	6,292	9	29,121
Ozaukee	2,990	2,392	1,676	8,952	4,263	—	20,335
Pepin	77	212	109	425	277	—	1,101
Pierce	926	869	667	1,377	1,506	1	5,357
Polk	774	967	489	2,360	2,014	3	6,607
Portage	2,436	3,136	1,775	3,924	2,326	8	13,633
Price	254	460	154	1,254	694	1	2,817
Racine	4,360	4,675	3,012	14,398	5,615	12	32,155
Richland	370	474	197	1,117	577	1	2,738
Rock	4,578	5,000	2,544	6,749	3,501	5	22,420

County vote for Wisconsin state treasurer, August 9, 2022 partisan primary, continued

	Democrat			Republican		Constitution	
	Gillian M. Battino	Aaron Richardson	Angelito Tenorio	John S. Leiber	Orlando Owens	Andrew Zuelke	Total
Rusk	207	368	160	1,286	710	1	2,734
Sauk	1,906	1,758	1,026	3,774	1,966	1	10,431
Sawyer	356	419	256	1,664	831	1	3,533
Shawano	480	736	346	4,208	2,026	—	7,796
Sheboygan	2,512	2,830	1,662	9,736	4,423	6	21,211
St. Croix	1,906	1,827	1,170	3,787	3,419	1	12,139
Taylor	163	349	125	2,018	892	1	3,548
Trempealeau	431	952	377	1,758	1,053	—	4,582
Vernon	740	970	582	2,176	1,272	—	5,748
Vilas	556	670	313	2,501	1,158	—	5,209
Walworth	2,191	2,147	1,216	9,137	4,301	7	19,060
Washburn	256	451	226	1,343	839	1	3,122
Washington	2,663	2,486	1,584	16,556	7,356	2	30,650
Waukesha	10,849	9,753	6,907	42,801	20,721	10	91,287
Waupaca	627	1,065	457	5,005	2,309	5	9,493
Waushara	335	541	252	2,428	1,080	—	4,636
Winnebago	3,384	4,505	2,473	9,611	5,219	4	25,272
Wood	1,380	2,155	914	5,448	2,657	6	12,579
Total	159,902	168,905	111,012	357,384	186,084	230	985,818

Note: County totals include scattered votes.
—Represents zero.
Source: Official records of the Wisconsin Elections Commission.

County vote for Wisconsin state treasurer, November 8, 2022 general election

	Aaron Richardson (Dem.)	John S. Leiber (Rep.)	Andrew Zuelke (Con.)	Total
Adams	3,570	5,973	273	9,817
Ashland	3,842	2,882	161	6,889
Barron	7,088	12,493	422	20,010
Bayfield	5,126	3,924	162	9,214
Brown	48,879	60,249	2,826	112,008
Buffalo	2,233	3,622	162	6,017
Burnett	2,790	5,208	169	8,167
Calumet	8,965	14,993	584	24,547
Chippewa	10,990	16,882	769	28,648
Clark	3,451	7,749	351	11,555
Columbia	12,756	13,284	731	26,782
Crawford	3,199	3,542	164	6,908
Dane	222,685	67,812	4,812	295,523
Dodge	12,115	25,121	1,001	38,237
Door	8,255	8,422	309	16,990
Douglas	10,119	7,922	421	18,477
Dunn	7,742	10,054	457	18,253
Eau Claire	26,029	20,406	1,249	47,709
Florence	605	1,856	33	2,494
Fond du Lac	15,019	29,297	1,139	45,465

County vote for Wisconsin state treasurer, November 8, 2022 general election, continued

	Aaron Richardson (Dem.)	John S. Leiber (Rep.)	Andrew Zuelke (Con.)	Total
Forest	1,339	2,649	93	4,081
Grant	8,314	10,936	459	19,717
Green	8,632	8,001	479	17,125
Green Lake	2,392	5,784	257	8,434
Iowa	6,314	4,835	279	11,430
Iron	1,210	1,987	39	3,236
Jackson	3,267	4,367	242	7,876
Jefferson	15,318	21,706	973	38,020
Juneau	3,717	6,656	313	10,688
Kenosha	30,260	33,360	1,351	65,003
Kewaunee	3,215	6,279	249	9,748
La Crosse	29,333	23,263	1,447	54,084
Lafayette	2,702	3,614	138	6,454
Langlade	2,733	5,921	234	8,888
Lincoln	4,775	8,144	352	13,273
Manitowoc	12,788	21,521	962	35,291
Marathon	22,967	36,143	1,527	60,655
Marinette	5,593	12,215	455	18,269
Marquette	2,426	4,564	226	7,220
Menominee	875	270	32	1,177
Milwaukee	232,370	100,787	5,712	339,202
Monroe	6,355	10,268	504	17,133
Oconto	5,373	13,370	503	19,248
Oneida	7,978	11,460	472	19,927
Outagamie	35,768	46,313	2,291	84,372
Ozaukee	20,738	29,926	812	51,509
Pepin	1,202	2,002	67	3,271
Pierce	7,531	9,965	460	17,962
Polk	7,124	12,696	513	20,333
Portage	16,765	15,447	858	33,080
Price	2,440	4,335	176	6,951
Racine	35,643	43,005	1,623	80,328
Richland	3,075	3,658	152	6,895
Rock	34,556	27,571	1,895	64,044
Rusk	2,028	4,147	162	6,338
Sauk	14,022	13,838	726	28,586
Sawyer	3,488	4,876	116	8,481
Shawano	5,311	11,997	405	17,713
Sheboygan	20,339	30,895	1,235	52,498
St. Croix	17,135	25,501	1,076	43,727
Taylor	2,097	6,237	239	8,573
Trempealeau	4,819	6,908	318	12,051
Vernon	6,092	6,519	378	12,991
Vilas	4,663	8,156	210	13,031
Walworth	16,706	27,516	1,003	45,248
Washburn	3,014	5,092	178	8,285
Washington	20,307	50,928	1,391	72,626
Waukesha	78,005	136,992	3,506	218,596
Waupaca	7,376	14,985	578	22,943
Waushara	3,390	7,365	376	11,131
Winnebago	32,965	37,843	2,162	73,016
Wood	12,646	19,049	934	32,635
Total	**1,254,949**	**1,293,553**	**57,333**	**2,607,103**

Note: County totals include scattered votes.
Con.–Constitution; Dem.–Democrat; Rep.–Republican.
Source: Official records of the Wisconsin Elections Commission.

County vote for Wisconsin secretary of state, August 9, 2022 partisan primary

	Democrat		Republican			Libertarian	
	Doug La Follette*	Alexia Sabor	Amy Lynn Loudenbeck	Justin D. Schmidtka	Jay Schroeder	Neil Harmon	Total
Adams	998	420	1,244	399	1,120	4	4,195
Ashland	1,069	583	324	142	395	3	2,524
Barron	1,493	814	1,695	889	2,060	6	6,966
Bayfield	1,747	901	688	246	747	3	4,341
Brown	11,001	6,442	10,127	3,556	10,456	34	41,686
Buffalo	517	250	906	340	891	5	2,912
Burnett	578	377	832	360	750	1	2,898
Calumet	1,945	1,153	2,718	883	3,180	15	9,909
Chippewa	2,779	1,414	2,899	1,324	3,180	8	11,622
Clark	868	339	1,322	526	1,672	3	4,732
Columbia	3,084	1,295	2,840	906	2,233	3	10,377
Crawford	1,091	424	511	242	551	—	2,820
Dane	56,939	34,760	14,226	3,918	8,581	76	118,787
Dodge	2,543	1,309	6,043	1,830	5,579	10	17,314
Door	2,272	1,207	1,530	418	1,622	8	7,064
Douglas	3,060	1,891	1,129	403	1,119	10	7,635
Dunn	1,896	1,134	1,247	603	1,576	1	6,457
Eau Claire	6,243	4,117	3,490	1,155	2,905	20	17,959
Florence	131	70	241	120	335	1	898
Fond du Lac	3,102	1,644	6,195	2,020	6,183	11	19,170
Forest	284	114	436	151	468	3	1,456
Grant	1,819	855	1,590	593	1,693	7	6,564
Green	2,336	1,025	1,721	482	1,100	5	6,683
Green Lake	580	269	1,228	361	1,103	2	3,543
Iowa	1,481	683	916	319	768	4	4,178
Iron	336	147	276	148	322	—	1,229
Jackson	971	454	705	299	668	4	3,103
Jefferson	3,407	1,836	4,736	1,423	3,658	9	15,099
Juneau	892	510	1,542	476	1,424	2	4,852
Kenosha	7,290	4,512	7,207	2,041	6,401	25	27,551
Kewaunee	715	369	1,155	352	1,323	2	3,923
La Crosse	7,829	4,602	3,910	1,229	3,078	17	20,693
Lafayette	641	210	601	255	552	4	2,263
Langlade	660	269	1,029	393	1,212	—	3,563
Lincoln	1,089	478	1,443	451	1,815	1	5,278
Manitowoc	3,028	1,509	4,373	1,398	3,819	11	14,167
Marathon	5,644	2,633	6,527	2,222	7,294	8	24,369
Marinette	1,354	550	2,551	961	2,605	8	8,042
Marquette	635	267	1,025	382	899	5	3,216
Menominee	105	41	57	16	51	—	272
Milwaukee	53,632	33,664	20,636	5,560	15,313	85	129,280
Monroe	1,735	816	1,965	575	1,592	6	6,694
Oconto	1,338	550	2,226	816	2,792	12	7,744
Oneida	1,960	869	2,328	686	1,951	4	7,809
Outagamie	7,477	4,533	7,496	2,562	8,850	23	30,941
Ozaukee	4,905	2,756	7,234	1,641	5,192	12	21,798
Pepin	267	161	256	151	312	—	1,148
Pierce	1,488	1,122	1,073	587	1,289	2	5,572
Polk	1,440	916	1,660	802	2,075	8	6,901
Portage	5,595	2,555	2,808	1,087	2,734	16	14,818
Price	693	252	894	303	834	2	2,978
Racine	7,907	4,735	9,965	2,713	8,237	30	33,661
Richland	850	300	711	231	803	3	2,901
Rock	8,799	4,304	8,364	1,199	2,346	20	25,071
Rusk	574	199	749	332	970	—	2,826

County vote for Wisconsin secretary of state, August 9, 2022 partisan primary, continued

	Democrat		Republican			Libertarian	
	Doug La Follette*	Alexia Sabor	Amy Lynn Loudenbeck	Justin D. Schmidtka	Jay Schroeder	Neil Harmon	Total
Sauk.	3,536	1,584	2,785	879	2,311	13	11,108
Sawyer	663	431	1,061	328	1,263	1	3,748
Shawano	1,062	555	2,573	897	2,949	10	8,046
Sheboygan. . . .	4,778	2,596	6,749	1,913	6,107	19	22,190
St. Croix.	2,828	2,280	2,764	1,302	3,412	13	12,614
Taylor	466	203	1,253	445	1,310	4	3,681
Trempealeau . .	1,341	545	1,206	497	1,200	1	4,796
Vernon	1,674	834	1,534	487	1,536	9	6,082
Vilas	1,169	509	1,871	461	1,521	1	5,545
Walworth.	3,545	2,284	9,599	1,434	3,938	13	20,853
Washburn	649	342	896	381	998	3	3,275
Washington . . .	4,530	2,588	11,394	3,263	10,472	21	32,268
Waukesha	18,672	10,814	34,461	8,074	25,294	58	97,577
Waupaca	1,583	733	3,363	1,014	3,280	9	10,009
Waushara.	873	356	1,630	521	1,455	3	4,838
Winnebago . . .	6,956	4,233	6,361	2,196	7,115	23	26,938
Wood	3,336	1,458	3,840	1,277	3,352	6	13,287
Total.	300,773	171,954	264,940	78,846	228,191	769	1,047,307

Note: County totals include scattered votes.
*Incumbent; —Represents zero.
Source: Official records of the Wisconsin Elections Commission.

County vote for Wisconsin secretary of state, November 8, 2022 general election

	Doug La Follette* (Dem.)	Amy Lynn Loudenbeck (Rep.)	Neil Harmon (Lib.)	Sharyl R. McFarland (Ind.)	Total
Adams	3,540	5,940	160	202	9,845
Ashland.	3,777	2,842	105	185	6,914
Barron.	7,079	12,322	378	276	20,059
Bayfield.	5,131	3,811	145	150	9,240
Brown.	49,962	58,303	2,582	1,822	112,708
Buffalo	2,216	3,645	115	112	6,089
Burnett	2,814	5,145	130	93	8,182
Calumet	9,331	14,572	503	325	24,734
Chippewa	11,190	16,519	694	457	28,868
Clark.	3,522	7,642	206	186	11,561
Columbia.	13,102	12,980	625	389	27,110
Crawford	3,226	3,484	130	102	6,944
Dane	222,397	63,324	6,034	5,788	297,676
Dodge	12,525	24,677	786	569	38,557
Door.	8,451	8,187	276	254	17,169
Douglas.	10,049	7,735	420	292	18,505
Dunn	7,655	9,950	433	347	18,385
Eau Claire.	25,742	19,906	1,261	1,009	47,935
Florence	615	1,833	35	17	2,500
Fond du Lac	15,684	28,803	839	664	45,994
Forest	1,364	2,573	87	74	4,099
Grant	8,496	10,634	431	317	19,885

County vote for Wisconsin secretary of state, November 8, 2022 general election, continued

	Doug La Follette* (Dem.)	Amy Lynn Loudenbeck (Rep.)	Neil Harmon (Lib.)	Sharyl R. McFarland (Ind.)	Total
Green	8,839	7,860	333	312	17,351
Green Lake	2,579	5,758	162	107	8,608
Iowa	6,431	4,662	247	175	11,520
Iron	1,208	1,951	39	42	3,240
Jackson	3,283	4,352	163	149	7,947
Jefferson	15,566	21,220	872	572	38,244
Juneau	3,706	6,599	185	173	10,665
Kenosha	30,360	32,650	1,355	1,028	65,419
Kewaunee	3,361	6,155	165	140	9,825
La Crosse	29,488	22,391	1,444	1,127	54,472
Lafayette	2,846	3,474	112	77	6,509
Langlade	2,794	5,904	154	108	8,960
Lincoln	4,948	7,953	258	192	13,353
Manitowoc	13,461	20,767	728	540	35,508
Marathon	23,789	35,496	1,122	807	61,230
Marinette	5,743	12,048	338	233	18,368
Marquette	2,523	4,534	127	92	7,276
Menominee	904	253	18	29	1,204
Milwaukee	232,340	95,754	6,774	6,453	341,589
Monroe	6,410	10,223	354	246	17,240
Oconto	5,611	13,059	446	244	19,365
Oneida	8,139	11,215	405	298	20,063
Outagamie	36,455	45,216	1,945	1,369	84,985
Ozaukee	21,275	28,882	1,059	553	51,795
Pepin	1,183	1,985	76	39	3,283
Pierce	7,418	9,752	461	361	17,994
Polk	7,068	12,576	438	330	20,412
Portage	16,865	15,127	659	651	33,310
Price	2,477	4,303	128	106	7,014
Racine	36,151	41,781	1,661	1,230	80,866
Richland	3,141	3,592	130	102	6,972
Rock	34,044	28,588	1,160	925	64,736
Rusk	2,072	4,098	101	101	6,374
Sauk	14,243	13,440	560	445	28,688
Sawyer	3,525	4,783	100	103	8,514
Shawano	5,400	11,772	362	274	17,808
Sheboygan	20,974	30,003	1,109	860	52,961
St. Croix	17,041	24,836	1,258	662	43,805
Taylor	2,190	6,150	160	118	8,618
Trempealeau	4,827	6,884	257	193	12,164
Vernon	6,101	6,443	307	247	13,101
Vilas	4,732	8,008	196	161	13,100
Walworth	16,507	27,641	871	606	45,641
Washburn	3,042	4,986	143	122	8,294
Washington	21,041	50,072	1,448	755	73,316
Waukesha	81,432	133,635	4,369	2,141	221,651
Waupaca	7,522	14,734	453	332	23,047
Waushara	3,547	7,336	184	190	11,257
Winnebago	33,431	36,811	2,070	1,270	73,619
Wood	12,847	18,767	572	512	32,703
Total	1,268,748	1,261,306	54,413	41,532	2,626,943

Note: County totals include scattered votes.
*Incumbent. Dem.–Democrat; Rep.–Republican; Lib.–Libertarian; Ind.–Independent.
Source: Official records of the Wisconsin Elections Commission.

District vote for Wisconsin state senators, partisan and special primaries

Senate district	Assembly districts	Party	Candidates	Vote
August 9, 2022 partisan primary				
1	1, 2, 3	Democratic	Andrea Gage-Michaels	11,519
		Republican	André Jacque*	20,968
3	7, 8, 9	Democratic	Tim Carpenter*	8,216
		Republican	Angel Sanchez	3,621
5	13, 14, 15	Democratic	Jessica Katzenmeyer	9,086
		Democratic	Tom Palzewicz	7,651
		Republican	Rob Brian Hutton	20,714
7	19, 20, 21	Democratic	Chris Larson*	19,784
		Republican	Red Arnold	4,209
		Republican	Peter Gilbert	5,080
9[1]	25, 26, 27	Democratic	Jeanette Deschene	2,431
		Republican	Devin LeMahieu*	16,963
		Republican	Ruth Villareal	4,342
11	31, 32, 33	Democratic	Steven J. Doelder	10,510
		Republican	Stephen Nass*	20,399
13	37, 38, 39	Republican	John Jagler*	23,630
15	43, 44, 45	Democratic	Mark Spreitzer	16,048
		Republican	Mark Trofimchuck	9,473
17	49, 50, 51	Democratic	Pat Skogen	10,092
		Republican	Howard Marklein*	17,008
19	55, 56, 57	Democratic	Kristin M. Alfheim	11,407
		Republican	Rachael Cabral-Guevara	11,905
		Republican	Andrew K. Thomsen	6,806
21	61, 62, 63	Republican	Jay Stone	6,831
		Republican	Van H. Wanggaard*	20,194
23[2]	67, 68, 69	Republican	Jesse James	10,411
		Republican	Sandra Scholz	2,588
		Republican	Brian Westrate	7,809
25	73, 74, 75	Democratic	Kelly Westlund	14,764
		Republican	Romaine Robert Quinn	16,643
27	79, 80, 81	Democratic	Dianne Hesselbein	25,352
		Republican	Robert Relph	10,074
29	85, 86, 87	Democratic	Bob Look	9,624
		Republican	Brent Jacobson	9,302
		Republican	Jon P. Kaiser	4,428
		Republican	Cory Tomczyk	10,419
31	91, 92, 93	Democratic	Jeff Smith*	13,896
		Republican	David Estenson	13,834
33	97, 98, 99	Republican	Chris Kapenga*	29,504
February 21, 2023 partisan primary				
8	22, 23, 24	Democratic	Jodi Habush Sinykin	17,670
		Republican	Janel Brandtjen	6,870
		Republican	Dan Knodl	13,996
		Republican	Van Mobley	3,743

*Incumbent.
1. Write-in candidate Jarrod Schroeder (Dem.) received 106 votes.   2. Write-in candidate Dan Hardy (Dem.) received 905 votes.
Source: Official records of the Wisconsin Elections Commission.

Statistics and Reference: Elections | 615

District vote for Wisconsin state senators, general and special elections

Senate district	Assembly districts	Party	Candidates	Vote	% of total[1]
November 8, 2022 general election					
1	1, 2, 3	Democratic	Andrea Gage-Michaels	35,363	40.45
		Republican	André Jacque*	52,009	59.49
3	7, 8, 9	Democratic	Tim Carpenter*	27,958	68.98
		Republican	Angel Sanchez	12,536	30.93
5	13, 14, 15	Democratic	Jessica Katzenmeyer	42,962	46.66
		Republican	Rob Hutton	49,025	53.24
7	19, 20, 21	Democratic	Chris Larson*	54,252	67.25
		Republican	Peter Gilbert	26,333	32.64
9	25, 26, 27	Democratic	Jarrod Schroeder (write-in)	1,237	2.00
		Republican	Devin LeMahieu*	57,836	93.64
11	31, 32, 33	Democratic	Steven J. Doelder	32,087	41.60
		Republican	Steve Nass*	44,974	58.31
13	37, 38, 39	Republican	John Jagler*	61,817	96.69
15	43, 44, 45	Democratic	Mark Spreitzer	46,192	61.38
		Republican	Mark Trofimchuck	29,006	38.54
17	49, 50, 51	Democratic	Pat Skogen	29,398	39.82
		Republican	Howard Marklein*	44,405	60.15
19	55, 56, 57	Democratic	Kristin M. Alfheim	36,447	45.94
		Republican	Rachael Cabral-Guevara	42,858	54.02
21	61, 62, 63	Republican	Van H. Wanggaard*	61,621	94.14
23	67, 68, 69	Republican	Jesse James	56,391	94.73
25	73, 74, 75	Democratic	Kelly Westlund	35,652	42.96
		Republican	Romaine Robert Quinn	47,293	56.99
27	79, 80, 81	Democratic	Dianne H. Hesselbein	65,618	67.97
		Republican	Robert Relph	30,863	31.97
29	85, 86, 87	Democratic	Bob Look	29,798	37.50
		Republican	Cory Tomczyk	49,602	62.43
31	91, 92, 93	Democratic	Jeff Smith*	38,936	50.42
		Republican	David Estenson	38,239	49.52
33	97, 98, 99	Republican	Chris Kapenga*	67,323	96.40
April 4, 2023 special election					
8	22, 23, 24	Democratic	Jodi Habush Sinykin	37,200	49.11
		Republican	Dan Knodl	38,492	50.81

*Incumbent.
1. Percentages do not add up to 100, as scattered votes have been omitted.
Source: Official records of the Wisconsin Elections Commission.

District vote for Wisconsin state representatives, partisan and special primaries

Assem. district	Party	Candidates	Vote
August 9, 2022 partisan primary			
1	Dem.	Roberta Thelen	4,692
	Rep.	Joel C. Kitchens*	6,893
	Rep.	Milt Swagel	1,992
2	Dem.	Renee Gasch	3,334
	Rep.	Shae Sortwell*	6,179
3	Rep.	Ron Tusler*	6,703
4	Dem.	Ashton Arndorfer	2,019
	Dem.	Derek Teague	2,121
	Rep.	David Steffen*	6,034
5	Dem.	Joseph Van Deurzen	2,669
	Rep.	Joy Goeben	3,153
	Rep.	Tim Greenwood	2,166
	Rep.	Kraig Knaack	548
6	Dem.	William J. Switalla	2,125
	Rep.	Matthew Kyle Albert	836
	Rep.	Craig Arrowood	1,076
	Rep.	David Kohn	1,255
	Rep.	Nathan J. Michael	1,813
	Rep.	Dean Martin Neubert	2,084
	Rep.	Peter Schmidt	2,155
7	Dem.	Daniel G. Riemer*	4,202
	Rep.	Zachary Marshall	2,262
8	Dem.	Sylvia Ortiz-Velez*	1,424
9	Dem.	Marisabel Cabrera*	2,356
	Rep.	Ryan Michael Antczak	905
10	Dem.	Bryan L. Kennedy	3,621
	Dem	Darrin Madison	5,069
11	Dem.	Dora Drake*	4,135
12	Dem.	LaKeshia N. Myers*	4,957
	Rep.	Greg Canady	1,123
13	Dem.	Sarah Harrison	5,035
	Rep.	Tom Michalski	4,958
	Rep.	Erik Ngutse	4,822
14	Dem.	Robyn Vining*	6,371
	Rep.	Keva Turner	3,425
15	Rep.	Dave Maxey	7,646
16	Dem.	Kalan Haywood*	3,704
17	Dem.	Supreme Moore Omokunde*	6,258
	Rep.	Abie Eisenbach	1,024
18	Dem.	Evan Goyke*	5,735
19	Dem.	Ryan Clancy	8,017
20	Dem.	Christine M. Sinicki*	6,909
	Rep.	Scott Hermann	2,868
21	Dem.	Nathan M. Jurowski	3,808
	Rep.	Jessie Rodriguez*	5,310
22	Dem.	Matt Brown	3,610
	Rep.	Janel Brandtjen*	10,205
23	Dem.	Deb Andraca*	8,392
	Rep.	Purnima Nath	4,557
24	Dem.	Bob Tatterson	3,756
	Rep.	Dan Knodl*	9,165
25	Rep.	Paul Tittl*	6,676
26	Dem.	Lisa Salgado	2,775
	Rep.	Terry Katsma*	7,367
27	Rep.	Amy Binsfeld	6,584
28	Dem.	Patty Schachtner	3,078
	Rep.	Gae Magnafici*	5,124
29	Dem.	Danielle Johnson	3,259
	Rep.	Clint Moses*	4,342
30	Dem.	Sarah Yacoub	3,667
	Rep.	Shannon Zimmerman*	4,681
31	Dem.	Brienne Brown	3,353
	Rep.	Jason Dean	1,977
	Rep.	Ellen Schutt	3,245
	Rep.	Maryann Zimmerman	2,405
32	Dem.	Adam Jaramillo	2,951
	Rep.	Tyler August*	6,201
	Rep.	Bart Williams	2,097
33	Dem.	Don Vruwink*	4,316
	Rep.	Scott Johnson	3,293
	Rep.	Dale W. Oppermann	3,087
34	Dem.	Eileen Daniel	4,043
	Rep.	Rob Swearingen*	8,860
35	Rep.	Calvin Callahan *	8,199
36	Dem.	Ben Murray	2,212
	Rep.	Jeffrey L. Mursau*	8,741
37	Dem.	Maureen McCarville	3,719
	Rep.	William Penterman*	6,539
38	Rep.	Barbara Dittrich*	7,633
39	Rep.	Mark L. Born*	9,220
40	Rep.	Kevin Petersen*	8,750
41	Dem.	William Fletcher (write-in)	144
	Rep.	Alex Dallman*	6,241
42	Dem.	Theresa Valencia	2,928
	Rep.	Jon Plumer*	7,053
43	Dem.	Jenna Jacobson	6,015
	Dem.	Matt McIntyre	1,251
	Rep.	Marisa Voelkel	3,759
44	Dem.	Sue Conley*	5,070
	Rep.	Spencer Zimmerman	2,964
45	Dem.	Clinton Anderson	2,431
	Dem.	Ben Dorsheid	1,329
	Rep.	Jeff Klett	2,894
46	Dem.	Syed Abbas	1,895
	Dem.	Analiese Eicher	1,178
	Dem.	Andrew Hysell	1,525

District vote for Wisconsin state representatives, partisan and special primaries, continued

Assem. district	Party	Candidates	Vote
	Dem.	Mike Jacobs	876
	Dem.	Melissa Ratcliff	3,112
	Rep.	Andrew McKinney	2,977
47	Dem.	Jimmy Anderson*	9,059
	Rep.	Lamonte Newsom	2,011
48	Dem.	Samba Baldeh*	11,217
49	Dem.	Lynne Parrott	2,929
	Rep.	Travis Tranel*	4,805
50	Dem.	Michael Leuth	3,026
	Rep.	Tony Kurtz*	6,731
51	Dem.	Leah Spicer	4,073
	Rep.	Todd Novak*	5,318
52	Dem.	Joe Lavrenz	2,534
	Rep.	Lawrence Foster	1,192
	Rep.	Donald R. Hannemann	1,292
	Rep.	Jerry L. O'Connor	4,342
	Rep.	Robert P. Thresher	929
53	Rep.	Michael Schraa*	7,017
54	Dem.	Lori Palmeri	3,864
	Rep.	Donnie Herman	3,817
55	Dem.	Stefanie A. Holt	3,716
	Rep.	Nate Gustafson	6,030
56	Dem.	Patrick Hayden	3,410
	Rep.	Dave Murphy*	6,630
57	Dem.	Lee Snodgrass*	4,335
	Rep.	Andrew Fox	3,396
58	Dem.	Mary Ann Rzeszutek	2,938
	Rep.	Rick Gundrum*	10,584
59	Rep.	Ty Bodden	7,891
	Rep.	Vinny Egle	4,447
60	Dem.	Daniel E. Larsen	3,417
	Rep.	Robert Brooks*	9,064
	Rep.	Samuel Krieg	2,179
61	Dem.	Max Winkels	3,298
	Rep.	Mike Honold	3,785
	Rep.	Amanda Nedweski	5,030
62	Dem.	Anthony Hammes	3,752
	Rep.	Robert Wittke*	7,656
63	Rep.	Robin J. Vos*	5,084
	Rep.	Adam Steen	4,824
64	Dem.	Tip McGuire*	4,522
	Rep.	Ed Hibsch	4,188
65	Dem.	Tod Ohnstad*	4,084
	Rep.	Frank Petrick	2,886
66	Dem.	Greta Neubauer*	3,340
	Lib.	Carl Hutton	8
67	Dem.	Jason D. Bennett	3,745
	Rep.	Rob Summerfield*	6,748
68	Dem.	Nate Otto	3,341

Assem. district	Party	Candidates	Vote
	Rep.	Chris Connell	1,451
	Rep.	Karen Hurd	3,557
	Rep.	Hillarie Roth	1,207
69	Dem.	Lisa Boero	2,886
	Rep.	Donna M. Rozar*	5,745
70	Dem.	Remy Gomez	3,536
	Rep.	Nancy Lynn VanderMeer*	6,269
71	Dem.	Katrina Shankland*	7,362
	Rep.	Robert Glisczinski	1,639
	Rep.	Scott Soik	4,334
72	Dem.	Criste Greening	3,564
	Rep.	Scott S. Krug*	7,294
73	Dem.	Laura R. Gapske	5,569
	Rep.	Scott Luostari	2,081
	Rep.	Angie Sapik	2,872
74	Dem.	John Adams	6,163
	Rep.	Chanz Green	4,327
	Rep.	John A. Schey	2,084
75	Rep.	David Armstrong*	6,460
76	Dem.	Francesca Hong*	8,097
77	Dem.	Shelia Stubbs*	11,537
78	Dem.	Lisa Subeck*	11,169
	Rep.	Matt Neuhaus	2,020
79	Dem.	Alex Joers	7,474
	Dem.	Brad Votava	2,356
	Rep.	Victoria Fueger	2,666
80	Dem.	Mike Bare	4,921
	Dem.	Anna Halverson	2,802
	Dem.	Chad Kemp	2,003
	Dem.	Doug Steinberg	132
	Dem.	Dale Edward Paul Yurs	460
	Rep.	Nathan Graewin	1,526
	Rep.	Jacob D. Luginbuhl	1,935
81	Dem.	Dave Considine*	5,776
	Rep.	Shellie Benish	2,826
	Rep.	Bob Wood	2,139
82	Dem.	Deborah Davis	4,185
	Rep.	Chuck Wichgers*	6,579
83	Rep.	Pat Goldammer	4,810
	Rep.	Nik Rettinger	6,645
84	Dem.	Lu Ann Bird	4,603
	Rep.	Laura Barker	459
	Rep.	Bob Donovan	4,887
	Rep.	David Karst	1,384
85	Dem.	Kristin Conway	3,830
	Rep.	Patrick Snyder*	5,796
86	Rep.	John Spiros*	7,805
87	Dem.	Elizabeth Riley	2,593
	Rep.	Michael Bub	3,563
	Rep.	James W. Edming*	6,121

District vote for Wisconsin state representatives, partisan and special primaries, continued

Assem. district	Party	Candidates	Vote
88	Dem.	Hannah Beauchamp-Pope	3,309
	Rep.	John Macco*	5,544
89	Dem.	Jane Benson	2,583
	Rep.	Elijah Behnke*	7,331
90	Dem.	Kristina Shelton*	3,283
	Rep.	Micah J. Behnke	2,469
91	Dem.	Jodi Emerson*	6,227
	Rep.	Josh Stanley	2,869
92	Dem.	Maria Bamonti	3,420
	Rep.	Ryan T. Owens	1,626
	Rep.	Treig E. Pronschinske*	5,655
93	Dem.	Alison H. Page	3,849
	Rep.	Warren Petryk*	4,960

Assem. district	Party	Candidates	Vote
94	Dem.	Steve Doyle*	5,689
	Rep.	Ryan Huebsch	5,325
95	Dem.	Jill Billings*	6,840
	Rep.	Chris Woodard	2,691
96	Dem.	Mark Fritsche	1,976
	Dem.	Jayne M. Swiggum	2,712
	Rep.	Holly Ottesen Liska	1,351
	Rep.	Loren Oldenburg*	5,439
97	Rep.	Scott Allen*	8,394
98	Dem.	Christina Barry	3,602
	Rep.	Adam Neylon*	7,767
99	Dem.	Alec Thomas Dahms	3,225
	Rep.	Cindi S. Duchow*	11,878

*Incumbent. Assem.–Assembly; Dem.–Democrat; Lib.–Libertarian; Rep.–Republican.
Source: Official records of the Wisconsin Elections Commission.

District vote for Wisconsin state representatives, general and special elections

Assembly district	Party	Candidates	Vote	% of total[1]
November 8, 2022 general election				
1	Democratic	Roberta Thelen	11,916	37.46
	Republican	Joel Kitchens*	19,864	62.45
2	Democratic	Renee Gasch	11,093	40.74
	Republican	Shae Sortwell*	16,112	59.18
3	Republican	Ron Tusler*	21,179	98.33
4	Democratic	Derek Teague	12,287	44.42
	Republican	David Steffen*	15,348	55.49
5	Democratic	Joseph Van Deurzen	10,258	40.17
	Republican	Joy Goeben	15,280	59.83
6	Democratic	William J. Switalla	7,694	29.08
	Republican	Peter Schmidt	14,710	55.60
	Republican	Dean Neubert (write-in)	4,050	15.31
7	Democratic	Daniel G. Riemer*	12,476	61.81
	Republican	Zachary Marshall	7,690	38.10
8	Democratic	Sylvia Ortiz-Velez*	6,573	98.10
9	Democratic	Marisabel Cabrera*	8,644	71.99
	Republican	Ryan Michael Antczak	3,345	27.86
10	Democratic	Darrin Madison	20,730	98.79
11	Democratic	Dora Drake*	14,311	99.00
12	Democratic	LaKeshia N. Myers*	13,770	78.79
	Republican	Greg Canady	3,688	21.10
13	Democratic	Sarah Harrison	14,523	43.66
	Republican	Tom Michalski	18,712	56.26
14	Democratic	Robyn Vining*	17,703	63.35

District vote for Wisconsin state representatives, general and special elections, continued

Assembly district	Party	Candidates	Vote	% of total[1]
14 (cont.)	Republican	Keva Turner	10,219	36.57
15	Republican	Dave Maxey	21,582	95.81
16	Democratic	Kalan Haywood*	14,158	98.75
17	Democratic	Supreme Moore Omokunde*	17,966	83.91
	Republican	Abie Eisenbach	3,410	15.93
18	Democratic	Evan Goyke*	17,306	98.45
19	Democratic	Ryan Clancy	24,193	98.26
20	Democratic	Christine Sinicki*	17,863	66.32
	Republican	Scott Hermann	9,043	33.57
21	Democratic	Nathan M. Jurowski	11,580	45.75
	Republican	Jessie Rodriguez*	13,712	54.18
22	Democratic	Matt Brown	12,210	35.38
	Republican	Janel Brandtjen*	22,278	64.55
23	Democratic	Deb Andraca*	21,236	62.73
	Republican	Purnima Nath	12,589	37.19
24	Democratic	Bob Tatterson	12,311	38.81
	Republican	Dan Knodl*	19,397	61.14
25	Republican	Paul Tittl*	19,344	97.11
26	Democratic	Lisa Salgado	9,492	37.12
	Republican	Terry A. Katsma*	16,061	62.80
27	Republican	Amy Binsfeld	17,132	64.41
	Independent	Chet Gerlach	9,373	35.24
28	Democratic	Patty Schachtner	9,901	37.51
	Republican	Gae Magnafici*	16,494	62.48
29	Democratic	Danielle Johnson	9,523	39.93
	Republican	Clint Moses*	14,321	60.05
30	Democratic	Sarah Yacoub	12,557	41.44
	Republican	Shannon Zimmerman*	17,719	58.48
31	Democratic	Brienne Brown	10,134	40.77
	Republican	Ellen Schutt	14,704	59.15
32	Democratic	Adam Jaramilo	9,269	37.00
	Republican	Tyler August*	15,757	62.89
33	Democratic	Don Vruwink*	13,462	49.49
	Republican	Scott Johnson	13,709	50.40
34	Democratic	Eileen Daniel	12,373	38.20
	Republican	Rob Swearingen*	20,004	61.77
35	Republican	Calvin Callahan*	19,481	69.79
	Independent	Todd Federick	8,403	30.10
36	Democratic	Ben Murray	8,262	29.53
	Republican	Jeffrey L. Mursau*	19,698	70.40
37	Democrat	Maureen McCarville	12,154	44.18
	Republican	William Penterman*	15,343	55.77
38	Republican	Barbara Dittrich*	21,399	95.26
39	Republican	Mark L. Born*	20,284	97.64
	Republican	Steve Rydzewski (write-in)	412	1.98
40	Republican	Kevin Petersen*	19,361	75.29
	Independent	Henry Fries	6,296	24.48
41	Republican	Alex Dallman*	18,736	96.88
42	Democratic	Theresa Valencia	10,969	39.75

District vote for Wisconsin state representatives, general and special elections, continued

Assembly district	Party	Candidates	Vote	% of total[1]
42 (cont.)	Republican	Jon Plumer*	16,608	60.18
43	Democratic	Jenna Jacobson	19,681	62.26
	Republican	Marisa Voelkel	11,903	37.66
44	Democratic	Sue Conley*	14,192	62.44
	Republican	Spencer Zimmerman	8,524	37.50
45	Democratic	Clinton Anderson	11,636	55.75
	Republican	Jeff Klett	9,221	44.18
46	Democratic	Melissa Ratcliff	20,710	69.65
	Republican	Andrew McKinney	9,001	30.27
47	Democratic	Jimmy Anderson*	23,843	79.90
	Republican	Lamonte Newsom	5,975	20.02
48	Democratic	Sambah Baldeh*	27,089	98.44
49	Democratic	Lynne Parrott	8,725	37.34
	Republican	Travis Tranel*	14,626	62.59
50	Democratic	Michael Leuth	8,524	35.45
	Republican	Tony Kurtz*	15,514	64.53
51	Democratic	Leah Spicer	11,546	43.87
	Republican	Todd Novak*	14,760	56.08
52	Democratic	Joe Lavrenz	9,108	37.67
	Republican	Jerry L. O'Connor	15,055	62.26
53	Republican	Michael Schraa*	20,336	97.63
54	Democratic	Lori Palmeri	12,124	53.79
	Republican	Donnie Herman	10,382	46.06
55	Democratic	Stefanie A. Holt	12,571	45.41
	Republican	Nate Gustafson	15,098	54.53
56	Democratic	Patrick Hayden	11,710	40.97
	Republican	Dave Murphy*	16,875	59.03
57	Democratic	Lee Snodgrass*	13,577	59.36
	Republican	Andrew Fox	9,282	40.58
58	Democratic	Mary Ann Rzeszutek	9,047	29.73
	Republican	Rick Gundrum*	21,381	70.27
59	Republican	Ty Bodden	25,716	99.36
60	Democratic	Daniel E. Larsen	11,636	35.20
	Republican	Robert Brooks*	21,396	64.72
61	Democratic	Max Winkels	9,851	35.94
	Republican	Amanda Nedweski	17,542	64.00
62	Democratic	Anthony Hammes	11,445	38.51
	Republican	Robert Wittke*	18,236	61.36
63	Democratic	Joel Jacobsen (write-in)	3,495	15.02
	Republican	Robin J. Vos*	16,977	72.98
	Republican	Adam Steen (write-in)	2,112	9.08
64	Democratic	Tip McGuire*	12,873	56.73
	Republican	Ed Hibsch	9,799	43.19
65	Democratic	Tod Ohnstad*	11,035	61.78
	Republican	Frank Petrick	6,803	38.08
66	Democratic	Greta Neubauer*	11,261	76.21
	Republican	Carl Hutton	3,338	22.61
67	Democratic	Jason D. Bennett	9,807	36.72
	Republican	Rob Summerfield*	16,889	63.23
68	Democratic	Nate Otto	9,273	39.25

District vote for Wisconsin state representatives, general and special elections, continued

Assembly district	Party	Candidates	Vote	% of total[1]
68 (cont.)	Republican	Karen Hurd	14,338	60.68
69	Democratic	Lisa Boero	8,345	35.68
	Republican	Donna M. Rozar*	15,032	64.27
70	Democratic	Remy Gomez	8,669	33.94
	Republican	Nancy Lynn VanderMeer*	16,856	65.99
71	Democratic	Katrina Shankland*	15,930	57.05
	Republican	Scott Soik	11,976	42.89
72	Democratic	Criste Greening	10,027	37.82
	Republican	Scott S. Krug*	16,473	62.14
73	Democratic	Laura R. Gapske	12,778	48.96
	Republican	Angie Sapik	13,268	50.83
74	Democratic	John Adams	14,276	47.13
	Republican	Chanz Green	16,006	52.84
75	Republican	David Armstrong*	20,730	96.56
76	Democratic	Francesca Hong*	27,702	98.39
77	Democratic	Shelia Stubbs*	27,839	98.70
78	Democratic	Lisa Subeck*	26,817	82.02
	Republican	Matt Neuhaus	5,845	17.88
79	Democratic	Alex Joers	24,469	74.11
	Republican	Victoria Fueger	8,514	25.79
80	Democratic	Mike Bare	23,380	69.66
	Republican	Jacob D. Luginbuhl	10,156	30.26
81	Democratic	David Considine*	17,490	58.90
	Republican	Shellile Benish	12,192	41.06
82	Democrat	Deborah Davis	12,715	43.19
	Republican	Chuck Wichgers*	16,705	56.74
83	Republican	Nik Rettinger	24,153	78.60
	Independent	Chaz Self	6,410	20.86
84	Democratic	Lu Ann Bird	12,653	48.95
	Republican	Bob Donovan	13,179	50.98
85	Democratic	Kristin Conway	10,659	43.76
	Republican	Patrick Snyder*	13,689	56.20
86	Republican	John Spiros*	22,224	97.14
87	Democratic	Elizabeth Riley	8,127	30.48
	Republican	James W. Edming*	18,532	69.49
88	Democratic	Hannah Beauchamp-Pope	10,384	41.78
	Republican	John Macco*	14,451	58.14
89	Democratic	Jane Benson	8,800	33.42
	Republican	Elijah Behnke*	17,514	66.52
90	Democratic	Kristina Shelton*	9,885	59.10
	Republican	Micah J. Behnke	6,818	40.77
91	Democratic	Jodi Emerson*	16,465	64.61
	Republican	Josh Stanley	8,995	35.30
92	Democratic	Maria Bamonti	9,053	36.58
	Republican	Treig E. Pronschinske*	15,680	63.36
93	Democratic	Alison H. Page	10,775	40.23
	Republican	Warren L. Petryk*	16,003	59.74
94	Democratic	Steve Doyle*	14,826	51.26
	Republican	Ryan Heubsch	14,070	48.67

District vote for Wisconsin state representatives, general and special elections, continued

Assembly district	Party	Candidates	Vote	% of total[1]
95	Democratic	Jill Billings*	16,897	66.83
	Republican	Chris Woodard	8,366	33.09
96	Democratic	Jayne M. Swiggum	10,483	41.42
	Republican	Loren Oldenburg*	14,814	58.53
97	Republican	Scott Allen*	20,691	96.14
98	Democratic	Christina Barry	11,304	40.72
	Republican	Adam Neylon*	16,439	59.22
99	Republican	Cindi S. Duchow*	24,196	69.55

*Incumbent.
1. Percentages do not add up to 100, as scattered votes have been omitted.
Source: Official records of the Wisconsin Elections Commission.

Personal data on Wisconsin legislators, 2013–23 sessions

	2013 Sen.	2013 Rep.	2015 Sen.	2015 Rep.	2017 Sen.	2017 Rep.	2019 Sen.	2019 Rep.	2021 Sen.	2021 Rep.	2023 Sen.	2023 Rep.[1]
Party affiliation												
Democratic	15	39	14	36	13	35	15	35	12	38	11	35
Republican	18	60	19	63	20	64	18	64	20	60	21	64
Previous legislative service												
Senate	30	—	27	—	30	—	28	—	24	—	25	—
Assembly	25	74	24	74	24	83	26	82	23	82	23	75
Most prior sessions in same house	25	13	26	14	27	12	28	10	17	11	18	12
Occupations												
Full-time legislator	12	35	11	34	24	56	22	48	15	35	12	32
Attorney	3	7	2	7	2	6	2	8	3	8	3	7
Farmer	2	4	1	6	1	7	1	6	1	8	2	9
Other	16	53	19	52	6	30	9	39	13	47	16	51
Education												
High school only	1	5	1	4	—	5	—	8	1	5	2	5
Beyond high school	32	94	32	95	33	94	33	91	31	93	30	94
Bachelor's or associate degree	28	72	28	69	28	74	26	72	26	65	26	72
Advanced degree	9	27	9	24	10	26	9	25	9	27	9	26
Experience on local governing body												
County board	7	18	9	19	9	26	7	19	5	21	8	24
Municipal board	11	30	9	29	16	49	14	41	6	35	8	37
Age (years)[2]												
Oldest	85	72	87	76	89	78	91	80	77	82	79	77
Youngest	32	25	34	24	36	26	31	19	32	21	32	23
Average	57	49	57	48	58	49	58	49	56	51	54	50
Veterans	2	10	3	7	7	10	7	9	6	9	4	10
Women	9	24	11	22	9	22	8	28	10	31	8	33

—Represents zero; Sen.–Senators; Rep.–Representatives.
1. Data do not include Senate District 8, which is vacant at the time of publication. 2. Ages for 2023 session calculated as of January 31, 2023.
Source: Data collected from legislative surveys by Wisconsin Legislative Reference Bureau, March 2023.

Political parties qualifying for Wisconsin ballot status as of November 2022
In the order they appear on the ballot

Democratic Party of Wisconsin

PO Box 1686, Madison, Wisconsin 53701; 608-255-5172; www.wisdems.org

Executive director . . . . Devin Remiker
Senior advisor. . . . . Katie Iliff
Operations director . . . . Sal Cornacchione
Senior digital director. . . . . Bhavik Lathia
Organizing director . . . . Gabbie Stasson
Political director . . . . Nicholas Truog
HR director. . . . . Katie Portis
Finance director . . . . Tina Ignosiak

State Administrative Committee
Party officers . . . . Ben Wikler, Madison, *chair*; Felesia Martin, Milwaukee, *first vice chair*;
Lee Snodgrass, Appleton, *second vice chair*; Meg Andrietsch, Racine, *secretary*;
Randy Udell, Madison, *treasurer*
National committee members. . . . . Martha Love, Milwaukee; Andrew Werthmann, Eau Claire;
Janet Bewley, Mason; Jason Rae, Glendale; Mahlon Mitchell, Fitchburg
College Democrats representative . . . . Margaret Keuler, Madison, *chair*
Young Democrats representative . . . . Kate Haga, Superior, *chair*
High School Democrats representative . . . . Henry Pahlow, Maribel, *chair*
Milwaukee County chair . . . . Chris Sinicki, Milwaukee
At-large members . . . . . . Michelle Bryant, Milwaukee; Michael Childers, La Pointe; Sean Elliot, Madison;
Haben Goitom, Fitchburg; Ryan Greendeer, Black River Falls; Wayde Lawler, Viola;
Matt Mareno, Waukesha; Lisa Noel, Greenleaf; Sherrie Richards-Francar, Manitowoc;
Patricia Ruiz-Cantu, Milwaukee; Kris Sadur, Brussels; Marcia Steele, Oshkosh;
Jessy Tolkan, Milwaukee; Rey Villar, Sturtevant; Yee Leng Xiong, Wausau
County Chairs Association chair. . . . . Sandy Rindy, New Glarus
Assembly representative . . . . Sara Rodriguez, Brookfield
Senate representative . . . . Janis Ringhand, Evansville
CD 1 representatives. . . . . James Foss, Janesville, *chair*; Sally Simpson, Kenosha
CD 2 representatives. . . . . Steve Hansberry, Sun Prairie, *chair*; Pat Skogen, Monroe
CD 3 representatives. . . . . Josefine Jaynes, Readstown, *chair*; Gary Hawley, Stevens Point
CD 4 representatives. . . . . Joshua Taylor, Milwaukee, *chair*; LaKeshia Myers, Milwaukee
CD 5 representatives. . . . . Alicia Halvensleben, Waukesha, *chair*; Justin Koestler
CD 6 representatives. . . . . Debra Dassow, Cedarburg, *chair*; Richard Baker, Poynette
CD 7 representatives. . . . . Kim Butler, Balsam Lake, *chair*; Steven Okonek, Marshfield
CD 8 representatives. Thomas Mandli, Peshtigo, *chair*; Gail Mandli, Peshtigo

Republican Party of Wisconsin

148 E Johnson Street, Madison, WI 53703; 608-257-4765; www.wisgop.org

Executive director . . . . Mark Jefferson
Data and political director . . . . Jordan Moskowitz
Communications director . . . . Rachel Reisner
Operations director . . . . Jordan Wileman
African American outreach director . . . . Khenzer Senat
Grassroots director. . . . . Leslie Hubert
Telemarketing manager. . . . . Rich Dickie

Executive Committee
Party officers . . . . Brian Schimming, Fitchburg, *chair*; Gerard Randall, Milwaukee, *first vice chair*;
Kathy Kiernan, Richfield; *second vice chair*; Jesse Garza, Hudson, *third vice chair*;
vacant, *fourth vice chair*; Tyler August, Lake Geneva, *party secretary*;
Brian Westrate, Fall Creek, *party treasurer*; Tom Schreibel, Madison, *national committeeman*;
Maripat Krueger, Menominee, *national committeewoman*
Immediate past chair . . . . Paul Farrow, Pewaukee
At-large member . . . . Will Martin, Racine

Political parties qualifying for Wisconsin ballot status as of November 2022, continued

Republican Party of Wisconsin, continued

Wisconsin African American Council chair . . . . .Gerard Randall, Milwaukee
Wisconsin Republican Labor Council chair . . . . Van Wanggaard, Racine
Wisconsin Hispanic Heritage Council chair . . . . Domingo Leguizamon, Hillpoint
CD 1 representatives. . . . . Nik Rettinger, Mukwonago, chair; Kim Travis, Williams Bay, vice chair
CD 2 representatives. . . . . .Kim Babler, Madison, chair; John Fandrich, Sylvester, vice chair
CD 3 representatives. . . . . Bill Feehan, La Crosse, chair; Hannah Testin, Stevens Point, vice chair
CD 4 representatives. . . . . Bob Spindell, Milwaukee, chair; Doug Haag, Milwaukee, vice chair
CD 5 representatives. . . . . Kathy Kiernan, Richfield, chair; John Macy, Oconomowoc Lake, vice chair
CD 6 representatives. . . . . .Darryl Carlson, Sheboygan, chair; Al Ott, Forest Junction, vice chair
CD 7 representatives. . . . . Jim Miller, Hayward, chair; Pam Travis, Sugar Creek, vice chair
CD 8 representatives. . . . . .Kelly Ruh, Green Bay, chair; Bill Berglund, Sturgeon Bay, vice chair

Libertarian Party of Wisconsin

608-571-2721; lpwi.org

State Committee
Party officers . . . . Stephen Ecker, chair; Tim Krenz, vice chair;
Elizabeth Hecht, treasurer; Tyler Danke, secretary
CD 1 representatives. . . . . Thomas Leary; Joe Kexel
CD 2 representatives. . . . . .Phil Anderson; Chris Nass
CD 3 representatives. . . . . Bryce Thon; Robert Holzberger
CD 4 representatives. . . . . Kristin Walker; Joe Hauer
CD 5 representatives. . . . . Jeff Kortsch; Meghan Wisner
CD 6 representatives. . . . . Michael Schisel; Jordan Hansen
CD 7 representatives. . . . . Bryan Voss
CD 8 representatives. . . . . .Jason Boris; Teresa Boris
At-large representatives . . . . Nathan Gall; Michael Chianese

Constitution Party of Wisconsin

PO Box 070344, Milwaukee, WI 53207; 608-561-7996; constitutionpartyofwisconsin@gmail.com; www.constitutionpartyofwisconsin.com

State Committee
Party officers . . . . .Andrew Zuelke, Ripon, chair; Michaeljon Murphy, Waukesha, vice chair;
Douglas Lindee, Deer Park, director of communications;
Mark Gabriel, Appleton, secretary; Robert DesJarlais, Mishicot, treasurer
CD 1 representatives. . . . . Dan Herro, Beloit; James Zimmerman, Whitewater
CD 2 representatives. . . . . vacant
CD 3 representatives. . . . . Mark Grimek, Onalaska; vacant
CD 4 representatives. . . . . Colin Hudson, Milwaukee; Arnold Lausevich, Milwaukee
CD 5 representatives. . . . . Don Hilbig, Muskego; vacant
CD 6 representatives. . . . . .vacant
CD 7 representatives. . . . . Joey Hewuse, Auburndale; vacant
CD 8 representatives. . . . . Phil Collins, De Pere, vacant
At-large representatives . . . . Carole Braun, Kewaunee

Note: Parties qualifying for ballot status are those that fulfill the definition of "recognized political party" under Wis. Stat. § 5.02 (16m). Independent candidates may list a party or principle along with their name on the ballot under Wis. Stat. § 5.64 (1) (e) 1. and (es).

CD–Congressional district.

Sources: Democratic Party of Wisconsin, Republican Party of Wisconsin, Libertarian Party of Wisconsin, Constitution Party of Wisconsin.

County vote for Wisconsin Supreme Court justice, February 21, 2023 spring primary

	Janet C. Protasiewicz	Daniel Kelly	Jennifer R. Dorow	Everett D. Mitchell	Total
Adams	1,222	1,119	737	125	3,205
Ashland	1,288	499	229	234	2,253
Barron	1,973	2,493	535	285	5,292
Bayfield	2,147	748	357	275	3,529
Brown	15,553	13,847	5,978	2,503	37,910
Buffalo	660	637	291	72	1,660
Burnett	659	846	310	127	1,942
Calumet	2,825	3,058	1,440	381	7,705
Chippewa	3,208	3,213	866	313	7,604
Clark	1,171	1,625	595	113	3,507
Columbia	4,950	2,702	1,870	467	9,989
Crawford	1,196	730	253	101	2,280
Dane	96,967	12,226	12,512	19,915	141,672
Dodge	4,013	4,364	4,074	421	12,872
Door	3,497	1,892	1,112	431	6,933
Douglas	2,699	1,288	651	417	5,057
Dunn	2,518	2,052	444	381	5,395
Eau Claire	8,426	3,952	1,183	1,164	14,732
Florence	203	346	146	22	717
Fond du Lac	4,696	5,333	4,316	652	14,997
Forest	341	497	204	46	1,089
Grant	2,997	1,954	1,244	345	6,542
Green	3,578	1,595	1,068	293	6,535
Green Lake	940	1,264	609	112	2,926
Iowa	2,780	867	670	154	4,474
Iron	420	312	152	58	943
Jackson	1,094	877	235	119	2,325
Jefferson	5,586	3,499	3,870	553	13,511
Juneau	1,336	1,256	671	111	3,374
Kenosha	10,054	5,771	5,295	1,292	22,424
Kewaunee	1,025	1,406	573	115	3,119
La Crosse	9,622	4,131	2,184	1,369	17,306
Lafayette	1,043	729	397	87	2,256
Langlade	905	1,323	455	99	2,782
Lincoln	1,518	1,508	861	160	4,171
Manitowoc	4,028	4,766	2,420	563	11,782
Marathon	7,717	7,082	4,744	891	20,442
Marinette	1,708	2,536	1,151	218	5,613
Marquette	941	1,067	576	92	2,677
Menominee	88	39	37	16	180
Milwaukee	73,777	13,360	29,094	18,187	134,505
Monroe	2,091	2,194	665	204	5,155
Oconto	1,721	2,755	1,308	228	6,013
Oneida	2,948	2,684	1,042	256	6,932
Outagamie	11,899	10,076	4,773	1,850	28,598
Ozaukee	8,770	4,546	7,873	875	22,074
Pepin	382	366	98	19	865
Pierce	2,074	1,434	471	293	4,272
Polk	1,942	2,338	669	329	5,278
Portage	6,221	3,089	2,205	883	12,408
Price	870	936	336	93	2,235
Racine	11,539	6,836	10,209	1,973	30,578
Richland	1,252	654	426	90	2,422
Rock	11,298	4,606	3,220	1,396	20,529
Rusk	722	1,034	199	72	2,032
Sauk	5,814	2,841	1,828	620	11,103
Sawyer	1,029	870	403	140	2,442

County vote for Wisconsin Supreme Court justice, February 21, 2023 spring primary, continued

	Janet C. Protasiewicz	Daniel Kelly	Jennifer R. Dorow	Everett D. Mitchell	Total
Shawano	1,512	2,364	1,034	196	5,106
Sheboygan	7,199	5,725	6,290	775	19,993
St. Croix	4,790	3,994	1,404	781	10,978
Taylor	705	1,409	550	73	2,737
Trempealeau	1,527	1,091	451	142	3,215
Vernon	2,379	1,535	509	221	4,646
Vilas	1,781	1,912	614	152	4,461
Walworth	6,107	4,988	4,425	637	16,163
Washburn	908	1,010	233	107	2,260
Washington	7,454	7,692	12,850	763	28,759
Waukesha	30,837	18,231	42,629	2,887	94,617
Waupaca	2,472	3,013	1,479	332	7,300
Waushara	1,192	1,606	921	118	3,837
Winnebago	10,896	7,985	3,893	1,470	24,258
Wood	4,703	4,128	2,684	641	12,172
Total	**446,403**	**232,751**	**210,100**	**71,895**	**961,665**

Note: County totals include scattered votes.
*Incumbent.
Source: Official records of the Wisconsin Elections Commission.

County vote for Wisconsin Supreme Court justice, April 4, 2023 spring election

	Janet C. Protasiewicz	Daniel Kelly	Total
Adams	3,242	4,192	7,465
Ashland	3,022	1,763	4,790
Barron	5,316	7,732	13,071
Bayfield	4,343	2,440	6,797
Brown	39,667	37,135	76,980
Buffalo	1,765	2,161	3,934
Burnett	2,083	3,261	5,344
Calumet	7,036	9,029	16,092
Chippewa	8,363	9,657	18,050
Clark	3,110	5,343	8,471
Columbia	10,884	8,884	19,798
Crawford	2,471	2,099	4,575
Dane	197,029	43,372	240,712
Dodge	9,896	16,460	26,356
Door	6,973	5,311	12,301
Douglas	6,968	4,403	11,384
Dunn	6,302	5,881	12,183
Eau Claire	21,141	11,897	33,081
Florence	472	1,100	1,572
Fond du Lac	11,966	18,001	29,989
Forest	1,005	1,548	2,561
Grant	7,049	6,662	13,740
Green	7,597	5,211	12,830
Green Lake	2,189	3,768	5,965
Iowa	5,454	3,108	8,579
Iron	965	1,089	2,057

County vote for Wisconsin Supreme Court justice, April 4, 2023 spring election, continued

	Janet C. Protasiewicz	Daniel Kelly	Total
Jackson	2,667	2,640	5,307
Jefferson	13,263	14,856	28,178
Juneau	3,051	4,052	7,115
Kenosha	22,946	19,558	42,583
Kewaunee	2,536	4,125	6,670
La Crosse	23,964	13,287	37,310
Lafayette	2,229	2,174	4,403
Langlade	2,339	3,958	6,297
Lincoln	3,609	4,869	8,508
Manitowoc	10,572	13,938	24,580
Marathon	18,669	23,686	42,468
Marinette	4,590	7,148	11,766
Marquette	2,125	3,043	5,178
Menominee	397	172	569
Milwaukee	170,540	63,056	234,153
Monroe	4,970	6,399	11,393
Oconto	4,425	7,997	12,451
Oneida	6,207	6,717	12,953
Outagamie	28,112	26,480	54,592
Ozaukee	18,528	20,341	38,936
Pepin	979	1,185	2,164
Pierce	5,867	5,781	11,659
Polk	5,465	7,731	13,196
Portage	13,908	9,993	23,944
Price	2,075	2,772	4,847
Racine	28,164	28,963	57,280
Richland	2,584	2,356	4,944
Rock	27,232	16,863	44,186
Rusk	1,640	2,666	4,313
Sauk	11,751	8,474	20,225
Sawyer	2,670	3,027	5,708
Shawano	4,003	6,921	10,939
Sheboygan	16,620	20,075	36,769
St. Croix	13,642	15,099	28,777
Taylor	1,653	3,946	5,599
Trempealeau	3,965	4,053	8,035
Vernon	5,374	4,364	9,756
Vilas	3,866	5,066	8,958
Walworth	14,199	17,074	31,364
Washburn	2,473	3,392	5,872
Washington	17,620	34,760	52,380
Waukesha	68,249	94,710	163,376
Waupaca	6,137	9,092	15,267
Waushara	2,867	4,971	7,838
Winnebago	26,244	22,250	48,593
Wood	10,528	12,804	23,404
Total	1,021,822	818,391	1,843,480

Note: County totals include scattered votes.
Source: Official records of the Wisconsin Elections Commission.

District vote for Wisconsin Court of Appeals judges, April 5, 2022 spring election

District II

County	Lori Kornblum*	Maria S. Lazar	Total
Calumet	4,087	4,519	8,606
Fond du Lac	6,736	6,813	13,550
Green Lake	1,529	1,443	2,976
Kenosha	13,760	12,964	26,809
Manitowoc	7,062	7,235	14,346
Ozaukee	10,062	10,969	21,076
Racine	12,694	13,266	26,015
Sheboygan	8,716	9,346	18,075
Walworth	7,269	8,668	15,967
Washington	9,930	17,324	27,254
Waukesha	36,803	54,195	91,140
Winnebago	13,225	11,555	24,840
Total	**131,873**	**158,297**	**290,654**

District III

County	Thomas M. Hruz*	Total
Ashland	1,964	1,980
Barron	6,094	6,120
Bayfield	2,666	2,699
Brown	27,361	27,674
Buffalo	1,661	1,672
Burnett	2,160	2,160
Chippewa	7,244	7,282
Door	4,376	4,419
Douglas	4,705	4,790
Dunn	5,072	5,139
Eau Claire	12,820	12,991
Florence	403	403
Forest	846	850
Iron	752	757
Kewaunee	3,363	3,382
Langlade	2,985	2,985
Lincoln	5,549	5,569
Marathon	19,036	19,255
Marinette	4,707	4,733
Menominee	516	516
Oconto	6,290	6,328
Oneida	5,605	5,672
Outagamie	18,237	18,237
Pepin	685	685
Pierce	5,468	5,519
Polk	6,668	6,668
Price	1,735	1,735
Rusk	2,030	2,048
Sawyer	2,604	2,625
Shawano	4,385	4,385
St. Croix	10,852	10,969
Taylor	3,932	3,937
Trempealeau	3,923	3,952
Vilas	3,354	3,371
Washburn	1,797	1,805
Total	**191,845**	**193,312**

District vote for Wisconsin Court of Appeals judges, April 5, 2022 spring election, continued

District IV

County	Brian Blanchard*	Total
Adams	1,988	2,016
Clark	3,531	3,554
Columbia	8,402	8,495
Crawford	1,420	1,428
Dane	61,024	61,618
Dodge	9,137	9,137
Grant	4,736	4,766
Green	5,512	5,571
Iowa	3,729	3,752
Jackson	2,106	2,106
Jefferson	9,702	9,841
Juneau	2,898	2,931
La Crosse	14,814	14,983
Lafayette	2,640	2,640
Marquette	1,843	1,858
Monroe	6,005	6,046
Portage	11,084	11,196
Richland	1,870	1,881
Rock	14,409	14,642
Sauk	8,306	8,306
Vernon	3,730	3,755
Waupaca	5,735	5,778
Waushara	2,921	2,933
Wood	10,640	10,721
Total	**198,182**	**199,954**

Note: County totals include scattered votes.
*Incumbent.
Source: Official records of the Wisconsin Elections Commission.

District vote for Wisconsin Court of Appeals judges, April 4, 2023 spring election

District I

County	William Brash	Sara Greenan	Total
Milwaukee	59,587	130,030	190,705
Total	**59,587**	**130,030**	**190,705**

District IV

County	Chris Taylor	Total
Adams	5,993	6,098
Clark	6,390	6,435
Columbia	13,854	14,021
Crawford	3,178	3,205
Dane	168,269	170,314
Dodge	18,415	18,415
Grant	10,047	10,111
Green	8,586	8,695
Iowa	6,199	6,250
Jackson	3,706	3,706

District vote for Wisconsin Court of Appeals judges, April 4, 2023 spring election, continued

District IV

County	Chris Taylor	Total
Jefferson	18,853	19,094
Juneau	5,350	5,395
La Crosse	25,046	25,419
Lafayette	3,333	3,333
Marquette	3,714	3,754
Monroe	8,274	8,422
Portage	15,837	15,993
Richland	3,540	3,559
Rock	29,998	30,355
Sauk	13,248	13,248
Vernon	6,782	6,854
Waupaca	11,575	11,718
Waushara	5,935	5,935
Wood	16,369	16,524
Total	**412,491**	**416,853**

Note: County totals include scattered votes.
Source: Official records of the Wisconsin Elections Commission.

Vote for Wisconsin Circuit Court judges, February 21, 2022 spring primary

Counties in circuit	Candidates	Vote
Kewaunee	Kimberly A. Hardtke	707
	John Peterson	663
	Jeffrey Ronald Wisnicky	1,219

Source: Official records of the Wisconsin Elections Commission.

Vote for Wisconsin Circuit Court judges, April 5, 2022 spring election

Counties in circuit	Branch	Candidates	Vote
Adams	2	Tania M. Bonnett	2,014
Barron	1	James C. Babler*	6,524
Crawford	—	Lynn Marie Rider*	1,521
Dane	3	Diane Schlipper	59,011
	4	Everett D. Mitchell*	59,312
	5	Nicholas J. McNamara*	58,155
	14	John D. Hyland*	58,064
	15	Stephen Ehlke*	58,090
Eau Claire	1	John Francis Manydeeds*	13,721
	6	Beverly Wickstrom	13,046
Fond du Lac	2	Laura Lavey	11,164
	4	Tricia L. Walker	10,854
	5	Douglas R. Edelstein	10,684
Iowa	—	Matt Allen	3,170
		Rhonda R. Hazen	1,689
Kewaunee	—	Kimberly A. Hardtke	1,628
		Jeffrey Ronald Wisnicky	2,720

Vote for Wisconsin Circuit Court judges, April 5, 2022 spring election, continued

Counties in circuit	Branch	Candidates	Vote
Lincoln	1	Galen Bayne-Allison	5,479
Marathon	1	Rick Cveykus	16,753
		William A. Harris	7,891
Milwaukee	5	Kristela L. Cervera*	89,969
	14	Christopher R. Foley, Sr.*	91,898
	25	Nidhi Kashyap	87,737
	31	Hannah C. Dugan*	89,206
	34	Glenn H. Yamahiro*	89,065
	44	Gwendolyn G. Connolly*	89,591
	45	Jean Marie Kies*	87,965
Monroe	2	Mark L. Goodman*	6,343
Oconto	2	Ed Burke	2,096
		Jay Conley*	5,822
Outagamie	4	Yadira J. Rein*	18,167
	7	Mark G. Schroeder*	18,352
Pierce	—	Elizabeth Rohl*	5,748
Portage	2	Louis John Molepske, Jr.	9,454
		Stephen W. Sawyer	7,357
	3	Trish Baker*	11,421
Racine	2	Eugene A. Gasiokiewicz*	18,273
	4	Mark F. Nielsen*	18,444
	5	Kristin M. Cafferty*	18,258
Rusk	—	Annette Barna	2,010
Sauk	1	Blake J. Duren	5,199
		Michael Screnock*	5,557
	2	Wendy J. N. Klicko*	8,446
St. Croix	4	R. Michael Waterman*	11,076
Vilas	1	Martha J. Milanowski*	3,766
	2	Meg Colleen O'Marro	2,017
		Daniel Overbey	2,597
Walworth	2	Daniel Johnson*	12,028
	4	David M. Reddy*	12,055
Waushara	2	Scott C. Blader	3,154
Winnebago	3	Bryan D. Keberlein	13,745
		Lisa Krueger	11,421
	4	Mike Gibbs	13,786
		LaKeisha D. Haase*	12,081
	5	John A. Jorgensen*	19,418

*Incumbent; — Means the circuit has only one branch.
Source: Official records of the Wisconsin Elections Commission.

Vote for Wisconsin Circuit Court judges, February 21, 2023 spring primary

Counties in circuit	Branch	Candidates	Vote
Grant	1	Lisa A. Riniker	2,676
		Jennifer Day	2,409
		Jeffrey W. Erickson	1,270
Oneida	1	Mary Burns*	3,107
		Michael W. Schiek	2,479
		Mike Fugle	1,072

*Incumbent.
Source: Official records of the Wisconsin Elections Commission.

Vote for Wisconsin Circuit Court judges, April 4, 2023 spring election

Counties in circuit	Branch	Candidates	Vote
Burnett	—	Melissia R. Mogen*	4,143
Clark	2	William Bratcher	4,194
		Jake Brunette	3,982
Columbia	2	W. Andrew Voigt*	14,159
Dodge	2	Martin J. De Vries*	18,530
Door	2	David L. Weber*	8,710
Grant	1	Lisa A. Riniker	6,873
		Jennifer Day	6,035
Green Lake	—	Mark Slate*	4,746
Jefferson	4	Bennett J. Brantmeier*	18,953
Kenosha	4	Anthony Milisaukas*	29,670
	7	Jodi L. Meier*	30,137
Manitowoc	3	Robert Dewane*	18,762
	4	Anthony A. Lambrecht	18,017
Marathon	4	Gregoy J. Strasser*	31,616
	5	Michael K. Moran*	31,329
Milwaukee	4	Michael J. Hanrahan*	140,875
	9	Paul Van Grunsven*	140,262
	10	Michelle Ackerman Havas*	140,678
	13	Ana Berrios-Schroeder	141,833
	18	Pedro A. Colon*	143,733
	21	Cynthia Davis*	141,995
	33	Carl Ashley*	141,787
	35	Frederick C. Rosa*	140,392
	47	Kristy Yang*	141,930
Oconto	1	Michael T. Judge*	10,332
Oneida	1	Michael W. Schiek	6,634
		Mary Burns*	5,967
Outagamie	1	Mark J. McGinnis*	38,221
Polk	1	Daniel J. Tolan*	10,451
	2	Jeff Anderson*	10,433
Portage	1	Michael Zell*	15,990
Richland	—	Lisa A. McDougal*	3,659
Rock	4	Ashley Morse*	30,048
	6	John M. Wood*	29,430
Sawyer	2	Monica M. Isham	4,161
Sheboygan	2	Natasha L. Torry	17,516
		James A. Haasch	15,808
	3	Angela W. Sutkiewicz*	25,874
	5	George Limbeck	16,284
		Cassandra Van Gompel	15,417
Trempealeau	—	Rian W. Radtke*	6,248
Vernon	—	Timothy J. Gaskell	4,785
		Angela Palmer-Fisher	4,605
Washington	1	Ryan J. Hetzel	27,512
		Russ Jones	18,850
	3	Michael S. Kenitz*	36,713
Waukesha	3	Ralph M. Ramirez*	103,459
	4	Lloyd V. Carter*	100,408
	7	Cody Horlacher	71,228
		Fred Strampe*	57,239
	11	William J. Domina*	99,727
Waupaca	1	Troy L. Nielsen*	11,834
Waushara	1	Guy Dutcher*	6,438
Winnebago	2	Scott C. Woldt*	23,463
		LaKeisha D. Haase	22,104

Vote for Wisconsin Circuit Court judges, April 4, 2023 spring election, continued

Counties in circuit	Branch	Candidates	Vote
	6	Daniel Bissett*.	33,567
Wood	4	Timothy Gebert.	12,722
		Craig Lambert.	9,031

*Incumbent. — Means the circuit has only one branch.
Source: Official records of the Wisconsin Elections Commission.

OFFICIALS AND EMPLOYEES

Wisconsin state officers appointed by the governor, May 15, 2023

911 Subcommittee
Brad Jorgenson. . . . . .expires 7/1/22
Steven R. Kutsch. 7/1/22
Kristina Page 7/1/22
Dena Clark. 7/1/24
John Cummings 7/1/24
Rodney D. Olson. 7/1/24
Jean M. Pauk 7/1/24
Mark Podoll 7/1/24
Marcie R. Rainbolt. 7/1/24
Andrew Faust. 7/1/25
Amanda Mulvey 7/1/25
Matt Sparks 7/1/25
Robert C. Whitaker 7/1/25
Melvin Frank 7/1/26
Daniel Hardman 7/1/26
Jamey Lysne. .7/1/26
Danielle Miller 7/1/26
Kinnyetta Patterson. 7/1/26
Gary Pelletier .7/1/26

Accounting Examining Board[1] ($25/day[2])
David K. Schlichting. . . . . .expires 7/1/22
Michael Friedman 7/1/23
Joan Phillips. .7/1/23
Susan Strautmann. 7/1/24
Thuy Barron 7/1/25
Robert Misey .7/1/25
John Reinemann 7/1/25

Adjutant General (group 6 salary[2])
Major Gen. Paul E. Knapp . . . . .expires 3/4/25

Administration, Department of, secretary[1] (group 8 salary[2])
Kathy K. Blumenfeld[3] expires at governor's pleasure

Adult Offender Supervision Board, Interstate
Mario White. . . . . .expires 5/1/25
Veronica Figueroa-Velez 5/1/27
Kari S. Ives. 5/1/27
LaKeshia Nicole Myers 5/1/27

Adult Offender Supervision Board, Interstate Compact Administrator
Joselyn Lopez. . . . . .expires 5/1/25

Aerospace Authority, Wisconsin[1] (inactive)

Affirmative Action, Council on
Janice Crump . . . . .expires 7/1/22
Joshua Hargrove. 7/1/22
Carlene Bechen. 7/1/25
Alenka Dries. .7/1/25
Fabiola Hamdan 7/1/25
Christopher Kilgour. 7/1/25
Dominic Ledesma 7/1/25
Angela Nash. .7/1/25
Devon Wilson. 7/1/25
Yee Leng Xiong. 7/1/25
Ankita Bharadwaj 7/1/26

Aging and Long-Term Care, Board on[1]
Dale B. Taylor . . . . .expires 5/1/25
Valerie A. Palarski[3]. 5/1/26
Abigail Lowery[3] 5/1/27
Tanya L. Meyer[3]. 5/1/27
Khyana Pumphrey[3] 5/1/27
James Surprise[3] 5/1/28
vacancy

Agriculture, Trade and Consumer Protection, Board of[1] (not to exceed $35/day nor $1,000/year[2])
Cindy Brown[3]. . . . . .expires 5/1/25
Daniel G. Smith. 5/1/25
Carla Washington 5/1/25
Clare Hintz. 5/1/27
Paul Palmby. 5/1/27
Doug Rebout .5/1/27
Paul M. Bauer[3] .5/1/29
Tina Hinchley[3] .5/1/29
Miranda Leis[3] 5/1/29

Agriculture, Trade and Consumer Protection, Department of, secretary[1] (group 6 salary[2])
Randy J. Romanski. . expires at governor's pleasure

Alcohol and Other Drug Abuse, State Council on
Sandy Hardie. . . . . .expires 7/1/23
Deb Kolste. 7/1/23
Terry Schemenauer 7/1/23
Kevin Florek. .7/1/25
Christina Malone. 7/1/25
Stacy Stone 7/1/25
Jessica Geschke. . . . expires at governor's pleasure
Christine A. Ullstrup. . . . . governor's pleasure

Architects, Landscape Architects, Professional Engineers, Designers, Professional Land Surveyors, and Registered Interior Designers, Examining Board of[1] ($25/day[2])
Daniel Fedderly . . . . .expires 7/1/13
Rosheen Styczinski 7/1/13
Steven Hook .7/1/14
Andrew Gersich 7/1/15
Kenneth D. Arneson. 7/1/18
Michael J. Heberling 7/1/19
Christina C. Martin. 7/1/19
Kristine Cotharn 7/1/21
Steven Wagner. 7/1/21
Gregory Douglas 7/1/23
Shawn Timothy Kelly 7/1/23
Colleen M. Scholl. 7/1/23
Jennifer Lynne Phillips 7/1/24
Laura Schade Stroik. 7/1/24
Steven Tweed. 7/1/24
Corissa D. Uselmann 7/1/24
Nathan Vaughn. 7/1/24
Melissa Mae Destree 7/1/25
Karl Linck 7/1/25
Dennis Myers .7/1/25
Christopher M. Sina 7/1/25

… | 635

Wisconsin state officers appointed by the governor, May 15, 2023, continued

Robin A. Stroebel 7/1/26
Roy Wagner[3] 7/1/27
7 vacancies

Artistic Endowment Foundation[1] (inactive)

Arts Board
John H. Potter. . . . . .expires 5/1/24
Gerard Randall .5/1/24
Rafael Francisco Salas. 5/1/24
Marcela Garcia .5/1/25
Karen A. Hoffman 5/1/25
Susan Lipp. 5/1/25
Dinorah Márquez Abadiano. 5/1/25
Mary K. Reinders. 5/1/25
Lynn Richie 5/1/25
Jennifer Schwarzkopf. 5/1/25
Matthew J. Wallock 5/1/25
Jayne Herring. .5/1/26
John William Johnson. 5/1/26
Brian Kelsey 5/1/26
William Mitchell 5/1/26

Athletic Trainers Affiliated Credentialing Board[1] ($25/day[2])
John J. Johnsen. . . . . .expires 7/1/21
Stephanie Atkins. 7/1/23
Kurt Fielding 7/1/23
Benjamin Wedro 7/1/23
Michael Moll 7/1/24
Jay J. Davide. 7/1/26

Auctioneer Board[1] ($25/day[2])
Heather Berlinski . . . . .expires 5/1/16
Jerry Thiel 5/1/18
Bryce L. Hansen 5/1/24
Randy L. Stockwell. 5/1/24
Stanley D. Jones[3]. 5/1/26
Deana M. Zentner[3] 5/1/27
vacancy

Banking Institutions Review Board[1] ($25/day, not to exceed $1,500/year[2])
Paul Adamski[3] . . . . .expires 5/1/24
Charles Schmalz[3] 5/1/25
Thomas E. Spitz[3] 5/1/26
John Brogan[3] 5/1/27
Jay McKenna[3]. 5/1/28

Bradley Center Sports and Entertainment Corporation, Board of Directors of the[1] (inactive)

Building Commission
Barb Worcester . . . . expires at governor's pleasure

Burial Sites Preservation Board ($25/day[2])
David Grignon . . . . .expires 7/1/23
Cynthia Stiles 7/1/23
Jennifer R. Haas. 7/1/24
Melinda Young .7/1/24
Katherine P. Stevenson 7/1/25
vacancy

Cemetery Board[1] ($25/day[2])
Bernard Schroedl . . . . .expires 7/1/21
Patricia Grathen 7/1/22

Edward G. Porter III 7/1/23
Izzy Marshall 7/1/24
John Reinemann. 7/1/24
vacancy

Child Abuse and Neglect Prevention Board
Molly J. Jasmer . . . . .expires 5/1/25
Jennifer Kleven 5/1/25
Michael McHorney 5/1/25
Michael Meulemans. 5/1/25
Teri B. Zywicki .5/1/25
Paula J. Breese .5/1/26
William Olivier .5/1/26
Vicki M. Tylka 5/1/26
Jameelah A. Love. . . expires at governor's pleasure
2 vacancies

Children and Families, Department of, Secretary[1] (group 6 salary[2])
Emilie Amundson[3]. . expires at governor's pleasure

Chiropractic Examining Board[1] ($25/day[2])
James M. Damrow . . . . .expires 7/1/23
Eugene Yellen-Shiring[3]. 7/1/23
Kathleen A. Hendrickson[3] 7/1/24
Kris Erlandson .7/1/25
Amy Heffernan .7/1/25
Daniel Meschefske[3] 7/1/25

Circus World Museum Foundation[1]
David Hoffman . . . expires at governor's pleasure

Claims Board
Mel Barnes. . . . . . . expires at governor's pleasure

College Savings Program Board[1]
Ashleigh Edgerson[3] . . . . .expires 5/1/24
LaTonya Johnson[3] 5/1/25
Kimberly Shaul[3] 5/1/25
Susan M. Bauer[3] 5/1/27
William L. Oemichen[3]. 5/1/27
vacancy

Commercial Building Code Council
Kevin Bierce . . . . .expires 7/1/17
Irina Ragozin 7/1/17
Steven Howard 7/1/18
Brian J. Rinke 7/1/18
Jennifer Emberson Acker. 7/1/22
Michael Adamavich. 7/1/22
Steven Harms. .7/1/22
William Hebert 7/1/22
Matthew Marciniak 7/1/22
Richard P. Paur .7/1/22

Controlled Substances Board
Subhadeep Barman. . . . . .expires 5/1/19
Alan Bloom 5/1/20

Conveyance Safety Code Council
Harold A. Thurmer. . . . . .expires 7/1/19
Steven L. Ketelboeter. 7/1/23
Ronald P. Mueller. 7/1/23
Jennie L. Macaluso. 7/1/24
Keith S. Misustin 7/1/24
Kenneth R. Smith 7/1/24

Wisconsin state officers appointed by the governor, May 15, 2023, continued

Paul S. Rosenberg 7/1/25
Mark Uy 7/1/25

Corrections, Department of, Secretary[1] (group 8 salary[2])
Kevin A. Carr[3] . . . . . expires at governor's pleasure

Cosmetology Examining Board[1] ($25/day[2])
Georgianna Halverson . . . . expires 7/1/23
Ann Hoeppner 7/1/23
Megan Jackson. 7/1/23
Kristin N. Lee 7/1/23
Daisy Quintal .7/1/23
Melissa Kay Blake 7/1/24
Kayla Cwojdzinski 7/1/24
2 vacancies

Credit Union Review Board[1] ($25/day, not to exceed $1,500 per year[2])
Sally Dischler . . . . expires 5/1/25
Liza Edinger 5/1/25
Sheila Schinke 5/1/26
Colleen Woggon[3] 5/1/27
Lisa M. Greco[3] 5/1/28

Crime Victims Rights Board
Nela Kalpic . . . . .expires 5/1/23

Criminal Penalties, Joint Review Committee on
Bradley Gehring . . . expires at governor's pleasure
Maury Straub . . . . governor's pleasure

Deaf and Hard of Hearing, Council for the
Christine Koemeter . . . . expires 7/1/23
Thomas O'Connor 7/1/23
Jonathan Petermon 7/1/23
Leia Sparks .7/1/23
Andrew Altmann. 7/1/25
Elizabeth Ermenc 7/1/25
Nicole Everson 7/1/25
Katy Hagmeyer. 7/1/25
David H. Seligman. 7/1/25

Deferred Compensation Board[1] ($25/day[2])
Terrance L. Craney . . . . expires 7/1/23
Connie Haberkorn. 7/1/24
Jason A. Rothenberg 7/1/25
William Stebbins 7/1/25
Kate M. Fleming[3]. 7/1/26

Dentistry Examining Board[1] ($25/day[2])
Herbert Michael Kaske . . . . expires 7/1/22
Deb Kolste. 7/1/24
Diana Whalen. 7/1/24
Troy Alton 7/1/25
Matthew R. Bistan 7/1/25
Joan Fox 7/1/25
Lisa Bahr[3] 7/1/26
Shaheda Govani[3] 7/1/26
Chris Kenyon[3]. 7/1/26
Katherine F. Schrubbe[3]. 7/1/26
Peter Sheild[3] 7/1/26

Developmental Disabilities, Board for People with ($50/day[2])
Gail M. Bovy . . . . expires 7/1/23

Kedibonye Carpenter 7/1/23
Pamela K. Delap 7/1/23
Patrick Friedrich 7/1/23
Desi Kluth 7/1/23
Stephenie J. Mlodzik 7/1/23
Nathan E. Ruffolo 7/1/23
Andy Thain 7/1/23
Christopher J. Wood. 7/1/23
Sydney Badeau. 7/1/24
Felicia Clayborne. 7/1/24
Cheryl Funmaker. 7/1/24
Jocelyn Osborne 7/1/24
Kelly Weyer 7/1/24
Marcia Perkins 7/1/25
Hector H. Portillo. 7/1/25
Julie Strenn 7/1/25
Tricia Thompson 7/1/25
Houa Yang. 7/1/25
Ashley Mathy .7/1/26
Gregory A. Meyer 7/1/26
George Zaske. 7/1/26

Dietitians Affiliated Credentialing Board[1] ($25/day[2])
David Joe . . . . expires 7/1/18
Tara LaRowe .7/1/22
Rebecca Kerkenbush 7/1/23
Jill D. Hoyt 7/1/25

Distance Learning Authorization Board
Russell Swagger . . . expires at governor's pleasure

Domestic Abuse, Council on[1]
Nela Kalpic . . . . .expires 7/1/23
Rosalind McClain 7/1/23
Abdul Shour[3] 7/1/23
Susan Sippel .7/1/23
Alena A. Taylor 7/1/23
Melissa Baldauff[3]. 7/1/25
Mildred I. Gonzales[3]. 7/1/25
Susan M. Perry[3]. 7/1/25
vacancy

Dry Cleaner Environmental Response Council (inactive)

Economic Development Corp. Authority, Wisconsin[1]
John J. Brogan . . . . expires at governor's pleasure
Eugenia Podestá Losada . . . . . governor's pleasure
Henry Newell . . . . governor's pleasure
Jack Salzwedel . . . . governor's pleasure
Thelma Sias . . . . governor's pleasure
vacancy

Economic Development Corporation Authority, Wisconsin, Chief Executive Officer[1]
Missy Hughes[4] . . . . expires at governor's pleasure

Education Commission of the States
Jennifer Collins . . . . expires at governor's pleasure
Camille Crary . . . . governor's pleasure
Zach Madden. . . . . governor's pleasure
Amy Traynor. . . . . governor's pleasure

Wisconsin state officers appointed by the governor, May 15, 2023, continued

Educational Communications Board[1]
Leah R. Lechleiter-Luke . . . . .expires 5/1/24
Anne Chapman[3] 5/1/25
Eric Fulcrum[3] .5/1/27
Alyssa Kenney[3] 5/1/27
Eileen Littig . . . . . . expires at governor's pleasure

Elections Commission[1] ($115/day[2])
Marge R. Bostelmann . . . . .expires 5/1/24
Joseph J. Czarnezki[3] 5/1/26

Electronic Recording Council
Margo C. Katterhagen . . . . .expires 7/1/21
Trista Mayer 7/1/23
Sara B. Andrew .7/1/25
Sandra Disrud 7/1/25
Michele Jacobs .7/1/25
Katharine Marlin 7/1/25
Sharon A. Martin 7/1/25

Emergency Management Division, Administrator of[1] (group 3 salary[2])
Greg Engle[3] . . . . . . expires at governor's pleasure

Emergency Medical Services Board
Michael Clark . . . . .expires 5/1/24
Christopher M. Eberlein 5/1/24
Brian Litza 5/1/24
Timothy A. Bantes 5/1/25
Jennifer Hernandez-Meier 5/1/25
Steven Zils 5/1/25
Christopher D. Anderson 5/1/25
Jerry R. Biggart 5/1/26
Justin Pluess 5/1/26
Dustin E. Ridings 5/1/26
Gregory Neal West 5/1/26

Employee Trust Funds Board[1] ($25/day[2])
Stephen Arnold . . . . .expires 5/1/23
Katy Lounsbury . . . expires at governor's pleasure

Employment Relations Commission[1] (group 5 salary[2])
James Daley . . . . .expires 3/1/23

Ethics Commission[1] ($115/day[2])
Timothy M. Van Akkeren . . . . .expires 5/1/24
Gerald P. Ptacek[3] 5/1/26

Federal-State Relations Office, Director (group 3 salary[2])
vacancy

Financial Institutions, Department of, Secretary[1] (group 6 salary[2])
Cheryll A. Olson-Collins[3] . . . . expires at governor's pleasure

Forestry, Council on
Heather Berklund . . expires at governor's pleasure
Matt Dallman . . . . governor's pleasure
Bradley Dorff . . . . governor's pleasure
Thomas Hittle . . . . governor's pleasure
James Hoppe . . . . governor's pleasure
Buddy Huffaker . . . . governor's pleasure
James R. Kerkman . . . . governor's pleasure

Rebekah Luedtke . . . . governor's pleasure
Jeffrey Mursau . . . . governor's pleasure
Romaine Quinn . . . . governor's pleasure
Erik Rantala . . . . governor's pleasure
Juris Repsa . . . . governor's pleasure
Adena Rissman . . . . governor's pleasure
Henry Schienebeck . . . . governor's pleasure
Katrina Shankland . . . . governor's pleasure
Jordan Skiff . . . . governor's pleasure
Jeff Smith . . . . governor's pleasure
William Van Lopik . . . . governor's pleasure
vacancy

Fox River Navigational System Authority[1]
H. Bruce Enke . . . . .expires 7/1/23
Jeffery Feldt 7/1/23
Tim Short 7/1/24
Ronald Van De Hey 7/1/24
John L. Vette[3] .7/1/25
vacancy

Funeral Directors Examining Board[1] ($25/day[2])
Eric Lengell . . . . .expires 7/1/16
Dawn Adams 7/1/23
Joseph B. Schinkten 7/1/23
Aziz Al-Sager 7/1/25
Mary Hoehne .7/1/25
Stephen P. Casey 7/1/26

Genetic Counselors Affiliated Credentialing Board[1] ($25/day[2])
Peter Levonian[3] . . . . .expires 7/1/23
Michael J. Muriello[3] 7/1/23
Jennifer Geurts[3] 7/1/24
Michael Patrick Mullane[3] 7/1/24
Jessica Grzybowski[3] 7/1/25
Stephanie Lynn Karwedsky[3] 7/1/25
Rebecca L. Pabst[3] 7/1/25

Geologists, Hydrologists and Soil Scientists, Examining Board of Professional[1] ($25/day[2])
Randall Hunt . . . . .expires 7/1/12
Stephanie Williams 7/1/17
Ann Hirekatur .7/1/24
Trevor Nobile .7/1/24
Prosper Gbolo .7/1/25
John Small 7/1/26
6 vacancies

Great Lakes Commission
Todd Ambs . . . . .expires 7/1/23
Melonee Montano 7/1/24
vacancy

Great Lakes Protection Fund[1]
Erin Deeley[3] . . . . . . expires at governor's pleasure
Demetria Smith[3] . . . . governor's pleasure

Groundwater Coordinating Council
Steve Diercks . . . . .expires 7/1/17

Group Insurance Board ($25/day[2])
Herschel Day . . . . .expires 5/1/25
Dan B. Fields 5/1/25
Erin Hillson 5/1/25

Wisconsin state officers appointed by the governor, May 15, 2023, continued

Walter E. Jackson. 5/1/25
Nancy L. Thompson 5/1/25
Nathan Ugoretz .5/1/25
Katy Lounsbury . . . expires at governor's pleasure

Health and Educational Facilities Authority, Wisconsin[1]
James K. Oppermann . . . . .expires 7/1/23
Renee E. Anderson 7/1/24
Tim K. Size 7/1/25
James Allen Dietsche 7/1/26
Robert Van Meeteren[3] 7/1/27
Billie Jo Higgins[3] 7/1/28
Pamela Stanick[3] 7/1/29

Health Care Liability Insurance Plan/Injured Patients and Families Compensation Fund Board of Governors ($50/day[2])
Carla Borda . . . . .expires 5/1/21
Jeffery Bingham 5/1/22
Gary Hebl 5/1/26
Gregory Schroeder 5/1/26

Health Services, Department of, Secretary[1] (group 8 salary[2])
Kirsten Johnson[3]. . . expires at governor's pleasure

Hearing and Speech Examining Board[1] ($25/day[2])
Thomas J. Krier . . . . .expires 7/1/21
Michael Harris 7/1/23
Kathleen A. Pazak 7/1/23
David H. Seligman 7/1/23
Robert R. Broeckert 7/1/24
Catherine Denison Kanter 7/1/24
Jason John Meyer 7/1/25
Justen Willemon 7/1/25
2 vacancies . . . .

Higher Educational Aids Board
Justin Wesolek . . . . .expires 5/1/22
Jeff Cichon. 5/1/23
Efrem Dana 5/1/23
Timothy Opgenorth. 5/1/23
Rosa Faustino. .5/1/24
Jennifer Garrett. 5/1/24
Susan Teerink 5/1/24
Stephen D. Willett 5/1/24
Jeff Neubauer. .5/1/26
Kyle M. Weatherly 5/1/26

Higher Educational Aids Board, Executive Secretary (group 3 salary[2])
Connie L. Hutchison. expires at governor's pleasure

Highway Safety, Council on
J. D. Lind .expires 7/1/18
Richard G. Van Boxtel 7/1/18
Joseph C. Gonnering 7/1/19
John P. Mesich .7/1/19
Yash Wadhwa. .7/1/19
Robert D. Hinds 7/1/20
William Neitzel .7/1/21
Brian Dean. 7/1/23
Donald Gutkowski. 7/1/24
Kurt Schultz 7/1/24

Historic Preservation Review Board
Carlen I. Hatala . . . . .expires 7/1/23
Daniel J. Joyce .7/1/23
Valentine Schute Jr. 7/1/23
Daniel J. Stephans 7/1/23
Donna Zimmerman 7/1/23
Sergio M. González 7/1/24
Carol McChesney Johnson 7/1/24
Neil Prendergast 7/1/24
Sissel Schroeder 7/1/24
Paul Wolter 7/1/24
Ray Reser 7/1/25
Matthew G. Sadowski. 7/1/25
Amy L. Scanlon .7/1/25
Peggy Veregin .7/1/25
Melinda J. Young. 7/1/25

Housing and Economic Development Authority, Wisconsin[1]
Jeffrey L. Skrenes. . . . . .expires 1/1/24
Ranell G. Washington 1/1/24
Raynetta R. Hill .1/1/26
Victoria Parmentier 1/1/26
Diane House[3] 1/1/27
vacancy

Housing and Economic Development Authority, Wisconsin, Executive Director[1] (group 6 salary[2])
Elmer Moore Jr.[3] . . . . .expires 1/3/23

Insurance, Commissioner of[1] (group 6 salary[2])
Nathan D. Houdek. . expires at governor's pleasure

Interagency Council on Homelessness
Sara Rodriguez . . . . expires at governor's pleasure

Interoperability Council
Kirk A. Gunderson . . . . .expires 5/1/25
Steven Hansen .5/1/25
Brian Uhl 5/1/25
James D. Formea 5/1/27
Matthew Joski .5/1/27
5 vacancies

Interstate Juvenile Supervision, State Board for
5 vacancies

Invasive Species Council
Mark Renz . . . . .expires 7/1/23
Douglas Cox 7/1/24
Jennifer A. Hauxwell. 7/1/24
Hannah Spaul. .7/1/24
Thomas Buechel 7/1/25
Thomas Bressner 7/1/27
Gregory Long 7/1/27

Investment and Local Impact Fund Board (inactive)

Investment Board, State of Wisconsin[1] ($50/day[2])
Esther Ancel. . . . . expires 5/1/2027
Barbara Nick 5/1/27
Clyde Tinnen 5/1/27
Jefferson DeAngelis[3] 5/1/29
Kristi Palmer[3] 5/1/29
vacancy

Wisconsin state officers appointed by the governor, May 15, 2023, continued

Judicial Commission[1] ($25/day[2])
Jane Foley[3] . . . . expires 8/1/23
Janet Jenkins[3]. 8/1/23
Mary Beth Keppel[3] 8/1/23
Judy K. Ziewacz[3] 8/1/23
Yulonda M. Anderson[3] 8/1/24

Judicial Council
William Gleisner . . . . .expires 7/1/24
Molly McNab .7/1/25
Christian Gossett . . expires at governor's pleasure

Kickapoo Reserve Management Board[1] ($25/day[2])
Reggie Nelson . . . . .expires 5/1/24
Luke Zahm 5/1/24
Tina Brown. .5/1/25
Travis M. Downing. 5/1/25
Julie Van Aman Hoel. 5/1/25
Adlai Mann .5/1/25
David M. Maxwell[3]. 5/1/25
Barbara Sarnowski. 5/1/25
Dan Goltz 5/1/26
Scott Lind 5/1/26
William L. Quackenbush 5/1/26

Labor and Industry Review Commission[1] (group 5 salary[2])
Michael Gillick[3]. . . . . .expires 3/1/25
Marilyn Townsend[3] 3/1/27
Katy Lounsbury[3] 3/1/29

Labor and Industry Review Commission, general counsel
Anita Krasno. . . . . . expires at governor's pleasure

Laboratory of Hygiene Board
Jessica Blahnik . . . . .expires 5/1/25
Jennifer M. Buchholz 5/1/25
Robert Corliss. 5/1/25
Christopher Strang 5/1/25
Gina Green-Harris 5/1/26
Jeffery A. Kindrai 5/1/26
vacancy

Lake Michigan Commercial Fishing Board
Charles W. Henriksen   expires at governor's pleasure
Richard R. Johnson . . . . governor's pleasure
Michael Le Clair . . . . governor's pleasure
Mark Maricque . . . . governor's pleasure
Dan Pawlitzke . . . . governor's pleasure
Brett Schwarz . . . . governor's pleasure
Todd Stuth . . . . governor's pleasure

Lake States Wood Utilization Consortium (inactive)

Lake Superior Commercial Fishing Board
Bryan Bainbridge . . expires at governor's pleasure
William Bodin . . . . governor's pleasure
Christopher Boyd . . . . governor's pleasure
Maurine Halvorson . . . . governor's pleasure
Craig Hoopman . . . . governor's pleasure

Land and Water Conservation Board[1] ($25/day[2])
Bobbie Webster . . . . .expires 5/1/23
Mark E. Cupp 5/1/24

Brian C. McGraw[3] 5/1/25
Andrew J. Buttles[3] 5/1/27
Ronald Grasshoff[3] 5/1/27

Law Enforcement Standards Board
Todd Delain . . . . .expires 5/1/24
Jean Galasinski 5/1/24
Denita Ball. .5/1/25
Timothy J. Gruenke 5/1/25
Nicole R. Miller 5/1/25
Kalvin Barrett 5/1/26
Jessie Metoyer 5/1/26
Katie Rosenberg 5/1/26
Benjamin Bliven 5/1/27
Charles A. Tubbs Sr. 5/1/27
vacancy

Library and Network Development, Council on
Terrence Berres . . . . .expires 7/1/23
Nick Dimassis 7/1/23
Miriam M. Erickson 7/1/23
Michael E. Otten 7/1/23
Joan Schneider 7/1/23
Charmaine Sprengelmeyer-Podein 7/1/23
Theresa L. Muraski 7/1/24
Dennis Myers .7/1/24
Isa Small 7/1/24
Amy Thornton 7/1/24
Amy Bahena-Ettner 7/1/25
Andi Cloud. .7/1/25
Jaime Healy-Plotkin 7/1/25
Joshua L. Klingbeil 7/1/25
Ellen Kupfer .7/1/25
Robert Lee Nunez II 7/1/25
Christinna Young Gene Swearingen. 7/1/25
Rachel E. Thomas 7/1/25
Kristi A. Williams 7/1/25

Lower Fox River Remediation Authority[1] (inactive)

Lower Wisconsin State Riverway Board[1] ($25/day[2])
Gretchen F. G. LaBudde. . . . . .expires 5/1/23
Meredith Beckman 5/1/24
Ritchie Brown. 5/1/24
Steve Wetter .5/1/24
Kim Cates 5/1/25
Dan Hillberry .5/1/25
Randall H. Poelma 5/1/25
Lara Czajkowski Higgins 5/1/26
vacancy

Marriage and Family Therapy, Professional Counseling, and Social Work, Examining Board of[1] ($25/day[2])
Tammy H. Scheidegger. . . . . .expires 7/1/20
Cynthia Adell .7/1/23
Andrea L. Simon 7/1/23
Christopher Webster 7/1/23
Sheng B. Lee Yang 7/1/23
Lindsey E. Marsh 7/1/24
Terrance C. Erickson 7/1/25
Marietta S. Luster 7/1/25
Tim Strait[3] 7/1/25
Patrick Stumbras. 7/1/25

Wisconsin state officers appointed by the governor, May 15, 2023, continued

Shawna Hansen[3]. 7/1/26
2 vacancies

Massage Therapy and Bodywork Therapy Affiliated Credentialing Board[1] ($25/day[2])
Robert Coleman Jr. . . . . .expires 7/1/23
Jaime Ehmer 7/1/23
Carla Hedtke .7/1/23
Jeff A. Miller 7/1/23
Gregory J. Quandt 7/1/23
Charisma Townsend-Davila 7/1/23
Ramona J. Trudeau 7/1/23

Medical College of Wisconsin, Incorporated, Board of Trustees of the[1]
Jon Hammes . . . . .expires 6/30/23
Ted Kellner[3] 6/30/27

Medical Education Review Committee (inactive)

Medical Examining Board[1] ($25/day[2])
Milton Bond Jr. . . . . .expires 7/1/23
Clarence Chou .7/1/23
Sumeet Goel .7/1/23
Michael Parish .7/1/23
Sheldon A. Wasserman 7/1/23
Diane Gerlach[3] 7/1/24
Stephanie Hilton[3] 7/1/24
Carmen Lerma[3]. 7/1/24
Lemuel G. Yerby III[3] 7/1/24
Emily Yu[3]. 7/1/24
Kris Ferguson[3] 7/1/25
Gregory Schmeling 7/1/25
Derrick Siebert[3] 7/1/25

Mental Health, Council on
Lynn A. Harrigan . . . . .expires 7/1/22
Jerolynn Bell-Scaggs 7/1/23
Wendy Henderson. 7/1/23
Kevin Kallas 7/1/23
Mary Madden. 7/1/23
Christine Barnard 7/1/24
Nic Dibble 7/1/24
Mark Eisner 7/1/24
Dennis Hanson. 7/1/24
Debra A. Lamboley 7/1/24
Pam Lano 7/1/24
Matthew MacLean. 7/1/24
Brian Michel. .7/1/24
Karen Odegaard 7/1/24
Kemba Banyard 7/1/25
Jessica Boling .7/1/25
Kimberlee M. Coronado 7/1/25
Svea Erlandson .7/1/25
Jennifer Farmbrough 7/1/25
Phung Nguyen .7/1/25
Tim Peerenboom. 7/1/25
Dawn Shelton-Williams. 7/1/25
Sheryl L. Smith 7/1/25
Ana Winton 7/1/25

Midwest Interstate Low-Level Radioactive Waste Commission, Wisconsin Commissioner[1] ($25/day[2])
Mark Paulson . . . . . expires at governor's pleasure

Midwest Interstate Passenger Rail Commission
Scott Rogers. . . . . .expires 1/2/23
vacancy

Midwestern Higher Education Commission
Connie L. Hutchison. . . . . .expires 7/1/23
Rebecca Larson. 7/1/23
Julie Underwood. . . . expires at governor's pleasure

Migrant Labor, Council on
John I. Bauknecht . . . . .expires 7/1/23
Aimee Jo Castleberry 7/1/23
Erica A. Kunze 7/1/23
Jose Martinez .7/1/23
Laura Waldvogel 7/1/23
Carolyn Flyte .7/1/25
Kate Lambert .7/1/25
Lupe G. Martinez 7/1/25
Ben Obregon .7/1/25
Erica L. Sweitzer-Beckman. 7/1/25
2 vacancies

Military and State Relations, Council on
Linda Fournier . . . . expires at governor's pleasure
vacancy

Milwaukee Child Welfare Partnership Council
Jameelah A. Love. . . . . .expires 7/1/22
Anthony E. Shields 7/1/22
Santana Lee 7/1/23
Linda Davis 7/1/24
Victor E. Barnett 7/1/25
Bria Grant 7/1/25
Christine Holmes. 7/1/25
Willie Johnson Jr. 7/1/25
Patti R. Logsdon 7/1/25
Mallory O'Brien 7/1/25
Kelly Pethke 7/1/25
Carmen M. Pitre 7/1/25
Sequanna Taylor 7/1/25

Mississippi River Parkway Commission
Jill Billings . . . . .expires 2/1/24
Jean Galasinski 2/1/24
Howard Marklein 2/1/24
Lee Nerison 2/1/24
Loren Oldenburg 2/1/24
Sherry Quamme 2/1/24
John J. Rosenow 2/1/24
Kris Sampson .2/1/24
Rosalie Schnick. 2/1/24
Jeff Smith 2/1/24
Kathleen Sweeney. 2/1/24
Thomas Vondrum 2/1/24

National and Community Service Board
Paula Horning . . . . .expires 5/1/24
Adam Riley 5/1/25
Christine Beatty 5/1/25
Anthony F. Hallman 5/1/25
David Moldavsky. 5/1/25
Margaret Jane Moore 5/1/25
Karen Pritchard. 5/1/25
Susan Schwartz. 5/1/25
Yolanda D. Shelton-Morris 5/1/25

Wisconsin state officers appointed by the governor, May 15, 2023, continued

Patricia Takamine 5/1/25
Theresa Clark 5/1/26
3 vacancies

Natural Resources, Department of, Secretary[1] (group 7 salary[2])
Adam N. Payne[3] . . . expires at governor's pleasure

Natural Resources Board[1]
William H. Smith . . . . .expires 5/1/25
Marcy West 5/1/25
Sharon Adams[3]. 5/1/27
Sandra Dee Naas[3] 5/1/27
R. Paul Buhr[3] 5/1/29
Dylan Jennings[3] 5/1/29
Jim VandenBrook[3] 5/1/29

Naturopathic Medicine Examining Board[1] ($25/day[2])
Robert Coleman Jr.[3]. . . . . .expires 7/1/23
Robyn Doege-Brennan[3] 7/1/23
Paul Ratté 7/1/23
Jill Crista[3]. 7/1/24
Kristine Nichols. 7/1/24
Allison Becker[3] 7/1/25
David Kiefer[3] 7/1/25

Nonmotorized Recreation and Transportation Trails Council
Rod Bartlow . . . . . expires at governor's pleasure
Stephen J. Clark . . . . governor's pleasure
Kirsten Finn . . . . governor's pleasure
William Johnson . . . . governor's pleasure
Anne Murphy . . . . governor's pleasure
William Pennoyer . . . . governor's pleasure
David Phillips . . . . governor's pleasure
Ben Popp . . . . governor's pleasure
Geoffrey Snudden . . . . governor's pleasure
Blake Theisen . . . . governor's pleasure
vacancy

Nursing, Board of[1] ($25/day[2])
Christian Saldivar Frias[3] 7/1/23
Linda Scott[3]. 7/1/23
Robert Weinman. 7/1/23
Emily Zentz 7/1/23
Janice Ann Edelstein[3]. 7/1/24
John Anderson[3] 7/1/25
Vera Guyton[3] .7/1/25
Rosalyn McFarland[3] 7/1/26
vacancy

Nursing Home Administrator Examining Board[1] ($25/day[2])
Lizzy Kaiser[3]. . . . . .expires 7/1/23
David L. Larson[3] 7/1/23
Patrick Shaughnessy[3]. 7/1/23
Diane Lynch-Decombsh[3] 7/1/24
Echo E. Bristol[3] 7/1/25
Jason Williams[3] 7/1/26
3 vacancies

Occupational Therapists Affiliated Credentialing Board[1] ($25/day[2])
Laura O'Brien . . . . .expires 7/1/19

Teresa L. Black. 7/1/23
Terry Erickson. .7/1/23
Randi Hanson. .7/1/23
Kari Inda 7/1/26
2 vacancies

Off-Highway Motorcycle Council
Craig A. Johnson. . . . . .expires 3/1/24
Robert B. McConnell 3/1/24
Bryan T. Much. 3/1/24
Phillip Smage. .3/1/24
Mitch Winder .3/1/26

Off-Road Vehicle Council
Rob McConnell . . . . .expires 3/1/24
Edward Slaminski 3/1/24
Michael Biese 3/1/25
Robert A. Donahue 3/1/25
Daniel Thole. 3/1/25
David Traczyk .3/1/26
James Wisneski 3/1/26

Offender Reentry, Council on
Robert P. Koebele . . . . .expires 7/1/19
Mary B. Davies .7/1/23
Emily Hynek 7/1/23
Sharlene Lopez. 7/1/23
Elizabeth Lucas. 7/1/23
Nicole R. Miller 7/1/23
Jon Padgham 7/1/23
Eric Boulanger .7/1/24
Marguerite Burns 7/1/24
Jeanne Geraci .7/1/24

Optometry Examining Board[1] ($25/day[2])
Mark Jinkins. . . . . .expires 7/1/16
Robert C. Schulz 7/1/20
Jeffrey J. Clark. 7/1/23
Lisa Slaby 7/1/23
Peter I. Sorce 7/1/23
Emmylou Wilson 7/1/23
vacancy

Parole Commission, Chairperson[1] (group 2 salary[2])
Jon Erpenbach[3]. . . . . .expires 3/1/25

Perfusionists Examining Council ($25/day[2])
David F. Cobb . . . . .expires 7/1/13

Pharmacy Examining Board[1] ($25/day[2])
Tony D. Peterangelo . . . . .expires 7/1/23
Tiffany O'Hagan[3] 7/1/24
Michael Walsh[3] 7/1/24
Susan Kleppin .7/1/25
Christa Wilson .7/1/25
John Weitekamp 7/1/26
vacancy

Physical Disabilities, Council on
Michael Conley-Kuhagen . . . . .expires 7/1/23
Artrell M. Mason 7/1/23
Charles H. Vandenplas 7/1/23
Roberto Escamilla II 7/1/24
Gabriel M. Schlieve 7/1/24
Benjamin Barrett 7/1/25
Ann Belisle. 7/1/25

Wisconsin state officers appointed by the governor, May 15, 2023, continued

Jeff Fox 7/1/25
Jason Glozier 7/1/25
Jackie Gordon. .7/1/25
Nicole Herda 7/1/25
Ramsey Lee 7/1/25
Karen E. Secor. 7/1/25
Emmakate Thelke . . expires at governor's pleasure

Physical Therapy Examining Board[1] ($25/day[2])
Shari Berry. . . . . .expires 7/1/20
John F. Greany .7/1/23
Barbara A. Carter. 7/1/25
Steven William Johnson[3]. 7/1/25
Todd McEldowney. 7/1/25

Physician Assistant Affiliated Credentialing Board[1] ($25/day[2])
Clark Collins. . . . . .expires 7/1/23
Jean Fischer 7/1/23
Cynthia Martin .7/1/23
Tara Streit 7/1/23
Eric Elliot. 7/1/24
Emelle Holmes-Drammeh. 7/1/24
Jennifer Jarrett .7/1/24
Robert Sanders. 7/1/24
Jacqueline Edwards 7/1/25

Podiatry Affiliated Credentialing Board[1] ($25/day[2])
Jack W. Hutter. . . . . .expires 7/1/23
Randal Kittleson 7/1/23
James Whelan[3] 7/1/24
vacancy

Prison Industries Board[1]
Tracey Griffith. . . . . .expires 5/1/24
James Meyer 5/1/24
Todd Spencer. .5/1/24
Mike Ervin 5/1/26
Kevin A. Carr[3] .5/1/27
David Hagemeier[3]. 5/1/27
Lenard Simpson[3]. 5/1/27
Aaron Zimmerman[3]. 5/1/27
vacancy

Psychology Examining Board[1] ($25/day[2])
Daniel Schroeder . . . . .expires 7/1/19
Peter I. Sorce 7/1/20
Marcus P. Desmonde 7/1/21
David Thompson. 7/1/22
John N. Greene. 7/1/23
John Small[3] 7/1/24

Public Defender Board[1]
Regina Dunkin . . . . .expires 5/1/22
James Brennan[3] 5/1/25
Anthony B. Cooper Sr.[3] 5/1/25
Ellen Thorn[3] 5/1/25
Mai N. Xiong[3] .5/1/25
Patrick Fiedler[3] 5/1/26
John J. Hogan[3] 5/1/26
Ingrid Jagers[3]. 5/1/26
Joseph T. Miotke[3] 5/1/26

Public Health Council
Terry Brandenburg . . . . expires 12/31/25
Sandra Brekke 12/31/25

Mary Dorn 12/31/25
Inshirah Farhoud. 12/31/25
Richard Ferrari Traner. 12/31/25
Elizabeth Giese. 12/31/25
Gary D. Gilmore 12/31/25
Kue Her. 12/31/25
William Keeton. 12/31/25
Eric Krawczyk. 12/31/25
Heather Le Monds. 12/31/25
G Lee 12/31/25
Robert Leischow 12/31/25
Angelique Lewis 12/31/25
Paula P. Morgen 12/31/25
Jordan-Lindsay Morris 12/31/25
Obiageli Nwabuzor 12/31/25
Shary Perez 12/31/25
Sarah Reed-Thryselius 12/31/25
Catoya M. Roberts 12/31/25
Alan Schwartzstein 12/31/25
Vipul Shukla. 12/31/25
Joan Theurer 12/31/25

Public Leadership Board
Scott R. Jensen . . . . .expires 5/1/23
Kimberly Liedl 5/1/23
Dean Stensberg 5/1/23
Jason Thompson. 5/1/23
Robin J. Vos 5/1/23

Public Records Board
James A. Friedman. . expires at governor's pleasure
Staci M. Hoffman. . . . . governor's pleasure
Julie A. Laundrie . . . . governor's pleasure
vacancy

Public Service Commission[1] (group 5 salary[2])
Rebecca Cameron Valcq . . . . .expires 3/1/25
Tyler Huebner[3] .3/1/27
Summer Strand[3] 3/1/29

Radiography Examining Board[1] ($25/day[2])
Paul J. Grebe . . . . .expires 7/1/23
Blas Berumen. 7/1/24
Rachael Julson 7/1/24
Timothy Peter Szczykutowicz 7/1/24
Donald Borst .7/1/25
2 vacancies

Railroads, Commissioner of[1] (group 5 salary[2])
Don Vruwink[3]. . . . . .expires 3/1/29

Real Estate Appraisers Board[1] ($25/day[2])
Jennifer M. Espinoza-Coates . . . . .expires 5/1/19
Dennis Myers .5/1/21
Thomas Kneesel 5/1/22
Christopher Krueger[3] 5/1/24
David J. Wagner[3] 5/1/26
Daniel Figurski[3] 5/1/26
Richard Rubow[3] 5/1/27

Real Estate Curriculum and Examinations, Council on
Robert G. Blakely . . . . .expires 7/1/20
Kathy S. Zimmerman 7/1/20
Anne M. Blood 7/1/23
3 vacancies

Statistics and Reference: Officials | 643

Wisconsin state officers appointed by the governor, May 15, 2023, continued

Real Estate Examining Board[1] ($25/day[2])
Dennis Pierce . . . . .expires 7/1/13
Sonya Mays 7/1/24
Gurmit Kaleka. 7/1/25
Cathy Lacy. 7/1/25
Jeffery Berry[3] 7/1/26
Elizabeth Anne Lauer[3] 7/1/26
Thomas J. Richie[3] 7/1/26

Recycling, Council on
Carsten Jarrod Holter . . . . .expires 1/5/24
David F. Keeling .1/5/24
David Pellitteri 1/5/24
Heidi Woelfel 1/5/24
Jeff Zillich 1/5/24
John Anderson .1/5/27
Mark A. Walter 1/5/27

Remote Notary Council
Jessica J. Shrestha . . . . .expires 5/1/24
Mark Ladd 5/1/25
Cheri Hipenbecker. 5/1/26
Philip Suckow. 5/1/26

Respiratory Care Practitioners Examining Council[1] ($25/day[2])
vacancy

Retirement Board, Wisconsin ($25/day[2])
Wayne E. Koessl . . . . .expires 5/1/09
Herbert Stinski 5/1/12
Mary Von Ruden 5/1/13
Julie Wathke 5/1/18
Angela Miller 5/1/24
Steven Wilding .5/1/24
Christy Schwan. .5/1/25
vacancy

Retirement Systems, Joint Survey Committee on
Michele Stanton . . . . expires 5/12/27

Revenue, Department of, Secretary[1] (group 7 salary[2])
Peter W. Barca . . . . . expires at governor's pleasure

Rural Health Development Council[1]
Hendrik Lai . . . . .expires 7/1/24
Rian Podein 7/1/24
Nicole Schweitzer 7/1/25
14 vacancies

Safety and Professional Services, Department of, Secretary[1] (group 6 salary[2])
Daniel Hereth[3] . . . . expires at governor's pleasure

Small Business Environmental Council
Amy Litscher . . . . .expires 7/1/23
Jody A. Jansen 7/1/24
vacancy

Small Business Regulatory Review Board
Hana Cutler . . . . .expires 5/1/25
Peggy Gunderson 5/1/25
Elizabeth Krause 5/1/25
Norah Leach 5/1/25
Alycann Taylor 5/1/25

Brian Cummins .5/1/26
Ruth Zahm 5/1/26

Snowmobile Recreational Council[1]
Gary Hilgendorf . . . . .expires 7/1/23
Samuel J. Landes 7/1/23
Robert B. Lang 7/1/23
Andrew F. Malecki 7/1/23
Leon Wolfe[3] 7/1/23
Lynsey Burzinski[3] 7/1/24
Joel Enking 7/1/24
Dale Mayo 7/1/24
Lee Van Zeeland 7/1/24
Beverly A. Dittmar[3] 7/1/25
Abigail Haas[3] 7/1/25
Michael F. Holden[3]. 7/1/25
Don Mrotek[3] 7/1/25
Sue Smedegard[3] 7/1/25
Erica Voelker[3] 7/1/25

Southeast Wisconsin Professional Baseball Park District Board[1]
Anthony Berndt . . . . .expires 7/1/23
Frank J. Busalacchi 7/1/23
Deb C. Dassow .7/1/23
Troy A. Dennhof 7/1/23
Timothy Sheehy 7/1/23
John T. Zapfel 7/1/23

Sporting Heritage Council
Reggie Hayes . . . . .expires 7/1/22

State Capitol and Executive Residence Board
Rafeeq Asad. . . . . .expires 5/1/26
Lesley Sager. 5/1/26
Ronald L. Siggelkow 5/1/26
John Fernholz 5/1/27
Arlan K. Kay 5/1/27
Janis Ringhand .5/1/27
Melissa Destree .5/1/29

State Employees Suggestion Board
Paul Ruby . . . . .expires 5/1/17
2 vacancies

State Fair Park Board[1] ($10/day, not to exceed $600/year[2])
Dan Devine . . . . .expires 5/1/24
Paul M. Ziehler .5/1/24
Kelly H. Grebe 5/1/25
John Yingling 5/1/25
Jayme L. Buttke .5/1/26
Kallie Jo Coates[3] 5/1/27
Susan Crane[3] 5/1/28

State Historical Society of Wisconsin Board of Curators[1]
Keene Winters . . . . .expires 7/1/23
Cate Zeuske 7/1/24
Sondy Pope . . . . . . expires at governor's pleasure
vacancy

State Trails Council
Steve Falter . . . . .expires 7/1/23
Randy Harden 7/1/24
Kristin Jewett 7/1/24

Wisconsin state officers appointed by the governor, May 15, 2023, continued

Luana Schneider 7/1/24
Holly Tomlanovich. 7/1/24
Ken Bates 7/1/25
Lacey Heward. .7/1/25
Bryan T. Much. .7/1/25
Kendal Neitzke .7/1/25
Ben L. Popp 7/1/25
Mike Repyak 7/1/25

State Use Board
Bill Smith . . . . expires 5/1/11
Amy C. Grotzke .5/1/21
Jana Steinmetz .5/1/21
Nickolas C. George Jr. 5/1/23
Tracy Nelson 5/1/23
3 vacancies

Tax Appeals Commission[1] (group 4 salary[2])
Elizabeth Kessler. . . . . .expires 3/1/25
Jessica Roulette. 3/1/27
Kenneth P. Adler[3] 3/1/29

Tax Exemptions, Joint Survey Committee on
Elizabeth Kessler . . . . expires 1/15/25

Teachers Retirement Board ($25/day[2])
David Schalow . . . . .expires 5/1/24
3 vacancies

Technical College System Board[1] ($100/year[2])
Janixa Franco Gonzalez[3] . . . . .expires 5/1/25
Douglas A. Holton Sr. 5/1/25
Daniel Sperberg .5/1/25
Mark Tyler 5/1/25
Daniel Klecker .5/1/27
Sara J. Rogers. 5/1/27
Lindsay Blumer[3] 5/1/29
Quincey Daniels Jr.[3] 5/1/29
Alex Lasry[3] 5/1/29
vacancy

Tourism, Council on
Deborah Carey . . . . .expires 7/1/23
Nathan Gordon. 7/1/23
Missy Tracy 7/1/23
Luke Zahm 7/1/23
Natalie Chin. 7/1/24
Robert Davis 7/1/24
Mary McPhetridge. 7/1/24
Denise Stillman. 7/1/24
Darren S. Bush 7/1/25
Genyne Edwards 7/1/25
Arlan Frels 7/1/25
Michelle Martin 7/1/25
Ben L. Popp 7/1/25
Krystal Westfahl 7/1/25

Tourism, Department of, Secretary[1] (group 6 salary[2])
Anne Sayers . . . . . . expires at governor's pleasure

Transportation, Department of, Secretary[1] (group 7 salary[2])
Craig M. Thompson[3]   expires at governor's pleasure

Transportation Projects Commission
Allison Bussler . . . . expires at governor's pleasure
Timothy M. Hanna . . . . governor's pleasure
Mark Servi . . . . governor's pleasure

Uniform Dwelling Code Council
Daniel E. Wald. . . . . .expires 7/1/19
Abe Degnan. 7/1/20
W. Scott Satula .7/1/20
Donald Brunner 7/1/22
Brian Juarez 7/1/22
Joseph Lotegeluaki 7/1/22
Dawn McIntosh 7/1/22
Virge Temme 7/1/22
Edmund Weaver Jr. 7/1/22
Mark Etrheim .7/1/23
Brian Wert 7/1/23

Uniform State Laws, Commission on
Vladlen David Zvenyach . . . . .expires 5/1/21
Fred Risser. 5/1/23

United States Semiquincentennial Commission, Wisconsin Commission for the
Robert Haglund[3] . . . . .expires 1/1/27
Shannon Holsey[3] 1/1/27
Zach Madden 1/1/27
Gena Selby[3] 1/1/27

University of Wisconsin Hospitals and Clinics Authority[1]
Karen Menéndez Coller . . . . .expires 7/1/24
Annette Miller .7/1/24
Candice Owley[3] 7/1/25
Paul Seidenstricker[3] 7/1/25
Barbara Lawton[3] 7/1/26
Sondy Pope[3] 7/1/27

University of Wisconsin System, Board of Regents of the[1]
Robert B. Atwell . . . . .expires 5/1/24
Michael T. Jones 5/1/24
Jennifer Staton[3] 5/1/24
Evan Brenkus[3] .5/1/25
Héctor Colón[3] .5/1/25
Cris Peterson 5/1/25
Edmund Manydeeds III. 5/1/26
Karen Walsh 5/1/26
Amy Blumenfeld Bogost[3] 5/1/27
Kyle M. Weatherly[3]. 5/1/27
John W. Miller[3] 5/1/28
Ashok Rai[3] 5/1/28
Angela Adams[3] 5/1/29
Dana Wachs[3] 5/1/29
Jim Kreuser[3] 5/1/30
Joan M. Prince[3] 5/1/30

Veterans Affairs, Board of[1]
Tonnetta D. Carter . . . . .expires 5/1/23
Chris J. Cornelius[3] 5/1/25
Christopher Hanson[3] 5/1/25
Robert Hesselbein[3] 5/1/25
Vern L. Larson[3] 5/1/25
Jason Maloney[3]. 5/1/25

Statistics and Reference: Officials | 645

Wisconsin state officers appointed by the governor, May 15, 2023, continued

Mark Mathwig[3]....................5/1/25
Pat Beggs[3].......................5/1/27
William R. Schrum[3]...............5/1/27

Veterans Affairs, Department of, Secretary[1] (group 6 salary[2])
James Bond[3] ..... expires at governor's pleasure

Veterinary Diagnostic Laboratory Board
Sandra C. Madland ....expires 5/1/23
Rebecca Suchla....................5/1/24
Laurence Baumann.................5/1/25
Barry Kleppe 5/1/25
Rory Meyer 5/1/26
Paul Kunde ...... expires at governor's pleasure

Veterinary Examining Board[1] ($25/day[2])
Hunter Lang................expires 7/1/23
Lisa Weisensel Nesson...............7/1/23
Lyn M. Schuh......................7/1/23
Arden M. Sherpe...................7/1/23
Karl Duane Solverson[3]..............7/1/23
Alan Holter 7/1/24
Amanda Reese....................7/1/24
Leslie Estelle 7/1/25

Waste Facility Siting Board[1] ($35/day[2])
James Schuerman........... expires 5/1/2013
Jeanette P. DeKeyser 5/1/18
Dale R. Shaver 5/1/20

Waterways Commission, Wisconsin[1]
Bruce J. Neeb[3] ....expires 3/1/24

Janeau Allman....................3/1/25
Korin Doering....................3/1/25
Roger E. Walsh[3]...................3/1/28
vacancy

Wetland Study Council
Tracy Hames................expires 7/1/24
Matthew Howard 7/1/25
Tim Andryk 7/1/26
Stacy Jepson.....................7/1/26
Thomas Larson...................7/1/27
Carol McCoy.....................7/1/27
Paul Kent.......................7/1/28
vacancy

Wisconsin Compensation Rating Bureau
Daniel Burazin .... expires at governor's pleasure
Michael W. Lester .... governor's pleasure

Women's Council
Gabrielle Aranda-Pino ....expires 7/1/23
Jolene Bowman 7/1/23
Rachel Fernandez.................7/1/23
Denise Gaumer-Hutchison 7/1/23
Rosalyn L. McFarland...............7/1/23
Nerissa Nelson...................7/1/23
Sara Rodriguez...................1/5/25

Workforce Development, Department of, Secretary[1] (group 7 salary[2])
Amy Pechacek[3].... expires at governor's pleasure

Note: List includes only appointments made by the governor. Additional members frequently serve ex officio or are appointed by other means. The governor also appoints members of intrastate regional agencies and nonstatutory committees and makes temporary appointments under Wis. Stat. ch. 17 to elected state and county offices when vacancies occur.

Terms are specified by the following statute sections or as otherwise provided by law: Wis. Stat. § 15.05 (1) - secretaries; Wis. Stat. § 15.06 (1)—commissioners; Wis. Stat. § 15.07 (1)—governing boards and attached boards; Wis. Stat. § 15.08 (1)—examining boards and councils; Wis. Stat. § 15.09 (1)—councils.

1. Nominated by the governor and appointed with the advice and consent of the senate. Senate confirmation is required for secretaries of departments, members of commissions and commissioners, governing boards, examining boards, and other boards as designated by statute. 2. Members of boards and councils are reimbursed for actual and necessary expenses incurred in performing their duties. In addition, examining board members receive $25 per day for days worked, and members of certain other boards under Wis. Stat. § 15.07 (5) receive a per diem as noted in the table. Wis. Stat. § 20.923 places state officials in one of 10 executive salary groups (ESG) for which salary ranges have been established. Group salary ranges for the period January 3, 2021, through June 17, 2023, are: Group 1: $65,416–$112,341; Group 2: $70,658–$121,326; Group 3: $76,315–$131,040; Group 4: $82,430–$141,544; Group 5: $89,045–$152,880; Group 6: $96,179–$165,131; Group 7: $103,875–$178,339; Group 8: $112,195–$192,608; Group 9: $121,181–$208,021; Group 10: $130,894–$224,661. 3. Nominated by governor but not yet confirmed by senate. 4. Compensation set by Economic Development Corporation Board.

Source: Appointment lists maintained by governor's office and received by the Legislative Reference Bureau on or before May 15, 2023.

Wisconsin Circuit Court judges, April 4, 2023

Counties in circuit	Branch	Court location	Judges	Term expires July 31
Adams	1	Friendship	Daniel Glen Wood	2027
	2	Friendship	Tania M. Bonnett................	2028
Ashland.........	—	Ashland	Kelly J. McKnight................	2024
Barron..........	1	Barron	James C. Babler.................	2028
	2	Barron	J. Michael Bitney	2026

Wisconsin Circuit Court judges, April 4, 2023, continued

Counties in circuit	Branch	Court location	Judges	Term expires July 31
	3	Barron	Maureen D. Boyle	2026
Bayfield	—	Washburn	John P. Anderson	2027
Brown	1	Green Bay	Donald R. Zuidmulder	2027
	2	Green Bay	Thomas J. Walsh	2024
	3	Green Bay	Tammy Jo Hock	2025
	4	Green Bay	Kendall M. Kelley	2027
	5	Green Bay	Marc A. Hammer[1]	2027
	6	Green Bay	John P. Zakowski	2024
	7	Green Bay	Timothy A. Hinkfuss	2025
	8	Green Bay	Beau G. Liegeois	2026
Buffalo, Pepin	—	Alma	Thomas W. Clark	2024
Burnett	—	Siren	Melissa R. Mogen[1]	2023
Calumet	1	Chilton	Jeffrey S. Froehlich	2024
	2	Chilton	Carey J. Reed	2027
Chippewa	1	Chippewa Falls	Steven H. Gibbs	2024
	2	Chippewa Falls	James M. Isaacson	2027
	3	Chippewa Falls	Benjamin J. Lane	2026
Clark[2]	—	Neillsville	Lyndsey Boon Brunette	2024
Columbia	1	Portage	Todd J. Hepler	2027
	2	Portage	W. Andrew Voigt[1]	2023
	3	Portage	Troy D. Cross	2024
Crawford	—	Prairie du Chien	Lynn Marie Rider	2028
Dane	1	Madison	Susan M. Crawford	2024
	2	Madison	Josann M. Reynolds[1]	2027
	3	Madison	Diane Schlipper	2028
	4	Madison	Everett Mitchell	2028
	5	Madison	Nicholas J. McNamara	2028
	6	Madison	Nia Trammell	2027
	7	Madison	Mario D. White	2027
	8	Madison	Frank D. Remington	2024
	9	Madison	Jacob B. Frost	2027
	10	Madison	Ryan Nilsestuen[3]	2024
	11	Madison	Ellen K. Berz	2024
	12	Madison	Chris Taylor	2027
	13	Madison	Julie Genovese	2027
	14	Madison	John D. Hyland	2028
	15	Madison	Stephen Ehlke	2028
	16	Madison	Rhonda L. Lanford	2025
	17	Madison	David Conway	2027
Dodge	1	Juneau	Brian A. Pfitzinger	2026
	2	Juneau	Martin J. De Vries[1]	2023
	3	Juneau	Joseph G. Sciascia	2025
	4	Juneau	Kristine A. Snow	2026
Door	1	Sturgeon Bay	D. Todd Ehlers	2024
	2	Sturgeon Bay	David L. Weber[1]	2023
Douglas	1	Superior	Kelly J. Thimm	2027
	2	Superior	George L. Glonek	2027
Dunn	1	Menomonie	James M. Peterson	2026
	2	Menomonie	Christina M. Mayer	2027
	3	Menomonie	Luke M. Wagner	2027
Eau Claire	1	Eau Claire	John F. Manydeeds	2028
	2	Eau Claire	Michael A. Schumacher	2026
	3	Eau Claire	Emily M. Long	2024
	4	Eau Claire	Jon M. Theisen	2024
	5	Eau Claire	Sarah Harless	2024
	6	Eau Claire	Beverly Wickstrom	2028
Florence, Forest	—	Crandon	Leon D. Stenz	2026
Fond du Lac	1	Fond du Lac	Anthony C. Nehls[3]	2024

Wisconsin Circuit Court judges, April 4, 2023, continued

Counties in circuit	Branch	Court location	Judges	Term expires July 31
	2	Fond du Lac	Laura J. Lavey	2028
	3	Fond du Lac	Andrew J. Christenson	2027
	4	Fond du Lac	Tricia L. Walker	2028
	5	Fond du Lac	Douglas R. Edelstein	2028
Grant	1	Lancaster	Robert P. Van De Hey[4]	2023
	2	Lancaster	Craig R. Day	2027
Green	1	Monroe	Faun Marie Phillipson	2027
	2	Monroe	Thomas J. Vale	2027
Green Lake	—	Green Lake	Mark Slate[1]	2023
Iowa	—	Dodgeville	Matthew C. Allen	2028
Iron	—	Hurley	Anthony J. Stella Jr.	2026
Jackson[3]	1	Black River Falls	Anna L. Becker	2027
	2	Black River Falls	Daniel S. Diehn	2027
Jefferson	1	Jefferson	William V. Gruber	2025
	2	Jefferson	William F. Hue	2025
	3	Jefferson	Robert F. Dehring Jr.	2024
	4	Jefferson	Bennett J. Brantmeier[1]	2023
Juneau	1	Mauston	Stacy A. Smith	2024
	2	Mauston	Paul S. Curran	2026
Kenosha	1	Kenosha	Gerad Dougvillo	2027
	2	Kenosha	Jason A. Rossell	2024
	3	Kenosha	Bruce E. Schroeder	2026
	4	Kenosha	Anthony J. Milisauskas[1]	2023
	5	Kenosha	David P. Wilk	2027
	6	Kenosha	Angelina Gabriele	2027
	7	Kenosha	Jodi L. Meier[1]	2023
	8	Kenosha	Chad G. Kerkman	2027
Kewaunee	—	Kewaunee	Jeffrey R. Wisnicky	2028
La Crosse	1	La Crosse	Ramona A. Gonzalez	2025
	2	La Crosse	Elliott Levine	2025
	3	La Crosse	Todd Bjerke	2025
	4	La Crosse	Scott L. Horne	2025
	5	La Crosse	Gloria L. Doyle	2027
Lafayette	—	Darlington	Duane M. Jorgenson	2027
Langlade	—	Antigo	John B. Rhode	2027
Lincoln	1	Merrill	Galen Bayne-Allison	2028
	2	Merrill	Robert R. Russell	2025
Manitowoc[2]	1	Manitowoc	Mark R. Rohrer	2025
	2	Manitowoc	Jerilyn M. Dietz	2024
	3	Manitowoc	Robert P. Dewane[1]	2023
Marathon	1	Wausau	Suzanne C. O'Neill	2027
	2	Wausau	Rick Cveykus	2028
	3	Wausau	LaMont K. Jacobson	2026
	4	Wausau	Gregory J. Strasser[1]	2023
	5	Wausau	Michael K. Moran[1]	2023
	6	Wausau	Scott M. Corbett	2027
Marinette	1	Marinette	Jane M. Sequin	2026
	2	Marinette	James A. Morrison	2025
Marquette	—	Montello	Chad A. Hendee	2025
Menominee, Shawano	1	Shawano	Katherine Sloma	2027
	2	Shawano	William F. Kussel Jr.	2024
Milwaukee	1	Milwaukee	Jack L. Dávila	2027
	2	Milwaukee	Milton L. Childs	2026
	3	Milwaukee	Katie Kegel	2027
	4	Milwaukee	Michael J. Hanrahan[1]	2023
	5	Wauwatosa	Kristela Cervera	2028
	6	Wauwatosa	Ellen R. Brostrom	2027
	7	Milwaukee	Thomas J. McAdams	2026

Wisconsin Circuit Court judges, April 4, 2023, continued

Counties in circuit	Branch	Court location	Judges	Term expires July 31
	8	Milwaukee	William Sosnay	2024
	9	Milwaukee	Paul R. Van Grunsven[1]	2023
	10	Milwaukee	Michelle A. Havas[1]	2023
	11	Milwaukee	David C. Swanson	2025
	12	Milwaukee	David L. Borowski	2027
	13	Milwaukee	Mary Triggiano[5]	2023
	14	Milwaukee	Christopher R. Foley	2028
	15	Milwaukee	Jonathan D. Watts	2027
	16	Wauwatosa	Brittany C. Grayson	2026
	17	Milwaukee	Carolina Maria Stark	2024
	18	Milwaukee	Pedro Colón[1]	2023
	19	Milwaukee	Kori L. Ashley	2027
	20	Milwaukee	Joseph R. Wall	2024
	21	Milwaukee	Cynthia M. Davis[1]	2023
	22	Milwaukee	Timothy M. Witkowiak	2027
	23	Milwaukee	Lindsey C. Grady	2024
	24	Milwaukee	Janet C. Protasiewicz[6]	2026
	25	Milwaukee	Nidhi Kashyap	2028
	26	Milwaukee	William S. Pocan	2025
	27	Milwaukee	Kevin E. Martens	2026
	28	Milwaukee	Mark A. Sanders	2024
	29	Milwaukee	Rebecca A. Kiefer	2026
	30	Milwaukee	Jonathan D. Richards	2027
	31	Milwaukee	Hannah C. Dugan	2028
	32	Milwaukee	Laura Gramling Perez	2026
	33	Milwaukee	Carl Ashley[1]	2023
	34	Milwaukee	Glenn H. Yamahiro	2028
	35	Milwaukee	Frederick C. Rosa[1]	2023
	36	Wauwatosa	Laura A. Crivello	2025
	37	Milwaukee	T. Christopher Dee	2027
	38	Milwaukee	Jeffrey A. Wagner	2024
	39	Milwaukee	Jane V. Carroll	2024
	40	Milwaukee	Danielle L. Shelton	2025
	41	Wauwatosa	Audrey K. Skwierawski	2025
	42	Wauwatosa	Reyna Morales	2027
	43	Wauwatosa	Marshall B. Murray	2024
	44	Wauwatosa	Gwendolyn G. Connolly	2028
	45	Milwaukee	Jean M. Kies	2028
	46	Milwaukee	David A. Feiss	2027
	47	Wauwatosa	Kristy Yang[1]	2023
Monroe	1	Sparta	Todd L. Ziegler	2025
	2	Sparta	Mark L. Goodman	2028
	3	Sparta	Rick Radcliffe	2024
Oconto	1	Oconto	Michael T. Judge[1]	2023
	2	Oconto	Jay N. Conley	2028
Oneida	1	Rhinelander	Mary L. R. Burns[3,7]	2023
	2	Rhinelander	Michael H. Bloom	2024
Outagamie	1	Appleton	Mark J. McGinnis[1]	2023
	2	Appleton	Emily I. Lonergan	2026
	3	Appleton	Mitchell J. Metropulos	2026
	4	Appleton	Yadira J. Rein	2028
	5	Appleton	Carrie A. Schneider	2024
	6	Appleton	Vincent Biskupic	2027
	7	Appleton	Mark G. Schroeder	2028
Ozaukee	1	Port Washington	Paul V. Malloy	2027
	2	Port Washington	Steven M. Cain	2025
	3	Port Washington	Sandy A. Williams	2027
Pierce	—	Ellsworth	Elizabeth Rohl	2028
Polk	1	Balsam Lake	Daniel J. Tolan[1]	2023

Wisconsin Circuit Court judges, April 4, 2023, continued

Counties in circuit	Branch	Court location	Judges	Term expires July 31
	2	Balsam Lake	Jeffery L. Anderson[1]	2023
Portage	1	Stevens Point	Michael D. Zell[1,3]	2023
	2	Stevens Point	Louis J. Molepske Jr.	2028
	3	Stevens Point	Patricia Baker	2028
Price	—	Phillips	Kevin G. Klein	2024
Racine	1	Racine	Wynne Laufenberg	2024
	2	Racine	Eugene A. Gasiorkiewicz	2028
	3	Racine	Maureen Martinez	2025
	4	Racine	Mark F. Nielsen	2028
	5	Racine	Kristin M. Cafferty	2028
	6	Racine	David W. Paulson	2027
	7	Racine	Jon E. Fredrickson	2025
	8	Racine	Faye M. Flancher	2027
	9	Racine	Robert S. Repischak	2024
	10	Racine	Timothy D. Boyle	2024
Richland	—	Richland Center	Lisa McDougal[1,3]	2023
Rock	1	Janesville	Karl R. Hanson	2025
	2	Janesville	Derrick A. Grubb	2025
	3	Janesville	Jeffrey S. Kuglitsch	2024
	4	Janesville	Ashley J. Morse[1,3]	2023
	5	Janesville	Michael A. Haakenson	2027
	6	Janesville	John M. Wood[1]	2023
	7	Janesville	Barbara W. McCrory	2024
Rusk	—	Ladysmith	Annette M. Barna	2028
St. Croix	1	Hudson	Scott J. Nordstrand	2026
	2	Hudson	Edward F. Vlack III	2025
	3	Hudson	Scott R. Needham	2024
	4	Hudson	R. Michael Waterman	2028
Sauk	1	Baraboo	Michael P. Screnock	2028
	2	Baraboo	Wendy J. N. Klicko	2028
	3	Baraboo	Patricia A. Barrett	2024
Sawyer[2]	—	Hayward	John M. Yackel	2027
Sheboygan	1	Sheboygan	Samantha R. Bastil	2027
	2	Sheboygan	Kent Hoffmann[8]	2023
	3	Sheboygan	Angela Sutkiewicz[1]	2023
	4	Sheboygan	Rebecca L. Persick	2027
	5	Sheboygan	Daniel J. Borowski[9]	2023
Taylor	—	Medford	Ann Knox-Bauer	2027
Trempealeau	—	Whitehall	Rian W. Radtke[1]	2023
Vernon	—	Viroqua	Darcy J. Rood[10]	2023
Vilas	1	Eagle River	Martha J. Milanowski	2028
	2	Eagle River	Daniel L. Overbey	2028
Walworth	1	Elkhorn	Phillip A. Koss	2024
	2	Elkhorn	Daniel S. Johnson	2028
	3	Elkhorn	Kristine E. Drettwan	2027
	4	Elkhorn	David M. Reddy	2028
Washburn	—	Shell Lake	Angeline E. Winton	2026
Washington	1	West Bend	Ryan J. Hetzel[1,3]	2023
	2	West Bend	James K. Muehlbauer	2026
	3	West Bend	Michael S. Kenitz[1,3]	2023
	4	West Bend	Sandra J. Giernoth	2027
Waukesha	1	Waukesha	Michael O. Bohren	2025
	2	Waukesha	Jennifer Dorow	2024
	3	Waukesha	Ralph M. Ramirez[1]	2023
	4	Waukesha	Lloyd V. Carter1	2023
	5	Waukesha	J. Arthur Melvin III	2026
	6	Waukesha	Brad D. Schimel	2025
	7	Waukesha	Frederick J. Strampe[3,11]	2023
	8	Waukesha	Michael P. Maxwell	2027

Wisconsin Circuit Court judges, April 4, 2023, continued

Counties in circuit	Branch	Court location	Judges	Term expires July 31
	9	Waukesha	Michael J. Aprahamian	2027
	10	Waukesha	Paul Bugenhagen Jr.	2027
	11	Waukesha	William Domina[1]	2023
	12	Waukesha	Laura Lau	2024
Waupaca	1	Waupaca	Troy L. Nielsen[1]	2023
	2	Waupaca	Vicki L. Clussman	2026
	3	Waupaca	Raymond S. Huber	2024
Waushara	1	Wautoma	Guy D. Dutcher[1]	2023
	2	Wautoma	Scott C. Blader	2028
Winnebago	1	Oshkosh	Teresa S. Basiliere	2024
	2	Oshkosh	Scott C. Woldt[1]	2023
	3	Oshkosh	Bryan D. Keberlein	2028
	4	Oshkosh	Michael Gibbs	2028
	5	Oshkosh	John A. Jorgensen	2028
	6	Oshkosh	Daniel J. Bissett[1]	2023
Wood[2]	1	Wisconsin Rapids	Gregory J. Potter	2026
	2	Wisconsin Rapids	Nicholas J. Brazeau Jr.	2024
	3	Wisconsin Rapids	Todd P. Wolf	2027

— Means the circuit has only one branch.

1. Reelected on April 4, 2023, for a six-year term to commence on August 1, 2023. 2. Under 2019 Act 184, four counties selected by the director of state courts may add new circuit court branches effective August 1, 2023. Judges were elected on April 4, 2023, for six-year terms to commence on August 1, 2023. William Bratcher was elected to serve as Clark County Circuit Court Judge Branch 2; Anthony D. Lambrecht was elected to serve as Manitowoc County Circuit Court Judge Branch 4; Monica M. Isham was elected to serve as Sawyer County Circuit Court Judge Branch 2; and Timothy Gebert was elected to serve as Wood County Circuit Court Judge Branch 4. 3. Appointed by Governor Tony Evers. 4. Lisa R. Riniker was newly elected on April 4, 2023, for a six-year term to commence on August 1, 2023. 5. Ana Berrios-Schroeder was newly elected on April 4, 2023, for a six-year term to commence on August 1, 2023. 6. Janet Protasiewicz was elected to the Wisconsin Supreme Court on April 4, 2023, for a ten-year term to commence on August 1, 2023. 7. Michael W. Schiek was newly elected on April 4, 2023, for a six-year term to commence on August 1, 2023. 8. Natasha L. Torry was newly elected on April 4, 2023, for a six-year term to commence on August 1, 2023. 9. George Limbeck was newly elected on April 4, 2023, for a six-year term to commence on August 1, 2023. 10. Timothy J. Gaskell was newly elected on April 4, 2023, for a six-year term to commence on August 1, 2023. 11. Cody Horlacher was newly elected on April 4, 2023, for a six-year term to commence on August 1, 2023.

Sources: 2021–2023 Wisconsin Statutes; Wisconsin Elections Commission, department data, April 2023; governor's appointment notices; Wisconsin Court System, Circuit court judges and court websites, April 2023.

Wisconsin county officers: county clerks, April 2023

	Clerk	Website
Adams	Liana Glavin (A)	www.co.adams.wi.us
Ashland	Heather Schutte (D)	www.co.ashland.wi.us
Barron	Jessica Hodek (A)	www.barroncountywi.gov
Bayfield	Lynn Divine (D)	www.bayfieldcounty.org
Brown	Patrick W. Moynihan, Jr. (R)	www.co.brown.wi.us
Buffalo	Roxann Halverson (D)	www.buffalocounty.com
Burnett	Wanda Hinrichs (D)	www.burnettcounty.com
Calumet	Beth Hauser (R)	www.co.calumet.wi.us
Chippewa	Jaclyn Sadler (D)	www.co.chippewa.wi.us
Clark	Christina Jensen (R)	www.clarkcounty.wi.gov
Columbia	Susan Moll (R)	www.co.columbia.wi.us
Crawford	Roberta Fisher (D)	www.crawfordcountywi.org
Dane	Scott McDonell (D)	www.countyofdane.com
Dodge	Karen Gibson (R)	www.co.dodge.wi.gov
Door	Jill Lau (R)	www.co.door.wi.gov
Douglas	Kaci Jo Lundgren (A)	www.douglascountywi.org
Dunn	Andrew Mercil (A)	www.co.dunn.wi.us

Wisconsin county officers: county clerks, April 2023, continued

	Clerk	Website
Eau Claire	Sue McDonald (D)	www.co.eau-claire.wi.us
Florence	Donna Trudell (R)	www.florencecountywi.com
Fond du Lac	Lisa Freiberg (R)	www.fdlco.wi.gov
Forest	Nora Matuszewski (R)	www.co.forest.wi.gov
Grant	Tonya White (R)	www.co.grant.wi.gov
Green	Arianna L. Voegeli (D)	www.co.green.wi.gov
Green Lake	Elizabeth Otto (R)	www.co.green-lake.wi.us
Iowa	Kristy Spurley (D)	www.iowacounty.org
Iron	Michael Saari (D)	www.co.iron.wi.gov
Jackson	Cindy M. Altman (D)	www.co.jackson.wi.us
Jefferson	Audrey McGraw (R)	www.jeffersoncountywi.gov
Juneau	Terri Treptow (R)	www.co.juneau.wi.gov
Kenosha	Regi Waligora (D)	www.co.kenosha.wi.us
Kewaunee	Jamie Annoye (D)	www.kewauneeco.org
La Crosse	Ginny Dankmeyer (D)	www.lacrossecounty.org
Lafayette	Carla Jacobson (R)	www.lafayettecountywi.org
Langlade	Judy Nagel (R)	www.co.langlade.wi.us
Lincoln	Christopher Marlowe (R)	www.co.lincoln.wi.us
Manitowoc	Jessica Backus (R)	www.co.manitowoc.wi.us
Marathon	Kim Trueblood (R)	www.co.marathon.wi.us
Marinette	Kathy Brandt (R)	www.marinettecounty.com
Marquette	Kiley Lloyd (R)	www.co.marquette.wi.us
Menominee	Laure Pecore (D)	www.co.menominee.wi.us
Milwaukee	George L. Christenson (D)	https://county.milwaukee.gov
Monroe	Shelley Bohl (R)	www.co.monroe.wi.us
Oconto	Kim Pytleski (R)	www.co.oconto.wi.us
Oneida	Tracy Hartman (R)	www.co.oneida.wi.us
Outagamie	Jeff King (R)	www.outagamie.org
Ozaukee	Karen Niemuth (A)	www.co.ozaukee.wi.us
Pepin	Audrey Bauer (R)	www.co.pepin.wi.us
Pierce	Jamie Feuerhelm (I)	www.co.pierce.wi.us
Polk	Shabana Lundeen (A)	www.co.polk.wi.us
Portage	Maria Davis (A)	www.co.portage.wi.us
Price	Jean Gottwald (D)	www.co.price.wi.us
Racine	Wendy Christensen (R)	https://racinecounty.com
Richland	Derek S. Kalish (A)	www.co.richland.wi.us
Rock	Lisa Tollefson (D)	www.co.rock.wi.us
Rusk	Connie Meyer (R)	www.ruskcounty.org
St. Croix	Christine Hines (A)	www.sccwi.gov
Sauk	Rebecca Evert (R)	www.co.sauk.wi.us
Sawyer	Lynn Fitch (R)	www.sawyercountygov.org
Shawano	Kara Skarlupka (A)	www.co.shawano.wi.us
Sheboygan	Jon Dolson (R)	www.sheboygancounty.com
Taylor	Andria Farrand (R)	www.co.taylor.wi.us
Trempealeau	Paul L. Syverson (D)	https://co.trempealeau.wi.us
Vernon	Jerry Pedretti (R)	www.vernoncounty.org
Vilas	Kim Olkowski (A)	www.vilascountywi.gov
Walworth	Susi Pike (A)	www.co.walworth.wi.us
Washburn	Alicia Swearingen (A)	www.co.washburn.wi.us
Washington	Ashley Reichert (R)	www.co.washington.wi.us
Waukesha	Meg Wartman (R)	www.waukeshacounty.gov
Waupaca	Kristy Opperman (A)	www.co.waupaca.wi.us
Waushara	Megan Kapp (R)	www.co.waushara.wi.us
Winnebago	Julie Barthels (A)	www.co.winnebago.wi.us
Wood	Trent Miner (R)	www.co.wood.wi.us

Note: County clerks are elected at the general election for four-year terms.
A–Appointed; D–Democrat; I–Independent; R–Republican.
Source: Data collected from county clerks by Wisconsin Legislative Reference Bureau, April 2023.

Wisconsin county officers: county board chair; executive (or alternative); treasurer, April 2023

	County board chair (# of supervisors)	Executive, administrator, administrative coordinator	Treasurer
Adams	John West (20)	Cynthia Haggard (AC)	Jani Zander (D)
Ashland	Richard Pufall (21)	Dan Grady (CA)	Tracey Hoglund (D)
Barron	Louie Okey (29)	Jeff French (CA)	Samantha Sommerfeld (A)
Bayfield	Dennis M. Pocernich (13)	Mark Abeles-Allison (CA)	Jenna Galligan (D)
Brown	Patrick J. Buckley (26)	Troy J. Streckenbach (CE)	Paul D. Zeller (R)
Buffalo	Dennis Bork (14)	Lee Engfer (AC)	Tina Anibas (R)
Burnett	Donald Taylor (21)	Nathan Ehalt (CA)	Sonja Rikkola (R)
Calumet	Alice Connors (21)	Todd Romenesko (CA)	Mike Schlaak (R)
Chippewa	Dean Gullickson (21)	Randy Scholz (CA)	Patricia Schimmel (D)
Clark	Wayne Hendrickson (29)	Christina Jensen (AC)	Renee Schoen (R)
Columbia	Chris Polzer (28)	Susan Moll (AC)	Stacy L. Opalewski (R)
Crawford	Tom Cornford (17)	Dan McWilliams (AC)	Deanne Lutz (D)
Dane	Patrick Miles (37)	Joe Parisi (CE)	Adam Gallagher (D)
Dodge	Dave Frohling (33)	Cameron Clapper (CA)	Kris Keith (A)
Door	David Lienau (21)	Ken Pabich (CA)	Ryan Schley (R)
Douglas	Mark Liebaert (21)	Ann Doucette (CA)	Carol Jones (D)
Dunn	Kelly McCullough (29)	Kris Korpela (CM)	Sifia Jevne (A)
Eau Claire	Nick Smiar (29)	Kathryn Schauf (CA)	Glenda J. Lyons (D)
Florence	Jeanette Bomberg (12)	Donna Trudell (AC)	Donna Liebergen (R)
Fond du Lac	Steven Abel (25)	Sam Kaufman (CE)	Brenda A. Schneider (R)
Forest	Cindy Gretzinger (21)	Nora Matuszewski (AC)	Christy Conley (R)
Grant	Robert C. Keeney (17)	Shane Drinkwater (AC)	Carrie Eastlick (R)
Green	Jerry Guth (31)	Arianna L. Voegeli (AC)	Sherri Hawkins (R)
Green Lake	David Abendroth (19)	Cate Wylie (AC)	Jessica McLean (A)
Iowa	John M. Meyers (21)	Larry Bierke (CA)	Debi Heisner (I)
Iron	Joe Pinardi (15)	Michael Saari (AC)	Clara Maki (D)
Jackson	Jeff Amo (19)	Cindy M. Altman (AC)	Tabitha Chonka-Michaud (D)
Jefferson	Steven J. Nass (30)	Ben Wehmeier (CA)	John E. Jensen (R)
Juneau	Timothy Cottingham (21)	None	Denise Giebel (R)
Kenosha	Gabe Nudo (23)	Samantha Kerkman (CE)	Teri Jacobson (D)
Kewaunee	Daniel A. Olson (20)	Scott Feldt (CA)	Michelle Dax (R)
La Crosse	Monica Kruse (30)	Jane Klekamp (CA)	Amy Twitchell (D)
Lafayette	Jack Sauer (16)	Jack Sauer (CA)	Lisa Black (R)
Langlade	Ben Pierce (21)	Jason Hilger (CA)	Tammy Wilhelm (D)
Lincoln	Don Friske (22)	Renee Krueger (AC)	Robbin Gigl (R)
Manitowoc	Tyler Martell (25)	Bob Ziegelbauer (CE)	Amy Kocian (R)
Marathon	Kurt Gibbs (38)	Lance Leonhard (CA)	Connie Beyersdorff (R)
Marinette	John M. Guarisco (30)	John Lefebvre (CA)	Bev A. Noffke (R)
Marquette	Ken Borzick (17)	Ron Barger (CA)	Jody Myers (R)
Menominee	Elizabeth Moses (7)	Jeremy Weso (AC)	Mary Beth Pecore (D)
Milwaukee	Marcelia Nicholson (18)	David Crowley (CE)	David Cullen (D)
Monroe	Cedric Schnitzler (16)	Tina Osterberg (CA)	Debra Carney (R)
Oconto	Alan Sleeter (31)	Erik Pritzl (CA)	Tanya Peterson (R)
Oneida	Scott Holewinski (21)	Lisa Charbarneau (AC)	Tara Ostermann (R)
Outagamie	Jeff Nooyen (36)	Tom Nelson (CE)	Trenten Woelfel (R)
Ozaukee	Lee Schlenvogt (26)	Jason Dzwinel (CA)	Sandra Tretow (A)
Pepin	Tom Milliren (12)	Pamela Hansen (AC)	Patricia Scharr (R)
Pierce	Jon Aubart (17)	Jason Matthys (CA)	Kathy Fuchs (R)
Polk	Jay Luke (15)	Vince Netherland (CA)	Amanda Nissen (D)
Portage	Allen Haga Jr. (25)	John Pavelski (CE)	Pamela R. Przybelski (D)
Price	Alan Barkstrom (13)	Nicholas Trimner (CA)	Lynn Neeck (D)
Racine	Thomas Roanhouse (21)	Jonathan Delagrave (CE)	Jeff Latus (R)
Richland	Marty Brewer (21)	Vacant	Jeffrey Even (A)
Rock	Richard Bostwick (29)	Joshua Smith (CA)	Michelle Roettger (D)
Rusk	Alan Rathsack (19)	Ashley Heath (AC)	Verna Nielsen (R)
St. Croix	Bob Long (19)	Ken Witt (CA)	Denise Anderson (R)
Sauk	Tim McCumber (31)	Brent Miller (CA)	Elizabeth Geoghegan (R)
Sawyer	Tweed Shuman (15)	Andy Albarado (CA)	Janeen Abric (A)

Wisconsin county officers: county board chair; executive (or alternative); treasurer, April 2023, continued

	County board chair (# of supervisors)	Executive, administrator, administrative coordinator	Treasurer
Shawano	Thomas Kautza (27)	James Davel (AC)	Debra Wallace (R)
Sheboygan	Vern Koch (25)	Alayne Krause (CA)	Laura Henning-Lorenz (D)
Taylor	Jim Metz (17)	Nicole Hager (AC)	Sarah Holtz (R)
Trempealeau	John Aasen (17)	Rick Niemeier (AC)	Laurie Halama (D)
Vernon	Lorn Goede (19)	Vacant (AC)	Karen DeLap (R)
Vilas	Gerald Burkett (21)	Kimberly Olkowski (AC)	Paulette Sarnicki (R)
Walworth	Rick Stacey (11)	Mark W. Luberda (CA)	Valerie Etzel (R)
Washburn	Dave Wilson (21)	Darci Peckman-Krueger (AC)	Nicole Tims (R)
Washington	Jeffrey Schleif (21)	Joshua Schoemann (CE)	Scott M. Henke (R)
Waukesha	Paul Decker (25)	Paul Farrow (CE)	Pamela Reeves (R)
Waupaca	Dick Koeppen (27)	Amanda Welch (AC)	Mark Sether (R)
Waushara	John Jarvis (11)	Melissa Pingel (CA)	Jessica Jaeger (R)
Winnebago	Thomas Egan (36)	Jon Doemel (CE)	Amber Hoppa (A)
Wood	Lance A. Pliml (19)	Lance A. Pliml (AC)	Heather Gehrt (D)

Note: The county board is composed of supervisors who are elected at the nonpartisan spring election for two-year terms. The county board elects one of its members to be its chair. County executives are elected at the nonpartisan spring election for four-year terms. In lieu of electing a county executive, a county can choose to appoint a county administrator or to designate a county official to serve as the county's administrative coordinator. Treasurers are elected at the general election for four-year terms.

A–Appointed to fill a vacancy; AC–Administrative coordinator; CA–County administrator; CE–County executive; CM–County manager; D–Democrat; I–Independent; R–Republican.

Source: Data collected from county clerks by Wisconsin Legislative Reference Bureau, April 2023.

Wisconsin county officers: clerk of circuit court; register of deeds; surveyor, April 2023

	Clerk of circuit court	Register of deeds	Surveyor[1]
Adams	Lori L. Banovec (D)	Julie Scholis (A)	Jerol Smart
Ashland	Sandra Paitl (D)	Julie Gleeson (D)	Patrick McKuen
Barron	Sharon Millermon (R)	Margo Katterhagen (R)	Catlon Phelps
Bayfield	Deidre Zifko (D)	Dan Heffner (D)	Patrick McKuen
Brown	John A. Vander Leest (R)	Cheryl A. Berken (R)	Dale E. Raisleger
Buffalo	Julie Vollmer (R)	Carol Burmeister (D)	Ron Jasperson
Burnett	Jacqueline O. Baasch (D)	Jeanine Chell (D)	Jason Towne
Calumet	LeAnne Karls (R)	Tamara Alten (R)	Bradley Buechel
Chippewa	Nathan A. Liedl (R)	Melanie K. McManus (D)	Sam Wenz
Clark	Heather Bravener (D)	Mary Denk (R)	Wade Pettit
Columbia	Julie Kayartz (R)	Lisa Krintz (R)	Jim Grothman
Crawford	Nancy Dowling (D)	Melissa Nagel (D)	Rich Marks
Dane	Carlo Esqueda (D)	Kristi Chlebowski (D)	Dan Frick
Dodge	Kelly Enright (R)	Chris Planasch (R)	Dave Addison
Door	Connie DeFere (R)	Carey Petersilka (R)	None
Douglas	Michele L. Wick (D)	Tracy Middleton (D)	Matt Johnson
Dunn	Katie Schalley (R)	Heather Kuhn (D)	Thomas Carlson
Eau Claire	Susan Schaffer (D)	Tina Pommier (D)	Dean Roth
Florence	Jessica McCoy (R)	Vacant	None
Fond du Lac	Ramona Geib (R)	James M. Krebs (R)	Peter Kuen
Forest	Penny Carter (D)	Cortney Britten Cleereman (D)	Jamie Anderson
Grant	Tina McDonald (R)	Andrea Noethe (R)	Jay P. Adams
Green	Barbara Miller (R)	Cynthia Meudt (R)	None
Green Lake	Amy Thoma (R)	Renee Thiem-Korth (R)	Don Lenz
Iowa	Lisa Leahy (R)	Taylor Campbell (D)	None
Iron	Karen Ransanici (D)	Daniel Soine (D)	Todd Maki
Jackson	Jean Sahr (D)	Shari Marg (D)	Cody Brommerich

Wisconsin county officers: clerk of circuit court; register of deeds; surveyor, April 2023, continued

	Clerk of circuit court	Register of deeds	Surveyor[1]
Jefferson	Cindy Hamre Incha (R)	Staci M. Hoffman (R)	Jim Morrow
Juneau	Alecia Kast (R)	Stacy Havill (R)	Gary Dechant
Kenosha	Rebecca Matoska-Mentink (D)	JoEllyn M. Storz (D)	Robert W. Merry
Kewaunee	Rebecca Deterville (D)	Germaine Bertrand (D)	Mau & Associates, LLP
La Crosse	Tammy Pedretti (D)	Robin L Kadrmas (A)	Bryan Meyer
Lafayette	Trisha Rowe (R)	Cathy Paulson (R)	Aaron Austin
Langlade	Tina M Wild (R)	Chet Haatvedt (D)	None
Lincoln	Thomas Barker (R)	Sarah Koss (R)	Anthony Dallman
Manitowoc	April R. Higgins (R)	Kristi L. Tuesburg (R)	Jason Bolz
Marathon	Kelly Schremp (R)	Dean Stratz (R)	Dave Decker
Marinette	Carrie Brazeau (R)	Renee Miller (R)	None
Marquette	Shari Rudolph (R)	Bette Krueger (R)	Jerry Smart
Menominee	Delsy Kakwich (D)	Menomin Hawpetoss (D)	None
Milwaukee	Anna Hodges (D)	Israel Ramón (D)	Robert W. Merry
Monroe	Laura Endres (R)	Deb Brandt (R)	Gary Dechant
Oconto	Trisha L. LeFebre (R)	Laurie Wusterbarth (R)	Brian Gross
Oneida	Brenda Behrle (R)	Kyle Franson (R)	Vacant
Outagamie	Barb Bocik (R)	Sarah R. Van Camp (R)	Terry Van Hout
Ozaukee	Connie Mueller (R)	Ronald A. Voigt (R)	None
Pepin	Audrey Lieffring (R)	Monica J. Bauer (R)	Cedar Corporation
Pierce	Kerry Feuerhelm (R)	Julie Hines (D)	James Filkins
Polk	Sharon Jorgenson (R)	Sally Spanel (D)	Steve Geiger
Portage	Lisa M. Roth (D)	Cynthia A. Wisinski (D)	Thomas J. Trzinski
Price	Lisa Walcisak (R)	Sylvia Kerner (D)	Alfred Schneider
Racine	Samuel A. Christensen (R)	Karie Pope (R)	None
Richland	Stacy Kleist (R)	Susan Triggs (R)	Todd Rummler
Rock	Susan Dahl	Sandy Disrud (D)	Brad Heuer
Rusk	Lori Gorsegner (R)	Mary Berg (R)	None
St. Croix	Kristi Severson (R)	Beth Pabst (D)	Corey Hughes
Sauk	Carrie Wastlick (R)	Brent Bailey (R)	Patrick Dederich (R)
Sawyer	Marge Kelsey (R)	Paula Chisser (R)	Dan Pleoger
Shawano	Ethan Schmidt (R)	Amy Dillenburg (R)	David Yurk
Sheboygan	Christine Koenig (R)	Ellen Schleicher (D)	Jeremy Hildebrand
Taylor	Jill Scheithauer (R)	Jaymi S. Kohn (R)	Robert Meyer
Trempealeau	Kari Tidquist (R)	Rose Ottum (D)	Joe Nelsen
Vernon	Sheila Olson (R)	Lindsey Formanek (R)	Laurence Johns
Vilas	Beth Soltow (R)	Sherry Bierman (R)	Thomas Boettcher (R)
Walworth	Kristina Secord (R)	Michele Jacobs (R)	SEWRPC
Washburn	Shannon Anderson (R)	Renee Bell (R)	Lucas Meier
Washington	Sarah Adjemian (R)	Sharon Martin (R)	Scott Schmidt
Waukesha	Monica Paz (A)	James Behrend (R)	Robert W. Merry
Waupaca	Yvette Kienert (R)	Michael Mazemke (R)	Joseph Glodowski
Waushara	Katrina Rasmussen (R)	Heather Schwersenska (R)	Jerry Smart
Winnebago	Tara Berry (R)	Natalie Strohmeyer (R)	None
Wood	Kimberly A. Stimac (R)	Tiffany Ringer (R)	Kevin Boyer

Note: Clerks of circuit court, registers of deeds, and surveyors are elected at the general election for four-year terms. In lieu of electing a surveyor, a county can choose to appoint one.

A–Appointed to fill a vacancy; D–Democrat; I–Independent; R–Republican.

1. Surveyors are appointed unless party designation is shown.

Source: Data collected from county clerks by Wisconsin Legislative Reference Bureau, April 2023.

Wisconsin county officers: district attorney; sheriff; coroner (or alternative), April 2023

	District attorney	Sheriff	Coroner/medical examiner
Adams	Rebecca Maki-Wallander (A)	Brent R. York (R)	Marilyn Rogers (ME)
Ashland	David Meany (I)	Brian Zupke (D)	Barbara Beeksma (D)
Barron	Brian Wright (R)	Chris Fitzgerald (D)	Nate Dunston (ME)
Bayfield	Kimberly Lawton (D)	Tony Williams (D)	Thomas Renz (D)
Brown	David L. Lasee (R)	Todd J. Delain (R)	Dr. Elizabeth Douglas (ME)
Buffalo	Tom Bilski (R)	Michael Osmond (R)	Cindy Giese (R)
Burnett	James Jay Rennicke (R)	Tracy Finch (I)	Jalene Scovell (ME)
Calumet	Nathan F. Haberman (R)	Brett Bowe (R)	Michael Klaeser (ME)
Chippewa	Wade C. Newell (R)	Travis Hakes (R)	Ronald Patten (D)
Clark	Melissa Inlow (D)	Scott Haines (R)	Clarissa Rochester (I)
Columbia	Brenda Yaskal (D)	Roger Brandner (R)	Madeleine Groenier (ME)
Crawford	Lukas Steiner (A)	Dale McCullick (R)	Joe Morovits (D)
Dane	Ismael R. Ozanne (D)	Kalvin Barrett (A)	Cristina Figueroa Soto (ME)
Dodge	Andrea Will (A)	Dale J. Schmidt (R)	Patrick Schoebel (ME)
Door	Colleen Nordin (R)	Tammy Sternard (D)	Elizabeth Douglas (ME)
Douglas	Mark Fruehauf (D)	Matt Izzard (D)	Sheila Keup (ME)
Dunn	Andrea Nodolf (R)	Kevin Bygd (R)	Marcie Rosas (ME)
Eau Claire	Peter J. Rindal (A)	Dave Riewestahl (D)	Marcie Rosas (ME)
Florence	Doug Drexler (D)	Dan Miller (R)	Jeff Rickaby (R)
Fond du Lac	Eric Toney (R)	Ryan F. Waldschmidt (R)	Adam Covach (ME)
Forest	Charles Simono (D)	Jeffery Marvin (R)	Crystal Schaub (ME)
Grant	Lisa Riniker (R)	Nate Dreckman (R)	Phyllis Fuerstenberg (R)
Green	Craig Nolen (R)	Jeff Skatrud (D)	Monica Hack (D)
Green Lake	Gerise Laspisa (A)	Mark Podoll (R)	Thomas Wastart II (ME)
Iowa	Zachary P. Leigh (A)	Michael Peterson (R)	Wendell F. Hamlin (R)
Iron	Matthew Tingstad (R)	Paul Samardich (R)	Robert Barnabo (R)
Jackson	Emily Hynek (A)	Duane Waldera (D)	Bonnie Kindschy (ME)
Jefferson	Monica J. Hall (D)	Paul Milbrath (R)	Nichol Tesch (ME)
Juneau	Kenneth Hamm (R)	Andrew Zobal (R)	Myron Oestreich (ME)
Kenosha	Michael D. Graveley (D)	David W. Zoerner (R)	Patrice Hall (ME)
Kewaunee	Andrew Naze (D)	Matthew Joski (R)	Rory Groessl (I)
La Crosse	Tim Gruenke (D)	John Siegel (D)	Elizabeth Lubinski (ME)
Lafayette	Jenna Gill (R)	Reginald Gill (R)	Linda Gebhardt (D)
Langlade	Kelly Hays (A)	Mark Westen (R)	Larry Shadick (R)
Lincoln	Kristopher Ellis (D)	Ken Schneider (R)	Valerie Caylor (R)
Manitowoc	Jacalyn LaBre (R)	Daniel Hartwig (R)	Curtis Green (D)
Marathon	Theresa Wetzsteon (D)	Chad Billeb (R)	Jessica Blahnik (ME)
Marinette	DeShea D. Morrow (R)	Randy Miller (R)	Kalynn Van Ermen (ME)
Marquette	Vacant	Joseph Konrath (R)	Thomas Wastart II (ME)
Menominee[1]	Gregory Parker (R)	Rebecca Smith (I)	Patrick Roberts (ME)
Milwaukee	John T. Chisholm (D)	Earnell R. Lucas (D)	Wieslawa Tlomak (ME)
Monroe	Kevin Croninger (R)	Wesley D. Revels (R)	Robert Smith (ME)
Oconto	Hannah N. Schuchart (A)	Todd Skarban (R)	Elizabeth Douglas (ME)
Oneida	Michael Schiek (R)	Grady Hartman (R)	Crystal Schaub (ME)
Outagamie	Melinda Tempelis (R)	Clint C. Kriewaldt (R)	Douglas A. Bartelt (R)
Ozaukee	Adam Y. Gerol (R)	Christy Knowles (R)	Luke Warnke (ME)
Pepin	Jon D. Seifert (R)	Joel D. Wener (R)	Jeff Doughty (A)
Pierce	Halle Hatch (D)	Chad Koranda (R)	John Worsing (ME)
Polk	Jeffrey L. Kemp (R)	Brent A. Waak (R)	John Dinnies (ME)
Portage	Cass Cousins (A)	Michael Lukas (D)	Heather Schultz (ME)
Price	Vacant	Brian Schmidt (R)	James Dalbesio, III (D)
Racine	Patricia J. Hanson (R)	Christopher Schmaling (R)	Kristan Binninger (ME)
Richland	Jennifer M. Harper (R)	Clay Porter (R)	James C. Rossing (I)
Rock	David J. O'Leary (D)	Curt Fell (D)	Agnieszka Rogalska (ME)
Rusk	Ellen Anderson (A)	Jeffery Wallace (R)	Annette Grotzinger (ME)
St. Croix	Karl Anderson (R)	Scott Knudson (R)	Patty Schachtner (ME)
Sauk	Michael X. Albrecht (I)	Chip Meister (R)	Greg L. Hahn (R)
Sawyer	Bruce R. Poquette (R)	Doug Mrotek (R)	John Froemel (ME)

Wisconsin county officers: district attorney; sheriff; coroner (or alternative), April 2023, continued

District attorney	Sheriff	Coroner/medical examiner
Shawano[1] . . . . . . Gregory Parker (R)	George Lenzner (R)	Brian Westfahl (R)
Sheboygan. . . . . . . Joel Urmanski (R)	Cory Roeseler (R)	Chris Nehring (ME)
Taylor . . . . Kristi Tlusty (D)	Larry Woebbeking (R)	Scott Perrin (ME)
Trempealeau . . . . John Sacia (D)	Brett Semingson (R)	Bonnie Kindschy (D)
Vernon . . . . Timothy Gaskell (R)	Roy R. Torgerson (R)	Betty Nigh (R)
Vilas . . . . Karl Hayes (A)	Joseph A. Fath (R)	Crystal Schaub (ME)
Walworth. . . . . . . Zeke Wiedenfeld (R)	Dave Gerber (R)	Gina Carver (ME)
Washburn . . . . . . Aaron Marcoux (D)	Dennis Stuart (R)	Angela Pank (R)
Washington . . . . . Mark Bensen (R)	Martin Schulteis (R)	Craig Garbisch (ME)
Waukesha . . . . . . Susan L. Opper (R)	Eric J. Severson (R)	Lynda Biedrzycki (ME)
Waupaca . . . . Kat Turner (A)	Timothy R. Wilz (R)	Catherine Wegener (ME)
Waushara. . . . . . . Matthew Leusink (R)	Walter Zuehlke (R)	Amanda Thoma (ME)
Winnebago . . . . . Eric Sparr (A)	John Matz (R)	Cheryl Brehmer (ME)
Wood . . . . Craig Lambert (I)	Shawn Becker (R)	Dave Patton (A)

Note: District attorneys, sheriffs, and coroners are elected at the general election for four-year terms. In lieu of electing a coroner, a county can choose to appoint a medical examiner.

A–Appointed to fill a vacancy; D–Democrat; I–Independent; ME–medical examiner; R–Republican.

1. Menominee and Shawano counties comprise a single prosecutorial unit, served by a single district attorney.

Source: Data collected from county clerks by Wisconsin Legislative Reference Bureau, April 2023.

Tribal chairs in Wisconsin, April 2023

Tribe and chair	Contact information
Bad River Band of Lake Superior Chippewa. . . . . Mike Wiggins Jr. (chair)	P.O. Box 39, Odanah 54861-0039 715-682-7111; https://badriver-nsn.gov
Forest County Potawatomi . . . . James Crawford (chair)	P.O. Box 340, Crandon 54520-0346 715-478-7200; https://fcpotawatomi.com
Ho-Chunk Nation . . . . Marlon WhiteEagle (president)	P.O. Box 667, Black River Falls 54615-0667 715-284-9343; https://ho-chunknation.com
Lac Courte Oreilles Band of Lake Superior Chippewa . . Louis Taylor, Sr. (chair)	13394 W. Trepania Road, Hayward 54843-2186 715-634-8934; https://lcotribe.com
Lac du Flambeau Band of Lake Superior Chippewa. . . . John Johnson (president)	P.O. Box 67, Lac du Flambeau 54538-0067 715-588-3303; https://ldftribe.com
Menominee Indian Tribe of Wisconsin . . . . Gena Kakkak (chair)	P.O. Box 910, Keshena 54135-0910 715-799-5114; https://menominee-nsn.gov
Oneida Nation . . . . Tehassi Hill (chair)	P.O. Box 365, Oneida 54155-0365 920-869-4481; https://oneida-nsn.gov
Red Cliff Band of Lake Superior Chippewa . . . . Christopher Boyd (chair)	88455 Pike Road, Bayfield 54814-0529 715-779-3700; https://redcliff-nsn.gov
St. Croix Chippewa Indians of Wisconsin . . . . William Reynolds (chair)	24663 Angeline Avenue, Webster 54893-9246 715-349-2195; https://stcroixojibwe-nsn.gov
Sokaogon Chippewa Community . . . . Robert VanZile Jr. (chair)	3051 Sand Lake Road, Crandon 54520-8815 715-478-7500; https://sokaogonchippewa.com
Stockbridge-Munsee Band of Mohican Indians . . . . . . Shannon Holsey (president)	P.O. Box 70, Bowler 54416-9801 715-793-4111; https://mohican.com

Sources: Wisconsin State Tribal Relations Initiative, http://witribes.wi.gov [April 2023] and individual tribal websites.

Wisconsin full-time equivalent state government positions

Type of funding	Number of positions[1]
General purpose revenue	34,199.58
Program revenue	20,809.59
Federal appropriations	10,972.56
Segregated funds	4,811.61
Total	**70,793.35**

1. Positions authorized by the legislature, or under procedures authorized by the legislature, as of June 30, 2022. Includes all branches of state government and the UW System.
Source: Wisconsin Department of Administration, Division of Executive Budget and Finance, departmental data, April 2023.

Wisconsin executive branch employees

Status	Number of employees[1]
Permanent	27,562
Unclassified	1,247
Limited term	4,016
Project	488
Seasonal	5
Elected	76
Total	**33,394**

1. Employees working on a full-time or part-time basis for the executive branch only, as of June 30, 2022.
Source: Wisconsin Department of Administration, Division of Executive Budget and Finance, departmental data, April 2023.

Wisconsin state and local government employment and payrolls, March 2021

Function	Full-time	Part-time	Full-time equivalent[1]	Total payroll ($1,000)
Air and water transport	386	59	405	2,172
Corrections	12,506	948	13,020	64,051
Education	134,428	90,755	168,238	799,640
Elementary and secondary	98,614	42,444	119,209	525,699
Higher education institutions	34,929	48,020	47,962	268,384
Other	885	291	1,067	5,557
Fire protection	4,372	5,219	4,999	30,586
Government administration	9,700	12,659	11,809	57,133
Health and hospitals	9,782	3,522	11,500	55,664
Highways	9,557	1,475	10,012	51,107
Housing and community development	1,018	358	1,156	5,129
Judicial and legal	5,413	1,087	5,818	32,693
Libraries	1,638	3,230	2,961	10,416
Natural resources	2,908	1,395	3,420	16,156
Parks and recreation	2,341	3,402	3,236	13,612
Police protection	15,111	2,812	15,936	96,102
Public welfare and social insurance administration	12,711	3,710	14,856	64,544
Sewerage	1,825	713	1,936	10,310
Solid waste management	1,335	995	1,445	6,415
Transit	1,870	155	1,959	8,365
Utilities (electric and water supply)	2,258	320	2,354	12,503

Wisconsin state and local government employment and payrolls, March, 2021, continued

	Number of employees			
Function	Full-time	Part-time	Full-time equivalent[1]	Total payroll ($1,000)
Other	6,735	3,669	7,477	38,677
Total	235,894	136,483	282,537	1,375,277

1. Full-time equivalent (FTE) is a derived statistic that provides an estimate of a government's total full-time employment by converting part-time employees to a full-time amount.

Source: U.S. Census Bureau, "2021 Government Employment and Payroll Tables," https://www.census.gov/programs-surveys/apes/data/datasetstables.html [October 28, 2022].

Wisconsin state and local government employment and payrolls

	Employees (full-time equivalents)[1]			Monthly payroll ($1,000)		
	State	Local	Total	State	Local	Total
2000	63,697	219,793	283,490	230,570	662,358	892,928
2005	70,189	223,523	293,712	275,824	725,374	962,942
2010	72,428	211,407	283,835	326,643	851,380	1,178,022
2015	74,383	211,442	285,825	357,334	901,925	1,259,259
2016	72,676	212,640	285,316	356,014	926,005	1,282,019
2017	73,073	213,021	286,094	363,732	958,789	1,322,521
2018	71,513	214,541	286,054	366,313	970,396	1,336,710
2019	71,907	212,799	284,706	382,513	1,002,811	1,385,324
2020	66,270	214,544	280,814	398,215	1,025,511	1,423,725
2021	67,828	209,955	277,783	413,709	1,033,613	1,447,321

1. Full-time equivalent (FTE) is a derived statistic that provides an estimate of a government's total full-time employment by converting part-time employees to a full-time amount.

Source: U.S. Census Bureau, "2021 Government Employment & Payroll Tables" and prior years at https://www.census.gov/programs-surveys/apes/data/datasetstables/2021.html [November 3, 2022].

Wisconsin state classified service profile, 2020

Category	Number	Percent
Permanent classified employees	28,808	100
Persons with disabilities[1]	1,686	5.8
Women	15,099	51.7
Racial/ethnic minorities	4,277	14.6
Black	2,053	7.0
Hispanic	1,017	3.5
Asian	812	2.8
American Indian /Alaska Native	145	0.5
Native Hawaiian/Pacific Islander	16	Z
Two or more races	176	0.6

Note: Data excludes unclassified, temporary, judicial, and legislative employees and employees in the UW System. Data may not be comparable to prior Blue Book tables.

Z—less than 0.01%.

1. Includes persons with severe disabilities. Disabilities are voluntarily self-reported.

Source: Wisconsin Department of Administration, Division of Personnel Management, *State of Wisconsin Classified Workforce & Affirmative Action Report: Fiscal Years 2019 and 2020*.

PUBLIC FINANCE

Wisconsin state revenues and expenditures

Fiscal year	General fund[1] Revenues ($1,000)	General fund[1] Expenditures ($1,000)	Other funds[2] Revenues ($1,000)	Other funds[2] Expenditures ($1,000)	Total—all funds Revenues ($1,000)	Total—all funds Expenditures ($1,000)	Net surplus or deficit[3] ($1,000)
1975...	2,966,532	3,148,968	1,252,422	924,455	4,218,954	4,073,423	78,120
1980...	4,900,275	5,027,130	2,481,324	1,809,840	7,381,599	6,836,970	72,627
1985...	7,160,174	7,237,716	4,908,582	2,743,287	12,068,756	9,981,002	314,084
1990...	9,418,918	9,464,483	5,483,442	3,287,809	14,902,360	12,752,292	306,452
1995...	13,259,772	13,094,450	9,823,810	4,963,553	23,083,582	18,058,003	400,881
2000...	18,185,980	18,333,634	14,687,330	8,111,005	32,873,310	26,444,639	574,416
2005...	21,191,600	21,488,178	15,827,541	10,772,231	37,019,141	32,260,409	-131,675
2010...	26,918,079	26,933,345	19,320,601	13,214,942	46,238,680	40,148,287	99,873
2011...	28,926,518	28,951,824	27,574,543	13,974,915	56,501,061	42,926,739	305,584
2012...	28,557,414	27,379,001	11,959,996	14,158,805	40,517,410	41,537,806	1,115,672
2013...	29,435,181	28,400,745	20,586,682	14,164,382	50,021,863	42,565,127	1,987,605
2014...	29,765,921	30,028,018	26,166,710	15,060,009	55,932,631	45,088,027	1,669,233
2015...	30,622,404	30,861,201	14,096,474	15,437,387	44,718,878	46,298,588	1,359,156
2016...	31,172,186	30,852,156	12,752,252	15,034,976	43,924,438	45,887,132	1,656,065
2017...	32,390,154	31,891,665	23,285,943	15,099,934	55,676,097	46,991,599	2,254,454
2018...	32,850,441	32,685,469	20,506,458	15,513,335	53,356,899	48,198,804	1,744,973
2019...	35,034,907	34,173,937	20,229,339	16,069,377	55,264,246	50,243,314	2,437,987
2020...	37,984,891	35,684,286	17,996,210	16,149,772	55,981,101	51,834,058	4,109,663
2021...	42,683,495	42,285,113	45,121,703	17,070,238	87,805,198	59,355,351	4,073,585
2022...	48,076,685	45,169,430	1,818,690	17,731,281	49,895,375	62,900,711	5,923,558

1. Includes general purpose revenue (GPR), program revenue, and federal funding. 2. Includes special revenue funds (such as conservation and transportation), federal funding, debt service, capital projects, pension and retirement funds, trust and agency funds, and others. 3. Unappropriated (unreserved) balance of the general fund for the fiscal year.
Source: Wisconsin Department of Administration, State Controller's Office, *2022 Annual Fiscal Report*, October 2022, and prior editions.

Wisconsin state budget allocations

Revenue type and allocation	Fiscal year 2021–22 ($1,000)	Fiscal year 2022–23 ($1,000)	Fiscal biennium ($1,000)	% of total budget allocations
GENERAL PURPOSE REVENUE.......	19,284,768.7	19,731,372.0	39,016,140.7	44.70
State operations	4,527,332.1	4,733,288.3	9,260,620.4	10.61
Local assistance.................	9,676,227.6	9,877,041.8	19,553,269.4	22.40
Aids to individuals and organizations ...	5,081,209.0	5,121,041.9	10,202,250.9	11.69
PROGRAM REVENUE.............	18,781,116.8	18,577,516.4	37,358,633.2	42.80
State operations	7,789,882.4	7,768,481.1	15,558,363.5	17.83
Local assistance.................	1,327,664.5	1,330,537.3	2,658,201.8	3.05
Aids to individuals and organizations ...	9,663,569.9	9,478,498.0	19,142,067.9	21.93
Program Revenue—federal........	11,943,494.5	11,727,336.2	23,670,830.7	27.12
State operations...............	2,593,445.3	2,581,782.6	5,175,227.9	5.93
Local assistance...............	1,251,832.1	1,254,344.9	2,506,177.0	2.87
Aids to individuals and organizations .	8,098,217.1	7,891,208.7	15,989,425.8	18.32
Program Revenue—service........	979,292.6	958,852.6	1,938,145.2	2.22
State operations...............	772,935.6	756,204.5	1,529,140.1	1.75
Local assistance...............	43,022.8	43,022.8	86,045.6	0.10
Aids to individuals and organizations .	163,334.2	159,625.3	322,959.5	0.37
Program Revenue—other.........	5,858,329.7	5,891,327.6	11,749,657.3	13.46
State operations...............	4,423,501.5	4,430,494.0	8,853,995.5	10.14

Wisconsin state budget allocations, continued

Revenue type and allocation	Fiscal year 2021–22 ($1,000)	Fiscal year 2022–23 ($1,000)	Fiscal biennium ($1,000)	% of total budget allocations
Local assistance	32,809.6	33,169.6	65,979.2	0.08
Aids to individuals and organizations	1,402,018.6	1,427,664.0	2,829,682.6	3.24
SEGREGATED REVENUE	**5,379,508.4**	**5,524,479.7**	**10,903,988.1**	**12.49**
State operations	2,684,312.3	2,720,844.3	5,405,156.6	6.19
Local assistance	1,684,155.4	1,503,460.3	3,187,615.7	3.65
Aids to individuals and organizations	1,011,040.7	1,300,175.1	2,311,215.8	2.65
Segregated Revenue—federal	**961,519.2**	**977,305.2**	**1,938,824.4**	**2.22**
State operations	763,475.4	779,261.4	1,542,736.8	1.77
Local assistance	191,755.1	191,755.1	383,510.2	0.44
Aids to individuals and organizations	6,288.7	6,288.7	12,577.4	0.01
Segregated Revenue—local	**115,325.6**	**115,325.6**	**230,651.2**	**0.26**
State operations	7,452.9	7,452.9	14,905.8	0.02
Local assistance	99,678.5	99,678.5	199,357.0	0.23
Aids to individuals and organizations	8,194.2	8,194.2	16,388.4	0.02
Segregated Revenue—service	**116,764.6**	**114,764.6**	**231,529.2**	**0.27**
State operations	114,764.6	112,764.6	227,529.2	0.26
Aids to individuals and organizations	2,000.0	2,000.0	4,000.0	0.00
Segregated Revenue—other	**4,185,899.0**	**4,317,084.3**	**8,502,983.3**	**9.74**
State operations	1,798,619.4	1,821,365.4	3,619,984.8	4.15
Local assistance	1,392,721.8	1,212,026.7	2,604,748.5	2.98
Aids to individuals and organizations	994,557.8	1,283,692.2	2,278,250.0	2.61
FEDERAL REVENUE	**12,905,013.7**	**12,704,641.4**	**25,609,655.1**	**29.34**
State operations	3,356,920.7	3,361,044.0	6,717,964.7	7.70
Local assistance	1,443,587.2	1,446,100.0	2,889,687.2	3.31
Aids to individuals and organizations	8,104,505.8	7,897,497.4	16,002,003.2	18.33
ALL SOURCES	**43,445,393.9**	**43,833,368.1**	**87,278,762.0**	**100.00**
State operations	15,001,526.8	15,222,613.7	30,224,140.5	34.63
Local assistance	12,688,047.5	12,711,039.4	25,399,086.9	29.10
Aids to individuals and organizations	15,755,819.6	15,899,715.0	31,655,534.6	36.27

Definitions: **General purpose revenue**—general taxes, miscellaneous receipts, and revenues collected by state agencies that are paid into the general fund, lose their identity, and are available for appropriation by the legislature. **Program revenue**—revenues paid into the general fund and credited by law to an appropriation used to finance a specific program or agency. **Segregated revenue**—revenues deposited, by law, into funds other than the general fund and available only for the purposes for which such funds were created. **Federal revenue**—money received from the federal government (may be disbursed either through a segregated fund or through the general fund). **Service revenue**—money transferred between or within state agencies for reimbursement for services rendered or materials purchased. **State operations**—amounts budgeted to operate programs carried out by state government. **Local assistance**—amounts budgeted as state aids to assist programs carried out by local governmental units in Wisconsin.

Source: Wisconsin Department of Administration, State Budget Office, departmental data, March 2023.

Wisconsin state annual appropriation obligations, 2022

Category	Amount of debt issued[1] ($1,000)	Amount outstanding December 15, 2022 ($1,000)
General Fund annual appropriation bonds	3,252,620	2,660,835
Master lease obligations	139,645	64,477
Total	**3,392,265**	**2,725,312**

Note: Appropriation obligations are not general obligations of the state, and they do not constitute "public debt" of the state as that term is used in the Wisconsin Constitution and in the Wisconsin Statutes. The payment of the principal of, and interest on, appropriation obligations is subject to annual appropriation. The state has no legal obligation to make these appropriations and incurs no liability to the owners of the appropriation obligations if it does not do so.

1. Amounts do not include refunding bonds, which do not count against the respective authorizations.

Source: Wisconsin Department of Administration, Division of Executive Budget and Finance, departmental data, March 2023.

Wisconsin state revenues, all funds

	Fiscal year 2019–20 ($1,000)	Fiscal year 2020–21 ($1,000)	Fiscal year 2021–22 ($1,000)
REVENUES FROM TAXES	18,760,189	20,683,340	21,818,909
General fund	17,558,529	19,600,872	20,578,238
General purpose revenues	17,532,124	19,572,791	20,548,425
Income taxes	10,350,139	11,843,536	12,174,429
Individual	8,742,266	9,283,388	9,214,407
Corporation	1,607,873	2,560,148	2,960,022
Sales and excise taxes	6,515,718	7,051,358	7,633,053
General sales and use	5,836,215	6,373,483	6,978,336
Cigarette	523,557	509,793	482,440
Other tobacco products	91,364	92,746	94,383
Vapor products	1,319	1,558	4,126
Liquor and wine	54,776	64,590	64,898
Malt beverage (beer)	8,487	9,188	8,870
Public utility taxes	357,152	356,256	383,597
Private light, heat, and power	225,411	225,671	248,803
Municipal light, heat, and power	2,729	2,764	2,969
Telephone	66,173	62,868	68,200
Pipeline	44,513	47,244	44,838
Electric cooperative	12,752	12,940	14,013
Municipal electric	4,445	4,265	4,084
Conservation and regulation	473	504	649
Other	656	—	41
Inheritance and estate taxes	41	—	3
Miscellaneous taxes	309,074	321,641	357,343
Insurance companies (premiums)	217,381	202,066	221,800
Real estate transfer fee	77,430	106,098	121,382
Lawsuits (courts)	14,263	13,392	14,132
Other	—	85	29
Program revenues	26,405	28,081	29,813
Fire dues	23,122	24,465	25,375
Pari-mutuel taxes	—	—	—
County expo tax administration	776	525	982
Baseball park administration fee	390	—	—
Business trust regulation fee	1,439	1,825	2,405
Other	678	1,266	1,051
Transportation fund			
Motor fuel tax	1,022,464	959,411	1,111,070
Air-carrier tax	7,047	7,772	3,517
Railroad tax	42,020	36,258	33,030
Aviation fuel tax	1,264	1,193	1,555
Other taxes	9,325	6,351	11,239
Conservation fund			
Forestry mill tax	-21	-16	-20
Forest crop taxes	514	519	1,232
Motor fuel tax	—	—	—
Dry cleaner fund	533	250	369
Mediation fund	1	1	1
Petroleum inspection tax	83,892	35,362	39,972
Historical Preservation Partnership Trust	—	—	—
Economic development fund temporary service charges	34,621	35,367	38,706
DEPARTMENT REVENUES	35,839,304	65,607,226	26,567,186
Intergovernmental revenue	15,033,737	16,830,533	19,817,036
Licenses and permits	1,960,681	2,058,298	2,030,047
Charges for goods and services	4,404,752	4,463,989	4,811,538
Contributions	3,831,957	3,994,094	4,094,824
Interest and investment income	5,511,010	32,175,734	-10,657,868
Gifts and donations	660,447	805,156	739,948

Wisconsin state revenues, all funds, continued

	Fiscal year 2019–20 ($1,000)	Fiscal year 2020–21 ($1,000)	Fiscal year 2021–22 ($1,000)
Proceeds from sale of bonds	1,052,808	1,102,142	614,288
Other revenues	3,006,119	3,261,835	3,311,214
Other transactions	377,793	915,445	1,806,159
TRANSFERS	1,381,608	1,514,632	1,509,280
TOTAL REVENUES	55,981,101	87,805,198	49,895,375

—Represents zero.
Source: Wisconsin Department of Administration, State Controller's Office, *2022 Annual Fiscal Report*, October 15, 2022.

Wisconsin state revenue bonds, 2022

Program funded	Amount of debt authorized ($1,000)	Amount issued[1] ($1,000)	Amount outstanding December 15, 2022 ($1,000)
Transportation facilities and highway projects	4,325,886	4,117,056	1,565,305
Clean Water/Environmental Improvement Fund	2,551,400	2,066,245	394,970
Petroleum environmental cleanup	436,000	387,550	—
Total	7,313,286	6,570,851	1,960,275

Note: Revenue bonds are issued for purposes and amounts specifically authorized by the legislature. This debt is not a legal obligation of the state and is not subject to existing debt limitations.
—Represents zero.
1. Amounts do not include refunding bonds, which do not count against the respective authorizations.
Source: Wisconsin Department of Administration, Division of Executive Budget and Finance, departmental data, March 2023.

Wisconsin state expenditures

	Fiscal year 2020–21 Amount ($1,000)	Percent	Fiscal year 2021–22 Amount ($1,000)	Percent
Executive	53,953,389	90.70	57,879,588	92.02
Administration	3,210,318	5.41	2,967,968	4.72
Agriculture, Trade and Consumer Protection	134,666	0.23	145,393	0.23
Board for People with Developmental Disabilities	1,828	0.00	1,912	0.00
Board on Aging and Long Term Care	3,599	0.01	3,757	0.01
Child Abuse and Neglect Prevention Board	3,086	0.01	4,072	0.01
Children and Families	2,443,013	4.12	2,353,381	3.74
Corrections	1,342,790	2.26	1,371,048	2.18
District attorneys	55,252	0.09	57,965	0.09
Educational Communications Board	17,520	0.03	19,134	0.03
Elections Commission	17,116	0.03	6,357	0.01
Employee Trust Funds	8,583,573	14.46	9,069,920	14.42
Employment Relations Commission	889	0.00	955	0.00
Environmental Improvement Program	62,366	0.11	62,313	0.10
Ethics Commission	1,161	0.00	1,138	0.00
Financial Institutions	17,529	0.03	18,415	0.03
Fox River Navigation System Authority	125	0.00	125	0.00
Governor	17,772	0.03	95,738	0.15
Health Services	16,547,673	27.88	18,142,619	28.84

Wisconsin state expenditures, continued

Function	Fiscal year 2020–21 Amount ($1,000)	Percent	Fiscal year 2021–22 Amount ($1,000)	Percent
Higher Education Aids Board	137,427	0.23	123,257	0.20
Historical Society	27,772	0.05	32,026	0.05
Insurance Commissioner	215,629	0.36	225,461	0.36
Investment Board	74,732	0.13	83,969	0.13
Justice	218,808	0.37	200,537	0.32
Kickapoo Reserve Management Board	1,075	0.00	1,436	0.00
Labor and Industry Review Commission	2,182	0.00	2,481	0.00
Lieutenant Governor	433	0.00	385	0.00
Lower Wisconsin Riverway	229	0.00	233	0.00
Medical College of Wisconsin	10,964	0.02	10,841	0.02
Military Affairs	160,547	0.27	474,216	0.75
Natural Resources	630,596	1.06	621,107	0.99
Public Defender	98,749	0.17	95,183	0.15
Public Instruction	7,691,287	12.96	8,405,199	13.36
Public Lands Board	1,619	0.00	1,552	0.00
Public Service Commission	55,742	0.09	130,007	0.21
Revenue	1,485,000	2.50	1,200,040	1.91
Safety and Professional Services	59,199	0.10	69,175	0.11
Secretary of State	269	0.00	280	0.00
State Fair Park	18,098	0.03	29,396	0.05
Technical College System Board	562,256	0.95	594,191	0.94
Tourism	34,036	0.06	22,622	0.04
Transportation	3,198,567	5.39	3,722,631	5.92
Treasurer	117	0.00	123	0.00
University of Wisconsin	6,249,760	10.53	6,871,641	10.92
Veterans Affairs	120,405	0.20	122,973	0.20
Wisconsin Economic Development Corporation	41,551	0.07	41,551	0.07
Workforce Development	396,066	0.67	474,866	0.75
Judicial	153,693	0.26	154,756	0.25
Legislative	77,769	0.13	81,703	0.13
Shared revenue and tax relief	2,862,136	4.82	2,949,787	4.69
Miscellaneous appropriations	174,405	0.29	221,630	0.35
Program supplements	49,762	0.08	-37,710	-0.06
Public debt	1,274,811	2.15	815,385	1.30
Building Commission	22,411	0.04	24,005	0.04
Building programs	786,976	1.33	811,566	1.29
Total	59,355,351	100.00	62,900,712	100.00

Source: Wisconsin Department of Administration, State Controller's Office, Appendix to *Annual Fiscal Report (Budgetary Basis)*, 2021 and 2022.

Debt of the state of Wisconsin

	Annual debt limit[1] ($1,000)	Amount incurred during calendar year Total ($1,000)	% of debt limit	Amount outstanding January 1 Total ($1,000)	Per capita ($)	% of state assessed value
1980	813,604	123,500	15.2	1,916,177	407	1.77
1985	922,661	440,955	47.8	2,153,152	508	1.96
1990	1,060,277	484,099	45.7	2,566,496	568	1.97
1995	1,511,536	368,322	24.4	3,244,079	637	1.64
2000	2,147,411	538,795	25.1	3,942,659	735	1.49
2005	3,209,502	571,990	17.8	5,116,439	924	1.27
2010	3,719,281	809,293	21.8	6,481,010	1,139	1.49

Debt of the state of Wisconsin, continued

	Annual debt limit[1] ($1,000)	Amount incurred during calendar year Total ($1,000)	% of debt limit	Amount outstanding January 1 Total ($1,000)	Per capita ($)	% of state assessed value
2011	3,651,482	896,260	24.5	7,407,431	1,298	1.62
2012	3,533,194	735,585	20.8	7,878,628	1,377	1.78
2013	3,506,269	642,295	18.3	8,385,973	1,462	1.78
2014	3,596,100	598,170	16.6	8,344,531	1,451	1.70
2015	3,679,519	750,475	20.4	8,134,099	1,412	1.68
2016	3,788,432	713,305	18.8	8,238,759	1,427	1.66
2017	3,944,844	607,975	15.4	8,389,198	1,448	1.55
2018	4,121,495	547,290	13.3	8,155,030	1,403	1.48
2019	4,356,545	539,415	12.4	8,212,806	1,411	1.41
2020	4,598,527	438,115	9.5	7,832,171	1,329	1.28
2021	4,911,153	433,360	8.8	7,654,755	1,298	1.16

1. The debt limit for each calendar year is derived through a formula specified in Wis. Stat. § 18.05.
Source: Wisconsin Department of Administration, Division of Executive Budget and Finance, departmental data, March 2023.

Debt of the state of Wisconsin, 2022

Type	Amount outstanding December 15, 2022 ($1,000)
Tax supported debt	4,962,362
General fund	3,512,680
Segregated funds[1]	1,449,682
Revenue supported debt[2]	1,857,753
Total	**6,820,115**

1. Includes the Transportation Fund and certain administrative facilities for the Wisconsin Department of Natural Resources.
2. Revenue supported debt includes debt that is issued with initial expectation that revenues and other proceeds from the operation of the programs or facilities financed will amortize the debt without recourse to the general fund.
Source: Wisconsin Department of Administration, Division of Executive Budget and Finance, departmental data, March 2023.

Debt of Wisconsin state authorities, 2022

Authority	Amount outstanding ($1,000)
Wisconsin Health and Educational Facilities Authority	9,341,966[1]
Wisconsin Housing and Economic Development Authority	1,892,064[2]

Note: State authority debt is not an obligation of the State of Wisconsin.
1. As of 6/30/22. 2. As of 12/31/22.
Source: Data provided by the respective authorities.

Debt of Wisconsin local governments

Year (Dec. 31)	Counties (mil. dol.)	Cities (mil. dol.)	Villages (mil. dol.)	Towns (mil. dol.)	Total (mil. dol.)
1965	192.5	548.1	22.5	9.2	772.3
1975	261.0	598.7	69.8	26.2	955.7
1985	532.5	1,320.4	227.6	75.2	2,155.7

Debt of Wisconsin local governments, continued

Year (Dec. 31)	Counties (mil. dol.)	Cities (mil. dol.)	Villages (mil. dol.)	Towns (mil. dol.)	Total (mil. dol.)
1995	1,221.6	2,082.8	418.7	193.8	3,916.9
2005	1,753.7	3,718.5	1,098.0	308.5	6,878.8
2010	2,444.8	4,468.2	1,440.1	374.6	8,727.7
2015	2,378.1	4,713.3	1,560.9	338.6	8,990.9
2016	2,352.8	5,026.9	1,632.0	341.0	9,352.6
2017	2,553.3	5,139.0	1,773.7	350.7	9,816.6
2018	2,590.6	5,399.0	1,858.9	376.9	10,225.5
2019	2,610.2	5,607.8	2,032.6	429.8	10,680.4
2020	2,686.5	5,974.8	2,110.1	472.3	11,243.7
2021	2,921.8	6,182.3	2,204.6	515.8	11,824.5

Sources: Wisconsin Department of Revenue, *Indebtedness 1981* and prior editions; Wisconsin Department of Revenue, Division of State and Local Finance, Bureau of Local Government Services, *County and Municipal Revenues and Expenditures 2021*, and prior editions.

Debt of Wisconsin school and technical college districts

Year (June 30)	School districts (mil. dol.)	Technical college districts (mil. dol.)	Total (mil. dol)
1965	336.6	X	336.6
1975	798.7	97.2	895.9
1985	448.7	64.7	513.4
1995	2,104.9	192.8	2,297.7
2005	5,335.5	461.4	5,796.9
2010	4,863.7	510.2	5,373.9
2015	4,916.4	886.4	5,802.8
2016	4,989.8	913.4	5,903.2
2017	5,763.2	916.2	6,679.4
2018	6,307.8	934.8	7,242.6
2019	7,468.5	908.8	8,377.4
2020	7,552.1	907.4	8,459.5
2021	7,789.3	934.5	8,723.8
2022	8,092.2	959.2	9,051.3

X–Not applicable. Technical college districts did not have authority to incur debt prior to 1967.
Sources: Wisconsin Department of Public Instruction, departmental data, March 2022; Wisconsin Technical College System Board, departmental data, March 2022.

Federal aids to Wisconsin

Agency administering aid	Aid received by Wisconsin ($1,000) Fiscal year 2020–21	Fiscal year 2021–22	Disbursed to local governments ($1,000) Fiscal year 2020–21	Fiscal year 2021–22	Aid to individuals and organizations ($1,000) Fiscal year 2020–21	Fiscal year 2021–22
Administration	2,189,111	1,756,685	244,229	318,428	46,803	33,889
Agriculture, Trade and Consumer Protection	15,169	15,917	—	—	—	—
Child Abuse and Neglect Prevention Board	315	781	—	—	235	592
Children and Families	715,082	827,694	113,507	120,938	581,149	615,038
Clean Water Fund Program[1]	—	—	53,301	53,716	—	—

Federal aids to Wisconsin, continued

Agency administering aid	Aid received by Wisconsin ($1,000) Fiscal year 2020–21	Fiscal year 2021–22	Disbursed to local governments ($1,000) Fiscal year 2020–21	Fiscal year 2021–22	Aid to individuals and organizations ($1,000) Fiscal year 2020–21	Fiscal year 2021–22
Corrections	365	675	—	—	—	—
District Attorneys	—	-491	—	—	—	—
Elections Commission	1,399	1,220	—	—	—	—
Environmental Improvement Program	53,301	53,716	—	—	—	—
Governor's Office	—	100,608	—	—	—	—
Health Services	9,313,863	11,853,546	170,110	180,286	9,040,510	10,608,718
Historical Society	1,314	1,234	—	—	—	—
Insurance, Commissioner of	127,726	141,955	—	—	—	—
Justice	71,763	60,434	53,054	54,747	1,576	1,560
Military Affairs	96,173	262,388	32,643	36,510	7,029	5,886
Natural Resources	139,533	154,907	10,185	11,135	—	—
People with Developmental Disabilities, Board for	1,832	1,866	—	—	605	527
Public Defender	5	488	—	—	—	—
Public Instruction	979,189	1,458,171	880,844	1,278,452	57,479	80,863
Public Lands Board	61	60	61	60	—	—
Public Service Commission	7,086	4,699	—	—	—	—
Safety and Professional Services	483	868	—	—	—	—
Supreme Court	453	997	—	—	—	—
Technical College System Board	30,126	30,520	26,303	25,580	595	591
Tourism	1,952	100	—	—	1,089	1,333
Transportation	980,611	1,035,168	166,902	243,377	7,308	6,505
University of Wisconsin System	1,797,700	1,921,800	—	—	—	—
Veterans Affairs	3,166	3,645	—	—	—	—
Workforce Development	196,966	232,236	—	—	55,208	86,549
Total	16,724,744	19,921,888	1,751,138	2,323,029	9,799,586	11,442,051

Note: Aid is not necessarily disbursed in the same fiscal year in which it is received by the agency. In some cases, aid is received as reimbursement for previous expenditures.
—Represents zero.
1. Federal aid received by Wisconsin for Clean Water Fund (Environmental Improvement Program, DOA) also includes safe drinking water loan program appropriations.
Source: Wisconsin Department of Administration, State Controller's Office, *Annual Fiscal Report—Appendix*, 2021 and 2022.

Wisconsin state payments to local units of government, fiscal year 2022

County[1]	School levy tax credit[2] ($)	Shared revenue payments[3] ($)	Exempt property aid[4] ($)	Personal property aid[5] ($)	Total ($)	Per capita[6] Amount ($)	Rank
Adams	4,116,407	1,271,237	35,167	121,890	5,544,701	266	66
Ashland	2,169,678	6,016,824	57,769	192,724	8,436,995	529	1
Barron	8,219,010	6,900,929	185,926	416,898	15,722,762	335	26
Bayfield	3,472,352	1,531,487	6,912	56,941	5,067,692	313	42
Brown	37,072,519	27,247,374	5,389,664	3,455,498	73,165,055	268	65
Buffalo	2,248,291	2,870,784	64,433	99,955	5,283,462	397	8
Burnett	3,708,102	1,174,037	20,970	50,632	4,953,742	299	50
Calumet	6,799,303	3,727,949	438,541	440,359	11,406,152	207	72
Chippewa	9,047,356	11,008,585	774,525	859,616	21,690,082	323	36
Clark	3,472,762	8,176,857	76,953	495,666	12,222,237	351	20
Columbia	10,090,872	8,006,996	202,007	657,860	18,957,736	323	35

Wisconsin state payments to local units of government, fiscal year 2022, continued

County[1]	School levy tax credit[2] ($)	Shared revenue payments[3] ($)	Exempt property aid[4] ($)	Personal property aid[5] ($)	Total ($)	Per capita[6] Amount ($)	Rank
Crawford....	2,203,708	3,554,383	100,133	291,555	6,149,778	381	10
Dane......	130,375,173	26,589,698	16,880,920	9,310,991	183,156,783	315	41
Dodge.....	11,547,970	12,775,901	442,012	1,536,806	26,302,688	296	51
Door.......	7,320,408	1,498,716	134,238	335,596	9,288,957	306	45
Douglas.....	6,266,166	11,120,500	129,904	718,915	18,235,485	409	6
Dunn......	5,184,302	8,109,262	187,514	956,395	14,437,473	318	39
Eau Claire....	14,082,847	13,346,699	1,213,018	1,293,692	29,936,256	277	61
Florence....	1,118,139	335,231	5,382	25,967	1,484,719	325	33
Fond du Lac..	12,823,539	15,153,777	1,090,943	1,544,356	30,612,615	294	53
Forest......	2,053,697	995,625	17,072	21,457	3,087,851	336	25
Grant......	6,277,348	12,258,563	157,665	364,087	19,057,663	372	13
Green......	6,089,061	3,774,945	600,642	551,929	11,016,577	294	52
Green Lake...	3,132,158	3,162,913	92,168	357,649	6,744,888	353	18
Iowa.......	4,161,797	2,459,155	625,567	610,778	7,857,297	328	29
Iron.......	1,228,566	1,375,109	4,202	35,678	2,643,555	432	5
Jackson.....	2,992,703	3,110,622	90,914	709,359	6,903,598	327	31
Jefferson....	13,069,510	9,402,208	924,640	785,778	24,182,136	279	60
Juneau.....	3,710,786	4,989,373	64,070	152,467	8,916,696	332	27
Kenosha....	26,448,578	20,413,026	2,981,053	5,200,731	55,043,388	323	37
Kewaunee...	2,838,404	3,127,569	60,847	200,797	6,227,617	302	49
La Crosse....	18,593,210	17,825,549	2,580,998	2,357,901	41,357,658	339	24
Lafayette....	2,271,380	4,994,138	23,040	266,801	7,555,360	454	3
Langlade....	2,515,834	4,126,709	108,831	116,972	6,868,346	353	19
Lincoln.....	4,086,869	5,704,163	194,788	225,750	10,211,570	359	15
Manitowoc...	8,697,342	18,015,545	601,487	777,278	28,091,653	345	23
Marathon....	19,680,830	19,977,164	2,311,040	2,121,419	44,090,454	317	40
Marinette....	6,139,227	9,965,390	220,810	442,710	16,768,138	400	7
Marquette...	2,381,240	1,055,742	55,358	88,205	3,580,546	229	70
Menominee..	517,806	644,698	3,058	2,395	1,167,956	274	62
Milwaukee...	114,246,144	312,954,095	31,267,186	9,597,606	468,065,032	498	2
Monroe.....	5,107,160	8,313,873	152,226	717,874	14,291,134	306	46
Oconto.....	6,393,839	4,512,866	78,954	250,199	11,235,858	286	56
Oneida.....	9,663,652	1,939,080	135,796	530,563	12,269,091	323	34
Outagamie...	24,315,042	22,603,494	2,649,092	2,447,955	52,016,283	270	64
Ozaukee....	20,005,878	6,588,291	810,708	732,420	28,137,297	304	48
Pepin......	1,271,685	1,372,788	15,550	119,645	2,779,668	378	11
Pierce......	6,324,421	5,176,394	104,317	348,731	11,953,863	282	58
Polk.......	8,258,951	4,262,755	89,493	503,144	13,114,343	289	54
Portage.....	8,990,375	7,801,001	1,094,696	875,724	18,761,797	264	67
Price	2,196,535	3,024,994	53,855	78,498	5,353,882	382	9
Racine......	28,751,695	34,650,702	3,287,441	2,476,157	69,165,996	349	21
Richland....	1,982,254	3,822,984	54,670	125,832	5,985,740	346	22
Rock.......	19,455,994	35,267,047	1,711,098	2,707,259	59,141,398	359	16
Rusk.......	2,304,810	3,847,231	70,867	118,985	6,341,893	446	4
St. Croix.....	17,938,156	3,759,606	281,731	840,336	22,819,828	237	68
Sauk.......	11,603,757	5,029,440	567,864	1,413,715	18,614,775	280	59
Sawyer.....	4,359,417	1,145,766	22,596	78,897	5,606,676	310	44
Shawano....	5,543,250	5,218,216	111,049	298,988	11,171,502	271	63
Sheboygan...	16,037,561	17,231,186	1,957,166	1,073,086	36,298,999	306	47
Taylor......	2,366,251	3,548,789	162,181	465,952	6,543,173	328	30
Trempealeau..	4,203,994	6,367,863	208,308	252,021	11,032,185	357	17
Vernon.....	3,502,082	5,989,244	119,846	324,176	9,935,349	321	38
Vilas.......	7,630,812	583,324	27,624	105,014	8,346,774	361	14
Walworth....	26,333,284	6,652,867	478,869	1,089,281	34,554,301	326	32
Washburn...	4,006,708	1,286,401	70,647	109,294	5,473,050	329	28

Wisconsin state payments to local units of government, fiscal year 2022, continued

County[1]	School levy tax credit[2] ($)	Shared revenue payments[3] ($)	Exempt property aid[4] ($)	Personal property aid[5] ($)	Total ($)	Per capita[6] Amount ($)	Rank
Washington..	23,617,562	5,505,497	1,060,569	1,459,619	31,643,248	229	71
Waukesha ...	94,292,543	11,149,624	6,242,177	6,999,116	118,683,460	289	55
Waupaca....	7,315,285	8,245,949	301,573	387,077	16,249,883	311	43
Waushara....	3,646,402	1,834,606	51,382	186,892	5,719,282	234	69
Winnebago ..	21,063,024	21,941,640	4,200,523	1,708,310	48,913,498	283	57
Wood	9,046,228	15,692,987	1,451,124	1,518,228	27,708,567	373	12
Total.......	940,000,000	895,116,033	98,047,059	78,193,047	2,011,356,139	338	X

X–Not applicable.

1. Some cities and villages are located in more than one county. In these cases, payments are attributed to the "primary" county, as determined by the Wisconsin Department of Revenue. For example, payments to the city of Appleton are attributed to Outagamie County even though parts of Appleton are located in Calumet and Winnebago Counties. 2. Distributed July 2022. 3. Total of amounts (excluding deductions) distributed July and November 2021. 4. Includes exempt computer aid distributed July 2019. 5. May 2022 payment. 6. Based on 2022 population estimates.

Sources: Wisconsin Department of Revenue, Division of State and Local Finance, Local Government Services Bureau, departmental data, March 2023; Wisconsin Department of Administration, Demographic Services Center, *Official Final Estimates, January 1, 2022*, October 2022.

Wisconsin general property assessments and tax levies

	Full-value assessment of all property (mil. dol.)	% change	Total state and local property taxes levied (mil. dol.)	% change	State property tax relief (mil. dol.)	Average full-value tax rate per $1,000	% change	Average net tax rate per $1,000 after state tax relief	% change
1900....	630	X	19	X	NA	31.00	X	NA	X
1910....	2,743	X	31	X	NA	11.18	X	NA	X
1920....	4,571	X	96	X	NA	21.06	X	NA	X
1930....	5,896	X	121	X	NA	20.49	X	NA	X
1940....	4,354	X	110	X	NA	25.26	X	NA	X
1950....	9,201	X	226	X	NA	24.52	X	NA	X
1960....	18,844	X	481	X	NA	25.55	X	NA	X
1970....	34,790	X	1,179	X	140	33.88	X	NA	X
1980....	108,480	X	2,210	X	309	20.37	X	NA	X
1990....	141,370	X	4,388	X	319	31.04	X	28.78	X
2000....	286,321	X	6,605	X	469	23.06	X	21.42	X
2010....	495,904	-3.1	10,365	2.6	747	20.90	5.9	19.39	6.1
2011....	486,864	-1.8	10,385	0.2	747	21.33	2.1	19.79	2.1
2012....	471,093	-3.2	10,470	0.8	747	22.22	4.2	20.63	4.3
2013....	467,503	-0.8	10,606	1.3	747	22.68	2.1	21.08	2.2
2014....	479,024	2.5	10,384	-2.1	747	21.67	4.4	20.11	4.6
2015....	490,603	2.4	10,620	2.3	853	21.65	0.1	19.91	1.0
2016....	505,124	3.0	10,792	1.6	853	21.37	1.3	19.68	1.2
2017....	525,985	4.1	11,016	2.1	940	20.94	2.0	19.16	2.6
2018....	549,533	4.5	11,199	1.7	940	20.38	-2.7	18.67	-2.6
2019....	580,873	5.7	11,618	3.7	940	20.00	-1.9	18.38	-1.6
2020....	613,137	5.6	12,017	3.4	940	19.60	-2.0	18.07	-1.7
2021....	654,820	6.8	12,208	1.6	940	18.64	-4.9	17.21	-4.8

NA–Not available; X–Not applicable.

Source: Wisconsin Department of Revenue, Division of State and Local Finance, *2021 Town, Village, and City Taxes: Taxes Levied 2021—Collected 2022*, and prior issues.

Wisconsin general property assessments, taxes, and rates, 2021

County	Full-value assessment[1] ($)	Total property tax[2] ($)	State property tax credit[3] ($)	Average full-value tax rate per $1,000[4] Gross ($)	Average full-value tax rate per $1,000[4] Net ($)
Adams	3,045,424,600	56,803,604	4,070,156	18.65	17.32
Ashland	1,294,573,200	30,044,665	2,123,351	23.21	21.57
Barron	5,008,571,400	90,641,151	8,104,529	18.10	16.48
Bayfield	2,922,293,700	40,325,020	3,327,025	13.80	12.66
Brown	26,708,662,500	483,296,902	36,854,256	18.10	16.72
Buffalo	1,315,831,200	25,743,566	2,228,285	19.56	17.87
Burnett	3,095,749,000	42,277,945	3,711,355	13.66	12.46
Calumet	5,083,636,000	91,572,706	6,791,782	18.01	16.68
Chippewa	7,010,535,800	104,081,956	9,189,539	14.85	13.54
Clark	2,434,706,700	50,410,674	3,453,184	20.71	19.29
Columbia	6,540,618,680	121,874,842	10,087,110	18.63	17.09
Crawford	1,407,875,700	31,059,994	2,164,406	22.06	20.52
Dane	76,889,801,300	1,626,198,098	134,207,699	21.15	19.40
Dodge	7,690,530,560	148,212,915	11,413,438	19.27	17.79
Door	8,556,994,600	113,184,097	7,574,480	13.23	12.34
Douglas	4,144,022,500	72,604,272	6,046,322	17.52	16.06
Dunn	3,836,605,100	72,841,896	5,097,652	18.99	17.66
Eau Claire	10,591,905,100	187,590,925	13,607,812	17.71	16.43
Florence	736,947,000	13,091,363	1,137,999	17.76	16.22
Fond du Lac	8,904,213,000	174,443,655	12,613,708	19.59	18.17
Forest	1,259,268,000	19,789,715	2,030,463	15.72	14.10
Grant	3,865,162,300	72,678,820	6,135,589	18.80	17.22
Green	3,691,417,980	77,174,592	6,002,860	20.91	19.28
Green Lake	2,577,954,200	45,366,775	3,047,123	17.60	16.42
Iowa	2,506,857,400	54,843,042	4,157,717	21.88	20.22
Iron	1,031,764,200	15,847,511	1,152,689	15.36	14.24
Jackson	1,849,553,600	35,078,118	2,928,754	18.97	17.38
Jefferson	8,726,940,700	169,312,904	13,302,059	19.40	17.88
Juneau	2,597,845,700	50,181,810	3,731,316	19.32	17.88
Kenosha	19,742,921,700	388,705,659	26,434,741	19.69	18.35
Kewaunee	1,929,833,700	39,130,061	2,871,821	20.28	18.79
La Crosse	12,238,688,900	236,875,002	18,238,946	19.35	17.86
Lafayette	1,364,211,000	28,975,935	2,206,102	21.24	19.62
Langlade	1,866,138,800	32,983,840	2,501,529	17.67	16.33
Lincoln	2,834,274,100	49,678,537	4,040,516	17.53	16.10
Manitowoc	6,385,053,700	122,131,749	8,708,986	19.13	17.76
Marathon	12,764,788,900	264,401,831	19,630,477	20.71	19.18
Marinette	4,365,485,300	72,022,851	6,044,517	16.50	15.11
Marquette	1,869,463,000	32,122,709	2,248,696	17.18	15.98
Menominee	395,192,300	6,744,159	523,520	17.07	15.74
Milwaukee	77,290,319,100	1,859,015,575	113,986,169	24.05	22.58
Monroe	3,934,664,700	71,144,729	5,064,039	18.08	16.79
Oconto	4,543,647,900	74,319,068	6,436,519	16.36	14.94
Oneida	7,797,473,900	95,508,395	9,410,822	12.25	11.04
Outagamie	19,041,095,200	331,267,356	24,281,932	17.40	16.12
Ozaukee	14,289,620,800	219,290,748	19,998,725	15.35	13.95
Pepin	721,544,900	14,284,348	1,216,433	19.80	18.11
Pierce	4,148,445,100	76,732,456	6,226,862	18.50	17.00
Polk	5,891,358,400	92,957,431	8,098,466	15.78	14.40
Portage	7,098,581,100	133,951,133	9,247,451	18.87	17.57
Price	1,503,796,700	30,639,992	2,189,001	20.38	18.92
Racine	19,576,633,100	394,804,365	28,987,246	20.17	18.69
Richland	1,348,098,200	28,972,140	1,917,063	21.49	20.07
Rock	14,617,256,450	316,468,771	19,909,813	21.65	20.29
Rusk	1,342,061,600	24,759,378	2,134,384	18.45	16.86
St. Croix	12,439,288,300	195,219,304	18,341,112	15.69	14.22

Wisconsin general property assessments, taxes, and rates, 2021, continued

County	Full-value assessment[1] ($)	Total property tax[2] ($)	State property tax credit[3] ($)	Average full-value tax rate per $1,000[4] Gross ($)	Net ($)
Sauk	8,639,095,500	155,719,738	11,625,472	18.03	16.68
Sawyer	3,995,635,200	45,014,889	4,288,356	11.27	10.19
Shawano	3,667,699,900	68,125,891	5,532,160	18.57	17.07
Sheboygan	11,530,754,800	213,456,854	15,890,793	18.51	17.13
Taylor	1,585,641,400	30,551,036	2,294,249	19.27	17.82
Trempealeau	2,673,075,300	55,416,621	4,165,954	20.73	19.17
Vernon	2,373,696,800	47,721,608	3,484,283	20.10	18.64
Vilas	7,883,730,900	77,154,143	7,514,240	9.79	8.83
Walworth	18,146,879,800	287,596,263	26,126,425	15.85	14.41
Washburn	3,002,427,600	43,818,867	4,014,100	14.59	13.26
Washington	18,282,260,200	266,747,351	23,882,307	14.59	13.28
Waukesha	66,686,337,700	970,574,922	93,325,432	14.55	13.15
Waupaca	4,807,805,200	92,044,734	6,965,648	19.14	17.70
Waushara	3,028,687,200	49,790,911	3,584,066	16.44	15.26
Winnebago	15,795,067,600	324,384,629	21,241,940	20.54	19.19
Wood	6,055,382,200	129,975,698	8,876,045	21.46	20.00
Total	**$654,820,375,870**	**$12,207,775,210**	**$940,000,016**	**18.64**	**17.21**

1. Reflects actual market value of all taxable general property, as determined by the Wisconsin Department of Revenue independent of locally assessed values, which can vary substantially from full value. 2. Includes taxes and special charges levied by schools, counties, cities, villages, towns, special purpose districts, and the State of Wisconsin. It does not include special assessments or other charges. 3. Total amount of school levy tax credit paid by the state to taxing districts and credited to taxpayers on their tax bills. The credit is considered part of the tax payment. 4. A county's average tax rate per $1,000 of assessed valuation (determined by dividing total taxes by equalized value and multiplying by 1,000) is the preferred figure for comparison purposes, rather than the general local property tax rate because the average is based on full market value. Net tax rate per $1,000 reflects the effect of state property tax relief.

Source: Wisconsin Department of Revenue, Division of State and Local Finance, *Town, Village, and City Taxes—2021: Taxes Levied 2021—Collected 2022.*

Municipal property taxes levied in Wisconsin

	Total (mil. dol.)	% Residential	% Commercial	% Manufacturing	% Agricultural	% Personal[1]	% Other[2]
1960	481.4	47.5	13.5	10.7	11.2	16.5	0.6
1965	664.1	48.4	14.4	10.3	10.6	15.8	0.6
1970	1,179.0	47.3	15.2	10.4	9.7	16.9	0.5
1975	1,601.3	50.5	16.8	5.7	10.1	16.2	0.7
1980	2,210.0	57.7	16.2	4.8	12.5	7.5	1.3
1985	3,203.5	58.9	17.7	4.7	12.4	4.8	1.6
1990	4,388.2	60.4	20.2	4.1	8.4	5.5	1.3
1995	5,738.9	64.8	18.8	3.6	6.7	4.9	1.1
2000	6,604.5	67.9	18.9	3.7	1.7	3.4	4.3
2005	8,326.7	71.0	18.7	3.0	0.5	2.6	4.2
2010	10,364.6	70.4	19.6	2.8	0.4	2.6	4.3
2011	10,384.8	70.2	19.7	2.8	0.4	2.5	4.3
2012	10,469.9	69.6	20.2	2.9	0.4	2.6	4.3
2013	10,605.5	69.0	20.5	3.0	0.4	2.7	4.3
2014	10,383.7	68.8	20.8	3.0	0.4	2.8	4.2
2015	10,620.2	68.6	21.0	3.0	0.4	2.7	4.2
2016	10,792.1	68.3	21.3	3.0	0.4	2.8	4.2
2017	11,016.1	68.1	21.7	3.0	0.4	2.7	4.1
2018	11,198.9	68.7	22.0	3.0	0.4	1.9	4.1

Municipal property taxes levied in Wisconsin, continued

	Total (mil. dol.)	% Residential	% Commercial	% Manufacturing	% Agricultural	% Personal[1]	% Other[2]
2019	11,618.2	68.8	22.0	3.0	0.4	1.9	4.0
2020	12,016.9	68.8	22.2	2.9	0.4	1.8	3.9
2021	12,207.8	68.9	22.4	2.8	0.4	1.7	3.8

Note: Percentages may not add up to 100 due to rounding.
1. An exemption for "Line A" business property was phased in beginning in 1977. "Line A" property was completely exempted by 1981. 2. Beginning in 1996, includes agricultural property not considered agricultural land for purposes of use-value assessment.
Sources: Wisconsin Department of Revenue, Division of State and Local Finance, Local Government Services, *2021 Town, Village and City Taxes: Taxes Levied 2021—Collected 2022*, and prior issues; for 1980, 1975, and 1970 data, *Property Tax*, 1981 and prior issues; 1960 and 1965 data are from the Wisconsin Department of Taxation.

Wisconsin general property tax levies, 2021

Type of property	Towns ($)	Villages ($)	Cities ($)	Total ($)
Real estate	3,418,300,620	2,276,308,485	6,304,608,275	11,999,217,380
Residential	2,702,392,835	1,692,187,869	4,018,137,256	8,412,717,960
Commercial	196,558,266	486,868,512	2,051,339,058	2,734,765,836
Manufacturing	30,042,149	82,703,365	229,605,936	342,351,450
Forest lands	122,589,338	2,173,639	770,778	125,533,755
Agricultural	41,440,800	1,185,287	512,617	43,138,704
Agricultural forest	56,444,177	1,064,862	470,028	57,979,067
Undeveloped	34,175,551	1,438,940	806,407	36,420,898
Other land and improvements	234,657,504	8,686,011	2,966,195	246,309,710
Personal property	23,170,976	34,807,233	150,579,741	208,557,950
Furniture, fixtures, equipment	7,319,991	18,754,055	82,635,151	108,709,197
Machinery, tools, patterns	5,442,676	8,541,026	28,955,513	42,939,215
Boats and other watercraft	152,494	40,337	175,888	368,719
All other personal property	10,255,815	7,471,815	38,813,189	56,540,819
Total general property taxes	3,441,471,596	2,311,115,718	6,455,188,016	12,207,775,330
Total state tax credit	322,100,461	180,604,551	437,295,004	940,000,016
Total effective taxes	3,119,371,135	2,130,511,167	6,017,893,012	11,267,775,314

Note: The sums of some columns and rows may differ slightly from the reported totals because the Department of Revenue truncates (rather than rounds) amounts under $1 for individual units of government.
Source: Wisconsin Department of Revenue, Division of State and Local Finance, *Town, Village, and City Taxes—2021: Taxes Levied 2021—Collected 2022.*

Wisconsin Conservation Fund revenues and expenditures

	FY 2019–20 ($)	FY 2020–21 ($)	FY 2021–22 ($)
Opening cash balance	132,085,902	150,257,626	172,530,217
Revenues	338,811,825	348,575,145	355,186,355
User fees (licenses, registrations, recreational fees)	115,386,597	130,121,935	125,993,259
GPR transfer for forestry mill tax[1]	98,574,101	104,049,333	111,123,018
Federal aids	66,183,985	51,853,263	60,764,768
Motor fuel tax formula	20,716,368	20,559,767	24,597,148
Gifts, donations and private support	1,462,418	1,369,408	1,090,385
Other revenues (sales, services)	36,488,356	40,621,439	31,617,777

Wisconsin Conservation Fund revenues and expenditures, continued

	FY 2019–20 ($)	FY 2020–21 ($)	FY 2021–22 ($)
Expenditures	320,640,101	326,302,554	336,196,504
Fish, wildlife, and parks—state	62,793,867	68,540,491	67,075,326
Fish, wildlife, and parks—federal	27,535,596	26,131,962	31,780,414
Forestry—state	54,761,432	56,291,833	56,580,815
Forestry—federal	1,651,113	2,471,809	3,756,043
Public Safety & Resource Protection—state	27,980,261	25,057,167	25,745,381
Public Safety & Resource Protection—federal	5,909,881	5,859,885	6,165,180
Environmental management—state	2,620,947	2,300,886	4,410,442
Conservation aids—state	33,709,146	38,685,926	37,245,883
Conservation aids—federal	8,528,438	8,347,400	9,746,622
Environmental aids—state	6,907,555	6,101,444	6,330,459
Development/debt service—state	25,182,892	24,138,853	22,968,598
Development/debt service—federal	1,496,042	2,497,462	3,427,428
Administration—state	3,457,124	3,829,723	3,938,562
Administration—federal	1,149,511	1,136,200	1,095,302
Internal and external services—state	36,343,776	35,335,050	36,428,155
Internal and external services—federal	5,541,017	6,474,811	7,400,362
Other activities—state	15,071,503	13,101,652	12,101,532
Fund balance	150,257,626	172,530,217	191,520,068

FY–Fiscal year.

1. The forestry mill tax sunset as of January 1, 2017, property tax assessments. 2017 Wisconsin Act 59 provides for a GPR transfer to the conservation fund in an amount comparable to what would have been provided from the tax.

Source: Wisconsin Department of Administration, Division of Executive Budget and Finance, State Controller's Office, *2022 Annual Fiscal Report (Budgetary Basis) Appendix*, and prior editions.

Wisconsin Transportation Fund revenues and expenditures

	Fiscal year 2020–21		Fiscal year 2021–22	
	State funds ($)	Federal, local, and agency funds ($)	State funds ($)	Federal, local, and agency funds ($)
Opening balance	505,631,376	-1,332,565,110	654,954,719	-1,321,239,760
Revenues	1,966,210,133	1,215,183,261	2,144,616,143	1,379,595,872
Motor fuel taxes	1,064,159,859	X	1,109,968,466	X
Vehicle registration[1]	716,144,069	X	708,194,057	X
Drivers license fees	40,674,208	X	39,013,730	X
Motor carrier fees	2,565,213	X	2,632,667	X
Other motor vehicle fees	24,106,458	X	26,728,267	X
Overweight/oversize permits	6,904,251	X	7,037,227	X
Investment earnings	590,718	X	1,932,828	X
Aeronautical taxes and fees	1,842,882	X	2,096,295	X
Public utility tax revenues (aeronautics and railroads)	44,030,293	X	36,546,964	X
Transfers-in[2]	60,676,662	X	202,481,038	X
Miscellaneous	4,515,520	-17,189,265	7,984,604	34,264,676
Service center operations	X	27,923,346	X	25,150,636
State and local highway facilities—federal	X	836,283,939	X	888,734,699
State and local highway facilities—local	X	92,612,146	X	175,540,001
Major highway development revenue bonds	X	88,801,610	X	67,495,964

Statistics and Reference: Public finance | 673

Wisconsin Transportation Fund revenues and expenditures, continued

	Fiscal year 2020–21 State funds ($)	Fiscal year 2020–21 Federal, local, and agency funds ($)	Fiscal year 2021–22 State funds ($)	Fiscal year 2021–22 Federal, local, and agency funds ($)
Highway administration and planning—federal	X	2,569,777	X	2,095,645
Aeronautics—federal	X	69,302,927	X	48,937,059
Aeronautics—local	X	29,853,758	X	29,422,333
Railroad assistance—federal	X	3,082,059	X	3,455,384
Railroad assistance—local	X	5,000,317	X	3,977,600
Railroad passenger service—federal	X	232,520	X	8,896,096
Railroad passenger service—local	X	-6,687	X	-19,617
Transit assistance—federal	X	32,393,993	X	19,014,517
Transit assistance—local	X	956,836	X	973,110
Congestion mitigation air quality—federal	X	2,553,816	X	986,771
Congestion mitigation air quality—local	X	14,716	X	-683,175
Harbors assistance—federal	X	31,721	X	—
Harbors assistance—local	X	637	X	—
Transportation facilities economic assistance and development—local	X	14,542	X	54
Transportation alternatives program—federal	X	6,368,742	X	6,921,938
Transportation alternatives program—local	X	4,749,811	X	3,260,244
General administration and planning—federal	X	23,007,369	X	51,809,079
General administration and planning—local	X	102,245	X	1,047,746
Administrative facilities—revenue bonds	X	1,701,982	X	3,569,126
Highway safety—federal	X	4,640,613	X	4,227,763
Gifts and grants	X	179,791	X	518,223
Total	**2,471,841,509**	**-117,381,849**	**2,799,570,862**	**58,356,112**
Expenditures[3]	**1,816,886,787**	**1,203,857,910**	**2,069,119,476**	**1,558,972,559**
Local assistance	745,959,976	249,371,449	734,576,629	409,330,411
Highway aids	522,690,695	—	526,145,036	—
Local bridge and highway improvement	65,547,796	177,659,472	57,699,861	252,908,123
Mass transit	131,856,911	5,193,567	121,590,099	11,186,123
Railroads	2,689,252	-816,570	2,802,275	-2,061,930
Aeronautics	11,780,796	62,694,212	11,526,108	145,989,680
Highway safety	—	4,564,910	—	4,167,031
Rail passenger service	4,860,721	—	11,526,108	45
Harbors	6,463,567	75,858	3,285,509	-2,858,661
Multimodal transportation studies	86,947	—	—	—
Transportation alternatives program	-16,709	—	1,633	—
Aids to individuals and organizations	7,209,920	13,671,823	5,693,164	9,349,969
Transportation facilities economic assistance and development	1,927,421	1,170,447	1,351,287	-633,074
Railroad crossings	4,404,924	3,346,411	3,894,995	5,184,937
Elderly and disabled	584,522	4,767,019	446,882	3,578,884
Freight rail	293,053	4,387,946	—	1,219,222
State operations	1,043,157,124	940,814,638	1,307,252,608	1,140,292,179
Highway improvements	385,334,282	825,780,114	644,677,176	888,333,073
Major highway development—revenue bonds	—	66,394,516	—	77,192,278
Highway maintenance, repair, and traffic operations	271,883,634	5,602,379	290,739,449	13,227,307

Wisconsin Transportation Fund revenues and expenditures, continued

	Fiscal year 2020–21		Fiscal year 2021–22	
	State funds ($)	Federal, local, and agency funds ($)	State funds ($)	Federal, local, and agency funds ($)
Highway administration and planning	12,804,765	2,707,007	13,199,393	1,914,307
Traffic enforcement and inspection...	73,549,108	6,620,532	77,456,568	7,058,808
Transportation safety	1,301,013	4,856,813	1,773,896	5,640,392
General administration and planning .	66,992,969	13,615,958	67,949,237	39,882,639
Administrative facilities—revenue bonds	—	-14,003,207	—	25,043,207
Vehicle registration and drivers licensing.	74,734,335	608,942	75,266,432	236,124
Vehicle inspection and maintenance . .	2,793,300	—	2,809,171	—
Debt repayment and interest[4]	152,008,122	—	131,099,789	—
Service centers	—	25,584,150	—	27,924,963
Congestion mitigation air quality	—	2,279,170	—	6,775,348
Miscellaneous	1,755,596	768,264	2,281,497	47,063,733
Conservation Fund transfers	20,559,767	—	21,597,075	—
Unreserved fund balance	**654,954,722**	**-1,321,239,759**	**730,451,386**	**-1,500,616,447**

X–Not applicable; — Represents zero.

1. Wis. Stat. § 84.59 provides that vehicle registration revenues derived under Wis. Stat. § 341.25 are deposited with a trustee in a fund outside the state treasury. Only those revenues not required for the repayment of Revenue Bond obligations are considered income to the Transportation Fund. The trustee retained $194.1 million during FY 2021 and $216.7 million during FY 2022. 2. Transfer-in amount for FY 2021 includes $44.1 million General Fund, $9.99 million Petroleum Inspection Fund, and $0.4 million Conservation Fund; and for FY 2022 includes $178 million General Fund, $7 million Petroleum Inspection Fund, and $0.3 million Conservation Fund. 3. The amounts exclude financial activity relating to General Obligation Bond funded projects that are reimbursed by the Capital Improvement Fund. 4. 2021 Wisconsin Act 58 (the 2021–23 biennial budget act) authorized General Obligation Bond proceeds funding for railroad and harbor improvements of $20.0 million for freight rail acquisitions and improvements and $15.3 million for harbor improvements. Debt service will be funded by the Transportation Fund.

Source: Wisconsin Department of Administration, Division of Executive Budget and Finance, State Controller's Office, *2022 Annual Fiscal Report (Budgetary Basis) Appendix.*

COMMERCE AND INDUSTRY

Value added by manufacturing in Wisconsin

Industry group	2018 ($1,000)	2019 ($1,000)	2020 ($1,000)	2021 ($1,000)
Food manufacturing	16,204,355	16,617,031	17,644,085	18,291,636
Machinery manufacturing	10,862,682	11,045,039	10,227,085	11,977,757
Fabricated metal product manufacturing	9,426,449	9,707,544	8,841,105	10,507,867
Paper manufacturing	6,324,080	7,140,160	7,027,774	7,276,387
Transportation equipment manufacturing	4,917,573	4,730,325	5,166,682	5,774,985
Plastics and rubber products manufacturing	5,499,361	5,578,957	4,881,263	5,620,231
Chemical manufacturing	4,675,909	4,997,210	4,769,707	5,109,853
Computer and electronic product manufacturing	4,211,280	4,161,033	3,710,207	4,548,900
Electrical equipment, appliance, and component manufacturing	4,459,958	4,534,653	3,737,614	3,909,508
Printing and related support activities	1,837,367	2,036,793	2,460,558	2,868,644
Primary metal manufacturing	2,857,374	2,849,974	2,622,302	2,728,377
Wood product manufacturing	2,832,312	2,536,222	1,951,729	2,630,748
Miscellaneous manufacturing	2,072,172	1,903,779	1,976,872	2,209,614
Nonmetallic mineral product manufacturing	1,975,016	1,960,938	1,837,525	2,155,978
Furniture and related product manufacturing	1,729,338	1,730,535	1,604,955	1,718,559
Beverage and tobacco product manufacturing	983,618	963,228	960,399	1,238,546
Petroleum and coal products manufacturing	195,485	215,100	232,220	219,665
Textile mills	215,066	212,370	134,166	D
Leather and allied product manufacturing	128,451	124,278	98,000	D
Textile product mills	107,567	78,856	66,523	D
Apparel manufacturing	40,796	45,796	37,370	D
Total [1]	81,556,209	83,169,821	79,988,141	89,226,568

D–Figure withheld to avoid disclosure.
1. Totals may not add due to the exclusion of manufacturing categories beneath the top 20 highest values.
Source: U.S. Census Bureau, "Annual Survey of Manufactures: Geographic Area Statistics: Summary Statistics for Industry Groups and Industries in the U.S. and States: 2018–2021" at https://www.census.gov/programs-surveys/asm.html [Dec. 29, 2022].

Value of Wisconsin exports by category

	2020 ($1,000)	2021 ($1,000)	2022 ($1,000)	% change 2021 to 2022
Top 20 categories[1] in 2022				
Industrial machinery	5,249,612	5,711,465	7,057,542	23.57
Electric machinery	2,023,065	2,123,396	2,581,158	21.56
Medical and scientific instruments	2,037,753	2,169,075	2,434,172	12.22
Vehicles and parts	1,337,271	1,658,849	1,683,204	1.47
Plastic products	1,146,331	1,447,351	1,603,350	10.78
Pharmaceutical products	315,763	1,939,398	1,106,337	-42.95
Aircraft, spacecraft, and parts	575,400	475,777	931,680	95.82
Paper products	723,358	766,187	909,168	18.66
Iron and steel products	385,486	503,873	630,107	25.05
Miscellaneous chemical products	538,708	594,366	513,750	-13.56
Organic chemicals	278,140	437,684	440,140	0.56
Miscellaneous edible preparations	343,231	389,336	438,493	12.63
Dairy, eggs, and honey	262,972	291,778	406,021	39.15
Beverages, spirits, and vinegar	186,023	291,778	385,556	24.69
Starch, glue, and enzymes	257,010	348,214	354,992	1.95
Furniture, bedding, and lamps	213,667	260,654	337,621	29.53
Prepared vegetables, fruits, and nuts	315,707	404,219	333,159	-17.58

Value of Wisconsin exports by category, continued

	2020 ($1,000)	2021 ($1,000)	2022 ($1,000)	% change 2021 to 2022
Wood products.	244,956	286,047	279,488	-2.29
Printed matter	245,664	301,563	279,252	-7.40
Essential oils and perfumes	231,831	259,559	267,876	3.20
All exports.	20,499,583	24,811,144	27,383,402	10.37

1. Export categories based on U.S. Census Bureau commodity codes.
Source: Data provided by the Wisconsin Economic Development Corporation, March 2023.

Value of Wisconsin exports by market

	2020 ($1,000)	2021 ($1,000)	2022 ($1,000)	% change 2021 to 2022
Top 20 markets in 2022				
Canada.	6,246,874	7,537,859	8,589,113	13.95
Mexico.	2,569,520	3,103,182	3,611,930	16.39
China.	1,552,173	1,798,056	1,805,033	0.39
Germany.	720,980	875,397	1,044,278	19.29
United Kingdom.	625,888	723,477	882,316	21.96
Australia.	563,672	597,887	761,748	27.41
Japan.	685,117	687,227	699,628	1.80
Belgium.	381,154	623,380	668,189	7.19
South Korea.	508,007	570,428	653,305	14.53
Netherlands.	428,258	473,775	563,588	18.96
Chile.	355,069	319,526	516,452	61.63
France.	371,186	450,763	492,276	9.21
Singapore.	252,138	332,141	421,341	26.86
Brazil.	302,413	792,271	395,737	-50.05
Thailand.	290,436	298,174	364,511	22.25
Italy.	262,107	241,409	326,573	35.28
Taiwan.	199,971	225,346	306,824	36.16
India.	206,749	256,959	295,407	14.96
Malaysia.	146,981	176,702	218,885	23.87
Indonesia.	100,697	208,085	203,629	-2.14
All markets.	20,499,583	24,811,144	27,383,402	10.37

Source: Data provided by the Wisconsin Economic Development Corporation, March 2023.

Basic data on Wisconsin corporations

	Transactions[1]				Fees ($)		
	Domestic				Fees ($)		
Fiscal year[2]	Articles of incorporation filed[3]	Amdts. and restated articles	Foreign corporations licensed	Fees for articles of incorporation	Fees for foreign corporation[4]	Other corporation fees[5]	Total fees collected
1975.	5,976	1,483	663	361,013	386,061	594,498	1,341,572
1980.	7,334	1,978	753	373,220	753,461	788,204	1,914,885
1985.	7,605	2,359	1,018	485,835	1,142,129	1,371,476	2,999,440
1990.	8,387	2,525	1,408	546,550	2,368,900	1,491,104	4,406,554
1995.	10,031	2,716	1,507	829,555	4,208,178	2,538,521	7,576,254
2000.	21,133	3,088	2,464	2,265,455	6,403,447	3,548,264	12,217,166
2005.	33,589	3,595	2,787	4,092,782	6,043,400	5,509,178	15,645,000

Basic data on Wisconsin corporations, continued

	Transactions[1]			Fees ($)			
	Domestic						
Fiscal year[2]	Articles of incorporation filed[3]	Amdts. and restated articles	Foreign corporations licensed	Fees for articles of incorporation	Fees for foreign corporation[4]	Other corporation fees[5]	Total fees collected
2010.....	27,349	2,231	2,495	5,247,361	8,311,900	5,291,939	18,851,200
2015.....	36,576	2,804	3,523	11,746,200	7,820,600	844,400	20,411,200
2016.....	38,304	3,203	3,701	13,643,500	6,659,700	748,700	21,051,900
2017.....	39,933	3,208	3,771	12,534,100	9,957,900	729,000	23,221,100
2018.....	43,179	3,430	4,116	13,165,800	9,822,300	782,700	23,770,800
2019.....	44,584	3,263	4,561	13,791,900	11,539,400	798,900	26,130,200
2020.....	45,943	3,080	4,283	14,489,000	9,416,100	946,500	24,851,600
2021.....	64,135	3,524	5,148	17,148,600	12,077,400	1,073,300	30,299,300
2022.....	64,413	3,724	5,743	17,465,300	12,197,300	1,214,700	30,877,800

Amdts.– Amendments.
1. Includes only corporate entities for which the reporting agency is the office of record. 2. Since 1975, data is computed on a fiscal year basis, ending June 30 of year shown. 3. Beginning in 1997, includes limited liability companies. 4. Since 1975, totals include fees for foreign corporation annual reports. 5. Includes fees for filing annual reports and corporation charter documents other than articles of incorporation.
Sources: Wisconsin Department of Financial Institutions, departmental data for 2000–20 [February 2021]; prior data from the Office of the Wisconsin Secretary of State.

Financial institutions operating in Wisconsin

Year[1]	Number	Total deposits (mil. dol.)	Year[1]	Number	Total deposits (mil. dol.)
1900...............	349	125	1980...............	634	24,764
1910...............	630	269	1990...............	504	37,589
1920...............	976	768	2000...............	365	75,379
1930...............	936	935	2010...............	299	126,660
1940...............	574	993	2020...............	216	179,312
1950...............	556	2,966	2021...............	210	200,854
1960...............	561	4,386	2022...............	205	205,894
1970...............	602	8,751			

1. Beginning in 1994, data include federal charter savings associations and state-chartered savings associations, supervised by the U.S. Office of Thrift Supervision, and institutions operating in Wisconsin but headquartered outside the state.
Sources: 1950 and earlier: Board of Governors of the Federal Reserve System, All-Bank Statistics, U.S., 1959; 1960: Wisconsin Commissioner of Banks, agency data, December 1965; 1970: Federal Deposit Insurance Corporation, Assets and Liabilities—Commercial and Mutual Savings Banks, June 1971; 1980: Federal Deposit Insurance Corporation, corporate data; 1990: Federal Deposit Insurance Corporation, Data Book: Operating Banks and Branches, Book 3, June 30, 1993; 2000 to date: Federal Deposit Insurance Corporation, Summary of Deposits, "State Totals by Charter Class for All Institution Deposits, Deposits of All FDIC-Insured Institutions Operating in Wisconsin," June 30, 2022, and prior issues.

Wisconsin financial institutions, June 30, 2022

		Headquartered in Wisconsin			Headquartered outside Wisconsin		
	Total deposits (mil. dol.)	Institutions	Offices	Deposits (mil. dol.)	Institutions	Offices	Deposits (mil. dol.)
Commercial banks.....	196,293	151	1,108	96,801	29	494	99,491
National charter.....	137,481	19	382	41,253	12	453	96,228
State charter........	58,812	132	726	55,548	17	41	3,264
FRS member......	13,104	15	102	12,505	3	6	599

Wisconsin financial institutions, June 30, 2022, continued

	Total deposits (mil. dol.)	Headquartered in Wisconsin Institutions	Offices	Deposits (mil. dol.)	Headquartered outside Wisconsin Institutions	Offices	Deposits (mil. dol.)
FRS nonmember	45,708	117	624	43,043	14	35	2,665
Savings institutions	9,601	22	135	9,483	3	5	118
Federal charter	5,288	9	69	5,171	3	5	118
State charter	4,312	13	66	4,312	X	X	X
Total	205,894	173	1,243	106,284	32	499	99,609

FRS—Federal Reserve System; X—Not applicable.

Source: Federal Deposit Insurance Corporation, Summary of Deposits, "Deposits of all FDIC-Insured Institutions: State Totals by Charter Class" at www.fdic.gov/regulations/resources/call/sod.html [June 30, 2022].

FDIC-insured institutions operating in Wisconsin, June 30, 2022

County	Commercial banks Institutions	Offices	Deposits (mil. dol.)	Savings institutions Institutions	Offices	Deposits (mil. dol.)
Adams	4	5	275	1	1	8
Ashland	4	8	515	—	—	—
Barron	9	19	1,157	1	1	183
Bayfield	4	10	407	—	—	—
Brown	16	57	9,922	1	6	176
Buffalo	4	10	392	—	—	—
Burnett	3	6	547	—	—	—
Calumet	7	11	729	1	1	38
Chippewa	10	21	1,080	1	1	53
Clark	6	9	623	2	5	225
Columbia	9	20	1,262	—	—	—
Crawford	5	11	514	—	—	—
Dane	31	134	21,855	3	3	1,382
Dodge	10	28	1,403	2	2	143
Door	3	10	1,004	1	2	110
Douglas	4	8	710	1	1	68
Dunn	8	14	518	—	—	—
Eau Claire	16	30	2,670	1	1	4
Florence	1	2	103	—	—	—
Fond du Lac	11	34	2,603	—	—	—
Forest	2	6	235	1	1	212
Grant	11	38	1,512	—	—	—
Green	7	16	1,219	—	—	—
Green Lake	6	13	993	—	—	—
Iowa	7	13	626	—	—	—
Iron	2	3	112	—	—	—
Jackson	3	6	270	—	—	—
Jefferson	11	25	1,766	—	—	—
Juneau	5	13	576	—	—	—
Kenosha	10	32	3,371	1	3	73
Kewaunee	2	8	543	—	—	—
La Crosse	15	38	3,540	—	—	—
Lafayette	7	12	444	—	—	—
Langlade	4	5	121	—	—	—
Lincoln	4	6	360	1	2	177
Manitowoc	7	8	356	—	—	—
Marathon	13	28	2,564	3	7	291
Marinette	9	19	1,880	—	—	—
Marquette	6	8	286	—	—	—

FDIC-insured institutions operating in Wisconsin, June 30, 2022, continued

County	Commercial banks Institutions	Offices	Deposits (mil. dol.)	Savings institutions Institutions	Offices	Deposits (mil. dol.)
Menominee	1	1	66	—	—	—
Milwaukee	18	173	63,465	8	43	2,491
Monroe	8	13	878	—	—	—
Oconto	4	7	298	1	3	64
Oneida	7	12	1,072	—	—	—
Outagamie	17	34	4,256	3	8	329
Ozaukee	12	31	3,340	3	4	155
Pepin	3	3	323	—	—	—
Pierce	8	12	762	—	—	—
Polk	10	12	807	—	—	—
Portage	12	22	2,103	2	2	54
Price	2	2	58	2	4	229
Racine	12	36	4,176	2	5	235
Richland	5	7	309	—	—	—
Rock	17	32	3,167	—	—	—
Rusk	4	5	281	1	1	70
St. Croix	13	22	1,948	—	—	—
Sauk	12	26	2,636	1	1	93
Sawyer	5	8	573	—	—	—
Shawano	8	13	634	—	—	—
Sheboygan	15	33	2,938	—	—	—
Taylor	3	3	331	2	2	193
Trempealeau	8	17	715	—	—	—
Vernon	7	15	619	—	—	—
Vilas	9	12	791	—	—	—
Walworth	14	32	2,332	—	—	—
Washburn	5	7	423	—	—	—
Washington	14	37	3,873	2	2	141
Waukesha	29	135	15,795	7	20	1,512
Waupaca	6	17	1,052	—	—	—
Waushara	7	8	356	—	—	—
Winnebago	13	28	2,564	2	2	71
Wood	9	19	1,880	4	6	820
Total[1]	180	1,602	196,293	25	140	9,601

— Represents zero.

1. Total number of institutions is an unduplicated total for institutions operating in more than one county. Deposit figures do not add to state totals due to rounding.

Source: Federal Deposit Insurance Corporation, "Deposits of all FDIC-Insured Institutions: State Totals by County," at www.fdic.gov/regulations/resources/call/sod.html [June 30, 2022].gov/regulations/resources/call/sod.html [June 30, 2022].

Wisconsin state-chartered credit unions

	Number of credit unions	Total members (% chg. from prior yr.)	Total assets (mil. dol.) (% chg. from prior yr.)
1930	22	4,659 (NA)	0.5 (NA)
1940	592	153,849 (NA)	11.2 (NA)
1950	542	193,296 (NA)	42.9 (NA)
1960	733	363,444 (NA)	206.4 (NA)
1970	766	628,543 (NA)	480.4 (NA)
1980	618	1,060,292 (NA)	1,403.8 (NA)
1990	440	1,485,109 (4.3)	4,148.7 (8.6)
2000	340	1,918,729 (1.7)	9,425.9 (7.9)
2010	223	2,186,471 (1.0)	20,685.4 (4.9)

Wisconsin state-chartered credit unions, continued

	Number of credit unions	Total members (% chg. from prior yr.)	Total assets in mil. dol. (% chg. from prior yr.)
2011	203	2,225,892 (1.8)	21,915.6 (5.9)
2012	187	2,264,788 (1.7)	23,353.8 (6.6)
2013	171	2,335,239 (3.1)	24,517.9 (5.0)
2014	160	2,460,025 (5.3)	26,324.6 (7.4)
2015	150	2,613,667 (6.2)	28,797.1 (9.4)
2016	143	2,790,644 (6.8)	31,453.3 (9.2)
2017	129	2,938,267 (5.3)	34,157.2 (8.6)
2018	125	3,081,193 (4.9)	37,012.0 (8.4)
2019	121	3,196,907 (3.8)	41,069.5 (11.0)
2020	118	3,307,029 (3.4)	49,524.8 (20.6)
2021	113	3,377,072 (2.1)	55,890.9 (12.9)
2022	110	3,490,300 (3.4)	60,746.0 (8.7)

NA–Not available.

Source: Wisconsin Department of Financial Institutions, Office of Credit Unions, 2022 Year End Credit Union Bulletin, at https://www.wdfi.org/_resources/indexed/site/fi/cu/QuarterlyReports/2022/2022YearendBulletin.pdf [March 2023], and prior editions.

Wisconsin's tribal gaming facilities

Casino	Location	Tribe
Legendary Waters Resort and Casino	Bayfield	Red Cliff Band (Lake Superior Chippewa)
Bad River Casino	Odanah	Bad River Band (Lake Superior Chippewa)
Lake of the Torches Resort Casino	Lac du Flambeau	Lac du Flambeau Band (Lake Superior Chippewa)
Sevenwinds Casino	Hayward	Lac Courte Oreilles Band (Lake Superior Chippewa)
St. Croix Casino Danbury	Danbury	St. Croix Band (Lake Superior Chippewa)
St. Croix Casino Hertel	Hertel	St. Croix Band (Lake Superior Chippewa)
St. Croix Casino Turtle Lake	Turtle Lake	St. Croix Band (Lake Superior Chippewa)
Mole Lake Casino	Crandon	Sokaogon Chippewa Community
Potawatomi Carter Casino and Hotel	Carter	Forest County Potawatomi Community
Menominee Casino Resort	Keshena	Menominee Indian Tribe
The Thunderbird Mini-Casino	Keshena	Menominee Indian Tribe
North Star Mohican Casino Resort	Bowler	Stockbridge-Munsee Community
Ho-Chunk Gaming Wittenberg	Wittenberg	Ho-Chunk Nation
Ho-Chunk Gaming Black River Falls	Black River Falls	Ho-Chunk Nation
Ho-Chunk Gaming Nekoosa	Nekoosa	Ho-Chunk Nation
Ho-Chunk Gaming Tomah	Tomah	Ho-Chunk Nation
Ho-Chunk Gaming Wisconsin Dells	Baraboo	Ho-Chunk Nation
Potawatomi Bingo Casino	Milwaukee	Forest County Potawatomi Community
Oneida Main Casino	Green Bay	Oneida Nation
IMAC Casino/Bingo	Green Bay	Oneida Nation
Oneida Mason Street Casino	Green Bay	Oneida Nation
Oneida One-Stop Packerland	Green Bay	Oneida Nation
Oneida Casino Travel Center	Oneida	Oneida Nation

Note: Only Class III gaming facilities regulated by tribal compact are included, pursuant to P.L. 100-497, the Indian Gaming Regulatory Act, which divides gambling into three classes. An additional Ho-Chunk casino in Madison offers Class II gaming. Class I games are social games played solely for prizes of minimal value or traditional forms of Indian gaming played in connection with tribal ceremonies or celebrations. Class II includes bingo or bingo-type games, pull-tabs and punch-boards, and certain nonbanking card games, such as poker. Class III covers all other forms of gaming.

Source: Wisconsin Legislative Fiscal Bureau, "Informational Paper 87: Tribal Gaming in Wisconsin," January 2023, at https://docs.legis.wisconsin.gov/misc/lfb/informational_papers/january_2023/0089_tribal_gaming_in_wisconsin_informational_paper_89.pdf.

■ ■ ■

EMPLOYMENT AND INCOME

Wisconsin employment trends

	Labor force (1,000)	Employed (1,000)	Unemployed (1,000)	Unemployment rate (%)	Total nonfarm employment (1,000)	Service providing (1,000)	Goods producing (1,000)	Manufacturing (1,000)	Trade, transportation, and utilities (1,000)
2000	2,985.6	2,884.7	100.9	3.4	2,832.3	2,107.6	724.7	595.8	551.1
2005	3,029.7	2,885.7	144.0	4.8	2,836.0	2,197.5	638.5	507.0	540.9
2010	3,082.9	2,820.6	262.3	8.5	2,725.0	2,194.6	530.5	433.0	505.5
2015	3,084.2	2,947.0	137.2	4.4	2,893.7	2,310.1	583.6	470.0	528.4
2016	3,110.5	2,988.7	121.7	3.9	2,929.3	2,345.3	584.0	467.7	536.4
2017	3,141.8	3,039.3	102.4	3.3	2,951.9	2,359.7	592.2	470.5	539.1
2018	3,123.9	3,030.7	93.2	3	2,980.1	2,373.5	606.7	479.6	540.1
2019	3,111.7	3,012.8	98.9	3.2	2,987.6	2,375.5	612.1	483.5	535.4
2020	3,094.7	2,897.4	197.3	6.4	2,823.8	2,237.1	586.7	459.1	520.2
2021	3,099.8	2,981.1	118.7	3.8	2,892.3	2,294.4	597.8	467.4	535.5
2022	3,082.1	2,992.1	90.1	2.9	2,965.0	2,348.8	616.2	481.2	549.3
2023	3,068.2	2,983.7	84.5	2.8	2,951.9	2,344.4	607.5	482.5	545.5

Note: Data are estimates that are revised monthly and annually and are seasonally adjusted. Industry classifications in this table are defined by the North American Industry Classification System (NAICS).

Sources: Wisconsin Department of Workforce Development, WisConomy, Wisconsin Labor Market Information Data Access, "Local Area Unemployment Statistics" and "Current Employment Estimates by Industry" at https://www.jobcenterofwisconsin.com/wisconomy/query [March 2023].

Wisconsin annual employment

Industry	2018	2019	2020	2021	2022
Labor force	3,123,898	3,111,729	3,094,716	3,099,768	3,082,128
Unemployment	93,239	98,901	197,294	118,698	90,079
Unemployment rate	3	3.2	6.4	3.8	2.9
Employment	3,030,659	3,012,828	2,897,422	2,981,070	2,992,049
Total nonfarm	2,980,100	2,987,600	2,823,800	2,892,300	2,965,000
Service providing	2,373,500	2,375,500	2,237,100	2,294,400	2,348,800
Goods producing	606,700	612,100	586,700	597,800	616,200
Trade, transportation, and utilities	540,100	535,400	520,200	535,500	549,300
Manufacturing	479,600	483,500	459,100	467,400	481,200
Private educational and health services	457,300	464,100	450,600	455,000	457,900
Professional and business services	328,200	326,600	309,900	319,200	327,800
Local government	285,300	282,900	266,500	268,900	273,800
Leisure and hospitality	282,400	285,500	227,800	250,200	267,000
Finance	153,000	154,500	153,000	155,700	158,700
Other services	152,200	152,700	142,800	143,400	145,800
Construction	122,300	124,500	124,100	127,000	131,300
State government	98,800	97,600	90,400	91,600	92,800
Information	47,200	47,100	45,000	45,100	46,300
Federal government	29,100	29,300	30,800	30,000	29,500
Mining and logging	4,700	4,200	3,500	3,500	3,700

Note: Industry classifications in this table are defined by the North American Industry Classification System (NAICS).

Source: Wisconsin Department of Workforce Development, WisConomy, Wisconsin Labor Market Information Data Access, "Local Area Unemployment Statistics" and "Current Employment Estimates by Industry" at https://www.jobcenterofwisconsin.com/wisconomy/query [March 2023].

Wisconsin manufacturing employment

Industry	2018	2019	2020	2021	2022
Durable goods	**287,200**	**289,100**	**269,200**	**274,500**	**283,400**
Fabricated metal product manufacturing	76,500	77,900	71,300	72,700	75,500
Machinery manufacturing	66,900	67,400	63,400	65,300	67,900
Transportation equipment manufacturing	26,200	26,000	24,000	24,800	25,500
Electrical equipment and appliances	24,300	24,900	24,100	25,100	25,500
Wood product manufacturing	17,900	17,700	16,900	17,000	17,400
Nondurable goods	**192,400**	**194,400**	**189,800**	**192,800**	**197,900**
Food manufacturing	72,800	74,500	75,000	76,300	79,100
Plastics and rubber products manufacturing	33,600	33,600	32,100	33,400	34,700
Paper manufacturing	29,600	29,300	28,000	27,400	27,200
Printing and related support activities	28,200	28,000	25,500	24,600	24,900
Total	**479,600**	**483,500**	**459,000**	**467,300**	**481,300**

Source: Wisconsin Department of Workforce Development, WisConomy, Wisconsin Labor Market Information Data Access, "Current Employment Estimates by Industry" at https://www.jobcenterofwisconsin.com/wisconomy/query [March 2023].

Wisconsin personal income, by industry

Industry	2017 (mil. dol.)	2018 (mil. dol.)	2019 (mil. dol.)	2020 (mil. dol.)	2021 (mil. dol.)
Services[1]	68,844	72,702	76,030	75,872	81,749
Manufacturing	35,713	37,373	38,102	38,036	39,955
Government and government enterprises	28,869	29,806	30,567	31,365	32,264
Finance and insurance	12,702	13,010	13,411	14,453	15,091
Retail trade	11,719	12,041	12,330	12,911	13,779
Construction	12,527	13,259	14,013	14,238	15,122
Wholesale trade	10,642	11,291	11,096	11,687	12,396
Transportation and warehousing	7,234	7,575	7,886	7,768	8,433
Information	4,589	4,832	5,283	5,273	5,735
Farm earnings	1,754	1,603	1,760	2,890	2,748
Real estate and rental and leasing	2,924	3,066	3,294	3,978	4,206
Utilities	1,644	1,656	1,532	1,435	1,381
Forestry, fishing, and related activities	642	615	605	D	671
Mining, quarrying, and oil and gas extraction	309	408	342	D	337
Total[2]	**284,576**	**298,257**	**311,019**	**329,623**	**351,551**

D—Figure withheld to avoid disclosure of confidential information.

1. Services includes the following NAICS classification categories: professional, scientific and technical services; management of companies and enterprises; administrative and waste management services; educational services; health care and social assistance; arts, entertainment, and recreation; accommodation and food services; and other services (except government).
2. Totals may not add due to rounding.

Source: U.S. Department of Commerce, Bureau of Economic Analysis, Regional Data, "Personal Income by Major Component and Earnings by Industry" at https://apps.bea.gov/itable/iTable.cfm?ReqID=70&step=1 [December 2022].

Wisconsin personal income

	Personal income (mil. dol.)[1]	Per capita personal income[2] Amount (dol.)	State rank	% of national average
1940	1,723.3	548	21	92
1945	3,527.0	1,191	22	96
1950	5,209.0	1,515	24	100

Wisconsin personal income, continued

	Personal income (mil. dol.)[1]	Per capita personal income[2] Amount (dol.)	State rank	% of national average
1955	6,955.7	1,891	21	98
1960	8,994.3	2,270	20	99
1965	11,798.4	2,788	22	98
1970	17,648.8	3,988	25	95
1975	27,872.0	6,099	26	96
1980	47,282.0	10,034	23	99
1985	66,276.7	13,960	27	95
1990	90,431.2	18,438	24	94
1995	119,327.1	23,015	21	98
2000	158,832.3	29,556	20	96
2005	191,047.1	34,447	23	96
2010	222,982.7	39,175	24	96
2015	269,703.9	46,548	25	96
2016	274,374.7	47,205	24	95
2017	284,576.5	48,758	25	95
2018	298,256.9	50,908	25	95
2019	311,019.0	52,893	25	94
2020	329,622.8	55,941	26	94
2021	351,551.3	59,626	27	93

1. Personal income includes all forms of income received by persons from business establishments; federal, state, and local governments; households and institutions; and foreign countries. Allowance is made for "in-kind" income not received as cash.
2. Per capita personal income is total personal income divided by total midyear population.
Source: U.S. Department of Commerce, Bureau of Economic Analysis, Regional Data, "County and MSA personal income summary: personal income, population, per capita personal income," 2021 and prior editions at https://apps.bea.gov/itable/iTable.cfm?ReqID=70&step=1 [December 2022].

Wisconsin adjusted gross income

County	per return AGI 2017 ($)	2018 ($)	2019 ($)	2020 ($)	2021 ($)	2021 AGI[1] ($)	2021 rank[2]
Adams	38,307	38,287	39,659	42,361	45,246	427,439,145	69
Ashland	38,219	41,038	41,616	42,236	46,208	351,507,702	68
Barron	46,537	49,036	48,424	47,875	53,018	1,254,610,500	51
Bayfield	46,050	52,404	51,205	51,453	55,545	438,192,734	42
Brown	62,528	65,652	68,385	69,107	73,234	10,000,837,570	7
Buffalo	41,796	43,518	48,778	47,693	51,147	349,484,518	57
Burnett	40,392	44,341	47,878	45,407	49,669	377,535,327	60
Calumet	63,548	66,857	71,461	69,706	74,577	1,771,802,960	6
Chippewa	51,372	54,180	53,308	55,325	59,555	1,877,338,323	33
Clark	45,156	47,758	49,056	52,882	57,921	869,274,877	37
Columbia	55,170	55,429	57,771	59,644	64,099	1,921,494,320	21
Crawford	43,320	45,035	43,704	47,580	47,393	371,418,316	67
Dane	72,928	75,399	79,597	79,933	86,457	25,178,979,581	3
Dodge	51,596	53,324	55,255	56,811	61,698	2,657,216,133	26
Door	54,808	57,215	59,608	61,058	68,091	1,102,867,271	13
Douglas	45,675	48,685	49,560	50,804	54,071	1,160,788,285	47
Dunn	50,807	53,201	54,061	57,424	60,513	1,250,253,060	30
Eau Claire	57,056	60,409	62,437	62,558	68,781	3,571,247,503	11
Florence	43,900	46,318	47,409	48,034	60,355	130,910,954	31
Fond du Lac	56,779	57,867	58,791	61,169	65,270	3,359,163,511	18
Forest	37,544	39,583	40,059	40,767	44,284	198,434,978	71
Grant	43,177	45,684	47,500	49,110	54,132	1,259,596,640	46

Wisconsin adjusted gross income, continued

	per return AGI						2021
County	2017 ($)	2018 ($)	2019 ($)	2018 ($)	2020 ($)	2021 AGI[1] ($)	rank[2]
Green	55,858	56,107	58,199	60,277	64,175	1,198,986,693	20
Green Lake	46,745	48,141	50,449	50,519	53,165	512,136,165	50
Iowa	52,209	54,019	57,041	59,715	65,636	787,834,025	17
Iron	39,836	41,191	45,037	42,703	48,692	155,766,100	64
Jackson	43,116	44,187	48,618	46,397	49,397	444,524,922	61
Jefferson	56,012	55,556	56,634	57,956	63,727	2,643,210,148	22
Juneau	41,147	42,821	44,586	46,480	51,237	654,043,464	56
Kenosha	53,570	56,076	57,680	58,273	63,099	5,291,138,881	23
Kewaunee	50,956	51,533	55,074	55,475	60,572	626,128,715	29
La Crosse	56,217	57,861	58,753	61,071	66,928	3,981,759,259	15
Lafayette	42,904	48,950	48,396	48,965	51,820	405,804,708	55
Langlade	41,182	43,061	44,696	44,840	48,027	474,118,069	65
Lincoln	46,158	48,081	49,279	50,027	54,291	793,411,809	45
Manitowoc	54,314	53,267	53,848	53,446	58,748	2,387,589,925	34
Marathon	57,099	59,993	62,278	63,637	67,121	4,650,210,645	14
Marinette	42,162	44,447	44,680	45,501	49,097	1,030,145,338	63
Marquette	42,631	44,876	46,701	47,715	49,184	389,588,687	62
Menominee	7,415	20,261	23,423	21,020	28,726	58,055,712	72
Milwaukee	50,516	53,380	54,920	52,751	57,444	26,515,607,892	38
Monroe	45,432	46,561	47,093	48,700	53,322	1,162,796,114	49
Oconto	49,069	51,963	53,700	55,819	59,857	1,125,853,044	32
Oneida	48,710	52,711	55,008	56,141	61,692	1,190,597,372	27
Outagamie	62,398	63,894	65,444	65,696	70,358	7,011,720,308	9
Ozaukee	102,425	107,155	111,890	108,658	119,305	5,554,119,155	1
Pepin	52,444	60,523	54,348	55,415	66,433	237,099,347	16
Pierce	58,999	63,918	64,867	66,043	71,548	1,434,244,832	8
Polk	47,955	50,873	52,135	53,692	58,681	1,308,299,406	35
Portage	52,738	54,930	56,738	57,599	60,898	2,126,084,341	28
Price	40,992	43,133	43,851	43,400	47,424	336,665,380	66
Racine	54,073	56,886	57,265	58,658	61,817	6,111,690,794	25
Richland	42,415	45,081	44,657	46,694	51,921	392,780,187	54
Rock	54,847	57,144	60,720	60,837	68,940	5,742,327,650	10
Rusk	37,534	39,993	39,475	39,903	44,510	290,648,646	70
St. Croix	70,628	75,912	75,165	78,582	86,368	4,022,757,318	4
Sauk	49,560	53,335	53,229	54,876	55,995	1,936,235,297	40
Sawyer	40,509	43,398	43,595	43,235	50,930	425,873,769	58
Shawano	44,768	45,731	47,222	47,881	52,165	1,024,830,293	53
Sheboygan	55,348	56,875	58,237	59,529	62,823	3,786,605,658	24
Taylor	45,345	46,552	47,915	52,192	55,227	511,236,119	43
Trempealeau	46,649	48,979	50,478	52,137	55,926	839,389,861	41
Vernon	43,827	45,477	47,052	49,563	53,780	735,166,359	48
Vilas	43,819	48,453	48,170	50,302	58,117	684,152,332	36
Walworth	55,567	58,923	60,527	61,470	68,104	3,566,328,255	12
Washburn	41,880	48,457	48,376	48,572	53,005	462,472,588	52
Washington	68,180	70,403	71,594	73,296	78,313	5,562,448,787	5
Waukesha	86,671	90,062	92,569	94,089	101,489	21,308,587,963	2
Waupaca	48,262	49,760	52,148	52,818	56,632	1,503,644,503	39
Waushara	42,483	43,253	45,280	46,592	50,469	579,584,525	59
Winnebago	59,145	58,908	60,701	62,243	64,881	5,548,659,038	19
Wood	48,470	50,108	51,573	52,317	55,159	2,122,073,450	44
Total[3]	56,698	59,423	61,003	61,518	66,369	210,839,144,342	

1. "Wisconsin adjusted gross income" (AGI) is Wisconsin income as reported to the Wisconsin Department of Revenue for income tax purposes and is based on the federal income tax definition of "gross income" as modified by certain additions and subtractions required by state law. 2. Rankings calculated by Wisconsin Legislative Reference Bureau. 3. State totals and state per return figures include amounts not allocated to a particular county.

Source: Wisconsin Department of Revenue, "Wisconsin Municipal Income Per Return Report for 2021" and prior reports at https://www.revenue.wi.gov/Pages/Report/WI-Muni-AGI.aspx [March 2023].

Distribution of Wisconsin business establishments, March 2020

Industry	Total employees[1]	Total establishments	1 to 19	20 to 49	50 to 99	100 to 249	250 to 499	500 or more
Agriculture, forestry, fishing, and hunting	3,765	524	499	16	3	5	Z	Z
Mining, quarrying, and oil and gas extraction	5,781	149	102	32	10	4	Z	Z
Utilities	12,724	364	248	55	31	22	4	4
Construction	124,079	14,053	12,880	789	240	99	31	12
Manufacturing	471,475	8,525	4,937	1,490	910	806	237	145
Wholesale trade	126,808	6,704	5,309	858	317	169	41	8
Retail trade	309,187	18,064	14,599	2,266	599	503	88	7
Transportation and warehousing	111,609	5,720	4,691	613	237	122	28	29
Information	54,591	2,527	2,171	195	75	58	18	10
Finance and insurance	145,598	8,775	7,965	456	166	101	54	33
Real estate and rental and leasing	28,178	5,246	5,001	179	40	23	3	Z
Professional, scientific, and technical services	114,960	11,392	10,332	693	200	131	22	14
Management of companies and enterprises	77,585	1,017	606	149	109	81	31	41
Administrative, support, waste management, and remediation services	145,588	7,572	6,453	570	275	177	66	31
Educational services	57,865	1,680	1,279	255	79	37	15	15
Health care and social assistance	415,712	16,677	13,072	2,198	744	440	134	89
Arts, entertainment, and recreation	45,281	2,835	2,368	285	98	58	21	4
Accommodation and food services	244,731	14,763	10,750	3,098	784	105	18	8
Other services (except public administration)	103,625	14,559	13,612	746	138	53	9	Z
Total	2,599,347	141,326	117,054	14,943	5,055	2,994	820	460

Note: Totals are provided by the U.S. Census Bureau and may not equal the sum of columns or rows due to incomplete data.

Z—Two or fewer establishments.

1. Number of employees for the week including March 12, 2020. Excludes most government and railroad employees and self-employed persons.

Source: U.S. Census Bureau, "County Business Patterns" at https://www.census.gov/programs-surveys/cbp.html [October 25, 2022].

■ ■ ■

SOCIAL SERVICES

Wisconsin Works (W-2) benefits

County	2021 Avg. mo. paid caseload	2021 Avg. mo. benefit payment ($)	2022 Avg. mo. paid caseload	2022 Avg. mo. benefit payment ($)
Adams	4	502	3	345
Ashland	15	486	6	549
Barron	19	544	11	535
Bayfield	6	539	3	388
Brown	102	542	92	435
Buffalo	1	207	2	268
Burnett	9	694	7	573
Calumet	9	557	9	539
Chippewa	26	564	19	561
Clark	7	584	2	421
Columbia	4	509	4	439
Crawford	3	522	4	490
Dane	130	454	113	424
Dodge	13	438	12	493
Door	9	511	5	502
Douglas	47	619	35	599
Dunn	26	581	23	518
Eau Claire	59	570	51	534
Florence	1	224	1	368
Fond du Lac	40	460	25	433
Forest	1	347	2	469
Grant	20	561	15	544
Green	3	462	3	476
Green Lake	7	433	5	521
Iowa	6	579	4	471
Iron	3	562	2	365
Jackson	3	605	2	438
Jefferson	10	500	14	390
Juneau	9	533	8	498
Kenosha	179	461	109	470
Kewaunee	5	712	5	475
La Crosse	22	468	21	417
Lafayette	2	487	3	469
Langlade	5	453	5	437
Lincoln	2	476	3	562
Manitowoc	21	481	27	460
Marathon	27	511	24	486
Marinette	5	589	7	480
Marquette	1	546	2	510
Menominee	4	401	2	295
Milwaukee	3,473	597	2,574	555
Monroe	5	484	7	418
Oconto	4	432	6	441
Oneida	7	509	5	409
Outagamie	54	480	47	524
Ozaukee	5	246	7	354
Pepin	1	477	1	356
Pierce	11	594	9	466
Polk	12	568	12	555
Portage	13	447	12	499
Price	2	355	1	464

Wisconsin Works (W-2) benefits, continued

County	2019 Avg. mo. paid caseload	2019 Avg. mo. benefit payment ($)	2020 Avg. mo. paid caseload	2020 Avg. mo. benefit payment ($)
Racine	254	481	162	427
Richland	11	585	8	525
Rock	69	533	58	500
Rusk	5	532	4	591
St. Croix	18	631	11	600
Sauk	4	358	3	250
Sawyer	6	553	3	515
Shawano	9	455	11	418
Sheboygan	49	489	35	475
Taylor	2	614	2	369
Trempealeau	5	499	4	416
Vernon	2	557	2	490
Vilas	3	409	2	558
Walworth	41	531	31	605
Washburn	5	532	2	508
Washington	15	373	17	435
Waukesha	108	536	89	536
Waupaca	11	574	9	544
Waushara	10	548	6	483
Winnebago	96	533	79	557
Wood	22	523	18	456
Total	**5,194**	**568**	**3,919**	**531**

Source: Wisconsin Department of Children and Families, departmental data, March 2023.

Wisconsin Works (W-2) expenditures

W-2 contract agency	Counties served	2021 expenditures ($)	2022 expenditures ($)
Ross IES (www.rossprov.com)	Northern Milwaukee	7,361,872	8,758,895
MAXIMUS (www.maximus.com)	West central Milwaukee	4,159,971	5,346,906
America Works of Wisconsin (www.americaworks.com)	East central Milwaukee	5,786,710	7,788,399
UMOS (www.umos.org)	Southern Milwaukee	5,065,684	4,927,883
Forward Service Corporation (www.fsc-corp.org)	Adams, Brown, Calumet, Columbia, Dane, Dodge, Door, Florence, Fond du Lac, Forest, Grant, Green, Green Lake, Iowa, Jefferson, Juneau, Kewaunee, Lafayette, Langlade, Lincoln, Manitowoc, Marathon, Marinette, Marquette, Menominee, Oconto, Oneida, Outagamie, Portage, Price, Richland, Rock, Sauk, Shawano, Sheboygan, Taylor, Vilas, Waupaca, Waushara, Winnebago, Wood	12,265,870	13,367,405
Equus (equusworks.com)	Kenosha, Ozaukee, Racine, Walworth, Washington, Waukesha	4,318,203	5,544,095
Workforce Connections (www.workforceconnections.org)	Buffalo, Crawford, Jackson, La Crosse, Monroe, Pepin, Trempealeau, Vernon	968,406	1,090,188

Wisconsin Works (W-2) expenditures, continued

W-2 contract agency	Counties served	2019 expenditures ($)	2020 expenditures ($)
Workforce Resource, Inc. (www.workforceresource.org)	Ashland, Barron, Bayfield, Burnett, Chippewa, Clark, Douglas, Dunn, Eau Claire, Iron, Pierce, Polk, Rusk, Sawyer, St. Croix, Washburn	1,985,044	2,568,814
Total		41,911,760	49,392,585

Source: Wisconsin Department of Children and Families, departmental data, March 2023.

Wisconsin Medicaid and BadgerCare

	Recipients[1]				Expenditures[2]			
County	Fiscal yr. 2021	Fiscal yr. 2022	% of 2022 population	Rank[3]	Fiscal yr. 2021 ($)	Fiscal yr. 2022 ($)	Per 2022 recipient Amount ($)	Rank[3]
Adams	5,708	6,184	29.68	17	33,938,443	39,234,402	6,344.50	59
Ashland	5,930	6,230	39.09	3	41,238,624	45,016,618	7,225.78	22
Barron	13,441	14,375	30.64	10	86,941,336	98,243,701	6,834.34	39
Bayfield	4,121	4,424	27.32	25	26,880,337	29,822,864	6,741.15	44
Brown	62,786	68,680	25.14	36	390,550,163	433,220,752	6,307.82	61
Buffalo	2,804	3,012	22.64	51	18,920,383	19,701,742	6,541.08	52
Burnett	4,726	5,027	30.31	13	27,038,942	27,411,331	5,452.82	71
Calumet	6,383	7,269	13.22	70	38,869,090	45,787,256	6,298.98	62
Chippewa	15,497	16,408	24.46	41	112,308,123	123,283,535	7,513.62	9
Clark	7,878	8,546	24.56	39	51,882,013	60,087,206	7,031.03	30
Columbia	11,079	11,826	20.17	60	79,265,829	88,505,815	7,484.00	11
Crawford	4,181	4,521	28.03	23	27,960,620	30,860,472	6,826.03	40
Dane	91,443	100,441	17.25	66	708,629,917	794,555,598	7,910.67	7
Dodge	16,811	18,329	20.64	59	121,468,758	137,238,683	7,487.52	10
Door	5,502	5,916	19.51	63	37,431,252	42,754,722	7,226.96	21
Douglas	11,655	12,320	27.66	24	77,929,845	85,825,347	6,966.34	32
Dunn	10,366	11,229	24.70	37	72,504,914	81,189,873	7,230.37	20
Eau Claire	24,469	26,523	24.55	40	151,449,387	165,915,534	6,255.53	63
Florence	1,125	1,182	25.84	30	6,983,445	7,118,836	6,022.70	67
Fond du Lac	20,857	22,695	21.79	57	144,168,634	160,830,578	7,086.61	26
Forest	3,053	3,368	36.65	4	18,438,388	19,604,930	5,820.94	69
Grant	10,432	11,390	22.26	53	70,403,967	80,314,171	7,051.29	29
Green	6,885	7,400	19.76	61	47,117,115	52,283,564	7,065.35	28
Green Lake	4,177	4,613	24.16	42	26,711,185	31,750,746	6,882.88	36
Iowa	4,322	4,645	19.41	64	28,196,401	31,084,085	6,691.95	46
Iron	1,746	1,853	30.25	14	12,724,359	13,257,486	7,154.61	23
Jackson	5,626	6,173	29.23	19	35,075,901	39,953,255	6,472.26	55
Jefferson	16,511	17,880	20.65	58	134,920,584	150,442,321	8,414.00	3
Juneau	7,801	8,314	30.97	8	53,395,894	56,104,514	6,748.20	43
Kenosha	44,592	48,056	28.22	22	287,868,406	320,500,245	6,669.31	48
Kewaunee	3,634	3,944	19.13	65	27,862,072	31,704,618	8,038.70	6
La Crosse	25,340	27,507	22.52	52	185,856,044	204,269,095	7,426.08	15
Lafayette	3,599	3,858	23.17	46	18,963,908	20,518,359	5,318.39	72
Langlade	6,352	6,718	34.53	7	39,629,113	42,422,917	6,314.81	60
Lincoln	6,647	7,170	25.22	35	49,615,978	52,665,297	7,345.23	17
Manitowoc	17,205	18,656	22.91	48	121,823,887	136,847,682	7,335.32	18
Marathon	30,450	33,309	23.93	43	201,537,657	222,224,806	6,671.61	47

Wisconsin Medicaid and BadgerCare, continued

County	Recipients[1] Fiscal yr. 2021	Recipients[1] Fiscal yr. 2022	% of 2022 population	Rank[3]	Expenditures[2] Fiscal yr. 2021 ($)	Expenditures[2] Fiscal yr. 2022 ($)	Per 2022 recipient Amount ($)	Rank[3]
Marinette...	11,382	12,479	29.77	16	75,480,435	85,472,686	6,849.32	38
Marquette..	3,842	4,082	26.11	28	25,989,067	28,883,418	7,075.80	27
Menominee.	2,972	3,119	73.11	1	19,521,951	20,094,368	6,442.57	57
Milwaukee..	391,873	416,205	44.30	2	2,727,622,508	2,964,188,414	7,121.94	24
Monroe.....	11,279	12,488	26.74	27	76,798,018	87,288,414	6,989.78	31
Oconto....	7,890	8,633	21.96	55	53,638,892	59,504,804	6,892.71	35
Oneida....	8,951	9,616	25.35	33	58,048,335	63,686,959	6,623.02	51
Outagamie..	34,585	38,090	19.74	62	223,969,146	259,925,750	6,823.99	41
Ozaukee...	9,593	10,406	11.23	72	85,160,648	91,640,156	8,806.47	2
Pepin.....	1,631	1,685	22.91	49	9,405,734	10,064,232	5,972.84	68
Pierce.....	6,660	7,239	17.07	67	44,674,457	49,681,136	6,862.98	37
Polk.......	10,844	11,636	25.66	31	69,530,025	75,124,387	6,456.20	56
Portage....	14,094	15,571	21.88	56	86,039,863	94,099,551	6,043.26	66
Price.....	3,941	4,286	30.56	11	27,544,271	32,064,269	7,481.16	12
Racine.....	56,902	61,161	30.87	9	409,622,331	456,210,174	7,459.17	13
Richland...	4,712	4,993	28.89	21	37,633,669	41,518,215	8,315.28	4
Rock.......	46,202	50,184	30.42	12	271,092,714	303,961,260	6,056.94	65
Rusk.......	4,812	5,200	36.56	5	30,283,425	33,921,873	6,523.44	53
St. Croix....	13,308	14,822	15.40	68	84,922,805	96,224,585	6,492.01	54
Sauk.......	14,994	16,358	24.60	38	99,989,721	113,785,452	6,955.95	33
Sawyer....	5,812	6,260	34.60	6	37,595,612	41,684,614	6,658.88	49
Shawano...	10,345	11,089	26.92	26	71,107,851	81,803,025	7,376.95	16
Sheboygan..	25,214	27,676	23.30	45	166,077,865	186,796,637	6,749.41	42
Taylor.....	4,693	5,050	25.28	34	28,383,484	31,304,818	6,198.97	64
Trempealeau	7,263	7,850	25.42	32	48,878,365	52,085,142	6,635.05	50
Vernon....	6,779	7,108	22.95	47	48,086,182	52,821,926	7,431.33	14
Vilas......	6,307	6,698	28.95	20	34,748,589	37,482,008	5,596.00	70
Walworth...	22,026	23,553	22.19	54	150,817,195	163,753,898	6,952.57	34
Washburn..	4,718	5,010	30.08	15	34,254,122	36,719,807	7,329.30	19
Washington.	17,893	19,742	14.28	69	137,472,517	153,750,631	7,788.00	8
Waukesha..	45,085	49,122	11.96	71	362,091,998	407,774,857	8,301.27	5
Waupaca...	11,418	12,350	23.61	44	99,251,442	111,185,005	9,002.83	1
Waushara...	5,876	6,394	26.11	29	36,404,269	41,162,142	6,437.62	58
Winnebago.	35,658	39,109	22.67	50	230,366,294	262,448,180	6,710.69	45
Wood.....	19,978	21,690	29.23	18	139,725,624	153,787,967	7,090.27	25
State.....	**1,414,666**	**1,526,945**	**25.67**	**X**	**9,758,730,339**	**10,804,453,714**	**7,075.86**	**X**

X–Not applicable.

1. If an individual resided in multiple counties during the year, the individual is counted only in the recipient tally for the last county of residence to avoid double-counting in the statewide total. 2. The expenditure totals include benefits issued and individuals eligible under BadgerCare+/MA and subprograms CORE, BASIC, Family Planning Only Services, and Medicaid Waiver. Costs include: Managed Care Capitation Payments, Fee For Service Payment to providers, and Long Term Care waiver program payments. 3. Rankings calculated by Wisconsin Legislative Reference Bureau.

Sources: Wisconsin Department of Health Services, departmental data, March 2023; Wisconsin Department of Administration, Division of Intergovernmental Relations, Demographic Services Center, *County Final Population Estimates, January 1, 2022*.

Wisconsin BadgerCare and Medical Assistance

Fiscal year	Long-term care — Nursing homes Amt. (mil. $)	% of total	State centers Amt. (mil. $)	% of total	Hospitals — Inpatient Amt. (mil. $)	% of total	Outpatient Amt. (mil. $)	% of total	Physicians and clinics Amt. (mil. $)	% of total	Drugs Amt. (mil. $)	% of total	Home care[1] Amt. (mil. $)	% of total	Managed care[2] Amt. (mil. $)	% of total	Other noninstitutional fee-for-service[3] Amt. (mil. $)	% of total	Total provider payments[4] Amt. (mil. $)	Annual % change
2000-01	916.2	27.8	115.3	3.5	297.8	9.0	58.7	1.8	72.4	2.2	373.6	11.4	522.2	15.9	523.6	15.9	280.1	8.5	3,291.8	8.1
2005-06	940.1	20.7	111.5	2.5	357.0	7.9	85.8	1.9	104.9	2.3	459.6	10.1	789.2	17.4	1,068.0	23.5	424.2	9.3	4,546.3	-4.8
2010-11	842.9	11.2	112.5	1.5	502.5	6.7	188.2	2.5	151.9	2.0	617.6	8.2	599.5	8.0	3,457.1	46.0	1,050.7	14.0	7,522.8	5.7
2011-12	818.8	11.7	127.1	1.8	440.0	6.3	196.3	2.8	166.8	2.4	610.6	8.7	659.0	9.4	2,691.3	38.5	1,288.5	18.4	6,998.4	-7.0
2012-13	819.4	10.8	133.5	1.8	580.6	7.7	208.6	2.8	143.9	1.9	625.8	8.3	784.4	10.4	3,024.3	40.0	1,207.0	16.0	7,553.1	7.9
2013-14	770.0	9.5	128.3	1.6	519.5	6.4	202.5	2.5	187.9	2.3	710.6	8.8	889.1	11.0	3,272.7	40.4	1,355.4	16.7	8,105.8	7.3
2014-15	762.8	9.0	112.5	1.3	564.1	6.6	230.0	2.7	158.3	1.9	876.0	10.3	925.5	10.9	3,531.5	41.5	1,350.5	15.9	8,511.2	5.0
2015-16	713.3	8.2	120.1	1.4	525.9	6.1	201.7	2.3	141.4	1.6	996.0	11.5	920.6	10.6	3,759.2	43.3	1,301.6	15.0	8,680.0	2.0
2016-17	708.0	8.3	108.4	1.3	567.0	6.6	206.8	2.4	170.2	2.0	1,061.9	12.4	903.3	10.6	3,909.4	45.7	917.4	10.7	8,552.5	-1.5
2017-18	685.7	7.7	114.5	1.3	576.4	6.5	194.7	2.2	158.9	1.8	1,139.2	12.8	978.0	11.0	4,043.0	45.4	1,019.6	11.4	8,910.1	4.2
2018-19	680.1	7.2	117.2	1.2	522.2	5.5	174.1	1.8	146.6	1.6	1,203.8	12.8	973.9	10.3	4,495.4	47.7	1,119.7	11.9	9,433.0	5.9
2019-20	672.4	6.3	120.8	1.1	519.7	4.9	177.1	1.7	168.7	1.6	1,355.1	12.7	1,057.5	9.9	5,512.8	51.6	1,091.9	10.2	10,676.1	13.2
2020-21	589.1	5.2	120.4	1.1	481.2	4.3	146.4	1.3	170.0	1.5	1,535.4	13.7	1,204.2	10.7	5,790.4	51.6	1,186.5	10.6	11,223.6	5.1
2021-22	634.9	5.3	134.4	1.1	505.7	4.2	151.3	1.3	178.0	1.5	1,768.4	14.8	1,321.7	11.0	5,906.3	49.4	1,361.3	11.4	11,962.0	6.6

Note: Enrollments in BadgerCare began in July 1999, and expenditures for the program are included in the Medical Assistance figures above. Medical Assistance expenditure data prior to BadgerCare can be found in previous editions of the *Wisconsin Blue Book*.

1. Home Care includes HCBS waivers. 2. Managed Care includes all capitated programs (BC/BS+, HMOs, CCF/WAM, SSI managed care, PACE/Partnership, Family Care). 3. All noninstitutional fee-for-service acute care not otherwise captured plus local government plus Medicare crossovers. 4. Total includes expenditures not listed separately but does not include offsetting recoveries and collections, such as estate recoveries, drug rebates, etc.

Source: Wisconsin Department of Health Services, departmental data, March 2023. Data prior to 2006 is from the Wisconsin Legislative Fiscal Bureau.

CORRECTIONAL AND TREATMENT FACILITIES

Wisconsin state corrections populations

	2022		Average daily population (fiscal year)					
Institutions	Avg. pop.	Capacity[1]	1970	1980	1990	2000	2010	2020
Maximum security (men)	4,317	3,838	1,709	1,833	2,986	4,513	5,161	5,228
Assessment and evaluation[2]	NA	904	NA	NA	NA	NA	1,214	NA
Columbia Correctional Institution	603	541	NA	NA	477	808	820	812
Dodge Correctional Institution[2]	1,490	1,165	NA	88	551	1,377	341	1,630
Green Bay Correctional Institution	916	749	755	658	832	1,002	1,089	1,066
Wisconsin Secure Program Facility	350	501	NA	NA	NA	101	461	478
Waupun Correctional Institution	958	882	954	1,087	1,126	1,225	1,237	1,242
Medium security	10,851	9,430	846	938	1,771	7,281	11,242	11,767
Fox Lake Correctional Institution	1,206	979	553	570	785	1,112	1,046	1,337
Jackson Correctional Institution	938	837	NA	NA	NA	971	977	985
Kettle Moraine Correctional Institution	1,076	783	293	368	542	1,233	1,160	1,177
New Lisbon Correctional Institution	987	950	NA	NA	NA	NA	1,009	1,036
Oshkosh Correctional Institution	1,948	1,494	NA	NA	444	1,859	2,031	2,035
Prairie du Chien Correctional Institution	475	326	NA	NA	NA	297	500	513
Racine Correctional Institution	1,529	1,171	NA	NA	NA	1,414	1,553	1,666
Racine Youthful Offender Correctional Facility	299	400	NA	NA	NA	395	445	447
Redgranite Correctional Institution	918	990	NA	NA	NA	NA	1,013	1,008
Stanley Correctional Institution	1,475	1,500	NA	NA	NA	NA	1,509	1,563
Minimum security	2,780	2,230	390	474	1,439	2,380	3,332	3,316
Chippewa Valley Correctional Treatment Center	390	450	NA	NA	NA	NA	465	455
Fox Lake Correctional Institution	NA	NA	NA	NA	NA	NA	280	NA
Oakhill Correctional Institution	678	344	NA	198	368	564	677	745
Sturtevant Transitional Facility	134	150	NA	NA	NA	NA	261	140
Wisconsin Correctional Center System (WCCS)	1,578	1,286	390	276	1,071	1,816	1,649	1,976
Detention facility	490	460	998	NA	NA	NA	956	924
Milwaukee Secure Detention Facility	490	460	998	NA	NA	NA	956	924
Wisconsin Women's Correctional System[3]	1,185	937	141	123	203	644	1,262	1,454
Taycheedah Correctional Institution (med./max.)	754	653	141	123	203	644	579	902
Correctional centers (min.)	431	284	NA	NA	NA	NA	683	552
Contract facilities	104	545	NA	NA	78	4,665	690	522
Intergovernmental contract	32	NA	NA	NA	NA	NA	30	32
In-state	72	NA	NA	NA	NA	NA	660	490
Other adults	63,192	NA	8,859	19,842	30,172	64,409	68,123	66,189
Community residential confinement	NA	NA	NA	NA	NA	48	NA	NA
Division of Intensive Sanctions	NA	NA	NA	NA	NA	412	NA	NA
Extended supervision and parole	23,445	NA	4,329	3,045	4,217	8,951	19,783	22,711
Probation	39,748	NA	4,530	16,797	25,907	55,046	48,340	43,478
Unknown offender type	NA	NA	NA	NA	NA	NA	NA	NA
Juvenile corrections	64	560	446	575	572	904	437	118
Copper Lake School[4]	11	29	NA	NA	NA	NA	NA	16
Ethan Allen School[5]	NA	NA	365	306	320	438	207	NA
Lincoln Hills School[4]	48	519	NA	245	252	330	176	98
Southern Oaks Girls School[5]	NA	NA	NA	NA	NA	87	49	NA

Wisconsin state corrections populations, continued

Institutions	2022 Avg. pop.	2022 Capacity[1]	1970	1980	1990	2000	2010	2020
Youth Leadership Training Center[6] . . .	NA	NA	NA	NA	NA	40	NA	NA
Sprite program[7].	NA	NA	NA	NA	NA	9	5	NA
Grow Academy[7]	5	12	NA	NA	NA	NA	NA	4
Juvenile correctional camp system. . .	NA	NA	81	24	NA	NA	NA	NA
Other juveniles.	75	NA	NA	NA	NA	308	265	80
Juvenile aftercare.	NA	NA	NA	NA	NA	NA	76	NA
Alternate care	18	NA	NA	NA	NA	174	49	20
Corrective sanctions	NA	NA	NA	NA	NA	134	140	NA
Home supervision	41	NA	NA	NA	NA	NA	NA	38
Alternate care supervision	16	NA	NA	NA	NA	NA	NA	22
Total.	83,058	NA	12,391	23,785	37,221	84,796	91,840	89,598

NA–Not available.

1. DOC "rated capacity" is the original design capacity, based on industry standards, plus modifications and expansions. It excludes beds and multiple bunking to accommodate crowding. 2. Dodge CI serves as the assessment and evaluation (A&E) center for sentenced adult male felons. 3. In July 2005, DOC designated the institutions for female offenders as the Wisconsin Women's Correctional System, which now includes Taycheedah CI and two of the minimum security correctional centers. Taycheedah CI serves as the A&E center for sentenced adult female felons. 4. Copper Lake opened in June 2011. 2017 Wis. Act 185 required the state to close Lincoln Hills and Copper Lake by July 1, 2020, and required DOC to establish new Type 1 juvenile correctional facilities. 5. Ethan Allen and Southern Oaks closed in June 2011. 6. Youth Leadership Training Camp program closed in February 2002 and became part of the program at Lincoln Hills. 7. The Sprite program was eliminated in March 2010. Grow Academy opened in June 2014.

Sources: Wisconsin Department of Corrections, Fiscal Year Summary Report of Population Movement for 1991 and prior issues, and departmental data, April 2023 and prior years.

Wisconsin state health service institutions populations

Institutions	2022 Avg. pop.	2022 Capacity[1]	1980	1990	2000	2010	2020	2021
Mental health institutions (MHI). . . .	1,171	1,365	666	693	1,053	1,273	1,185	1,146
Mendota MHI	282	308	202	266	238	240	287	266
Winnebago MHI	178	185	310	266	279	291	168	185
Mendota Juvenile Treatment Center . .	26	29	NA	NA	43	29	23	19
Sand Ridge Secure Treatment Center .	278	400	NA	NA	72	286	310	295
Central State Hospital	NA	NA	154	NA	NA	NA	NA	NA
Wisconsin Resource Center.	407	443	NA	161	421	427	397	381
Centers for developmentally disabled (CDD)	288	440	2,142	1,677	843	448	324	298
Central Wisconsin CDD	171	255	731	606	380	258	189	176
Northern Wisconsin CDD	11	25	676	495	189	12	13	12
Southern Wisconsin CDD	106	160	735	576	274	178	122	110
Total.	1,459	1,805	2,808	2,370	1,896	1,721	1,509	1,444

NA–Not available.

1. FY22 capacity is defined as follows: Mendota and Winnebago Mental Health Institutes—staffed capacity; Sand Ridge Secure Treatment Center and the Wisconsin Resource Center—building design capacity; Central, Northern and Southern Wisconsin Center—number of licensed beds.

Source: Wisconsin Department of Health Services, departmental data, May 2023 and prior years.

MILITARY AND VETERANS AFFAIRS

Wisconsin veterans benefits

		Grants			Loans	
Fiscal year	Total benefits ($)	Economic ($)	Educational ($)	Economic assistance ($)	Personal loans[2] ($)	General obligation bond housing loans ($)
1995.........	114,984,938[1]	552,893	754,052	2,544,584	X	111,133,409
2000.........	143,192,551	3,226,128	1,786,205	X	10,802,068	127,378,150
2005.........	37,428,288	413,564	5,698,107	X	2,271,942	29,044,675
2010.........	15,859,166	426,535	1,726,307	X	3,133,961	10,572,363
2011.........	4,011,393	682,235	1,271,083	X	2,058,075	X
2012.........	2,531,220	577,061	1,044,751	X	909,397	X
2013.........	1,242,884	443,312	799,572	X	NA	X
2014.........	1,181,380	713,279	468,101	X	NA	X
2015.........	2,450,024	2,005,365	444,659	X	NA	X
2016.........	2,099,056	1,843,991	255,065	X	NA	X
2017.........	2,459,211	2,074,031	385,180	X	NA	X
2018.........	2,674,808	2,562,378	112,430	X	NA	X
2019.........	2,560,050	2,503,224	56,826	X	NA	X
2020.........	2,475,928	2,420,420	55,508	X	NA	X
2021.........	2,844,914	2,793,954	50,960	X	NA	X
2022.........	2,924,406	2,886,362	38,044	X	NA	X

NA–Not available; X–Not applicable.
1. Includes $11,024,956 in consumer loans under the Veterans Trust Fund stabilization provision of 1993 Wisconsin Act 16.
2. Personal Loan Program replaced economic assistance loans.
Source: Wisconsin Department of Veterans Affairs, departmental data, April 2023.

Wisconsin Veterans Homes membership

	Spanish-American		World War I		World War II		Korean Conflict		Vietnam		Other eras[1]		
	Vets.	Deps.	Vets.	Deps.	Vets.	Deps.	Vets.	Deps.	Vets.	Deps.	Vets.	Deps.	Total
1975......	1	18	272	171	198	40	3	2	—	—	—	—	705
1980......	1	8	242	144	241	36	5	1	—	—	—	—	678
1985......	—	4	129	102	329	54	28	—	5	—	—	—	651
1990......	—	2	49	65	431	76	62	8	10	1	3	—	707
1995......	—	1	8	31	484	84	99	12	16	2	1	—	738
2000......	—	—	—	10	423	94	132	12	47	4	21	2	745
2005......	—	—	—	2	350	103	144	15	71	3	40	2	730
2006......	—	—	—	1	407	119	164	17	87	5	50	4	854
2007......	—	—	—	1	475	135	173	26	100	8	3	—	921
2008......	—	—	—	1	417	123	177	26	115	7	4	—	870
2009......	—	—	—	1	389	130	193	21	122	8	8	—	947
2010......	—	—	—	1	356	127	176	22	122	8	10	—	892
2011......	—	—	—	1	339	124	170	19	154	12	12	—	904
2012......	—	—	—	1	330	121	180	32	178	11	19	2	953
2013......	—	—	—	1	412	145	286	53	276	16	44	2	1,235
2014......	—	—	—	1	259	128	215	34	262	11	98	4	1,012
2015......	—	—	—	—	308	114	269	49	338	11	43	1	1,133
2016......	—	—	—	—	248	107	255	46	364	14	45	3	1,082
2017......	—	—	—	—	207	93	217	49	376	17	39	9	1,007
2018......	—	—	—	—	157	79	224	46	382	13	44	2	947

Wisconsin Veterans Homes membership, continued

	Spanish-American		World War I		World War II		Korean Conflict		Vietnam		Other eras[1]		Total
	Vets.	Deps.	Vets.	Deps.	Vets.	Deps.	Vets.	Deps.	Vets.	Deps.	Vets.	Deps.	
2019......	—	—	—	—	85	26	144	26	222	11	94	8	616
2020......	—	—	—	—	44	31	101	23	281	10	118	8	616

Note: The Wisconsin Veterans Home at King was established in 1887, the home at Union Grove opened in 2001, and the home at Chippewa Falls opened in 2013.
—Represents zero. Deps.–Dependents; Vets.–Veterans.
1. Other periods of hostilities for which expeditionary medals were awarded.
Source: Wisconsin Department of Veterans Affairs, departmental data, March 2021.

Wisconsin National Guard

JOINT UNITS
Joint Force Headquarters Wisconsin
Joint Force Headquarters Detachment Madison
54th Civil Support Team (WMD)–Madison

ARMY UNITS
Headquarters, Wisconsin Army National Guard–Madison

Joint Force Headquarters Separate Units
Recruiting and Retention Battalion–Madison
Det. 1, Recruiting and Retention Battalion–Madison
Det. 2, Recruiting and Retention Battalion–Milwaukee

32nd Infantry Brigade Combat Team
Headquarters and Headquarters Company–Camp Douglas

1st Battalion, 120th Field Artillery
Headquarters and Headquarters Battery*–Wisconsin Rapids
Det. 1, Headquarters and Headquarters Company–Berlin
Battery A–Marshfield
Battery B–Stevens Point
Battery C–Oconomowoc

3rd Battalion, 126th Infantry (Michigan Army National Guard)
Headquarters and Headquarters Co.–Wyoming, MI
Company A–Detroit, MI
Company B– Wyoming, MI
Company C–Dowagiac, MI
Company D–Cadillac, MI

2nd Battalion, 127th Infantry
Headquarters and Headquarters Company*–Appleton
Det. 1, Headquarters Company–Clintonville
Company A*–Waupun
Det. 1, Company A–Ripon
Company B–Green Bay
Company C–Fond du Lac
Company D–Marinette

1st Battalion, 128th Infantry
Headquarters and Headquarters Co.*–Eau Claire
Det. 1, Headquarters Company–Abbotsford
Company A–Menomonie
Company B*–New Richmond
Det. 1, Company B–Rice Lake
Company C*–Arcadia
Det. 1, Company C–Onalaska
Company D–River Falls

132nd Brigade Support Battalion
Headquarters and Headquarters Co.–Portage
Company A* (Distribution)–Janesville
Det. 1, Company A–Elkhorn
Company B (Maintenance)–Mauston
Company C (Medical)–Racine
Company D (Forward Support)–Madison
Company E (Forward Support)–Antigo
Company F (Forward Support)–Mosinee
Company G (Forward Support)–Waupaca
Company H (Forward Support)–Neillsville
Company I (Forward Support)–Wyoming, MI (MIARNG)

173rd Brigade Engineer Battalion
Headquarters and Headquarters Co.–Wausau
Company A*–Tomahawk
Det. 1, Company A–Rhinelander
Company B–Onalaska
Company C (Signal)–Camp Douglas
Company D* (Military Intelligence)–Madison
Det. 1, Company D (TUAS)–Camp Douglas

1st Squadron, 105th Cavalry (Reconnaissance, Surveillance and Target Acquisition)
Headquarters and Headquarters Troop–Madison
Troop A–Fort Atkinson
Troop B–Watertown
Troop C–Reedsburg

64th Troop Command
Headquarters–Madison
Wisconsin Medical Detachment–Camp Douglas

732nd Combat Sustainment Support Battalion
Headquarters and Headquarters Company–Tomah

Statistics and Reference: Military | 695

Wisconsin National Guard, continued

107th Maintenance Company*–Sparta
Det. 1, 107th Maintenance Company–Viroqua
1157th Transportation Company–Oshkosh
1158th Transportation Company*–Beloit
Det. 1, 1158th Trans. Company–Black River Falls
3561 Quartermaster Platoon–Tomah

1st Battalion, 147th Aviation Regiment
Headquarters and Headquarters Co.*–Madison
Company A–Madison
Det. 1, Company C–Madison
Company D*–Madison
Company E*–Madison
Det. 1, Company B, 248th Aviation Support Battalion–West Bend
Company C* 1st Battalion, 168th Aviation–West Bend
Det. 1, Company G, 2nd Battalion, 104th Aviation–West Bend
Det. 2, Company D, 1st Battalion, 112th Aviation Regiment–West Bend
Det. 5, Company A, 2nd Battalion, 641st Aviation–Madison
54th Civil Support Team–Madison

641st Troop Command Battalion
Headquarters and Headquarters Detachment/Wisconsin CERFP Command and Control Element–Madison
135th Medical Company–Waukesha
1967th Contingency Contracting Team–Camp Douglas
273rd Engineer Company (Wheeled Sapper)/CERFP Search and Extraction–Medford
457th Chemical Company/CERFP Decontamination*–Hartford
Det. 1, 457th Chemical Company–Burlington
112th Mobile Public Affairs Det.–Madison
132nd Army Band–Madison
Det. 1, Cyber Protection Team–Madison
505th Trial Defense Team–Madison

157th Maneuver Enhancement Brigade
Headquarters and Headquarters Co.–Milwaukee
32nd Military Police Company*–Milwaukee
924th Engineer Det. (Facilities)– Milwaukee
357th Signal Network Support Co.– Milwaukee

1st Battalion, 121st Field Artillery (HIMARS)
Headquarters and Headquarters Battery (HIMARS), 121st Field Artillery – Oak Creek
Battery A (HIMARS)–Sussex
Battery B (HIMARS)–Plymouth
108th Forward Support Company–Sussex

724th Engineer Battalion
Headquarters and Headquarters Company–Chippewa Falls
Company A (Forward Support Company)–Hayward

106th Engineer Det. (Quarry Team)–Baraboo
229th Engineer Co.* (Horizontal)–Prairie du Chien
Det. 1, 229th Engineer Company–Platteville
824th Engineer Det. (Concrete)– Baraboo
829th Engineer Company (Vertical)*–Spooner
Det. 1, 829th Engineer Company–Ashland 950th Engineer Company (Clearance)–Superior

426th Regiment–Regional Training Institute (Wisconsin Military Academy)
Headquarters and Headquarters Det.–Fort McCoy
1st Battalion, 426th Regiment (Field Artillery)–Fort McCoy
2nd Battalion, 426th Regiment (Modular Training)–Fort McCoy

AIR UNITS
Headquarters, Wisconsin Air National Guard–Madison

115th Fighter Wing–Truax Field, Madison
115th Operations Group
176th Fighter Squadron
115th Operations Support Squadron
115th Maintenance Group
115th Aircraft Maintenance Squadron
115th Maintenance Squadron
115th Maintenance Operations Flight
115th Mission Support Group
115th Logistics Readiness Squadron
115th Security Forces Squadron
115th Force Support Squadron
115th Civil Engineer Squadron
115th Communications Flight
115th Medical Group
Detachment 1–CERFP Medical

128th Air Refueling Wing–Mitchell Field, Milwaukee
128th Operations Group
126th Air Refueling Squadron
128th Operations Support Squadron
128th Maintenance Group
128th Aircraft Maintenance Squadron
128th Maintenance Squadron
128th Maintenance Operations Flight
128th Mission Support Group
128th Logistics Readiness Squadron
128th Security Forces Squadron
128th Force Support Squadron
128th Civil Engineer Squadron
128th Communications Flight
128th Medical Group

Volk Field Combat Readiness Training Center–Camp Douglas
128th Air Control Squadron–Camp Douglas
128th Weather Flight–Camp Douglas

Bold Face–Major Command
*Headquarters of a split unit
Co.–Company
Det.–Detachment
Trans.–Transportation

CERFP–Chemical, Biological, Radiological, Nuclear Enhanced Response Force Package
HIMARS–High-Mobility Artillery Rocket System
TUAS–Tactical Unmanned Aircraft System
WMD–Weapons of mass destruction

Source: Wisconsin Department of Military Affairs, departmental data, May 2023.

Wisconsin's military service

Military action	Number served	Number killed
Civil War	91,379[1]	12,216
Spanish–American War	5,469	134[2]
Mexican Border Service	4,168	NA
World War I	122,215	3,932
World War II	332,200	8,390
Korean Conflict	132,000	729
Vietnam	165,400	1,239
Lebanon/Grenada	400	1
Panama	520	1
Operations Desert Shield/Desert Storm	10,400	11
Somalia	426	2
Bosnia/Kosovo	678	NA
Military and civilian personnel deployed since September 11, 2001	36,941[3]	128[4]

Note: Includes Wisconsin residents who served on active duty during declared wars and officially designated periods of hostilities.

NA–Not available.

1. Total includes some who enlisted more than once. The net number of soldiers recruited in Wisconsin was about 80,000. 2. Casualties only from Wisconsin 1st, 2nd, 3rd, and 4th Regiments. No details available for Wisconsin residents serving in federal units. 3. Includes the total personnel deployed through December 2018. The U.S. Department of Defense stopped reporting the number of personnel deployed from a particular state after that date. 4. Includes one killed in attack on Pentagon on September 11, 2001.

Sources: U.S. Veterans Administration; U.S. Department of Defense; and Wisconsin Department of Military Affairs, departmental data, April 2021.

EDUCATION

University of Wisconsin System fall enrollment

	2017	2018	2019	2020	2021	2021 detail Female	Male
Main campuses	**162,908**	**161,895**	**160,289**	**158,355**	**157,308**	**87,492**	**69,816**
Eau Claire	10,825	10,905	10,730	10,592	10,158	6,201	3,957
Undergraduate	10,104	10,189	10,065	9,885	9,458	5,812	3,646
Graduate	721	716	665	707	700	389	311
Green Bay	7,178	7,383	7,975	8,056	8,771	6,050	2,721
Undergraduate	6,815	7,006	7,579	7,600	8,248	5,721	2,527
Graduate	363	377	396	456	523	329	194
La Crosse	10,534	10,579	10,604	10,543	10,330	6,025	4,305
Undergraduate	9,691	9,708	9,649	9,573	9,393	5,412	3,981
Graduate	843	871	955	970	937	613	324
Madison	43,450	44,116	44,993	45,483	47,824	25,215	22,609
Undergraduate	31,872	32,381	33,165	33,542	35,386	18,571	16,815
Graduate	11,578	11,735	11,828	11,941	12,438	6,644	5,794
Milwaukee	25,381	24,933	23,992	23,001	22,583	12,764	9,819
Undergraduate	20,750	20,256	19,362	18,492	18,164	9,995	8,169
Graduate	4,631	4,677	4,630	4,509	4,419	2,769	1,650
Oshkosh	13,935	14,216	13,942	13,998	13,157	8,094	5,063
Undergraduate	12,412	12,903	12,688	12,751	11,961	7,249	4,712
Graduate	1,523	1,313	1,254	1,247	1,196	845	351
Parkside	4,308	4,325	4,420	4,465	4,143	2,307	1,836
Undergraduate	4,168	4,090	3,938	3,804	3,376	1,921	1,455
Graduate	140	235	482	661	767	386	381
Platteville	8,558	8,106	7,762	7,217	6,486	2,386	4,100
Undergraduate	7,621	7,274	6,970	6,562	5,979	2,144	3,835
Graduate	937	832	792	655	507	242	265
River Falls	6,110	6,139	5,977	5,862	5,410	3,590	1,820
Undergraduate	5,678	5,725	5,581	5,428	5,003	3,287	1,716
Graduate	432	414	396	434	407	303	104
Stevens Point	8,208	7,760	7,307	7,385	7,329	4,220	3,109
Undergraduate	7,880	7,445	6,812	6,781	6,689	3,749	2,940
Graduate	328	315	495	604	640	471	169
Stout	9,401	8,748	8,393	7,970	7,692	3,551	4,141
Undergraduate	8,116	7,555	7,289	6,889	6,631	2,814	3,817
Graduate	1,285	1,193	1,104	1,081	1,061	737	324
Superior	2,590	2,601	2,608	2,559	2,609	1,736	873
Undergraduate	2,368	2,294	2,257	2,164	2,200	1,431	769
Graduate	222	307	351	395	409	305	104
Whitewater	12,430	12,084	11,586	11,224	10,816	5,353	5,463
Undergraduate	11,128	10,747	10,158	9,657	9,121	4,405	4,716
Graduate	1,302	1,337	1,428	1,567	1,695	948	747
Branch campuses	**11,608**	**9,741**	**7,399**	**6,411**	**5,672**	**3,010**	**2,662**
Baraboo/Sauk County (UW–Platteville)	461	494	360	225	216	128	88
Barron (UW–Eau Claire)	512	642	454	423	401	234	167
Fond du Lac (UW Oshkosh)	563	579	444	394	281	144	137
Fox Cities (UW Oshkosh)	1,286	1,629	1,134	925	714	309	405
Manitowoc (UW–Green Bay)	334	311	237	287	341	180	161
Marinette (UW–Green Bay)	289	306	203	215	240	140	100
Marshfield (UW–Stevens Point)	541	545	431	395	346	239	107
Richland (UW–Platteville)	273	366	159	108	75	24	51
Rock County (UW–Whitewater)	908	975	862	771	644	347	297
Sheboygan (UW–Green Bay)	560	581	381	411	447	241	206

University of Wisconsin System fall enrollment, continued

	2017	2018	2019	2020	2021	2021 detail Female	Male
Washington County (UW–Milwaukee)	730	744	605	500	387	201	186
Waukesha (UW–Milwaukee)	1,740	1,767	1,542	1,221	1,049	523	526
Wausau (UW–Stevens Point)	779	802	587	536	531	300	231
UW Colleges Online	2,632	—	—	—	—	—	—
System total	**174,516**	**171,636**	**167,688**	**164,766**	**162,980**	**90,502**	**72,478**

— Represents zero.

Source: University of Wisconsin System, Office of Policy Analysis and Research, Education Reports and Statistics, "Enrollment" at https://www.wisconsin.edu/education-reports-statistics/enrollments [March 2022].

University of Wisconsin System budgeted faculty positions, 2022–23

Institution	Professor	Associate professor	Assistant professor	Instructor	Total faculty
Eau Claire	149	93	101	—	343
Green Bay	41	91	63	—	194
La Crosse	115	130	128	7	380
Madison	1,164	472	616	1	2,253
Milwaukee	241	325	102	—	668
Oshkosh	135	120	68	3	325
Parkside	33	58	44	—	135
Platteville	102	83	55	—	240
River Falls	91	32	76	—	198
Stevens Point	133	101	55	1	289
Stout	100	44	86	—	230
Superior	37	21	32	—	90
Whitewater	109	167	108	—	384
System total	**2,448**	**1,736**	**1,533**	**12**	**5,729**

Notes: Full-time equivalent (FTE) data used. Positions at branch campuses are included with their affiliated university. Includes vacant positions. Does not include student assistants. Totals may not add due to rounding.

—Represents zero.

Source: University of Wisconsin System, Office of Budget and Planning, departmental data, 2022–23 Annual Operating Budget approved by Board of Regents June 2022.

Wisconsin private institutions of higher education fall enrollment

Institution (location)	2017	2018	2019	2020	2021
Universities and colleges	**48,403**	**55,350**	**54,400**	**62,512**	**61,865**
Alverno College (Milwaukee)	1,942	1,851	1,744	1,876	1,822
Beloit College (Beloit)	1,402	1,275	1,143	978	1,011
Cardinal Stritch University (Milwaukee)	2,355	2,148	1,896	1,646	1,365
Carroll University (Waukesha)	3,452	3,352	3,449	3,452	3,397
Carthage College (Kenosha)	2,860	2,872	2,742	2,763	2,746
Concordia University Wisconsin (Mequon)	7,288	6,374	5,777	5,492	5,204
Edgewood College (Madison)	2,221	2,190	2,038	2,014	1,894
Lakeland University (Sheboygan)	2,679	2,497	2,511	2,753	2,094
Lawrence University (Appleton)	1,467	1,463	1,387	1,430	1,483
Marian University (Fond du Lac)	1,971	1,819	1,656	1,593	1,445

Wisconsin private institutions of higher education fall enrollment, continued

Institution (location)	2017	2018	2019	2020	2021
Marquette University (Milwaukee)	11,426	11,605	11,819	11,550	11,320
Mount Mary University (Milwaukee)	1,399	1,339	1,246	1,200	1,273
Northland College (Ashland)	635	582	609	570	531
Ripon College (Ripon)	756	807	787	816	810
St. Norbert College (De Pere)	2,165	2,228	2,081	1,939	2,009
Silver Lake College (Manitowoc)[1]	475	444	448	NA	NA
Viterbo University (La Crosse)	2,796	2,598	2,592	2,516	2,520
Wisconsin Lutheran College (Milwaukee)	1,114	1,248	1,148	1,166	1,147
Technical and professional	**8,208**	**8,658**	**9,272**	**9,379**	**9,897**
Bellin College (Green Bay)	440	477	649	626	697
Columbia College of Nursing[2]	122	122	122	NA	NA
Herzing University[3] (WI campuses)	2,700	2,994	3,327	3,569	3,942
Medical College of Wisconsin (Milwaukee)	1,385	1,413	1,477	1,506	1,538
Milwaukee Institute of Art & Design (Milwaukee)	660	756	870	925	898
Milwaukee School of Engineering (Milwaukee)	2,823	2,820	2,746	2,673	2,747
Wisconsin School of Professional Psychology (Milwaukee)	78	76	81	80	75
Theological seminaries	**1,321**	**1,220**	**1,147**		
Maranatha Baptist University (Watertown)	1,139	1,035	985	916	1,066
Nashotah House (Nashotah)	73	65	57	X	X
Sacred Heart Seminary and School of Theology (Franklin)	109	120	105	98	111
Tribal colleges	**496**	**468**	**530**	**451**	**497**
College of Menominee Nation (Keshena)	285	237	191	173	191
Lac Courte Oreilles Ojibwa Community College (Hayward)	211	231	339	278	306
Total	**58,428**	**65,696**	**65,349**	**72,342**	**72,259**

NA–Not Available; X–Not Applicable.
1. Closed in August 2020.   2. Closed in June 2020 and became an additional location for Alverno College.   3. For-profit institution.
Sources: National Center for Education Statistics, Integrated Postsecondary Education Data System at https://nces.ed.gov/ipeds/datacenter; U.S. Department of Education, Office of Postsecondary Education, Database of Accredited Postsecondary Institutions and Programs, accredited by the Higher Learning Commission of the North Central Association of Colleges and Schools at https://www.hlcommission.org/Directory-of-HLC-Institutions.html [March 2023].

Wisconsin Technical College System enrollment

School year	Total[1]	Associate arts & associate science[2]	Applied associate degree[3]	Technical diploma	Vocational adult	Non-post secondary	Community services
2010–11	383,671	28,052	149,249	36,911	167,135	72,176	13,181
2011–12	378,240	27,796	148,017	35,401	166,463	65,506	14,112
2012–13	362,252	26,532	148,548	34,546	149,628	61,552	14,929
2013–14	348,747	25,590	144,915	32,416	143,943	51,902	15,339
2014–15	329,407	23,996	140,380	32,164	134,203	50,782	12,704
2015–16	326,153	22,729	135,593	31,406	134,796	48,794	13,831
2016–17	307,607	21,721	134,543	30,789	119,921	45,885	11,804
2017–18	314,835	21,103	137,562	31,359	124,974	43,325	12,121
2018–19	307,849	21,543	140,767	32,134	114,970	41,771	11,672
2019–20	286,381	20,862	138,658	31,397	98,484	41,090	9,313
2020–21	248,534	18,167	129,203	28,389	82,976	28,978	3,352
2021–22	274,203	17,122	133,838	30,378	99,301	33,554	4,553

1. Unduplicated student headcount.   2. Includes courses that transfer to four-year institutions. Prior to 2019, the Technical College System labeled this column "Liberal arts transfer."   3. In the 2019 *Wisconsin Blue Book* and prior editions, this column was labeled "Associate degree."
Source: Wisconsin Technical College System, *Fact Book: Student Data 2021–2022*, November 2022, at https://www.wtcsystem.edu/impact/publications/fact-book-student-data/ [November 2022] and prior issues.

Wisconsin Technical College enrollment, 2021–22

	Total[1]	Associate arts & associate science[2]	Applied associate degree[3]	Technical diploma	Vocational adult	Non-post secondary	Community services
Blackhawk	8,198	—	5,055	811	2,583	693	36
Chippewa Valley	16,465	1,223	10,447	2,380	3,608	2,729	—
Fox Valley	49,655	—	15,718	3,396	30,611	1,704	722
Gateway	17,835	—	11,688	3,398	3,193	1,791	—
Lakeshore	8,947	—	4,088	1,026	3,784	927	14
Madison Area	24,722	7,254	13,192	2,300	4,465	3,420	1,181
Mid-State	7,923	—	4,339	973	2,120	2,743	288
Milwaukee Area	27,733	6,739	15,289	2,734	3,582	5,423	103
Moraine Park	13,525	—	5,897	1,839	4,720	2,038	848
Nicolet Area	3,756	693	1,248	302	1,788	771	—
Northcentral	18,566	—	8,724	1,131	8,043	3,448	613
Northeast Wisconsin	24,780	—	13,266	3,721	9,281	789	175
Northwood	14,427	50	3,903	1,685	9,007	687	355
Southwest Wisconsin	6,606	—	3,087	812	3,176	532	—
Waukesha County	17,343	—	9,056	2,144	6,779	1,433	218
Western	13,722	1,163	8,841	1,729	2,561	4,426	—
Total	274,203	17,122	133,838	30,378	99,301	3,354	4,553

—Represents zero.

1. Unduplicated student headcount. 2. Includes courses that transfer to four-year institutions. Prior to 2019, the Technical College System labeled this column "Liberal arts transfer." 3. In the 2019 *Wisconsin Blue Book* and prior editions, this column was labeled "Associate degree."

Sources: Wisconsin Technical College System, *Fact Book: Student Data 2021–2022* at https://www.wtcsystem.edu/impact/publications/fact-book-student-data, November 2022, and prior issues.

Wisconsin public high school completion rates, 2021–22

	Students (rate)			Student detail by race[1] or Hispanic origin					
CESA[2]	Total[3]	Female	Male	American Indian	Asian	Black	Hispanic	White	2 or more
1	16,368 (85.4)	8,162 (87.9)	8,206 (83.0)	17	718	2,640	2,733	9,138	625
2	11,490 (92.8)	5,651 (93.9)	5,838 (91.7)	NA	339	539	1,480	8,016	406
3	1,457 (94.7)	721 (95.0)	711 (94.4)	NA	NA	NA	9	549	4
4	2,534 (93.7)	1,230 (95.3)	1,304 (92.3)	27	77	17	137	1,821	48
5	3,710 (92.9)	1,847 (94.0)	1,863 (91.8)	NA	48	17	160	2,521	58
6	7,094 (92.7)	3,450 (93.7)	3,644 (91.7)	6	201	113	504	5,666	120
7	6,021 (92.1)	2,945 (93.9)	3,066 (90.4)	82	223	142	650	4,103	164
8	1,381 (93.1)	651 (94.2)	709 (92.2)	109	NA	NA	21	787	16
9	2,450 (93.5)	1,192 (94.3)	1,252 (92.8)	31	151	NA	83	1,865	54
10	2,521 (92.2)	1,277 (93.5)	1,231 (90.8)	NA	70	12	47	1,596	54
11	3,633 (93.4)	1,845 (93.9)	1,788 (92.8)	NA	28	14	76	2,722	55
12	1,025 (92.7)	483 (94.9)	511 (90.9)	57	NA	14	6	649	32
Total	59,690 (90.5)	29,510 (92.1)	30,179 (89.1)	563	2,379	4,029	6,618	43,923	2,139
Rate				-81.7	-92.6	-71.1	-82.6	-94.5	-87.7

Notes: Percent completion calculated by number of combined completions (diplomas, HSED, certificate) divided by number of students in the 4-year cohort. This table is based on 4-year adjusted cohort completion rates, as required by federal law, and may not be comparable to tables in prior Blue Books. Details may not sum to totals due to privacy rules.

NA–Not available. Includes only students who are identified by race in DPI report. Not all students can be identified by race due to privacy rules relating to small groups.

1. Pacific Islander state total (rate): 38 (88.4). 2. Cooperative Educational Service Agency. 3. Includes students who have completed high school with a diploma, HSED, or other method.

Source: Wisconsin Department of Public Instruction, Wisconsin Information System for Education Data Dashboard at https://dpi.wi.gov/wisedash/download-files [March 2023].

Enrollment in Wisconsin elementary and secondary public schools

Grade level	2013–14	2014–15	2015–16	2016–17	2017–18	2018–19	2019–20	2020–21	2021–22	2022–23
Pre-kindergarten[1]	56,777	55,830	55,907	55,435	55,186	56,096	56,338	47,126	51,208	50,612
Kindergarten	61,522	60,424	58,078	57,331	56,832	56,915	56,756	53,961	54,458	53,432
1	62,479	61,498	60,459	58,224	57,517	57,236	56,992	55,037	54,749	55,233
2	60,999	62,311	61,405	60,523	58,370	57,706	57,345	55,579	55,415	55,140
3	60,697	60,885	62,322	61,749	60,783	58,744	57,949	56,227	55,843	55,767
4	61,393	60,795	60,999	62,407	61,911	61,157	59,044	56,975	56,392	56,235
5	60,768	61,459	60,924	61,207	62,743	62,329	61,357	58,194	57,059	56,761
6	60,505	60,843	61,677	61,264	61,549	63,275	62,482	60,555	58,179	57,320
7	61,814	60,795	61,047	62,170	61,582	62,193	63,739	61,928	60,789	58,727
8	62,721	62,029	61,077	61,428	62,353	61,964	62,455	63,374	62,040	61,180
9	67,985	68,043	67,036	65,847	65,959	66,758	65,849	65,807	67,878	66,556
10	64,958	65,290	65,841	65,137	64,298	64,687	65,459	64,702	64,186	66,388
11	65,450	65,019	64,546	65,269	64,505	63,643	63,903	64,842	64,243	63,656
12	66,346	65,431	65,819	65,832	66,542	66,130	65,291	65,628	66,704	65,797
Total[2]	874,414	870,652	867,137	863,823	860,130	858,833	854,959	829,935	829,143	822,804

1. Includes K3 and K4. 2. Totals do not include students with unknown grade levels.

Source: Wisconsin Department of Public Instruction, Wisconsin Information System for Education Data Dashboard at http://dpi.wi.gov/wisedash/download-files [March 2023].

Enrollment in Wisconsin elementary and secondary private schools

Grade level	2013–14	2014–15	2015–16	2016–17	2017–18	2018–19	2019–20	2020–21	2021–22	2022–23
Pre-kindergarten[1]	14,204	14,516	14,226	13,572	14,456	14,153	14,150	11,965	12,924	13,477
Kindergarten	9,841	9,796	9,529	9,336	9,346	9,381	9,259	9,525	9,817	10,161
1	9,600	9,929	9,658	9,459	9,198	9,384	9,258	9,285	9,830	9,912
2	9,325	9,822	9,855	9,532	9,327	9,201	9,314	9,146	9,490	9,949
3	9,327	9,541	9,769	9,733	9,432	9,347	9,069	9,147	9,383	9,620
4	9,153	9,494	9,425	9,677	9,609	9,444	9,133	8,973	9,313	9,522
5	9,139	9,285	9,403	9,291	9,481	9,598	9,251	8,993	9,046	9,372
6	9,012	9,114	9,105	9,142	9,164	9,400	9,349	9,129	9,075	9,204
7	8,750	8,853	8,827	8,723	8,782	9,030	8,922	9,169	8,910	8,972
8	8,702	8,802	8,747	8,711	8,547	8,731	8,667	8,781	9,077	8,862
9	6,026	6,328	6,389	6,313	6,410	6,406	6,321	6,474	6,802	7,037
10	5,766	5,926	6,072	6,039	6,010	6,177	6,200	6,052	6,220	6,413
11	5,590	5,682	5,795	5,844	5,781	5,889	5,885	5,804	5,726	5,954
12	5,190	5,233	5,250	5,344	5,505	5,536	5,352	5,460	5,567	5,390
Ungraded elem. and secondary	176	783	1,087	784	788	863	575	959	549	602
Total	119,801	123,104	123,137	121,500	121,836	122,540	120,705	118,862	121,729	124,447

1. Includes K4.

Source: Wisconsin Department of Public Instruction, Wisconsin Information System for Education Data Dashboard at http://dpi.wi.gov/wisedash/download-files [March 2023].

Number of Wisconsin school districts, all grades

# of pupils[1]	2013–14	2014–15	2015–16	2016–17	2017–18	2018–19	2019–20	2020–21	2021–22	2022–23
1–499	125	129	130	123	125	126	124	128	137	136
500–999	123	116	117	117	118	120	118	121	118	120
1,000–1,999	96	97	96	98	98	94	100	98	98	96
2,000–2,999	31	31	32	31	29	32	27	26	26	27
3,000–3,999	29	29	29	28	30	26	29	27	25	24
4,000–4,999	13	13	11	12	10	13	13	12	13	13
5,000–9,999	22	22	23	23	23	23	23	24	25	25
10,000 and above	10	10	10	10	10	10	9	8	8	8
Total	449	447	448	442	443	444	443	444	450	449

1. Enrollment data includes charter schools not sponsored by a school district.

Source: Wisconsin Department of Public Instruction, Wisconsin Information System for Education Data Dashboard data at https://dpi.wi.gov/wisedash/download-files [March 2023].

Number of Wisconsin school districts, grades 9–12

# of pupils[1]	2013–14	2014–15	2015–16	2016–17	2017–18	2018–19	2019–20	2020–21	2021–22	2022–23
0[2]	64	64	65	60	61	59	57	57	59	55
1–299	181	179	173	178	178	182	180	180	187	189
300–499	64	67	71	64	66	65	67	66	67	67
500–999	71	66	63	64	63	63	62	65	63	64
1,000–1,999	47	48	51	52	51	50	53	52	50	51
2,000 and above	22	23	25	24	24	25	24	24	24	23
Total	449	447	448	442	443	444	443	444	450	449

1. Enrollment data includes nondistrict-sponsored charter schools. 2. This group includes the K3-8 districts, which do not have secondary level students.

Source: Wisconsin Department of Public Instruction, Wisconsin Information System for Education Data Dashboard at https://dpi.wi.gov/wisedash/download-files.

Wisconsin public school salaries

	Instructional staff Number	Instructional staff Average salary ($)	Teachers Number	Teachers Average salary ($)
2010–11	63,948	58,171	58,041	54,207
2015–16	62,986	58,485	56,937	54,115
2016–17	59,866	55,641	54,401	51,439
2017–18	65,976	59,632	55,172	58,007
2018–19	66,722	60,027	55,850	58,277
2019–20	67,048	61,177	55,960	59,431
2020–21	67,679	61,776	56,446	59,992
2021–22[1]	67,976	62,116	56,490	60,453

1. These figures are estimates based on projections made with data from the Wisconsin Department of Public Instruction.

Source: National Education Association, *Rankings of the States 2021 and Estimates of School Statistics 2022* at http://www.nea.org/rankings-and-estimates, June 2022 and prior issues.

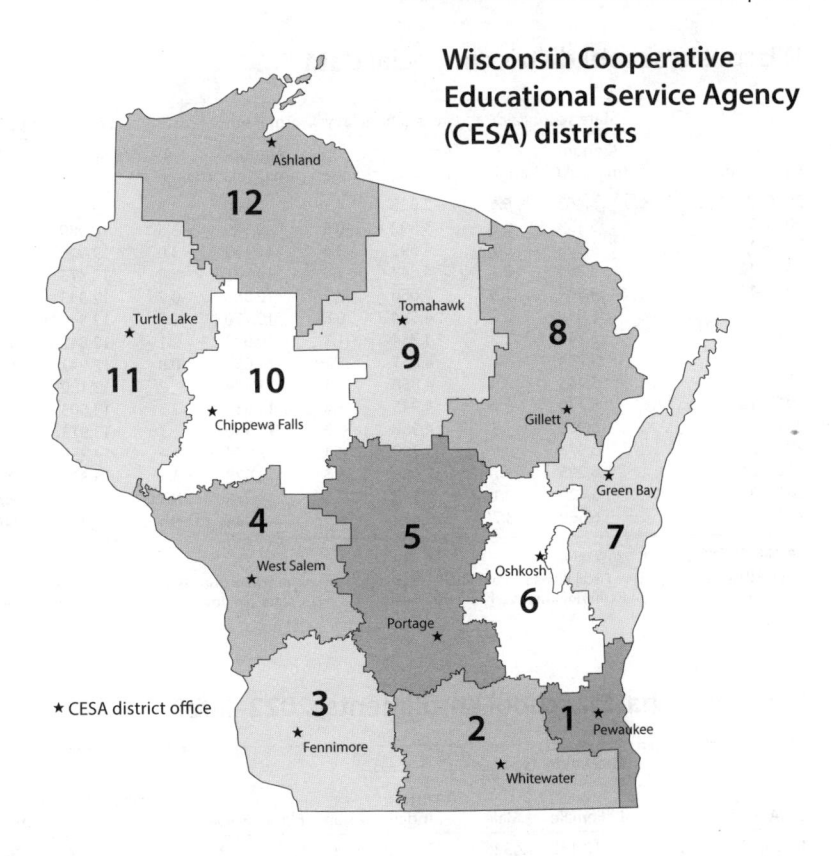

Wisconsin Cooperative Educational Service Agency (CESA) districts

★ CESA district office

Wisconsin state and local expenditures for public education

Agency/program	2017–18 (mil. dol.)	2018–19 (mil. dol.)	2019–20 (mil. dol.)	2020–21 (mil. dol.)	2021–22 (mil. dol.)
Public elementary and secondary schools[1]	11,557.2	11,900.0	12,184.6	12,628.1	13,415.4
Department of Public Instruction	137.8	139.5	131.6	218.6	205.4
University of Wisconsin System	6,201.7	6,498.9	6,406.8	6,248.8	6,872.0
Wisconsin Technical College System Board	551.1	551.2	562.9	562.3	594.2
Public libraries (local expenditures)[2]	291.0	297.0	303.0	303.0	NA
Other:					
Educational Communications Board	19.3	18.0	17.8	17.5	19.1
Higher Educational Aids Board	142.0	141.5	137.1	137.4	123.3
Medical College of Wisconsin, Inc. (state funding)	9.8	10.1	10.4	11.0	10.8
State Historical Society	27.5	29.8	27.9	27.8	32.0
Total	18,937.4	19,289.0	19,479.1	20,154.5	NA
Per capita expenditures[3] (dollars)	3,275	3,316	3,349	3,420	NA

NA–Not available.
1. Includes the gross costs of general operations, special projects, debt service, and food service; the net capital projects; and the costs of CESA and County Children with Disabilities Education Board operations. 2. Expenditures are for calendar year ending in the fiscal year shown. 3. Based on total state population. Wisconsin population estimate for 2017: 5,783,278; 2018: 5,816,231; 2019: 5,843,443; 2020: 5,893,718.

Sources: Wisconsin Department of Administration, *Annual Fiscal Report, Appendix (Budgetary Basis)* 2022, and previous issues; Wisconsin Department of Administration, Demographic Services Center, Time Series Population Estimates: County Totals [October 2022]; 2020 US Census; Wisconsin Department of Public Instruction, Library Service Data 2017, and previous data; Wisconsin Department of Public Instruction, departmental data.

Wisconsin school district financial data

Fiscal year	State school aid Amount (mil. dol.)	% change	Gross school levy Amount (mil. dol.)	% change	Total school costs Amount (mil. dol.)	% change	Cost per pupil Amount ($)	% change
2000–01	4,463	5.6	2,928	4.7	7,900	4.8	9,087	4.7
2005–06	5,159	6.2	3,592	-0.5	9,539	3.5	10,989	3.6
2010–11	5,325	0.2	4,693	3.4	11,162	3.0	13,020	3.1
2011–12	4,894	-8.1	4,647	-1.0	10,585	-5.2	12,375	-5.0
2012–13	4,964	1.4	4,656	0.2	10,568	-0.2	12,343	-0.3
2013–14	5,079	2.3	4,694	0.8	10,750	1.7	12,546	1.6
2014–15	5,242	3.2	4,754	1.3	10,972	2.1	12,842	2.4
2015–16	5,244	—	4,855	2.1	11,058	0.8	12,942	0.8
2016–17	5,445	3.8	4,858	0.1	11,274	2	13,182	1.9
2017–18	5,730	5.2	4,945	1.8	11,557	2.5	13,505	2.5
2018–19	5,900	3	4,988	0.9	11,900	3	13,913	3
2019–20	6,073	2.9	5,209	4.4	12,184	2.4	14,259	2.5
2020–21	6,295	3.7	5,380	3.3	12,628	3.6	15,329	7.5
2021–22	6,429	2.1	5,398	0.3	NA	NA	NA	NA
2022–23	6,669	3.7	5,477	1.5	NA	NA	NA	NA

NA–Not available; —Represents zero.

Source: Wisconsin Legislative Fiscal Bureau, Informational Paper #28, *State Aid to School Districts*, January 2023, at https://docs.legis.wisconsin.gov/misc/lfb/informational_papers/january_2023/0028_state_aid_to_school_districts_informational_paper_28.pdf.

Wisconsin charter school enrollments, 2022–2023

CESA[1] district	Total	Female	Male	American Indian	Asian	Black	Hispanic	Pacific Islander	White	2 or more
1	25,240	12,135	12,326	59	2,181	8,773	7,825	18	5,480	904
2	7,033	3,525	2,404	47	154	932	1,289	—	4,044	567
3	72	29	31	—	1	3	3	—	62	3
4	1,228	593	601	10	14	36	76	—	1,012	80
5	1,690	740	826	11	8	16	55	1	1,531	68
6	4,811	2,364	2,252	20	293	157	485	2	3,587	267
7	2,431	1,258	1,134	27	63	111	518	—	1,548	164
8	197	88	74	49	—	1	13	—	113	21
9	1,848	939	870	10	44	29	103	4	1,562	96
10	1,877	958	817	13	34	43	99	3	1,577	108
11	1,772	982	702	23	13	79	129	1	1,432	95
12	783	389	358	30	4	3	24	2	690	30
Total	48,982	24,000	22,395	299	2,809	10,183	10,619	31	22,638	2,403

Note: Totals may not add due to redacted data.
—Represents zero.
1. Cooperative Educational Service Agency.

Source: Wisconsin Department of Public Instruction, Wisconsin Information System for Education Data Dashboard at https://dpi.wi.gov/wisedash/download-files [March 2023].

Wisconsin home-based private educational enrollments

Grade level	2012–13	2013–14	2014–15	2015–16	2016–17	2017–18	2018–19	2019–20	2020–21	2021–22
1	1,158	1,197	1,183	1,175	1,214	1,304	1,210	1,196	2,739	1,784
2	1,060	1,144	1,144	1,084	1,133	1,199	1,142	1,150	2,438	1,711

Wisconsin home-based private educational enrollments, continued

Grade level	2012–13	2013–14	2014–15	2015–16	2016–17	2017–18	2018–19	2019–20	2020–21	2021–22
3	1,106	1,077	1,160	1,136	1,147	1,228	1,114	1,112	2,285	1,692
4	1,062	1,095	1,136	1,081	1,191	1,211	1,179	1,130	2,146	1,668
5	1,123	1,087	1,095	1,037	1,118	1,247	1,077	1,177	2,030	1,616
6	1,085	1,089	1,171	1,046	1,131	1,206	1,242	1,174	1,838	1,598
7	1,102	1,035	1,171	1,069	1,119	1,167	1,154	1,207	1,674	1,608
8	1,018	1,053	1,078	983	1,068	1,134	1,165	1,104	1,555	1,453
9	989	996	1,080	933	1,071	1,144	1,076	1,098	1,260	1,453
10	1,030	996	1,041	936	1,017	1,135	1,056	1,043	1,188	1,334
11	840	993	964	845	1,034	1,104	1,092	1,053	1,079	1,297
12	769	717	820	727	794	886	906	936	951	1,037
Ungraded .	6,122	6,625	6,807	6,698	7,325	7,668	8,164	8,264	10,695	11,151
Total.	18,464	19,104	19,850	18,750	20,362	21,633	21,577	21,644	31,878	29,402

Note: A home-based private educational program is a program of educational instruction provided to a child by a child's parent or guardian or by a person designated by the parent or guardian. These programs must provide at least 875 hours of instruction each school year and must offer a sequentially progressive curriculum of fundamental instruction in reading, language arts, mathematics, social studies, science, and health.

Source: Wisconsin Department of Public Instruction, Home-Based Private Educational Program Statistics, "Enrollment by Grade" at https://dpi.wi.gov/sms/home-based/statistics [August 2022].

AGRICULTURE

Wisconsin's comparative agricultural production, 2021

Commodity	Unit (1,000)	United States Production	Leading state	Wisconsin Production	% of U.S.	U.S. rank
All commodities	Dol	435,797,834	California	12,853,127	2.9	10
Livestock and livestock products	Dol	195,791,687	Texas	8,108,235	4.1	8
Crops	Dol	240,006,147	California	4,744,892	2	16
Dairy						
Milk production	Lbs	226,258,000	California	31,702,000	14	2
Cheese, total (excluding cottage cheese)	Lbs	13,706,566	Wisconsin	3,474,483	25.3	1
American	Lbs	5,567,561	Wisconsin	1,078,229	19.4	1
Cheddar	Lbs	3,933,303	Wisconsin	732,528	18.6	1
Hispanic	Lbs	351,501	California	111,209	31.6	2
Italian	Lbs	5,752,159	Wisconsin	1,649,447	28.7	1
Mozzarella	Lbs	4,487,636	California	1,050,775	23.4	2
Dry whey, human food	Lbs	911,502	Wisconsin	311,836	34.2	1
Livestock and poultry						
Cattle and calves, all[1]	Head	91,902	Texas	3,500	3.8	9
Milk cows[1]	Head	9,375	California	1,275	13.6	2
Hogs and pigs, all[2]	Head	74,446	Iowa	365	0.5	18
Sheep[1]	Head	5,065	Texas	82	1.6	18
Milk goats[1]	Head	410	Wisconsin	74	18	1
Chickens[2]	Head	522,704	Iowa	8,829	1.7	16
Broilers	Head	9,130,700	Georgia	55,900	0.6	20
Eggs	Eggs	110,728,700	Iowa	2,182,000	2	15
Mink	Pelts	1,444	Wisconsin	579	40.1	1
Honey	Lbs	126,466	North Dakota	1,974	1.6	17
Crops						
Corn for grain	Bu	15,115,170	Iowa	547,200	3.6	10
Corn for silage	Tons	130,317	Wisconsin	19,135	14.7	1
Soybeans	Bu	4,435,232	Illinois	113,850	2.6	13
Oats	Bu	39,836	Minnesota	3,782	9.5	4
Wheat, winter	Bu	1,277,365	Kansas	18,375	1.4	19
Forage (dry equivalent), all	Tons	81,624	Texas	7,817	9.6	2
Hay (dry only), all	Tons	120,196	Texas	3,520	2.9	13
Potatoes, all	Cwt	409,671	Idaho	29,113	7.1	3
Cherries, tart	Lbs	172,100	Michigan	10,500	6.1	4
Cranberries	Bbl	7,074	Wisconsin	4,165	58.9	1
Maple syrup	Gals	3,721	Vermont	365	9.8	4
Carrots, all	Cwt	31,587	California	1,479	4.7	3
Green peas, all	Cwt	4,536	Washington	1,197	26.4	3
Pumpkins, all	Cwt	16,663	Illinois	276	1.7	13
Snap beans, all	Cwt	15,123	Wisconsin	6,693	44.3	1
Sweet corn, all	Cwt	57,714	Washington	9,576	16.6	3

Note: Wisconsin is also a leading state in the production of turkeys, ducks, and ginseng; Wisconsin's rank is not available for these commodities.

Bbl–Barrels; Bu–Bushels; Cwt–Hundredweight; Dol–Dollars; Gals–Gallons; Lbs–Pounds.

1. January 1, 2022 inventory. 2. December 1, 2021.

Sources: U.S. Department of Agriculture, National Agriculture Statistics Service, "2022 Wisconsin Agricultural Statistics" and U.S. Department of Agriculture, Economic Research Service, "Annual cash receipts by commodity, U.S. and States 2008–2022F" at https://www.ers.usda.gov/data-products/farm-income-and-wealth-statistics/data-files-us-and-state-level-farm-income-and-wealth-statistics.

Wisconsin's net farm income

	2017	2018	2019	2020	2021
Value of agricultural sector production[1] ($1,000)	**12,616,321**	**11,977,500**	**12,357,927**	**12,706,907**	**14,413,359**
Value of crop production	3,233,167	3,365,005	2,967,079	3,634,870	4,916,517
Value of animals and products production	7,787,646	7,307,118	7,873,338	7,778,439	8,171,366
Farm-related income	1,595,508	1,305,377	1,517,510	1,293,598	1,325,476
Less: Intermediate product expenses[2]	7,157,586	6,571,583	6,963,701	7,166,392	7,697,938
Less: Contract labor expenses	34,138	23,320	48,193	35,359	7,425
Less: Property taxes	380,000	400,000	380,000	425,000	460,000
Less: Motor vehicle registration and licensing fees	16,238	12,614	14,997	17,011	19,562
Plus: Direct government payments	134,422	300,846	501,461	1,569,350	822,354
Equals: Gross value added	**5,162,781**	**5,270,830**	**5,452,498**	**6,632,495**	**7,050,787**
Less: Capital consumption (depreciation)	1,251,208	1,074,589	997,754	1,013,305	906,316
Equals: Net value added[3]	**3,911,573**	**4,196,241**	**4,454,744**	**5,619,189**	**6,144,472**
Less: Payments to stakeholders[4]	2,069,247	2,116,623	2,168,232	1,936,704	2,009,459
Equals: Net farm income[5]	**1,842,326**	**2,079,618**	**2,286,511**	**3,682,485**	**4,135,013**
Number of farms	64,800	64,800	64,900	64,400	64,100
Average net farm income per farm ($)	28,431	32,093	35,231	57,181	64,509

1. Value of agricultural sector output is the gross value of the commodities and services produced within a year. 2. Includes purchases of feed, livestock, poultry, and seed; outlays for fertilizers and lime, pesticides, fuel and electricity; capital repair and maintenance; and marketing, storage, transportation, and other expenses. 3. Net value added is the sector's contribution to the national economy and is the sum of the income from production earned by all factors of production, regardless of ownership. 4. Includes compensation for hired labor, net rent paid to landlords, and interest payments. 5. Net farm income is the farm operators' share of income from the sector's production activities.

Sources: U.S. Department of Agriculture, Economic Research Service, "Value added by U.S. agriculture (includes net farm income)" at https://www.ers.usda.gov/data-products/farm-income-and-wealth-statistics/data-files-us-and-state-level-farm-income-and-wealth-statistics [December 2022]; U.S. Department of Agriculture, National Agriculture Statistics Service, "2022 Wisconsin Agricultural Statistics" at https://www.nass.usda.gov/Statistics_by_State/Wisconsin/Publications/Annual_Statistical_Bulletin [December 2022].

Wisconsin's agricultural cash receipts

Commodity	2018 ($1,000)	2019 ($1,000)	2020 ($1,000)	2021 ($1,000)
All commodities	**10,929,825**	**11,168,466**	**11,361,774**	**12,853,127**
Livestock, dairy, and poultry	**7,340,192**	**7,848,713**	**7,754,751**	**8,108,235**
Meat animals	1,875,008	1,772,785	1,624,522	1,769,169
Cattle and calves	1,754,534	1,633,874	1,485,841	1,581,642
Hogs	120,474	138,911	138,681	187,527
Dairy products, milk	5,002,800	5,702,980	5,763,366	5,912,788
Poultry and eggs	340,563	254,742	256,880	301,084
Broilers	127,899	110,905	80,729	118,955
Farm chickens	262	219	106	78
Eggs	176,103	104,750	132,165	129,357
Miscellaneous livestock	121,821	118,206	109,983	125,194
Honey	6,770	6,486	6,998	5,547
Trout	1,493	1,525	1,424	660
Mink pelts	27,414	22,071	14,260	24,048
Wool	198	187	155	160
Crops	**3,589,634**	**3,319,754**	**3,607,022**	**4,744,892**
Food grains	67,956	54,200	44,192	89,030
Wheat	59,576	47,630	39,819	84,242
Feed crops	1,587,319	1,508,889	1,333,519	2,221,993
Barley	294	610	816	671

Wisconsin's agricultural cash receipts, continued

Commodity	2018 ($1,000)	2019 ($1,000)	2020 ($1,000)	2021 ($1,000)
Corn	1,465,229	1,364,148	1,204,139	2,098,784
Hay	112,838	133,352	117,322	112,528
Oats	8,958	10,779	11,243	10,010
Oil crops	**876,156**	**655,184**	**1,024,064**	**1,135,094**
Soybeans	876,156	655,184	1,024,064	1,135,094
Vegetables and melons	**432,797**	**460,764**	**489,249**	**569,189**
Potatoes	283,795	294,772	326,549	344,188
Beans, snap	47,877	42,254	35,291	52,274
Cabbage	14,912	20,976	34,451	65,349
Carrots	7,092	28,874	8,483	8,054
Corn, sweet	40,181	33,470	49,507	52,967
Cucumbers	21,141	16,277	17,544	23,103
Pumpkins	2,791	12,869	3,203	5,087
Peas, green	11,811	11,272	14,221	18,167
Fruits and nuts	**156,787**	**163,578**	**178,153**	**170,841**
Cherries, tart	1,928	934	5,189	6,510
Cranberries	154,859	162,644	172,964	164,331
All other crops	**468,619**	**477,138**	**537,845**	**558,745**
Maple products	7,290	8,775	7,712	12,082
Peppermint oil	3,565	NA	NA	NA
Mushrooms	2,527	NA	NA	NA

Note: Bold figures indicate category totals of the commodities immediately following and indicate categories included in next higher level of aggregation. Category totals may include amounts for specific commodities not listed separately or that are not listed to provide confidentiality to large producers in concentrated industries. Prior year's numbers have been revised to reflect updated source data.

NA–Not available.

Source: U.S. Department of Agriculture, Economic Research Service, "Annual Cash Receipts by Commodity, U.S. and States, 2008–2022F" at https://www.ers.usda.gov/data-products/farm-income-and-wealth-statistics/data-files-us-and-state-level-farm-income-and-wealth-statistics/.

Wisconsin's agricultural cash receipts, 2021

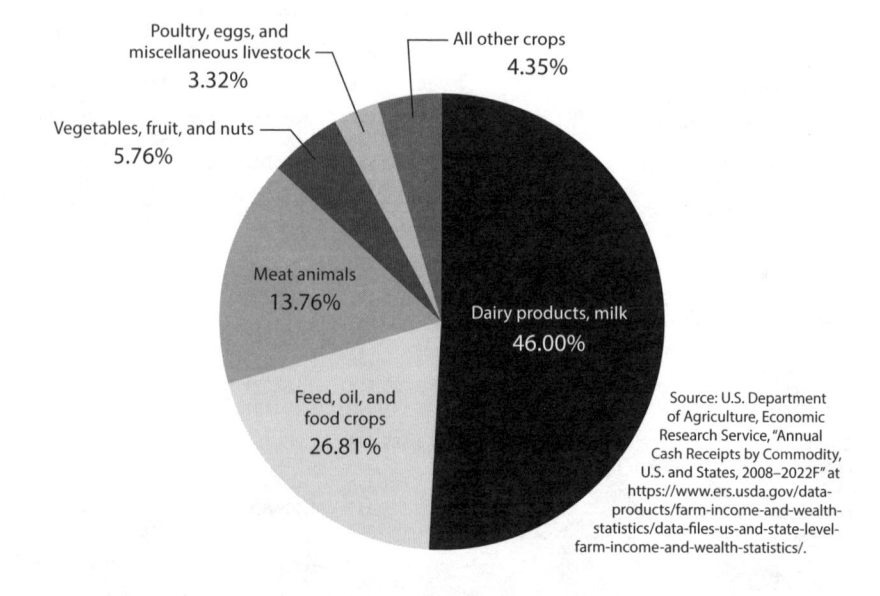

- Poultry, eggs, and miscellaneous livestock: 3.32%
- All other crops: 4.35%
- Vegetables, fruit, and nuts: 5.76%
- Meat animals: 13.76%
- Dairy products, milk: 46.00%
- Feed, oil, and food crops: 26.81%

Source: U.S. Department of Agriculture, Economic Research Service, "Annual Cash Receipts by Commodity, U.S. and States, 2008–2022F" at https://www.ers.usda.gov/data-products/farm-income-and-wealth-statistics/data-files-us-and-state-level-farm-income-and-wealth-statistics/.

Number, size, and value of farms in Wisconsin

	Number of farms	Farm land (1,000 acres)	Avg. farm size (acres)	Total (mil. dol.)	Avg. per farm ($)	Avg. per acre ($)
1935	200,000	23,500	117	1,246	6,228	53
1940	187,000	22,900	123	1,191	6,368	52
1945	178,000	23,600	133	1,440	8,088	61
1950	174,000	23,600	136	2,100	12,071	89
1955	155,000	23,200	150	2,343	15,117	101
1960	138,000	22,200	161	2,953	21,396	133
1965	124,000	21,400	173	3,317	26,750	155
1970	110,000	20,100	183	4,663	42,393	232
1975	100,000	19,300	193	8,376	83,762	434
1980	93,000	18,600	200	18,674	200,800	1,004
1985	83,000	17,900	216	16,898	203,586	944
1990	80,000	17,600	220	14,098	176,220	801
1995	80,000	16,800	210	17,472	218,400	1,040
2000	77,500	16,000	206	27,200	350,968	1,700
2005	76,500	15,400	201	43,890	573,725	2,850
2010	73,200	14,700	201	53,655	732,992	3,650
2015	66,600	14,400	216	65,520	983,784	4,550
2016	65,700	14,400	219	65,088	990,685	4,520
2017	64,800	14,300	221	69,641	1,074,707	4,870
2018	64,800	14,300	221	70,070	1,081,327	4,900
2019	64,900	14,300	220	70,785	1,090,678	4,950
2020	64,400	14,300	222	69,355	1,076,941	4,850
2021	64,100	14,200	222	73,698	1,149,735	5,190

Notes: "Farm" is currently defined as a place that sells, or would normally sell, at least $1,000 of agricultural products during the year. The actual number of farms in Wisconsin peaked at 199,877 in 1935.
Source: U.S. Department of Agriculture, National Agricultural Statistics Service, "2022 Wisconsin Agricultural Statistics" and prior editions at https://www.nass.usda.gov/Statistics_by_State/Wisconsin/Publications/Annual_Statistical_Bulletin [December 2022].

Wisconsin nonirrigated cropland cash rents

County	2017 ($/acre)	2022 ($/acre)	% change	County	2017 ($/acre)	2022 ($/acre)	% change
Adams	77.00	91.00	18.2	Fond du Lac	173.00	163.00	-5.8
Ashland	D	34.00	D	Forest	D	19.50	D
Barron	83.50	95.50	14.4	Grant	185.00	217.00	17.3
Bayfield	D	28.50	28.5	Green	164.00	180.00	9.8
Brown	165.00	210.00	27.3	Green Lake	133.00	169.00	27.1
Buffalo	131.00	134.00	2.3	Iowa	169.00	185.00	9.5
Burnett	46.00	57.00	23.9	Iron	D	D	D
Calumet	134.00	171.00	27.6	Jackson	108.00	137.00	26.
Chippewa	117.00	102.00	-12.8	Jefferson	148.00	167.00	12.8
Clark	105.00	D	D	Juneau	90.50	102.00	12.7
Columbia	189.00	184.00	-2.6	Kenosha	139.00	159.00	14.4
Crawford	134.00	123.00	-8.2	Kewaunee	D	194.00	D
Dane	180.00	206.00	14.4	La Crosse	152.00	134.00	-11.8
Dodge	199.00	D	D	Lafayette	230.00	235.00	2.2
Door	D	100.00	D	Langlade	79.00	114.00	44.3
Douglas	D	23.50	D	Lincoln	56.00	59.00	5.4
Dunn	102.00	122.00	19.6	Manitowoc	158.00	193.00	22.2
Eau Claire	88.50	107.00	20.9	Marathon	95.50	86.50	-9.4
Florence	D	24.00	D	Marinette	66.50	120.00	80.5

Wisconsin nonirrigated cropland cash rents, continued

County	2017 ($/acre)	2022 ($/acre)	% change	County	2017 ($/acre)	2022 ($/acre)	% change
Marquette	75.50	76.50	1.3	Sauk	127.00	139.00	9.4
Menominee	D	D	D	Sawyer	41.50	56.50	36.1
Milwaukee	D	101.00	D	Shawano	99.00	109.00	10.1
Monroe	130.00	130.00	0.0	Sheboygan	108.00	123.00	13.9
Oconto	119.00	119.00	0.0	Taylor	78.00	89.50	14.7
Oneida	D	52.00	D	Trempealeau	124.00	124.00	0.0
Outagamie	124.00	158.00	27.4	Vernon	140.00	137.00	-2.1
Ozaukee	D	111.00	D	Vilas	D	D	D
Pepin	144.00	143.00	-0.7	Walworth	184.00	198.00	7.6
Pierce	152.00	157.00	3.3	Washburn	51.00	59.00	15.7
Polk	77.00	85.50	11.0	Washington	108.00	135.00	25.0
Portage	66.00	55.50	-15.9	Waukesha	128.00	137.00	7.0
Price	35.00	35.00	0.0	Waupaca	79.00	104.00	31.6
Racine	128.00	146.00	14.1	Waushara	53.00	71.00	34.0
Richland	107.00	124.00	15.9	Winnebago	91.50	99.50	8.7
Rock	161.00	178.00	10.6	Wood	104.00	86.50	-16.8
Rusk	70.00	74.00	5.7	**Total**	**133.00**	**145.00**	**9.0**
St. Croix	98.00	136.00	38.8				

D–Data withheld to avoid disclosing details of individual operators.

Source: U.S. Department of Agriculture, National Agriculture Statistics Service, "2022 Wisconsin Agricultural Statistics" and prior editions at https://www.nass.usda.gov/Statistics_by_State/Wisconsin/Publications/Annual_Statistical_Bulletin [December 2022].

Wisconsin agricultural land sales

	Land continuing in agricultural use				Agricultural land diverted to other uses			
	Transactions		Avg. cost per acre ($)		Transactions		Avg. cost per acre ($)	
County[1]	2020	2021	2020	2021	2020	2021	2020	2021
Adams	6	6	3,314	2,988	2	NA	2,879	NA
Ashland	4	3	1,212	1,791	1	NA	577	NA
Barron	22	35	3,018	3,438	NA	1	NA	2,983
Bayfield	7	9	1,320	1,790	NA	NA	NA	NA
Brown	23	13	9,503	9,028	7	3	26,762	19,690
Buffalo	19	13	3,940	4,382	2	1	3,874	5,129
Burnett	2	6	1,874	2,243	NA	NA	NA	NA
Calumet	14	16	9,046	9,335	2	NA	19,473	NA
Chippewa	28	19	3,523	4,117	2	6	3,128	7,593
Clark	22	25	4,007	4,176	NA	NA	NA	NA
Columbia	18	18	7,810	7,977	4	1	12,838	10,426
Crawford	14	11	3,731	4,308	NA	NA	NA	NA
Dane	33	32	9,081	10,963	5	1	22,084	14,500
Dodge	23	30	7,328	8,314	1	NA	12,359	NA
Door	1	13	3,996	5,054	NA	NA	NA	NA
Douglas	1	3	1,026	1,493	NA	NA	NA	NA
Dunn	25	35	3,728	4,291	2	2	3,036	4,051
Eau Claire	20	24	4,063	4,335	NA	1	NA	4,914
Florence	1	2	2,000	1,574	NA	NA	NA	NA
Fond du Lac	25	46	6,168	7,049	5	1	12,121	7,550
Forest	2	3	1,478	1,251	NA	NA	NA	NA
Grant	31	35	5,476	6,983	NA	NA	NA	NA
Green	32	29	6,237	5,761	NA	1	NA	12,636
Green Lake	12	12	9,587	8,021	1	NA	9,600	NA

Wisconsin agricultural land sales, continued

	Land continuing in agricultural use				Agricultural land diverted to other uses			
	Transactions		Avg. cost per acre ($)		Transactions		Avg. cost per acre ($)	
County[1]	2020	2021	2020	2021	2020	2021	2020	2021
Iowa	28	32	6,386	6,623	NA	NA	NA	NA
Jackson	16	8	2,930	3,530	NA	NA	NA	NA
Jefferson	15	18	7,525	6,676	1	2	4,500	8,726
Juneau	12	11	3,839	3,881	NA	NA	NA	NA
Kenosha	3	9	8,709	10,867	4	9	14,677	89,763
Kewaunee	14	6	5,369	5,604	NA	NA	NA	NA
La Crosse	12	10	5,868	4,655	NA	NA	NA	NA
Lafayette	24	30	7,644	9,321	NA	1	NA	7,800
Langlade	6	16	3,266	2,672	NA	NA	NA	NA
Lincoln	11	3	2,092	2,846	2	5	2,235	2,161
Manitowoc	28	25	6,269	7,934	NA	NA	NA	NA
Marathon	40	31	3,852	4,329	4	NA	4,908	NA
Marinette	3	1	4,157	4,977	NA	NA	NA	NA
Marquette	8	5	3,807	3,601	NA	1	NA	6,500
Milwaukee	NA	1	NA	12,600	NA	NA	NA	NA
Monroe	25	21	3,375	3,880	3	NA	2,794	NA
Oconto	15	10	4,019	4,070	NA	NA	NA	NA
Oneida	NA	1	NA	1,694	NA	NA	NA	NA
Outagamie	23	36	7,266	7,745	7	2	21,518	7,880
Ozaukee	8	9	8,351	9,312	1	4	10,200	18,154
Pepin	8	6	4,201	4,704	NA	NA	NA	NA
Pierce	16	12	4,819	6,070	3	2	5,530	9,505
Polk	20	23	3,299	3,787	6	NA	2,568	NA
Portage	8	13	3,539	3,346	1	1	3,500	4,600
Price	4	6	1,045	1,298	NA	NA	NA	NA
Racine	7	10	9,403	8,632	4	2	7,883	109,496
Richland	22	15	3,774	4,660	NA	NA	NA	NA
Rock	26	15	8,038	8,353	2	4	18,220	29,330
Rusk	7	3	1,842	2,291	1	1	1,500	2,010
St. Croix	36	37	4,751	5,609	2	1	4,111	22,446
Sauk	23	27	4,367	5,002	1	NA	12,132	NA
Sawyer	2	3	1,275	2,163	1	2	2,400	2,062
Shawano	13	21	5,788	6,756	NA	1	NA	6,000
Sheboygan	23	32	6,680	8,419	NA	NA	NA	NA
Taylor	11	26	2,730	2,657	1	2	2,000	1,374
Trempealeau	14	14	3,600	3,597	NA	1	NA	3,500
Vernon	31	20	3,949	4,274	1	NA	19,640	NA
Vilas	NA	NA	NA	NA	NA	1	NA	3,700
Walworth	33	29	8,284	9,804	2	4	14,355	12,998
Washburn	3	8	2,007	2,392	NA	NA	NA	NA
Washington	19	28	9,212	9,876	2	3	12,331	14,145
Waukesha	7	10	14,756	11,288	1	11	19,297	42,370
Waupaca	14	11	4,002	5,937	NA	NA	NA	NA
Waushara	11	12	4,184	4,124	NA	1	NA	3,795
Winnebago	11	19	5,367	6,520	3	3	5,038	8,831
Wood	11	26	2,496	3,498	NA	NA	NA	NA
Total	1,072	1,147	5,579	6,202	87	82	12,458	32,158

NA–Not available.
1. Iron and Menominee Counties had no agricultural sales in years shown.
Source: U.S. Department of Agriculture, National Agricultural Statistics Service, "2022 Wisconsin Agricultural Statistics" and prior versions at https://www.nass.usda.gov/Statistics_by_State/Wisconsin/Publications/Annual_Statistical_Bulletin [September 2022].

CONSERVATION

Fish and game harvested in Wisconsin, 2021–22

Fish[1]	
Great Lakes trout	131,434
Great Lakes salmon	191,898
Game and fowl[2]	
Wild turkey	41,237
Pheasant	224,098
Ruffed grouse	155,234
Gray partridge	—
Bobwhite quail	—
Woodcock	54,598
Squirrel	197,647
Cottontail rabbit	61,230
Snowshoe hare	3,624
Doves	41,874
Raccoon	70,424
Red fox	4,657
Gray fox	1,665
Coyote	41,621
Deer (with guns)	209,288
Deer (with bows)	99,141
Elk	7
Bear	3,847
Duck	318,700
Canada goose	111,505
Furbearers[2]	
Woodchuck	965
Muskrat	135,215
Mink	4,230
Beaver	15,351
River otter	1,784
Bobcat	1078
Opossum	6,718
Skunk	3,692
Fisher	641

—Represents zero.
1. Based on the 2014–15 diary survey, the DNR estimates the total number of fish caught as 51,704,570 and the total number harvested at 13,436,401. These are underestimates, because they do not include fish caught or harvested by unlicensed anglers, short-term license holders, or senior citizen discount license holders. 2. Deer, bear, turkey, bobcat, otter, and fisher data are all from hunter-registered harvest. Remaining data are from hunter surveys.
Source: Wisconsin Department of Natural Resources, departmental data, April 2023.

Fish and game stocked in Wisconsin, 2021–22

Game farm pheasants released	79,542
Warmwater fish produced and distributed (includes fry)	52,325,334
Coldwater fish	7,895,524

Source: Wisconsin Department of Natural Resources, departmental data, April 2023.

Fish and game licenses and recreation permits issued in Wisconsin

	2017	2018	2019	2020	2021	2022
Boats actively registered	630,134	619,319	609,957	625,273	628,423	618,782
Snowmobiles actively registered	223,938	214,661	211,624	229,118	231,513	226,981
All-terrain vehicles actively registered	382,029	400,285	418,345	447,917	473,433	488,103
Off-highway motorcycles actively registered[1]	2,245	3,608	4,209	5,234	6,738	7,320
Gun deer hunting and license tags (including nonresident)[2]	488,826	472,370	460,314	454,394	447,172	437,901
Small game hunting license tags (including nonresident)[2]	120,103	109,155	109,943	120,213	113,514	112,265
Spring turkey licenses (including nonresident)[2]	93,689	87,429	86,047	90,313	89,405	85,080
Fall turkey licenses (including nonresident)[2]	15,298	21,767	21,114	25,240	22,931	23,297

Fish and game licenses and recreation permits issued in Wisconsin, continued

	2017	2018	2019	2020	2021	2022
Resident annual fishing licenses[3]	686,253	652,561	647,672	738,472	671,640	643,576
Resident husband and wife fishing licenses	190,994	187,471	179,962	201,922	189,714	176,798
1-day resident fishing licenses	10,566	9,767	9,616	10,912	10,402	9,830
Nonresident annual fishing licenses	120,563	113,594	113,380	132,288	133,317	121,313
Nonresident family annual fishing licenses	54,324	53,548	53,080	58,883	61,197	57,244
15-day nonresident family fishing licenses	23,282	22,424	22,109	21,082	21,583	19,615
15-day nonresident fishing licenses	24,956	24,973	24,326	22,622	25,297	23,381
4-day nonresident fishing licenses	52,288	51,184	50,804	46,555	52,360	47,538
1-day nonresident fishing licenses	64,394	60,211	59,675	58,926	61,453	56,212
Resident sports licenses	44,567	48,140	48,700	56,003	52,819	51,288
Nonresident sports licenses	3,147	3,403	3,344	3,630	3,640	3,551
2-day Great Lakes fishing licenses	37,837	36,174	34,412	32,947	39,067	35,053
Resident archer's licenses[2]	143,244	130,524	119,785	125,075	114,845	108,978
Nonresident archer's licenses[2]	8,928	8,782	9,452	10,879	10,009	9,733
Guide licenses (residents only)	1,592	1,789	1,790	2,019	2,121	1,995
Conservation patron licenses	51,889	52,633	52,590	55,805	61,264	62,717
Nonresident patron licenses	1,213	1,039	857	1,026	1,045	1,040
Resident crossbow licenses[4]	70,855	77,988	93,681	112,905	104,440	107,757
Nonresident crossbow licenses[4]	2,093	2,453	3,042	3,514	4,158	4,539
Elk licenses[5]	NA	5	5	5	4	4

NA–Not available.
1. DNR began registering off-highway motorcycles in 2016. 2. Includes mentored licenses. 3. Includes senior and junior fishing licenses. First-time buyer junior and senior licenses were created in 2020. 4. Includes mentored licenses. Does not include upgrades. 5. The first Wisconsin elk season was held in 2018, Wisconsin issued permits only.
Source: Wisconsin Department of Natural Resources, departmental data, March 2023.

Wisconsin Department of Natural Resources funding sources

	2016–17 ($1,000)	2017–18 ($1,000)	2018–19 ($1,000)	2019–20 ($1,000)	2020–21 ($1,000)	2021–22 ($1,000)
Segregated funds	**432,415**	**427,135**	**455,533**	**453,397**	**461,976**	**462,874**
All-terrain vehicle registration fees	3,954	5,471	4,174	6,340	7,010	6,673
Boat registration fees	5,165	5,573	5,380	5,428	4,873	6,239
Dry cleaner fund	576	572	928	437	426	323
Endangered resources voluntary payments	1,688	1,422	271	650	693	317
Environmental improvement fund	1,408	1,729	1,752	1,661	701	881
Environmental management account	48,057	44,353	47,984	46,991	48,177	47,061
Federal aids	103,659	104,553	123,313	112,367	114,909	124,852
Fishing, hunting licenses and permits	59,181	60,932	57,476	66,822	66,048	68,783
Forestry mill tax	109,699	98,883	103,166	101,948	107,002	104,856
Gifts and donations	641	932	953	798	1,618	522
Heritage State Parks and Forests Trust Fund	94	33	183	35	222	41
Nonpoint source account	15,866	15,055	14,960	14,646	13,914	12,694
Park stickers and fees	19,068	21,605	23,001	22,590	23,527	23,830
Petroleum storage environmental cleanup fund	10,964	12,351	14,403	11,442	10,866	6,816
Program revenue[1]	35,280	36,634	39,724	43,526	44,149	40,397
Snowmobile registration fees	3,737	3,873	4,370	4,162	5,212	6,225
Waste management fund	18	438	307	134	113	49
Water resources account	12,893	12,306	12,744	12,991	12,037	11,831
Wisconsin Natural Resources Magazine	467	420	444	429	479	484
General funds	**164,092**	**158,356**	**176,422**	**165,944**	**168,673**	**166,158**
General purpose revenue	106,900	97,746	113,768	98,444	99,223	100,956
Program revenues	20,227	22,983	20,978	22,866	23,315	20,342
Program revenue—services	9,455	7,860	10,464	12,899	12,544	12,320

Wisconsin Department of Natural Resources funding sources, continued

	2016–17 ($1,000)	2017–18 ($1,000)	2018–19 ($1,000)	2019–20 ($1,000)	2020–21 ($1,000)	2021–22 ($1,000)
Federal aids	27,510	29,767	31,212	31,735	33,591	32,540
Total	596,507	585,491	631,955	619,341	630,649	629,032

—Represents zero.
1. Includes all segregated expenditures in assigned or dedicated appropriations.
Source: Wisconsin Department of Natural Resources, departmental data, March 2023.

Wisconsin Department of Natural Resources expenditures

Program	2016–17 ($1,000)	2017–18 ($1,000)	2018–19 ($1,000)	2019–20 ($1,000)	2020–21 ($1,000)	2021–22 ($1,000)
Fish, wildlife, and parks (FWP)	87,401	85,706	93,519	93,547	98,509	102,848
Wildlife management	21,248	24,285	27,854	26,819	27,910	29,732
Southern forests	5,540	5,455	5,823	5,783	6,387	6,322
Fisheries management	25,509	26,322	26,441	27,943	28,200	29,655
Parks	17,720	17,842	17,802	17,256	19,637	19,528
Endangered resources	6,648	6,939	8,210	8,288	7,249	8,322
Facilities and lands	9,438	—	—	—	—	—
Property management	—	3,744	6,168	6,275	7,781	7,497
FWP program management	1,298	1,119	1,221	1,183	1,345	1,792
Forestry	61,655	53,403	58,092	56,441	59,222	59,420
Public safety and resource protection (PSRP)	40,425	36,145	35,315	39,378	37,374	37,315
Law enforcement	31,230	35,383	34,598	39,378	37,374	37,315
Integrated science services	8,356	—	—	—	—	—
Enforcement/science program management	839	762	717	*—	—	—
Environmental management (EM)	69,667	72,080	75,960	79,291	82,239	79,503
Drinking and groundwater	13,464	13,755	14,952	15,498	15,784	16,312
Water quality	22,922	23,299	27,044	27,104	24,829	25,428
Air management	13,366	10,911	13,166	13,009	13,365	12,782
Waste and materials management	7,106	7,159	7,376	7,225	8,094	8,068
Remediation and redevelopment	10,529	15,689	12,159	14,985	18,869	15,673
EM program management	2,280	1,267	1,263	1,470	1,298	1,240
Conservation aids	43,735	44,718	47,270	48,501	50,339	56,472
Fish and wildlife aids	1,367	848	1,862	1,516	2,329	2,356
Forestry aids	8,571	8,005	9,611	8,091	8,724	8,913
Recreational aids	12,105	13,825	13,694	16,422	15,961	18,342
Aids in lieu of taxes	16,975	17,140	17,229	17,325	17,937	20,764
Enforcement aids	2,277	2,277	2,277	2,532	2,532	2,913
Wildlife damage aids	2,440	2,623	2,597	2,615	2,856	3,184
Environmental aids	35,803	35,669	38,090	33,961	33,656	29,135
Water quality aids	6,839	6,260	6,307	6,269	8,696	8,329
Solid and hazard waste aids	21,103	20,829	20,162	20,411	20,000	20,000
Environmental aids	5,912	6,509	9,011	5,677	4,508	303
Environmental planning aids	294	365	303	285	452	503
Nonpoint aids	1,655	1,706	2,307	1,319	—	—
Debt service	116,781	105,634	123,473	105,167	102,627	98,686
Resource	87,567	79,399	93,821	79,788	80,786	78,237
Environmental	4,856	4,093	4,470	4,077	4,050	3,854
Water quality	20,766	18,737	21,282	17,901	14,352	12,891
Administrative facility	3,592	3,405	3,900	3,401	3,439	3,704
Acquisition and development	9,479	9,690	9,276	9,873	8,705	8,403
Wildlife	995	741	1,497	2,176	2,582	1,306
Fish	752	314	552	220	227	185
Forestry	1,572	285	314	1,070	625	643

Wisconsin Department of Natural Resources expenditures, continued

Program	2016–17 ($1,000)	2017–18 ($1,000)	2018–19 ($1,000)	2019–20 ($1,000)	2020–21 ($1,000)	2021–22 ($1,000)
Southern forests	379	327	233	475	722	707
Parks	2,310	1,639	3,492	2,649	2,457	3,166
Endangered resources	320	254	85	121	55	57
Facilities and lands	3,142	5,530	1,529	1,657	966	1,532
Property management	—	600	1,574	1,505	1,070	807
Law Enforcement	4	—	—	—	1	—
Water resources	5	—	—	—	—	—
Administration	**21,986**	**24,191**	**22,180**	**23,751**	**26,012**	**23,916**
Administration	1,906	1,437	1,486	1,593	1,510	1,668
Legal services	2,158	2,210	2,439	2,450	2,539	2,638
Management and budget	427	640	446	612	562	384
Facility rental	7,651	7,498	7,676	7,524	7,646	7,570
Nonbudget accounts[1]	9,844	12,406	10,133	11,572	13,755	11,656
Internal services (IS)	**20,287**	**31,193**	**32,312**	**32,884**	**32,450**	**34,053**
Finance	6,837	6,893	6,329	6,396	6,487	7,073
Facilities and lands	—	9,164	8,064	8,338	8,318	8,719
Technology services	9,691	8,840	10,812	11,601	11,284	11,716
Human resources	3,759	2,686	2,900	2,645	2,694	2,354
IS program management	—	3,610	4,207	3,904	3,667	4,191
External Services (EX)	**89,170**	**87,062**	**96,464**	**96,527**	**99,515**	**99,280**
Watershed management	14,455	14,321	16,490	17,505	20,134	9,283
Waterways	—	—	—	—	—	10,621
Office of communication	923	723	728	1,246	1,224	1,213
Community financial assistance	56,611	55,920	61,365	60,714	60,581	60,705
Customer & outreach services	11,143	9,957	10,473	10,047	10,017	9,513
Environmental analysis & sustainability	3,084	5,123	5,795	6,104	6,523	6,984
EX program management	2,954	1,018	1,613	911	1,036	961
Total	**596,389**	**585,491**	**631,951**	**619,321**	**630,648**	**629,031**

Note: Subtotals and total do not add due to rounding.
—Represents zero.
1. Includes gifts, donations, and non-budget appropriations.
Source: Wisconsin Department of Natural Resources, departmental data, March 2023.

Wisconsin Department of Natural Resources land acquisition acres

Fiscal year	Northern forests	Southern forests	Natural areas	Parks	Wild rivers	Wildlife mgt.	Fisheries mgt.	Other	Total
2000[1]	496	110	3,301	3,705	16,135	11,800	2,808	136	38,489
2005	6,578	475	7,477	3,842	10,692	5,385	2,308	329	37,086
2010	8,547	37	3,498	1,000	818	3,767	785	73	18,525
2015	14,446	10	455	1,049	81	1,404	843	218	18,506
2016	22,340	92	245	358	4	6,671	358	85	30,152
2017	7,285	44	1,040	359	146	990	355	12	10,230
2018	20,816	1	4	17	21	844	444	3	22,150
2019	14,392	—	—	108	—	356	339	10	15,205
2020	—	—	—	412	69	322	182	—	985
2021	843	—	51	287	29	399	166	—	1,775
2022	11,720	—	25	916	104	2,919	91	—	15,775
Total	**336,949**	**7,462**	**78,120**	**42,072**	**106,791**	**128,618**	**47,548**	**6,883**	**754,443**

—Represents zero.
1. The Stewardship 2000 program replaced the Warren Knowles-Gaylord Nelson Stewardship Program in 2000.
Source: Wisconsin Department of Natural Resources, Bureau of Facilities and Lands, departmental data, April 2023.

Wisconsin Department of Natural Resources land acquisition cost

Fiscal year	Northern forests ($1,000)	Southern forests ($1,000)	Natural areas ($1,000)	Parks ($1,000)	Wild rivers ($1,000)	Wildlife mgt. ($1,000)	Fisheries mgt. ($1,000)	Other ($1,000)	Total ($1,000)
2000[1]	550	403	3,472	2,734	12,633	9,061	2,861	352	32,066
2005	2,418	3,050	4,993	16,693	3,591	8,164	5,034	401	44,345
2010	5,867	272	5,448	2,881	2,119	6,693	2,232	122	25,634
2015	1,154	30	782	884	899	2,315	1,390	40	7,493
2016	189	660	719	1,273	7	1,328	682	40	4,896
2017	213	250	2,148	74	520	192	369	—	3,767
2018	3	—	—	—	—	60	71	—	134
2019	4,341	—	—	86	—	176	462	1,100	6,165
2020	—	—	—	693	186	635	528	—	2,042
2021	666	—	87	1,300	379	272	278	—	2,982
2022	4,649	187	46	1,714	54	842	203	—	7,695
Total	149,946	32,878	69,025	92,799	97,468	131,494	70,340	11,418	655,367

—Represents zero.

1. The Stewardship 2000 program replaced the Warren Knowles-Gaylord Nelson Stewardship Program in 2000.

Source: Wisconsin Department of Natural Resources, Bureau of Facilities and Lands, departmental data, April 2023.

TRANSPORTATION

Wisconsin road mileage, January 1, 2022

County	Total miles	State trunk system	County trunk system	Local roads City	Local roads Village	Local roads Town	Other roads[1]
Adams	1,450.17	91.39	226.57	22.57	7.68	1,101.96	0.00
Ashland.	1,134.56	119.53	91.26	78.28	6.50	793.98	45.01
Barron.	2,000.84	141.93	290.90	137.44	42.57	1,387.67	0.33
Bayfield.	2,200.43	155.16	172.75	40.65	2.61	1,734.60	94.66
Brown.	2,376.89	190.10	362.95	525.64	613.48	672.02	12.70
Buffalo	1,041.73	147.99	317.85	57.26	6.66	508.04	3.93
Burnett	1,574.95	106.34	220.05	0.00	37.26	1,170.34	40.96
Calumet	882.12	94.73	130.92	131.61	135.93	388.93	0.00
Chippewa . . .	2,152.01	210.28	489.17	188.96	108.29	1,137.19	18.12
Clark.	2,192.07	157.37	300.98	97.12	23.94	1,565.68	46.98
Columbia. . . .	1,739.95	277.83	357.20	120.20	72.81	911.91	0.00
Crawford	1,089.53	182.73	132.48	49.35	66.15	653.12	5.70
Dane	4,268.30	401.19	512.76	1,317.69	510.82	1,516.34	9.50
Dodge	2,075.82	238.13	538.56	214.70	85.38	982.53	16.52
Door.	1,269.03	101.62	295.55	77.41	45.79	748.66	0.00
Douglas.	2,095.71	161.60	336.72	190.66	82.35	1,228.75	95.63
Dunn	1,760.98	205.41	425.25	94.77	43.02	992.53	0.00
Eau Claire. . . .	1,608.99	150.08	420.58	383.69	14.30	620.84	19.50
Florence	554.56	66.90	49.12	0.00	0.00	379.38	59.16
Fond du Lac . .	1,795.89	199.47	384.12	236.57	58.91	916.24	0.58
Forest	1,114.40	152.41	109.06	25.48	0.00	755.66	71.79
Grant	2,132.33	259.19	310.36	139.98	76.98	1,343.67	2.15
Green	1,263.97	122.36	277.84	100.34	41.10	722.33	0.00
Green Lake. . .	703.17	69.88	228.27	70.64	6.35	328.03	0.00
Iowa.	1,321.28	169.74	366.83	58.16	54.14	672.41	0.00
Iron	801.67	113.57	67.26	29.39	0.00	528.28	63.17
Jackson.	1,478.25	185.97	231.11	29.42	23.53	983.38	24.84
Jefferson	1,447.15	179.65	256.30	246.50	38.70	724.22	1.78
Juneau	1,530.40	192.03	234.17	54.41	35.63	1,002.05	12.11
Kenosha	1,111.08	116.83	248.59	324.81	333.75	84.94	2.16
Kewaunee . . .	829.32	61.80	219.04	42.51	22.88	483.09	0.00
La Crosse	1,219.96	156.51	281.02	286.78	95.02	399.51	1.12
Lafayette	1,160.70	126.79	272.23	29.65	34.79	697.24	0.00
Langlade	1,159.21	143.36	271.04	56.85	7.69	672.06	8.21
Lincoln	1,321.80	155.44	270.74	104.20	0.00	764.17	27.25
Manitowoc. . .	1,663.01	154.66	283.60	240.85	51.51	932.39	0.00
Marathon. . . .	3,390.30	276.67	614.26	293.56	429.67	1,769.66	6.48
Marinette. . . .	2,362.51	154.31	334.28	116.58	36.15	1,487.19	234.00
Marquette . . .	860.59	87.44	237.22	9.50	31.60	494.76	0.07
Menominee . .	455.02	40.74	36.51	0.00	0.00	81.67	296.10
Milwaukee . . .	3,028.60	254.53	140.20	2,325.56	308.31	0.00	0.00
Monroe	1,649.14	238.33	344.01	107.73	36.77	920.20	2.10
Oconto	2,055.82	149.83	318.59	73.55	10.99	1,457.47	45.39
Oneida	1,722.95	159.52	171.18	56.54	0.00	1,294.81	40.90
Outagamie. . .	2,040.16	186.89	343.70	386.05	251.51	864.51	7.50
Ozaukee	953.57	82.38	155.51	325.19	118.76	271.73	0.00
Pepin	462.27	48.58	154.72	14.49	11.25	233.23	0.00
Pierce	1,321.97	164.19	248.68	73.06	53.71	774.55	7.78
Polk	1,989.61	159.22	331.37	44.47	108.66	1,335.60	10.29
Portage.	1,906.49	157.82	433.85	143.31	147.72	1,023.79	0.00
Price	1,442.96	155.25	220.05	38.11	20.04	1,000.67	8.84
Racine.	1,333.92	152.57	163.09	294.15	501.33	222.78	0.00
Richland	1,130.65	150.12	296.49	29.61	20.76	633.14	0.53

Wisconsin road mileage, January 1, 2022, continued

County	Total miles	State trunk system	County trunk system	City	Village	Town	Other roads[1]
Rock.......	2,099.56	255.65	211.06	591.44	26.41	1,014.96	0.04
Rusk.......	1,243.10	105.32	255.05	34.45	37.50	787.66	23.12
St. Croix.....	1,963.05	205.07	334.42	176.02	112.40	1,133.46	1.68
Sauk.......	1,835.27	221.19	309.10	124.09	125.88	1,049.01	6.00
Sawyer.....	1,510.10	161.32	228.94	23.86	17.95	1,052.63	25.40
Shawano....	1,766.27	178.83	293.58	57.95	68.68	1,125.73	41.50
Sheboygan...	1,570.32	166.75	449.14	266.94	94.89	591.58	1.02
Taylor......	1,458.67	110.22	248.42	30.74	28.06	1,023.07	18.16
Trempealeau..	1,371.43	176.46	291.59	79.28	36.12	779.21	8.77
Vernon.....	1,657.04	214.02	285.22	60.14	42.73	1,052.41	2.52
Vilas.......	1,556.74	136.21	204.25	24.68	0.00	1,106.57	85.03
Walworth....	1,539.38	216.08	193.19	173.22	159.31	796.99	0.59
Washburn...	1,417.32	137.16	198.90	52.59	22.05	907.78	98.84
Washington..	1,549.97	182.82	176.61	208.31	370.95	611.28	0.00
Waukesha...	3,134.67	220.33	404.54	1,130.02	770.38	609.40	0.00
Waupaca....	1,664.26	197.38	333.46	141.52	27.75	964.15	0.00
Waushara....	1,331.46	132.36	333.40	18.70	56.25	790.75	0.00
Winnebago..	1,584.76	168.08	217.05	457.86	119.86	621.91	0.00
Wood......	1,799.93	185.92	324.22	307.66	62.71	906.52	12.90
Total.......	115,682.06	11,749.53	19,819.05	14,095.47	7,053.63	61,294.97	1,669.41

1. Includes county forest, U.S. Forest Service, U.S. Fish and Wildlife Service, U.S. National Park Service, U.S. Army Corps of Engineers, and university and campus roads.

Source: Wisconsin Department of Transportation, Division of Transportation Investment Management, departmental data, January 2023.

Wisconsin road surfaces, January 1, 2022

Surface	Miles	Percent
Bituminous or higher[1].	92,572	80.0
Gravel[2] or soil-surfaced.	15,593	13.5
Sealcoat[3].	5,760	5.0
Graded and drained.	1,641	1.4
Unimproved.	116	0.1
Total.	115,682	100

1. Includes paved roads made of asphalt, concrete, or brick. 2. Includes unpaved roads made of gravel without an asphalt sealcoat. 3. Includes unpaved gravel roads treated with an asphalt sealcoat.

Source: Wisconsin Department of Transportation, Division of Transportation Investment Management, departmental data, January 2023.

Wisconsin motor vehicles by type

Fiscal year (ending June 30)	Total	Autos	Trucks[1]	Trailers, semi-trailers	Motor homes	Buses	Motor-cycles	Mopeds	Auto-Cycles[2]
1930.....	819,718	700,251	115,883	X	X	554	3,030	X	X
1940.....	874,652	741,583	123,742	5,144	X	675	3,508	X	X
1950.....	1,157,221	921,194	209,083	14,124	X	2,465	10,355	X	X
1960.....	1,598,693	1,303,679	246,353	31,502	X	5,184	11,975	X	X
1970.....	2,205,662	1,762,681	317,096	64,065	X	8,178	53,642	X	X
1980.....	3,417,748	2,509,904	558,840	102,256	17,071	13,775	205,786	10,116	X

Statistics and Reference: Transportation | 719

Wisconsin motor vehicles by type, continued

Fiscal year (ending June 30)	Total	Autos	Trucks[1]	Trailers, semi-trailers	Motor homes	Buses	Motor-cycles	Mopeds	Auto-Cycles[2]
1990	3,834,608	2,456,175	1,045,583	123,061	21,095	15,081	149,268	24,345	X
2000	4,652,048	2,405,408	1,813,385	214,344	24,427	15,587	160,920	17,977	X
2010	5,525,794	2,333,029	2,416,295	426,092	19,615	13,376	269,316	48,071	X
2011	5,564,794	2,300,243	2,445,056	434,782	18,792	13,745	296,808	55,368	X
2012	5,551,411	2,274,596	2,473,072	447,195	18,535	14,169	274,553	49,291	X
2013	5,671,185	2,276,007	2,548,029	460,542	18,187	10,598	301,477	56,345	X
2014	5,697,808	2,255,966	2,609,402	479,237	18,584	12,615	275,120	46,884	X
2015	5,823,555	2,229,199	2,703,329	502,301	18,766	13,324	303,577	53,059	X
2016	5,870,311	2,192,295	2,802,029	525,513	18,760	13,739	274,787	43,188	X
2017	5,985,094	2,132,984	2,919,745	546,535	18,779	14,138	303,541	49,372	X
2018	6,047,860	2,080,739	3,050,820	571,827	19,005	10,164	275,301	40,004	X
2019	6,195,594	2,019,545	3,197,066	596,396	19,282	12,525	305,278	45,502	X
2020	6,072,320	1,886,351	3,245,480	604,370	18,199	12,896	269,335	35,593	96
2021	6,205,260	1,803,318	3,392,950	633,315	19,694	12,947	301,689	40,688	659
2022	6,373,249	1,780,279	3,570,020	671,017	20,760	13,350	281,039	35,957	827

X–Not applicable.
1. "Trucks" includes minivans and sport utility vehicles. 2. An autocycle is a motor vehicle that has 3 wheels, a steering wheel, and seating that does not require a driver or passenger to straddle or sit astride it and is manufactured to meet certain safety standards for motorcycles.
Sources: Wisconsin Secretary of State, *Biennial Report—1928–30*; Wisconsin Highway Commission, *Biennial Reports—1933–35, 1938–40*; Wisconsin Motor Vehicle Department, *Wisconsin Motor Vehicle Registrations—Fiscal Years 1944–45* through *1964–65*; Wisconsin Department of Transportation, *Wisconsin Motor Vehicle Registrations—Fiscal Year 1979–80, 1980*, and prior issues, and *Wisconsin Transportation Facts* (periodical); departmental data, March 2023.

Wisconsin motor vehicle crashes

	Total licensed drivers	Crashes[1] Total	Fatal	Injury	Persons killed	Persons injured	Miles traveled (millions)	Fatality rate[2]	Fatal crash rate[3]
2000	3,667,497	139,510	718	43,145	801	63,890	57,266	1.4	1.25
2005	4,049,450	125,174	700	37,515	801	53,462	60,018	1.33	1.17
2010	4,114,622	108,808	517	29,380	562	40,889	59,420	0.95	0.87
2015	4,206,700	121,615	513	29,846	555	41,655	62,140	0.89	0.83
2016	4,250,018	129,051	524	31,066	588	43,669	63,870	0.92	0.82
2017	4,286,263	139,870	539	30,614	594	42,178	65,324	0.91	0.83
2018	4,288,173	144,212	517	29,959	575	41,125	65,884	0.87	0.78
2019	4,296,646	145,288	511	28,791	551	39,723	66,341	0.83	0.77
2020	4,315,892	114,697	540	23,747	592	32,374	57,571	1.03	0.94
2021	4,361,931	128,296	546	26,209	595	35,676	65,003	0.92	0.84

1. A motor vehicle crash is defined as an event caused by a single variable or chain of variables. The property damage threshold for a reportable crash was raised from $500 to $1,000, effective January 1, 1996. 2. Number of fatalities per 100 million vehicle miles traveled. 3. Number of fatal crashes per 100 million vehicle miles traveled.
Source: Wisconsin Department of Transportation, *2021 Wisconsin Traffic Crash Facts*; departmental data, January 2023.

Wisconsin fatal crashes by road type

	Total	Interstate	State	County	Local
2000	718	39	311	143	225
2005	700	42	284	163	211
2010	517	32	230	105	150

Wisconsin fatal crashes by road type, continued

Year	Total	Interstate	State	County	Local
2015	513	36	223	93	161
2016	524	31	211	110	172
2017	539	36	230	111	162
2018	517	40	223	124	130
2019	511	45	226	115	125
2020	540	32	223	125	160
2021	546	51	223	129	143

Source: Wisconsin Department of Transportation, *2021 Wisconsin Traffic Crash Facts*; departmental data, December 2023.

Wisconsin drivers involved in crashes, 2021

Age of drivers	Total licensed drivers Number	% of drivers	Drivers involved in crashes Number[1]	% of total crashes	Fatal	Injury	Property damage
14 and under	—	—	185	0.1	3	60	122
15–24	524,753	12.00%	43,408	22.1	155	10,287	32,966
25–34	706,721	16.20%	37,570	19.1	167	9,289	28,114
35–44	706,709	16.20%	29,784	15.1	149	7,106	22,529
45–54	654,544	15.00%	24,136	12.3	121	5,783	18,232
55–64	777,366	17.80%	23,455	11.9	139	5,468	17,848
65–74	618,431	14.20%	14,192	7.2	89	3,381	10,722
75–84	284,910	6.50%	6,403	3.3	38	1,521	4,844
85 and over	88,497	2.00%	1,649	0.8	19	412	1,218
Unknown	—	—	16,060	8.2	11	1,617	14,432
Total	**4,361,931**		**196,842**		**891**	**44,924**	**151,027**

—Represents zero.

1. Figure indicates the number of times a driver in this age group was involved in a crash. If a driver had more than one crash, the driver would be counted more than once.

Source: Wisconsin Department of Transportation, *2021 Wisconsin Traffic Crash Facts*; departmental data, January 2023.

Wisconsin motorcycle crashes

	Total registered motorcycles	Motorcycle crashes Total	Fatal	Personal injury	Property damage	Motorcyclist fatalities[1] Total[2]	No helmet	Helmet
2000	175,486	2,078	76	1,760	242	78	57	15
2005	239,938	2,680	91	2,277	312	92	69	22
2010	343,878	2,426	97	1,959	370	98	72	23
2015	365,878	2,221	80	1,724	417	81	62	14
2016	334,950	2,250	78	1,733	439	82	63	16
2017	363,094	2,206	73	1,741	392	76	45	27
2018	331,356	1,967	76	1,511	380	81	52	28
2019	358,964	1,806	81	1,369	356	82	53	28
2020	336,935	2,104	110	1,616	378	113	81	32
2021	321,872	2,082	115	1,575	392	120	83	35

1. Number of motorcyclists killed includes both drivers and passengers. 2. Includes fatalities where there is no data on whether the motorcyclist was wearing a helmet.

Source: Wisconsin Department of Transportation, *2021 Wisconsin Traffic Crash Facts*; departmental data, January 2023.

Possible contributing circumstances to Wisconsin motor vehicle crashes, 2021

	Crashes			
	Total	Fatal	Injury	Property damage
Driver				
Failure to control	19,315	154	5,628	13,533
Failed to yield right-of-way	16,956	68	5,859	11,029
Operated motor vehicle in inattentive, careless, negligent, or erratic manner	11,139	69	3,430	7,640
Following too close	9,614	9	2,525	7,080
Speed too fast for conditions	9,597	74	2,366	7,157
Looked but did not see	8,352	18	1,673	6,661
Failed to keep in designated lane	7,836	99	2,159	5,578
Other contributing action	7,626	37	2,010	5,579
Ran off roadway	5,836	81	2,005	3,750
Unsafe backing	5,314	3	212	5,099
Exceed speed limit	3,757	120	1,591	2,046
Operated motor vehicle in aggressive/reckless manner	3,326	61	1,146	2,119
Disregarded red light	2,976	12	1,343	1,621
Improper turn	2,860	4	450	2,406
Disregarded stop sign	2,151	36	934	1,181
Over-correcting/over-steering	1,398	23	483	892
Swerved or avoided due to wind, slippery surface, motor vehicle, object, non-motorist in roadway, etc.	1,218	12	338	868
Wrong side or wrong way	1,044	31	395	618
Improper overtaking / passing left	985	16	230	739
Disregarded other traffic control	869	7	296	566
Improper overtaking / passing right	679	2	150	527
Disregarded other road markings	566	5	164	397
Racing	98	5	38	55
Unknown	21,753	165	3,226	18,362
Highway				
Road surface condition (wet, icy, snow, slush, etc.)	7,063	28	1,297	5,738
Backup due to regular congestion	2,504	3	660	1,841
Work zone (construction/maintenance/utility)	952	6	249	697
Backup due to prior crash	589	2	153	434
Backup due to prior non-recurring incident	410	1	114	295
Obstruction in roadway	314	4	57	253
Visibility obscured	314	1	101	212
Other debris	150	3	20	127
Debris prior to crash	131	1	23	107
Loose gravel	120	1	56	63
Rut, holes, bumps	93	1	35	57
Traffic control device inoperative, missing, or obscured	83	—	28	55
Narrow shoulder	50	—	10	40
Soft shoulder	29	—	15	14
Rough pavement	27	1	9	17
Low shoulder	24	—	13	11
Non-highway work	12	—	4	8
Sign obscured/missing	12	—	4	8
Narrow bridge	3	—	1	2
Worn, travel-polished surface	3	—	1	2
Toll booth/plaza related	1	—	—	1
Other	378	2	84	292
Vehicle				
Tires	1,079	8	268	803
Brakes	981	2	280	699
Body, doors	615	3	155	457

Possible contributing circumstances to Wisconsin motor vehicle crashes, 2021, continued

	Crashes			
	Total	Fatal	Injury	Property damage
Steering	408	1	108	299
Vehicle, continued				
Wheels	378	2	89	287
Head lamps	209	3	64	142
Power train	209	2	68	139
Windows/wind shield	206	1	64	141
Other disabled	170	1	52	117
Suspension	138	—	46	92
Coupling device/trailer hitch/safety chains	110	—	19	91
Turn signals	96	1	30	65
Mirrors	67	1	19	47
Tail lamps	65	1	20	44
Stop lamps	49	—	16	33
Disabled due to prior crash	46	1	10	35
Exhaust system	29	—	10	19
Wipers	24	—	5	19
Other	642	3	110	529

Note: Numbers represent the number of times a possible contributing circumstance was cited and not the total number of accidents.
—Represents zero.
Source: Wisconsin Department of Transportation, departmental data, January 2023.

Wisconsin urban transit systems

	Revenue miles (1,000)	Revenue passengers (1,000)	Operating revenue[1] ($1,000)
1950	53,362	288,996	22,692
1960	34,950	130,299	20,665
1970	28,371	80,172	22,078
1980	33,943	88,756	29,631
1990	33,685	78,215	39,594
2000	42,447	89,821	58,785
2010	52,579	74,717	87,288
2011	52,316	77,533	82,640
2012	51,214	75,290	83,005
2013	50,973	74,694	83,522
2014	52,003	72,281	76,310
2015	53,268	67,281	71,737
2016	52,816	63,346	68,149
2017	54,078	59,955	68,422
2018	52,834	57,913	71,368
2019	53,202	54,046	69,426
2020	44,366	31,618	39,441
2021	46,086	29,708	42,740

1. As recognized by the Wisconsin Department of Transportation.
Sources: Wisconsin Department of Transportation, departmental data through February 2023; (former) Division of Transportation Assistance *Wisconsin Urban Bus System Annual Report 1989* and prior issues.

Wisconsin mass transit systems, January 2023

Urban bus	Rural/commuter bus	Shared-ride taxi[1]	
Appleton	Bay Area Rural Transit	Baraboo	Ozaukee County
Beloit	Dunn County	Beaver Dam	Plover
Eau Claire	Kenosha County[2]	Berlin	Prairie du Chien
Fond du Lac	Lac du Flambeau Tribe	Black River Falls	Prairie du Sac/
Green Bay	La Crosse County[2]	Chippewa Falls	Sauk City
Janesville	Manitowoc[5]	Clark County/Neillsville	Reedsburg
Kenosha	Menominee Regional Transit	Clintonville	Rhinelander
Madison	Merrill	Door County	Richland Center
Milwaukee County[2]	Oneida Tribe	Edgerton	Ripon
Monona[2]	Oneida-Vilas Counties Transit	Fitchburg	River Falls
Oshkosh	Commission	Fort Atkinson	Shawano
Racine[3]	Ozaukee County Express[3]	Grant County	Stoughton
Sheboygan	Platteville[3]	Hartford	Sun Prairie[5]
Superior[4]	Racine Commuter[3]	Jefferson	Tomah
Waukesha (city)[2]	Rusk County	La Crosse County	Viroqua/Westby
Waukesha County[2]	Sawyer County	Lake Mills	Walworth County
Wausau	Stevens Point	Marinette	Washington County
	Verona	Marshfield	Watertown
	Washington County Express[2]	Mauston	Waupaca
		Medford	Waupun
		Monroe	West Bend
		New Richmond	Whitewater
		Onalaska	Wisconsin Rapids

1. Taxi services are privately contracted except for Grant County and the City of Hartford, where they are publicly owned and operated. 2. Privately contracted. (Note: Waukesha (city) and Waukesha (county) jointly own the inter-urban Waukesha Metro Transit.) 3. Privately managed. 4. Contracted with Duluth Transit Authority. 5. Sun Prairie also providing commuter bus service through contract with Madison Metro.
Source: Wisconsin Department of Transportation, Division of Transportation Investment Management, departmental data, February 2023.

Wisconsin railroad mileage, usage, and revenue

	No. of rail-roads	Mileage operated in Wisconsin[1] Road[2]	Track[3]	Freight traffic Tons (1,000)	Ton-miles[4] (1,000)	Revenue ($1,000)	Passenger traffic Passengers (1,000)	Miles[5] (1,000)	Revenue ($1,000)
1920....	35	7,546	11,615	100,991	9,052,084	92,826	20,188	960,569	28,646
1930....	27	7,231	11,583	83,672	6,908,656	78,747	4,799	466,154	14,071
1940....	22	6,646	10,484	87,980	6,910,647	69,941	3,952	445,938	8,201
1950....	20	6,337	10,000	121,576	10,850,178	141,762	5,575	646,353	14,933
1960....	18	6,195	9,625	93,475	9,096,855	134,065	3,127	383,457	9,800
1970....	15	5,965	9,127	97,130	13,432,055	191,764	1,463	138,572	4,264
1980[6]...	21	5,192	7,990	101,008	14,727,522	453,977	174	1,122	54
1990....	15	4,415	6,125	116,099	14,436,776	455,541	112	783	63
2000....	12	3,548	4,956	151,573	21,321,266	580,678	NA	NA	NA
2010....	10	3,408	4,594	108,206	21,394,264	771,203	NA	NA	NA
2011....	10	3,402	4,606	106,527	24,891,634	971,369	NA	NA	NA
2012....	9	3,482	4,669	111,472	25,972,105	1,146,602	NA	NA	NA
2013....	9	3,489	4,676	126,154	28,734,278	1,288,345	NA	NA	NA
2014....	9	3,482	4,668	135,210	30,455,440	1,511,135	NA	NA	NA
2015....	9	3,005	4,176	130,219	29,220,895	1,237,662	NA	NA	NA
2016....	9	3,018	4,189	114,986	27,804,936	994,275	NA	NA	NA
2017....	9	2,995	4,111	138,393	31,589,253	1,155,539	NA	NA	NA
2018....	9	3,044	4,166	148,156	32,570,938	1,157,136	NA	NA	NA
2019....	9	3,036	4,156	135,129	31,242,722	1,140,078	NA	NA	NA
2020....	9	2,974	4,094	111,892	27,800,617	859,461	NA	NA	NA

Wisconsin railroad mileage, usage, and revenue, continued

	No. of rail- roads	Mileage operated in Wisconsin[1] Road[2]	Track[3]	Freight traffic Tons (1,000)	Ton-miles[4] (1,000)	Revenue ($1,000)	Passenger traffic Passengers (1,000)	Miles[5] (1,000)	Revenue ($1,000)
2021....	9	3,021	4,156	117,171	28,775,369	984,802	NA	NA	NA

NA–Not available.

1. In order to avoid duplication, mileage shown is exclusive of trackage rights. 2. Road mileage is the measurement of stone roadbed in miles. 3. Track mileage is the measurement of track (2 steel rails) on roadbeds in miles. 4. A ton-mile is the movement of one ton (2,000 pounds) of cargo over the distance of one mile. 5. Passenger miles are the combination of the number of passengers carried on Wisconsin trains and the miles traveled by the passengers while within Wisconsin boundaries. 6. Intercity passenger service operated by Amtrak after May 1, 1971.

Source: Office of the Wisconsin Commissioner of Railroads, departmental data, March 2021.

Wisconsin harbor commerce tonnage, 2020

Harbors[1]	Coal and lignite	Petroleum and petroleum products	Chemi- cals and related products	Crude materials- inedible (except fuels)	Primary mfd. goods	Food and farm products	Mfd. equipment, machinery, and products	Total
Lake Superior	4,965,639	188,192	64,092	18,190,707	151,804	1,369,342	170,373	25,100,149
Duluth- Superior	4,965,639	186,108	64,092	18,190,162	151,804	1,369,342	143,963	25,071,110
Bayfield.....	—	1,042	—	535	—	—	13,285	14,862
La Pointe....	—	1,042	—	10	—	—	13,125	14,177
Lake Michigan	222,034	306,768	39,842	2,804,171	1,592,339	198,128	16,860	5,180,142
Milwaukee	—	80,469	14,245	1,501,637	981,219	198,128	2,461	2,778,159
Green Bay	222,034	224,519	25,597	1,144,482	397,479	—	8,289	2,022,400
Manitowoc	—	—	—	101,251	153,015	—	—	254,266
Marinette- Menominee	—	—	—	47,593	59,267	—	80	106,940
Detroit Harbor[2]	—	1,780	—	—	—	—	4,932	6,712
Kenosha	—	—	—	5,690	—	—	420	6,110
Kewaunee	—	—	—	3,518	—	—	—	3,518
Sturgeon Bay	—	—	—	—	1,359	—	658	2,017
Sheboygan	—	—	—	—	—	—	20	20
Total.......	5,187,673	494,960	103,934	20,994,878	1,744,143	1,567,470	187,233	30,280,291

Note: Tonnage reported in short tons (one short ton equals 2,000 pounds).
— Represents zero; Mfd–Manufactured.

1. Harbors with reported commerce. 2. Washington Island.

Source: U.S. Army Corps of Engineers, Navigation Data Center, Ports and Waterways (database), Calendar Year 2020, Region 3, at http://cwbi-ndc-nav.s3-website-us-east-1.amazonaws.com/files/wcsc/webpub/#/?year=2020&regionId=3 [May 2023].

Wisconsin airport usage by certified air carriers

	2019 Passen- gers	Enplaned freight (lb.)	2020 Passen- gers	Enplaned freight (lb.)	2021 Passen- gers	Enplaned freight (lb.)
General Mitchell International (Milwaukee)............	3,374,073	75,874,000	1,309,967	74,298,000	2,231,010	606,695,536
Dane County Regional (Madison)...............	1,162,024	13,061,697	95,753	188,370,514	699,167	183,122,476

Wisconsin airport usage by certified air carriers, continued

	2020 Passengers	2020 Enplaned freight (lb.)	2021 Passengers	2021 Enplaned freight (lb.)	2022 Passengers	2022 Enplaned freight (lb.)
Green Bay-Austin Straubel International (Green Bay)	386,737	10,805,803	190,282	8,203,186	352,006	112,098,150
Appleton International (Appleton)	347,263	174,403	144,316	165,176	269,025	225,790
Central Wisconsin (Mosinee)	141,123	619,262	56,782	638,756	98,087	1,763,711
La Crosse Municipal (La Crosse)	97,069	X	44,050	X	82,683	X
Chippewa Valley Regional (Eau Claire)	27,203	1,420,686	13,652	1,419,884	26,252	861,321
Rhinelander-Oneida County (Rhinelander)	24,268	X	10,086	X	19,860	X
Total	5,559,760	101,955,851	1,864,888	273,095,516	3,778,090	904,766,984

Note: A certified air carrier is an airline that is registered by the Federal Aviation Administration.
X–Not applicable.
Source: Wisconsin Department of Transportation, departmental data, March 2023.

Number of landing facilities in Wisconsin

Type	2019	2020	2022
Airports in the State Airport System (public use)[1]	97	97	97
Privately owned, public use airports	31	30	31
Private use airports	426	420	283
Heliports[2]	155	109	111
Seaplane bases[2]	27	16	16

1. Eligible for federal and/or state funding. 2. Public and private.
Source: Wisconsin Department of Transportation, departmental data, March 2023.

Wisconsin automobile and truck registrations by fuel type

	Total	Gasoline	FFV or ethanol[1]	Diesel	Gas-electric	Electric	Other[2]	Unknown[3]
2013	4,850,998	4,083,715	404,073	188,114	43,858	316	4,203	126,719
2014	4,904,992	4,067,474	459,092	196,861	50,327	447	4,047	126,744
2015	4,966,820	4,079,094	500,574	201,660	54,573	587	3,632	126,700
2016	5,027,775	4,096,159	539,764	205,331	59,588	828	3,514	122,591
2017	5,118,517	4,146,597	570,581	213,193	65,523	1,723	3,087	117,813
2018	5,175,153	4,173,498	592,190	219,703	70,872	2,940	2,728	113,222
2019	5,238,318	4,207,511	606,183	233,482	76,850	4,460	2,418	107,414
2020	5,216,311	4,180,089	604,686	241,706	82,177	6,109	2,194	99,350
2021	5,181,106	4,152,046	592,155	239,252	93,448	8,909	2,014	93,282

Note: Trucks include heavy trucks, pick-ups, vans, and most SUVs.
FFV–Flexible fuel vehicles.
1. FFVs are capable of using either gasoline or ethanol blends up to 85% ethanol (E-85 fuel). A small number (fewer than 1,000 for a given year) of the motor vehicles reported under this category are designed to run on pure ethanol. 2. "Other" fuels include compressed natural gas (CNG), propane, and methanol. 3. Fuel type not specified because it could not be decoded from the Vehicle Identification Number (VIN) or was otherwise unavailable. Applicant disclosure of fuel type is not required.
Source: Wisconsin Department of Transportation, Division of Motor Vehicles. https://wisconsindot.gov/Pages/about-wisdot/newsroom/statistics/veh-info.aspx.

NEWS MEDIA

Correspondents covering the 2023 Wisconsin Legislature

Organization	Correspondents
Print/web	
Associated Press	Scott Bauer, Todd Richmond, Harm Venhuizen
Capital Times	Jack Kelly
Daily Reporter/Wisconsin Law Journal	Ethan Duran
Isthmus	Judith Davidoff
MacIver News Service	Bill Osmulski, Heather Smith
Milwaukee Journal Sentinel	Molly Beck, Laura Schulte, Jessie Opoien
Spectrum News	Anthony DaBruzzi
Up North News	Christina Lorey, Pat Kreitlow, Cherita Booker
Wheeler Report	Gwyn Guenther, Trevor Guenther
Wisconsin Examiner	Ruth Conniff, Erik Gunn, Isiah Holmes, Henry Redman, Baylor Spears
Wisconsin State Journal	Mitchell Schmidt, Alexander Shur
Wispolitics.com	JR Ross, Adam Kelnhofer, Kate Morton
Radio	
Wisconsin Public Radio	Shawn Johnson, Anya van Wagtendonk
Wisconsin Radio Network	Bob Hague, Raymond Neupert, Ted Ehlen
Television	
WDJT-TV (CBS 58) Milwaukee/ Telemundo Wisconsin	Emilee Fannon
WisconsinEye	Jon Henkes, Lisa Pugh, John Schroeder, Matthew Peters
Wisconsin Public Television	Frederica Freyberg, Zac Schultz, Marisa Wojcik, Steven Potter, Nathan Denzin, Murv Seymour, Kristian Knutsen
WISC-TV (CBS 3) (Madison)	Naomi Kowles, Will Kenneally
WKOW-TV (ABC 27) (Madison)	Tony Galli

Source: Data collected by the Wisconsin Legislative Reference Bureau with the assistance of the Wisconsin Capitol Correspondents Association, January 2023.

■ ■ ■

THE WISCONSIN CONSTITUTION

Last amended at the April 2023 election

PREAMBLE

ARTICLE I—Declaration of rights
Section
1. Equality; inherent rights
2. Slavery prohibited
3. Free speech; libel
4. Right to assemble and petition
5. Trial by jury; verdict in civil cases
6. Excessive bail; cruel punishments
7. Rights of accused
8. Prosecutions; double jeopardy; self-incrimination; bail; habeas corpus
9. Remedy for wrongs

9m. Victims of crime

10. Treason
11. Searches and seizures
12. Attainder; ex post facto; contracts
13. Private property for public use
14. Feudal tenures; leases; alienation
15. Equal property rights for aliens and citizens
16. Imprisonment for debt
17. Exemption of property of debtors
18. Freedom of worship; liberty of conscience; state religion; public funds
19. Religious tests prohibited
20. Military subordinate to civil power
21. Rights of suitors
22. Maintenance of free government
23. Transportation of school children
24. Use of school buildings
25. Right to keep and bear arms
26. Right to fish, hunt, trap, and take game

ARTICLE II—Boundaries
Section
1. State boundary
2. Enabling act accepted

ARTICLE III—Suffrage
Section
1. Electors
2. Implementation
3. Secret ballot
4. Repealed
5. Repealed
6. Repealed

ARTICLE IV—Legislative
Section
1. Legislative power
2. Legislature, how constituted
3. Apportionment
4. Representatives to the assembly, how chosen
5. Senators, how chosen
6. Qualifications of legislators
7. Organization of legislature; quorum; compulsory attendance
8. Rules; contempts; expulsion
9. Officers
10. Journals; open doors; adjournments
11. Meeting of legislature
12. Ineligibility of legislators to office
13. Ineligibility of federal officers
14. Filling vacancies
15. Exemption from arrest and civil process

16. Privilege in debate
17. Enactment of laws
18. Title of private bills
19. Origin of bills
20. Yeas and nays
21. Repealed
22. Powers of county boards
23. Town and county government
23a. Chief executive officer to approve or veto resolutions or ordinances; proceedings on veto
24. Gambling
25. Stationery and printing
26. Extra compensation; salary change
27. Suits against state
28. Oath of office
29. Militia
30. Elections by legislature
31. Special and private laws prohibited
32. General laws on enumerated subjects
33. Auditing of state accounts
34. Continuity of civil government

ARTICLE V—Executive
Section
1. Governor; lieutenant governor; term
1m. Repealed
1n. Repealed
2. Eligibility
3. Election
4. Powers and duties
5. Repealed
6. Pardoning power
7. Lieutenant governor, when governor
8. Secretary of state, when governor
9. Repealed
10. Governor to approve or veto bills; proceedings on veto

ARTICLE VI—Administrative
Section
1. Election of secretary of state, treasurer and attorney general; term
1m. Repealed
1n. Repealed
1p. Repealed
2. Secretary of state; duties, compensation
3. Treasurer and attorney general; duties, compensation
4. County officers; election, terms, removal; vacancies

ARTICLE VII—Judiciary
Section
1. Impeachment; trial
2. Court system
3. Supreme court: jurisdiction
4. Supreme court: election, chief justice, court system administration
5. Court of appeals
6. Circuit court: boundaries
7. Circuit court: election
8. Circuit court: jurisdiction
9. Judicial elections, vacancies
10. Judges: eligibility to office
11. Disciplinary proceedings
12. Clerks of circuit and supreme courts
13. Justices and judges: removal by address
14. Municipal court
15. Repealed
16. Repealed
17. Repealed
18. Repealed
19. Repealed
20. Repealed
21. Repealed

22. Repealed
23. Repealed
24. Justices and judges: eligibility for office; retirement

Article VIII—Finance
Section

1. Rule of taxation uniform; income, privilege and occupation taxes
2. Appropriations; limitation
3. Credit of state
4. Contracting state debts
5. Annual tax levy to equal expenses
6. Public debt for extraordinary expense; taxation
7. Public debt for public defense; bonding for public purposes
8. Vote on fiscal bills; quorum
9. Evidences of public debt
10. Internal improvements
11. Transportation fund

Article IX—Eminent domain and property of the state
Section

1. Jurisdiction on rivers and lakes; navigable waters
2. Territorial property
3. Ultimate property in lands; escheats

Article X—Education
Section

1. Superintendent of public instruction
2. School fund created; income applied
3. District schools; tuition; sectarian instruction; released time
4. Annual school tax
5. Income of school fund

6. State university; support
7. Commissioners of public lands
8. Sale of public lands

Article XI—Corporations
Section

1. Corporations; how formed
2. Property taken by municipality
3. Municipal home rule; debt limit; tax to pay debt
3a. Acquisition of lands by state and subdivisions; sale of excess
4. General banking law
5. Repealed

Article XII—Amendments
Section

1. Constitutional amendments
2. Constitutional conventions

Article XIII—Miscellaneous provisions
Section

1. Political year; elections
2. Repealed
3. Eligibility to office
4. Great seal
5. Repealed
6. Legislative officers
7. Division of counties
8. Removal of county seats
9. Election or appointment of statutory officers
10. Vacancies in office
11. Passes, franks and privileges
12. Recall of elective officers
13. Marriage

Article XIV—Schedule
Section
1. Effect of change from territory to state
2. Territorial laws continued
3. Repealed
4. Repealed
5. Repealed
6. Repealed
7. Repealed
8. Repealed
9. Repealed
10. Repealed
11. Repealed
12. Repealed
13. Common law continued in force
14. Repealed
15. Repealed
16. Implementing revised structure of judicial branch

PREAMBLE

We, the people of Wisconsin, grateful to Almighty God for our freedom, in order to secure its blessings, form a more perfect government, insure domestic tranquility and promote the general welfare, do establish this constitution.

ARTICLE I—Declaration of rights

Equality; inherent rights. Section 1. All people are born equally free and independent, and have certain inherent rights; among these are life, liberty and the pursuit of happiness; to secure these rights, governments are instituted, deriving their just powers from the consent of the governed.

Slavery prohibited. Section 2. There shall be neither slavery, nor involuntary servitude in this state, otherwise than for the punishment of crime, whereof the party shall have been duly convicted.

Free speech; libel. Section 3. Every person may freely speak, write and publish his sentiments on all subjects, being responsible for the abuse of that right, and no laws shall be passed to restrain or abridge the liberty of speech or of the press. In all criminal prosecutions or indictments for libel, the truth may be given in evidence, and if it shall appear to the jury that the matter charged as libelous be true, and was published with good motives and for justifiable ends, the party shall be acquitted; and the jury shall have the right to determine the law and the fact.

Right to assemble and petition. Section 4. The right of the people peaceably to assemble, to consult for the common good, and to petition the government, or any department thereof, shall never be abridged.

Trial by jury; verdict in civil cases. Section 5. The right of trial by jury shall remain inviolate, and shall extend to all cases at law without regard to the amount in controversy; but a jury trial may be waived by the parties in all cases in the manner prescribed by law. Provided, however, that the legislature may, from time to time, by statute provide that a valid verdict, in civil cases, may be based on the votes of a specified number of the jury, not less than five-sixths thereof.

Excessive bail; cruel punishments. Section 6. Excessive bail shall not be required, nor shall excessive fines be imposed, nor cruel and unusual punishments inflicted.

Rights of accused. Section 7. In all criminal prosecutions the accused shall enjoy the right to be heard by himself and counsel; to demand the nature and cause of the accusation against him; to meet the witnesses face to face; to have compulsory process to compel the attendance of witnesses in his behalf; and in prosecutions by indictment, or information, to a speedy public trial by an impartial jury of the county or district wherein the offense shall have been committed; which county or district shall have been previously ascertained by law.

Prosecutions; double jeopardy; self-incrimination; bail; habeas corpus. Section 8. (1) No person may be held to answer for a criminal offense without due process of law, and no person for the same offense may be put twice in jeopardy of punishment, nor may be compelled in any criminal case to be a witness against himself or herself.

(2) All persons, before conviction, shall be eligible for release under reasonable conditions designed to assure their appearance in court, protect members of the community from serious harm as defined by the legislature by law, or prevent the intimidation of witnesses. Monetary conditions of release may be imposed at or after the initial appearance only upon a finding that there is a reasonable basis to believe that the conditions are necessary to assure appearance in court, or if the person is accused of a violent crime as defined by the legislature by law, only upon a finding that there is a reasonable basis to believe that the conditions are necessary based on the totality of the circumstances, taking into account whether the accused has a previous conviction for a violent crime as defined by the legislature by law, the probability that the accused will fail to appear in court, the need to protect members of the community from serious harm as defined by the legislature by law, the need to prevent the intimidation of witnesses, and the potential affirmative defenses of the accused. The legislature may authorize, by law, courts to revoke a person's release for a violation of a condition of release.

(3) The legislature may by law authorize, but may not require, circuit courts to deny release for a period not to exceed 10 days prior to the hearing required under this subsection to a person who is accused of committing a murder punishable by life imprisonment or a sexual assault punishable by a maximum imprisonment of 20 years, or who is accused of committing or attempting to commit a felony involving serious bodily harm to another or the threat of serious bodily harm to another and who has a previous conviction for committing or attempting to commit a felony involving serious bodily harm to another or the threat of serious bodily harm to another. The legislature may authorize by law, but may not require, circuit courts to continue to deny release to those accused persons for an additional period not to exceed 60 days following the hearing required under this subsection, if there is a requirement that there be a finding by the court based on clear and convincing evidence presented at a hearing that the accused committed the felony and a requirement that there be a finding by the court that available conditions of release will not adequately protect members of the community from serious bodily harm or prevent intimidation of witnesses. Any law enacted under this subsection shall be specific, limited and reasonable. In determining the 10-day and 60-day periods, the court shall omit any period of time found by the court to result from a delay caused by the defendant or a continuance granted which was initiated by the defendant.

(4) The privilege of the writ of habeas corpus shall not be suspended unless, in cases of rebellion or invasion, the public safety requires it.

Remedy for wrongs. Section 9. Every person is entitled to a certain remedy in the laws for all injuries, or wrongs which he may receive in his person, property, or character; he ought to obtain justice freely, and without being obliged to purchase it, completely and without denial, promptly and without delay, conformably to the laws.

Victims of crime. Section 9m. (1) (a) In this section, notwithstanding any statutory right, privilege, or protection, "victim" means any of the following:

1. A person against whom an act is committed that would constitute a crime if committed by a competent adult.

2. If the person under subd. 1. is deceased or is physically or emotionally unable to exercise his or her rights under this section, the person's spouse, parent or legal guardian, sibling, child, person who resided with the deceased at the time of death, or other lawful representative.

3. If the person under subd. 1. is a minor, the person's parent, legal guardian or custodian, or other lawful representative.

4. If the person under subd. 1. is adjudicated incompetent, the person's legal guardian or other lawful representative.

(b) "Victim" does not include the accused or a person who the court finds would not act in the best interests of a victim who is deceased, incompetent, a minor, or physically or emotionally unable to exercise his or her rights under this section.

(2) In order to preserve and protect victims' rights to justice and due process throughout the criminal and juvenile justice process, victims shall be entitled to all of the following rights, which shall vest at the time of victimization and be protected by law in a manner no less vigorous than the protections afforded to the accused:

(a) To be treated with dignity, respect, courtesy, sensitivity, and fairness.

(b) To privacy.

(c) To proceedings free from unreasonable delay.

(d) To timely disposition of the case, free from unreasonable delay.

(e) Upon request, to attend all proceedings involving the case.

(f) To reasonable protection from the accused throughout the criminal and juvenile justice process.

(g) Upon request, to reasonable and timely notification of proceedings.

(h) Upon request, to confer with the attorney for the government.

(i) Upon request, to be heard in any proceeding during which a right of the victim is implicated, including release, plea, sentencing, disposition, parole, revocation, expungement, or pardon.

(j) To have information pertaining to the economic, physical, and psychological effect upon the victim of the offense submitted to the authority with jurisdiction over the case and to have that information considered by that authority.

(k) Upon request, to timely notice of any release or escape of the accused or death of the accused if the accused is in custody or on supervision at the time of death.

(L) To refuse an interview, deposition, or other discovery request made by the accused or any person acting on behalf of the accused.

(m) To full restitution from any person who has been ordered to pay restitution to the victim and to be provided with assistance collecting restitution.

(n) To compensation as provided by law.

(o) Upon request, to reasonable and timely information about the status of the investigation and the outcome of the case.

(p) To timely notice about all rights under this section and all other rights, privileges, or protections of the victim provided by law, including how such rights, privileges, or protections are enforced.

(3) Except as provided under sub. (2) (n), all provisions of this section are self-executing. The legislature may prescribe further remedies for the violation of this section and further procedures for compliance with and enforcement of this section.

(4) (a) In addition to any other available enforcement of rights or remedy for a violation of this section or of other rights, privileges, or protections provided by law, the victim, the victim's attorney or other lawful representative, or the attorney for the government upon request of the victim may assert and seek in any circuit court or before any other authority of competent jurisdiction, enforcement of the rights in this section and any other right, privilege, or protection afforded to the victim by law. The court or other authority with jurisdiction over the case shall act promptly on such a request and afford a remedy for the violation of any right of the victim. The court or other authority with jurisdiction over the case shall clearly state on the record the reasons for any decision regarding the disposition of a victim's right and shall provide those reasons to the victim or the victim's attorney or other lawful representative.

(b) Victims may obtain review of all adverse decisions concerning their rights as victims by courts or other authorities with jurisdiction under par. (a) by filing petitions for supervisory writ in the court of appeals and supreme court.

(5) This section does not create any cause of action for damages against the state; any political subdivision of the state; any officer, employee, or agent of the state or a political subdivision of the state acting in his or her official capacity; or any officer, employee, or agent of the courts acting in his or her official capacity.

(6) This section is not intended and may not be interpreted to supersede a defendant's federal constitutional rights or to afford party status in a proceeding to any victim.

Treason. Section 10. Treason against the state shall consist only in levying war against the same, or in adhering to its enemies, giving them aid and comfort. No person shall be convicted of treason unless on the testimony of two witnesses to the same overt act, or on confession in open court.

Searches and seizures. Section 11. The right of the people to be secure in their persons, houses, papers, and effects against unreasonable searches and seizures shall not be violated; and no warrant shall issue but upon probable cause, supported by oath or affirmation, and particularly describing the place to be searched and the persons or things to be seized.

Attainder; ex post facto; contracts. Section 12. No bill of attainder, ex post facto law, nor any law impairing the obligation of contracts, shall ever be passed, and no conviction shall work corruption of blood or forfeiture of estate.

Private property for public use. Section 13. The property of no person shall be taken for public use without just compensation therefor.

Feudal tenures; leases; alienation. Section 14. All lands within the state are declared to be allodial, and feudal tenures are prohibited. Leases and grants of agricultural land for a longer term than fifteen years in which rent or service of any kind shall be reserved, and all fines and like restraints upon alienation reserved in any grant of land, hereafter made, are declared to be void.

Equal property rights for aliens and citizens. Section 15. No distinction shall ever be made by law between resident aliens and citizens, in reference to the possession, enjoyment or descent of property.

Imprisonment for debt. Section 16. No person shall be imprisoned for debt arising out of or founded on a contract, expressed or implied.

Exemption of property of debtors. Section 17. The privilege of the debtor to enjoy the necessary comforts of life shall be recognized by wholesome laws, exempting a reasonable amount of property from seizure or sale for the payment of any debt or liability hereafter contracted.

Freedom of worship; liberty of conscience; state religion; public funds. Section 18. The right of every person to worship Almighty God according to the dictates of conscience shall never be infringed; nor shall any person be compelled to attend, erect or support any place of worship, or to maintain any ministry, without consent; nor shall any control of, or interference with, the rights of conscience be permitted, or any preference be given by law to any religious establishments or modes of worship; nor shall any money be drawn from the treasury for the benefit of religious societies, or religious or theological seminaries.

Religious tests prohibited. Section 19. No religious tests shall ever be required as a qualification for any office of public trust under the state, and no person shall be rendered incompetent to give evidence in any court of law or equity in consequence of his opinions on the subject of religion.

Military subordinate to civil power. Section 20. The military shall be in strict subordination to the civil power.

Rights of suitors. Section 21. (1) Writs of error shall never be prohibited, and shall be issued by such courts as the legislature designates by law.

(2) In any court of this state, any suitor may prosecute or defend his suit either in his own proper person or by an attorney of the suitor's choice.

Maintenance of free government. Section 22. The blessings of a free government can only be maintained by a firm adherence to justice, moderation, temperance, frugality and virtue, and by frequent recurrence to fundamental principles.

Transportation of school children. Section 23. Nothing in this constitution shall prohibit the legislature from providing for the safety and welfare of children by providing for the transportation of children to and from any parochial or private school or institution of learning.

Use of school buildings. Section 24. Nothing in this constitution shall prohibit the legislature from authorizing, by law, the use of public school buildings by civic, religious or charitable organizations during nonschool hours upon payment by the organization to the school district of reasonable compensation for such use.

Right to keep and bear arms. Section 25. The people have the right to keep and bear arms for security, defense, hunting, recreation or any other lawful purpose.

Right to fish, hunt, trap, and take game. Section 26. The people have the right to fish, hunt, trap, and take game subject only to reasonable restrictions as prescribed by law.

ARTICLE II—Boundaries

State boundary. Section 1. It is hereby ordained and declared that the state of Wisconsin doth consent and accept of the boundaries prescribed in the act of congress entitled "An act to enable the people of Wisconsin territory to form a constitution and state government, and for the admission of such state into the Union," approved August sixth, one thousand eight hundred and forty-six, to wit: Beginning at the northeast corner of the state of Illinois—that is to say, at a point in the center of Lake Michigan where the line of forty-two degrees and thirty minutes of north latitude crosses the same; thence running with the boundary line of the state of Michigan, through Lake Michigan, Green Bay, to the mouth of the Menominee river; thence up the channel of the said river to the Brule river; thence up said last-mentioned river to Lake Brule; thence along the southern shore of Lake Brule in a direct line to the center of the channel between Middle and South Islands, in the Lake of the Desert; thence in a direct line to the head waters of the Montreal river, as marked upon the survey made by Captain Cramm; thence down the main channel of the Montreal river to the middle of Lake Superior; thence through the center of Lake Superior to the mouth of the St. Louis river; thence up the main channel of said river to the first rapids in the same, above the Indian village, according to Nicollet's map; thence due south to the main branch of the river St. Croix; thence down the main channel of said river to the Mississippi; thence down the center of the main channel of that river to the northwest corner of the state of Illinois; thence due east with the northern boundary of the state of Illinois to the place of beginning, as established by "An act to enable the people of the Illinois territory to form a constitution and state government, and for the admission of such state into the Union on an equal footing with the original states," approved April 18th, 1818.

Enabling act accepted. Section 2. The propositions contained in the act of congress are hereby accepted, ratified and confirmed, and shall remain irrevocable without the consent of the United States; and it is hereby ordained that this state shall never interfere with the primary disposal of the soil within the same by the United States, nor with any regulations congress may find necessary for securing the title in such soil to bona fide purchasers thereof; and in no case shall nonresident proprietors be taxed higher than residents. Provided, that nothing in this constitution, or in the act of congress aforesaid, shall in any manner prejudice or affect the right of the state of Wisconsin to 500,000 acres of land granted to said state, and to be hereafter selected and located by and under the act of congress entitled "An act to appropriate the proceeds of the sales of the public lands, and grant pre-emption rights," approved September fourth, one thousand eight hundred and forty-one.

ARTICLE III—Suffrage

Electors. Section 1. Every United States citizen age 18 or older who is a resident of an election district in this state is a qualified elector of that district.

Implementation. Section 2. Laws may be enacted:
 (1) Defining residency.
 (2) Providing for registration of electors.
 (3) Providing for absentee voting.
 (4) Excluding from the right of suffrage persons:
 (a) Convicted of a felony, unless restored to civil rights.
 (b) Adjudged by a court to be incompetent or partially incompetent, unless the judgment specifies that the person is capable of understanding the objective of the elective process or the judgment is set aside.
 (5) Subject to ratification by the people at a general election, extending the right of suffrage to additional classes.

Secret ballot. Section 3. All votes shall be by secret ballot.

ARTICLE IV—Legislative

Legislative power. Section 1. The legislative power shall be vested in a senate and assembly.

Legislature, how constituted. Section 2. The number of the members of the assembly shall never be less than fifty-four nor more than one hundred. The senate shall consist of a number not more than one-third nor less than one-fourth of the number of the members of the assembly.

Apportionment. Section 3. At its first session after each enumeration made by the authority of the United States, the legislature shall apportion and district anew the members of the senate and assembly, according to the number of inhabitants.

Representatives to the assembly, how chosen. Section 4. The members of the assembly shall be chosen biennially, by single districts, on the Tuesday succeeding the first Monday of November in even-numbered years, by the qualified electors of the several districts, such districts to be bounded by county, precinct, town or ward lines, to consist of contiguous territory and be in as compact form as practicable.

Senators, how chosen. Section 5. The senators shall be elected by single districts of convenient contiguous territory, at the same time and in the same manner as members of the assembly are required to be chosen; and no assembly district shall be divided in the formation of a senate district. The senate districts shall be numbered in the regular series, and the senators shall be chosen alternately from the odd and even-numbered districts for the term of 4 years.

Qualifications of legislators. Section 6. No person shall be eligible to the legislature who shall not have resided one year within the state, and be a qualified elector in the district which he may be chosen to represent.

Organization of legislature; quorum; compulsory attendance. Section 7. Each house shall be the judge of the elections, returns and qualifications of its own members; and a majority of each shall constitute a quorum to do business, but a smaller number may adjourn from day to day, and may compel the attendance of absent members in such manner and under such penalties as each house may provide.

Rules; contempts; expulsion. Section 8. Each house may determine the rules of its own proceedings, punish for contempt and disorderly behavior, and with the concurrence of two-thirds of all the members elected, expel a member; but no member shall be expelled a second time for the same cause.

Officers. Section 9. (1) Each house shall choose its presiding officers from its own members.

(2) The legislature shall provide by law for the establishment of a department of transportation and a transportation fund.

Journals; open doors; adjournments. Section 10. Each house shall keep a journal of its proceedings and publish the same, except such parts as require secrecy. The doors of each house shall be kept open except when the public welfare shall require secrecy. Neither house shall, without consent of the other, adjourn for more than three days.

Meeting of legislature. Section 11. The legislature shall meet at the seat of government at such time as shall be provided by law, unless convened by the governor in special session, and when so convened no business shall be transacted except as shall be necessary to accomplish the special purposes for which it was convened.

Ineligibility of legislators to office. Section 12. No member of the legislature shall, during the term for which he was elected, be appointed or elected to any civil office in the state, which shall have been created, or the emoluments of which shall have been increased, during the term for which he was elected.

Ineligibility of federal officers. Section 13. No person being a member of congress, or holding any military or civil office under the United States, shall be eligible to a seat in the legislature; and if any person shall, after his election as a member of the legislature, be elected to congress, or be appointed to any office, civil or military, under the government of the United States, his acceptance thereof shall vacate his seat. This restriction shall not prohibit a legislator from accepting short periods of active duty as a member of the reserve or from serving in the armed forces during any emergency declared by the executive.

Filling vacancies. Section 14. The governor shall issue writs of election to fill such vacancies as may occur in either house of the legislature.

Exemption from arrest and civil process. Section 15. Members of the legislature shall in all cases, except treason, felony and breach of the peace, be privileged from arrest; nor shall they be subject to any civil process, during the session of the legislature, nor for fifteen days next before the commencement and after the termination of each session.

Privilege in debate. Section 16. No member of the legislature shall be liable in any civil action, or criminal prosecution whatever, for words spoken in debate.

Enactment of laws. Section 17. (1) The style of all laws of the state shall be "The people of the state of Wisconsin, represented in senate and assembly, do enact as follows:".
    (2) No law shall be enacted except by bill. No law shall be in force until published.
    (3) The legislature shall provide by law for the speedy publication of all laws.

Title of private bills. Section 18. No private or local bill which may be passed by the legislature shall embrace more than one subject, and that shall be expressed in the title.

Origin of bills. Section 19. Any bill may originate in either house of the legislature, and a bill passed by one house may be amended by the other.

Yeas and nays. Section 20. The yeas and nays of the members of either house on any question shall, at the request of one-sixth of those present, be entered on the journal.

Powers of county boards. Section 22. The legislature may confer upon the boards of supervisors of the several counties of the state such powers of a local, legislative and administrative character as they shall from time to time prescribe.

Town and county government. Section 23. The legislature shall establish but one system of town government, which shall be as nearly uniform as practicable; but the legislature may provide for the election at large once in every 4 years of a chief executive officer in any county with such powers of an administrative character as they may from time to time prescribe in accordance with this section and shall establish one or more systems of county government.

Chief executive officer to approve or veto resolutions or ordinances; proceedings on veto. Section 23a. Every resolution or ordinance passed by the county board in any county shall, before it becomes effective, be presented to the chief executive officer. If he approves, he shall sign it; if not, he shall return it with his objections, which objections shall be entered at large upon the journal and the board shall proceed to reconsider the matter. Appropriations may be approved in whole or in part by the chief executive officer and the part approved shall become law, and the part objected to shall be returned in the same manner as provided for in other resolutions or ordinances. If, after such reconsideration, two-thirds of the members-elect of the county board agree to pass the resolution or ordinance or the part of the resolution or ordinance objected to, it shall become effective on the date prescribed but not earlier than the date of passage following reconsideration. In all such cases, the votes of the members of the county board shall be determined by ayes and noes and the names of the members voting for or against the resolution or ordinance or the part thereof objected to shall be entered on the journal. If any resolution or ordinance is not returned by the chief executive officer to the county board at its first meeting occurring not less than 6 days, Sundays excepted, after it has been presented to him, it shall become effective unless the county board has recessed or adjourned for a period in excess of 60 days, in which case it shall not be effective without his approval.

Gambling. Section 24. (1) Except as provided in this section, the legislature may not authorize gambling in any form.

(2) Except as otherwise provided by law, the following activities do not constitute consideration as an element of gambling:

(a) To listen to or watch a television or radio program.

(b) To fill out a coupon or entry blank, whether or not proof of purchase is required.

(c) To visit a mercantile establishment or other place without being required to make a purchase or pay an admittance fee.

(3) The legislature may authorize the following bingo games licensed by the state, but all profits shall accrue to the licensed organization and no salaries, fees or profits may be paid to any other organization or person: bingo games operated by religious, charitable, service, fraternal or veterans' organizations or those to which contributions are deductible for federal or state income tax purposes. All moneys received by the state that are attributable to bingo games shall be used for property tax relief for residents of this state as provided by law. The distribution of moneys that are attributable to bingo games may not vary based on the income or age of the person provided the property tax relief. The distribution of moneys that are attributable to bingo games shall not be subject to the uniformity requirement of section 1 of article VIII. In this subsection, the distribution of all moneys attributable to bingo games shall include any earnings on the moneys received by the state that are attributable to bingo games, but shall not include any moneys used for the regulation of, and enforcement of law relating to, bingo games.

(4) The legislature may authorize the following raffle games licensed by the state, but all profits shall accrue to the licensed local organization and no salaries, fees or profits may be paid to any other organization or person: raffle games operated by local religious, charitable, service, fraternal or veterans' organizations or those to which contributions are deductible for federal or state income tax purposes. The legislature shall limit the number of raffles conducted by any such organization.

(5) This section shall not prohibit pari-mutuel on-track betting as provided by law. The state may not own or operate any facility or enterprise for pari-mutuel betting, or lease any state-owned land to any other owner or operator for such purposes. All moneys received by the state that are attributable to pari-mutuel on-track betting shall be used for property tax relief for residents of this state as provided by law. The distribution of moneys that are attributable to pari-mutuel on-track betting may not vary based on the income or age of the person provided the property tax relief. The distribution of moneys that are attributable to pari-mutuel on-track betting shall not be subject to the uniformity requirement of section 1 of article VIII. In this subsection, the distribution of all moneys attributable to pari-mutuel on-track betting shall include any earnings on the moneys received by the state that are attributable to pari-mutuel on-track betting, but shall not include any moneys used for the regulation of, and enforcement of law relating to, pari-mutuel on-track betting.

(6) (a) The legislature may authorize the creation of a lottery to be operated by the state as provided by law. The expenditure of public funds or of revenues derived from lottery operations to engage in promotional advertising of the Wisconsin state lottery is prohibited. Any advertising of the state lottery shall indicate the odds of a specific lottery ticket to be selected as the winning ticket for each prize amount offered. The net proceeds of the state lottery shall be deposited in the treasury of the state, to be used for property tax relief for residents of this state as provided by law. The distribution of the net proceeds of the state lottery may not vary based on the income or age of the person provided the property tax relief. The distribution of the net proceeds of the state lottery shall not be subject to the uniformity requirement of section 1 of article VIII. In this paragraph, the distribution of the net proceeds of the state lottery shall include any earnings on the net proceeds of the state lottery.

(b) The lottery authorized under par. (a) shall be an enterprise that entitles the player, by purchasing a ticket, to participate in a game of chance if: 1) the winning tickets are randomly predetermined and the player reveals preprinted numbers or symbols from which it can be immediately determined whether the ticket is a winning ticket entitling the player to win a prize as prescribed in the features and procedures for the game, including an opportunity to win a prize in a secondary or subsequent chance drawing or game; or 2) the ticket is evidence of the numbers or symbols selected by the player or, at the player's option, selected by a computer, and the player becomes entitled to a prize as prescribed in the features and procedures for the game, including an opportunity to win a prize in a secondary or subsequent chance drawing or game if some or all of the player's symbols or numbers are selected in a chance drawing or game, if the player's ticket is randomly selected by the computer at the time of purchase or if the ticket is selected in a chance drawing.

(c) Notwithstanding the authorization of a state lottery under par. (a), the following games, or games simulating any of the following games, may not be conducted by the state as a lottery: 1) any game in which winners are selected based on the results of a race or sporting event; 2) any banking card game, including blackjack, baccarat or chemin de fer; 3) poker; 4) roulette; 5) craps or any other game that involves rolling dice; 6) keno; 7) bingo 21, bingo jack, bingolet or bingo craps; 8) any game of chance that is placed on a slot machine or any mechanical, electromechanical or electronic device that is generally available to be played at a gambling casino; 9) any game or device that is commonly known as a video game of chance or a video gaming machine or that is commonly considered to be a video gambling machine, unless such machine is a video device operated by the state in a game authorized under par. (a) to permit the sale of tickets through retail outlets under contract with the state and the device does not determine or indicate whether the player has won a prize, other than by verifying that the player's ticket or some or all of the player's symbols or numbers on the player's ticket have been selected in a chance drawing, or by verifying that the player's ticket has been randomly selected by a central system computer at the time of purchase; 10) any game that is similar to a game listed in this paragraph; or 11) any other game that is commonly considered to be a form of gambling and is not, or is not substantially similar to, a game conducted by the state under par. (a). No game conducted by the state under par. (a) may permit a player of the game to purchase a ticket, or to otherwise participate in the game, from a residence by using a computer, telephone or other form of electronic, telecommunication, video or technological aid.

Stationery and printing. Section 25. The legislature shall provide by law that all stationery required for the use of the state, and all printing authorized and required by them to be done for their use, or for the state, shall be let by contract to the lowest bidder, but the legislature may establish a maximum price; no member of the legislature or other state officer shall be interested, either directly or indirectly, in any such contract.

Extra compensation; salary change. Section 26. (1) The legislature may not grant any extra compensation to a public officer, agent, servant or contractor after the services have been rendered or the contract has been entered into.

(2) Except as provided in this subsection, the compensation of a public officer may not be increased or diminished during the term of office:

(a) When any increase or decrease in the compensation of justices of the supreme court or judges of any court of record becomes effective as to any such justice or judge, it shall be effective from such date as to every such justice or judge.

(b) Any increase in the compensation of members of the legislature shall take effect, for all senators and representatives to the assembly, after the next general election beginning with the new assembly term.

(3) Subsection (1) shall not apply to increased benefits for persons who have been or shall be granted benefits of any kind under a retirement system when such increased benefits are provided by a legislative act passed on a call of ayes and noes by a three-fourths

vote of all the members elected to both houses of the legislature and such act provides for sufficient state funds to cover the costs of the increased benefits.

Suits against state. Section 27. The legislature shall direct by law in what manner and in what courts suits may be brought against the state.

Oath of office. Section 28. Members of the legislature, and all officers, executive and judicial, except such inferior officers as may be by law exempted, shall before they enter upon the duties of their respective offices, take and subscribe an oath or affirmation to support the constitution of the United States and the constitution of the state of Wisconsin, and faithfully to discharge the duties of their respective offices to the best of their ability.

Militia. Section 29. The legislature shall determine what persons shall constitute the militia of the state, and may provide for organizing and disciplining the same in such manner as shall be prescribed by law.

Elections by legislature. Section 30. All elections made by the legislature shall be by roll call vote entered in the journals.

Special and private laws prohibited. Section 31. The legislature is prohibited from enacting any special or private laws in the following cases:

(1) For changing the names of persons, constituting one person the heir at law of another or granting any divorce.

(2) For laying out, opening or altering highways, except in cases of state roads extending into more than one county, and military roads to aid in the construction of which lands may be granted by congress.

(3) For authorizing persons to keep ferries across streams at points wholly within this state.

(4) For authorizing the sale or mortgage of real or personal property of minors or others under disability.

(5) For locating or changing any county seat.

(6) For assessment or collection of taxes or for extending the time for the collection thereof.

(7) For granting corporate powers or privileges, except to cities.

(8) For authorizing the apportionment of any part of the school fund.

(9) For incorporating any city, town or village, or to amend the charter thereof.

General laws on enumerated subjects. Section 32. The legislature may provide by general law for the treatment of any subject for which lawmaking is prohibited by section 31 of this article. Subject to reasonable classifications, such laws shall be uniform in their operation throughout the state.

Auditing of state accounts. Section 33. The legislature shall provide for the auditing of state accounts and may establish such offices and prescribe such duties for the same as it shall deem necessary.

Continuity of civil government. Section 34. The legislature, in order to ensure continuity of state and local governmental operations in periods of emergency resulting from enemy action in the form of an attack, shall (1) forthwith provide for prompt and temporary succession to the powers and duties of public offices, of whatever nature and whether filled by election or appointment, the incumbents of which may become unavailable for carrying on the powers and duties of such offices, and (2) adopt such other measures as may be necessary and proper for attaining the objectives of this section.

ARTICLE V—Executive

Governor; lieutenant governor; term. Section 1. The executive power shall be vested in a governor who shall hold office for 4 years; a lieutenant governor shall be elected at the same time and for the same term.

Eligibility. Section 2. No person except a citizen of the United States and a qualified elector of the state shall be eligible to the office of governor or lieutenant governor.

Election. Section 3. The governor and lieutenant governor shall be elected by the qualified electors of the state at the times and places of choosing members of the legislature. They shall be chosen jointly, by the casting by each voter of a single vote applicable to both offices beginning with the general election in 1970. The persons respectively having the highest number of votes cast jointly for them for governor and lieutenant governor shall be elected; but in case two or more slates shall have an equal and the highest number of votes for governor and lieutenant governor, the two houses of the legislature, at its next annual session shall forthwith, by joint ballot, choose one of the slates so having an equal and the highest number of votes for governor and lieutenant governor. The returns of election for governor and lieutenant governor shall be made in such manner as shall be provided by law.

Powers and duties. Section 4. The governor shall be commander in chief of the military and naval forces of the state. He shall have power to convene the legislature on extraordinary occasions, and in case of invasion, or danger from the prevalence of contagious disease at the seat of government, he may convene them at any other suitable place within the state. He shall communicate to the legislature, at every session, the condition of the state, and recommend such matters to them for their consideration as he may deem expedient. He shall transact all necessary business with the officers of the government, civil and military. He shall expedite all such measures as may be resolved upon by the legislature, and shall take care that the laws be faithfully executed.

Pardoning power. Section 6. The governor shall have power to grant reprieves, commutations and pardons, after conviction, for all offenses, except treason and cases of impeachment, upon such conditions and with such restrictions and limitations as he may think proper, subject to such regulations as may be provided by law relative to the manner of applying for pardons. Upon conviction for treason he shall have the power to suspend the execution of the sentence until the case shall be reported to the legislature at its next meeting, when the legislature shall either pardon, or commute the sentence, direct the execution of the sentence, or grant a further reprieve. He shall annually communicate to the legislature each case of reprieve, commutation or pardon granted, stating the name of the convict, the crime of which he was convicted, the sentence and its date, and the date of the commutation, pardon or reprieve, with his reasons for granting the same.

Lieutenant governor, when governor. Section 7. (1) Upon the governor's death, resignation or removal from office, the lieutenant governor shall become governor for the balance of the unexpired term.

(2) If the governor is absent from this state, impeached, or from mental or physical disease, becomes incapable of performing the duties of the office, the lieutenant governor shall serve as acting governor for the balance of the unexpired term or until the governor returns, the disability ceases or the impeachment is vacated. But when the governor, with the consent of the legislature, shall be out of this state in time of war at the head of the state's military force, the governor shall continue as commander in chief of the military force.

Secretary of state, when governor. Section 8. (1) If there is a vacancy in the office of lieutenant governor and the governor dies, resigns or is removed from office, the secretary of state shall become governor for the balance of the unexpired term.

(2) If there is a vacancy in the office of lieutenant governor and the governor is absent from this state, impeached, or from mental or physical disease becomes incapable of performing the duties of the office, the secretary of state shall serve as acting governor for the balance of the unexpired term or until the governor returns, the disability ceases or the impeachment is vacated.

Governor to approve or veto bills; proceedings on veto. Section 10. (1) (a) Every bill which shall have passed the legislature shall, before it becomes a law, be presented to the governor.

(b) If the governor approves and signs the bill, the bill shall become law. Appropriation bills may be approved in whole or in part by the governor, and the part approved shall become law.

(c) In approving an appropriation bill in part, the governor may not create a new word by rejecting individual letters in the words of the enrolled bill, and may not create a new sentence by combining parts of 2 or more sentences of the enrolled bill.

(2) (a) If the governor rejects the bill, the governor shall return the bill, together with the objections in writing, to the house in which the bill originated. The house of origin shall enter the objections at large upon the journal and proceed to reconsider the bill. If, after such reconsideration, two-thirds of the members present agree to pass the bill notwithstanding the objections of the governor, it shall be sent, together with the objections, to the other house, by which it shall likewise be reconsidered, and if approved by two-thirds of the members present it shall become law.

(b) The rejected part of an appropriation bill, together with the governor's objections in writing, shall be returned to the house in which the bill originated. The house of origin shall enter the objections at large upon the journal and proceed to reconsider the rejected part of the appropriation bill. If, after such reconsideration, two-thirds of the members present agree to approve the rejected part notwithstanding the objections of the governor, it shall be sent, together with the objections, to the other house, by which it shall likewise be reconsidered, and if approved by two-thirds of the members present the rejected part shall become law.

(c) In all such cases the votes of both houses shall be determined by ayes and noes, and the names of the members voting for or against passage of the bill or the rejected part of the bill notwithstanding the objections of the governor shall be entered on the journal of each house respectively.

(3) Any bill not returned by the governor within 6 days (Sundays excepted) after it shall have been presented to the governor shall be law unless the legislature, by final adjournment, prevents the bill's return, in which case it shall not be law.

ARTICLE VI—Administrative

Election of secretary of state, treasurer and attorney general; term. Section 1. The qualified electors of this state, at the times and places of choosing the members of the legislature, shall in 1970 and every 4 years thereafter elect a secretary of state, treasurer and attorney general who shall hold their offices for 4 years.

Secretary of state; duties, compensation. Section 2. The secretary of state shall keep a fair record of the official acts of the legislature and executive department of the state, and shall, when required, lay the same and all matters relative thereto before either branch of the legislature. He shall perform such other duties as shall be assigned him by law. He shall receive as a compensation for his services yearly such sum as shall be provided by law, and shall keep his office at the seat of government.

Treasurer and attorney general; duties, compensation. Section 3. The powers, duties and compensation of the treasurer and attorney general shall be prescribed by law.

County officers; election, terms, removal; vacancies. Section 4. (1) (a) Except as provided in pars. (b) and (c) and sub. (2), coroners, registers of deeds, district attorneys, and all other elected county officers, except judicial officers, sheriffs, and chief executive officers, shall be chosen by the electors of the respective counties once in every 2 years.

(b) Beginning with the first general election at which the governor is elected which occurs after the ratification of this paragraph, sheriffs shall be chosen by the electors of the respective counties, or by the electors of all of the respective counties comprising each combination of counties combined by the legislature for that purpose, for the term of 4 years and coroners in counties in which there is a coroner shall be chosen by the electors of the respective counties, or by the electors of all of the respective counties comprising each combination of counties combined by the legislature for that purpose, for the term of 4 years.

(c) Beginning with the first general election at which the president is elected which occurs after the ratification of this paragraph, district attorneys, registers of deeds, county clerks, and treasurers shall be chosen by the electors of the respective counties, or by the electors of all of the respective counties comprising each combination of counties combined by the legislature for that purpose, for the term of 4 years and surveyors in counties in which the office of surveyor is filled by election shall be chosen by the electors of the respective counties, or by the electors of all of the respective counties comprising each combination of counties combined by the legislature for that purpose, for the term of 4 years.

(2) The offices of coroner and surveyor in counties having a population of 500,000 or more are abolished. Counties not having a population of 500,000 shall have the option of retaining the elective office of coroner or instituting a medical examiner system. Two or more counties may institute a joint medical examiner system.

(3) (a) Sheriffs may not hold any other partisan office.

(b) Sheriffs may be required by law to renew their security from time to time, and in default of giving such new security their office shall be deemed vacant.

(4) The governor may remove any elected county officer mentioned in this section except a county clerk, treasurer, or surveyor, giving to the officer a copy of the charges and an opportunity of being heard.

(5) All vacancies in the offices of coroner, register of deeds or district attorney shall be filled by appointment. The person appointed to fill a vacancy shall hold office only for the unexpired portion of the term to which appointed and until a successor shall be elected and qualified.

(6) When a vacancy occurs in the office of sheriff, the vacancy shall be filled by appointment of the governor, and the person appointed shall serve until his or her successor is elected and qualified.

ARTICLE VII—Judiciary

Impeachment; trial. Section 1. The court for the trial of impeachments shall be composed of the senate. The assembly shall have the power of impeaching all civil officers of this state for corrupt conduct in office, or for crimes and misdemeanors; but a majority of all the members elected shall concur in an impeachment. On the trial of an impeachment against the governor, the lieutenant governor shall not act as a member of the court. No judicial officer shall exercise his office, after he shall have been impeached, until his acquittal. Before the trial of an impeachment the members of the court shall take an oath or affirmation truly and impartially to try the impeachment according to evidence; and no person shall be convicted without the concurrence of two-thirds of the members present. Judgment in cases of impeachment shall not extend further than to removal from office, or removal from office and disqualification to hold any office of honor, profit or trust under the state; but the party impeached shall be liable to indictment, trial and punishment according to law.

Court system. Section 2. The judicial power of this state shall be vested in a unified court system consisting of one supreme court, a court of appeals, a circuit court, such trial courts of general uniform statewide jurisdiction as the legislature may create by law, and a municipal court if authorized by the legislature under section 14.

Supreme court: jurisdiction. Section 3. (1) The supreme court shall have superintending and administrative authority over all courts.

(2) The supreme court has appellate jurisdiction over all courts and may hear original actions and proceedings. The supreme court may issue all writs necessary in aid of its jurisdiction.

(3) The supreme court may review judgments and orders of the court of appeals, may remove cases from the court of appeals and may accept cases on certification by the court of appeals.

Supreme court: election, chief justice, court system administration. Section 4. (1) The supreme court shall have 7 members who shall be known as justices of the supreme court. Justices shall be elected for 10-year terms of office commencing with the August 1 next succeeding the election. Only one justice may be elected in any year. Any 4 justices shall constitute a quorum for the conduct of the court's business.

(2) The chief justice of the supreme court shall be elected for a term of 2 years by a majority of the justices then serving on the court. The justice so designated as chief justice may, irrevocably, decline to serve as chief justice or resign as chief justice but continue to serve as a justice of the supreme court.

(3) The chief justice of the supreme court shall be the administrative head of the judicial system and shall exercise this administrative authority pursuant to procedures adopted by the supreme court. The chief justice may assign any judge of a court of record to aid in the proper disposition of judicial business in any court of record except the supreme court.

Court of appeals. Section 5. (1) The legislature shall by law combine the judicial circuits of the state into one or more districts for the court of appeals and shall designate in each district the locations where the appeals court shall sit for the convenience of litigants.

(2) For each district of the appeals court there shall be chosen by the qualified electors of the district one or more appeals judges as prescribed by law, who shall sit as prescribed by law. Appeals judges shall be elected for 6-year terms and shall reside in the district from which elected. No alteration of district or circuit boundaries shall have the effect of removing an appeals judge from office during the judge's term. In case of an increase in the number of appeals judges, the first judge or judges shall be elected for full terms unless the legislature prescribes a shorter initial term for staggering of terms.

(3) The appeals court shall have such appellate jurisdiction in the district, including jurisdiction to review administrative proceedings, as the legislature may provide by law, but shall have no original jurisdiction other than by prerogative writ. The appeals court may issue all writs necessary in aid of its jurisdiction and shall have supervisory authority over all actions and proceedings in the courts in the district.

Circuit court: boundaries. Section 6. The legislature shall prescribe by law the number of judicial circuits, making them as compact and convenient as practicable, and bounding them by county lines. No alteration of circuit boundaries shall have the effect of removing a circuit judge from office during the judge's term. In case of an increase of circuits, the first judge or judges shall be elected.

Circuit court: election. Section 7. For each circuit there shall be chosen by the qualified electors thereof one or more circuit judges as prescribed by law. Circuit judges shall be elected for 6-year terms and shall reside in the circuit from which elected.

Circuit court: jurisdiction. Section 8. Except as otherwise provided by law, the circuit court shall have original jurisdiction in all matters civil and criminal within this state and such appellate jurisdiction in the circuit as the legislature may prescribe by law. The circuit court may issue all writs necessary in aid of its jurisdiction.

Judicial elections, vacancies. Section 9. When a vacancy occurs in the office of justice of the supreme court or judge of any court of record, the vacancy shall be filled by appointment by the governor, which shall continue until a successor is elected and qualified. There shall be no election for a justice or judge at the partisan general election for state or county officers, nor within 30 days either before or after such election.

Judges: eligibility to office. Section 10. (1) No justice of the supreme court or judge of any court of record shall hold any other office of public trust, except a judicial office, during the term for which elected. No person shall be eligible to the office of judge who shall not, at the time of election or appointment, be a qualified elector within the jurisdiction for which chosen.

(2) Justices of the supreme court and judges of the courts of record shall receive such compensation as the legislature may authorize by law, but may not receive fees of office.

Disciplinary proceedings. Section 11. Each justice or judge shall be subject to reprimand, censure, suspension, removal for cause or for disability, by the supreme court pursuant to procedures established by the legislature by law. No justice or judge removed for cause shall be eligible for reappointment or temporary service. This section is alternative to, and cumulative with, the methods of removal provided in sections 1 and 13 of this article and section 12 of article XIII.

Clerks of circuit and supreme courts. Section 12. (1) There shall be a clerk of circuit court chosen in each county organized for judicial purposes by the qualified electors thereof, who, except as provided in sub. (2), shall hold office for two years, subject to removal as provided by law.

(2) Beginning with the first general election at which the governor is elected which occurs after the ratification of this subsection, a clerk of circuit court shall be chosen by the electors of each county, for the term of 4 years, subject to removal as provided by law.

(3) In case of a vacancy, the judge of the circuit court may appoint a clerk until the vacancy is filled by an election.

(4) The clerk of circuit court shall give such security as the legislature requires by law.

(5) The supreme court shall appoint its own clerk, and may appoint a clerk of circuit court to be the clerk of the supreme court.

Justices and judges: removal by address. Section 13. Any justice or judge may be removed from office by address of both houses of the legislature, if two-thirds of all the members elected to each house concur therein, but no removal shall be made by virtue of this section unless the justice or judge complained of is served with a copy of the charges, as the ground of address, and has had an opportunity of being heard. On the question of removal, the ayes and noes shall be entered on the journals.

Municipal court. Section 14. The legislature by law may authorize each city, village and town to establish a municipal court. All municipal courts shall have uniform jurisdiction limited to actions and proceedings arising under ordinances of the municipality in which established. Judges of municipal courts may receive such compensation as provided by the municipality in which established, but may not receive fees of office.

Justices and judges: eligibility for office; retirement. Section 24. (1) To be eligible for the office of supreme court justice or judge of any court of record, a person must be an attorney licensed to practice law in this state and have been so licensed for 5 years immediately prior to election or appointment.

(2) Unless assigned temporary service under subsection (3), no person may serve as a supreme court justice or judge of a court of record beyond the July 31 following the date on which such person attains that age, of not less than 70 years, which the legislature shall prescribe by law.

(3) A person who has served as a supreme court justice or judge of a court of record may, as provided by law, serve as a judge of any court of record except the supreme court on a temporary basis if assigned by the chief justice of the supreme court.

ARTICLE VIII—Finance

Rule of taxation uniform; income, privilege and occupation taxes. Section 1. The rule of taxation shall be uniform but the legislature may empower cities, villages or towns to collect and return taxes on real estate located therein by optional methods. Taxes shall be levied upon such property with such classifications as to forests and minerals including or separate or severed from the land, as the legislature shall prescribe. Taxation of agricultural land and undeveloped land, both as defined by law, need not be uniform with the taxation of each other nor with the taxation of other real property. Taxation of merchants' stock-in-trade, manufacturers' materials and finished products, and livestock need not be uniform with the taxation of real property and other personal property, but the taxation of all such merchants' stock-in-trade, manufacturers' materials and finished products and livestock shall be uniform, except that the legislature may provide that the value thereof shall be determined on an average basis. Taxes may also be imposed on incomes, privileges and occupations, which taxes may be graduated and progressive, and reasonable exemptions may be provided.

Appropriations; limitation. Section 2. No money shall be paid out of the treasury except in pursuance of an appropriation by law. No appropriation shall be made for the payment of any claim against the state except claims of the United States and judgments, unless filed within six years after the claim accrued.

Credit of state. Section 3. Except as provided in s. 7 (2) (a), the credit of the state shall never be given, or loaned, in aid of any individual, association or corporation.

Contracting state debts. Section 4. The state shall never contract any public debt except in the cases and manner herein provided.

Annual tax levy to equal expenses. Section 5. The legislature shall provide for an annual tax sufficient to defray the estimated expenses of the state for each year; and whenever the expenses of any year shall exceed the income, the legislature shall provide for levying a tax for the ensuing year, sufficient, with other sources of income, to pay the deficiency as well as the estimated expenses of such ensuing year.

Public debt for extraordinary expense; taxation. Section 6. For the purpose of defraying extraordinary expenditures the state may contract public debts (but such debts shall never in the aggregate exceed one hundred thousand dollars). Every such debt shall be authorized by law, for some purpose or purposes to be distinctly specified therein; and the vote of a majority of all the members elected to each house, to be taken by yeas and nays, shall be necessary to the passage of such law; and every such law shall provide for levying an annual tax sufficient to pay the annual interest of such debt and the principal within five years from the passage of such law, and shall specially appropriate the proceeds of such taxes to the payment of such principal and interest; and such appropriation shall not be repealed, nor the taxes be postponed or diminished, until the principal and interest of such debt shall have been wholly paid.

Public debt for public defense; bonding for public purposes. Section 7. (1) The legislature may also borrow money to repel invasion, suppress insurrection, or defend the state in time of war; but the money thus raised shall be applied exclusively to the object for which the loan was authorized, or to the repayment of the debt thereby created.

(2) Any other provision of this constitution to the contrary notwithstanding:

(a) The state may contract public debt and pledges to the payment thereof its full faith, credit and taxing power:

1. To acquire, construct, develop, extend, enlarge or improve land, waters, property, highways, railways, buildings, equipment or facilities for public purposes.

2. To make funds available for veterans' housing loans.

(b) The aggregate public debt contracted by the state in any calendar year pursuant to paragraph (a) shall not exceed an amount equal to the lesser of:

1. Three-fourths of one per centum of the aggregate value of all taxable property in the state; or

2. Five per centum of the aggregate value of all taxable property in the state less the sum of: a. the aggregate public debt of the state contracted pursuant to this section outstanding as of January 1 of such calendar year after subtracting therefrom the amount of sinking funds on hand on January 1 of such calendar year which are applicable exclusively to repayment of such outstanding public debt and, b. the outstanding indebtedness as of January 1 of such calendar year of any entity of the type described in paragraph (d) to the extent that such indebtedness is supported by or payable from payments out of the treasury of the state.

(c) The state may contract public debt, without limit, to fund or refund the whole or any part of any public debt contracted pursuant to paragraph (a), including any premium payable with respect thereto and any interest to accrue thereon, or to fund or refund the whole or any part of any indebtedness incurred prior to January 1, 1972, by any entity of the type described in paragraph (d), including any premium payable with respect thereto and any interest to accrue thereon.

(d) No money shall be paid out of the treasury, with respect to any lease, sublease or other agreement entered into after January 1, 1971, to the Wisconsin State Agencies Building Corporation, Wisconsin State Colleges Building Corporation, Wisconsin State Public Building Corporation, Wisconsin University Building Corporation or any similar entity existing or operating for similar purposes pursuant to which such nonprofit corporation or such other entity undertakes to finance or provide a facility for use or occupancy by the state or an agency, department or instrumentality thereof.

(e) The legislature shall prescribe all matters relating to the contracting of public debt pursuant to paragraph (a), including: the public purposes for which public debt may be contracted; by vote of a majority of the members elected to each of the 2 houses of the legislature, the amount of public debt which may be contracted for any class of such purposes; the public debt or other indebtedness which may be funded or refunded; the kinds of notes, bonds or other evidence of public debt which may be issued by the state; and the manner in which the aggregate value of all taxable property in the state shall be determined.

(f) The full faith, credit and taxing power of the state are pledged to the payment of all public debt created on behalf of the state pursuant to this section and the legislature shall provide by appropriation for the payment of the interest upon and instalments of principal of all such public debt as the same falls due, but, in any event, suit may be brought against the state to compel such payment.

(g) At any time after January 1, 1972, by vote of a majority of the members elected to each of the 2 houses of the legislature, the legislature may declare that an emergency exists and submit to the people a proposal to authorize the state to contract a specific amount of public debt for a purpose specified in such proposal, without regard to the limit provided in paragraph (b). Any such authorization shall be effective if approved by a majority of the electors voting thereon. Public debt contracted pursuant to such authorization shall thereafter be deemed to have been contracted pursuant to paragraph (a), but neither such public debt nor any public debt contracted to fund or refund such public debt shall be considered in computing the debt limit provided in paragraph (b). Not more than one such authorization shall be thus made in any 2-year period.

Vote on fiscal bills; quorum. Section 8. On the passage in either house of the legislature of any law which imposes, continues or renews a tax, or creates a debt or charge, or makes, continues or renews an appropriation of public or trust money, or releases, discharges or commutes a claim or demand of the state, the question shall be taken by yeas and nays, which shall be duly entered on the journal; and three-fifths of all the members elected to such house shall in all such cases be required to constitute a quorum therein.

Evidences of public debt. Section 9. No scrip, certificate, or other evidence of state debt, whatsoever, shall be issued, except for such debts as are authorized by the sixth and seventh sections of this article.

Internal improvements. Section 10. Except as further provided in this section, the state may never contract any debt for works of internal improvement, or be a party in carrying on such works.

(1) Whenever grants of land or other property shall have been made to the state, especially dedicated by the grant to particular works of internal improvement, the state may carry on such particular works and shall devote thereto the avails of such grants, and may pledge or appropriate the revenues derived from such works in aid of their completion.

(2) The state may appropriate money in the treasury or to be thereafter raised by taxation for:

(a) The construction or improvement of public highways.

(b) The development, improvement and construction of airports or other aeronautical projects.

(c) The acquisition, improvement or construction of veterans' housing.

(d) The improvement of port facilities.

(e) The acquisition, development, improvement or construction of railways and other railroad facilities.

(3) The state may appropriate moneys for the purpose of acquiring, preserving and developing the forests of the state. Of the moneys appropriated under the authority of this subsection in any one year an amount not to exceed two-tenths of one mill of the taxable property of the state as determined by the last preceding state assessment may be raised by a tax on property.

Transportation Fund. Section 11. All funds collected by the state from any taxes or fees levied or imposed for the licensing of motor vehicle operators, for the titling, licensing, or registration of motor vehicles, for motor vehicle fuel, or for the use of roadways, highways, or bridges, and from taxes and fees levied or imposed for aircraft, airline property, or aviation fuel or for railroads or railroad property shall be deposited only into the transportation fund or with a trustee for the benefit of the department of transportation or the holders of transportation-related revenue bonds, except for collections from taxes or fees in existence on December 31, 2010, that were not being deposited in the transportation fund on that date. None of the funds collected or received by the state from any source and deposited into the transportation fund shall be lapsed, further transferred, or appropriated to any program that is not directly administered by the department of transportation in furtherance of the department's responsibility for the planning, promotion, and protection of all transportation systems in the state except for programs for which there was an appropriation from the transportation fund on December 31, 2010. In this section, the term "motor vehicle" does not include any all-terrain vehicles, snowmobiles, or watercraft.

ARTICLE IX—Eminent domain and property of the state

Jurisdiction on rivers and lakes; navigable waters. Section 1. The state shall have concurrent jurisdiction on all rivers and lakes bordering on this state so far as such rivers or lakes shall form a common boundary to the state and any other state or territory now or hereafter to be formed, and bounded by the same; and the river Mississippi and the navigable waters leading into the Mississippi and St. Lawrence, and the carrying places between the same, shall be common highways and forever free, as well to the inhabitants of the state as to the citizens of the United States, without any tax, impost or duty therefor.

Territorial property. Section 2. The title to all lands and other property which have accrued to the territory of Wisconsin by grant, gift, purchase, forfeiture, escheat or otherwise shall vest in the state of Wisconsin.

Ultimate property in lands; escheats. Section 3. The people of the state, in their right of sovereignty, are declared to possess the ultimate property in and to all lands within the jurisdiction of the state; and all lands the title to which shall fail from a defect of heirs shall revert or escheat to the people.

ARTICLE X—Education

Superintendent of public instruction. Section 1. The supervision of public instruction shall be vested in a state superintendent and such other officers as the legislature shall direct; and their qualifications, powers, duties and compensation shall be prescribed by law. The state superintendent shall be chosen by the qualified electors of the state at the same time and in the same manner as members of the supreme court, and shall hold office for 4 years from the succeeding first Monday in July. The term of office, time and manner of electing or appointing all other officers of supervision of public instruction shall be fixed by law.

School fund created; income applied. Section 2. The proceeds of all lands that have been or hereafter may be granted by the United States to this state for educational purposes (except the lands heretofore granted for the purposes of a university) and all moneys and the clear proceeds of all property that may accrue to the state by forfeiture or escheat; and the clear proceeds of all fines collected in the several counties for any breach of the penal laws, and all moneys arising from any grant to the state where the purposes of such grant are not specified, and the 500,000 acres of land to which the state is entitled by the provisions of an act of congress, entitled "An act to appropriate the proceeds of the sales of the public lands and to grant pre-emption rights," approved September 4, 1841; and also the 5 percent of the net proceeds of the public lands to which the state shall become entitled on admission into the union (if congress shall consent to such appropriation of the 2 grants last mentioned) shall be set apart as a separate fund to be called "the school fund," the interest of which and all other revenues derived from the school lands shall be exclusively applied to the following objects, to wit:

(1) To the support and maintenance of common schools, in each school district, and the purchase of suitable libraries and apparatus therefor.

(2) The residue shall be appropriated to the support and maintenance of academies and normal schools, and suitable libraries and apparatus therefor.

District schools; tuition; sectarian instruction; released time. Section 3. The legislature shall provide by law for the establishment of district schools, which shall be as nearly uniform as practicable; and such schools shall be free and without charge for tuition to all children between the ages of 4 and 20 years; and no sectarian instruction shall be allowed therein; but the legislature by law may, for the purpose of religious instruction outside the district schools, authorize the release of students during regular school hours.

Annual school tax. Section 4. Each town and city shall be required to raise by tax, annually, for the support of common schools therein, a sum not less than one-half the amount received by such town or city respectively for school purposes from the income of the school fund.

Income of school fund. Section 5. Provision shall be made by law for the distribution of the income of the school fund among the several towns and cities of the state for the support of common schools therein, in some just proportion to the number of children and youth resident therein between the ages of four and twenty years, and no appropriation shall be made from the school fund to any city or town for the year in which said city or town shall fail to raise such tax; nor to any school district for the year in which a school shall not be maintained at least three months.

State university; support. Section 6. Provision shall be made by law for the establishment of a state university at or near the seat of state government, and for connecting with the same, from time to time, such colleges in different parts of the state as the interests of education may require. The proceeds of all lands that have been or may hereafter be granted by the United States to the state for the support of a university shall be and remain a perpetual fund to be called "the university fund," the interest of which shall be appropriated to the support of the state university, and no sectarian instruction shall be allowed in such university.

Commissioners of public lands. Section 7. The secretary of state, treasurer and attorney general, shall constitute a board of commissioners for the sale of the school and university lands and for the investment of the funds arising therefrom. Any two of said commissioners shall be a quorum for the transaction of all business pertaining to the duties of their office.

Sale of public lands. Section 8. Provision shall be made by law for the sale of all school and university lands after they shall have been appraised; and when any portion of such lands shall be sold and the purchase money shall not be paid at the time of the sale, the commissioners shall take security by mortgage upon the lands sold for the sum remaining unpaid, with seven per cent interest thereon, payable annually at the office of the treasurer. The commissioners shall be authorized to execute a good and sufficient conveyance to all purchasers of such lands, and to discharge any mortgages taken as security, when the sum due thereon shall have been paid. The commissioners shall have power to withhold from sale any portion of such lands when they shall deem it expedient, and shall invest all moneys arising from the sale of such lands, as well as all other university and school funds, in such manner as the legislature shall provide, and shall give such security for the faithful performance of their duties as may be required by law.

ARTICLE XI—Corporations

Corporations; how formed. Section 1. Corporations without banking powers or privileges may be formed under general laws, but shall not be created by special act, except for municipal purposes. All general laws or special acts enacted under the provisions of this section may be altered or repealed by the legislature at any time after their passage.

Property taken by municipality. Section 2. No municipal corporation shall take private property for public use, against the consent of the owner, without the necessity thereof being first established in the manner prescribed by the legislature.

Municipal home rule; debt limit; tax to pay debt. Section 3. (1) Cities and villages organized pursuant to state law may determine their local affairs and government, subject only to this constitution and to such enactments of the legislature of statewide concern as with uniformity shall affect every city or every village. The method of such determination shall be prescribed by the legislature.

(2) No county, city, town, village, school district, sewerage district or other municipal corporation may become indebted in an amount that exceeds an allowable percentage of the taxable property located therein equalized for state purposes as provided by the

legislature. In all cases the allowable percentage shall be 5 percent except as specified in pars. (a) and (b):

(a) For any city authorized to issue bonds for school purposes, an additional 10 percent shall be permitted for school purposes only, and in such cases the territory attached to the city for school purposes shall be included in the total taxable property supporting the bonds issued for school purposes.

(b) For any school district which offers no less than grades one to 12 and which at the time of incurring such debt is eligible for the highest level of school aids, 10 percent shall be permitted.

(3) Any county, city, town, village, school district, sewerage district or other municipal corporation incurring any indebtedness under sub. (2) shall, before or at the time of doing so, provide for the collection of a direct annual tax sufficient to pay the interest on such debt as it falls due, and also to pay and discharge the principal thereof within 20 years from the time of contracting the same.

(4) When indebtedness under sub. (2) is incurred in the acquisition of lands by cities, or by counties or sewerage districts having a population of 150,000 or over, for public, municipal purposes, or for the permanent improvement thereof, or to purchase, acquire, construct, extend, add to or improve a sewage collection or treatment system which services all or a part of such city or county, the city, county or sewerage district incurring the indebtedness shall, before or at the time of so doing, provide for the collection of a direct annual tax sufficient to pay the interest on such debt as it falls due, and also to pay and discharge the principal thereof within a period not exceeding 50 years from the time of contracting the same.

(5) An indebtedness created for the purpose of purchasing, acquiring, leasing, constructing, extending, adding to, improving, conducting, controlling, operating or managing a public utility of a town, village, city or special district, and secured solely by the property or income of such public utility, and whereby no municipal liability is created, shall not be considered an indebtedness of such town, village, city or special district, and shall not be included in arriving at the debt limitation under sub. (2).

Acquisition of lands by state and subdivisions; sale of excess. Section 3a. The state or any of its counties, cities, towns or villages may acquire by gift, dedication, purchase, or condemnation lands for establishing, laying out, widening, enlarging, extending, and maintaining memorial grounds, streets, highways, squares, parkways, boulevards, parks, playgrounds, sites for public buildings, and reservations in and about and along and leading to any or all of the same; and after the establishment, layout, and completion of such improvements, may convey any such real estate thus acquired and not necessary for such improvements, with reservations concerning the future use and occupation of such real estate, so as to protect such public works and improvements, and their environs, and to preserve the view, appearance, light, air, and usefulness of such public works. If the governing body of a county, city, town or village elects to accept a gift or dedication of land made on condition that the land be devoted to a special purpose and the condition subsequently becomes impossible or impracticable, such governing body may by resolution or ordinance enacted by a two-thirds vote of its members elect either to grant the land back to the donor or dedicator or his heirs or accept from the donor or dedicator or his heirs a grant relieving the county, city, town or village of the condition; however, if the donor or dedicator or his heirs are unknown or cannot be found, such resolution or ordinance may provide for the commencement of proceedings in the manner and in the courts as the legislature shall designate for the purpose of relieving the county, city, town or village from the condition of the gift or dedication.

General banking law. Section 4. The legislature may enact a general banking law for the creation of banks, and for the regulation and supervision of the banking business.

ARTICLE XII—Amendments

Constitutional amendments. Section 1. Any amendment or amendments to this constitution may be proposed in either house of the legislature, and if the same shall be agreed to by a majority of the members elected to each of the two houses, such proposed amendment or amendments shall be entered on their journals, with the yeas and nays taken thereon, and referred to the legislature to be chosen at the next general election, and shall be published for three months previous to the time of holding such election; and if, in the legislature so next chosen, such proposed amendment or amendments shall be agreed to by a majority of all the members elected to each house, then it shall be the duty of the legislature to submit such proposed amendment or amendments to the people in such manner and at such time as the legislature shall prescribe; and if the people shall approve and ratify such amendment or amendments by a majority of the electors voting thereon, such amendment or amendments shall become part of the constitution; provided, that if more than one amendment be submitted, they shall be submitted in such manner that the people may vote for or against such amendments separately.

Constitutional conventions. Section 2. If at any time a majority of the senate and assembly shall deem it necessary to call a convention to revise or change this constitution, they shall recommend to the electors to vote for or against a convention at the next election for members of the legislature. And if it shall appear that a majority of the electors voting thereon have voted for a convention, the legislature shall, at its next session, provide for calling such convention.

ARTICLE XIII—Miscellaneous provisions

Political year; elections. Section 1. The political year for this state shall commence on the first Monday of January in each year, and the general election shall be held on the Tuesday next succeeding the first Monday of November in even-numbered years.

Eligibility to office. Section 3. (1) No member of congress and no person holding any office of profit or trust under the United States except postmaster, or under any foreign power, shall be eligible to any office of trust, profit or honor in this state.

(2) No person convicted of a felony, in any court within the United States, no person convicted in federal court of a crime designated, at the time of commission, under federal law as a misdemeanor involving a violation of public trust and no person convicted, in a court of a state, of a crime designated, at the time of commission, under the law of the state as a misdemeanor involving a violation of public trust shall be eligible to any office of trust, profit or honor in this state unless pardoned of the conviction.

(3) No person may seek to have placed on any ballot for a state or local elective office in this state the name of a person convicted of a felony, in any court within the United States, the name of a person convicted in federal court of a crime designated, at the time of commission, under federal law as a misdemeanor involving a violation of public trust or the name of a person convicted, in a court of a state, of a crime designated, at the time of commission, under the law of the state as a misdemeanor involving a violation of public trust, unless the person named for the ballot has been pardoned of the conviction.

Great seal. Section 4. It shall be the duty of the legislature to provide a great seal for the state, which shall be kept by the secretary of state, and all official acts of the governor, his approbation of the laws excepted, shall be thereby authenticated.

Legislative officers. Section 6. The elective officers of the legislature, other than the presiding officers, shall be a chief clerk and a sergeant at arms, to be elected by each house.

Division of counties. Section 7. No county with an area of nine hundred square miles or less shall be divided or have any part stricken therefrom, without submitting the question to a vote of the people of the county, nor unless a majority of all the legal voters of the county voting on the question shall vote for the same.

Removal of county seats. Section 8. No county seat shall be removed until the point to which it is proposed to be removed shall be fixed by law, and a majority of the voters of the county voting on the question shall have voted in favor of its removal to such point.

Election or appointment of statutory officers. Section 9. All county officers whose election or appointment is not provided for by this constitution shall be elected by the electors of the respective counties, or appointed by the boards of supervisors, or other county authorities, as the legislature shall direct. All city, town and village officers whose election or appointment is not provided for by this constitution shall be elected by the electors of such cities, towns and villages, or of some division thereof, or appointed by such authorities thereof as the legislature shall designate for that purpose. All other officers whose election or appointment is not provided for by this constitution, and all officers whose offices may hereafter be created by law, shall be elected by the people or appointed, as the legislature may direct.

Vacancies in office. Section 10. (1) The legislature may declare the cases in which any office shall be deemed vacant, and also the manner of filling the vacancy, where no provision is made for that purpose in this constitution.

(2) Whenever there is a vacancy in the office of lieutenant governor, the governor shall nominate a successor to serve for the balance of the unexpired term, who shall take office after confirmation by the senate and by the assembly.

Passes, franks and privileges. Section 11. No person, association, copartnership, or corporation, shall promise, offer or give, for any purpose, to any political committee, or any member or employe thereof, to any candidate for, or incumbent of any office or position under the constitution or laws, or under any ordinance of any town or municipality, of this state, or to any person at the request or for the advantage of all or any of them, any free pass or frank, or any privilege withheld from any person, for the traveling accommodation or transportation of any person or property, or the transmission of any message or communication.

No political committee, and no member or employee thereof, no candidate for and no incumbent of any office or position under the constitution or laws, or under any ordinance of any town or municipality of this state, shall ask for, or accept, from any person, association, copartnership, or corporation, or use, in any manner, or for any purpose, any free pass or frank, or any privilege withheld from any person, for the traveling accommodation or transportation of any person or property, or the transmission of any message or communication.

Any violation of any of the above provisions shall be bribery and punished as provided by law, and if any officer or any member of the legislature be guilty thereof, his office shall become vacant.

No person within the purview of this act shall be privileged from testifying in relation to anything therein prohibited; and no person having so testified shall be liable to any prosecution or punishment for any offense concerning which he was required to give his testimony or produce any documentary evidence.

Notaries public and regular employees of a railroad or other public utilities who are candidates for or hold public offices for which the annual compensation is not more than three hundred dollars to whom no passes or privileges are extended beyond those which are extended to other regular employees of such corporations are excepted from the provisions of this section.

Recall of elective officers. Section 12. The qualified electors of the state, of any congressional, judicial or legislative district or of any county may petition for the recall of any incumbent elective officer after the first year of the term for which the incumbent was elected, by filing a petition with the filing officer with whom the nomination petition to the office in the primary is filed, demanding the recall of the incumbent.

(1) The recall petition shall be signed by electors equalling at least twenty-five percent of the vote cast for the office of governor at the last preceding election, in the state, county or district which the incumbent represents.

(2) The filing officer with whom the recall petition is filed shall call a recall election for the Tuesday of the 6th week after the date of filing the petition or, if that Tuesday is a legal holiday, on the first day after that Tuesday which is not a legal holiday.

(3) The incumbent shall continue to perform the duties of the office until the recall election results are officially declared.

(4) Unless the incumbent declines within 10 days after the filing of the petition, the incumbent shall without filing be deemed to have filed for the recall election. Other candidates may file for the office in the manner provided by law for special elections. For the purpose of conducting elections under this section:

(a) When more than 2 persons compete for a nonpartisan office, a recall primary shall be held. The 2 persons receiving the highest number of votes in the recall primary shall be the 2 candidates in the recall election, except that if any candidate receives a majority of the total number of votes cast in the recall primary, that candidate shall assume the office for the remainder of the term and a recall election shall not be held.

(b) For any partisan office, a recall primary shall be held for each political party which is by law entitled to a separate ballot and from which more than one candidate competes for the party's nomination in the recall election. The person receiving the highest number of votes in the recall primary for each political party shall be that party's candidate in the recall election. Independent candidates and candidates representing political parties not entitled by law to a separate ballot shall be shown on the ballot for the recall election only.

(c) When a recall primary is required, the date specified under sub. (2) shall be the date of the recall primary and the recall election shall be held on the Tuesday of the 4th week after the recall primary or, if that Tuesday is a legal holiday, on the first day after that Tuesday which is not a legal holiday.

(5) The person who receives the highest number of votes in the recall election shall be elected for the remainder of the term.

(6) After one such petition and recall election, no further recall petition shall be filed against the same officer during the term for which he was elected.

(7) This section shall be self-executing and mandatory. Laws may be enacted to facilitate its operation but no law shall be enacted to hamper, restrict or impair the right of recall.

Marriage. Section 13. Only a marriage between one man and one woman shall be valid or recognized as a marriage in this state. A legal status identical or substantially similar to that of marriage for unmarried individuals shall not be valid or recognized in this state.

ARTICLE XIV—Schedule

Effect of change from territory to state. Section 1. That no inconvenience may arise by reason of a change from a territorial to a permanent state government, it is declared that all rights, actions, prosecutions, judgments, claims and contracts, as well of individuals as of bodies corporate, shall continue as if no such change had taken place; and all process which may be issued under the authority of the territory of Wisconsin previous to its admission into the union of the United States shall be as valid as if issued in the name of the state.

Territorial laws continued. Section 2. All laws now in force in the territory of Wisconsin which are not repugnant to this constitution shall remain in force until they expire by their own limitation or be altered or repealed by the legislature.

Common law continued in force. Section 13. Such parts of the common law as are now in force in the territory of Wisconsin, not inconsistent with this constitution, shall be and continue part of the law of this state until altered or suspended by the legislature.

Implementing revised structure of judicial branch. Section 16. **(4)** The terms of office of justices of the supreme court serving on August 1, 1978, shall expire on the July 31 next preceding the first Monday in January on which such terms would otherwise have expired, but such advancement of the date of term expiration shall not impair any retirement rights vested in any such justice if the term had expired on the first Monday in January.

INDEX

Accounting Examining Board, 226, 634
Acts, Wisconsin (Session Laws), 137, 164, 229
  significant enactments of the 2021 Legislature, 364–84
Adjutant general, 209, 634
Administration, Department of, 177–85, 359
Administrative rules, 152
Administrative Rules, Joint Committee for Review of, 143
Administrators, county, 340–41, 652–53
Adoption and Medical Assistance, Interstate Compact on, 259
Adult Offender Supervision, Interstate Compact for, 259, 634
Adult Offender Supervision Board, Interstate, 191, 634
Aerospace Authority, Wisconsin, 245, 634
Affirmative Action, Council on, 178, 634
Agard, Melissa, senator, 21, **67**, 124, 494
Aging and Long-Term Care, Board on, 179, 634
Agricultural Producer Security Council, 186
Agricultural Safety and Health, UW Center for, 238
Agriculture, Trade and Consumer Protection
  Board, 185, 634
  Department of, 185–87
  significant legislation, 2021 session, 364
  statistics, 706–11
Alcohol and Other Drug Abuse, State Council on, 167, 634
Alcohol and Other Drug Abuse Programs, State Superintendent's Advisory Council on, 219
Allen, Scott, representative, **118**, 618, 622
Amendments to the constitution, historical table, 509–14
American Family Field, 251
Anderson, Clinton, representative, **66**, 616, 620
Anderson, Jimmy, representative, **68**, 617, 620
Andraca, Deb, representative, **44**, 616, 619
Appeals, court of, 263–65
  district map, 264
  election results, 628–30
  judges, 263–65
  significant decisions, July 2020–July 2022, 385–421
Appointments by governor, 167, 634–45
Apprenticeship Advisory Council, Wisconsin, 243
Architects, Landscape Architects, Professional Engineers, Designers, Professional Land Surveyors, and Registered Interior Designers, Examining Board of, 227, 634–35
Area Health Education Centers, 237
Armstrong, David, representative, **95**, 617, 621
Artistic Endowment Foundation, Wisconsin, 247, 635
Arts Board, 231, 635
Assembly
  caucus chairs, 124
  chief clerk, 21, 124, 127, 131, 494–96
  committees, 128–30, 139–142
  district maps, 22–118
  election results, 616–22
  employees, 124, 131
  majority leader, 21, 124, 127, 493–94
  majority leader, assistant, 21, 124
  members, biographies and photos, 23–120
  minority leader, 21, 124, 127, 493–94
  minority leader, assistant, 21, 124, 127, 493–94
  officers, 21, 124, 127, 128
  political composition, 496–98
  sergeant at arms, 21, 122, 124, 127, 494–96
  sessions, 126, 131, 422–34, 435–52, 498–502, 506–7
  speaker, 21, 124, 127, 129, 490–92
  speaker pro tempore, 21, 124, 127
  term of office, 125
Assessors, State Board of, 224
Athletic Trainers Affiliated Credentialing Board, 226, 635
Attorney general, 207–8
  biography and photo, 5
  list of, 485–86

Auctioneer Board, 226, 635
Audit Bureau, Legislative, 160–62
Audit Committee, Joint Legislative, 149–50
August, Tyler, representative, 21, **53**, 124, 494, 616, 619, 623
Authorities, 244–46, 664
Autism, Council on, 171
Automatic Fire Sprinkler System Contractors and Journeymen Council, 225

Baldeh, Samba, representative, **69**, 617, 620
Baldwin, Tammy, U.S. senator, **12**, 520, 524
Ballweg, Joan, senator, **61**, 124
Banking Institutions Review Board, 197, 635
Bar Examiners, Board of, 270–71
Bar of Wisconsin, State, 275–76
Bare, Mike, representative, **101**, 617, 621
Baseball Park District, Southeast Wisconsin Professional, 251, 346, 643
Bay-Lake Regional Planning Commission, 248
Behnke, Elijah, representative, **110**, 618, 621
Beverages, significant legislation, 2021 session, 364
Bicycle Coordinating Council, 170
Billings, Jill, representative, **116**, 124, 618, 622, 640
Bills, how become a law, 131–37
Binsfeld, Amy, representative, **48**, 616, 619
Birth Defect Prevention and Surveillance, Council on, 199
Birth to Three Early Intervention Interagency Coordinating Council, 170
Blazel, Edward (Ted) A., assembly chief clerk, 21, **122**, 124, 496
Blind and Visual Impairment Education Advisory Council, 218
Blindness, Council on, 199
Board chairs, county, 652–53
Board of Commissioners of Public Lands, 220
Bodden, Ty, representative, **80**, 617, 620
Born, Mark L., representative, **60**, 616, 619
Bradley, Ann Walsh, supreme court justice, **8**, 490
Bradley, Marc Julian, senator, **103**
Bradley, Rebecca Grassl, supreme court justice, **9**, 490

Bradley Center Sports and Entertainment Corporation, 246–47, 635
Brandtjen, Janel, representative, **44**, 614, 616, 619
Broadband Access, Governor's Task Force on, 173–74
Brooks, Robert, representative, **81**, 617, 620
Budget, state, 357–63
 allocations, 659–60
 executive budget, 359–61
 legislative process, 357–63
Building Commission, State of Wisconsin, 158–59, 635
Building Program, State of Wisconsin, 158–59
Burial Sites Preservation Board, 204, 635
Business and consumer law, significant legislation, 2021 session, 364
Business Development, Office of, 182
Byers, Anne Tonnon, assembly sergeant at arms, 21, **122**, 124, 496

Cabral-Guevara, Rachael, senator, **76**, 614, 615
Cabrera, Marisabel, representative, **30**, 616, 618
Callahan, Calvin, representative, **56**, 616, 619
Campaign finance, 332–38. *See also* Ethics Commission
Capital Area Regional Planning Commission, 248
Capitol and Executive Residence Board, State, 182–84, 643
Carpenter, Tim, senator, **28**, 614, 615
Cartographer, Office of the State, 238
Caucuses, legislative, 127
 chairs, 124
Cemetery Board, 226, 635
Certification Standards Review Council, 178
CESA districts, 703
Charter schools, 351–53, 704
Chief clerks, legislature, 21, 121, **122**, 124, 127, 131, 494–96
Child Abuse and Neglect Prevention Board, 188–89, 635
Children, Interstate Compact on the Placement of, 260
Children, significant legislation, 2021 session, 364–65

Children and Families, Department of, 187–89
Chiropractic Examining Board, 226, 635
Circuit court, 265–69
    administrative districts, 265–66
    clerks, 653–54
    election results, 630–33
    judges, 265–66, 645–50
Circus World Museum Foundation, 203, 635
Cities
    government, 320, 342–44
    population, 537–58, 566–68
Claims Board, 180, 635
Clancy, Ryan, representative, **41**, 616, 619
Clean Energy and Environmental Innovation, Governor's Green Ribbon Commission on, 172–73
Clerks, chief, of the legislature, 21, 121, 122, 124, 127, 131, 494–96
Clerks, circuit court, 653–54
Clerks, county, 326–28, 341, 650–51
Coastal Management Council, Wisconsin, 175
Coat of arms, state, 454
College Savings Program Board, 197, 635
Commerce and industry, statistics, 675–80
Commercial Building Code Council, 225, 635
Committees
    governor's special, 169–76
    Joint Legislative Council study, 151, 154–56
    legislative, 128–30, 137–58
Congress, U.S., Wisconsin members, biographies and photos, 12–18
    election results, 570–79
Congressional district map, 13
Conley, Sue, representative, **65**, 616, 620
Conservation, statistics, 712–16
Conservation Congress, 216
Considine, Dave, representative, **102**, 617, 621
Constitution, Wisconsin,
    amendments, historical table, 509–14
    significant legislation, 2021 session, 384
    text, 727–62
Constitution Party of Wisconsin, 624
Controlled Substances Board, 225, 635
Conveyance Safety Code Council, 225, 635–36

Coroners, 655–56
Correctional and treatment facilities, 691–92
Corrections
    Department of, 189–92
    significant legislation, 2021 session, 365–66
    statistics, 691–92
Corrections Compact, Interstate, 259
Corrections System Formulary Board, 190
Cosmetology Examining Board, 226, 636
Counties
    area, 533–35
    clerks, 326–38, 341, 650–51
    county seats, 533–35
    creation date, 533–35
    executives, 340–41, 652–53
    government, 340–41
    officers, 652–56
    population, 533–35, 537–55
Courts
    administrative districts, circuit courts, 268
    appeals, court of, 263–65
    circuit courts, 265–69, 630–33, 645–50, 653–54
    commissioners, 261, 268–69
    director of state courts, office of, 275
    election results, 625–33
    judges, 264–70, 628–33
    justices, 8–11, 261–63, 489–90, 625–27
    Law Library, David T. Prosser Jr. State, 271
    municipal courts, 269–70
    significant decisions, July 2020–July 2022, 385–421
    significant legislation, 2021 session, 366–67
    supreme court, 8–11, 261–63, 489–90, 625–27
Cowles, Robert L., senator, **25**
Credit Union Review Board, 197, 636
Credit Unions, Office of, 197, 679–80
Crime, significant legislation, 2021 session, 367–68
Crime Victims Council, 208
Crime Victims Rights Board, 208, 636
Criminal Justice Coordinating Council, 171
Criminal Penalties, Joint Review Committee on, 157, 636

Dallet, Rebecca Frank, supreme court justice, **9**, 490
Dallman, Alex, representative, **62**, 616, 619
Deaf and Hard of Hearing, Council for the, 199, 636
Deaf and Hard-of-Hearing Education Council, 219
Deferred Compensation Board, 194, 636
Democratic Party of Wisconsin, 623
Dentistry Examining Board, 227, 636
Detainers, Interstate Agreement on, 259
Developmental Disabilities, Board for People with, 179, 636
Dietitians Affiliated Credentialing Board, 227, 636
Disabilities
  Blind and Visual Impairment Education Council, 218
  Blindness, Council on, 199
  Deaf and Hard of Hearing, Council for the, 199, 636
  Deaf and Hard-of-Hearing Education Council, 219
  Developmental Disabilities, Board for People with, 179, 636
  Disabilities, Governor's Committee for People with, 171
  Physical Disabilities, Council on, 201, 641–42
  Special Education, Council on, 219
  vocational rehabilitation, 176, 242
Disability Board, 168
Distance Learning Authorization Board, 202, 636
District attorneys, 655–56
Districts, legislative, 20
Dittrich, Barbara, representative, **59**, 616, 619
Domestic Abuse, Governor's Council on, 188, 636
Domestic relations, significant legislation, 2021 session, 368–69
Donovan, Bob, representative, **105**, 617, 621
Doyle, Steve, representative, **116**, 618, 621
Drake, Dora, representative, **32**, 616, 618
Dry Cleaner Environmental Response Council, 212, 636
Duchow, Cindi S., representative, **120**, 124, 618, 622
Dwelling Code Council, Uniform, 226, 644

Early Childhood Advisory Council, 171
Early College Credit Program, 350–51
East Central Wisconsin Regional Planning Commission, 248
Eau Claire campus, UW System, 235
Economic development, significant legislation, 2021 session, 369
Edming, James W., representative, **108**, 617, 621
Education,
  Commission of the States, 252, 636
  significant legislation, 2021 session, 369–71
  statistics, 697–705
  See also Public education; Public Instruction, Department of; Schools; Private schools; Charter schools
Educational Communications Board, 192, 637
Elections,
  absentee voting, 332
  attorney general, 605–7
  campaign finance, 332–38
  circuit court judges, 630–33
  Congress, U.S., 118th, 570–79
  constitutional amendments, 2021 session, 384
  constitutional amendments, historical table, 509–14
  county clerk duties, 326–27
  court of appeals, 628–30
  Elections Commission, 192–93, 326, 637
  Ethics Commission, 195–96, 637
  general election, 318–19, 323–24
  gubernatorial, 579–81, 481–84, 585–604
  judges, 628–33
  lieutenant governor, 582–604
  municipal clerk duties, 327–28
  nonpartisan, 320–21
  nonpartisan primary, 321–22
  partisan, 318–19
  partisan primary, 319–20
  political parties, 319–20, 623–24
  polling place, 331–32
  presidential election, 322–24, 517–19
  presidential preference primary, 322–23
  recall, 325
  referenda, 325–26, 515–16
  representatives, state, 616–22
  representatives, U.S., 574–79
  secretary of state, 611–13

senators, state, 614–15
senators, U.S., 570–74
significant legislation, 2021 session, 371
special election (to fill midterm vacancy), 324–25
spring election, 320–21
spring primary, 321–22
statistical tables, 570–633
supreme court justices, 625–27
treasurer, 608–10
voter eligibility, 328
voter registration, 329–30
when held, 318–25
Elections Commission, 192–93, 326, 637
Electronic Recording Council, 181, 637
Emergency Management, Division of, Department of Military Affairs, 209, 211, 637
Emergency Management Assistance Compact, 259
Emergency Management Assistance Compact, Northern, 259–60
Emergency Medical Services Board, 201, 637
Emerson, Jodi, representative, 113, 618, 621
Employee Trust Funds
  Board, 193–94, 637
  Department of, 193–95
Employees Suggestion Board, State, 179, 643
Employment
  significant legislation, 2021 session, 371–72
  statistics, 681–85
Employment Relations
  Commission, 243, 637
  Joint Committee on, 144–45
Engels, Tom, senate sergeant at arms, 21, 121, 124, 496
Environment, significant legislation, 2021 session, 372
Environmental Education, Wisconsin Center for, 238
Ethics Commission, 195–96, 637
Evers, Tony, governor, 4, 480, 484, 487, 579–81, 585–604
Executive officers, state, 4–7, 579–613
Executives, county, 340–41, 652–53
Extension, UW System, 235
Extraordinary sessions of the legislature, 130–31, 435–52, 506–7

Fairs. *See* State Fair Park Board
Farm to School Council, 186
Farmland Advisory Council, 223
Felzkowski, Mary J., senator, 55
Fertilizer Research Council, 186
Feyen, Dan, senator, 21, 73, 124
Finance, Joint Committee on, 145–47, 361–62
Finance, public, 659–74. *See also* Budget, state
Financial aid, student, 202, 230
Financial Institutions
  Department of, 196–97
  significant legislation, 2021 session, 372
Financial Literacy and Capability, Governor's Council on, 172
Fire Department Advisory Council, 213–14
Fiscal Bureau, Legislative, 162–63, 361–62
Fitzgerald, Scott, U.S. representative, 16, 493–94, 521, 524, 575, 578
Flag, state, 454
Football Stadium District, Professional, 250, 346–47
Forestry, Council on, 212, 637
Fox River Navigational System Authority, 244, 637
Funeral Directors Examining Board, 227, 637

Gallagher, Mike, U.S. representative, 17, 521, 525, 576, 579
Genetic Counselors Affiliated Credentialing Board, 227, 637
Geological and Natural History Survey, 237
Geologist, state, 237
Geologists, Hydrologists, and Soil Scientists, Examining Board of Professional, 227, 637
Godlewski, Sarah, secretary of state, 7, 488, 570–72
Goeben, Joy, representative, 26, 616, 618
Governor, 166–76
  appointments by, 167, 634–45
  biography and photo, 4
  elections, 481–84, 579–81, 585–604
  list of, 480
  role in state budget, 359–61
  special committees, 169–76
  vetoes, 125, 137, 167, 358, 363, 498–502, 508

Goyke, Evan, representative, **39**, 616, 619
Great Lakes Commission, 252–53, 637
Great Lakes Protection Fund, 253, 637
Great Lakes-St. Lawrence River Basin Water Resources Council, 253
Great Lakes-St. Lawrence River Water Resources Regional Body, 254
Green, Chanz, representative, **95**, 617, 621
Green Bay campus, UW System, 235
Green Ribbon Commission on Clean Energy and Environmental Innovation, Governor's, 172–73
Grothman, Glenn, U.S. representative, **16**, 521, 524, 575–76, 578
Groundwater Coordinating Council, 214, 637
Group Insurance Board, 194, 637–38
Gundrum, Rick, representative, **80**, 617, 620
Gustafson, Nathaniel Lee, representative, **77**, 617, 620

Hagedorn, Brian, supreme court justice, **10**, 490
Handicapped. *See* Disabilities
Haywood, Kalan, representative, 21, **38**, 124, 616, 619
Health and human services, significant legislation, 2021 session, 373–74
Health Care Liability Insurance Plan, Wisconsin, 206, 638
Health Care Provider Advisory Committee, 242
Health Services, Department of, 198–201
Hearing and Speech Examining Board, 227, 638
Hearings and Appeals, Division of, Department of Administration, 180
Herbarium, Wisconsin State, 238
Hesselbein, Dianne, senator, **100**, 124, 614, 615
Higher Education Commission, Midwestern, 256–57, 640
Higher Educational Aids Board, 201–2, 638
Highway Safety, Council on, 233, 638
Historic Preservation Review Board, 204–5, 638
Historical Museum, Wisconsin, 203
Historical Records Advisory Board, 174
Historical Society of Wisconsin, State, 202–5
  Curators, Board of, 643

History of Wisconsin
  historical lists, 480–525
  significant events, 460–79
Homeland Security Council, 174
Homelessness, Interagency Council on, 181, 638
Hong, Francesca, representative, **98**, 617, 621
House of Representatives, U.S., *See* Representatives, U.S., from Wisconsin
Housing, significant legislation, 2021 session, 374
Humanities Council, Wisconsin, 168
Hurd, Karen, representative, **89**, 617, 621
Hutton, Rob, senator, **34**, 614, 615
Hygiene Board, Laboratory of, 238–39, 639

Incorporation Review Board, 181
Independent Living Council of Wisconsin, 174–75
Information Policy and Technology, Joint Committee on, 147
Information Technology Executive Steering Committee, Governor's, 173
Injured Patients and Families Compensation Fund, 205, 206, 207
  Board of Governors, 206, 638
  Peer Review Council, 206
Insurance
  Office of the Commissioner of, 205–6
  significant legislation, 2021 session, 374
Insurance Product Regulation Commission, Interstate, 255
Insurance Security Fund, Board of Directors of the, 205–6
Interoperability Council, 211, 638
Interstate Adult Offender Supervision Board, 191, 634
Interstate Compacts, 252–60
Interstate Juvenile Supervision, State Board for, 191–92, 638
Invasive Species Council, 215, 638
Investment and Local Impact Fund Board, 224, 638
Investment Board, State of Wisconsin, 206–7, 638

Jacobson, Jenna, representative, **65**, 616, 620
Jacque, André, senator, **22**, 614, 615

Jagler, John, senator, **58**, 614, 615
James, Jesse, senator, **88**, 614, 615
Joers, Alex, representative, **101**, 617, 621
Johnson, LaTonya, senator, **37**, 635
Johnson, Ron, U.S. senator, **12**, 520, 570–72, 573–74
Johnson, Scott, representative, **54**, 616, 619
Joint Committee on Finance, 145–47, 361–62
Joint Legislative Council, 150–52
 permanent committees, 152–53
 staff, 162
 study committees, 154–56
Judges
 appeals, court of, 263–65, 628–30
 circuit court, 265–69, 645–50
 election results, 628–33
 municipal court, 269–70
 supreme court (*see* Justices, supreme court)
Judicial
 administrative districts, 267–68
 Commission, 271–72, 639
 Conduct Advisory Committee, 272
 Conference, 272–73
 Council, 273, 639
 Education Committee, 273–74
 Planning and Policy Advisory Committee, 275
 Selection Advisory Committee, Governor's, 173
 See also Courts; Judges; Justices, supreme court
Justice, Department of, 207–9
Justices, supreme court
 biographies and photos, 8–11
 election results, 625–27
 list of, 489–90
 See also Supreme court
Juvenile Justice Commission, Governor's, 173
Juvenile Supervision, State Board for Interstate, 191–92, 638
Juveniles, Interstate Commission for, 254

Kapenga, Chris, senator, 21, **118**, 124, 492, 614, 615
Karofsky, Jill J., supreme court justice, **10**, 490
Katsma, Terry, representative, **47**, 616, 619

Kaul, Joshua L., attorney general, 5, 486, 605–7
Kickapoo Reserve Management Board, 232, 639
Kitchens, Joel C., representative, **23**, 616, 618
Knodl, Dan, senator, **43**, 614, 615, 616, 619
Krug, Scott S., representative, **93**, 617, 621
Kurtz, Tony, representative, **71**, 617, 620

La Crosse campus, UW System, 235
La Follette, Douglas J., secretary of state, 487–88, 611–13
La Follette (Robert M.) School of Public Affairs, 238
Labor. *See* Employment Relations
Labor and Industry Review Commission, 181, 639
Laboratories, state
 Hygiene, 238–39, 639
 Soils and Plant Analysis, 238
 Veterinary Diagnostic, 239–40, 645
Lake Michigan Commercial Fishing Board, 215, 639
Lake Superior Commercial Fishing Board, 215, 639
Lambeau Field, 250, 346
Land and Water Conservation Board, 186–87, 639
Lands, Board of Commissioners of Public, 220
Larson, Chris, senator, **40**, 124, 494, 614, 615
Law enforcement, significant legislation, 2021 session, 374–75
Law Enforcement Standards Board, 208–9, 639
Law Library, David T. Prosser Jr. State, 271
Law Revision Committee, 153
Laws of Wisconsin. *See* Acts, Wisconsin
Lawyer Regulation System, 274
Legislation, summary, 2021 session, 364–84
Legislative Audit Bureau, 160
Legislative Audit Committee, Joint, 149–50
Legislative Council, Joint, 150–52
 permanent committees, 152–53
 staff, 162
 study committees, 154–56
Legislative districts, 20
 maps, 20, 22–118
 population, 536–37

Legislative Fiscal Bureau, 162–63, 361–62
Legislative Organization, Joint Committee on, 148–49
Legislative Reference Bureau, 137, 163–65, 360, 362
Legislative Technology Services Bureau, 165
Legislature
  biographies and photos, 22–120
  budget, 357–63
  caucus chairs, 124
  chief clerks, 21, 121, 122, 124, 127, 131, 494–96
  commissions, 142–43, 158–60
  committees, 128–30, 137–58
  districts, 20
  election results, 614–22
  employees, 124, 131
  extraordinary sessions, 130–31, 435–52, 506–7
  hearings, 128, 132
  how a bill becomes a law, 131–37
  legislation, summary of 2021 significant, 364–84
  majority leaders, 21, 124, 127, 493–94
  majority leaders, assistant, 21, 124, 127
  maps of districts, 20, 22–118
  minority leaders, 21, 124, 127, 493–94
  minority leaders, assistant, 21, 124, 127
  officers, 21, 124, 127–28
  personal data of legislators, 622
  political composition, 496–98
  president, senate, 21, 124, 127, 490–92
  president pro tempore, senate, 21, 124, 127, 490–92
  publications, 151, 161, 162, 164
  representatives, state, 23–120, 616–22
  rules, 126
  schedule, 126, 130–31
  senators, state, 22–118, 614–15
  sergeants at arms, 21, 121, 122, 124, 127, 494–96
  service agencies, 160–65
  sessions, 126, 130–31, 422–34, 435–52, 498–507
  speaker, assembly, 21, 124, 127, 129, 490–92
  speaker pro tempore, assembly, 21, 124, 127
  special sessions, 131, 422–34, 502–6
Legislatures, former, historical lists
  chief clerks, 494–96
  majority leaders, 493–94
  minority leaders, 493–94
  political composition, 496–98
  presidents, senate, 490–92
  presidents pro tempore, senate, 490–92
  sergeants at arms, 494–96
  sessions, 498–507
  speakers of the assembly, 490–92
Leiber, John, state treasurer, **6**, 488, 608–10
LeMahieu, Devin, senator, 21, **46**, 124, 494, 614, 615
Library, David T. Prosser Jr. State Law, 271
Library and Network Development, Council on, 219, 639
Licensing of trades and occupations. *See* Safety and Professional Services, Department of
Lieutenant governor, 176–77
  biography and photo, 5
  election results, 582–604
  list of, 484–85
Livestock Facility Siting Review Board, 187
Local government, 340–47
  cities, 320, 342–44, 555–58, 566–68
  counties, 326–28, 340–41, 533–35, 537–55, 652–56
  finances, 664–65
  metropolitan sewerage districts, 345–46
  professional sports team stadium districts, 346–47
  school districts, 320, 328, 345, 348–56
  significant legislation, 2021 session, 375–76
  special purpose districts, 344–47
  technical college districts, 345
  towns, 320, 340, 341–42, 344, 537–55, 568–69
  villages, 320, 321, 340, 342–44, 537–55, 559–68
Lower Fox River Remediation Authority, 244, 639
Lower St. Croix Management Commission, 256
Lower Wisconsin State Riverway Board, 215–16, 639
Low-Level Radioactive Waste Commission, Midwest Interstate, 256, 640

Macco, John J., representative, **110**, 618, 621
Madison campus, UW System, 236

Madison Jr., Darrin B., representative, **32**, 616, 618
Magnafici, Gae, representative, **50**, 616, 619
Majority leaders, 21, 124, 127, 493–94
Majority leaders, assistant, 21, 124, 127
Malpractice insurance, medical, 205, 206, 275
Manufactured Housing Code Council, 226
Maps
   assembly districts, 22–118
   CESA districts, 703
   court of appeals districts, 264
   judicial administrative districts, 268
   population change, 535
   regional planning commission areas, 249
   state senate districts, 20, 22–118
   U.S. congressional districts, 13
Marklein, Howard, senator, **70**, 614, 615, 640
Marriage and Family Therapy, Professional Counseling and Social Work Examining Board, 227, 639–40
Massage Therapy and Bodywork Therapy Affiliated Credentialing Board, 227, 640
Maxey, Dave, representative, **36**, 616, 619
McGuire, Tip, representative, **86**, 617, 620
Medicaid Pharmacy Prior Authorization Advisory Committee, 200
Medical Assistance (Medicaid), 198, 200
   significant legislation, 2021 session, 373–74
   statistics, 688–89
Medical College of Wisconsin, Inc., 168, 640
Medical examiners, 655–56
Medical Examining Board, 227–28, 640
Medical Licensure Compact Commission, Interstate, 255
Medical malpractice insurance, 205, 206, 275
Mendota Mental Health Institute, 198, 692
Mental Health, Council on, 199–200, 640
Mental Health, Interstate Compact on, 259
Mental health institutions, 198, 692
Metallic Mining Council, 212
Michalski, Tom, representative, **35**, 616, 618
Midwest Interstate Low-Level Radioactive Waste Commission, 256, 640
Midwest Interstate Passenger Rail Commission, 256, 640

Midwestern Higher Education Commission, 256–57, 640
Migrant Labor, Governor's Council on, 242, 640
Military Affairs
   Department of, 209–11
   statistics, 693–96
Military and State Relations, Council on, 167, 640
Military Interstate Children's Compact Commission, 257
Milwaukee campus, UW System, 236
Milwaukee Child Welfare Partnership Council, 189, 640
Mining, 212, 216, 224
Minority leaders, 21, 124, 127, 493–94
Minority leaders, assistant, 21, 124, 127
Mississippi River Parkway Commission, 257, 640
Mississippi River Regional Planning Commission, 248
Moore, Gwendolynne S., U.S. representative, **15**, 522, 524, 575, 577
Moore Omokunde, Supreme, representative, **38**, 616, 619
Moses, Clint, representative, **50**, 616, 619
Municipal Best Practices Reviews Advisory Council, 161–62
Municipal court, 269–70
Murphy, Dave, representative, **77**, 617, 620
Mursau, Jeffrey L., representative, **57**, 616, 619, 637
Myers, LaKeshia N., representative, **33**, 616, 618, 623, 634

Nass, Stephen L., senator, **52**, 614, 615
National and Community Service Board, 182, 640–41
National Guard, 156, 167, 209–10, 694–95
Natural Areas Preservation Council, 212
Natural Resources
   Board, 211, 641
   Department of, 211–16, 713–16
   significant legislation, 2021 session, 376–77
   statistics, 713–16
Naturopathic Medicine Examining Board, 228, 641
Nedweski, Amanda, representative, **83**, 617, 620

772 | Index

Neubauer, Greta, representative, 21, **87**, 124, 494, 617, 620
Newborn Screening Advisory Group, 200–201
News media, 726
Neylon, Adam, representative, **119**, 618, 622
Nonmotorized Recreation and Transportation Trails Council, 212, 641
Nonprofit corporations, 246–47
North Central Wisconsin Regional Planning Commission, 248
Northwest Regional Planning Commission, 249
Novak, Todd, representative, **72**, 617, 620
Nurse Licensure Compact Administrators, Interstate Commission of, 254–55
Nursing, Board of, 226, 641
Nursing Home Administrator Examining Board, 228, 641

Occupational regulation, significant legislation, 2021 session, 377–79
Occupational Therapists Affiliated Credentialing Board, 228, 641
Occupational Therapy Compact Commission, 257–58
O'Connor, Jerry, representative, **74**, 617, 620
Offender Reentry, Council on, 191, 641
Off-Highway Motorcycle Council, 212, 641
Officials and employees, state, 634–58
Off-Road Vehicle Council, 212–13, 641
Ohnstad, Tod, representative, **86**, 617, 620
Oldenburg, Loren, representative, **117**, 618, 622, 640
Optometry Examining Board, 228, 641
Ortiz-Velez, Sylvia, representative, **29**, 616, 618
Oshkosh campus, UW System, 236

Palmeri, Lori, representative, **75**, 617, 620
Pardon Advisory Board, Governor's, 173
Parental choice programs, 353–54, 356
Parkside campus, UW System, 236
Parole, 180, 190, 191, 254, 259
   Commission, 191, 641
Parties, political, 319–20, 623–24
Passenger Rail Commission, Midwest Interstate, 256, 640

Patients Compensation Fund. *See* Injured Patients and Families Compensation Fund
Payroll Fraud and Worker Misclassification, Joint Enforcement Task Force on, 175
Penterman, William, representative, **59**, 616, 619
Perfusionists Examining Council, 641
Petersen, Kevin David, representative, 21, **62**, 124, 616, 619
Petryk, Warren, representative, **114**, 618, 621
Pfaff, Brad, senator, **115**, 574–75, 577
PFAS Action Council, Wisconsin, 175–76
Pharmacy Examining Board, 228, 641
Physical Disabilities, Council on, 201, 641–42
Physical Health and Wellness, Governor's Council on, 172
Physical Therapy Compact Commission, 258
Physical Therapy Examining Board, 228, 642
Physician Assistant Affiliated Credentialing Board, 228, 642
Physicians' licenses. *See* Medical Examining Board
Placement of Children, Interstate Compact on, 260
Planning, emergency, 211
Planning and Policy Advisory Committee (judicial agency), 275
Planning commissions, regional, 247–50
Platteville campus, UW System, 236
Plumbers Council, 226
Plumer, Jon, representative, 21, **63**, 124, 616, 620
Pocan, Mark, U.S. representative, **14**, 522, 524, 574, 577
Podiatry Affiliated Credentialing Board, 228, 642
Political parties, 319–20, 623–24
Population and political subdivisions, 526–69
   cities, 537–58, 566–68
   counties, 533–35, 537–55
   legislative districts, 536–37
   state, 526–33
   towns, 537–55, 568–69
   villages, 537–55, 559–68
President, senate, 21, 124, 127, 490–92

Index | 773

President pro tempore, senate, 21, 124, 127, 490–92
Presidential elections, U.S., 322–24, 517–19
Prison Industries Board, 191, 642
Private schools, 353–56, 701
Probation, 180, 190, 254, 259
Professional Baseball Park District, Southeast Wisconsin, 251, 346, 643
Professional Football Stadium District, 250, 346–47
Professional Standards Council, 219
Pronschinske, Treig E., representative, **113**, 124, 618, 621
Protasiewicz, Janet, supreme court justice, **11**, 490, 625–26, 626–27, 648
Psychiatric Health-Emotions Research Institute, 238
Psychology Examining Board, 228, 642
Psychology Interjurisdictional Compact Commission, 258
Public Defender, Office of the State, 217
Public Defender Board, 217, 642
Public education, 348–56
   CESA districts, 703
   charter schools, 351–53, 704
   Early College Credit Program, 350–51
   open enrollment, 349–50
   parental choice programs, 353–54, 356
   school districts, 320, 328, 345, 348–56
   significant legislation, 2021 session, 369–71
   Special Needs Scholarship Program, 354–56
   statistics, 697–705
   Technical College Dual Credit, 351
   See also Education; Public Instruction, Department of; Schools
Public finance statistics, 659–74
Public Health Council, 200, 642
Public Instruction
   Department of, 217–19
   state superintendent of, 6, 217, 320, 486–87
   See also Education; Public education; Schools
Public Lands, Board of Commissioners of, 220
Public Leadership Board, 239, 642
Public Records Board, 182, 642
Public Service Commission (PSC), 220–23, 642

Public utilities, significant legislation, 2021 session, 379

Qualification of Educational Personnel, Interstate Agreement on, 260
Quality Assurance and Improvement Committee, 201
Queensland, Michael J., senate chief clerk, 21, **121**, 124, 496
Quinn, Romaine, senator, **94**, 614, 615, 637

Radiography Examining Board, 228, 642
Rail Commission, Midwest Interstate Passenger, 256, 640
Railroads, Office of the Commissioner of, 222–23, 642
Ratcliff, Melissa, representative, **68**, 617, 620
Rate Regulation Advisory Committee, 188
Real Estate
   Appraisers Board, 228, 642
   Examining Board, 228, 643
   James A. Graaskamp Center for, 237
   significant legislation, 2021 session, 379–80
Recall elections, 325
Recycling, Council on, 214–15, 643
Reference Bureau, Legislative, 137, 163–65, 360, 362
Referenda, 325–26
   historical list, 515–16
Regional planning commissions, 247–50
Registers of deeds, county, 653–54
Rehabilitation Council, Wisconsin, 176
Remote Notary Council, 197, 643
Representatives, state. *See* Assembly
Representatives, U.S., from Wisconsin
   biographies and photos, 14–18
   district map, 13
   election results, 574–79
   list of, 520–525
Republican Party of Wisconsin, 623
Retirement, public employees, 157–58, 194, 195
Retirement Board, Teachers, 194–95, 644
Retirement Board, Wisconsin, 195, 643
Retirement Security, Governor's Task Force on, 174
Retirement Systems, Joint Survey Committee on, 157–58, 643

Rettinger, Nik, representative, **104**, 617, 621, 624
Revenue, Department of, 223–24
Riemer, Daniel G., representative, **29**, 616, 618
River Falls campus, UW System, 236–37
Rodriguez, Jessie, representative, **42**, 616, 619
Rodriguez, Sara, lieutenant governor, 5, 485, 582–604, 623, 638, 645
Roys, Kelda Helen, senator, 97
Rozar, Donna, representative, **90**, 617, 621
Rules, legislative, 126
Rural Health Development Council, 239, 643
Rustic Roads Board, 233–34

Safety and Professional Services, Department of, 224–28
Sapik, Angie, representative, **95**, 617, 621
Schmidt, Peter, representative, **27**, 616, 618
School District Boundary Appeal Board, 219
Schools
 charter, 351–53, 704
 districts, 320, 328, 345, 348–56
 private, 353–56, 701
 public (*see* Public education)
 technical colleges (*see* Technical College System)
 University of Wisconsin (*see* University of Wisconsin System)
 See also Education; Public Instruction, Department of; Financial aid
Schraa, Michael, representative, **74**, 617, 620
Schutt, Ellen, representative, **53**, 616, 619
Seal, state, 454
Secretary of state, 229
 biography and photo, 7
 election results, 611–13
 list of, 487–88
Self-Insurers Council, 242
Senate, Wisconsin
 caucus chairs, 124
 chief clerk, 21, 121, 124, 127, 131, 494–96
 committees, 128–30, 137–39
 election results, 614–15
 employees, 124, 131
 majority leader, 21, 124, 127, 129, 493–94

majority leader, assistant, 21, 124, 127
maps of districts, 20, 22–118
members, biographies and photos, 22–118
minority leader, 21, 124, 127, 493–94
minority leader, assistant, 21, 124, 127
officers, 21, 124, 127–28
political composition, 496–98
president, 21, 124, 127, 490–92
president pro tempore, 21, 124, 127, 490–92
sergeant at arms, 21, 121, 124, 127, 494–96
sessions, 126, 131, 422–34, 435–52, 498–502, 506–7
term of office, 125–26
Senators, U.S., from Wisconsin
 biographies and photos, 12–13
 elections, 570–74
 list of, 519–20
Sergeants at arms, legislature, 21, 121, 122, 124, 127
 list of, 494–96
Service agencies, legislative, 160–65
Sessions, legislative, 126, 131, 422–34, 435–52, 498–507
Shankland, Katrina, representative, **92**, 617, 621, 637
Shared revenue, significant legislation, 2021 session, 380
Shared Services Executive Committee, Wisconsin, 176
Shelton, Kristina, representative, **111**, 124, 618, 621
Sheriffs, 328, 655–56
Sinicki, Christine, representative, **41**, 616, 619, 623
Small Business, Veteran-Owned Business and Minority Business Opportunities, Council on, 179
Small Business Environmental Council, 213, 643
Small Business Regulatory Review Board, 182, 643
Smith, Jeff, senator, 21, **112**, 124, 614, 615, 637, 640
Snodgrass, Lee, representative, **78**, 124, 617, 620, 623
Snowmobile Recreational Council, 213, 643
Snyder, Patrick, representative, **107**, 617, 621

Social services
    statistics, 686–90
    See also Children and Families,
        Department of
Soils and Plant Analysis Laboratory, State, 238
Sortwell, Shae, representative, **23**, 616, 618
Southeast Wisconsin Professional Baseball Park District, 251, 346, 643
Southeastern Wisconsin Regional Planning Commission, 250
Southwestern Wisconsin Regional Planning Commission, 250
Speaker of the assembly, 21, 124, 127, 129, 490–92
Speaker pro tempore of the assembly, 21, 124, 127
Special Education, Council on, 219
Special purpose districts, 344–47
Special sessions of the legislature, 131, 422–34, 502–6
Spiros, John, representative, **107**, 617, 621
Sporting Heritage Council, 213, 643
Spreitzer, Mark, senator, **64**, 614, 615
Stafsholt, Rob, senator, **49**
State Bar of Wisconsin, 275–76
State budget. *See* Budget, state
State Capitol and Executive Residence Board, 182–84, 643
State Fair Park Board, 232–33, 643
State government
    employees and officials, 634–58
    significant legislation, 2021 session, 380–81
State Law Library, David T. Prosser Jr., 271
State of Wisconsin Investment Board (SWIB), 206–7, 638
State superintendent of public instruction, 217, 320
    biography and photo, 6
    list of, 486–87
State Trails Council, 213, 643–44
State treasurer, 229
    biography and photo, 6
    election results, 608–10
    list of, 488
State-Tribal Relations, Special Committee on, 152
    Technical Advisory Committee, 152–53
State Use Board, 184, 644
Statutes, 153, 164, 165

Steffen, David, representative, **26**, 616, 618
Steil, Bryan, U.S. representative, **14**, 523, 524, 574, 577
Stevens Point campus, UW System, 237
Stout campus, UW System, 237
Stroebel, Duey, senator, **79**
Stubbs, Shelia, representative, **98**, 617, 621
Student financial aid, 202, 230
Subeck, Lisa, representative, **99**, 124, 617, 621
Suggestion Board, State Employees, 179, 643
Summerfield, Rob, representative, **89**, 124, 617, 620
Superintendent of public instruction, state, 217, 320
    biography and photo, 6
    list of, 486–87
Superior campus, UW System, 237
Supreme court, 261–63
    election results, 625–27
    justices, biographies of current, 8–11
    justices, list of, 489–90
    significant decisions, July 2020–July 2022, 385–421
Surveyors, county, 318, 653–54
Swearingen, Rob, representative, **56**, 616, 619
Symbols, state, 454–59

Tax Appeals Commission, 184, 644
Tax Exemptions, Joint Survey Committee on, 158, 644
Taxation, significant legislation, 2021 session, 381–82
Taylor, Lena C., senator, **31**
Teachers Retirement Board, 194–95, 644
Technical College System, 229–30
    Board, 229–30, 644
    districts, 345
    Dual Credit program, 351
    statistics, 665, 699–700
Technology Committee, Wisconsin, 176
Technology Services Bureau, Legislative, 165
Telecommunications Relay Service Council, 175
Testin, Patrick, senator, 21, **91**, 124, 582–84
Tiffany, Tom, U.S. representative, **17**, 523, 524, 576, 578–79

Tittl, Paul, representative, **47**, 616, 619
Tomczyk, Cory, senator, **106**, 614, 615
Tourism
　Council on, 232, 644
　Department of, 230–33
Towns
　government, 320, 340, 341–42, 344
　population, 537–55, 568–69
Trade and consumer protection, significant legislation, 2021 session, 382
Trades and occupations. *See* Safety and Professional Services, Department of
Traffic Citations and Complaints, Council on Uniformity of, 233
Trails Council, State, 213, 643–44
Tranel, Travis, representative, **71**, 617, 620
Transportation
　Department of, 233–34
　Projects Commission, 159–60, 644
　significant legislation, 2021 session, 382–83
　statistics, 717–25
Trauma Advisory Council, 200
Treasurer, state, 229
　biography and photo, 6
　election results, 608–10
　list of, 488
Treasurers, county, 652–53
Tribal chairs, 656
Tribal gaming facilities, 680
Trust Lands and Investments, Division of, Department of Administration, 180–81
Tusler, Ron, representative, **24**, 616, 618

Underly, Jill, state superintendent of public instruction, **6**, 487
Unemployment Insurance Advisory Council, 243
Uniform Dwelling Code Council, 226, 644
Uniform State Laws, Commission on, 142–43, 644
Uniformity of Traffic Citations and Complaints, Council on, 233
United States Semiquincentennial Commission, Wisconsin Commission for the, 241, 644
Universal Service Fund Council, 222
University of Wisconsin System, 234–40
　Board of Regents, 234, 644

Extension, 235
　four-year campuses, 235–37
　Hospitals and Clinics Authority, 244–45, 644
　statistics, 697–98
Upper Mississippi River Basin Association, 258–59
Urban Education, Institute for, 237
Urban Forestry Council, 214
U.S. presidential elections, 322–24, 517–19
U.S. representatives from Wisconsin. *See* Representatives, U.S., from Wisconsin
U.S. senators from Wisconsin. See Senators, U.S., from Wisconsin

Van Orden, Derrick, U.S. representative, **15**, 523, 524, 574–75, 577
VanderMeer, Nancy Lynn, representative, **92**, 124, 617, 621
Veterans Affairs
　Board, 240, 644–45
　Department of, 240–41
　Museum, Wisconsin Veterans, 240
　statistics, 693–94
Veterans and military affairs, significant legislation, 2021 session, 383
Veterans Employment, Council on, 167
Veterans Programs, Council on, 240–41
Veterinary Diagnostic Laboratory Board, 239–40, 645
Veterinary Examining Board, 186, 645
Veterinary Medicine, School of, 238
Vetoes, governor's, 125, 137, 167, 358, 363, 498–502, 508
Victims rights
　Crime Victims Council, 208
　Crime Victims Rights Board, 208, 636
Villages
　government, 320, 321, 340, 342–44
　population, 537–55, 559–68
Vining, Robyn Dorianne Beckley, representative, **35**, 616, 618
Vos, Robin J., representative, 21, **84**, 124, 492, 617, 620, 642
Voting, 328–32

Wanggaard, Van H., senator, **82**, 124, 614, 615, 624
Waste Facility Siting Board, 184, 645

Waterways Commission, Wisconsin, 216, 645
West Central Wisconsin Regional Planning Commission, 250
Wetland Study Council, 213, 645
Whitewater campus, UW System, 237
Wichgers, Chuck, representative, **104**, 617, 621
Wildlife Violator Compact Board of Administrators, Interstate, 255–56
Wimberger, Eric, senator, **109**
Wind Siting Council, 220
Winnebago Mental Health Institute, 198, 692
Wirch, Robert W., senator, **85**
Wisconsin Aerospace Authority, 245, 634
Wisconsin Apprenticeship Advisory Council, 243
Wisconsin Center District, 247, 251–52, 347
Wisconsin Constitution,
  amendments, historical table, 509–14
  significant legislation, 2021 session, 384
  text, 727–62
Wisconsin Economic Development Corporation (WEDC), 245, 636
Wisconsin Health and Educational Facilities Authority (WHEFA), 245–46, 638
Wisconsin Historical Museum, 203
Wisconsin Historical Society. *See* Historical Society of Wisconsin, State
Wisconsin Housing and Economic Development Authority (WHEDA), 246, 638
Wisconsin PFAS Action Council (WISPAC), 175–76
Wisconsin Retirement Board, 195, 643
Wisconsin Veterans Museum, 240
Wittke Jr., Robert O., representative, **83**, 617, 620
Women's Council, 184–85, 645
Worker's Compensation Advisory Council, 243
Workforce Development, Department of, 241–43
Workforce Investment, Governor's Council on, 172

Zimmerman, Shannon, representative, **51**, 616, 619

Ziegler, Annette, supreme court chief justice, **8**, 490